THE COMPUTER SCIENCE PROBLEM SOLVER ®

REGISTERED TRADEMARK

Staff of Research and Education Association,

Dr. M. Fogiel, Director

Research and Education Association
505 Eighth Avenue
New York, N. Y. 10018

THE COMPUTER SCIENCE PROBLEM SOLVER ®

Printed in the United States of America

Library of Congress Catalog Card Number 81-50900

International Standard Book Number 0-87891-525-7

Revised Printing, 1986

PROBLEM SOLVER is a registered trademark of
Research and Education Association, New York, N. Y. 10018

WHAT THIS BOOK IS FOR

Computer science with its many languages and complex operational procedures, has become a difficult subject for students to understand and learn. Despite the publication of hundreds of textbooks in this field, each one intended to provide an improvement over previous textbooks, students continue to remain perplexed as a result of the numerous conditions that must often be remembered and correlated in solving a problem. Various possible interpretations of terms used in computer science have also contributed to much of the difficulties experienced by students.

In a study of the problem, REA found the following basic reasons underlying students' difficulties with computer science taught in schools:

(a) No systematic rules of analysis have been developed which students may follow in a step-by-step manner to solve the usual problems encountered. This results from the fact that the numerous different conditions and principles which may be involved in a problem, lead to many possible different methods of solution. To prescribe a set of rules to be followed for each of the possible variations, would involve an enormous number of rules and steps to be searched through by students, and this task would perhaps be more burdensome than solving the problem directly with some accompanying trial and error to find the correct solution route.

(b) Textbooks currently available will usually explain a given principle in a few pages written by a professional who has an insight in the subject matter that is not shared by students. The explanations are often written in an abstract manner which leaves the students confused as to the application of the principle. The explanations given are not sufficiently detailed and extensive to make the student aware of the wide range of applications and different aspects of the principle being studied. The numerous possible variations of principles and their applications are usually not discussed, and it is left for the students to discover these for themselves while doing the exercises. Accordingly, the average student is expected to rediscover that which has been long known and practiced, but not published or explained extensively.

(c) The examples usually following the explanation of a topic are too few in number and too simple to enable the student to obtain a thorough grasp of the principles involved. The explanations do not provide sufficient basis to enable a student to solve problems that may be subsequently assigned for homework or given on examinations.

The examples are presented in abbreviated form which leaves out much material between steps, and requires that students derive the omitted material themselves. As a result, students find the examples difficult to understand--contrary to the purpose of the examples.

Examples are, furthermore, often worded in a confusing manner. They do not state the problem and then present the solution. Instead, they pass through a general discussion, never revealing what is to be solved for.

Examples, also, do not always include diagrams/graphs, wherever appropriate, and students do not obtain the training to draw diagrams or graphs to simplify and organize their thinking.

(d) Students can learn the subject only by doing the exercises themselves and reviewing them in class, to obtain experience in applying the principles with their different ramifications.

In doing the exercises by themselves, students find that they are required to devote considerably more time to computer science than to other subjects of comparable credits, because they are uncertain with regard to the selection and application of the theorems and principles involved. It is also often necessary for students to discover those "tricks" not revealed in their texts (or review books), that make it possible to solve problems easily. Students must usually resort to methods of trial-and-error to discover these "tricks," and as a result they find that they may sometimes spend several hours to solve a single problem.

(e) When reviewing the exercises in classrooms, instructors usually request students to take turns in writing solutions on the boards and explaining them to the class. Students often find it difficult to explain in a manner that holds the interest of the class, and enables the remaining students to follow the material written on the boards. The remaining students seated in the class are, furthermore, too occupied with copying the material from the boards, to listen to the oral explanations and concentrate on the methods of solution.

This book is intended to aid students in computer science to overcome the difficulties described, by supplying detailed illustrations of the solution methods which are usually not apparent to students. The solution methods are illustrated by problems selected from those that are most often assigned for class work and given on examinations. The problems are arranged in order of complexity to enable students to learn and understand a particular topic by reviewing the problems in sequence. The problems are illustrated with detailed step-by-step explanations, to save the student the large amount of time that is often needed to fill in the gaps that are usually found between steps of illustrations in textbooks or review/outline books.

The staff of REA considers computer science a subject that is best learned by allowing students to view the methods of analysis and solution techniques themselves. This approach to learning the subject matter is similar to that practiced in various scientific laboratories, particularly in the medical fields.

In using this book, students may review and study the illustrated problems at their own pace; they are not limited to the time allowed for explaining problems on the board in class.

When students want to look up a particular type of problem and solution, they can readily locate it in the book by referring to the index which has been extensively prepared. It is also possible to locate a particular type of problem by glancing at just the material within the boxed portions. To facilitate rapid scanning of the problems, each problem has a heavy border around it. Furthermore, each problem is identified with a number immediately above the problem at the right-hand margin.

To obtain maximum benefit from the book, students should familiarize themselves with the section, "How To Use This Book," located in the front pages.

To meet the objectives of this book, staff members of REA have selected problems usually encountered in assignments and examinations, and have solved each problem meticulously to illustrate the steps which are usually difficult for students to comprehend. Gratitude is expressed to the many participants in this program including Garfield Dunn, Nicholas Fuller, Simon Halapir, R. Kannan, Eugene Ostrovsky, Mansur Paghdiwala, Dennis Riney, Paras Shah, Joel Stern, M. Suavi, David Taylor, and Mark Tilly.

Gratitude is also expressed to the many persons involved in the difficult task of typing the manuscript with its endless changes, and to the REA art staff who prepared the numerous detailed illustrations together with the layout and physical features of the book.

The difficult task of coordinating the efforts of all persons was carried out by Carl Fuchs. His conscientious work deserves much appreciation. He also trained and supervised art and production personnel in the preparation of the book for printing.

Finally, special thanks are due to Helen Kaufmann for her unique talents to render those difficult border-line decisions and constructive suggestions related to the design and organization of the book.

Max Fogiel, Ph.D.
Program Director

HOW TO USE THIS BOOK

This book can be an invaluable aid to students in computer science as a supplement to their textbooks. The book is subdivided into 24 chapters, each dealing with a separate topic. The subject matter is developed beginning with fundamental computer concepts and extending through computer architecture, data structures, and program development. The important computer languages are covered in detail. The topics include an extensive number of illustrated problems involving practical applications to business, industry, and research.

TO LEARN AND UNDERSTAND
A TOPIC THOROUGHLY

1. Refer to your class text and read there the section pertaining to the topic. You should become acquainted with the principles discussed there. These principles, however, may not be clear to you at that time.

2. Then locate the topic you are looking for by referring to the "Table of Contents" in front of this book, "The Computer Science Problem Solver."

3. Turn to the page where the topic begins and review the problems under each topic, in the order given. For each topic, the problems are arranged in order of complexity, from the simplest to the more difficult. Some problems may appear similar to others, but each problem has been selected to illustrate a different point or solution method.

To learn and understand a topic thoroughly and retain its contents, it will generally be necessary for students to review the problems several times. Repeated review is essential in order to gain experience in recognizing the principles that should be applied, and to select the best solution technique.

TO FIND A PARTICULAR PROBLEM

To locate one or more problems related to a particular subject matter, refer to the index. In using the index, be certain to note that the numbers given there refer to problem numbers, not to page numbers. This arrangement of the index is intended to facilitate finding a problem more rapidly, since two or more problems may appear on a page.

If a particular type of problem cannot be found readily, it is recommended that the student refer to the "Table of Contents" in the front pages, and then turn to the chapter which is applicable to the problem being sought. By scanning or glancing at the material that is boxed, it will generally be possible to find problems related to the one being sought, without consuming considerable time. After the problems have been located, the solutions can be reviewed and studied in detail. For this purpose of locating problems rapidly, students should acquaint themselves with the organization of the books as found in the "Table of Contents."

In preparation for an exam, it is useful to find the topics to be covered in the exam from the "Table of Contents," and then review the problems under those topics several times. This should equip the student with what might be needed for the exam.

CONTENTS

CHAPTER 1

FUNDAMENTAL COMPUTER CONCEPTS

BASIC DESCRIPTIONS, DEFINITIONS, AND TERMINOLOGY

● PROBLEM 1-1

Define the following terms:

    A) Program
    B) Heuristic programming
    C) Time sharing
    D) Computer language
    E) Data processing

Solution: A) The computer program is a set of instructions telling the computer what to do.
    B) Heuristic programming is the kind of programming which encourages a computer to learn.
    C) Time sharing is the simultaneous use of a single computer by many users.
    D) The computer language is the set of rules, according to which the computer program is written, and which must be followed by the computer as the program progresses.
    E) Data processing is the collecting, processing, and distributing of facts and figures to achieve a desired result.

● PROBLEM 1-2

Give a brief family history of the three generations of computers. What do you think the next generation has in store for us?

Solution: First generation computers are classified as those which used the vacuum tube as the functional unit of electronic circuitry. This period of development, also called the Introductory Period, ranged from about 1953 to 1958. Before this time, there were several types of computational machines with some input/output features and a primitive mercury delay line memory. The first generation's real hallmark

1

was the transition from a single-purpose, electromechanical calculator to a general-purpose, electronic stored program device. UNIVAC I (UNIVersal Automatic Computer) was the father of this new generation in the sense that directly after it, came the major breakthrough: magnetic core storage.

The second generation spawned with the development of transistors instead of vacuum tubes. In 1959, the Commercial Period began as manufacturers could now produce economic and relatively efficient computers for business use. These computers were less expensive, more reliable, less bulky, and more powerful. International Business Machines Corporation entered the forefront of their creation.

Not only did IBM develop commercial data processors, but they also expanded the scientific market. Included in this market were the Department of Defense and the fledgeling aerospace program. Other companies joined the competition, striving to reduce the size of the machines and increase the speed of their operation.

By 1964, the second generation was coming to a close. The new difficulties arising at this time entailed problems of standardization, software support (especially in the area of programming languages), and compatibility among computers. All of these problems were significant as the third generation drew closer to reality.

Strictly speaking, however, the third generation was marked by the development of integrated circuitry and micro-miniaturization of components. Solid-state parts permitted even further reduction of storage capability, faster retrieval time, and more economic computing power. Also called the Expansion Period, this era of computers saw major advances in the "family" concept of computers. IBM's 360 and 370 series, UNIVAC's 9000 series, Honeywell's 200 series, and various other companies' families of computers increased the universality of computer applications to accomodate both the business and scientific communities.

As far as a fourth generation of computers is concerned, we are, probably, in the midst of its adolescence right now. With the mercurial rise of pocket calculators, mini-and micro-computers, photographic emulsion techniques, the latest innovation in storage, and bubble memory, we are certainly far beyond the days of the late 60's and early 70's.

● **PROBLEM** 1-3

A) List and describe briefly the steps of program development.
B) Define the term "debugging".

Solution: A) Computer programming is the task of program development. While not being too difficult most of the time, it must be done carefully. It involves much more than just writing instructions. Several program-development steps must be carried out each time a problem is intended to be solved by a computer. These steps are:

2

1. Defining the problem - Describing the problem, the input data for it, and the desired results in everyday language as clearly and completely as possible.
2. Planning a solution algorithm - Deciding on the directions in solving the problem; breaking the task into specific operations that the computer can perform.
3. Coding the solution - Writing a set of directions (a program) for the computer to perform the operations identified in the solution algorithm.
4. Checking out the program - Debugging and testing the solution algorithm and its computer-program form of representation to ensure that the desired results are provided in the output.

B) When something does not work the way it should, we say that it has "bugs." The programs seldom work the way they should the first time we run them. The longer they are, the more likely they are to have "bugs." The entire procedure of troubleshooting a program, removing its "bugs," and making it work, is therefore called debugging.

● **PROBLEM** 1-4

Define the following words, making clear the distinctions between them: a) bit b) byte c) word.

Solution: a) The bit is the elementary functional unit of computer manipulation. Inside the computer's memory there are minute "doughnuts" composed mostly of iron. Each one of these doughnuts is called a core. Because they contain iron, these cores can conduct magnetism. This is significant, in that the computer can recognize the magnetic lines of force, directed clockwise or counterclockwise through the doughnut. The mathematical convention adopted to make use of this feature is that a clockwise flow corresponds to zero, and a counterclockwise flow corresponds to one.

b) To avoid a discussion of the actual hardware, suffice it to say that the computer represents everything in terms of groups of these bits. A byte is such a group of bits. The size of a byte varies with the different brands of machines. (Usually, 8 bits form a byte.) It is advisable to ask your instructor or the consultants who work at your computer center for the byte size of your machine.

c) A word is a similarly relative term in computer applications. In terms of core memory, each vertical string of doughnuts is considered a word. Another definition, which applies to machine language, is that a word is 5 bytes plus a sign bit (positive or negative). Words are generally thought of as being larger than bytes. This consideration was applied in the development of the IBM System/360, in which a 32-bit word was used to give a higher degree of precision than before. In the 360, four bytes, each of which can be addressed directly, make up one word. However, in the DEC-20, the term byte is abandoned; we speak of words, each having a length of 36 bits. Again, these conventions differ from machine to machine.

3

Give the list and define the symbols of system (not program!) flowcharting.

Solution:

⬜— PUNCHED CARD	⬜— PUNCHED TAPE, (PAPER OR PLASTIC)
⬜— DOCUMENT	⬜— TRANSMITTAL TAPE
◯— MAGNETIC TAPE	⬜— ONLINE STORAGE
▽— OFFLINE STORAGE	◁— DISPLAY
⬜— MANUAL INPUT	◯— SORTING, COLLATING
⬜— CLERICAL OR MANUAL OPERATION	☐— AUXILIARY OPERATION
⬜— KEYING OPERATION	⇄— COMMUNICATION LINKS

Describe the usage of the various columns on the standard 80-column computer card.

Solution: The usage of the 80-columns of the standard computer input card varies with the particular language and purpose for which the card is being used. As an example, we will give the field specifications for a typical FORTRAN statement card.

```
Column 1      :  reserved for carriage control
Columns 2-5   :  used for statement numbers
Column 6      :  used to indicate the continuation of the
                 statement from the previous card that is too
                 long for one card
Columns 7-72  :  used for recording statements, comments, etc.
Columns 73-80 :  used for comments, ignored by compiler
```

SYSTEMS' CLASSIFICATIONS AND STRUCTURES

Name the two basic types of modern electronic computers. Give their similarities and differences.

Solution: The two basic types of modern electronic computers are ANALOG and DIGITAL computers.

Analog computers operate with quantities, such as voltages of currents, which stand for (are analogs for) other quantities, such as pressure, mass, and so on. This fact can be explained by the argument that often one equation can apply to many different processes or operations. Here is a simple example of the validity of this argument:

1 man	+ 1 man	= 2 men,
1 volt	+ 1 volt	= 2 volts,
1 reacted chemical	+ 1 reacted chemical	= 2 reacted chemicals

and so on. The general formula for all three equations is

$$1 + 1 = 2$$

A more complicated example uses the general equation of oscillation and applies it to mechanical and electrical systems. The mechanical system is shown in Fig. 1.

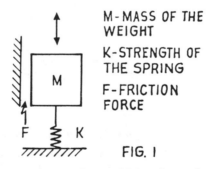

M-MASS OF THE WEIGHT

K-STRENGTH OF THE SPRING

F-FRICTION FORCE

FIG. 1

The general equation of oscillation for this system is:

$$(MD + F + \frac{1}{KD})X = 0,$$

where D is called the differential operator, and X is the position of the weight at any moment.

The corresponding electrical circuit is shown in Fig. 2.

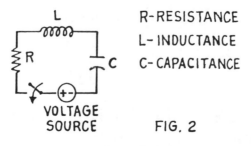

R-RESISTANCE

L-INDUCTANCE

C-CAPACITANCE

VOLTAGE SOURCE

FIG. 2

After the switch is closed, the equation of electrical oscillation will take the following form:

$$(LD + R + \frac{1}{CD})I = 0,$$

where I is the current at any moment. Note that these two equations are identical, except for some of the letters used. Therefore, the behavior of the two systems will also be identical.

In this way the analog computer is extremely helpful in studying any physical system, the behavior of which can be described by an equation. But it has some disadvantages. For one, the accuracy of the analog computer depends on how well we can duplicate the equation, and how accurately we can then measure the results. For example, if we used an analog computer to calculate the interest on a million-dollar loan, the result could easily be off by at least a few dollars, while the bank accountant has to account for every penny.

Another disadvantage of the analog computer is that often we cannot write an exact equation to describe the problem, or the given equation cannot be easily duplicated. These discomforts are easily eliminated by the digital computer.

The digital computer deals with numbers (digits) rather than quantities. This makes it less useful in studying the structure of a process, but it results in other advantages. First, we can make the results as accurate as we desire. Second, the digital computer can handle letters as well as numbers. Third, the digital computer can make decisions, based on some of the fed-in data. Another great advantage of the digital computer is that it can be easily programmed by inputting the sets of instructions. An analog computer is not really programmed. Instead, connections are made with cables to set up the circuit required to duplicate a given equation.

● **PROBLEM** 1-8

Define the terms hardware, software, and firmware. List and briefly explain the four types of functional units of an EDP (Electronic Data-Processing) system. List and briefly discuss the functions of the three major parts of the CPU (Central Processing Unit).

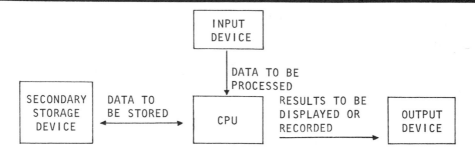

Solution: Hardware, software, and firmware are the three

6

components of the modern EDP system. Hardware is the machinery that performs the mechanics of operations; software is the prewritten sequences of instructions, that direct those operations; firmware is the name for special stored-program instructions, which control the basic operations, such as multiplication, division, etc.

Even though different computers have different features and may include different operational devices, an EDP system typically consists of four types of functional units: the central processing unit, secondary-storage devices, input devices, and output devices. The interrelationships of these units are shown on the diagram below:

The central processing unit is the "brain" of the entire system. It contains a control section, an arithmetic/logic unit, and an internal storage unit (also called primary storage or main storage). The control section of the CPU directs and coordinates the operations of the EDP system according to a prewritten sequence of instructions (firmware) stored within it. The control section selects instructions, interprets them, and generates signals and commands that cause other system units to perform required operations at appropriate times.

The arithmetic/logic unit performs arithmetic and logical operations. It calculates, shifts numbers to the right or left, sets the algebraic sign of a result, rounds, compares algebraically, and so on.

The internal storage unit can be compared with a post office containing a huge number of numbered mail boxes. Each "box," or location, is capable of holding data or instructions. Each such storage location has an assigned address. Using the addresses, the control section of the CPU can locate data and instructions as needed.

● **PROBLEM** 1-9

Briefly describe some commonly used types of input-output (I/O) units.

Solution: Input Section:
The input section differs from computer to computer, and depends on the computer's size and use. One input source is the console keyboard. It is the most direct way of inserting material into the computer, because it is an electric typewriter with keys electrically connected to the computer. Information is transmitted via a console keyboard as rapidly as it is typed in. Since the speed of the fastest human typist is extremely slow compared to the speed of information transmission within the computer, this method of input is usually reserved for use by an operator of a large computer system. Programs and data are usually prepared off-line, that is on a separate machine not actually connected to the computer itself. It is then entered into the input mechanism connected to the computer.

The keypunch machine is a device used to record the input information in a form that can be read by a computer on the computer input cards. The keyboard of the keypunch machine has the standard alphanumeric and punctuation characters of a typewriter, several additional operators (includ-

ing arithmetic), and necessary control keys. When the keys
are hit, a card is punched with holes, which represent an
encoding of characters. The coding used will depend on the
model of the keypunch machine used. The punched cards are
put into a card reader, which is connected to the computer
and can read hundreds of cards per minute into the computer.

A faster input mechanism is the punched paper tape
reader, which can read about 50,000 characters per minute
into the computer. Faster still is the magnetic tape drive.
Although more expensive than the paper tape reader, the magnetic tape drive is capable of reading hundreds of thousands
of characters per minute into the computer. It can also be
used as an output device by recording on tape. These tapes
can then be stored for later use. In addition, the magnetic
tape can easily be cleared and reused, while the punched tape
is used only once.

Another useful input device in a modern computer is a
"data transmission unit" which can connect the computer to a
telephone line. Using the telephone line, the computer can
then communicate with another computer miles away. Another
common use of the data transmission unit is connecting the
computer to thousands of remote typewriters, card readers,
and other input-output devices. One common I/O device used
with the data transmission unit is the Cathode-Ray Tube (CRT)
terminal. This is the familiar keyboard attached to a screen,
similar to a television screen.

Output Section:

The console keyboard mentioned above is also a printer
and used for output. But because the fastest typewriter today can only type about fifteen letters or numbers a second,
which is much too slow compared to the computer's output
speed, the console printer is used only for short communication between the computer and the operator.

One of the most popular output devices is the high-speed
printer, which prints on paper, much like a typewriter. But
by printing an entire line at a time rather than just a letter at a time, the printer can print up to a thousand or more
lines per minute (around 130 characters per line). However,
the computer can attain much higher output speed than this.
In order to use the computer at its full capability, output
information from the computer is often recorded on magnetic
tape at speeds of thousands of characters per second, and
later changed into printed information off line on a tape-
to-printer converter, which can read the magnetic record
produced by the computer and produce written records.

Another type of computer output device is the card
puncher, which records the information by punching holes in
the computer cards with the same code and format used by the
input keypunch machine. The card puncher, however, performs
this task much faster.

Another commonly used output device is the X-Y plotter.
This is the machine which draws graphs and drawings under
control of the computer.

● **PROBLEM** 1-10

Explain the function of the INTERPRETER in the computer
system.

Solution: An interpreter is a program that treats the statements in the programming language as data. In processing the program, the interpreter reads the statements in the programming language into memory. When executing the program, the interpreter scans through the statements, decides what operations to perform, and performs them.

Since the interpreter is written in machine-executable instructions, the CPU (Central Processing Unit) is actually executing instructions only from within the interpreter itself. By executing these instructions within the interpreter, however, the CPU effectively decodes the statements in the programming language. Depending upon the nature of the statement, different instructions within the interpreter are executed in order to effectively perform the operations specified by the programming language itself.

● **PROBLEM** 1-11

Define the terms random access, direct access, and sequential access. Give examples of each.

Solution: Random access refers to the characteristics of certain storage media, such as magnetic cores. In core, each separate location, or address, can be reached as easily and as quickly as any other location. This type of memory is extremely fast, but often more expensive than other types.

An example of a direct access device is the magnetically sensitive disk drive. Magnetic recording heads, analagous to a phonograph stylus, move across the disk rapidly until reaching the desired spot. Information is then read/written from/onto the disk by the recording head. This medium is less expensive than core memory, but it is also considerably slower.

Sequential access is the least expensive storage medium, but it can also be the most tedious. A typical sequential access medium is the magnetic tape. To find a piece of information located near the end of the tape, the tape drive must scan all the characters that precede the desired ones. Thus, it takes extra time to look at many irrelevant characters, making the tape drive inefficient for some purposes. Other types of sequential media include paper tape and punched cards.

● **PROBLEM** 1-12

Briefly describe the properties of the different storage media used in the memory section.

Solution: The program and data are inserted into the memory through the input section. While the program is running, the program instructions and data might continually pass back and forth between the CPU and memory. After the program is finished, the data is taken out of the computer through the output section.

The most important storage unit in a modern computer is "core memory." The cores in a typical computer are strung out on hair-thin wires. Electric current passing through the wires magnetizes the cores, and the diagonal wires through each core "sense" which cores are magnetized and which are not. The presence or absence of magnetization can correspond to a 1 or 0. (On some of the older hardware, the direction of magnetization around the cores, either clockwise or counterclockwise, indicated the value of the bit.) That is, each core stores one binary digit (or bit, as it is usually called). The cores are arranged in planes with 32, 64, 128, or 256 cores in both directions; and the planes are stacked one on top of the other. The bits are grouped into "words." Usually the number of planes determines the number of bits per word, and the number of cores in a plane determines the number of words in the memory unit. For example, a 128 by 128 unit 36 planes deep stores $128 \times 128 = 16,384$ (or 16 K for short) 36-bit words. Core memory is divided into separate "locations" and each location is given a unique "address." The time of access to a location is independent of the location in core memory. The time needed to access 100 word stored sequentially is the same as the time needed to access 100 words that have their addresses selected at random. For this reason, core memory is called a "random access memory."

Another type of memory is magnetic tape. A one-inch strip of tape can accommodate 800 rows of information, each row storing a 6-bit character. Information is stored in blocks, and gaps (sometimes called inter-record gaps). About 3/4 of an inch must be left between blocks to allow for stopping and starting between blocks. Magnetic tape devices have no addressing mechanism. Once the tape is set in motion, a required block is identified by counting the blocks that pass the reading head, or by reading identifying data stored within the blocks themselves. For this reason, magnetic tape storage is called "sequential storage." If data has to be accessed in a more or less random manner, long access time makes tapes completely useless. Since a tape's capacity is much larger than core memory's capacity, however, tapes can be used for permanent storage of bulky records and temporary storage of programs which can be brought into core memory to be run.

A magnetic "disk memory" consists of a number of disks in continuous rotation about an axis through their centers with their flat surfaces coated with magnetic material. The surfaces are divided into rings, called "tracks." Magnetic recording heads read and write information on the disk. Access to a particular region of the surface is gained by bringing the head in close contact with the region by mechanical means. By contrast, the accessing mechanism of core memory is electronic. Consequently, access times for disk memory are longer than for core storage. But the "direct access" method used by disks is still much faster than tapes.

● **PROBLEM** 1-13

What are the basic differences between a computer designed for scientific use and one designed for business use? Elaborate on the differences of the requirements of the CPU's

and other devices. Also mention the differences between
FORTRAN, COBOL, and PL/I as they apply to science and business needs.

Solution: The scientific use of computers deals with the
solution of equations, numerical approximation methods, simulation techniques, and the like. Business applications
are more concerned with data processing and information retrieval: handling of data in a highly organized fashion
with minimal amounts of numerical calculation.

The scientific computer is designed to be extremely
fast and accurate. It is designed primarily for numerical
computations, rather than for letter and word manipulation.
As for the business machine, it need not have a very powerful arithmetic section. It must house a substantial memory
along with a rapid control section in its CPU. These are
necessary (1) to store vast amounts of information, and (2)
to input and output this information quickly.

As you may know, different computer languages have been
developed for different applications. Although there exist
literally hundreds of different languages, each having a
specific purpose, we will mention only the three major languages involved in the scientific-business dichotomy.

FORTRAN (derived from FORmula TRANslator) is, perhaps,
the most well-known scientific language. It is fundament-
ally designed to be written in a mathematics-type format,
which lends itself to the scientist and engineer.

COBOL, an acronym for COmmon Business Oriented Language,
is specified in sentences and structured for commerical use
and application. This readability of COBOL by non-technical
personnel is a nice feature, since not all business people
are computer specialists. Its strong points include variability of input-output procedures and development of report
generators.

PL/I (Programming Language/I) is an attempt to unite
the computing problems of the scientific and business worlds
into a single, general-purpose language. Two advantages to
this language are (1) the economic utilization of storage
by writing statements as blocks, and (2) the easy adaptabil-
ity of PL/I statements to the tenets of structured programming.

COMPUTER LANGUAGES AND SYSTEMS' ORGANIZATION

● **PROBLEM** 1-14

Describe the hierarchy of the various computer languages.
Differentiate between six levels of accessibility.

Solution: The highest level of computer language is the
specialized, or problem-oriented, language. This is a
source language oriented to the description of a narrowly
defined class of problems. It consists of macro-instruc-
tions, high-level commands that consist of many machine
language instructions. Examples include FORTRAN, PL/I,

11

ALGOL, and COBOL. Even more specific are SIMSCRIPT - a simulation language, LISP - a list processor, SNOBOL - a character string manipulator, and CHEBO - a language that mirrors social interaction.

Next down the list we have generators. These are routines whose input defines the action to be taken by the computer. The input becomes the language, for the generating program constructs a new program to complete the task at hand. In business applications, RPG (Report Generator Program) is a generator that takes the user's specifications, writes a program to satisfy these specifications, and outputs a result.

Compilers are used to produce routines that translate source programs into several machine instructions. A compiler goes beyond an assembler, in that it expands greatly the source program into many micro-instructions.

Assemblers operate on symbolic input data and produce machine instructions which carry out such functions as storage assignation, translation of symbolic-operation codes into computer-operating instructions, and computation of absolute addresses from symbolic addresses. Assembler language is symbolic: there exists a one-to-one correspondence between each assembler instruction and a single machine language instruction. The symbols it uses are called mnemonic-operation codes, such as ADD for addition, CLR for clear storage, and SQR for square root.

Interpreter programs reside in the machine as subroutines. They assist the running of the main program by controlling and interpreting certain statements. On some machines, an interpreter takes care of double-precision arithmetic. The interpreter is loaded in the computer concurrently with the main program, and it translates to the computer in sequence those instructions which would have no meaning to the computer otherwise.

Finally, we have the absolute machine language. Computer circuitry is designed to recognize this language so that it can be readily translated into electrical signals. Composed of zeros and ones, this language is exceedingly difficult to program. But on the hardware level, the computer recognizes the code as a series of on and off switches When several million of these are strung together, meaningful operations can be performed.

● **PROBLEM** 1-15

Explain briefly the background and applications of ALGOL language.

Solution: ALGOL (ALGOrithmic Language). Being particularly oriented toward ease of expression of algorithms, ALGOL has enjoyed widespread use as a standardized language in which algorithms can be expressed in the published literature. Ordinary mathematical expressions and English words are incorporated in such a manner that it is a powerful language yet simple to use. Oriented toward the scientific community, ALGOL competes directly with FORTRAN, but FORTRAN certainly dominates in this country. One reason is that implementations of ALGOL have generally fallen short of the published standards for the language. Another is that in the late 1950's FORTRAN was enthusiastically promoted by IBM, which dominates the computer market in this country. ALGOL has fared much better in the European market, which is not so dominated by IBM.

● PROBLEM 1-16

What is the difference between time-sharing and multiprogramming? Discuss the advantages and disadvantages of each as applied to the central processing unit (CPU).

Solution: Multiprogramming involves the running of several programs in the computer at the same time. Actually, only one program runs at a time, but if this one program pauses for a fraction of a second, the monitor, a supervisory program that controls the allocation of CPU facilities, will halt the first program and begin another. Thus, the monitor jumps back and forth between programs so quickly that it seems to be running them simultaneously.

For example, say we have two programs, one - a scientific calculation requiring a lot of computation, and the other - a business program which needs mostly input-output devices. The monitor will start the scientific problem first, with periodic interruptions for the processing of the business program. Because the business program has the capability of interrupting the scientific one, we refer to the business program as the foreground program, while the scientific one becomes the background program.

Timesharing is slightly different. Here a programmer or another computer may communicate directly with the time sharing device. Communication may be achieved via a remote typewriter or teletype machine. The user may feed his program directly to the machine, run the program, and receive results almost immediately. This is executed with the help of input-output buffers. Buffers compensate for the difference between slower I/O devices and rapid CPU speeds by using the overlapping operations. They collect information from the remote typewriter slowly, dump it into the processor for rapid execution, and then return answers slowly once again.

Multiprogramming is designed to increase the effective utilization of computing resources by dividing the main memory into smaller partitions, each large enough to accommodate a problem program. As each program is read into storage, the related resources (such as I/O devices) needed for processing are allocated to it before execution is initiated. For example, if two programs, each requiring four tape drives, were encountered, the first would be allowed to process to completion before the other was started. This could tie up the rest of the system if the first program has many computations and little I/O activity.

Two ways of avoiding this difficulty are priority control and time-slicing. Priority control allows the operator, before a program is run, to assign a value which indicates to the CPU what order of precedence the program should have. Time slicing allows a program, residing in some location, to be processed for a predetermined length of time. Control is automatically passed to another location at the end of the time segment.

Time sharing is slightly different. One main advantage
is the alleviation of difficulties in the sequential mode of
batch processing. In addition, the software utilized in
time-sharing systems is generally user-oriented and conversational in style. Availability to small users, quick and
easy access, and efficient CPU usage are other advantages.
    The disadvantages that have been voiced over time
sharing include security problems, unreliable servicing,
noise invading the transmission wires between user and CPU,
and wasted usage of computer time. Perhaps more intelli-
gently designed time sharing systems will eliminate these
seemingly trivial problems.

● **PROBLEM** 1-17

Explain the terms RUN, WAIT, READY, SUBMIT, HOLD and COM-
PLETE and depict the life cycle of a process.

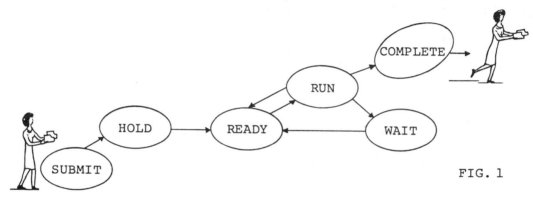

FIG. 1

Solution: RUN: - The process has been assigned a processor
and its programs are presently being executed.
    WAIT: - The process is waiting for some event (e.g. an
I/O operation to be completed).
    READY: - The process is "ready to run," but there are
more processes than processors and it must wait for its turn
on a processor.
    SUBMIT: - A user submits a job to the system; the sys-
tem must respond to the user's request.
    HOLD: - The user's job has been converted into internal
machine readable form, but no resource have been assigned to
the process.
    COMPLETE: - The process has completed its computation
and all its assigned resources may be reclaimed.
    The user submits his job to the system, by placing his
card deck in the card reader. The spooling routine reads
the job and places it onto a disk (hold state).
    Some time later, the job scheduling routine picks the
job. In picking a job, the scheduler will call memory management to determine if sufficient main memory is available,
and call device management to determine whether the devices
requested by job are available. Once the job scheduler decides that the job is to be assigned resources, the traffic
controller creates associated process information. The
job is loaded into memory (ready state).
    When a processor becomes free, the process scheduler
scans the list of ready processes, and assigns processor to

14

it (running state).

If the running process requests access to information (e.g. read a file), information management calls device management to initiate reading of file. The process is in wait state.

When I/O is completed, the traffic controller places the process back into the ready state.

Should the process complete its computation when run again, it is placed into completed states and all allocated resources are freed.

The process state of fig. (1) represents one possible view of the life cycle of a process. This is a simplified example. More states exist in complex operating systems.

● **PROBLEM** 1-18

Describe how the operating system acts as resource manager and classify the management functions it has to execute.

Solution: The operating system must keep track of the status of each resource. It must also decide which process is to get how much of each resource and when. Finally, it must allocate and eventually reclaim the resources. Thus the operating system can be viewed as a resource manager. Its functions are classified under four management activities:

I Memory Management function: -

1) Keep track of memory: What parts are in use and by whom? What parts (of memory) are not in use?

2) If multiprogramming, decide which process gets memory, when it gets it and how much.

3) Allocate the memory when process requests it.

4) Reclaim the resource when the process no longer needs it or has been terminated.

II Processor Management functions: -

1) Keep track of the processor and the status of process. The program that does this has been called the 'traffic controller.'

2) Decide who will have a chance to use the processor; the 'job scheduler' chooses from all the jobs submitted to system. If multiprogramming, decide which process gets the processor, when and for how long; this is called the 'processor scheduler.'

3) Allocate the resource to a process by setting up necessary hardware registers; this is often called dispatcher.'

4) Reclaim processor when process terminates, or exceeds allowed amount of usage.

III Device Management functions: -

1) Keep track of the devices, channels, control units; this is typically called "I/O traffic controller.'

2) Decide what is the most efficient way to allocate the device. If it is to be shared, then decide who gets it and for how long. This is called 'I/O scheduling.'

3) Allocate the device and initiate I/O operation.

4) Reclaim.

IV Information Management functions: -

1) Keep track of information: its location, use, status, etc. These facilities are often called 'file system.'

2) Decide who gets to use the file, enforce protection and provide accessing routines.
3) Allocate the file i.e. 'open a file.'
4) Reallocate the file i.e. 'close a file.'
Thus, all the resource-management functions of an operating system fall into the above-mentioned categories.

● **PROBLEM** 1-19

Explain the difference between truncation and rounding. How can one operation be made to perform the functions of another?

Solution: Consider the number 5.6158, which contains a fractional part, 0.6158. This number can be converted to an integer in one of two ways. First, the fractional part could be simply deleted or chopped off to give, in this case, the integer 5. This process is known as truncation. Second, we might note, that the integer whose value is closest to 5.6158 is 6, a process known as rounding.

Suppose it is known in advance that a particular computer truncates all the numbers to which the integer conversion function is applied. But you want all the numbers to be rounded. What should you do? Just insert in the main program a function, which ADDS 0.5 to every number to be rounded. Now the truncated increased value will be equal to the initial rounded value. For example:

$$1 \begin{cases} 5.6158 \ (ROUND) = 6 \\ 5.6158 + 0.5 = 6.1158 \ (TRUNC) = 6 \end{cases}$$

$$2 \begin{cases} 2.3042 \ (ROUND) = 2 \\ 2.3042 + 0.5 = 2.8042 \ (TRUNC) = 2 \end{cases}$$

If the computer rounds, but you need the truncated values, insert a function which subtracts 0.5 from every number.

CHAPTER 2

NUMBER REPRESENTATIONS

BASE CONVERSIONS

● **PROBLEM** 2-1

Perform the following conversions:
a) $1 1 0 1 1 1 0 1 1_2$ into base 10

b) $4 5 7_8$ into base 2

c) $7 B 3_{16}$ into base 8

d) $1 2 4 2 5_{10}$ into base 16

Solution: We will develop programs for these conversions later. For this exercise, you should figure out the conversions by hand.
$1 1 0 1 1 1 0 1 1_2$ may be converted into base 10 by considering this fact: Each digit in a base two number may be thought of as a switch, a zero indicating "off", and a one indicating "on". Also note that each digit corresponds, in base 10, to a power of two. To clarify, look at the procedure:

2^8	2^7	2^6	2^5	2^4	2^3	2^2	2^1	2^0
1	1	0	1	1	1	0	1	1_2

$(1 \times 256)+(1 \times 128)+(0 \times 64)+(1 \times 32)+(1 \times 16)+(1 \times 8)+(0 \times 4)+(1 \times 2)+(1 \times 1)$ = 443.

If the switch is "on", then you add the corresponding power of two. If not, you add a zero. Follow the next conversion closely.

b) 457_8 may be converted into base two by using the notion of triads.

Triads are three-bit groups of zeros and ones which correspond to octal (base 8) and decimal (base 10) numbers. This table can, with some practice, be committed to memory:

Binary (2)	Octal (8)	Decimal (10)	Hexadecimal (16)
0 0 0	0	0	0
0 0 1	1	1	1
0 1 0	2	2	2
0 1 1	3	3	3
1 0 0	4	4	4
1 0 1	5	5	5

```
1 1 0              6              6              6
1 1 1              7              7              7
```

So, taking each digit of 457_8 separately, we get:

$$4_8 = 100_2$$
$$5_8 = 101_2$$
$$7_8 = 111_2$$

which becomes $100101111_2 = 457_8$

c) $7B3_{16}$ is a hexadecimal number. Letters are needed to replace numbers, since the base here is 16. The following chart will help:

BINARY	OCTAL	DECIMAL	HEXADECIMAL
1 0 0 0	10	8	8
1 0 0 1	11	9	9
1 0 1 0	12	10	A
1 0 1 1	13	11	B
1 1 0 0	14	12	C
1 1 0 1	15	13	D
1 1 1 0	16	14	E
1 1 1 1	17	15	F
1 0 0 0 0	20	16	10

It may be easier to follow if we convert $7B3_{16}$ into decimal first. We get:

$$16^2 \qquad 16^1 \qquad 16^0$$
$$7 \qquad\quad B \qquad\quad 3_8$$
$$(7 \times 256) + (11 \times 16) + (3 \times 1) = 1971_{10}$$

Now, convert to octal using this procedure: Divide 8, the base to be used, into 1971. Find the remainder of this division and save it as the first digit of the new octal number. Then divide 8 into the quotient of the previous division, and repeat the procedure. The following is an illustration:

```
8 | 1971
   -1968                    246 x 8 = 1968
      3  →  3

    246
   -240                     30 x 8 = 240
      6  →  6

     30
    -24                     3 x 8 = 24
      6  →  6
      3  →  3               3 ÷ 8 ≠ an integer.
```

$$7B3_{16} = 1971_{10} = 3663_8$$

d) $1 2 4 2 5_{10}$ may be converted to base 16 by this method: Take the highest power of 16 contained in 12425. Then, subtract that value and try the next lowest power. Continue the process until all the digits are accounted for.

$$\begin{array}{r} 1\ 2\ 4\ 2\ 5 \end{array}$$

$$16^3 \times 3 = \underline{1\ 2\ 2\ 8\ 8}$$
$$1\ 3\ 7$$

$$16^1 \times 8 = \underline{1\ 2\ 8}$$
$$9$$

$$16^0 \times 9 = \underline{9}$$
$$0$$

Answer: $12425_{10} = 3089_{16}$

● **PROBLEM** 2-2

Perform the following conversions from

a) 1 0 0 1 1 0 1 0
b) 1 0 1 . 1 0 1
c) 0 . 0 0 1 1

base 2 to base 8, 10, and 16 .

Solution: a) To convert base 2 to base 8, we use the triad method where three digits are taken together and converted to equivalent decimal value; this results in base 8 conversion

$$\lfloor 0\ 1\ 0 \rfloor\ \lfloor 0\ 1\ 1 \rfloor\ \lfloor 0\ 1\ 0 \rfloor_2 = 232_8$$

Similarly for hexadecimal conversion 4 bits are taken together. Zeros are assumed for most significant grouping.

$$\lfloor 0\ 0\ 0\ 0 \rfloor\lfloor 1\ 0\ 0\ 1 \rfloor\lfloor 1\ 0\ 1\ 0 \rfloor = 9A_{16}$$

For binary to decimal conversion

$$\begin{array}{cccccccc} 1 & 0 & 0 & 1 & 1 & 0 & 1 & 0 \end{array}$$
$$1{\times}2^7 + 0{\times}2^6 + 0{\times}2^5 + 1{\times}2^4 + 1{\times}2^3 + 0{\times}2^2 + 1{\times}2^1 + 0{\times}2^0$$

$$128 + 0 + 0 + 16 + 8 + 0 + 2 + 0 = 154_{10}$$

b) i) $101\ .\ 101_2 = 5\ .\ 5_8$

   ii) $\dfrac{0101}{5}\ .\ \dfrac{1010_2}{A} = 5\ .\ A_{16}$

   iii) $101\ .\ 101_2$

$$(1{\times}2^2 + 0{\times}2^1 + 1{\times}2^0)\ .\ (1{\times}2^{-1} + 0{\times}2^{-2} + 1{\times}2^{-3})$$

$$= 4 + 0 + 1 + 0.5 + 0 + 0.125 = 5\ .\ 625_{10}$$

c) i) $0\ .\ 0011 = \lfloor 000 \rfloor.\lfloor 001 \rfloor\lfloor 100 \rfloor = 0\ .\ 14_8$

   ii) $0\ .\ 0011 = \lfloor 0000 \rfloor\ .\ \lfloor 0011 \rfloor = 0\ .\ 3_{16}$

   iii) $0\ .\ 0011 = .\ (0{\times}2^0 + 0{\times}2^{-1} + 0{\times}2^{-2} + 1{\times}2^{-3} + 1{\times}2^{-4})$

$$= 0 + 0 + 0 + 0.125 + 0.0625$$

$$= 0 \cdot 1875_{10}$$

Perform the following conversions from decimal to binary, octal and hexadecimal systems.

a) 17_{10} b) 1321_{10} c) 360_{10} d) $.75_{10}$ e) $.390625_{10}$ f) $.9_{10}$

Solution: a) (i) The conversion for integer part consists of dividing by the desired base (e.g. 2) repeatedly and saving the remainder:

$$2\,\overline{\big|17} \qquad 2\,\overline{\big|8} \qquad 2\,\overline{\big|4} \qquad 2\,\overline{\big|2} \qquad 2\,\overline{\big|1}$$

$2\,\big|\overline{17}$	$2\,\big|\overline{8}$	$2\,\big|\overline{4}$	$2\,\big|\overline{2}$	$2\,\big|\overline{1}$
$\frac{8}{}$	$\frac{4}{}$	$\frac{2}{}$	$\frac{1}{}$	$\frac{0}{}$
16	8	4	2	1 (save)
1 (save)	0 (save)	0 (save)	0 (save)	

Writing the remainders from right to left we have   10001
$$17_{10} = 10001_2$$

Another format is the top-down division method as shown below:

```
2  |17 |
   | 8 | 1
   | 4 | 0
   | 2 | 0
   | 1 | 0
   | 0 | 1  ↑  =  10001
```

(ii) Proceeding in the same way for octal conversion

```
8  |17 |
   | 2 | 1
   | 0 | 2  ↑  21₈
```
$$17_{10} = 21_8$$

(iii)
```
16  |17 |
    | 1 | 1
    | 0 | 1  ↑  =  11₁₆
```
$$17_{10} = 11_{16}$$

As the binary, octal and hexadecimal systems can easily be converted from one form to another, it is only necessary to convert in any one of them and use the triad or quartet methods to obtain the results for remaining bases. Thus, $17_{10} = 10001_2 = \lfloor 010 \rfloor \lfloor 001 \rfloor = 21_8$ or

$$17_{10} = 10001 = \lfloor 0001 \rfloor \lfloor 0001 \rfloor = 11_{16}$$

b) 1321_{10} to octal

```
8  |1321 |
   | 165 | 1
   |  20 | 5
   |   2 | 4
   |   0 | 2  ↑   1321₁₀ = 2,451₈
```

$$1321_{10} = 2451_8 = 010\ 100\ 101\ 001_2$$

$$1321_{10} = 010\ 100\ 101\ 001_2 = 0101\ 0010\ 1001_2 = 529_{16}$$

c) 360_{10} to octal

```
8 | 360
    45    0
     5    5
     0    5  ↑
```

Thus $360_{10} = 550_8$. Now $550_8 = 101\ 101\ 000_2$ and $101\ 101\ 000_2 =$
$0001\ 0110\ 1000_2 = 168_{16}$

d) (i) The fraction conversion procedure is exactly the opposite of
the integer procedure

$$.75_{10}\ \text{ to octal}$$

```
 .75
 x8
6.00
```

Take the digit 6, and save it; it's the first digit of the octal number. Now take the decimal part .00 and again multiply it by 8. We get
all 0's and hence

$$0.75_{10} = 0.60_8 = 0.110_2$$

(ii) The binary conversion can be obtained directly or from converted
octal numbers as shown above.

Direct method:
```
        .75
        x2
  = 1.50
        x2
  = 1.00
        x2
  = 0.00
```

$$.75_{10} = .110_2$$

(iii) $.75_{10} = .110_2$
and

$$.110_2 = .1100_2 = .c_{16}$$

e) (i) $.390625_{10} = X_8$

```
    .390625
        x8
  3.125000
        x8
  1.000000
        x8
  0.000000
```

Thus $.390625_{10} = .31_8$

$$.31_8 = .011\ 001_2$$

(ii) $\quad .390625_{10} = .011001_2$

(iii) $\quad .390625_{10} = ?_{16}$

$$.011001_2 = .\underline{|0110|}\ \underline{|0100|}_2 = .64_{16}$$

f) $\quad 0.9_{10} = ?_8$

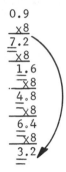

Observe that the arrow connecting the 7.2, in the third line and the 3.2 in the eleventh line points out that after multiplying by 8 we shall have a repetition pattern of 1463. Hence, to convert $.9_{10}$ to X_8, the precision must be known, say, up to the 9th digit after the decimal point. Hence, $.9_{10} = (.7\ 1463\ 1463\ \ldots)_8$.

ii) The same will be the case for binary conversion. We convert to binary from the obtained octal number

$$.9_{10} = (.71463\ldots)_8 = (.111\ 001\ 100\ 110\ 011\ldots)_2$$

For direct conversion

$$\begin{array}{r}
.9 \\
\times 2 \\
\hline
1.8 \\
\times 2 \\
\hline
1.6 \\
\times 2 \\
\hline
1.2 \\
\times 2 \\
\hline
0.4 \\
\times 2 \\
\hline
0.8 \\
\times 2 \\
\hline
1.6 \\
\times 2 \\
\hline
1.2 \\
\times 2 \\
\hline
0.4 \\
\times 2 \\
\hline
0.8 \\
\end{array} \quad = .11100\ 1100\ldots$$

iii) Now, to convert 0.9_{10} into hexadecimal base, use the binary form already obtained.

$$0.9_{10} = 0.1\ 1100\ 1100\ 1100\ 11\ldots_2$$

$$= 0. \ 1110 \ 0110 \ 0110 \ 0110 \ldots_2$$

(grouping by four bits)

$$= 0.E666 \ldots_{16}$$

$$= 0.\dot{E}66\dot{6}_{16} \ \text{(up to } 4_{10} \text{ places after the point)}$$

● **PROBLEM 2-4**

Describe the procedures involved in adding and subtracting hexadecimal numbers.

Solution: The process of adding and subtracting hexadecimal (Hex) digits is almost identical to that of adding and subtracting Arabic digits. Actually, there are a few ways in which these calculations may be performed. The most efficient one is the method used in the decimal calculations. The operations will be done from right to left. In using this method, each Hex symbol will be translated to a decimal digit before the calculations, then, upon completion of the calculations, each resulting decimal digit will be retranslated to a corresponding Hex symbol.

Addition: In decimal calculations, as we go from one column to the next, we carry units of tens. For example:

col 2	col 1	col ∅
1	2	8
	8	8
2	1	6

In Hex addition, instead of carrying units of ten, we carry units of sixteen. Example 1

col 3	col 2	col 1	col ∅
6	E	8	8
+	1	D	3

For col ∅:

Hex →	Decimal →	Decimal Sum →	Hex Sum
8	8	8	
3	3	3	
		11	→ B

Note in this column the decimal sum is less than 16, and no units of sixteen are carried.

For col 1:

Hex →	Decimal →	Decimal Sum →	Hex Sum
8	8	8	
D	13	13	
		21	→ 16 + 5

Here the decimal sum is greater than 16. After factoring out the units of sixteen (here only one), the remaining digit should be placed in this column.

For col 2:
```
Hex → Decimal → Decimal Sum → Hex Sum
 E       14           14
 1        1            1
                      ──
                      15
                    + 1 (from col 1)
                      ──
                      16  →   16 + ∅
```

One unit of sixteen can be factored out, leaving zero as the remaining digit for col 2.

For col 3:
```
Hex → Decimal → Decimal Sum → Hex Sum
 6       6           6
                     ──
                     6
                   + 1 (from col 2)
                     ──
                     7 →        7
```

Thus, the final result is:
```
      6 E 8 8
    + 1 D 3
    ─────────
      7 0 5 B
```


Subtraction: In the subtraction procedure the units of sixteen are borrowed instead of being carried.

Example 2:
```
          col 2     col 1     col ∅
            3         5         E
    -       2         B         8
          ──────────────────────────
```


For col ∅
```
   Hex → Decimal → Decimal Difference - Hex Difference
    E       14           14
    8        8          - 8
                        ──
                         6  →  6
```


For col 1:
```
   Hex → Decimal → Decimal Difference → Hex Difference
    5       5        (5)+16 (Borrowed unit from col 2)
    B      11          11
                       ──
                       10   →               A
```

The difference in col 2 is zero since one unit was borrowed from 3. The final result is:
```
        2      +16
        3̶       5       E
    -   2       B       8
      ──────────────────────
               A        6
```

24

RADIX COMPLEMENTS

Obtain the 1's and 2's complements of the following binary numbers:
a) 1010101
b) 0111000
c) 0000001
d) 10000
e) 0000

<u>Solution</u>: Forming complements is useful when one wants to perform subtraction without borrowing from another column. This is because subtraction is the same as adding the two's complement.

a) The 1's complement of 1010101_2 is found by subtracting it from 1111111 . Thus

$$\begin{array}{r} 1111111 \\ -1010101 \\ \hline 0101010 \end{array}$$

The two's complement is formed by subtracting 1010101_2 from 10000000. Thus,

$$\begin{array}{r} 10000000 \\ - \ 1010101 \\ \hline 00101011 \end{array}$$

Forming the two's complement by binary subtraction is difficult.

b) Since the base, or radix, of the binary system is 2, the one's complement is referred to as the radix minus one complement. Similarly, the two's complement is called the radix complement. The radix minus one complement of 0111000_2 is

$$\begin{array}{r} 1111111 \\ -0111000 \\ \hline 1000111 \end{array}$$

The radix complement of 0111000_2 is

$$\begin{array}{r} 10000000 \\ - \ 0111000 \\ \hline 1001000 \end{array}$$

While examining a) and b), note that finding the radix minus one complements of the two given numbers is equivalent to changing 0's to 1's and 1's to 0's in the given numbers.

c) The radix minus one complement of 0000001 is 1111110. The radix complement is

$$\begin{array}{r} 10000000 \\ - \ 0000001 \\ \hline 1111111 \end{array}$$

Examining the radix complements of a), b) and c) observe that

$$\text{Radix complement}(X)_2 = \text{Radix complement minus one}(X)_2 + 1 \qquad (1)$$

where X is a binary number.

25

d) The one's complement of 10000 is 01111 or 1111. The two's complement, using (1) is

$$
\begin{array}{r}
1111 \\
+\ \ \ 1 \\
\hline
10000
\end{array}
$$

or, the number itself.

e) The radix minus one complement of 0000 is 1111 and the radix complement is

$$
\begin{array}{r}
1111 \\
+\ \ \ 1 \\
\hline
10000
\end{array}
$$

To illustrate the advantage of representing numbers by their radix complements, suppose we wish to store the negative of d), i.e., -10000, in a 12-bit word. The left-most bit has value 1 to represent the minus sign:

$$1000\ 0001\ 0000$$

Now suppose word size is increased to 16 bits. This is most easily done by adding 4 bits with zero value on the left. But the left-most bit must be changed to 1 and the 1 in the third quartet of bits (third from the left) must be changed to zero:

$$1000\ 0000\ 0001\ 0000$$

Suppose , instead, that the radix complement of -10000 is in a 12-bit storage. The radix complement of -10000 in a 12-bit storage is

$$
\begin{array}{r}
111111111111 \\
-\ \ \ \ \ \ \ \ 10000 \\
\hline
111111101111 \\
+\ \ \ \ \ \ \ \ \ \ \ \ 1 \\
\hline
111111110000
\end{array}
$$

Now, if word length is to be extended to 16 bits, simply add a quartet of 1's. No special provisions need be made for the sign bit. In other words, when word size is increased, simply copy the sign bit into all the bits to its left.

Finally, the two's complement representation is preferred to the one's complement because +0 $\neq$ -0 in the one's complement, but +0 = -0 in the 2's complement.

● **PROBLEM 2-6**

Explain the subtraction function using the complementing system as in decimal and in binary number system.

Solution: To understand the complementing system in computers and why this system is used, consider the following example:

$$12\ +\ 7\ =\ 19$$

$$-12\ +\ 7\ =\ -5$$

Each of these is defined as an addition between two operands (numbers), but because one of the numbers is actually negative in the latter case, it is really a subtraction. This means that, even though we instructed the computer to do an addition, it would first have to examine the numbers and, if one of them is negative, do a subtraction instead. This makes the job of the computer harder, because it has to examine the numbers, make a decision on what to do, and then do it. For this reason the complementing system was developed, so that addition could work for both positive and negative numbers.

For decimal numbers there are two complementing systems - 10's and 9's. 10's complement system: Consider the example

$$5 - 3 = 2$$
$$\equiv 5 + 10 - 3 - 10 = 2$$
$$\equiv 5 + (10 - 3) - 10 = 2$$
$$\equiv 5 + 7 - 10 = 2$$
$$\equiv 12 - 10 = 2$$

i.e., for -3, take its 10's complement, 10 - 3 = 7. Now add 7 to 5 = 12 and drop the last 1. This gives $\cancel{1}2 = 2$, the necessary answer.

9's complement method: Here we subtract the negative number from 9. Perform addition and the last digit is again added back to the result.

$$5 - 3 = 2$$

1st step $9 - 3 = 6$

2nd step $5 + 6 = 11$

3rd step $11 = 1 + 1 = 2$
                  $+1$

One of the methods for constructing a 1's complement for a binary number is the interchange of zeros and ones. e.g.,

decimal	subtraction
5	101
-3	-011
2	010 = 2

Now the 1's complement of 011 = 100. Thus,

$$\begin{array}{r} 5 \\ -3 \\ \hline 2 \end{array} \equiv \begin{array}{r} 101 \\ +100 \\ \hline 1001 \\ \llcorner\!\!\rightarrow 1 \\ \hline 010 \end{array} = 2$$

This is equivalent to the 9's complement in decimal. Similarly, there is a 2's complement method equivalent to the 10's complement method. Here we take the complement of a binary number and add one to it.

$$011 = \begin{array}{r} 100 \\ +1 \\ \hline 101 \end{array} \quad \begin{array}{l} \text{1st step complement} \\ \\ \text{2nd step add 001 to it} \end{array}$$

Now

$$\begin{array}{r} 5 \\ -3 \\ \hline 2 \end{array} \equiv \begin{array}{r} 101 \\ +101 \\ \hline \cancel{1}010 \end{array} \quad \text{drop out last bit as in}$$

10's complement method.

Now consider the case where the result of the subtraction is negative. For example,

$$\begin{array}{r} 6 \\ -7 \\ \hline -1 \end{array} \quad \text{(decimal subtraction)}$$

Or, 6 = 0110 in binary, and, 7 = 0111 in binary.

27

1's complement of 7 in binary = 1000. Hence,

$$\left.\begin{matrix} 6 \\ -7 \\ \hline -1 \end{matrix}\right\} \quad = \quad \left\{\begin{matrix} 0110 \\ +1000 \\ \hline 1110 \end{matrix}\right.$$

As no carry is generated in the last stage, it means the result is negative. Hence, take the complement

$$1110 \rightarrow 0001$$

Hence, the answer is: -0001, i.e., -1 (binary). Also, 2's complement of 7 in binary = 1000

$$\begin{matrix} +\quad 1 \\ \hline 1001 \end{matrix}$$

$$\left.\begin{matrix} 6 \\ -7 \\ \hline -1 \end{matrix}\right\} \quad = \quad \left\{\begin{matrix} 0110 \\ 1001 \\ \hline 1111 \end{matrix}\right.$$

$$\begin{matrix} 0000 \leftarrow \text{complement} \\ +\quad 1 \leftarrow \text{add 1} \\ \hline 0001 \leftarrow \text{result} \end{matrix}$$

Hence, the answer = -0001, i.e., -1.

● **PROBLEM** 2-7

Perform the following operations (using 1's and 2's complement where necessary).
(i) 21 + 7 ; (ii) 45 - 33 ; (iii) -15 + 6

<u>Solution</u>: i)
$$\begin{matrix} 21 \\ +\ 7 \\ \hline 28 \end{matrix} \qquad \begin{matrix} 10101 \\ +\ 00111 \\ \hline 11100 \end{matrix}$$

ii)
$$\begin{matrix} 45 \\ -33 \\ \hline 12 \end{matrix} \qquad \begin{matrix} 101101 \\ -100001 \\ \hline 001100 \end{matrix}$$

Now to do binary subtraction using 1's complement, take the complement of 33: 100001 = 011110. Next add it to 45

$$\begin{matrix} 101101 \\ 011110 \\ \hline 1001011 \\ \longrightarrow +1 \\ \hline 001100 \end{matrix} \quad = \quad 12$$

Similarly, for the 2's complement method, take the complement of 33 and add binary one to it.

$$33 \ = \ 100001 \quad \text{binary equivalent}$$

$$\begin{matrix} 011110 \leftarrow \text{1's complement of it} \\ +1 \\ \hline 011111 \leftarrow \text{2's complement} \end{matrix}$$

Then

$$\begin{matrix} (+\ 45) \equiv & 101101 \\ +\ (-\ 33) & 011111 \\ \hline 12 & 1001100 \end{matrix} \quad = \quad 12 \quad \text{drop last digit}$$

28

iii)   -15
              + 6
              ─────
               -9

        15 = 1111   binary equivalent

                      0000   1's complement
                       +1
                      ─────
                      0001   2's complement
        6 = 0110   binary equivalent

        -15   10000
    +   +6   00110   1's complement
    ─────   ─────
        -9   0110

Now as no carry is generated the answer is negative and is in 1's complement form. Taking back its complement, we get the answer in binary equivalent form.

              0110 = 1001 ≡ 9   the correct answer.

        -15   -10001
      + 6   +00110   2's complement
    ──────   ───────
        -9   -10111

Again, as no carry is generated at the most significant bit position, the answer is negative and is in 2's complement form. Complement and add binary one to obtain the answer in binary equivalent form.

              0111 = 1000
                       +1
                      ─────
                      1001 = -9

Obtain the 9's and 10's complements of the following decimal numbers:
(a)   13579
(b)   90090
(c)   09900
(d)   10000
(e)   0000

Solution: The nine's and ten's complements of a given decimal number X are found by subtracting it from a sequence of nine's and from the power of ten greater than X respectively.
(a) The nine's complement of 13579 is:

                      99999
                     -13579
                     ──────
                      86420

The ten's complement is:

                      100000
                     - 13579
                     ──────
                      86421

(b) The nine's complement of 90090 is:

                      99999
                     -90090
                     ──────
                      09909

29

The ten's complement is:

$$
\begin{array}{r}
100000 \\
-\ 90090 \\
\hline
09910
\end{array}
$$

From (a) and (b) note that

Ten's complement (X) = Nine's complement (X) + 1

(c)   The nine's complement of 09900 is:

$$
\begin{array}{r}
99999 \\
-09900 \\
\hline
90099
\end{array}
$$

The ten's complement is 90099 + 1 = 90100 .

(d)   When numbers are represented in decimal form, the number ten is called the base or radix of the decimal system. Then, forming the radix complement of a decimal number means finding its ten's complement representation and the radix minus one complement is equal to the nine's complement. The radix complement of 10000 is:

$$
\begin{array}{r}
100000 \\
-\ 10000 \\
\hline
90000
\end{array}
$$

The radix minus one complement is 89999.

(e)   The radix minus one complement of 0000 is:

$$
\begin{array}{r}
9999 \\
-0000 \\
\hline
9999
\end{array}
$$

Hence, the radix complement is 10000. Radix complement representations of numbers are useful for subtracting two numbers. For example, suppose (c) is to be subtracted from (b).

$$
\begin{array}{r}
90090 \\
-09900 \\
\hline
80190
\end{array}
$$

In performing this subtraction, we had to borrow twice from the next column. To eliminate the need for borrowing, the subtraction may be performed as follows:

   i)   Form the nines complement of (c) (09900):

90099

   ii)   Add 1 to obtain the ten's complement:

90099 + 1 = 90100

   iii) Add (b) (90090) to the result:

90100 + 90090 = 180190

   iv)   Subtract 100000 from iii) to obtain the final answer

180190 - 100000 = 80190

● **PROBLEM 2-9**

Obtain the 7's and 8's complement of the following octal numbers: 770, 1263, 00010 and 0000.

Solution: In the octal system, $8 = 10$, $8^2 = 100$, $8^3 = 1000$, etc.   Thus, the octal system contains only the numbers 0,1,2,3,4,5,6,7.

a) The seven's complement of 770 is

$$\begin{array}{r} 777 \\ -770 \\ \hline 007 \end{array}$$

The eight's complement is then

$$007 + 1 = 010$$

This could also have been obtained directly:

$$\begin{array}{r} 1000 \\ -\ 770 \\ \hline 010 \end{array}$$

b) The seven's complement is:

$$\begin{array}{r} 7777 \\ -1263 \\ \hline 6514 \end{array}$$

The eight's complement is:

$$6514 + 1 = 6515$$

according to the relationship

Radix complement (X) = Radix complement minus one (X) + 1

(In base eight arithmetic, 8 is the radix and the radix complement of a number equals

$$X_1 X_2 \ldots X_n = 1 \underbrace{0000 \ldots 00}_{n \text{ zeros}} \quad \text{minus one}).$$

c) The radix minus one complement of 00010 is:

$$\begin{array}{r} 77777 \\ -00010 \\ \hline 77767 \end{array}$$

and the radix complement is:

$$77770$$

Note that although 00010 = 10, the radix complements are different. In the computer, numbers are stored in words of length 12 - 36 bits. In a 12-bit word, the number 10 would be stored as

$$000000000010$$

The radix complement is:

$$777777777770$$

d) The radix complement of 0000 is:

$$\begin{array}{r} 10000 \\ -\ 0000 \\ \hline 10000 \end{array}$$

and the radix minus one complement is:

$$10000 - 1 = 7777$$

Obtain the 15's and 16's complement of the following hexadecimal
numbers:
a) FF0
b) 1234
c) ABCD
d) 0000

Solution: Hexadecimal numbers arise frequently in computer applications because 16 is the fourth power of 2. This means that each
hexadecimal digit can be represented uniquely by four bits.

a) The 15's complement of FF0 is found by subtracting it from FFF.

$$\begin{array}{r} FFF \\ -FF0 \\ \hline 00F \end{array}$$

Since radix complement = radix complement minus one + 1, the 16's
complement here is:

$$00F + 1 = 010 \ .$$

b) The 15's complement of 1234 is:

$$\begin{array}{r} FFFF \\ -1234 \\ \hline EDCB \end{array}$$

The 16's complement is then EDCB + 1, or EDCC.
   To make this more comprehensible, convert into the decimal system:

$$10000_{16} = 16^4 + 0 \times 16^3 + 0 \times 16^2 + 0 \times 16^1 + 0 \times 16^0$$

$$= 65,536_{10}$$

$$1234_{16} = 1 \times 16^3 + 2 \times 16^2 + 3 \times 16^1 + 4 \times 16^0$$

$$= 4660_{10}$$

Then the 16's complement (decimal equivalent) is:

$$\begin{array}{r} 65,536 \\ -\ 4,660 \\ \hline 60,876 \end{array}$$

Now,

$$EDCC_{16} = 14 \times 16^3 + 13 \times 16^2 + 12 \times 16^1 + 12 \times 16^0$$

$$= 60,876_{10} \quad \text{as above.}$$

Thus $EDCC_{16}$ is the 16's complement of 1234_{16} .

c) The radix minus one complement of ABCD is:

$$\begin{array}{r} FFFF \\ -ABCD \\ \hline 5432 \end{array}$$

The radix complement of ABCD is 5433.

d) The radix complement of 0000 is 10000 while the radix complement
minus one is FFFF.

FRACTIONS MANIPULATIONS

Perform the following multiplications:

a) $3652_8 \times 24_8$

b) $11.01_2 \times 1.01_2$

c) $5AB_{16} \times F5A_{16}$

<u>Solution</u>: a) When doing multiplication in a base other than base 10, there are two common approaches. The first is to multiply the numbers together with base 10 multiplication, get an answer in base 10, and then encode the answer into the desired base. The other method is a direct one; you need to know the multiplication tables for the particular base. In this example, we have each line as a partial product. After the products are obtained, we add them together as base 8 numbers. Thus,

$$
\begin{array}{r}
3652 \\
\times \quad 24_8 \\
\hline
10 \\
24 \\
30 \\
14 \\
124 \\
14 \\
6 \\
\hline
114510_8
\end{array}
$$

b) Binary numbers can also be multiplied via partial products.

$$
\begin{array}{r}
11.01_2 \\
\times \quad 1.01_2 \\
\hline
1101 \\
0000 \\
1101 \\
\hline
100.0001_2
\end{array}
$$

As in base 10, the total number of digits in the multiplier and multiplicand to the right of the binary point must equal to the number of digits to the right of the binary point in the product.

c) Hexadecimal multiplication is often confusing because letters are used to signify numbers. Although it is possible to use the partial product method, it is far simpler to convert the hexadecimal numbers to decimal numbers and then perform the multiplication.

$$5AB_{16} = (5 \times 16^2) + (A \times 16^1) + (B \times 16^0)$$

Remembering that $A_{16} = 10_{10}$ and $B_{16} = 11_{10}$, you can write

$$= (5 \times 16^2) + (10 \times 16^1) + (11 \times 16^0)$$

$$= 1280 + 160 + 11$$

$$5AB_{16} = 1451_{10}$$

$$F5A_{16} = (F \times 16^2) + (5 \times 16^1) + (A \times 16^0)$$

Also recall that $F_{16} = 15_{10}$, so that

$$F5A_{16} = (15 \times 16^2) + (5 \times 16^1) + (10 \times 16^0)$$

$$= 3840 + 80 + 10$$

$$F5A_{16} = 3930_{10}$$

Now the multiplication is simple:

$$
\begin{array}{r}
1451_{10} \\
\times \quad 3930_{10} \\
\hline
43530 \\
13059 \\
4353 \quad\quad \\
\hline
5702430_{10}
\end{array}
$$

To convert back to hexadecimal, you can subtract powers of 16. The value of 16^5 is 1,048,576. Multiply this by 5, and you will get 5,242,880, which is less than 5,702,430. Subtract and look at the answer. Check the value of 16^4 and do the same as above. Continue the process until all digits have been accounted for. The example will show the correct procedure.

16^5	16^4	16^3	16^2	16^1	16^0
1048576	65536	4096	256	16	1

		Digits of Hex Number
5702430		
− 5242880	($= 5 \times 16^5$)	5
459550		
− 458752	($= 7 \times 16^4$)	7
798		
− 000	(16^3 is too big)	0
798		
− 768	($= 3 \times 16^2$)	3
30		
− 16	($= 1 \times 16^1$)	1
14		
− 14	($= 14 \times 16^0$)	D

The answer is $57031D_{16}$.

● **PROBLEM 2-12**

Verify the following equalities:
a) $.1_{10} = (.19999\ldots)_{16}$

b) $.875_{10} = (.513)_6$

c) $.2_{10} = (.001100110011\ldots)_2$

Solution: a) To convert fractions from decimal to hexadecimal, we begin the following procedure: Multiply the base you want (in this case 16) by the fraction to be converted.

$$.100 \times 16 = 1.600$$

34

Now, the first digit to the left of the decimal point becomes the first digit to the right of the hexadecimal point. Thus, we begin constructing our hexadecimal fraction with .1 .

Subtract the first digit from the product obtained above.

$$\begin{array}{r} 1.600 \\ -1.000 \\ \hline .600 \end{array}$$

Repeat the multiplication process. Then you will have obtained the next digit of the hexadecimal fraction.

$$.600 \times 16 = 9.600$$

The digit 9 becomes the next digit on the right side of the hexadecimal point. Do the subtraction as before and you will see that our fraction is now .19. The process will repeat infinitely because there will always be a remainder left from the subtraction. Hence, we prove the original equality.

b) In general, we can express a fraction f converted to base b as the following:

$$f = a_{-1} \times b^{-1} + a_{-2} \times b^{-2} + a_{-3} \times b^{-3} + \ldots$$

where a_{-1}, a_{-2},... are digits from 0 to b - 1. If we do this for $.875_{10}$, we get these three steps: Multiplying .875 by 6 yields the integer 5 plus the fraction .250.

Multiplying .250 by 6 yields the integer 1 plus the fraction .500. Multiplying .500 by 6 yields the integer part 3 plus the fraction .000.

Putting this all together, we prove that $.875_{10} = (.513)_6$.

c) Conversions from decimal to binary are simple, but the student often gets caught up in the tedium of writing only 1's and 0's. For this example, we will bore you only with the first four steps, since the digits repeat after that anyway:

Multiplying .2 by 2 yields the integer 0 plus the fraction .4.
Multiplying .4 by 2 yields the integer 0 plus the fraction .8.
Multiplying .8 by 2 yields the integer 1 plus the fraction .6.
Multiplying .6 by 2 yields the integer 1 plus the fraction .2.

Another notation for repeating digits is to draw a line over those digits which repeat. Hence, $.2 = (.00\overline{1100}11)_2$.

RELATED PROGRAMS

• PROBLEM 2-13

Write a program which converts a number in base ten [with value $\leq 2^{20}$] into the corresponding representation in base two.

Solution: The method upon which our solution is based is to subtract off the highest power of two contained in the given number. The remainder then becomes the new number and we continue subtracting off powers of two until the exponent of the power of two subtracted off is zero. Thus, if N, the original number, is given by

$$N = I * (2**E) + R$$

$$(I = \text{integer quotient, } R = \text{remainder}),$$

then we can calculate I from

$$I = INT(N/(2**E)),$$

so that

$$R = N - I*(2**E).$$

R becomes N in the next iteration.

```
1Ø          READ N
2Ø          PRINT N; "BASE TEN = ";
3Ø          FOR  E = 2Ø  TO  Ø  STEP - 1
4Ø          LET  I = INT(N/2↑E)
5Ø          PRINT I;
6Ø          LET  R = N - I*2↑E
7Ø          LET  N = R
8Ø          NEXT E
85          PRINT "BASE TWO"
86          PRINT
9Ø          GO TO 1Ø
1ØØ         DATA 999999., 16
11Ø         END
```

● **PROBLEM** 2-14

Write a subprogram in FORTRAN to add two numbers in any base K. Use the arrays L(I) and M(I) for I = 2,3,4...30 to store the digits of the numbers, saving L(1) and M(1) for the sign. Also let N(I) hold the answer, with N(1) for the sign.

Solution: First you must decide which way the digits are to be added. In other words, you could enter the sum of 4379 + 2512 as either:

	L(2)	L(3)	L(4)	L(5)
	4	3	7	9
+	M(2)	M(3)	M(4)	M(5)
	2	5	1	2

or as

	L(30)	L(29)	L(28)	L(27)
	9	7	3	4
+	M(30)	M(29)	M(28)	M(27)
	2	1	5	2

We will use the latter example, because it leaves us room for an overflow on the final digit. Hence, we need a decrementing loop. Also notice that the maximum number of digits we can have is 28 because of this overflow problem.

```
            SUBROUTINE ADD(L,M,N,K)
            INTEGER L(3Ø), M(3Ø), N(3Ø), K
            NN = 3Ø
            DO 2Ø  J = 2, NN
            I = NN - J + 1
15          N(I) = L(I) + M(I)
            IF (N(I). LT.K) GO TO 2Ø
            N(I) = N(I) - K
            N(I - 1) = L(I - 1) + M(I - 1) + 1
            I = I - 1
            GO TO 15
2Ø          CONTINUE
```

36

Write a FORTRAN subroutine and an accompanying calling program to perform conversions from base 10 to base M, where M ≤ 36.

Solution: We initialize an array, NB, with all the possible characters needed for the different bases. The subprogram runs through the division process for converting between bases (developed earlier), each time calculating a quotient IQUOT and a remainder IREM. The first dividend is the absolute value of N_{10}, placed in location NDIVID. The remainders, integers in base 10 between 0 and n - 1 inclusive, are identified with a corresponding alphanumeric character from NB, as shown by the statement NA(J) = NB(IREM + 1). Then we test the quotient: if it is not zero, it becomes the new dividend NDIVID, and the loop continues.

As written, the subroutine uses remainders to identify with alphanumeric characters. Suppose the remainder is 5 (IREM = 5 when J = 14). Then the statement NA(J) = NB(IREM + 1) causes the contents of NB(6) to be placed in NA(14). The rightmost digits are placed at the higher positions in array NA.

The program looks as follows:

```
          DIMENSION NA(16)
10        READ(2,100) M,N
100       FORMAT(I2,I8)
          IF(M - 1) 15,15,20
15        GO TO 66
20        CALL CONVRT (M,N,NA)
          WRITE(3,101) N, (NA(I), I = 1,16),M
101       FORMAT(1Hb, I6, 13Hb (BASE 10) =, 16A1,7Hb,BASE b,2,1H))
          GO TO 10
          END
          SUBROUTINE CONVRT(M,N,NA)
          DIMENSION NA(16), NB(36)
          DATA NBLANK, MINUS/' ', '-'/
          DATA NB/'0','1','2','3','4','5','6','7','8','9','A','B',
     1    'C','D','E','F','G','H','I','J','L','M','N','O','P','Q',
     2    'R','S','T','U','V','W','X','Y','Z','$'/
          NDIVID = IABS(N)
          J = 16
25        IQUOT = NDIVID/M
          IREM = NDIVID - M*IQUOT
          NA(J) = NB(IREM + 1)
          J = J - 1
          IF (IQUOT) 30,45,30
30        NDIVID = IQUOT
          GO TO 25
45        IF (N) 50,55,55
50        NA(J) = MINUS
          IF (J - 1) 65,65,52
52        J = J - 1
55        DO 60 I = 1,J
          NA(I) = NBLANK
60        CONTINUE
65        RETURN
66        END
```

CHAPTER 3

BOOLEAN ALGEBRA

BOOLEAN ALGEBRA LAWS

● **PROBLEM** 3-1

Translate the following Boolean expressions into Venn diagrams:
a) A + B   (Inclusive OR)
b) A ∘ B   (AND)
c) ~ A   (NOT)

<u>Solution</u>: Venn diagrams offer a pictorial representation of logical
relations. When translating from Boolean algebra, sometimes the notation changes. We will give the diagrams and the alternate notations:
a) The expression A + B is an OR function, also known as the union
of two sets. Elements can be in A, or in B, or in both A and B.
In the Venn diagram of Fig. 1, the shaded area is the area of interest.

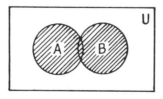

FIG. I

A + B can also be written as AUB, using set notation.

b) The AND function of Boolean algebra is given by A ∘ B. This may
also be considered to be the intersection of sets A and B, written
as A∩B . By definition, an intersection is the set of all elements
contained in both A and B simultaneously. Using a Venn diagram,
we represent it as shown in Fig. 2.

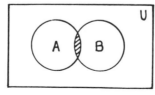

FIG. 2

Again, the shaded area is the part described by the relation A ∘ B
(or A∩B).
c) The NOT function, ~ A, is also known as the complement of a set A.
The complement of a set A includes all elements in the universe that
are not in A. We can write the complement as Ā, and our Venn diagram

is shown in Fig. 3. The shaded area represents Ā.

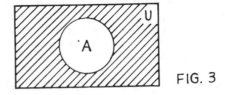

FIG. 3

• **PROBLEM** 3-2

State the basic laws of Boolean algebra.

<u>Solution</u>: If A, B and C are Boolean variables, then the basic laws of Boolean algebras are (where + and • are binary operators representing OR (inclusive) and AND respectively):

1A: A + A = A [Idempotent law for +]
1B: A ∘ A = A [Idempotent law for •]
2A: A + B = B + A [Commutative law for +]
2B: A ∘ B = B ∘ A [Commutative law for •]
3A: A + (B+C) = (A+B) + C [Associative law for +]
3B. A ∘ (B•C) = (A∘B) • C [Associative law for •]
4A: A • (B+C) = (A∘B) + (A•C) [Distributive law for • over +]
4B: A + (B•C) = (A+B) ∘ (A+C) [Distributive law for + over •]
5A: A + 1 = 1 (Law of Union)
5B: A ∘ 0 = 0 (Law of Intersection)
6A: A ∘ 1 = A [1 is the identity element for ∘]
6B: A + 0 = A [0 is the identity element for +]

The laws of ∼ :

7 : ∼(∼ A) = A   [Double Negative Law or Involution Law]
8A: A + ∼A = 1 $\}$
8B: A ∘ ∼ A = 0 $\{$ Law of Complement
9A: ∼(A+B) = ∼ A ∘ ∼ B [deMorgan's law]
9B: ∼(A∘B) = ∼ A + ∼ B [deMorgan's law]

10: $\tilde{1}$ = 0 and $\tilde{0}$ = 1

Any system obeying these laws is known as Boolean algebra. A set with its subsets and the subset operations union and intersect (+ and • , respectively) is a Boolean algebra. The one-to-one correspondence between Boolean expressions and switching circuits suggests that a switching algebra is a Boolean algebra. In fact, 1A - 3B obviously holds true for switching circuits. The switching analog of 4A claims that Fig. 1,

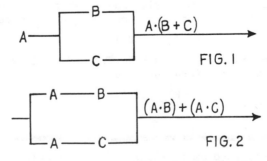

FIG. 1

FIG. 2

and Fig. 2 are equivalent circuits. Since both circuits conduct unless A is open or both B and C are open, they are, in fact, equivalent. Therefore, 4A holds true for switching circuits. And similarly, 4B - 10

can be shown to hold for switching circuits by exhibiting the switching
circuits representing the left and right sides of the equation and showing that the two are equivalent. Once it is shown that all 18 laws hold
for switching circuits, they can be used for simplifying circuits. For
example, 4A and 4B reduce four-switch circuits to three-switch circuits. Actually all 18 laws are not a minimal set of Boolean algebra
laws, since laws 1A, 1B, 3A, 3B, 5A, 5B, 7, 9B and 10 can be derived
from the other laws. For example, once this fact is established, only
8 properties need be satisfied to determine a Boolean algebra, since
the other ten follow immediately. Since the gate elements OR, AND
and NOT are representations of the operations $+$, $\cdot$ and $\sim$ respectively, it follows that a gating algebra is a Boolean algebra. This
fact can be used for simplifying gating circuits. For instance 4A
and 4B reduce 3-gate circuits to 2-gate circuits.

● **PROBLEM** 3-3

Simplify the following expressions according to the commutative law.

a) $A\bar{B} + \bar{B}A + CDE + \bar{C}DE + E\bar{C}D$

b) $AB + AC + BA$

c) $(LMN)(AB)(CDE)(MNL)$

d) $F(K+R) + SV + W\bar{X} + VS + \bar{X}W + (R+K)F$

Solution: The commutative law states that

$$AB = BA \ ; \ A+B = B+A$$

Thus, when logic symbols are ANDed or ORed, the order in which they
are written does not affect their value.

a) Notice that $A\bar{B}$ and $\bar{B}A$ are equal to each other and $\bar{C}DE$ and

$E\bar{C}D$ are equal to each other since only their order is changed. The
idempotent law states that $A+A = A$; $AA = A$. Thus, any term ANDed
or ORed with itself will be equal to itself. The equation is rewritten as

$$A\bar{B} + CDE + \bar{C}DE$$
$$\underbrace{A\bar{B} + \bar{B}A} \quad \underbrace{\bar{C}DE + E\bar{C}D}$$

b) Similarly AB and BA are combined to form AB. Therefore, we get

$$AB + AC$$

c) Remember that the commutative and indempotent laws are also true for
the AND operation. Thus LMN and MNL combine to form LMN

$$(LMN)(AB)(CDE)$$

d) In this case: $F(K+R) = (R+K)F$, $SV = VS$, and $W\bar{X} = \bar{X}W$, again by the
commutative law. Therefore our result is:

$$F(K+R) + SV + W\bar{X}$$

● **PROBLEM** 3-4

Apply DeMorgan's theorem to the following equations:

a) $F = \overline{V + A + L}$

b) $F = \bar{A} + \bar{B} + \bar{C} + \bar{D}$

40

c) $F = \overline{WXYZ}$

d) $F = \overline{ABC} + D$

Solution: DeMorgan's theorem states that a logical expression can be complemented by complementing all its variables and exchanging AND ($\cdot$) operations with OR (+) operations. For example the complement of

$$F = AB$$

is

$$\overline{F} = \overline{A} + \overline{B} .$$

Another expression for F is found by complementing $\overline{F}$.

$$F = \overline{\overline{F}} = \overline{\overline{A} + \overline{B}}$$

Thus

$$\overline{\overline{A} + \overline{B}} = AB$$

a) Complementing variables V,A, and L and changing + to $\cdot$, we get

$$\overline{F} = \overline{V} \cdot \overline{A} \cdot \overline{L} \quad \text{(note } AB = A \cdot B)$$

Complement the entire expression to find F,

$$F' \overline{\overline{F}} = \overline{\overline{V}\ \overline{A}\ \overline{L}} = \overline{V}\ \overline{A}\ \overline{L}$$

Thus,

$$\overline{V + A + L} = \overline{V}\ \overline{A}\ \overline{L}$$

b) Again, complementing A,B,C, and D and changing + to $\cdot$ we get

$$\overline{F} = ABCD$$

$$F = \overline{\overline{F}} = \overline{ABCD}$$

c) This time exchanging $\circ$ for +, we have

$$\overline{F} = \overline{W} + \overline{X} + \overline{Y} + \overline{Z}$$

$$F = \overline{\overline{F}} = \overline{\overline{W} + \overline{X} + \overline{Y} + \overline{Z}}$$

d) This time split the function into two parts

$$F = X + D$$

where $X = \overline{ABC}$. Apply DeMorgan's theorem to X.

$$\overline{X} = \overline{A} + \overline{B} + \overline{C}$$

thus,

$$X = \overline{\overline{A} + \overline{B} + \overline{C}}$$

$$F = \overline{\overline{A} + \overline{B} + \overline{C}} + D$$

● **PROBLEM 3-5**

Simplify the following expressions

a) $A = ST + VW + RST$

b) $A = TUV + XY + Y$

c) $A = F(E + F + G)$

d) $A = (PQ + R + ST)TS$

e) $A = \overline{D}\ \overline{D}\ E$

f) $A = Y(W + X + \overline{\overline{Y} + \overline{Z}})Z$

g) $A = (BE + C + F)C$

Solution: We need the following laws to simplify the expressions:

Idempotent law: $AA = A$
$A + A = A$

Distributive law: $A(B+C) = AB + AC$
$A + BC = (A+B)(A+C)$

Law of Absorption: $A(A+B) = A$
$A + AB = A$

DeMorgan's law : $\overline{AB} = \overline{A} + \overline{B}$
$\overline{A+B} = \overline{A}\ \overline{B}$

a) $A = ST + VW + RST$ is equal to $ST + RST + VW$ by the associative law.
$A = ST(1 + R) + VW$ by distributive law but $1 + R = 1$ by law of union. So,
$$A = ST + VW$$

b) $A = TUV + XY + Y$
Use the law of absorption on XY and Y.
$$A = TUV + Y$$

c) $A = F(E + F + G)$
Use the distributive law,
$$A = FE + FF + FG$$
Use the idempotent law on FF.
$$A = FE + F + FG$$
Use the law of absorption.
$$A = F$$

d) $A = (PQ + R + ST)TS$
Use the distributive law
$$A = TSPQ + TSR + STTS$$
Use the idempotent law on $STTS$.
$$A = TSPQ + TSR + TS$$
Use the law of absorption.
$$A = TS$$

e) $A = \overline{\overline{D}\ \overline{D}\ E}$
Use DeMorgan's law
$$A = D + D + \overline{E}$$
Use the idempotent law on $D + D$.
$$A = D + \overline{E}$$

f) $A = Y(W + X + \overline{\overline{Y} + \overline{Z}})Z$
Use DeMorgan's law on $\overline{\overline{Y} + \overline{Z}}$.

$A = Y(W + X + YZ)Z$
Use the distributive law
$$A = YZW + YZX + YZYZ$$

Use the idempotent law on YZYZ.
$$A = YZW + YZX + YZ$$

Use the law of absorption
$$A = YZ$$

g) A = (BE + C + F)C
Use the distributive law
$$A = CBE + CC + CF$$

Use the idempotent law
$$A = CBE + C + CF$$

Use the law of absorption

$$A = C$$

Although the law of absorption enables us to solve problems somewhat faster, it generally takes the new reader some time to familiarize himself with it. In such cases, even though it may take an extra step or two, you will certainly find that it is less confusing to use the Law of distribution.

• PROBLEM 3-6

Use the laws of Boolean algebra to simplify the following Boolean expression:

$$[(A+B) + (A+C) + (A+D)] \cdot [A \cdot \sim B] \cdot (1)$$

+ is the inclusive OR, · is AND and N is NOT.

Show the switching and gate representations of the resulting expression.

Solution: One suggested plan of attack is to eliminate redundancy in the expression. Since A appears four times, we try to simplify the terms using A. The law that allows each step is given on the right:

$[(A+B) + (A+C) + (A+D)] \cdot [A \cdot \sim B]$

$= [(B+A) + (A+C) + (A+D)] \cdot [A \cdot \sim B]$ Comm. of +

$= [B + (A+A) + C + (A+D)] \cdot [A \cdot \sim B]$ Assoc. of +

$= [B + A + C + (A+D)] \cdot [A \cdot \sim B]$ Idempotent law

$= [B + C + A + (A+D)] \cdot [A \cdot \sim B]$ Comm. of +

$= [B + C + (A+A) + D] \cdot [A \cdot \sim B]$ Assoc. of +

$= [B + C + A + D] \cdot [A \cdot \sim B]$ Idempotent law (1)

Working on B and $\sim$ B,

$(1) = [B + C + A + D] \cdot [\sim B \cdot A]$ Commutativity of ·

$= [(B + C + A + D) \cdot \sim B] \cdot A$ Associativity of ·

$= [(B \cdot \sim B) + (C \cdot \sim B) + (A \cdot \sim B) + (D \cdot \sim B)] \cdot A$

Distributive law of · over +

$= [0 + (C \cdot \sim B) + (A \cdot \sim B) + (D \cdot \sim B)] \cdot A$ Law of complement

43

$$= [(C \cdot \sim B) + (A \cdot \sim B) + (D \cdot \sim B)] \cdot A \quad \text{Identity of} \quad \cdot$$

$$= [(C + A + D) \cdot \sim B) \cdot A \quad \text{Dist. law of} \quad \cdot \quad \text{over} \quad + \quad (2)$$

The switching representation of (2) would be as shown in Fig. 1.

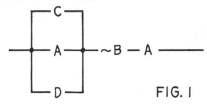

FIG. I

Note that the circuit conducts if and only if both A and $\tilde{B}$ are closed, regardless of the settings of C and D.

The gate representation of (2) would be as shown in Fig. 2.

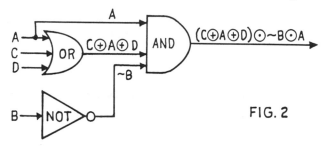

FIG. 2

The reduction of statement (1) to statement (2) was tedious but straightforward. It allows an eight-switch circuit to be replaced by a five-switch circuit, or a seven-gate circuit to be replaced by a three-gate circuit. However, the reduction method depended on observation and a "feel" for algebraic manipulation. Fortunately, minimization algorithms exist which do not depend on such subjective methods and can, in fact, be implemented on a computer.

● **PROBLEM 3-7**

It can be shown that the set of operations $S = \{ +, \cdot, \sim \}$ is functionally complete. That is, every Boolean function can be represented by a form $f(x_1, \ldots, x_n)$ in variables $x_1, \ldots, x_n$ and operations $+$, $\cdot$, $\sim$. Equivalently, the set of gates $S^1 = \{OR, AND, NOT\}$ is functionally complete. Show that:

(a) $S_1 = \{ +, \sim \}$

(b) $S_0 = \{ \cdot, \sim \}$

(c) $S_3 = \{\uparrow\}$ where $x_1 \uparrow x_2 = \sim(x_1 \cdot x_2)$ (1)

(d) $S_4 = \{\downarrow\}$ where $x_1 \downarrow x_2 = \sim(x_1 + x_2)$ (2)

are functionally complete.

Solution: (a) It is sufficient to show that we can construct the $\cdot$ operation from S_1, since we know that $S = \{ +, \cdot, \sim \}$ is functionally complete. DeMorgan's law suggests itself here:

$$\sim(A \cdot B) = \sim A + \sim B \qquad 9B$$

44

Applying the $\sim$ operator to both sides and using the involution law for the left side, we get:

$$A \cdot B = \sim [\sim (A \cdot B)] = \sim [\sim A + \sim B]$$

Hence, $S_1 = \{+, \sim\}$ is functionally complete. The gate representation of

$$A \cdot B = \sim [\sim A + \sim B]$$

is shown in figure 1

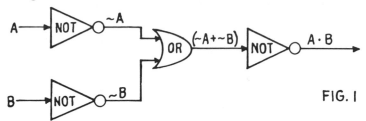

FIG. I

This means that every gating function can be implemented by a network of OR and NOT gates, by substituting the network of fig. 1 for any AND gate in the original OR-AND-NOT network.

(b) It is sufficient to show that we can construct the $+$ operation from S_2. But DeMorgan's law states that:

$$\sim(A + B) = \sim A \cdot \sim B$$

Applying the $\sim$ operator to both sides and using the involution law for the left side, we get:

$$A + B = \sim[\sim(A + B)] = \sim[\sim A \cdot \sim B]$$

Hence, $S_2 = \{\cdot, \sim\}$ is functionally complete. The gate representation of

$$A + B = \sim[\sim A \cdot \sim B]$$

is shown in fig. 2 .

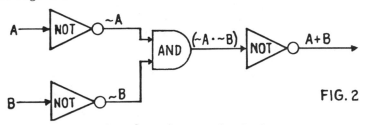

FIG. 2

This means that every gating function can be implemented by a network of AND and NOT gates.

(c) The $\uparrow$ operator is called the Shaeffer stroke function and its associated gate is a NAND(for NOT-AND) gate. It is sufficient to show that we can construct $S_2 = \{\cdot, \sim\}$ from the stroke function alone, since it has already been shown that S_2 is functionally complete. The idempotent law for $\cdot$ allows substitution of $x_1 \cdot x_1$ for x_1 so that:

$$\sim x_1 = \sim(x_1 \cdot x_1)$$

But from the definition of the stroke function, equation (1), we have:

$$\sim(x_1 \cdot x_1) = x_1 \uparrow x_1$$

Therefore, $\sim x_1 = x_1 \uparrow x_1$. $\qquad\qquad$ (3)

To obtain $\cdot$ from the stroke function, recall that the involution law allows us to write:

$$x_1 \cdot x_2 = \sim[\sim(x_1 \cdot x_2)]$$

But from the definition of the stroke function, equation (1), we have:

$$\sim[\sim(x_1 \cdot x_2)] = \sim[x_1 \uparrow x_2]$$

Using the result obtained in equation (3), we can write:

$$\sim[x_1 \uparrow x_2] = (x_1 \uparrow x_2) \uparrow (x_1 \uparrow x_2)$$

Therefore, $$x_1 \cdot x_2 = (x_1 \uparrow x_2) \uparrow (x_1 \uparrow x_2) \qquad (4)$$

and S_3 is functionally complete. The gate representation of equation (3) is shown in fig. 3.

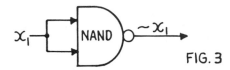

FIG. 3

The gate representation of equation (4) is shown in fig. 4.

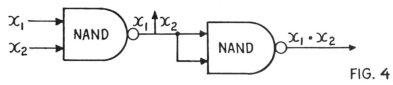

FIG. 4

This means that every gating function can be implemented by a network of NAND gates only.

(d)   The $\downarrow$ operator is called the NOR (from NOT-OR) function and its associated gate is a NOR gate. It is sufficient to show that we can construct the $S_1 = \{ + , \sim \}$ from the NOR function alone. Using the idempotent law for $+$ and the definition of the NOR function, equation (2), we can write:

$$\sim x_1 = \sim(x_1 + x_1)$$
$$= x_1 \downarrow x_1 \qquad (5)$$

To obtain $+$ from the NOR function, we apply the involution law and use the definition of the NOR function and equation (5):

$$x_1 + x_2 = \sim[\sim(x_1 + x_2)]$$
$$= \sim[x_1 \downarrow x_2]$$
$$= [x_1 \downarrow x_2] \downarrow [x_1 \downarrow x_2] \qquad (6)$$

Hence, $S_4 = \{\downarrow\}$ is functionally complete. The gate representation of equation (5) is shown in fig. 5

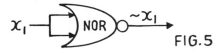

FIG. 5

The gate representation of equation (6) is shown in fig. 6

46

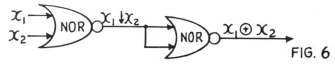

FIG. 6

Every gating function can be implemented by a network of NOR gates only: Though, for simplicity, only two variables were used in showing the functional completeness of $S_1 - S_4$, the results can be shown to be true for any number of variables by a simple induction argument.

EQUIVALENCE & EXCLUSIVE-OR FUNCTIONS

● **PROBLEM** 3-8

Obtain expressions for the exclusive-OR and the equivalence functions of two variables A and B.

Solution: The Exclusive-OR function is defined as a function which gives an output 1 whenever either A or B is 1, but gives an output 0 whenever A and B are both 1 or both 0.

The equivalence function of two variables A and B is defined as a function which gives an output 1 whenever both A and B are equal (both 1 or both 0), but gives an output 0 whenever A and B are unequal.

These two functions can be represented by a Truth Table as follows: If A and B are binary variables, they can be represented in 4 different ways, giving us the 4 rows in the Truth Table. The Truth Table is shown in figure 1.

Col. 1		Col. 2	Col. 3
VARIABLES		EXCLUSIVE-OR	EQUIVALENCE
A	B	$A \times B$	$A \equiv B$
0	0	0	1
0	1	1	0
1	0	1	0
1	1	0	1

We note from the Truth Table of fig. 1 that the exclusive-OR:and the equivalence functions are complements of each other.

Also, from the Truth Table, we can write the equations:

a)   Expressions for exclusive-OR

$A \times B = A' \cdot B + A \cdot B'$. (This is a sum of products form of the expression obtained by considering entries of column 2 which are equal to 1). Also,

$A \times B = (A+B) \cdot (A'+B')$. (This is a product of sums form, obtained by considering entries of column two which are equal to 0.)

b)   Expressions for Equivalence:

$A \equiv B = A' \cdot B' + A \cdot B$ (Sum of products form)

$A \equiv B = (A+B') \cdot (A'+B)$. (Product of sums form)

We shall now realize the exclusive-OR and the equivalence functions, using a)   NAND gates only, and, b) NOR gates only.

(a)

$$[A\cdot(A\cdot B)']' = A' + A\cdot B = A' + B = (A\cdot B')'$$

$[(A\cdot B)'\cdot B)]' = A\cdot B + B' = A + B' = (A'\cdot B)'$

$$[(A\cdot B')'\cdot(A'\cdot B)']'$$
$$= A\cdot B' + A'\cdot B$$
(EXCLUSIVE-OR)

$$[A\cdot B' + A'\cdot B]' = (A\cdot B')'\cdot(A'\cdot B)'$$
$$= (A'+B)\cdot(A+B')$$
(EQUIVALENCE)

(b)

$$[A + (A+B)']' = A'\cdot(A+B) = A'\cdot B$$

$[(A+B)'+B)]' = (A+B)\cdot B' = A\cdot B'$

$$[A'\cdot B + A\cdot B']'$$
$$= (A'\cdot B)'\cdot(A\cdot B')'$$
$$= (A+B')\cdot(A'+B)$$
(EQUIVALENCE)

$$[A'\cdot B + A\cdot B']$$
(EXCLUSIVE-OR)

● **PROBLEM 3-9**

The equivalence (also called biconditional) function of x_1, x_2, written
$x_1 \equiv x_2$ (or $x_1 \Leftrightarrow x_2$), is defined as:

$$x_1 \equiv x_2 = (\sim x_1 + x_2)\cdot(x_1 + \sim x_2) \tag{1}$$

a) The + operator denotes the inclusive OR function here; · represents
AND and ~ representes the negation operator. Set up the truth table
for the equivalence function.

b) Use AND, OR and NOT gates to evaluate the equivalence function.

Solution: (a)   The truth table is set up by first specifying the possible combinations of values of x_1 and x_2 . There are $2^2 = 4$ of
them and they represent the numbers 0 to 3 in the binary system.
The next step is to evaluate the terms of statement (1):

x_1	x_2	$\sim x_1$	$\sim x_2$	$\sim x_1 + x_2$	$x_1 + \sim x_2$
0	0	1	1	1	1
0	1	1	0	1	0
1	0	0	1	0	1
1	1	0	0	1	1

Now transfer columns 1,2,5, and 6 to a truth table evaluating statement
(1):

x_1	x_2	$\sim x_1 + x_2$	$x_1 + \sim x_2$	$x_1 \equiv x_2 = (\sim x_1 + x_2)\cdot(x_1 + \sim x_2)$
0	0	1	1	1
0	1	1	0	0
1	0	0	1	0
1	1	1	1	1

Note that $x_1 \equiv x_2 = 1$ if and only if $x_1 = x_2$, which is why it is called the equivalence function.

(b) Recall that variables which are operands of the + operation are inputs to an OR gate and a variable that is the operand of the ~ operation is the input to a NOT gate. Thus, the gate representations of the terms in parentheses are as shown in Fig. 1.

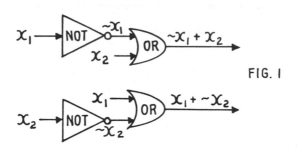

FIG. 1

Since each term is an operand of the · operation, each of the above gate circuits is an input to an AND gate. Thus, the gating circuit of statement (1) is as shown in Fig. 2.

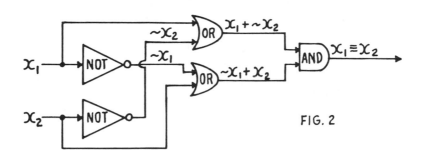

FIG. 2

Note that the output of this network is 1 if and only if $x_1 = x_2$.

Thus, the network acts as a comparing device. Specifically, it is the circuit for an equality comparator. An equality comparator compares one bit, x_1, with another bit, x_2. If two strings of bits are to be compared, they could be compared serially. That is, compare a bit in the first position of the first string with a bit in the first position of the second string, then compare a bit in the next position of the first string with a bit in the next position if the second string and continue until either a zero is output, indicating the strings are not equal, or all positions have been compared, indicating the strings are equal. Or they could be compared in parallel. That is, a parallel comparing device that inputs two strings of length n would have n equality comparators. An output of a string of ones indicates that the two inputs are equal. The advantage of parallel comparing is its higher speed compared with series comparison. It will always require k time units to compare strings where k is the operation time of the equality comparator. The series comparator requires n·k time units at worst and k time units at best. The advantage of the series comparator is its economy. But since gates can be manufactured inexpensively, no commercial computer would use a series comparator, since every instruction must be identified by using the comparator and hence, there would be a serious loss of speed.

49

Represent the exclusive-OR function, using
a) NAND gates only
b) NOR gates only
Sketch the circuit realizations in each case.

Solution: a) Exclusive-OR realization using NAND gates only:
The exclusive-OR function can be written as

$$A \times B = A \cdot B' + A' \cdot B \qquad \text{[Using the Sum of Products form]}$$

$$= [(\underline{A \cdot B}' + \underline{A' \circ B})']' \quad \text{[Complementing Twice]}$$

$$= [(A \cdot B')' \cdot (A' \circ B)']' \quad \text{[Applying deMorgan's Rules on the inner primed bracket]}$$

$$= [(A \uparrow B') \uparrow (A' \uparrow B)] \quad \text{[Using the Shaeffer stroke notation]}.$$

We assume that both unprimed variables (A,B) and primed variables
(A',B') are available as inputs. Note that the outer bracket represents
a NAND function of the two inner brackets. Each inner bracket is a
NAND function of two variables each.

The circuit realization is shown in figure 1.

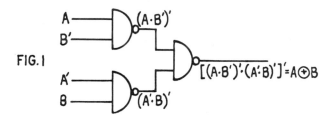

FIG. I

b) Exclusive-OR realization using NOR gates only. We can write:
$$A \times B = (A+B) \cdot (A'+B') \qquad \text{[Using a Product of Sums form]}$$

$$= [((A+B) \cdot (A'+B'))']' \quad \text{[Complementing twice]}$$

$$= [(A+B)' + (A'+B')']' \quad \text{[Applying DeMorgan's Rules on the inner primed bracket]}$$

$$= [(A \downarrow B) \downarrow (A' \downarrow B')] \quad \text{[Using the Pierce Arrow notation]}.$$

Observe that in the last two steps the outer square bracket represents
a NOR function of the two inner brackets, each of which is a NOR
function of two variables.

The circuit realization using NOR gates only is shown in figure 2.

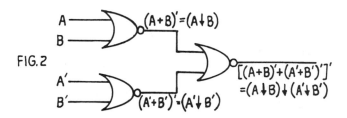

FIG. 2

50

Represent the equivalence function circuit realizations, using:
a)   NAND gates only
b)   NOR gates only

Solution: a)   Using NAND gates:
  The equivalence function can be written as:

$A \equiv B = A \cdot B + A' \cdot B'$ [Using the Sum of Products form]

  $= [(A \cdot B + A' \cdot B')']'$ [Complementing twice]

  $= [(A \cdot B)' \circ (A' \cdot B')']'$ [Applying DeMorgan's Rules]

  $= (A {\uparrow} B) {\uparrow} (A' {\uparrow} B')$ [Using the Shaeffer stroke notation]

The circuit realization is shown in fig. 1 .

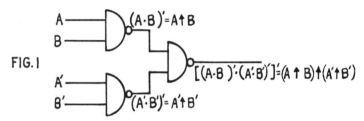

FIG. 1

b)   Using NOR gates:

  We can write

$A \equiv B = (A + B') \cdot (A' + B)$ [Using the Product of Sums form]

  $= [((A + B') \circ (A' + B))']'$ [Complementing twice]

  $= [(A + B')'; + (A' + B)']'$ [Applying DeMorgan's rule to the inner primed bracket]

  $= [(A {\downarrow} B') {\downarrow} (A' {\downarrow} B)]$.

The circuit realization is shown in figure 2.

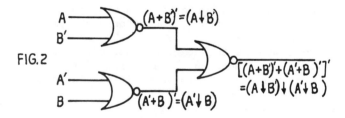

FIG. 2

TRUTH TABLES

(a)   Set up the truth table for each of the following Boolean expressions:

  (i) $\sim A$

  (ii)   A + B   (inclusive or)

  (iii) A $\cdot$ B   (and)

<u>Solution</u>: (a) A truth table is set up by specifying all the possible combinations of values of the Boolean variables, then evaluating each term according to the rule of relation of the operation. There are 2 possible values for each variable: 0 or 1. Then, if there are n variables, there will be 2^n possible combinations of the variables, and therefore, the truth table will have 2^n rows of entries.

(i)   Since there is only one variable, the truth table has only $2^1 = 2$ rows of entries.

A	$\sim$ A
0	1
1	0

The $\sim$ operation (called complement or invertion) changes 0 to 1 or 1 to 0.

(ii)   Since there are 2 variables, the truth table has $2^2 = 4$ rows of entries:

A	B	A + B
0	0	0
0	1	1
1	0	1
1	1	1

The + operation (called disjunction) yields a value of 0 if and only if both variables have a value of 0. Otherwise, it yields a value of 1.

(iii)   Since there are 2 variables, the truth table has $2^2 = 4$ rows of entries.

A	B	A $\cdot$ B
0	0	0
0	1	0
1	0	0
1	1	1

The $\cdot$ operation (called conjunction) yields a value of 1 if and only if both variables have a value of 1. Otherwise, it yields a value of 0.

(b) There is a one-to-one correspondence between Boolean expressions and switching circuits. An open switch or nonconductor can represent the 0-condition and a closed switch or conductor can represent the 1-condition.

Boolean algebra can be used to determine what circuits are necessary to perform a specific logic function. The action of a two-position switch with an open position and a closed position can be represented by a Boolean variable.

(i) If A represents a switch in the closed position, then $\sim$ A would represent the same switch in the open position, as shown in figure 1.

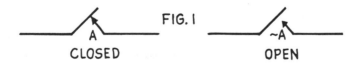

FIG. I

CLOSED   OPEN

(ii) The + operation yields a value of 0 if and only if both variables have a value of 0. Therefore, the switching circuit needed to perform the + operation must be open (nonconducting) if and only if both switches are open. The parallel connection is the switching circuit realization of the + operation; as shown in figure 2.

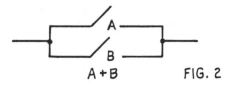

A + B   FIG. 2

(iii) The · operation yields a value of 1 if and only if both variables have a value of 1. The switching circuit needed to perform the · operation, therefore, must be closed (conducting) if and only if both switches are closed. The series connection is the switching circuit realization of the · operation, as shown in figure 3.

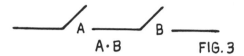

A·B   FIG. 3

(c) Gates are switches that are sensitive to high and low voltages. If 0 represents a low voltage and 1 represents a high voltage, the output of a gate is either 0 or 1, depending on the type of gate.

(i) The ~ operation changes 0 to 1 and 1 to 0. The gate needed to perform the ~ operation, therefore, must output a 1 for a 0 input and output a 0 for a 1 input. This is the operation of a NOT gate shown in figure 4.

FIG. 4

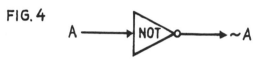

(ii) An OR-gate outputs a 0 if and only if all inputs are 0. Otherwise, it outputs a 1. This corresponds to the + operation and is shown in figure 5.

FIG. 5

FIG. 6

(iii) An AND-gate outputs a 1 if and only if all inputs are 1. Otherwise, it outputs a 0. This corresponds to the · operation; shown in figure 6.

● **PROBLEM** 3-13

(a) Evaluate the following statement by using a truth table:

$$[(A + B) + (A + C) + (A + D)] \cdot [A \cdot \sim B] \tag{1}$$

The + operator denotes the inclusive OR function and the · operator denotes the AND function. NOT is represented by ~ .

(b) Change statement (1) into its equivalent switching circuit.

(c) Show the gate representation of statement (1).

Solution: (a) Set up the truth table by specifying all possible combinations of A,B,C, and D and evaluating the terms of the statement for each combination. Since there are 4 variables, the truth

53

table has $2^4 = 16$ rows of entries as shown in figure 1. First, evaluate the innermost terms:

A	B	~B	C	D	A + B	A · ~ B	A + C	A + D
0	0	1	0	0	0	0	0	0
0	0	1	0	1	0	0	0	1
0	0	1	1	0	0	0	1	0
0	0	1	1	1	0	0	1	1
0	1	0	0	0	1	0	0	0
0	1	0	0	1	1	0	0	1
0	1	0	1	0	1	0	1	0
0	1	0	1	1	1	0	1	1
1	0	1	0	0	1	1	1	1
1	0	1	0	1	1	1	1	1
1	0	1	1	0	1	1	1	1
1	0	1	1	1	1	1	1	1
1	1	0	0	0	1	0	1	1
1	1	0	0	1	1	0	1	1
1	1	0	1	0	1	0	1	1
1	1	0	1	1	1	0	1	1

Fig. 1

Now, transfer the results in columns 6,8, and 9 to a second truth table, shown in figure 2 which evaluates the first bracketed term.

A + B	A + C	A + D	(A + B)+(A + C) + (A + D)
0	0	0	0
0	0	1	1
0	1	0	1
0	1	1	1
1	0	0	1
1	0	1	1
1	1	0	1
1	1	1	1
1	1	1	1
1	1	1	1
1	1	1	1
1	1	1	1
1	1	1	1
1	1	1	1
1	1	1	1
1	1	1	1

Fig. 2

Finally, transfer the result in the last column of this truth table and the result in column 7 of the first truth table to a third truth table, shown in figure 3, which evaluates the entire statement (1).

A · ~ B	(A + B) + (A + C) + (A + D)	Statement (1)
0	0	0
0	1	0
0	1	0
0	1	0
0	1	0
0	1	0
0	1	0
0	1	0

1	1	1
1	1	1
1	1	1
1	1	1
0	1	0
0	1	0
0	1	0
0	1	0

Fig. 3

The entry in each row of column 3 is the result of performing the ·
operation on the entries in columns 1 and 2 of that row.

(b)   The switching circuit equivalent to statement (1) is obtained
by connecting, in parallel, variables which are operands of the +
operation and connecting, in series, variables which are operands of
the · operation.   First, find equivalent switching circuits for
the innermost terms.   These are shown in figure 4.

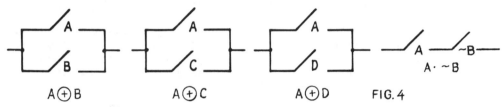

A⊕B   A⊕C   A⊕D   FIG.4

The switching circuit equivalent to the first bracketed term is a
parallel connection of the three parallel circuits A + B, A + C,
A + D, as shown in figure 5.

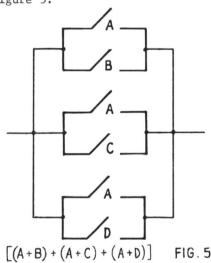

$[(A+B) + (A+C) + (A+D)]$ FIG. 5

The switching circuit equivalent to statement (1) is a series connection of the parallel circuit

$$[(A + B) + (A + C) + (A + D)]$$

and the series circuit $[A \cdot \sim B]$.   The complete switching circuit
is shown in figure 6.

$$[(A + B) + (A + C) + (A + D)] \cdot [A \cdot \sim B]$$

Note that the circuit conducts if and only if A is closed and B is
open, regardless of the settings of C and D.   This agrees with the
truth table, since statement (1) has value if and only if A = 1 and
B = 0.

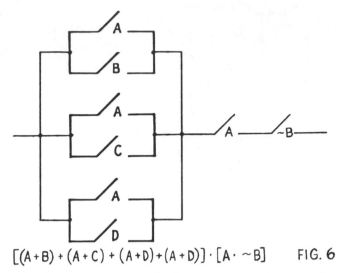

$$[(A+B)+(A+C)+(A+D)+(A+D)]\cdot[A\cdot\sim B]\qquad\text{FIG. 6}$$

(c) Variables which are operands of the + operation are inputs to an OR gate. Variables which are operands of the · operation are inputs to an AND gate. A variable that is the operand of the ~ operation is the input to a NOT gate. The gate representation of the terms in parentheses are shown in figure 7.

FIG. 7

The composition of 2 operations is done by plugging the output of 1 gate into the input of another, so that the gate representation of [A · ~ B] is shown in figure 8.

FIG.8

Finally, by the same reasoning, the complete gate representation of

$$[(A + B) + (A + C) + (A + D)] \cdot [A \cdot \sim B]$$

is shown in figure 9.

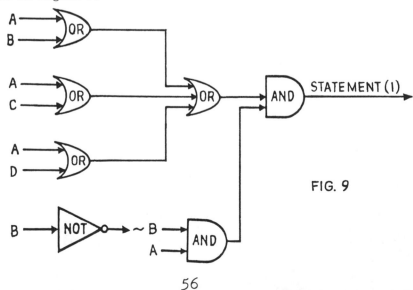

FIG. 9

Explain the properties of NAND gates, and use NAND gates to generate
AND, OR, and NOT operations. Draw the symbol diagrams, and give truth
tables for each operation.

FIG. 1

Solution: The NAND gate is a combination of an AND gate followed by a
NOT gate. In fig. 1 the structure of a NAND gate is shown. The key to
understanding a NAND gate is to notice that the output is 0 if and
only if its inputs are simultaneously 1.
The Truth table of the NAND gate is given in fig. 2.

a	b	a b	f(a,b)
0	0	0	1
0	1	0	1
1	0	0	1
1	1	1	0

$$f(a,b) = \overline{ab}$$

Fig. 2

NAND gates are usually represented as in fig. 3 when used in circuit
diagrams;
Several other interesting properties of NAND gates are;

$$f(a,b) = \overline{ab} = \bar{a} + \bar{b} \qquad \text{(DeMorgan's Law)}$$

$$f(a,a) = \bar{a} + \bar{a} = \bar{a}$$

$$f(\bar{a},\bar{b}) = \overline{\bar{a}\bar{b}} = a + b \qquad \text{(DeMorgan's Law)}$$

(NAND GATE)

FIG. 3

A NAND gate with both of its inputs the same acts like a NOT gate.
This idea is illustrated in fig. 4. Truth table for the gate illustrated
in fig. 4 is shown in fig. 5.

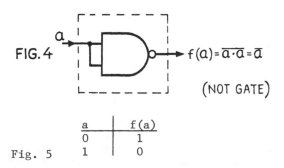

FIG. 4

$$f(a) = \overline{a \cdot a} = \bar{a}$$

(NOT GATE)

a	f(a)
0	1
1	0

Fig. 5

Use of NAND gates to generate AND operations;

Two NAND gates connected as shown in fig. 6 generate an AND operation
at the output. Since AND gates have the truth table shown in fig. 7.

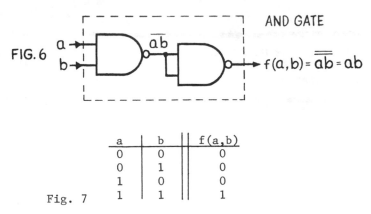

FIG. 6   AND GATE

$$f(a,b) = \overline{\overline{ab}} = ab$$

a	b	f(a,b)
0	0	0
0	1	0
1	0	0
1	1	1

Fig. 7

It can easily be verified that the output in fig. 4 has the same operation. When inputs a and b are both 0, output of the first NAND gate is 1. This output is the input of the second NAND gate, therefore both inputs to the second NAND gate are 1. The output of this NAND gate then is found to be 0, from the definition of NAND gates.

The OR gate can be obtained from three NAND gates, connected as shown in fig. 8.

OR GATE OPERATION

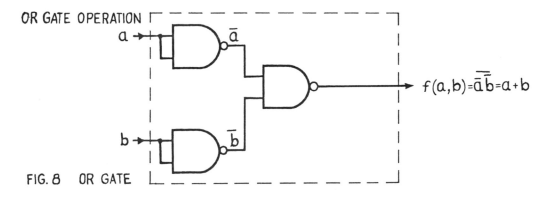

$$f(a,b) = \overline{\overline{a}\,\overline{b}} = a + b$$

FIG. 8   OR GATE

When inputs a and b are both 0, the input to the third NAND gate is 1 1 and its output is 0. In all the other input combinations the output will be 1. The truth table of the OR gate is given in fig. 9.

a	b	f(a,b)
0	0	0
0	1	1
1	0	1
1	1	1

Fig. 9

● **PROBLEM** 3-15

Explain the operation of NOR gates, and generate OR, NOT, and AND operations using NOR gates. Draw symbol diagrams, and explain the functions of each system with the help of truth tables.

Solution: The NOR gate is derived by combining the functions of an OR operator followed by a NOT operator. The key to remembering the function of a NOR gate is the first row of the truth table of fig. 1;

a	b	a + b	f(a,b)
0	0	0	1
0	1	1	0
1	0	1	0
1	1	1	0

Fig. 1

$$f(a,b) = \overline{a+b}$$

The output of a NOR gate is 1 if and only if both inputs are simultaneously 0. The block diagram of a NOR gate is shown in fig. 2.

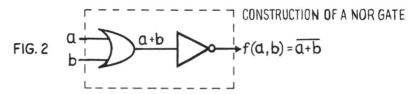

CONSTRUCTION OF A NOR GATE

FIG. 2

NOR gates may also be used to generate AND, OR, and NOT operations. As seen in fig. 3, an OR gate can be constructed using two NOR gates.

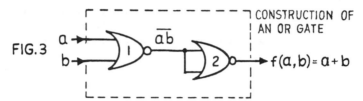

CONSTRUCTION OF AN OR GATE

FIG. 3

When the inputs a and b into gate 1 are both 0, the output of gate 1 (which is the input of gate 2) is 1. Therefore, the output of gate 2 is 0, following the truth table given for NOR gates. When one or both inputs are 1 the output of the OR gate is 0. The truth table of fig. 3(a) illustrates this principle throughly;

a	b	f(a,b)
0	0	0
0	1	1
1	0	1
1	1	1

Fig. 3(a)

$$f(a,b) = a + b$$

Construction of a NOT gate using NOR gates:

FIG. 4 NOT GATE

$$f(a) = \overline{a+a} = \overline{a}$$

Operation of the circuit in fig. 4 is illustrated by its truth table given in fig. 5;

a	f(a)
0	1
1	0

Fig. 5

Fig. 6 shows the construction of an AND gate using NOR gates. 1st and 2nd NOR gates act as NOT gates and supply $\overline{a}$, and $\overline{b}$ into the third NOR gate. The output of this gate is then; $f(a,b) = \overline{\overline{a} + \overline{b}} = ab$, by the use of DeMorgan's Law.

59

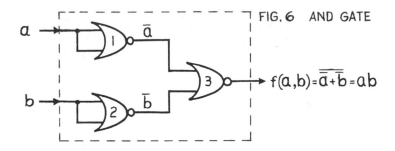

FIG.6 AND GATE

$$f(a,b)=\overline{\overline{a}+\overline{b}}=ab$$

MINIMIZATION

● **PROBLEM** 3-16

a) Carefully examine the given switching network, find its output, and explain each operation.
b) Draw an equivalent network which will give the same output function as in part (a), using the minimum amount of gates.

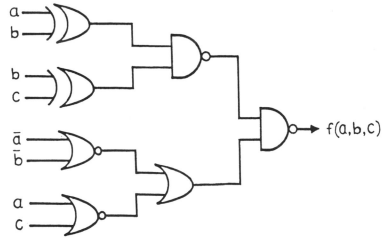

$$f(a,b,c)$$

Solution: The circuit and the output of each gate is shown in fig. 1. Gates 1 and 2 are EXCLUSIVE OR gates, 3 and 4 are NOR gates, 5 is an OR gate, 6, and 7 NAND gates.
     The output of gate 7 is determined by the use of outputs of gates 5, and 6, and according to the definition of NAND gates (i.e., $f(a,b) = \overline{ab}$). Therefore the output function $f(a,b,c)$ is:

$$f(a,b,c) = \overline{(a\oplus b)(b\oplus c) \cdot \overline{\overline{a} + \overline{b} + \overline{a + c}}}$$.

By the use of Boolean algebra theorems, this function can be reduced as follows:

$$f(a,b,c) = \overline{(a\oplus b)(b\oplus c)} + \overline{\overline{\overline{a} + \overline{b}} + \overline{a + c}} \quad \text{(DeMorgan's Law)}$$

$$= \overline{(a\oplus b)(b\oplus c)} + (\overline{a} + \overline{b})\cdot(a + c) \quad \text{(DeMorgan's Law)}$$

$$= (a\overline{b} + \overline{a}b)(b\overline{c} + \overline{b}c) + (\overline{a} + \overline{b})(a + c) \quad \text{(Definition of Exclusive OR function)}$$

$$= a\overline{b}b\overline{c} + a\overline{b}\overline{b}c + \overline{a}bb\overline{c} + \overline{a}b\overline{b}c + (\overline{a} + \overline{b})(a + c) \quad \text{(Distributive Property)}$$

60

$$= 0 + a\underline{bc} + \overline{ab}\overline{c} + 0 + \overline{b}a + \overline{b}c + \overline{a}c \quad \text{(Negation Laws)}$$

$$= a\underline{bc} + \overline{ab}\overline{c} + \overline{a}c + a\overline{b} \quad \text{(Identity Laws)}$$

$$= \overline{b}c + \overline{ab}\overline{c} + \overline{a}c + a\overline{b} \quad \text{(DeMorgan's Law)}$$

$$= \overline{b}c + \overline{a}b + \overline{a}c + a\overline{b} \quad \text{(DeMorgan's Law)}$$

$$= \overline{b}c + \overline{a}b + a\overline{b} \quad \text{(DeMorgan's Law)}$$

$$= \overline{b}c + a \oplus b \quad \text{(Definition of exclusive OR)}$$

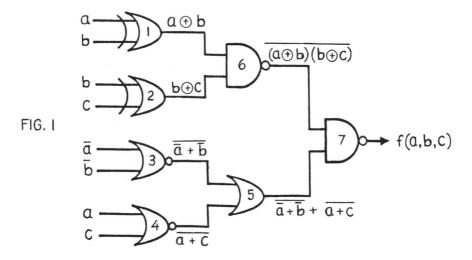

FIG. I

This final function can now be translated into a switching network by
the use of AND, OR, and EXCLUSIVE OR gates.

The first term $\overline{b}c$ can be obtained by an AND gate, and the second
term with an Exclusive OR gate. These functions then must be added by
the use of an OR gate. The equivalent switching network and its truth
table is given in fig. 2. Note that original and the equivalent
circuits both give the same results, only the latter is in reduced form.

a	b	c	$\overline{b}c$	$a \oplus b$	$f(a,b,c)$
0	0	0	0	0	0
0	0	1	1	0	1
0	1	0	0	1	1
0	1	1	0	1	1
1	0	0	0	1	1
1	0	1	1	1	1
1	1	0	0	0	0
1	1	1	0	0	0

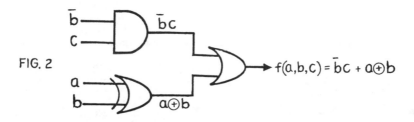

FIG. 2

Given the function f(x,y,z) below, write f(x,y,z) as a sum of minterms.

$$f(x,y,z) = x\bar{z} + y\bar{z} + xyz$$

<u>Solution</u>: If a switching function is given in Sum of Products form, it may be expanded to the canonical Sum of Products through repeated use of the Theorem below.

THEOREM 1: $ab + a\bar{b} = a$

Therefore given the function $f(x,y,z) = x\bar{z} + y\bar{z} + xyz$, $f(x,y,z) = xy\bar{z} + x\bar{y}\bar{z} + y\bar{z} + xyz$ can be obtained, by using theorem 1, and saying $x\bar{z} = xy\bar{z} + x\bar{y}\bar{z}$. Using Theorem 1 a second time and making the equality $y\bar{z} = xy\bar{z} + \bar{x}y\bar{z}$, the function f(x,y,z) becomes:

$$f(x,y,z) = xy\bar{z} + x\bar{y}\bar{z} + xy\bar{z} + \bar{x}y\bar{z} + xyz$$

At this point a second theorem may be used to reduce the number of terms present;

THEOREM 2: $a + a = a$

In the final form of the function it can easily be seen that the first and the third terms are in the same form, $xy\bar{z}$. Using Theorem 2 these terms can be reduced as follows;
$$xy\bar{z} + xy\bar{z} = xy\bar{z}$$

then the final form of the function is;
$$f(x,y,z) = xy\bar{z} + x\bar{y}\bar{z} + \bar{x}y\bar{z} + xyz .$$

After the desired reduced form is obtained where each term has the same number of variables, a special minterm code is used to CODE the function. Minterm code is basically giving a value of 1 for each true variable, and a value of 0 for each false variable. Taking this definition and applying it to the function gives;

$$xy\bar{z} + x\bar{y}\bar{z} + \bar{x}y\bar{z} + xyz$$

$$110 \quad 100 \quad 010 \quad 111 \qquad \text{(minterm code)}$$

In decimal arithmetic these terms represent the numbers 6,4,2, and 7. Therefore the desired Sum of Minterms form is written as;

$$f(x,y,z) = m_6 + m_4 + m_2 + m_7$$

or

$$f(x,y,z) = \Sigma m\ (2,4,6,7)$$

Given the function f(x,y,z) below, write f(x,y,z) as a product of maxterms.
$$f(x,y,z) = (z + \bar{x})(y + \bar{z})(x + y + z)(\bar{x} + \bar{y})$$

<u>Solution</u>: If a switching function is specified in Product of Sum form, then it may be expanded to canonical PS form by repeatedly using the theorem given below.

THEOREM: $(a + b)(a + \bar{b}) = a$

Note: in the original function $f(x,y,z)$, the first, second, and the fourth terms can be changed using the theorem defined above. These changes will be;

$$(z + \bar{x}) = (\bar{x} + y + z)(\bar{x} + \bar{y} + z)$$

$$(y + \bar{z}) = (x + y + \bar{z})(\bar{x} + y + \bar{z})$$

$$(\bar{x} + \bar{y}) = (\bar{x} + \bar{y} + z)(\bar{x} + \bar{y} + \bar{z})$$

then the function $f(x,y,z)$ becomes;

$$f(x,y,z) = (\bar{x} + y + z)(\bar{x} + \bar{y} + z)(x + y + \bar{z})$$

$$\cdot \; (\bar{x} + y + \bar{z})(\bar{x} + \bar{y} + z)(\bar{x} + \bar{y} + \bar{z})$$

$$\circ \; (x + y + z)$$

this is the desired final form of the function, now it can be translated into MAXTERM code by assigning 1's to false variables, and 0's to true variables. This procedure of coding MAXTERMS is illustrated below using the function $f(x,y,z)$;

$$f(x,y,z) = (\bar{x} + y + z)(\bar{x} + \bar{y} + z)(x + y + \bar{z})$$
$$\qquad\qquad\quad 1 \quad 0 \quad\;\; 0 \quad 1 \quad 1 \quad\; 1 \quad 0 \quad\; 0 \quad 1$$

$$(\bar{x} + y + \bar{z})(\bar{x} + \bar{y} + z)(\bar{x} + \bar{y} + \bar{z})$$
$$\; 1 \quad 0 \quad 1 \quad 1 \quad\; 1 \quad 0 \quad 1 \quad\; 1 \quad 1$$

$$(x + y + z)$$
$$\; 0 \quad 0 \quad 0$$

In decimal arithmetic each code group represents numbers such as 4,7,1,5,6,0, with the redundant 7 being used only once, and the solution can be written as;

$$f(x,y,z) = M_4 \; M_7 \; M_1 \; M_5 \; M_6 \; M_0$$

or

$$f(x,y,z) = \prod M(0,1,4,5,6,7)$$

● **PROBLEM** 3-19

Minimize the given minterm function $f(A,B,C,D)$ via the Karnaugh map.

$$f(A,B,C,D) = \Sigma m(0,1,3,8,9,11,13,14)$$

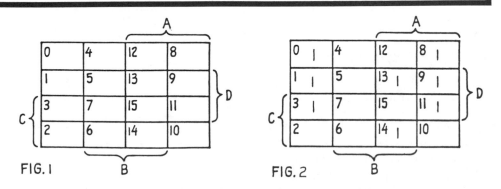

FIG. 1   B   FIG. 2   B

Solution: We are given the function $f(A,B,C,D) = \Sigma m(0,1,3,8,9,11,13,14)$ which consists of minterms to be minimized. The first step in obtaining the solution is to plot the function on the K-map.

In figure #1 a K-map for four variables is given. These maps are standard for each problem, however they change size according to the number of variables in the function.

To plot the given function into the K-map, 1's are put into the boxes which number matches with the given minterm variable. The final K-map with the variables plotted looks as shown in figure 2. Secondly, the number of adjacencies for each minterm is counted.

The number of adjacencies for each minterm is shown in the lower right-hand corner of the minterm block of figure 3.

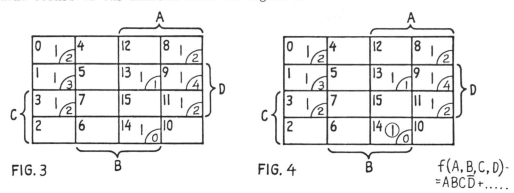

FIG. 3

FIG. 4

$f(A,B,C,D)-$
$=ABC\bar{D}+\ldots$

Now the map is ready for the simplification process. This is done by choosing first the minterm m_{14} which has no adjacencies, as in figure 4.

This minterm must be taken as a group itself; hence the first term in the minimized function is $ABC\bar{D}$ since minterm box #14 is not covered by variable D.

Next, minterms with one adjacency are examined; m_{13} is the only one. Consequently, m_{13} has one way of being grouped and that is with m_9. This is illustrated in figure 5.

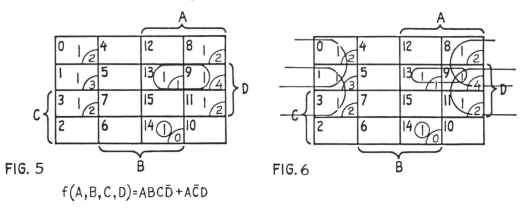

FIG. 5

FIG. 6

$f(A,B,C,D)=ABC\bar{D}+A\bar{C}D$

Note that minterms m_{13} and m_9 have the following variables:

$m_{13} = AB\bar{C}D$, $m_9 = A\bar{B}\bar{C}D$, therefore, B (in m_{13}), and $\bar{B}$(in m_9) may be cancelled according to Boolean algebra theorems. Continuing the solution; four minterms with two adjacencies are taken into account. These are m_0, m_3, m_8 and m_{11} . One of these is picked to group at random. If m_3 is picked (it is adjacent to m_1, and m_{11}), since m_9) is also available (any minterm may be used as many times as it is needed), a large group of four minterms may be formed. Note that

$$m_1 = \bar{A}\ \bar{B}\ \bar{C}\ D$$

$$m_3 = \bar{A}\ \bar{B}\ C\ D$$

$$m_{11} = A\ \bar{B}\ C\ D$$

$$m_9 = A\ \bar{B}\ \bar{C}\ D$$

in these four minterms A, and $\bar{A}$ terms also C, and $\bar{C}$ terms cancel each other, using Boolean theorems $a \cdot \bar{a} = 0$, therefore the minimized form of minterm m_1, m_3, m_{11}, and m_9 is $\bar{B}D$. The function now becomes $f(A,B,C,D) = ABC\bar{D} + A\bar{C}D + \bar{B}D$.

Finally there are still two minterms which have not been accounted for. These two, m_0 and m_8, can be grouped with m_1 and m_9 respectively, to form a last group of four minterms as shown in figure 6. This last group adds the final product term $\bar{B}\bar{C}$ to the function $f(A,B,C,D)$, and hence: $f(A,B,C,D) = ACB\bar{D} + A\bar{C}D + \bar{B}D + \bar{B}\bar{C}$.

● **PROBLEM** 3-20

Minimize the following minterm function containing 'don't cares' using the Karnaugh-Map.

$$f(A,B,C,D) = \Sigma m(5,6,7,8,9) + d(10,11,12,13,14,15)$$

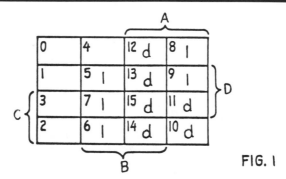

FIG. 1

Solution: $f(A,B,C,D) = \Sigma m(5,6,7,8,9) + d(10,11,12,13,14,15)$. In the design of digital circuits one often encounters cases in which the switching function is not completely specified. In other words, a function may be required to contain certain minterms, omit certain minterms, with the remaining minterms being optional; that is certain minterms may be included in the logic design if they help simplify the logic circuit. A minterm which is optional is called a don't care minterm.

The plotting of the given function $f(A,B,C,D)$ is shown in fig. 1 .

In the use of don't cares there is one additional rule which may be used in mapping. Recall that the don't cares by definition can be either 0 or 1. Hence in minimizing terms in Sum of Product form, the don't cares may be chosen to be 1 if in doing so the set of blocks on the map which can be grouped together is larger than would otherwise be possible without including the don't cares. In other words, with regard to don't cares one can take it or leave it, depending on whether they do or do not aid in the simplification of the function.

In the map of fig. 1 the following minterms and don't cares may be grouped.

$$m_8 = A \; \bar{B} \; \bar{C} \; \bar{D}$$

$$m_9 = A \; \bar{B} \; \bar{C} \; D$$

$$d_{11} = A \; \bar{B} \; C \; D$$

$$d_{10} = A \; \bar{B} \; C \; \bar{D}$$

$$d_{12} = A \; B \; \bar{C} \; \bar{D}$$

$$d_{13} = A \; B \; \bar{C} \; D$$

$$d_{15} = A \; B \; C \; D$$

$$d_{14} = A \; B \; C \; \bar{D}$$

and by the use of Boolean theorem $A \cdot \bar{A} = 0$, terms B,C, and D are eliminated. The result from this group would be A.

The next group is minterms 5 and 7, and don't cares 13 and 15.

$$m_5 = \bar{A} \; B \; \bar{C} \; D$$

$$m_7 = \bar{A} \; B \; C \; D$$

$$d_{13} = A \; B \; \bar{C} \; D$$

$$d_{15} = A \; B \; C \; D$$

With the same argument, the eliminated terms are A and C. Leaving the resulting terms BD.

The third and the last group consists of minterms 7 and 6, and don't cares 15 and 14.

$$m_6 = \bar{A} \; B \; C \; \bar{D}$$

$$m_7 = \bar{A} \; B \; C \; D$$

$$d_{14} = A \; B \; C \; \bar{D}$$

$$d_{15} = A \; B \; C \; D$$

Giving the result BC. The resulting total function can now be written as the sum of reduced terms that are found, namely;

$$f(A,B,C,D) = A + BD + BC \; .$$

Note that this function is much simpler to deal with than it would have been without the inclusion of don't cares.

● **PROBLEM** 3-21

Simplify F together with its don't care condition d in
(a)   sum-of-products form and
(b)   product-of-sums form.

$$F(A,B,C,D) = \Sigma \; (0,1,2,8,9,12,13)$$

$$d(A,B,C,D) = \Sigma \; (10,11,14,15)$$

<u>Solution</u>: F is simplified with a four-variable K map. Each don't care minterm can be treated as a 0 or a 1, whichever can help minimize F the most.
(a) The **K**-map is drawn in fig. 1 with X's representing don't cares. F minterms of 8,9,12 and 13 and don't cares treated as 1's at

66

10,11,14 and 15 combine to form A. F minterms at 0,1,8, and 9 combine to form $\overline{B}\overline{C}$. F minterms at 0,2, and 8 and a don't care treated as a 1 at 10 combine to form $\overline{B}\overline{D}$. Thus using sum-of-products:

$$F = A + \overline{B}\overline{C} + \overline{B}\overline{D}$$

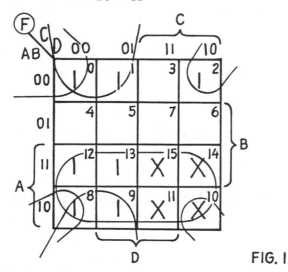

FIG. I

(b) Use the K-map of fig. 2, which is the same as fig. 1, but now minimize $\overline{F}$ with the aid of the don't cares and then use DeMorgan's Law to change F to the product-of-sums form. $\overline{F}$ minterms which are 0's for the product-of-sums case, at 4,5,6, and 7 combine to form $\overline{A}B$. $\overline{F}$ minterms at 3 and 7 and don't cares treated as 0's at 11 and 15 combine to form CD. Thus

$$\overline{F} = \overline{A}B + CD$$

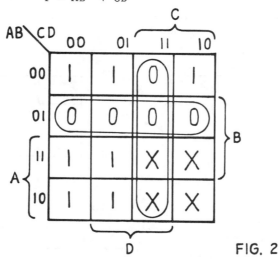

FIG. 2

Applying DeMorgan's Law gives the product-of-sums form

$$F = (A + \overline{B}) \cdot (\overline{C} + \overline{D})$$

● **PROBLEM** 3-22

Using the timing diagram given in fig. 1, obtain a minimum two-level NOR network.

Using the timing diagram given, a function in minterm list form may be derived.

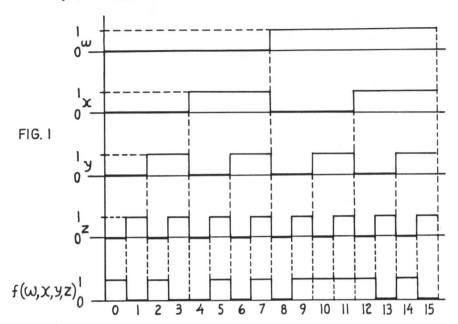

FIG. I

First it is observed from the timing diagram that the function needed has four variables w,x,y, and z. The values that each variable takes when f(w,x,y,z) is 1 are also shown in the diagram. Therefore the minterms found when f(w,x,y,z) = 1 are used to create the minterm function

$$f(w,x,y,z) = \sum m(0,2,5,7,9,10,11,12,14)$$

Using the Karnough Map for the given function and plotting the minterms into the map gives the table of fig. 2, from the definition of

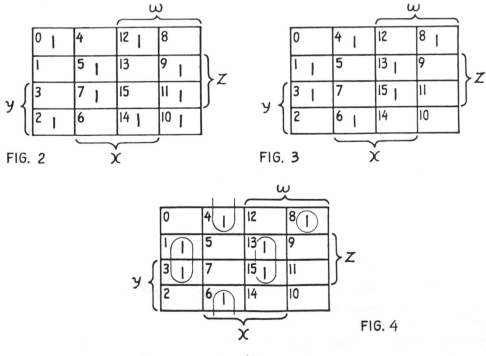

FIG. 2   FIG. 3

FIG. 4

68

NOR networks, it is known that a NOR gate gives the complement of the sum of inputs, therefore the NOR network gives the "Product of the Sum" form as ouput. The complement of the function $f(w,x,y,z)$ therefore is needed. The K-map for $\bar{f}(w,x,y,z)$ (complement) is given in fig. 3.

The next step now is to minimize the map obtained using $\bar{f}$ (complement). Going through the standard Karnough map minimizing techniques on the terms that are contained in K-map of fig. 2, we group the terms as in the K-map of fig. 4.

The resulting minimized function is obtained as follows;

From $m_1 = \bar{w}\ \bar{x}\ \bar{y}\ z$

$m_3 = \bar{w}\ \bar{x}\ y\ z$

total (term 1) $= \bar{w}\ \bar{x}\ z$

from $m_{13} = w\ x\ \bar{y}\ z$

$m_{15} = w\ x\ y\ z$

total (term 2) $= w\ x\ z$

from $m_4 = \bar{w}\ x\ \bar{y}\ \bar{z}$

$m_6 = \bar{w}\ x\ y\ \bar{z}$

total (term 3) $= \bar{w}\ x\ \bar{z}$

from $m_8 = w\ \bar{x}\ \bar{y}\ \bar{z}$

and the function $\bar{f}(w,x,y,z)$ is;

$$\bar{f}(w,x,y,z) = w\bar{x}\bar{y}\bar{z} + wxz + \bar{w}\bar{x}z + \bar{w}x\bar{z}$$

this function is the minimized form of the complement of $f(w,x,y,z)$ given initially. To find $f = \bar{\bar{f}}$ in "Product of Sum" form $\bar{f}(w,x,y,z)$ must be complemented.

$$f = \bar{\bar{f}} = \overline{w\bar{x}\bar{y}\bar{z} + wxz + \bar{w}\bar{x}z + \bar{w}x\bar{z}}$$

using DeMorgan's Law;

$$f = \bar{\bar{f}} = (\bar{w}+x+y+z)(\bar{w}+\bar{x}+\bar{z})(w+x+\bar{z})(w+\bar{x}+z)$$

Once this function is obtained, to get the NOR network involution may be used.

$$f = \bar{\bar{f}} = \overline{\overline{(\bar{w}+x+y+z)(\bar{w}+\bar{x}+\bar{z})(w+x+\bar{z})(w+\bar{x}+z)}}$$

$$f = \bar{\bar{f}} = \overline{\overline{w+x+y+z}+\overline{\bar{w}+\bar{x}+\bar{z}}+\overline{w+x+\bar{z}}+\overline{w+\bar{x}+z}}$$

and the logic diagram for this function is shown in fig. 5

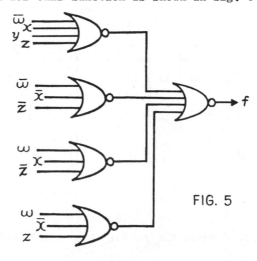

FIG. 5

69

Plot the following function on a K-map and simplify in SOP and POS forms.

$$F(A,B,C,D) = \Sigma(0,2,5,8,10,13,14,15) + X(1,11,12).$$

By using the simplified expression, determine the output when a redundant input occurs.

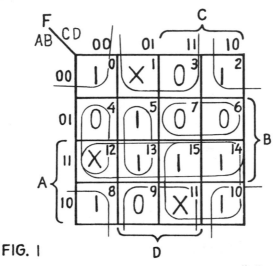

FIG. I

Solution: The K-map is shown in figure 1. The "X" mark at locations one, eleven, and twelve denotes the redundancies.

First simplify in the SOP form. Minterms at 13,14, and 15 and the redundancy at 12 combine to form AB. Minterms at 0,2,8, and 10 combine to form $\bar{B}\bar{D}$. Minterms at 5 and 13 combine to form $B\bar{C}D$. The SOP form is:

$$F = AB + \bar{B}\bar{D} + B\bar{C}D$$

To simplify F into the POS form, simplify $\bar{F}$ in SOP form and then use DeMorgan's Law. From the K-map it is seen that the 0's at 6 and 7 combine to form $\bar{A}BC$. The 0 at 4 and the redundancy at 12 combine to form $B\bar{C}\bar{D}$. The 0's at 3 and 9 and the redundancies at 1 and 11 combine to form $\bar{B}D$. The SOP of $\bar{F}$ is

$$\bar{F} = \bar{A}BC + B\bar{C}\bar{D} + \bar{B}D$$

	A	B	C	D	F SOP	POS
X_1	0	0	0	1	1	0
X_{11}	1	0	1	1	1	0
X_{12}	1	1	0	0	1	0

FIG. 2

Apply DeMorgan's Law to $\bar{F}$ gives the POS form of F.

$$F = (A+\bar{B}+\bar{C})(\bar{B}+C+D)(B+\bar{D})$$

The table of fig. 2 shows the output when redundancies occur.

Use Quine-McCluskey Method to minimize the function f(A,B,C,D).

f(A,B,C,D) = Σm(2,4,6,8,9,10,12,13,15)

Solution: To begin the Quine-McCluskey minimization technique the minterms are grouped according to the number of 1's in the binary representation of the minterm number. This grouping of items is illustrated in fig. 1.

Minterms	A	B	C	D
2	0	0	1	0
4	0	1	0	0
8	1	0	0	0
6	0	1	1	0
9	1	0	0	1
10	1	0	1	0
12	1	1	0	0
13	1	1	0	1
Fig. 1 15	1	1	1	1

Minterms 2,4, and 8 form the first group since they both contain a single 1 in their binary representation form. Minterms 6,9,10 and 12 form the second group hence they contain two 1's in their binary representations. The third group which consists of three 1's is the minterm 13. And the fourth group with four 1's, minterm 15. Once this method is formed, using the table obtained, adjacent minterms are found and combined into minterm lists in a minimizing table.
  In the following tables this procedure is illustrated;

Minterm	A	B	C	D	
2	0	0	1	0	Group 1
4	0	1	0	0	
8	1	0	0	0	
6	0	1	1	0	Group 2
9	1	0	0	1	
10	1	0	1	0	
12	1	1	0	0	
13	1	1	0	1	Group 3
Fig. 2 15	1	1	1	1	Group 4

In fig. 2 all 4 groups are given. Note here that two terms can be combined if and only if they differ in a single literal. Hence, in Fig. 2 group 1 terms can only be combined with group 2 terms, to form the list given in fig. 3.

Minterms	A	B	C	D	
2,6	0	-	1	0	PI_2
2,10	-	0	1	0	PI_3
4,6	0	1	-	0	PI_4
4,12	-	1	0	0	PI_5
8,9	1	0	0	-	✓
8,10	1	0	-	0	PI_6
8,12	1	-	0	0	✓
9,13	1	-	0	1	✓
12,13	1	1	0	-	✓
Fig. 3 13,15	1	1	-	1	PI_7

Note here that in forming fig. 3 several minterms are combined together. Such as m_2 of group 1, and m_6 of group 2. In these two minterms only the term B differs, and is therefore dropped.

Minterm 2 of group 1, and 10 of group 2 differ in A, Minterms 4 of group 1, and 6 of group 2 differ in C; Minterms 4 of group 1, and 12 of group 2 differ in A; Minterms 8 of group 1, and 9 of group 2 differ in D; Minterms 8 of group 1, and 10 of group 2 differ in C; Minterms 8 of group 1, and 12 of group 2 differ in B.

When all the combinations between the groups 1 and 2 have been made and they have been entered in the list, a line is drawn under these combinations, and combination of terms in group 2 with those in group 3 starts, following the same logic.

Next, using the list of fig. 3, the list in fig. 4 is obtained.

Minterms	A	B	C	D	
8,9,12,13	1	-	0	-	PI_1

Fig. 4

As before, two terms in list 2 can be obtained only if they differ in a single literal, only terms which have the same literal missing can possibly be combined. Note that in fig. 3 minterm combinations 8, 12 and 9,13 also 8,9 and 12,13 can be combined to yield terms 8,9,12,13 in fig. 4. These terms are checked off in the table of fig. 3 and all the other terms are labeled as Prime Implicants.

To determine the smallest number of Prime Implicants required to realize the function, a Prime Implicant Chart is formed as in fig. 5.

	2	4	6	8 ✓	9 ✓	10	12 ✓	13 ✓	15 ✓
PI_1				X	⊗		X	X	
PI_2	X		X						
PI_3	X					X			
PI_4		X	X						
PI_5		X					X		
PI_6				X		X			
PI_7								X	⊗

FIG. 5

The double line through the chart between PI_1 and PI_2 is used to separate prime implicants which contain different number of literals.

An examination of the minterm columns indicates that minterms 9 and 15 are covered by only one prime implicant. Therefore prime implicants PI_1 and PI_7 must be chosen, and hence they are essential prime implicants. Note that in choosing these two prime implicants, minterms 8,9,12,13, and 15 are also covered. These minterms are shown checked in the table.

To cover the remaining minterms 2,4,6, and 10 a reduced prime implicant chart is formed as in fig. 6.

Prime implicants PI_5 and PI_6 may be omitted because they are covered by PI_4 and PI_3 respectively. Hence ignoring PI_5 and PI_6 for the moment minterms 2,4,6, and 10 can be most efficiently covered by choosing PI_3 and PI_4 .

Therefore a minimal realization of the original function would be;

$$f(A,B,C,D) = PI_1 + PI_3 + PI_4 + PI_7$$

$$f(A,B,C,D) = 1 - 0 - + - 0\ 1\ 0 + 0\ 1 - 0 + 1\ 1 - 1$$

and using the variable coding;

$$f(A,B,C,D) = A\bar{C} + \bar{B}C\bar{D} + \bar{A}B\bar{D} + ABD$$

	2	4	6	10
PI_2	X		X	
PI_3	X			X
PI_4		X	X	
PI_5		X		
PI_6				X

FIG.6

CIRCUIT DESIGN

● **PROBLEM** 3-25

A combinational system is to receive a decimal value encoded according to code I. It also receives a control signal, J, that affects the output of the system. When J is TRUE, the input is converted to its equivalent in code II. When J is FALSE the output is chosen from code III. Design the combinational system for implementing this process. Consider both sum of products (SOP) and product of sums (POS) forms.

Minterm	Code I A B C D	Code II W X Y Z	Code III W X Y Z
1	0 0 0 1	0 0 0 0	0 0 1 1
2	0 0 1 0	0 0 0 1	0 1 0 0
4	0 1 0 0	0 0 1 0	0 1 0 1
8	1 0 0 0	0 0 1 1	0 1 1 0
9	1 0 0 1	0 1 0 0	0 1 1 1
10	1 0 1 0	0 1 0 1	1 0 0 0
12	1 1 0 0	0 1 1 0	1 0 0 1
13	1 1 0 1	0 1 1 1	1 0 1 0
14	1 1 1 0	1 0 0 0	1 0 1 1
15	1 1 1 1	1 0 0 1	1 1 0 0

<u>Solution</u>: A five variable K-map is used to minimize each output. Notice that there are don't care minterms, namely, 0,3,5,6,7, and 11. Half of the K-map is used for J = 1 and the other half for J = 0. A K-map is drawn for each output W,X,Y, and Z.

It is seen from the W K-map that $W = \bar{J}AB + BC + \bar{J}AC$ and in the POS form:

$$W = (A)(\bar{J} + \bar{A} + C)(\bar{A} + B + C)(\bar{J} + D + B)\ .$$

Similarly:

$$X = \bar{J}\ \bar{A}\ \bar{D} + A\ \bar{B}\ D + \bar{J}\ C\ D + J\ A\ B\ \bar{C} + J\ A\ B\ C\ \bar{D} + J\ A\ B\ \bar{C}$$

$$X = (\bar{J}+A)(A+\bar{D})(J+\bar{A}+\bar{B}+C)(J+\bar{A}+\bar{C}+D)$$
$$(\bar{J}+B+C+D)(\bar{J}+\bar{A}+B+\bar{C})$$

$$Y = \bar{J}\ \bar{C}\ D + J\ B\ \bar{C} + A\ \bar{B}\ \bar{C}\ \bar{D} + \bar{J}\ B\ C\ \bar{D}$$

$$Y = (\bar{J}+\bar{C})(\bar{C}+\bar{D})(B+\bar{C})(\bar{J}+B+C+\bar{D})(\bar{J}+\bar{B}+C+D)$$

$$Z = JBD + JA\bar{B}\bar{D} + J\bar{B}C\bar{D} + \bar{J}BD + \bar{J}B\bar{D}$$

$$Z = (J+\bar{B}+\bar{D})(J+\bar{A}+D+B)(J+B+\bar{C}+D)(\bar{J}+B+\bar{D})(\bar{J}+\bar{B}+D)$$

73

To decide which method would be cheapest to implement, SOP or POS, we will look at the number of gates required for implementation. The table of fig. 1 shows the number of gates needed to implement the SOP and the POS form of each variable.

It is seen from fig. 1 that W and Y are best expressed in the SOP form because the SOP form takes the least amount of gates. X and Z can be expressed in either SOP or POS form as both require the same number of gates. We will express X in POS form and Z in SOP form.

Figure 2 shows the circuit implementation with W,Y, and Z expressed in the SOP form and X in the POS form.

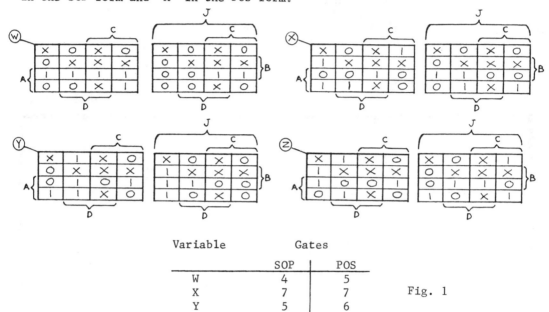

Variable	Gates	
	SOP	POS
W	4	5
X	7	7
Y	5	6
Z	6	6

Fig. 1

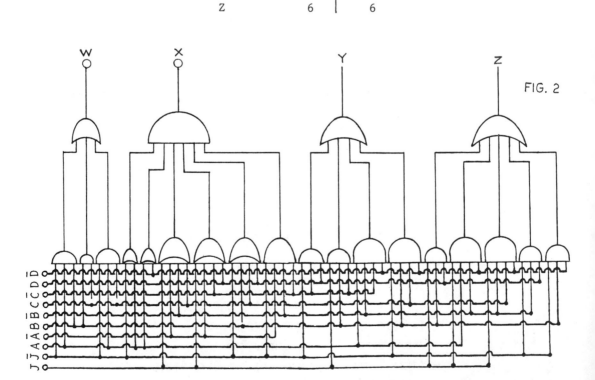

FIG. 2

74

CHAPTER 4

SWITCHING CIRCUITS

COMBINATIONAL CIRCUIT ANALYSIS

Using positive logic, determine the logic function represented by the diode circuit of figure 1.

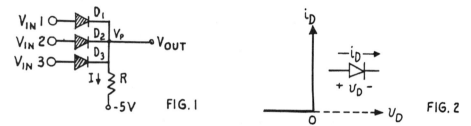

FIG. 1   FIG. 2

<u>Solution</u>: The ideal voltage-current characteristic of a diode is shown in fig. 2. The diode conducts when V_D is positive and acts as an insulator when V_D is negative. Hence, the diode is similar to a valve which lets current flow in only one direction.

As can be seen in fig. 1, when all inputs are high (greater than -5V) the diodes conduct, there is a large positive current in R, and the output voltage is greater than -5V.

When only one or two inputs are high; those diodes corresponding to the high inputs conduct and those diodes corresponding to the low inputs (less than or equal to -5V) act as insulators. The conducting diode(s) pass current to the resistor R, forming a voltage drop. Hence, the output voltage is greater than -5V.

When all inputs are low (less than or equal to -5V) all the diodes act as insulators and there is no current in resistor R, hence, the output voltage is -5V. From this information it is seen that the output is low only when all of the inputs are low. Tabulating this result, we get:

$V_{IN\ 1}$	$V_{IN\ 2}$	$V_{IN\ 3}$	V_{OUT}
L	L	L	L
L	L	H	H
L	H	L	H
L	H	H	H
H	L	L	H
H	L	H	H
H	H	L	H
H	H	H	H

It is evident that this table represents an OR gate.

● **PROBLEM** 4-2

Using Positive Logic, show that the Diode circuit of fig. 1 represents a three-input AND gate.

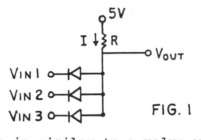

FIG. 1

Solution: A diode is similar to a valve which lets current flow in only one direction. In fig. 1 it is seen that when all inputs are low (0V) all diodes conduct. This action brings V_{out} to the same voltage as $V_{in\ N}$, hence V_{out} is low.

When one or two inputs are high ($\geq$ 5V), any diodes corresponding to the low inputs conduct and any diodes corresponding to the high inputs act as insulators. Hence the diodes that conduct bring V_{out} to the low voltage.

The diodes that are insulators have no effect on the output voltage. When all inputs are high, all of the diodes act as insulators and only then will the output voltage be high.

From this information, it is seen that the output is high only when all of the inputs are high. Using positive logic, this is seen to be an AND gate.

● **PROBLEM** 4-3

Show that a NOT gate can be achieved with the transistor inverter of fig. 1.

Solution: The transistor in figure 1 operates in the fol-

76

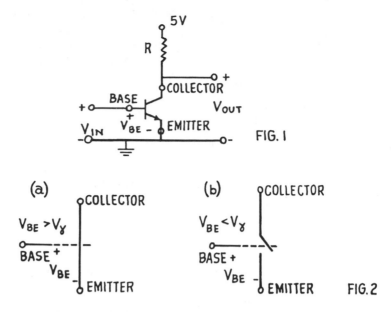

FIG. I

FIG. 2

lowing manner: If a voltage, V_{BE} , is impressed at the emitter with respect to the base; and V_{BE} is greater than a threshold voltage V_{γ} , then the collector-emitter junction of the transistor becomes a conductor, or a closed switch as shown in fig 2a. If V_{BE} is less than V_{γ} , then the collector-emitter junction becomes an insulator, or an open switch as shown in fig 2b. Thus the transistor behaves as a switch which can be opened or closed by varying V_{BE} . It is seen from the circuit of fig. 1 that $V_{BE} = V_{in}$; hence when

$$V_{in} < V_{\gamma} \quad : \text{ switch open}$$

$$V_{in} > V_{\gamma} \quad : \text{ switch closed}$$

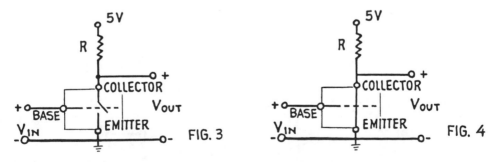

FIG. 3

FIG. 4

In many transistors V_{γ} is approximately 0.7V; thus when $V_{in} < 0.7$V the circuit of figure 1 is seen as the circuit of figure 3. Assuming a negligible voltage drop across resistor R, the output voltage, V_{out} , is 5V. When $V > 0.7$V fig. 1 is seen as the circuit of fig. 4. In this case V_{out} is seen to be 0V. In reality however, there is

a small voltage, V_{CESAT} , between collector and emitter
which is approximately 0.2V. This occurs because the
transistor is not an ideal switch. From the information
gathered so far, a circuit function table is made

V_{in}	V_{out}
< 0.7V	5V
> 0.7V	0.2V

If logic 1 is assigned to any voltage above, say, 3V and
logic O is assigned to any voltage below 0.7V, the truth
table will be:

Input	Output
0	1
1	0

The truth table proves that the circuit of figure 1 is a
logic inverter or a NOT gate.

● **PROBLEM** 4-4

Using positive logic, show that the diode-transistor
circuit of fig. 1 represents a three-input NAND gate.

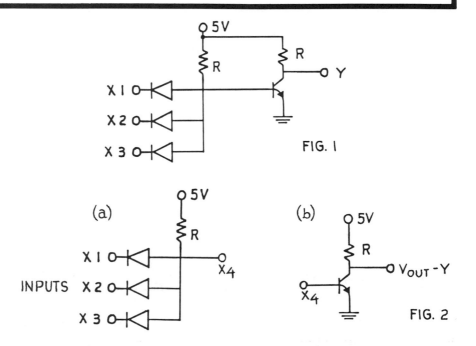

FIG. 1

(a)

INPUTS

(b)

FIG. 2

Solution: The circuit is broken down into two "sub-
circuits"; fig. 2(a) and (b).

In sub-circuit a, fig. 2(a), if any of the inputs are
low(or), its corresponding Diode will conduct, pulling the
output X_4 Low. If all the inputs are high ($\geq$ 5V), none of

78

the diodes will conduct, leaving the output X_4 high (5V). The truth table of figure 3 illustrates subcircuit a's action, that of an AND gate.

Inputs	Output
X_1 X_2 X_3	X_4
L L L	L
L L H	L
L H L	L
L H H	L
H L L	L
H L H	L
H H L	L
H H H	H

Fig. 3

  In sub-circuit b, figure 2(b), the transistor acts as a switch, conducting when X_4 is high ($> \cdot 7V$), and open when X_4 is low (OV). When X_4 is high the transistor is conducting and the output Y is pulled low. When X_4 is low the transistor is open and Y floats to 5V (high). Thus, sub-circuit b acts as an inverter and the whole circuit, whose truth table is shown in fig. 4, acts as a NAND gate.

INPUTS			X_4	Y (OUTPUT)
X_1	X_2	X_3		
L	L	L	L	H
L	L	H	L	H
L	H	L	L	H
L	H	H	L	H
H	L	L	L	H
H	L	H	L	H
H	H	L	L	H
H	H	H	H	L

Fig. 4

● **PROBLEM** 4-5

Show that a two input NOR gate can be achieved with two transistor inverters in parallel as shown in figure 1.

<u>Solution</u>: A transistor operates as a switch. When the base voltage is high, > .7V base to emitter, the collector-emitter junction forms a closed switch and when the base

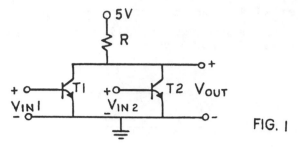

FIG. I

voltage is low, < .7V base to emitter, the collector-emitter junction forms an open switch.

Hence, when $V_{in\ 1}$ and $V_{in\ 2}$ are low, both switches are open, preventing current from flowing through T_1 or T_2, and the output voltage is high ($\sim$ 5V). When $V_{in\ 1}$ (or $V_{in\ 2}$) is high and other input is low, then Tl (T2) is closed. In this case the output voltage is low, because current flows through one of the switches, connecting V_{out} to ground. When $V_{in\ 1}$ and $V_{in\ 2}$ are high, switches Tl and T2 close, connecting V_{out} to ground.

This circuit behavior can be tabulated as follows:

$V_{in\ 1}$	$V_{in\ 2}$	V_{out}
L	L	H
L	H	L
H	L	L
H	H	L

Using positive logic, this table is seen to be the truth table for a NOR gate.

● **PROBLEM** 4-6

What is wrong with each of the following gate representations?

(a)
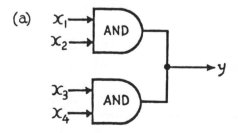

<u>Solution</u>: a) This is an example of the incorrect assumption that a single variable may be controlled simultaneously from two or more elements whose outputs are inconsistent.

80

Even though the definition of a gate structure is fulfilled --a set of elements with given behaviors and a set of couplings between elements--the contradictions inherent in the structure make its analysis meaningless. For example, if $X_1 = X_2 = 0$ and $X_3 = X_4 = 1$, then Y could be either 1 or 0.

b) Although a circuit may contain dependency loops, this circuit contains a closed loop of inconsistent dependency in which a variable Y depends upon another variable X in such a way that two different values of Y are required simultaneously. This example fails for Y = 0 and X = 1 because Y must also equal 1 now.

(b)

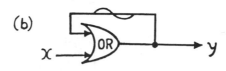

(c)

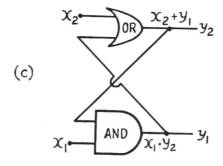

c) Let us represent the output in terms of a pair of simultaneous Boolean equations:

$$Y_1 = X_1 \cdot Y_2$$
$$Y_2 = X_2 + Y_1$$

When solving these equations for Y_1 and Y_2 by substitution, we obtain either of two sets of equations:

$$Y_1 = Y_2 \cdot X_1$$
$$Y_2 = X_2$$

(a)

or

$$Y_1 = X_1$$
$$Y_2 = X_2 \cdot X_1$$

(b)

If we begin with $X_2 = 0$ and $X_1 = 1$, set (a) gives $Y_1 = Y_2 = 0$, but set (b) gives $Y_1 = Y_2 = 1$. With this state, the response of the circuit is ambiguous.

● **PROBLEM** 4-7

In the proceding problem what would be correct forms for the circuits in parts a) and b)?

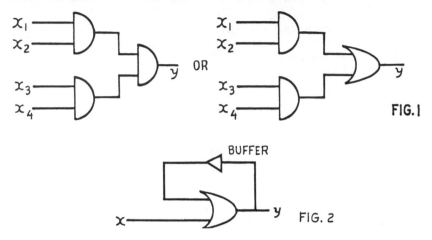

OR

FIG. 1

BUFFER

FIG. 2

Solution: a) For this circuit we could feed the outputs of the two AND-gates into a second level AND- or OR-gate as shown in Fig. 1.

b) For this circuit the output Y of the OR-gate can be fed back into one of its inputs by passing the output Y through a better amplifier. The advantages of using the buffer (with amplification >1 or <1) are listed below:

    i) It matches the output impedance of the OR-gate, to the input impedance of the OR-gate.

    ii) It balances any phase differences in the signals between the output side and the input side of the gate.

    iii) It also facilitates amplification or attenuation of the signal fed back from the output to the input so that the amount of signal fed back is the right amount. The possible circuit as shown in Fig. 2.

COMBINATIONAL CIRCUIT DESIGN

● **PROBLEM** 4-8

Design a combinational circuit that accepts a three-bit number and generates an output binary number equal to the square of the input number.

Solution: The largest number to be squared is decimal seven or 111_2. With decimal seven as an input the output

82

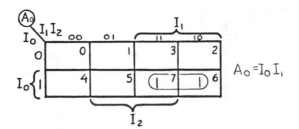

$A_0 = I_0 I_1$

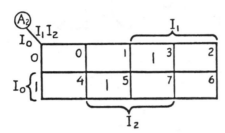

$A_1 = I_0 \bar{I}_1 + I_0 I_2$

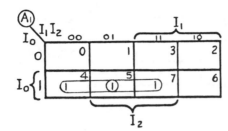

$A_2 = I_0 \bar{I}_1 \ I_2 + \bar{I}_0 I_1 I_2$

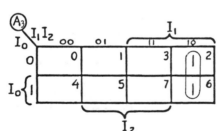

$A_3 = I_1 \bar{I}_2$

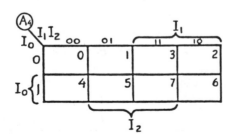

$A_4 = 0$

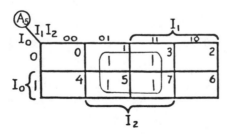

$A_5 = I_2$

83

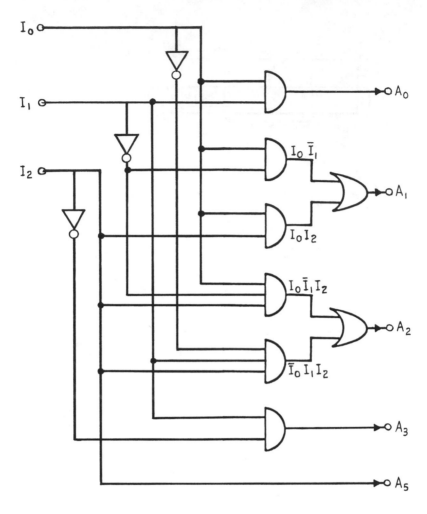

LOGIC "0"o————————————————→oA4   FIG. I

will be 49_{10} or 110001_2 hence there will be three inputs, one for each bit, and six outputs. A truth table is made with inputs I_0 , I_1, I_2 and outputs A_0 , A_1 ,A_2 , A_3 , A_4 , A_5 . I_0 and A_0 are the most significant bits.

minterms	Inputs				Outputs					
	I_0	I_1	I_2		A_0	A_1	A_2	A_3	A_4	A_5
0	0	0	0		0	0	0	0	0	0
1	0	0	1		0	0	0	0	0	1
2	0	1	0		0	0	0	1	0	0
3	0	1	1		0	0	1	0	0	1
4	1	0	0		0	1	0	0	0	0
5	1	0	1		0	1	1	0	0	1
6	1	1	0		1	0	0	1	0	0
7	1	1	1		1	1	0	0	0	1

From the truth table it is seen that

$$A_0 \ (I_0 \ , \ I_1 \ , I_2) \ = \ \textstyle\sum 6, \ 7$$

$$A_1 \ (I_0 \ , \ I_1 \ , I_2) \ = \ \textstyle\sum 4, \ 5, \ 7$$

$$A_2 \ (I_0 \ , \ I_1 \ , I_2) \ = \ \textstyle\sum 3, \ 5$$

$$A_3 \ (I_0 \ , \ I_1 \ , I_2) \ = \ \textstyle\sum 2, \ 6$$

$$A_4 \ (I_0 \ , \ I_1 \ , I_2) \ = \ \textstyle\sum \text{none - connect to Logic 0}$$

$$A_5 \ (I_0 \ , I_1 \ , I_2) \ = \ \textstyle\sum 1, \ 3, \ 5, \ 7$$

Use 3-variable K-maps to simplfy the expressions

$$A_0 = I_0 \ I_1$$

$$A_1 = I_0 \ \overline{I_1} + I_0 \ I_2$$

$$A_2 = I_0 \ \overline{I_1} \ I_2 + \overline{I_0} \ I_1 \ I_2$$

$$A_3 = I_1 \ \overline{I_2}$$

$$A_4 = 0$$

$$A_5 = I_2$$

A logical diagram is drawn from the minimized equations.
Figure 1 shows the combinational circuit.

● **PROBLEM** 4-9

A light emitting diode (LED) used to display a number in decimal form has the following 7-segment configuration.

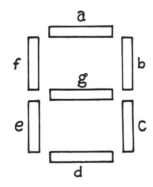

Segment a lights up when input a is at logic level 1 and, segment b lights up when input b is at logic level 1, etc. Design a decoder which will accept a 3 bit number and decode it to a seven bit number to be accepted by the LED. The LED will then display the decimal form of the three bit number.

Solution: To design this decoder we can begin by setting up a table of the input possibilities. Let the 3 bit input number be represented by ABC, C being the least significant digit.

INPUT	EQUIVALENT DECIMAL	SEGMENTS NEEDED TO LIGHT UP						
A B C	NUMBER	a	b	c	d	e	f	g
0 0 0	0	1	1	1	1	1	1	0
0 0 1	1	0	1	1	0	0	0	0
0 1 0	2	1	1	0	1	1	0	1
0 1 1	3	1	1	1	1	0	0	1
1 0 0	4	0	1	1	0	0	1	1
1 0 1	5	1	0	1	1	0	1	1
1 1 0	6	1	0	1	1	1	1	1
1 1 1	7	1	1	1	0	0	0	0

Note: 3 bits can give you a maximum of 8 possibilities.

Next we find which numbers light up a given segment, in other words, which numbers are common to a given segment.

From the table we find:

a = $\sum$ (0, 2, 3, 5, 6, 7) or a = $\sum$ (000, 010, 011, 101, 110, 111)

b = $\sum$ (0, 1, 2, 3, 4, 7) or b = $\sum$ (000, 001, 010, 011, 100, 111)

c = $\sum$ (0, 1, 3, 4, 5, 6, 7) or

$\qquad$ c = $\sum$ (000, 001, 011, 100, 101, 110, 111)

d = $\sum$ (0, 2, 3, 5, 6) or d = $\sum$ (000, 010, 011, 101, 110)

e = $\sum$ (0, 2, 6) or e = $\sum$ (000, 010, 110)

f = $\sum$ (0, 4, 5, 6) or f = $\sum$ (000, 100, 101, 110)

g = $\sum$ (2, 3, 4, 5, 6) or g = $\sum$ (010, 011, 100, 101, 110)

Next we minimize the logic for each segment a through g using K-maps:

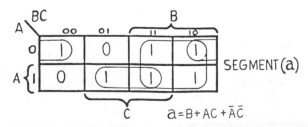

$a = B + AC + \bar{A}\bar{C}$

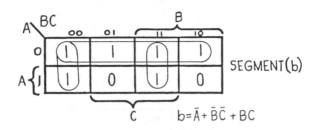

SEGMENT(b)

$$b = \bar{A} + \bar{B}\bar{C} + BC$$

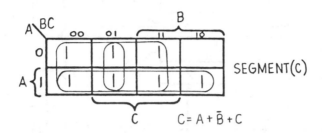

SEGMENT(c)

$$C = A + \bar{B} + C$$

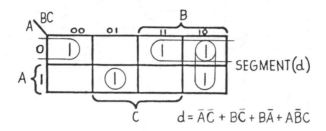

SEGMENT(d)

$$d = \bar{A}\bar{C} + B\bar{C} + B\bar{A} + A\bar{B}C$$

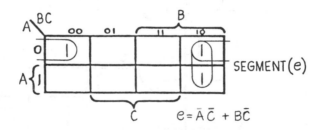

SEGMENT(e)

$$e = \bar{A}\bar{C} + B\bar{C}$$

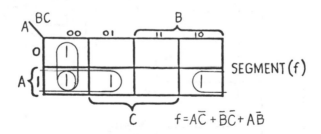

SEGMENT(f)

$$f = A\bar{C} + \bar{B}\bar{C} + A\bar{B}$$

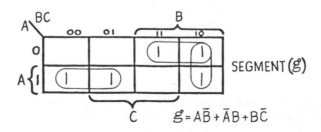

SEGMENT(g)

$$g = A\bar{B} + \bar{A}B + B\bar{C}$$

87

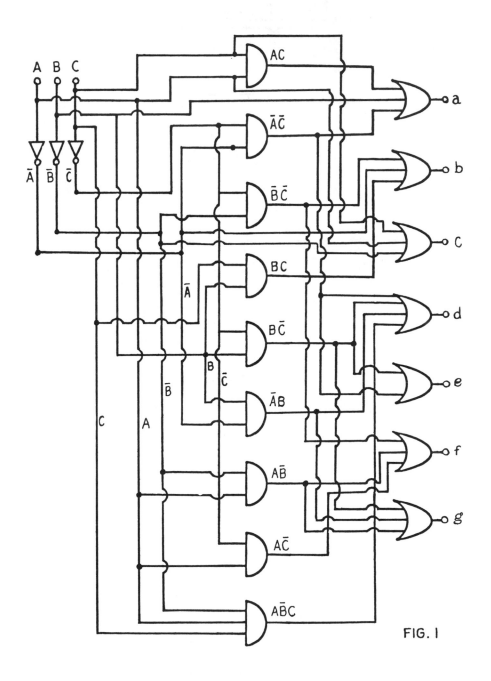

FIG. I

Now the logic diagram of figure 1 is synthesized using the simplified segment equations a through g.

88

An LED used to display a decimal number has the following configuration.

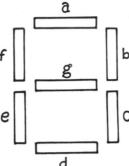

Design a decoder which will accept a four bit binary number, whose value will range from 0_{10} to 9_{10} , and decode it to a seven bit number to be accepted by the LED. the LED will then display the decimal form of the four bit number.

Solution: Begin designing the decoder by listing a truth table. The inputs to the decoder will be A, B, C and D with A the most significant bit. The outputs are a, b, c, d, e, f and g.

decimal number	Input A	B	C	D	Output a	b	c	d	e	f	g
0	0	0	0	0	1	1	1	1	1	1	0
1	0	0	0	1	0	1	1	0	0	0	0
2	0	0	1	0	1	1	0	1	1	0	1
3	0	0	1	1	1	1	1	1	0	0	1
4	0	1	0	0	0	1	1	0	0	1	1
5	0	1	0	1	1	0	1	1	0	1	1
6	0	1	1	0	1	0	1	1	1	1	1
7	0	1	1	1	1	1	1	0	0	0	0
8	1	0	0	0	1	1	1	1	1	1	1
9	1	0	0	1	1	1	1	1	0	1	1
10	1	0	1	0	X	X	X	X	X	X	X
11	1	0	1	1	X	X	X	X	X	X	X
12	1	1	0	0	X	X	X	X	X	X	X
13	1	1	0	1	X	X	X	X	X	X	X
14	1	1	1	0	X	X	X	X	X	X	X
15	1	1	1	1	X	X	X	X	X	X	X

Notice that all of the inputs greater than 9_{10} have

don't-care outputs. This is possible because the inputs will not be greater than 9_{10}. The don't care states will help in minimizing the expressions.

Evaluate the sum of products form for each output.

$a(A, B, C, D) = \sum (0, 2, 3, 5, 6, 7, 8, 9) + d$

$b(A, B, C, D) = \sum (0, 1, 2, 3, 4, 7, 8, 9) + d$

$c(A, B, C, D) = \sum (0, 1, 3, 4, 5, 6, 7, 8, 9) + d$

$d(A, B, C, D) = \sum (0, 2, 3, 5, 6, 8, 9) + d$

$e(A, B, C, D) = \sum (0, 2, 6, 8) + d$

$f(A, B, C, D) = \sum (0, 4, 5, 6, 8, 9) + d$

$g(A, B, C, D) = \sum (2, 3, 4, 5, 6, 8, 9) + d$

where d represents the don't care conditions

$$d(A, B, C, D) = \sum 10, 11, 12, 13, 14, 15$$

Construct a 4 variable K-map to minimize each Boolean expression.

Note: X corresponds to don't care conditions

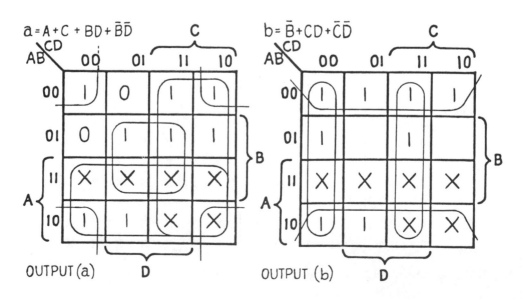

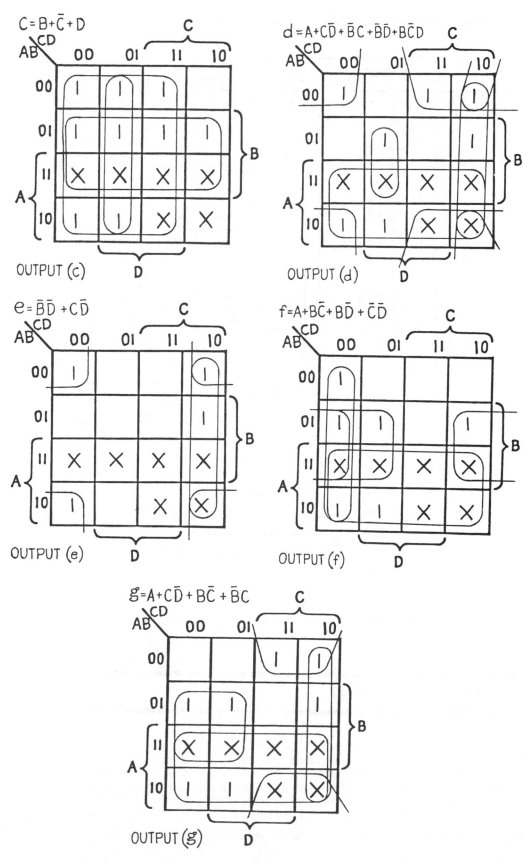

OUTPUT (c)

$C = B + \bar{C} + D$

OUTPUT (d)

$d = A + C\bar{D} + \bar{B}C + \bar{B}\bar{D} + B\bar{C}D$

OUTPUT (e)

$e = \bar{B}\bar{D} + C\bar{D}$

OUTPUT (f)

$f = A + B\bar{C} + B\bar{D} + \bar{C}\bar{D}$

OUTPUT (g)

$g = A + C\bar{D} + B\bar{C} + \bar{B}C$

91

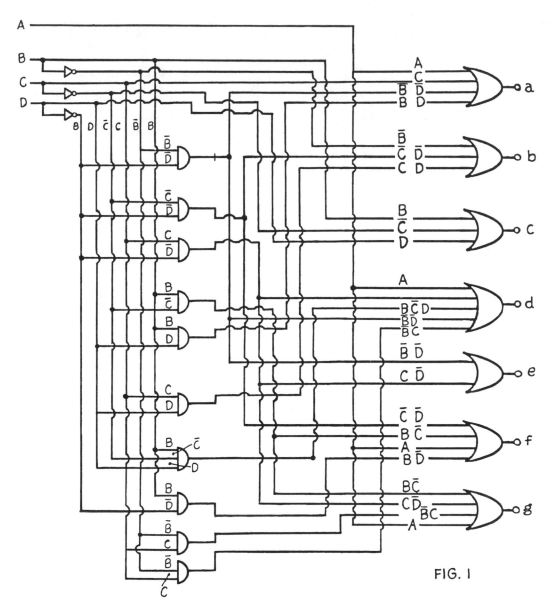

FIG. 1

The logic diagram of figure 1 is constructed from the minimized expressions a through g.

● **PROBLEM** 4-11

Design an 8 x 3 encoder.

Solution: An encoder is a device with 2^n input lines (in this case eight) and n output lines (in this case 3). Only one of the input lines can be excited at any one time. The encoder generates on its output lines a code corresponding to the input line that was excited. The truth table for the 8 x 3 encoder is shown in figure 1. Bits I_0 through I_7 are the input lines and bits A_0 through A_2 are the

| | | | Inputs | | | | | | | Outputs | |
I_0	I_1	I_2	I_3	I_4	I_5	I_6	I_7		A_0	A_1	A_2
1	0	0	0	0	0	0	0		0	0	0
0	1	0	0	0	0	0	0		0	0	1
0	0	1	0	0	0	0	0		0	1	0
0	0	0	1	0	0	0	0		0	1	1
0	0	0	0	1	0	0	0		1	0	0
0	0	0	0	0	1	0	0		1	0	1
0	0	0	0	0	0	1	0		1	1	0
0	0	0	0	0	0	0	1		1	1	1

Fig. 1 - truth table

output lines. A_0 is most significant output bit; A_2 is least significant output bit. From the truth table it is seen that

$$A_0 = I_4 + I_5 + I_6 + I_7$$

$$A_1 = I_2 + I_3 + I_6 + I_7$$

$$A_2 = I_1 + I_3 + I_5 + I_7$$

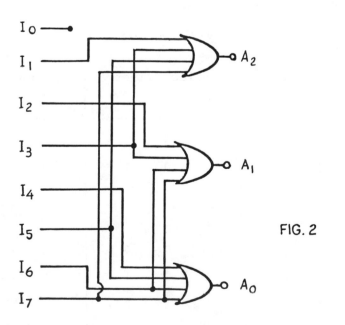

FIG. 2

The logic diagram of the encoder is obtained from these equations. Figure 2 shows the encoder.

93

Design an 8 x 1 multiplexer.

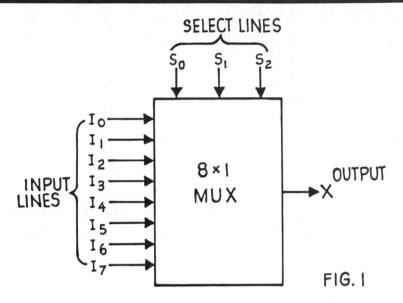

SELECT LINES

S_0 S_1 S_2

INPUT LINES

I_0
I_1
I_2
I_3
I_4
I_5
I_6
I_7

8 × 1
MUX

OUTPUT
X

FIG. 1

Solution: A multiplexer is a device that receives binary information from 2^n (in this case eight) input lines and transmits the information, selected from one input line, on a single output line. N (in this case 3) control lines, called select lines, determine which of the eight input lines will be selected.

The block diagram of an 8 x 1 multiplexer is shown in fig. 1.

Select lines			Output
S_0	S_1	S_2	X
0	0	0	I_0
0	0	1	I_1
0	1	0	I_2
0	1	1	I_3
1	0	0	I_4
1	0	1	I_5
1	1	0	I_6
1	1	1	I_7

Fig. 2

The truth table for the multiplexer is shown in figure 2.

From the truth table it is seen that

$$X = I_0 \, \bar{S}_0 \, \bar{S}_1 \, \bar{S}_2 + I_1 \, \bar{S}_0 \, \bar{S}_1 \, S_2 + I_2 \, \bar{S}_0 \, S_1 \, \bar{S}_2 + I_3 \, \bar{S}_0 \, S_1 \, S_2$$

$$+ \, I_4 \, S_0 \, \bar{S}_1 \, \bar{S}_2 + I_5 \, S_0 \, \bar{S}_1 \, S_2 + I_6 \, S_0 \, S_1 \, \bar{S}_2 + I_7 \, S_0 \, S_1 \, S_2$$

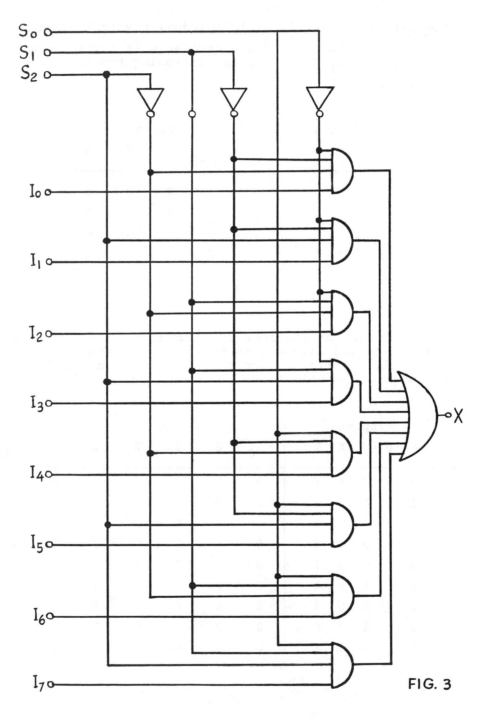

FIG. 3

The logic diagram of the 8 x 1 multiplexer can be derived from this equation. Figure 3 shows the logic diagram.

Design a 5 x 32 decoder using four 3 x 8 decoders (with enable inputs) and one 2 x 4 decoder.

<u>Solution</u>: a decoder is a digital device with n input lines and 2^n output lines. A 2 x 4 decoder with inputs X and Y and outputs Z_0 Z_1 Z_2 Z_3 has the following truth table, shown in figure 1.

Inputs		Outputs			
X	Y	Z_0	Z_1	Z_2	Z_3
0	0	1	0	0	0
0	1	0	1	0	0
1	0	0	0	1	0
1	1	0	0	0	1

Fig. 1

Hence, for each of the four combinations of 1's and 0's there is one and only one output line that assumes the value of 1. Similarly, the truth table for a 3 x 8 decoder with an enable input is shown in figure 2.

Inputs				Outputs							
enable	W	X	Y	Z_0	Z_1	Z_2	Z_3	Z_4	Z_5	Z_6	Z_7
0	X	X	X	0	0	0	0	0	0	0	0
1	0	0	0	1	0	0	0	0	0	0	0
1	0	0	1	0	1	0	0	0	0	0	0
1	0	1	0	0	0	1	0	0	0	0	0
1	0	1	1	0	0	0	1	0	0	0	0
1	1	0	0	0	0	0	0	1	0	0	0
1	1	0	1	0	0	0	0	0	1	0	0
1	1	1	0	0	0	0	0	0	0	1	0
1	1	1	1	0	0	0	0	0	0	0	1

Fig. 2

Note: X denotes "don't care"

The 5 x 32 decoder is shown in fig. 3.

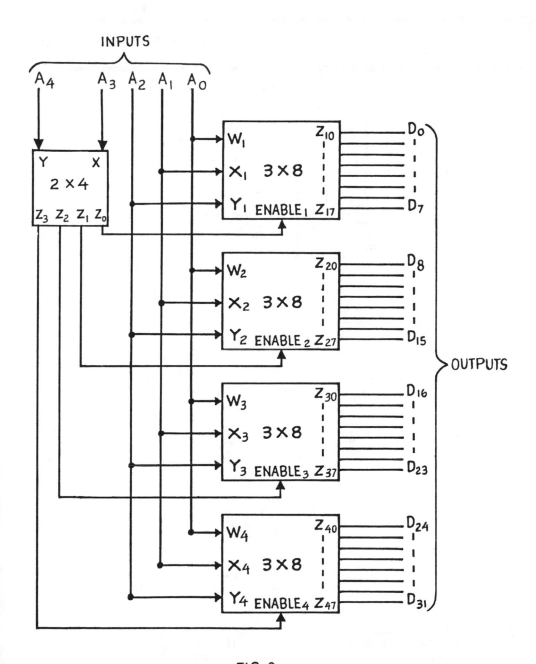

FIG. 3

The 2 x 4 decoder decodes bits A_3 and A_4 and ensures that only one of the 3 x 8 decoders is enabled. Hence bits A_3 and A_4 determine which of the 3 x 8 decoders to enable and bits A_0, A_1, and A_2 determine which output of the enabled decoder will become 1.

SEQUENTIAL CIRCUIT ANALYSIS

What type of flip-flop does the diode-transistor circuit of fig. 1 represent?

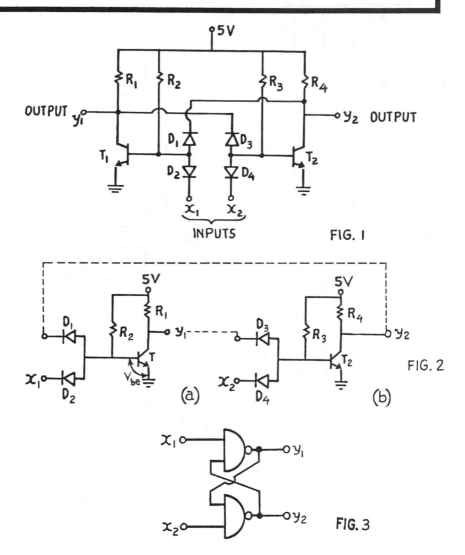

FIG. I

FIG. 2

FIG. 3

Solution: The circuit of fig. 1 is broken down into two identical "sub-circuts" in fig. 2(a) and (b). In sub-circuit (a) if either or both of the input diodes are connected to OV (200), current flows through R2. This makes V_{be} = OV and the transistor does not conduct, leaving its output Y_1 high (5V). If both diodes are connected to 25V (high), no current flows through R2. This makes V_{be} = 5V and the transistor conducts, pulling V_1 low (OV). Thus, each sub-circuit is a NAND gate and the output of each gate is connected to the input of the opposite gate. The logic diagram of fig. 1 is shown in fig. 3.

The truth table for fig. 3 is shown in Fig. 4.

Inputs		Present State		Next State	
X_1	X_2	Y_1	Y_2	Y_1	Y_2
0	0	0	1	not used	
0	0	1	0	not used	
0	1	0	1	1	0
0	1	1	0	1	0
1	0	0	1	0	1
1	0	1	0	0	1
1	1	0	1	0	1
1	1	1	0	1	0

Fig. 4

This truth table is similar to that of an S-R flip-flop except in this case

$$X_1 = \overline{S}; \quad X_2 = \overline{R} .$$

Hence, this is an $\overline{S}$ - $\overline{R}$ flip-flop.

● **PROBLEM** 4-15

What type of flip-flop does the transistor circuit of fig. 1 represent?

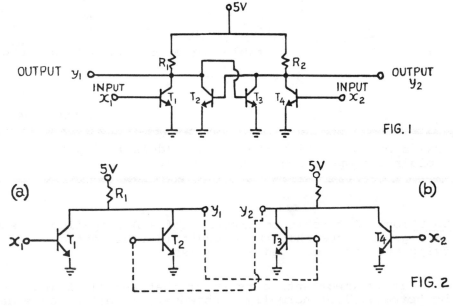

FIG. 1

FIG. 2

Solution: The circuit of fig. 1 is broken down into two identical "sub-circuits" in fig. 2(a) and (b).

99

In sub-circuit (a), if either or both of the transistor bases are connected to 5V (high), current will flow through R_1 to ground and the output Y will be low (0V). If both bases are connected to low (0V), no current will flow and Y_1 will float up to 5V (high). Thus, each sub-circuit is a NOR gate and the output of each gate is connected to the input of the opposite gate. The logic diagram of fig. 1 is shown in fig. 3.

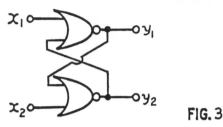

FIG. 3

The truth table for fig. 3 is shown in fig. 4.

Input		Present State		Next State	
X_1	X_2	Y_1	Y_2	Y_1	Y_2
0	0	0	1	0	1
0	0	1	0	1	0
0	1	0	1	0	1
0	1	1	0	0	1
1	0	0	1	1	0
1	0	1	0	1	0
1	1	0	1	not used	
1	1	1	0	not used	

Fig. 4

This is the same truth table for an S-R flip-flop, hence,

$$X_1 = S, \ X_2 = R, \ Y_2 = Q, \ Y_1 = \overline{Q}$$

● **PROBLEM** 4-16

Draw a circuit realization of a D (delay) flip-flop, explain the operation of the device.

Solution: A circuit realization of a D flip-flop is shown in fig. 1. Note that the circuit is implemented by modifying the cross coupled NAND gates.

It is important to remember that the clock input can be normally 1 or normally 0; however, in either case data is always clocked to the output Q on a 0 to 1 transition of the clock input C.

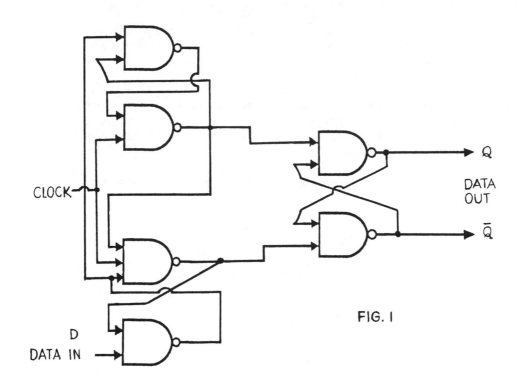

FIG. I

Inputs		Present State	Next State	
D(t)	C(t)	Q(t)	Q(t + E)	
0	0 → 0, 1 → 1, 1 → 0	0	0	No
0	0 → 0, 1 → 1, 1 → 0	1	1	change
0	0 → 1	0	0	Data is
0	0 → 1	1	0	clocked in
1	0 → 0, 1 → 1, 1 → 0	0	0	No
1	0 → 0, 1 → 1, 1 → 0	1	1	change
1	0 → 1	0	1	Data is
1	0 → 1	1	1	clocked in

Fig. 2

Inputs DC				
Present state	00	01	11	10
0	0	0	1	0
1	1	0	1	1

Next state

Fig. 3   State-table of D F-F.

The characteristics of the device are summarized by
the truth table, shown in figure 2, and the state table
shown in figure 3.

● **PROBLEM** 4-17

Draw a circuit realization of a clocked JK flip-flop. Explain the operation of the device, give timing diagram, and
truth tables for clocked, and static operations. What is
the logic symbol for a clocked JK flip-flop?

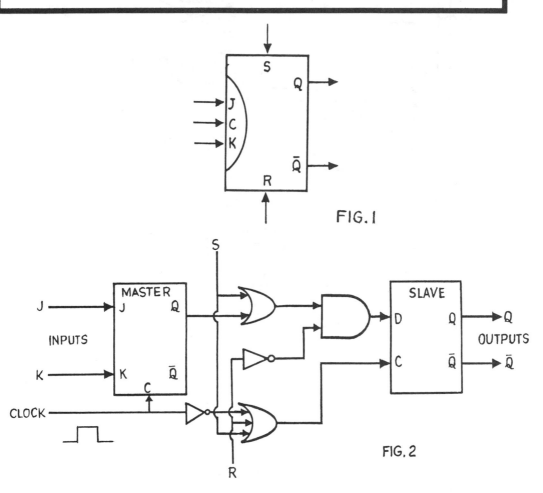

FIG. 1

FIG. 2

Solution: The clocked JK flip-flop, for which the logic
symbol is given in Fig. 1, has five input signals J, K, S,
R, and C. J, C, and K are used for synchronous, clocked
operation of the device. In this mode the set (S), and
reset (R) inputs are held at zero.

To initiate a state change in the device a $0 \to 1 \to 0$
clock pulse must occur, because internally this flip-flop
consists of two flip-flops in a master-slave configuration.
This property is shown in the circuit realization of the JK
flip-flop in Fig. 2.

The first clock transition, $0 \to 1$, causes the master

flip-flop to operate, while the second, 1 → 0, transfers data from the master to the slave.

The outputs Q and $\overline{Q}$ come from the slave flip-flop.

The truth table for clocked operation (when S = R = 0) is shown in figure 3.

Inputs		clock	Present state	
J(t)	K(t)	C(t)	Q(t)	Q(t + E)
0	0	0→1→0	0	0 No change
0	0	0→1→0	1	1
0	1	0→1→0	0	0 Reset
0	1	0→1→0	1	0
1	0	0→1→0	0	1 Set
1	0	0→1→0	1	1
1	1	0→1→0	0	1 Complement
1	1	0→1→0	1	0

Fig. 3 Truth Table - Synchronous operation

(S = R = 0)

Note that when either S or R are NOT EQUAL to zero there will be a STATIC OPERATION.

The truth table for static operation is shown in figure 4.

S(t)	R(t)	Q(t)	Q(t + E)
0	0	0	? Clocked
0	0	1	? Operation
0	1	0	0 Reset
0	1	1	0
1	0	0	1 Set
1	0	1	1
1	1	0	d Not allowed
1	1	1	d

Fig. 4 Truth Table - static operation

Note: J and K inputs don't matter in static operation.

103

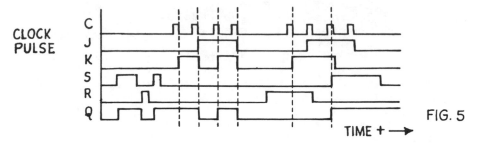

CLOCK PULSE

FIG. 5

TIME + →

The clocked JK flip-flop timing diagram is shown in Figure 5.

● **PROBLEM** 4-18

For a T type (toggle) clocked, master-slave flip-flop, give
a) the block diagram, b) the timing diagram, c) the Karnaugh Map, d) the excitation equation, e) the state table,
and f) the state diagram.

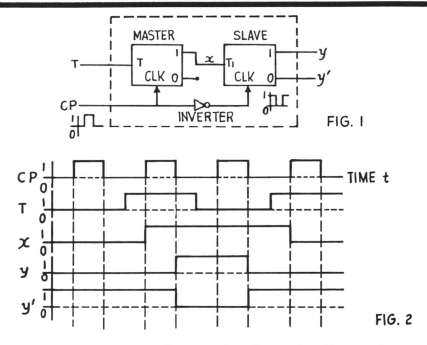

FIG. 1

FIG. 2

Solution: a) The block diagram is shown in figure 1.

The slave gets a clock pulse which is a complement of the
master's clock pulse.

The input to the slave is taken from the x-output of the
master. (It could be taken from the x'-output, too.)

b) The timing diagram is shown in Figure 2.

Note that the transitions take place in x at the leading
edge of the clock pulse, while transitions in Y take place
at the trailing edge of the clock pulse. This is because

104

of the Inverter which is incorporated inside the master slave flip-flop.

c) The Karnaugh Map of the T flip-flop is shown in figure 3.

KARNAUGH MAP FOR $\vec{y}$ FIG. 3

d) The excitation equation of the T flip-flop is obtained from the Karnaugh Map as follows:

$$\vec{y} = Ty' + T'y .$$

e) The State Table, shown in figure 4, is obtained from the excitation equation:

T	y	$\vec{y}$	REMARKS
0	0	0	NO
0	1	1	CHANGE
1	0	1	FLIPS
1	1	0	

FIG. 4

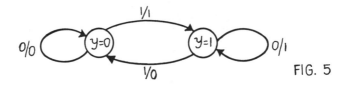

FIG. 5

f) The state diagram, drawn from the Karnaugh Map is shown in fig. 5.

● **PROBLEM** 4-19

For a D type (delay), clocked, master-slave flip-flop, give: a) a block diagram, b) a timing diagram, c) a Karnaugh Map, d) an excitation equation, e) a state table, and f) a state diagram.

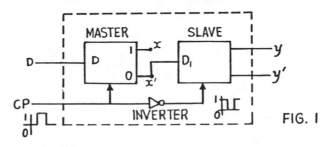

FIG. 1

Solution: The block diagram is shown in figure 1. The slave gets the inverted clock pulse. The input to the slave is taken from the x'-output of the master.

b) The timing diagram is shown in figure 2.

Normally a D flip-flop behaves simply as a delay line. However, here we have fed x' of the master as the input to the slave. Hence, our master-slave combination gives an inversion plus a delay (see D and Y).

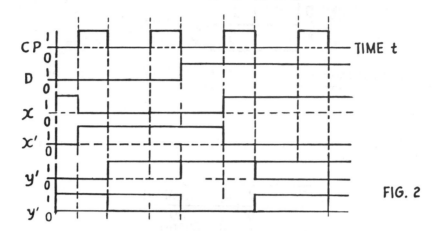

FIG. 2

c) The Karnaugh Map is drawn as shown in figure 3.

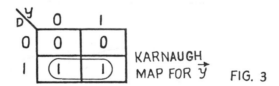

KARNAUGH MAP FOR $\vec{y}$ FIG. 3

d) From the Karnaugh Map, we write down the excitation equation as:

$$\vec{y} = D .$$

e) The state table can be prepared as shown in figure 4:

D	y	$\vec{y}$	REMARKS
0	0	0	$\vec{y}$ IS SAME AS D
0	1	0	
1	0	1	$\vec{y}$ IS SAME AS D
1	1	1	

FIG. 4

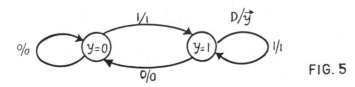

FIG. 5

f) The state diagram is also plotted with the help of the Karnaugh Map as shown in figure 5.

Describe, by means of block diagrams, how an S-C type flip-flop can be derived using NOR-gates and delay-lines, and then obtain an excitation equation for the S-C flip-flop.

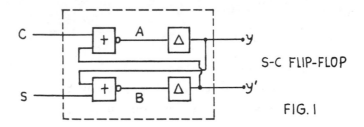

S-C FLIP-FLOP

FIG. 1

Solution: The S-C (i.e., set-clear) type flip-flop can be obtained using NOR-gates and Delay-lines as in fig. 1. From figure 1:

$$A = (y' + C)'$$

and,

$$B = (y + S)' .$$

Also, after a time-delay Δ, when steady state is reached, the next states $\vec{y}$ and $\vec{y}'$ of the outputs y and y' respectively, are given by the equations:

$$\vec{y} = A = (y' + C)' ,$$

and,

$$\vec{y}' = B = (y + S)' .$$

To show that the circuit is indeed a flip-flop we substitute different combinations of values of S and C into the next state equations for $\vec{y}$ and $\vec{y}'$.

i) Put S = 0 and C = 0

$$\therefore \vec{y} = (y' + 0)' = (y')' = y$$

and,

$$\vec{y}' = (y + 0)' = (y)' = y'$$

Thus, there is no change in the circuit.

ii) Put S = 1 and C = 0

$$\therefore \vec{y} = (y' + 0)' = (y')' = y$$

and,

$$\vec{y}' = (y + 1)' = (1)' = 0$$

And, as $\vec{y}' = 0$ therefore $\vec{y}$ becomes $= 1$.

Thus, the flip-flop sets

iii) Put $S = 0$ and $C = 1$

$$\therefore \vec{y} = (y' + 1)' = (1)' = 0$$

and,

$$\vec{y}' = (y + 0)' = y' = 1$$

Thus, the flip-flop clears.

iv) The condition $S = 1$ and $C = 1$ is not allowed because it leads to ambiguity in the outputs $\vec{y}$ and $\vec{y}'$:

$$\vec{y} = (y' + 1)' = (1)' = 0$$

and,

$$\vec{y}' = (y + 1)' = (1)' = 0$$

But both $\vec{y}$ and $\vec{y}'$ cannot be equal to zero because $\vec{y}$ and $\vec{y}'$ must be complements of each other.

Hence, for an S-C type flip-flop, there must always be a constraint on the input, i.e., $S \cdot C = 0$, so that both S and C cannot be $= 1$.

The above conditions can be plotted on a Karnaugh map. The constraint condition (S=1, C=1) gives rise to 'don't-care' states "d", because they will never occur in actual working of the flip-flop.

Hence, the Karnaugh map is shown in figure 2.

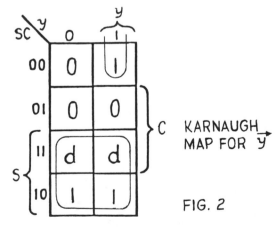

KARNAUGH MAP FOR $\vec{y}$

FIG. 2

This Karnaugh Map now allows us to write down the excitation equation as follows:

$$\vec{y} = S + C'y$$

$$= S \times y' + C'y \text{ (equivalent statement)}$$

$$\therefore \vec{y} = Sy' + C'y$$

108

Give: a) the block diagram, b) the timing diagram, c) the
Karnaugh Map, d) the excitation equation, e) the state
table, and f) the state diagram, for an S-C type, clocked,
master-slave flip-flop.

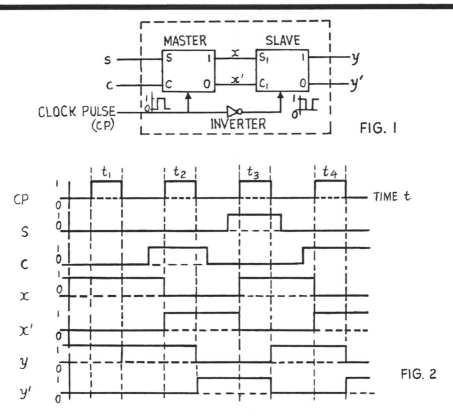

FIG. 1

FIG. 2

<u>Solution</u>: a) The block diagram of a clocked, master-slave
SC type flip-flop is shown in figure 1.

The master-slave flip-flop is a combination of two flip-flops,
the master getting the direct clock pulse and the slave getting the inverted clock pulse. The input condition is that
the Boolean product S·C = 0.

b) The timing diagram is shown in figure 2.

Timings for four clock pulses t_1 , t_2, t_3 and t_4 are shown.
We assume that initially, before t_1 arrives, x and y are
each = 1.

Note that x and x' change state, whenever required to do
so, at the leading edge of the clock pulse, but y and y'
change state at the trailing edge of the clock pulse due
to the inverter.

c) The Karnaugh Map of the master-slave SC flip-flop is
shown in figure 3.

The Karnaugh Map in figure 3 is for $\vec{y}$, where $\vec{y}$ denotes the
next state of y. Note also that as the input with both

S=1 and C=1 is not allowed, and hence does not ever occur,
we insert a 'd' in the squares for S,C=1,1. The 'd' represents a "don't care" condition.

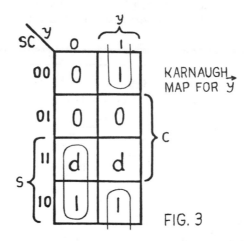

FIG. 3

d) The Karnaugh Map leads to the formulation of the excitation equation, i.e., the equation for $\vec{y}$ in terms of S, C
and y.

$$\therefore \vec{y} = Sy' + C'y .$$

e) The Karnaugh helps us to draw the state table, Figure 4.

S	C	y	$\vec{y}$	REMARKS
0	0	0	0	NO
0	0	1	1	CHANGE
0	1	0	0	CLEARS
0	1	1	0	
1	0	0	1	SETS
1	0	1	1	
1	1	0	d	NOT
1	1	1	d	ALLOWED

FIG. 4

f) The state diagram is drawn in Figure 5:

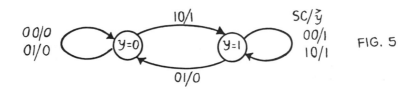

FIG. 5

Note in the above that the input condition 11 does not
occur at all.

110

For a J-K type, clocked, master-slave flip-flop, give a) a block diagram, b) a timing diagram, c) the Karnaugh Map, d) the excitation equation, e) the state table, and, f) the state diagram.

Solution: a) The block diagram is as shown below.

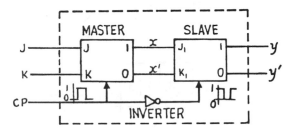

The slave gets the inverted clock pulse of what the master gets. The J-K flip-flop differs from the SC flip-flop in that the J-K flip-flop does not have the restriction that the S-C type flip-flop has, i.e., both the inputs of the S-C type flip-flop cannot simultaneously be equal to one. In the J-K type flip-flop, it is permissible to have both the J and K inputs 1.

b) The timing diagram is given in Figure 1 for 5 clock pulses up to t_5 .

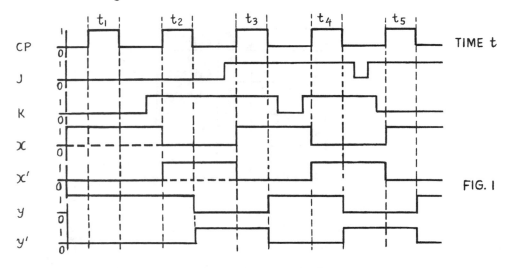

FIG. 1

    Note that y does at the trailing edge of the clock pulse exactly what x does at the leading edge of the clock pulse. Also note that x' and y' are just the reciprocals of x and y respectively.

c) The Karnaugh Map for the J-K flip-flop is plotted in Figure 2.

The entries in the Map represent the next state $\vec{y}$ for a given combination of y, i.e., the present state, and the inputs J and K.

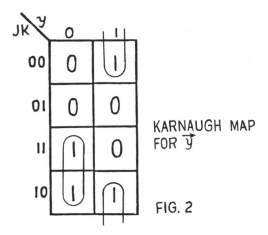

KARNAUGH MAP
FOR $\vec{y}$

FIG. 2

d) The excitation equation is obtained from the Karnaugh map of figure 2, as follows, for the next state $\vec{y}$

$$\vec{y} = Jy' + K'y .$$

e) The Karnaugh Map also helps us to prepare the state table as given in figure 3:

J	K	y	$\vec{y}$	REMARKS
0	0	0	0	NO
0	0	1	1	CHANGE
0	1	0	0	CLEARS
0	1	1	0	CLEARS
1	0	0	1	SETS
1	0	1	1	SETS
1	1	0	1	FLIPS
1	1	1	0	FLIPS

FIG. 3

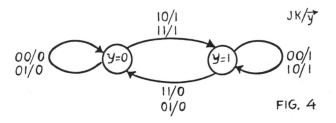

FIG. 4

f) The state diagram is drawn in figure 4.

112

Analyze the synchronous sequential circuit given below. Assume the inputs are binary levels and that the following state assignment is used.

$$y = 0 \equiv A$$

$$y = 1 \equiv B$$

Use Karnaugh maps to find

a) the state table

b) the state diagram

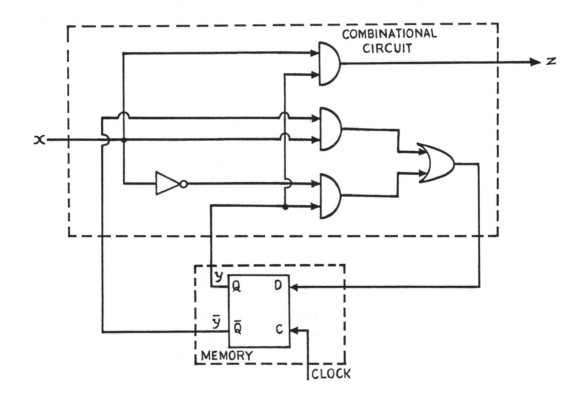

Solution: The given sequential circuit is built of AND, OR, and NOT gates and a memory device called a D Flip-Flop. Having an external clock connected to the circuit means that the memory changes state only during a clock pulse.

The operation of a D Flip-Flop goes like this: When the clock pulse goes from 0 to 1, data enters the flip-flop. When the clock pulse returns to 0 from 1 the output state changes may occur. Flip-flops which work under these conditions are called EDGE-TRIGGERED.

This sequential circuit has only one Flip-flop and hence only two states, A and B.

The best way to examine the behavior of the given sequential circuit is by drawing the timing diagram.

The timing diagram for the memory circuit is given in Figure 1;

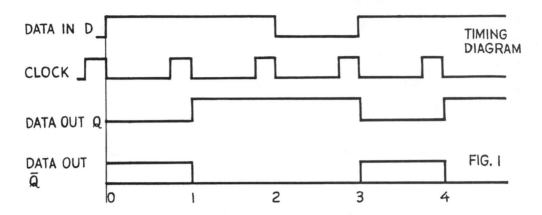

TIMING DIAGRAM

FIG. I

In general, the operation of the sequential circuit given may be completely defined by a state-table which lists all possible operating conditions, as shown in figure 2.

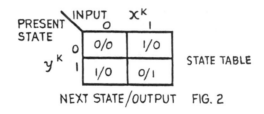

STATE TABLE

NEXT STATE/OUTPUT   FIG. 2

The logic followed in the construction of the state-table is as follows:

To fill in the upper left hand corner assume a present state $y^k = 0$ and the input $x^k = 0$. Folloiwng these signals through the combinational circuit it is found that the next state is $y^k = 0$ and that the output is $j = 0$. Hence the entry in the upper left block is 0/0 .

The initial conditions for the upper right block is $y^k = 0$, and $x^k = 1$. Applying these signals to the combinational circuit given yields the output $j = 0$. So that the entry in this block is 1/0.

To obtain the completed state diagram the states which the circuit assumes must be identified.

Identification may be done as follows:

$$y = (0) \equiv A$$

$$y = (1) \equiv B$$

114

The completed state table is shown in Fig. 3:

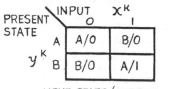

PRESENT STATE	INPUT x^k 0	1
A	A/0	B/0
y^k B	B/0	A/1

NEXT STATE/OUTPUT   FIG. 3

b) To construct the state diagram, the state table is used. Examination of the state table reveals that these are the only two states, A and B, which the circuit may assume. These states are represented in a state diagram as shown in figure 4.

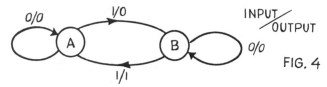

FIG. 4

Note that assuming an initial state, $y^k = 0$ and $x^k = 0$, the output is zero and the next state is still A. When $y^k = 0$ and $x^k = 1$ the next state is the state B and the output is y = 0.

When $x^k = 0$ is applied to state B the next state is again state B and output is y = 0. When $x^k = 1$ state B changes to state A with an output of j = 1.

SEQUENTIAL CIRCUIT DESIGN

● **PROBLEM** 4-24

Describe how J-K, T and D type flip-flops can be derived starting from the S-C type flip-flop, and obtain excitation equations for them from the excitation equation of the S-C type flip-flop.

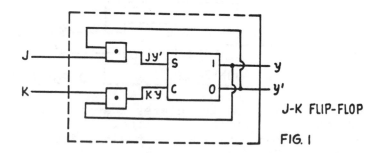

J-K FLIP-FLOP

FIG. I

Solution: a) J-K type flip-flop can be obtained from an S-C type flip-flop by adding two AND-gates as shown in fig. 1.   The input constraint S·C = 0 of the S-C flip-flop

115

is automatically achieved in the J-K flip-flop, as shown in figure 1, because of the AND-gates.

And thus, the J and K inputs need not worry about any input constraints. Both J and K can be = 1.

The excitation equation of the J-K flip-flop is obtained by substitution in the excitation equation for the S-C flip-flop as follows:

$$\vec{Y} = SY' + c'Y$$

$$\vec{Y} = (JY')Y' + (KY)'Y \quad \text{(substitution)}$$

$$\vec{Y} = JY'Y' + (K' + Y')Y \quad \text{(by DeMorgans law)}$$

$$\vec{Y} = JY' + K'Y + Y'Y \quad \text{(distributive law)}$$

$$\vec{Y} = JY' + K'Y$$

b) A T type flip-flop is obtained by shorting together the J and K inputs of the J-K flip-flop obtained in (a) as shown. in fig. 2.

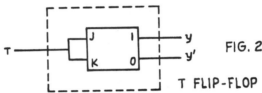

FIG. 2

T FLIP-FLOP

The excitation equation of the T flip-flop is obtained from the excitation equation of the J-K flip-flop by putting J = K = T

$$\therefore \vec{Y} = JY' + K'Y \qquad \text{(Now put J=K=T)}$$

$$\therefore \vec{Y} = TY' + T'Y$$

$$= T + Y$$

c) A D type flip-flop can be obtained from an S-C type flip-flop by giving mutually inverted inputs to the S and C inputs, as shown in Figure 3:

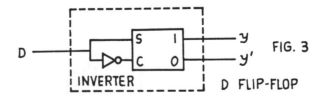

FIG. 3

INVERTER

D FLIP-FLOP

The inverter automatically ensures that both S and C will never be equal to 1 at the same time.

The excitation equation is obtained from the excitation equation of the S-C flip-flop as follows:

$$\vec{y} = Sy' + C'y = Dy' + (D')'y$$

$$\therefore \vec{y} = Dy' + Dy = D(y' + y) = D \cdot 1 = D \ .$$

Using a clocked JK flip-flop construct a:

a) D flip-flop.

b) T flip-flop.

c) Clocked T flip-flop.

d) SR flip-flop.

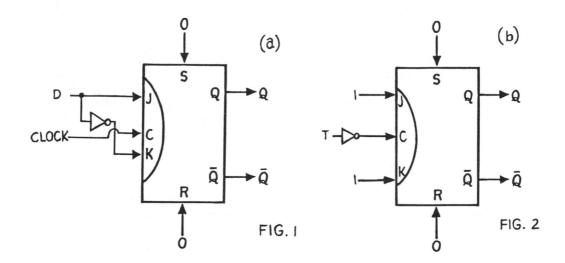

FIG. 1   FIG. 2

Solution: The construction shown in fig. 1 gives a D flip-flop realization.   Note that both S and R inputs are zero, and the circuit obeys the truth table given below;

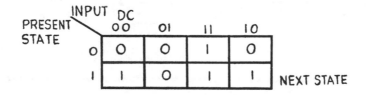

PRESENT STATE	INPUT DC 00	01	11	10
0	0	0	1	0
1	1	0	1	1	NEXT STATE

b) By applying 0 to both inputs S and R and 1 to inputs J and K, a T flip-flop may be constructed as shown in fig. 2. Note that the C (clock) input becomes the $\bar{T}$ input and the circuit constructed obeys the truth table of a T flip-flop.

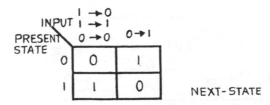

PRESENT STATE	INPUT $1 \to 0$, $1 \to 1$, $0 \to 0$	$0 \to 1$
0	0	1
1	1	0	NEXT-STATE

c) Shown in figure 3 is a realization of the clocked T

117

flip-flop. The control signal T_c allows the clock pulses to be selectively applied to the input terminal. Each clock pulse that arrives at T causes the flip-flop to a state change.

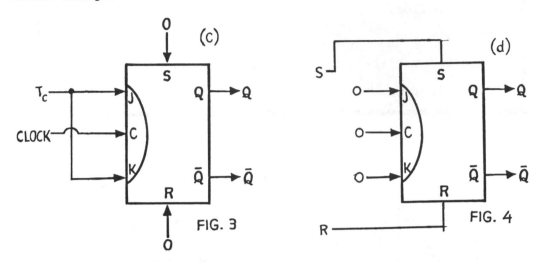

FIG. 3   FIG. 4

d) Applying 0 to J, K, and Clock inputs gives an SR flip-flop realization, shown in fig. 4.

● **PROBLEM** 4-26

Convert the following sequential machine which uses T type flip-flops into one using S-C type flip-flops only.

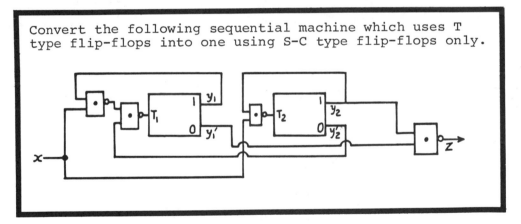

Solution: Step I.

First, write out all the outputs and inputs of all the gates and flip-flops in terms of x and the flip-flop outputs y_1 , y_1' , y_2 , y_2' , as follows:

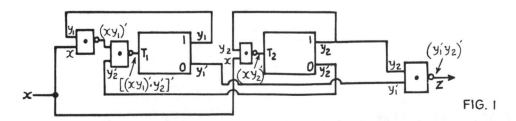

FIG. I

118

Hence, we find that $T_1 = [(xy_1)' \cdot y_2']'$ (from the figure).

$$\therefore T_1 = (xy_1) + y_2 \text{ (using De Morgan's laws).}$$

Also,

$$T_2 = (xy_2)' = x' + y_2' \text{ (by De Morgan's laws)}$$

and,

$$Z = (y_1' \, y_2)' = y_1 + y_2' \text{ (by DeMorgan's laws).}$$

Step II.

Now, we plot each equation T_1 and T_2 into a Karnaugh Map for $y_1 y_2$ and x, as follows:

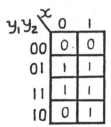

KARNAUGH MAP FOR T_1 KARNAUGH MAP FOR T_2

FIG. 2

Now, in order to convert a T flip-flop into an S-C flip-flop, we make the following observations:

i) The excitation equations of the T and S-C type flip-flops, for $\vec{y}_1$ are:

$$\vec{y}_1 = T_1 \cdot y_1' + T_1' \cdot y_1$$

and,

$$\vec{y}_1 = S_1 \cdot y_1' + C' \cdot y_1$$

ii) On putting $y_1 = 0$ (and hence $y_1' = 1$), in both the above equations, we get:

$$\vec{y}_1 = T_1 \cdot 1 + T_1' \cdot 0 = T_1$$

and,

$$\vec{y}_1 = S_1 \cdot 1 + C_1' \cdot 0 = S_1 .$$

Hence we see that in our Karnaugh Map for T_1, the first two rows (viz., for $y_1 y_2 = 00$ and 01, i.e., for which $y_1 = 0$), correspond to T_1 or S_1.

119

iii)   Similarly, on putting $y_1 = 1$ (and hence $y_1' = 0$) in the above equations, we get:

$$\vec{y}_1 = T_1 \cdot 0 + T_1' \cdot 1 = T_1' ,$$

and,

$$\vec{y}_1 = S_1 \cdot 0 + C_1' \cdot 1 = C_1' .$$

$$\therefore (\vec{y}_1)' = T_1 ,$$

and,

$$(\vec{y}_1)' = C_1 \quad \text{(complementing both sides in the above equation).}$$

Hence, we see that the last two rows of our Karnaugh Map for T_1, viz., $y_1y_2 = 11$ and 10 are the complements of $\vec{y}_1$, and correspond to the remainder of T_1 in a T flip-flop, or to C_1 in an S-C flip-flop.

Step III.

In view of the observations i), ii), and iii), we can now split up T_1 into its components for S_1 and C_1.

FIG. 3

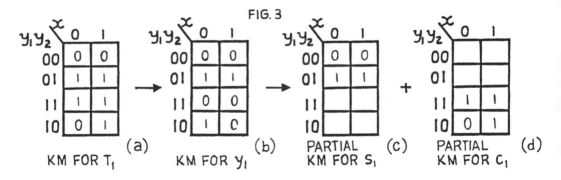

The fig. (3a) for T_1 leads to fig. (3b) for $\vec{y}_1$ by complementing the entries for $y_1y_2 = 11$ and 10 from fig. (3a), as explained in observation iii) before.

Fig. (3b) is now split up into two parts corresponding to $y_1 = 0$ and $y_1 = 1$ in fig. (3c) and fig. (3d), respectively. Note that fig. (3d) uses the complements of the entries in fig. (3b).

We could have split up fig. (3a) directly into the figs. (3c) and (3d) without worrying about the fig. (3b) for $\vec{y}_1$, and the complements. But this intervening step was used in the example only to illustrate the reasoning involved.

Step IV.

Now complete the partial Karnaugh Maps of figs. (3c) and (3d) by making use of any special properties of the type of flip-flop used. For example, for changing over to J-K flip-flops, all the remaining entries would be don't care conditions, "d". But, an SC type flip-flop, must satisfy the condition $S \cdot C = 0$. Hence, fill up the empty blanks such that the product of corresponding blanks in the Maps for S_1 and $C_1 = 0$.

This is done as follows, in fig. (4):

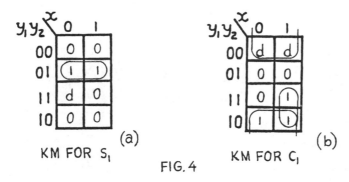

(a)

KM FOR S_1

FIG. 4

KM FOR C_1

(b)

Where a zero already exists in one of the partial Karnaugh Maps, a 'd' can be entered in the corresponding square in the other Karnaugh Map. This is because the product of $S_1 = 0$ and $C_1 = 0$ or 1 will always be 0. For example, note that a 0 already exists in the Karnaugh Map for S_1 in the square for $y_1 y_2$ x equal to 00 0. Hence, a 'd' can be entered in the corresponding square for $y_1 y_2$ x equal to 00 0 in the Map for C_1 because $S_1 \cdot C_1$ will equal 0. Similarly, a 'd' is entered in the square for $y_1 y_2$ x equal to 00 1 in the Map for C_1 because there is a 0 in the square for $y_1 y_2$ x equal to 00 1 in the Map for S_1.

But, the squares for $y_1 y_2$ x equal to 01 0 and 01 1 are entered with zeroes in the Map for C_1 because there are 1's in the corresponding squares in the Map for S_1.

Similarly, fill up the lower half of the Map for S_1 with d's or 0's according to whether there are 0's or 1's in the corresponding squares in the Map for C_1 .

Step IV.

We now write out equations for S_1 and C_1

$$S_1 = y_1' y_2 \qquad \text{(from fig. (4a).)}$$

$$C_1 = y_2' + y_1 x . \left(\text{from fig. (4b)} \right)$$

121

Step V.

We repeat the Steps III to V for T_2 to get S_2 and C_2 .

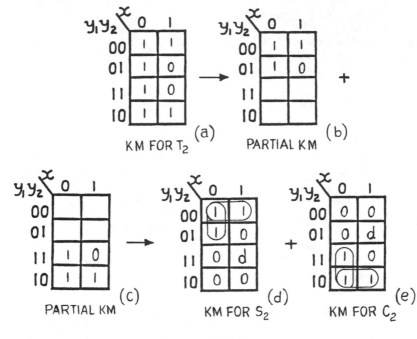

FIG. 5

$$\therefore S_2 = y_1'x' + y_1'y_2' = y_1' \cdot (x' + y_2') \qquad \text{(from fig. (5d).)}$$

and

$$C_2 = y_1x' + y_1y_2' = y_1(x' + y_2') \qquad \text{(from fig. (5e).)}$$

Step VI.

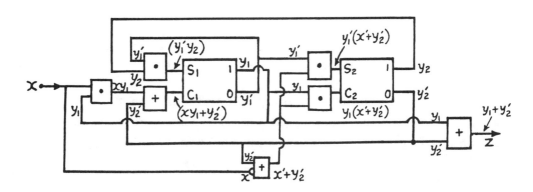

We now draw a circuit diagram with two SC type
flip-flops, and draw necessary input gates to satisfy the
inputs S_1 , C_1 , S_2 , C_2 of the flip-flops obtained above.

Draw the logic diagram of a four-bit register using S-R
flip-flops.

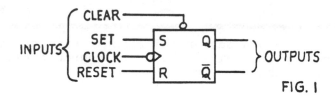

FIG. 1

Solution: Figure 1 shows the inputs and outputs of an S-R
flip-flop.

When clear is 0 the flip-flop is cleared sequentially (without the clock pulse requirement). The clear input must go
to 1 during the normal clocked operation.

Figure 2 shows the block diagram of the four-bit
register. The data inputs are I_1 , I_2 , I_3 , and I_4 .
The control inputs are CP (clock pulse), load, and clear.
The data outputs are A_1 , A_2 , A_3 , and A_4 .

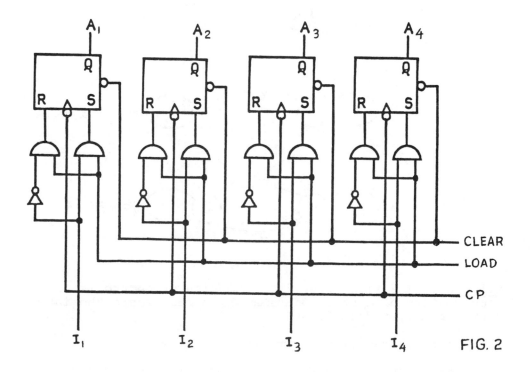

FIG. 2

The clock pulse is common to all four flip-flops and
consists of continuous pulses. The circle under the triangle in each flip-flop indicates that flip-flop transitions occur during the falling edge of each clock pulse.

The Load input is connected to all four flip-flops via the AND gates. When Load is 0 the inputs to S and R are 0, and Q remains in the previous state. When Load is 1 the inputs to S and R are I and $\bar{I}$, respectively; thus the output Q will show the value of I.

● **PROBLEM** 4-28

Design a synchronous sequential circuit with one input and one output that recognizes the input sequence 01. For example, if the input sequence is

$$x = 0101000111101$$

then the output sequence will be

$$Z = 0101000100001$$

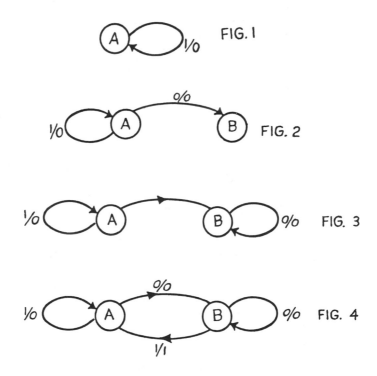

FIG. 1

FIG. 2

FIG. 3

FIG. 4

Solution: The first step in the design procedure is the construction of a state diagram which represents the input-output behavior described.

The diagram is constructed as follows:

First it is assumed that the machine is in some starting state A and the first input is a 1. Since a 1 is not the first element in the input string to be considered, the machine remains in state A and yields an output z = 0. This is shown in fig. 1.

If the machine is in the initial state A and the input is 0, then because this input is the first input symbol in the string to be recognized, the machine moves to a new state B and yields an output z = 0, shown in figure 2.

Now the machine is in state B and the next input symbol is a 0. Because this is not the second symbol in the sequence 01 the machine remains in state B and gives an output z = 0, as shown in figure 3.

Finally, if the machine is in state B and the next input symbol is a 1, then the machine moves to state A and produces an output z = 1, shown in figure 4.

The relationship between the number of states (N_s) and the number of flip-flops (N_{FF}) is given by the expression

$$2^{N_{FF}-1} < N_s \leq 2^{N_{FF}}$$

State Assignment is arbitrarily chosen to be A = 0 B = 1

The state table, figure 5, now can be drawn as the transition table, Figure 6.

	x	
	0	1
0=A	B/0	A/0
1=B	B/0	A/1

STATE TABLE
FIG. 5

y^k \ x	0	1
0	1	0
1	1	0

y^{k+1}

FIG. 6

Transition tables: y^k, denotes the present state of the circuit which is the current output of the flip-flop. y^{k+1} denotes the next state of the machine, which is the output of the flip-flop after a transition has occurred.

Using the clocked SR flip-flop input tables, figure 7, the excitation tables for the problem are derived, figures 8 and 9.

Input		Present State	Next State
S	R	y^k	y^{k+1}
0	0	0	0
0	0	1	1
0	1	0	0
0	1	1	0
1	0	0	1
1	0	1	1
1	1	0	Not used
1	1	1	Not used

Fig. 7

As an example of derivation, consider the upper left

hand corner of the transition table given in Fig. 6. Here $y^k = 0$, $x = 0$, and $y^{k+1} = 1$. To effect a state change from $y^k = 0$ to $y^{k+1} = 1$, the signals which must appear on the Set and Reset lines, found from figure 7, are $S = 1$ and $R = 0$. Hence, these signals appear in the corresponding positions in the excitation maps of Figs. 8 and 9.

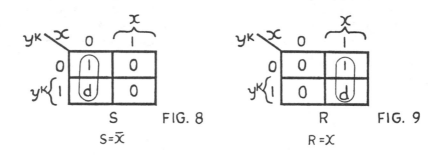

FIG. 8   FIG. 9

$S = \bar{x}$ $R = x$

Next consider the state transition in the upper right hand corner of the transition table where $y^k = 0$, $x = 1$, and $y^{k+1} = 0$. Since no change in state must occur, the signal, found from figure 7, on the set line must be 0, while the reset line doesn't matter.

From the state diagram of figure 4 the Karnaugh map of the output z is constructed, as shown in fig. 10.

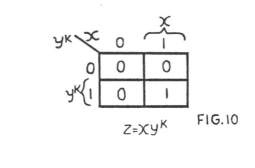

FIG. 10

$z = xy^k$

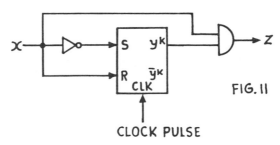

FIG. 11

CLOCK PULSE

The combinational circuit of figure 11 is created from the simplified equations $s = \bar{x}$, $R = x$, $z = xy^k$

126

Design a synchronous sequential circuit with one input line and one output line that recognizes the input string x = 1111.

The circuit is also required to recognize overlapping sequences such that if the input string is

x = 110111111010

then the output string should be

z = 000000111000

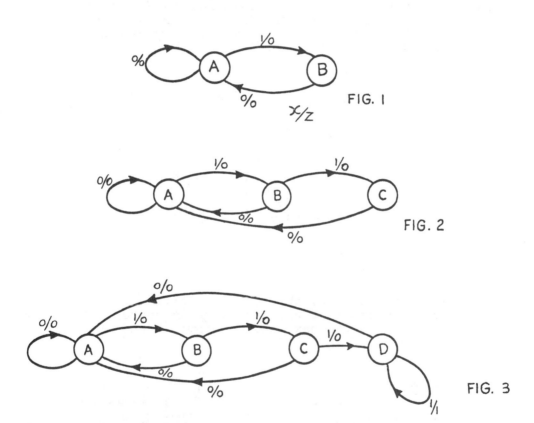

FIG. 1

FIG. 2

FIG. 3

Solution: The first step in the design procedure is to draw a state diagram which represents the behavior of the circuit, which in this case happens to be a sequence 1111 detector. First you assume that the machine is in some starting state A and the first input is a 0. Since 0 is not part of our sequence, the machine remains in state A with an output of 0, 'waiting' for a 1. As soon as a 1 occurs at the input, the machine jumps into state B. The output is still 0, because our sequence has not yet been completed. See fig. 1.

If an input of 0 occurs while the machine is in state B, the 1111 sequence is interrupted and the machine must

go back to state A to start all over again. See fig. 1.
However, if an input of 1 occurs, the machine jumps from
state B to state C, meaning that the second '1' of the
sequence was detected. See fig. 2. If the next input is
a 0, the 1111 sequence is again interrupted, and the
machine must go from C back to A to start all over again;
also in fig. 2; but if the input is a 1, while in state
C, the machine jumps into state D, meaning that it has
just detected the third '1' of the 1111 sequence; see
fig. 3. If the next input is a 0, the sequence is again
interrupted, and the machine must go back to state A; however, if the input is a 1, the machine has just detected
the last '1' of the 1111 sequence, and the output finally
becomes 1. See fig. 3 again.

Note in fig. 3 that when the machine is in state D,
the '1/1' loop will continue giving outputs of 1 as long
as the inputs remain 1; thus ensuring the detection of
overlapping 1111 sequences. Fig. 3 is the complete state
diagram. The next step is to set up a state table from
the state diagram. See fig. 4.

STATE TABLE

P.S. \ x	0	1
A	A/0	B/0
B	A/0	C/0
C	A/0	D/0
D	A/0	D/1

N.S./Z

X = INPUT

Z = OUTPUT

P.S. PRESENT-
    STATE

N.S. NEXT-
    STATE

FIG. 4

Note, for example, that the top, right-hand box of the
state table means that when the present state is A and input becomes a 1, the next state becomes B and the output
is 0.

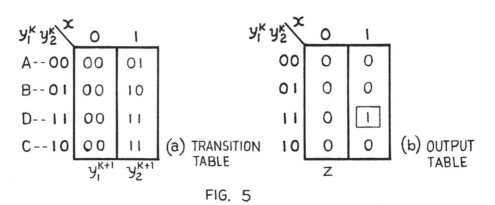

$y_1^k y_2^k$ \ x	0	1
A--00	00	01
B--01	00	10
D--11	00	11
C--10	00	11

$y_1^{k+1} y_2^{k+1}$

(a) TRANSITION TABLE

$y_1^k y_2^k$ \ x	0	1
00	0	0
01	0	0
11	0	1
10	0	0

Z

(b) OUTPUT TABLE

FIG. 5

Now we choose arbitrary state assignments as follows:

128

$$A = 00$$

$$B = 01$$

$$C = 10$$

$$D = 11$$

This results in a transition table, and an output table (which is simply extracted from the state table). See fig. 5. Note that states D and C have been interchanged to facilitate the use of K-maps.

The next step is to pick a memory element. We shall pick the JK flip-flop. Note that we will need two memory elements, since

$$Log_2 \text{ (no. of states)} \leq \text{No. of memory elements .}$$

Y^K	Y^{K+1}	J	K
0	0	0	d
1	1	d	0
0	1	1	d
1	0	d	1

NOTE: d MEANS "DON'T CARE"

FIG. 6

To work with flip-flop logic, an application table is extremely helpful. This table is easily derived from the truth table of the particular flip-flop. See fig. 6.

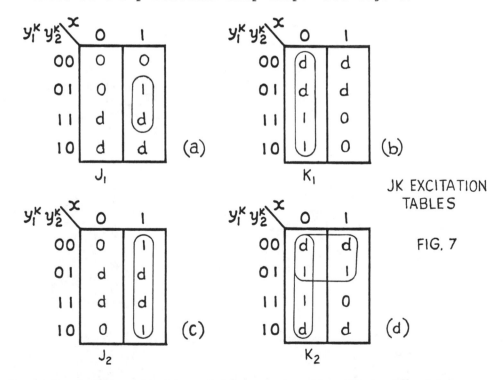

JK EXCITATION TABLES

FIG. 7

Next we form JK excitation tables using the JK application

129

table, and the transition table.

See fig. 7a,b,c,d.

Note that J_1K_1 corresponds to the y_1^{k+1} column on the transition table.

Now we solve for the logic equations using the excitation tables as K-maps:

$$J_1 = Y_2X \qquad\qquad K_1 = \overline{X}$$

$$J_2 = X \qquad\qquad K_2 = \overline{X} + \overline{Y}_1$$

$$Z = XY_1Y_2$$

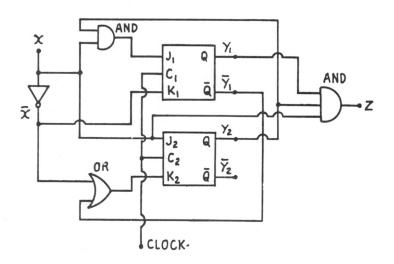

FIG. 8 LOGIC DIAGRAM
FOR THE COMPLETE
CIRCUIT.

From the logic equations we can now build the actual circuit which will perform the desired function; in this case a 1111 sequence detector. See Fig. 8.

CHAPTER 5

COMPUTER ARCHITECTURE

HARDWARE

Explain the terms: Memory cell, Registers, Decoders, Multiplexers.

Solution: The memory cell is the basic unit of memory. It can store 1 bit of information (i.e. it can have value "1" in it or value "0" in it). The cell may be either a core memory or a flip-flop.

Registers: A group of flip-flops constitutes a Register. A 4 bit Register is made up of 4 flip-flops and holds 4 bits of information. Registers can be used in various ways; for example, as counters, shift registers, Increment/Decrement counters with parallel load, etc. These are temporary storage devices used in the internal storage of intermediate data in the CPU.

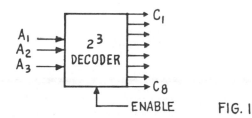

FIG. I

Decoders: Decoders are devices by which we can divide n number of input lines to it into 2^n output lines; see Figure 1. The decoder is used in conjunction with a truth table, Figure 2. From the truth table we can find the decoder's output for any combination of the imputs; enable and bits A_1, A_2, A_3.

INPUTS				OUTPUTS							
Enable	A_1	A_2	A_3	C1	C2	C3	C4	C5	C6	C7	C8
0	0	0	0	0	0	0	0	0	0	0	0
1	0	0	0	1	0	0	0	0	0	0	0
1	0	0	1	0	1	0	0	0	0	0	0
1	0	1	0	0	0	1	0	0	0	0	0
1	0	1	1	0	0	0	1	0	0	0	0
1	1	0	0	0	0	0	0	1	0	0	0
1	1	0	1	0	0	0	0	0	1	0	0
1	1	1	0	0	0	0	0	0	0	1	0
1	1	1	1	0	0	0	0	0	0	0	1

Fig. 2.   Truth Table for 3 line to 8 line decoder

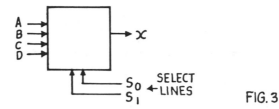

FIG. 3

Multiplexer: This is just the reverse of the Decoder.
Given 2^n input lines there will be only one output line,
see Figure 3. Here, which input lines proceed to output
depends on the bit combination of the n select lines.

The truth table for the 4 line to 1 line multiplexer,
shown in Figure 3, is given in Figure 4.

INPUTS		OUTPUT
S_0	S_1	X
0	0	A
0	1	B
1	0	C
1	1	D

Fig. 4

● **PROBLEM** 5-2

What is meant by "coincident current" in a computer's
core memory? How does this relate to binary states?

Solution: A single unit of core can take on a value of
1 or 0, depending upon whether the direction of its magnetization is clockwise or counterclockwise. If all the
cores were strung on a single wire, each time current was
passed down the wire, all the cores would become magnetized in the same direction. This would render the use
of core inefficient.

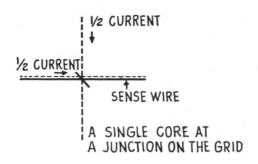

½ CURRENT

½ CURRENT

SENSE WIRE

A SINGLE CORE AT
A JUNCTION ON THE GRID

To avoid this possibility, the method of coincident current is used. Three wires are strung through each core
to mediate control of the direction of magnetization.
One entire plane of cores resembles a grid with cores at
each intersection. Two of the three wires are current
wires, while the third is called a sense wire.

Let us present an example of the procedure necessary to
have a single core represent the binary digit 1. Each of
the current wires sends only one-half the necessary current to make the core become magnetized in a clockwise
direction. The core located where the current wires intersect will become magnetized in a clockwise direction;
all other cores along the lines remain unaffected. The
sense wire is a feedback device which can determine at
any time if a particular core is representing a binary 1
or a binary 0.

● **PROBLEM** 5-3

Using the S-R (set-reset) flip-flop, design a memory cell
with the following inputs: Data-in, Read/Write, Select.
Output: Data-out.

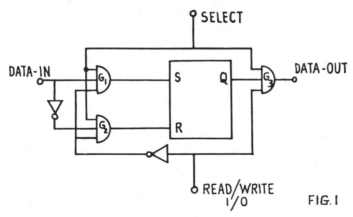

FIG. 1

Solution: The memory cell, which is the basic building
block of the memory unit in a computer, is capable of
storing one bit of information. The memory cell is
shown in Figure 1. The memory cell is used to store
information (Write) or recall information (Read).

To store information, connect the Select line to logic
level 1, the Data-in line to the logic level to be

stored, and the Read/Write line to logic level 0. Under
these conditions gates G_1 and G_2 are enabled and gate G_3
is disabled. The values of the S and R inputs of the
flip-flop are the Data-in and $\overline{\text{Data-in}}$, respectively.
Since the S and R inputs are complements of each other,
the output of the flip-flop, Q, has the same logic level
as the S input. Hence data has been written into the
memory cell. After writing in the data, the Select line
is connected to logic level 0. This disables all the
gates so that changes in the Data-in line no longer
affect the inputs to the flip-flop. Also, when the Select
line is 0, both inputs to the flip-flop are 0 and the
flip-flop is in its "memory" state, that is Q retains
the previous value of S.

To read data from the memory cell, the Select line and
the Read/Write line are connected to logic level 1.
Under these conditions gates G_1 and G_2 are disabled and
G_3 is enabled. Hence, the value of Q appears at the
Data-out line. After reading the data the Select line is
connected to logic level 0.

● **PROBLEM** 5-4

Design a 4 x 3 random access memory (RAM) using one-bit
memory cells, OR gates, and a decoder.

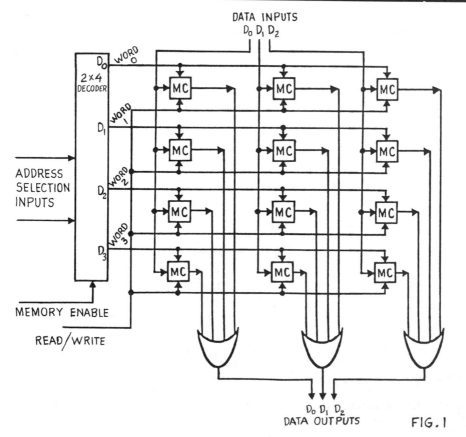

FIG. 1

134

Solution: Figure 1 is the configuration of a 4 x 3 RAM.
Each box labeled M.C. is a one-bit memory cell whose
inputs and output are designated in Figure 2.

The enable input of the decoder is used as a Memory enable
line. When the line is 0 the decoder is disabled and
none of the memory words are selected. When the Memory
enable line is 1 the decoder is enabled and one of the
four words is selected, depending upon the address.

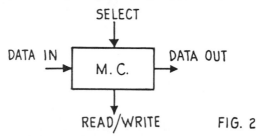

FIG. 2

The Read/Write control is connected to every M.C. When
it is 1, the outputs of the selected M.C.s pass through
the three OR gates to the Data-output terminals. The
outputs of the non-selected M.C.s are 0, having no effect
on the OR gates.

When the Read/Write control is 0 the information on the
data-input lines is transferred into the flip-flops of
the selected word. The M.C.s in the non-selected words
are disabled by the selection line so their values remain
unchanged.

● **PROBLEM** 5-5

(a)   Use a truth table to show that the sum (disregarding
the carry) of two binary digits x and y is given by the
Boolean expression:

$$(x \cdot \sim y) + (\sim x \cdot y) \qquad \text{(Statement 1)}$$

(b)   Write a Boolean expression for the carry.
(c)   Set up a circuit to find the sum and carry of two
binary digits, using AND, OR and NOT gates.

Solution: Recall that the rule of addition of two binary
digits is given in the truth table of Figure 1.

First addend	Second addend	Sum digit	Carry digit
0	0	0	0
0	1	1	0
1	0	1	0
1	1	0	1

Fig. 1

(a) Since x and y each could be either 0 or 1, there are 2^2 = 4 possible combinations of values of x and y. Evaluating the terms in parentheses of Statement 1, and then Statement 1 itself, the truth table of Figure 2 is created.

x	y	∿x	∿y	x·∿y	∿x·y	(x·∿y) + (∿x·y)
0	0	1	1	0	0	0
0	1	1	0	0	1	1
1	0	0	1	1	0	1
1	1	0	0	0	0	0

Fig. 2

We see that the entries in the last column of the truth table match the corresponding entries (that is, given the same values for x and y) in the sum-digit column. Therefore, the Boolean sum (that is, disregarding the carry) of x and y can be represented by the logical expression given in Statement (1). Statement (1) is also called the nonequivalence function of x, y, written

$$x \not\equiv y = (x·∿y) + (∿x·y).$$

Note that x ≢ y = 1 if and only if x ≡ y = 0, that is, when x ≠ y, which is why it is called the nonequivalence function. It is also known as the EXCLUSIVE-OR function.

(b) Note that the carry digit is one if and only if both addends, x and y, are 1. But this is the definition of the AND function. Therefore, the carry digit can be represented by x·y.

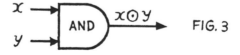

FIG. 3

(c) The circuit for the carry is simply the gate representation for x·y (see Figure 3). Using the rule that operands of the + operation are inputs to an OR gate, operands of the · operation are inputs to an AND gate and the operand of the ∿ operation is the input to a NOT gate, we can represent the terms in parentheses as shown in Figure 4.

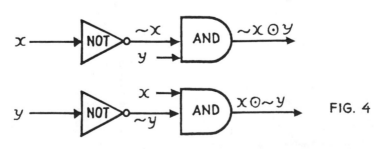

FIG. 4

Since each term in parentheses is an operand of the +
operation, each of the above gate circuits is an input
to an OR gate. Running the carry circuit in parallel to
the sum circuit would complete the network.

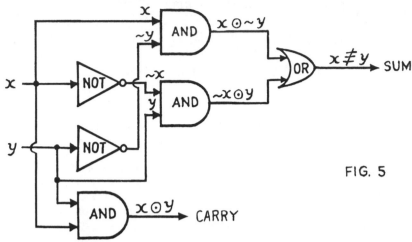

FIG. 5

The network in Figure 5 is known as a half-adder. The half-
adder has two inputs, corresponding to the two addends,
and it will have two outputs, one giving the sum digit
and the other giving the carry digit. It performs only
half the task for full addition, since it provides neither
for a previous carry nor for placing the carry bit to
the next column. For complete addition two half-adders
are required. Methods for addition may be classified as
either parallel or serial. In parallel addition each
column is added simultaneously by a separate full-adder.
In serial addition each column to be added is transmitted
one digit at a time, beginning with the digit in lowest
position. The carry bit is retained to be combined with
the addition results of the next column. The sum is
given as a sequential output.

● **PROBLEM** 5-6

(a)   If the inputs to half-adder are x and y, show that
the sum output could be given by the Boolean expression:

$$(x+y) \cdot (\sim x + \sim y) \tag{1}$$

and the carry output could be given by:

$$\sim(\sim x + \sim y) \tag{2}$$

(b)   Set up a new circuit for a half-adder using the
alternate expressions for sum and carry, given by (1)
and (2) and OR, AND and NOT gates.

(c)   Show that $(x+y) \cdot \sim(x \cdot y)$ $\qquad$ (3)

is equivalent to (1) and set up a new half-adder circuit
using $x \cdot y$ as the expression for the carry output and
(3) as the expression for the sum output.

Solution: (a) To show that the sum output is given by
expression (1) and the carry output is given by expression (2), we could set up their truth tables and note
that the results agree with the addition table. But
since this approach is used to show that the sum output
could be given by:

$$(x \cdot \sim y) + (\sim x \cdot y) \tag{4}$$

and that the carry output could be given by:

$$x \cdot y \tag{5}$$

we will use the laws of Boolean algebra to show that (1)
is equivalent to (4) and (2) is equivalent to (5):

$$(x+y) \cdot (\sim x + \sim y) = [x \cdot (\sim x + \sim y)] + [y \cdot (\sim x + \sim y)]$$

      Distributive law of • over +

$$= [(x \cdot \sim x) + (x \cdot \sim y)] + [(y \cdot \sim x) + (y \cdot \sim y)]$$

      Distributive law of • over +

$$= [0 + (x \cdot \sim y)] + [(y \cdot \sim x) + 0]$$

      Law of the excluded middle

$$= (x \cdot \sim y) + (y \cdot \sim x)$$

      Identity of +

$$= (x \cdot \sim y) + (\sim x \cdot y)$$

      Commutativity of •

To show that (2) is equivalent to (5):

$$\sim (\sim x + \sim y) = \sim (\sim x) \cdot \sim (\sim y)$$

      de Morgan's Law

$$= x \cdot y \qquad\qquad \text{Involution Law}$$

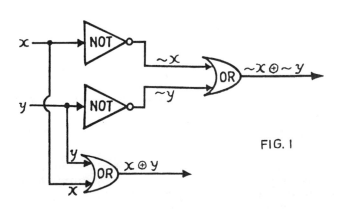

FIG. I

(b)   Setting up the terms in parentheses of equation 1
first, we create the circuit of Figure 1.   Since both
x+y and $\sim$x + $\sim$y are operands of the • operation they will
be inputs to an AND gate whose output is the sum digit.
Using $\sim$x + $\sim$y as input to a NOT gate gives an output
that is the carry digit.   The complete implementation
of equation (4) is shown in Figure 2.

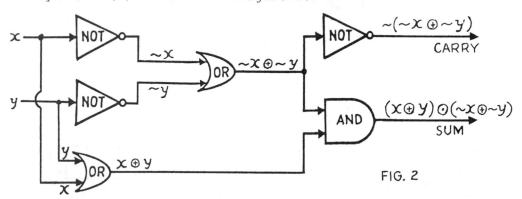

FIG. 2

(c)   De Morgan's law allows us to write:

$$(x+y) \cdot \sim(x \cdot y) = (x+y) \cdot (\sim x + \sim y)$$

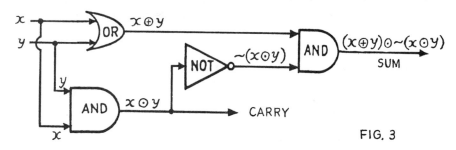

FIG. 3

The left and right terms in parentheses of (3) are simply
outputs of OR and AND gates, respectively, where x and y
are the inputs.   But x•y is also the expression for the
carry digit.   So the complete half-adder circuit using
(3) is the simplest of those we've constructed.   (See
Figure 3).

● **PROBLEM** 5-7

(1)   Obtain the SUM and CARRY functions for a FULL ADDER
and give its circuit implementation.

(2)   Obtain the Difference and Borrow functions for the
FULL SUBTRACTOR and give its circuit implementation.

Solution: In a FULL-ADDER we have to add three bits, the
Augend bit, Addend bit and previous carry bit.   Using the
rules for addition in binary, create the truth table
shown in Figure 1.

A	B	C_{i-1}	SUM	CARRY
0	0	0	0	0
0	0	1	1	0
0	1	0	1	0
0	1	1	0	1
1	0	0	1	0
1	0	1	0	1
1	1	0	0	1
1	1	1	1	1

Fig. 1

Now use the Karnaugh Maps of Figure 2 to find the logic expressions.

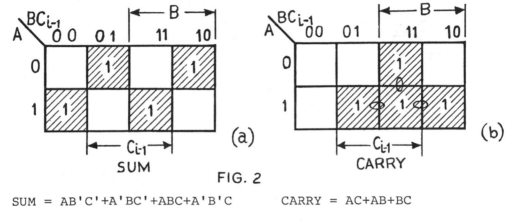

FIG. 2

SUM = AB'C'+A'BC'+ABC+A'B'C   CARRY = AC+AB+BC

= (AB'+A'B)C' + (AB+A'B')C   = AB + (A'B+AB')C
(Distributive Law)

= (A+B)C' + (A+B)'C   = AB + (A+B)C
(NOR definition)

= A+B+C   (NOR definition)

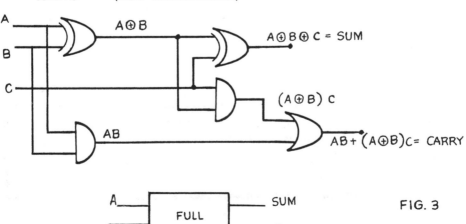

FIG. 3

BLOCK DIAGRAM

The Circuit Implementation of a full adder is shown in Figure 3.

FULL SUBTRACTOR: A full subtractor is a combinational circuit that performs a subtraction between two bits while taking into account the fact that a 1 may have been borrowed by a lower significant position. The three inputs A,B,C denote the minuend, subtrahend, and previous borrow, respectively. The two outputs D and K represent the difference and next borrow, respectively. The truth table for the circuit is shown in Figure 4.

A	B	C	Diff	Borrow
0	0	0	0	0
0	0	1	1	1
0	1	0	1	1
0	1	1	0	1
1	0	0	1	0
1	0	1	0	0
1	1	0	0	0
1	1	1	1	1

Fig. 4

Now use the Karnaugh's Maps of Figure 5 to find the logic equations.

Difference = AB'C' + A'BC'

$\qquad$ + ABC + A'B'C

$\qquad$ = A + B + C
(same as full-adder)

Borrow = A'B'C + A'BC'

$\qquad$ + BC

$\qquad$ = A'[B'C + BC']

$\qquad$ + BC

$\qquad$ = A'(B+C) + BC

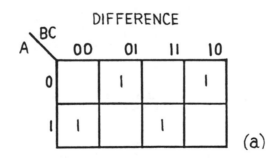

DIFFERENCE

(a)

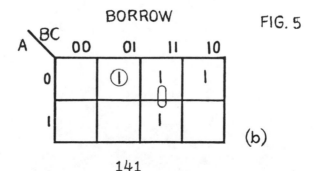

BORROW

FIG. 5

(b)

141

The Circuit Implementation of a full subtractor is shown in Figure 6.

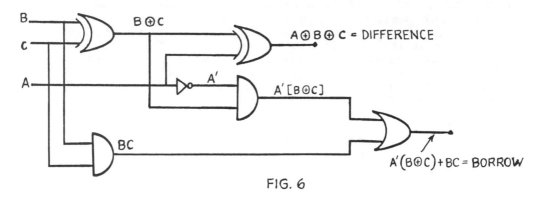

FIG. 6

Realize a circuit which acts as a full adder and a full sub-tractor.

Solution: The truth table of a full adder is shown in Figure 1. A and B are the bits to be added, C_{i-1} is the carry bit from a previous addition.

A	B	C_{i-1}	SUM	CARRY
0	0	0	0	0
0	0	1	1	0
0	1	0	1	0
0	1	1	0	1
1	0	0	1	0
1	0	1	0	1
1	1	0	0	1
1	1	1	1	1

Fig. 1

The truth table shown in Figure 2 is that of a full sub-tractor. B is the bit subtracted from A, C is the borrow bit from a previous subtraction.

A	B	C	DIFF.	BORROW
0	0	0	0	0
0	0	1	1	1
0	1	0	1	1
0	1	1	0	1
1	0	0	1	0
1	0	1	0	0
1	1	0	0	0
1	1	1	1	1

Fig. 2

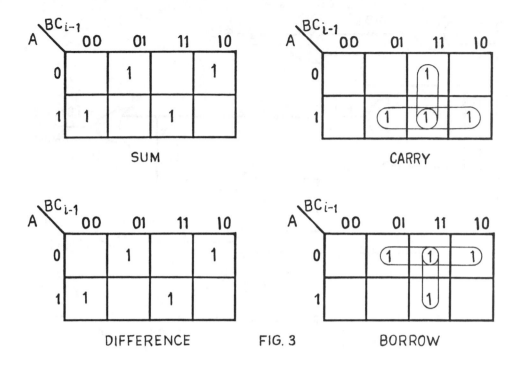

SUM   CARRY

DIFFERENCE   FIG. 3   BORROW

The Karnaugh Maps for sum, carry, borrow and difference are shown in Figure 3.

The Sum and Carry functions of a Full Adder are given by:

SUM = AB'C' + A'BC' + ABC + A'B'C = (AB'+A'B)C' + (AB+A'B')C

SUM = (A+B)C' + (A + B)'C = A + B + C

CARRY = A·B + A·C + B·C = A·[B+C] + B·C

The Difference and Borrow functions of a full subtractor are given by:

Difference = A + B + C (same as sum)

Borrow = A'·B + A'·C + B·C = A'·[B+C] + BC

It can be easily seen that Sum and Difference functions are the same and that the Carry and Borrow functions require little manipulation. The combinational circuit is shown in Figure 4.

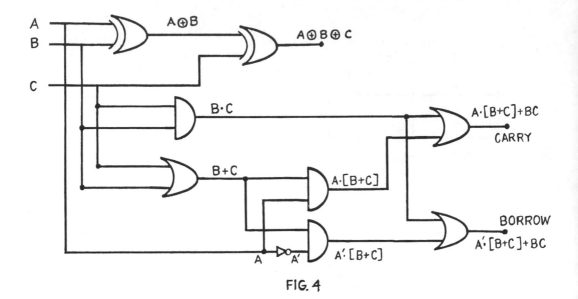

FIG. 4

An alternate manipulation of Borrow and Carry gives further reduction in the above circuitry. First let us redraw the Karnaugh Maps of the Borrow and Carry functions, as shown in Figure 5.

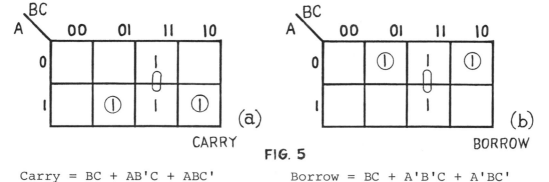

FIG. 5

Carry = BC + AB'C + ABC'

= BC + A[B+C]

Borrow = BC + A'B'C + A'BC'

= BC + A'[B+C]

The combinational circuit implementing the simplified expressions is shown in Figure 6.

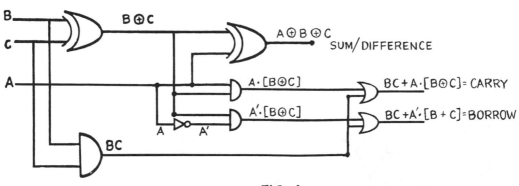

FIG. 6

Show how you would use the Full Adder for adding and
subtracting two 4 bit numbers.

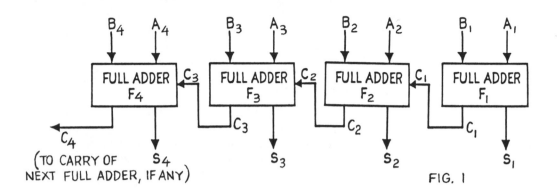

FIG. I

Solution: To add two 4 bit numbers, $A = A_4 A_3 A_2 A_1$ and
$B = B_4 B_3 B_2 B_1$, take four full adders F_4, F_3, F_2 and F_1
and connect at the input of the four full adders A_4B_4,
A_3B_3, A_2B_2, and A_1B_1 to F_4, F_3, F_2 and F_1 respectively.
Also, the output carry from the previous full adder is
connected to the input carry of the next full adder.
The complete circuit is shown in Figure 1.

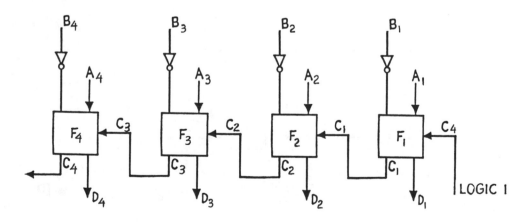

FIG. 2

For implementing subtraction using Full Adders, we use
2's complement technique, i.e. take a complement of the
subtrahend, add it to the minuend, and add 1 in the least

significant position of the result, i.e. Difference. For
example

$$
\begin{array}{rrrl}
8 & 1000 & 1000 & \text{1's complement method} \\
\underline{-5} & \underline{-0101} & \underline{1010} & \\
3 & 0011 & \overline{10010} & \\
& & \underline{+1} & \\
& & \overline{0011} & \\
\end{array}
$$

$$
\begin{array}{lrrr}
\text{or} & 8 & 1000 & 1000 \\
& \underline{-8} & \underline{1000} & \underline{0111} \\
& 0 & & \overline{1111} \\
& & & \underline{+1} \\
& & & \overline{0000} \\
\end{array}
$$

The subtraction circuit is shown in Figure 2.

In Figure 3 a circuit realizing adding and subtracting
functions is shown depending on the control line state.

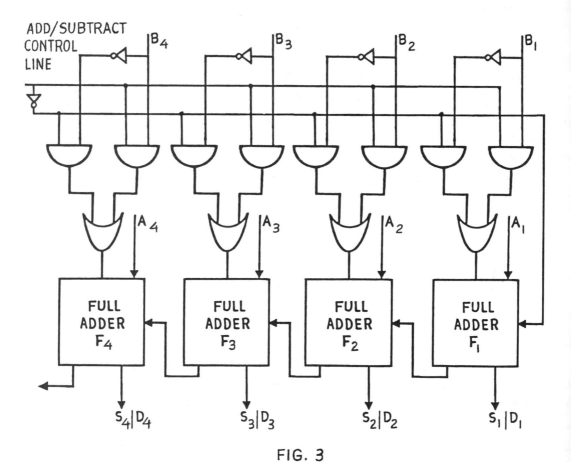

FIG. 3

If 1 is placed on the control line, the two numbers are
added, and if a 0 is placed on the control line, the
two numbers are subtracted.

Explain bus transfer of data. Show the circuit elements involved in parallel bus transfer and the symbolic representation of data transfer.

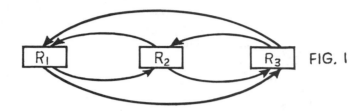

FIG. I

Solution: In a system with many registers, the transfer from one register to another requires that lines be connected from the output of each flip-flop in one register to input of each flip-flop in another register. Consider for example, the requirement for transfer among three registers as shown in Figure 1. There are six data paths between registers. If each register consists of F flip-flops, there is need of 6F lines for parallel transfer from one register to another. As the number of registers goes to n, there will be $(2^n - 2)$ x F lines (where F is number of flip-flops in each register). This greatly enhances the complexity of connections and cost per bit transfer. The idea of bus transfer is analogous to a central transportation system. Instead of each commuter using his own private car to go from one location to another, a bus system is used with each commuter waiting in line until transportation is available.

A bus system is formed with multiplexer and decoder circuit elements. Consider Figure 2 where there are four registers (each register has four flip-flops) and four 4 x 1 multiplexers. The four inputs to M1 are A_1, B_1, C_1 and D_1. Similarly, for M_2, M_3 and M_4, each multiplexer is connected to the same two selection lines x and y. When xy = 00, I_0 line of all four multiplexers gets selected and at output we have $A_1A_2A_3A_4$. Similarly xy = 01 selects $B_1B_2B_3B_4$. When xy = 10 the selection is $C_1C_2C_3C_4$, and xy = 11 selects $D_1D_2D_3D_4$.

Figure 2 is symbolically represented as Figure 3.

Thus, by proper selection of x and y select lines, we have the desired data on Bus. Now, the question is: How do we transfer the data on bus to the desired register? The technique is to use a Decoder whose output is used to enable the desired register in which the data is to be transferred. As shown in Figure 4, we have a 2 x 4 Decoder whose output is connected to the enable input of the registers.

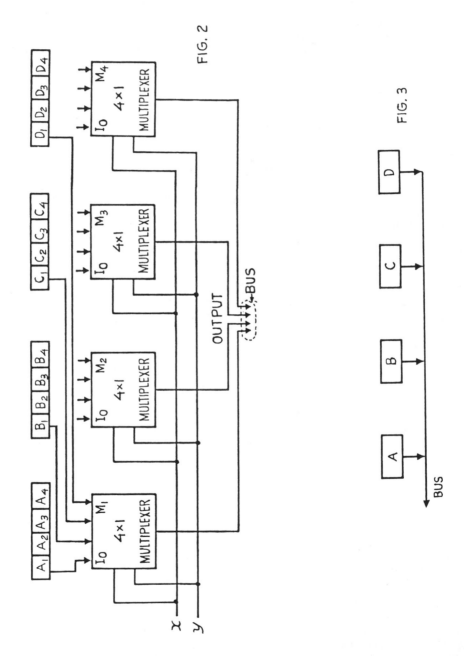

FIG. 2

FIG. 3

148

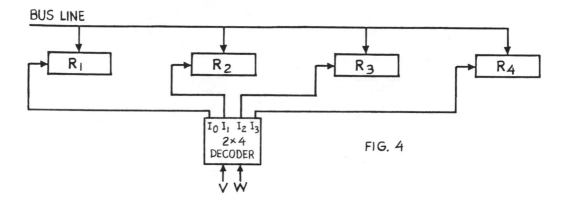

BUS LINE

FIG. 4

The Bus line carries four output wires from multiplexer.
These wires, in the form of a bus, are connected to all
four registers R_1, R_2, R_3 and R_4. On selection of xy =
00 we have $A_1A_2A_3A_4$ on the bus line; all these are going
as input to the four registers of Figure 4. Yet the data
is not transferred to them until they are enabled. Enabling the register is done by the 2 x 4 decoder, depending
on the input v and w. If vw = 00, I_0 is on and register R_1
gets enabled. Similarly, if vw = 01, I_1 is on, vw = 10, I_2
is on and if vw = 11, I_3 is on, enabling registers R_2, R_3
and R_4 respectively. Hence the data from register A is
transferred to register R_2 by making xy = 00 and vw = 01.
Symbolically, this is represented as

$\overline{xy}$:   BUS <—— A

$\overline{vw}$:   R2 <—— BUS

where $\overline{xy}$ or $\overline{vw}$ before the colon (:) represent conditions
and the transfer occurs only if the conditions are true.

ORGANIZATION

● **PROBLEM 5-11**

What are the main parts of the CPU? What tasks must the
CPU perform during each instruction cycle?

Solution: Figure 1 shows the main parts of the CPU.

The CPU performs the following tasks during each instruction cycle.

1. It places the address of the instruction on the address bus.

2. It takes the instruction from the input data bus and
decodes it.

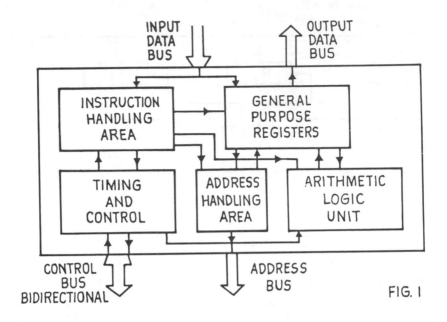

INPUT DATA BUS

OUTPUT DATA BUS

INSTRUCTION HANDLING AREA

GENERAL PURPOSE REGISTERS

TIMING AND CONTROL

ADDRESS HANDLING AREA

ARITHMETIC LOGIC UNIT

CONTROL BUS BIDIRECTIONAL

ADDRESS BUS

FIG. I

3. It fetches the address and data required by the instruction.

4. It performs the operation specified by the operation code. The instruction may be a logical or arithmetic function, a data transfer, or a management function.

5. It provides appropriate responses to incoming control signals, such as interrupts.

6. It provides status, timing, and control signals to the memory and I/O sections.

● **PROBLEM** 5-12

The arithmetic logic unit (ALU) in Figure 1 can add the contents of A and B, complement the contents of A or B, and logically AND the contents of A and B.

Show how the ALU can:
a) Increment
b) Decrement
c) Subtract
d) Logically OR
e) Shift left
f) Clear

Solution: (a) The contents of register A can be incremented by clearing register B and letting $C_i = 1$.   When the addition operation is performed the value of sum becomes $A + B + C_i = A + C_i = A + 1$.   Thus, A is incremented.

150

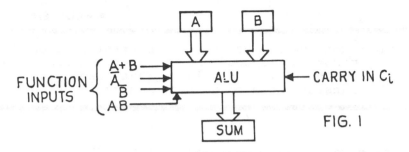

FIG. 1

(b)   The contents of A can be decremented by adding negative ones. Negative one in two's complement is all 1's;
thus, to decrement A: let the contents of B be all 1's,
C_i = 0, and add.

(c)   Subtraction is simply adding a negative number. Thus,
to form A - B, get the two's complement of B and add to A.
The two's complement of a number is found by complementing
the number and adding one. Thus, to subtract B from A:
complement B through the ALU using the $\bar{B}$ function input.
The complement function will place the result ($\bar{B}$) in
storage area SUM. Put the contents of SUM back into B.
Then, to complete the complementing process, add 1 to the
new B by zeroing A and making C_i = 1. Again, this result
will be placed in SUM. This new number in SUM now represents the fully complemented B (or -B). With this, we can
store the complement in Register B. Let us now place the
number which B (or more precisely, the contents of B) is
to be subtracted from in Register A. Hence, by adding
the contents of the two registers, we obtain the difference of the two numbers, represented in two's complement form.

(d)   Logically ORing A and B can be carried out using
DeMorgan's Law.

$$A + B = \overline{\bar{A} \cdot \bar{B}}$$

Thus, to OR A and B: complement A and put the result
back into A, complement B and put the result back into B,
AND A and B and put back in A, then complement A.

(e)   Shifting-left is the same as multiplying by two in
base two, just like shifting left is the same as multiplying by ten in base ten. Instead of multiplying by
two, however, just add A to A. Thus, to shift the contents of register A left: put the contents of A into B
(registers A and B now hold the same numbers), let C_i = 0
and add.

(f)   Clearing a register (making it all zero's) is done
by the following formula:

$$0 = A\bar{A}$$

Thus, to clear register A: complement A through the ALU
and put back into B, AND registers A and B, put sum
(which is zero) into A.

151

Draw the inter-connections between the control section
(CPU) and the memory section of the computer and state
the purpose of each inter-connection. What takes place
when the CPU transfers data to or from memory?

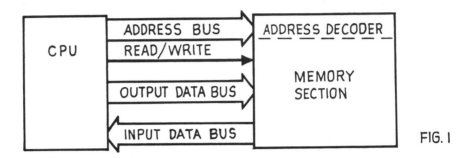

FIG. 1

Solution: Figure 1 shows the inter-connections between
the CPU and memory section of the computer.

The address bus transfers the address of the location to
be read from, or written into, the memory section

The read/write line designates whether data is to be read
from memory or written into memory. The output data bus
is used to transmit data to be written into memory. The
input data bus is used to transmit data read from memory.
Many times a single data bus is used for more than one
purpose. However, more control lines are needed to
designate the purpose of the bus. Such multifunction
buses are said to be "time shared" or "multiplexed."

The CPU transfers data to the memory section as follows:

1. The CPU sends the address to the memory section via
the address bus.

2. The CPU sends the data to the memory section via
the output data bus.

3. The CPU signals a Write operation to the memory section via the Read/Write line.

The CPU transfers data from memory as follows:

1. The CPU sends the address to the memory section via
the address bus.

2. The CPU signals a Read operation to the memory section via the Read/Write line.

3. The CPU waits, then the data is sent out to the CPU
via the input data bus.

What is the advantage of using DMA? When is DMA used?

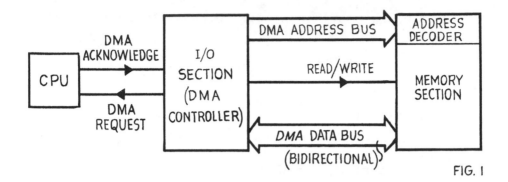

FIG. 1

Solution: Computers with the DMA (direct memory access)
feature have a direct link between the memory section
and the I/O section. Thus, data can be transmitted to
and from peripherals without intervention by the CPU.

The advantage of using DMA is that the time to transfer
data is limited only by the memory access time (usually
less than one microsecond). Data transfer to the CPU of
a computer without DMA requires several instruction
cycles and takes ten to twenty times longer.

Figure 1 shows the connections required for direct memory
access. The DMA controller located in the I/O section
handles data transfers just like the CPU. The "DMA
request" control signal ensures that the CPU retains
control of memory usage. The Address bus and data bus
shown can be the same busses that connect the CPU to
memory.

The DMA is used with high-speed peripherals such as magnetic disk, high-speed communication lines, and CRT
displays.

● **PROBLEM** 5-15

Define buffer and interrupt. What is the distinction
between the two?

Solution: In both input and output of data or physical
records, the memory has reserved buffers. These are
areas of core memory outside the main processor's memory
used to compensate for the discrepancy between the relatively quick speed of the processor and the slower electromechanical I/O devices such as printers or card readers.

An economical use of buffers is through logical switching.
Say we have two fixed-length buffers, one each for input

and output. We want to output some records that are
presently sitting in an input buffer by using an output
buffer. If the status of the output buffer is idle, and
if it has adequate length, a simple change of machine
addresses, giving the output buffer the input buffer's
address, will send the input into the output stream.
There is no physical movement of data across memory space,
but only an address switch, hence the name logical switching. This concept is used in multiprogramming systems.

An interrupt is an internal control signal that diverts
the machine's attention away from one task and causes
it to perform another. These interrupts are associated
with various priorities within the CPU. If the interrupt
facility is disabled, the interrupt request will be ignored. If the output of an important program is expected, the other programs in the system will be temporarily
halted until the important one is completed. It is
through the interrupt that this task of halting is performed.

Buffers and interrupts are both features of time-sharing
and multiprogramming systems. The reason for their
implementation is so that no part of the CPU or I/O
accessories will be left idle.

● **PROBLEM** 5-16

List the common types of registers used in the computer
and state their purpose.

Solution: There are nine types of registers in the
computer.

1. Program Counter: This register holds the address of
the instruction to be executed. As the name implies, it
is also a counter since instructions are listed in memory
sequentially (for the most part).

2. Instruction Register: This register holds the binary
code of the instruction to be executed.

3. Memory Address Register (MAR): This register holds the
address of any type of data (instruction, operand, etc.)
to be stored in, or recalled from, memory.

4. Memory Buffer Register (MBR): This register holds
the data written from memory until the appropriate
register is ready to accept it. The MBR also stores
information that is to be transferred from a register
into main memory.

5. Accumulator: This register stores temporary data
during calculations. The accumulator always holds one
of the operands in arithmetic operations.

6. General Purpose Registers: These registers usually
serve as temporary storage for data and addresses. In

some computers, the user may specify them as accumulators
or program counters. If he wishes, the programmer may
also use these registers for arithmetic calculations.

7. Index Register: This register holds a relative
address which, when added to the memory address, forms
an effective address, that states the actual location
of data. Thus, if the contents of the Index Register are
changed, the same instructions can be used to handle data
from different locations. Generally, the contents of the
index register (XR or X) are added to the numerical address of a symbol to calculate its absolute (actual)
address in main memory. This numerical address is com-
prised of a displacement and the contents of a base
register. The base register holds the address at which
the program was stored in main memory upon its entry.
The displacement is the distance (i.e. the number of
bytes) which an instruction is from the start of the
program. Thus, by adding the contents of the index
register, the contents of the base register, and the displacement, the absolute address of an instruction can be
calculated.

8. Condition Code Register: This register holds one-
bit flags which represent the state of conditions inside
the CPU. The states of these flags are the basis for
computer decision making in conditional instructions such
as "Jump to Location 31 if Accumulator is greater than
zero."

9. Stack Pointer: This register contains the address
of the top of the stack. It can be incremented or decremented depending upon whether data is put onto, or taken
off of, the stack.

● **PROBLEM** 5-17

What are the basic flags incorporated into a condition
code register? State the purpose of each flag.

Solution: Each flag in the condition code register
designates a certain condition inside the CPU. The flags
are the basis for computer decision-making in conditional
instructions such as "Jump to location 31 if the Accumulator is Zero." When the computer reads such an instruction it will check the flag in the condition code register
which designates a zero accumulator. If the flag is 1
the accumulator is zero and the computer jumps to location 31. If the flag is 0 the accumulator is not zero
and the computer reads the next instruction. As can be
seen, the more flags a computer has in its condition
code register, the stronger the computer will be in its
decision-making.

The basic flags incorporated into a condition register
are:

1. Carry: This flag is set to 1 if the last operation

generated a carry from the most significant bit.

2. Zero: This flag is set to 1 if the last operation resulted in a zero. This flag is often used in loop control and searching for a certain data value.

3. Overflow: This flag is set to 1 if the last operation produced a 2's complement overflow.

4. Sign: This flag is set to 1 if the most significant bit of the result of the last operation was 1, designating a negative two's complement number.

5. Parity: This flag is set to 1 if the result of the last operation contains an even number of 1's (sometimes called Even Parity).

6. Half-Carry: This flag is set to 1 if the last operation generated a carry from the lower half word to the upper half word.

7. Interrupt Enable: This flag is set to 1 if an interrupt is allowed, 0 if not. A computer may have several interrupt enable flags if it has several interrupt inputs or levels.

● **PROBLEM** 5-18

If the last operation performed on a computer with an 8-bit word was an addition in which the operands were 2 and 3, what would be the values of the following flags?

(a)   Carry
(b)   Zero
(c)   Overflow
(d)   Sign
(e)   Even Parity
(f)   Half-carry

What if the operands were -1 (two's complement) and +1?

Solution: The addition operation of 2 and 3 is:

```
    +2:    0000|0010
    +3:    0000|0011
    +5:    0000|0101
bit #      7654|3210
```

(a)   The Carry flag is 1 if there is a carry from the most significant bit position (bit 7). Since there is no carry from bit 7 the contents of the Carry flag is 0.

(b)   The Zero flag is 1 if the result is zero. Since the result is not zero the contents of the Zero flag is 0.

(c)   The Overflow flag is 1 if the two operands in an

156

addition have the same sign but the result has the opposite sign. As an example:

```
+64:  01000000
+64:  01000000
      10000000
```

This answer is incorrect if the numbers are signed because the answer is negative. Thus, this result is too large for 8-bit two's complement notation and the Overflow flag would be set to 1. Another example:

```
-96:  10100000
-64:  11000000
      01100000
```

This answer is also incorrect because it is positive and thus the Overflow flag would be set to 1. In the addition of 2 and 3 the sign bit is correct so the contents of the Overflow flag is 0.

(d)   The Sign flag is 1 if the most significant bit (bit 7) is 1 (corresponding to a negative number). Thus the contents of the Sign flag is 0 since bit 7 is 0.

(e)   The Even Parity flag is set to 1 if the result of the last operation contained an even number of 1's. The addition of 2 and 3 produced two 1's and hence the contents of the Even Parity flag is 1.

(f)   The Half-carry flag is set to 1 if the last operation produced a carry from the lower half word (bits 0-3). The addition of 2 and 3 produced no carry from bit 3 so the contents of the Half-carry flag is 0.

The addition of -1 and +1 is:

```
     -1:  1111|1111
     +1:  0000|0001
      0: 10000|0000
bit #    7654|3210
```

(a)   A carry was generated from bit 7 so the content of the Carry flag is 1. When binary numbers of different signs are being added, the computer will indicate a carry and not an overflow, if the result extends outside of its storage field, as is the case in this example.

(b)   The addition of -1 and +1 produced zero so the contents of the Zero flag is 1.

(c)   There is no overflow so the contents of the Overflow flag is 0.

(d)   The sign bit (bit 7) is 0 so the contents of the Sign flag is 0.

(e)   There are no 1's in the result so the contents of the Even Parity flag is 1 (zero is an even number).

(f) A carry was generated from bit 3 so the contents of the Half-carry flag is 1.

Explain how the stack area of a computer's memory operates.

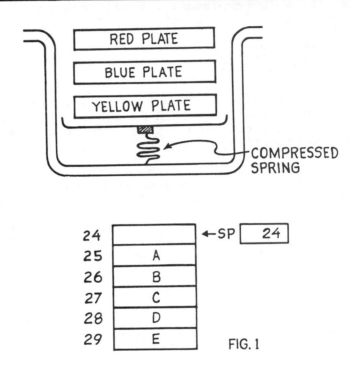

FIG. 1

Solution: The stack is similar to a plate dispenser in a cafeteria. Figure 1 shows a plate dispenser with yellow, blue, and red plates. Notice that plates can only be put in or taken from the top of the stack. If someone wants the yellow plate, the red and then the blue plate must be removed before the yellow plate. Notice that the last plate in is always the first plate out. This "last in-first out" (LIFO) rule is characteristic of all computer stacks.

Most computers have a specific section in memory which is used as a stack and a specific register called the stack pointer. The stack pointer (SP) contains the address of the first "empty" memory location in the stack. Figure 2 shows the stack with contents A, B, C, D and E at memory locations 25, 26, 27, 28 and 29 respectively. To remove A the POP instruction is used and the SP is incremented. With A removed the SP still contains the first empty position. To insert F a PUSH instruction is used; the SP is decremented, and F goes into the stack at location 25.

When using the stack, care must be taken to ensure that

the stack is not in "over fill." If too many Push
instructions are used, the stack will grow upward and
interfere with a main program. The programmer must
always keep track of what is at the top of the stack
and how many items are in the stack, otherwise errors
will be made. Also, care must be taken to see that not
too many items are removed from a stack, since it is impossible to "pop" an "empty" stack.

● **PROBLEM** 5-20

What are the major tasks performed by the linking
loader? Explain the term relocation.

Solution: The function of the linking loader is to load
a program that has been compiled into machine code into
memory for direct execution by the CPU. The linking
loader's major tasks are:

1. to determine the operational locations of the program;

2. to process and to remove the external symbol dictionaries;

3. to translate all relative addresses of data and
instructions to their absolute forms and to remove the
internal relocation symbol dictionaries;

4. to make certain determinations relative to channel,
input and output unit assignment;

5. to make certain determinations relative to the number, location, and assignment of buffers; and

6. to make the initial placement of data and instruction
in the main memory so that the program may be properly
executed.

Functionally, tasks (1), (2) and (3) are concerned with
program relocation and memory utilization; tasks (4) and
(5) are concerned with input and output device utilization and task (6) is loading.

In addition to these basic facilities, a linking loader
may have some new capabilities. For example, chaining,
which enables a large collection of programs to be over-
layed in a small memory space, and dynamic loading, which
enables the loading of a subroutine during execution of
the calling program.

The linking loader performs the process of translating
all the program references (e.g. relative address, external symbols, internal relocation symbols and entries)
into their absolute form. Absolute form is the form by
which the CPU can decode. Such a process is known as
relocation.

Describe the organization of the PDP-8 computer, giving the various registers, memory, etc. Also explain the terms "address and "operation code."

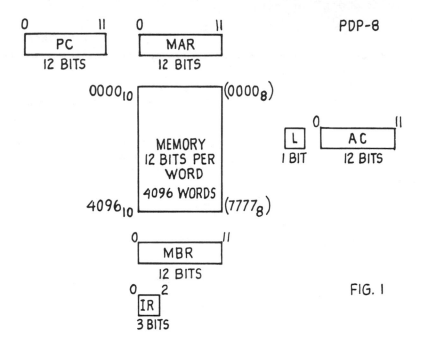

FIG. 1

Solution: The block diagram of Figure 1 shows the various elements of the PDP-8 computer.

As shown in Figure 1, the PDP-8 memory has 4096 words or locations. Each word of the memory has 12 bits.

Memory Address: Each word of the memory is numbered sequentially from 0 to 4095. This number associated with a word is called the "address" of the word. Thus, the "address" of a word shows the physical location of the word in memory.

Actually, the PDP-8 uses the octal number system rather than the decimal number system. Hence, the address of a memory word (in octal) can be anything from 0 to 7777_8. To see this note that

$$4095 = 2^{12} - 1 = 111111111111_2$$

$$= 111\ 111\ 111\ 111_2$$

$$= 7\ 7\ 7\ 7_8$$

Thus, if the address of a word is 7777_8, the word is located at the last physical location in the memory.

And, if the address of a word is 0, it is located at the first physical location in the memory.

PC: The PDP-8 has a Program Counter (PC). The PC stores the address of the instruction to be executed (i.e., carried out) by the computer. At any given time the PC contains the address of the next instruction to be carried out, after the completion of the instruction which is presently being executed. The PC has 12 bits.

MAR: The PDP-8 has a register called Memory Address Register (MAR). The MAR is used whenever any information is to be read from or written into the memory. The procedures are as follows: If there is a memory location from which information is to be read from or written into, then the address of this location must be entered into the MAR. The MAR then communicates with the memory and the MBR to get the information transferred as desired.

The MAR holds 12 bits. The number of bits in MAR depends on the size of the program counter. In this case the program counter has 12 bits. Therefore the number of bits in MAR is 12.

MBR: The PDP-8 has another register called Memory Buffer Register (MBR). Any information which is read from the memory is read into the MBR first. Then, from the MBR the information can be sent to wherever it is needed. Similarly, any information which is to be written into the memory must first be placed into the MBR. Then, from the MBR the information is written into the memory. In many instances, the main function of the MBR is to momentarily store data that is being transferred between the general purpose registers and main memory. Registers manipulate data much faster than memory devices, and as such, memory buffer registers (MBR) were created to bridge the timing gap between registers and main memory. The outstanding feature of the MBR is that it can regulate its speed. When information is to be passed to memory, the MBR accepts this information from the high-speed registers and passes it at a slower speed to the memory device. The reverse is done when information is to be transferred from memory to a register. The MBR accepts this information from the low speed memory device and passes it at a higher speed to the register. Thus, MBR acts as a buffer between the memory and other registers in the computer.

The bit size of the MBR depends on the bit size of one computer word. In the case of the PDP-8 one word is 12 bits long so MBR is also 12 bits long.

IR: The PDP-8 has a register called Instruction Register (IR). At any given time the IR contains the Operation Code (OP) of the instruction which is presently being executed by the computer. The Operation Code present in the IR is coded information telling the computer what is to be done with the various data present in the different registers of the computer. The IR has 3 bits.

AC: The PDP-8 has a general purpose register called
the Accumulator (AC). The computer carries out addition,
subtraction, multiplication, division, etc. by storing
the intermediate and final operands and sums in the accumulator. The AC has 12 bits.

L: The PDP-8 has a 1-bit register called a Link Register
(L). The Link register works in association with AC.
Sometimes, the Link register and the AC are referred to
by the combined mnemonic LAC, forming a combined 13-bit
register.

The Link register (normally referred to as the Link bit)
can be set to 1 or cleared to 0 independently of the AC.
But, while doing register shift-left and shift-right
operations, the L bit works in association with the 12-
bit AC, as LAC, to store the bit shifted into or out of
the AC register.

● **PROBLEM** 5-22

Describe the flow of data from the Program Counter to
the Accumulator in a PDP-8 computer.

Solution: The Program Counter (PC) contains the address
of the next instruction. So after executing the previous
instruction the PC starts as follows:

The contents of the PC are transferred to the memory address register (MAR). The PC is then incremented in
anticipation of the next instruction to be executed.

Now, the MAR has the address where an instruction is
stored. Therefore, the instruction corresponding to this
address is read from the memory into the memory buffer
register (MBR).

Next, the contents of the MBR are treated as follows:

The first three bits (bits 0 to 2) are sent to the IR.
These 3 bits represent the OP code.

Now, bit No. 4 of the MBR is examined. If this bit is 0,
then the MAR is cleared to 0. (All bits of the MAR
become 0.) But, if this bit is 1, then the MAR is not
cleared.

After this, bits Nos. 5 to 11 of the MBR are transferred
to bits Nos. 5 to 11 of the MAR. As a result, at this
stage the MAR contains information which is either one
of the following:

> Bits 0 to 4: all 0's; Bits 5 to 11: same as
>   Bits 5 to 11 of MBR

or,   Bits 0 to 4: same as originally in the MAR; Bits
>   5 to 11: same as Bits 5 to 11 of MBR.

Next, Bit No. 3 of the MBR is examined. This bit signifies whether the instruction uses direct or indirect
addressing.

i) If Bit No. 3 is 0, the instruction utilizes direct addressing, and the contents of the memory location corresponding to the new value in the MAR are read into the MBR. The MBR now contains an operand. Hence, the contents of the MBR can be transferred to the AC to carry out the operation corresponding to the op-code stored in the IR.

ii) If Bit No. 3 is 1, then the contents of the memory location corresponding to the new value in the MAR are read into the MBR. Now, the contents of the MBR are transferred again to the MAR, and the contents of the memory location, corresponding to the latest MAR contents, are read into the MBR. (This mode of addressing is called Indirect Addressing.)

The contents of the MBR are now finally transferred to the AC to be processed according to the op-code stored in the IR.

TIMING AND CONTROL

A computer has the following Instruction formats:

Memory Reference Instructions:

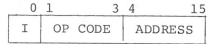

Register-Reference Instruction (Indirect):

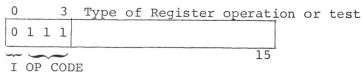

Input Output Instruction:

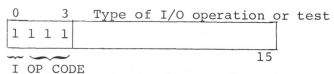

The computer operates in four different cycles:

      Fetch Cycle (read instruction)
      Indirect cycle (read address of operand)
      Execute cycle (read operand)
      Interrupt

where each cycle will execute no more than four steps.

Design a block diagram of the control unit for this computer.

<u>Solution:</u> The control unit is shown in Figure 1.

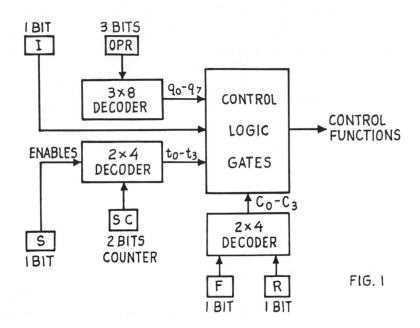

FIG. 1

The F and R registers are used to denote which of the four cycles the computer is operating in. The 2 x 4 decoder associated with these registers generates four control signals C_0 - C_3. Each cycle has its own control signal specified by the table of Figure 2.

Registers F R		Decoder Output	Computer Cycle
0	0	C_0	Fetch Cycle
0	1	C_1	Indirect Cycle
1	0	C_2	Execute Cycle
1	1	C_3	Interrupt Cycle

Fig. 2

Each cycle is divided into four steps. Each step is designated by the output of the two-bit binary step counter, SC. The counter starts at 00 when the computer enters a cycle and the computer stays in this cycle until the counter reaches 11. At this point, the computer enters another cycle and the counter returns to 00. Each step is decoded into one of four timing signals, t_0 - t_3.

The S bit is used to start and stop the computer. The user starts the computer by putting a logic level 1 in the S register. This enables the SC decoder and the timing signals.

The user stops the computer by putting the S register to 0. This disables the decoder and all the timing signals $t_0 - t_3$.

The OPR register contains the three bit op-code specified in the instruction format. Each of the eight possible op-codes is decoded into eight separate control signals $q_0 - q_7$. Each signal specifies one of eight instructions from the instruction set of the computer.

The I bit is bit 1 of the instruction format. It is used to designate whether the instruction is: (1) Indirect addressing (I = 1), when $q_7 = 0$ (op-code $\neq$ 111); (2) Register reference (I = 0), or I/O (I = 1), when $q_7 = 1$ (op-code = 111).

All of these signals ($C_0 - C_3$; $t_0 - t_3$; $q_0 - q_7$; I) go to the control logic section which then carries out the actual Instruction through the control functions.

● **PROBLEM** 5-24

Write the micro-operations for the Fetch Cycle. Assume that the computer has the following registers and control signals:

```
      M - memory
     PC - program counter
    MAR - memory address register
    MBR - memory buffer register
    OPR - op-code register
    F }
    R } - cycle identification registers
      I - indirect register
```

The cycle code is shown in Figure 1.

Cycle ID Registers F R	Cycle code	Cycle description
0 0	C_0	Fetch cycle
0 1	C_1	Indirect cycle
1 0	C_2	Execute cycle
1 1	C_3	Interrupt cycle

Fig. 1

Each cycle consists of four steps t_0, t_1, t_2, t_3.

Solution: During the fetch cycle, the instruction is read from memory. The memory location which contains the instruction is specified in the PC register. In

165

most computers, the instructions are stored in memory sequentially. That is, the next instruction is at the location of the previous instruction plus one; hence, the PC will be incremented during each fetch cycle. The fetch cycle is designated by the C_0 control signal.

A step is specified when the control signal expression to the left of the colon is true (Logical 1).

$$C_0 t_0: \qquad MAR \longleftarrow [PC] \qquad\qquad (Step \; 1)$$

$$Note: \quad [\;] \; means \; "contents \; of"$$

In the first step of the fetch cycle, the contents of the PC, which contains the location of the next instruction to be read from memory, are transferred to the MAR.

$$C_0 t_1: \qquad PC \longleftarrow [PC]+1 \; ; \; MBR \longleftarrow [M<MAR>] \quad (Step \; 2)$$

Two operations take place in the second step of the fetch cycle: (1) The PC is incremented so that it will specify the location of the next instruction when the next fetch cycle occurs. (2) The contents of memory, whose address is specified by the MAR, is transferred to the MBR; hence, the MBR contains the instruction code. These two operations occur simultaneously with both operations having equal importance.

$$C_0 t_2: \qquad I \longleftarrow [MBR]_0 \; ; \qquad OPR \longleftarrow [MBR]_{1-3} \quad (Step \; 3)$$

Again, two operations take place in the third step of the fetch cycle: (1) The contents of bit 0 of the MBR is transferred to I. This bit specifies whether or not the data in the instruction will be indirectly addressed. (2) The contents of bits 1 through 3 of the MBR are transferred to the OPR. Once the op-code is in the OPR, it will be decoded into one of eight possible signals, $q_0 - q_7$.

$$q_7 I c_0 t_3: \qquad R \longleftarrow 1$$

$$(Step \; 4)$$

or $\qquad (q_7 + \bar{I}) c_0 t_3: \; F \longleftarrow 1$

Different operations take place in the fourth step of the fetch cycle, depending on the status of several control signals. q_7 is excited when the op-code is 111 (an I/O or register-reference instruction) and I is excited when there is an indirect instruction; hence, the first statement states that when there is an indirect memory reference instruction, go to the indirect cycle. The computer goes to the indirect cycle by letting the R-register become 1 and leaving the F-register 0. When F and R are decoded, the c_1 control line is excited, which designates the indirect cycle.

The second statement states that when there is a memory-reference or I/O instruction, go to the execute cycle.

The computer goes to the execute cycle by letting the F register become 1 and leaving the R register 0. When F and R are decoded, the c_2 control line, which designates the execute cycle, is excited.

● **PROBLEM** 5-25

Write the micro-operations for the indirect cycle of the computer whose registers and control signals are specified as follows:

> PC - program counter
> MAR - memory address register
> MBR - memory buffer register
> OPR - op-code register
> F
> R   } - cycle identification registers
> I - indirect register
> M - memory

The cycle code is shown in Figure 1.

Cycle ID registers F R	Cycle code	Cycle description
0 0	C_0	Fetch cycle
0 1	C_1	Indirect cycle
1 0	C_2	Execute cycle
1 1	C_3	Interrupt cycle

Fig. 1

Each cycle consists of four steps T_0, T_1, T_2, T_3.

Solution: The difference between a direct memory reference instruction and an indirect memory reference instruction is explained with the use of Figure 2.

In a direct memory-reference instruction the address portion of the instruction format (bits 4 through 15) contains the address of the operand; hence, when the fetch cycle is completed, bits 4 through 15 of the MBR contain the address of the operand. The operand is not taken from memory until the execution cycle.

In an indirect memory-reference location the address portion of the instruction format contains the location of the address of the operand; hence, after the fetch cycle the address of the operand must still be found. Thus, an extra cycle called the indirect cycle is used during an indirect memory reference instruction to fetch the address of the operand.

The indirect cycle is designated by the control signal

167

Instruction format:

0	1	3	4	15
I	OP-CODE		ADDRESS	

Direct address instruction:

address   Memory

	I	OPCODE	ADDRESS	
2_8	0_2	101_2	1406_8	Instruction
$\vdots$				
1406_8	0_2	101_2	0023_8	Operand

Indirect address instruction:

address   Memory

	I	OPCODE	ADDRESS	
2_8	0_2	101_2	1366_8	Instruction
$\vdots$				
1366_8	0_2	000_2	1406_8	Address of operand
$\vdots$				
1406_8	0_2	101_2	0023_8	Operand

Fig. 2

c_1 (F = 0, R = 1). A step is specified when the control signal expression to the left of the colon is true (Logical 1).

$$c_1 t_0: \quad MAR \longleftarrow [MBR]_{4-15} \quad \text{(Step 1)}$$

Note: [ ] means "contents of"

In the first step of the indirect cycle the address portion of the fetched instruction is transferred to the MAR; thus, the computer is preparing to fetch the address of the operand.

$$c_1 t_1: \quad MBR \longleftarrow [M<MAR>] \quad \text{(Step 2)}$$

After the second step, the address of the operand has been fetched. The only thing that remains to be done is to go to the execute cycle.

$$c_1 t_2: \quad\quad\quad\quad\quad \text{(Step 3)}$$

$$c_1 t_3: \quad F \longleftarrow 1, \quad R \longleftarrow 0 \quad \text{(Step 4)}$$

The execute cycle control signal cannot be set until the last step. If it were set on step three, control would go to the fourth step of the execute cycle rather than the first step of the execute cycle. (In other words, the computer would skip three steps in the execute cycle.)

Write the micro-operations for the execute cycles of the
Memory reference instructions of Figure 2 using these
registers and control signals.
  M - memory
  PC - program counter
  MAR - memory address register
  MBR - memory buffer register
  OPR - op-code register
  F,R - cycle identification registers
  E - carry bit register
The cycle code is shown in Figure 1.

Cycle ID registers F	R	Cycle code	Cycle description
0	0	c_0	Fetch cycle
0	1	c_1	Indirect cycle
1	0	c_2	Execute cycle
1	1	c_3	Interrupt cycle

Fig. 1

Each cycle consists of four steps t_0, t_1, t_2, t_3.

Instruction Symbol	Op-Code	Control Signal	Effective Address	Memory Word	Symbolic Designation
AND	000	q_0	m	M	AC← [AC]∧M
ADD	001	q_1	m	M	EAC← [AC]+M
LDA	010	q_2	m	M	AC← [M]
STA	011	q_3	m	M	M← [AC]
BUN	100	q_4	m	–	PC←m
BSA	101	q_5	m	M	M← [PC], PC←m+1
ISZ	110	q_6	m	M	M←M+1, if M+1=0, then PC←[PC]+1

Fig. 2

Solution: At the beginning of the execute cycle the
registers contain the following information:

[PC] = The address of the instruction about to be exe-
    cuted; incremented by one.
$[MBR]_{4-15}$ = The address of the operand (effective
    address).
[OPR] = The op-code part of the instruction format (this
    was decoded into one of eight control signals
    $q_0 - q_7$)

169

$$\left.\begin{array}{l} [F] = 1 \\ [R] = 0 \end{array}\right\} \text{ decoded to excite } c_2$$

A step is specified if the control signal expression to the left of the colon is true (logic 1).

AND: This instruction logically "ands" the contents of the accumulator and the operand. The result is stored back in the accumulator.

Note: [ ] means "contents of"; < > means "addressed by."

$q_0 c_2 t_0$:   MAR←[MBR]$_{4-15}$ ⎫

$q_0 c_2 t_1$:   MBR←[M<MAR>]   ⎬   Fetch operand

$q_0 c_2 t_2$:   AC←[AC]∧[MBR]   AND with AC, store result in AC

$q_0 c_2 t_3$:   F←0   Go to Fetch cycle (c_0 is excited)

ADD: This instruction adds the contents of the AC and the operand. The result is stored in the AC. If there is a carry, it is stored in E.

$q_1 c_2 t_0$:   MAR←[MBR]$_{4-15}$ ⎫

                                 ⎬   Fetch operand

$q_1 c_2 t_1$:   MBR←[M<MAR>]   ⎭

$q_1 c_2 t_2$:   EAC←[AC]+[MBR]   Add to AC, store result in AC and E

$q_1 c_2 t_3$:   F←0   Go to Fetch cycle

LDA: This instruction loads the operand into the AC.

$q_2 c_2 t_0$:   MAR←[MBR]$_{4-15}$ ⎫

                                 ⎬   Fetch operand, clear AC

$q_2 c_2 t_1$:   MBR←[M<MAR>]; AC←0 ⎭

$q_2 c_2 t_2$:   AC←[AC]+[MBR]   Add to AC

$q_2 c_2 t_3$:   F←0   Go to Fetch cycle

STA: This instruction stores the contents of the AC into the memory location specified by [MBR]$_{4-15}$.

$q_3 c_2 t_0$:   MAR←[MBR]$_{4-15}$ Store address in MAR

$q_3 c_2 t_1$:   MBR←[AC]   Store [AC] in MBR

$q_3 c_2 t_2$:   M<MAR>←[MBR]   Load into memory

$q_3 c_2 t_3$:   F←0   Go to Fetch cycle

BUN (branch unconditionally): This instruction is similar
    to the JUMP or GO TO statement in FORTRAN. The address
    of the next instruction is specified by the address
    portion of the MBR. The execute cycle is:

$q_4 c_2 t_0$:   PC←[MBR]$_{4-15}$ Transfer next address
                                                         to PC

$q_4 c_2 t_1$:   Do nothing

$q_4 c_2 t_2$:   Do nothing

$q_4 c_2 t_3$:   F←0   Go to Fetch cycle

BSA (branch and save return address): This instruction
    stores the contents of the PC in the memory location
    specified by the effective address and then control
    branches to the next higher location of the effective
    address.

$q_5 c_2 t_0$:   MAR←[MBR]$_{4-15}$

                  MBR$_{4-15}$←[PC]   Load effective address
                                               into PC
                  PC←[MBR]$_{4-15}$

$q_5 c_2 t_1$:   [M<MAR>]←MBR   Load old PC into
                                               effective address

$q_5 c_2 t_2$:   PC←[PC]+1   Increment PC

$q_5 c_2 t_3$:   F←0   Go to Fetch cycle

The BUN and BSA instructions are very useful when branching to and from subroutines.

ISZ (increment and skip-if-zero): This instruction incre-
    ments the operand and then tests to see if the operand
    is zero. If the operand is not zero then the program
    flows normally. If the operand is zero then the next
    instruction is skipped and control resumes at the
    instruction after the skipped instruction.

$q_6 c_2 t_0$:   MAR←[MBR]$_{4-15}$
                                               Fetch operand
$q_6 c_2 t_1$:   MBR←[M<MAR>]

$q_6 c_2 t_2$:   MBR←[MBR]+1   Increment operand

$q_6 c_2 t_3$:   M<MAR>←[MBR]   Store new operand;
                  if [MBR]=0 then PC=PC+1   Increment PC if
                                                operand is zero;
                  F←0   Go to Fetch cycle.

171

Explain how the BSA and BUN instructions can be used for subroutine call and return.

Solution: Figure 1 demonstrates the use of the BSA and BUN instructions in writing subroutines. The actual subroutine in Figure 1 starts at location m+1 and continues to location m+z.

After fetching the BSA instruction from memory the contents of the PC are 026. During the execute cycle the contents of the PC are stored in location m and the address m+1 is stored in the PC. Thus, the computer jumps to the subroutine and saves the return address in location m. The computer then executes all of the instructions in the subroutine.

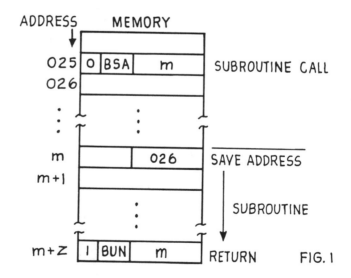

Finally the computer reads the BUN instruction at the end of the subroutine. Notice, however, that BUN is an indirect instruction (specified by the 1 in bit I of the instruction). During this instruction the address specified in location m is stored in the PC; hence the PC contains the return address and returns to location 026 after executing the BUN instruction.

Write the micro-operations for the execute cycles of the following register-reference instructions.

Instruction Symbol	Hexadecimal Code	Definition
CLA	7800	Clear Accumulator
CLE	7400	Clear E register
CMA	7200	Complement Accumulator
CME	7100	Complement E register
INC	7020	Increment Accumulator
HLT	7001	Halt Computer

Solution: All register reference instructions are specified by an op-code of 111 and a 0 in the I register; thus the control signal specifying the register-reference instruction is $q_7 \bar{I} c_2$ and a particular step is specified when $q_7 \bar{I} c_2 t_j [MBR]_i$ is true (logic 1).

CLA: This instruction is specified by $q_7 \bar{I} c_2$ and when the MBR appears as

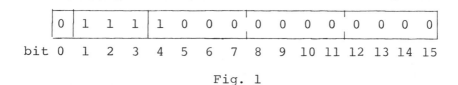

0	1	1	1	1	0	0	0	0	0	0	0	0	0	0	0

bit 0 1 2 3 4 5 6 7 8 9 10 11 12 13 14 15

Fig. 1

or $[MBR]_4 = 1$

The instruction may be executed during only one timing signal, t_3; hence,

$$q_7 \bar{I} c_2 t_3 [MBR]_4: \quad AC \leftarrow 0$$
$$F \leftarrow 0$$

The first micro-instruction clears the AC and the second one sets the fetch cycle control signal. The rest of the micro-instructions are found in a similar manner.

CLE:
$$q_7 \bar{I} c_2 t_3 [MBR]_5: \quad E \leftarrow 0$$
$$F \leftarrow 0$$

CMA:
$$q_7 \bar{I} c_2 t_3 [MBR]_6: \quad AC \leftarrow [\overline{AC}]$$
$$F \leftarrow 0$$

CME:
$$q_7 \bar{I} c_2 t_3 [MBR]_7: \quad E \leftarrow [\bar{E}]$$
$$F \leftarrow 0$$

173

INC:

$$q_7\bar{I}c_2t_3[MBR]_{10}: \qquad EAC\leftarrow[AC]+1$$
$$F\leftarrow 0$$

HLT: The S register designates whether or not the computer is running. If s = 1, the computer is on and
if s = 0, the computer is stopped; hence, a 0 is
stored in S to halt the computer.

$$q_7\bar{I}c_2t_3[MBR]_{15}: \qquad S\leftarrow 0$$
$$F\leftarrow 0$$

● **PROBLEM** 5-29

Write the micro-instructions for the execute cycles of the
following register reference instructions.

Instruction Symbol	Hexadecimal Code	Definition
CIR	7080	Circulate right E and AC
CIL	7040	Circulate left E and AC
SPA	7010	Skip if AC is positive
SNA	7008	Skip if AC is negative
SZA	7004	Skip if AC is zero
SZE	7002	Skip if E is zero

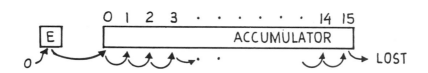

Solution: Each register-reference instruction is specified when the expression $q_7\bar{I}c_2t_3[MBR]_i$ is true (logical 1)
where the i_{th} bit of the MBR is the high bit specified
by each instruction. All the instructions can be executed during one timing signal t_3.

CIR: The circulate right instruction is explained with
the use of Figure 1. The content of each bit is shifted
to the next higher bit, E is shifted to bit 0 of the AC,
and bit 15 of the AC is lost.

$$q_7\bar{I}c_2[MBR]_8t_3: \qquad n\leftarrow 15$$
$$AC_n\leftarrow[AC]_{n-1}; \text{ for } 1 \leq n \leq 15$$
$$A_{c_0}\leftarrow[E]$$
$$E\leftarrow 0$$
$$F\leftarrow 0$$

CIL: This is just the opposite of the CIR instruction,
with E getting the bit shifted off the end.

174

$$q_7 \bar{I} c_2 t_3 [MBR]_9: \quad n \leftarrow 0$$
$$AC_n \leftarrow [AC]_{n+1}; \text{ for } 0 \leq n \leq 14$$
$$AC_{15} \leftarrow E$$
$$E \leftarrow AC_0$$
$$F \leftarrow 0$$

SPA: The PC is incremented only if the AC is positive. The AC is positive when bit 0 is 0 and the AC is negative when bit 0 is 1 (2's complement notation). Note that when the AC is zero it is also positive (zero is treated as a positive number).

$$q_7 \bar{I} c_2 t_3 [MBR]_{11} [\overline{AC}]_0: \quad PC \leftarrow [PC]+1$$
$$F \leftarrow 0$$

or $\quad q_7 \bar{I} c_2 t_3 [MBR]_{11} [AC]_0: \quad F \leftarrow 0$

The SNA and SZA micro-instructions are written in a similar manner.

SNA:
$$q_7 \bar{I} c_2 t_3 [MBR]_{12} [AC]_0: \quad PC \leftarrow [PC]+1$$
$$F \leftarrow 0$$

or $\quad q_7 \bar{I} c_2 t_3 [MBR]_{12} [\overline{AC}]_0: \quad F \leftarrow 0$

SZA: The AC is zero when $A_0 A_1 \cdots A_{15} = 0$.

$$q_7 \bar{I} c_2 t_3 [MBR]_{13} [\overline{A_0 + A_1 + \cdots + A_{15}}]: \quad PC \leftarrow [PC]+1$$
$$F \leftarrow 0$$

or $\quad q_7 \bar{I} c_2 t_3 [MBR]_{13} [A_0 + A_1 + \cdots + A_{15}]: \quad F \leftarrow 0$

SZE: The PC is incremented if E = 0.

$$q_7 \bar{I} c_2 t_3 [MBR]_{14} \bar{E}: \quad PC \leftarrow [PC]+1$$
$$F \leftarrow 0$$

or $\quad q_7 \bar{I} c_2 t_3 [MBR]_{14} E: \quad F \leftarrow 0$

● **PROBLEM** 5-30

A computer with a teletype as an I/O device has the following I/O registers

INPR: Input Register - 8 bits
OUTR: Output Register - 8 bits
FGI: Input Flag - 1 bit
FGO: Output Flag - 1 bit
IEN: Interrupt Enable - 1 bit

Describe how each register is used.

Solution: The teletype is able to encode and decode an

alpha-numeric symbol to an eight bit word. The eight
bit word is stored in the Input Register (INPR) if it is
going from the teletype to the computer. The eight bit
word is stored in the output register (OUTR) if it is
going from the computer to the teletype. The input flag
(FGI) is set (1) when an eight bit word enters the input
register from the teletype. The computer is constantly
checking the FGI. When the FGI is set, the computer
transfers the eight bit word from the INPR to the AC,
and the FGI is cleared (0). The INPR will not accept a
word from the teletype until the FGI is clear.

The output flag, FGO, is originally set. When the computer wants to send data out to the terminal it checks
the FGO to see if it is set. If the FGO is set, the
computer sends the contents of the AC to the OUTR and
clears the FGO. The FGO remains cleared until the 8 bit
word is decoded and printed. The teletype clears the
FGO after the word is printed. The computer cannot send
a word to the OUTR when the FGO is cleared because this
condition indicates that the teletype is still in the
process of printing the previous character.

The Input/Output process just described is very wasteful
because the computer, which operates much faster than the
teletype, cannot perform any useful operations while the
teletype is operating. Thus, the computer wastes time
checking the state of the flags.

With the IEN, however, the computer does not have to
check the teletype because the teletype can now tell the
computer when it is ready to accept or send information.
Thus, the computer can run other tasks when previously it
had to wait. The IEN can be set or cleared by the programmer's instruction. When IEN is cleared the computer
cannot be interrupted by the flags. When IEN is set
the flags can interrupt the computer.

● **PROBLEM** 5-31

Write the micro-instruction for the execute cycles of
the following I/O instructions:

Symbol	Hexadecimal Code	Description
INP	F800	Input character to lower eight bits of AC
OUT	F400	Output character from lower eight bits of AC
SKI	F200	Skip on input flag
SKO	F100	Skip on output flag
ION	F080	Interrupt on
IOF	F040	Interrupt off

Solution: The I/O instructions are specified when the
control signal $q_7 I c_2 [MBR]_i$ is true (logic 1), where the

i^{th} bit of the MBR is the high bit specified by each instruction. All of the I/O instructions can be executed during one timing signal t_3.

INP: This instruction transfers the eight bit word from the INPR to the AC. After transferring the word, the FGI flag must be cleared so the teletype can insert another word in the INPR, if it needs to.

$$q_7 I c_2 t_3 [MBR]_4: \quad AC_{8-15} \leftarrow [INPR]$$
$$FGI \quad \leftarrow 0$$
$$F \quad \leftarrow 0$$

The first micro-instruction transfers the data to the AC. The second micro-instruction clears the FGI. The third micro-instruction sets the fetch cycle control signal.

OUT: This instruction transfers the word from the AC to the OUTR and clears the FGO flag so that the OUTR cannot be changed while the teletype is printing.

$$q_7 I c_2 t_3 [MBR]_5: \quad OUTR \leftarrow [AC]_{8-15}$$
$$FGO \leftarrow 0$$
$$F \leftarrow 0$$

SKI: This instruction increments the PC when the FGI flag is set.

$$q_7 I c_2 t_3 [MBR]_6 [FGI]: \quad PC \leftarrow [PC]+1$$
$$F \leftarrow 0$$

or $\quad q_7 I c_2 t_3 [MBR]_6 [\overline{FGI}]: \quad F \leftarrow 0$

SKO: This instruction increments the PC when the FGO flag is set.

$$q_7 I c_2 t_3 [MBR]_7 [FGO]: \quad PC \leftarrow [PC]+1$$
$$F \leftarrow 0$$

or $\quad q_7 I c_2 t_3 [MBR]_7 [\overline{FGO}]: \quad F \leftarrow 0$

ION: This instruction turns the interrupt on. The interrupt is on when the IEN flag is set.

$$q_7 I c_2 t_3 [MBR]_8: \quad IEN \leftarrow 1$$
$$F \leftarrow 0$$

IOF: This instruction turns the interrupt off.

$$q_7 I c_2 t_3 [MBR]_9: \quad IEN \leftarrow 0$$
$$F \leftarrow 0$$

Design the block diagram of the accumulator and code the micro-operations that go into it.

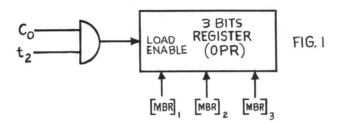

FIG. I

Solution: Each micro-operation and its associated control function describes what logic operations need to be carried out. For example, the statement:

$$c_0 t_2: \quad OPR \leftarrow [MBR]_{1-3}$$

implies that a two-input AND gate and a three bit register (called OPR) are needed. Figure 1 shows the block diagram implementation of this statement.

To design the block diagram of the accumulator, a list is made of all the micro-operations whose results go into the AC and their associated control functions.

Control function	Micro-operation	Definition
$q_0 c_2 t_2$:	$AC \leftarrow [AC] \wedge [MBR]$	AND with MBR
$q_1 c_2 t_2 + q_2 c_2 t_2$:	$AC \leftarrow [AC] + [MBR]$	Add
$q_2 c_2 t_1 + q_7 \bar{I} c_2 t_3 [MBR]_4$:	$AC \leftarrow 0$	Clear
$q_7 \bar{I} c_2 t_3 [MBR]_6$:	$AC \leftarrow [\overline{AC}]$	Complement
$q_7 \bar{I} c_2 t_3 [MBR]_8$:	$AC_{n+1} \leftarrow [AC]_n, \ AC_0 \leftarrow [E]$	Shift-right
$q_7 \bar{I} c_2 t_3 [MBR]_9$:	$AC_{15} \leftarrow [E]; \ AC_{n-1} \leftarrow [AC]_n$	Shift-left
$q_7 \bar{I} c_2 t_3 [MBR]_{10}$:	$AC \leftarrow [AC] + 1$	Increment
$q_7 I c_2 t_3 [MBR]_4$:	$AC_{8-15} \leftarrow [INPR]$	Transfer INPR

Figures 2 and 3 show the block diagram of the accumulator. Two figures are used to simplify the circuit, however, the total circuit is the combination of Figures 2 and 3.

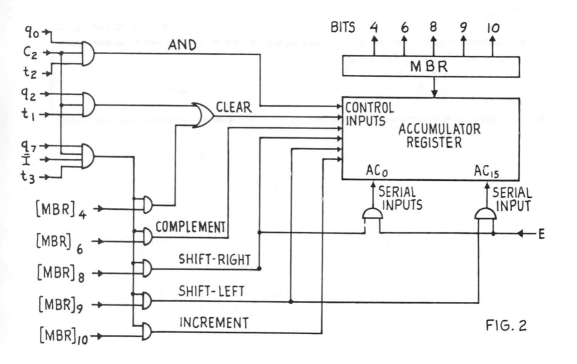

FIG. 2

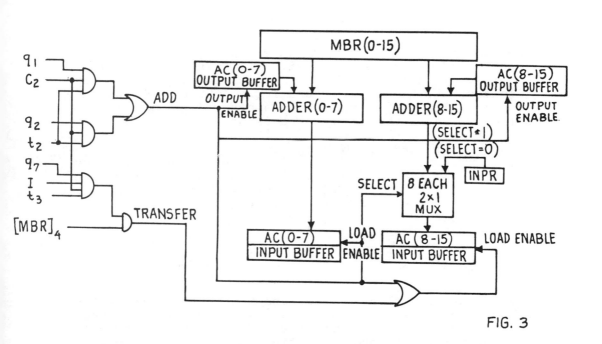

FIG. 3

The accumulator register is an integrated circuit package capable of storing, shifting, complementing, incrementing and clearing a sixteen bit number. The add and transfer operations are shown in Figure 3.

179

Write the micro-instructions for the interrupt cycle of the computer. What changes must be made in the execute cycle of the previous instruction to accommodate the interrupt cycle?

Solution: Previously, after executing the instruction the F register would be cleared and control would then go to the fetch cycle. To facilitate the interrupt capability, however, the IEN flag must be checked at the end of each execute instruction. If IEN = 0 the interrupt capability is not used and control then goes to the fetch cycle. If IEN = 1 the FGO and FGI flags must be checked to see if the teletype needs service. If FGO and FGI are both clear (zero), then control goes to the fetch cycle, but if FGO or FGI are set, then control must go to the interrupt cycle. Hence, the end of the execute cycle must be changed from this:

$$c_2 t_3: \quad F \leftarrow 0$$

to this: $\quad c_2 t_3 \{ [IEN] \cdot [[FGI] + [FGO]] \}: \quad R \leftarrow 1$

$$c_2 t_3 \overline{\{ [IEN] \cdot [[FGI] + [FGO]] \}}: \quad F \leftarrow 0$$

When the computer enters the interrupt cycle it goes to a subroutine specifically designed for interrupts. The return address is stored in a special location in memory (location 0), that can be recalled at the end of the subroutine. The IEN is cleared so another interrupt will not occur until the present one is dealt with.

$$c_3 t_0: \quad MBR_{4-15} \leftarrow [PC]$$
$$PC \quad \leftarrow 0$$

$$c_3 t_1: \quad MAR \quad \leftarrow [PC]$$
$$PC \leftarrow [PC] + 1$$

$$c_3 t_2: \quad M<MAR> \leftarrow [MBR]$$
$$IEN \leftarrow 0$$

Go to Interrupt Subroutine at location 1, Save return address in location 0, Clear IEN.

$$c_3 t_3: \quad F \leftarrow 0$$
$$R \leftarrow 0$$

Go to fetch cycle

The FGO and FGI flags will be checked in the interrupt subroutine to determine if data must enter or leave the AC. After the teletype is serviced the IEN is set to 1 and control leaves the subroutine at the BUN instruction. The computer then fetches the instruction addressed by the PC contents saved in location 0.

CHAPTER 6

CODING

INTRODUCTION TO THE COMMON CODES

● PROBLEM 6-1

Explain the concept of coding and give the general characteristics of the most widely used codes.

Solution: Coding is representation of the characters via a character code in which each character is assigned a unique combination of bits. The three most popular codes are BCDIC–Binary Coded Decimal Interchange code, EBCDIC–Extended Binary Coded Decimal Interchange code, and ASCII–American Standard Code for Information Interchange.

The BCDIC was widely used until the advent of the IBM System/360 and similar to it systems. Being a six-bit character code, BCDIC can accumulate as much as 64 (2^6) characters assigning 000 000 to the first and 111 111 to the last character. This is sufficient for the 26 upper-case letters, 10 digits, and 28 special characters such as period, comma, etc. If, however, distinction is to be made between the upper-case and the lower-case letters, 64 characters are not enough.

The 256 (2^8) "spaces" of the eight-bit codes, such as EBCDIC and ASCII, are more than enough to accomodate all the needed characters. BCDIC and EBCDIC are very similar except that the second code contains more characters.

Table 1 ; illustrates these three character codes.

Table 1.

Character	BCDIC[a]	EBCDIC	ASCII
0	001 010	1111 0000	0011 0000
1	000 001	1111 0001	0011 0001
2	000 010	1111 0010	0011 0010
3	000 011	1111 0011	0011 0011
4	000 100	1111 0100	0011 0100
5	000 101	1111 0101	0011 0101
6	000 110	1111 0110	0011 0110
7	000 111	1111 0111	0011 0111
8	001 000	1111 1000	0011 1000
9	001 001	1111 1001	0011 1001

A	110 001	1100 0001	0100 0001
B	110 010	1100 0010	0100 0010
C	110 011	1100 0011	0100 0011
D	110 100	1100 0100	0100 0100
E	110 101	1100 0101	0100 0101
F	110 110	1100 0110	0100 0110
G	110 111	1100 0111	0100 0111
H	111 000	1100 1000	0100 1000
I	111 001	1100 1001	0100 1001
J	100 001	1101 0001	0100 1010
K	100 010	1101 0010	0100 1011
L	100 011	1101 0011	0100 1100
M	100 100	1101 0100	0100 1101
N	100 101	1101 0101	0100 1110
O	100 110	1101 0110	0100 1111
P	100 111	1101 0111	0101 0000
Q	101 000	1101 1000	0101 0001
R	101 001	1101 1001	0101 0010
S	010 010	1110 0010	0101 0011
T	010 011	1110 0011	0101 0100
U	010 100	1110 0100	0101 0101
V	010 101	1110 0101	0101 0110
W	010 110	1110 0110	0101 0111
X	010 111	1110 0111	0101 1000
Y	011 000	1110 1000	0101 1001
Z	011 001	1110 1001	0101 1010
blank	010 000	0100 0000	0010 0000
=	001 011	0111 1110	0011 1101
+	110 000	0100 1110	0010 1011
−	100 000	0110 0000	0010 1101
*	101 100	0101 1100	0010 1010
/	010 001	0110 0001	0010 1111
(	011 100	0100 1101	0010 1000
)	111 100	0101 1101	0010 1001
,	011 011	0110 1011	0010 1100
.	111 011	0100 1011	0010 1110
$	101 011	0101 1011	0010 0100
'		0111 1101	0010 0111
<	111 010	0100 1100	0011 1100
>	101 111	0110 1110	0011 1110
:		0111 1101	0011 1010
;		0101 1110	0011 1011
"	111 111	0111 1010	0010 0010

METHODS OF TRANSMISSION ERROR DETECTION

● **PROBLEM** 6-2

(a) Explain what is meant by error detection through redundancy.

For each of the following words, determine if it is a "legal" code word for the
(b) binary-coded decimal (BCD) system.
(c) excess-3(X-3) code system.

(i) 0 1 0 1   (ii) 0 1 0 0   (iii) 1 1 0 0

Solution: (a) All information within a computer is represented as bits of 1's and 0's. The flow of this information within, to and from the computer occurs along some form of transmission line. A basic physical characteristic of any transmission line is the presence of disturbances which introduce the possibility of errors occurring in the information transmitted on this line. Let us represent a transmission system by letting the transmitted information be the binary n-tuple $(x_1, x_2, \ldots, x_n)$ which moves along n parallel data lines, forming n independent networks. Thus, one faulty line can influence only a single bit, and therefore, at worst, introduce the error of complementing one of the n-tuple components in the output:

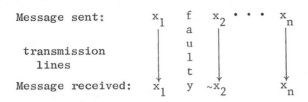

This independent error representation of transmission lines characterizes data buses (bidirectional communication lines between the CPU, memory, and I/O devices, which carry instructions and transfer data). A simplifying assumption that will be useful is that, in a data word consisting of n bits, only one bit will be incorrect. Probability theory can be used to show that for an error rate of one in 1000 transmitted bits, the odds of having two erroneous bits in a 5-bit word (n = 5) are less than one in 100,000. So the single-error approximation is a reasonable, though simplistic, assumption. Computers are supplied with automatic error detectors. An error can be detected by redundancy, which is the inclusion of extra information with each transmission. This extra information helps the receiver to decide if the received message has been altered in transmission. The simplest error detecting system, conceptually, would be duplicate transmission of each data unit. Thus, if the first transmission doesn't match the second transmission, the receiver can signal that an error has occurred. If we are willing to surrender a degree of certainty in exchange for efficiency, better methods are available. One such method is the binary-coded decimal (BCD) code system. In the BCD system, four bits are used to code the decimal digits 0-9 in their binary representation.

Decimal	BCD
0	0000
1	0001
2	0010
3	0011
4	0100
5	0101
6	0110
7	0111
8	1000
9	1001

From these 10 digits any positive decimal integer can be constructed. In BCD the binary representations for the numbers 10-15 are not used and, if they show up at a receiver, they can be detected as "illegal" by checking the received datum with a "legal word" list:

Messary received: x_1 x_2 x_3 x_4
                     ↓   ↓   ↓   ↓

Comparing device	Equality Comparator	Equality Comparator	Equality Comparator	Equality Comparator	OUT PUT →

                     ↑   ↑   ↑   ↑

Legal word list   0   0   ¦   0   0

                     1   0   0   1

(b) Since the legal BCD word list consists of the binary representations of the decimal digits 0-9, any received 4 bit word whose decimal equivalent is greater than 9 is illegal.
  (i)   Since binary 0101 = decimal 5, 0101 is a legal BCD code word.
  (ii)   Since binary 0100 = decimal 4, 0100 is a legal BCD code word.
 (iii)   Since binary 1100 = decimal 12 is greater than 9, 1100 is not a legal BCD code word.

(c) The excess-3 (X-3) code is obtained by adding binary 0011 to the BCD codes:

Decimal	BCD	Excess-3
0	0000	0011
1	0001	0100
2	0010	0101
3	0011	0110
4	0100	0111
5	0101	1000
6	0110	1001
7	0111	1010
8	1000	1011
9	1001	1100

Note that X-3 does not allow 0000 or 1111. Thus, every legal X-3 word contains at least one 0 and at least one 1, which provides the receiver with the information that the data channel is active and transmitting. Again, the error-detection algorithm involves table look-up and comparison. Since 0101, 0100, and 1100 are all on the legal word list, they are all legal X-3 code words.

● **PROBLEM** 6-3

Describe the zoned and packed formats of the binary coded decimal (BCD) representation of the characters and represent the decimal numbers 493 and -493 in both formats using EBCDIC.

Solution: Each of the representations of the digits in the eight-bit character codes consists of two fields: a four-bit zone field followed by a four-bit digit field. For digits in EBCDIC the zone field is represented by 1111. The digits 4, 9, and 3 in decimal are 0100, 1001, and 0011 respectively. Thus, the number 493 in BCD representation looks as follows: 0100 1001 0011, and in zoned BCD representation: 1111 0100 1111 1001 1111 0011 . The equivalents for plus and minus signs in EBCDIC are 1100 and 1101 respectively. To indicate the sign of a number in the zoned format, the sign equivalent is placed in the zone field of the rightmost digit. Thus,

               1111 0100 1111 1001 1100 0011

and

               1111 0100 1111 1001 1101 0011

represent +493 and -493 respectively in the zoned format (many systems also consider a 1111 in the sign field to be plus, thereby making unsigned numbers positive).

While the zone fields are necessary to represent the characters, they are not necessary when numbers are being manipulated internally. The packed format leads to more efficient memory utilization.

To obtain the packed representation from the zoned, two changes have to be made:
1) all zone fields have to be removed
2) the sign field has to be transposed to the rightmost byte.
Thus,

        0100 1001 0011 1100

and

        0100 1001 0011 1101

represent +493 and -493 respectively in the packed format.

● **PROBLEM** 6-4

(a) Explain what is meant by a parity check;
(b) Encode the decimal digits 0-9 into their
   (i) 7421 code
  (ii) two-out-of-five code
 (iii) biquinary code
representations.

Solution: (a) A parity check is simply the technique of counting the number of 0's or 1's in a data word. In some systems, the result then determines the value assigned to an extra "parity bit", which is carried along as a check.
(b) (i) Codes are sometimes identified by their positional values. The binary code may be referred to as the 8421 code (since a 1 in the leftmost position has a value of 8, a 1 in the rightmost position has a value of 1, etc.) The 7421 code is identical to the 8421 code for the first seven digits, but the high-order bit is used to represent decimal 7 rather than decimal 8 as in 8421 code. The codes are shown in fig. 1.

Decimal	8421	7421
0	0000	0000
1	0001	0001
2	0010	0010
3	0011	0011
4	0100	0100
5	0101	0101
6	0110	0110
7	0111	1000
8	1000	1001
9	1001	1010

Fig. 1

Note that no legal 7421 word has more than two 1's. Therefore, if a parity check indicated that a received word had three or four 1's, an error condition would be signalled.
(ii) The two-out-of-five code can be obtained from the 7421 code by adding a fifth bit. This new bit, added in the least significant position, is called the parity byt. If the 7421 code representation of a particular decimal integer has a single 1 bit, the parity bit

is 1. If the 7421 code for a decimal integer has zero or two 1 bits,
the parity bit is 0. The two-out-of-five code is shown in fig. 2.

Decimal	7421	Two-out-of-five
0	0000	00000
1	0001	00011
2	0010	00101
3	0011	00110
4	0100	01001
5	0101	01010
6	0110	01100
7	1000	10001
8	1001	10010
9	1010	10100

Fig. 2

Note that every legal two-out-of-five code word has a pair of 1's,
except 00000. Thus, the presence of a single 1 bit or more than
two 1 bits would signal an error.

(iii) The problem with the two-out-of-five code is that there is no
parity check for zero, since zero is represented by a code consisting
only of zeros. If a digit is being transmitted and for some reason
the 1's are suppressed, the result will be 00000, and the computer
has no way of knowing if this is an error or the number is supposed to
be zero. In the biquinary code, zero is indicated as 01 00001. The
value of each succeeding integer is increased by 1 by moving the 1
left one column until decimal 5 is reached. Decimal 5 is represented
as 1000001. The values of decimals 6-9 are obtained by moving the 1
to the left, again. The biquinary code is shown in fig. 3.

Decimal	Bi	quinary
0	01	00001
1	01	00010
2	01	00100
3	01	01000
4	01	10000
5	10	00001
6	10	00010
7	10	00100
8	10	01000
9	10	10000

Fig. 3

Every legal biquinary code word must contain a pair of 1's. Thus, the
presence of a single 1 bit or more than two 1 bits would signal an
error.

● **PROBLEM** 6-5

(a) Explain what is meant by even parity and odd parity.
(b) Decode the following under the odd parity 8421 redundant
     (8421 R) code and determine if an error has occurred:
     (i) 00011   (ii) 01011   (iii) 01001 .
(c) Decode the following four-digit number under the horizontal
     and vertical odd parity 8421 R coding scheme and determine
     if it had been correctly transmitted:
                 01101
                 00101

186

```
                        01011
                        00100
                        1101
```

<u>Solution</u>: (a) The even parity system adds a 1-bit to a data word
if the word has an odd number of 1-bits or adds a 0-bit if the word
has an even number of 1-bits. Thus, in an even parity system every
legal code word has an even number of 1-bits. The odd parity system
adds a 1-bit to a data word if the word has an even number of 1-bits,
or adds a 0-bit if the word has an odd number of 1-bits. Thus, in an
odd parity system every legal code word has an odd number of 1-bits.
In an odd parity system it is also true that every legal code word
has at least one 1-bit and at least one 0-bit, thus yielding additional
information on whether or not the transmission line is operative.

(b) When a parity bit is added to an 8421 code, it is sometimes known
as the 8421 redundant (8421 R) code. The parity bit here is called
a redundancy bit. In an odd parity system, this parity bit would be
1 if the 8421 code word had an even number of 1's and 0 if the
8421 code word had an odd number of 1's. Thus, with the addition
of the parity bit, every number in the odd parity 8421 R code has
either one 1-bit or three 1-bits. If a received word has two or no
1-bits, an error has occurred. In decoding, the rightmost bit is
not used, and the other four bits are decoded as regular 8421 code
representation.
  (i) Since 00011 has two 1-bits, an error has occurred.
 (ii) Since 01011 has three 1-bits the word has been correctly trans-
     mitted.
     01011 in 8421 R = 0101 in 8421 = decimal 5 .
(iii) Since 01001 has two 1-bits, an error has occurred.
(c) With odd parity, the presence of an even number of 1-bits indicates
an error, but the precise faulty bit is not known. This can be overcome by checking for parity in columns as well as rows. This procedure is called horizontal and vertical odd parity check. Thus, if
the received message is: 01101 ◄── first row
                        00101 ◄── second row
                        01011 ◄── third row
                        00100 ◄── fourth row
                        1101
               / ↑
     first column   fourth column

the rightmost bits of the first four rows are row parity bits, and
the last row consists of column parity bits. The first, third and
fourth rows contain an odd number of 1-bits, so no error has occurred
in those rows. But the second row has two 1-bits, indicating an
error in that row. To determine which bit in that row is faulty,
check the column parity bits. The first, second and third columns
contain an odd number of 1-bits, so no error has occurred in those
columns. But the fourth column has two 1-bits, indicating an error
in that column. Therefore, the bit in the fourth column and the
second row is in error. Note that this system not only has error-
detecting capabilities, but error correcting capabilities as well,
since, once the faulty bit is located, it can be corrected by changing
it to its complement. (Recall that a bit in error is the complement
of the input value and hence, complementing it again would yield the
original input value, by the involution law.) The amount of redundancy in an error-correcting code must be much higher than in a mere
error-detecting code. Also, note that although the regular parity
(8421 R) system cannot pick up two errors occurring in the same data
word (since the first error would result in an even number of 1-bits

and the second error would result in an odd number of 1-bits, thus allowing the received word to pass the parity check), the horizontal and vertical parity system will indicate an error if a double error has occurred. The ability to detect the faulty bit is lost, however. Again, this encoding, decoding and error-correcting scheme is automatically implemented by the machine hardware.

HAMMING CODE SYSTEM

Use the Hamming code system to:
(a) encode decimal 11
(b) determine if each of the following received words was transmitted correctly, and then decode the word:
  (i)   0110011
  (ii) 0110001
  (iii) 0010011

Solution: The Hamming system is a type of the parity check system. For a four-bit datum, for example, the Hamming system, generates three check bits. Let the datum be given by (D_0, D_1, D_2, D_3) and the check bits be given by (C_1, C_2, C_3). Then, if $+_2$ represents mod 2 addition (exclusive-OR sum), then

$$C_1 = D_0 +_2 D_2 +_2 D_3 \qquad (1)$$

$$C_2 = D_0 +_2 D_1 +_2 D_3 \qquad (2)$$

$$C_3 = D_0 +_2 D_1 +_2 D_2 \qquad (3)$$

The check and data bits must be interspersed in the correct manner for the decoding and verification to occur correctly. The check digit C_i is placed in bit position $2^{(i-1)}$.

Bit Position: 1   2   3   4   5   6   7

Occupying bit: C_1 C_2 - C_3 - - -

The remaining bit positions are filled sequentially by filling the lowest unfilled bit position with the data bit of highest index:

Bit Position: 1   2   3   4   5   6   7

Occupying bit: C_1 C_2 D_3 C_3 D_2 D_1 D_0

A received word is checked by generating the associated syndrome. For a 4-bit datum encoded into a seven-bit word, the syndrome will be 3 bits (S_3, S_2, S_1), such that

$$S_1 = C_1 +_2 (D_0 +_2 D_2 +_2 D_3) \qquad (4)$$

$$S_2 = C_2 +_2 (D_0 +_2 D_1 +_2 D_3) \qquad (5)$$

$$S_3 = C_3 +_2 (D_0 +_2 D_1 +_2 D_2) \qquad (6)$$

Substituting equations (1)-(3) into (4)-(6), respectively, one sees that:

$$S_1 = (D_0 +_2 D_2 +_2 D_3) +_2 (D_0 +_2 D_2 +_2 D_3) = 0$$

$$S_2 = (D_0 +_2 D_1 +_2 D_3) +_2 (D_0 +_2 D_1 +_2 D_3) = 0$$

$$S_3 = (D_0 +_2 D_1 +_2 D_2) +_2 (D_0 +_2 D_1 +_2 D_2) = 0$$

if no error has occurred. (Recall that in mod 2 addition if $a = b$, then $a +_2 b = 0$). If an error has occurred, changing either a data or check bit, then one or more of the syndrome bits would not be 0. Equations (4)-(6) can be written as the matrix equation:

$$S = Y \cdot H \qquad\qquad (7)$$

where S is the vector $[S_3\ S_2\ S_1]$, Y is the received word vector $[C_1\ C_2\ D_3\ C_3\ D_2\ D_1\ D_0]$, $\cdot$ is matrix multiplication (using mod 2 addition), and

$$H = \begin{bmatrix} 001 \\ 010 \\ 011 \\ 100 \\ 101 \\ 110 \\ 111 \end{bmatrix}$$

is the parity check matrix. Note that the rows of the parity check matrix are simply the binary representations of decimals 1-7, written in sequence.

(a) The four-bit binary representation of decimal 11 is 1011.

Substituting into equations (1)-(3) with $(D_0, D_1, D_2, D_3) = (1,1,0,1)$, one gets:

$$C_1 = 1 +_2 0 +_2 1 = 0$$

$$C_2 = 1 +_2 1 +_2 1 = 1$$

$$C_3 = 1 +_2 1 +_2 0 = 0$$

Therefore, the Hamming code word for decimal 11 is:

Bit Position:	1	2	3	4	5	6	7
Occupying bit:	0	1	1	0	0	1	1

or 0110011.

(b) (i) Substituting into equation (7), with $Y = [0110011]$, one gets:

$$S = [0\ 1\ 1\ 0\ 0\ 1\ 1] \cdot \begin{bmatrix} 0\ 0\ 1 \\ 0\ 1\ 0 \\ 0\ 1\ 1 \\ 1\ 0\ 0 \\ 1\ 0\ 1 \\ 1\ 1\ 0 \\ 1\ 1\ 1 \end{bmatrix}$$

$$= [0\ 0\ 0]$$

indicating that the message was transmitted correctly. To decode the message, the information bits from the code word must be extracted. Remembering that bit positions 1, 2 and 4 contain the check bits, we extract the information bits from bit positions 3,5,6 and 7 as 1011 = decimal 11. Checking this with the answer obtained in part (a), one can see that the received word was indeed transmitted correctly.

(ii) Substituting into equation (7), with $Y = [0\ 1\ 1\ 0\ 0\ 0\ 1]$, one gets:

$$S = \begin{bmatrix} 0 & 1 & 1 & 0 & 0 & 0 & 1 \end{bmatrix} \cdot \begin{bmatrix} 0 & 0 & 1 \\ 0 & 1 & 0 \\ 0 & 1 & 1 \\ 1 & 0 & 0 \\ 1 & 0 & 1 \\ 1 & 1 & 0 \\ 1 & 1 & 1 \end{bmatrix}$$

$$= \begin{bmatrix} 1 & 1 & 0 \end{bmatrix} \neq \begin{bmatrix} 0 & 0 & 0 \end{bmatrix}$$

indicating that an error has occurred. Since this error has effected both S_3 and S_2 but not S_1, the error bit must be the one that occurs in both the computations of S_3 and S_2 but not S_1. Looking at equations (4)-(6) one sees that the only bit that appears in (5) and (6) but not (4) is D_1. Hence the error bit must be D_1. Note that D_1 is in bit position 6. If $S = \begin{bmatrix} 1 & 1 & 0 \end{bmatrix}$ is taken as the binary representation of a decimal integer, then binary $1\ 1\ 0 =$ decimal 6. If an error has occurred, the syndrome will always point to the bit position of the error. Complementing the bit in position 6, yields:

received word: 0 1 1 0 0 0 1

corrected word: 0 1 1 0 0 1 1

The corrected word is decoded by extracting bits 3,5,6, and 7 as the information bits and converting from binary to decimal:

binary 1 0 1 1 = decimal 11.

Comparing this result with that of part (i), one sees that, if this were the transmitted word, an error in bit 6 would indeed yield the word received.

(iii) Substituting into equation (7), with $Y = \begin{bmatrix} 0 & 0 & 1 & 0 & 0 & 1 & 1 \end{bmatrix}$, one gets:

$$S = \begin{bmatrix} 0 & 0 & 1 & 0 & 0 & 1 & 1 \end{bmatrix} \cdot \begin{bmatrix} 0 & 0 & 1 \\ 0 & 1 & 0 \\ 0 & 1 & 1 \\ 1 & 0 & 0 \\ 1 & 0 & 1 \\ 1 & 1 & 0 \\ 1 & 1 & 1 \end{bmatrix}$$

$$= \begin{bmatrix} 0 & 1 & 0 \end{bmatrix} \neq \begin{bmatrix} 0 & 0 & 0 \end{bmatrix}$$

indicating that an error has occurred. Since binary 0 1 0 = decimal 2, the error is in bit position 2, the bit containing C_2. Thus, even errors in the check digits can be detected and corrected. Complementing the bit in position 2, yields:

received word: 0 0 1 0 0 1 1

corrected word: 0 1 1 0 0 1 1

Extracting bits 3,5,6 and 7 as the information bits and converting from binary to decimal one gets:

binary 1 0 1 1 = decimal 1 1.

Comparing this result with that of part (i), one sees that if this was the transmitted word, an error in bit 2 would indeed yield the word received. Again, the encoding, decoding and error-correcting scheme is automatically implemented by the machine hardware.

Calculate the number of parity bits required in order to code an information consisting of one binary bit on each input line, into the Hamming code, if each input information has: a) 8 bits, and, b) 4 bits.

Solution: The number of parity bits K, required to be added to n information lines is calculated as follows: with K parity bits, the total number of combinations of 0's and 1's that one can have is 2^K . Out of these 2^K combinations, one must reserve one combination to denote a no-error condition when the lines are received at the receiver. The other $(2^K - 1)$ combinations can be used to identify each one of the incoming lines, so that one can point out which incoming line has developed an error.

Now, the number of incoming lines

$$= n + k$$

i.e., sum of the n information-bits lines plus the k parity-bits lines that were added at the transmitter. Hence, one must satisfy the condition that

$$2^k \geq n + k + 1 .$$

a) As there are 8 information bits or lines, $n = 8$.

$$\therefore 2^k \geq 8 + k + 1 .$$

i.e., $2^k \geq 9 + k$

Now, k can be found by a trial and error method. Let k = 5

therefore, $2^k = 2^5 = 32.$
And
$$9 + k = 9 + 5 = 14 .$$

Hence,
$$32 \geq 14 .$$

The condition is satisfied, but maybe a more "economical" number can be found.

     Let   k = 4

       then $2^k = 2^4 = 16 .$
And,
$$9 + k = 9 + 4 = 13 .$$

$$16 \geq 13 .$$

Again the condition is satisfied. But if k = 3, the condition will no longer be satisfied. Hence, k = 4 is the correct answer. i.e., 4 parity bits must be added.

b) If there are 4 information bits or lines, n = 4. Again, k is selected by trial and error method until the condition is just satisfied (i.e., the least possible k). Let k = 3

$$\therefore 2^k = 2^3 = 8 .$$

And, n + k + 1 = 4 + k + 1 = 5 + k = 5 + 3 = 8

$$8 \geq 8 .$$

the condition is satisfied, while k = 2 leads to the incorrect comparision $4 \geq 7$. Thus, with n = 4 information bits, one must have k = 3 parity bits.

Produce a circuit for coding a binary coded decimal digit input into the Hamming code.

FIG. 1

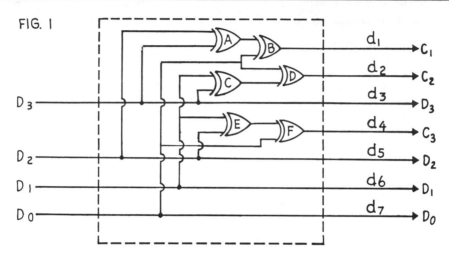

$\underline{Solution}$: A binary coded decimal digit has four input lines D_0, D_1, D_2, D_3.

The number K of parity bits required with 4 information input lines = 3 (see the previous problem). Let these 3 parity check bits be C_1, C_2, C_3. Hence, the coded information will be of the type:

C_1 C_2 D_3 C_3 D_2 D_1 D_0 (see problem 3 of this chapter). And, let us name these 7 lines as: d_1 d_2 d_3 d_4 d_5 d_6 d_7. Now, by the theory of Hamming code, one must have an even parity between

$$C_1, \ D_0, \ D_2, \ D_3 \ ;$$

$$C_2, \ D_0, \ D_1, \ D_3 \ ;$$

and $\qquad C_3, \ D_0, \ D_1, \ D_2 \ .$

In other words, one must ensure that the exclusive-or sum of each of the four variables in the above 3 sets equals to 0.

i.e.,
$$C_1 \oplus D_0 \oplus D_2 \oplus D_3 = 0 \ ,$$

$$C_2 \oplus D_0 \oplus D_1 \oplus D_3 = 0 \ ,$$

$$C_3 \oplus D_0 \oplus D_1 \oplus D_2 = 0 \ .$$

The circuit for generating C_1, C_2, and C_3 can now be conceived by noting that the parity check bit should be a 1 if the exclusive-or of the other three variables = 1 (i.e., there is an odd number of variables which are equal to 1), and the parity check bit should be = 0 if the exclusive-or of the other three variables = 0. Hence, the circuit can be drawn as shown in Fig. 1.

Note in the above figure, that all gates A to F are 2-input exclusive-or gates. Gate A gives the exclusive-or of D_2 and D_3.

Output of gate A is 1 if only one of D_2 or D_3 is a 1. This output is again exclusive-ored with D_0. If the output of A was a 1, then, if D_0 is 1, the output of B will be 0, i.e., $C_1 = 0$, as required. In each case it can be verified that the check bits C_1, C_2, C_3 take on values 0 or 1 so as to maintain an even-parity in their respective groups.

CHAPTER 7

DATA STRUCTURES

POLISH NOTATION

● **PROBLEM** 7-1

Define the following terms as they relate to Polish string notation:

a) infix

b) prefix

c) postfix

     Then, convert the following tree into the three types of expressions just defined.

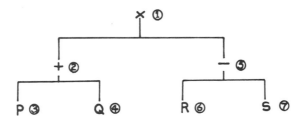

Solution: Infix notation refers to the way we normally write expressions, namely, with the operators between the two operands. This is also known as algebraic notation, which is different from Polish notation.

     Prefix notation refers to the fact that the operator precedes the expression in the string. So, if we have the string ÷ XY, it means that the division operator acts to divide X by Y.

     One inconvenience with prefix notation is that to understand the string, you must read from end to beginning. Postfix notation avoids this difficulty. For the string above, postfix notation would be XY ÷ . The meaning is the same as above, but the operator comes after the two operands.

The infix translation of the tree diagram is then (P + Q) x (R - S). This is obvious if you follow the tree up from the terminal nodes to the root node.

Prefix translation yields x + PQ - RS. By simply looking at the numbering of the individual nodes, you can see that they correspond with the order of the string. In other words, you can write the following to highlight the correspondence:

X + PQ - RS

①②③④⑤⑥⑦

Postfix notation looks somewhat different. For this tree, we get PQ + RS - x. This may be read from beginning to end as "add P and Q, then subtract S from R, then multiply the sum and the difference together."

● **PROBLEM** 7-2

Convert (a) - (c) from Infix to Prefix and Postfix expressions and (d) - (f) from Prefix to Infix and Postfix expressions.

(a) A + B * C/D
(b) A - C & D + B↑E
(c) X↑Y↑Z
(d) + * - ABCD
(e) + mA * BmC
(f) ↑X + * YZW

Solution: For conversion from Infix to Prefix and Postfix forms we need to recollect the hierarchy and associativity rule. The former says that ↑ has highest priority, then *, / and then +, - . The latter says that at the same level of priority associativity applies from left to right.

e.g. A-B-C = (A-B) - C

(a) A + B * C/D

Conversion to Prefix form: Scanning from left to right we observe the operators +, * and/ · As *, and/ have higher priority than + and * precedes/, BC becomes the operand followed by /D. Thus the whole second operand takes the form /*BCD. A is the first operand and + is the operator between them.
A + B * C / D   = + A/*BCD

Postfix form: — we have BC* then BC*D/ & finally ABC*D/+
A + B*C/D = ABC * D/+

(b) A-C * D + B↑E   scan left to right

First step   B↑E = ↑BE, BE↑ ↑has highest priority

Second step   C*D = *CD, CD*   * has 2nd highest priority

195

Third step   A-C*D = - A*CD, ACD+-   - and + are on the
                  same level

Final step   A-C*D + B↑E = + - A*CD↑BE, ACD* - BE ↑ +

   (c)   X↑Y↑Z   both ↑ on same level

                    Infix   Prefix   Postfix

First step   X↑Y   =   ↑XY   ,   XY↑

Final step   X↑Y↑Z   =   ↑↑XYZ   ,   XY↑Z↑

     Conversion from Prefix to Infix and Post fix expression.

   (d)   + * - A B C D

                  Prefix   Infix   Postfix

1st step   - AB   =   (A-B)   ,   AB -

2nd step   * -ABC   =   (A-B)*C   ,   AB-C*

Final step   + * - ABCD = (A-B)*C+D ,   AB-C*D+

   (e)   + m A * B m C   m is unary operator acting
                                   on immediate operand with
                                   - sign & parenthesis.

                  Prefix   Infix   Postfix

1st step   mC   =   (-C)   ,   Cm

2nd step   &B mC   =   B&(-C)   ,   BCm*

Final step   +mA&BmC =   (-A) + B&(-C), AmBCm*+

   (f)   ↑X + * YZW/

                  Prefix   Infix   Postfix

1st step   *Y Z   =   Y*Z   ,   YZ*

2nd step   +*YZW   =   Y*Z + W   ,   YZ*W+

Final step   ↑X+*YZW   =   X↑Y*Z+W   ,   XYZ*W+↑

● **PROBLEM** 7-3

Convert the following logical expressions to reverse Polish
string notation:

a) (Z↓((((X̄) ⊙ Y)/(X ⊙ (Z̄))) > ((Ȳ) ≡ X)))

b) (X/Y)/((X/X)/(Y/Y))

Solution: Polish notation is a way of representing logical
and algebraic expressions without using parentheses, unless

196

parentheses represent some variables or operators in the particular expression. If you think about it, the purpose of parentheses is to override the natural hierarchy of the operators. Polish notation does away with that notion. All operators have the same precedence: their position in the string determines their order of evaluation.

With reverse Polish notation, also called Polish postfix, the operator is written after its two operands. For example, the usual logical equation A $\oplus$ B would be written AB $\oplus$ in postfix notation. It is possible to use trees to evaluate Polish strings, but we will not do so here.

a) As we can see in this example, the abundance of parentheses makes this expression look formidable. We will proceed step-by-step, enclosing in brackets each portion of the expression that has been converted.

Step 1. First, we will take care of the negations. We use the symbol ¬ for this operator.

(Z↓((([X¬] ⊙ Y)/(X ⊙ [Z¬])) > ([Y¬] ≡ X)))

Step 2. We consider next the innermost partial expressions and convert them.

(Z↓(([X¬Y ⊙]/[XZ¬⊙]) > [Y¬X≡]))

Step 3. Now we include the NAND operator/to complete the innermost partial expression.

(Z↓([X¬Y ⊙ XZ¬⊙ /] > [Y¬X≡]))

Step 4. We evaluate the operator >, inserting it at the end of the string.

(Z↓[X¬Y ⊙ XZ¬⊙ / Y¬X ≡ >])

Step 5. Finally, we add the NOR operator ↓ to the end of the string. The final reverse Polish string is

ZX¬Y ⊙ XZ¬⊙ / Y¬X≡>↓

b) This problem uses solely the NAND operator/and several parentheses. We will proceed as before, evaluating the innermost parentheses first.

Step 1. The two inner expressions on the right side get translated and bracketed first.

(X/Y)/([XX/]/[YY/])

Step 2. Next we merge the two bracketed expressions together over the NAND operator.

(X/Y)/[XX/YY//]

Step 3. Now we convert the right side.

[XY/]/[XX/YY//]

Step 4. Finally, the entire expression, translated into a reverse Polish string looks like this.

    XY/XX/YY///

Describe what is known as the shunting-yard algorithm for converting infix (or algebraic) notation into the Polish postfix notation. Enumerate the five rules of priority that must be applied to the input string in order to explain the algorithm.

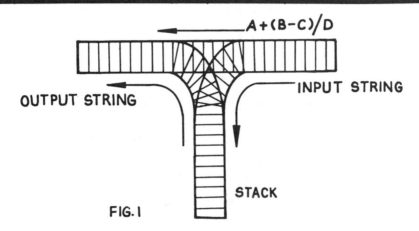

A+(B-C)/D

OUTPUT STRING

INPUT STRING

STACK

FIG. I

Solution: The metaphor of the shunting-yard is an appropriate one for this algorithm. We can think of a string of variables and operators as the cars of a train. The shunting-yard is the place where cars are added, removed, and rearranged.

In programming terminology, the shunting-yard can be represented by a stack. This stack can be likened to a rail-road track siding, as shown in Figure 1.

As the string is moved from right to left, each symbol is evaluated. A symbol will be placed either in the stack or directly into the output string, contingent upon the following rules of priority:

1) Operands at the front of the input string are moved directly to the output string.

2) A left parenthesis at the front of the input string is pushed onto the stack.

3) A right parenthesis at the front of the input string causes all operators to be popped up from the stack into the output string until a left parenthesis (if necessary) appears. The parentheses are then discarded from the output string.

4) Operators at the front of the input string cause operators in the stack to be popped up and into the output string until the top item in the stack is one of lower priority

198

than the operator in the front of the input string.
Priority is assigned to items according to the following
table:

Item	Priority
(	low
+ , -	high
* , /	higher

If the stack is empty, or if the item at the top of
the stack is one of lower priority, an operator at the
front of the input string is pushed onto the stack.

5) When the input string becomes empty, all items in the
   stack are popped up and into the output string sequentially.

Let us now "walk through" this algorithm, showing the
movement of the items in the string and stating the rules
to be applied at each step.

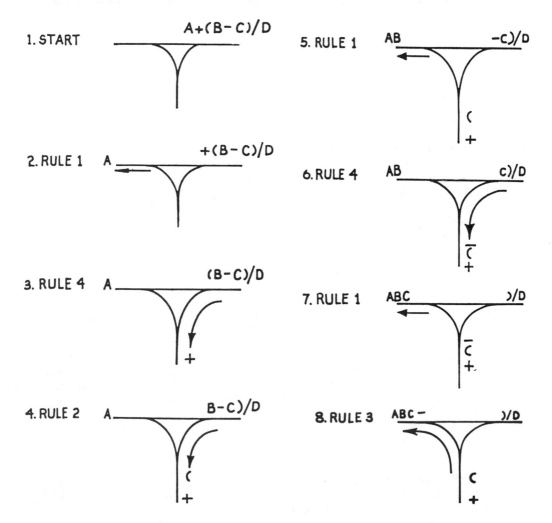

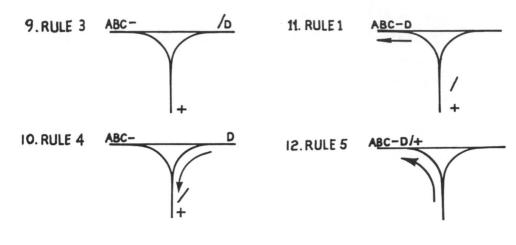

9. RULE 3 ABC— /D

10. RULE 4 ABC— D +

11. RULE 1 ABC—D +

12. RULE 5 ABC—D/+

• **PROBLEM** 7-5

Define stack, queue, and deque. What characteristics of these three list structures make each of them useful for different applications?

<u>Solution</u>: A queue is a type of list structure with the limitation that items may be added or deleted at either end, but not in the middle. The term queue is also used in connection with computer memory to mean a group of items chained together sequentially by addresses. But here, we will discuss the queue as a way of entering data at the macro level.

Queue is a general term which describes several types of lists. One type of queue is known as a FIFO queue, which stands for "first-in-first out." Items that are added to a FIFO queue at one end are removed at the other. The other type of queue is a LIFO queue, which stands for "last-in-first-out." This type of queue is known as a stack. Stacks have the property that the items are removed in the reverse of the order in which they are entered. In addition, a stack allows insertions and deletions to take place only at one end.

The term deque is an acronym for "double-ended queue", in which items may be added to, or deleted from, either end. This type of list may be constructed with a double set of pointers, one to keep track of items moving up the list, and one to keep track of items moving down the list.

One sample application of queues is in the simulation of customer arrival at a ticket window. New customers coming up to the window can be placed at one end of a queue which represents the line of prospective ticket buyers. When the tickets are bought, the customer is removed from the list at the opposite end. Using this concept, the owner of the ticket booth can simulate the flow of customers and plan his business activities accordingly.

Stacks are especially useful in processing data structures such as trees. Stacks can also be used when converting expressions in algebraic notation to Polish expressions.

Recursive procedures, sometimes found in PL/l programs, use the notion of stacks to allocate additional memory space for themselves.

Deques, since they can be constructed with two sets of pointers, are ideal for two-way, or undirected, lists. This allows the user to search a list back and forth from either end.

How can the stack be used with subroutines?

Solution: The stack can be used to store return addresses and any other contents of registers that need to be saved before going to a subroutine. Consider a computer with accumulator ACC and general purpose registers X and Y. The program in fig. l shows how the stack is used to call a subroutine which will store the sum of the contents of the ACC and register X into register Y. The main program includes steps 14 through 18.

Registers	Instruction	Memory	Stack
after instruction 16	15	Push ACC	after instruction 15
ACC [20]	16	Jump to Subroutine 1	80
X [5]	17	Pop ACC	81 PC = 17
pC [57]	18		82 ACC = 20
SP [80]			
after 59	57	Start of Subroutine 1	after 60
ACC [25]	58	Add AC and X	80
X [5]	59	Store ACC in Y	81
Y [25]	60	Return	82 ACC = 20
PC [60]			
SP [80]			after 17
after 17			80
ACC [20]			81
X [5]			82
Y [25]			
PC [18]			

SP [82]

and subroutine 1 starts at step 57 and stops at step 60.
At location 15 the ACC contents is pushed into the stack.
Note that the value of the ACC remains unchanged even though
it was pushed on the stack. During the Jump to Subroutine 1
the return address is stored in the stack. At location 58
the sum of [ACC] + [X] is stored in the ACC. At location
60 the return address is taken off of the stack and put back
in the PC, thus the computer has "returned" to the main program. After returning, the ACC is popped, hence the ACC contains its previous value.

As you can see stacks are a valuable tool for storing
registers while they are temporarily being used for other
purposes.

● **PROBLEM** 7-7

Write a PL/I Program to initialize stacks or queues and to
make insertions or deletions in stacks or queues.

Solution: In PL/I, since we don't have data structures for
stacks and queues we shall use an array of one dimension,
along with pointers to simulate the stack and queue operations.

DCL STACK (20) type / * type in the type of data items
to be stored in stack; this statement creates a one dimensional array called STACK of 20 elements */.

DCL STACK_PTR FIXED DEC (2);
/*Pointer is required to know whether stack is empty or
full */.

Insert an item.

If STACK_PTR=20 THEN (go to error routine)(Stack is full)
    ELSE   STACK_PTR=STACK_PTR+1
    STACK(STACK_PTR)= X /* Item */

We have thus stored a data item X in the location in the
stack denoted by STACK (STACK_PTR), i.e., if for example,
the value of STACK_PTR=6, we insert X in the position
STACK(6) in the stack. Deletion of an item.

If STACK_PTR = 0 THEN (go to error routine)(Stack is
    empty)
ELSE   X = STACK(STACK_PTR)   (Delete)
        STACK_PTR = STACK_PTR -1

After reading out the value of the position STACK(STACK_PTR)
into a memory location X, we decrement the STACK_PTR by 1
to keep track of the number of elements still left in the
stack.

```
          END;
```

Queue:-- Queue is a data structure of type FIFO (First in
First out). That is, data is inserted at one end, say the
tail, & removed from the other end (head). For this purpose
we shall need two pointers and a one dimensional array.

```
    /* QUEUE: ONE DIMENSIONAL ARRAY */
    /* QUEUE SIZE IS 2φ */
    /* PNTR1:  POINTS TO THE TOP ELEMENTS */
    /* PNTR2:  POINTS TO THE NEXT AVAILABLE SPACE */
    /* INITIALIZE */
    DCL QUEUE (20) CHAR(5);
    DCL (PNTR1, PNTR2)      BIN FIXED (15);
    PNTR1 = 1 ;
    PNTR2 = 1 ; FLAG = φ; /* FLAG = φ INDICATES EMPTY */
    /* INSERT AN ELEMENT */
    IF  PNTR1 = PNTR2 & FLAG = 1 THEN [go to error
          routine]
           /* QUEUE FULL */
           ELSE Do;
                      FLAG = 1;
          QUEUE (PNTR2) = new element;
          IF PNTR2 = 2φ   THEN PNTR2 = 1  ;
/* THIS IS THE CASE WHEN THE NEXT AVAILABLE SPACE REACHES
THE BOTTOM.  THE NEXT AVAILABLE WILL GO BACK TO THE TOP */
       ELSE PNTR2 = PNTR2 + 1  ;
           END;
    /*DELETION OF AN ELEMENT */
IF FLAG = φ[go to error routine] ; /* QUEUE EMPTY */
     Element = QUEUE (PNTR1); /* DELETE ELEMENT */
     PNTR1 = PNTR1 + 1;

IF PNTR1 > 20 THEN PNTR1 = 1; /*CIRCLE AROUND */
IF PNTR2 = PNTR1 THEN FLAG = φ /* QUEUE EMPTY */
END;
```

TREES

● **PROBLEM** 7-8

**Construct a tree which represents the Polish prefix expres-
sion +XA-B12÷C4. Remember that in Polish notation, all operators have the same precedence; only their position is significant to the order of operations.**

Solution: Trees are useful to display the way in which the
computer translates the algebraic form of an expression (the
way in which you generally enter various formulae) into
Polish notation during the process of compiling a program.

     As a general rule, a tree will have operators $(+,-,x,
÷,↑)$ in its nonterminal nodes and operands (constants or
variables) in its terminal nodes. The root node is the
exception; it may be thought of as representing the middle
operator of an expression.

In Polish prefix notation, however, the middle operator actually comes at the beginning of the string. To begin constructing the tree, we number each element to correspond with the number of the node it will occupy. Hence,

+ × A − B 12 ÷ C 4

1 2 3 4 5 6 7 8 9

The first element (+) will be the root node. We see that the next element is (×). Remembering that trees are always constructed left to right, this element becomes the left subnode of the root. Since it is also an operator, we will neglect the right subnode for a moment in order to find the two operands which appear on either side of the (×). (See Figure 1.)

The following figures should illustrate the growth of the tree in a clearer fashion:

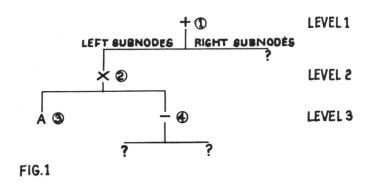

FIG.1

At this point, we need to find the operands which should appear on either side of the (−). B and 12, since they are the next two elements, will be those operators. Fig. 2 shows that the left side of the tree is complete:

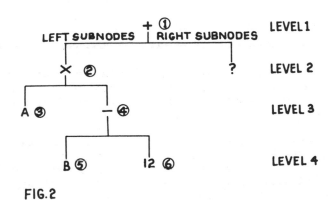

FIG.2

204

Finally, we notice that the next operator is (÷). The two operands, C and 4, follow directly, so we have the completed tree in Figure 3.

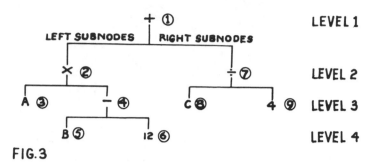

FIG.3

● PROBLEM 7-9

Evaluate the following tree expressions:

(a)

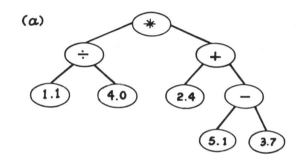

(b)

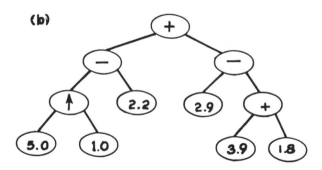

Solution: To begin evaluating trees, we look for terminal nodes, those which contain numerical values or variables at the end of the tree. Then, the rule becomes "left node, right node, operator." Starting at the leftmost node, we begin combining operands with their operators. The tree begins to lose its leaves as the process of combination continues.

a) Let us evaluate the first tree, combining nodes as we go along. Starting with the leftmost node, we see that /./ is to be divided by 4.0. After evaluation, we get the following tree:

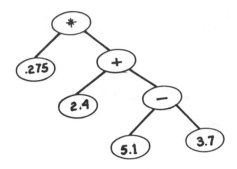

Note that the left side is now complete. Turning to the
right side, we may combine 5.1 and 3.7 under the subtraction
operator to obtain 1.4. A new node is created containing
1.4 because of this operation.

Moving up the tree from the right, we can combine 2.4
and 1.4 under the addition operator to obtain 3.8. The tree
now has the following shape:

To complete it, we simply perform the multiplication to
obtain the final answer 1.045.

b) This tree introduces the ↑ operator, which signifies
the exponential operation. Starting once again from the
left, we have 5.0 raised to the 1st power, which yields 5.0.
Then, we move up the tree to find that the next task to be
done is to subtract 2.2 from 5.0, which yields 2.8. At this
stage, the tree is

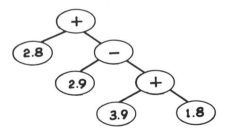

We now start with the right side to find that we must
add 3.9 to 1.8, giving us the answer 5.7. We take this
answer and move up to the next node, which indicates that we
are to subtract 5.7 from 2.9. After this operation, we
have

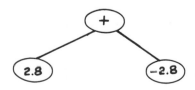

which evaluates to zero.

Write a FORTRAN function subprogram that determines whether
a particular item is contained in an ordered binary tree.
All items in the tree are assumed to be integers.

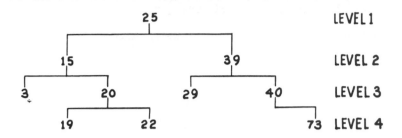

		LEVEL 1

Solution: A binary tree is said to be ordered if the following properties hold: For each node in the tree, all numbers
contained in the left subtree are less than the number at
the node being considered. All numbers contained in the right
subtree of a node are greater than the number at that node.

When a search is begun, we start at the root, turning
left if the number being searched is smaller, or turning
right if the number is greater. Consider the tree below:

We must set up a linked list, complete with two pointers
at each node, one for each branch. We also require a pointer
for the root node. To implement this in FORTRAN, we use a
two-dimensional array called TREE (100,3). We are searching
the tree for an integer between 0 and 100, hence the size of
the first parameter. The second parameter refers to the data
for each node and the two pointers which check, respectively,
the left and right subtrees. The following table shows the
initial status of the array:

I	TREE(I,1)	TREE(I,2)	TREE(I,3)
1	3	0	0
2	15	1	4
3	19	0	0
4	20	3	5
5	22	0	0
6	25	2	8
7	29	0	0
8	39	7	9
9	40	0	10
10	73	0	0
Array Component	Node Data	Left Subtree	Right Subtree

The values of the pointers represent row numbers in the
array. We take the root of the tree to be 6.

The strategy used involves logical variables. We declare the function to return a value of .TRUE. if the element
is in the tree, and to return a value of .FALSE. if the element is not found. Nodes are checked in succession. If the

value is not found at a particular node, the left branch is investigated first. Then the right branch is checked. If the node is terminal (i.e., having no branches), we exit from the program. The value of K is used to indicate the node under current consideration.

The steps are given as follows. Comments will illuminate the modular structrue of the program.

```
       LOGICAL FUNCTION SEARCH (TREE, ROOT, ITEM)
       INTEGER TREE (100,3), ROOT, ITEM, K
       K=ROOT
C      LOOP BEGINS HERE
   10  CONTINUE
C      IF NODE IS FOUND, SET SEARCH = .TRUE. AND EXIT
       IF (TREE (K,1).NE. ITEM) GO TO 20
       SEARCH = .TRUE.
       GO TO 99
   20  CONTINUE
C      TRY SEARCHING THE BRANCHES, STARTING WITH
C      THE LEFT
       IF (TREE(K,1).LT. ITEM) GO TO 30
C      IF THIS NODE IS TERMINAL,SET SEARCH = .FALSE. AND EXIT
       IF (TREE (K,2) . NE. 0) GO TO  40)
       SEARCH=.FALSE.
       GO TO 99
   40  CONTINUE
       K = TREE (K,2)
       GO TO 98
C      NOW TRY THE RIGHT BRANCH; IF NODE IS
C      TERMINAL, SET SEARCH=.FALSE. AND EXIT
       IF (TREE(K,3).NE.0) GO TO 50
       SEARCH=.FALSE.
       GO TO 99
   50  CONTINUE
       K=TREE (K,3)
   98  CONTINUE
       GO TO 10
C      END LOOP
   99  CONTINUE
       RETURN
       END
```

● **PROBLEM** 7-11

Give a pseudo code to do a tree search, using an ALGOL-like language.

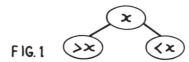

FIG. 1

Solution: We make the following assumptions:

Each node n of the tree has 3 fields

1st field is: Data [n], i.e., the number or data in the sort list.

2nd field is: Left [n], i.e., pointer to the root of the left sub-tree.

(the pointer = 0 if there is no left sub-tree)

3rd field is: Right [n], i.e., pointer to the root of the right sub-tree

(the pointer = 0 if there is no right sub-tree)

The placement of the different data items in the tree is as follows:

If the first data item is x, then, if the second data item in the list is greater than x it is placed in the left subtree, and if the second item is less than x it is placed in the right sub-tree.

i.e., Data [n] < Data [x] for all nodes x which are elements of the left sub-tree (n), and,

Data [n] > Data [x] for all nodes x which are elements of the right sub-tree (n)

We are now ready to form a strategy to search a tree, as follows:

1) Begin the search of the sort tree at the root for a node whose data field contains the argument, i.e., the value or number which we want to search

2) If there is such a node, set m to point to it and set a variable 'treesearch' to the value 'True'

3) Otherwise, if there is no such node then set the variable 'treesearch' to 'false'.

The ALGOL-like pseudo-code is given below:--

```
procedure Treesearch (root, arg, m)

    /* arg is the data we are searching for, and m
    is a pointer to the node we are on */
if root = 0 then Treesearch := false
    /* we are checking if there is still any root
    at all */
    else
          begin
    d:= Data [root]
      if arg = d then
          begin
              m: = root
                  Treesearch: = True
              end;
          else
          if arg > d then
      Treesearch: = Treesearch (left (root), arg, m);
          else
      Treesearch: = (right (root), arg, m)
          end;
```

What is the maximum number of entries that can be stored in a binary tree if the longest path from the root to any node does not exceed N? Find the general equation for the average search time for any entry in a tree with N levels.

Solution: If the longest path is N, the tree will have N levels below the root node. At most, one node can be at the root, two nodes at the next level, four nodes at the next, etc. This expands geometrically, until the total number of nodes possible is

$$1 + 2 + 4 + \ldots 2^{N-1} = 2^N - 1$$

If we want to search the nodes for a particular entry, each time we descend to the next level, we must perform another comparison. For example, if we have 3 levels, the following distribution of search times is realized:

1 node takes 1 comparison

2 nodes take 2 comparisons

4 nodes take 3 comparisons

The average over the seven nodes is given simply by multiplying nodes by comparisons, taking the sum, and dividing by the total number of nodes. Hence,

$$(1 \times 1 + 2 \times 2 + 4 \times 3)/7 = 2.43$$

We do not include the unit of time here, for it could be milli-, micro-, or nanoseconds, according to the machine doing the comparisons.

The general equation for N levels is given by

$$N-1 + (N/(2^N - 1))$$

ARRAYS

Assume X and Y are two arrays, each already sorted in ascending order, with M and N elements respectively. Merge X and Y into a single sorted array Z.

Solution: One method is to compare the first elements of each array. The smaller of the two will become the first member of the new array, while the greater of the two will come next. This picture will illustrate the idea:

The flow chart is as follows:

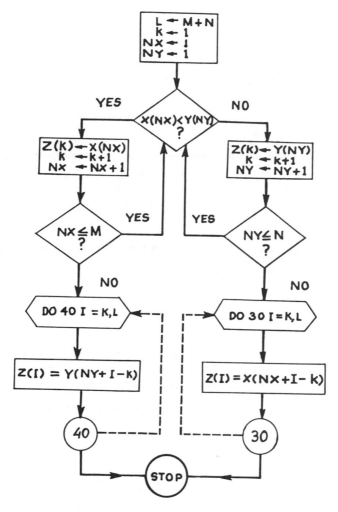

```
        INTERIOR L,M,N,K,NX,NY,X(M),Y(N)
        L=M+N
        K=1
        NX=1
        NY=1
     20 IF (X(NX).LT.Y(NY)) GØ TØ 50
C       THIS SECTIØN EXECUTES ALL STATEMENTS
C       ØN THE RIGHT SIDE ØF THE FLØW CHART.
        Z(K)=Y(NY)
        K=K+1
        NY=NY+1
        IF (NY.LE.N) GØ TØ 20
        DØ 30 IY=K,L
```

```
          Z(I)=X(NX+IY-K)
   30     CØNTINUE
          GØ TØ 90
C         THIS SECTION EXECUTES ALL STATEMENTS ØN THE
C         LEFT SIDE OF THE FLØWCHART.
   50     Z(K)=X(NX)
          K=K+1
          NX=NX+1
          IF (NX.LE.M) GØ TØ 20
          DØ 40 IX=K,L
          Z(I)=Y(NY+IX-K)
   40     CØNTINUE
   90     STØP
          END
```

[Note: Merge sorts of this type are used frequently in
business applications, in which large files must be updated
with new material.]

● **PROBLEM** 7-14

Design a BASIC program to sort 50 random numbers by a
method known as radix sorting. This method sorts numbers
by examining individual digits, starting with the units
column. For this problem, generate random numbers with no
more than 4 digits.

Solution: To understand radix sorting, consider the following example:

     3192, 4365, 6702, 13, 357, 3999,
     4132, 1872, 6345, 582.

At the first pass, the computer sorts the numbers according
to the right-most digits. If two numbers have the same units
digit, their order will be unchanged in the new list.

     3192, 6702, 4132, 1872, 582, 13, 4365, 6345,
     357, 3999

At the next pass - second right-most digits

     6702, 0013, 4132, 6345, 0357, 4365, 1872,
          0582, 3192, 3999.

Similarly, on the third pass the computer compares third
digits from the right in every number:

     0013, 0357, 0582, 4132, 3192, 6345, 4365,
     6702, 1872, 3999.

At the fourth pass, the numbers are finally sorted into
ascending order.

     0013, 0357, 0582, 1872, 3192, 3999,
          4132, 4365, 6345, 6702.

For solving this problem, we need two arrays: one to hold

the unsorted random numbers, and the other to hold the sorted list. Once the random numbers are generated, you check each column in succession, from units to thousands. To print the array after each pass, we will need four separate executions of the PRINT statement. The values can be printed out using the MAT PRINT command. Notice the parameters of the DIM statement in line 240. This means that there will be 10 rows and 5 columns. The reason for the parameters being (9,4) is that since we started our loop at zero, a place must be saved for the zeroth value.

```
15 REM RADIX SORT: DIGIT-BY-DIGIT COMPARISON
20 DIM R(49), S(49)
21 LET V=0
25 REM FILL ARRAY R WITH 4-DIGIT RANDOM NOS.
30 FOR J=0 TO 49
40 LET R(J)=INT(10000*RND(X))
50 NEXT J
60 LET L=0
70 LET M=0
80 FOR J=0 TO 49
85 REM IF 1 IS THE FIRST ELEMENT, LEAVE IT ALONE
90 IF R(J)=1 THEN 200
100 LET H=R(J)
110 FOR K=0 TO V
120 LET Z=INT(H/10)
125 REM G IS THE RIGHTMOST DIGIT
130 LET G=H-10*Z
140 LET H=Z
150 NEXT K
160 IF G<>M THEN 200
165 REM STORE R(J) IN SORTED ARRAY S(L)
170 LET S(L)=R(J)
180 LET R(J)=1
190 LET L=L+1
200 NEXT J
210 LET M=M+1
220 IF M<10 THEN 80
230 PRINT
240 MAT(S)=DIM(9,4)
250 PRINT
255 REM PRINT SORTED ARRAY S AFTER EACH PASS
260 MAT PRINT S
270 MAT S=DIM(49)
280 MAT R=S
290 LET V=V+1
295 REM WHEN 4 DIGITS HAVE BEEN CHECKED, END
300 IF V<4 THEN 60
310 END
```

● **PROBLEM** 7-15

What arrangement of the integers 1,2,3,4, and 5 in a five-element array will yield the longest sort time (also known as the worst-case sort time) for the insertion sort? Generalize the answer you obtain for N integers.

Solution: As developed earlier, in the insertion sort

213

method, the list is scanned until an element is found to be out of order. The unordered element is stored temporarily, and the scan reverses direction until it reaches the place where the unordered element should be. The rest of the list's elements are moved up one place, and the sort continues.

If the list of integers is presented initially in reverse order, the insertion sort will have to make the greatest number of comparisons. Let us walk through the steps that must be taken:

after 1st pass   4,5,3,2,1

after 2nd pass   4,3,5,2,1

after 3rd pass   3,4,5,2,1

after 4th pass   3,4,2,5,1

after 5th pass   3,2,4,5,1

after 6th pass   2,3,4,5,1

after 7th pass   2,3,4,1,5

after 8th pass   2,3,1,4,5

after 9th pass   2,1,3,4,5

after 10th pass   1,2,3,4,5

Ten comparisons must be made to get the list in order.

We can generalize from this result to obtain a worst-case equation for the insertion sort. The maximum number of comparisons for the insertion sort is

$$N(N-1)/2$$

This can be seen by writing the series in the order given and in the reverse order:

$(N-1)+(N-2)+(N-3)+ \ . \ . \ . \ + 3 + 2 + 1$

$1 + 2 + 3 + \ . \ . \ . \ +(N-3)+(N-2)+(N-1)$

Adding term by term, we find that twice the sum of the series is

$N+N+N+ \ ... \ +N+N+N$

Since N-1 terms are in the series above, we can say that twice the sum of the series is $N(N-1)$, so, dividing by 2, the sum of the series is $N(N-1)/2$.

● **PROBLEM** 7-16

Write a program using PL/I, to sort an integer array into ascending order using a bubble sort.

Solution: BUBBLE_SORT Program

```
      INTEGER I,J,K,ID(N), TEMP /* THE CONTENTS OF
THE ARRAY ID AND ITS DIMENSION N ARE ASSUMED GIVEN */
        I=N;
        K=1;   /*K IS FLAG ≠0 ON THE FIRST PASS AND
WHEN SWITCHES ARE MADE ON THE PREVIOUS PASS */
     DO WHILE (I≥2) AND K≠0;
        J=1;
        K=0;
        DO WHILE (J≤I-1);
            IF ID(J) > ID(J+1) THEN DO,
        TEMP = ID(J);
        ID(J) = ID(J+1);
        ID(J+1) = TEMP;      /* SWITCH ENTRIES ID(J) &
                                       ID(J+1)*/
        K=1;
        END If;
J=J+1;
END DO;
I = I-1;    /* COUTER I DECREMTED FROM N TO 2 ON SUCCESSIVE
                PASSES */
END DO;
END BUBBLE_SORT;
```

● **PROBLEM** 7-17

Develop a FORTRAN program segment to arrange in ascending
order a set of N elements, trying to use the least number of
passes possible.

Solution: One efficient method is known as a bubble sort.
With this method, each pair of adjacent elements is compared.
If they are in the proper order, they are left alone. If not,
the terms are reversed in order before going on to the next
pair. The integers are represented in the array ID(N), where
N is the total number of elements to be sorted. The variable
K permits the termination of the loop: if K is still zero
at the beginning of the pass, the outer loop terminates, indicating that no switches had to be made, so that the array
is sorted. If K equals one, another pass through the list
must be made. The program segment is given below:

```
        INTERGER I,J,N,ID(N),TEMP.
        DIMENSION ID(N)
        K=1
        DO 30 I=N,2,-1
        IF (K.EQ.0) GO TO 50
        K=0
        DO 40 J=1,I-1
        IF (ID(J).LE.ID(J+1)) GO TO 30
        TEMP = ID(J)
        ID(J) = ID(J+1)
        ID(J+1) = TEMP
        K=1
        GO TO 30
40      CONTINUE
30      CONTINUE
50      DO 60 m = 1,N
```

```
          WRITE (5,100) ID(N)
100          FORMAT (IX,I4)
 60     CONTINUE
```

Write a FORTRAN program which reads 100 data cards, each
consisting of four letters, and stores them in a vector
WORD. Then sort these words into alphabetical order.

Solution: Characters are represented internally by a numeric
code whose ordering preserves alphabetic precedence. Thus if
the integer variables X and Y each contain character data,
the expression X.LT.Y will have the value .TRUE. if and only
if the character string stored in X precedes in alphabetical
order the character string stored in Y.

The basic method of the program is to compare successive
pairs of four-letter words. Two successive words are interchanged in the vector if they are not in alphabetical order,
i.e., the first is not "less than" the second. After the entire vector has been processed, the last word in alphabetical
order has been pushed to the end of the vector. The vector
is then processed again, and as a result the "second-largest"
word appears in the second to last position. After (at most)
99 passes over the data in the vector, the words are arranged
in alphabetic order. Note that the logical variable SWT is
used to measure whether or not any words are interchanged.
If after a given pass an interchange occurs, the sort is not
finished and SWT is true. Otherwise, SWT is False, no interchange occurs, and the sort is complete.

```
INTEGER WORD (1ØØ)
LOGICAL SWT
DO 1   I=1,1ØØ
1 READ2, WORD(I)
2 FORMAT (A4)
    N=99
    DO 3 I=1,99
    SWT= .FALSE.
    DO 4 J=1,N
    IF (WORD (J).LE.WORD(J+1)) GO TO 4
    ITEMP = WORD (J)
    WORD(J) = WORD(J+1)
    WORD(J+1) = ITEMP
    SWT = .TRUE.
    4 CONTINUE
      IF (.NOT. SWT) GO TO 5
    3 N=N-1
    5 PRINT7, WORD
    7 FORMAT ('ф',1фA6)
        STOP
        END
```

Write a BASIC program to alphabetize a list of names.
Assume that the name is fifteen letters or less.

<u>Solution</u>:   A flowchart giving the program logic is given
below.

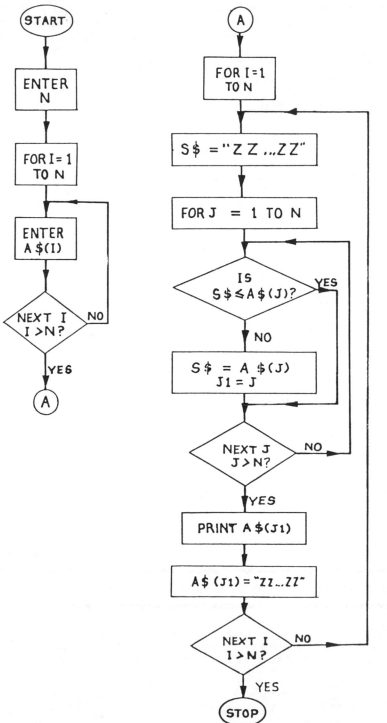

Consider the operation of this program. Statements 2∅ to 8∅ provide for the entering of the names in arbitrary order. Next a pair of nested loops is set up. The outer one runs from statement 9∅ to statement 18∅, and the inner one runs from 11∅ to 15∅. In statement 1∅∅, we set

    S$ = "ZZZZZZZZZZZZZZZ"

Since we assume all names are 15 letters or less, S$ represents the largest possible numerical representation of a name. Now consider the inner loop. The variable with the smallest numerical value corresponds to the first name of the alphabetical list. Thus after the inner loop is completely cycled, J1 will be the number of the name that is alphabetized to be first. That is, A$(J1) will be the first name in the alphabetical list. After control leaves the inner loop, A$(J1) is printed. Next, we set

    A$(J$) = "ZZZZZZZZZZZZZZZ"

and cycle the loop again. The first name in the alphabetical list has now been moved to the end. Now, when the inner loop is cycled again, the second name in the alphabetical list will be printed. Hence, when the outer loop goes through a complete cycle, the complete list will be printed in alphabetical order.

```
1∅     REM ALPHABETIZING PROGRAM
2∅     DIM A$(100)
3∅     PRINT "ENTER TOTAL NUMBER"
4∅     INPUT N
5∅     PRINT "ENTER NAMES"
6∅     FOR I = 1 TO N
7∅     INPUT   A$(I)
8∅     NEXT I
9∅     FOR I = 1 TO N
1∅∅    LET S$ = "ZZZZZZZZZZZZZZZ"
11∅    FOR J=1 TO N
12∅    IF S$<=A$(J) THEN 15∅
13∅    LET S$=A$(J)
14∅    LET J1=J
15∅    NEXT J
16∅    PRINT A$(J1)
17∅    LET A$(J1) = "ZZZZZZZZZZZZZZZ"
18∅    NEXT I
999    END
```

● **PROBLEM** 7-20

Develop a program in FORTRAN for the merge sort.

Solution: Say we have two arrays, A and B, and we wish to merge them into one master array C. Assume that A and B are already sorted in ascending order. For example,

A(I)	B(J)	I	J
2	6	1	1
3	11	2	2

4	13	3	3
5	14	4	4
12	19	5	5

To merge the two, you must first compare A(1) with B(1). The smaller of the two will go in position C(1). If they are equal, a random device can decide which element goes first. Next, compare A(2) with B(1) to find the smaller element. This process continues until all of the elements have been compared. The following pseudocode illustrates the algorithm. For simplicity, let us assume that A and B are 6 elements long; C will contain 12 elements:

```
    I=6, J=6, N=1
  II=I; JJ=J
  do while N< (length of array C)
    if (elements of A have been sorted into C)
        C(N) = B(JJ)
        JJ = JJ+1
    if (elements of B have been sorted into C)
        C(N) = A(II)
        II = II+1
  else  C(N) = B(JJ)
        JJ = JJ+1
  end if
  N = N+1
  end do while
  end program
```

The FORTRAN version of this algorithm is presented below. Appropriate comments have been placed throughout the program. As it is written, the program assumes the data has already been stored in the arrays A and B.

```
      DIMENSION A(6), B(6), C(12)
      INTEGER A,B,C
      DATA II, JJ, N/6, 6, 1/
C     DO WHILE N LESS THAN OR EQUAL TO 12
20    IF (N.GT.12) GO TO 98
C     IF FINISHED WITH ARRAY A, THEN
      IF (II.LE.6) GO TO 25
        C(N)=B(JJ)
        JJ=JJ+1
        GO TO 40
25    CONTINUE
C     IF FINISHED WITH ARRAY B, THEN
      IF (JJ.LE.6) GO TO 30
      C(N) = A(II)
      II = II+1
      GO TO 40
30    CONTINUE
C     IF A(II) LESS THAN B(JJ), THEN
      IF (A(II).GE.B(JJ)) GO TO 35
        C(N)=A(II)
        II=II+1
        GO TO 40
C     ELSE
35    CONTINUE
      C(N)=B(JJ)
      JJ=JJ+1
```

```
C     ENDIF
40    N=N+1
      GO TO 20
C     END DO-WHILE
98    WRITE (5,100)(C(N),N=1,12)
100   FORMAT (12(2x,I3))
```

● **PROBLEM** 7-21

Trace the movement of the integers 4,3,5,1,2 as they are
sorted in ascending order with the bubble sort. Can you
give a general formula for the time needed for sorting N
numbers in the best case? In the worst case?

Solution: The bubble sort compares each pair of adjacent
elements in a list. If in the proper order, the pair is
left alone, and the next pair is examined. If out of order,
the items are switched, and the next pair is examined. In
this fashion, the larger elements are "bubbled" down the
list, while the smaller elements move to the head of the
list. Of course, if the list is to be sorted in descending
order, the opposite process will occur.

Let us illustrate the steps necessary to arrange the
integers in ascending order:

1st comparison   3,4,5,1,2   Compare 3 and 4, no switch

2nd comparison   3,4,5,1,2   Compare 4 and 5, no switch

3rd comparison   3,4,1,5,2   Compare 5 and 1, switch them

4th comparison   3,4,1,2,5,   Compare 5 and 2, switch -
                               end of 1st pass

5th comparison   3,1,4,2,5   Compare 4 and 1, switch

6th comparison   3,1,2,4,5   Compare 4 and 2, switch -
                               end of 2nd pass

7th comparison   1,3,2,4,5   Compare 3 and 1, switch

8th comparison   1,2,3,4,5   Compare 3 and 2, switch -
                               end of 3rd pass

In the best case, i.e., when the data are already in
order, the bubble sort makes only one pass through the list.
No sorting method can do any better than this.

However, in the worst case, the bubble sort makes a
maximum of $N(N-1)/2$ comparisons, just like other sequential
sorting methods. The worst case is realized when the data are
in the opposite order from the order you wish to have. For
example, if we wish to sort the integers 5,4,3,2,1 into
ascending order, the bubble sort will make 10 switches.

    4,3,2,1,5   4 switches
    3,2,1,4,5   3 switches

220

```
2,1,3,4,5    2 switches
1,2,3,4,5    1 switch
             ___
            10 switches total
```

Develop a FORTRAN subroutine that sorts a list of N elements and arranges them in ascending order.

Solution: This method is called a selection sort. It is not the most efficient method in terms of computer time, but it is simple to understand. It compares the first value of the array Y(N) to each successive value. If the first value is greater than the Nth value, they are interchanged. Then, the second value is compared to the others in succession, and so on. The subroutine is as follows:

```
      SUBROUTINE SORT (Y,N)
      DIMENSION Y(1)
C     Y IS THE ARRAY TO BE SORTED
      N1=N-1
      DO 10 I=1,N1
      J=I+1
      DO 20 K=J,N
      IF (Y(I).LE.Y(K)) GO TO 20
      TEMP = Y(I)
      Y(I) = Y(K)
      Y(K) = TEMP
20    CONTINUE
10    CONTINUE
      RETURN
      END
```

Suppose we have a list consisting of people's names, sexes, eye colors, heights, weights, and telephone numbers. Suppose in addition that we wish to look up the telephone numbers of three particular people, namely Robert J. Coyle, Mary Holmes, and Victor E. Lee. Write a computer program in PL/I to accomplish this.

Solution: We use mnemonic notation for the alphanumeric data in the problem by using identifiers like NAME, SEX, and COLOR. We abbreviate phone numbers as NUMBER, and we designate the height of the person by H and the weight by W.

The program proceeds as follows. We start by declaring our four character strings and then transmitting the data to the program. Notice that in the GET LIST statement, we transmit to the program all 6 variables, even though we want only the name and phone number of that person. In the next three statements in the program, we make tests to determine if the name is Coyle, Holmes, or Lee. Note that the names must be

221

put in quotation marks. If any of the tests yield TRUE, we go to PRINT where the desired message is printed. If any of the tests fail, we drop through to the next step.

```
        /* PHONE NUMBERS */
    DECLARE NAME CHARACTER (15),
        SEX CHARACTER (7),
        COLOR CHARACTER (6),
        NUMBER CHARACTER (9);
START: GET LIST (NAME, SEX, COLOR, H, W, NUMBER);
    IF NAME = 'ROBT J. COYLE' THEN GO TO PRINT;
    IF NAME = 'MARY HOLMES' THEN GO TO PRINT;
    IF NAME = 'VICTOR E. LEE' THEN GO TO PRINT;
    GO TO START;
    PRINT: PUT EDIT ('PHONE NO. OF', NAME,'IS',
        NUMBER)(A(20), A(15), A(3), A(9));
    PUT SKIP (2);
    GO TO START;
```

● **PROBLEM** 7-24

Find a general formula to give information about the number of passes through the loop in both the best case and the worst case for the selection sort. Express in terms of N elements.

Solution: Take the worst case first. For the integers 5,4,3,2,1, the selection sort will take the following actions:

1. Find the smallest entry and interchange it with the element in the first position.

    1,4,3,2,5

2. Sort the remaining N-1 elements in positions 2 through N of the array

    1,2,3,4,5

If you refer back to the program, notice that on the first pass through the outer loop, the inner loop is executed for K from 2 to N; on the second pass, from 3 to N, and so on. The total number of passes through the inner loop is $(N-1)+(N-2)+(N-3)+...3+2+1$, which comes to $N(N-1)/2$ passes through the inner loop. Unfortunately, the same number of passes is required in the best case to check the list.

The best way to understand the formula above is to write the series in the order given and in reverse:

$(N-1)+(N-2)+(N-3)+ ... +3+2+1$

$1 + 2 + 3 + ... + (N-3)+(N-2)+(N-1)$

Adding term by term, we get twice the sum of the series, which is

$N+N+N+ ... +N+N+N$

Since there are N-1 terms in the above series, twice the sum of the series may be written as N(N-1). Dividing by 2 gives us the sum of the series, or N(N-1)/2.

Write a PL/I program to initialize, search, insert and delete items in a one-way list.

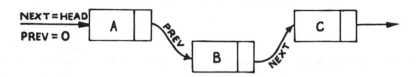

Solution: To simulate a one-way list in PL/I we shall use two dimensional array. The first column stores the Data and second column the pointers to next OWL element.

ONE-WAY LIST

```
/* OWL: TWO DIMENSIONAL ARRAY */
/* 1st ENTRY OF OWL IS DATA, 2nd ENTRY IS THE POINTER */
/* TO THE NEXT OWL ELEMENT, HEAD IS PNTR */

/*TO THE HEAD OF LIST */
      /* INITIALIZE */


DCL OWL (1Ø, 2) FIXED (5);
DCL HEAD FIXED (5) INIT (φ);

/* INITIAL CHECK AND FIRST INSERT */
IF HEAD = φ THEN DO;   /* OWL IS EMPTY */
             HEAD = J; /* J CAN HAVE A VALUE FROM 1 TO 10 */
             OWL (J,1) = X; /* INSERT X IN OWL (J,1) */
             OWL (J,2) = φ; /* REARRANGE THE PNTR   */
/* SEARCH AND INSERT */
/* SEARCH OWL ELEMENT KEY AGAINST THE INSETING ELEMENT,
     INSERT   */
/* AFTER KEY REARRANGE THE POINTERS */
     NEXT = HEAD;
     DO WHILE OWL (NEXT,1)¬= KEY;   /* SEARCH FOR KEY */
     NEXT = OWL (NEXT,2);      /* GOES ON MATCHING DOWN */
     IF NEXT = φ THEN [go to error routine]; /*THE LIST,
        φ PTR INDICATES LAST ELEMENT */
     END;
     OWL [Insert,2] = OWL [NEXT,2]; /* PTR OF KEY ELEMENT
IS TO BE ASSIGNED TO INSERT   */
     OWL (NEXT,2)=INSERT   /* NOW OWL (NEXT,2) POINTS TO INSERT */
     /* SEARCH AND DELETE   */
```

Initially NEXT points to the top element and there is no previous pointer. But as the search proceeds NEXT points out the next element and PREV points to the element having pointer NEXT. We want to delete B. The goal is to make PREV point to C and if the match is successful for the 1st element A we want to change the value of the head.

```
      NEXT=HEAD;
      PREV=0
      DO WHILE (OWL (NEXT,1)¬=KEY);   /* SEARCH */
      PREV = NEXT
      NEXT = OWL (N,2)   /* LOOPING TO SEARCH NEXT ELEMENT */
      IF NEXT = φ THEN [go to error routine]; /* NO MATCH */
      END;
      IF PREV=0 THEN HEAD = OWL (NEXT,2) /* MATCH SUCCEEDS AT
                                              FIRST ELEMENT */
      ELSE OWL (PREV,2) = OWL (NEXT,2);   /* MATCH SUCCEEDS
                                              IN THE LIST
      END;             AND REARRANGE POINTERS   */
```

● **PROBLEM** 7-26

Develop a sorting subroutine that compares elements that
are separated by a distance K. In your algorithm, try to
make exchanges between elements such that each exchange
moves an element close to its final position.

<u>Solution</u>: This method is known as a Shell sort. Compari-
sons are made between an element X_i and element x_{i+k} . For
the bubble and insertion sorts, K is always 1. With the
shell sort, you set K at the largest power of two that is
less than N, N being the total number of elements. Therefore

$$2^K < N \le 2^{K+1}$$

Once K is chosen, a pass is made through the array. Each
successive pass results in the division of K by 2. Finally,
for the last pass, K=1 and the procedure becomes an ordinary
bubble sort.

      This variety of exchange sort functions best when the
size of the array is relatively small, viz., less than 25
elements. However, if you are not too concerned about speed
and efficiency, this sort is conceptually simple and short.

```
      SUBROUTINE SHELL (X,N)
      DIMENSION X(N)
      MIDPT=N
1Ø    MIDPT = MDPT/2
      IF (MIDPT.LE.0) RETURN
      LIMIT = N-MIDPT
      DO 20 J=1,LIMIT
      IJ=J
3Ø    IM = IJ+MIDPT
      IF (X(IM).GE.X(IJ)) GO TO 20
      TEMP = X(IJ)
      X(IJ) = X(IM)
      X(IM) = TEMP
      IJ = IJ-MIDPT
      IF (IJ.GE.1)GO TO 30
20    CONTINUE
      GO TO 1Ø
      END
```

Write a FORTRAN program containing four subroutines to
initialize a list, insert a name in alphabetical order,
delete a name, and output the list in order. You will
need to use pointers to create this data structure, known
as a chained or linked list.

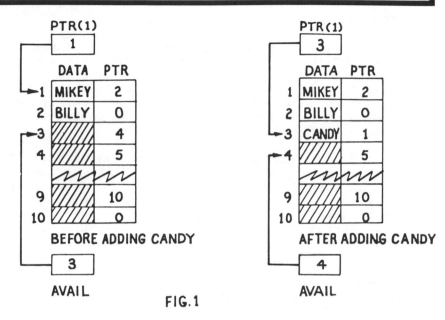

FIG.1

Solution: For this project, you should construct the main
program so that it has a case structure, enabling the user
to choose whether he would like to insert or delete a name.
The main program should consist only of type declarations,
a DO-WHILE loop to choose the case the user wants, and
statements to call the subroutines. Since this part is
perhaps the easiest, we will do it first and then explain
the meaning of the variables. Maximum name length is five
letters.

```
      INTEGER CHOICE, PTR, DATA, AVAIL, N, NAME
      DIMENSION DATA(10), PTR(10)
      N=10
      CALL INIT (PTR,N,AVAIL)
C       DO WHILE CHOICE NOT EQUAL TO 'STOP'
10    IF (CHOICE.EQ.'STOP') GO TO 99
      WRITE (5,100)
100   FORMAT (5X,'TYPE INSRT,DELET,OR STOP')
      READ (5,101) CHOICE
101   FORMAT(A5)
C     IF CHOICE IS INSRT, THEN
      IF (CHOICE.NE.'INSRT') GO TO 20
      WRITE (5,102)
102   FORMAT (5X, 'TYPE THE NAME, PLEASE')
      READ (5,103) NAME
103   FORMAT (A5)
      CALL INSERT (DATA, PTR, N, AVAIL, NAME)
      CALL PRINT (DATA, PTR, N)
      GO TO 10
```

```
C      IF CHOICE IS DELET, THEN
20     IF (CHOICE.NE.'DELET') GO TO 30
       WRITE (5, 102)
       READ (5,103) NAME
       CALL DELETE (DATA, PTR, N, AVAIL, NAME)
       CALL PRINT (DATA, PTR, N)
30     GO TO 10
C      END DO-WHILE
99     STOP
       END
```

DATA(N) is the array which contains the names to be put
in order. PTR(N) is the array containing pointers which can
be manipulated to accommodate insertions and deletions. The
mechanics of pointers will be explained as the problem develops, but for now remember that pointers permit the accessing of data in memory without performing an actual search-
and-sort routine.

Continuing with the main program, the variable CHOICE
can take on three possibilities: INSRT if you want to insert a name, DELET if you want to delete a name, STOP to
end the session. The program will keep looping back to the
beginning, allowing you to adjust the list until you type
in STOP. Notice also that after each insertion or deletion,
the subroutine PRINT allows you to see the elements of the
list.

Subroutine INIT sets up the linked list. N is the total number of names (in this case, 10). AVAIL is the address of the first available location in the storage area
DATA. PTR(1), known as the list head, is set to zero.
This means that DATA(1) is not used, a necessary precaution
that avoids complications in the special case of an empty
list. PTR(2) through PTR(9) are initialized such that
PTR(2)=3, PTR(3)=4, and so on until PTR(9)=10. Finally,
PTR(10) is also set to zero.

Let us now begin to fill DATA with names to illustrate
the activity of the pointers. (See Figure 1.)

Subroutine INSERT will go down the list, search for the
first available storage location in DATA, insert the name,
and most important, rearrange the pointers so that they will
cause the list to be printed in alphabetical order. The
comparison for alphabetizing is done at statement 23, but
the ordering of the pointers is accomplished by the statements following statement 33. Let us "walk through" these
statements to discover what is happening at each step:

J becomes 3

AVAIL becomes PTR(3), which is 4

PTR(3) becomes PTR (1), which is 1

DATA (3) becomes 'CANDY'

PTR(1) becomes 3

226

Now, let us turn to the case where we want to delete a name, say BILLY. The list starts off as it is in Figure 1, after the addition of 'CANDY'. (See Figure 2.)

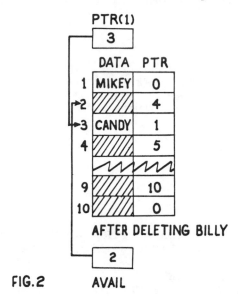

FIG.2

The storage location at DATA(2) is saved in the variable AVAIL; only the pointers are rearranged. In subroutine DE-LETE, statement 14 does the table lookup of the name to be deleted. If it is present, control is passed to statement 34, where the pointers are rearranged to eliminate the de-sired name. A "walk through" yields the following:

JD becomes 2

PTR(1) becomes PTR(2), which is 3

PTR(2) becomes 4

AVAIL becomes 2

```
      SUBROUTINE INIT (PTR,N,AVAIL)
      INTEGER I,N, PTR(N), AVAIL
C     INITIALIZE LIST HEAD AND START OF FREE LIST
      AVAIL = 2
      PTR(1) = 0
C     SET POINTERS FOR FREE LIST
      DO 12 I=2, N-1
      PTR(I) = I+1
12    CONTINUE
C     SET NULL POINTER AT END OF FREE LIST
      PTR(N) = 0
      RETURN
      END
      SUBROUTINE INSERT (DATA, PTR, N, AVAIL, NAME)
      INTEGER II, J, N, PTR(N), DATA(N), NAME
      IF (AVAIL.NE.0) GO TO 13
      WRITE (5,104)
104   FORMAT (5X, 'NO STORAGE LEFT')
      GO TO 53
13    II=1
C     SEARCH LIST FOR INSERTION POINT
```

```
C      DO-WHILE PTR(II) NOT EQUAL TO ZERO
C      AND DATA(PTR(II)) LESS THAN NAME
23     IF (PTR(II).EQ.0.OR.DATA(PTR(II)).GE.NAME)
1      GO TO 33
       II=PTR(II)
       GO TO 23
33     CONTINUE
C      END DO-WHILE
C      ALLOCATE SPACE FROM FREE LIST FOR
C      NEW ENTRY AND INSERT IT FOLLOWING
C      ENTRY II BY SETTING POINTERS
       J=AVAIL
       AVAIL=PTR(J)
       PTR(J)=PTR(II)
       DATA(J)=NAME
       PTR(II)=J
53     CONTINUE
       RETURN
       END
       SUBROUTINE DELETE (DATA, PTR, N, AVAIL, NAME)
       INTEGER ID, JD, N, PTR(N), AVAIL, DATA(N)
       ID=1
C      FIND NAME TO BE DELETED
C      DO WHILE PTR(ID) NOT EQUAL TO ZERO AND
C      DATA (PTR(ID)) NOT EQUAL TO NAME
14     IF (PTR(ID).EQ.0.OR. DATA (PTR(ID)).EQ. NAME)
1      GO TO 24
       ID=PTR(ID)
       GO TO 14
24     CONTINUE
C      END DO-WHILE
       IF (PTR(ID).NE.0) GO TO 34
       WRITE (5,105) NAME
105    FORMAT (5x, A5, 'NOT PRESENT IN LIST')
       GO TO 54
C      ENTRY FOLLOWING ID NOW CONTAINS
C      NAME. DELETE IT FROM DATA LIST AND
C      PUT IT ON FREE LIST.
34     JD=PTR(ID)
       PTR(ID)=PTR(JD)
       PTR(JD)=AVAIL
       AVAIL=JD
54     CONTINUE
       RETURN
       END
       SUBROUTINE PRINT (DATA, PTR, N)
       INTEGER IP, N, PTR(N), DATA(N)
       IP=PTR(1)
C      DO WHILE IP NOT EQUAL TO ZERO
15     IF (IP.EQ.0) GO TO 25
       WRITE (5,107) DATA(IP)
107    FORMAT (1X,A5)
       GO TO 15
25     CONTINUE
C      END DO-WHILE
       RETURN
       END
```

On some systems, the DO-WHILE constructs in INSERT and
DELETE may cause problems because of a reference to DATA(0).

To amend that difficulty, you may substitute the following:

(for INSERT)
```
23    IF (PTR(II).EQ.0) GO TO 33
      IF (DATA(PTR(II)).GE.NAME) GO TO 53
```

(for delete)
```
14    IF (PTR(ID).EQ.0) GO TO 24
      IF (DATA(PTR(ID)).EQ.NAME) GO TO 54
```

● **PROBLEM** 7-28

Write a program to sort an integer array into ascending
order using a selection sort.

Solution:
```
            SORT: PROC OPTION(MAINS);
                DCL (ARRAY(N),SMALL, N) FIXED (3.0);
      /* IT IS ASSUMED THE CONTENTS OF ARRAY AND ITS DIMENSION
      ARE GIVEN */
          K=1;
      DO WHILE K≤N-1   /* ASSUME FIRST K-1 ELEMENTS ARE IN
ORDER FIND SMALLEST REMAINING ELEMENT AND MOVE IT TO POSITION
K*/
      I=K;
      SMALL = ARRAY(K);
      J = K+1;
      DO WHILE J≤N
      IF ARRAY (J) < SMALL THEN DO;
      I=J;
      SMALL = ARRAY(J);
      END;
      J=J+1;
      END;
    ARRAY(I) = ARRAY(K);
    ARRAY(K) = SMALL;
    K = K+1;
  END;
END SORT;
```

● **PROBLEM** 7-29

Develop a sorting program that arranges the elements of
the array A(1:N) in ascending order. Use your knowledge
of binary trees and heaps to complete the problem.

Solution: A sort of this type is referred to as a heap
sort. While not as conceptually accessible as the insertion
sort or bubble sort, the heap sort is most efficient, having
a run time proportional to $n\log_2 n$.

A binary tree is based on principles similar to those
which are used in the creation of a family tree. The tree
consists of nodes (the uncircled numbers in Fig. 1) and
branches (the lines connecting individual nodes). At the
top of the tree, we have the root node. Two is the maximum
number of branches that can originate from any single node.

Each node is labeled (the cirled integers in Fig. 1).
The notation for the labels is NODE(I), where I is the en-
circled integer. In this example, NODE(1)=6, NODE(3)=5,
and NODE(8)=1.

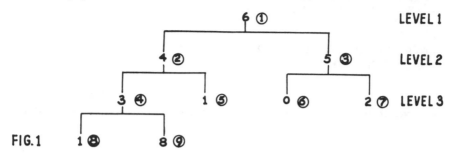

FIG. 1

Remaining consistent with the idea of a family tree, we
may say that any node from which branches originate is a
father. The father may have right and left sons, which are
the elements which emanate from the father. You can probably
guess that each node can have ancestors and descendants. The
root node, however, may be considered Adam, since it has no
ancestors.

Notice the method of labeling in the tree. The root
node is always NODE(1). After that, the rule is: If a node
has label I, its left son is always 2I, and its right son is
always 2I+1. Another restriction on the tree is that there
are no holes. In other words, if NODE(I) exists, then so do
nodes 1,2, ..., I-1.

To translate a binary tree into a heap, remember the
following caveat: A binary tree is a heap only if for any
node I, NODE (each ancestor of I) $\geq$ NODE(I). Now, to calculate fathers and sons, we recognize the following:

FATHER$\big($A(I)$\big)$ is B(FLOOR(I/2))

LEFTSON$\big($A(I)$\big)$ is B(2I)

RIGHTSON$\big($A(I)$\big)$ is B(2I+1)

First, we must make B(N) into a heap, and then we must
sort the heap in ascending order. Notice that nodes 1-8
are already in order. Node 9, however, is out of order
because its value, 8, is larger than the value in node 4,
which is 3. We must move the unordered value up the tree
until the order is restored. This is accomplished by swapping values of father and son until the condition NODE
(each ancestor of I) $\geq$ NODE(I) is satisfied.

This is the swapping algorithm, written in PL/1, which
makes A(N) into a heap:

```
/* TRANSLATION OF BINARY TREE INTO HEAP */
   HEAP_IT: DO I=1 TO N BY 1;
/* MAKE A(1:I) INTO A HEAP, ASSUMING */
/* A (1:I-1) IS ALREADY HEAPED */
DO WHILE (J>1);
    FATHER_J=FLOOR (J/2EO);
    IF A(FATHER_J) > = A(J) THEN GO TO TERM;
```

230

```
      SWAP_TEMP = A(FATHER_J);
      A(FATHER_J) = A(J);
      A(J) = SWAP_TEMP;
      J = FATHER_J; END;
TERM:; END HEAP_IT;
```

Consider the number of times the DO WHILE loop is executed. Each time the loop is traversed, the unordered value is moved up one level in the tree. Hence, the maximum number of executions possible is the number of levels minus one. On reflection, you can see that the level is exactly FLOOR(LOG2(I))+1. For a given value of I, the maximum number of loops is LOG2(I). times. The total number of times the inner loop body is executed is LOG2(1)+LOG2(2)+ ... +LOG2(N), a sum which has as an upper bound N*LOG2(N).

Now, the heap A satisfies the relation A(FATHER(I)) $\geq$ A(I). To output a sort in ascending order, we want A to satisfy the relation A(I) $\leq$ A(I+1). In other words, the largest value must be put in the last node of the tree. This will destroy the heap relation, such that only the value A(I) will disrupt the heap.

```
/* SORT HEAP A(1:N). */
      I = N;
SWAP: DO WHILE (I>1);
      TEMP = A(1);
      A(1) = A(I);
      A(I) = TEMP;
      I = I-1;
/* MAKE A(1:I) INTO A HEAP, WITH THE */
/* VALUE A(1) THE ONLY DISRUPTER OF THE HEAP */
         J=1; /* K is J's */
         K=2*J; /* LARGER SON */
         DO WHILE (K< = I);
         If K<I THEN IF A(K)<
      A(K+1) THEN K=K+1;
        If A(J)> = A(K) THEN GO TO DUMMY_END;
         A_TEMP = A(J);
         A(J) = A(K);
         A(K) = A_TEMP;
         J=K;
         K=2*J; END;
DUMMY_END:; END SWAP;
```

● **PROBLEM** 7-30

Explain what is meant by a Hash Table, and a Hashing function. Explain various methods of inserting entries in the table.

Solution: A Hash Table is a type of data structure in the computer memory. Stocks, lists, arrays, etc., are other examples of data structures.

The advantage of a hash table over many other types of data structures is that the operations of insertion, deletion, searching, etc., are much more efficient, especially when the number of elements to be inserted in the structure is extremely large or initially the number of elements is not known.

In essence, a Hash Table is a sequential block of memory space set aside for the table. Let us assume we reserve 1000 memory words for the Hash Table.

Now, in order to determine where we should insert a particular data item, within any one of the 1000 words, we make use of a Hashing function.

A Hashing function can be any arbitrary function selected by us, which operates on the given data item, and extracts from it a memory address, within our reserved block of storage.

For example, if our data items are names of persons, we could define our Hashing Function arbitrarily as follows:

a) Give weights in ascending order from 1 to 26 to each of
   the letters of the alphabet from A to Z.i.e., A=1, B=2,
   ..., Y=25, Z=26.

b) Add up the weights of the letters in a given data item
   (Eg., if our data item is the name NANCY the sum of weights
   is : N+A+N+C+Y = 14+1+14+3+25 = 57).

c) Divide the sum by 7.

d) Multiply by 10.

e) Round off to the nearest integer, to get the value of the
   Hashing function.

Thus, once a value of the Hashing function is obtained, this corresponds to the position, within our reserved block of memory, into which the data item is to be stored.

Observe that the important aspect about hashing functions is not how it is devised, but whether it distributes the different data items quite uniformly within our reserved memory block.

Conversely, if we want to search whether a given data item is in the Hash Table or not, we subject the data item to the same Hashing Function and obtain an address. We can then immediately access the address thus found and check if the data item we are looking for is in that location.

Many times it happens that the Hashing function calculates the same memory address for more than one data item. Thus, when we go to the address location, we may find that there already is some other data item there. Or, while searching, we may find that there is some other data item at the location calculated instead of the one which we are searching for. In this case we adopt any one of three methods:

a) We multiply the data item by a pre-determined fixed
   constant and re-evaluate the Hashing Function, and see

if now we find an empty location for insertion, or the given data item while searching. We repeat the process till success, using a set of pre-determined constants.

b) Beginning at the calculated location, start a sequential scan up or down the table till we either succeed or come to the end of the table.

c) Bucket Hashing: Associated with each of the memory words in our Hash Table is a pointer. When a Hash function calculates an address and we find that the addressed location is already full, we search for any other vacant memory location, say within the general storage area of the memory, outside the Hash Table block. Data is stored in the first empty location and its address is stored into the pointer position of our calculated hash table address.

e.g., NANCY and FRED has the same hash function, say 10. NANCY was previously stored in location 10. Now to store FRED with hash function 10 we search for vacant storage. Store FRED in that location and the address of that location is placed in the pointer position of NANCY. We now store our data item in this empty location. If a third data item also happens to have the Hash Table address, we search for another empty location in the general storage area, store the data in it, and move the pointer of the second data item to this third data item, forming a long list or bucket. While searching too, we search down the bucket.

● PROBLEM 7-31

Write a program to create, initialize, insert, delete, search, etc., a Hash Table, using PL/I.

Solution: PL/I has no Hash Table as a standard data structure type. Hence, we shall use a two-dimensional array to simulate a Hash Table.

Creation of Hash Table:

    DCL   HASHTAB(N,2)CHAR(6) VAR,
          MARKER FIXED (3);

/* We have created an array named HASHTAB of N, say, 180 data items each of which can be a character variable, of upto 6 characters. This is our Hash Table. */

/* The variable MARKER will be useful later as a pointer */

/* For any location J of the Table, the first element HASHTAB(J,1) will store a data item and the second element HASHTAB(J,2) will store a pointer, if necessary, to the next linked element having the same HASH address. */

Search and Insert:

/* Assume that the value of the HASHING function has turned out to be J */

233

```
    IF J<1|>N THEN GO TO ('recalculate' error routine);

/* We check if the Hashed address is within bounds of our
table */

    DO WHILE HASHTAB(J,1)¬=0; /* We check if location is
empty */
    MARKER = J
    J = J+1; /* If not empty, look at the next location */
    IF J=N THEN J=1; /* If we reach the end then we go round
        to the top of the array */
    If J= MARKER THEN GO TO (table full error routine);
    /* We come back around to the starting point again,
    which indicates the Table has no empty spaces left */
        HASHTAB(MARKER,2) = J; /*Pointer of location calculated
    by the hashing function points to the new location J, */
    End; /* End of DO WHILE */
    HASHTAB(J,1) = DATA; /* If we find the new location
        HASHTAB(J,1) to be empty we do not enter the
        DO WHILE block, and jump to this statement, where
        we insert the data item. */
```

Search and Read Out:

```
/* Assume that we are looking for a data item denoted by KEY,
and whose HASH function value has been calculated as J*/

    DO WHILE HASHTAB(J,1)¬= KEY;
    MARKER = J /* We store the original value of J in
            the variable MARKER */
    J=HASHTAB(J,2); /* We change the value of J to that
            pointed to by the pointer part of J */
    If J = 0 THEN GO TO ('not available' error routine);
/* This means there are no more linkages to search, and the
data item is not in the table */.
End; /* End of DO WHILE */
Y = HASHTAB(J,1); /* If the position denoted by J is equal
to the Key, we do not enter the DO WHILE, but come to this
statement, and read out the value written in the location
into some required location Y */

HASHTAB(MARKER,2) = HASHTAB(J,2); /* We now complete the
pointer linkages of the chain by making the pointer of the
previous element, stored in Marker, to point to the next
element to the deleted element */
    End;
```

GRAPHS

● PROBLEM 7-32

Classify the following graphs according to the following
criteria:

a) directed or undirected

b) connected or unconnected

c) planar or nonplanar

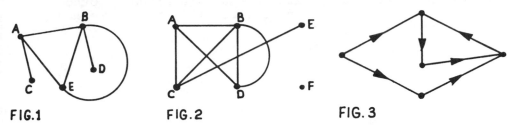

FIG.1   FIG.2   FIG. 3

Solution: Figure 1 is an example of an undirected, connected, planar graph. Undirected graphs contain no arrows:
there is no particular direction associated with any of the
branches. This graph is connected, since each node has at
least one branch leading to it. Also, the graph is planar,
because we can draw it on a plane so that none of the
branches overlaps.

Figure 2 is an undirected, unconnected, nonplanar graph.
It is unconnected because node F is not attached to any
branch. In addition, it is a nonplanar graph because of
the overlapping of the various branches. There is no way
to redraw this graph on a plane without running into overlaps.

Finally, Figure 3 is a connected, directed, and planar
graph. Notice the arrow along the branches, giving direc-
tionality to it. We say it is a digraph, an abbreviated
form of directed graph.

● **PROBLEM** 7-33

Develop a pseudocoded program that converts the nodes of the
following undirected graph into an adjacency matrix.

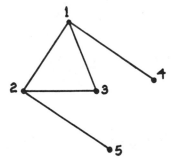

Solution: A graph is a collection of nodes and branches in
which each branch links one node to another. The particular
graph above is called an undirected graph because there is
no particular direction associated with any of the branches.
As you can see, the nodes are numbered. Two nodes that are
connected by branches may be represented by pairs; for this
graph, we notice the pairs:(1,2), (1,3), (1,4), (2,3), and
(2,5).

235

One way of representing the graph is to use a list of the branches as defined by the pairs of nodes. We will look at the representation of the graph through an adjacency matrix. We define an adjacency matrix as one whose (i,j)th element is nonzero if nodes i and j are joined by a branch. Otherwise, the (i,j)th element is zero. For this graph, we have the adjacency matrix below:

$$\begin{pmatrix} 0 & 1 & 1 & 1 & 0 \\ 1 & 0 & 1 & 0 & 1 \\ 1 & 1 & 0 & 0 & 0 \\ 1 & 0 & 0 & 0 & 0 \\ 0 & 1 & 0 & 0 & 0 \end{pmatrix}$$

Notice that the nonzero elements are found at both the (i,j)th elements and the (j,i)th elements. This is because the graph is undirected: nodes may be accessed along branches from either side.

For this simple graph, we store nodes in a 5 by 5 array. Other data structures may be used to represent graphs; a chained list could be used if the nodes are to be changed often.

The pseudocode is presented below. After the array is filled with zeros, the (i,j)th elements and the (j,i)th elements are changed to ones.

```
C     TO CONVERT FROM PAIRS TO THE ADJACENCY MATRIX,
C     ASSUME THE BRANCHES ARE GIVEN AS PAIRS A(K), B(K)
          integer A,B,I,J,K,m(5,5)
          INPUT (A(1),B(1)),(A(2),B(2)), ..., (A(5),B(5))
          do for I←1 to 5
              do for J←1 to 5
                  m(I,J)←0
              end do for
          end do for
C     NOW CHANGE ELEMENTS TO NONZERO FOR PAIRS A(K),B(K)
C     FOR EACH PAIR
```

K indicates the branch number and A and B the nodes of that branch.

```
      do for K←1 to 5
          m(A(K),B(K))←1
          m(B(K),A(K))←1
      end do for
      output m(K,K)
      end program
```

CHAPTER 8

PROGRAM DEVELOPMENT

STRUCTURED PROGRAMMING

● **PROBLEM** 8-1

Define the following symbols as they are used in flowcharting:

Solution: These symbols have very specific meanings for flowcharting procedures. The following explanations come from the American National Standards Institute:

a)  Input or output using a line printer or a terminal

b)  Two or more actions may follow from this point, based upon the response to the question raised

c)  Input or output using the standard 80-column card

d)  Commentary on a particular section of the algorithm, used to explain ambiguous actions

e) Usually with a number inside the circle, it connects flowlines when going to or coming from another spot on the same page or another page

● **PROBLEM** 8-2

What are the three fundamental logical structures used in computer programming? Give a brief example of each by drawing flowcharts.

Solution: The three cornerstones of structured programming are:

1) Simple sequencing
2) Decision-making
3) Repetition or looping

By implementing these concepts in the form of distinct modules, you will find that your program can be understood readily and, if problems occur, you will be able to debug your program with greater ease.

SIMPLE SEQUENCE

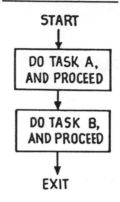

DECISION-MAKING

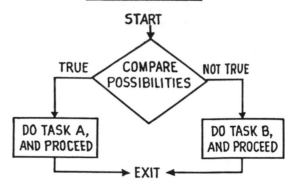

REPETITION OR LOOPING

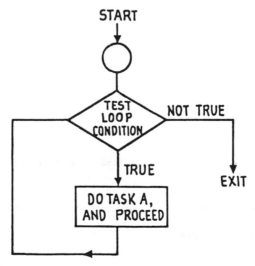

The looping construct is also known as a DO-WHILE structure. The looping continues while some condition remains satisfied. When the condition is violated, the loop terminates.

What is modular programming? Name the six functional modules of a structured program.

<u>Solution</u>: Modular programming is a term which describes a disciplined means of writing computer programs. By writing program segments which perform specific tasks, you will find that it is easier to debug your program. This concept is a step to take some of the "art" out of computer programming and to replace it with more logical, intelligent, and efficient techniques.

There are six types of modules needed in almost every type of program. The table below gives an overview of these modules.

FUNCTIONAL MODULE	DESCRIPTION
1) INPUT	Performs the input of data necessary to accomplish the task
2) INPUT DATA VALIDATION	Checks the validity of the incoming data and diagnoses what type of error if any, has occurred
3) PROCESSING	Completes the basic task requested of the algorithm
4) OUTPUT	Performs output of information needed by the user
5) ERROR SPECIFICATION	Analyzes problematical points in the execution of the program and takes appropriate action
6) CLOSING	Finalizes program execution

The above modules should stand alone in their meaning. That is, if defined thoroughly enough, the module should be readily adaptable to another program with only minor changes in variable names. In addition, each module should have only one point of entry and one point of exit. Multiple returns and branches, if used excessively, tend to bewilder the reader of your program.

The term robustness is used in programming to mean the degree of completeness a program offers. A robust algorithm takes care of almost all possibilities with swift and precise action. The idea of modular programming, if followed carefully, yields robustness.

● **PROBLEM** 8-4

Define top-down structured programming. Also define bottom-up structured programming. What importance does each of these terms have in relation to the computer implementation of an algorithm?

<u>Solution</u>:   The top-down design technique is the offspring of the idea of refinement. This technique requires that the programmer define the algorithm coarsely, in plain English or with some sort of code. Next, a structured language or a flow chart should be used to explain the parts of the algorithm that need greater clarification. This process

of writing more and more detailed descriptions continues until the
algorithm is sufficiently documented. Thereafter, the translation of
the algorithm into a standard computer language, such as COBOL or
FORTRAN, becomes a simple mechanical procedure.

This technique is especially useful when a team of programmers is
working on a specific problem. If each programmer is assigned a small
part of a large task, the parts can be combined easily by assembling
the codes from each part. If the modular programming rule of one-entry-
one-exit per module is followed as well, the sections of code become
like interchangeable parts of a machine. Any other programmer can
pick up your section of code and substitute it into a program that
needs what you have written.

Bottom-up design is just the opposite. It refers to the creation of
the program in a highly detailed fashion before coding or documentation
is begun. This is sometimes bad practice when writing programs because
the programmer is prone to miss important details. Also, it is both
time-saving and economical to iron out errors in the coding stage before
typing out a program for computer execution. This idea of program-
first, code-second may be used if one wants to debug a program. By
looking at a program first, you might be able to find syntactical errors
that cause problems. After this is done, then a look at the code allows
you to debug any logical errors.

● **PROBLEM** 8-5

Analyze the following flowchart and ask yourself these questions:
a)   Is the flowchart a structured one?
b)   Can you write pseudocode to structure it?
c)   What difficulties or inconveniences could arise when coding?

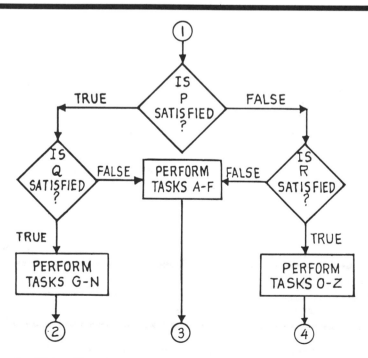

Solution: a) This flowchart is somewhat fictitious, and it does not
satisfy the one-entry one-exit rule of modules in structured programming. We will assume that this flowchart represents a program segment,
since we are not shown where the four nodes (written as circles en-

closing numbers) lead. The problem lies in the module for tasks A-F.
It has two points of entry, an unstructured means of transferring
program control.
b) Recalling the three logical structures of programming -- sequencing,
decision-making, and looping -- you should recognize that the flowchart can be rendered into proper pseudocode easily. We need the
IF-THEN-ELSE construct, along with some kind of nesting of decisions.
The pseudocode is rather straightforward:

> if (P)
>> then if (Q)
>> then tasks G-N
>> else tasks A-F
>> else if (R)
>>> then tasks O-Z
>> else tasks A-F
> end if then else

c) Notice that tasks A through F are referenced twice in the program.
If these tasks take up many lines of instructions, it would be tedious
to write out all of these instructions twice. As an alternative, you
may want to call a subroutine to perform these tasks. By doing this,
you need write out tasks A through F only once.

● **PROBLEM** 8-6

Give examples of the following control constructs as they would be
rendered in FORTRAN:
a)   IF-THEN-ELSE
b)   DO-WHILE
c)   REPEAT-UNTIL
d)   DO-FOR

Solution: Although FORTRAN is not a structured language as such, these
constructs can be rendered with the use of a few simple statements,
including the GO-TO statement.
a) The IF-THEN-ELSE construct can be rendered with the following
statements. A verbal description is "IF X > Y, then J = J + 1. Otherwise, if X ≤ Y, J = J - 1".

```
10      IF (X.LE.Y) GO TO 40
C       IF X IS NOT LESS THAN OR EQUAL TO Y THEN WE GO TO STEP 20
20      J = J + 1
30      GO TO 50
C       ELSE, J = J - 1
40      J = J - 1
C       END OF IF-THEN-ELSE
50      CONTINUE
```

b) The Do-WHILE construct uses an IF statement in the first line of
the construct. The last line is a GO TO statement, which creates a loop.
This loop terminates only when the condition in the IF statement is
satisfied. This example may be described by the following:

241

```
C         DO WHILE X NOT EQUAL TO ZERO
20        IF (X.EQ.O.) GO TO 30
C         IF X IS EQUAL TO ZERO WE EXIT FROM THE LOOP
          X = X - Y
          Y = Y**2
          GO TO 20
C         END DO-WHILE
30        CONTINUE
```

c) The REPEAT-UNTIL construct is similar to the DO-WHILE in that an IF statement is used to control the loop. Because the REPEAT-UNTIL construct requires that the statements contained within it must be executed at least once, we place the IF statement at the bottom of the loop.

```
C         REPEAT UNTIL X BECOMES GREATER THAN 50
20        CONTINUE
          X = Y + 2
          Y = Y * Z
          IF (X.LE.50.) GO TO 20
30        CONTINUE
C         END OF REPEAT-UNTIL
```

d) FORTRAN has a special statement to render the DO-FOR construct. The simple DO statement has the following format:

```
DO                20           I   =   1,      25,     2

statement number at           index     initial  final   increment
end of construct                        value    value   value
```

If the increment value is to be 1, you may omit it. The final statement number is usually either an assignment statement or a CONTINUE statement.

```
C         DO FOR I FROM 1 TO 25
1∅        DO 2∅ I = 1, 25
          J = I * 2
          WRITE (5,*) J
2∅        CONTINUE
C         END DO-FOR
```

● **PROBLEM** 8-7

Since PL/I can be treated as a modular language, it is very adaptable to the tenets of structured programming. One of the tenets is the reduction, sometimes even abolition, of the use of the GO TO statement. With this in mind, redesign the following program segments so that the GO TO statements are not necessary:

a)   IF X = X + Y ** 2 THEN GO TO FIRST; ELSE GO TO NEXT;
        FIRST: X = X - 1;
               T = T + X;
        PUT DATA (T);
        GO TO FINAL;
        NEXT: PUT DATA (X,Y);
        FINAL: C = C + T;

b)   GET DATA (T);
        T1 = 0; S = 0;
        SUM: T1 = T1 + S;

```
             S = S + 2;
      IF T1 = T THEN GO TO B;
      GO TO SUM;
B:    PUT DATA (T,T1,S);
```

Solution: The way to solve this problem is just by moving segments of
statements around. For example, a) may be rewritten thus:

```
      IF X = X + Y ** 2  THEN DO;
      X = X - 1;
      T = T + X;
      PUT DATA (T);
      END;
      ELSE PUT DATA (X);
FINAL: C = C + T;
```

The procedure names NEXT and FIRST are unnecessary, so we
simplify the code by rendering a simple IF-THEN-ELSE construct.
The next program segment can be modified with the use of the
DO WHILE:

```
      GET DATA (T);
          T1 = 0; S = 0;
          DO WHILE (T > T1);
          T1 = T1 + S;
          S = S + 2;
          END;
B:    PUT DATA (T,S);
```

As before, the procedure names are not always necessary.

FLOWCHARTS

• **PROBLEM** 8-8

State what is wrong with the following flowchart entries, and suggest
better ways of writing them:

Solution: a) When writing flowcharts, it is bad practice to use the
equal sign to mean "store the integer 7 in location B." You should

use equal signs only in decision boxes when comparing two quantities. Instead, a better way of writing this box requires an arrow; thus we have

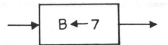

b) As written, this decision box is meaningless. When the question "Is Q odd?" is asked, an appropriate answer would be "yes" or "no", or perhaps "true" or "false". Equal signs should be used when two things are compared, not when you question the status of one item.

c) This box has a trivial error, but one that should be clarified. The author of this statement probably meant "store the integer 3 in location N." To correct this, write the following:

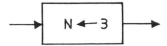

d) The colon is used in flowcharts to compare two items. The possibilities are M > N, M ≥ N, M = N, M < N, or M ≤ N, and these cases should be taken into consideration. One possible interpretation is the following:

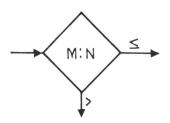

● **PROBLEM** 8-9

Write a flowchart describing how one would design a computer program to print a multiplication table. You need only print 12 rows of products.

Solution: To accomplish this task, you will need a nested loop. The inner, or nested, loop outputs one number for each time the loop is executed. Because there are 12 × 12 = 144 numbers in the table, the nested loop is used 144 times. The outer loop, or nest, is executed 12 times: each execution of this loop causes one row to be printed.

    This flowchart is not well-refined. Although it does describe thoroughly the actions that must take place in order to obtain the table, it does not detail the calculations necessary to produce the

products. The point is that if the calculations were exceedingly complex, you might waste a lot of time worrying about the calculation and
forget about the printing of the table. This is a familiar case in
programming, in which the student, to put it colloquially, cannot see
the forest for the trees. If you can understand how to print a table,
it is a relatively simple matter to adjust the calculations of the
elements to be put into it.

   The flowchart is mostly self-explanatory. The dotted line indicates
the boundaries of the nested loop.

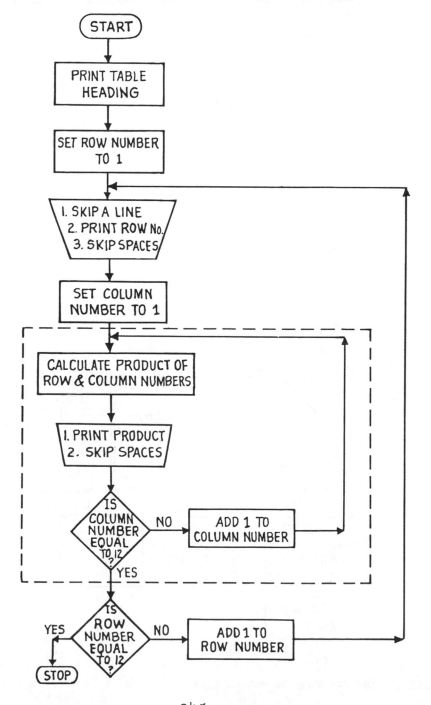

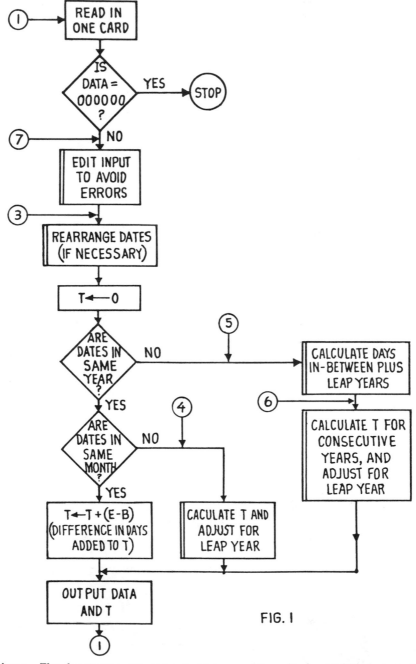

You are handed a deck of punched cards with each card bearing two dates in the twentieth century. The format for June 13, 1979, for example, is 061379. Design a generalized flowchart with instructions to output the two dates along with the number of days elapsed between them. It should not matter which of the punched dates comes earlier. Also, remember to account for leap years and errors in the data. A card containing all zeros signifies the end.

READ IN ONE CARD

IS DATA = 000000 ? — YES → STOP

NO

EDIT INPUT TO AVOID ERRORS

REARRANGE DATES (IF NECESSARY)

T ← 0

ARE DATES IN SAME YEAR ? — NO → CALCULATE DAYS IN-BETWEEN PLUS LEAP YEARS

YES

CALCULATE T FOR CONSECUTIVE YEARS, AND ADJUST FOR LEAP YEAR

ARE DATES IN SAME MONTH ? — NO → CACULATE T AND ADJUST FOR LEAP YEAR

YES

T ← T + (E-B) (DIFFERENCE IN DAYS ADDED TO T)

OUTPUT DATA AND T

FIG. I

Solution: The best way to attack this problem is by writing a series of

246

flowcharts, each being more detailed than the previous one. The concept of refinement is used here, because there are many subtasks that must be accomplished throughout.

The first flowchart to be written is only a skeleton of the entire algorithm and is shown in figure 1. We include annotation nodes where the subsequent flowcharts should fit in.

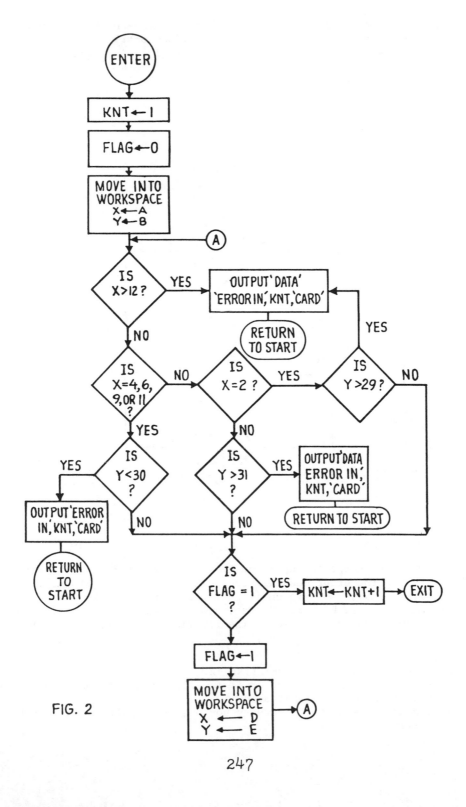

FIG. 2

Let us call the six input items A,B,C,D,E, and F. Assume that the two dates are June 1, 1978 and May 15, 1979. Then, A,B, and C are 06, 01 and 78 respectively and D,E, and F are 05,15 and 79 respectively. To find intervening days in a single month, control passes to the box containing $T \leftarrow T + (E - B)$. To find longer periods of time, you must write more complicated instructions.

First, let us examine node 7. This section evaluates the number of days in the month given. February is set aside until we have to adjust for leap years. The flowchart for node 7 is given in figure 2.

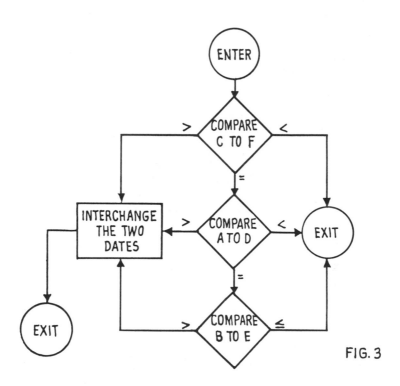

FIG. 3

This section checks the data for all types of errors. The variable KNT is used in the error messages to indicate that the KNTth card is wrong. FLAG remains at zero until both pairs of dates, (A and B, D and E) are checked on each card. X and Y store the dates temporarily while error testing is done. The following relations are checked; if there is an error, a message is output.

1) No month code can be greater than 12.
2) If the month code is 4,6,9, or 11 (April, June, September, or November), a maximum of 30 days is allowed.
3) If the month is neither February nor one of the above, it must have a maximum of 31 days.

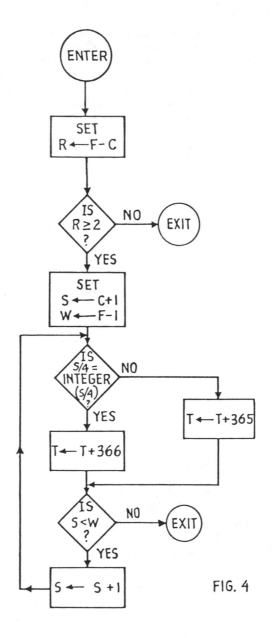

FIG. 4

The flag must be raised to 1 before control passes to the next card. When the next pair of dates is examined through the flowchart, KNT is increased by 1, and the main program continues.

Node 3 rearranges the dates if the first group ABC follows DEF on the calendar. Year, month, and day are evaluated in that order, and appropriate action is taken. The flowchart for node 3 is given in figure 3.

Node 5 calculates the number of days if the dates are not in the same year. Leap years are taken into account by adding 366 days to the elapsed time. Further refinements for the elapsed months and days will come in node 6. The flowchart for node 5 is shown in figure 4.

To explain the next node, we must first introduce the following data table. It gives the month codes, the elapsed days in a year starting with the first of each month(s), the days remaining in a year starting with the last day of each month (W), and the number of days in each month (Z). For leap years, the entries in the table are adjusted in the program. The table is shown in figure 5 and the flowchart in figure 6.

Month	S	W	Z
1	0	334	31
2	31	306	28
3	59	275	31
4	90	245	30
5	120	214	31
6	151	184	30
7	181	153	31
8	212	122	31
9	243	92	30
10	273	61	31
11	304	31	30
12	334	0	31

fig. 5

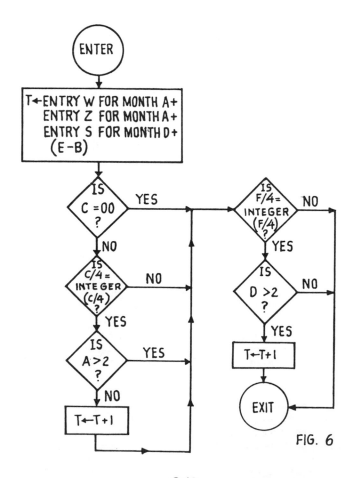

FIG. 6

Finally, if the dates are in the same year but not in the same month, we turn to node 4. The data table is used in this section to adjust the dates accordingly. The flowchart of node 4 is given in figure 7.

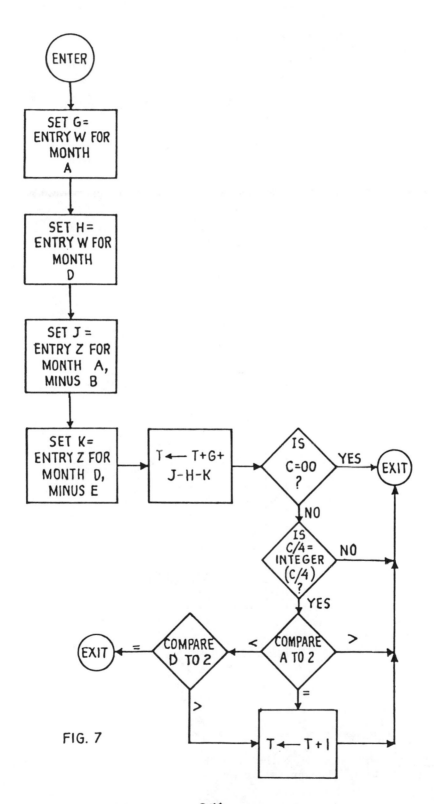

FIG. 7

251

Construct a flowchart for the following PL/I program:

```
SINCALC:    PROC;
            X = 2.5;
            N = 1;
    F1:     FACT = 1;
    F2:     POWER_X = X;
            SINX_2 = 0;
  REPEAT:   SINX_2 = SINX_2 + POWER_X/FACT;
    F3:     POWER_X = -POWER_X*X*X;
    F4:     N = N + 2;
    F5:     FACT = FACT * (N-1) * N;
            GO TO REPEAT;
  DONE:     END;
```

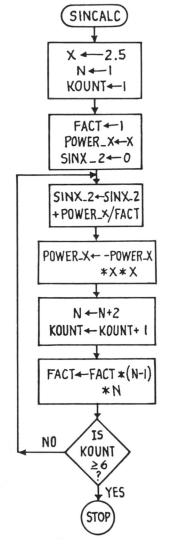

<u>Solution</u>: This program calculates the sine function as represented by a power series. The general formula is:

252

$$\sin(X) = \frac{X}{1!} - \frac{X^3}{3!} + \frac{X^5}{5!} - \ldots = \sum_{n=0}^{\infty} (-1)^n \frac{X^{2n+1}}{(2n+1)!}$$

The variable POWER_X is introduced to calculate the powers of x appearing in the series. Statement F2 initializes POWER_X and SINX·2. Statement F3 has two functions:
1) It increases the power of X by multiplying POWER_X twice by X, giving the odd exponents X^3, X^5, X^7, etc.

2) The unary operator (-) alternates the sign of POWER_X. This is necessary to the definition of the function.

As the program is written, we have an infinite loop. Execution of the statement REPEAT will continue indefinitely, since there is no way to reach the END statement. Let us insert control statements in the flowchart to amend this oversight. The programmer who designed this program neglected to choose an upper bound on the number of terms to be computed. We will write the flowchart so that only six terms are computed. To do this, we insert the variable KOUNT: when KOUNT is 6, control passes out of the loop.

PSUEDOCODE

● **PROBLEM** 8-12

PROBLEM: Write pseudocode and flowcharts to represent the LOOP-EXIT IF-ENDLOOP construct. What rudimentary control constructs are used to build this larger construct?

Solution: In pseudocode, we have the following rendition:

                do for I = 1 through J
                    tasks A - M
                    if (X) then exit do for
                    tasks N - Z
                end do for

A DO-FOR loop is set up, in which tasks A through M are executed. Then, an IF-THEN construct interrupts the program flow to evaluate some condition X. If X is satisfied, no more looping needs to be done, so program control jumps out of the loop. The following flowchart will help you visualize the process:

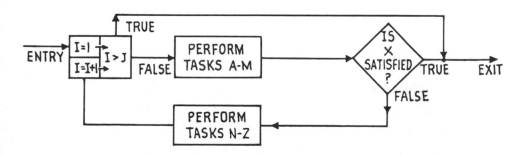

Render the following "nonsense" pseudocode into FORTRAN, including appropriate comments. Name the law of propositional logic you need to render the DO-WHILE and IF-THEN-ELSE constructs:

```
            input  L, J, KOUNT, N
            I ← 1
            do while L < J**3 and  I < KOUNT
            KOUNT ← KOUNT + 2
            if  J < 0  or  L < 0
            then  J ← J + 1
            else  L ← L + 1
            endif
            I ← I + 1
            end do-while
            output KOUNT, J, L
            end program
```

Solution: The name of the law required is often referred to as DeMorgan's Law, which is stated thus:

$$\text{not } (P \text{ and } Q) \equiv \text{not } P \text{ or not } Q$$

Actually, DeMorgan's law includes the Boolean equation

$$P \text{ or } Q \equiv \text{not } [\text{not } P \text{ and not } Q]$$

Here, the two constructs use the former equivalence.

```
            INTEGER L,J,KOUNT,N
            READ (5,100) L,J,KOUNT,N
100         FORMAT (4 I 5)
            I = 1
C           DO WHILE  L  LESS THAN  J**3 AND
C           I IS GREATER THAN KOUNT
10          IF (L.GE.J**3.OR.I.GE.KOUNT) GO TO 20
            KOUNT = KOUNT + 2
C           IF  J LESS THAN 0  OR  L  GREATER
C           THAN ZERO THEN DO
            IF (.NOT.(J.GE.0.AND.L.LE.0)) GO TO 30
C           ELSE DO
            L = L + 1
            GO TO 40
30          J = J + 1
40          CONTINUE
C           ENDIF
            I = I + 1
            GO TO 10
C           END DO-WHILE
20          CONTINUE
            STOP
            END
```

254

Write a pseudocode and a flowchart describing how you would go about analyzing the distribution of sales in a retail store. This will require several program paths, so use the case structure in your description.

Solution: Let us divide the types of sales into 5 categories, assuming that no sale exceeds $2000:

less than $500	Case 1
$500 to $999.99	Case 2
$1000 to $1499.99	Case 3
$1500 to $1999.99	Case 4

Pseudocode is another word describing a structured language. It is a precise account of the steps needed to expedite the solution of a problem. We want to add up the number of sales that have taken place within each case, and obtain a percentage for each. Our pseudocode reads:

        Initialize counters C1, C2, C3, C4, TOTAL
        Read initial value of SALE
            If out of data, go to END
            If error in data-type, write ERROR, and END

Divide SALE by 500.00, add 1, and take the integer of this calculation. Store it in K.
Choose case K and evaluate:

            If K = 1, then C1 = C1 + 1
            If K = 2, then C2 = C2 + 1
            If K = 3, then C3 = C3 + 1
            If K = 4, then C4 = C4 + 1

Read next value of SALE, and continue until SALE has no more elements. Also, increment TOTAL to TOTAL = TOTAL + 1 for each value of sale.

To get percentages:

            For C1, divide C1 by TOTAL then multiply by 100 and place
            in P1
            For C2, divide C2 by TOTAL then multiply by 100 and place
            in P2
            For C3, divide C3 by TOTAL then multiply by 100 and place
            in P3
            For C4, divide C4 by TOTAL then multiply by 100 and place
            in P4

Output P1, P2, P3, P4.
   Now we can write a flowchart which may highlight the pseudocode:
   The pseudocode and flowcharts presented here are general. Keep in mind that there are other forms of pseudocode with stricter rules. What we have presented as pseudocode is a rough draft of the problem. To get from the pseudocode to the flowchart, we used the concept of refinement. This term refers to the development of an algorithm in stages, beginning at a very high and very crude level and systematically refining parts of the algorithm until, finally, it is sufficiently explicated for computer implementation. An analogous procedure in mathematics is the proof of a theorem in stepwise fashion; these steps are called subtheorems or lemmas. In computer programming, these steps are referred to as subprograms.

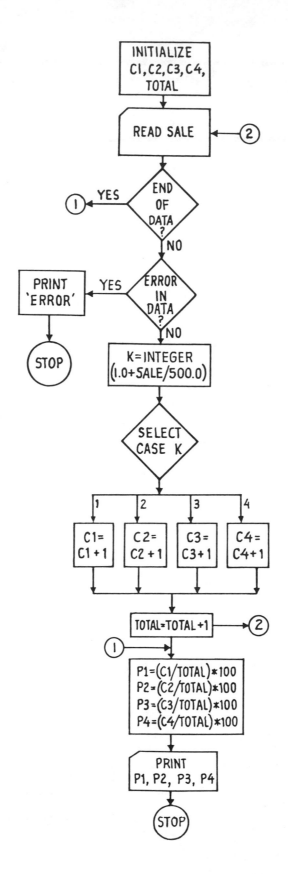

Translate the following flowchart into a pseudocoded program and a BASIC program:

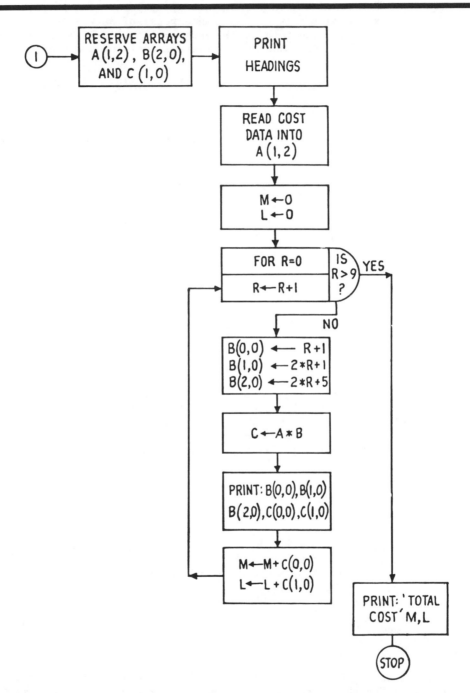

Solution: You probably don't know what this flowchart means at this point. Actually, if you can understand the flowchart symbols alone, you could render the flowchart into pseudocode without understanding the meaning of the problem. This is not advisable, but sometimes programmers are asked to write programs without being given the theory

behind the algorithm. If you are familiar with the three basic control
constructs - sequencing, looping, decision-making - you can design programs
to execute many kinds of tasks.

In this example, the logic is straightforward, but the idea behind
it may not be so. This flowchart illustrates a program that determines
how many of each part is needed for a specific purpose. The process
uses the term explosion matrix to find the expense of materials and
labor if a contractor plans to build 6 ranches, 11 split-levels, and
15 Tudors in the next year. Assume the average building costs are as
given in the table:

Expenses	Ranches	Split-Levels	Tudors
material	17500	16200	12400
labor	6200	5500	4900

We can write the table above and the desired number of homes as the product
of two matrices. Thus:

$$\begin{pmatrix} 17500 & 16200 & 12400 \\ 6200 & 5500 & 4900 \end{pmatrix} \begin{pmatrix} 6 \\ 11 \\ 15 \end{pmatrix} = \begin{pmatrix} \text{materials} \\ \text{labor} \end{pmatrix}$$

The program outputs the answers in the following format:

Ranches	Splits	Tudors	Materials	Labor
1	1	5		
2	3	7		
3	5	9		
.	.	.		
.	.	.		
10	19	23		

TOTAL COSTS

First, we present the pseudocoded version. Notice that we have
referenced array elements with zero subscripts. This was done to accommodate this convention in the BASIC language.

```
real A(1,2), B(2,0), C(1,0)
output headings: 'RANCHES   SPLITS   TUDORS   MATERIALS
                 LABOR'
input data into A
M ← 0.0
L ← 0.0
do for R = 0 to 9
B(0,0) ← R + 1.
B(1,0) ← 2. * R + 1.
B(2,0) ← 2. * R + 5.
C ← A * B  (A,B, and C refer to entire matrices)
output B(0,0), B(1,0), B(2,0), C(0,0), C(1,0)
m ← m + C(0,0)
L ← L + C(1,0)
end do for
output  'TOTAL COSTS', M,L
end program
```

In BASIC, we add DATA statements and MAT instructions to calculate
the product. The BASIC program is given below:

```
10          DIM A(1,2), B(2,0), C(1,0)
12          PRINT
14          PRINT "RANCHES", "SPLITS", "TUDORS", "MATERIALS", "LABOR"
15          PRINT
```

```
20          MAT READ A
25          LET M = 0
26          LET L = 0
30          FOR  R = 0  TO  9
34          LET B(0,0) = R + 1.
36          LET B(1,0) = 2. * R + 1.
38          LET B(2,0) = 2. * R + 5.
40          MAT C = A * B
45          PRINT
50          PRINT B(0,0), B(1,0), B(2,0), C(0,0), C(1,0)
54          LET M = M + C(0,0)
58          LET L = L + C(1,0)
60          NEXT R
62          PRINT
70          PRINT "TOTAL COST = ", M,L
80          STOP
82          DATA 17500, 16200, 12400
84          DATA 6200, 5500, 4900
99          END
```

● **PROBLEM** 8-16

Write pseudocode to describe an algorithm to find a particular sub-array in a larger array of characters.

Solution: Suppose that the main array is $M(I)$, $I = 1,2,3,...,N$ and the subarray is $S(I)$, $I = 1,2,3,...,K$, where $K \leq N$. The idea is to compare successive elements of $M(I)$ with $S(1)$ until a match is found. If so, then the subsequent values of $M(I)$ must be compared with $S(2)$, $S(3),...,S(K)$ to find the entire subarray.

It is assumed that both the main array and the subarray have already been read in. The program will output "yes" if the subarray is found, "no" if not found. A logical flag is used to indicate if a match has been found. The beginning and end of nests are indicated by a dotted line.

```
            do for     I = 1 to N - K + 1 by 1
               if  M(I) = S(1)  then do
                  FLAG ← 'TRUE'
                  do for  J = I + 1 to I + K - 1 by 1
                     if M(J) ≠ S(J - I + 1)
                        then FLAG←'FALSE' exit do for
                     end if
                  end do for
                  if FLAG = 'TRUE' exit do for
               end if
            end do for
            if FLAG = 'TRUE'
               then output "YES, SUBARRAY FOUND"
               else output "NO, SUBARRAY NOT FOUND"
               end if then else
               end program
```

259

Look at the following pseudocoded program. Can you think of an instance in which the program would get stuck in an infinite loop? Modify the program to deal with this possibility.

```
integer  N, NSUM
NSUM ← 0
input  N
do while  N ≠ 0
    NSUM ← NSUM + N
    N ← N - 1
end do while
output NSUM
end program
```

Solution: A problem arises if N is a negative number. Say we input for N the value -6. On the initial pass through the loop, NSUM takes on a value of -6. But when the next statement is encountered, N becomes -7. The loop will continue to decrement the value of N so that N will never equal 0. Hence, the loop is infinite as written.

Probably the programmer wants to sum the digits between -6 and 0. To accomplish this, we can include an IF-THEN-ELSE clause in the DO-WHILE construct:

```
do while  N ≠ 0
    NSUM ← NSUM + N
    if  N < 0
        then N ← N + 1
        else N ← N - 1
    end if
end do while
```

Now the program can handle both positive and negative values of N.

Give examples, in pseudocode or with flowcharts, of the following control constructs:
a)   DO-WHILE
b)   DO-FOR
c)   IF-THEN-ELSE

Solution: Control constructs are program segments which interrupt the sequencing of the entire program to perform some specific task. These constructs may consist of decision instructions, loops, or a combination of both. If rendered faithfully, these constructs will make your program efficient and readable. The DO-WHILE construct requires the continued execution of a sequence of statements, as long as a given condition is satisfied. A pseudocode description looks something like this:

```
do while (X)
    tasks A - Z
end do while
    X  is some logical expression.
```

The loop is repeated until X is no longer satisfied. Program control drops out of the loop and on to the next statement. A flowchart of the situation is as shown in Fig. 1

The DO-FOR construct differs from the DO-WHILE construct in that it

specifies explicitly the number of times the loop should be executed.
When the desired number of loops has been executed, control passes
out of the loop. Here are pseudocode and flowchart descriptions of the
DO-FOR: (see Fig. 2)

```
do for  I = 1  through  N
    tasks  A - Z
end do for
```

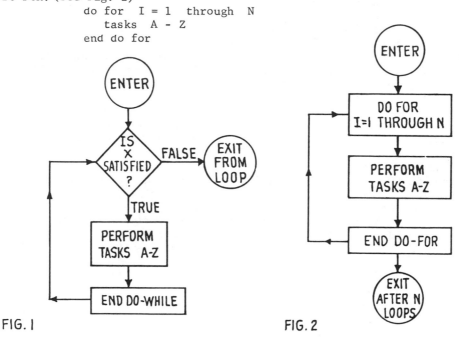

FIG. 1   FIG. 2

When translated into a high-level language, the loop will contain
some statement that declares the value of N. Exit from the loop is
contingent upon N executions. It should be noted that there are two
distinct types of DO-FOR loops. The PL/1 implementation of a DO-FOR
loop is as shown in Fig. 1(a).

If N = 0, the body of the loop (tasks A - Z) will not be performed.
The FORTRAN implementation of a DO-FOR loop is described by the flowchart
see Fig. 2(b).

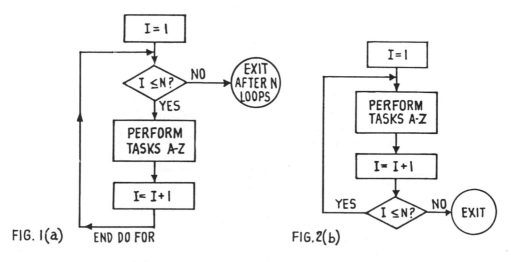

FIG. 1(a)   END DO FOR   FIG. 2(b)

Note that the body of the loop (tasks A - Z) will always be performed
at least once in a FORTRAN DO-loop, even if N = 0. An unwary student
might look at the flowchart given for a DO-FOR loop and think that it
describes FORTRAN's DO-loop, but actually it does not.

Note also that DO FOR constructs may be nested inside each other, such as in the following pseudocode:

```
do for  I = 1 through N
   do for  J = 1 through  M
          tasks A - Z
   end do for  J
end do for  I
```

Tasks A - Z will be performed M × N times. Notice two important conventions in this example. First, in both the DO FOR and DO WHILE constructs, only the first and last statements are left-justified; all other statements within the loop are indented. This is purely a stylistic convention, but it serves to clarify the difference between the loop's control statements and its task-performing, or assignment, statements. Second, realize that you may not terminate a nested loop outside the bounds of the "nest". In the example above, because the DO-FOR J loop is the nested loop, you must terminate it before terminating the DO-FOR I loop. A violation of this rule will cause serious logical errors.

The IF-THEN-ELSE construct is a decision-rendering construct. If the given condition is satisfied, then a certain sequence of statements is executed. If the condition is not satisfied, a different sequence is followed. In pseudocode we have

```
If (x)
   then tasks A - M
   else tasks N - Z
end if then else
```

with x as the given condition. Notice again that the first and last statements are not indented, while the others are. See flowchart Fig. 3.

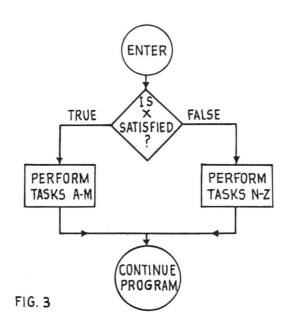

FIG. 3

The true condition corresponds to the THEN part of the construct, while the false condition is interpreted as the ELSE part.

Give an example, in pseudocode, of the REPEAT-UNTIL construct. Compare it to the DO-WHILE construct. Are there any similarities? differences?

<u>Solution</u>:   In pseudocode, the REPEAT-UNTIL construct is rendered as

```
repeat
    tasks  A - Z
until(X)
```

The condition X can be either logical or numerical. When condition X is satisfied, program control passes out of the loop. Notice also that no matter what the status of the condition X, the enclosed statements (tasks A - Z) are executed at least once.

Let us write out the REPEAT-UNTIL construct again, but this time we will include the DO-WHILE construct alongside for comparison.

```
repeat                      do while (X)

    tasks A - Z                 tasks A - Z

until (X)                   end do while
```

When program control passes into a DO-WHILE construct, the condition, or predicate, is tested before the enclosed statements are executed. The REPEAT-UNTIL construct, as previously mentioned, allows the enclosed statements to be executed at least once. A flowchart representation clasifies the structure:

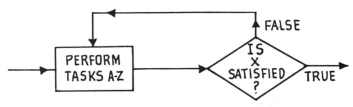

The DO-WHILE construct, on the other hand, has this flowchart representation:

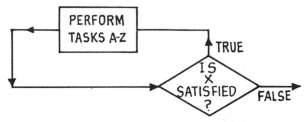

A general rule can be derived from the similarity of the two constructs: any REPEAT-UNTIL construct can be coded using the DO-WHILE construct plus a Boolean variable. For example, suppose that condition X in the earlier pseudocode is a logical variable TEST. Before entering the loop, TEST = FALSE. To exit, the loop TEST must become TRUE. However, tasks A through Z must be executed at least once, a requirement of the REPEAT-UNTIL construct. To render these notions into a pseudocoded DO-WHILE, we can write:

```
TEST = FALSE
do while ~ (TEST)
    tasks A - Z
    TEST = Q
end do while
```

The variable Q is dependent upon the execution of tasks A through Z. After evaluating tasks A through Z, Q can become either TRUE or FALSE. The loop is terminated when Q is true; the condition ∼ (TEST) is not satisfied.

DEBUGGING

● **PROBLEM** 8-20

Construct a flowchart describing the problem-solving procedure. Include a description of debugging the program.

Solution: The novice is apt to imagine that bugs crawl into the program only during the process of converting the written program to a form acceptable to the computer. In fact, errors can arise even during the phase when one is formulating a mathematical solution to the problem. Hence, the process of debugging a program should properly start by studying, once again, the algorithm for solving the problem and then proceed to checking the written program. Finally, the input medium (cards, C.R.T.,etc.) should be checked for typographical errors.
    A typical flowchart of the problem-solving procedure might be as follows:

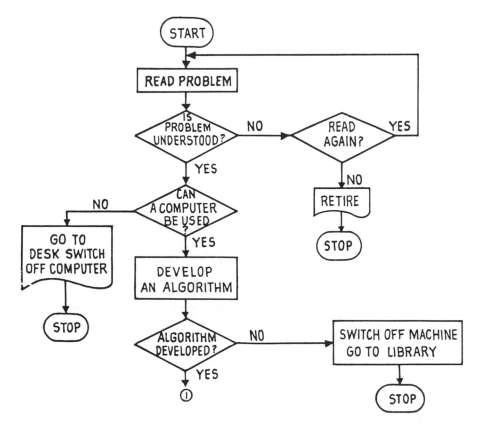

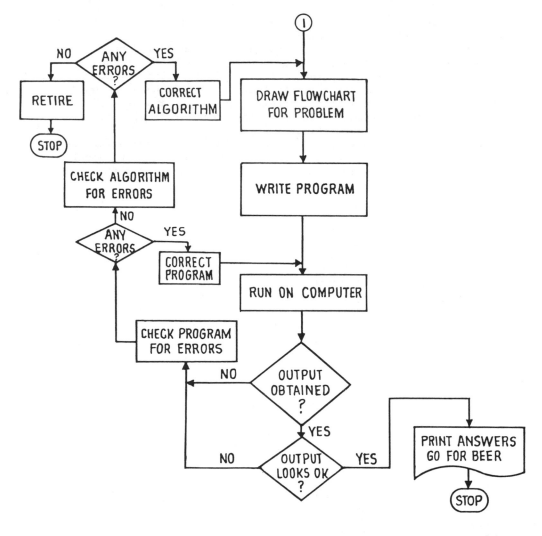

Illustrate using flowcharts the need for debugging when dealing with improper loop sequences.

Solution: Most beginners have some difficulty understanding and applying the rules dealing with loops. Consequently, many of their debugging concentrates on the proper construction of a loop.

Consider the flowchart of figure 1 that develops an algorithm for finding the factors of a number.

Now, suppose the instruction

$$NUMBER \leftarrow K$$

is omitted from the inner loop, leaving the (partial) flowchart of figure 2.

Suppose NUMBER is 12. The loop begins with J = 2. Since 2 divides 12, K will be an integer. The computer prints 2 IS A FACTOR and returns to the start of the loop. Since the value of NUMBER has not been changed, the computer repeats exactly the same computations on the second pass around the loop. 2 IS A FACTOR is printed and the computations repeated.

The computer is in a loop for which the normal exit condition will never be satisfied. The program must be aborted.

The error here can be easily recognized since 2 or 3 pages of '2 IS A FACTOR' indicate that the value of NUMBER is not changing.

Now, suppose that the print statement has also been omitted. In this case there is no output to tell the user that he has constructed an infinite loop. He will not receive any output and so may assume that the system is 'down'. In fact, the computer is slaving away trying to exit out of an infinite loop.

In this case, the system will also abort the program before it is complete. The lack of output tells the programmer that he should include some PRINT instructions in his loops to find what caused the program to abort.

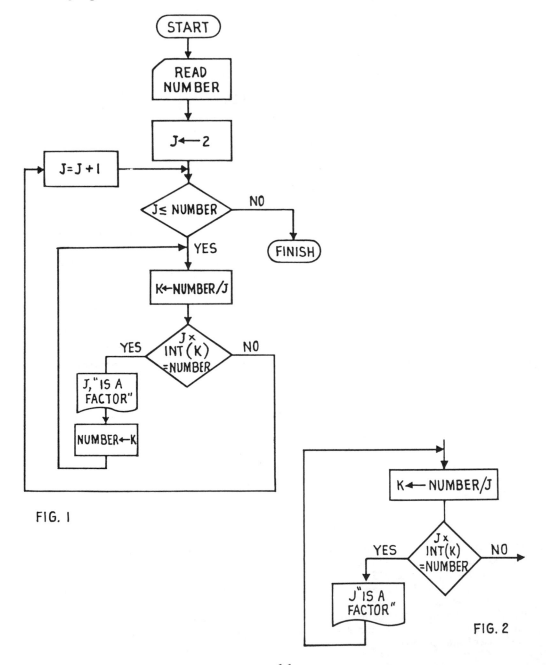

FIG. I

FIG. 2

CHAPTER 9

ASSEMBLER LANGUAGE PROGRAMMING

IBM 360 and 370 Assembler

ADDRESSING

● PROBLEM 9-1

Briefly explain the significance of the ASSEMBLER language.

Solution: Any high level-language, such as BASIC, FORTRAN,
COBOL, and others, is a very convenient and relatively
simple set of instructions that a programmer uses to record
a program needed to be executed. However, these languages
are not readable by a computer, and have to be translated
into an intermediate language, which, in turn, is
changed into binary code before the actual execution process starts.
      This intermediate language is called the ASSEMBLER
language.
      It is not a mandatory rule to use a high level-language
for writing a program. A program can be written in assembler language. This saves a computer some execution time by
eliminating the process of translation of the high-level instructions into assembly instructions. It adds, however,
the procedure of checking the input assembly program for
syntax errors. But the loss of time from this check is
minimal compared to the gain of time from eliminating the
translation step.
      Being the next step from high-level language coding to
the actual execution process, the assembler language is
called a low-level programming language.

● PROBLEM 9-2

In writing a basic assembler language program, our first and
foremost concern is that of housekeeping. What is housekeeping and why is it necessary?

Solution: The first six or so instructions of the IBM/360-
370 assembly language are the housekeeping instructions.

267

In almost all programs, there is some housekeeping to be done. These instructions provide standard linkage between the program and the operating system. In general, these instructions are:

```
LABEL   START φ
        SAVE   (14,12)
        BALR   3,0
        USING  *,3
        ST     13, SAVE+4
        LA     13, SAVE
```

These housekeeping instructions have three basic functions:

1. They provide standard operating system (OS) program linkage. This is done by means of the SAVE, ST and LA instructions.

2. They load and identify the base register for the program. The BALR and USING statements perform this task.

The third function is not of fundamental concern to the BAL programmer. This step involves preparation of the units and materials needed by the main processing part of the program. In most instances, the task is to open input and output files, a task which the system itself usually fails to perform.

Let us now consider the basic functions of each instruction:

LABEL START φ: The label is usually the name of the program. START φ gives the system a location in memory where the program should be stored. The address coded is almost never obtained so a zero is substituted, later to be replaced by the assembler.

SAVE (14,12): Here, the contents of 15 (Register 13 excluded) of the system's 16 general purpose registers are saved. It is important to save the contents of these registers since they may hold information pertinent to the system's operation. The save area generally has a length of 18 fullwords, and saving of the registers starts in the fourth word.

Let us now discuss the 'ST 13, SAVE+4' and 'LA 13, SAVE' instructions. Because of some system operations which the programmer doesn't need to concern himself with presently, it was found to be convenient to store the contents of Register 13 in the second fullword, (SAVE+4), of the SAVE area. The 'LA 13, SAVE' simply places the address of the SAVE area in Register 13. This is done so that the area can be referred to, and the contents of the register restored at the end of the program.

Now, going back, we can look at the 'BALR 3,0' and the 'USING *,3' instructions. The BALR sets up the base register for the program in Register 3. It then stores the base address (or just the address) of the program. The 'USING *,3', in effect confirms that Register 3 is the base register of the program. It tells the computer that starting at that point (indicated by *-asterick) the base register of this program is Register 3. The way these two instructions are coded indicates the natural order of these two instructions in most assembly language housekeeping procedures. The choice of the base register, of course, is left up to the programmer.

From the above discussion we can clearly see why house-keeping is of foremost concern to the programmer. It allows the computer to preserve, for later use, the present contents of its registers, and it enables the assembler to properly place the users program in core.

● **PROBLEM** 9-3

Explain and discuss why the branch and link register (BALR) instruction is usually one of the most important instructions of the IBM/360-370 computers?

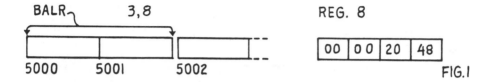

FIG.1

Solution: The branch-and-link register instruction has the register-to-register (RR) format, and as such, it has a single register for each of its operands. When this instruction is executed, it places the address of the next instruction in storage in the register specified as the first operand, and then branches of the address are specified in the second register. To illustrate the function of this instruction, let us assume that the instruction is stored in bytes 5000 and 5001 (the instruction is 2 bytes long). As the first operand we have Register 3 and as the second - Register 8, which contains the binary equivalent of 2048. When this instruction is executed, the address 5002 is placed in Register 3 and the computer then goes to location 2048, the address specified by Register 8. Execution now proceeds from this location.

However, if a zero is specified as the second operand of the BALR instruction, no branching takes place. The address of the next instruction in memory is placed in operand 1 as usual, but since the operand 2 is zero, no branching takes place. Instead, processing of the next sequential instruction occurs. For example, let's use the addresses of Fig. 1 for Fig. 2.

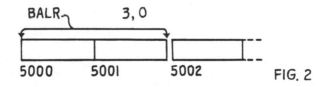

FIG. 2

On execution, address 5002 is placed in Register 3, and processing of the next sequential instruction begins. As we can see this instruction also begins at location 5002. It is this feature of the BALR instruction that makes it one of the IBM/360-370 computers' most important instructions. By this procedure a base address is loaded into the base register of the program. In the example (2), Register 3 is the base register.

269

If a program is loaded into storage and a proper address is not loaded into the base register, the program will not be executed as intended. As a result, a BALR instruction with zero as its second operand is normally the first executable instruction of a program.

● **PROBLEM** 9-4

Discuss and illustrate the meaning of absolute and relative addressing.

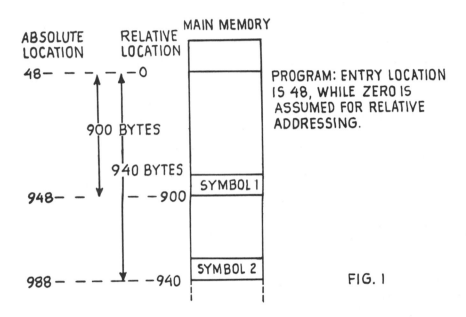

FIG. 1

Solution: One does not need an in depth knowledge of computer science to realize that any program loaded into the main memory of a computer is stored at a particular address. In basic assembler language, by means of a BALR instruction, the address of the first instruction of the program is always placed in a base register. We can safely say that this address never has location "zero." This is so because the first section of the computer's memory is reserved for the operating system. If we call the address at which the program is loaded its ENTRY address, then, in general, to calculate the address of any of the program's symbols, we must add the distance (number of bytes) that is between the symbol and the ENTRY address to the ENTRY address. For example if the ENTRY address' location is 925 and the symbol is 48 bytes away, then the address of the symbol is 925+48=973; the symbol is at location 973. The ENTRY address and the process of adding the displacement dictate what is known as the absolute address of the program and its symbols. In fact, the absolute address of a symbol is its actual location in main memory.

In relative addressing however, we are only interested in the positions which statements occupy relative to the beginning of the program. As a result of this we do not

concern ourselves with the contents of the base register
(since it is constant for all statements in the program) in
calculating this address. The relative address is merely
the distance of a particular statement from the beginning
of the program. Both relative and absolute addressing are
illustrated by the example in Fig. 1.

● **PROBLEM** 9-5

Explain the basic functions of a base register, and describe
how it affects the location of a program segment in the main
memory of the IBM/360-370 computers.

Solution: The IBM/360-370 computers have 16 general-purpose
registers consisting of 32 bits each. Any one of these general-purpose registers can be used as a base register. When
a register is used as a base register, the 24 rightmost bits
are used as a base address. Only 24 bits are needed for a
base address since the main memory of the computer has approximately 2^{24} storage locations, and each of our 24 bits
represents a power of two. This base is the location at
which the program segment was loaded into main memory. Since
the base register stores the address of a program in main
memory, the location of an entire program may be changed just
by altering the contents of this register. Thus, a base register aids in the relocation of a program.

Sometimes it is necessary to use more than one base register in a program. This may happen in the implementation
of a subroutine. When different base registers are used to
address different program segments, the process is referred
to as the use of Multiple Base Registers.

● **PROBLEM** 9-6

One of the most outstanding features of any assembler language is its close association with the main memory of a
computer. Discuss the uses of explicit addresses and state
the importance of checking the format of an instruction before coding it.

Solution: The process of explicit addressing generally involves replacing a symbol in a program by its displacement,
its length, and a substitute base register, not necessarily
in this order. Going from left to right, the displacement
indicates what portion, (how many bytes) of a symbol is to
be ignored in the calculations. The length tells how many
of the remaining bytes are to be used in the calculations,
and the substitute base register gives the address of the
symbol relative to the start of the program in main memory.
The address of this symbol usually has to be loaded into a
register before it is used in an explicit address. The register is referred to as a substitute base register because
it is generally not the main base register of the program.
To illustrate this we will add two packed decimal fields,
PKDAYS and PKHRS. We will assume PKDAYS to be 8 bytes long
and PKHRS to be 6 bytes long. Our intentions are to add

271

the last 3 bytes of PKHRS to the last 4 bytes of PKDAYS:

        AK 3(4,14), 2(3,7)

The above instruction accomplishes our task. Operand 1 is
PKDAYS and operand 2 is PKHRS. In each operand, the number
outside the parentheses is the displacement D, the one following it is the length, L and the last is the substitute
base register, B. Therefore, the general format is
D(L,B). One should be especially careful when coding the
displacement. Note that we are operating on the last 4
bytes of PKDAYS and on the last 3 bytes of PKHRS, but we
have used a displacement of 3 and 2 respectively. This is
so because the first byte of the symbol is not included in
D.
      As you can see, explicit addressing enables us to op-
erate on desired portions of a field. This method of coding is especially useful when table handling is to be done.
For example, let us place zeros in a 16 byte table. Each
entry in the table will be 4 bytes long, therefore, our
zeroing symbol, ZTAB, will be 4 bytes in length. We will
name our table TABZERO.

Example

      L   9,=F'16'   STORING LENGTH OF TABLE
      LA   6,TABZERO   LOAD ADDRESS OF TABLE
ZERO ZAP 0(4,6),ZTAB   ZERO 4 BYTES OF TABLE
      S   9,=F'4'   4 BYTES JUST SET TO ZERO, SO ADJUST
                         REG. 9 TO AMOUNT LEFT
      C   9,=F'0'   SEE IF ZEROING IS COMPLETED
      BE   OUT
      A   6,=F'4'   GO TO NEXT 4 BYTES OF TABLE IF NOT
                         FINISHED
      B   ZERO   CONTINUE ZEROING

As you can see, through explicit addressing, we are able to
operate on a table with great ease. The general operational
rules for string handling and mathematics also apply to explicit coding. Thus, we should be careful of such things as
overflows.
      When coding explicit operands you must remember that
different instructions have different formats, and so, what
can be coded in some instructions cannot be coded in others.
Each explicit value is critical to the resulting object code,
so the formats must be checked to make sure each explicit
value means the right thing.

● **PROBLEM** 9-7

If it were not for Arithmetic Registers like the accumulator (AC), we would find it almost impossible to do effective
programming. Using illustrations, indicate the basic properties of the Accumulator.

Solution: Memory units, such as fullwords, are quite valuable, but if we are unable to alter or operate on them, they
become quite useless. The accumulator facilitates this.

Let's for the moment assume that each unit of memory can hold four decimal digits. The Accumulator may be regarded as a special unit of memory in the computer. For simplicity, we will also assume that it also holds four decimal digits.

1) The AC has the power to copy data from any word in memory without destroying the word's contents. This process is analogous to making a photostat copy. This copy can then be used in other operations. The CLA (clear and add) instruction will do this copying. It first clears the accumulator and then adds the contents of the specified location to it, as shown in Example 1.

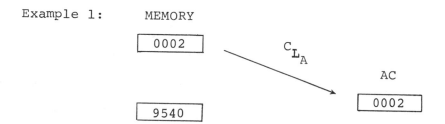

Example 1:

2) The AC can also reverse the above process; ;it can store (STO) its contents in a specified word, with the use of the STO instruction.

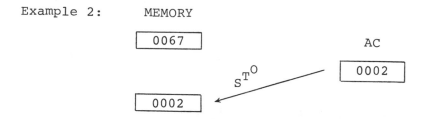

Example 2:

3) The AC also performs arithmetic instructions. Thus, an ADD (add) instruction adds the contents of any specified word to the contents of the AC and retains the accumulated sum in the AC.

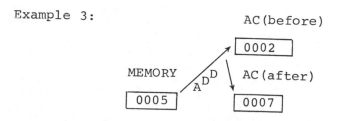

Example 3:

To enable the AC to perform some other task, the new sum is then stored in a convenient location. Storage may be done as shown in Example 2. Since subtraction is merely another form of addition, the AC can also be used in subtractions.

273

Using the SUB(subtract) instruction, this calculation may be
done as in Example 4.

Example 4:

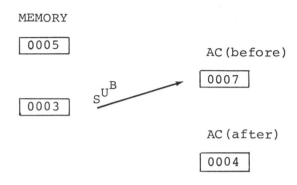

MEMORY

Once again, the sum will be stored in a convenient location
of memory.
The above are the basic properties of the accumulator.
But the great flexibility that results from the AC can be
seen in much more depth by studying its use in conjunction
with another arithmetic register referred to as an MQ. The
Multiply Quotient (MQ) register is generally combined with
the AC when multiplications and divisions are to be done.
If we assume that each register has a length of 17 bits,
then in a multiplication or division, they merge to form a
simple 34-bit field. In this 34-bit field, the MQ occupies
the low order 17 bits. After a multiplication or division,
the result is stored starting with the MQ register. In
other words, the results are right-justified. In the case
of division, the remainder is stored in the AC field.

SPECIALIZED INSTRUCTIONS

● **PROBLEM** 9-8

Describe in general the use of the Data Control Block (DCB)
in basic assembler language of IBM/360-370 computers.

Solution: In writing a basic assembler language program,
files have to be used. Each file used in the program must
be defined in a Data Control Block (DCB). These files can
be output files, input files, and so forth. In coding the
Data Control Block, the mnemonic DCB is used to indicate
the operation code. Like any other operation code this is
written in columns 10-14. The operands following it are
the file specifications. These operands are keywords which
designate the specific characteristics of the file. Many
keywords may be required, which means continuation cards
may be used, if the program is punched on cards. The general format of a DCB statement (file specification) is:

```
Col 1-9  10-12 16→
FILENAME DCB   KEYWORD=SPECIFICATION, KEYWORD=...
```

The keywords used are determined by the kind of input/output
device to be used (card reader, printer, magnetic tape, disc,
optical character reader, etc.) and by the organization of
the records in this file (sequential, random, or otherwise).

To illustrate a DCB we will code one for a program
punched on cards. The card and printer files are sequential
files, which means processing of these files is done in the
order in which they are written.

Example

```
*THE CARD FILE DEFINITION
CARDIN  DCB     DSORG=PS, RECFM=F,            X
                MACRF=GM, BLKSIZE=80,         X
                LRECL=80, DDNAME=CRDIN,       X
                EODAD=CRDEOF
```

In this example we have used 4 cards to code the DCB. The
X, which is in column 72, is a continutation character.
The label CARDIN is the filename, it is generally up to 8
alphanumeric characters in length. DCB is the instruction
code. DSORG=PS indicates that the data set is sequential
(actually physical sequential). This entry determines what
kind of access method will be used for the file and what
input/output modules ('SUBPROGRAMS') will be required.
RECFM=F: RECFM, which stands for record format, indicates
that the records (cards) are of fixed length. (A card's
length is always fixed). MACRF (macro form)=GM indicates
what form of input or output instruction will be coded for
this file. To read cards, the GET instruction (GM) is used.
BLKSIZE and LRECL indicate block and record size. Each 80
byte (one byte for each of the 80 columns) card forms a
LRECL, therefore, both are 80. DDNAME gives the name of
the file, which was previously written as the label of the
DCB instruction. Finally, we have EODAD which means end of
data address. EODAD=CRDEOF: CRDEOF is the label in the program which the computer must branch to when no more data is
found.

The above is a general description of the format of a
DCB. The keywords of the instruction will vary with the
input/output devices and the files being used. But as you
can observe, the DCB precisely defines a file to be used
by a program.

● **PROBLEM** 9-9

What is the difference between a basic assembler language
macro instruction and a machine or imperative instruction.
Indicate what, if any, relationship exists between them.

Solution: In assembler language, as in any other computer
language, we often find it necessary to repeat a contiguous
group or block of instructions. This block, of course, may
consist of any combination of codes permitted by the assembler. Having to do repetition, the assembler language programmer will find a macro instruction facility useful.
Macro instructions (or just Macros) are single abbreviations
for groups of instructions. So in writing a macro instruction, the programmer in effect defines a single line of

275

code to represent a group of instructions. Each time this line occurs in the program, the macro facility will substitute the block of instructions. This process is similar to calling a subroutine in a high level language. After the substitution, this block of code is translated to machine language. Hence, unlike the assembler instruction, which is translated directly to object code, the macro must first be expanded (substituting the block of code for the macro is referred to as expanding the macro) before its translation to object code.

Although the macro may contain other types of instructions, we can clearly see that the assembler instruction is usually a subset of the macro.

● **PROBLEM** 9-10

For earlier computer systems, the storage of data in main memory was done by means of magnetic cores (donut-like structures [◎] whose diameter is a fraction of an inch). To represent these cores, we use the binary digits (Bits) 0 and 1. In the interpretation of bits, what are the rules used by the IBM/360-370 computers to make distinction between their fixed point integer and packed decimal representations?

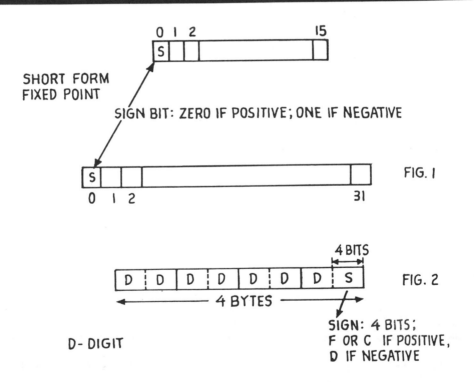

SHORT FORM
FIXED POINT

SIGN BIT: ZERO IF POSITIVE; ONE IF NEGATIVE

FIG. I

4 BITS

D- DIGIT

4 BYTES

SIGN: 4 BITS;
F OR C IF POSITIVE,
D IF NEGATIVE

FIG. 2

Solution: The IBM/360-370 processors have many ways of interpreting groups of bits stored in memory. When storing fixed point integers, these computers use two forms; a short form and a long form. In the short form, two bytes (16 bits) are used to store the integer; for the long form, four bytes (32 bits) are used. In either case, if the processor de-

termines that it has encountered an integer, the sign of
this integer is indicated by using the leftmost bit of the
2 or 4 byte field. If the integer is positive this bit is
zero, if it is negative the bit is one.

The computers store packed decimal numbers by placing
two decimal digits in each byte (8 bits) field. This is
done for all the bytes of the field with the exception of
the rightmost. For this byte, the rightmost four bits indicate the sign of the number. If the number is positive,
the sign is an 'F' or a 'C', if negative, it is a 'D'.

The length of a packed decimal field can be between 1
and 16 bytes. Assuming this, the field can be a minimum of
1 digit and a sign or a maximum of 31 digits and a sign.

● **PROBLEM** 9-11

Discuss the fullword multiplication (M or MR) and the division (D or DR) instructions of IBM/360-370 computers. Can
these two instructions be said to have anything in common?

Solution: The Multiplication Instruction (M or MR):
Both types of this instruction have a register for the
first operand. But the M-instruction is of register to in-
dex (RX) format and has a fullword as its second operand.
In contrast, the MR instruction is of register to register
(RR) format and has a register as its second operand.

Once more let us consider the first operand of the M
and MR instructions. In writing the instruction a single
register appears as the first operand, but in actuality we
are employing two registers. In both cases the register
designated as operand 1 must be an even (i.e. 2, 4, 6 etc.)
register. Since two registers are employed, by IBM convention, the even register designates the beginning of a
"single" field. This 'single' field can be said to have
resulted from a conceptual merger of the two 4-byte registers to form a single 8-byte field. Since we perform multiplication from right to left, the number to be multiplied
is stored in the low order (right) bytes of the mergered
field. Storing is done starting with the rightmost byte of
the odd register since this register constitutes the 4 low
order bytes of the 8-byte field. In doing multiplication
the odd register is first loaded with the number to be multiplied (the multiplicand). The resulting product replaces
the multiplicand of the 8-byte field. In many cases the
product is small enough to be contained in the 4 low order
bytes of the 8-byte field. This is so since 4 bytes can
contain 32 binary digits (bits) and each bit represents a
power of two. As a result of this, a single register can
contain a decimal number as large as four and a third billion. These 4 bytes are of course the odd register. Thus,
in storing the product at a convenient location in core,
the contents of the odd register is stored. It must be
noted that the procedure of storing the single register is
done at the discretion of the programmer.

Example 1

L   7,MULCAN   STORING NUMBER TO BE MULTIPLIED IN LOW
                        8 BYTES

277

```
M    6,MLTPLYR          MULTIPLYING REGISTERS 6 AND 7 BY MULTPLYR
                        (FULLWORD)
STM  6,7,DOUBLE         STORING REGISTERS 6 AND 7 IN A DOUBLE
                        WORD
OR THE LAST STATEMENT CAN BE REPLACED BY:
ST   7,FULL             STORES ONLY THE SINGLE REGISTER.
```

Interpretation of: M 6,MLTPLYR
    This instruction may be seen as:

    BEFORE

    REG 6

| 00 | 00 | 00 | 00 |

←―4 bytes―→

                                        MLTPLYR

                                | 00 | 00 | 00 | 09 |

                                ←― 4 bytes ―→

    REG 7

| 00 | 00 | 00 | 08 |

←― 4 bytes ―→

    WITH

    M   6,MLTPLYR

WE HAVE

    REG 6   MERGING   REG 7
    ┌──────────────┐ ─ ─ →   ← ─ ─ ┌──────────────┬────┐
    │   │   │   │ 08 │
    └──────────────┘   └──────────────┴────┘
        4 bytes   4 bytes

    REG 6   REG 7
    ┌──────────────────┬──────────────────┬────┐
    │   │   │ 08 │
    └──────────────────┴──────────────────┴────┘
              8 byte MERGER

    OR, NOW JUST

    REG 6
    ┌──────────────────────────────────────┬────┐
    │   │ 08 │
    └──────────────────────────────────────┴────┘
                  8 bytes

    AFTER

    REG 6   REG 7
| 00 | 00 | 00 | 00 | 00 | 00 | 00 | 72 |
                  MERGER

    MULTPLYR
| 00 | 00 | 00 | 09 |

The Division Instruction (D or DR):
    The operands here are similar in form to those of the
multiplication instruction. The D-instruction is of RX-

format and takes a register for the first operand and a full-word for the second. The DR instruction is of RR format and has registers as both operands. The aforementioned conceptual merger also occurs. The number to be divided (the dividend) is also stored starting with the rightmost byte of the 8 byte field. After the calculation, the quotient is stored as a fullword in the odd register, and the remainder, which takes the sign of the divider, is stored in the even register. If any of these results do not fit into the registers, a fixed-point exception occurs, and the program is usually cancelled.

It is not difficult to see that the common feature of the IBM 360-370 multiply and divide instructions is that of the conceptual merger. It is this aspect of these instructions that may provide problems for the programmer. If we see these instructions as operations on 8 byte fields designated by an even register we should find coding these instructions quite simple. The main idea behind the merger is to have a field large enough to contain the resulting data. It should be noted that the information in the registers are stored in binary form although the examples indicate decimal digits.

● PROBLEM 9-12

High-level languages specifically provide us with subroutines to lessen repetitious coding. How does a simple subroutine of FORTRAN compare to a basic assembler language subroutine? What specifically does assembler language use for repetitious procedures?

Solution: Although both are referred to as subroutines, the subroutine of the high-level language and that of assembler show no noteworthy similarities. We will not be concerned with the functions of the two subroutines that are used as examples, for this is not relevant to our discussion. Our attention will be primarily focused on the manner in which these subroutines are called, the passing of parameters, and ending procedure. Let us consider the subroutine of FORTRAN This subroutine is initiated by a 'CALL' statement in the main program. This CALL statement has parameters that are passed to the subroutine. In general, it is only through the CALL statement that a subroutine can be accessed. In addition the subroutines may be said to be completely dependent on the operands passed to it by the main program.

Now on inspecting the subroutine of the IBM/360-370 computers, we find something completely different. The subroutine is not called but is branched to as if the computer was branching to any other part of the main program. There are no operands passed in this branching process and hence, the subroutine is not dependent on the main program. In fact, the subroutine of the 360-370 computer could quite easily be mistaken for just another part of the main program.

The subroutine of the high-level language requires an 'END' statement whereas that of assembler does not. When the end of the high-level subroutine is found, control automatically returns to the instruction that comes immediately after the call of the subroutine. With the assembler sub-

routine, the computer has to be directed (branch) to this
instruction. The high-level subroutine is generally placed
outside of the main program but, the subroutine of the assembler language is almost like another part of the main
program. The following example will clearly illustrate the
difference between the two subroutines:

Example 1A

FORTRAN:

CALL LARGER(DATA1,DATA2,MAXI)
.
.
.
C THIS SUBROUTINE FINDS THE LARGER OF TWO NUMBERS
SUBROUTINE LARGER(FIRST,SECOND,RESULT)
INTEGER FIRST,SECOND,RESULT
IF(FIRST.GT.SECOND)RESULT=FIRST
IF(SECOND.GT.FIRST)RESULT=SECOND
RETURN
END

Example 1B (Basic Assembler Language Subroutine)

Assembly:

```
          BAL      11, LCNTRT 1
           .
           .
           .
*LINE    COUNTING AND PRINTING SUBROUTINE
LCNTRT1 CP          LINECNT,=P'50'
        BL          LCNTRT2
        OUT         PRTOUT,HDGLINE
        ZAP         LINECNT,=P'0'
        MV1         WORKAREA,C'0'
LCNTRT2 PUT         PRTOUT,WORKAREA
        AP          LINECNT,=P'1'
        BR          11
```

For FORTRAN:
     The CALL statement initiates the subroutine, and passes
operands DATA1, DATA2 and MAXI to it. This data is accepted
by FIRST, SECOND and RESULT respectively. Note, the data is
'accepted' in the order in which it is passed, so DATA1 is
accepted by FIRST, DATA2 by SECOND and MAXI by RESULT. Incidentally, 'LARGER' is the name of this routine, and its
end is indicated by the END statement. At this point the
computer goes back to the instruction following CALL LARGER
(DATA1,DATA2,MAXI) statement.
For Assembler:
     The BAL statement tells the computer to branch to the
label LCNTRT1, but before doing this, it must store the address of the next instruction in register 11. Going to
LCNTRT1, the assembler processes the instructions until it
comes to the BR 11 instruction. Here, the computer branches
to the address previously stored in register 11. This is
the address of the instruction follwoing the BAL 11, LCNTRT1
instruction.

So, as you can see, these two subroutines have almost
nothing in common. The subroutine of a high-level language
is comparable to that of an assembler MACRO. The calling
procedure and operand passing are quite similar, as the following example illustrates.

Example 2

```
SUMWDS     5, WORDA,WORDB
  .
  .
  .
MACRO
SUMWDS,  ER1,EW1,EW2
   SR     ER1,ER2
   A      ER1,EW1
   A      ER1,EW2
MEND
```

In the main program the name of the macro (SUMWDS) calls
the macro. The operands following the name are passed to
the macro and accepted exactly like those illustrated in
example 1A. The word MACRO indicates the start of the
macro. The end is indicated by MEND. At this point control
goes back, in the main program, to the instruction immediately following the call (SUMWDS 5, WORDA,WORDB).

● **PROBLEM** 9-13

A sign of a good computer programmer is the ability to write
a program which minimizes storage usage. The IBM 360/370
computers provide us with the DSECT and CSECT statements.
How do they enable us to become better programmers?

Solution: The DSECT (Dummy Section) is actually an indicator that tells the assembler that the following code defines
a dummy section. This facility enables us to define and use
many variables in our program without actually allocating
storage space for them all at one time. This may sound
somewhat strange but the procedure is rather simple. The
DSECT is an assembler instruction, and it generates no machine code. It tells the assembler that the storage definitions which follow forms a dummy section. The CSECT (Control
Section) instruction indicates the end of the dummy section.
     For the DSECT a substitute base register is used. The
register to be used is generally specified in a 'USING'
statement at the beginning of the program. When the DSECT
is encountered, the displacements of the labels within it
are assigned, not from the beginning of the program, but
from the DSECT statement. The CSECT instruction indicates
the end of the dummy section. With this, the substitute
base register is restored (freed), the location counter proceeds as if the DSECT instruction was not there. It has the
value it had previous to encountering the DSECT instruction.
     Instead of having storage allocation for the 'running-
life' of the program, the symbols of a DSECT are allocated
space as they are encountered in the body of the program.
This space is then freed when usage is completed.

By placing a label in the label field of the DSECT instruction, the dummy section can be named. The label field of the SCECT statement must contain the name of the program, this name is taken from the label field of the start instruction. Coding of the section is generally done as follows

```
          USING CRDMAP,5
          AP    TOTSUM,SLSREG
CRDMAP    DSECT
SLSCARD   DS    OCL80
SLSNBR    DS    CL4
SLSNAM    DS    CL20
SLSREG    DS    CL2
SLSQTY    DS    CL6
          DS    CL48
PROGNAME CSECT
```

The 'USING' statement is generally coded after the program's base register 'USING' statement. The AP statement adds a number previously placed in SLSREG to TOTSUM.

The DSECT is usually coded for repetitive procedures. In many instances it is used to replace explicit coding. This is done because DSECT is considered easier to code and there are less changes of addressing errors.

It is important to note that since DSECT is a dummy section only storage space can be defined in it and not constants. Thus, only the 'DS' statement is used for the labels.

PROGRAMS

● **PROBLEM** 9-14

Write an assembler language program in BAL to add 20 numbers from main storage.

Solution: Let AA denote the starting location of the numbers A_i to be added together. We assume these numbers occupy consecutive full words in main storage (i.e. 4 bytes per word). If the address of the A_i just added to the sum is kept in a register, the number 4 can be added to the contents of that register; the result is the address of the next number to be added. Suppose register 7 is initialized to AA, the address of A_0. Each time the adjustment step is executed, the quantity in register 7 is increased by 4. Hence the second time the instruction A 8,ϕ(7) is executed, the address in register 7 is 4 greater than the address of A_0; thus it is the address of A_1. The third time the body of the loop is executed, the address of register 7 has been increased again, so A_2 is growing to sum. The process of adding on A_i and adjusting the address continues until execution of the loop is terminated. We exit from the loop when the contents of register 9 is 20.

```
* A SEGMENT TO ADD 20 NUMBERS FROM
* CONSECUTIVE FULL WORDS IN MAIN STORAGE
* INITIALIZATION
```

```
        LA   8,φ  SUM= φ

        LA   9,φ  I= φ

        LA   7,AA ADDRESS OF FIRST A
*       BODY: ADD A(SUBI) TO SUM
LOOP A  8,φ(7)
        LA   9,1(9)  INCREASE I
        LA   7,4(7)  GET ADDRESS OF NEXT A
        C    9,=F'2φ'
        BNE  LOOP    BRANCH BACK IF I NOT YET 20, LV LOOP IF I=2φ
```

● **PROBLEM** 9-15

Write a program to read in a man's earning for the day, calculate his salary for the week and print it.

Solution:

```
        AP      WKDAYS,=P'0'        INITIALIZE COUNTER
READ    READCARD CARDIN,CRDEOF      READS IN EARNINGS FOR DAY
                                    GOES TO LABEL 'CRDEOF' WHEN
                                    NO MORE DATA IS FOUND.
        PACK    WKERN, CRDERN       CONVERT EBCDIC DATA TO PACK
                                    DECIMAL FOR CALCULATIONS
        AP      WKSUM, WKERN        ADDS DAY'S EARNINGS TO SALARY
        AP      WKDAYS,=P'1'        ADDS 1 TO NUMBER OF DAYS
                                    WORKED
        CP      WKDAYS,=P'6'        MAN WORKS 6 DAYS PER WEEK
        BE      SALFND
        B       READ
                                    *If the program reaches this
                                     statement it means the pre-
                                     vious test has failed, it
                                     tells the computer that days
                                     worked does not yet equal 6,
                                     therefore another card must
                                     be read.
*AT THIS POINT SALARY FOR WEEK IS FOUND
SALFND ZAP  WKDAYS,=P'0'            RESET WKDAYS TO ZERO
        MVC  PRTSUM,WKSUM           PREPARE TO PRINT SALARY FOR
                                    THE WEEK
     PRINTLIN PRTSAL,132            PRINT SALARY
        .
        .
        .
CRDEOF   ...                        END OF DATA; DO END OF FILE
                                    PROCEDURES
*THE DATA DEFINITION FOR THE INPUT AREA
CARDIN  DS      φCL80
CRDERN  DS      CL4
        DS      CL76
*THE DATA DEFINITION FOR THE PRINT AREA.
PRTSAL  DS      φCL132
PRTSUM  DS      CL6
        DS      126C''
*DATA DEFINITION FOR WORK AREAS
WKERN   DS      PL3
WKSUM   DS      PL4
WKDAYS  DS      PL2
```

READCARD CARDIN, CRDEOF: The first operand of this instruction specifies the name of the data definition for this area. The data definition indicates how the data should be read in. On a card, the data must be punched exactly in the format specified by the data definition. You should also observe that there is a data definition for the print area.

PACK WKERN, CRDERN: The data is read in in EBCDIC form and cannot be operated on in this form. Hence, we convert it to packed decimal which is an operable form.

ZAP WKDAYS,=P'0': The man has worked for six days, so after the sixth day we reset WKDAYS by zeroing it.

MUC PRTSUM,WKSUM: Here the salary WKSUM is moved into the print area prior to printing. It is generally a good idea to edit (convert back to EBCDIC) data in packed decimal before printing it.

PRTLIN PRTSAL,132: PRTSAL is the name of the data definition for the print area, and 132 is the length of the print area. You should note that the general format of a data definition is NAME DS ϕCLX. The ϕ indicates that the symbols that follow are sub-area of the field. X is the length of the field, 80 for card, 132(or 133) for a print line.

● PROBLEM 9-16

Write a basic assembler language program to compute a woman's weekly work hours in fixed point binary, and convert the result back to decimal.

Solution:

```
                L    4,=F'6'         PLACE NO. OF DAYS WORKED
                                     IN REGISTER 4.
                SR   5,5             CLEAR REGISTER 5 - IT WILL
                                     STORE TOTAL HOURS WORKED
NXTHRS          READCARD CRDIN,CRDEOF READ HOURS WORKED EACH DAY
                PACK DBLE,CRDHRS     CONVERT EBCDIC DATA TO
                                     PACKED DECIMAL IN DOUBLE-
                                     WORD AREA
                CVB 7,DBLE           CONVERT PACKED DECIMAL TO
                                     BINARY IN REGISTER 7
                AR  5,7              STORE SUM OF HOURS IN RE-
                                     GISTER 5
                BCT 4,NXTHRS         DECREASE REGISTER 4 BY 1
                                     AND GO TO INSTRUCTION LA-
                                     BELLED NXTHRS.
                CVD 5,DBLE           CONVERT BINARY HOURS BACK
                                     TO DECIMAL.
                ZAP WKHRS,DBLE       STORE HOURS IN AREA CALLED
                                     WKHRS
CRDEOF
  .
  .
  .
*DATA DEFINITION FOR INPUT AREAS
CARDIN          DS       φCL80
CRDHRS          DS       CL3
                DS       CL77
```

```
*DATA DEFINITION FOR WORK AREAS
DBLE            DS        D
WKHRS           DS        DC3
```

You should note that the CVB (convert to binary) and
the CVD (convert to decimal) instructions must have a
double word (indicated by D in data definition) as the second operand. For the CVB instruction the data in the
doubleword is converted to binary and then placed in the
register specified as operand 1. The reverse is done for
the CVD instruction where data in the register is converted
to packed decimal form and placed in the doubleword. The
BCT (branch and count) instruction will decrement the contents of Register 4 by one each time it is encountered. It
will then branch to the label specified as operand 2. When
Register 4 finally contains a zero, control will go to the
next sequential instruction; the CVD instruction. At this
point we have found the total sum of the hours worked for
that week.

● **PROBLEM** 9-17

Write a program, using IBM/360 Assembly language, to check
if a number, greater than 2, is a prime number. Make use
of the flowchart of Fig. 1.

Solution:

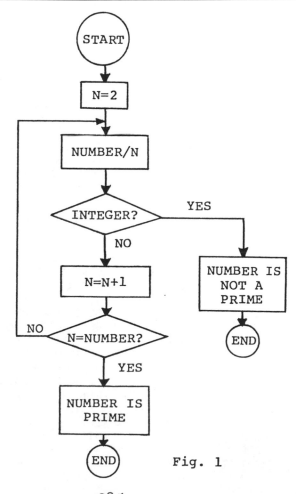

Fig. 1

285

On examining the flow chart, we see that we shall need the following registers:

A register for storing the variable N : say, Register 2.
A register for the NUMBER to be checked: say, Register 3.
A register for storing the constant '1': say, Register 4.
A register for storing the constant '0': say, Register 5.
Registers for multiplication and division: say, Registers 6 and 7.
A utility register : say, Register 8.

With these registers alloted, we can now write the program as follows.

```
MAIN     START     0
         PRINT     NOGEN
         INITIAL
         L         2,=F'2'   SET REGISTER 2 TO '2',FOR AN
                             INITIAL VALUE OF N=2
         L         4,=F'1'   SET REGISTER 4 TO '1'
         L         5,=F'0'   SET REGISTER 5 TO '0'
         RWD       3         READ THE VALUE OF THE NUMBER
*                            TO BE CHECKED INTO REGISTER 3
LOOP     L         7,4       LOAD REG. 7 WITH CONTENTS OF
                             REG. 4
         MR        6,3       MULTIPLY CONTENTS OF REGS. 6 &
                             7 BY REG. 3 (i.e., MULTIPLY 1
                             BY NO. TO BE CHECKED) & STORE
                             THE RESULT IN REG. 6 AND REG.
                             7, AS A COUBLE-WORD.
         DR        6,2       DIVIDE CONTENTS OF REG. 6 & 7,
*                            i.e., THE NUMBER, BY CONTENTS
*                            OF REG. 2, i.e., N.  (THE QUO-
*                            TIENT GETS STORED IN REG. 7 &
*                            THE REMAINDER IN REG. 6)
         CR        5,6       COMPARE REMAINDER WITH '0'
         BM        CHK       IF NEGATIVE, BRANCH TO LABEL
                             CHK
         WWD       4         IF NOT NEGATIVE, REMAINDER IS
*                            ZERO, HENCE, NUMBER IS NOT A
*                            PRIME, HENCE, WRITE '1' AS AN
                             INDICATION
         B         OUT       BRANCH TO END THE PROGRAM
CHK      AR        2,4       ADD CONTENTS OF REGISTERS 2 &
                             4, i.e., INCREMENT N TO N+1.
         LR        8,2       LOAD INCREMENTED 'N' IN REG. 8
         SR        8,3       SUBTRACT 'NUMBER' FROM 'N'
         BM        LOOP      IF NEGATIVE, IT MEANS 'NUMBER'
*                            IS GREATER THAN 'N'.  HENCE,
*                            REPEAT THE LOOP.
         WWD       3         IF NOT NEGATIVE, IT MEANS 'NUM-
                             BER'='N'; HENCE, 'NUMBER' IS A
*                            PRIME NUMBER, AND HENCE, PRINT
*                            THE 'NUMBER' ITSELF AS AN IN-
*                            DICATION.
OUT      EXIT
         END       MAIN
```

Using basic assembler language, write a program to determine
if the number 313791 is a prime number.

Solution A prime number is a number that can only be divided by 1 and itself. To determine if a number is prime, we
divide it by other numbers, starting with the divisor 2 and
incrementing it by 1 until there is no remainder or the divisor is equal to the number.

Program:

```
        L     2,=F'2'     LOAD STARTING DIVISOR
        L     3,=F'1'     LOAD INCREMENT TO BE USED IF THERE IS A
                          REMAINDER
        RWD   4           READ NUMBER AND PLACE IT IN REGISTER 4
LOOP    SR    8,8         CLEAR REGISTERS FOR
        SR    9,9         THE DIVISION
        LR    9,4         PLACE NUMBER IN REGISTER 9
        DR    8,2         DIVIDE NUMBER NOW STORED IN REGISTERS
                          8 & 9, ALTHOUGH ONLY REGISTER 8 IS
                          CODED AS OPERAND-1
        C     8,=F'0'     COMPARE REMAINDER STORED IN REGISTER 8
                          WITH ZERO
        BE    NTPRME      IF REMAINDER IS ZERO, THEN NUMBER IS
                          NOT PRIME
        AR    2,3         INCREMENT DIVISOR BY 1
        CR    2,4         CHECK IF THE DIVISOR IS EQUAL TO THE
                          NUMBER
        BEE   PRIME       NUMBER IS PRIME IF DIVISOR EQUALS IT
        B     LOOP        REPEAT DIVISION PROCESS IF TEST FAILS
NTPRME  WWD   3           WRITE 1 FROM REGISTER 3 TO INDICATE
                          NUMBER IS NOT PRIME AND GO TO END OF
        B     OUT         PROGRAM.
PRIME   WWD   4           WRITE NUMBER FROM REGISTER 4 TO INDI-
                          CATE NUMBER IS PRIME
OUT     END   MAIN
```

You have been given an unordered table to search for a particular entry. When this entry is found you are to replace
it with an updated piece of data.

Solution: Since the table is not ordered it would be best
to use a linear search in which all the elements of the
table are inspected.
    To do this problem we will assume that the table has
100 entries and each entry is 14 bytes long.

Program:

```
RDCD        READCARD DATA,CRDEOF
            LA     4,SYMTBL         STORE ADDRESS OF TABLE
SEARCH      CLC    0(14,4),SYMBOL   COMPARE ENTRY WITH ITEM TO
                                    BE SEARCHED FOR (SYMBOL)
            BE     SYMFOUND         IF EQUAL WE'VE FOUND SYMBOL
```

```
          C       4,LAST           'LAST' HOLDS THE ADDRESS OF
                                   THE LAST ENTRY IN THE TABLE
          BE      NOTFOUND         HERE, IF EQUAL AND THE SYM-
                                   BOL IS NOT FOUND, THEN IT
                                   IS NOT IN THE TABLE

          A       4,=F'14'         GO TO NEXT ENTRY IF SYMBOL
                                   IS NOT FOUND

          B       SEARCH           CONTINUE TO SEARCH
NOTFOUND  .
          .
          .
          .
          .
          .
          .
SYMFOUND  MVC     0(14,4),NUDATA   REPLACE ENTRY WITH UPDATED
          .                        DATA
          .
CRDEOF---------
*DATA DEFINITION FOR WORK AREAS
SYMTBL    DS      100CL14          ALLOCATE SPACE FOR A HUN-
                                   DRED 14-BYTE ENTRIES.
SYMBOL    DS      CL14             HOLDS SYMBOL BEING CHECKED.
LAST      DC      A(FINDAT)        STORES ADDRESS OF FINAL
                                   DATA IN TABLE.
*DATA DEFINITION FOR INPUT AREA
DATA      DS      ¢CL80
NUDATA    DS      CL14
          DS      CL66
```

Comments:

The 'NOTFOUND' segment of this program would usually involve printing a message which indicates the data was not in the table. This is always a good procedure, since when we do any table searching there is the possiblility that the given data won't be found. For the 'LAST DC A(FINDAT)' instruction, the 'A' indicates that the address of the symbol in the parentheses should be stored in the location represented by the symbol in the label field. In other words, this instruction tells the computer to store the address of 'FINDAT' in the location denoted by LAST. In coding the table, in our program, we would attach the the label 'LAST' to the final piece of data in the table.

On reaching the label 'CRDEOF', program execution would have generally been completed, and as such, we would restore the contents of the registers stored at the beginning of our program.

● **PROBLEM** 9-20

Write a Basic Assembler Language program to compute and print out the first twenty numbers of the Fibonacci Sequence.

Solution: The Fibonacci numbers are a sequence of numbers beginning with 0 and 1. To compute the following numbers of the series one adds the previous two to form the next. For example, the third number of the series is 0+1=1. The next is 1+1=2, the next 1+2=3, the sixth is 2+3=5 and so on.

This simple number sequence is easily programmed in assembler language. We will start off by loading the first two numbers of the sequence into two registers. Next we fall into a loop which prints out the two registers and then adds each register to the other creating the next two numbers of the sequence. These next two numbers are printed out when the program goes back to the top of the loop and the procedure is repeated.

The program follows below:

```
         BALR       2,0 ⎫        ESTABLISHES BASE REGISTER
         USING      *,2 ⎭
         LA         1,0          REGISTER 1 CONTAINS NUMBER TO BE
                                 INCREMENTED BY LOOP
         LA         4,1          REGISTER 4 CONTAINS INCREMENT
         LA         5,9          REGISTER 5 CONTAINS LIMIT
         L          7,=F'0' ⎫    LOADS FIRST TWO NUMBERS OF SEQUENCE
         L          8,=F'1' ⎭
LOOP     PRINTOUT   7 ⎫          PRINT NUMBERS OF SEQUENCE
         PRINTOUT   8 ⎭
         AR         7,8 ⎫        CREATES NEXT TWO NUMBERS OF SE-
         AR         8,7 ⎭        QUENCE
         AR         1.4          ADDS INCREMENT TO INDEX
         CR         4,5          COMPARE INDEX TO END
         BLE        LOOP         RETURN FOR NEXT PART OF SERIES
                                 IF NOT PAST END
         END
```

● **PROBLEM** 9-21

You are given groups of numbers. Using Basic Assember Language. You are to compute the following:

1. N = the number of elements in a group

2. $\sum_{i=1}^{N} x_i$ = the sum of the numbers in the group.

3. Average = SUM/N

4. Variance = $\dfrac{\sum_{i=1}^{N} (x_i)^2 - \left(\sum_{i=1}^{N} x_i \right)^2}{N - 1}$

Also: $\sum (x_i)^2$ = sum of the squares of each number and

$\left(\sum x_i \right)^2$ = the square of the sum of the numbers.

5. MAX = maximum x_i in each group

6. MIN = minimum x_i in each group.

The input deck of cards containing each group will be divided from each other by means of an E card. The E is to
be placed in the first column of each partition card. The
number cards have the integers right justified in columns
1-3 of the card.

The output must be labelled as follows:

#(GROUP NUMBER) N   SUM   AVG   VAR   MAX   MIN

This is to be printed on a new page, with two spaces between
each output line.

Solution

	Col 1-8	Col 10-14	16-71	
1	VARIANCE	START	0	
2		SAVE	(14,12)	SAVE REGISTERS
3		BALR	3,0	STORE BASE ADDRESS
4		USING	*,3	USING REGISTER 3 AS BASE REGISTER
5		ST	13,SAVE+4	
6		LA	13,SAVE	STORE ADDRESS OF SAVE AREA
7		PRINTLIN	HEADING,132	PRINTING THE LABELS
8		AP	WRKGPNBR,=P'1'	FIRST GROUP NUMBER
9	RDCD	READCARD	CARDINPA,CRDEOF	READ IN A NUMBER,X;
10		CLI	CRDATA,C'E'	CHECK TO SEE IF NUM-BER IS A DIVISOR
11		BE	CALQUE	IF 'E', THEN END OF A GROUP
		AP	WRKGPCNT,=P'1'	COUNT ELEMENTS OF GROUP
12		PACK	WRKDATA,CRDATA	CONVERT NUMBER TO PACKED DECIMAL
13		AP	WRKSUM,WRKDATA	FINDING SUM OF GROUP
14		ZAP	WKDATASQ,WRKDATA	PLACE NUMBER IN AN-OTHER AREA
15		MP	WKDATASQ,WRKDATA	SQUARE NUMBER
16		AP	WRKSUMSQ,WKDATASQ	FINDING SUM OF THE SQARES
17		ZAP	WKDATASQ,ZERO	ZERO AREA USED FOR SQUARING
18		CP	WRKDATA,WRKMAX	FINDING MAX
19		BH	GPHIGH	STORE MAX
20		CP	WRKDATA,WRKMIN	FINDING MIN
21		BL	GPLOW	STORE MIN
22		B	RDCD	GET NEXT NUMBER IN THE GROUP
23	GPLOW	ZAP	WRKMIN,WRKDATA	STORE NEW MIN

	1-8	10-14	16-71	
23A		B	RDCD	
24	CALQUE	MVC	PRTGPNBR,PATT1	PREPARE GROUP
25		ED	PRTGPNBR,WRKGPNBR	NUMBER FOR THE PRINT LINE
26		MVC	PRTGPCNT,PATT1	PREPARE N FOR
27		ED	PRTGPCNT,WRKGPCNT	PRINT LINE
28		MVC	PRTSUM,PATT2	PREPARE SUM FOR

29		ED	PRTSUM,WRKSUM	PRINT LINE
30		ZAP	WRKSUMST,WRKSUM	GET COPY OF SUM
31		MP	WRKSUMST,WRKSUM	FINDING THE SQUARE
				OF THE SUM
32		DP	WRKSUMST,WRKGPCNT	DIVIDE THE SQUARE
				OF THE SUM BY N
33		SP	WRKSUMSQ,WRKSUMST(5)	CALCULATE THE
				NUMERATOR OF
				VARIANCE
34		SP	WRKGPCNT,=P'1'	FIND DENOMINATOR
				OF VARIANCE
35		DP	WRKSUMSQ,WRKGPCNT	FINDING VARIANCE
36		AP	WRKGPCNT,=P'1'	RESTORE N TO FIND
				AVERAGE
37		DP	WRKSUM,WRKGPCNT	FIND AVERAGE
38		MVC	PRTAVER,PATT2	PREPARING THE
39		ZAP	WRKSUM,WRKSUM(2)	AVERAGE FOR THE
40		ED	PRTAVER,WRKSUM	PRINT LINE
41		MVC	PRTVAR,PATT2	PREPARING VARIANCE
42		ZAP	TEMPHOLD,WRKSUMSQ+V(4)	FOR THE
43		ED	PRTVAR,TEMPHOLD	PRINT LINE
44		MVC	PRTMAX,PATT2	PREPARING TO PRINT
45		ED	PRTMAX,WRKMAX	GROUP'S MAX
46		MVC	PRTMIN,PATT2	PREPARING TO PRINT
47		ED	PRTMIN,WRKMIN	GROUP'S MIN
48		PRINTLIN	PRTDETL,133	PRINT OUTPUT LINE
49		AP	WRKGPNBR,=P'1'	INCREMENT GROUP
				NUMBER
50		ZAP	WRKGPCNT,ZERO	
51		ZAP	WRKGPCNT,ZERO	
52		ZAP	WRKSUMSQ,ZERO	
53		ZAP	WRKMAX,=P'0000'	
54		ZAP	WRKMIN,=P'9999'	
55		B	RDCD	
56	GPHIGH	ZAP	WRKMAX,WRKDATA	STORE NEW MAX
57		CP	WRKDATA,WRKMIN	
58		BL	GPLOW	
59		B	RDCD	
60	CRDEOF	L	13,SAVE+4	
60A		RETURN	(14,12)	RESTORE REGISTERS
*	DATA DEFINITION FOR THE CARD INPUT AREA			
62	CRDINPA	DS	0CL80	
63	CRDDATA	DS	CL3	
64		DS	CL77	
*	DATA DEFINITION FOR THE WORK AREAS			
66	SAVE	DS	18F	USE TO SAVE THE
				CONTENTS REGIS-
				TERS
67	WRKDATA	DS	PL3	
68	ZERO	DC	PL4'0'	
69	WRKSUM	DC	PL3'0'	
70	WKDATASQ	DS	PL6	
71	WRKSUMSQ	DC	PL6'0'	
72	WRKSUMST	DS	PL6	
73	WRKGPNBR	DC	P'0'	
74	WRKGPCNT	DC	P'0'	
75	WRKMAX	DC	PL3'0'	
76	WRKMIN	DC	PL3'9'	
77	TEMPHOLD	DS	PL4	
78	PATT1	DC	X'40202020'	

```
79 | PATT2      DC        | X'402020212020202020'
*  | DATA DEFINITION FOR THE HEADING
81 | HEADING    DS        | φCL133
```

	1-8	10-14	16-71	72
82	PRTCC1	DC	C'1'	
82A		DC	19C' '	
83		DC	C'# N SUM AVG VAR	X
83A			MAX MIN'	
84		DC	57C' '	

```
*  DATA DEFINITION FOR THE PRINTER WORK AREA
 86 | PRTDETL  | DS  | φCL133
 87 | PRTCC2   | DC  | C'-' SKIP TWO SPACES
 88 |          | DC  | 19C' '
 89 | PRTGPNBR | DS  | CL2
 90 |          | DC  | 3C' '
 91 | PRTGPCNT | DS  | CL2
 92 |          | DC  | 4C' '
 93 | PRTSUM   | DS  | CL6
 94 |          | DC  | 4C' '
 95 | PRTAVER  | DS  | CL6
 96 |          | DC  | 4C' '
 97 | PRTVAR   | DS  | CL8
 98 |          | DC  | 6C' '
 99 | PRTMAX   | DS  | CL6
100 |          | DC  | 6C' '
101 | PRTMIN   | DS  | CL6
102 |          | DC  | 50C' '
103 |          | END | VARIANCE
```

Comments:

For the beginning assembler language programmer, the calculations in his program will generally be done in either of two forms of arithmetic, packed decimal or fixed point binary. Our VARIANCE program written above is an example of an assembler language program which uses only packed decimal arithmetic. It should be understood that both forms of arithmetic can be done simultaneously, and, in fact, this is what is done on most occasions.

We must first point out that the numbers, as written in the leftmost edge of the program, are simply placed there for the purposes of reference, and are not in any way related to the program itself.

The calculations involved in our program have been done in an order corresponding to the listing of our question, and as such, we do not think it necessary to explain the logic of the program. In our explanation, we will discuss only those instructions we think would pose problems for the student.

The first six instructions of our program constitute the housekeeping procedures required. The label in Columns 1-8 of Line 1 is the name of the program. The other instructions we will consider are:

7. PRINTLIN HEADING, 132 - The label 'HEADING' is the name of a print area. The format of this print area is dictated by a data definition (Lines 80-84) given by the programmer. The length of a print area is, in most cases, specified as the length of a print line (132 or 133 spaces) on an output

page. This print area usually contains carriage controls (Column 1), output information (whether defined as constants or moved into the area), and blanks. It is good assembler programming practice to fill up unused portions of a print area with blanks since the computer has a tendency to print undesired characters in 'unblanked' spaces.

The above discription given for the "heading' print area applies, in general, to all print areas defined by a data definition. Variations of these areas lie only in their names (chosen by the programmer) and in the fact that data to be printed may be explicitly defined in the area (DC statement), moved into it (MVC statement) or a combination of both.

The coding procedures for the way data is to be read from a card are quite similar to those of printing. The only differences are that the length of the input area is 80 bytes (80 columns on a card), and instead of placing blanks in the unused fields, we just define them (DS statement - Line 64).

10. CLI CRDATA,C'E' - This instruction determines if the card read in has an 'E' in Column 1. If so, we are at the beginning of a new group, but we must first process (find the variance of) the old group before commencing this one.

Lines 14-15 and 30-31 illustrate the technique used in multiplying (and squaring) two packed decimal numbers. The multiplicand is placed in a field twice as long as that of the multiplier. When the calculation is done, the result will replace the multiplicand. Thus, in making its area twice as long as that of the multiplier, we quard against overflow.

In general, when calculations are done in assembler language, Operand-1 is replaced by the result, so one should always check to see that this area is large enough to receive the largest (most spacious) possible result. For example, in the DP instructions of Lines 32 and 35, Operand-1 was made large enough to store the resulting quotients and their remainders. The length of these fields can be checked by inspecting them in their various data definitions. Incidentally, it is good programming practice to somehow indicate in which data definition a particular symbol maybe found. This is usually achieved by allowing the first (or last) two or three letters of the symbol to correspond to the name of the data definition. For example, 'CRDDATA' is to be found in the data definition for the card input area, and 'PRTSUM' is located in the definition for the print area.

The only other instructions we think necessary to discuss are those involved in the EDITING (ED) of packed decimal results to be printed. It is imperative that we edit packed decimal results prior to printing, since our output will not be what we expect unless this is done. Our problem here is one of translation. When the computer reads in our data, it does so in EBCDIC code. This process involves replacing each character of our data with two EBCDIC digits.

For example, it reads 1 (data) as F1(ECDIC), E as C5, and so forth. Now, in printing it does the reverse; the information to be printed is taken as EBCDIC and translated back to 'readable' code. For example, the packed decimal number 406F, taken as EBCDIC, would be translated as

| � | ? | instead of | 4 | 0 | 6 |.

Having pointed out the importance of editing, we will now illustrate the way in which it is done. A packed decimal number has the form:

| 00 | 09 | 8F |

This is a representation of the number in memory. Two decimal digits are stored per byte, except for the rightmost byte, which has a sign factor in its last four bits. The integers are those of our actual answer. As you can see, the storage space alotted a pack decimal number is usually such that unused high order locations are packed with zeros.

By first placing a lexadecimal pattern in a print area, a packed number will be translated to the correct EBCDIC code before printing is done. The first byte of this pattern usually contains a hexadecimal 40, which causes suppression of high order zeros. In general, the length of the pattern field is twice that of the packed decimal field. The aforementioned 40 of the pattern field may be said to replace the sign factor of the packed decimal field, but it will be in the first byte instead of the last. Each integer in the packed field will then be replaced by a DIGIT SELECTOR (HEX 20) in the pattern field. For example, let us consider the following instructions:

        MVC   PRTSUM, PATTERN
        ED   PRTSUM, WRKSUM

Before MVC and ED instructions

PRTSUM   PATTERN
| | | | | | | | 40 | 20 | 20 | 20 | 20 | 20 |

WRKSUM
| 00 | 09 | 8F |

After instructions:

1. MVC PRTSUM, PATTERN

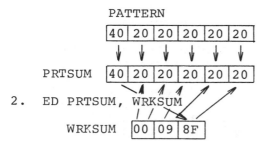

2. ED PRTSUM, WRKSUM

        WRKSUM | 00 | 09 | 8F |

Finally

PRTSUM

| FO | FO | FO | FO | F9 | F8 | EBCDIC

OUTPUT OF PARTSUM:
98

PATTERN

| 40 | 20 | 20 | 20 | 20 | 20 | HEX

WRKSUM

| 00 | 09 | 8F | PACKED DECIMAL

The main idea behind editing is to place a hexadecimal pattern in the print field, to ensure correctness of the packed decimal data to be printed. The pattern used can be longer than the print field since it will be truncated on the right. Although this means less coding and simple editing, it should not be done unless the portion to be truncated is of no importance. One should also note that since there are two digits per byte for a packed decimal field the print field should be at least twice as long.

As long as our intentions are to print only the integers from the packed field, it is okay to make the pattern, and hence the printfield, twice as long. But if we intend to place decimal points, commas, and/or any special characters in our output, we must use a pattern and a printfield that are more than twice the length of the packed field. Lines 83 and 83A of our program illustrate how a literal is continued from one card to another in a data definition. The X in column 72 of the card is a continuation character.

Our variance program is one coded to completion. It lacks only the JCL cards and the actual data. But after studying this program, the student should not find it difficult to write a program which uses the packed decimal instructions.

● **PROBLEM** 9-22

An efficient method of organizing an unordered set of records is by means of a HASH (or SCATTER) FILE. A HASH FILE works as follows: A specified set of arithmetic operations are performed on a data element (also called a key) of a record. The result of this operation is then used as the HASH address for that key. Using this HASH address we can store and locate the record. It should be noted that different records may have the same HASH address. Our program will analyze how well a HASH function (the arithmetic operations on a key) performs for a sample input file.

We will use as our key element the ID number of the record. The arithmetic operation will be to divide the key by 50, and use the remainder as the HASH address. Thus, our addresses will range from 0 to 49 (possible remainders). Finally, we will set up and print the following tables:

1. One containing key elements and HASH addresses

2. Another containing HASH addresses and the number of keys hashed to each address. We will assume that no more than 999 keys will be hashed to one address. So, for example, if the key (ID number) is 81564, then the HASH address is

$$81564 \div 50 = REMAINDER\ 14\ (HASH\ ADDRESS)$$

Table Entries:

1. | KEY | HASH-ADDRESS |
   |-----|--------------|
   | 81564 | 14 |

2. | HASH-ADDRESS | COUNT |
   |--------------|-------|
   | 14 | 1 |

Solution:

```
 1  HASHFILE  START      0
 2            SAVE       (14,12)
 3            BALR       3,0
 4            ST         13,SAVE+4
 5            LA         13,SAVE
*  THE LOADING OF TABLE 2
*  BY INCREMENTING REGISTER 5 BY 1 AND STORING
*  THE RESULT IN CONTIGUOUS FULLWORDS.
 9            LA         6,ASHTABLE
10            L          5,=F'0'       FIRST HASH-ADDRESS OF TABLE
11            L          10,=F'50'     LOOP CONTROL FOR REMAINDERS
12  LOAD      CVD        5,CONVERT
13            PACK       0(2,6),0(2,6)
14            ZAP        0(2,6),CONVERT+6(2)   STORING POSSIBLE
                                              REMAINDERS
15            PACK       2(2,6),2(2,6)

17            LA         6,4(6)        GOTO NEXT WORD OF ASHTABLE
18            A          5,=F'1'       NEXT REMAINDER FOR ASH-
                                       TABLE
19            CR         5,10          DO WE HAVE REMAINDERS 0-
                                       49?
20            BL         LOAD
*PROCESSING THE KEY AFTER READING IT IN
22  GETKEY READ CARD CARDINPA, CRDEOF
23            CLC        CRDIDNO,=C'9999'  END OF FILE CARD
24            BE         PRTHEAD2
25            PACK       WRKKEY,CRDIDNO
26            ZAP        CONVERT,WRKKEY
27            CVB        9,CONVERT     REGISTER 9 HOLDS ID# PRIOR
                                       TO DIVISION.
28            SR         8,8           CLEAR REGISTER 8.

29            D          8,FINDHASH    REMAINDER DETERMINES
                                       HASH ADDRESS
30            CVD        8,CONVERT     CONVERT REMAINDER IN
                                       REGISTER 8 TO DECIMAL
*PRINTING THE ID NUMBER AND ITS HASH-ADDRESS
```

```
32              MVC      PRTKEY,CRDIDNO
33              ZAP      REM,CONVERT    STORE REMAINDER
34              MVC      PRTHASH1,PATT1
35              ED       PRTHASH1,REM
36      PRINTLIN PRTDETL,133
*INCREMENTING THE COUNT FOR AN ADDRESS
38              LA       6,ASHTABLE
39              LR       9,8
40              SR       8,8
41              M        8,POSITION
42              AR       6,9            GOTO REMAINDER IN ASH-
                                        TABLE
43              ZAP      CONVERT,2(2,6) STORE COUNT IN 'CON-
                                        VERT'
44              CVB      7,CONVERT      PLACE COUNT IN REGIS-
                                        TER 7
45              A        7,=F'1'        INCREMENT COUNT
46              CVD      7,CONVERT
47              ZAP      2(2,6),CONVERT+6(2)
48              B        GETKEY
49 PRTHEAD2     PRINTLIN HEADING2,133
*PRINTING HASH-ADDRESS AND THEIR COUNTS
51              LA       6,ASHTABLE
52              LA       5,50
53 PRINTHASH    MVC      PRTHASH2,PATT1
54              ZAP      TEMPHOLD,0(2,6)
55              ED       PRTHASH2,TEMPHOLD
56              MVC      PRTCOUNT,PATT1
57              ZAP      TEMPHOLD,2(2,6)
58              ED       PRTCOUNT,TEMPHOLD
59      PRINTLIN PRTTABLE,133
60              LA       6,4(6)
61              BCT      5,PRINTASH
62 CRDEOF       L        13,SAVE+4
63              RETURN   (14,12)

*DATA DEFINITION FOR CARD INPUT AREA

64 CARDINPA     DS       ϕCL80
65 CRDIDNO      DS       CL5
66              DS       CL75

*DATA FOR KEY AND ITS ADDRESS

67 HEADING1     DS       ϕCL133
68 PRTCC1       DC       C'1'           CARRIAGE CONTROL-RE-
                                        SULTS IN PRINTING ON
                                        NEW PAGE
69              DC       20C' '
70              DC       C'KEY HASH-ADDRESS'
71              DC       92C' '
*DATA DEFINITION FOR PRINT AREA
72 PRTDETL1     DS       ϕCL133
73              DC       C'0'           CARRIAGE CONTROL
74              DC       19C' '
75 PRTKEY       DS       CL5
76              DC       8C' '
77 PRTHASH1     DS       CL4
78              DC       96C' '
*DATA DEFINITION FOR HEADING OF HASH-ADDRESS AND COUNT
```

297

```
79 HEADING2    DS      φCL133
80 PRTCC2      DC      C'1'

81             DC      20C' '
82             DC      C'HASH-ADDRESS COUNT'
83             DC      92C' '
*DATA DEFINITION FOR ASHTABLE

84 PRTTABLE    DS      φCL133
85             DC      C'0'
86             DC      25C' '
87 PRTHASH2    DS      CL4
88             DC      10C' '
89 PRTCOUNT    DS      CL4
90             DC      89C' '
*DATA DEFINITION FOR WORK AREAS
91 SAVE        DS      18F
92 ASHTABLE    DC      50F'0'
93 WRKKEY      DS      PL4
94 POSITION    DS      F'4'
95 CONVERT     DS      D
96 FINDHASH    DC      F'50'           THE DIVISOR
97 REM         DS      PL2
98 TEMPHOLD    DS      PL2
99 PATT1       DC      X'4020212020'
100            END     HASHFILE
```

In general, the format of our program is as follows:
The table to contain the hash-addresses, and the a-
mount of records hashed to each address (count), is defined
as having a length of 50 fullwords. By use of Register 5,
the set of all possible remainders (0-49) are placed in the
first two bytes of the words, each of the words containing
one possible remainder, increasing from one to 50. The
latter two bytes of each word will then store the 'count'
for each corresponding hash-address.

As each address is found, it is printed along with its
key. This constitutes the first table of the program. After printing the key and its address, we then increment the
count of this address in the 'address-count' table (ASH-
TABLE). When no more key elements are found (keys 99999),
the contents of the second table are printed.

It is to be observed that, in the case of 'ASHTABLE',
we manipulate 2 bytes of each word at a time and not the
complete word. We first load all the remainders in the
first two bytes of each word in the 50-word area. This is
accomplished by means of:

```
    13.  PACK  0(2,6),0(2,6)
and 14.  ZAP   0(2,6),CONVERT+6(2)
```

The pack instruction of Line 13 simply converts the contents
of the location addressed by 0(2,6) to packed decimal. The
location addressed by 0(2,6) is a part of ASHTABLE, and
since ASHTABLE is defined as having zeroes, this location
also contains zeroes. The contents of this location are
then replaced by a possible remainder. This is done by the
ZAP instruction of Line 14.

Using the LA instruction of Line 17 we can address the
next word of ASHTABLE.

LA 6,4(6): Coded in such a manner, this instruction adds a displacement of 4 bytes to the present address in Register 6. Hence, if Register 6 contains 1080, the new address after LA 6,4(6) would be 1084. This technique enables us to use just the two instructions of Lines 13 & 14 to load the table. Incidentally, Operand-2 of Line 14 is an example of the combination of implicit and explicit addressing. Since the ZAP instruction proceeds from right to left, this coding was not really necessary, but it indicates how the two types of addresses can be combined. ZAP 0(2,6),CONVERT+6(2) tells the computer to place the last two bytes of the doubleword 'CONVERT' into Operand-1. The following figure indicates 'CONVERT+6(2)'.

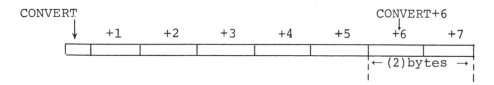

As is always the case, the location of the first byte of a field represents the address of the field in main memory. By 'ADDING' integers to the field (symbol), we can reference a particular byte in the field. Furthermore, if we also specify a length factor, we are able to reference a particular set of bytes in the field. So in the combination of both types of addresses, we have

```
Symbol   Addition  Length Factor
  ↓         ↓           ↓
CONVERT    +6         (2).
```

Note, you should be careful not to make references outside the field, since this will result in error messages from the computer or unintended executions.

Interestingly enough, we can also reference previous bytes in memory by "subtracting" integers from our symbol. For example, ZAP ANY,SYM-6. If 'SYM' were at location 1848, then the contents of location (1848-6) 1842 would be placed in 'ANY'. Once again, you should check to be certain that your intentions are carried out.

Let us now backtrack our steps a little. The PACK instruction of Line 15 prepares the latter two bytes of each of the 50 words for the count. In Lines 38-47, each count is incremented when it is found. The technique involved in the incrementing of the table is one that should be given some thought. If our HASH-address (remainder) is 37 after dividing, we cannot simply increment the count at the 37th position in the table. The count to be incremented will not be at this position, but at the location of the 37th fullword of the table. So in order to get to the 37th count, we must multiply 37 (HASH-address) by 4, the length of a fullword. By adding this result to the address of ASHTABLE, we obtain the desired count. This task is performed by the following instructions:

```
41.  M    8,POSITION
42.  AR   6,9
```

Remember that two registers are needed for a multiplication in fixed point binary arithmetic and that the result is usually small enough to be stored in one (the odd) register.

We will now turn our attention to the LA instruction. The general format of this instruction is:

```
    (a)  LA   R,SYMBOL
or  (b)  LA   R,D(L,B)
```

Let us concentrate on Case (b). Operand-1 is a register, and Operand-2 specifies a displacement D, a length L, and base register B. Coded like this, the instruction loads the address specified by Operand-2 into the register. Now, if we were to code the instruction with the length (L) and base register (B) absent (Line 52), it takes on a somewhat different meaning. Instead of loading an actual address, the instruction loads the number specified as a displacement into the register. For example, Line 52,

```
    LA   5,50
```

The number 50 is loaded into Register 5. Such a method provides us with a simple way of loading numbers into registers. Many programmers prefer this technique since it is easier to code than that of the L (load) instruction.

Our program coded here is a good example of calculations which involve the combination of packed decimal and fixed point binary arithmetic. Incidentally, if you are not clear on the matter, fixed point binary arithmetic is the name given to calculations in which any of the sixteen general purpose registers are used. Many times, the operands involved in these calculations must be registers or fullwords. As our program mostly worked on two bytes at a time, we found it rather difficult to directly increment the elements of ASHTABLE using fixed point binary arithmetic. Thus, like most computer features, binary arithmetic can be restrictive at times.

DEBUGGING

● **PROBLEM** 9-23

Describe the interrelations between the Basic Assembler Language (BAL) Cross Reference Table and its Post Execution Storage Dump.

Solution: Along with other types of information, the Cross Reference Table provides the location of all the symbols used within the program. By finding this address in the Post Execution Storage Dump, the contents of a symbol can be easily found. In the Cross Reference Table, the address of the symbols are coded in hexadecimal (HEX). Not only are these addresses coded in hexadecimal in the Post Executional Storage Dump, but so is all other data found in this Dump. The leftmost column of the Dump contains addresses that consecutively increase by 32 bytes; here it is important to remember the dump is coded in HEX. To the right of

300

the addresses are rows of 32 bytes. These bytes represent
the contents of 32 consecutive bytes in core. The first
byte of each row represents the content of the location
listed in the address column to the left of it.

Let's represent a location in the address column by
the letters 'DCA'. By hexadecimally adding 1 to 'DCA' we
can determine the content of the second byte in this specific row.

For example

```
ADDRESS COLUMN            CORE  CONTENT
      ↓                         ↓
    DCA            90 ECDOOC . . . 02185A  CO
                    ↓                        ↓
                  1st byte              32nd byte
                  of row                of row
```

so

DCA	CONTAINS	90
DCA+1	CONTAINS	EC
DCA+2	CONTAINS	DO
DCA+30	CONTAINS	5A

and

DCA+31	CONTAINS	CO

Thus, by adding the required amount, the contents of any
byte in the row can be determined. It should be noted again
that the addition is a hexadecimal one.

In summation, we can determine the contents of a symbol
by obtaining its address and length from the Cross Reference
Table and then locating the content of this symbol in the
Post Execution Storage Dump. When the address is found in
the Dump, the number of bytes to be observed is dictated by
the length of the symbol.

It should be noted that in the Dump the addresses are
generally denoted by six hexadecimal digits, but on most
occasions we need only concern ourselves with the last
three.

Also, to the right of the dump we usually find a standard (English) translation of each hexadecimal row of the
Dump. This translation confirms the contents of the Dump
and makes it more comprehensible.

● PROBLEM 9-24

You have just received a Basic Assembler Language program
you ran. As you turn to the execution page to check the
printout, you find that every fourth line of the program
reads, for example, PSW=...00004F17B4C4. What is the PSW
and what information does it provide? In addition, what
information is provided in the three lines following the
PSW statement?

Solution: PSW is a mnemonic that stands for Program Status
Word. The PSW has a length of 64 bits (8 bytes), and in

301

general, contains the value of the location counter, system
protection information, and program interrupt status. The
system protection information protects the operating system
(data needed by the computer) from errors that could be de-
trimental to the system. This feature is an imperative one,
since quite often programmers unknowingly make critical
system errors. The interrupt status indicates the condition of the Central Processing Unit (CPU) at the time of
the interruption. When an interruption occurs, the processor (CPU) places specific interrupt information in the PSW.
In a simplified manner, we can say that when an interrupt
occurs, the PSW stores the address of the next instruction
to be executed; we may say the PSW 'looks-ahead'. The address of this instruction is indicated by the location
counter portion of PSW. Thus, it is this part of the PSW
that the beginning assembler language programmer should
concern himself with.

When an interrupt occurs, starting with the third byte
of the 8-bytes PSW, the contents of the PSW are printed on
the execution page of the program. It is printed in hexadecimal notation. To find the instruction about to be executed when the interrupt occured, the programmer need only
concern himself with the rightmost four digits of the PSW.
Using these digits, he can find the instruction in the body
of the program. As this is the instruction that was to be
executed when the interruption occured, it is the instruction immediately preceding it that caused the problem. By
closely inspecting this instruction, the cause of the interrupt can be found.

The three lines following the PSW statement display
the contents of the system's registers at the time of interruption. The first two lines contain the 16 general purpose
registers; this is indicated by the GPR (GPR 0-7; GPR 8-F)
statement at the beginning of the line. The third line
holds the Floating Point Registers (FPR).

It should be noted that each time an interrupt occurs,
the system prints the contents of the PSW. The program
will be terminated if the number of allowed program interruptions is exceeded.

● **PROBLEM** 9-25

You have just received the output from one of your Basic
Assembly Language (BAL) programs, but to your dismay, the
output is not what you had hoped for. To debug this program,
your first reaction is to check the contents of your storage
locations. What procedures would you follow in this process
of debugging?

Solution: It is the default of the computer's operating
system to provide a Cross Reference Table and a P/P Storage
Dump with each program listing. Among other things, the
Cross Reference Table yields the names of all variables and
labels used in the program and their corresponding locations
in memory. The variables and labels of this table are generally displayed in alphabetical order. Thus, finding any
member of this table is comparable to obtaining a word from
the page of a dictionary. When this variable is found the

table provides us with the amount of space it occupies in memory (LEN), where it is defined in the listing (DEFN), where it is referenced in the listing, and most important, the location of the variable in memory (value). The order of the information in the table will not necessarily be as stated above.

For our present purpose all we need to concern ourselves with is the value (address) that the table indicates for the symbol. Going to the P/P Storage Dump, we match our symbol value with the address we are searching for and also the contents of this address. By the use of this procedure we are able to check the contents of any symbol in our program.

There are two points to be noted:

1. Depending on the computer, the Cross Reference Table will probably produce more information than presented here.

2. Some computers will refer to the P/P Store Dump by a slightly different name, for example, Post Execution Storage Dump.

● **PROBLEM** 9-26

What are the rules of Assembler Language? Explain them in detail with an illustrative example.

Solution: A programming language is defined by a set of rules. Almost every commercial computer has its own particular assembly language. The basic unit of an assembly language program is a line of code. The general rules for writing a mnemonic assembler language for the basic computer are given below.

Rules of the language - each line of an assembly language program is arranged in three fields. The fields specify the following information.

1. The label field may be empty or it may specify a symbolic address.

2. The instruction field specifies a machine instruction or a pseudo-instruction.

3. The comment field may be empty or it may include a comment.

In the label field a symbolic address consists of one, two, or three, but not more than four alphanumeric characters. The first character must be a letter; the next two may be letters or numerals. A symbolic address in the label field is terminated by a comma so it will be recognized by the assembler as a label.

The instruction field in an assembly language program specifies one of the following items.

1. A memory-reference instruction (MRI).

2. A register-reference or input-output instruction (non-MRI).

3. A pseudo-instruction with or without an operand.

A memory-reference instruction occupies two or three symbols separated by spaces. The first must be a three-letter symbol defining an MRI operation. The second is a symbolic address. The third symbol, which may or may not be present, is the letter I, depending on direct or indirect address instruction situation.

A non-MRI is defined as an instruction that does not have an address part. A non-MRI is recognized in the instruction field of the program by one three-letter symbol.

A pseudo-instruction is not a machine instruction but rather an instruction to the assembler giving information about some phase of the translation.

The following is an illustration of the symbols that may be placed in the instruction field of program.

```
CMA         non MRI
ADD  OPR    direct address MRI
AND  PTR I  indirect address MRI
ORG         pseudo instruction
```

A memory reference instruction, such as ADD, must be followed by a symbolic address. The letter I may or may not be present. A symbolic address in the instruction field specifies the memory location of an operand. This location must be defined somewhere in the program by appearing again as a label in the first column; it is absolutely necessary that each symbolic address that is mentioned in the instruction field must occur again in the label field.

The third field in a program is reserved for comments. It must be preceeded by a slash for the assembler to recognize the beginning of a comment field.

Example 1

```
        ORG 100     /ORIGIN OF PROGRAM IN LOCATION 100.
        LDA SUB     /LOAD SUBTRAHEND TO AC (MRI)
        CMA         /COMPLEMENT AC. (NON MRI)
        INC         /INCREMENT AC.  (NON MRI)
        ADD MIN     /ADD MINUEND TO AC  (MRI)
        STA DIFF    /STORE DIFF   (MRI)
        HLT         /END OF INSTRUCTIONS
MIN,    DEC 50      /MINUED.  MIN IS LABEL
SUB,    DEC -10     /SUBTRAHEND
DIFF,   HEX 0       /DIFFERENCE STORED HERE
        END         /END OF SYMBOLIC PROGRAM
```

● **PROBLEM** 9-27

What is a One-to-One Assembler?

Solution: One to One Assembler: - The most direct approach to interpreting each line of an assembler language program is as one machine word during assembly. The assembler can be a one pass or two pass assembler. Often, when we hear the term one-to-one, the thought of correspondence comes to mind, in particular, one-to-one correspondence. This is also the case with the One-to-One Assembler; it makes a one-to-one correspondence. This correspondence stems from the fact that a One-to-One assembler translates each line of an assembler language program into one machine word during assembly. The translation is done on a sequential basis; an instruction is "mapped" into a machine word as it is encountered, with the assembler making one or two passes over each instruction, depending on its type. The following is an example of how a One-to-One Assembler may do its translation.

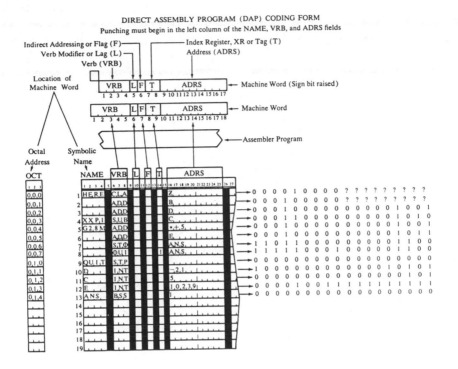

DIRECT ASSEMBLY PROGRAM (DAP) CODING FORM
Punching must begin in the left column of the NAME, VRB, and ADRS fields

The One-to-One Assembler is an example of one of the simplest assemblers. Actually, it forms the foundations on which most practical assemblers are built. For the assembler to translate assembly language into machine code the following rules must be observed:

For naming locations:
1. No name may exceed four characters in length.
2. The first character must be alphabetic, but the remaining ones, if any, may be alphabetic or numeric in any desired mixture. Any other character, such as a comma, is illegal. No character of the name may be a blank.
3. No two locations may be given the same name.
4. No name may be written in address fields unless it is also written exactly once in the NAME field.
5. The punching of all names in the NAME field must begin in Column 1.
6. The NAME field may be left blank, if desired.
7. If Column 1 is blank, then the leftmost non-blank character is taken to be the start of the command field.

In general, the rules pertaining to a One-to-One Assembler are quite similar to those of most assemblers. This is not surprising since the One-to-One Assembler forms the basis for most assemblers.

D.E.C. PDP-8 Assembler

Explain the general meaning of assembler and its basic functions.

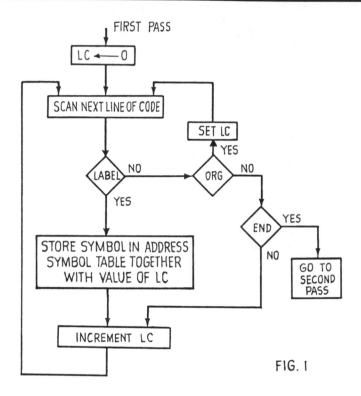

FIRST PASS

LC ←— 0

SCAN NEXT LINE OF CODE

SET LC

LABEL — NO — ORG — NO

YES (ORG) — YES (SET LC)

YES (LABEL)

END — YES — GO TO SECOND PASS

NO

STORE SYMBOL IN ADDRESS
SYMBOL TABLE TOGETHER
WITH VALUE OF LC

INCREMENT LC

FIG. I

Solution: An assembler is a program that accepts a symbolic
language and produces its binary machine language equivalent. The input symbolic program is called the source program and the resulting binary program is called the object
program. The assembler is a program that operates on character strings and produces an equivalent binary interpretation. An assembler must know the arrangment of the characters in memory so it can distinguish between symbols and
lines.
    The symbolic program constitutes the input data for
the assembler.
    Now we shall see how a two pass assembler translates
the symbolic program of the previous problem.
    First Pass: A two pass assembler scans the entire sym-
bolic program twice. During the first pass, it generates a
table that correlates all user defined address symbols with
their binary equivalent value. The binary translation of
the program is done during the second pass. In order to
keep track of the location of instructions, the assembler
uses a memory word called location counter (LC). The ORG
pseudo instruction initializes the LC to the value of the
first location; in case ORG is missing LC is set to 0

initially. The tasks performed by the assembler during the first pass are described in the flow chart of Fig. 1.

LC is initially set to 0. A line of symbolic code is scanned to see if it has a label (by presence of comma). If the line of code has no label, the assembler checks in the instruction field. If it contains ORG, it sets LC to the number followed by ORG. If it is END pseudo instruction, the assembler terminates the first pass and goes to the second pass. If the line of code has a label, it is stored in the address symbol table together with its binary equivalent number specified by LC.

Label	LC
MIN	100
SUB	107
DIFF	108

Fig. 2

On the first pass, the assembler encounters ORG in the example program (previous problem) and sets the LC to 100. It then scans the next line. If it has neither label nor END, LC is incremented by 1 to 101 & proceeds until HLT, when LC has value of 105. Now LC is incremented by 1 to 106. Upon scanning, it finds label MIN, then SUB and DIFF. The address symbol table is shown in Fig. 2. On encountering the last instruction, END, the assembler goes to second pass.

Second Pass: - Machine instructions are translated during the second pass by means of table-lookup procedures. A table lookup procedure is a search of table entries to determine whether a specific item matches one of the items stored in the table. The assembler uses four tables. 1) Pseudo-instruction table. 2) MRI table. 3) Non-MRI table. 4) Address-symbol table. The way the assembler proceeds in the second pass is described in the flow chart of Fig. 3.

LC is initially set to 0. Labels are neglected during the second pass, so the assembler goes immediately to the instruction field. It first checks the pseudo-instruction table. For a match with ORG, the assembler sets LC to numbers followed by ORG. A match with END terminates the translation process. An operand pseudo instruction causes a conversion of the operand into binary. This operand(e.g. DEC 50 from the previous problem)converted into its binary value is placed in the memory location specified by contents of LC i.e. at location 106. The LC is incremented by 1 and the assembler continues to analyze the next line of code.

If the symbol encountered is not a pseudo-instruction, the assembler refers to the MRI table. If the symbol is not found in this table, the assembler refers to the non-MRI table e.g. in a scan of the second line, the symbol is CMA with LC=101. The assembler stores the bit code of CMA

into a memory location specified by LC i.e. at place 101.
Again LC is incremented by 1 and a new line is analyzed.

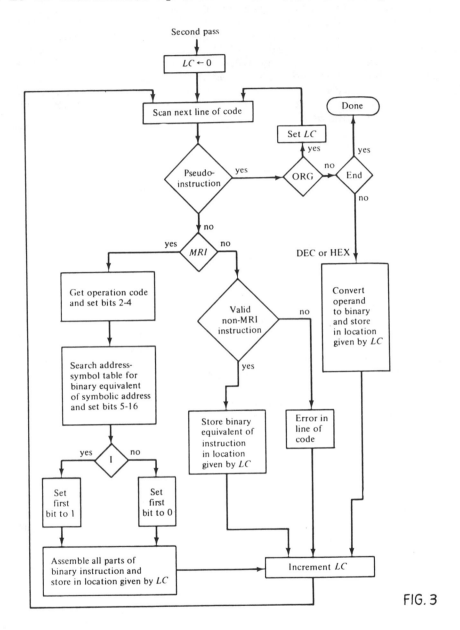

FIG. 3

When a symbol is found in the MRI table, the assembler extracts its equivalent code and inserts it in, say, bits 2-4 of the memory location specified by LC. The corresponding second symbol is an address. This is converted to binary by searching the address symbol table. The first bit of instruction is set to 0 or 1, depending on whether the letter I is absent or present. For example the first line from the previous problem is LDA SUB. LDA is an MRI and its equivalent 3 bit code, say, 010 is set in bit position 2-4, SUB is searched in the address symbol table and is found to be at location 107. I is not present, therefore,

LDA SUB has the HEX code 2107; its equivalent binary is stored in memory location specified by LC=100. Therefore memory location 100 contains 2107. One important task of an assembler is to check for possible errors in the symbolic program.

This was just the basics of how an assembler performs translation. A practical assembler is much more complicated.

● **PROBLEM** 9-29

The computer is a PDP-8. The program counter (PC) is at 400. The contents of the various memory locations are as follows:

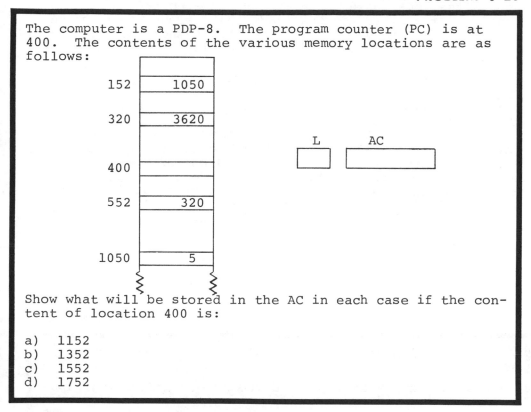

Show what will be stored in the AC in each case if the content of location 400 is:

a) 1152
b) 1352
c) 1552
d) 1752

Solution: a) The instruction is 1152. This instruction is in octal. Writing it out in binary, we get

001 001 101 010.

The first bit on the left hand side is bit #0. The rightmost bit is bit #11. Bit #4 is 0. This means the address is on Page 0. Hence, the last 7 bits give the address =152. Bit #5 is also 0. This means that it is direct addressing. Hence, location 152 contains the operand. Thus, the AC gets the value of location 152, which is 1050.

b) The instruction is 1352, in octal. Hence, in binary the instruction is: 001 011 101 010. Bit #4 is 1. This means that the address is on the same page as the instruction. But, the instruction is in location 400, i.e., on Page 2. Hence, the address is also on Page 2.

Hence, the address is given by the first five bits of the PC concatenated with the last seven bits of the instruction. The program counter contains 0400, i.e.,

000 100 000 000.

And, the instruction is: 001 011 101010. Hence, the address is 00010 1101 010, i.e., 0552. Now, the contents of
location 552 are 320. Therefore 320 gets stored in the AC.
     c) The instruction 1552 means: 001 101 101 010. Bit
#4 is 0, therefore address is on Page 0. Thus, the ad-
dress is: 00000 1101 010
       = 000 001 101 010
       = 0 152
And, the Bit #3 is 1. This means it is Indirect Addressing.
Hence, the location 0152 on Page 0 contains not the operand
itself, but another address where the operand can be found.
    The content 1050 of location 152 is therefore an add-
ress. And hence, the content of location 1050, viz., 5 is
the operand which goes to the AC.
    d) The instruction is 1752, i.e., 001 111 101 010.
The #4 bit is 1. Therefore it indicates the same page as
the instruction at 400, i.e., at 000 100 000 000. Hence,
the address is: 00010 1101 010
        = 000 101 101 010 = 0552.
Now, the #3 bit is 1. Therefore it means indirect addressing, and the content of 552 is an address of the operand. The content of 552 is: 320. Hence, 320 is the
address of the operand. Now, the content of 320 is 3620.
Hence, 3620 is the operand which goes to the AC.
    Hence the AC contains the following:

    a)   1050
    b)   320
    c)   5
    d)   3620.

● **PROBLEM** 9-30

As you know 9 bits can address 512 words. Show how on a
PDP-8 machine with 4096_{10} words in memory, any word can be
addressed using 9 bits (extend the memory addressing capabilities).

Solution: When there were 512_{10} words in memory, 9 bits
were required to address any word location in the memory.
Hence the Instruction Counter register (IC) and Memory
Address Register (MAR) were to store 9 bits. The word
length we want is 12 bits long therefore, the Memory Buffer
Register (MBR) is 12 bits long. The scheme was as follows:

```
0     2 3                        11
┌──────┬───────────────────────────┐
│OP-CODE│                          │
│BITS   │ 9-ADDRESS BITS           │
└──────┴───────────────────────────┘
```

    When a word had an instruction in it, the first three
bits specified operation code and the remaining 9 bits were
sufficient. Now as there are 4096 words IC and MAR have to
be of 12 bits. The MBR is of 12 bits as word length is 12
bits. Direct addressing of any word in the 4096 words will
use a total 12 bits of word and no room (bits) is left for
the OP-CODE.
    The scheme to extend the memory addressing capabilities

is that the 4096_{10} words memory is divided into pages. Each page has 128_{10} (200_8) words. This is a logical division and not a physical division of memory as shown in Fig. 1.

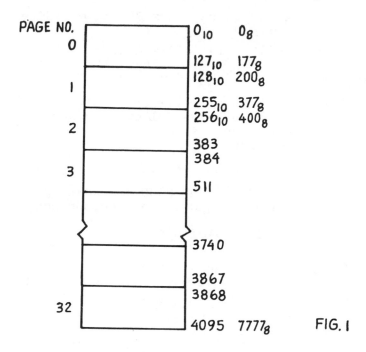

FIG. 1

As each page has 128_{10} words, 7 bits can address any word on the same page, but as there are 32 pages we need 5 bits to address a page.

5 bits for page + 7 bits for words on page = 12 bits

and we end up still with the same problem of having only a total of 12 bits where the first 3 bits are for the OP-CODE and only 9 bits for address.

To solve this, two bits, bit 3 and bit 4 are used as I bit and P bit respectively - as illustrated in Fig. 2.

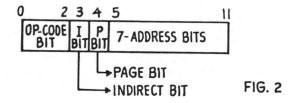

FIG. 2

When the P bit is 1, the word is on the current page, where the instruction was, and the next address is found by concatenating the 7 address bits and the first five bits of the instruction counter.

For example, if we are on page 2 with the IC pointing to 0410_8, the instruction at this location is 1352:

1352 = 001 011 101 010.

311

The first three bits 001 specify the ADD instruction to the accumulator; the address of the operand is found by observing bits. Bit 4=1 i.e. P bit is 1, hence the operand is on the current page and its address is:

first 5 bits IC concatenate 7 bits of address
0410_8 = 000 100 001 000

Address = 00010 1 101 010 = 0552_8

and 552_8 is the word which is on page 2.

If P bit=0, the page referred is always Page 0 and the address is formed by 5 zeros followed by a 7 bit address in MBR. As an example, assume we are in page 2 with IC pointing to 0410_8. Now suppose the instruction at this location was 1152_8 i.e. 1152_8 = 001 001 101 010. Since P bit = 0, it references page 0, the OP-CODE 001 part specifies the ADD instruction and the address of the operand is

000 001 101 010 = 0152_8

where this a word on page 0.

By doing the above we have extended our addressing capabilities to address 256_{10} words, 128 word on page 0 + 128 words on any current page. Yet the memory has 4096 words. A mechanism to address from one page to another is established using bit 3 as an indirect bit.

When I=0 it is Direct address and the address is obtained, depending on the P bit and the 7-address bits.

When I=1 it is Indirect address, i.e. the address specified by the address bit is not the address of the operand but the contents of the given address (location) are the address of the operand. For example, suppose data 25_{10} is stored in location 100_{10} and 100_{10} is stored at 15_{10}. Then indirect addressing will be

ADD I 15

I being present, data at location 15 i.e. 100 is not to be added to accumulator; rather, the data of 100 has to be used as an address. At this address data=25 is stored; this is to be added to accumulator.

Now in the PDP-8 when I bit = 1 there are two conditions of the P bit. If I=1, P=0 then the page is zero page.

0	2 3 6 5		11
OP CODE	I 1	P 0	7- ADDRESS BIT

On page zero, go to the location specified by 7-address bits. The contents of this location, a 12 bit word, is the address of the operand.

If I=1, P=1 then the page is the current page as given

312

by instruction counter IC. Suppose we are on page 2 where the IC is pointing to 0410_8 brought in the MBR instruction 1752_8

$1752_8 = 001\ 111\ 101\ 010$

OP-CODE=001 is the ADD instruction.
I bit = 1, P bit = 1

As in indirect addressing, the location specified by address bits has the address of the operand we need to find the location specified.

As P=1 the address of the location = first 5 bits of IC concatenated with 7 address bits = $00010\ 1\ 101\ 010 = 0552_8$.

Now location 0552_8 has the full 12 bit address of operand.

These 12 bits can be the location of any of the 4096 words in memory. Thus by using the concept of I bit and P bit the addressing capability of memory is increased.

● **PROBLEM** 9-31

Write a program in the PDP-8 computer Assembler Language to find the factorial of numbers. The program should use Subroutine jumps. The numbers are stored in an array starting at location 300_8. The results, i.e., the values of the factorials are to be stored in another array starting at location 200_8. The end of the numbers array is indicated by the occurrence of a negative number. The program is to start at location 400_8.

Solution: The mathematical background for this problem is as follows:

Factorial 0 = 0! = 1
Factorial 1 = 1! = 1
Factorial 5 = 5! = 5×4×3×2×1 (= 120).
Factorial n = n! = n×(n-1)×(n-2)×...×3×2×1.

The strategy to be used for solving this problem is as follows:

A number will be obtained first from the array. It will be tested to see if it is negative. If it is indeed negative, then it will indicate an end of the array, and the program will stop.

Next, the number will be tested to see if it is equal to zero. If it is indeed zero, then the value of its factorial will immediately be entered in the results-array as equal to one.

After this, the number will be tested to see if it is equal to 1. If it is indeed equal to 1 then the value of its factorial will be written down as 1 also.

If the number was neither negative, nor zero nor equal to one, then it means that it is a positive number n (≥ 2). In this case we jump to a subroutine which does some calculations and returns a value of n!

313

Of course, the way the program is written for this example, it will be seen that the factorial subroutine itself calls a multiplication subroutine to do the various multiplications required to be done in obtaining the value of n!

The program is written as follows. It should be noted that the main program starts at location 400_8, a factorial subroutine starts at location 440_8 and a multiplication subroutine starts at location 450_8. Each instruction is to be punched on one card, starting at column 2. A comment is indicated by a slash (/). Everything on the card following a / is regarded as a comment.

```
*400              /INDICATES TO THE COMPUTER THE STARTING
                   LOCATION OF THE PROGRAM
LOOP1,ISZ ARYADR  /LOOP1 IS A LABEL TO THIS STATEMENT.
                   ARYADR IS THE NAME OF A LOCATION WHICH
                   STORES A VALUE (277₈), i.e., THE STARTING
                   ADDRESS (LESS 1) OF THE NUMBER-ARRAY.
                   ISZ INCREMENTS THE CONTENT OF 277₈ BY 1
                   TO 300₈ AT THE START.
ISZ RESADR        /RESADR IS THE NAME OF A LOCATION WHERE
                   AN ADDRESS IS STORED.  THIS ADDRESS IN
                   TURN IS THE LOCATION WHERE THE RESULT OF
                   A FACTORIAL COMPUTATION IS TO BE STORED
CLA CLL           /INITIALLY CLEAR THE AC AND THE LINK L
DCA I RESADR      /CLEAR THE CONTENT OF RESADR.  NOTE THAT
                   INDIRECT ADDRESSING IS TO BE USED BECAUSE
                   THE LOCATION OF THIS STATEMENT IS 403₈,
                   i.e., ON PAGE 2.  BUT THE LOCATION OF
                   RESADR IS ON A DIFFERENT PAGE.  RESADR IS
                   IN LOCATION 200₈ WHICH IS ON PAGE 1.
TAD I ARYADR      /LOAD THE NUMBER INTO THE AC
SPA               /CHECK IF THE NUMBER IS ≥0.  SKIP IF IT IS.
HLT               /HALT IF THE NUMBER IS NOT ≥0
SNA               /SKIP IF THE AC CONTENT IS NOT 0.
JMP LOOP2         /THE PROGRAM COMES TO THIS STEP IF THE AC IS
                   0.  THEN IT JUMPS TO LOOP 2.
DCA A             /THE NUMBER IS STORED IN LOCATION A.  AS A IS
                   ON THE SAME PAGE DIRECT ADDRESSING CAN BE
                   USED RATHER THAN INDIRECT ADDRESSING REQUIRED
                   FOR ARYADR.  DIRECT ADDRESSING SAVES TIME.
TAD A             /THE NUMBER IS AGAIN LOADED INTO THE AC.
CMA IAC           /THE TWO'S COMPLEMENT OF THE NUMBER IS FORMED.
IAC               /THE TWO'S COMPLEMENT IS INCREMENTED BY 1.
SNA               /CHECK IF THE INCREMENTATION RESULTS IN A ZERO.
                   THIS WOULD HAPPEN IF THE NUMBER WAS ORIGINALLY
                   1.
JMP LOOP2         /JUMP TO LOOP 2 IF THE VALUE IS ZERO.
DCA B             /IF THE NUMBER ISN'T NEGATIVE, OR 0 OR 1 THEN
                   STORE THE NEGATIVE OF THE NUMBER INTO B.
JMS FCTRL         /GO TO THE SUBROUTINE TO CALCULATE FACTORIALS.
TAD A             /LOAD THE AC WITH THE FACTORIAL OF THE NUMBER
                   FROM A.
DCA I RESADR      /STORE THE VALUE OF THE FACTORIAL INTO RESADR.
JMP LOOP1         /GO BACK TO LOOP1 TO FETCH A NEW NUMBER.
LOOP2,IAC         /COMES TO THIS STEP IF THE NUMBER IS 0 OR 1.
```

```
                       THE AC IS 0.  THEREFORE IAC MAKES AC=1.
DCA I RESADR          /THE VALUE 1 GETS STORED IN RESADR IN THIS
                       CASE.
JMP LOOP1             /GO BACK TO LOOP 1 TO FETCH A NEW NUMBER.
*430                  /INDICATES START OF A NEW MEMORY BLOCK TO BE
                       USED BY THE PROGRAM.
ARYADR,277            /SHOWS THAT ARYADR LOCATED IN 430_8 CONTAINS A
                       VALUE 277_8.
RESADR,177            /RESADR, LOCATED IN 431_8 CONTAINS 177_8.
A, 0                  /A, IN LOCATION 432_8 CONTAINS 0
B, 0                  /B HAS 0.
C, 0                  /C HAS 0.
*440                  /START OF A NEW BLOCK.
FCTRL, 0              /FIRST LOCATION OF THE SUBROUTINE FCTRL.  THIS
                       LOCATION HAS A VALUE 0.  WHEN THE SUBROUTINE
                       WILL BE CALLED, THE RETURN ADDRESS WILL BE
                       STORED IN THIS LOCATION.
LOOP3,TAD B           /THE NEGATIVE OF THE NUMBER IS LOADED INTO THE
                       AC FROM B.
DCA C                 /THE SAME VALUE IS STORED IN C.
JMS MLTPLY            /GO TO A SUBROUTINE TO MULTIPLY 2 NUMBERS.
ISZ B                 /INCREMENT B AND CHECK IF RESULT IS ZERO.
JMP LOOP3             /REPEAT LOOP 3 IF B IS NOT ZERO.
JMP I FCTRL           /IF B IS ZERO, PROGRAM COMES TO THIS STEP,
                       WHICH INDICATES THAT THE VALUE OF THE FACTORIAL
                       IS READY.  THEREFORE A JUMP IS PERFORMED TO THE
                       CALLING PROGRAM VIA THE ADDRESS STORED IN LO-
                       CATION CALLED FCTRL.
*450                  /START OF A NEW MEMORY BLOCK.
MLTPLY, 0             /FIRST LOCATION IN THE SUBROUTINE MLTPLY.
LOOP4, TAD A          /ADD THE NUMBER FROM A INTO AC.
ISZ C                 /INCREMENT C AND CHECK IF IT IS ZERO.
JMP LOOP4             /IF C IS NOT ZERO THEN GO BACK TO LOOP 4 TO
                       ADD A ONCE AGAIN TO AC.
DCA A                 /WHEN C IS ZERO, IT SIGNIFIES THAT THE MULTI-
                       PLICATION IS OVER.  AND THEREFORE STORE THE
                       CONTENTS OF AC INTO A.

JMP I MLTPLY          /RETURN TO THE CALLING FCTRL ROUTINE, VIA THE
                       ADDRESS STORED IN MLTPLY.
*300                  /START OF A NEW BLOCK.
+6                    /A NUMBER +6, STORED IN LOCATION 300_8.  THIS
                       IS THE FIRST NUMBER IN THE NUMBERS-ARRAY.
0                     /ANOTHER NUMBER IN THE NUMBERS-ARRAY.
1                     /ANOTHER NUMBER IN THE NUMBERS-ARRAY.
-2                    /A NEGATIVE NUMBER IN THE NUMBERS-ARRAY TO
                       INDICATE THE END OF THE NUMBERS-ARRAY.
$                     /INDICATES END OF PROGRAM.
```

● **PROBLEM** 9-32

Explain what is Computer-assisted numerical machine control.
Explain the advantages, and describe how a program may be
written.

Solution: Numerical machine control is the automatic contol of machines by numerical data, on punched cards or tapes. The advantage of this method is that when an item is to be produced, all the minute details and operations are planned out in the office. Then the cards or tapes are punched out, and from the moment the tape is taken to the shop floor and installed in the machine, production starts as pre-planned. Thus, management flexibility, and efficiency are both achieved.

Computers come in to assist when the problems become too complex to be handled manually. For example, when the tools have to move along continuous paths which form arcs of circles, parabolas, etc., the paths have to be calculated, given only a few individual points. The computer also has a number of built-in functions and subroutines, so that complicated operations just have to be called by their name, and the computer carries out all the details. In fact, some computer languages have been developed (e.g., APT) which use English-like words and abbreviations to write programs to carry out different machining operations.

For simpler position control machining, the program must specify the starting and ending positions of various tools, the spindles to be used, the speeds and feed rates, various auxiliary functions such as whether coolant fluid should be on, etc. For example, the Avery Machine Tool Company programming system uses commands such as:

Command	Description
G80	CANCEL ALL PREVIOUS INSTRUCTIONS.
G81	MOVES SPINDLE DOWN FOR DRILLING AND THEN RAISES UP AGAIN.
G82	DRILLS AS ABOVE, BUT DWELLS FOR A WHILE BEFORE RAISING UP.
G84	SPINDLE DESCENDS, DOES A TAPPING OPERATION, RISES UP AGAIN.
F	SPECIFIES SPINDLE FEED RATE, e.g., F02 (IT COULD, e.g., MEAN 3"/MIN.).
S	SPECIFIES SPINDLE SPEED, e.g., S07 (IT COULD, e.g., MEAN 300 RPM).
T	SPINDLE SELECTION, e.g., T01 (i.e., SPINDLE NO. 1 TO BE OPERATIVE).
X...	MOVE IN THE DIRECTION OF X-AXIS BY AMOUNT SPECIFIED.
Y...	MOVE IN THE DIRECTION OF Y-AXIS BY AMOUNT SPECIFIED.
Z...	MOVE IN THE DIRECTION OF Z-AXIS BY AMOUNT SPECIFIED.
R...	MOVE IN THE DIRECTION OF THE Z-AXIS BY THE AMOUNT SPECIFIED, BUT AT A RAPID TRAVERSING RATE. THE REST OF THE DISTANCE (Z-R) IS TO BE TRAVERSED AT THE RATE SPECIFIED BY F.
M06	COOLANT ON.
M30	END OF TAPE REWIND TAPE TO STARTING POINT.
ETC.	ETC.

The above commands can be used to write out programs for the machining of various workpieces.

Write a program to drill the 3 holes in the workpiece shown, and tap the hole #3 with a 3/4"-10 TAP, using a programmable turret drilling machine.

Assume that the spindle speeds available are: S01, S02 and S03, viz., 250, 375 and 440 rpm., and the spindle feed rates available are F01, F02 and F03, viz., 2", 1" and 1/2" per min., resp. The tools are mounted as follows: spindle T01 carries a 1" drill, T02 carries a 41/64" drill, T03 carries a 3/4"-10 TAP, and T04 carries a 1/4" drill. The rest position of the spindles has a Z-offset of 2", but assume that X and Y offsets are zero.

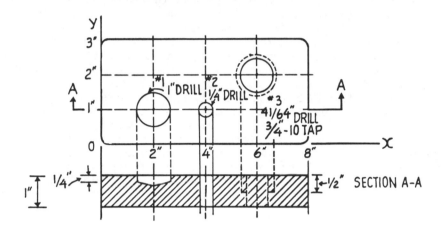

Solution: Zero offsets for X and Y mean that the tools are at the origin 0 at the start. A Z-offset of 2" means that the tools are 2" above the workpiece in their idle positions.

From the data given, obviously, hole #1 requires spindle T01 carrying the 1" drill. We select a slower speed for this large hole, say S02, i.e., 375 rpm. The feed rate is taken as F02, i.e., 1" per min.

The hole #2 requires spindle T04 carrying a 1/4" drill. The speed can be faster, say, S03, i.e., 440 rpm., and the spindle feed rate can be F01, i.e., 2".

The hole #3 requires spindle T02 first, and then spindle T03 for the tap. While tapping, we will also require a coolant fluid feature, which is obtained by specifying M06.

The program for the machining of the workpiece can be written as follows:

OP.NO.	'G'	'X'	'Y'	'R'	'Z'	Auxiliaries
N001	G80	X02000	Y01000			S02 F02 T01
	G82			R01750	Z02250	
N002	G80	X04000	Y01000			S01 F03 T04
	G81			R01750	Z03500	
N003	G80	X06000	Y02000			S02 F04 T02
	G81			R01750	Z03500	
N004	G80	X06000	Y02000			S03 F03 T03 M06
	G84			R01750	Z02500	
	G80	X00000	Y00000			M30

In step No. 001, the G80 clears any stray instructions lying about in the storage. The spindle T01, holding a 1" drill moves to the X and Y coordinates. The G82 command makes the spindle rotate at the specified speed S and the spindle descends at a rapid rate by 1-75", so that it is still 1/4" above the workpiece. The spindle then descends at a programmed feed rate F02, for a distance of 1/2" (Z-R = 2.25 - 1.75 = 0.5").

In operation #N002, we perform a G80, change the spindle to T04, move to the X and Y specified, and lower the spindle as specified by R and Z. We perform a G81 drilling operation which differs from the G82 in that in G81 the spindle is withdrawn immediately rather than dwelling at the end of the drilling as in G82.

In N003, we again do a drilling operation, but by using the T02 spindle which carries a 41/64" drill. Note that as Z = 3.5", the drill goes completely through the 1" thick workpiece and comes out 0.5" on the other side.

In N004 we keep X and Y same, and so, perform a tapping operation using spindle T03. Note that the M06 starts the coolant during the tapping operation.

Finally, the G80 in the last step clears all previous commands, and moves the spindle to the edge of the workpiece so as to facilitate removal of the workpiece.

The M30 command signifies an end of the tape on which the program will be punched, and is also a command to the tape reader on which the tape will be later mounted, to rewind the tape to the starting position so that it is ready to be re-run for the machining of the next workpiece.

CHAPTER 10

BASIC

BASIC CONCEPTS

● **PROBLEM** 10-1

Explain briefly the background and applications of BASIC computer language.

<u>Solution</u>: BASIC (Beginner's All-purpose Symbolic Instruction Code).

In the early 1960's, a project was undertaken at Dartmouth College to make the computer more accessible and easy to use by both students and faculty. One of the objectives was to develop a language that could be quickly learned but powerful enough to be used in solving most small to medium scale problems in any discipline. The result of this effort was BASIC, and it more than met its objective.

Since BASIC provides the opportunity for someone with little or no previous computer experience to quickly begin writing programs and using the computer, it is commonly available on time sharing systems.

BASIC's statements and operands are, probably, the closest to actual English language and algebra respectively and the easiest to comprehend, which ensures its huge popularity in almost every field of science, business, and engineering.

● **PROBLEM** 10-2

Give some examples of valid and invalid variable names in BASIC. Explain briefly the differences.

<u>Solution</u>: Variable names in BASIC can be represented by a single letter of the alphabet, or a single letter followed by a single digit. For example:

VALID	INVALID
C	5N (starts with a digit)
F	BG4 (too many letters)
K1	M28 (too many digits)
L9	

319

List the arithmetic operators used in BASIC and state their priorities of execution in a statement. Also give a list and briefly explain the functions of the most popular statements.

Solution: Arithmetic operations in BASIC are represented by the following symbols:

$$+ \quad - \quad \text{ADDITION}$$
$$- \quad - \quad \text{SUBTRACTION AND NEGATION}$$
$$* \quad - \quad \text{MULTIPLICATION}$$
$$/ \quad - \quad \text{DIVISION}$$
$$** \text{ or } \uparrow \quad - \quad \text{EXPONENTIATION}$$

Exponentiation has the highest priority of execution; multiplication and division are executed next; addition and subtraction are done last. If 2 or more equally "powerful" operators are present in the statement, their execution goes from left to right.

Operations in parenthesis are always done first.
The most popular BASIC statements are:

LET variable = expression
(The arithmetic assignment statement)
INPUT variable list
(Statement for data entry from terminal into a program during the execution phase)
READ variable, variable, etc.
(Statement for data entry from the DATA statement)
DATA constant, constant, etc.
(Information supplier statement for READ statement)
PRINT variable, constant, "junk", etc.
(Primary output statement)
REM comments
(Comments, insertion statement)
GO TO n
("Sends" the computer to the statement labelled n)
More complicated statements will be explained in later problems.

Write a program in BASIC to find and print the sum of two complex numbers, inputted from the terminal. You may treat a single complex number as an ordered pair of real numbers.

Solution: If Z_1 and Z_2 are two complex numbers given by $a + bi$ and $c + di$ respectively where $i = \sqrt{-1}$, we define $Z_1 + Z_2 = (a + c) + (b + d)i$. In terms of ordered pairs of real numbers, $Z_1 = (a,b)$, $Z_2 = (c,d)$, and $Z_1 + Z_2 = (a+c, b+d)$, where a,b,c and d are the coordinates of the two points representing given numbers:

a and c are on the real axis,
b and d are on the imaginary axis
The program below used the input of a particular number 999 to terminate the program.
This is done by means of an IF ... THEN statement, which has the form

        IF variable = expression THEN label AND works as fol-
lows: If the value of given variable equals the given expression,
then the next statement to be executed is the one with the label
following the word THEN. Otherwise, the computer goes to the next
statement.

```
1Ø              PRINT "THIS PROGRAM ADDS TWO COMPLEX";
15              PRINT "NUMBERS IN  A,B  FORM"
2Ø              PRINT
3Ø              PRINT "TYPE IN THE FIRST NUMBER"
4Ø              INPUT  A,B
5Ø              IF  A = 999  THEN  999
6Ø              PRINT "TYPE IN THE SECOND NUMBER"
7Ø              INPUT  C,D
8Ø              PRINT "THE SUM Z1 + Z2 = (";A + C; ",";B + D;")"
9Ø              GO TO 2Ø
999             END
```

● **PROBLEM** 10-5

Write a BASIC program to find and print the difference, product, and
quotient for pairs of complex numbers which are inputted from a terminal. Again, treat a single complex number as an ordered pair of
real numbers.

Solution: We use the same notation developed in the previous problem
for adding complex numbers. If Z_1 = (a,b) and Z_2 = (c,d), then the
difference, product, and quotient of Z_1 and Z_2 are respectively

$$Z_1 - Z_2 = (a-c, b-d)$$

$$Z_1 * Z_2 = (ac - bd, ad + bc)$$

$$Z_1 / Z_2 = ((ac+bd)/(c^2+d^2), (bc - ad)/(c^2 + d^2))$$

```
1Ø              PRINT "THIS PROGRAM FINDS THE DIFFERENCE,";
15              PRINT "PRODUCT, AND QUOTIENT OF TWO";
17              PRINT "COMPLEX NUMBERS IN  A,B  FORM";
2Ø              PRINT
3Ø              PRINT "TYPE IN THE FIRST NUMBER"
4Ø              INPUT  A,B
5Ø              IF  A = 999  THEN  999
6Ø              PRINT "TYPE IN THE SECOND NUMBER"
7Ø              INPUT  C,D
8Ø              PRINT "THE DIFFERENCE IS (";  A-C;",";B-D;")"
9Ø              PRINT "THE PRODUCT IS (";
95              PRINT  A*C - B*D;",";A*D+B*C;")"
96              PRINT "THE QUOTIENT IS (";
98              PRINT (A*C+B*D)/(C↑2+D↑2);",";(B*C-A*D)/(C↑2+D↑2);")"
99              GO TO 2Ø
999             END
```

321

Write a BASIC program which calls for the input of an arbitrary number, and then prints out whether the number read in is positive, negative, or zero.

Solution: This problem represents an aspect of elementary decision making. The implementation of these decisions is best handled by use of several IF ... THEN clauses.

```
100     REM DETERMINE IF  X  IS POSITIVE, NEGATIVE
110     REM OR ZERO
120     PRINT "WHEN I ASK, YOU ENTER A NUMBER AND";
130     PRINT "I WILL TELL YOU WHETHER YOUR NUMBER";
140     PRINT "IS POSITIVE, NEGATIVE, OR ZERO."
150     PRINT
160     PRINT "WHAT IS YOUR NUMBER?";
170     INPUT  X
180     IF  X > 0  THEN 190
181     IF  X < 0  THEN 210
182     IF  X = 0  THEN 230
190     PRINT X;  "IS POSITIVE"
200     GO TO 150
210     PRINT X; "IS NEGATIVE"
220     GO TO 150
230     PRINT X; "IS ZERO"
240     GO TO 150
999     END
```

FOR - NEXT LOOPS

Calculate and print out the area of a rectangle whose width and length vary in integral steps from 1 to 4.

Solution: In this problem a "FOR - NEXT" loop is being introduced. It has a general form of:

$$\text{FOR variable} = \text{expr}_1 \text{ TO expr}_2 \text{ STEP expr}_3$$

$$\text{NEXT variable}$$

where expr_1 is the initial value of the variable, expr_2 - the final value, and expr_3 indicates the value by which the variable has to be incremented after each pass through the loop. If the STEP part is omitted, it is assumed to be 1. We use two nested "FOR ... NEXT" loops as shown below.

```
10      REM CALCULATES RECTANGLE'S AREA
20      FOR  W = 1  TO  4
30      FOR  L = 1  TO  4
40      PRINT "L ="; L; "W = "; W; "A = "; L*W
50      NEXT  L
60      NEXT  W
70      END
```

Write a BASIC program to calculate the sum of cubes of integers from 1 to 100.

Solution: This can be accomplished by an elementary FOR ... NEXT loop. A more sophisticated approach could be based on the formula

$$\sum_{i=1}^{K} i^3 = \frac{K^2 (K+1)^2}{4} \quad ,$$

where

$$\sum_{i=1}^{K} i^3 = 1^3 + 2^3 + 3^3 + \ldots + K^3 \quad .$$

PROGRAM # 1

```
100      REM SUM OF CUBES
110      LET  S = 0
120      FOR  I = 1  TO  100
130      LET  S = S + I ↑ 3
140      NEXT I
150      PRINT  S
160      END
```

PROGRAM # 2

```
100      LET  K = 100
110      LET  S = K*K*(K+1)*(K+1)/4
120      PRINT  S
130      END
```

LIBRARY FUNCTIONS

Write a BASIC program to calculate the hypotenuse of a right triangle. Your program should read in values of the two sides A and B, and calculate the hypotenuse C according to the Pythagorean theorem. Illustrate the results when A = 3, B = 4; A = 6, B = 8; A = B = 1.

Solution: This program illustrates the use of Library Functions in BASIC. It executes function SQR (Square Root) for determining the hypotenuse. The hypotenuse C is calculated from the formula

$$C = \sqrt{A^2 + B^2} \quad .$$

The program follows:

```
10      REM CALCULATES THE HYPOTENUSE
20      REM OF A RIGHT TRIANGLE
30      PRINT "SIDE A", "SIDE B", "HYPOTENUSE C"
40      READ  A,B
50      LET  C = SQR(A ↑ 2 + B ↑ 2)
60      PRINT  A,B,C
70      GO TO 40
80      DATA  3, 4, 6, 8, 1, 1
90      END
```

```
                          OUTPUT:
        SIDE A            SIDE B                 HYPOTENUSE C
        3                 4                      5
        6                 8                      1Ø
        1                 1                      1.41...
```

● **PROBLEM** 10-10

Write a BASIC program to round numbers of the form XX.X to the nearest integer. Your program should read in the numbers from a DATA statement and print out the original number and the rounded number.

Solution: This program introduces the library function INT(X), which returns the integer part of the input number X. We need one elementary result from numerical analysis, namely that the rounded value of X is given by INT(X + 0.5) to the nearest integer.

```
1Ø        REM ROUNDS NUMBERS
2Ø        PRINT "NUMBER", "ROUNDED #"
3Ø        FOR A = 1  TO  8
4Ø        READ X
5Ø        LET  Y = INT(X + Ø.5)
6Ø        PRINT X,Y
7Ø        NEXT A
8Ø        DATA 16.6, 14.8, 25.6, 4.8, 87.8, 67.2, 35.1, 93.2
9Ø        END
```

It is not needed to add Ø.5 to X (statement 5Ø) for those systems where command INT(X) rounds off, instead of just cutting the fractional part of X.

● **PROBLEM** 10-11

Write a BASIC program which converts inches to feet and inches.

Solution: Use the INT function

```
1Ø        READ I
2Ø        LET  F = INT(I/12)
3Ø        LET  I1 = I - F*12
4Ø        PRINT  I "INCHES = "; F;"FEET"; I1;"INCHES"
45        GO TO 1Ø
5Ø        DATA 9, 86, 47, 37, 947, 48Ø
6Ø        END
```

● **PROBLEM** 10-12

Write a program to find the remainder of the quotient of two integer numbers. Test the program with sample data.

Solution: The remainder is given by

$$R = N - INT(N/D)*D$$

where N = numerator, D = denominator, and integer quotient is INT(N/D).
       (This statement will work properly only on those systems where

324

INT(X) function determines the largest integer number that does not exceed X. For a few systems where INT(X) just truncates fractional parts of X, the statement would need some modification.)

```
5       PRINT "NUMERATOR", "DENOM", "REMAINDER", "INT QUOT"
10      READ N,D
15      REM FIND REMAINDER WHEN 'N' IS DIVIDED BY 'D'
20      LET R = N - INT(N/D)*D
30      PRINT N,D,R, INT(N/D)
40      GO TO 10
50      DATA 93, 12, 100, 25, 365, 52, 365, 7
60      END
```

Sample Output:

NUMERATOR	DENOM	REMAINDER	INT QUOT
93	12	9	7
100	25	4	0
365	52	1	7
365	7	1	52

● **PROBLEM** 10-13

Write a program to find the greatest factor of an integer.

Solution: Here, a trick is used based on the application of the INT function. If the quotient of two integers is also an integer, the denominator must be a factor (i.e., if $N/D = K = INT(N/D)$, then both D and K are factors of N). The smallest D which satisfies this condition will give us the desired value of the greatest factor $K = N/D$. What values of D should be tried? The first guess would be 2 to N - 1. A refinement of this guess would be to observe that 2 is the smallest possible factor, while N/2 is the largest. Moreover, since $\sqrt{N}\,\sqrt{N} = N$, it is best to examine all D's = $2,3,\ldots,\sqrt{N}$ as possible factors.

```
10      READ N
20      FOR  D = 2  TO  SQR(N)
30      IF  N/D = INT(N/D)  THEN 70
40      NEXT D
50      PRINT N; "IS PRIME"
60      GO TO 10
70      PRINT N/D; "IS THE GREATEST FACTOR OF"; N
80      GO TO 10
90      DATA 1946, 1949, 1009, 1003
100     DATA 11001, 240,
110     END
```

● **PROBLEM** 10-14

Write a BASIC program to reduce a fraction to lowest terms. Test your program with sample data.

Solution: We make use of the INT function to find the largest factor of an integer. What we need to do is find the largest common factor

325

of the numerator and denominator. A flowchart illustrating the program
logic is given below:

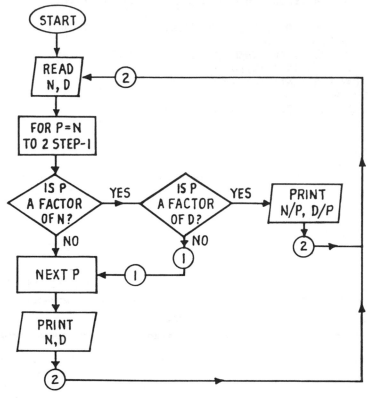

```
1Ø      READ  N,D
2Ø      FOR P = N  TO  2 STEP - 1
3Ø      IF  N/P = INT(N/P) THEN 7Ø
4Ø      NEXT  P
5Ø      PRINT  N"/"D
6Ø      GO TO 1Ø
7Ø      IF  D/P = INT(D/P) THEN 9Ø
8Ø      GO TO 4Ø
9Ø      PRINT  N"/"D" ="N/P"/"D/P
1ØØ     GO TO 1Ø
11Ø     DATA  5,6
12Ø     DATA  82, 48
13Ø     END
```

Note that the absence of commas in both PRINT statements tells the
computer to write the numerical values of the variables and the arithmetic operators right after each other, not leaving any blank space in
between.

● **PROBLEM** 10-15

Plot the graph of a sine curve with points at $15°$ intervals.

<u>Solution</u>: The TAB function is useful here. By specifying the appropriate
coordinates, it causes the printer to place an X in the correct column.
We use column 40 to correspond to the X-axis so that there will be room
to plot negative values.

In the program, C = $\pi/180$. It converts from degrees to radians. The PRINT statement, however, represents the points in 15° steps, as given by the FOR ... NEXT construct. The program is given below:

```
1Ø      REM A PLOT OF THE SINE CURVE
2Ø      LET  C = 3.14159/18Ø.Ø
3Ø      FOR  A = Ø  TO  36Ø  STEP 15
4Ø      LET  R = C*A
5Ø      PRINT  A; "DEG"; TAB(4Ø.Ø + 25*SIN(R)); "X"
6Ø      NEXT  A
7Ø      END
```

SIN $\pi/2$ = +1

SIN π = 0

SIN $\frac{3}{2}\pi$ = -1

```
                    -1                      0                   +1
 Ø      DEG                                 X
15      DEG                                    X
3Ø      DEG                                       X
45      DEG                                          X
6Ø      DEG                                             X
75      DEG                                                X
9Ø      DEG                                                   X
1Ø5     DEG                                                      X
12Ø     DEG                                                X
135     DEG                                             X
15Ø     DEG                                          X
165     DEG                                       X
18Ø     DEG                                    X
195     DEC                                 X
21Ø     DEG                              X
225     DEG                           X
24Ø     DEG                        X
255     DEG                     X
27Ø     DEG                  X
285     DEG                     X
3ØØ     DEG                        X
315     DEG                           X
33Ø     DEG                              X
345     DEG                                 X
36Ø     DEG                                    X
```

STRING VARIABLES

● **PROBLEM** 10-16

Write a BASIC program to search a data statement for a given name which is typed in when the program is executed.

Solution: This problem introduces the notion of string variables and of comparisons between strings. String variables are denoted by any valid variable name with $ at the end, for example: A$, B$, C1$,..., etc. One can test strings for equality by means of the ' = ' and '< >' operators. When the search is finished, if the user wishes to search for another name, the RESTORE statement is used.

```
10      REM PROGRAM SEARCHES THE DATA STATEMENT
20      REM FOR A CERTAIN NAME
30      PRINT "TYPE NAME, THEN HIT RETURN"
40      INPUT A$
50      FOR  J = 1  TO  5
60      READ  B$
70      IF  B$ = A$  THEN 110
80      NEXT  J
90      PRINT "CAN'T FIND NAME"
100     GO TO 120
110     PRINT  B$; "WAS FOUND"
120     PRINT "TO CONTINUE TYPE YES; ELSE - NO."
130     INPUT  C$
140     IF  C$ < > "YES" THEN 180
150     DATA "JOHN", "BOB", "JILL", "MARY", "FRED"
160     RESTORE
170     GO TO 30
180     END
```

● **PROBLEM** 10-17

Write a BASIC program which compares two strings according to their alphabetic ordering. Output both strings and their relationship to each other.

Solution: In this problem string variables are denoted by A$ and B$. They can be compared to each other using the relational operators <, =, or > .

```
100     REM COMPARES STRINGS FOR ORDER
110     PRING "A$";
120     INPUT A$
130     IF  A$ = "STOP" THEN 240
140     PRINT  "B$";
150     INPUT  B$
160     IF  A$ < B$  THEN  220
170     IF  A$ = B$  THEN  200
180     PRINT  A$; "IS GREATER THAN"; B$
190     GO TO 100
200     PRINT  A$; "IS EQUAL TO"; B$
210     GO TO  100
220     PRINT  A$; "IS LESS THAN"; B$
230     GO TO 100
240     END
```

FUNCTIONS

Define a BASIC function which takes on the value $\sqrt{x^2 - y^2}$ if $x^2 \geq y^2$, but $\sqrt{y^2 - x^2}$ if $y^2 > x^2$.

Solution: A multiline function which takes into account the sign of $x^2 - y^2$ is needed for solving this problem. The multiline function starts with a defining statement. It does not include an assignment statement (unlike the DEF statement of a single line function), just the function name and a list of "dummy" variables. BASIC statements defining the calculation of the function follow. Also, there must be a function ending command. It is the same for all multiline functions and consists of a statement number followed by the word FNEND.

Note that the multiline function can be placed anywhere in the program. As in the case of a single line function, it is good programming practice to place all functions at the beginning (or end) where they can be kept track of by the programmer.

See the program below:

```
100     DEF FNA(X,Y)
110     LET  X1 = X↑2 - Y↑2
120     IF  X1 > = 0  then  140
130     LET  X1 = -X1
140     LET FNA = X1↑0.5
150     FNEND
```

Write a general purpose BASIC program which prints a table of values for any function.

Solution: The solution uses the notion of string variables and user-defined functions. This program also makes use of the STOP statement, which, in BASIC, essentially terminates the execution of the program in the same fashion as the END statement. A term with $ following a single letter is used to record character data.

```
10      REM PRINTS A TABLE OF VALUES FOR ANY FUNCTION
20      DEF FNA(X) = X
30      PRINT "TO DEFINE A NEW FUNCTION TYPE Y; ELSE TYPE N."
40      INPUT A$
50      IF  A$ = "N" THEN 110
60      PRINT "TYPE YOUR FUNCTION AS A FUNCTION OF X, AFTER YOU TYPE"
70      PRINT "20 DEF FNA(X) ="
80      PRINT "THEN HIT THE RETURN KEY AND FINALLY";
90      PRINT "TYPE THE COMMAND RUN"
100     STOP
110     PRINT "WHAT ARE THE MINIMUM, MAXIMUM, AND INCREASE IN X"
120     INPUT  X1, X2, D
130     FOR  I = X1  TO  X2  STEP D
140     PRINT "X ="; I; "F(X) ="; FNA(I)
150     NEXT  I
160     END
```

329

Obtain polar solutions for the following polar equations, in which the ordered pair (R,T) is interpreted as R = length of the vector going from the origin to the point R, and T = angle between polar axis and that vector:
a) R = 1 - 2 sin T
b) R = 2 + 2 sin T
c) R = 1 + 2 cos T - sin² T

Solution: Although it is not absolutely necessary, we can make use of the defined statement function. The value of T will be incremented by 15 degrees each time by establishing a loop. Conversion to radians is accomplished with k = π/180. The output will appear in tabular form, with values rounded to the nearest hundredth:

```
1Ø      REM SOLVING POLAR EQUATIONS IN 15 -
2Ø      REM DEGREE STEPS
3Ø      LET  K = 3.14159/18Ø.Ø
4Ø      PRINT "ANGLE", "1-2SIN(T)", "2+2SIN(T)", "1+2COS(T) - SIN(T)↑2"
5Ø      DEF FNR(X) = INT(X*1ØØ)/1ØØ
6Ø      DEF FNA(X) = 1 - 2*SIN(K*X)
7Ø      DEF FNB(X) = 2 + 2*SIN(K*X)
8Ø      DEF FNC(X) = 1 + 2*COS(K*X) - SIN(K*X)↑2
9Ø      FOR  T = Ø  TO 3ØØ STEP 15
1ØØ     PRINT T, FNR(FNA(T)), FNR(FNB(T)), FNR(FNC(T))
11Ø     NEXT  T
12Ø     END
```

[Note: a variety of polar equations can be evaluated with this program by making minor adjustments.]

Devise a BASIC program to calculate the first N numbers of the FIBONACCI series.

Solution: The FIBONACCI series is defined recursively by F(1) = 1, F(2) = 1, and for I greater or equal to 3, F(I) = F(I - 1) + F(I - 2). It is convenient to tabulate the functional values in an array dimensioned to be, say, 50. DIM (dimension) statement is used for this purpose. BASIC automatically provides for 10 places in its memory cells for any one dimensional array (11 places in those systems, which accept 0 subscript). If one desires N ≠ 10 places to be reserved, he can use the statement of the form:
$$DIM V(N)$$
where V can be any valid variable. Thus the program will handle N up to 50.

```
1Ø      DIM F(5Ø)
2Ø      INPUT  N
3Ø      LET  F(1) = 1
4Ø      LET  F(2) = 1
45      PRINT  F(1), F(2),
5Ø      FOR  I = 3  TO N
6Ø      LET  F(I) = F(I - 1) + F(I - 2)
7Ø      PRINT  F(I),
8Ø      NEXT  I
1ØØ     END
```

USING THE RANDOM NUMBER GENERATOR

● **PROBLEM** 10-22

Design a program using BASIC to simulate the rolls of a die.

Solution: For this problem, the random number generator RND can be used. This function generates random numbers between 0 and 1. We want to generate integers from 1 to 6 inclusive, and find out how many 6's appeared after 100 tosses. A counter S is set up to sum the number of times a 6 is encountered.

```
1∅      REM DIE THROWING SIMULATION
2∅      LET  S = ∅
3∅      FOR  X = 1  TO  1∅∅
4∅      LET  D = INT(1 + 6*RND)
5∅      IF  D = 6  THEN  8∅
6∅      GO TO 1∅∅
7∅      REM  S  COUNTS SIXES
8∅      LET  S = S + 1
9∅      NEXT  X
1∅∅     PRINT
11∅     PRINT  S; "SIXES OUT OF 100 ROLLS"
12∅     END
```

● **PROBLEM** 10-23

In BASIC the RND function is used to generate a random number between 0 and 1. What statements would you use to:
(a) generate integral random number between 0 and X - 1?
(b) generate integral random number between 1 and X?
(c) simulate the toss of a cubical die?
(d) simulate a binary random choice taking values 1 or 2?

Solution: (a) 1∅ LET T = INT(X*RND)
(b) 2∅ LET V = INT(1 + X*RND)
(c) 3∅ LET W = INT(1 + 6*RND)
(d) 4∅ LET N = INT(1 + 2*RND)

● **PROBLEM** 10-24

Write a BASIC program which generates and prints out an inputted number of random digits (0 through 9 inclusive).

Solution: We use the RND function. [Some texts use RND with an argument; others use no argument. Consult your BASIC manual for details of your particular implementation.] Since $0 < RND < 1$, $0 < 10*RND < 10$, and thus INT(10*RND) takes values 0, 1, 2,...,9

```
1∅∅     REM RANDOM DIGITS
11∅     PRINT "HOW MANY RANDOM DIGITS DO YOU WANT";
12∅     INPUT  N
13∅     PRINT
14∅     FOR  K = 1  TO  N
```

```
150      PRINT INT(1Ø*RND)
160      NEXT  K
170      PRINT
180      GO TO 11Ø
999      END
```

Write a program to simulate a coin toss experiment of 50 tosses. Repeat
the experiment ten times. Count the number of heads in each experiment
and print out this value.

Solution: We know that if we say

$$LET \quad F = INT(2*RND + 1)$$

then F takes on values of 1 and 2 randomly corresponding to heads
and tails. Hence we will loop through this statement to produce the
required simulation:

```
2        FOR  Y = 1  TO  1Ø
5        LET  C = Ø
1Ø       FOR  X = 1  TO  5Ø
2Ø       LET  F = INT(2*RND + 1)
3Ø       IF  F = 1  THEN 6Ø
4Ø       PRINT "T";
5Ø       GO TO 1ØØ
58       REM  C  COUNTS THE NUMBER OF HEADS
6Ø       LET  C = C + 1
7Ø       PRINT "H";
1ØØ      NEXT  X
11Ø      PRINT
12Ø      PRINT C; "HEADS OUT OF 5Ø FLIPS"
125      NEXT  Y
13Ø      END
```

In 1773, Comte de Georges Louis Leclerc Buffon proposed a method of
finding an approximation to π . He dropped a needle of length L on
a flat piece of paper ruled with horizontal, parallel lines which were
separated by the length 2L. By repeating the drops over a large
number of trials, he was able to demonstrate that the probability of
the needle landing across one of the lines is 1/π . Design a program
using BASIC to simulate this procedure to find an approximation to π.

Solution: First, we present a pictorial description of the situation:

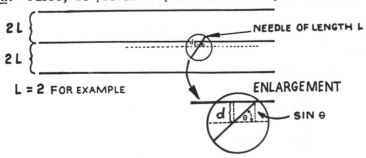

Let D = the distance from the center of the needle to the nearest horizontal. Let θ = the angle between the needle and an imaginary horizontal (dotted line) through the needle's center. Also, notice that the distance from the head of the needle to the dotted line can be represented as $\sin \theta$.

Notice that D takes on values between 0 and 2, while θ takes on values between $0°$ and $180°$. In order for the needle to touch a line, D must be less than or equal to $\sin \theta$. Consider the following diagram:

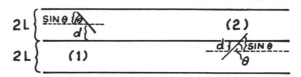

In case (1), $D > \sin \theta$, and the needle is not touching the line. Case (2) shows the situation where $D \leq \sin \theta$: the needle is touching the line (The case of $D = \sin \theta$ will occur when the head of the needle lies on the line.)

Now, we show a geometrical model of $D \leq \sin \theta$:

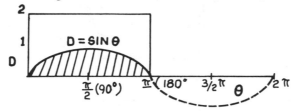

If we pick a point (θ, d) at random within the bounds of the rectangle $(0 \leq D \leq 2, 0 \leq \theta \leq \pi)$, the probability that $D \leq \sin \theta$ is:

$$P(\theta) = \frac{\int_0^\pi \sin \theta \; d\theta}{2\pi} \quad \frac{\text{(area under } D = \sin \theta)}{\text{(total area of rectangle)}}$$

which simplifies to:

$$\frac{-\cos \theta \Big|_0^\pi}{2\pi} = \frac{(-\cos \pi) - (-\cos 0)}{2\pi}$$

$$= \frac{1 - (-1)}{2\pi}$$

$$= \frac{2}{2\pi}$$

$$= \frac{1}{\pi}$$

Taking the reciprocal, you get a value for π.

Our strategy for the program will be to generate random numbers for D and θ, decide whether they fall under the condition $D \leq \sin \theta$, calculate the probability, and take its reciprocal.

```
10      REM BUFFON'S NEEDLE PROBLEM
15      LET  T1 = 0
16      LET  T2 = 0
20      FOR  K = 1  TO  1000
30      LET  D = 2*RND
40      LET  T = 3.14159*RND
50      D1 = SIN(T)
60      T1 = T1 + 1
```

```
7Ø      IF  D > D1  THEN 9Ø
8Ø      T2 = T2 + 1
9Ø      NEXT  K
1ØØ     P = T1/T2
11Ø     PRINT "APPROXIMATION TO  PI  IS"; P
12Ø     END
```

● **PROBLEM** 10-27

Write a pseudocoded program to find an approximation of pi using the
Monte Carlo method. This method is an example of a system which uses
random digits to solve a problem that does not, by itself, have randomness.

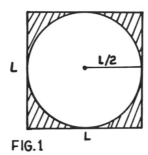

FIG.1

Solution: First, we must assume that there is a subprogram called
RANDOM available in the user's compiler. Different compilers have
different means of obtaining random digits, so we omit a discussion
of the actual process of randomization.

Monte Carlo methods typically use random digits to solve problems
which have no inherently random properties. For the approximation of
pi, we need the dart board analogy. We have a square board with an
inscribed circle, as in Fig. 1. Suppose we have monkeys that have been
trained to toss darts at the board. Now, assuming all the darts land
somewhere on the board, and assuming that a dart can land anywhere
with equal likelihood, we ask: what is the probability that a dart
will land inside the circle?

If you remember the equations for the areas of a circle and a
square $(A = \pi(L/2)^2$ and $A = L^2$, respectively), you can discover that
the probability equals the ratio of the circle's area to the square's
area, or $\pi/4$, which is about 0.7854. For our example, we do not
know π. However, if we could get the monkeys to throw a large number
of darts at the board, we could compute the proportion of hits falling
inside the circle. From this proportion, we can find an approximation
for π.

The following pseudocode generates randomly the X- and Y-
coordinates of each "dart" thrown at the board. Since these coordinates
lie between 0 and 1, darts appear only in the positive quadrant of
the square (the top right corner). However, the full figure can be
built from four identical pieces, so the result remains the same. We
just multiply $\pi/4$ by 4 to get the desired result.

Also note that if we increase the number of darts thrown, the
degree of deviation from the expected result decreases. This axiom
is called in statistics the "law of large numbers". We are testing
for 4-digit accuracy in this problem. Our output consists of the
number of darts, the approximate value of π, and the deviation from
the expected result.

```
INTEGER        I, M, N, KOUNT
REAL           APPROX, X, Y
               N ← 0
               KOUNT ← 0
               OUTPUT MESSAGE 'INPUT M: NUMBER OF DARTS TO BE TOSSED'
               INPUT M
               DO WHILE  M > 0
               DO FOR  I ← 1  TO M
               X ← RANDOM
               Y ← RANDOM
C              CHECK TO SEE IF THE DART HAS LANDED INSIDE CIRCLE
               IF(X*X) + (Y*Y) < 0
               THEN KOUNT ← KOUNT + 1
               END IF - THEN
               END DO FOR  I
               N ← N + M
               APPROX ← FLOAT(KOUNT)/FLOAT(N)*4.0
               OUTPUT N,APPROX, APPROX - 3.1416
               OUTPUT MESSAGE  'IF YOU WISH TO TOSS MORE DARTS,
               INPUT  M'
               INPUT  M
               END DO WHILE
END PROGRAM
```

CHAPTER 11

COBOL

COBOL VOCABULARY

● **PROBLEM** 11-1

Explain briefly the background and applications of the
COBOL programming language.

Solution: On May 28 and 29, 1959, a meeting was called in
the Pentagon for the purpose of considering the desirability
and feasibility of establishing a common language for programming of electronic computers in business data processing.
As a result, in a short period of time, a new computer language COBOL (COmmon Business Oriented Language) was developed.

Since that time COBOL has definitely become the most
popular and useful language inside the business community.

The basic language element in COBOL is the "word." As
in the English language, COBOL contains many types of words
with which meaningful thoughts are formed. This makes the
language intelligible for many people who do not have much
programming experience and only use the computer occasionally for solving problems.

Every COBOL program is divided into four parts:

1. The Identification Division - identifies the program.

2. The Environment Division - specifies the input-output
    devices to be used.

3. The Data Division - describes the data to be used in the
    program.

4. The Procedure Division - includes the instructions that
    the system will follow in solving the problem.

Such a division provides greater simplicity of understanding
and analysis of a COBOL program.

These are only a few of the factors that account for the constantly growing popularity of the COBOL language in the business world.

What are the types of simple conditional expressions and compound conditional expressions? Give their formats and any conditions if necessary.

Solution: The Simple Conditional Expression: A simple condition reducing to the value true or false can be expressed in the following types of simple conditional expression:

    i) a relation

    ii) a condition-name

   iii) a sign condition

    iv) a class condition

    v) a switch status condition.

Any of the above are used in a decision-making operation to select different paths of control in a program.

1) The Relational Condition: This condition causes a comparison of magnitude between two quantities. The general form is:

$$\begin{Bmatrix} \text{identifier - 1} \\ \text{literal - 1} \\ \text{arithmetic expression - 1} \end{Bmatrix} \text{Operator} \begin{Bmatrix} \text{identifier - 2} \\ \text{literal - 2} \\ \text{arithmetic expression - 2} \end{Bmatrix}$$

Note: {} means choose one.

The first quantity is called the subject and the second is referred to as the object of the condition. A relational operator must be preceded and followed by a space. The list of relational operators are GREATER, LESS, EQUAL. The word, NOT, before an operator specifies the opposite of what the operator normally specifies.

e.g.,   AGE IS GREATER THAN 21

              SUM IS NOT LESS THAN 100

              A+B IS EQUAL TO A+M

The words IS and THAN are optional and do not alter the meaning of the expression.

e.g.,   AGE GREATER 21

   is equivalent to

AGE IS GREATER THAN 21.

2) The Condition-Name condition: A condition name is a name, assigned in the Data Division, to one of the values a conditional variable assumes. The variable is tested to determine whether or not its value is equal to a value associated with a particular condition name.

e.g.,   02. MARITAL-STATUS;   (condition variable)

88 SINGLE VALUE IS 1   (condition name)

88 MARRIED VALUE is 2 ⎫   condition names

88 DIVORCED VALUE is 3 ⎭

Using an IF statement, the test to determine marital status may appear as follows:

IF MARRIED THEN .....

which is equivalent to

IF MARITAL-STATUS IS EQUAL TO 2 THEN .....

NOT is used to specify the opposite of what the condition-name test would normally specify.

e.g.,   IF NOT SINGLE .....

    is equivalent to

IF MARITAL-STATUS IS NOT EQUAL TO 1 ......

3) Sign Condition: This condition determines whether a numeric quantity is less than, equal to, or greater than zero. The general format is:

Note: [ ] means optional

$$\begin{Bmatrix} \text{identifier} \\ \text{arithmetic expression} \end{Bmatrix} \text{is [NOT]} \begin{Bmatrix} \text{POSITIVE} \\ \text{NEGATIVE} \\ \text{ZERO} \end{Bmatrix}$$

e.g., A + B * C IS POSITIVE

The identifier in a numeric status test must always represent a numeric value.

4) Class Condition: The class condition test determines whether a quantity is purely numeric or alphabetic. The general format of this conditional expression is as follows:

$$\text{identifier is [NOT]} \begin{Bmatrix} \text{NUMERIC} \\ \text{ALPHABETIC} \end{Bmatrix}$$

338

The test must be consistent with data description of the item being tested. That is, only the NUMERIC test may be used for data which has been described as numeric and only the ALPHABETIC test for alphabetic data either may be used for alpha numeric data. The usage of the identifier must be defined, either explicitly or implicitly, as DISPLAY.

5) The Switch Status Condition: This condition is used to determine whether a particular hardware switch is off or on.

The Compound Conditional Expression

A conditional expression having a single condition is referred to as a simple conditional expression. One containing more than one condition is referred to as a compound conditional expression. The various conditions are connected by the logical operators AND and OR and the format is:

$$\text{simple conditional expression} \left\{ \begin{array}{l} \text{AND [NOT]} \\ \text{OR [NOT]} \end{array} \right\} \begin{array}{l} \text{simple-conditional} \\ \text{expression} \end{array}$$

For example:

A IS EQUAL TO B OR C IS LESS THAN D AND E IS GREATER THAN F

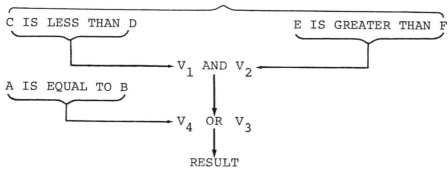

Implied Subject: In a compound conditional expression it is possible for several consecutive conditions to have the same subject.

e.g., SUM IS GREATER THAN 100 OR SUM IS LESS THAN 1000

ie equivalent to

SUM IS GREATER THAN 100 OR LESS THAN 1000.

Implied Operator: Operators, as well as subjects may be implied in a compound condition consisting of a consecutive series of relational expressions.

e.g., SALES IS EQUAL TO 25 OR EQUAL TO 66 OR EQUAL TO 85

is equivalent to

SALES IS EQUAL TO 25 OR 66 OR 85

339

Implied operators must only be used in expressions where
the subjects are also implied.

● **PROBLEM** 11-3

When is a condition expression used in COBOL? Give the
rules for comparison of numeric or nonnumeric items.

Solution: Conditional Expressions: Conditional expressions are expressions used in situations where need of testing any condition arises. The outcome of a test determines
the next logical step to be performed. The conditional
expression reduces to a single value, "true" or "false."
The truth or falsity is determined by a relational test.
This test is based on a comparison of characters.

        Rules of Comparison: Characters are compared and
evaluated on the basis of a computer collating sequence
in which the characters have a specified order of magnitude.
This collating sequence varies from machine to machine.
As an example, the ordering scheme of fig. 1 will be used
in the following discussions.

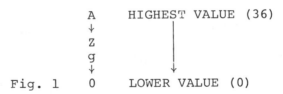

A   HIGHEST VALUE (36)

↓

Z

g

↓

Fig. 1   0   LOWER VALUE (0)

Items declared numeric in the DATA DESCRIPTION section
cannot be compared with items declared to be nonnumeric.

        Comparison of Numeric Items: The comparison of numeric
items is based on respective values of the item considered
purely as algebraic values. The item length, in terms of
the number of digits is not itself significant.

e.g., comparison of +00003 with +03 results in an equal
condition, and +01 is greater than -155.

        Comparison of Nonnumeric Items: For two nonnumeric
items, possibly containing numeric characters, a comparison
results with respect to the ordered character set. There
are two cases:

a) Equal Length Items: If items are of equal length,
comparison proceeds by comparing characters in corresponding
character positions. Starting from the high-order end, comparison continues until either a pair of unequal characters
is encountered or the lower order end of the item is reached.

        As an example, consider:

1   ABCD and ABBD results in inequality

     ABBD > ABCD.

2   SAM and SAM results in equality.

3   NAME 1 and NAME 2 results in inequality,

NAME 1 < NAME 2.

b) Unequal Length Items: If the items are of unequal length, comparison proceeds as above. If the process exhausts the characters of the shorter item without detection of difference, the shorter item is Less Than the longer item.

e.g.,   comparing   ABC & ABCD,

every character A, B and C of the first item equals every character of the later item but due to the shorter length of ABC the result is ABC < ABCD.

● **PROBLEM** 11-4

Define 'Expressions' in COBOL language.   What are arithmetic expressions and how are they evaluated?

Solution: Expressions: An expression in the COBOL language may be defined as a combination of data-names, literals, and operators which may be reduced to a single value.

Arithmetic Expressions: They are data names, identifiers, or numeric literals or, a series of data-names, identifiers and literals separated by arithmetic operators, which define a single numeric value.

The format of arithmetic expressions using arithmetic operators is as follows:

data name

or

identifier

or

literal

or

$$\begin{Bmatrix} \text{data name} \\ \text{literal} \\ \text{Identifier} \end{Bmatrix} \quad \text{operator} \quad \begin{Bmatrix} \text{data name} \\ \text{literal} \\ \text{Identifier} \end{Bmatrix}$$

The arithmetic operators are:

Operation	Operators
Addition	+
Subtraction	-
Multiplication	*

341

```
Division              /

Exponentiation        * *
```

The normal precedence rule (from high to low) is:

```
1) Exponentiation
2) Multiplication and Division
3) Addition and Subtraction
```

When operators are all on the same hierarchical level, evaluation occurs in left to right order. Parentheses are used to alter the normal rules of precedence. In COBOL, parentheses are defined as having a higher order of precedence than any operator

e.g., $\dfrac{A + B}{C - D}$

cannot be expressed in COBOL as A + B/C - D as this represents the formula

$A + \dfrac{B}{C} - D.$

Using parentheses it can be accurately expressed as

(A + B)/(C - D).

Operations within parentheses have precedence over any other in a calculation;

e.g., calculate A + B * A - C/2.

with   A = 4, B = 3 and C = 6.

The expression will be evaluated as follows:

Multiplication and division are on the same level, so first

B*A = 12 and then C/2 = 3 and thus

it reduces to

A + 12 - 3.

Now + and - are on the same level.

A + 12 = 16 is first evaluated and then 16 - 3 = 13 is the final evaluation.

If we use parentheses instead:

((A + B) * A - C)/2

the sequence of evaluation is as follows

1. A + B = 7

2. 7 * A = 28

3. 28 - C = 22

4. 22/2 = 11 (RESULT).

PROGRAM DIVISIONS

● **PROBLEM** 11-5

Write a complete IDENTIFICATION DIVISION for a COBOL
program which calculates the weekly paychecks of the
employees of a company.

Solution: IDENTIFICATION DIVISION is the first part of any
COBOL program. Its main purpose is to identify the program
to the computer, and then it can also be used to explain to
the reader what the program does.

The first statement in this part of the program is the
IDENTIFICATION DIVISION. In format form the statement
starts from the eighth column and ends with a full stop
mark (.).

PROGRAM-ID. This is the second mandatory statement
of IDENTIFICATION DIVISION; it also starts from the eighth
column and ends with a full stop mark. Leaving one empty
space and continuing on the same line program-name follows
the PROGRAM-ID statement. Program name could be any name
except the reserved words such as IF, GO TO, DATA, and a
hyphen must be used to separate two or more words. So,
call the program PAYROLL-LIST.

The third, fourth and fifth statements are not mandatory. It is up to the programmer to decide whether the name
of the author, date-written, and any extra remarks would be
included or not.

Following those steps, the IDENTIFICATION DIVISION.
takes the complete form of fig. 1.

CONT	A	B	COBOL STATEMENT										
7 8	12	16	20	24	28	32	36	40	44	48	52	56	
	IDENTIFICATION DIVISION.												
	PROGRAM-ID. PAYROLL-LIST.												
	AUTHOR. GREGORY STEIN												
	DATE-WRITTEN. MARCH 31, 1981												
	REMARKS. THIS PROGRAM IS WRITTEN TO												
	CALCULATE WEEKLY PAYCHECKS.												

All of the actual remarks in the REMARKS. section must come
after margin B.

Write and explain ENVIRONMENT DIVISION, and section headers, along with the two paragraphs, to compile a program on a Honeywell 200, and then execute it on an IBM System/360 Model 40.

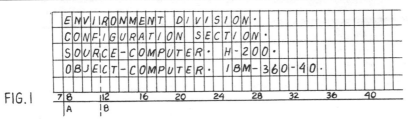

FIG. 1

Solution: ENVIRONMENT DIVISION describes the environment, or equipment, on which the program will be run. Entries in this division depend on the computer available to the programmer.

All ENVIRONMENTAL DIVISION entries begin with margin A, and end with a period.

The computer names used in the configuration section are not optional or created by the programmer; they are the official names given to the computers available. In practice the ENVIRONMENT DIVISION will be constant in programs for the same installation. To allow a program to be used on different computers, the CONFIGURATION SECTION. heading allows for specification of the compilation and execution computers.

To define the computer which will be used to compile the program, ENVIRONMENT DIVISION. uses the statement SOURCE-COMPUTER. In this case the SOURCE-COMPUTER. is H-200.

OBJECT-COMPUTER. is where the program gets executed, and in this problem it is given to be IBM-360-40. The complete ENVIRONMENT SECTION is given in fig. 1.

● **PROBLEM** 11-7

When files are used in a COBOL program, the physical environment of the program changes. Write a complete ENVIRONMENT DIVISION for a COBOL program which will make the usage of the file called MEDICAL-DATA possible, using a card reader.

Solution: When files are used in COBOL programming the INPUT-OUTPUT SECTION must be included in the ENVIRONMENT DIVISION.

INPUT-OUTPUT SECTION follows the CONFIGURATION SECTION, it also begins with Margin A.

FILE-CONTROL, which is the first statement and paragraph header in INPUT-OUTPUT SECTION begins with margin A. The two clauses that make the FILE-CONTROL paragraph are the words SELECT and ASSIGN, which must begin on margin B. The file-name specified in the SELECT clause must be the one the programmer will call in the program.

The ASSIGN clause describes to the computer exactly what physical equipment is required for that file.

The general formats for ASSIGN, and SELECT are,

ASSIGN system-name

SELECT file-name

Fig. 1 shows the complete ENVIRONMENT DIVISION with INPUT-OUTPUT SECTION entries included.

FIG. 1

Variables UR-S-CARDX. following the ASSIGN clause indicate that the file is used for card input (which is a reading device) with external name CARDX. These variables change from system to system and each device has its own code name.

● **PROBLEM 11-8**

Using COBOL language write a DATA DIVISION. There are four independent data items in the program, namely FIRST-NAME, eight characters; LAST-NAME, ten characters; TEL-NO, twelve characters; and STATE, twenty characters.

Solution: DATA-DIVISION is the third division of the COBOL program. It describes the data to be used in the procedure division. Input data, output data, and working data must all be described.

DATA-DIVISION has two sections 1) File Section, 2) Working-Storage Section. When files are not used one can omit the File-Section.

In the Working-Storage section independent and subdivided items can be described. An item which is not subdivided is called an independent item. Social security number is a good example of an independent item. It can not be subdivided. On the other hand ADDRESS is a subdivided, group item. An address consists of a combination of elements such as street, house number, etc.

Independent data items which are not subdivided are always given level number 77, which must be entered in the A margin. Any other level number can be used to describe subdivided items.

In COBOL, describing data means specifying a level number, giving a data-name, and giving a PICTURE (PIC) description. The PICTURE clause tells the computer how many characters are in the data item, and what kind of characters they are.

The most widely used picture character is X; this character is used to tell the computer that the corresponding data item might be any character in the standard character set. A Standard character could be a number, letter, $, or any of the special characters.

When PICTURE XX., or PICTURE X(2). is written, its meaning to the computer is that the data item is two characters long and both of them are standard characters. Given in Fig. 1 is the DATA DIVISION for the program described.

FIG. 1

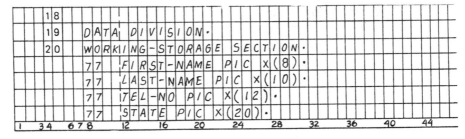

● **PROBLEM** 11-9

A variable to be used in a program is called BIRTH-DATE. This variable is not an independent variable, that is to say it has subdivisions such as MONTH, which is three characters long, DAY, which is two characters long, and YEAR, which is four characters long. Write group and elementary items to describe this variable.

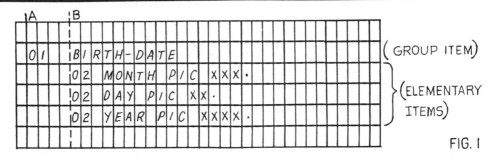

FIG. 1

Solution: The variable BIRTH-DATE will be described in DATA DIVISION with level number 01, which refers to the

346

highest level of a data item, and coded with margin A.

Following this, using margin B and level number 02 (actually any level number from 02-49 could be used) the subdivisions are defined as shown in fig. 1.

PIC stands for Picture and describes the length and type of the item. Each X corresponds to one character in the elementary item descriptions, thus YEAR is 4 characters long.

The use of the X in the item description means that the item is alphanumeric, it can be any combination of characters, numbers and special characters.

● **PROBLEM 11-10**

Examine the DATA DIVISION of Fig. 1 and explain the usage and effects of File Description entries.

FIG. 1

Solution: The DATA DIVISION of a COBOL program is divided into sections such as WORKING-STORAGE section, and the FILE Section.

The File Section always precedes the Working-Storage Section and includes descriptions of all the files and their associated records. File Section header begins with margin A.

In the given example program FD means File Description and it describes 2 files, PARTS-FILE and OUTFILE. Both

347

PARTS-FILE and OUTFILE must have been specified in an ENVIRONMENT DIVISION SELECT Statement. Following this, LABEL and DATA records are also included and are very important in the FD section. Every FD entry must include a LABEL RECORDS clause. Many files use labels to tell the computer where the particular file begins and ends. These records may by unique to that file, they may be standard, or in some files they may be omitted. For unit record files, such as card files or printer files, the label clause reads LABEL RECORDS ARE OMITTED. The DATA RECORD clause specifies the record name associated with the file being described. The DATA RECORD clause is not required in most computer systems since the description of the associated data record must directly follow each FD entry. However, the LABEL RECORDS clause is always required for every FD entry. The data records P_RECORD and SUMMARY are used in the PROCEDURE DIVISION to store the data read into or out of their associated files.

● **PROBLEM** 11-11

Give the formation of a Procedure in COBOL and explain in brief the terms statements, sentences, paragraph and section as applied to COBOL.

Solution: Procedure Formation: Procedures are formed by combining one or more sentences into a paragraph and one or more paragraphs into a section. Each paragraph or section must be preceded by a procedure name. These may be either numeric, alphabetic, or alphanumeric. If numeric, leading zeros are significant (i.e., 18 is not the same as 018). All precedure names must start at position A (column 8) on the COBOL programming form, be a maximum of 30 characters in length and be followed by a period.

e.g., 010200 PROCEDURE DIVISION.

       030000 CHECK-STOCK-NUMBER.

       060100 FINISH-MASTER.

The characters underlined by the break lines are procedure names.

       Statements and Sentences: Statements form the basic functional component of COBOL procedures. Just as clauses make up sentences in normal English-language construction, so statements make up COBOL sentences. A sentence may contain one or more statements.

       The rules governing formation of sentences are:

a) Each sentence may be made up of one or more statements.

b) Each sentence must be terminated by a period.

c) Separators are optional and used to enhance readability. The allowable separators are:

ɓ (space, blank)
; (semicolon)
, (comma)

d) Two contiguous separators are not permissible.

e) Separators may be used in the following places:

- Between statements

e.g., ADD A TO B GIVING C; PERFORM 180 THRU 198

- Between a condition and statement-1 in a condition sentence.

e.g., IF condition; statement–1

- Between statement-1 and ELSE in a conditional statement.

e.g., statement-1; ELSE statement 2.

Paragraphs: One or more sentences may be combined to form a paragraph. Essentially, a paragraph expresses a single procedure to be carried through in the main program. Each paragraph must be preceded by a procedure name. Whenever reference is made, it is to an entire paragraph and not to individual sentences contained therein. If reference is made to a single sentence, that sentence must be defined as a complete paragraph and must be preceded by a procedure name.

Sections: One or more paragraphs can be grouped into a section. The section is the largest unit in COBOL to which a procedure-name may be assigned. This is done by writing a procedure-name, followed by a key word SECTION, followed by a period; the remainder of the line must be left blank.

● PROBLEM 11-12

Categorize the various procedural verbs used in COBOL.

Solution: Procedural Verbs: Verbs specify action to be performed. In COBOL, each verb built into the system causes a specific series of events to occur when the program is running. The various verbs in COBOL are categorized in the following manner.

Input/Output	OPEN
	CLOSE
	READ
	WRITE
	ACCEPT
	DISPLAY
Arithmetic	ADD
	SUBTRACT
	MULTIPLY

349

```
                              DIVIDE
                              COMPUTE

Data Movement and
Manipulation                  MOVE
                              EXAMINE

Sequence Control              GO TO
                              ALTER
                              PERFORM
                              STOP

Compiler Directing            ENTER
                              NOTE
                              EXIT
```

COBOL PROGRAMS

Describe in words the function and the output of the
following COBOL program.

IDENTIFICATION DIVISION

PROGRAM-ID. ID-DISPLAY.

ENVIRONMENT DIVISION.

CONFIGURATION SECTION.

SOURCE-COMPUTER. H-200.

OBJECT-COMPUTER. IBM-360-40.

DATA DIVISION

WORKING-STORAGE SECTION.

77 ID PIC X(20).

PROCEDURE DIVISION.

FIRST-PARA.

    DISPLAY "ENTER OPERATORS ID"

UPON CONSOLE.

ACCEPT ID FROM CONSOLE.

DISPLAY "THANK YOU," ID UPON CONSOLE.

DISPLAY ID.

STOP RUN.

Solution: This is an introductory computer program written

with COBOL language (COmmon Business-Oriented Language).
COBOL was specifically created for handling the masses of
data that are necessary in business data processing.

Specific features of COBOL language are as follows:

1) Identification Division entries

IDENTIFICATION DIVISION. (header) This part is used
to identify the program to the computer.

PROGRAM-ID. This is a special paragraph which belongs
to IDENTIFICATION DIVISION. It appears in the format as
follows;

PROGRAM-ID. program-name

The program-name identifies the program, in this case it is
called ID-DISPLAY.

2) Environment Division entries:

ENVIRONMENT DIVISION. header

CONFIGURATION SECTION. header

SOURCE-COMPUTER. computer-name entry.

OBJECT-COMPUTER. computer-name entry.

Environment division describes the environment, or
equipment, on which the program will be run. Entries in
this division will vary depending on the computer available.
As specified in line 5 of the example program, the source
computer is a Honeywell 200. (program compiler), and the
object computer is an IBM-360-40 (program executer.).

3) Data Division entries:

DATA DIVISION header

WORKING-STORAGE SECTION header

Level number 77

PICTURE clause

Picture character X

The third division of the COBOL program describes the
data to be used in the procedure division. Input data,
output data, and working data must all be described. In the
actual format, the level number and Picture appear as follows:

77 data-name PIC picture.

In this format, the level number and PIC are required
parts and must be used as specified. The programmer fur-
nishes the data-name, in this case ID, and the actual pic-

351

ture. The PICTURE clause tells the computer how many characters are in the data item, and what kind of characters
they are.

The most useful all purpose Picture character is X,
which is used to tell the computer that the corresponding
character in the data item might be anything--at least any
character in the standard character set. Thus when PIC
X(20) is written it tells the computer the data item is 20
characters long and they are all standard characters.

4) Procedure Division entries:

PROCEDURE DIVISION. (header)

DISPLAY statement

ACCEPT statement

DISPLAY statement

DISPLAY statement

STOP RUN. statement

In the procedural part of the program the programmer
tells the computer exactly how to solve a problem.

For the PROCEDURE DIVISION there should be a paragraph-
name. This paragraph-name may be referred to during the
execution of the program, or it may be used for documentation,
to explain the program to a reader. In the example given
the paragraph-name is FIRST-PARA.

Programs usually require some kind of input and output
data. In COBOL, the ACCEPT statement is used to handle low
volume input from either the card reader or the console keyboard, and the DISPLAY statement is used to handle low-volume
output to either the printer or the console.

With the UPON CONSOLE option, as shown in the
example program, DISPLAY will cause the message to be
printed on the console typewriter or be displayed on the
cathode ray tube, depending on the system hardware. Formats for both statements are given below.

DISPLAY $\left\{ \begin{array}{l} \text{literal} \\ \text{data-name} \end{array} \right\}$ [UPON CONSOLE.]

ACCEPT   data-name   [FROM CONSOLE.]

Restrictions:

1. Brackets [ ] indicate optional clause.

2. Braces { } indicate choose one.

3. Literal must be exactly what you want displayed, enclosed
   in quotes.

4. Data-name must have been described in Data Division.

STOP RUN. This statement is used to end every program.

The given example program can now be explained with more detail.

After identifying the program as ID-DISPLAY, the programmer defines the machinery to be used in handling the problem, namely a Honeywell-200 to compile the program, and an IBM 360 Model 40 to solve, or rather, execute it.

In DATA DIVISION, the variable ID is identified as an independent variable with the use of level number 77. Therefore the identified variable ID has no subdivisions in itself, and has 20 characters from the standard character set.

Procedure division header is followed immediately by the paragraph name FIRST-PARA, then the computer is instructed to ask for the operators ID by displaying "Enter Operators ID" on either the cathode ray tube or console typewriter. The computer places the operators ID in the variable ID.

Then the sentence "THANK YOU" followed by the operators ID will appear on the screen or on the typewriter (depending on the setup). The computer will then print the ID on the standard output device, usually a printer, because the DISPLAY ID statement did not specify an output device. The machine then stops execution with the STOP RUN statement.

● **PROBLEM** 11-14

Follow the flow chart and the group of items given to write a program called DATA-ALTERATION. You may omit the Configuration Section, but use the required division header. Use two independent data items, LAST-NAME, which is fifteen characters long, and SOCIAL-SEC, which is nine characters long.

FIRST-NAME		STUDENT-RECORD		
INIT	REST-OF-NAME	STUDENT-NO.	STUDENT-NAME	S-INIT
1 character	8 characters	9 characters	12 characters	1 character

In the above, note that FIRST-NAME, STUDENT-RECORD, INIT, REST-OF-NAME, STUDENT-NO., STUDENT-NAME, and S-INIT are variables used in the program to be written.

Solution: In following the flow chart, the START statement covers the IDENTIFICATION and ENVIRONMENT DIVISION. In reality a programmer who works for a company almost always uses the same IDENTIFICATION and ENVIRONMENT divisions, keeping in mind that changes such as DATE-WRITTEN and DATE-COMPILED are essential.

In DATA-DIVISION the programmer is required to use two independent data items. In COBOL independent data items are identified by level number 77; therefore the required

```
                                        COBOL STATEMENT
IDENTIFICATION DIVISION.
PROGRAM-ID. DATA-ALTERATION.
AUTHOR. GREGORY STEIN
DATE-WRITTEN. MARCH 31, 1981
REMARKS. THIS IS A SAMPLE PROGRAM FOR
         DATA ALTERATION.
ENVIRONMENT DIVISION.
DATA DIVISION.
WORKING-STORAGE SECTION.
77  LAST-NAME PIC X(15).
77  SOCIAL-SEC PIC X(9).
01  FIRST-NAME.
    02 INIT PIC X(1).
    02 REST-OF-NAME PIC X(8).
01  STUDENT-RECORD.
    02 STUDENT-NO PIC X(9).
    02 S-INIT PIC X(1).
    02 STUDENT-NAME X(12).
PROCEDURE DIVISION.
FIRST-PARA.
    DISPLAY "ENTER LAST NAME" UPON CONSOLE.
    ACCEPT LAST-NAME FROM CONSOLE.
    DISPLAY "ENTER FIRST NAME" UPON CONSOLE.
    ACCEPT FIRST-NAME FROM CONSOLE.
    DISPLAY "ENTER YOUR SOCIAL SEC. NO."
    UPON CONSOLE.
    ACCEPT SOCIAL-SEC FROM CONSOLE.
    MOVE SOCIAL-SEC TO STUDENT-NO.
    MOVE LAST-NAME TO STUDENT-NAME.
    MOVE INIT TO S-INIT.
    DISPLAY STUDENT-RECORD.
LAST-PARA.
    DISPLAY "THANK YOU, THATS ALL." UPON
    CONSOLE.
    STOP RUN.
```

FIG. 1

items may be written as:

    77 LAST-NAME PIC X(15).

    77 SOCIAL-SEC PIC X(9).

Observe that the first item has 15, and the second item has

9 characters from the standard character set.

Examining the group of items given in the question, it is clear that there are two group items each with their own subdivisions, namely, FIRST-NAME, and STUDENT-RECORD.

In format, these group items get identified by level numbers 01 through 49, the first one being the highest level of the data item, and starting from Margin A. The rest of the level numbers are called secondary and start from margin B. Following these rules, the given group of items may be formatted as:

```
A    B

01   FIRST-NAME.
     02 INIT PIC X(1).
     02 REST-OF-NAME PIC X(8).
01   STUDENT-RECORD
     02 STUDENT-NAME X(12)
     02 STUDENT-NO PIC X(9).
     02 S-INIT PIC X(1)
```

Now having finished the IDENTIFICATION, ENVIRONMENT, and DATA DIVISIONS the flow chart may be followed to write the PROCEDURE DIVISION.

Step by step examination of the given flow-chart will enable the programmer to write the required statements.

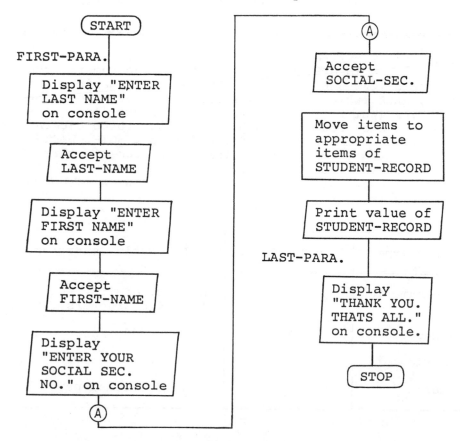

There are two paragraph names given in the flow-chart; FIRST-PARA, and LAST-PARA.

The first paragraph consists of the following operations:

1) Display the sentence "ENTER LAST NAME" on console (screen or typewriter); after the name is entered by the user, accept it from typewriter or screen.

2, 3) Do the same for FIRST NAME, and SOCIAL SECURITY Number.

4) Take these accepted items and move them to their appropriate places in Student-RECORD

5) Print the STUDENT-RECORD on the standard ouput device.

In the last paragraph the computer is told to display the sentence "THANK YOU THATS ALL" on screen or on the typewriter and stop the execution.

Following these rules and explanations the complete program is given in fig. 1.

● **PROBLEM** 11-15

Write a program to read input variables length, width, and height and compute the area and the volume using those variables. At the end of the program print values found.

Solution: To write this program we need four independent data items: INPUT-VARIABLE (which is nine numeric characters long), VOLUME (which is nine numeric characters long), AREA (which is six numeric characters long), and PERIMETER (which is four numeric characters long). We also need one group item subdivided into three elementary data items: DIMENSIONS subdivided into LENGTH, WIDTH, and HEIGHT. Each of these elementary data items is three numeric characters long, with the decimal point at the rightmost end. Note the character types used in COBOL language are shown in figure 1.

Data Type	Picture Char.	Allowable Characters
Alphanumeric	X	Letters, digits, spaces, special characters
Alphabetic	A	Letters and spaces only
Numeric	9	Digits 0 - 9 only
Numeric	V	Implied decimal point

Fig. 1

Arithmetic Operations:

The formats for arithmetic operations are very straight-forward, and the four standard ADD, SUBTRACT, MULTIPLY, and DIVIDE statements are very similar. Either numeric data-names or numeric literals can be specified in these four statements.

ADD statement format:

```
ADD {data-name  }  TO {data-name  }  GIVING data-name
    {num-literal}     {num-literal}
```

SUBTRACT statement format:

```
SUBTRACT {data-name  }  FROM {data-name  } GIVING data-name
         {num-literal}       {num-literal}
```

MULTIPLY statement format:

```
MULTIPLY {data-name  }  BY  {data-name  } GIVING data-name
         {num-literal}      {num-literal}
```

DIVIDE statement format:

```
DIVIDE {data-name  } {BY  } {data-name  } GIVING data-name
       {num-literal} {INTO} {num-literal}
```

COMPUTE STATEMENT: This statement has several uses. It can be used in much the same way as the other arithmetic statements we have seen so far.

Compute statement format:

```
                          { data-name - 2          }
COMPUTE data-name - 1 =   { numeric-literal         }
                          { arithmetic-expression   }
```

357

Relational Operator	Symbol
GREATER THAN	>
NOT GREATER THAN	NOT >
LESS THAN	<
NOT LESS THAN	NOT <
EQUAL TO	=
NOT EQUAL TO	NOT =

Fig. 2

format for GO TO statement:

```
GO TO paragraph-name.
```

GO TO statement speci-
fies a paragraph name

to which control is transferred.

format for IF statement:

```
IF condition statement - 1
```

the IF statement allows execution of statement - 1 if the
condition is true.

Relation Condition Operators are shown in fig. 2

Data values can be moved around in the Procedure
section. One way to do this is to use the MOVE statement.
This statement causes the data to be copied from one data
location to another.

format for MOVE statement:

```
MOVE {data-name - 1} TO data-name - 2
     {literal       }
```

Using the data, information, and the statements given
we write the program as shown in fig. 3.

358

COBOL Coding Form

SYSTEM				PUNCHING INSTRUCTIONS				PAGE 1 OF 2
PROGRAM ARITHMETIC-PRACTICE			GRAPHIC			*		IDENTIFICATION
PROGRAMMER GREGORY STEIN	DATE 3/31	PUNCH		CARD FORM #				73 [80]

SEQUENCE (PAGE) (SERIAL)	CONT	A B	COBOL STATEMENT
3 4	6 7 8	12 16 20 24 28 32 36 40 44 48 52 56 60 64 68
0 1		IDENTIFICATION DIVISION.
0 2		PROGRAM-ID. ARITHMETIC-PRACTICE.
0 3		AUTHOR. GREGORY STEIN.
0 4		DATE-WRITTEN. MARCH 31, 1981.
0 5		ENVIRONMENT DIVISION.
0 6		CONFIGURATION SECTION.
0 7		SOURCE-COMPUTER. H-200
0 8		OBJECT-COMPUTER. IBM-370-135
0 9		DATA DIVISION.
1 0		WORKING-STORAGE SECTION.
1 1		77 INPUT-VARIABLE PIC 9(9).
1 2		77 VOLUME PIC 9(9).
1 3		77 AREA PIC 9(6).
1 4		77 PERIMETER PIC 9(4).
1 5		01 DIMENSIONS.
1 6		02 LENGTH PIC 999 USAGE COMP.
1 7		02 WIDTH PIC 999 USAGE COMP.
1 8		02 HEIGHT PIC 999 USAGE COMP.
1 9		PROCEDURE DIVISION.
2 0		PARAGRAPH-1

FIG. 3

359

COBOL Coding Form

SYSTEM			PUNCHING INSTRUCTIONS			PAGE 2 OF 2
PROGRAM	ARITHMETIC - PRACTICE		GRAPHIC		*	IDENTIFICATION
PROGRAMMER	GREGORY STEIN	DATE 3/31	PUNCH	CARD FORM #		73 ⌐ 80

COBOL STATEMENT

SEQUENCE (PAGE) / (SERIAL)	CONT	A	B	COBOL STATEMENT
01			DISPLAY "ENTER INPUT VARIABLE" UPON
02			CONSOLE.
03			ACCEPT INPUT-VARIABLE FROM CONSOLE
04			IF INPUT VARIABLE EQUAL TO 000000000
05			GO TO ENDING PARAGRAPH.
06		CALCULATIONS.
07			MOVE INPUT-VARIABLE TO DIMENSIONS.
08			COMPUTE PERIMETER = (LENGTH + WIDTH) * 2.
09			MULTIPLY LENGTH BY WIDTH GIVING AREA.
10			COMPUTE VOLUME = LENGTH * WIDTH * HEIGHT.
11		DISPLAY-PARAGRAPH.
12			DISPLAY "LENGTH OF PERIMETER IS"
13			PERIMETER.
14			DISPLAY "AREA IS" AREA.
15			DISPLAY "VOLUME IS" VOLUME.
16			GO TO PARAGRAPH-1.
17		ENDING-PARAGRAPH.
18			STOP RUN.
19			
20			

FIG. 3

Using the information of fig. 1, write a program called
PRINT-A-RECORD, which will read an input card file and
prepare and print a report containing C-CODE, PAYCODE and
PRESENT-DUE.

CARD RECORD							
C-COED	PERSONAL-DATA			CREDIT DATA			
	C-NAME	C-ADDRESS	C-PHONE	YR-OPENED	MAX-CREDIT	PRESENT DUE	PAYCODE
9 digits	21 char.	25 char.	10 char.	2 digits	6 digits 2 rt. of dec.	6 digits 2 rt. of dec.	1 digit

PRINT-LINE	133 character positions

HEADING-LINE							
FILLER	H1 "CUSTOMER CODE"	FILLER	H2 "PAYMENT HISTORY"	FILLER	H3 "CURRENT BALANCE"	FILLER
1	10 spaces		10 spaces		10 spaces		to fill line

INFO-LINE							
FILLER	C-CODE	FILLER	PAYCODE	FILLER	PRESENT-DUE	FILLER
1	12 spaces	9 digits	19 spaces	1 char.	21 spaces	print 6 digits, use $ and dec.	to fill line

fig. 1,

Solution: All the information needed to write the program
is given in the group of diagrams supplied with the prob-

361

lem. This program will read an input card file and prepare
and print a report containing some of the data from the
cards. ASSIGN clause requirements vary with the system,
the general format for the ASSIGN clause is:

```
ASSIGN system-name.
```

An FD (FILE DESCRIPTION) entry must be included in
the File section for each file. The entry must include
FD with the file-name, a LABEL RECORDS clause, and
may include a DATA RECORD clause.

The characters in a file must all be accounted for in
its record description entry. The FILLER item is thus used
to refer to unused spaces in the printer file. For the
PROCEDURE DIVISION new WRITE and MOVE statements are
introduced. The WRITE statement accomplishes a MOVE and
WRITE in a single COBOL operation.

```
WRITE record-name FROM data-name.
```

This format accomplishes both moving of data-name to
record-name and writing of the record to its associated
file. The MOVE CORRESPONDING statement;

```
MOVE CORRESPONDING data-name-1 TO data-name-2
```

moves elementary data items from the data group of
data-name-1 to elementary data items, with the exact same
name, of the data group data-name-2. As an example, in
this problem the statement: MOVE CORRESPONDING CARD-
RECORD TO INFO-LINE. will move only the data items C-
CODE, PAYCODE, PRESENT-DUE in CARD-RECORD to the corresponding items C-CODE, PAYCODE, PRESENT-DUE in INFO-LINE.

In the following program, the new concepts introduced
in this problem are demonstrated thoroughly.

COBOL Coding Form

SYSTEM PRINT-A-REPORT

PROGRAM GREGORY STEIN DATE 3/31

PUNCHING INSTRUCTIONS

GRAPHIC

PUNCH

CARD FORM #

PAGE 1 OF 4

IDENTIFICATION
73 | 80

SEQUENCE		CONT.	A	B	COBOL STATEMENT
(PAGE) 1 3	(SERIAL) 4	6 7 8		12 16 20 24 28 32 36 40 44 48 52 56 60 64 68	
	01		IDENTIFICATION DIVISION.		
	02		PROGRAM-ID. PRINT-A-REPORT.		
	03		ENVIRONMENT DIVISION.		
	04		INPUT-OUTPUT SECTION.		
	05		FILE-CONTROL.		
	06		SELECT CARD-FILE ASSIGN READ001.		
	07		SELECT PRINT-FILE ASSIGN PRINT0001.		
	08		DATA DIVISION.		
	09		FILE SECTION.		
	10		FD CARD-FILE.		
	11		LABEL RECORDS ARE OMITTED.		
	12		DATA RECORD IS CARD-RECORD.		
	13		01 CARD-RECORD.		
	14		02 C-CODE PIC 9(9).		
	15		02 PERSONAL DATA.		
	16		03 C-NAME PIC X(21).		
	17		03 C-ADDRESS PIC X(25).		
	18		03 C-PHONE PIC X(10).		
	19		02 CREDIT-DATA.		
	20		03 YR-OPENED PIC 99.		
			03 MAX-CREDIT PIC 9999V99.		

FIG. 2

COBOL Coding Form

SYSTEM				PUNCHING INSTRUCTIONS			
PROGRAM	PRINT-A-REPORT			GRAPHIC		CARD FORM #	*
PROGRAMMER	GREGORY STEIN		DATE 3/31	PUNCH			IDENTIFICATION 73

COBOL STATEMENT

```
       03  PRESENT-DUE PIC 9999V99.
       03  PAYCODE PIC 9.
   FD PRINT-FILE.
       LABEL RECORDS ARE OMITTED.
   01  PRINT-LINE PIC X(133).
   WORKING STORAGE SECTION.
   01  HEADING-LINE.
       02  CCTL PIC X.
       02  FILLER PIC X(10) VALUE IS SPACES.
       02  H1 PIC X(13) VALUE IS
           "CUSTOMER CODE".
       02  FILLER PIC X(10) VALUE IS SPACES
       02  H2 PIC X(15) VALUE IS
           "PAYMENT HISTORY".
       02  FILLER PIC X(10) VALUE IS SPACES.
       02  H3 PIC X(15) VALUE IS
           "CURRENT BALANCE".
       02  FILLER PIC X(59) VALUE IS SPACES.
   01  INFO-LINE.
       02  CCTL2 PIC X.
```

364

COBOL Coding Form

SYSTEM		PUNCHING INSTRUCTIONS					
PROGRAM *PRINT-A-REPORT*		GRAPHIC			CARD FORM #		*
PROGRAMMER *GREGORY STEIN*	DATE *3/31*	PUNCH					

IDENTIFICATION [73] [80]

SEQUENCE (PAGE) (SERIAL)	CONT	A	B	COBOL STATEMENT
0 1			02 FILLER PIC X(12) VALUE IS SPACES.
0 2			02 C-CODE PIC X(9).
0 3			02 FILLER PIC X(19) VALUE IS SPACES.
0 4			02 PAYCODE PIC X.
0 5			02 FILLER PIC X(21) VALUE IS SPACES
0 6			02 PRESENT-DUE PIC $9999.99.
0 7			02 FILLER PIC X(62) VALUE IS SPACES.
0 8			
0 9		PROCEDURE DIVISION.	
1 0		FIRST-PARA.	
1 1			OPEN INPUT CARD-FILE OUTPUT PRINT-FILE.
1 2			MOVE 1 TO CCTL.
1 3			WRITE PRINT-LINE FROM HEADING-LINE.
1 4			MOVE 0 TO CCTL2.
1 5		PROCESS-PARA.	
1 6			READ CARD-FILE AT END GO TO END-PARA.
1 7			MOVE CORRESPONDING CARD-RECORD TO
1 8			INFO-LINE.
1 9			WRITE PRINT-LINE FROM INFO-LINE.
2 0			GO TO PROCESS-PARA.

COBOL Coding Form

SYSTEM					PAGE 4 OF 4
PROGRAM PRINT-A-REPORT		PUNCHING INSTRUCTIONS		*	IDENTIFICATION
PROGRAMMER GREGORY STEIN	DATE 3/31	GRAPHIC		CARD FORM #	73 ⎿⎽⎽⎽ 80
		PUNCH			

SEQUENCE		CONT.		COBOL STATEMENT
(PAGE) 1 2	(SERIAL) 3 4	6 7 8 A	B 12	16 20 24 28 32 36 40 44 48 52 56 60 64 68
0 1			END	PARA.
0 2				CLOSE CARD-FILE PRINT-FILE.
0 3				STOP RUN.
0 4				
0 5				
0 6				
0 7				
0 8				
0 9				
1 0				
1 1				
1 2				
1 3				
1 4				
1 5				
1 6				
1 7				
1 8				
1 9				
2 0				

Examine the following COBOL program and describe in words the function of each section.

Solution: We have the first three divisions (IDENTIFICATION DIVISION, ENVIRONMENT DIVISION, and DATA DIVISION) of the program LIST-REPORT given.

The IDENTIFICATION DIVISION gives the program name, who wrote it and when it was written, and may include remarks about the program.

The ENVIRONMENT DIVISION consists of two sections. In the CONFIGURATION SECTION the compiling (source) and executing (object) computers are specified. In this program both compilation and execution of the program is done on an IBM-370. The INPUT-OUTPUT section specifies the interface between the program files and the actual external devices. In this program the actual file associated with the identifier TAPE-FILE is the UT-S-TAP01 tape reader. Similarly, CARD-FILE is associated with the UR-S-CAR01 card reader and PRINT-FILE is associated with the UR-S-PRINT01 printer.

The DATA DIVISION is also composed of two sections. The File Section describes the structure of the files used in the program. Every file selected in the INPUT-OUTPUT SECTION of the Environment Division must have an FD (File description) entry in this section. Every FD contains:

1) a file-name

2) a LABEL RECORDS clause. The label record can be either STANDARD or OMITTED. OMITTED is used when there is no label record, STANDARD is used when the label is a standard system label.

3) A description of the record associated with the file-name. As an example of an FD, the file TAPE-FILE will be used from our program. In this file the label records are standard. The statement BLOCK CONTAINS 10 RECORDS. means that the tapereader UT-S-TAP01 sends data to the computer in the form of Data Blocks, each block containing 10 records of the type described in TAPE-RECORD.

The WORKING STORAGE SECTION describes the independent or group variables which will be used for data storage and manipulation in the PROCEDURE SECTION of a program.

367

COBOL Coding Form

SYSTEM				PUNCHING INSTRUCTIONS				
PROGRAM	LIST - REPORT			GRAPHIC		CARD FORM #		*
PROGRAMMER	FRANK HARRISON	DATE 3/3		PUNCH				IDENTIFICATION

IDENTIFICATION 73 80

SEQUENCE (PAGE) 3 4 (SERIAL)	CONT 6 7	A 8	B 12	COBOL STATEMENT 16 20 24 28 32 36 40 44 48 52 56 60 64 68
0 1		IDENTIFICATION DIVISION.		
0 2		PROGRAM-ID. LIST-REPORT.		
0 3		AUTHOR. FRANK HARRISON.		
0 4		DATE-WRITTEN. MARCH 3, 1981.		
0 5				
0 6		ENVIRONMENT DIVISION.		
0 7		CONFIGURATION SECTION.		
0 8		SOURCE-COMPUTER. IBM-370.		
0 9		OBJECT-COMPUTER. IBM-370.		
1 0		INPUT-OUTPUT SECTION.		
1 1		FILE-CONTROL.		
1 2			SELECT TAPE-FILE ASSIGN UT-S-TAPO1.	
1 3			SELECT CARD-FILE ASSIGN UR-S-CARO1.	
1 4			SELECT PRINT-FILE ASSIGN UR-S-PRINTO1.	
1 5				
1 6		DATA DIVISION.		
1 7		FILE SECTION.		
1 8		FD TAPE-FILE.		
1 9			LABEL RECORDS ARE STANDARD	
2 0			BLOCK CONTAINS 10 RECORDS.	
2 1		01	TAPE-RECORD.	
2 2			02 C-CODE PIC 9(9).	
2 3			02 PERSONAL DATA.	
2 4			03 C-NAME PIC X(21).	

COBOL Coding Form

SYSTEM							PUNCHING INSTRUCTIONS				
PROGRAM	LIST-REPORT				GRAPHIC				*	CARD	
PROGRAMMER	FRANK HARRISON		DATE 3/3		PUNCH					FORM #	

IDENTIFICATION
73 ▯ 80

SEQUENCE		CONT.	A	B	COBOL STATEMENT
(PAGE)	(SERIAL)				
	01			03	C-ADDRESS PIC X(30).
	02			03	C-PHONE PIC X(10).
	03				
	04			02	CREDIT-DATA.
	05			03	YR-OPENED PIC 99.
	06			03	MAX-CREDIT PIC 9999V99.
	07			03	PRESENT-DUE PIC S9999V99.
	08			03	PAYCODE PIC 9.
	09				88 BAD VALUE IS 1.
	10				88 POOR VALUE IS 2.
	11				88 AVERAGE VALUE IS 3.
	12				88 GOOD VALUE IS 4.
	13				88 EXCELLENT VALUE IS 5.
	14				88 NONE VALUE IS 6.
	15		FD	CARD-FILE	
	16			LABEL RECORDS ARE OMITTED.
	17		01	CUSTOMER-ACTIVE.
	18			02	CUST-NO PIC 9(9).
	19			02	FILLER PIC X(71).
	20		FD	PRINT-FILE	
				LABEL RECORDS ARE OMITTED.
			01	ONE-LINE PIC X(133).
			WORKING-STORAGE SECTION.	

369

COBOL Coding Form

SYSTEM			PUNCHING INSTRUCTIONS			PAGE 3 OF 3
PROGRAM	LIST-REPORT		GRAPHIC		*	IDENTIFICATION
PROGRAMMER	FRANK HARRISON	DATE 3/3	PUNCH	CARD FORM #		[73]____[80]

SEQUENCE (PAGE) 1 3	(SERIAL) 4 6	CONT 7	A 8	B 12		COBOL STATEMENT							
					16	20	24	28	32	36	40	44
0 1			0 1	HEAD-LINE.								
0 2				02	FILLER	PIC	X(59)	VALUE	SPACES.			
0 3				02	HEADING	PIC	X(16)	VALUE	IS			
0 4				"MISSING	PAYCODES".							
0 5				02	FILLER	PIC	X(58)	VALUE	SPACES.			
0 6			0 1	DATA LINE								
0 7				02	FILLER	PIC	XX	VALUE	SPACES.			
0 8				02	C-CODE	PIC	9(9).					
0 9				02	FILLER	PIC	X(10)	VALUE	SPACES.			
1 0				02	C-NAME	PIC	X(21).					
1 1				02	FILLER	PIC	X(10)	VALUE	SPACES.			
1 2				02	C-ADDRESS	PIC	X(30).					
1 3				02	FILLER	PIC	X(51)	VALUE	SPACES.			
1 4												
1 5												
1 6												
1 7												
1 8												
1 9												
2 0												

370

Write a PROCEDURE DIVISION for the DESCRIPTION, ENVIRON-
MENT and DATA divisions of the previous problem. The
program should print the customer code, name, and address
of the active customers listed in the CARD-FILE. The
customer information is located in the file TAPE-FILE.
Both CARD-FILE and TAPE-FILE are sequentially ordered by
Customer-code.

Solution: Procedure division is used in this record-
matching problem to produce a report. Notice that a new
tape is not being created here. When the card file ends,
the program can be ended. If the tape file happens to
end first, we display an error message and end the
program.

    In the first paragraph, inputs to TAPE and CARD
files, and output to PRINT file are opened, allowing
data to be passed to and from these files.

    In paragraphs named PARA2, and RTAPE the CARD and TAPE
files are read and an ERROR message displayed if the tape
file runs out.

    In COMPARE, the Customer number is compared with
C-CODE. Using decision statements the computer is instructed to go to R-TAPE if Customer number is greater than
C-CODE, this means we haven't found the correct customer
and will keep searching the tape file until we do. Note
that C-CODE is identified in the DATA DIVISION of the
previous problem.

    If the C-CODE is equal to Customer number the com-
puter is instructed to go to the paragraph named WRITE-
LINE. Here we have found the correct customer information
in tape file and thus this paragraph prints the required
information. If the CUST-NO does NOT fit these two conditions it is an invalid CUST-NO and an error message is
displayed. This whole procedure is now repeated until the
CARD-FILE or TAPE-FILE is exhausted, whereupon all files
are closed and execution is stopped.

COBOL Coding Form

SYSTEM

PROGRAM LIST-REPORT (PROCEDURE DIV.)

PROGRAMMER JOHN C. DOE   DATE 3/13

PUNCHING INSTRUCTIONS

GRAPHIC   PUNCH

CARD FORM #

PAGE 1 OF 2

IDENTIFICATION
73 [   ] 80

SEQUENCE (PAGE) (SERIAL)	CONT.	A B	COBOL STATEMENT
0 1			PROCEDURE DIVISION.
0 2			PARA1.
0 3			OPEN INPUT TAPE-FILE CARD-FILE,
0 4			OUTPUT PRINT-FILE.
0 5			WRITE ONE-LINE FROM HEAD-LINE.
0 6			PARA2.
0 7			READ CARD-FILE AT END GO TO ENDING.
0 8			R-TAPE.
0 9			READ TAPE-FILE AT END DISPLAY "ERROR"
1 0			GO TO ENDING.
1 1			COMPARE.
1 2			IF CUST-NO GREATER THAN C-CODE GO TO
1 3			R-TAPE.
1 4			IF CUST-NO EQUAL TO C-CODE GO TO
1 5			WRITE-LINE.
1 6			DISPLAY "ERROR" CUST-NO.
1 7			READ CARD-FILE AT END GO TO ENDING.
1 8			GO TO COMPARE.
1 9			
2 0			

372

COBOL Coding Form

SYSTEM

PROGRAM LIST REPORT (PROCEDURE DIV.)

PROGRAMMER JOHN C. DOE   DATE 3/13

PUNCHING INSTRUCTIONS

| GRAPHIC | | | |
| PUNCH | | | |

CARD FORM #

PAGE   OF

IDENTIFICATION
73 [   ] 80

COBOL STATEMENT

SEQUENCE (PAGE)	(SERIAL)	CONT	A B	COBOL STATEMENT
	01		WRITE-LINE.	
	02		MOVE CORRESPONDING TAPE-RECORD TO	
	03		DATA-LINE.	
	04		WRITE ONE-LINE FROM DATA-LINE.	
	05		GO TO PARA2.	
	06		ENDING.	
	07		CLOSE TAPE-FILE CARD-FILE PRINT-FILE.	
	08		STOP RUN.	
	09			
	10			
	11			
	12			
	13			
	14			
	15			
	16			
	17			
	18			
	19			
	20			

373

Working-Storage entries describing two heading lines are shown in fig. 2. Description of report items, including data-names and starting columns to line up with the headings, are given in the table of fig. 1. Use these descriptions of edited items to write a record description for TRANS-LINE.

Solution: In writing the record description of fig. 3, defined in WORKING STORAGE SECTION and the data table, the VALUE clause is used to specify the appearance of spaces. Observe that the solution is following the data table step by step. The editing characters used in the PICTURE of each data item are described in fig. 4.

Data-Name	Starting Column	Description
C-NUMB	9	6 digits; insert 0 between sets of two
C-NAME	26	20 characters; insert blank bet. 12th. and 13th.
C-CODE	55	1 digit
C-AMT	64	6 digits, 2 to right of decimal point; all digits replaced with blanks if zero.
C-NEW-BAL	79	6 digits, 2 to right of decimal point; comma in appropriate position, fixed dollar sign, sign if value negative, item all asterisks if zero.
C-DUE	96	5 digits, 2 to right of decimal point; dollar sign just before first nonzero digit. Blank if zero.
C-DATE	110	3 sets of two-digit numbers; insert blanks between sets.

Fig. 1

COBOL Coding Form

SYSTEM	PUNCHING INSTRUCTIONS	PAGE 1 OF 1
PROGRAM WORKING-STORAGE ENTRIES	GRAPHIC / CARD FORM # *	IDENTIFICATION 73–80
PROGRAMMER SUAVI USLUCA — DATE 9/12	PUNCH	

```
SEQUENCE  A   B                         COBOL STATEMENT
 01       WORKING-STORAGE SECTION.
 02       01  HEADING-1.
 03           02  FILLER PIC X(58) VALUE SPACES.
 04           02  HEADI PIC X(18) VALUE
 05               "DAILY TRANSACTIONS".
 06           02  FILLER PIC X(57) VALUE SPACES.
 07       01  HEADING-2.
 08           02  FILLER PIC X(6) VALUE SPACES.
 09           02  COLA PIC X(15) VALUE
 10               "CUSTOMER NUMBER".
 11           02  FILLER PIC X(4) VALUE SPACES.
 12           02  COLB PIC X(4) VALUE "NAME".
 13           02  FILLER PIC X(25) VALUE SPACES.
 14           02  COLC PIC X(4) VALUE "CODE".
 15           02  FILLER PIC X(5) VALUE SPACES.
 16           02  COLD PIC X(6) VALUE "AMOUNT".
 17           02  FILLER PIC X(9) VALUE SPACES.
 18           02  COLE PIC X(11) VALUE "NEW BALANCE".
 19           02  FILLER PIC X(6) VALUE SPACES.
 20           02  COLF PIC X(7) VALUE "DUE NOW".
 21           02  FILLER PIC X(7) VALUE SPACES.
 22           02  COLG PIC X(4) VALUE "DATE".
 23           02  FILLER PIC X(20) VALUE SPACES.
```

FIG. 2

COBOL Coding Form

SYSTEM

PROGRAM RECORD-DESCRIPTIONS

PROGRAMMER SUAVI USLUCA   DATE 9/12

PUNCHING INSTRUCTIONS
GRAPHIC
PUNCH
CARD FORM #

PAGE 1 OF 1
IDENTIFICATION 73 [80]

COBOL STATEMENT

SEQUENCE (PAGE)	(SERIAL)	CONT	A	B	COBOL STATEMENT
	01		01		TRANS-LINE.
	02			02	FILLER PIC X(8) VALUE SPACES.
	03			02	C-NUMB PIC XXOXXOXX.
	04			02	FILLER PIC X(9) VALUE SPACES.
	05			02	C-NAME PIC X(12) BX(8).
	06			02	FILLER PIC X(8) VALUE SPACES.
	07			02	C-CODE PIC 9.
	08			02	FILLER PIC X(8) VALUE SPACES.
	09			02	C-AMT PIC ZZZZ.ZZ.
	10			02	FILLER PIC X(8) VALUE SPACES.
	11			02	C-NEW-BAL PIC $*,***.**-.
	12			02	FILLER PIC X(7) VALUE SPACES.
	13			02	C-DUE PIC $$$$.$$.
	14			02	FILLER PIC X(7) VALUE SPACES.
	15			02	C-DATE PIC XXBXXBXX.
	16			02	FILLER PIC X(16) VALUE SPACES.
	17				
	18				
	19				
	20				

FIG. 3

376

Examples

		data	PICTURE	printed
0	Inserts a zero at this position	5432	9099	50432
B	Inserts a blank at this position	AB26	XXB9(2)	AB 26
Ƶ	Replaces leading zeros with blanks up to the amount of Ƶ's used.	00265 00023	Ƶ9(5) ƵƵƵƵƵ	0265 23
.	Inserts a decimal point in this position	265	9.99	2.65
$	Inserts dollar sign at this position if just one, or at farthest right position for more than one, suppressing leading zeros.	125 0026 00015	$9(4) $$$$ $$9(5)	$125 $26 $015
*	Replace leading zeros with asterisks up to the amount of asterisks	0003 0002	$**** **	$***3 **02

Fig. 4

● **PROBLEM** 11-20

Write a complete COBOL program to update an indexed sequential file that contains records of customers who have
charge accounts at a department store. The update information will include new customer records to be added to
the file, charges to be added to customer's accounts, and
credits to be subtracted from others.

   a) Write the complete division to identify the program.

Solution: IDENTIFICATION DIVISION. In the COBOL program
this identifies the program to the user, and the computer.
Besides the mandatory section header and program-ID.
sentences, the programmer may use optional sentences such
as DATE-WRITTEN., AUTHOR., DATE-COMPILED., and REMARKS,
which may be used to clarify the program's main idea to
any future users.

COBOL Coding Form

SYSTEM					PUNCHING INSTRUCTIONS			PAGE	OF
PROGRAM *INDEXED SEQUENTIAL FILE*				GRAPHIC		CARD FORM #	*		IDENTIFICATION
PROGRAMMER *ROBERT C. PUIG*	DATE *3/31*			PUNCH					73 80

COBOL STATEMENT

SEQUENCE (PAGE) (SERIAL)	CONT	A	B																
	34	67 8	12	16	20	24	28	32	36	40	44	48	52	56	60	64	68		
01		IDENTIFICATION DIVISION.															
02		PROGRAM-ID. INDEXED SEQ FILES.															
03		AUTHOR. ROBERT C. PUIG.															
04		DATE-WRITTEN MARCH 31, 1981.															
05		REMARKS. INDEXED SEQUENTIAL FILES THAT															
06		CONTAIN RECORDS OF CUSTOMERS WHO															
07		HAVE CHARGE ACCOUNTS AT A DEPARTMENT															
08		STORE.															
09																	
10																	
11																	
12																	
13																	
14																	
15																	
16																	
17																	
18																	
19																	
20																	

Using the previous problem, write the complete ENVIRON-
MENT DIVISION. The SOURCE-COMPUTER is a Honeywell 200,
and the system on which the program will be executed is
an IBM System/360 Model 40 (IBM-360-40).

Solution: Use the system flowchart given in fig. 1 to
describe the equipment for a program to randomly update
an indexed sequential file. The program uses card input
and print output in addition to the random access file.

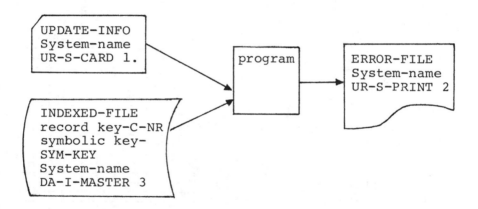

Fig. 1

The indexed file requires 2 extra clauses, RECORD KEY and
SYMBOLIC KEY if the file is used for random access. The
RECORD KEY, C-NR in this program, is used by the computer
to search the file for the specific record requested in
a program. The SYMBOLIC KEY, SYM-KEY in this program,
must be specified if the file is used for output. The
variable associated with SYMBOLIC key must be defined in
the WORKING STORAGE SECTION. The clause, ACCESS IS RANDOM,
sets up the file so that records may be located randomly
by their key, C-NR in this program.

379

COBOL Coding Form

SYSTEM					PUNCHING INSTRUCTIONS				PAGE	/	OF	/
PROGRAM	INDEXED SEQUENTIAL FILE				GRAPHIC			*	IDENTIFICATION			
PROGRAMMER	ROBERT C. PUIG	DATE 3/31			PUNCH		CARD FORM #		73			80

SEQUENCE (PAGE) (SERIAL)	A	B	COBOL STATEMENT
0 1		ENVIRONMENT DIVISION.
0 2		CONFIGURATION SECTION.
0 3		SOURCE-COMPUTER. H-200.
0 4		OBJECT-COMPUTER. IBM-360-40
0 5		INPUT-OUTPUT SECTION.
0 6		FILE-CONTROL.
0 7		SELECT UPDATE-INFO ASSIGN UR-S-CARD1.
0 8		SELECT ERROR-FILE ASSIGN UR-S-PRINT2.
0 9		SELECT INDEXED-FILE
1 0		ASSIGN DA-I-MASTER3
1 1		RECORD KEY IS C-NR
1 2		SYMBOLIC KEY IS SYM-KEY
1 3		ACCESS IS RANDOM.
1 4		
1 5		
1 6		
1 7		
1 8		
1 9		
2 0		

Write a complete DATA-DIVISION for the previous two problems.

Open a FILE-SECTION named UPDATE-INFO using a printer. There will be one unindependent variable called UPDATE-RECORD, which will contain the following units:

Transaction Code: 1 digit
Card Number: 6 standard characters.
New-Name: 21 standard characters.
New-Address: 30 standard characters.
Year: 2 standard characters.
Maximum Credit: 6 numerical characters with a decimal
                 point between 4th and 5th digits. Or
                 4 standard characters.
Action: 6 numerical characters with a decimal point
         between 4th and 5th digits. Or 4 standard
         characters.

Open an ERROR-FILE. Use printer for records.

Open an INDEXED-FILE. Let label records be created by the system.

Define a group item variable called BAS-REC.

For the indexed file.

Subdivide this variable into PERSONAL, and HISTORY, and also subdivide PERSONAL into NAME with 21 standard characters, Customer Number with 6 standard characters, and Customer Address with 30 standard characters. Subdivide HISTORY into OPERATIONAL YEARS with 2 standard characters, MAXIMUM CREDIT with 6 numerical characters (decimal point between 4th and 5th digits), MAXIMUM BILL with 6 numerical characters with a decimal point between 4th and 5th digits, BALANCE DUE--same format as MAXIMUM CREDIT and MAXIMUM BILL and PAYCODE--one numerical character.

In the WORKING STORAGE SECTION define two independent variables called SYM-KEY, and AMOUNT, and an unindependent variable called LISTING with subdivisions CARRIAGE: 1 standard character, PROBLEM: 80 standard characters, and E-MESSAGE: 52 standard characters.

Solution: The DATA DIVISION is shown in fig. 1. The statement BLOCK CONTAINS 5 RECORDS in the INDEXED file description means that the record BAS-REC will be stored in the indexed file in blocks of 5. This allows more efficient searching for the unique keys requested in the program. The computer handles all the details of record storage and retrieval.

COBOL Coding Form

SYSTEM

PROGRAM INDEXED SEQUENTIAL FILE

PROGRAMMER JOHN DOE   DATE 3/30

PUNCHING INSTRUCTIONS   GRAPHIC   PUNCH   CARD FORM #

PAGE 1 OF 2

IDENTIFICATION 73 [80]

COBOL STATEMENT

SEQUENCE	CONT	A	B — COBOL STATEMENT
01			DATA DIVISION.
02			FILE SECTION.
03		FD	UPDATE-INFO
04			LABEL RECORDS ARE OMITTED.
05		01	UPDATE-RECORD.
06			02 TRANSACTION-CODE PIC 9.
07			02 CARDNO PIC X(6).
08			02 NEW-NAME PIC X(21).
09			02 NEW-ADDR PIC X(30).
10			02 YEAR PIC XX.
11			02 MAX-CREDIT PIC 9999V99.
12			02 FILLER PIC X(4).
13			02 ACTION PIC 9999V99.
14			02 FILLER PIC X(4).
15		FD	ERROR-FILE
16			LABEL RECORDS ARE OMITTED.
17		01	ERROR-LIST PIC X(133).
18		FD	
19		FD	INDEXED FILE
20		01	LABEL RECORDS ARE STANDARD

FIG. 1

382

COBOL Coding Form

SYSTEM	PUNCHING INSTRUCTIONS	PAGE 2 OF 2
PROGRAM INDEXED SEQUENTIAL FILE	GRAPHIC / PUNCH / CARD FORM # *	IDENTIFICATION 73–80
PROGRAMMER JOHN DOE — DATE 3/30		

SEQUENCE (PAGE) 1–3 (SERIAL) 4–6 | CONT. 7 | A 8 | B 12 | COBOL STATEMENT

```
 01       BLOCK CONTAINS 5 RECORDS.
 02   01  BAS-REC.
 03       02 PERSONAL.
 04           03 NAME PIC X(21).
 05           03 C-NR PIC X(6).
 06           03 C-ADDR PIC X(30).
 07       02 HISTORY.
 08           03 OP-YR PIC XX.
 09           03 MAXIM PIC 9999V99.
 10           03 MAX-BILL PIC 9999V99.
 11           03 BAL-DUE PIC 9999V99.
 12           03 PAYCODE PIC 9.
 13   WORKING STORAGE SECTION.
 14   77  SYM-KEY PIC X(6).
 15   77  AMOUNT PIC 9999V99.
 16   01  LISTING.
 17       02 CARRIAGE PIC X.
 18       02 PROBLEM PIC X(80).
 19       02 E-MESSAGE PIC X(52).
 20
```

Complete the program defined earlier in the previous three problems by writing the PROCEDURE DIVISION. The transaction records for this program each contain a TRANSACTION-CODE based on the type of transaction. A code of 1 indicates a new customer's record is to be added to the file. A code of 2 indicates a charge to the customer's account, and a 3 indicates a credit, either from payment or return. The program must specify different paths for each transaction. In coding your solution, write the three routines ADD-RECORD, ADD-CHARGE, and SUBTRACT-CREDIT first. Then write the basic program branching to and from routines as necessary. Any time an INVALID KEY clause is activated while a record is being replaced in the file, display "INVALID KEY", C-NR, then transfer control to READ-UPDATE-INFO. Refer back to the Data Division as needed.

COBOL Coding Form

SYSTEM		PUNCHING INSTRUCTIONS		
PROGRAM *INDEXED SEQUENTIAL FILE*	GRAPHIC			CARD
PROGRAMMER *JOHN C. DOE* DATE *3/31*	PUNCH			FORM #

SEQUENCE		COBOL STATEMENT
0 1		PROCEDURE DIVISION.
0 2		OPENING.
0 3		OPEN INPUT UPDATE-INFO, OUTPUT
0 4		ERROR-FILE, I-O INDEXED-FILE.
0 5		READ-UPDATE-INFO.
0 6		READ UPDATE-INFO AT END GO TO FINISH.
0 7		MOVE CARDNO TO SYM-KEY.
0 8		GO TO ADD-RECORD ADD-CHARGE
0 9		SUBTRACT-PAYMENT DEPENDING ON
1 0		TRANSACTION CODE.
1 1		MOVE " INCORRECT CODE" TO E-MESSAGE.
1 2		ERROR-LISTING.
1 3		MOVE UPDATE-RECORD TO PROBLEM.
1 4		WRITE ERROR-LIST FROM LISTING.
1 5		GO TO READ-UPDATE-INFO.
1 6		
1 7		ADD-RECORD.
1 8		MOVE CARDNO TO C-NR.
1 9		MOVE NEW-NAME TO NAME.
2 0		MOVE NEW-ADDR TO C-ADDR.

Fig. 1

Solution: The complete procedure division is shown in fig. 1. In the OPENING paragraph Indexed-file is opened

as I/O, allowing us to write data to and from it.   The
statement is a conditional Go To statement.   In this program paragraph 1 (ADD RECORD) is specified when TRANSACTION-
CODE is a 1, paragraph 2 (ADD-CHARGE) is specified when
TRANSACTION-CODE is a 2, etc.   The statements after
INVALID KEY are executed whenever there is an error while
writing or reading from an indexed file.   The error
messages are printed using the ERROR-LISTING PARAGRAPH,
which displays the error message and the record which
contained the error.

COBOL Coding Form

SYSTEM		PUNCHING INSTRUCTIONS		
PROGRAM INDEXED SEQUENTIAL FILE	GRAPHIC			CARD
PROGRAMMER JOHN C. DOE DATE 3/31	PUNCH			FORM #

```
01          MOVE YEAR TO OP-YR.
02          MOVE MAX-CREDIT TO MAXIM.
03          WRITE BAS-REC INVALID KEY MOVE
04          " DUPLICATE KEY" TO E-MESSAGE GO TO
05          ERROR-LISTING.
06          GO TO READ-UPDATE INFO.
07
08      ADD-CHARGE.
09          READ INDEXED-FILE INVALID KEY MOVE
10          "NOT IN FILE" TO E-MESSAGE GO TO
11          ERROR-LISTING.
12          MOVE ACTION TO AMOUNT.
13          ADD AMOUNT TO BAL-DUE
14
15          IF BAL-DUE GREATER THAN MAX-BILL
16          MOVE BAL-DUE TO MAX-BILL.
17          IF MAX-BILL LESS THAN MAXIM GO TO ADD2.
18          MOVE " VERIFY CREDIT STANDING " TO
19          E-MESSAGE
20          MOVE UPDATE-RECORD TO PROBLEM.
            WRITE ERROR-LIST FROM LISTING.
```

Fig. 1 (part 2)

COBOL Coding Form

SYSTEM				PUNCHING INSTRUCTIONS		PAGE 3 OF 3
PROGRAM	INDEXED SEQUENTIAL FILE		GRAPHIC		CARD FORM #	IDENTIFICATION
PROGRAMMER	JOHN C. DOE	DATE 3/31	PUNCH			73 ⎯ 80

COBOL STATEMENT

```
02  ADD 2L.
03  WRITE BAS-REC INVALID KEY DISPLAY
04  "INVALID KEY" C-NR GO TO
05  READ-UPDATE-INFO.
06  GO TO READ-UPDATE-INFO.
07  SUBTRACT-CREDIT.
08  READ INDEXED-FILE INVALID KEY MOVE
09  "NOT IN FILE" TO E-MESSAGE GO TO
10  ERROR-LISTING.
11  MOVE ACTION TO AMOUNT.
12  SUBTRACT AMOUNT FROM BAL-DUE.
13  WRITE BAS-REC INVALID KEY DISPLAY
14  "INVALID KEY" C-NR.
15  GO TO READ-UPDATE-INFO.
16  FINISH.
17  DISPLAY "NORMAL ENDING" UPON CONSOLE
18  WIND-UP.
19  CLOSE UPDATE-INFO ERROR-FILE
20  INDEXED FILE.
21  STOP RUN.
```

Fig. 1 (part 3)

Input records for a sales agency include, along with
identifying information for each salesman, commission sales
for each of the last six months. Write a procedure division
to read these cards, select the largest of six commission
payments, and print out the salesman's name and his highest
commission payment over the months. The commission is
described as COM OCCURS 6 TIMES PIC 9(4)V99. Start your
program with a flowchart.

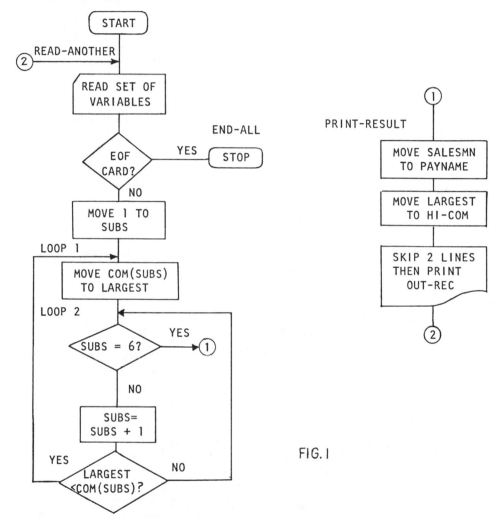

FIG.1

Solution: This problem requires the computer to read a
set of cards, find the largest commission paid to each
salesman, and print the particular salesman's name and
commission.

The flowchart can be started by the read statement,
that is a command should be put into the computer to cause
it to read the set of variables. To prevent an error a
conditional statement should also be used immediately so
that when there are no more variables to read the process
will come to halt.

A complete flowchart of the problem is given in fig. 1.

It should be noted that each programmer has his or her own methods in programming. Therefore flowcharts also vary from person to person, depending on the method of approach to the problem. In the flowchart given, the programmer uses a set of conditional statements to find the largest commission and once it is found, the card or the group of variables is taken out of the deck and certain information contained in it is printed.

Once the flowchart is done, the rest of the work is purely mechanical, and depends on the ability to use the technical knowledge related to the particular programming language, COBOL in this case. In Fig. 2 is the procedure division of the program. Note that adding the remaining three divisions IDENTIFICATION, ENVIRONMENT, and DATA would make this program complete and ready to run. The use of the OCCURS clause sets up a table of 6 com elements. To index a certain element a statement of the form:

$$\text{COM} \left(\left\{ \begin{array}{l} \text{literal} \\ \text{data name} \end{array} \right\} \right)$$

is used. As an example, the statement COM (subs) where subs=4 gives com the value of the fourth com element in the table.

SYSTEM		PUNCHING INSTRUCTIONS	
PROGRAM SALES COMMISSIONS		GRAPHIC	CA
PROGRAMMER JOHN C. DOE	DATE 3/31	PUNCH	FO

```
SEQUENCE  CONT  A  B        COBOL STATEMENT
01    PROCEDURE DIVISION.
02    BEGINNING.
03        OPEN INPUT INFILE, OUTPUT OUTFILE.
04    READ-ANOTHER
05        READ INFILE AT END GO END-ALL.
06        MOVE 1 TO SUBS.
07    LOOP-1.
08        MOVE COM (SUBS) TO LARGEST.
09    LOOP-2.
10        ADD 1 TO SUBS.
11        IF SUBS EQUAL TO 6 GO TO PRINT-RESULT.
12        IF LARGEST LESS THAN COM (SUBS)
13            GO TO LOOP-1.
14        GO TO LOOP-2.
15    PRINT-RESULT.
16        MOVE SALESMN TO PAYNAME.
17        MOVE LARGEST TO HI-COM.
18        WRITE OUT-REC AFTER ADVANCING 2 LINES.
19        GO TO READ-ANOTHER.
20    END-ALL.
          CLOSE INFILE, OUTFILE.
          STOP RUN.
```

Fig. 2

388

CHAPTER 12

FORTRAN

FORTRAN VOCABULARY

● **PROBLEM** 12-1

Explain briefly the background and applications of FORTRAN Computer
Programming Language.

Solution: In 1957, a revolutionary new concept of scientific programming became available to users of the IBM-704 computer. It was called
"FORTRAN" (FORmula TRANslation), or, more formally, the FORTRAN Automatic Coding System for the IBM-704.
Since its introduction, features have been steadily added to the
language. The latest version is FORTRAN V. FORTRAN is a digital
computer programming language which resembles elementary algebra,
augmented by certain English words such as DO, GO TO, READ, WRITE,
IF, etc. Because of its similarity to ordinary algebra, the FORTRAN
language is particularly well suited for solving problems in science,
mathematics, and engineering. However, use of the language is by no
means restricted to these areas. FORTRAN is also applied to a wide
variety of problems in business, economics, psychology, medicine,
library science - virtually any area which might require extensive
manipulation of numerical data or character information. Such a huge
number of areas of application, together with simplicity of learning
and usage, make FORTRAN, probably, the most popular digital computer
language. Although more powerful and flexible languages exist, the
popularity of FORTRAN will probably continue for many years to come.

● **PROBLEM** 12-2

Each of the following is not a correct FORTRAN statement. Give reasons
in each case.
a)   READ (2,1) K, L, M + 1
b)   K + 5 = 37 * I - J * 13
c)   WRITE (3,13) I, J, K, L.
d)   K = 2 $\times$ I
e)   Z ** Y ** W

Solution: a) The only acceptable characters in a variable name in any
FORTRAN statement are the twenty-six letters of the alphabet and the ten
digits 0 to 9 (some systems also accept the $ included in the variable

name). Algebraic signs cannot be included, and therefore M + 1 is an invalid variable.

b) For FORTRAN statements involving arithmetic operations, we use the following symbols:

-   for subtraction
+   for addition
** for exponentiation
*   for multiplication
/   for division

No arithmetic operations are allowed on the left side of the "=" sign.

c) In the WRITE statement the first number (3) indicates the device that is to be used to print the values obtained at the end of the program. (Typewriter, printer). The second number (13) is the number of the corresponding FORMAT statement (will be discussed in later chapters). The listing of the variables should not be followed by a period. This is an error.

d) FORTRAN has no symbol "χ" (presumably we mean multiplication, in which case the correct FORTRAN statement is K = 2 * I .

e) The expression is ambiguous. It could mean

$$(Z^Y)^W \quad \text{or} \quad (Z)^{(Y^W)} .$$

These are not always equal. For example, if Z = 2, Y = 3, W = 4:

$$(2^3)^4 \neq 2^{(3^4)} .$$

● PROBLEM 12-3

Find the mistakes in the following FORTRAN expressions.
a) (A - (B - (C + D(4.7))
b) ((A/B)
c) V = 1.63 * /D

Solution: a) In FORTRAN any constant or variable in an expression, unless it is the first constant or variable of that expression, must be preceded immediately by one of the following:

a left parenthesis
one of the operators +, -, *, /, or ** .

Any constant or variable in an expression, unless it is the last constant or variable of that expression, must be followed by one of the following:

a right parenthesis
one of the operators +, -, *, /, or ** .

The number of opened and closed parenthesis must be equal. Therefore the correct expression is (A - (B - (C + D(4.7)))).

b) For the same argument as was used in part (a), the correct expressions are (A/B) or (A)/(B).

c) The statement is incorrectly formed, and has no meaning. Except for the unary minus, each operator +, *, /, or ** must have a term or factor both to its left and to its right, in order for an expression to be correctly formed.

・ **PROBLEM** 12-4

Pick out the errors in the following FORTRAN statements and explain
briefly why they are incorrect:
a) RESULT = SUM/FLOAT(NUM) + 2ERR
b) IF (M*(N/M) = N) GO TO 20
c) INTEGER CAPITAL, COST, INCOME
d) AREA = LENGTH * WIDTH
e) TAU = BETA/-3.0

Solution: a) FORTRAN variable names cannot begin with numbers, so
2ERR is an invalid variable.
b) In an IF statement, comparisons are made by using relational
operators. An equality sign, which is used only in FORTRAN assignment
statements, should be replaced by .EQ. TERM.
c) CAPITAL is a seven-letter word. FORTRAN allows a maximum of six
characters in each variable name.
d) In FORTRAN, variables beginning with letters I through N are
integer unless specified otherwise. Since WIDTH and AREA are real
variable names, LENGTH cannot be used in order to avoid mixed mode
multiplication.
e) Two arithmetic operators may not be juxtaposed in a FORTRAN assignment statement.

・ **PROBLEM** 12-5

Using FORTRAN rules what would be the value of sum in each case.

a) SUM = 3 - 1 + 5 * 2/2
b) SUM = (4 - 2) ** 2
c) SUM = 9 ** 2 + 9/2 ** 2
d) SUM = (((1 + 2)/2 * 5) * 10/2 + 7)/3

Solution: The rules adopted by the creators of FORTRAN state that
evaluation of arithmetic operations is conducted from left to right,
except when the succeeding operation has a higher "binding power"
than the one currently being considered.

The binding power of "+" and "-" is the lowest in strength;
operators "*" and "/" are of middle strength, and raising to a power
(**) has the highest priority.

The concept of parenthesizing subexpressions was added to
the rules to achieve a sequence in operations different from the rules
of binding power of operators.

Therefore, using this knowledge we find the solutions to be :
a) First division 2/2, then multiplication by 5, followed by adding
to -1 and to 3. The result is 7.
b) First, solving the expression inside the brackets, then using
exponent 2. The answer is 4. Note that the operation was done from
left to right and exponent binding power wasn't taken into consideration
because of the priority of parenthesis.

c) Using the binding power rule, 9**2 is 81 and 2**2 is 4. The third
operation is division: 9/4 - which is 2.25. The last operation is
addition. The result is 83.25.
d) The result is 14.833.

Give a list of the built-in single-precision mathematical functions that can be used in FORTRAN language.

Solution:

NAME	FUNCTION	TYPE OF ARGUMENT	TYPE OF RESULT
ABS(X)	Absolute value of X	real	real
IABS(I)	Absolute value of I	integer	integer
SQRT(X)	Square root of X	real	real
SIN(X)	Sine of X	real	real
COS(X)	Cosine of X	real	real
ATAN(X)	Principal value of arc Tangent of X	real	real
ATAN(X,Y)	Arc-tangent of X/Y	real	real
ASIN(X)	Principal value of arc sine of X	real	real
ACOS(X)	Principal value of arc cosine of X	real	real
TAN(X)	Tangent of X	real	real
COT(X)	Cotangent of X	real	real
ALOG(X)	Natural logarithm of X	real	real
ALOG 10(X)	Common logarithm of X	real	real
EXP(X)	e^x	real	real
GAMMA(X)	Gamma function of X	real	real
INT(X)	Integer part of X	real	integer
FLOAT(I)	Converts integer to real	integer	real
IFIX(X)	Converts real to integer	real	integer
AMOD(X,Y)	Remainder of X/Y	real	real
MOD(I,J)	Remainder of I/J	integer	integer
SIGN(X,Y)	Sign of Y times ABS(X)	real	real
ISIGN(I,J)	Sign of J times IABS(I)	integer	integer
DIM(X,Y)	Difference between X and the smaller of X and Y	real	real
IDIM(I,J)	Difference between I and the smaller of I and J	integer	integer
ERF(X)	Error function of X	real	real
ERFC(X)	Complement error function of X	real	real
AMAX 1(U,V,X...)	Largest of real constants	real	real
MAX 0(I,J,K...)	Largest of integer constants	integer	integer
AMIN 1(U,V,X...)	Smallest of real constants	real	real
MIN 0(I,J,K...)	Smallest of integer constants	integer	integer

USER-DEFINED FUNCTIONS AND SUBROUTINES

Describe the output of the following program.

```
      L = 0
      DO 1 K = 1, 25
1     L = L + K * K
      WRITE (3,2) L
2     FORMAT (1X, I 11)
      STOP
```

Solution: This problem is a good example of the usage of the CONTROL STATEMENT "DO". DO statements are always of the form

DO r i = j,k , or
DO r i = j, k, ℓ, where
r-statement number, i - variable name, j,k,ℓ-variable names or positive integers.

A DO statement is interpreted as follows: do all FORTRAN statements down to and including the one numbered r, first using the value of i = j, then i = j + ℓ, i = j + 2ℓ, and so on, until i becomes larger than k. If ℓ is missing, it is assumed that ℓ = 1.

Therefore, the program takes L = 0 and K = 1 as initial values and then, according to DO statement, executes the formula L = L + K*K 25 times with the value of K being increased by 1 each time. The program then writes the value of L which is finally obtained.

Arithmetical execution of the program is as follows:

$$L = 0 + 1 \cdot 1 = 1$$
$$L = 1 + 2 \cdot 2 = 5$$
$$L = 5 + 3 \cdot 3 = 14$$
$$L = 14 + 4 \cdot 4 = 30$$
$$L = 30 + 5 \cdot 5 = 55$$
$$L = 55 + 6 \cdot 6 = 91$$
$$L = 91 + 7 \cdot 7 = 140$$
$$L = 140 + 8 \cdot 8 = 204$$
$$L = 204 + 9 \cdot 9 = 285$$
$$L = 285 + 10 \cdot 10 = 385$$
$$L = 385 + 11 \cdot 11 = 506$$
$$L = 506 + 12 \cdot 12 = 650$$
$$L = 650 + 13 \cdot 13 = 819$$
$$L = 819 + 14 \cdot 14 = 1015$$
$$L = 1015 + 15 \cdot 15 = 1240$$
$$L = 1240 + 16 \cdot 16 = 1496$$
$$L = 1496 + 17 \cdot 17 = 1785$$
$$L = 1785 + 18 \cdot 18 = 2109$$
$$L = 2109 + 19 \cdot 19 = 2470$$
$$L = 2470 + 20 \cdot 20 = 2870$$
$$L = 2870 + 21 \cdot 21 = 3311$$
$$L = 3311 + 22 \cdot 22 = 3795$$
$$L = 3795 + 23 \cdot 23 = 4324$$
$$L = 4324 + 24 \cdot 24 = 4900$$
$$L = 4900 + 25 \cdot 25 = 5525$$

5525 is the desired result, which will be printed.

Examine the following program and explain the usage of Subprograms
(i.e., Subroutines)

```
      COMPLEX X1, X2
      COMMON/QUADR/X1, X2, A,B,C
      DATA INPUT /60/
1     READ (INPUT, 11) A,B,C
11    FORMAT ( 3E20.9)
      IF (A. EQ. 0.)  GO TO 7
      CALL ROOTS
      PRINT 2, A, B, C, X1, X2
2     FORMAT (13H1 COEFFICIENTS/3E22.9/10X, 4E22.9)
      GO TO 1
7     STOP
      END
      SUBROUTINE ROOTS
      COMPLEX X1, X2, W
      COMMON/QUADR/X1, X2, C1, C2, C3
      W = C2 ** 2 - 4.0 * C1 * C3
      W = W ** 0.5
      X1 = (-C2 + W)/(2.0 * C1)
      X2 = (-C2 - W)/(2.0 * C1)
      RETURN
      END
```

Solution: This is a complete program which consists of a MAIN PART and
a SUBPROGRAM. The MAIN part reads in data for the coefficients of a
quadratic equation and then calls upon a subprogram to find its roots.

The following points are significant in examining the program.

1)   The MAIN program assigns five variables X1, X2, A,B,C to the
common block named QUADR.
2)   The subprogram (ROOTS) names the constituents of common region
QUADR - X1, X2, C1, C2, and C3. Getting into a more detailed explanation of Subprograms:

Every subroutine program begins with a statement of the form
SUBROUTINE NAME. There should be at least one blank space between the
word SUBROUTINE and its name. The name of the subroutine must not appear
anywhere else within the subprogram. Every subprogram has END as its
last statement, and must contain at least one RETURN statement in order
to continue the execution of the MAIN program from the next statement
after the one that called this subroutine.

A subroutine is entered from another program unit (main program or
a different program) by means of a CALL statement. The general form of
the CALL statement is:

CALL name of the subroutine
A subroutine may assign values to one or more of its arguments in
order to "return" results to the main part of the program. Furthermore,
there is the possibility of storing results in COMMON AREA so that values
obtained in a subprogram could be available to other program units.

Determine the output of the following program.

```
        READ (2,3) I,J
3       FORMAT (2 I11)
        IF  (I - J) 5,6,6
6       WRITE (3,10) I
10      FORMAT (1X, I11)
        GO TO 7
5       WRITE (3,10) J
7       STOP
```

Solution: To analyze the program, start from the top. The READ statement tells the computer to use the "card reader" for reading in the values I and J which are specified by the following FORMAT statement, identified by the number 3.

The FORMAT statement states that there are eleven columns used on the card for recording each number input (i.e., 2I11). Every blank space among eleven reserved is equivalent to zero. Naturally, zeros before the first digit of the number have no effect on the number, while each blank space at the end increases the number ten times.

"IF", is a CONTROL statement. In this problem it has the form IF(e)a,b,c, where e is an expression to be evaluated (in this case: I - J), and a,b,c are three statement numbers. The meaning of such statement is as follows:

(1) If the value of the expression is negative, the next statement to be executed is the one labelled a.

(2) If the value of the expression is zero, the next statement to be executed is the one labelled b.

(3) If the value of the expression is positive, the next statement to be executed is the one labelled c. Therefore, in the program, if the value of I - J is negative, the next statement to be executed is the one numbered 5, which causes the output of J. Following this the STOP statement is executed.

If the value of I - J is zero or positive, the next statement to be executed is the one numbered 6,which causes the output of the value of I. The statement following this is another control statement "GO TO". This statement causes a jump in program execution and program pointer goes directly to the statement which is specified by a number following GO TO statement.

Therefore it is clear that the program finds and prints out the largest of two numbers.

a)   Suppose that the statement IF(I - J) 5,6,6 is replaced by
                        IF(I - J) 6,5,5
      in the program of the previous problem. Explain the effect of this change.

b)   Explain what happens if the same statement is replaced by
                        IF(J - I) 6,5,5

c)   Explain what happens if the statement GO TO 7 is omitted in the program of the previous problem.

Solution: a) If we use the statement IF(I - J) 6,5,5, then whenever the value of I - J is negative the computer will go to statement number 6, which causes the output of the value of I, followed by the end of the program (i.e., STOP statement).

On the other hand, if the value I - J is zero or positive, statement number 5 will be executed. Therefore, the program is written to find the smallest of two numbers.
b) If the statement is replaced by IF(J - I) 6,5,5 execution will happen exactly as it did in a), except that the values of I and J will be interchanged. At the end of the output will be the largest of two numbers.
c) If the GO TO 7 statement is omitted, there are two possible cases:

    I.   If I - J < 0 (i.e., I < J), the computer will go to statement 5 and print the value of J.

    II.   If I - J ≥ 0 (i.e., I ≥ J), the computer will go to statement 6 and first print the value of I, and then the value of J.

● **PROBLEM** 12-11

Describe in words the function and the output of the following subroutine.

```
      SUBROUTINE GCD (I,J,K)
      IF (I - J) 1,4,2
    1 L = J
      J = I
      I = L
    2 L = I-(I/J)*J
      IF(L) 3,4,3
    3 I = J
      J = L
      GO TO 2
    4 K = J
      RETURN
      END
```

Solution: The program is written to find the greatest common divisor K of two positive integers I and J. Following the first IF statement, the program pointer will go directly to 1 if the value I - J is negative, to 4 if the value is zero, and 2 if the value is positive. Statement number 1 and the following two statements interchange the values of I and J; therefore prior to statement 2, I is greater than or equal to J. Statement 2 seems useless at first glance. But do not forget that I,J,K and L represent integer variables. Therefore (I/J)*J may not be equal to I. For example: Let I = 4 and J = 3. I/J then will be equal to 1.25, but will be truncated by the computer into integer 1. Then, after multiplying it by J = 3 the computer will get 3 as the result, not 4 as it had originally.

In the second IF statement using the same argument as above, the program pointer will go to statements 3 or 4. Statement 3 and the following statement replace J with I and L with J. Then the computer goes back to the statement 2 and repeats the calculations. This goes on until I will be divided by J with no remainder left to truncate. In that case value of L will become zero, and the computer will go to statement 4, equate K to J and store this value under K as the desired divisor.

Change the Subroutine of the previous problem into a FUNCTION SUBPROGRAM and explain the procedure.

Solution: In FORTRAN, there is another kind of subprogram, called the FUNCTION SUBPROGRAM. The Function Subprogram may replace the subroutine if the result obtained by the SUBROUTINE is a single value.

In order to get a function subprogram from the subroutine of the previous problem, 3 changes have to be made.
1) The first statement should be replaced by
        FUNCTION IGCD(I,J)
that is, the word SUBROUTINE is replaced by FUNCTION. Parameter K is not being used anymore because the name of the function will be assigned the value of the greatest common divisor.

The divisor value obtained by the subprogram is an integer; there-fore the name of the FUNCTION subprogram must begin with the corresponding letter (i.e., I,J,...,N).
2) Variable K must be replaced by the name of the function-IGCD each time it appears in the statement, i.e., statement 4, (K = J), has to be changed into IGCD = J.
3) Function Subprograms must not change values of any of their parameters. It was observed in the Subroutine program GCD that the values of I and J were changed, therefore some modifications must be made before this subroutine can become a function subprogram. The simplest modification would be to assign the values of I and J to two independent variables, say M and N, and then use them in place of I and J. Therefore, the modified FUNCTION SUBPROGRAM will take the following form:

```
FUNCTION   IGCD (I,J)
M = I
N = J
IF (M - N)1,4,2
1 L = N
N = M
M = L
2 L = M - (M/N)*N
IF(L)3,4,3
3 M = N
N = L
GO TO 2
4 IGCD = N
RETURN
END
```

Using either the Subroutine Subprogram or Function Subprogram of the previous two problems obtain the greatest common divisor of L1 and L2, and add it to NN. Assume the Main Program is written, and integer values are assigned to L1, L2, and NN.

Solution: This is a good example of some of the advantages of using FUNCTION SUBPROGRAMS. We could use the following statements for the Subroutine:

```
CALL GCD(L1, L2, M)
NN = NN + M
```

However, for the FUNCTION SUBPROGRAM we only need one statement:

$$NN = NN + IGCD(L1, L2)$$

Notice that the function subprogram is used in expressions wherever needed, in a way similar to the built-in functions such as SQRT (square root), IABS(Absolute Value of I),etc.

● **PROBLEM** 12-14

Write the necessary statement function(s) to compute the area of a triangle, given 3 sides. Use Hero's formula.

Solution: The area of a triangle of sides a,b, and c is given by

$$Area = \sqrt{s(s-a)(s-b)(s-c)} \text{ where } s = \tfrac{1}{2}(a+b+c)$$

Hence, using one statement function to define s and a second to define Area, we get:

```
S(A,B,C) = 0.5 * (A + B + C)
X = S(A,B,C)

AREA(A,B,C,X) = SQRT(X*(X-A)*(X-B)*(X-C))
```

DIMENSION

● **PROBLEM** 12-15

(a) A FORTRAN program contains the statement:

DIMENSION A(10,15,7)

Assuming that elements of arrays are stored in lexicographic order of their indices, find the displacement of the location of the element A(5,7,4) relative to the location of A(1,1,1).

(b) If A is a three-dimensional FORTRAN array of dimension $n_1 \times n_2 \times n_3$, find the location of the element A(I,J,K) in terms of the location of A(1,1,1) and I, J and K, where I, J and K are simple integer variables. Assume that elements are stored in lexicographic order of their indices.

Solution: (a) All conventional computers require a multidimensional array to be stored as a linear sequence of elements. The compiler must, therefore, contain a procedure that computes the actual location of an element in an array from its specification in terms of indices. The mapping from the multidimensional array to the linear array is not unique. However, if we assume that the elements of the multidimensional array are stored in the lexicographic order of their indices, we cay say that A(5,7,4) comes in the fourth column of the seventh row of the fifth plane of the array; i.e., it is preceded by four planes, six rows and three elements. But the FORTRAN statement

DIMENSION A(10,15,7)

allocates a storage area equivalent to 10 planes of 15 rows with 7 elements in each row. Each of the 10 planes, therefore, contains 15×7 elements. If loc(X) is the location of element A(X), then
loc(5,7,4) = loc(1,1,1) + 4(15·7) + 6(7) + 3 = loc(1,1,1) + 420 + 42 + 3 = loc(1,1,1) + 465.

Hence, the displacement of the location of the element A(5,7,4) relative to the location of A(1,1,1) is 465.

(b) Generalizing the reasoning of part (a), we can say that A(I,J,K) comes in the K-th column of the J-th row of the I-th plane of the array, i.e., it is preceded by (I-1) planes, (J-1) rows, and (K-1) elements. But A's dimensions are $n_1 \times n_2 \times n_3$, which means that each plane contains n_2 rows and n_3 columns, or $n_2 n_3$ elements. Therefore,

$$\text{loc}(I,J,K) = \text{loc}(1,1,1) + (I-1)n_2 n_3 + (J-1)n_3 + (K-1)$$

The part played by array dimensions n_1, n_2, n_3 in storage mapping is one reason why FORTRAN (and most other programming languages) require the actual dimensions of arrays to be declared. Some compilers, e.g., the WATFIV FORTRAN compiler, generate a code that determines during execution of the program whether a reference to a subscripted variable lies outside the declared array bounds. If it does, and were to remain undetected, the information might get recorded in locations that house other data, or even in the program itself, altering the program and, hence, its behavior. Since such compilers as WATFIV are used for program testing, the increase in execution time due to these tests is well worth it.

● **PROBLEM** 12-16

A FORTRAN program contains the statement:

DIMENSION A(10,10,10)
Assuming that elements of the array are stored in lexicographic order of their indices, find displacements of the locations of:
(a) A(5,6,7)　　(b) A(10,9,8)　　(c) A(1,5,9)
relative to the location of A(1,1,1).

Solution: In the previous problem, it was shown that if A has dimensions $n_1 \times n_2 \times n_3$, the location of any element A(I,J,K) is given by:

$$\text{loc}(I,J,K) = \text{loc}(1,1,1) + (I-1)n_2 n_3 + (J-1)n_3 + (K-1),$$

assuming that elements are stored in lexicographic order of their indices. The displacement of the location of the element A(I,J,K) relative to the location of A(1,1,1), therefore, is given by:

$$\text{disp}(I,J,K) = \text{loc}(I,J,K) - \text{loc}(1,1,1)$$

$$= (I-1)n_2 n_3 + (J-1)n_3 + (K-1) \qquad (1)$$

We are given that $n_1 = n_2 = n_3 = 10$.

(a) Here I = 5, J = 6, K = 7. Substitution into equation (1) yields:

$$\text{disp}(5,6,7) = (5-1)(10 \cdot 10) + (6-1)10 + (7-1)$$

$$= (4)100 + (5)10 + 6 = 456$$

(b) Here I = 10, J = 9, K = 8. Substituting into equation (1) gives us:

$$\text{disp}(10,9,8) = (10-1)(10 \ 10) + (9-1) \ 10 + (8-1)$$

$$= (9)100 + (8)10 + 7 = 987$$

(c) Here I = 1, J = 5, K = 9. Substituting into equation (1), we have:

$$\text{disp}(1,5,9) = (1-1)(10 \cdot 10) + (5-1)10 + (9-1)$$

$$= (0)(100) + (4)(10) + 8 = 48$$

What is the output for the following FORTRAN program?

```
        DIMENSION A(8), PTR (8)
        DATA A/'A', 'S', 'E', 'Q', 'N', 'U', 'T', '1'/
        DATA PTR/4,7,2,6,6,3,0,5/
        I = PTR (1)
   20   IF (I.EQ.0) GO TO 30
        WRITE (5,100) A (I)
  100   FORMAT (1X,A1)
        I = PTR (I)
        GO TO 20
   30   CONTINUE
        STOP
        END
```

Solution: This is an elementary problem using pointers. The object is to introduce pointers in a simple way by allowing you to "walk" through the program to find the output.

The first executable statement puts the first value of the array PTR in the variable I. If you look at the DATA statement for PTR, you will notice that PTR (1) is 4. I is not equal to zero, so control passes to the WRITE statement, which indicates that the element in A(4) should be outputted. This, as indicated by the DATA statement for A, is represented by the letter Q. Next, the value contained in PTR (4) replaces the initial value of I. The number 6 is in the position of PTR (4) now. Control then passes back to statement 20, and the loop continues until PTR (I) reaches a value of zero. Notice that termination will occur when PTR (7) stores 0 in I.

The final output requires only five passes until termination. Follow the program and you will see that your "quest" for the answer will not be difficult at all.

I^{th} element of A(I)	PTR(I)	A(I)
4th	4	Q
6th	6	U
3rd	3	E
2nd	2	S
7th	7	T

Write a pseudocoded program to set up a simple system of computer-aided instruction (CAI). It should keep track of the student's grades for each lesson.

Solution: Computer teaching methods are used in many schools and businesses. It allows students to study when they want, and it eliminates some of the distractions of the classroom.

The cathode ray tube (CRT) is a very useful device for these systems. This device, which looks like a TV screen, lets a student see segments of a lesson, a few at a time. After a sufficient amount of material has been presented, a short quiz of one question appears. The student types in his choice of answer, and the computer evaluates it. If the answer is correct, the lesson continues. If incorrect, a message pointing out the mistake comes on the tube.

The structure of a lesson is a series of pages. Each page has a question associated with a set of possible answers. The answer selected determines what page will appear next.

The organization of a simple CAI system is outlined below. Pages are numbered 1 to M. The page following a correct answer J is given in the array element PAGE (I,J). We store O in PAGE (I,J) if J corresponds to the end of the session. We could also say that PAGE (I,J) equals -1 if J is the wrong answer. The array SCORE keeps track of the student's performance throughout the course.

```
Integer  I,J,K,L,M,N, STUD - SCORE, SCORE(M,N), PAGE (M,N)
STUD-SCORE ← 0
I ← 1
do while  I ≠ 0
    output K ← -1 PAGE I
    do while K = -1
    input response  J
    K ← PAGE (I,J)
If  K = -1, output 'TRY AGAIN, PLEASE'
end do while
STUD-SCORE ← STUD-SCORE + SCORE (I,J)
I ← K
end do while
end program
```

PROGRAMS IN FORTRAN

● **PROBLEM** 12-19

Write a function to evaluate $f(x) = e^{-x^2}(1 - x^3/3)$. Show calculation of $f(3)$.

Solution: The simplest type of function is the so-called statement function. Making use of this concept, we can immediately write:

```
F(x) = EXP(-X*X)*(1. - (X**3)/3.)
Y = F(3.0)
```

● **PROBLEM** 12-20

A business law class of 25 students takes a midterm exam that has 100 true-or-false questions. The instructor, who is also a computer fanatic, wants to devise a program to obtain a printout with the student's name, score, and letter grade, according to the following schedule:

50	or below	F
51 - 55		D
56 - 60		C-
61 - 65		C
66 - 70		C+
71 - 75		B-
76 - 80		B
81 - 85		B+
86 - 90		A-
91 - 95		A
96 - 100		A+

In addition, the instructor wants to include the total number of students scoring each of the 11 possible grades.
How would you use the FORTRAN language to solve his problem?

Solution: We need four arrays in this problem. The array KOUNT stores the number of times a grade is achieved by students; eleven cells are to be reserved, one for each grade. The array NGRADE stores the numerical upper limits of the corresponding letter grades. To initialize NGRADE, we use the first data card, filled out in the following format:

     50   55   60   65   70   75   80   85   90   95   100

The third array, LETTER, is a two-dimensional array with 11 rows and 2 columns. It stores the 11 possible letter grades. When the grades are to be outputted, LETTER provides the data. As in NGRADE, we use a data card for initialization:

     F   D   C- C   C+ B- B   B+ A- A   A+

We set up a DO loop to read in the remaining 25 cards, one for each student. Another loop is nested within the first one to categorize the scores into the proper letter grade range. We output each student's name (the first 20 characters of it) the numerical score, and the letter grade. Finally, the counts for the number of occurrences of each letter grade are printed.

```
          DIMENSION KOUNT (11), NGRADE (11), LETTER (2,11),
1         NAME (20)
C         INITIALIZE KOUNT AND READ TWO
C         INITIAL DATA CARDS FOR NGRADE AND LETTER
          DO 5  I = 1,11
          KOUNT (I) = 0
5         CONTINUE
          READ (5,100) NGRADE
100       FORMAT (11I3)
          READ (5,101) LETTER
101       FORMAT (22A1)
C         READ MASTER CARD DECK
          DO 10  J = 1,25
          READ (5,102) NAME, ISCORE
102       FORMAT (20A1, I4)
          DO 20  K = 1,11
          IF (ISCORE.LT.NGRADE (K)) GO TO 15
20        CONTINUE
          GO TO 98
15        WRITE (6,103) NAME, ISCORE, (LETTER (K,
1         J),  K = 1,2)
103       FORMAT (1X,20A1, I4, 1X, 2A1)
          KOUNT (J) = KOUNT (J) + 1
10        CONTINUE
          WRITE (6,104) KOUNT
104       FORMAT (11(2X,I3))
          GO TO 99
98        WRITE (6,105)
105       FORMAT (1X,'DATA ERROR IN DECK')
99        STOP
          END
```

The Riverdell Englewoods, a Little League team of the future, is offering a prize to anyone who can write a FORTRAN program to keep track of the box scores of their games. An underfinanced team, the Englewoods have an ancient card-punching machine in the dugout. Each time an Englewood comes to bat, the scorekeeper prepares a card with the following items:
1) the player's number (2 digits)
2) the result of his at-bat (0 for out, 1 for a single, etc., up to 4 for a home run)
3) whether the player scored a run (either 0 or 1)
4) the number of runs batted in
   The manager wants the program to output the player's number, the number of at-bats, hits, runs scored, and runs batted in for each game. After the last player has been listed, compute and output the team totals.

Solution: We assume that there is a total of 20 players on the team numbered 1 through 20. Thus, we need a loop to compute the required statistics for each player. After each computation, we store the elements in arrays so that team totals may be computed at the end.

Variable names are chosen to match closely the baseball terminology. The program stores each player's totals until a card containing all zeros is encountered. This signifies the end of the deck, whereupon the output procedure begins, completed with appropriate headings.

```
C          BOX SCORES FOR ENGLEWOODS
           INTEGER PLAYNO, EFORT, RUNSCO, RBI
           INTEGER ATBAT, HITNO, RUNNO, RBINO
           INTEGER TOTBAT, TOTHIT, TOTRUN, TOTRBI
           DIMENSION ATBAT(20), HITNO(20), RUNNO(20), RBINO(20)
C          INITIALIZE ALL VARIABLES TO ZERO
           DATA PLAYNO, EFORT, RUNSCO, RBI/0,0,0,0/
           DATA ATBAT, HITNO, RUNNO, RBINO/20*0, 20*0, 20*0, 20*0/
           DATA TOTBAT, TOTHIT, TOTRUN, TOTRBI/0,0,0,0/
C          READ CARDS
10         READ (2,100) PLAYNO, EFORT, RUNSCO, RBI
100        FORMAT (12,3I1)
C          DO WHILE PLAYNO IS NOT EQUAL TO ZERO
           IF (PLAYNO. EQ. 0) GO TO 20
           ATBAT (PLAYNO) = ATBAT (PLAYNO) + 1
           IF (EFORT. NE. 0) HITNO (PLAYNO) = HITNO (PLAYNO) + 1
           RUNNO(PLAYNO) = RUNNO(PLAYNO) + RUNSCO
           RBINO(PLAYNO) = RBINO(PLAYNO) + RBI
           GO TO 10
C          PRINT HEADINGS
           WRITE (6,101)
101        FORMAT(1X,'PLAYER NUMBER',5X,'AT BATS',5X,
1          'HITS',5X,'RUNS',5X,'RBIS')
20         DO 25  J = 1,20
           IF (ATBAT (J).EQ. 0) GO TO 25
           WRITE (6,102) J, ATBAT (J), EFORT, RUNSCO, RBI
102        FORMAT (7X,I2,13X,I1,11X,I1,2(8X,I1)/)
           TOTBAT = TOTBAT + ATBAT (J)
           TOTHIT = TOTHIT + HITNO (J)
           TOTRUN = TOTRUN + RUNNO (J)
           TOTRBI = TOTRBI + RBINO (J)
25         CONTINUE
           WRITE (6,103) TOTBAT, TOTHIT, TOTRUN, TOTRBI
103        FORMAT (1X,'TEAM TOTALS',9X,I2,11X,I2,2(8X,I2))
           STOP
           END
```

Write a FORTRAN program that outputs the customer's name and account
number, the number of message units used, the arrears, and the total bill.
The rate schedule should be 10 cents per message unit up to 75, and 8
cents per message unit beyond 75.

Solution: This is a telephone billing scheme which excludes long-
distance calls. We read in the cards, each of which contains the
following information:

variable	description	number of spaces per card
NAME	customer name	12
NUMCUS	customer number	7
MSGS	message units	5
ARREAR	arrears	6

Program control is managed by a loop through which each card is read.
If a blank space appears in the first space of NAME, control passes
out of the loop, and the program terminates. The rest of the logic is
a straightforward computation of the billing rates described above.
Appropriate messages and headings will be contained in the output.
Integer arithmetic is used for simplicity's sake.

```
          INTEGER NAME (12), NUMCUS, MSGS, BLANK,
1         TOTBIL
          BLANK = ' □ '
5         READ (2,101)NAME, NUMCUS, MSGS, ARREAR
101       FORMAT(12A1,I7,2X,I5,7X,I6)
C         IF FIRST COLUMN IS BLANK, ENDPROGRAM
          IF (NAME (1).EQ.BLANK)GO TO 25
C         10 CENTS PER MESSAGE UNIT PLUS ARREARS
          TOTBIL = 10*MSGS + ARREAR
C         DISCOUNT FOR MSGS OVER 75
          IF (MSGS.GT.75) TOTBIL  =  TOTBIL - 8*(MSGS - 75)
          WRITE (6,102) NAME, NUMCUS, MSGS, ARREAR, TOTBIL
102       FORMAT (1X,12A1,2X,I7/I7,'MSG  UNITS',3X,I6,
1         'CENTS ARREARS'/'AMOUNT DUE',I7,'CENTS'/)
          GO TO 5
25        CONTINUE
          STOP
          END
```

Write a FORTRAN program to set up a direct-access file with one record
for each of 1,869 students in a school. Assume that the students have
been assigned identification numbers from 1 to 1,869. Allow some extra
space for expansion of student population as well as for expansion of
items within a student record.

Solution: This problem introduces the DEFINE FILE statement along with
the associated WRITE statement. This statement takes the form
          DEFINE FILE N1 (NREC, NRECL, E, INT)
where N1 is a unit number (for restrictions on N1 see your computer
installation manual), NREC is the number of records, NRECL is the
record length in bytes, E stands for format control, and INT is an
associated variable which is the index to the next sequential record

in the file following a READ or WRITE operation.

The form of the WRITE statement is

WRITE (UNIT, INDEX, FMT) LIST

UNIT is an integer variable, or integer constant four spaces long, which has a value between 1 and 99 and which corresponds to the file to be written. This file must have been previously defined with a DEFINE FILE statement.

The INDEX is an integer expression whose value indicates the index of the record to be written.

FMT is a statement number which refers to the FORMAT statement to be used.

Finally, LIST defines the data to be written, and usually contains one or more FORTRAN variable names separated by commas.

```
          INTEGER STUDNO, NAME (5)
          DEFINE FILE 12(2000, 150, E, INT)
          DO 22  I = 1, 1869
          READ 3, STUDNO, NAME
22        WRITE (12 , STUDNO, 4) NAME
3         FORMAT (I4, 5A4)
4         FORMAT (5A4)
          STOP
          END
```

● **PROBLEM** 12-24

You are handed a stack of IBM cards, each of which is supposed to contain a number between 0 and 50. Write a FORTRAN program to sum the results of the following operations on these numbers:
a) Multiply numbers between 0 and 10 inclusive by 3
b) Divide numbers between 11 and 30 inclusive by 2
c) Subtract 5 from all numbers from 31 to 50 inclusive.
Also have the program sum the number of errors in the input deck, i.e., how many cards contain numbers outside the specified range. The program should terminate when the value 99.9 is encountered in the deck.

Solution: A flowchart outlines the structure of the algorithm to be used:

The idea is to check each number to find out the range in which it lies. The specified operation is performed upon every number; each answer (stored in the variable TEMP) is added to the final answer - the sum of all the adjusted numbers. Control passes to the output stage when the number 99.9 is reached.

```
          DATA ERRSUM, SUM, TEMP/0.0, 0.0, 0.0/
10        READ (2,100) X
100       FORMAT (F3.1)
          IF (X.EQ. 99.9) GO TO 98
          IF (X. LT.0..OR.X.GT.50.)  GO TO 20
20        ERRSUM = ERRSUM + 1
          GO TO 10
          IF (X.GE.0. AND.X.LE.10.) GO TO 30
30        TEMP = X*3.0
          SUM = SUM + TEMP
```

405

```
          GO TO 10
          IF (X.GE.11.AND.X.LE.30.) GO TO 40
40        TEMP = X/2.0
          SUM = SUM + TEMP
          GO TO 10
          TEMP = X - 5.0
          SUM = SUM + TEMP
          GO TO 10
98        WRITE (6,101) SUM, ERRSUM
101       FORMAT (1X ,'SUM =', F8.4,'   ERRORS   IN   DECK = ',F4.0)
          STOP
          END
```

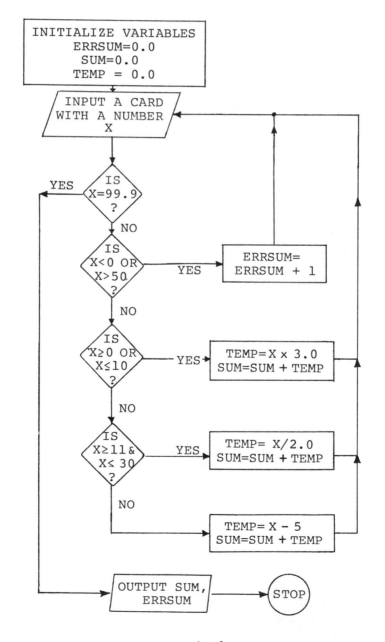

Write a FORTRAN program to analyze a population according to these three genetic criteria:
1) Hair color
2) Eye color
3) Skin color
The program should read a deck of cards, each of which contains for one individual the integers, 1, 2, or 3 to identify the three criteria. Output should consist of the number of individuals found to have the corresponding set of genetic factors.

Solution: We will need a three-dimensional array to store hair, eye, and skin data. These will be in the form of five-digit integers; e.g., black hair = 01111, blue eyes = 02100, green skin = 03999. As each card is read, the program should add 1 to the appropriate cell of the array. In the output, we want to print the number of individuals that have the same set of genetic factors. Note that we are not interested in the individual cases, but only in the number of matches found in the population.

The variable IEND appears at the end of each card; the program terminates when a card is encountered where IEND is nonzero.

```
           DIMENSION KOUNT (3,3,3)
           DO 10  I = 1,3     /*INITIALIZING ARRAY*/
           DO 20  J = 1,3
           DO 30  K = 1,3
           KOUNT (I,J,K) = 0
30         CONTINUE
20         CONTINUE
10         CONTINUE
40         READ (2,100) IHAIR, IEYES, ISKIN, IEND
100        FORMAT (4I5)
           IF (IEND.NE.0)  GO TO 50
           KOUNT(IHAIR,IEYES,ISKIN) = KOUNT(IHAIR,IEYES,
1          ISKIN) + 1
           GO TO 40
50         CONTINUE
           DO 60  I = 1,3
           DO 61  J = 1,3
           DO 62  K = 1,3
           WRITE (6,100) KOUNT (I,J,K)
62         CONTINUE
61         CONTINUE
60         CONTINUE
           STOP
           END
```

Assume that a gasoline company has a computer facility to take care of billing customers when they buy gasoline with credit cards. The computer is used to make out the check to the station, prepare a master list and create mailing lists and bills. Each customer's information is punched on the card, which contains the gas station number and name, the customer's number and name, and certain billing codes. Can you think of any things that could happen that would make the program useless?

Solution: Although this doesn't sound like a complicated computer problem, in reality programmers tend to forget about "trivial" details that often

become troublesome. For example:
a)   What if the customer dies? The program must be able to accommodate uncollectable bills.
b)   What if a customer moves? The program should be able to alter addresses.
c)   What if a customer sends invalid checks?
d)   What if the customer loses his bill and wants a duplicate?
e)   What if a customer changes his or her name?

   Appropriate actions should be taken in these special cases. If the program doesn't take these possibilities into account, the output will be meaningless when these eventualities arise.

● **PROBLEM** 12-27

A suburban housewife, who lives at location A of the town street plan in Figure 1, drives to fill up her automobile at the local gas station, located at B. For some reason, all of the horizontal streets run from left to right, and all the vertical streets run from bottom to top. She is curious as to how many possible routes exist between her and the gas station. Write a FORTRAN program to solve her dilemma.

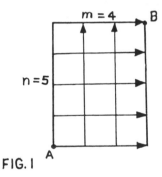

FIG. I

Solution: From the definition of the street plan, the direction of movement from each corner can be either up or to the right. Any particular path can be written as a sequence of u's and r's (ups and rights), in which the total number of u's and r's can be written as n and m, respectively. Hence, the total number of possible paths is

$$(m + n)! \ / \ n! \ m!$$

We can write a program to generalize this problem for a street plan of n and m dimensions. The use of the FACT (factorial) function will make the program shorter and easier to understand.

```
         INTEGER N,M
         READ (5,*) N,M
C        COMPUTE NUMBER OF POSSIBLE PATHS
C        FROM CORNER TO CORNER
         PATHS = FACT(M+N)/FACT(N)*FACT(M)
         WRITE (5,100) N,M, PATHS
100      FORMAT (1X,'NUMBER OF POSSIBLE PATHS
1        FROM CORNER TO CORNER IN AN',I2,'BY',
2        I2, 'MATRIX =',I4)
         STOP
         END
```

Given the coordinates of three points (X_1, Y_1), (X_2, Y_2), and (X_3, Y_3), develope a program which outputs a message regarding their collinearity. (Three points are collinear if they all lie on the same line.) Include statements that will take into account round-off errors.

Solution: The solution to the problem rests on the fact that three points P_1, P_2, and P_3 are collinear if and only if the slopes of the segments P_1P_2 and P_2P_3 are equal. This implies

$$\frac{Y_2 - Y_1}{X_2 - X_1} = \frac{Y_3 - Y_2}{X_3 - X_2}$$

where (X_1, Y_1), (X_2, Y_2) and (X_3, Y_3) are the coordinates of three points.

Instead of calculating slopes, we can test the expressions $(Y_2 - Y_1) \times (X_3 - X_2)$ and $(Y_3 - Y_2) \times (X_2 - X_1)$, for equality. If they are equal, the three points are collinear, and an appropriate message is output. This expression may also be used to establish the degree of round-off error. One way of doing this is with the statement

        ABS((Y2 - Y1)*(X3 - X2) - (Y3 - Y2)*(X2 - X1))

If this quantity is very small, say, less than .0001, we can accept the accuracy of collinearity. If this condition is not met, a message indicates that there is an unacceptable accuracy in the determination.

We use a format-free READ statement in the program for simplicity's sake, a feature available on some machines.

```
C               COLLINEARITY PROGRAM
                READ (5,*) X1, Y1, X2, Y2, X3, Y3 ,ACCUR
C               ARE THEY COLLINEAR?
                IF((Y2 - Y1)*(X3 - X2). NE. (Y3 - Y2)*(X2 - X1)) GO TO 30
                WRITE (5,100) X1, Y1, X2, Y2, X3, Y3
100             FORMAT (1X,'THE PAIRS OF POINTS  ', 3(1X,2(1X,F7.5)),'ARE
1               COLLINEAR')
                TEST = ABS((Y2 - Y1)*(X3 - X2) - (Y3 - Y2)*(X2 - X1))
                IF (TEST. GE. ACCUR)  GO TO 25
                WRITE (5,101) ACCUR
101             FORMAT(1X,'WITH DESIRED ACCURACY TO  ', F7.5)
                GO TO 99
25              WRITE (5,101) ACCUR
101             FORMAT (1X 'WITHOUT ACCURACY OF', F7.5)
30              WRITE (5,102)
102             FORMAT (1X,'POINTS ARE NOT COLLINEAR')
99              STOP
                END
```

The formula
$$Z = \left(\frac{e^{ax} - e^{-ax}}{2}\right) \sin(x+b) + a \log\left(\frac{b + x}{2}\right)$$
is to be evaluated for all combinations of   x: 1.0(0.1) 2.0
                                            a: 0.10(0.05)0.80
                                            b: 1.0(1.0) 10.0

where   x: 1.0(0.1) 2.0 means   x = 1.0, 1.1, 1.2,...,2.0   and so on.
(There are 11 $\times$ 15 $\times$ 10 = 1650 combinations.) For each combination
a line giving x,a,b, and Z values is to be written. Write a program
containing three DO loops to carry out this computation.

Solution: We need to obtain integral subscripts for our DO loops. This
is no problem for b. For x, though, note that 10*X takes on values
10., 11.,...,20. Thus if I = 10, 11,...,20, X = FLOAT(I)/10. Similarly,
100*A takes on values
$$10.0, \ 15.0, \ 20.0,...,80.0$$
in steps of 5. Let J = 10, 15, 20,...,80. So A = FLOAT(J)/100.
[Remember that the library function FLOAT changes an integer number into
a real number.] Hence we obtain the program below.

```
         DO 100 I = 10,20
         X = FLOAT (I)/10.0
         DO 100 J = 10,80,5
         A = FLOAT(J)/100.0
         DO 100 K = 1,10
         B = FLOAT(K)
         Z = 0.5*(EXP(A*X) - EXP(-A*X))*SIN(X+B)
1            + A*ALOG ((B+X)/2.)
         WRITE (6,10) A,B,X,Z
10       FORMAT (4X,3(2X,F6.3), E13.7)
100      CONTINUE
         STOP
         END
```

● **PROBLEM** 12-30

The screen at the Bijou theatre is 20 feet high with its lower edge 10
feet above the observer's eyelevel. The angle θ at the observer's eye
subtends the entire screen. This angle varies with the distance x of
the observer from the plane of the screen. At what distance x is the
angle θ greatest?

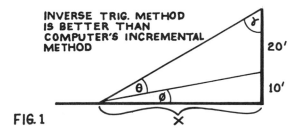

INVERSE TRIG. METHOD
IS BETTER THAN
COMPUTER'S INCREMENTAL
METHOD

FIG. 1

Solution: The problem is a very practical one, for the value obtained
for x turns out to be the distance at which the observer gets the best
view of the movie. One method involves inverse trigonometric functions.
Notice that we can use the triangles constructed in Figure 1 to say:

$$COT \ \emptyset = X/10$$

and $\qquad COT(\emptyset + \theta) = X/30$

or $\qquad \emptyset = ARCCOT \ X/10$

and $\qquad \emptyset + \theta = ARCCOT \ X/30$

Combining terms, we get

$$\theta = ARCCOT(X/30) - \emptyset$$
$$\theta = ARCCOT(X/30) - ARCCOT \ X/10$$

To find x for the largest θ, we take derivatives. Remembering that

$$\frac{d}{dz} \text{ arccot } z = - \frac{1}{1+z^2}$$

for $0 < Z < \pi$, we can express $d\theta/dx$ in terms of x as:

$$\frac{d\theta}{dx} = - \frac{1}{1 + (x/30)^2} \left(\frac{1}{30}\right) - \left(- \frac{1}{1 + (x/10)^2} \left(\frac{1}{10}\right)\right)$$

$$= - \frac{30}{900(1 + x^2/900)} - \left(- \frac{10}{100(1 + x^2/100)}\right)$$

$$= \frac{-30}{900 + x^2} + \frac{10}{100 + x^2}$$

To find x, we set $d\theta/dx = 0$ and solve for x:

$$0 = \frac{-30}{900 + x^2} + \frac{10}{100 + x^2}$$

$$\frac{30}{900 + x^2} = \frac{10}{100 + x^2}$$

$$30(100 + x^2) = 10(900 + x^2)$$
$$3000 + 30x^2 = 9000 + 10x^2$$

$$30x^2 = 6000 + 10x^2$$

$$\frac{20x^2 = 6000}{20}$$

$$x^2 = 300$$

$$x = \sqrt{300} = 17.35$$

```
                    READ (5,1) A,B
1                   FORMAT (    )
                    CALL XFIN (X)
                    PHI = ATAN(B/X)
                    ALPHA = ATAN(A/X)
                    THETA = ALPHA - PHI
                    WRITE (6,2) THETA
2                   FORMAT (    )
                    STOP
                    SUBROUTINE XFIN(X1(I), A,B)
                    I = 1
                    DO 4 X = 1,30,0.1
                    DALPHA = A/(A**2+X1(I)**2)
                    DPHI = B/(B**2+X1(I)**2)
                    ZERO(I) = DALPHA - DPHI
                    IF (ZERO(I).LT.ZERO(I - 1)) GO TO 5
4                   I = I + 1
5                   WRITE (6,6) X1(I)
6                   FORMAT (    )
                    RETURN
                    END
```

SIMULATION IN FORTRAN

● **PROBLEM** 12-31

A lead ball, initially at rest, is dropped from a certain height.
Assume it takes the ball 5 seconds to reach the ground. Develop a
program segment to give position and velocity at one-second intervals.

<u>Solution:</u>   The initial velocity v_0 is zero. The formula for the change
of position is $y = (1/2)gt^2$, where $g = -9.8$ meters/sec^2 . We include
the negative sign since the ball travels in the negative y-direction.
Now, with a constant acceleration, the instantaneous velocity is
$V_n = V_0 + at$, where n = 1,2,3,4,5. By iteration, we can simulate the
ball's motion.

```
          WRITE (5,100)
100       FORMAT (1X,'POSITION', 5X, 'VELOCITY')
          DO 20  NT = 1,5
          Y = 0.5 * -9.8 *(NT**2)
          V = -9.8 * (NT)
          WRITE (5,101) Y,V
101       FORMAT (1X, F10.4, 5X, F10.4)
20        CONTINUE
```

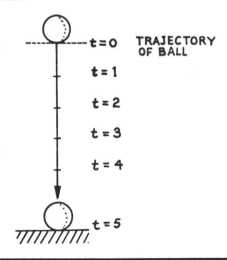

TRAJECTORY
OF BALL

● **PROBLEM** 12-32

A rocket blasts off from Earth at 12 noon. The original mass of the
rocket is M_0, and the exit velocity of the fuel jet is V_e . Assume
that fuel is burned at a constant rate, dm/dt. How high will the rocket
be at 12:15 PM? (assuming a straight-line trajectory). Write a FORTRAN
program to find the height at intervals of 0.5 minutes.

<u>Solution:</u> Force may be expressed as the change of momentum, as given by
Newton's second law: F = dp/dt. Now, we establish that positive y is
the vertical direction upwards. If M_0 is the total mass of rocket and
fuel before the launch, and m is the mass of the exiting fuel jet, then the
rate of change in momentum is given by:

$$F = \left(d/dt \right)(MV) + (V - V_e)\left(dm/dt \right)$$

We must also take into account the force of gravity, which is acting against
the motion of the rocket. The formula will not be derived step-by-step

here; a text on differential equations will have the thorough explanation. However, all variables will be explained, after presenting the general equation.

The initial condition $V = 0$ at $t = 0$ yields the equation:

$$V = -gt - V_e \ln\left[\frac{m_0 - ut}{u}\right]$$

then, by integrating, the equation of motion is obtained, which expresses the height y as a function of time t:

$$y = -\left(1/2\right)gt^2 + V_e\left[t + \frac{m_0 - ut}{u} \ln \frac{m_0 - ut}{m_0}\right]$$

The variables are as follows: y = vertical height; $-(1/2)gt^2$ = the effect of gravity pulling the rocket downward; hence the use of the negative sign.

V_e = the exit velocity of the fuel jet

M_0 = original mass of the rocket plus the unburned fuel

$u = dm/dt$ = the rate of change of the mass of the unburned fuel

Note that as the rocket rises, the mass of the fuel, and ultimately, the total mass of the rocket is decreasing. Also notice that in the program, a decision should be made upon appropriate values for M_0, μ, and V_e. It is assumed that these have already been read in.

Also, since g is defined in meters per sec^2, it may be best to use the MKS system of units.

```
C                 SIMULATE THE VERTICAL ASCENT OF AN
C                 UNCONTROLLED ROCKET FOR 15 MINUTES
C                 AT 30-SECOND INTERVALS
                  Y = 0.0
                  G = 9.80616
                  WRITE (5,100)
100               FORMAT (1X,'TIME', 5X, 'HEIGHT')
                  DO 20  I = 1,30
                  T = 0.5 * FLOAT(I)
                  Y = -0.5*G*(T**2) + (VE*(T + (RMO -(RMU*
1                 T))/RMU)*LOG((RMO - RMU)*T/RMO))
                  WRITE (5,101) T,Y
101               FORMAT (2X, F5.2, 4X, F12.4)
20                CONTINUE
                  STOP
                  END
                  SAMPLE OUTPUT:
                       TIME              HEIGHT
                       0.50
                       1.00
                       1.50
                       2.00
```

A mass M is connected to a linear spring of stiffness K. The mass-spring system is initially at rest. At time $t = t_0$, the system is displaced a distance of x_0, and released. It can be shown that the motion of the system is described by the following differential equation:

$$M\ddot{x} + Kx(t) = 0$$

where $x(t)$ is the displacement of the mass and $\ddot{x}$ is the second derivative of x with respect to time. If v_0 is the initial velocity, construct a model of this system and devise a digital program which simulates the motion of the system from time $t = t_0$ to time $t = t_f$.

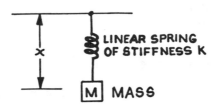

LINEAR SPRING
OF STIFFNESS K

x

M MASS

Solution: The general procedure for developing a model for simulation purposes can be summarized as follows:
1. Definition of the problem and the system that is being studied.
2. Making simplifying assumptions concerning the components of the system.
3. Determining the factors outside the system's environment (exogenous factors) that will affect it.
4. Formulation of a mathematical model (if possible).
5. Compiling the relevant data.
6. Construction of a computer program of the model.

Applying these steps to this particular problem:
1. The system consists of the mass and the spring. The problem of following the motion of the system can be viewed through the change in displacement, x. So essentially, the problem is to solve the given differential equation and record samples of the values x assumes from $t = t_0$ to $t = t_f$.
2. The differential equation given, results from assuming that M and K are time invariant (constant). Also, the mass of M is considered "lumped" at a single point.
3. The differential equation does not include the effect of air resistance for simplicity.
4. The differential equation is a dynamic mathematical model of the system.
5. The data available is, t_0, t_f, $x(t_0) = x_0$; $v(t_0) = v_0$, K and M.
6. Although analytical methods exist for solving second-order linear differential equations with constant coefficients such as the one given, digital simulation is applicable even when no analytical method applies. The numerical method used here is called the Euler predictor-corrector method (slow, but straightforward and very general). To use it we must transform the equation to a system of simultaneous first-order equations; using the substitution $v = \dot{x}$:

$$\dot{x} = v(t) \qquad (1)$$
$$\dot{v} = -(K/M) * x(t) \qquad (2)$$

The flow-chart for the subroutine is as follows.

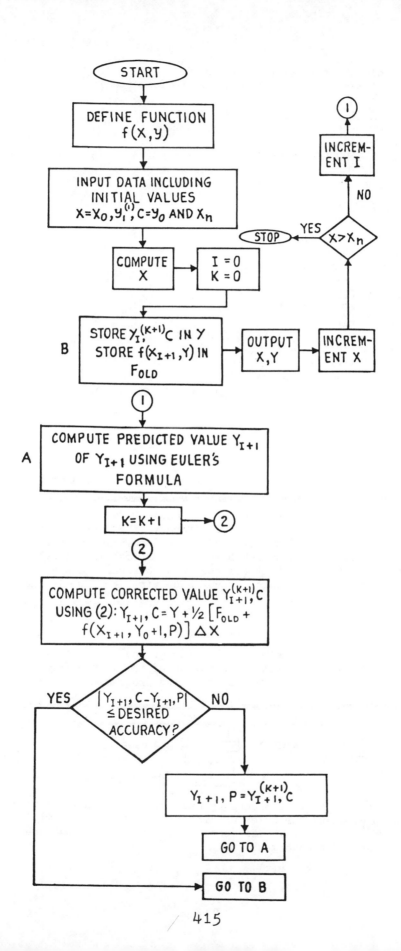

START

DEFINE FUNCTION
$f(X, y)$

INPUT DATA INCLUDING
INITIAL VALUES
$X = X_0, y_1^{(i)}, C = y_0$ AND X_n

COMPUTE
X

$I = 0$
$K = 0$

B STORE $Y_I^{(K+1)} C$ IN Y
STORE $f(X_{I+1}, Y)$ IN
F_{OLD}

OUTPUT
X, Y

INCREM-
ENT X

$X > X_n$

YES → STOP

NO

INCREM-
ENT I

1

A COMPUTE PREDICTED VALUE Y_{I+1}
OF Y_{I+1} USING EULER'S
FORMULA

$K = K+1$ → 2

2

COMPUTE CORRECTED VALUE $Y_{I+1}^{(K+1)} C$
USING (2): $Y_{I+1}, C = Y + \frac{1}{2} [F_{OLD} +
f(X_{I+1}, Y_0 +1, P)] \Delta X$

$|Y_{I+1}, C - Y_{I+1}, P|
\leq$ DESIRED
ACCURACY?

YES   NO

$Y_{I+1}, P = Y_{I+1}^{(K+1)}, C$

GO TO A

GO TO B

415

The program closely follows the flow chart:
    (I/O statements can be appropriately formatted):

```
      REAL  K,M,N
      READ K,M,N,T,TFIN, XCOR, VCOR, ACCVR
C     N IS THE NUMBER OF SAMPLES TO BE CHOSEN
      DT = (TFIN - T)/N
C     DT IS THE INCREMENT SIZE
50    X = XCOR
      V = VCOR
      A = -(K/M)*X
      PRINT T,X
      T = T + DT
      IF (T.GT.TFIN) STOP
      XPRED  = X + V * DT
      VPRED = V + A * DT
100   XDOT = VPRED
C     EQUATION (1)
      VDOT = -(K/M) * XPRED
C     EQUATION (2)
      XCOR = X + 0.5 * (V + XDOT) * DT
      VCOR = V + 0.5 * (A + VDOT) * DT
      XDIF = ABS (XCOR - XPRED)
      VDIF = ABS(VCOR - VPRED)
      IF = (XDIF.LE.ACCUR.AND.VDIF.LE.ACCUR) GO TO 50
      XPRED = XCOR
      VPRED = VCOR
      GO TO 100
      END
```

● **PROBLEM** 12-34

A damper (or dashpot) is connected to the mass M of the previous
problem. This could represent air resistance. The entire system
could be a simple model of an automobile wheel suspension system
(assuming the automobile body immobile in a vertical direction).
Then the damper acts as a shock absorber. As before, the system is
displaced and released and $x(t_0) = x_0$ and $v(t_0) = v_0$. It can be
shown that the motion of the system is described by the following differential equation:
$$M\ddot{x} + D\dot{x} + Kx(t) = 0$$
where D is the damping factor of the dashpot and $\dot{x} = v(t) \equiv$ velocity
at time t . Model and simulate the motion of the system from time
$t = t_0$ to $t = t_f$, using a digital computer program, FIG. 1

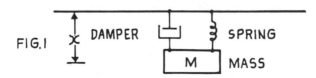

FIG.1 X DAMPER SPRING M MASS

Solution: Repetition of the procedure used in the previous problem
leads to step 6, where the Euler predictor-corrector method will be
used again. Transforming the differential equation to a simultaneous
system of first-order equations:

$$\dot{x} = v(t) \tag{1b}$$

$$\dot{v} = -[D*v(t) + K*x(t)]/M \tag{2b}$$

This relation can be diagrammed as shown in FIG. 2

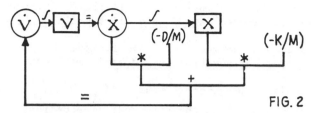

FIG. 2

The only change in the program needed is substitution of the new
expression for acceleration. Since this expression appears in two
lines and is fairly long, a statement function is used. This has the
additional effect of making the program more general. It can be applied
to any second-order differential equation. Only the statement function
definition and the I/O statements vary. The program:

```
        REAL   K,M,N
        F(Y,Z) = -(D*Y + K*Z)/M
        READ K,M,N,T,TFIN,XCOR,VCOR,ACCUR,D
        DT = (TFIN - T)/N
50      X = XCOR
        V = VCOR
        A = F(V,X)
        PRINT T,X
        T = T + DT
        IF(T.GT.TFIN) STOP
        XPRED = X + V * DT
        VPRED = V + A * DT
100     XDOT = VPRED
        VDOT = F(V,XPRED)
        XCOR = X + 0.5 *(V + XDOT) * DT
        VCOR = V + 0.5 *(A + VDOT) * DT
        XDIF = ABS(XCOR - XPRED)
        VDIF = ABS(VCOR - VPRED)
        IF(XDIF.LE.ACCUR.AND.VDIF.LE.ACCUR) GO TO 50
        XPRED = XCOR
        VPRED = VCOR
        GO TO 100
        END
```

● **PROBLEM** 12-35

A capacitor with capacitance C and initial charge q_0 and an inductor
with inductance L are connected in series. At time $t = t_0$, the switch
S is closed. If $q(t)$ is the charge on the capacitor at time t it
can be shown that the behavior of the circuit is governed by the following
differential equation: $L\ddot{q} + (1/C)q(t) = 0$ where $\ddot{q} = d^2q/dt^2$. If
i_0 is the initial current, construct a model of this circuit and devise
a digital program which simulates the behavior of the circuit from time
$t = t_0$ to $t = t_f$.

Solution: Following the steps of the general procedure outlined in the
two previous problems:
1. If the given differential equation can be solved, and samples of
the values q assumes from $t = t_0$ to $t = t_f$ recorded, we will have
a model which effectively simulates the given system, i.e., the circuit,

2. The assumption that L and C are linear and time-invariant has
already been included in the model, through the derivation of the given
equation. Similarly, the assumption that all the capacitance of the
circuit is considered "lumped" at C and all inductance "lumped" at L
has already been made.

3. Circuit resistance is neglected for simplicity.

4. The given differential equation is a dynamic mathematical model of
the system.

5. The input data is t_0, t_f, $q(t_0) = q_0$, $i(t_0) = i_0$, L and C.

6. The equation given here and the differential equation of the previous
two problems appear to be similar. In fact, using the equivalences:

$$q \rightarrow x, \; i = \dot{q} \rightarrow v = \dot{x}, \; \ddot{q} \rightarrow a = \dot{v} = \ddot{x}, \; L \rightarrow M, \; (1/C) \rightarrow K$$

the differential equation of harmonic motion can be constructed from
the equation of this problem. Hence, the programmer needs only to
substitute his input data as follows:

```
USE THE VALUE (1/C) AS  K
USE THE VALUE  L  AS  M
USE THE VALUE  q₀  AS  XCOR
USE THE VALUE  i₀  AS  VCOR
```

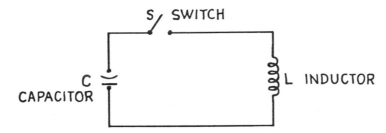

● **PROBLEM** 12-36

A resistor with resistance R is connected in series with the circuit
of the previous problem. As before, q_0 is the initial charge on the
capacitor and the switch is closed at time $t = t_0$. It can be shown
that the behavior of the circuit is governed by the following differential equation:

$$L\ddot{q} + R\dot{q} + (1/C)q(t) = 0$$

where $\dot{q} = i(t) \equiv$ current at time t. If i_0 is the initial current,
model and simulate the behavior of the circuit from time $t = t_0$ to
$t = t_f$, using a digital computer program.

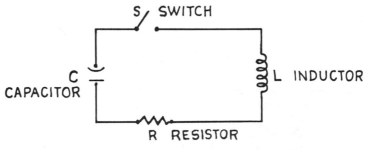

Solution: As in the previous problem, a similarity can be noticed

418

between the given differential equation and that of a differential equation describing harmonic motion (damped). Using the same equivalences with the addition of $R \to D$, the equation of the damped system can be constructed from the equation of this problem. The programmer needs only to substitute the following as input data in the previous program:

USE THE VALUE   R   as D
USE THE VALUE (1/C) as K
USE THE VALUE (q_0) as XCOR
USE THE VALUE (i_0) as VCOR

● **PROBLEM** 12-37

Consider again the RCL circuit of the previous problem, or, analogously, an automobile suspension system discussed before. Suppose a voltage source is connected with the circuit [In the case of the automobile suspension system, suppose an external force is applied to the system. The road would be such a force.] At time $t = 0$, S is closed. If $E(t)$ is the voltage at time t, it can be shown that the behavior of the circuit is governed by the following differential equation:

$$L\ddot{q} + R\dot{q} + (1/C)q(t) = E(t)$$

where $q(t)$ is the charge on the capacitor, $\dot{q}$ is the current at time t and $\ddot{q}$ is the rate of change of current. [If $E(t)$ is the external force on the suspension system at time t, then:

$$M\ddot{x} + D\dot{x} + Kx(t) = E(t)]$$

If $q_0(0) = i_0(0) = 0$ [if the suspension system is at equilibrium, so that $x_0(0) = i_0(0) = 0$], write a digital computer program that models and simulates the behavior of the system from time $t = 0$ to $t = t_f$, for the following test inputs:

(i) $E_1(t) = h$ where h is constant

(ii) $E_2(t) = \begin{cases} 0 & \text{if } t < t_1 \\ h & \text{if } t_1 \leq t < t_2 \\ 0 & \text{if } t \geq t_2 \end{cases}$

$E_2(t)$ is a pulse of height h and width $(t_2 - t_1)$. $[E_2(t)$ can be used to simulate a bump in the road.] (See Fig. 1)

(iii) $E_3(t) = A_1 \sin wt$ where w and A_1 are constants. $[E_3(t)$ could represent a hilly road.]

(iv) $E_4(t) = \begin{cases} 0 & \text{if } t < t_1 \\ h & \text{if } t_1 \leq t < t_1 + w \\ 0 & \text{if } t_1 + w \leq t < t_1 + 2w \end{cases}$

and $E_4(t + 2w) = E_4(t)$
  $E_4(t)$ is a pulse train. (See Fig. 2)

Solution: Using the variables associated with the automobile suspension system, we call upon the variable $v(t) = \dot{x}$ again to transform the

419

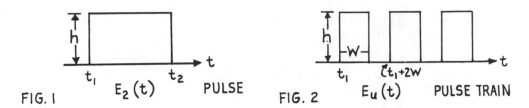

FIG. I $E_2(t)$ PULSE   FIG. 2 $E_u(t)$ PULSE TRAIN

equation to a simultaneous system of first-order equations to be used in the Euler predictor-corrector program:

$$x = v(t) \tag{1}$$

$$\dot{v} = [E(t) - D\ddot{x} - Kx(t)]/M \tag{2}$$

(See Fig. 3)

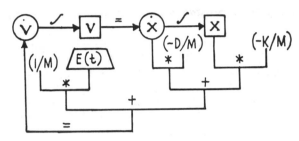

FIG. 3

Since E(t) varies with time, it is given a different symbol (trapezoid). Writing equation (2) as a statement function definition, using it at the correct time in the program, substituting the new initial values (T = XCOR = VCOR = 0) and changing I/O statements, complete the solution:

(i)
```
        REAL K,M,N, T/0.0/, XCOR/0.0/,VCOR/0.0/
        F(Y,Z) = (H - D*Y - K*Z)/M
        READ K,M,N,TFIN,ACCUR,D,H
        DT = (TFIN - T)/N
                  ⋮
```

Missed segment of the problem is similar to the ones in the previous problems.

(ii)
```
        REAL K,M,N,T/0.0/, XCOR/0.0/, VCOR/0.0/
        F(Y,Z) = (H - D*Y - K*Z)/M
        G(R,S) = -(D*R + K*S)/M
        READ K,M,N,TFIN,ACCUR,D,H,T1,T2
        DT = (TFIN - T)/N
50      X = XCOR
        V = VCOR
        A = G(V,X)
        IF (T.GE.T1.AND.T.LT.T2)A = F(V,X)
75      PRINT T,X
        T = T + DT
        IF (T.GT.TFIN) STOP
        IF (T.LT.T1) GO TO 75
        XPRED = X + V*DT
        VPRED = V + A*DT
100     XDOT = VPRED
        VDOT = F(V,XPRED)
        IF (T.GE.T2)VDOT = G(V,XPRED)
        XCOR = X + 0.5*(V + XDOT)*DT
                  ⋮
```

420

Missed segment of the problem is similar to the ones in the previous problems.

```
(iii)              REAL K,M,N,T/0.0/,XCOR/0.0/,VCOR/0.0/
                   F(TIME,Y,Z) = (A1*SIN(OMEGA*TIME) - D*X - K*Z)/M
                   READ K,M,N,TFIN,ACCUR,D,A1,OMEGA
                   DT = (TFIN - T)/N
50                 X = XCOR
                   V = VCOR
                   A = F(T,V,X)
                   PRINT T,X
                   T = T + DT
                   IF (T.GT.TFIN) STOP
                   XPRED = X + V*DT
                   VPRED = V + A*DT
100                XDOT = VPRED
                   VDOT = F(T,V,XPRED)
                   XCOR = X + 0.5*(V + XDOT)*DT
                                   .
                                   .
                                   .
```

Missed segment of the problem is similar to the ones in the previous problems.

```
(iv)               REAL K,M,N,T/0.0/,XCOR/0.0/,VCOR/0.0/
                   F(Y,Z) = (H - D*Y - K*Z)/M
                   G(R,S) = -(D*R + K*S)/M
                   READ K,M,N,TFIN,ACCUR,D,H,T1,W,
                   DT = (TFIN - T)/N
                   PER = T1 + 2W
C                  PER = TIME OF COMPLETION OF FIRST PERIOD
                   HPER = T1 + W
C                  HPER = TIME OF COMPLETION OF FIRST HALF-PERIOD
                   TIME = T
50                 X = XCOR
                   V = VCOR
                   A = G(V,X)
                   IF (TIME.GE.T1.AND.TIME.LT.HPER)A = F(V,X)
75                 PRINT T,X
                   T = T + DT
                   IF (T.GT.TFIN) STOP
                   TIME = T
                   IF (T.GE.PER) TIME = T - 2*W
                   IF (TIME.LT.T1) GO TO 75
                   XPRED = X + V*DT
                   VRED = V + A*DT
100                XDOT = VPRED
                   VDOT = F(V,XPRED)
                   IF (TIME.GT.HPER)VDOT = G(V,XPRED)
                   XCOR = X + 0.5*(V + XDOT)*DT
                                   .
                                   .
                                   .
```

Missed segment of the problem is similar to the ones in the previous problems.

Modify the automobile suspension program of part i) of the previous problem so that it is possible to find a value for D - the damping coefficient, that will not allow the displacement of the mass x(t) to exceed 1.6, given K = 400.0, M = 2.0, E(t) = h = 1.0. Start with D = 6.0 and increase it by one unit whenever it is found that x(t) > 1.6, until the desired damping is found.

Solution: The modification is made when the value of XCOR is found with desired accuracy. We test to see if XCOR ≤ 1.6. If so, the program proceeds as in part i) of the previous problem. If not, D is increased by 1 and variables are reinitialized so that the algorithm may begin again using the new value of D. The program follows:

```
            REAL K/400.0/,M/2.0/,N,T/0.0/,XCOR/0.0/,
                VCOR/0.0/,H/1.0/,D/6.0/
            F(Y,Z) = (H - D*Y - K*Z)/M
            READ N, TFIN, ACCUR
            DT = (TFIN - T)/N
50          X = XCOR
            V = VCOR
            A = F(V,X)
            PRINT T,X,D
            T = T + DT
            IF (T.GT.TFIN) STOP
            XPRED = X + V*DT
            VPRED = V + A*DT
100         XDOT = VPRED
            VDOT = F(V,XPRED)
            XCOR = X + 0.5*(V + XDOT)*DT
            VCOR = V + 0.5*(A + VDOT)*DT
            XDIF = ABS(XCOR - XPRED)
            VDIF = ABS(VCOR - VPRED)
            IF (XDIF.LE.ACCUR.AND.VDIF.LE.ACCUR) GO TO 110
            XPRED = XCOR
            VPRED = VCOR
            GO TO 100
110         IF (XCOR.LE.1.6) GO TO 50
            D = D + 1.0
            T = 0.0
            XCOR = 0.0
            VCOR = 0.0
            GO TO 50
            END
```

Water flows into a tank at a constant rate Q. Q is determined by the position of a valve connected to the inflow pipe. Write a digital computer program to simulate this system from time t = 0 to t = t_f if V(0) = V_0 . (Consider the walls to be of infinite height, so that overflow is not possible.)

Solution: Following the steps outlined in the previous problems:

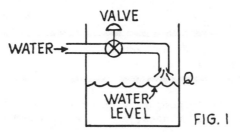

FIG. 1

1. Changes in this system's state can be viewed through changes in the volume V of water in the tank.

2 & 3. Once the valve position is set, Q is determined and will remain unchanged. Thus, it can be considered external to the system consisting of water in the tank and water flowing into the tank. Q is changed only when a new simulation run is being made with a new parameter Q.

4. Using the notation of the preceding problems, the behavior of the system can be diagrammed as shown in Fig. 2 $\textcircled{Q} \rightarrow \boxed{v}$ Fig. 2

V is the accumulation of the rate of change Q (when Q has units of Volume/time). To conform more closely with notation previously developed, let $\dot{V}$ = the constant Q, and since accumulation of rates of change is mathematically expressed as integration, the complete diagram is shown in Fig. 3

$$(Q) = \textcircled{$\dot{V}$} \overset{\int}{\rightarrow} \boxed{V} \quad \text{Fig. 3}$$

From this, the equation can be written:

$$\dot{V} = Q \quad \text{or} \quad dV/dt = Q \tag{1}$$

5. Since the solution of (1) can easily be seen to be: $V(t) = Q * T + V_0$ (2) a simple program would just substitute values of t into (2) and output V. A more general program would use the Euler predictor-corrector algorithm to solve the first-order differential equation (1). But since the rate of change is constant, the corrected value would always equal the predicted value. The method used here directly simulates the behavior of the system according to observed changes in V for small, discrete changes in t:

$$V_{new} = V_{old} + V_{added} \tag{3}$$

where:

$$V_{added} = Q * \text{Change in time}$$
$$= Q * (t_{new} - t_{old})$$
$$= Q * \Delta t$$

This is the original Euler's method (generally, it is less accurate than predictor-corrector method). Thus V_N is calculated from V_{N-1}. If V_0 is always used for V_{old} and $t_0 = 0$ is always used for t_{old} equation (3) would be reduced to equation (2). The program is as follows:

```
        DATA T/0.0/
        READ N, TFIN,Q,VOL
        PRINT T, VOL
        REALN = N
C       USING REALN AVOIDS MIXED-MODE ARITHMETIC
        DT = (TFIN - T)/REALN
        DO 50 I = 1,N
        T = T + DT
        VOL = VOL + Q * DT
        PRINT T, VOL
50      CONTINUE
        STOP
        END
```

423

Modify the program of the previous problem to handle overflow if the capacity of the tank is finite.

Solution: Each time VOL is computed, check to see if it exceeds the given capacity CAP. If it does, indicate this and stop the simulation:

```
          DATA T/0.0/
          READ N, TFIN, Q, VOL, CAP
          PRINT T, VOL
          REALN = N
          DT + (TFIN - T)/REALN
          DO 50 I = 1,N
          T = T + DT
          VOL = VOL + Q * DT
          IF(VOL.GT.CAP) GO TO 60
          PRINT T, VOL
50        CONTINUE
          STOP
60        PRINT 'OVERFLOW'
          STOP
          END
```

Suppose a hole is punched into the bottom of the tank of the previous problem. If the water flows out at a constant rate, Q_1, modify the program of the previous problem to simulate this system.

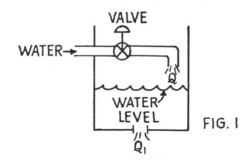

FIG. I

Solution: Since Q_1 is the rate of flow out of the tank, it tends to decrease V; therefore we give it a negative sign. V is the accumulation of the net flow,

$$Q + (-Q_1) :$$

FIG. 2

From this, the equation can be written:

$$\dot{V} = Q - Q_1 \tag{1}$$

424

Since both Q and Q_1 are constant, $Q - Q_1$ is constant too and equation (1) can be written:

$$V = Q_2 \quad \text{where} \quad Q_2 = Q - Q_1$$

Hence, the programmer needs only to substitute the value of Q_2 for Q in his input data.

CHAPTER 13

PL/I

INTRODUCTION TO PL/I

● **PROBLEM** 13-1

Explain briefly the background and applications of the PL/I programming language.

Solution: PL/I (Programming Language One) was developed by the International Business Machines (IBM) corporation for its System/360 series of computers. PL/I is a multipurpose programming language—it is designed to be used by both scientific and commercial programmers and to give these programmers language features powerful enough to handle all their problems. PL/I is constructed so that the individual programmer can move and operate easily at his own level of experience, whether this level is low or high. The language has many automatic and default conditions to assist the beginning programmer, while the specialist with extensive experience may detail each step of his complicated program.

Being a high-level language, PL/I lets the user describe complicated procedures in simple, easy to understand terms. This virtually frees the programmer from having to learn the machine organization.

Although the notation of PL/I is not identical to conventional algebraic notation, it is close enough to be easily read by anyone knowing algebra.

All these features make PL/I one of the most powerful and and flexible languages in Computer Science today.

● **PROBLEM** 13-2

Give a list of the character set used in PL/I. Also define the term 'variable', and explain what is meant by an 'assignment statement'.

Solution: Altogether, 60 different characters constitute the PL/I character set, all or only some of them may appear in a

426

specific PL/I program. In PL/I there is a choice of the 26
capital letters A through Z, the 10 digits 0 through 9, and
also 24 special characters. The graphics and names by which
these 24 special characters are represented are as follows:

=	Equal or assignment symbol
+	Plus symbol
−	Minus symbol
*	Asterik or multiply symbol
/	Slash or divide symbol
(	Left parenthesis symbol
:	Colon symbol
¬	NOT symbol
&	AND symbol
|	OR symbol
>	Greater than symbol
<	Less than symbol
)	Right parenthesis symbol
,	Comma symbol
.	Period or decimal point symbol
'	Quotation mark symbol
%	Percent symbol
;	Semicolon symbol
−	Break character symbol
?	Question mark symbol
$	Currency symbol
@	"at" symbol
#	Number sign symbol
∅	Blank (space, no graphic)

Recognition of a blank character is important. The
blank character has no graphic representation; it represents
spacing. Often one wrongly considers the blank character as
an unessential character for a language. But consider the
following:

THESEATHADANICECOVER

The above statement, without blanks, could either mean:

        The seat had a nice cover,   or,
        The seat had an ice cover.

Hence, it can be seen that blanks are very important in a
language.
    To understand what is meant by 'assignment statements'
take a simple example as follows:

                X = A + B;

The semicolon indicates to the PL/I machine the end of an instruction. The symbol "=" has the function of a directed
equality sign. It states that the quantity on the left-hand
side is defined by the formula on the right-hand side. Or,
more precisely, the value created by addition of the two
variables on the right-hand side is taken on by the variable
X on the left-hand side. One can say that the newly calculated value (i.e. sum of A & B) is "assigned" to the variable
X. The complete structure is called 'assignment statement.'
It is necessary that the variables A and B, at the instant

of calculation, have well defined values. This is not necessary for X on the left-hand side. If X does not appear in
any previous statements its value will be undefined before
execution of the assignment statement. After execution, the
value of X will be equal to the sum of the values of A & B.
If there is any previous assignment, say X = 5, before X =
A + B, the effect of the assignment statement is as follows:
Any previous value of X is lost; a new value of X is defined;
the old value is replaced by the new value.

We have used the term 'variable' for A, B and X while
explaining the term 'assignment statement'. The term 'variable' is used to indicate that a value attached to the quantity may "vary" during the calculations performed by the
PL/I machine.

● **PROBLEM** 13-3

Give the set of arithmetic operators used in PL/I. Explain
what is meant by the priority rule. Explain how the expression A + B - C * D/F ** G is evaluated. Also, find the value
of the above expression if A = 7, B = 2, C = 3, D = 8, F = 2,
and G = 3.

Solution: Every language has some fixed set of arithmetic
operators. The normal algebraic operations are all available
in PL/I. Arithmetic operators are symbols used to indicate
these operations. The following operators are available:

   a) Infix Operators:

         + addition   - subtraction
         * multiplication / division
         ** exponentiation

   b) Prefix Operators

         + plus
         - negation or minus

The operators are shown in two groups above. Operators
in group a) are called infix operators because they operate
on two operands. For example,

   A+B, 2*3, X**Y, I-1, u/v, etc.

The operators in group b) are called prefix operators
because they operate on single operands. For example,

         +10, -52, -(A+B)

Notice that in the -(A+B), the + sign is for an infix operator, between two operands A and B. But, the - sign is a prefix operator. The complete parentheses, (A+B), acts as a
single operand for the prefix - operator.

Now consider the given expression:

      A+B-C*D/F**G.

428

Notice that if parentheses are omitted as in the above, the expression will evaluate to different answers, depending on the order in which the different operations are carried out.

To avoid any ambiguity on the evaluation process, PL/I has a set of Precedence Rules. The Precedence Rule says that an operator at a higher level of priority is executed first, and then an operator at a lower level of priority is executed. The various operators are set at different priority levels. An operator having a higher priority level is executed first. The priority set for the operators are as follows:

```
First level  **, Negation    (highest priority)
Second level *  , /          (second highest priority)
Third level  +, -            (lowest priority).
```

If two operators at the same level of priority are encountered, then PL/I applies a left to right associativity, e.g. A-B-C is considered as (A-B)-C.

Arithmetic expressions are analyzed as follows:

1. The expression is examined from right to left in search of the two first level operators. The operations specified by them are performed as the operators are encountered.
2. All subsequent scans take place from left to right. During the first of these left to right scans, * and / operations are performed as they occur.
3. The final left to right scan carries out calculations involving infix + and - operations.

Using the above rules of Precedence and Associativity, ambiguity is eliminated.

Hence, consider the given expression, viz.,

A+B-C*D/F**G.

In the above, it can be seen that there is an exponentiation operator **, which has the highest priority from amongst all the operators in the given expression. Hence, F**G is evaluated first.

The expression therefore reduces as shown below:

A+B-C*D/(F**G).

The highest priority for the remaining operators belongs to * and /. Now, both * and / are on the same level of priority. Hence, the left to right Associativity Rule is applied. Thus, C*D is evaluated first. The expression thus reduces as shown below:

A+B-(C*D)/(F**G).

Now, the / operation is performed. The expression then reduces as shown below:

A+B-(C*D/F**G).

Now remains the + and - operators. Both are again at the same level of priority. Hence, the left to right Associativity rule is again applied, and A+B is carried out first.

This reduces the expression to that shown below:

$$(A+B)-(C*D/F**G).$$

Now, the subtraction is finally carried out, completing the evaluation of the expression.

Using the numeric values of the various variables, the expression becomes as follows:

```
        7+2-3*8/2**3.
    = 7+2-3*8/(2**3)
    = 7+2-3*8/(8)
    = 7+2-(3*8)/(8)
    = 7+2-(24)/(8)
    = 7+2-(24/8)
    = 7+2-(3)
    = 7+2-3
    = (7+2)-3
    = (9)-3
    = 9-3
    = 6
```

DATA DEFINITION

● **PROBLEM** 13-4

Explain what you understand by the DECLARE statement and list how it is used for Numeric and Non numeric Variables.

Solution: The DECLARE statement, abbreviated as DCL, in PL/I allows for proper storage allocation of programmers' variable. It lets the compiler know in what form the variable will be stored by declaring its name followed by a list of its attributes.

Numerical variables: PL/I has a wide variety of DCL statement forms for declaring numeric variables.

a) Fixed Decimal Point variables: - The general form is as follows:

        DECLARE name scale attribute base attribute (precision
                attribute);

For example,

        DECLARE Y FIXED DECIMAL (6,3);

The above could be followed by a statement as follows:

        Y=12·4;

Thus, the stored result will be equivalent to 012·400.

Zeros are added on both sides of 12·4 because Y was declared to have 6 digits in all, but with 3 digits after the decimal point. Similarly, if the variable had a lesser total number of digits declared, compared to the precision and the value of the variable, a truncation of the number takes

430

place. This truncation must be regarded as an error. As an example

DECLARE A FIXED DECIMAL (5,2);
GET DATA (A);
PUT DATA (A).

If A=5218·79, in view of the precision of (5,2) declared above, A in storage = 218·79. Hence, the PUT DATA statement will lead to a print-out of A=218·79. A truncation of the left-most bit exceeding the precision attribute, has taken place.

Similarly if A=6179, then, A in storage will be 179·00. In this case, the PUT DATA (A); statement will lead to a print-out of A=179·00; (Totally there should be five digits, with two digits after the decimal point.).

b) Float decimal point variables: - The basic declaration reads as follows:

DECLARE name FLOAT DECIMAL (W);

The precision is specified by W, i.e., the total number of digits to be accomodated in the floating point number. For example,

DECLARE Y FLOAT DECIMAL (8);

The above could be followed up with a statement as follows:

Y=112·4357;

Hence the stored result will be as follows:

0·11243570E+3.

If the value of the variable is specified using more digits than the declaration provides PL/I will truncate, just as for fixed point variables, as illustrated below: For example:

DCL A FLOAT DECIMAL (5);

If A=317·04 at input, then A=3·1704E+02 at output.
If A=0·0278 at input, then A=2·7800E-02 at output.
If A=8241·356 at input, then A=8·2413E+03 at output.

c) Similar to declarations for fixed and floating point decimal variables, there are declarations for Binary variables. For example,

DECLARE name FIXED BINARY (w,d);

e.g., DCL C BINARY FIXED (8,3);

PL/I requires a 'B' immediately following a binary constant, to distinguish it from decimal constants, because otherwise, 101·10 can be a decimal constant as well as a binary constant. Now consider the following:

DCL C BINARY FIXED (8,3);

The above will accomodate a value of C as follows, for example,

C=10011·000B;   (=19 decimal).

But, if B is not present, the PL/I compiler takes it to be 10011·000 decimal and will then convert it to binary according to normal practice, producing a value 10011100011011. (As can be verified by continuously dividing 10011 by 2, thus converting 10011 to a binary form). For the floating point representation of BINARY numbers we can have a declaration ofthe type illustrated below:

DECLARE name FLOAT BINARY (W);

d) Non-Numeric Variables: - The allocation of storage for non-numeric variables must always be explicit.
i) CHARACTER STRINGS: - For character strings, the declaration is as follows:

DECLARE name CHARACTER (length);

'length' is a decimal integer specifying the number of characters to be accomodated. Character strings have to be shown between single quotation marks for instance

DECLARE X CHARACTER (5)
X='PARIS'

As a result of the above declaration, the compiler saves 5 storage locations for X, & the five character 'PARIS' will be placed in X. When a string length differs from the storage area made available by the declaration, PL/I either pads or truncates the string, as necessary. For example, consider the following Declare statement:

DECLARE B CHARACTER (7);
Now, if B='VANØGOGH', then, the stored value for B=VANØGOG
If B='KUGEL', then, the stored value for B=KUGELØØ.
ii) BIT STRINGS: - When a variable is declared with a statement as follows, viz.,

DECLARE name BIT (length);

then, that variable is treated as a bit string, consisting of only ones and zeros. Bit strings are handled in the same way as character strings.
Multiple Declarations: - It is not necessary to allocate storage for each variable in separate Declare statements. For example, consider the following four separate declare statements:

DCL A FLOAT (6);
DCL B FIXED BINARY (18);
DCL C CHARACTER (12);
DCL X FIXED (7,2);

The above can be combined together as illustrated below:

DCL A FLOAT(6), B FIXED(18), C CHARACTER(12),
    X FIXED(7,2);

Factored Declarations: - When storage is to be allocated for several variables that have a common set of attri-

432

butes, it is possible to condense them, as shown below:

DCL A FIXED(5,2), B CHAR(5), C FIXED(5,2), D FLOAT(7);

can be written as follows:

DCL (A,C) FIXED(5,2), B CHAR(5), D FLOAT(7);

In the above, the FIXED(5,2) attribute of both A and C has been factored out, leading to a condensed form of the declare statement. Note that no more factoring is possible now in the above statement.

● **PROBLEM** 13-5

Write Declare statements for the following variables or constants, making use of the rules of PL/I regarding attributes. Also explain the reasons why you selected the particular attributes. The variables are given as follows:

a) A variable named PERCENT which takes values from 0·00 to 100·00. PERCENT is an array of 8 elements.
b) A variable named AMOUNT which represents dollars and cents, from 0·00 to 1 million dollars.
c) A variable named NUMBER which represents Avogadro's number = $6·022 \times 10^{23}$
d) A variable named TOTAL which represents integer numbers from 1 to 4000, to be stored in a binary form.

Solution: a) We can Declare PERCENT as follows:

DCL PERCENT(1:8) FIXED(5,2) REAL DEC;

Here, the parentheses (1:8) shows that PERCENT is an array. FIXED specifies the Scale. (5,2) specifies the precision, which is of the form

XXX·XX.

REAL specifies the Mode
DEC specifies the Base.
b) We can Declare AMOUNT as follows:

DCL AMOUNT FIXED(9,2) DEC REAL;

In the above, the words FIXED, DEC and REAL specify the scale, the Base and the Mode respectively. Also, (9,2) can represent numbers from -9,999,999·99 to +9,999,999·99. Thus, our range of 0·00 to 1,000,000·00 can be easily accomodated in this range.
c) We can Declare NUMBER as follows:

DCL NUMBER FLOAT(4) REAL DECIMAL;

In the above, the value of the variable NUMBER is equal to $6·022 \times 10^{23}$. Hence, if we tried to use the FIXED Scale, we would have to specify its scale and precision as follows:

FIXED(26,3).

This huge number of almost all digits of zero, is very cumbersome to use, store, etc.

Hence, we use instead the Floating point scale as above. The specification Float(4) means that the number is of the form X·XXX, i.e., 4 digits, with the remaining multiplier of powers of ten implicitly provided. A printout of the NUMBER would be: 6·022E+23.

d) We declare TOTAL as follows:

DCL TOTAL FIXED(12) BINARY REAL;

In the above, we have specified the Scale as FIXED, the Mode as REAL, and, the Base as BINARY. The reason for specifying the precision as (12) is as follows: We are given that the variable TOTAL takes values from 0 to 4000. And we observe that a number $2^{11}=2048, 2^{12}=4096, 2^{13}=8192$. Hence, a precision of 2^{12} is just right to represent a range from 0 to 4000.

● **PROBLEM** 13-6

What is meant by character string variables, character string constants? Give and explain the rules governing declaration, value acquisition (GET) and value disposition (PUT).

Solution: Consider the following PL/I statement

DECLARE STUDENT_NAME CHARACTER (15);
GET LIST (STUDENT_NAME);

On the data card there is: 'JIMMY∅CARTER∅', 'TED∅KENNEDY∅', 'RICHARD∅NIXON∅'.

The declaration specifies STUDENT_ NAME as the name of a character string variable. A character string variable has character string data as its value. The GET LIST statement acquires the value 'JIMMY∅CARTER∅' as the value of the variable STUDENT_NAME. This constant has a length of only 13 characters, but the variable is declared a length of 15 characters. Therefore 2 blanks characters will be added. The storage will therefore contain:

JIMMY∅CARTER∅∅∅

A character string variable must always be explicitly declared in a program. There are no default rules to associate character string variables. The character attribute is the word CHARACTER followed by a decimal integer enclosed in parentheses. The integer value denotes the length of the character string.

e.g.   CHARACTER(10)
         CHAR(18)
         CHAR

If no length is specified in the attribute as above, the PL/I machine assumes a length of one. The keyword CHARACTER may also be used in abbreviated form CHAR as shown above.

In addition to the character attribute, the attribute VARYING may be used to indicate that the length specification shows the maximum possible length. But the variable may actually take any length up to the maximum. An abbreviation of VARYING is VAR.

e.g.   DECLARE STUDENT_NAME CHARACTER(15) VARYING;
          GET LIST (STUDENT_NAME);

The above GET LIST statement, with the same DATA card as before acquires the constant

        JIMMYɸCARTERɸ

The length is 13. But now the 2 extra blanks are not added in the storage because of the specification of the VARYING attribute.

If the length attribute specified in the declaration is less than the length of the character string constant, then the right-most excess characters are truncated.

e.g.   DECLARE CITY_NAME CHAR(5);
          GET LIST (CITY_NAME);

The information punched on the data card is 'CHICAGO' which is 7 characters long. But as the length attribute is 5, CITY_NAME acquires the value CHICA. Note that the GET and PUT statements are the same as for numeric variables but the character string constants on the data card must be enclosed within quotes.

Also, when we want to output a character string constant which is not declared in the declare statement, it must be enclosed within quotes

e.g.   PUT LIST ('THE VALUE IS', ---);
        PUT LIST ('CUSTOMERS NAME', 'NEW PURCHASE', 'BALANCE');

● **PROBLEM** 13-7

How is an ARRAY declared in PL/I? Explain using examples.

Solution: Every identifier to be used as an array name requires explicit declaration. The declaration must also define the subscripting to be used when the array elements are referenced. For declaration of an array variable, the declaration has the following format:

    DCL ARRAY NAME(DIMENSION ATTRIBUTES) DATA ATTRIBUTES;

Array names can be any variable names and every element within the array is referenced by the array name declared.

The use of the dimension attribute in an array declaration is governed by the following rules.

1. The dimension attribute has the form of one or more boundary specifications enclosed within a pair of parentheses. If two or more boundary specifications are used in the list,

they are separated by commas. The number of boundary specifications in the dimension attribute establishes dimensional-
ity of the array variable.

2. A boundary specification is composed of two, possibly signed, decimal integer constants, separated by a colon.
The first integer value specifies the lower bound and the
second the upper bound of that particular dimension.
For example

DECLARE A (-1:2, 8:10);

In the above, A is the name of the array. It could have been
any other name too, e.g., NANCY, PETE, POOR, etc.. But the
same name cannot be used to refer to more than one data structure or data item. Also note that in the above, A is a two
dimensional array as there are two boundary specifications.
The first subscript may assume any one of the integer values
-1, 0, 1, or 2. The second subscript may assume any one of
the integer values in the range of 8 through 10. Thus, in
the first subscript there are 4 elements and the second subscript has 3 elements so the array A contains 4×3=12 elements.

3. In a boundary specification, the lower bound must
have its value less than or equal to the value of the upper
bound. The dimension attributes,

e.g.,   (3:5), (-3:0, 0:3), (9:9, 1:1),

are well formed.

But, (5:3) is not well formed because the lower bound
is greater than the higher bound. If the lower bound is not
specified it is assumed to have a numeric value of one. For
example, the dimension attributes

(17,26,5) and (1:17, 1:26, 1:5)

are equivalent.

4. The dimension attribute must always appear as the
first attribute following the variable name declared.

Using the above 4 rules a well-formed declare statement
can be written. E.g., consider the following declare statement:

DECLARE B(5,12) FIXED DEC(8,3);

The above statement is a well-formed declare statement. It
establishes a two dimensional array B, with upper bounds 5
and 12. The elements are fixed decimal numbers with precision of the type XXXXX.XXX. However, the following declare
statement is wrong.

DECLARE B FIXED(5,12) DEC(8,3);

The machine would be unable to distinguish between dimension
and precision attributes when written as above. The declarations for more than one array can sometimes be condensed.
For example, consider the following:

DECLARE (A,B,MATRIX) (10, 1:9, -2:5) FLOAT;
DECLARE (X FIXED, Y FLOAT) (17,20);

This is how the array structure is declared. In the

above, A, B and MATRIX are 3-dimensional arrays with 10×9×8=720 elements in each. All the elements have a Floating Point number representation.

X and Y are both 2-dimensional arrays, each of 17×20=340 elements. But, the elements of X have a Fixed Point representation, and the elements of Y have a Floating Point representation.

● **PROBLEM** 13-8

Explain what the computer takes as the attributes of the following variables by Default Rules of PL/I, if full explicit declarations are not provided by the programmer.

a) A variable named: PERCENT(1:8),
b) A variable named: AMOUNT FIXED,
c) A variable named: NUMBER COMPLEX,
d) A variable named: TOTAL BINARY,
e) A variable named: INCANT

Solution: a). First of all note that the name of the variable, PERCENT starts with a P. The letter P does not lie between the letters I and N (inclusive). Hence, PERCENT is assigned the following:

PERCENT(1:8)DEC, REAL, FLOAT(6);
b) The variable AMOUNT has the scale declared as FIXED. Hence, the computer completes the attributes as follows:

AMOUNT FIXED(5) DEC, REAL.

In the above, the precision is made equal to 5, i.e., (5,0). The Base and Mode are supplied as DEC and REAL.
c) The variable NUMBER has the mode specified as COMPLEX. Hence, the following remaining attributes are supplied by the computer:

Scale : FIXED
Base : DEC
Precision: (5), i.e., (5,0)

Hence, the variable looks like that given below.

NUMBER FIXED(5) DEC COMPLEX.

d) The missing attributes are supplied for TOTAL BINARY as follows, according to the Default rules:

TOTAL FLOAT (21) BINARY REAL;

e) The missing attributes are supplied for INCANT as follows:

INCANT FIXED(15) BIN, REAL;

It should be noted in which order the attributes following a variable name are declared, especially the Scale and Precision. The Precision attribute should always follow the Scale attribute, and never vice versa.

437

Explain what is meant by Initialization or Initial Attributes. Explain how a variable is initialized. Also, explain how initialization is done, and what is stored in the computer memory by the following statement:

DCL A FIXED(3,2) INITIAL(1·5), B FIXED(2,1)INIT(2·25),
   C FLOAT(4)INIT(170), J INIT(10010B), P INIT(-11E2).

<u>Solution</u>: It is often necessary that a variable appearing in a program have a value before it is used in expressions in the program. This value is given to the variable by explicitly assigning an initial value or initial attribute to the variable. The assigning of an initial attribute is called Initialization.
   Initialization can be done by means of a statement as follows:

     A=3·2; B=-4E-1; C=2

In the above, A is given an initial value of 3·2. B is initialized to a floating point value of -0·4, and the initial value of C is 2.
   Initialization can be done anywhere within the body of the program, but it must be done before the variable appears in an expression in the program.
   A good place to do the initialization of the variables in a program is immediately following the DECLARE statements.
   A better and shorter way is to initialize the variables simultaneously as they are declared, that is, do the initialization in the DECLARE statement itself. This is done as illustrated below:

     DCL A FIXED(3,2) INITIAL(1·5),
        B FIXED(2,1) INIT (2·25),
        C FLOAT(4) INIT(170),
        J INIT(10010B),
        P INIT(-11E2);

In the above, INIT is a short form for INITIAL. A is declared as FIXED(3,2) with an initial value of 1·5. Hence, the initial value stored in memory for A is 1·50. B is declared as FIXED(2,1) with an initial value of 2·25. Therefore, the value stored for B is as follows: 2·2. Notice the 5 is truncated because the declaration FIXED(2,1) specifies only one position to the right of the decimal. C is declared as FLOAT(4) with an initial value of 170. Therefore, the value stored for C is as follows: 0·1700E+03. If a PUT DATA(C) statement were used in the program before the value of C was changed, the print out for C would be as follows:

     C=1·700E+02.

For J, except for the initial value, no other attributes are declared. Hence, by Default Rules, J receives the following attributes: BIN REAL FIXED(15,0). The initial value of J is 10010B, which is stored in memory.

A PUT DATA(J) statement would print out as below:

J=000000000010010B

For P, by Default Rules, the attributes are as follows:

DEC REAL FLOAT(6).

Hence, the value of P stored in memory is as follows:
-0·110000E+04. A PUT DATA(P) statement will cause a print
out as follows:

P=-1·10000E+03

● **PROBLEM** 13-10

Explain how initialization is done for array variables. Can
the statement DCL A(8) FIXED(3) INIT(0) initialize the elements of the array A?

Solution: In the case of an array, each element of the array
must be explicitly initialized. For example,

DCL A(8) FIXED(3) INIT((8)0);

In the above statement ((8)0) means that all 8 elements are
initialized to zero.
    The given statement DCL A(8) FIXED(3) INIT(0); cannot
initialize all the elements of the array A. It means that
only the first element is initialized to 0. The remaining
seven elements have no specified initial value.

DCL A(2:6, 3:5) FLOAT(3) INIT((9),2);

means that the first 9 elements are initialized to a value
of 2 in the floating point form. That is, the initial
values of the first nine elements are stored in the computer
memory as 0·200E+01. Now, the array A(2:6, 3:5) has a total
number of elements

$$= (6-(2-1)) \times (5-(3-1))$$
$$= (6-1) \times (5-2) = 5 \times 3 = 15 \text{ elements.}$$

This means that the remaining (15-9)=6 elements have no initial values specified.
    Moreover, if a ROW MAJOR ORDER is followed in numbering
the array elements, as is usual, then,

Elements   A(2,3),A(2,4),A(2,5),
           A(3,3),A(3,4),A(3,5),
           A(4,3),A(4,4),A(4,5),

each have an initial value of 0·200E+01. And,

Elements   A(5,3),A(5,4),A(5,5),
           A(6,3),A(6,4),A(6,5),

have no initial values specified for them.

439

Finally, consider the following array declaration:

DCL B(2,3,2) FIXED(2) INIT((5)0,(4)1,(3)2);

In the above, array B is a 2×3×2=12 element array. The elements have a FIXED(2) attribute. The initial values of the first 5 elements are stored as 00; of the next 4 elements as 01; and of the last 3 elements as 02.
That is, B(1,1,1),B(1,1,2),B(1,2,1),B(1,2,2) and B(1,3,1) have an initial value of 0. And, B(1,3,2),B(2,1,1), B(2,1,2) and B(2,2,1) have an initial value of 1, while B(2,2,2),B(2,3,1) and B(2,3,2) have an initial value of 2.

● **PROBLEM** 13-11

Explain how the elements of a structure are initialized. In addition, list the initial values of each of the elements of each of the structures given below.

```
a)   DCL   1 A,
              2 B FLOAT(3) INIT(2•5E0),
              2 C,
                 3 D FIXED(4,2) INIT(4),
                 3 E CHAR(2) INIT(BA),
              2 F LIKE C;

b)   DCL   1 A(4),
              2 B(3) FLOAT(3) INIT((3)2•5E0),
              2 C(2),
                 3 D(2) FIXED(4,2) INIT(0,3),
                 3 E CHAR(2) INIT(BA)
              2 F LIKE C;
```

Solution: Each structure consists of a Major Structure containing a few Minor Structures. Each Minor Structure consists of other Minor Structures and Elements. The Elements are the items of a structure which can have arithmetic or character-string attributes. Hence, it is the Elements only which can have initial values. The rules regarding the assignment of initial values to the elements of a structure are the same as that for the assignment of ordinary variables in a program.
Moreover, each Item of a structure, whether Major, Minor or an Element, can be an array. In this case, rules regarding initialization of array elements apply to the arrays in the structure.

a) The various elements of the structure and their initial values are listed below.

Elements of the Structure	Initial Value stored in the memory
A•B	0•250E+01
A•C•D	04•00
A•C•E	BA
A•F•D	04•00
A•F•E	BA

b) Here, the Item A of the structure is an array of 4 elements. The following table gives the initial values for the elements of the structure corresponding to the element A(1) of the array. The rest of the elements of the structure corresponding to the elements A(2), A(3) and A(4) of the array can be obtained by simply substituting for A(1) in the Table.

Elements of the Structure	Initial Value stored in the memory
A(1)·B(1)	0·250E+01
A(1)·B(2)	0·250E+01
A(1)·B(3)	0·250E+01
A(1)·C(1)·D(1)	00·00
A(1)·C(1)·D(2)	03·00
A(1)·C(2)·D(1)	00·00
A(1)·C(2)·D(2)	03·00
A(1)·C(1)·E	BA
A(1)·C(2)·E	BA
A(1)·F·D(1)	00·00
A(1)·F·D(2)	03·00
A(1)·F·E	BA

Note in the above table that when the LIKE C attribute is used for F, the dimensions of the array C are not copied. So F becomes a one element array, i.e., a simple variable having a minor structure of 3D(2) and 3E. If F was required to be an array of 2 elements like C, the declaration statement would have to be modified to

        2F(2) LIKE C

instead of   2F LIKE C   as given.

● **PROBLEM** 13-12

A PL/I program has variables U, V, W, X, Y, Z which are declared as follows:

        DCL U BIT(4) , V FIXED(4,1),
            W CHAR(5) , X FLOAT(4),
            Y CHAR(3) , Z FIXED(3);

The Data Card for the same program contains the following information: U='1101'B, V=981·2;

U='1101'B, V=123·4, W='123·4', X=·1052E+02, Y='PQR', Z=-249;

a) Show what will be entered into memory storage in the computer as a result of the statements: GET DATA; followed a little later in the program by the statement:
GET DATA(Z,V,W,Y,U,X);

b) In the same program at a later stage, the contents of the memory locations corresponding to U, V, W, X, Y and Z were changed to

```
              0100
               769·2
               144·7
              ·0129E-03
              BOG
              -47
```

respectively. Show what will be printed out by the following
statements:

```
        PUT DATA(U,Y);
        PUT SKIP DATA(X);
        PUT SKIP DATA(W,V,Z);
```

Solution: a) The GET DATA; statement reads in the values
of all the variables available up to the first semi-colon on
the card. Hence, the memory storage is filled in with contents as follows:

Name of memory location	Content of the memory location
U	1101
V	981·2
W	
X	
Y	
Z	

The next statement, which is GET DATA(U,V,W,X,Y,Z); will read
in the values of the variables up to the next semicolon on the
data card. If the new values of the variables are different,
the memory contents will be changed accordingly. Hence, the
latest memory contents are as follows:

Name of memory location	Content of memory location
U	1101
V	123·4
W	123·4
X	·1052E+02
Y	PQR
Z	-249

b) As a result of the PUT DATA statements, the following is
printed out:

```
U='0100'B            Y='BOG';
                          (BLANK LINE)
X=·0129E-03;
                          (BLANK LINE)
W='144·7'            V=769·2      Z=-47;
```

442

A PL/I program uses the EDIT form of input. The declare statement of the program is as follows:

    DCL (A,B,C,D,E,F) FIXED(5,2);

        G CHAR(15)VAR, H CHAR(4);

A data card used by the program has the following information punched on it (Note: The symbol ∅ denotes a blank space).

col.8   col.34
↓   ↓
AB-123·45∅123·459123·456∅∅12345∅18·345912345B2G∅CARS

Show what will be stored in the memory locations corresponding to A, B, C, D, E, F, G and H when the following statement is executed:

GET EDIT(A,B,C,D,E,F,G,H)(COL(10),F(7,2),F(7,2),X(2),F(4,1), COL(34),F(5,2),X(1),F(6,3),F(1,1),X(5),A(3),X(1),A(4));

Solution: As a result of the GET EDIT statement, the data card will be read in the following manner: All entries on the data card up to col. 10 are ignored. Starting from col. 10, a numerical field F(7,2) is read off, for A. Thus, a value -123·45 is stored for A. This brings the computer to col. 17 of the card. Next, a numeric field F(7,2) for B is read off. Thus, a value 123·45 is stored for B. This brings the computer to col. 24 of the card. The next instruction is X(2), i.e., skip 2 columns. Hence the computer ignores the 91, and goes to col. 26 of the card. Now, it must read a numeric field of F(4,1) corresponding to C. Thus, a value 23·4 is read off, and the computer comes to col. 30 of the card. However, C is declared as FIXED(5,2). Therefore, the value 23·4 which is read from the card is stored as 023·40 in the memory location corresponding to C.

The next 4 columns of the card are to be skipped because the program must jump to col. 34 of the card according to the next instruction.

Starting from col. 34, a numeric field of F(5,2) is to be read. Thus, 12345 are read off from the card and assigned to D. And, as D is specified a format of F(5,2), therefore 12345 is stored for D as 123·45. The program comes to col. 39

Column 39 is skipped due to X(1), and the program reaches col. 40. The next instruction is F(6,3) corresponding to E. So, 1·8345 are read from the card and assigned to E. However, E is specified a format of F(6,3). The format specifications wants E to be of the form XX·XXX. In case of a conflict between the format specification and the value read from the card, the value read from the card gets preference. Hence, E becomes 1·8345.

Now, E is declared as FIXED(5,2). Thus, the memory allocated for E on the basis of the declare statement (DCL) expects E to be of the form XXX·XX.

Hence, the value stored in memory for E is 001·83. Note that the extra two decimal places to the right of 3 are truncated.

Next to be read is a field F(1,1) corresponding to F which is declared as FIXED(5,2). Thus, F(1,1) reads off a single digit, 9, from the card. The value of F stored is 000·90.

The next 5 card columns are skipped due to X(5). The next instruction specifies A(3). This means a character field of 3 characters is to be read off from the card corresponding to G. Thus, B2G is stored for G. (2 is treated as a character). The next card column is to be skipped because of X(1). Finally, a value CARS is read off for H, corresponding to the specification A(4).

The contents of the memory locations are shown below:

Name of the memory location	Content of the memory location
A	-123·45
B	123·45
C	023·40
D	123·45
E	001·83
F	000·90
G	B2G
H	CARS

● **PROBLEM** 13-14

As part of a certain program, there is a declare statement as follows:

    DCL (A,C) FIXED(5,2), B CHAR(5) VAR, D FIXED(2,1),
        E CHAR(4), F BIT(7) VAR, G FIXED(3,2);

Also, as part of the same program, there is an EDIT-directed output statement as follows:

PUT EDIT(A,B,C,D,E,F,G)(LINE(40), COL(15), F(7,2),

        PAGE, A(3), F(6,2), LINE(10), F(7,3), X(3),

        A(5), COL(30), B(6), SKIP(7), X(5), F(3,1));

Show what will be printed out, if the contents of the memory storage are as follows:

Name of Memory location	Contents
A	-123·45
B	B2GL¢
C	123·45
D	-1·8
E	CARS
F	1011¢¢¢
G	-7·94

Note: ¢ is a symbol used to denote a blank space.

Solution: The PUT EDIT statement states that the values for the variables A, B, C, D, E, F and G are to be printed out.

The format in which these are to be printed out is given in the second set of parentheses ( ). The first format instruction is LINE(40). Hence, the printer skips to line (40) on the current page. This assumes that the printer did not pass line 40 already. If the printer was indeed past line 40, e.g., on line 45, then, the printer skips the rest of the page and goes to line 40 on the next page. Now, the next format instruction says COL(15), which is a short form for COLUMN(15). This is an instruction to the printer to go to column 15 on the current line, which is line 40.

However, if in case column 15 has already been passed as a result of carrying out some previous format instruction, the printer then skips to col. 15 on the next line. That is, it would skip to column 15 on line 41 in this case if the present position of the printer was, for example, column 59 on line 40.

Thus, after having moved to the correct page, line and column, the computer reads the next format instruction which specifies F(7,2). This specification of F(7,2) corresponds to the first element A in the data list of the PUT EDIT statement.

Therefore, the computer retrieves the value for A from its memory. This value is -123·45, and it agrees with the specification of the F(7,2) format, which requires a number of the type XXXX·XX. Hence, starting from column 15, of the current line (say, line 40), the printer prints out -123·45.

After this printing, the printer is on column 22 (15+7=22). The minus sign and the decimal point also count as one column position in -123·45.

Now the computer wants to print out the next data item, which is B. Therefore, it checks the format list and sees that the next format instruction says PAGE. This causes the printer to leave blank the rest of the current page and go to the first line, first column of a new page.

Next comes the instruction A(3), which means, that the data item B has a character field of 3 characters to be printed. Thus, the value of B, which is, B2GLØ is retrieved from memory and as only 3 characters are to be printed, the printer prints B2G. The L is cut off, and the printer now has come to column 4 of the first line of the new page.

The next format instruction F(6,2) is for the third item C from the data list of the PUT EDIT statement. Therefore the value of C is fetched from memory as 123·45. The format specification requires a form XXX·XX. Hence, 123·45 is printed out from column 4 onwards, and the printer comes to column 10.

Next comes the turn for item D. For this, the first format instruction specifies LINE(10). Therefore the printer jumps from the current LINE(1) to LINE(10). The next format instruction is F(7,3). The value for D from memory is -1·8 now, F(7,3) requires a form XXX·XXX. Therefore -1·8 is converted to 0-1·800. Now, the print out is: Ø-1·800, starting at column 1. Note that the leading zero is suppressed. This brings the printer to column 8.

Now, the next item on the data list, which is, E is to be printed out. The first format instruction for E says X(3). This means that 3 columns are to be skipped. The printer now skips from the present column 8 to column 11. Now, a character field A(5) is specified. The value fetched

445

for E from memory is CARS, which has only 4 characters,
therefore a blank is added at the end of CARS to make up the
5 characters specified by the format. The printer now prints
out CARSβ (note that the 5th character is a blank). The
printer thus comes as a result to column 16 of line 10. Next,
the item F is to be printed. For this, the format first
specifies COL(30); as a result the printer jumps from column
16 to column 30 of the same line 10. Then, the computer
reads the specification B(6), which means that a Binary bit
string is to be printed out from memory. The value for F is
obtained as 1011βββ. This string has 4 characters, and 3
blanks, but the format specification, B(6), requires 6 bits
to be printed out. Hence, zeroes are filled in to make up
the required string length, and the printer prints out 101100.

Now, the last item on the data list, which is G is to be
printed out.

The format specification for G specifies first a SKIP(7).
This causes the printer to jump 7 lines from the present line
10 to line 17. The next format specification says X(5). Hence,
the printer jumps 5 columns from column 1 of line 17 to column
6 on the same line 17.

The next format instruction specifies F(3,1) for G. The
value for G as obtained from memory is -7.94. But the format
specification requires a form X·X. Hence, the value of G is
truncated at both ends, and the printer prints out 7·9. Note
that the minus sign and the digit 4 have been truncated. The
truncation of the decimal place (digit 4) is not very serious.
At most is affects the accuracy of the number. However, the
truncation of the minus sign from the left is very serious.
It changes a negative number into a positive number. Truncation from the left can also cut off the higher order digits.

Hence, the computer is programmed to regard truncation
of a number from the left as an error condition. This error
is called a SIZE condition. Also, the printer prints out a
warning that a SIZE condition has occurred.

To summarize, the print-out for this problem would be
as shown in fig. 1.

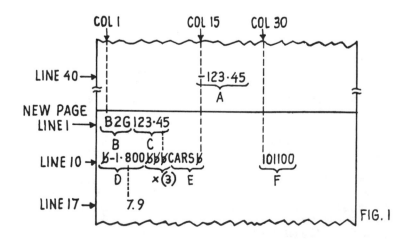

FIG. 1

446

Explain with illustrations how data are read in (acquired),
Written out (disposed of) and referred to in array structures.

Solution: A matrix (i.e. a two dimensional array) is declared by the statement

          DCL X[9,9] FIXED DECIMAL(4);

Now if a problem requires that the values of the main diagonal of the matrix be read in, there are two techniques for
doing it. i) Use of a single get statement of the form
given below:

GET LIST (X(1,1), X(2,2), X(3,3), X(4,4), X(5,5), X(6,6),
          X(7,7), X(8,8), X(9,9)),

or, ii) the iterative DO group illustrated below:

          DO I = 1 TO 9 BY 1;

          GET LIST X[I,I];

          END;

The first method has the disadvantage that a long data
specification is required. The second method is short and
flexible.
     One of the ways to acquire data for one dimensional
arrays is as follows:

               GET LIST(N);
               DO I = 1 TO N BY 1;
               GET LIST(A(I));
               END;

If it is a two dimensional array then the following program
segment can be used:

               GET LIST(M,N);
               DO I = 1 TO M;
               DO J = 1 TO N;
               GET LIST(X(I,J));
               END;
               END;

This method can be generalized to a multidimensional array:
Take the upper bounds of all the dimensions. Then set DO
loops with the most frequently varying dimension at the innermost position and the least frequently varying dimension
at the outermost position.
     There is another technique provided by the PL/I machine,
called repetitive data specification, which reads in an entire array in just one GET statement. This is shown below:

     GET LIST(N,(X(I) DO I=1 TO N));

Because of the left to right order, the variable N will

be acquired before execution of the DO-loop, where it is
used as the upper limiting value.

If it is a two dimensional array, for example
X(10,4) the statement will be as follows:

GET LIST((X(I,J) DO J=1 TO 4) DO I=1 TO 10);

The repetitive specification consists of the following:
a) the data item to be used during execution of the
DO portion (e.g., X(I), Y(I,J));
b) the control information which determines the number
of times the data item is to be used for reading/writing
values of the elements. (e.g. DO I=1 TO N BY 1);
c) a pair of parentheses that enclose the repetitive
specification.

Similarly, to write out (dispose of) array elements, the
repetitive data specification can also be used e.g.,

DECLARE (A,B)(10) FLOAT DECIMAL(5);
PUT LIST((B(I), A(I) DO I=1 TO 10)) SKIP;

The value of B(1) is printed out first, followed by A(1),
and then a line is skipped. After testing the limiting condition, iteration continues and outputs B(2), A(2) and so on.

e.g.,   DCL (A(100,4), B (100)) FIXED BIT(8);
PUT DATA ((B(J),(A(J,K) DO K=1 TO 4) DO J=1 TO 100));

The put statement produces an output stream as follows:

B(1)=XXX   A(1,1)=XXX   A(1,2)=XXX   A(1,3)=XXX   A(1,4)=XXX
B(2)=XXX   A(2,1)=XXX   A(2,2)=XXX   A(2,3)=XXX   A(2,4)=XXX
  •   •   •   •   •
  •   •   •   •   •
  •   •   •   •   •

To refer to an element of array the following is done:
a) A subscripted reference, also termed a subcripted
name, is used.
b) The subscript list must contain as many subscripts
as there are dimensions declared for the array.
c) A subscripted reference consists of the name of the
array followed by a list of one or more subscripts enclosed
in parentheses.
d) The integer value resulting from a subscript evaluation must fall within the bounds declared by the corresponding boundary specification.

To understand clearly the above rules of referring to an
element of an array, consider the example given below:

DECLARE A(10,10) FIXED DECIMAL(10,2), B(-1:5,-5:0,10:98)

The subscript references

A(3,5)
A(1,2×5-2)
B(2,-3,40)
B(-(-6+3),0,90)

are all well formed and valid. Elements of the array A are

referred by the array name A. Since A is a two dimensional
array, the subscript reference has two subscripts and the integer value of the subscript is within the bounds declared
for the array. So is the case for a reference made to array
B. Now observe the following:
The subscript references

        A(1,2,3)
        A(5)
        A(12,-3)

are not valid. In the first case, A(1,2,3), there are three
subscripts, alluding to a three dimensional array. But array A is declared as 2 dimensional. The same goes for the
second case, but here, the subscript reference has only one
dimension instead of the 2 which are required. In the third
case, there are two subscripts and array A is also of two dimensions. However, both the dimensions of array A have a
lower bound of 1 and a higher bound of 10. Hence, 12, the
first subscript element is greater than the higher bound, and
-3, the second subscript element is less than the lower bound
1. This is not permissible.

● **PROBLEM** 13-16

Write a procedure in PL/I that gives information about under-
graduate alumni for a university's records. Your input will
be a deck of 80-column cards, each card specified to the following format:

Columns	Contents	Specifications
1-15	Last name	Characters
16-30	First name	Characters
31-34	Year entered	Fixed-point
35-38	Year graduated	Fixed-point
39-40	Empty	
41-60	GPI for each year	Fixed-point
61-80	Empty	

Your output should contain the alumnus' name, years of attendance, and final GPI. Input is terminated by a card with a
blank last name field.

Solution: This is a simple data processing routine which
contains some interesting format specifications. In the
first PUT EDIT statement, the options PAGE and LINE(3) are
executed prior to the transmission of data. The A specifications allow 15 spaces for each of the headings. X specifications insert blanks, and the COL(40) option jumps the
preceding heading to the fortieth column of the page.
The GET statement acquires the first and last names as
characters, but unlike the list-directed and data-directed
formats, it does not require that the characters be in
quotes.
Now let us look at a sample card from the input stream
to illustrate the possible defaults that could occur:

```
     ANDERSON JON 19761980 2.9 31273.6123.7

     ↑           ↑   ↑         ↑
     1           16  31        43
```

The specification 4F(5,3) denotes usage of format for the
four yearly averages. These rules will clarify the way in
which data is taken into this program.

First, if an explicit decimal point appears in the input stream, it overrides the instructions specified in the F
format item, as is the case of 2.9. If there is no explicit
decimal point, the decimal point is placed implicitly by the
format statement. Hence the digits 3127 are read in as
3.127. If an explicit decimal point appears, the value may
appear anywhere within the field width, as shown by the last
two values 3.612 and 3.7.

The rest of the program is apparent, and is presented
below:

```
LIST:   PROC OPTIONS(MAIN);
        DCL(LAST,FIRST) CHAR(15), (ENTER,GRAD) FIXED,
          (AVER(4),SUM) FIXED DECIMAL(4,3);
/* WRITE LIST HEADINGS */
    PUT EDIT('LAST NAME', 'FIRST NAME', 'YEAR ENTERED',
            'YEAR GRADUATED', 'FINAL AVERAGE')
            (PAGE,LINE(3),A(15),X(1),A(15),COL(40),A(15),
            X(2),A(15),X(2),A(15));
    PUT SKIP(1);
    NEW:  GET EDIT(LAST, FIRST, ENTER, GRAD, AVER)
            (A(15),A(15),2F(4),X(2),4F(5,3));
    IF LAST=' ' THEN GO TO FINISHED;
    SUM=0;
    DO I=1 TO 4;
        SUM=SUM+AVER(I);
    END;
    PUT EDIT(LAST, FIRST, ENTER, GRAD, SUM/4)
            (SKIP,A(15),X(1),A(15),COL(40),
            2(X(4),F(4),X(9)),X(5),F(5,3));
    GET SKIP;
    GO TO NEW;
    FINISHED:  END LIST;
```

BUILT-IN FUNCTIONS

● PROBLEM 13-17

Describe the operations and built-in functions used for character string manipulations.

<u>Solution</u>: One of the most useful operations on character
strings is called concatenation. Concatenation is used to
join two character string operands, giving a single character
string as a result. For example,

        'JANEϷ' || 'FONDA' = 'JANEϷFONDA'

The concatenation operator must connect the character

string JANEø with the character string FONDA. The string
JANEøFONDA will result.

The concatenation operator is represented by ‖ . The
string resulting from the execution of a concatenation operation has a length equal to sum of the lengths of the two
operands (character strings). To understand the processing
of variable length and fixed length string data, consider
the following example.

```
DECLARE ((FIRST_NAME, LAST_NAME) CHAR(10),
         STUDENT_NAME CHAR(15)) VARYING;
GET LIST (FIRST_NAME, LAST_NAME);
STUDENT_NAME = FIRST_NAME ‖ ø ‖ LAST_NAME;
```

If on the data card we have

'JANE', 'FONDA'

then the GET statement creates the following:

Variable	Value	Current length
FIRST_NAME	JANE	4
LAST_NAME	FONDA	5

but due to the varying attribute, no blanks are added, and

STUDENT_NAME = JANEøFONDA

but if the varying attribute is not specified then the GET
statement creates the following:

Variable	Value	Current length
FIRST_NAME	JANEøøøøøø	10
LAST_NAME	FONDAøøøøø	10

Hence STUDENT_NAME = JANEøøøøøøFONDAøøøøø. It has a length
of 21 characters. But the declared length is 15 so the last
6 characters will be truncated, and hence the following is
obtained:

STUDENT_NAME = JANEøøøøøøFOND

Condition Testing and Comparison Operations:

All eight comparison operators (>,>=,=,<=,<,¬>,¬=,¬<),
together with the condition-testing IF statement can be used
with character type operands.

Comparison can only be made with character strings of
the same length. If the operands are of different lengths,
the shorter character string value is expanded at the right
with blank characters. If two character strings of length
zero (i.e., null strings) are compared, the result of the
'=' comparison is true. All other comparison operators return a false when applied to two null-string operands.
Character strings of more than one character are compared,

character by character, in a left-to-right order.

STRING BUILT-IN FUNCTIONS:

For string manipulations, three built-in functions are provided in PL/I.

      1)   LENGTH built-in function
      2)   SUBSTR built-in function
      3)   INDEX built-in function

LENGTH Built-in function: The length of character string variables declared with varying attributes may change during the execution of the PL/I progrma. It may be necessary to utilize the current length of a character string during calculations.

The built-in function 'LENGTH' returns an integer value which is the current length of the character string.

e.g.   STUDENT_NAME = 'JERRY'
            N = LENGTH (STUDENT_NAME);

LENGTH returns a value of 5 as the length of the character string.

The SUBSTR Built-in function: The substring function extracts a segment of a string (i.e. a substring) from a given character string. The function reference uses three arguments.

e.g.   TAR = SUBSTR (CHAR-STRING, i,j)

1. The first argument CHAR-STRING identifies the character string from which the selection process is to take place.

2. The second argument 'i' identifies the starting position in the character string from where extraction of the substring is to be done. It is always an integer value. If k is the current length of a character string, then,

$$0 < i \leq k.$$

3. The third argument 'j' specifies the length of the substring extracted. 'j' is also always an integer. If the value of j is zero, the substring built-in function returns a null string. It is not necessary that this argument, viz., 'j' always be specified explicitly.

e.g.   STUDENT_NAME = !TOMɄANUTH'.
            LAST_NAME = SUBSTR(STUDENT_NAME,5,3)

Then from the character string STUDENT_NAME a substring has to be extracted and assigned to the variable LAST_NAME. Here i=5 which indicates that the substring begins from the 5th position i.e. A. Also, j=3 which gives the length of the substring to be extracted. Hence LAST_NAME = ANU.

If j was not specified

e.g.   LAST_NAME = SUBSTR(STUDENT_NAME,5).

then the substring returned starts from the 5th place, and

extends up to the end of the character-string.

Thus, LAST_NAME = ANUTH.

The substring built-in function may also appear on the left-hand side of the assignment operator (=). In these cases, the built-in function is used as a pseudo-variable. The purpose is to replace a part of a character string item with a new value. For example, consider the following:

```
STUDENT_NAME = 'JAMESβCOOK'
SUBSTR(STUDENT_NAME,1,5) = 'HARRY'
```

produces a new value for the variable STUDENT_NAME. Thus, STUDENT_NAME = HARRYβCOOK.

The INDEX Built-in function: The INDEX built-in function tests a given character string value for the occurrence of a specific substring, and returns an integer value. The search is performed from left-to-right and the integer value returned specifies the leftmost position in the first substring matched. If no match is found, the value zero is returned.

e.g.
```
STUDENT_NAME = 'TOMβPETERSON'
K = INDEX[STUDENT_NAME,'β']
```

A search for β is made and an integer value of 4 is returned because a β appears in the 4th position in the character string 'TOMβPETERSON'. Thus, K = 4.

These three built-in functions, along with the concatenation operation provide us with a powerful tool to operate on character string data.

● **PROBLEM** 13-18

A corporate executive who is slowly embezzling money from the company's pension fund has instructed his partner in crime, an investment banker, to send all correspondence in code. The computer operators on his staff type the correspondence on cards, each card containing 60 characters.

To decode the message, you must first divide up the string into 5 blocks containing 12 characters each, with every twelfth character used to build a word. In addition, each letter is to be replaced with the letter six ahead of it in the alphabet. Thus, A becomes G, B becomes H, and U becomes A, V becomes B, and so on.

Write a procedure in PL/I to read the characters from cards, decode the characters of each card, and print the 12 output words, four per line. The program should terminate when a card contains all consonants (consider Y to be a consonant).

Solution: To complete this program, we make use of the INDEX, VARYING and SUBSTR functions, three built-in routines useful for handling characters. We shall go through the program, explaining the implementation of each of these functions in the program.

In the declaration section, we use the VARYING attribute to adjust the length of the string. Based on the number of

characters in the string, each element in the array having
less than 5 characters will not be padded with blanks. If
WORD(12) were 'QOR', it would be stored just as is. Without
the VARYING (VAR for short) attribute, WORD(12) would contain
'QOR '.

After this we have a section which determines if the message is complete. Here we use the INDEX function. This is a
powerful tool which searches a character string to determine
whether a specified character or combination of characters is
contained there. The five IF statements check to see if any
vowels are contained in the strings. If not found, a value
of 0 is returned to the program, and the next step is executed. If it is found, INDEX returns a single integer indicating
the number of the character where the match begins. This
section causes the program to terminate if the card contains
all consonants.

The statement in which characters are replaced deserves
special attention. First, the double bar symbol stands for
the concatenation operation. Its function is to connect two
character strings to form a single, longer one. In this
statement, WORD(J) is attached to a lengthy expression, beginning with the substring function SUBSTR.

Let us digress for a moment to explain the SUBSTR function. The general form of this function is SUBSTR(a,n) where
a is the name of a character string variable, and n is any
numerical expression that produces a positive integer. It
examines the string in a, reaches the nth character, and pulls
from the string all characters, including the nth one, to the
right. Say we have stored in WORD the characters 'WDPSO'.
If we write NEWWORD = SUBSTR(WORD,3), the variable NEWWORD
will contain the substring 'PSO'. We can even insert a third
argument into the SUBSTR function, which has the same restrictions as n, to indicate the last character we wish to remove.

Now, the section of the statement following the ∥ symbol
can be explained. Character string ALP is the string which
contains the master code. The INDEX function determines the
number of the character to be moved, while the inner SUBSTR
function finds the character in the string. The integer 6 is
added to the number returned by the INDEX function to assign
a letter six ahead of it in the alphabet. This is done to
each character in sequence.

The output is given in tabular form with four words per
row.

```
DECODE:  PROC OPTIONS(MAIN);
    DCL MESSAGE CHAR(60), WORD(12) CHAR(5) VARYING,
        ALP CHAR(32) INIT('ABCDEFGHIJKLMNOPQRSTUVWXYZABCDEF');
/* READ STRING TO DETERMINE IF MESSAGE IS COMPLETE */
LOOP:  GET DATA(MESSAGE);
        IF INDEX(MESSAGE,'A')=0 THEN
          IF INDEX(MESSAGE,'E')=0 THEN
            IF INDEX(MESSAGE,'I')=0 THEN
              IF INDEX(MESSAGE,'O')=0 THEN
                IF INDEX(MESSAGE,'U')=0 THEN GO TO FINISH;
/* INITIALIZE ARRAY AND COUNTER */
    WORD=''; K=0;
/* NEST WORD LOOP INSIDE LETTER LOOP */
LETTERS:  DO I=1 TO 5;
  WORDS:  DO J=1 TO 12;
/* NOW INCREMENT COUNTER, DETERMINE REPLACEMENT FOR LETTER,
    AND ADD REPLACEMENT TO WORD */
```

```
      K=K+1;
      WORD(J)=WORD(J)||SUBSTR(ALP,INDEX(ALP,SUBSTR
         (MESSAGE,K,1))+6,1);
   END WORDS;
END LETTERS;
/* PRINT DECODED WORDS */
PRINTIT:  DO I=1 TO 12 BY 4;
   PUT SKIP DATA(WORD(I),WORD(I+1),WORD(I+2),WORD(I+3));
END PRINTIT;
GO TO LOOP;
FINISH:  END DECODE;
```

Suppose you are given 3 sides of a triangle. Write a program
in PL/I to compute the perimeter, the largest side, the
samllest side, the area, the inscribed radius, the circumscribed radius, and the three angles.

Solution: We need some facts from plane geometry. Suppose
the 3 sides of the triangle are denoted by S_1, S_2, and S_3.
Then the perimeter is given by $P = S_1 + S_2 + S_3$. Let $h \triangleq P/2$.
Then the area is given by

$$\text{Area} = \sqrt{h(h-S_1)(h-S_2)(h-S_3)}.$$

The radius of the inscribed circle is given by

$$\rho = \text{Area}/h.$$

The radius of the circumscribed circle is given by

$$R = S_1 S_2 S_3/4a.$$

The three angles are determined from the trigonometric relationships:

$$\tan \alpha_1 = \rho/(h-S_1)$$
$$\tan \alpha_2 = \rho/(h-S_2)$$
$$\tan \alpha_3 = \rho/(h-S_3)$$

     In the computer program we denote the sides of the tri-
angle by S1, S2, and S3; the perimeter by P; the auxiliary
variable by H; the area by A; the radius of the inscribed
circle by RI; the radius of the circumscribed circle by RC;
and the three angles by A_1, A_2, A_3.
     The program uses the built-in functions MAX and MIN to
get the longest and shortest sides of the triangle. The a-
bove formulas are used to compute inscribed and circumscribed
radii, and the built-in function ATAND computes the angle
from the tangent in degrees.
     Formatting of the output is handled through the PUT EDIT
statement.

```
TRIANGLE:  PROC OPTIONS(MAIN)
RPT:  GET LIST(S1,S2,S3);
```

```
            P=S1+S2+S3;
            H=P/2;
            B=MAX(S1,S2,S3);
            S=MIN(S1,S2,S3);
            A=SQRT(H*(H-S1)*(H-S2)*(H-S3));
         RI=A/H;
         RC=S1*S2*S3/(4*A);
         A1=2*ATAND(RI/(H-S1));
         A2=2*ATAND(RI/(H-S2));
         A3=2*ATAND(RI/(H-S3));
PUT EDIT('SIDES OF TRIANGLE ARE:',S1,S2,S3,
         '3 ANGLES ARE:'A1,A2,A3,
         'THE PERIMETER IS:',P,
         'THE AREA IS:',A,
         'INSCRIBED RADIUS:',RI,
         'CIRCUMSCRIBED RADIUS:',RC,
         'THE BIGGEST SIDE IS:',B,
         'THE SMALLEST SIDE IS:',S)
         (2(A(30),3E(15,5),X(25),6(A(30)),E(15,5),SKIP));
PUT SKIP(2);
GO TO RPT;
END TRIANGLE;
```

EXECUTION SEQUENCE CONTROL

● **PROBLEM** 13-20

Explain the need for STOP JOB CARDS, and list the different methods used in computers to bring about a proper end of the program.

Solution: The computer is just a machine without any intelligence of its own. It only does exactly what is has been programmed to do, i.e., told, to do.

When an instruction is given to the computer to get some kind of data, say, from a punched card, the computer keeps on getting the data till it is explicitly told again to stop getting any more data.

When a computer is taking in data as part of a program, there must be some means of telling the computer how many data items to expect, especially when the appropriation of data is part of an iterative loop. If the computer tries to continously read in data it will eventually not find any more data. The computer now assumes there is an error, and either terminates the program, or gives out an error message. To eliminate this problem we must have some ways of telling the computer just how much data to expect or what to do (other than bombing the program!) when the data runs out.

There are normally four ways to do this:

1) Header Card method,   2) Trailer Card method,
3) End-File condition method, 4) Count and compare method

Explain the Header Card method of stopping a computer job, i.e., a program.

Solution: In this, the first executable statement in the program is a statement which reads in the value of some variable, say N, the value of which denotes the number of data items which will follow. If the program is punched out on cards, the value of the variable N is punched on the first card of the data section of the deck of cards. This method is useful when during different re-runs of the same program, the set of data that is to be used in the program changes.

We have no advance knowledge, while writing the program, how much data will be in each set of data, and what will be their range of values. Hence, while writing the program, we just use the variable N. Later, just before running the program, we punch out a card with the value of N for the particular set of data we have. We call this card the 'Header Card', and place it as the first card of the data cards.

Below is a program to illustrate the use of the Header Card Method.

```
SUM:    PROC OPTIONS(MAIN);
DCL (N,X,Y)FIXED(3)INIT(0),SUM FIXED(4)INIT(0);
GET LIST(N);
/* WE READ THE VALUE OF N FROM THE HEADER CARD */
LOOP:   GET LIST(X)
/* WE READ THE VALUE OF X FROM A DATA CARD */
        SUM=SUM+X;
        Y=Y+1; /*Y IS INCREMENTED BY 1 */
        IF Y=N THEN GOTO FINISH;
        GOTO LOOP; /* IF Y IS NOT EQUAL TO N THEN WE GO
                    BACK TO LOOP AND GET ONE MORE
                    VALUE OF X */
FINISH:  PUT LIST(SUM);
END SUM;
```

Explain the TRAILER CARD method of stopping a computer job, i.e., a program.

Solution: In this method, we use a certain unique number on the last card in the data section of a program card deck. This last card is called the Trailer Card.

The unique number selected is such that it is different in value, or number of digits, etc., from all the other authentic data on the other preceding data cards of the program deck. For example, if we know that all our data consists of positive numbers, we could use a negative number on the Trailer Card. Or, if we know that all the data is non-zero, we could use a value of zero on the Trailer Card. Then, in the body of the program we insert a statement which tells the computer to end the job when the value which we have put on the Trailer Card is encountered.

The Trailer Card method is most useful in cases where different re-runs of a given program will have different amounts of data, which cannot be known in advance. Hence, instead of modifying the program each time the data changes, we use the same program, but take advantage of the Trailer Card to tell the computer when to end the program.

We give below a program to illustrate the use of the Trailer Card method.

```
SUM:  PROC OPTIONS(MAIN);
DCL(X,SUM)FIXED(4)INIT(0);
LOOP:  GET LIST(X); /* WE READ ONE DATA VALUE */
       SUM=SUM+X;
       IF X=0000 THEN GO TO FINISH;
/* WE READ A VALUE OF 0000 FOR X, WHICH IS ON THE TRAILER
CARD, AND, AS THE TRAILER CARD IS THE LAST DATA CARD, WE GO
OUT OF THE LOOP TO LABEL FINISH.  HERE WE ASSUME NONE OF THE
DATA NORMALLY HAS A VALUE '0000' */
       GOTO LOOP; /* IF THE TRAILER CARD IS NOT REACHED, WE
                    REPEAT THE LOOP */
FINISH:  PUT LIST(SUM);
END SUM;
```

● **PROBLEM** 13-23

Explain what is known as the 'Count and/or Compare' method of stopping a computer job.

Solution: Sometimes, computer programs may be such that the computer will enter into a segment of the program which makes the computer do an endless number of loops. This will happen because the programmer has not provided the instructions which control the exit from the loop. In such a case the program will be terminated by the operating system when the alloted time for the job has been exhausted.

The careful programmer always watches out for these pitfalls in his program, and if there is a possibility of endless loopings (e.g., in a program that calculates the sum of all even numbers greater than one), he normally places a maximum limit to the amount times the loop is carried out, or, a maximum limit to the value of the result of his program.

When this maximum limit is reached, the computer is instructed to exit the loop and carry out the remainder of the program.

This method is illustrated in the program below:

```
SUM:  PROC OPTIONS(MAIN);
DCL (X,SUM)FIXED(4)INIT(0);
LOOP:  GET LIST(X);
/* A VALUE OF X IS READ OFF A CARD */
SUM=SUM+X;
IF SUM>100 THEN GOTO FINISH;
/* HERE, WE SET A MAXIMUM LIMIT OF 100 TO THE VALUE THAT THE
SUM OF ALL THE DIFFERENT NUMBERS 'X' WHICH ARE READ FROM THE
CARD/CARDS, CAN REACH */
  GOTO LOOP;
FINISH:  PUT LIST(SUM);
END SUM;
```

Explain the 'END OF FILE Condition' method of ending a program in PL/I.

Solution: The end-file condition occurs when an attempt is
made to acquire data from the input file after the last data
from the file has already been read. Hence, this end of the
file condition has to be specified for the computer by using
the key-word ENDFILE, followed by parentheses containing the
name of the file.
    The file in question could be a deck of cards being
read in through a card reader, in which case we will use the
form: ON ENDFILE(SYSIN)...
    This way we tell the computer what to do when the end-
file condition is reached.
    For example, the statement:

        ON ENDFILE(SYSIN) GOTO FINISH;

tells the computer to go to a statement labelled 'FINISH'
when the ENDFILE condition is reached on the SYSIN FILE.
    The following program illustrates the use of this state-
ment:

```
SUM:  PROC OPTIONS(MAIN);
DCL (X,SUM)FIXED(4)INIT(0);
ON ENDFILE(SYSIN) GOTO FINISH;
LOOP:  GET LIST(X);
SUM=SUM+X;
GOTO LOOP;
FINISH:  PUT LIST(SUM);
/* WE KEEP REPEATING THE LOOP, UNTIL FINALLY WE FIND THAT
WHEN THE GET LIST(X) STATEMENT IS EXECUTED, THERE IS NO MORE
DATA X LEFT TO BE FETCHED.  NOW THE COMPUTER REMEMBERS THAT
BEFORE IT HAD STARTED EXECUTING THE LOOPS, IT HAD ALREADY
BEEN TOLD THAT ON ENDFILE CONDITION, IT SHOULD GO TO THE
STATEMENT LABELLED 'FINISH'.  SO THIS IS WHAT IT DOES */
END SUM;
```

Note: The best place for inserting the ENDFILE condition
statement is after the DCL statement but before the GET LIST
statement, so that the computer will read it before it does
any GET LIST.

Explain the features of the following program.
```
EXAMPLE:  PROC OPTIONS(MAIN);
          DCL BIT_STRING BIT(4) VARYING;
          GET LIST(BIT_STRING);
          IF BIT_STRING ¬=0 THEN PUT LIST(BIT_STRING, 'NOT ALL
                                          BITS ARE ZERO');
                           ELSE PUT LIST(BIT_STRING,'ALL BITS
                                          ARE ZERO');
          END EXAMPLE,
```

Solution: The program illustrates the features of bit strings
in PL/I.

In the declare statement BIT_STRING is the name of a bit string variable. A bit string variable can take bit string data as values, just as arithmetic variables take on numerical values.

A bit string constant consists of a sequence of one or more of the digits 0 and 1. The constant is enclosed within quotes. The terminating quotes symbol is immediately followed by the letter B indicating a bit string.

e.g.   '111'B means that 111 is a bit string.
        (3)'101'B means that 101101101 is a bit string.
          ' 'B   means a null length bit string.

Any bit string variable must always be explicitly declared as in the given example. The bit attribute consists of the keyword BIT followed by an integer enclosed in parentheses indicating the length of the bit string. Hence (4) in the DCL statement specifies the length of the variable named as BIT_STRING. The attribute VARYING specifies that the variable BIT_STRING is of varying length, and its maximum length is 4. The bit string variable can also be initialized using the attribute INITIAL.

e.g. DECLARE INTEREST VARYING BIT(5) INITIAL('011'B);

initializes the variable INTEREST to the bit string value 011.
The second statement in the given program is a value acquisition statement. The rules regarding value acquisition are that all data on the data card (input stream) be in the form of bit string constants without repetition factors. If the value in the input is longer in length than the declared length, truncation occurs and the rightmost excess digits are deleted.

e.g. If on the data card we have '001100'B then, the value acquired will be BIT_STRING=0011.

Thus, the last two bits are truncated.
Similarly, if the value specified in the input is shorter in length than the declared length, padding, by means of zero bits occurs at the right.

e.g. If on the data card the value is '01'B then, the value acquired by the BIT_STRING is equal to 0100.

No padding occurs if the VARYING attribute is used.
The third statement in the given program is of decision making, using ø bit strings. The variable which is named as BIT_STRING is tested, in order to arrive at a certain decision.
For decision-making, the PL/I machine accepts a bit string of arbitrary length. The True path is taken if the bit string contains at least one bit with the value 1. The False path is taken if none of the bits in the string has the value one. The null string ' 'B does not contain any bit; the False path is taken if a null string is present.
In the same third statement the second part involves value disposition (PUT statement). It prints out the value of BIT_STRING and also prints out the remark depending on the decision which is made.

Thus, bit-string processing is quite like character-string processing, and has the facility of using the same built-in functions (SUBSTR, LENGTH, INDEX), concatenation and comparison operators as for character-strings.

Write a PL/I program that reads in pairs of points on a Cartesian coordinate system and classifies them according to the quadrant in which they lie. Make sure you take care of the possibility that one of the pairs lies on the axes of the coordinate system.

<u>Solution</u>: To solve this problem, we will use three if statements, each taking care of a specific task. The first, labeled IF1, decides whether the calculation should terminate by going to the statement FINISHED, or if the coordinate point lies on the Y-axis. IF2, the second if statement, looks for points that lie on the X-axis. Finally, IF3 classifies all remaining points by quadrant location.

As a refresher, the following coordinate system will point out the X- and Y-axes and the quadrant names:

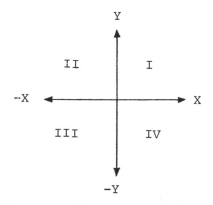

Assume that the program ends when the origin point is encountered, which is when X=0. and Y=0. Output is in tabular form.

```
POINT_CLASSIFY:  PROC OPTIONS(MAIN);
    PUT PAGE LIST('0','CLASSIFYING POINTS');
    PUT SKIP(2) LIST('X-COORDINATE','Y-COORDINATE',
                'CLASSIFICATION');
SEARCH:  GET DATA(X,Y)
    IF1:  IF X=0
            THEN IF Y=0
                THEN GO TO FINISHED;
                ELSE DO;
                    PUT LIST(X,Y,'Y-AXIS')SKIP;
                    GO TO SEARCH;
                    END;
        IF2:  IF Y=0 THEN DO;
                    PUT LIST(X,Y,'X-AXIS')SKIP;
                    GO TO SEARCH;
                    END;
        IF3:  IF X>0
```

461

```
                THEN IF Y>0
                    THEN PUT LIST(X,Y,'I')SKIP;
                    ELSE PUT LIST(X,Y,'IV')SKIP;
                ELSE IF Y>0
                    THEN PUT LIST(X,Y,'II')SKIP;
                    ELSE PUT LIST(X,Y,'III')SKIP;
                GO TO SEARCH;
      FINISHED:  PUT LIST('ORIGIN ENCOUNTERED:  DONE')SKIP;
                END POINT_CLASSIFY;
```

● **PROBLEM** 13-27

Write a PL/I program to find the roots of a quadratic equation and print out an appropriate message.

Solution: The Quadratic equation is given by the formula

$$Ax^2 + Bx + C = 0$$

where A, B, and C are coefficients. Roots of the equation are given by the expression

$$Roots = \frac{-B \pm \sqrt{B^2 - 4AC}}{2A}$$

Now before directly evaluating the roots, we need to calculate the value of B^2-4AC as this may be a negative value

e.g. $A = B = C = 1$ or, $\sqrt{B^2-4AC} = \sqrt{1-4\times1\times1} = \sqrt{-3}$

and a negative sqrt cannot be calculated unless we assume an imaginary number i where $i^2 = -1$ and $\sqrt{-3} = \sqrt{3i^2}$

```
ROOTS:  PROCEDURE OPTION(MAINS);
/* THIS PROGRAM FINDS ROOTS OF QUADRATIC EQUATIONS*/
DCL (A,B,C) REAL DEC FIXED(5,2)(ROOT1,ROOT2,IMAG,QUAD)
    FIXED(5,2);
GET LIST(A,B,C);
QUAD=B**2-4*A*C
IF QUAD<0 THEN DO;
            QUAD=-QUAD;IMAG=(SQRT(QUAD))/2*A;
    PUT LIST('THE ROOTS ARE COMPLEX','ROOT1=',-B/2*A,
            '-I',IMAG,'ROOT2=',-B/2*A,'+I',IMAG);
ELSE IF QUAD=0 THEN PUT LIST('THE ROOTS ARE EQUAL','ROOTS='
                    -B/2*A);
    ELSE PUT LIST('THE ROOTS ARE UNEQUAL','ROOT1='(-B+SQRT
            (QUAD))/2*A
            'ROOT2='(-B-SQRT(QUAD))/2*A);
END ROOTS;
```

● **PROBLEM** 13-28

Given pairs (x,y) on data cards, write a PL/I program to test x,y and decide in which quadrant they lie. Also find the distance from the origin. If the distance from origin is less than 10 classify as small; if distance is less than 20 classify as medium and all other cases classify as large. Your program should not to have any GOTO except for the one GOTO needed for repetitive input.

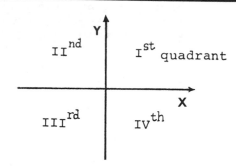

Solution: This is an exercise in IF THEN and IF ELSE control statements. The program reads in the values of X & Y from each data card. To obtain the information about the quadrants consider the figure.

Test for X and Y   Quadrant the point lies

Test for X and Y	Quadrant the point lies
X>0, Y>0	Ist quadrant
X>0, Y<0	IVth quadrant
X<0, Y<0	IIIrd quadrant
X<0, Y>0	IInd quadrant
X=0	Y axis
Y=0	X axis
X=0, Y=0	Origin

Distance from origin to the point with coordinates (X,Y) is given by

$$\text{Distance} = \sqrt{X^2 + Y^2}$$

The program is as follows.

```
        TABLE:  PROCEDURE OPTIONS(MAIN);
/* THIS PROGRAM GIVES THE LOCATION OF THE POINT AND THE
        DISTANCE FROM THE ORIGIN */
        DCL(X,Y,DIST) FIXED REAL DEC(6,2);
PUT LIST('X CO-ORD','Y CO-ORD','QUADRANT','DISTANCE',
        'CLASSIFICATION');
/* THIS PROVIDES A HEADING FOR EACH COLUMN */
PUT SKIP(2);
REPEAT:  GET LIST(X,Y);
        IF X=1000,Y=1000 THEN STOP;/* THE LAST CARD HAS
THIS VALUE OF X,Y THIS IS A WAY TO END LOOPING AND EXIT */
PUT LIST(X,Y);
```

Note that in the following, the brackets {} have been used to delineate the THEN clause and the ELSE clause.
        IF condition THEN expression 1;
                     ELSE expression 2;
It should be borne in mind that the use of the {} brackets is limited only for purposes of explanation of this example. The {} brackets are not a standard PL/I feature.

```
IF X=0 THEN{IF Y=0 THEN PUT LIST('ORIGIN');
                 ELSE PUT LIST('Y AXIS');}
      ELSE{IF Y=0 THEN PUT LIST('X AXIS');
                 ELSE;}
IF X>0 THEN{IF Y>0 THEN PUT LIST('FIRST QUADRANT');
                 ELSE PUT LIST('THIRD QUADRANT');}
      ELSE{IF Y>0 THEN PUT LIST('SECOND QUADRANT');
                 ELSE PUT LIST('FOURTH QUADRANT');}
DIST=SQRT(X*X+Y*Y);
PUT LIST(D);
IF D<10 THEN{PUT LIST('SMALL');}
       ELSE{IF D<20 THEN PUT LIST('MEDIUM');
                 ELSE PUT LIST('LARGE');}
PUT SKIP(2);
GO TO REPEAT;
END TABLE;
```

Illustrate transfer of control in a PL/I program, using GO TO statements.

Solution: The PL/I machine has an implicitly defined sequential execution. The execution of statements is normally a sequential process, however, a special statement, the GOTO statement can alter the processing sequence of the PL/I machine. This GOTO statement discontinues the normal sequential execution and processing resumes at a point that is indicated by a label. Examples of well formed GOTO statements are given below:

```
1)  SUM:  A = B+C;
          .
          .
          .
          GOTO SUM:
2)        GOTO NEXT;
          .
          .
          .
          NEXT:  X=Y*Z;
3)  JUMP:  GOTO TERMINATE;
          .
          .
          .
             TERMINATE:  END;
```

The following are a few examples of not well-formed GOTO statements.

```
a)  JOE:  PROCEDURE OPTIONS(MAIN);
          .
          .
          .
          GOTO JOE;
```

The above is wrong due to the fact that the control can only be transferred within the body of the main program. In other words, GOTO cannot transfer control to the starting point of a procedure as above.

b)   GOTO END_1
.
.
.
.
END END_1

The above is wrong because there is no label END_1 anywhere in the body of the program. END_1 is used as a part of another statement, but END_1 is not a label of any statement in the program body.

● **PROBLEM** 13-30

Write a program to sum up 50 numbers each on individual data cards. The program halts if sum is greater than 1000 or 50 numbers have been summed. Use GOTO statements for transfer of control. Explain all steps in the program with appropriate comments.

Solution: ADD: PROCEDURE OPTIONS(MAIN);
DECLARE(SUM,X,N)DEC FIXED(6,2);
SUM=0; /* INITIALIZE THE SUM VARIABLE */
N=0; /* N IS USED AS COUNTER, TO COUNT
ADDING OF 50 NOS */.

LOOP: GET LIST(X); /* READ IN DATA FROM DATA
CARD */
SUM=SUM+X;
N=N+1; /* INCREMENT THE COUNTER */
IF SUM>1000 OR N=50 GOTO EOJ; /* HERE WE TEST THE
CONDITION IMPOSED IN THE PROBLEM, WHETHER SUM>
1000 OR N=50. IN THAT CASE WE WISH TO TRANSFER
CONTROL FURTHER DOWN IN THE PROGRAM */
GOTO LOOP; /* WE COME TO THIS INSTRUCTION
WHEN THE ABOVE TEST FAILS, THAT IS SUM IS ⩽1000
OR TOTAL NOS ADDED IS ≠50. WE WANT TO BRANCH
BACK TO GET A VALUE ON DATA CARD */
EOJ: PUT LIST(SUM,N);
END ADD;

Notice that the first GOTO statement takes us down the program to the PUT LIST statement, while the second GOTO statement transfers control to the upper part of the program.

For the following PL/I program,

a) Explain how a condition known as 'SIZE CONDITION' arises,
b) Show what the computer will print out if the program is run,
c) Write out a corrected program to avoid errors due to this condition, using ON SIZE condition, and,
d) Show what will be printed out by the corrected program.

```
EXAMPLE:    PROC OPTIONS(MAIN);
            DCL A(5) FIXED(3), (X,Y,Z) FIXED(2);
            GET LIST(Z);
            DO I=1 TO Z;
            GET LIST(X,Y);
            A(I)=X*Y;
            PUT LIST(I,A(I));
            END;
            END EXAMPLE;
```

The Data Card contains the following DATA:

    5, 10, 10, 5, 3, 20, 49, 90, 80, 7, 8

Solution: a). Notice from the program that each element of the array A has been declared as FIXED(3). This means that each element can be a numeral with 3 digits to the left and 0 digits to the right of the decimal point.

The GET LIST(Z) statement reads a value 5 from the DATA CARD. This value 5 of Z becomes the upper limit of the loop head statement: 'DO I=1 TO Z'. In the body of the loop, X and Y are read from the DATA CARD, and then A(I) is calculated. Thus, in the first loop, X and Y are obtained as 10 and 10. And hence, as A(I)=X*Y,

$$A(1)=10*10=100.$$

As Z=5, the loop is performed 5 times. In the fourth loop, the values of X and Y obtained are 90 and 80, respectively. Hence, the value of X*Y is calculated as:

$$X*Y=90*80=7200.$$

However, the array A(5) is declared as FIXED(3). Hence, each array element can consist of 3 digits only. And so, the computer throws away the fourth digit, viz., 7, and stores only 3 digits in the array element A(4). Thus A(4)= 200. This condition, where extra digits are thrown away is known as a SIZE CONDITION. But this throwing away of extra digits can lead to serious errors by the user of the program if he is not aware that the computer has dropped some digits, and that the 200 in A(4) should really have been 7200, for example.

Thus, the computer is programmed to print out a message indicating that a SIZE CONDITION occurred in a particular statement number whenever it does.

b) The print out of the computer for the given program will be as follows:

```
1     100
2      15
3     980
4     200
5      56
```

c) The program can be corrected by adding '(SIZE):' as a prefix to the first statement of the program, and then inserting a statement 'ON SIZE ....' inside the body of the program. A good place for inserting this statement is just after the DCL statement so that the computer reads it before it starts with the calculations, etc.

Thus, the corrected program is given as:

```
(SIZE):   EXAMPLE:   PROC OPTIONS(MAIN);
                     DCL A(5) FIXED(3),(X,Y,Z) FIXED(2);
                     ON SIZE X*Y=999;
                     GET LIST(Z);
                     DO I=1 TO Z;
                     GET LIST(X,Y);
                     A(I)=X*Y;
                     PUT LIST(I,A(I));
                     END;
                     END EXAMPLE;
```

Note that in the above program, the computer has been instructed that if a SIZE CONDITION occurs it must put X*Y=999. Hence, in any loop, whenever the values of X and Y are such that X*Y becomes a number with more than 3 digits, the computer makes X*Y=999. This means the old, larger value of X*Y, is replaced by 999. And thus, the value of the corresponding element of A(I) becomes 999.

It is assumed that the programmer knows that whenever there is a print out of 999, it means he should not consider that value as it is the result of a SIZE CONDITION.

d) The print out of the corrected program will be as follows:

```
1     100
2      15
3     980
4     999
5      56
```

A computer message stating that a SIZE CONDITION had occurred in a particular statement will also be printed out.

Note in the above printout that the value of A(I) corresponding to I=4 has been affected by the SIZE CONDITION.

● **PROBLEM** 13-32

For the following PL/I program,

a) Explain how a condition known as 'STRINGRANGE CONDITION' arises.
b) Show what will be printed out if the program is run.
c) Write a corrected program to avoid errors due to this condition.
d) Show what the print out will be from the corrected program.

467

```
      EXAMPLE:  PROC OPTIONS(MAIN);
                DCL (B(6),C) CHAR(4),Z FIXED(2);
                GET LIST(Z,C);
                DO I=1 TO Z;
                B(I)=SUBSTR(C,1,I);
                PUT LIST(I,B(I));
                END;
                END EXAMPLE;

The DATA CARD holds data as follows:  6, ROVE.
```

Solution: a) The purpose of the above program is to illus-
trate a type of condition known as 'STRINGRANGE CONDITION'.
    In the program, the array B is declared as having 6 ele-
ments.
    The GET LIST statement gets the value of Z from the DATA
CARD as Z=6. Also, the value of C is obtained from the DATA
CARD as C='ROVE'.
    In the next statement, viz., DO I=1 TO Z, the value of
Z=6 gets substituted. Hence, the DO loop statement becomes
DO I=1 TO 6;.
    This means that the DO loop will be performed 6 times.
Each time, the value of an array element B(I) is calculated.
    This value of B(I)=SUBSTR(C,1,I) means that from C, i.e.,
from 'ROVE', starting from the first character, select I
characters. These selected I characters are to be assigned
to B(I).
    Thus, for example, if I=2, then SUBSTR(C,1,2) gives
B(2)='RO'.
    In the given program, as Z=6, the loop will be perform-
ed 6 times. But, during the 5th loop, on substituting values
of I and C in the equation: B(I)=SUBSTR(C,1,I), gives:
B(5)=SUBSTR('ROVE',1,5).
    The above statement tries to find a substring of 'ROVE',
starting from the first character up to (and including) the
fifth character. However, 'ROVE' has only 4 characters.
Hence, the computer will just print the available characters.
The programmer must be informed. Hence, the computer is programmed to print out a message stating that the STRINGRANGE
CONDITION had occurred in a certain program statement of the
program.
b) The printout of the program will be as follows:

1	'R'
2	'RO'
3	'ROV'
4	'ROVE'
5	'ROVE'
6	'ROVE'

c) The program can be corrected as follows: The computer
must be told that it must look out for the STRINGRANGE CON-
DITION. This is done by using a word within parentheses,
viz., (STRINGRANGE):, as a prefix to the first program statement, as shown below. Also, in the body of the program, a
statement such as: On STRINGRANGE GOTO ....., must be included. A good place for inserting this statement is just
after the DCL statement so that the computer reads it before it enters the loop.

The corrected program can now be written as shown below:

```
(STRINGRANGE):   EXAMPLE:   PROC OPTIONS(MAIN);
                            DCL(B(6),C) CHAR(4), Z FIXED(2);
                            ON STRINGRANGE B(I)='0000';
                            GET LIST(Z,C);
                            DO I=1 TO Z;
                            B(I)=SUBSTR(C,1,I);
                            PUT LIST(I,B(I));
                            END;
                 FINISH:    END EXAMPLE;
```

In the above program the program is made to go to the FINISH
label, which is the end of the program when the STRINGRANGE
CONDITION arises. But as a matter of fact any valid instruction could be given to the computer instead of the 'GOTO
FINISH' instruction.

d) The print-out of the corrected program is as follows:

```
            1        'R'
            2        'RO'
            3        'ROV'
            4        'ROVE'
            5        '0000'
            6        '0000'
```

The computer will also print out a STRINGRANGE CONDITION message. It is assumed that the user of the program knows that
whenever '0000' is printed out it means that a STRINGRANGE
CONDITION has occurred at that stage.

● **PROBLEM** 13-33

For the following PL/I program,

a) Explain how a condition known as 'SUBSCRIPTRANGE CONDI-
    TION' arises.
b) Show what will be printed out if the program is run.
c) Write out a corrected program to avoid errors due to
    this condition.
d) Show what the corrected program will print out.

```
      EXAMPLE:   PROC OPTIONS(MAIN);
                 DCL A(5) FIXED(3),(X,Y,Z) FIXED(2);
                 GET LIST(Z);
                 DO I=1 TO Z;
                 GET LIST(X,Y);
                 A(I)=X*Y;
                 PUT LIST(I,A(I));
                 END;
                 END PROGRAM;
```

Data: 6, 10, 10, 5, 3, 20, 40, 30, 30, 7, 8, 15, 2.

Solution: a) The purpose of this example is to illustrate
a type of condition in which an array subscript is calculated beyond the declared range for that array.

     Notice from the DCL statement that a storage space for
an array A of 5 elements is to be reserved.

469

The 'GET LIST(Z)' statement fetches 6 from the DATA CARD as a value for Z. Now, this value of Z becomes the upper limit of the DO loop of the next statement.

In the body of this DO loop, a value for X and a value for Y are read from the DATA CARD, and the array element A(I) is computed.

The program looks straight forward. However, an examination of the program reveals the occurrence of a condition known as the 'SUBSCRIPTRANGE CONDITION'.

Note that the value of Z obtained from the card is 6. The DO loop will be performed 6 times. Thus, 6 elements of the array A(I) will be computed.

But the DCL statement declared the array A(I) as consisting of 5 elements only. Hence, the program may use additional storage declared under some other name, destroying its previous contents. This is undesireable, because those storage elements may have contained some precious data which is now destroyed.

b) The printout of the computer will be as follows:

```
100
 15
800
900
 56
 30
```

Notice that the computer calculated 6 elements for array A(5), even though A(5) should have had only 5 elements.

c) The error due to this condition can be avoided by specially instructing the computer to regard this as a condition to look out for. The instruction is given to the computer by attaching a 'KEYWORD' prefix to the first statement of the program, as shown in the corrected program below. Also, the program body must contain an additional statement telling the computer what to do if the given condition does arise. For example, the computer could be told to go to some 'error routine' if the SUBSCRIPTRANGE CONDITION arises, as is done below.

The corrected program is as follows:

```
(SUBSCRIPTRANGE):  EXAMPLE:  PROC OPTIONS(MAIN);
                             DCL A(5) FIXED(3);
                             ON SUBSCRIPTRANGE GOTO (ERROR
                                 ROUTINE);
                             GET LIST(Z);
                             DO I=1 TO Z;
                             GET LIST(X,Y);
                             A(I)=X*Y;
                             PUT LIST(A(I));
                             END;
                             END EXAMPLE;
```

d) The computer will now continuously check if the number of array elements computed is within the bounds declared for the array.

Consequently, now, only 5 elements will be computed and printed out, as follows:

```
                       100
                        15
                       800
                       900
                        56
```

The program will end now. But, an error message will also
be printed out, informing the programmer that a SUBSCRIPT-
RANGE CONDITION had occurred during the program.

● **PROBLEM** 13-34

For the following PL/I program,

a) Explain how a condition called ENDFILE CONDITION' arises.
b) Show what will be printed out if the program is run.
c) Write out a corrected program to avoid errors due to this
    condition.
d) Show what the printout from the corrected program will be.

```
EXAMPLE:   PROC OPTIONS(MAIN);
           DCL(X,Y,Z) FIXED(3) INIT(0);
           GET LIST(Z);
           DO I=1 TO Z;
           GET LIST(X);
           Y=Y+X;
           PUT LIST(I,Y);
           END;
           PUT LIST(2I,Y);
           END EXAMPLE;
```

The DATA CARD contains the following data:

        8, 0, 1, 2, 3, 4, 5, 6

Solution: a) The purpose of the above program is to illustrate a condition known as ENDFILE CONDITION.
     In this program, the GET LIST(Z) statement reads a value
for Z from the DATA CARD. Hence, Z=8. This value of Z becomes the upper limit for the loop of the next statement.
Hence, the loop statement becomes:

        DO I=1 TO 8.

     During each loop, a value of X is read from the card and
the sum Y=Y+X is calculated.
     Now, observe that there are only 7 values of X (0 to 6)
punched on the DATA CARD. Hence, when the program enters the
eighth loop, the computer finds that the data have run out
and terminates the program. This condition of data running
out is known as an ENDFILE CONDITION.
b) The printout of the computer is as follows:

```
            1        0
            2        1
            3        3
            4        6
            5       10
            6       15
            7       21
```

471

After the seventh loop, I gets a value of 8. Now the program
tries to execute GET LIST(X). But since there is no 8th value
of X, the program halts giving out an error message. So there
is no chance for executing the other PUT LIST statement which
follows outside the loop.

c) The program can be corrected by inserting an ON statement
of the general form

        ON ENDFILE (FILE NAME) ACTION;

The above statement prevents termination of the program abrupt-
ly on the occurrence of the ENDFILE CONDITION.
     Inside the parentheses, the name of the file, which is to
be used, should be specified. For example, if punched cards
are being used for input, the name of the input file is
(SYSIN).
     'ACTION' in the above statement means some sort of in-
struction to the computer telling it what to do if the data
on the file run out. The corrected program can therefore be
written as follows:

        EXAMPLE: PROC OPTIONS(MAIN);
                  DCL (X,Y,Z) FIXED(3), INIT(0);
                  ON ENDFILE(SYSIN) GOTO A;
                  GET LIST(Z);
                  DO I=1 TO Z;
                  GET LIST(X);
                  Y=Y+X;
                  PUT LIST(I,Y);
                  END;
              A: PUT LIST(2I,Y);
                  END EXAMPLE;

d) The printout from the corrected program will be:

              1   0
              2   1
              3   3
              4   6
              5   10
              6   15
              7   21
             16   21

Note that after the seventh loop is completed, the computer
goes back to the loop head, viz.,

        DO I=1 TO Z.

As Z=8, therefore I is incremented by 1 from 7 to 8. Now,
on trying to execute the next statement, viz., GET LIST(X),
the computer finds that an ENDFILE CONDITION has occurred on
the SYSIN file. Hence, the program goes to the statement
labelled 'A'. This statement is PUT LIST(2I,Y);. The latest values of I and Y lying in the program are 7 and 22 respectively; therefore 16 and 22 are printed out. The program now goes to the next statement END EXAMPLE which is a
normal end of the program.

472

DO STATEMENTS

● **PROBLEM** 13-35

> Explain the various features of DO statements used for iter-
> ation.

Solution: By means of condition testing, one can execute
only a single statement. There is a DO statement which allows a group of statements to be executed on condition testing. This is called a THEN DO statement. It is illustrated
by the following example.

```
IF A>0 THEN DO;
        SUM=SUM+X;
        A=A+1;
        B=SUM/Y;
        PUT LIST(SUM,B);
        END;
```

Observe that four statements are executed when the condition
tested is true as compared to only one statement that would
be executed without the use of the DO statement. This DO
statement allows a grouping of statements. The DO statement
must have as its last statement an END statement. The DO and
END statement pair do not influence the execution of the PL/I
machine but has an editing function in the program. The pair
identifies the loop more explicitly.

Besides the simple DO group, there is also an iterative
DO group. The format of the iterative DO statement is as
follows:

DO CONTROL VARIABLE=INITIAL VALUE TO LIMIT VALUE BY INCRE-
MENT VALUE.

Control variable is a variable name whose value will change
according to control specifications. The variable is followed by an assignment symbol (=), which in turn is followed
by a control specification. The control specification may
consist of up to three elements as follows:
a)   Initial value, which is the value assigned to the
control variable initially. The initial quantity must always
be specified in the DO statement. Also, this initial quantity must be the first item to be specified on the right hand
side of the (=) sign in the DO statement.
b)   The TO clause describes the limiting value to be
used by the loop control variable. Once the value of the
control variable exceeds the limiting value, no statement
within the loop is executed and the next statement immediately outside the loop is executed.
c)   The BY clause describes the increment value to be
used in the loop control mechanism. Every time the loop is
executed the value of the control variable is incremented by
the increment value. The new value of the control variable
is tested against the limiting value and the loop is executed if the control variable's value is less than or equal
to the limiting value. For example, consider the following:

```
DO I=-5 TO 5 BY 2;
    STATEMENT 1;
    STATEMENT 2;
          .
          .
          .
    STATEMENT N;
    END;
    STATEMENT X;
```

I is the control variable, its initial value is -5. As -5 is less than the limiting value of 5, statements 1 to n are executed, then the value of I is incremented by the increment value 2. Hence, the value of the control variable is -3. Still it is less than 5, and again the loop is executed. Once again I is incremented by 2, tested against the limiting value of 5, and so on. When I=5, still I is not greater than the limit value of 5 and therefore the loop is executed once again. Now I=7 which is greater than 5 and exit from the loop to statement X is performed. With regard to DO loops, the points to remember are as follows:

a)   If the increment value is positive, the limiting value must be greater than the initial value.

b)   If the increment value is negative, the limiting value must be less than the initial value.

c)   The BY and TO clauses are optional and may be omitted.

i)   When the BY clause is omitted: If no BY clause is found, but the TO clause is present then, by default the PL/I machine assumes

            BY 1

(increment by one). That is, PL/I assumes that the following statements

```
DO I=1 TO 70 BY 1,        and,
DO I=1 TO 70;
```

are completely equivalent.

ii)   When the TO clause is omitted: If the DO statement has the form given below:

```
DO X=2 BY 3,
```

it can be seen that the TO clause is omitted. But there are no default rules to supply a TO clause in PL/I. Instead, the PL/I machine proceeds without testing the limiting value when the TO clause is omitted. Hence, a mechanism must be provided within the body of the loop to exit out of the loop, otherwise infinite looping will result.

```
e.g.   LOOP:  DO I=1 BY 1;
               SUM=SUM+I;
               IF SUM>10 THEN GOTO LABEL;
               END LOOP;
       LABEL:  PUT LIST(I,SUM);
               END;
```

In the above, exit from the loop is achieved when the value of SUM exceeds 10.

If the TO clause and the BY clause are both omitted, for instance,

    DO J=3.

The DO statement will be executed only once as a result of the above.

The While Clause In the Specification of a DO Group:

The flexibility and power of the DO statement is further enhanced by using a WHILE clause in the control specification of the DO statement. The format is as follows:

    DO WHILE (CONDITION)
        STATEMENT 1
        STATEMENT 2
            .
            .
            .
        STATEMENT N
    END

In the above, processing of the DO group is terminated as soon as the CONDITION specified in the WHILE clause is not satisfied anymore.

There are various formats and features of DO statements used for iteration. The DO statements are extensively used for iteration purposes as compared to GOTO statements. For a DO statement, the following segmented flowchart symbol is used:

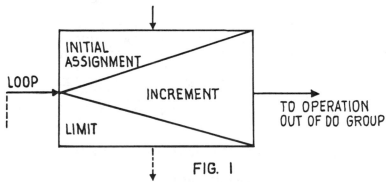

FIG. 1

● **PROBLEM 13-36**

Write a PL/I program to determine whether a given integer between 0 and 1000 (exclusive) is prime or composite.

Solution: As we know a prime is any positive integer p greater than 1 whose only positive divisors are 1 and p. Integers greater than 1 which are not prime are called composite. According to the fundamental theorem of arithmetic, every composite number n has at least two prime factors p and q such that 1<p<n and 1<q<n. Since p and q cannot both be greater than $\sqrt{n}$ (otherwise pq would be greater than n) we have "If an integer n>1 has no prime factor less than or equal to $\sqrt{n}$, then n is prime." Thus we have an algorithm to determine whether a given number n is prime or composite: Divide n successively by the primes 2, 3, 5, 7, ... p_n, where p_n denotes the largest prime that does not exceed $\sqrt{n}$, if none of these primes divides n, then n is prime, otherwise n is composite.

In our example to test integers less than 1000 we will need to divide by the primes less than $\sqrt{1000}=31\cdot6$. These are 2, 3, 5, 7, 11, 13, 17, 19, 23, 29 & 31. We can now detail the steps that our program is to perform.

1. Place the eleven primes into memory.
2. Read an integer n into memory.
3. (a) If 1<n<1000, proceed to step 4. (b) If n=1, or if n≥1000, print an error message. (c) Terminate if n is not positive.
4. Calculate $[\sqrt{n}]$, the largest integer not exceeding the real number $\sqrt{n}$.
5. Divide n successively by primes. (a) If all eleven primes are found not to divide n. n is prime; else it is a composite number.

```
        PRIME:  PROCEDURE OPTIONS(MAIN);
/* THIS PROGRAM DETERMINES WHETHER INTEGERS BETWEEN 1 TO
   1000 ARE PRIME OR COMPOSITE */
   DCL NPR(11) FIXED(2,0),(LIMIT,N) FIXED(3,0);
   GET LIST(NPR(I) DO I=1 TO 11); /* INPUT ELEVEN PRIMES */
LABEL:  GET LIST N; /* READ IN INTEGER TO BE TESTED */
        IF N<0 THEN STOP;
            ELSE IF N=1 OR N≥1000 THEN PUT LIST('OUT OF
                                             RANGE');
            ELSE;  /* CHECK THAT N IS WITHIN RANGE */
        RN=N; /* CONVERT N TO REAL NUMBER */
   NROOT=SQRT(RN);  /* CALCULATE SQUARE ROOT */
   DO I=1 TO 11;
      IF (NPR(I)-NROOT)>0 THEN PUT LIST(N,'THE NO IS PRIME');
```

This statment is followed by comment /* IS CURRENT PRIME GREATER THAN SQUARE ROOT */

```
        ELSE IF(N/NPR(I)*NPR(I)-N)=0 THEN PUT LIST(N,'THE
                                        NO IS COMPOSITE');
/* WE CHECK IF THE CURRENT PRIME DIVIDES N */
        ELSE;
/* THIS IS A NULL ELSE AND SIGNIFIES THAT IF NEITHER OF THE
   ABOVE POSSIBILITIES HOLD, THEN THE LOOP IS TO BE REPEATED
   AND A NEW VALUE OF NPR IS TO BE OBTAINED */
GOTO LABEL;
END PRIME;
```

● **PROBLEM** 13-37

Compute and print out a table of the function $Y=1/(4-X^2)$ in the range 0<X<2 using a variable step interval. Start out with a step width of $0\cdot1$ (i.e. X=0,$0\cdot1$,$0\cdot2$...$1\cdot9$). Reduce the step width by a factor of 10 whenever X would reach 2 during next iteration, or whenever two successive values differ by more than 10. Stop the tabulation when Y reaches 100.

Details of printout: The X and Y values are to be printed in two parallel columns, in the 2nd and 4th field. Headings are to be printed as shown below. An extra blank line is to be inserted whenever the step interval is changed.

FUNCTION TABLE OF F(X)=1/(4-X**2)

2 blank lines → {

VALUE OF X   VALUE OF F(X)

2 blank lines {

0·00000E+00   2·50000E-01
.   .
.   .
.   .
.   .

Solution: This problem deals with two aspects.
(1) Formatting the output in desired form. Using LIST-directed input-output methods, assuming that at this point we are unaware of the EDIT form of input output.
(2) Computation of Y.
1) Formatting: The first heading FUNCTION TABLE OF F(X)=1/(4-X**2) has to be placed in the center of page. We can have 132 letters printed in a single line. 132 characters are divided in five or six fields. Assuming a division of five fields each field has 26 characters; the center of the page would be at the 132/2=66th character. Now, the heading is to be centered and it has 37 characters including blanks. Hence the 19th character i.e. letter F of F(X) must be at the center. The heading will be between the 2nd and 3rd fields. Leaving the first field, we are left with 40 characters to the center i.e. 66-26=40. Out of 40, 18 characters are towards the left i.e. the second field as used by the heading. So we have to insert 40-28=22 blanks in the PUT statement. Using SKIP(0) and the same number of blanks followed by (37) — will underline the heading. As two blanks are required between heading & subheading, use SKIP(2) statement. The value of X and value of F(X) are to be in the 2nd and 4th fields. Hence, in the PUT statement we SKIP the 1st & 3rd field by using the null string i.e. ' '
2) To compute Y, we are given Y=1/(4-X**2). Use the DO loop to have different values of X between 0≤X<2.

First we increment X in steps of 0·1. At every step we store the calculated value of Y in Y_OLD. Increment X and compute Y. Take the difference of (Y-Y_OLD). If this difference is ≤10 we store this Y as computed Y in Y_OLD, increment X and proceed. At the same time we check for X<2. When X=2 or (Y-Y_OLD)>10, reduce the step width by a factor of 10. Also we check if Y<100. When this fails we exit the loop and end the program.

The program is as follows.

```
TABLE:  PROCEDURE OPTIONS(MAIN);
DCL((X,Y,XINT,Y_OLD) INIT(0),(X1,XFIN,S)) FIXED(9,5);
PUT LIST(' ','         FUNCTION TABLE OF F(X)=1/(4-X**2)');
PUT LIST(' ','      --------------------------------')
                                                 SKIP(0);

PUT SKIP(2);
PUT LIST(' ','       VALUE OF X',' ',' VALUE OF F(X)');
PUT LIST(' ','      ----------',' ',' -------------')
                                                 SKIP(0);
PUT SKIP(2);          /* WITH ABOVE STATEMENTS WE FORM THE
                                                 TABLE */

XFIN=2;
S=0·1;     /* S IS INCREMENT STEP OF X */
LOOP1:  DO WHILE (Y<100);
LOOP2:  DO X=XINT TO (XFIN-S) BY S WHILE((Y-Y_OLD)≤10);
        Y_OLD=Y;  /* STORE PREVIOUS VALUE OF Y */
        Y=1/(4-X*X); /* COMPUTE Y */
        IF Y>100 THEN STOP;
        PUT LIST(' ',X,' ',Y) SKIP;
        X1=X;
        END LOOP2;
        S=S/10;   /* REDUCE S BY FACTOR OF 10)
        XINT=X1+S  /* REINITIALIZE XINT */
        Y_OLD=Y;
        PUT SKIP;  /* EXTRA BLANK INSERTED WHEN STEP
                        INTERVAL IS CHANGED */
        END LOOP1;
        END TABLE;
```

During the first run XINT=0, S=0·1, XFIN-S=1·9 therefore LOOP2: DO X=0 TO 1·9 BY 0·1 WHILE ((Y-Y_OLD)≤10).
    We go out of this loop either when X=2 or Y-Y_OLD)>10.
Now X1 holds the value of X, when we exit from the loop.
Say for the first run X1=1·9, X became = 2 & we exit out
of LOOP2. Now S=S/10=·01.

                XINT=X1+S=1·91

ENTER LOOP2 again whence

        LOOP2: DO X=1·91 TO 2 BY ·01 WHILE ((Y-Y_OLD)<10);

and go on until Y becomes ≥ 100. We go out of LOOP1 and
proceed to END;

● **PROBLEM** 13-38

Write a program which uses as input character strings of up
to 200 characters, consisting of left parentheses and right
parentheses only (assume there are no blanks separating
them), and determine whether the strings are "well formed".

    A well-formed set of parentheses is one where

    1) There are equal numbers of left and right parentheses.
    2) For every right parenthesis, there must be a left
        parenthesis which appears earlier in the string.
    Print out the following message as applicable.

(a)   WELL FORMED
(b)   UNMATCHED RIGHT PARENTHESES
(c)   TOO MANY LEFT PARENTHESES.

Solution: This problem deals with the manipulation of character strings. SUBSTR, INDEX and LENGTH are built-in functions used for solving problems on character strings.

The program for the above problem has logical steps as
1)   Read in parentheses
2)   Find the Index of right parenthesis, i.e. position of first right parenthesis in string of parentheses.
3)   If index (say) N=1 then increment the count of right parenthesis; else increment count of left parenthesis.
4)   Compare: If R_count > L_count then there is an unmatched right parenthesis.
5)   Otherwise find the length L, of string parentheses.
6)   If L=1 compare R_count & L_count. If they are equal, then the string is well-formed. If L_count > R_count, then the string has too many left parentheses.
7)   If L≠1 remove the first left or right parenthesis from the character string of parentheses and call this new reduced character string as parentheses itself using PAR= SUBSTR[PAR,2]. Loop back to (2).

The program is as follows.

```
STRING:  PROCEDURE OPTIONS(MAIN);
         ON ENDFILE(SYSIN) STOP;
/* R_COUNT COUNTS RIGHT PAR, L_COUNT COUNTS LEFT PAR, L_LENGTH,
   N_INDEX NUMBER */
   DCL(KEY,R_COUNT,L_COUNT,L,M,N) FIXED DEC(3),PAR CHAR(200)VAR;
   PUT LIST('STRING','            MESSAGE');
   PUT LIST('------','            -------') SKIP(0);
   PUT SKIP(2);
LOOP_1:  DO WHILE(1=1);
         GET LIST(PAR);
         PUT LIST(PAR);
         R_COUNT,L_COUNT,KEY=0;
LOOP_2:  DO WHILE(KEY=0);
         N=INDEX(PAR,')'); /* FINDS POSITION OF FIRST RIGHT
PARENTHESIS */
         IF N=1 THEN R_COUNT=R_COUNT+1;
                ELSE L_COUNT=L_COUNT+1;
/* INCREMENTING R_COUNT OR L_COUNT DEPENDING ON VALUE OF N */
         IF R_COUNT>L_COUNT THEN DO;
                PUT LIST('UNMATCHED RIGHT PARENTHESES');
                KEY=1;
                END;
         L=LENGTH(PAR);
         IF L=1 THEN K=1;
LOOP_3:  DO WHILE(L¬=1);
         PAR=SUBSTR(PAR,2);
         L=1;
         END LOOP_3;
   END LOOP_2;
M=IL-IR;
IF IR=IL THEN PUT LIST ('     WELL FORMED');

IF IR<IL THEN PUT LIST(M||'TOO MANY LEFT PARENTHESES');
   PUT SKIP(2);
   END LOOP_1;
   END STRING;
```

479

Sometimes there is more than one way to write a program. Maybe one method is more efficient than another. Demonstrate this by rewriting the program which uses a character string of up to 200 parentheses as input. The program is to determine whether the input string is 'well formed', has too many right parentheses, or, too many left parentheses.

Solution: The program can be written as follows:

```
      STRING:  PROC OPTIONS(MAIN);
               DCL (R,L,T,M) FIXED(3),INIT(0),PAR CHAR(200)VAR;

/* R IS THE COUNT OF THE NUMBER OF RIGHT PARENTHESES, L IS
THE COUNT OF THE NUMBER OF LEFT PARENTHESES, T REPRESENTS
THE LENGTH OF THE CHARACTER STRING PAR, M IS A VARIABLE TO
BE USED IN THE PROGRAM */
      PUT LIST('STRING', '        MESSAGE');
      PUT LIST('------', '        -------') SKIP(0);
      PUT SKIP(2);
      DO WHILE(1=1);
      GET LIST(PAR);
      PUT LIST(PAR);
      DO WHILE(R¬>L&T¬= 1);
              T=LENGTH(PAR);
              IF INDEX(PAR,')')=1 THEN R=R+1;
                                ELSE L=L+1;
              IF T¬= 1 THEN PAR=SUBSTR(PAR,2);
      END;
      M=L-R
      IF M<0 THEN PUT LIST('UNMATCHED RIGHT PARENTHESES');
            ELSE IF M>0
                  THEN PUT LIST(M,'TOO MANY LEFT PARENTHESES');
                  ELSE PUT LIST('WELL FORMED');
      END;
      PUT SKIP(2);
      END STRING;
```

Write a program which handles a credit card operation. For simplicity, assume that there are only six customers. The first set of six data cards is

511	'MARIAN GREEN'	0·00
128	'WILLIAM BROWN'	-5·89
094	'GARY WHITE'	48·50
407	'JUDY GREY'	234·00
351	'ALLEN BLACK'	0·00
013	'JOHN GREEN'	127·14

where the first (three digit) integer is an account number, the second item is the customer's name, and the third number is the unpaid balance of previous purchases. The minus sign means BROWN overpaid and has positive balance.
    The second set of data cards is

```
        013        127·14        83·25    ⎧Your program must be
        407        100·00         0·0     ⎪able to handle up to
        511          0·0         141·50   ⎨6 sets of data
        128          0·0          47·10   ⎩here
```

where the first integer is again an account number, the second number represents the payment since the last bill, and the third number represents new purchases made with the credit card.

Write a PL/I program which reads in this data and prints out a five column table showing, for each customer, the account number, name, previous unpaid balance, the new unpaid balance, and the word DELINQUENT in a case where the payment made is less than one half the previous balance.

Print out the above table in numerical order by account number with the lowest number first:

Solution: This is a program which requires the use of arrays. The program illustrates how to use DECLARE, GET LIST, manipulate data and PUT LIST statements. The problem also involves sorting. There are various ways of sorting, list; one technique is dealt with in the program. The program is as follows.

Let the arrays be A - ACCOUNT NUMBER
                  B - NAME OF CUSTOMER
                  C - PREVIOUS UNPAID BALANCE
                  G - NEW UNPAID BALANCE
                  H - FOR REMARK

Arrays A, C, G consist of numeric values and arrays B, H have character strings as its element.
                  D - SPECIFIES ACCOUNT NUMBER
                  E - PAYMENT MADE FOR PREVIOUS BILL
                  F - IS NEW PURCHASES MADE.

These three D, E and F are not arrays, but simple variables as designated. S1, S2, S3, S4, S5 are simple variables used for sorting the credit card operation in ascending order.

The new unpaid balance G[I] = Previous unpaid balance C[I] + Purchases F - Payment E.
To check for condition of 'DELINQUENT' payment made

$$E < \frac{1}{2} \text{ Previous unpaid balance} \left\{ - \frac{C(I)}{2} \right\}$$

In sorting, the procedure applied here is to compare two adjacent elements, A[J] and A[J+1].

If A[J]>A[J+1] i.e. the number in A[J+1] is less than number in A[J], hence switch these two numbers. For example A[1]=5, A[2]=3.
Since A[1] > A[2]
therefore 3 must be placed in A[1] and 5 in A[2] to have ascending sequence order.

```
CREDIT_CARD:   PROCEDURE OPTIONS(MAIN);
               DCL(((A,C,G)(6)) FIXED(6,2)),(B,H)(6)CHAR(15)
                                                          VAR;
               DCL(D,E,F,S1,S3,S4) FIXED DEC(6,2),(S2,S5)
                                       CHAR(15) VAR;
```

481

```
/* FORMS THE HEADING */
   PUT LIST('ACCOUNT NUMBER','NAME','PRE UNPAID BAL','NEW
            UNPAID BAL','REMARK');
   PUT LIST('--------------','----','--------------','---
            ----------','------');
   GET LIST((A(M),B(M),C(M) DO M=1 TO 6)); /* TAKES IN THE
      FIRST SET OF CARDS */
/* INITIALIZE ELEMENTS OF ARRAY H TO DELINQUENT EXCEPT FOR
      C[I]≤0 */
   DO K=1 TO 6;
   IF ([K]>0)THEN H[K]='DELINQUENT';
   END;
/* CALCULATES NEW UNPAID BAL, CHECKS FOR DELINQUENT */
   DO WHILE[1=1];
   ON ENDFILE(SYSIN) GOTO LABEL;
   GET LIST[D,E,F];
   DO I=1 TO 6;
   IF D=A[I] THEN DO;
            G[I]=C(I)+F-E;
            IF E<C(I)/2 THEN H[I]='DELINQUENT';
                       ELSE H[I]='           ';
                       END;

            END;
            END;
/* SORTING PROCEDURE */
LABEL:  DO J=1 TO 5;
        IF A(J)>A(J+1) THEN DO;
                       S1=A(J);
                       A(J)=A[J+1];
                       A[J+1]=S1;
                       S2=B(J);
                       B(J)=B[J+1];
                       B[J+1]=S2;
                       S3=C[J];
                       C[J]=C[J+1];
                       C[J+1]=S3;
                       S4=G(J);
                       G[J]=G(J+1);
                       G(J+1)=S4;
                       S5=H(J);
                       H(J)=H(J+1);
                       H(J+1)=S5;
                       J=0;
                       END;
                       END;
        DO N=1 TO 6;
        PUT LIST(A(N),B(N),C(N),G(N),H(N)) SKIP(2);
        END;
        END CREDIT_CARD;
```

PROCEDURES

● **PROBLEM** 13-41

Given the following program segment, evaluate which elements
of the array A(I) will be a part of the product.

```
PRODUCT=1; J=1; N=12;
```

```
      DO I=1 BY J TO N;
         PRODUCT=PRODUCT*A(I);
         J=3I-J; N=N-J;
```

Assume, for purposes of the iteration head, either case a),
b),c) or d).

a) J and N are only evaluated once on initial entry into
    the loop,
b) J is evaluated only once but N is re-evaluated at each
    entry into the loop,
c) J is re-evaluated at each entry into the loop, but N is
    evaluated only once, and,
d) Both J and N are re-evaluated at each entry into the
    loop.

Solution: The working of this program segment can be best
illustrated by the following tables.

a)

Values stored in the ITERATION HEAD			Values obtained during execution of the program		
J	N	I=I+J	PRODUCT	J=3I-J	N=N-J
1	12	1	1×A(1)	3×1 - 1 = 2	12 - 2 = 10
1	12	2	1×A(1)×A(2)	3×2 - 1 = 5	10 - 5 = 5
1	12	3	1×A(1)×A(2)×A(3)	3×3 - 1 = 8	5 - 8 = -3
1	12	4	1×A(1)×...×A(4)	3×4 - 1 = 11	-3 - 11 = -14
1	12	5	1×A(1)×...×A(5)	3×5 - 1 = 14	-14 - 14 = -28
1	12	6	1×A(1)×...×A(6)	3×6 - 1 = 17	-28 - 17 = -45
1	12	7	1×A(1)×...×A(7)	3×7 - 1 = 20	-45 - 20 = -65
1	12	8	1×A(1)×...×A(8)	3×8 - 1 = 23	-65 - 23 = -88
1	12	9	1×A(1)×...×A(9)	3×9 - 1 = 26	-88 - 28 = -116
1	12	10	1×A(1)×...×A(10)	3×10- 1 = 29	-116 -29 = -145
1	12	11	1×A(1)×...×A(11)	3×11- 1 = 32	-145 -32 = -177
1	12	12	1×A(1)×...×A(12)	3×12- 1 = 35	-177 -35 = -212
1	12	13			

Note that a new value of J and N is computed on each pass
through the loop, however these computed values are not
entered in the Iteration head which always keeps the values
J=1 and N=12 which were obtained on the first initial entry
into the loop.
     Thus the Product=1×A(1)×...×A(12),i.e., all the 12 ele-
ments of the array are multiplied out.
     Thus here, J is entered in the Iteration Head only the
first time. Therefore J is always equal to 1. But N is re-
evaluated each time in the Head. The looping ends when I>N.
     Therefore the first three elements of the array are
multiplied out.

b)

Values stored in the ITERATION HEAD		Values obtained during execution of the program			
J	N	I=I+J	PRODUCT=PRODUCT$_\times$A(I)	J=3I-J	N=N-J
1	12	1	$1_\times$A(1)	$3_\times 1 - 1 = 2$	$12 - 2 = 10$
1	10	2	$1_\times$A(1)$_\times$A(2)	$3_\times 2 - 1 = 5$	$10 - 5 = 5$
1	5	3	$1_\times$A(1)$_\times$A(2)$_\times$A(3)	$3_\times 3 - 1 = 8$	$5 - 8 = -3$
1	-3	4			

c)

Values stored in the ITERATION HEAD		Values obtained during execution of the program			
J	N	I=I+J	PRODUCT=PRODUCT$_\times$A(I)	J=3I-J	N=N-J
1	12	1	$1_\times$A(1)	$3_\times 1 - 1 = 2$	$12 - 2 = 10$
2	12	3	$1_\times$A(1)$_\times$A(3)	$3_\times 3 - 1 = 7$	$10 - 7 = 3$
7	12	10	$1_\times$A(1)$_\times$A(3)$_\times$A(10)	$3_\times 10 - 1 = 29$	$3 - 29 = -26$
29	12	39			

d)

Values stored in the ITERATION HEAD		Values obtained during execution of the program			
J	N	I=I+J	PRODUCT=PRODUCT$_\times$A(I)	J=3I - J	N=N-J
1	12	1	$1_\times$A(1)	$3_\times 1 - 1 = 2$	$12 - 2 = 10$
2	10	3	$1_\times$A(1)$_\times$A(3)	$3_\times 2 - 1 = 5$	$10 - 5 = 5$
5	5	8			

Here, J is re-evaluated in the iteration head after each loop. The product=A(1)×A(3)× A(10).

Both J and N are re-evaluated in the Iteration Head after each loop. The product includes only two terms A(1)×A(3).

● **PROBLEM 13-42**

Explain what a procedure is, and what are the different types of procedures.

Solution: If a certain set of calculations or a certain set of expressions to be executed occur often in a program, it becomes convenient to use a procedure for the given set. PL/I provides this very important facility.

A procedure that is contained in some other procedure is called an iternal procedure and a procedure that is not included within another procedure is said to be an external procedure.

A reference in the program to the name of a procedure is called a procedure-reference.

A procedure can be a function procedure or a subroutine procedure.

A function procedure is like a built-in function and initiates an evaluation of the procedure. The result value produced will be used for further calculations in the program.

What are the rules regarding the specification of a procedure?

Solution: The rules for the specification of a procedure are as follows.

1.   The procedure block may appear in any part of the PL/I program body in which a Declare statement is allowed.

2.   Each procedure block must start with a procedure statement which contains at least one name for the procedure. E.g.,

        GRAVY: BREAD: PROCEDURE;

In the above, BREAD and GRAVY are names of the procedure.

3.   Each procedure block must end with an END procedure-name statement. E.g.,

        END BREAD;

4.   When a procedure statement is encountered by the program control during execution, the program control bypasses the whole procedure block up to the end statement of the procedure.

5.   Program control will execute the procedure only when the procedure is invoked by a procedure reference. A procedure reference may be a function reference or a subroutine reference. E.g.,

        CALL BREAD;
        Y=U*SHIP(X,Y);

In the above, BREAD and SHIP are procedures which are explicitly invoked as part of a program. The procedures will then be executed.

Explain the action of the following procedure which includes a subroutine procedure within itself.

```
VERIFY_TEST_VALUES:  PROCEDURE;
      DCL LENGTH FIXED DEC(3);



      CALL GET_AND_TEST_INPUT;
             .
             .
             .
             .
      CALL GET_AND_TEST_INPUT'
             .
             .
             .
             .
GET_AND_TEST_INPUT:  PROCEDURE;
      AGAIN:  GET LIST(LENGTH);
              IF LENGTH=0 THEN GOTO L;
              IF LENGTH<0|LENGTH>90 THEN DO;
                     PUT LIST('ERROR',LENGTH);
                     GOTO AGAIN;
                     END; /* END OF DO GROUP */

              END GET_AND_TEST_INPUT;
             .
             .
             .
             .
             .
      CALL GET_AND_TEST_INPUT;
      L:END VERIFY_TEST_VALUES;
```

Solution: From three different points in the program, the subroutine procedure is called.

This is called a subroutine procedure because no result value is produced. This is what differentiates a subroutine procedure from a function procedure, which initiates an evaluation of a result to be later used by the main program.

Each time the subroutine is invoked in the above example, it acquires a new value length from the data card. Then, the subroutine checks if each length value is between 0 and 90.

If the value is <0 or >90 then the PUT LIST statement is executed, and the control goes to the statement labelled 'AGAIN'. Thus, a new value for length is obtained. If a value of zero is obtained for length, it is an indication that data is over and the program returns to the statement labelled FINISH in the calling program. But, if the value of length lies between 0 and 90, then the program does not

go to the statement labelled FINISH, nor does it enter the
DO group. Instead, the program control goes to the next
statement after the DO group, which happens to be the last
statement of the subroutine procedure. From here, control
is transferred back to the calling procedure, which continues with the other steps of the program.

● **PROBLEM** 13-45

Explain the action of the following procedure which includes
a function procedure within itself.

```
SALES:    PROCEDURE;
          DCL 1 SALES_FORCE(500);
               2 NAME;
                  3 FIRST_NAME CHAR(10),
                  3 LAST_NAME CHAR(20),
               2 BASE_SALARY FIXED(6,2)
               2 PERCENT_COMMISSION FIXED(2,0),
          A:  IF BASE_SALARY(SALESMAN_INDEX)=
                        BASE_SALARY(SALESMAN_INDEX) THEN GOTO L;
                                                    ELSE GOTO A;
              SALESMAN_INDEX:  PROCEDURE;
               GET LIST(F_NAME, L_NAME);
               DO I=1 TO 500 WHILE(F_NAME(I)¬=FIRST_NAME(I)|
                               L_NAME(I)¬=LAST_NAME(I));
               END;
              IF I>500 THEN DO;
               PUT LIST(F_NAME‖L_NAME,'ᵇ NOT FOUND')
               GOTO ERROR;
               END;
              RETURN(I);
              END SALESMAN_INDEX;
          L:  END SALES;
```

Solution: In the above program, 'SALES' is the label of the
main procedure.
     The declaration shows that the variable SALES_FORCE is
a 500 element array. The first executable statement of the
program is labelled 'A'. But, in order to evaluate this
statement expression, the computer comes across the variable
'SALESMAN_INDEX' on the left hand side of the expression of
the statement labelled 'A'. Now, SALESMAN_INDEX is not in
the DCL statement. Therefore, the computer checks to see if
it is a procedure reference. On looking down, it sees that
there is a procedure called 'SALESMAN_INDEX'. Hence, the
program jumps to that label.
     As a part of this procedure, the computer reads the
data card for values of variables F_NAME and L_NAME. Then,
if I is evaluated, it returns the value of I, say I_1 as a
consequence of the statement RETURN(I). That is, the value
of the variable SALESMAN_INDEX in the statement labelled A
is made equal to the value of I. Now, the program comes to
the right hand side of the statement labelled 'A'. Once a-
gain it sees the function procedure reference SALESMAN_INDEX.
Hence, the program again goes to the procedure SALESMAN_INDEX
and evaluates a new value of I, say, I_2. This new value of I
is returned to the right hand side of the statement labelled
'A'.

Now we have all the information required to evaluate the conditional part of statement 'A',

A: IF BASE_SALARY(I_1)=BASE_SALARY(I_2) THEN ...

The program is, given a list of F_NAME and L_NAME, it checks whether the person having particular F_NAME, L_NAME is in sales force and if so we go to L. Here L is labelled to end but we can transfer control to any other computation e.g., calculation of commission, etc. by labelling that computation as L. Hence, if the above condition is satisfied then we go to the statement labelled L, which is the END SALES statement. But, if the above condition is not satisfied, then we go to the ELSE part of the statement, which asks us to go back to A. This means we evaluate all over again the function procedure SALESMAN_INDEX for new values of F_NAME and L_NAME read from data cards, and continue as before.

● **PROBLEM** 13-46

What is recursion? Why does PL/I have a recursive procedure while FORTRAN does not?

Solution: In pure mathematics, the Fibonacci sequence is a recursive procedure. If you recall, Fibonacci numbers are generated by using prceding numbers to continue the sequence. For example,

$$F_0 = 0$$
$$F_1 = 1$$
$$F_n = F_{n-1} + F_{n-2} \quad \text{for} \quad n = 2,3,...$$

is the method for obtaining Fibonacci numbers.
    In computer science, recursion takes on a slightly different meaning. We may want, in the course of a program, a certain procedure to invoke itself by means of a CALL statement. By repeating the calling procedure, you are actually reducing the size of the program. For example, in this PL/I code segment, we want to store values in the array VALUE. We are assuming that we are filling the array from top to bottom by decrementing the variable KOUNT. When KOUNT is 0, we want to terminate.

```
STORAGE:  PROC RECURSIVE
          IF KOUNT>=1
          THEN DO;
          VALUE(KOUNT)=INDEX;
          KOUNT=KOUNT-1;
          CALL STORAGE;
          END;
END STORAGE;
```

In this procedure, each stage of processing contains all subsequent stages, i.e., the first stage is incomplete until the final stage has been completed.
    Using recursion, one can streamline the code, cutting down on repeated lines of information. At the machine level,

488

recursive procedures must save their addresses for subsequent invocations. This is generally accomplished by a stacking procedure, in which addresses are pushed onto the stack after an invocation and popped up each time the procedure is invoked again.

There is a danger when using recursive procedures, the danger being related to the saving of machine addresses. Each time a procedure is invoked recursively, the memory space used to save the addresses contains all of the previous information from the other invocations. If a recursive procedure is not terminated correctly, the memory block will grow indefinitely, consuming valuable space in the machine.

● **PROBLEM** 13-47

What are the various methods by which PL/I debugs or notes defects in a program while processing it?

Solution: After a program has been compiled, it enters the execution stage. Here, many situations exist that can cause errors and prevent execution. PL/I has facilities for monitoring program executions.

1) The CONVERSION condition

Suppose Y is defined as a numeric variable, but the input format specification is non-numeric. In this case the system stops the program at this point and a CONVERSION message is printed out.

2) Overflow and underflow:

These conditions occur when a numerical value turns out to be too large or too small to be accomodated in the machine. If a fixed point number has more than 15 digits, the computer prints FIXEDOVERFLOW. With floating point numbers the OVERFLOW condition is raised. This means the computer notes the error and automatically increases the limit on the size of that number, and continues the program. Finally if a very small value is divided by a very large number and the number is less (in absolute value) than 10^{-75}, UNDERFLOW occurs and an appropriate message is printed.

3) Division by zero is a special type of overflow. When it is attempted, the ZERODIVIDE condition is printed and the program stops. For example, if X, Y are variables and X = Y, then the instruction SQRT(40*(Y-W)/(X-Y)) will stop the program.

4) The usual method of indicating the end of input data is to insert a trailer card with a value that cannot be in the data set. An instruction to exit when this value is read is inserted in the main program. If some indication for the termination of processing is not included, the system will respond with an ENDFILE condition.

5) Suppose we expect an execution-halting error but wish the processing to continue after it has occurred. This is done through PL/I's ON statement whose general form is

ON condition action   (1)

In (1), 'condition' is some keyword (UNDERFLOW, ENDFILE, etc.). 'action' is some instruction to be performed when

489

the stated condition occurs. Thus, if we want to make sure that $SQRT\left(\frac{Y}{X}\right)$ is executed even when X = 0, we insert the statement, ON ZERODIVIDE X = 9999.

This should be placed before computations involving X are executed.

In (1) the action specified can be any single statement except DECLARE, IF, PROCEDURE, END, DO or another ON. Except for the ON statement which is a part of the program, the other conditions discussed above abort the program. But PL/I also gives a diagnosis as to why the abortion occurred. The next creative run may well produce a normal program.

● **PROBLEM** 13-48

Debug the following PL/I program. The program is given as a source listing i.e. a written record of the PL/I program supplied by the computer.

```
STNT
  1            PROCEDURE OPTION(MAIN);
  2            DECLARE(A(10),B(10))FIXED(5),(X,Y,Z)FIXED(4),
               C CHARACTER(5);
  3            PUTPAGE; PUT SKIP(3)EDIT('C','X','Y','Z','W',
               'V','A','R')(COL(20),A,COL(30),A,COL(40),A,
               COL(50),A,COL(60),A,COL(70),A,COL(85),A,COL(95),A;
  5            GET EDIT(X,Y,C,W)(X(2),F(4),X(3),F(4),X(7),A(5),
                    F(2));
  6            GET SKIP;
  7            IF X=0 & Y=0 THEN GOTO NOMORE;
  8            IF X>Y THEN Z=2*X+Y;ELSE Z=2*(X+Y)-18;
  9            V=SQRT(40)(Y-2)-W*X)/(X-Y);
 10    L|:     DO I=| TO W;
 11            A(I)=X+Y+3*I; B(I)=X - Y-3*I;
 12            IF I=1 PUT SKIP(2)EDIT; EDIT(C,X,Y,Z,
 13            W,V,A(I),B(I))(COL(20),A(5),COL(30),F(4),COL(40),
               F(4),COL(50),F(4),COL(60),F(2),COL(70),E(13,6)
               COL(85),F(6),COL(95),F(6));
 14            ELSE PUT SKIP EDIT(A(I),B(I))(COL(85),F(5),
               COL(95),F(5));
 15            FIND L1;
 16            GO   TO IN;
 17            NOMORE; END BUGS;
```

Solution: This program reads sets of edit-directed data, performs some calculations and prints the results.

The written program contains the following errors:
1) Statement 1: The procedure has no name
2) Statement 1: OPTION should be OPTIONS
3) Statement 3: There should be a blank between PUT and PAGE.
4) Statement 7: There should be a blank between GO and TO.
5) Statement 9: There is no arithmetic operator between the constant 40 and the term (Y-2).
6) Statement 10: The 1 has been mispunched as |.
7) Statement 11: The minus sign in X-Y is misplaced.

490

8) Statement 12: The keyword THEN is omitted from the IF statement.
9) Statement 16: There is no statement in the program labelled IN.
10) Statement 17: BUGS appears nowhere else.

● **PROBLEM 13-49**

In reference to the previous problem, classify the bugs as a) severe errors b) errors c) warnings. What action would PL/I take with respect to these errors?

Solution: PL/I allows several errors (through default options) that other languages (FORTRAN for example) would find intolerable. Thus, in spite of all the errors in the program above, PL/I will compile it by changing the program in such a way that it can be compiled.

If a program has bugs (in the etymological, not entomological sense), its output will differ from what the user desires. The changes in the program depend on the magnitude of the error. PL/I makes the following distinctions:

a) A statement containing a severe error cannot be executed or complied without a major change. PL/I makes the change to produce the program. But execution is doubtful.

b) Errors cause improper execution. After an error has been modified by PL/I, the resulting output is highly suspect.

c) Warnings notify the programmer of certain standard actions taken by PL/I in the absence of explicit specifications in the program. These are not really errors and the output of the program is not affected. Hence, no action is required.

Statement 1: The missing label is filled in by PL/I. This is a severe error. Since OPTIONS is misspelt, the compiler deletes everything beyond PROCEDURE and then inserts a semi-colon. Thus Statement 1 reads

1 DUMMY PROCEDURE;

This means the procedure can be used only as part of another program and not as a PROCEDURE MAIN.

Statement 3: PUTPAGE is identified as part of an assignment statement. PL/I adds an equal sign and an error signal.

Statement 7: GOTO is recognized as GO TO and no correction is noted.

Statement 9: SQRT(40(Y-2)-W*X)/(X-Y) is shortened to SQRT(40. PL/I expects some operator to come between 40 and Y. Since nothing is there, everything after 40 is ignored. PL/I supplies ")" and ";" to obtain

9 SQRT(40);

This is a severe error.

Statement 10: The | is interpreted as a + and TO is interpreted as a name. The W is truncated and a ; is inserted.

491

Statement 11: The minus sign is correctly identified although misplaced.

Statement 12: PL/I spots the missing keyword THEN and makes the appropriate insertion.

Statement 16: Since the branch destination is unknown and cannot be found, the entire statement is removed from the program. This is a severe error.

Statement 17: The nonexistent label on the END statement is noted. The END statement cannot be linked with any PROCEDURE or DO statement. This is a severe error.

CHAPTER 14

APL

INTRODUCTION, BASIC OPERATIONS AND VECTOR MANIPULATIONS

● **PROBLEM** 14-1

Explain briefly the background and applications of APL programming.

Solution: APL (A Programming Language) is an extremely powerful, simple to learn, easy to use computer language, which lends itself to many applications. Widely recognized as a scientific language, APL is equally useful in business and in education. APL is one of the best-suited languages for special applications, such as computer aided instruction (CAI), operations research, and simulation.

Being a versatile language, it can be used in either execution or definition modes. In execution mode the language enables you to operate the terminal as though it were a desk calculator. In definition mode you are able to enter, store, execute, and debug programs.

APL is efficient. When compared with other languages: it takes the least amount of programming effort to accomplish a given job.

When in execution mode, APL has immediate diagnostics. The system reports errors as soon as they are made and gives their type and location.

All these features make APL a strong tool in solving a wide range of complicated problems.

● **PROBLEM** 14-2

A vector in APL is entered as follows: V ← 3 4 2 -1. Find the result of the following operations.
    a) |V , b) ⌈V , c) ⌊V.

Solution: a) The symbol |, when written as a monadic function, as |V, specifies the absolute value of V.

V is a vector, which consists of the elements 3 4 2 -1. The absolute value of V is 3 4 2 1 i.e., |V is equal to 3 4 2 1.

b) The symbol ⌈ represents a maximum function. When used with the Reduction Operator /, the maximum function selects the largest from among all the elements of the vector, V in this case. Thus, if V consists of 3 4 2 -1, then ⌈/V is equivalent to the following:

$$3⌈4⌈2⌈-1$$
$$i.e.,\quad 3⌈4⌈2$$
$$i.e.,\quad 3⌈4$$
$$i.e.,\quad 4$$

In the above, using the right to left rule of APL for evaluating an expression, the elements of V are compared two by two from the right. The maximum is selected at each comparison. Thus, finally when the whole string has been checked out, the largest element is obtained.

c) The symbol ⌊ represents a minimum function. When used with the Reduction Operator /, the minimum function selects the least from among all the elements of the vector (V in this case). Thus, if V consists of 3 4 2 -1, then ⌊/V is equivalent to the following:

$$3⌊4⌊2⌊-1$$
$$i.e.,\quad 3⌊4⌊-1$$
$$i.e.,\quad 3⌊-1$$
$$i.e.,\quad -1.$$

In the above, using the right to left rule, the elements of V are compared two by two, and the minimum is selected.

● **PROBLEM** 14-3

Explain what is meant by reduction of vectors. Also explain the rule for APL arithmetic. Evaluate the expression: $6 + ((5 + 2 × 11 - 2) - 3 + 2) ÷ 2 × 3$.

Solution: Reduction of a vector, in APL, is equivalent to placing a dyadic operator between each element of the vector and evaluating the resulting expresssion. Examples of dyadic operators are plus +, minus -, multiply ×, divide ÷, exponentiation *, etc.

The symbol for reduction is a right-tilting slash, e.g., /.

The use of the smybol is illustrated below for a vector V.

+/V, -/V, ×/V, ÷/V, */V, etc.

If V is defined by V ← 1 2 3 then each of the above reductions is equivalent to the following, respectively.

+/V   is equivalent to   1 + 2 + 3
-/V   is equivalent to   1 - 2 - 3
×/V   is equivalent to   1 × 2 × 3

```
÷/V   is equivalent to   1 ÷ 2 ÷ 3
*/V   is equivalent to   1 * 2 * 3
```

The rule for APL arithmetic is a right to left rule. That is, the arithmetic operations are performed on a string of operators from right to left.

Items enclosed within parentheses are evaluated first, and the whole parenthesized content acts as a single operator. The given expression evaluates as follows:

$$
\begin{aligned}
\text{Expression} &= 6 + ((5 + 2 \times 11 - 2) - 3 + 2) \div 2 \times 3 \\
&= 6 + ((5 + 2 \times 9) - 3 + 2) \div 2 \times 3 \\
&= 6 + ((5 + 18) - 3 + 2) \div 2 \times 3 \\
&= 6 + ((23) - 3 + 2) \div 2 \times 3 \\
&= 6 + (23 - 3 + 2) \div 2 \times 3 \\
&= 6 + (23 - 5) \div 2 \times 3 \\
&= 6 + (18) \div 2 \times 3 \\
&= 6 + 18 \div 2 \times 3 \\
&= 6 + 18 \div 6 \\
&= 6 + 3 \\
&= 9 \qquad\qquad \text{Answer}
\end{aligned}
$$

Note that the innermost pair of brackets is evaluated out first using the right to left rule inside the brackets. Then the outer pair of brackets is evaluated using the right to left rule inside the brackets. Then, after all the brackets have been eliminated, the whole expression is evaluated using the right to left rule. Also note that the effect of a reduction operation performed on the vector V is to reduce it to a scalar quantity, which is the evaluated value of the resulting expression.

Now, a vector has a dimension of 1. And, a scalar has a dimension of 0. Thus, the reduction operation has reduced the dimension of the variable V from 1 to 0.

In general, it is found that for an n-dimensional array, a reduction operation reduces the dimension of the array by 1, from n to n-1.

Finally, note that the arithmetical operations are not ordered in a hierarchy unlike FORTRAN, where multiplications and divisions are performed before additions and subtractions.

● **PROBLEM** 14-4

The elements of a vector V are entered as follows on an APL computer.

$$V \leftarrow 3\ 4\ 2\ -1.$$

Show what will be displayed as a result of each of the following statements:

a) ×/V ,   b) ÷/V ,   c) */V,
d) -/V ,   e) +/V.

Solution: a) The value of ×/V is obtained as follows:

$$2 \times (-1) = -2$$
$$4 \times (-2) = -8$$
$$3 \times (-8) = -24.$$

Therefore -24 is displayed.
b) The value of ÷/V is obtained as follows:

$$2 \div (-1) = \frac{2}{-1} = -\frac{2}{1} = -2$$

$$4 \div (-2) = \frac{4}{-2} = -\frac{4}{2} = -2$$

$$3 \div (-2) = \frac{3}{-2} = -\frac{3}{2} = -1.5.$$

Therefore -1.5 is displayed
c) The value of */V is obtained as follows:

$$2 * (-1) = 2^{-1} = \frac{1}{2^1} = \frac{1}{2} = 0.5$$

$$4 * 0.5 = 4^{0.5} = \sqrt{4} = 2.$$
$$3 * 2 = 3^2 = 9.$$

Therefore 9 is displayed.
d) The value of -/V is obtained as follows:

$$2 - (-1) = 2 + 1 = 3$$
$$4 - 3 = 1$$
$$3 - 1 = 2.$$

Therefore 2 is displayed.
e) The value of +/V is obtained as follows:

$$2 + (-1) = 2 - 1 = 1$$
$$4 + 1 = 5$$
$$3 + 5 = 8.$$

Therefore 8 is displayed.

● **PROBLEM** 14-5

Write a single APL statement that gives values for the current, according to Ohm's Law, where I = E/R. I is current, E is voltage, and R is resistance. You can assume that E and R are vectors of four elements each. If E ← 4 8 9 12 and R ← 2 4 3 4, find I.

Solution: Since E and R are vectors of equal length, one can write: I ← E ÷ R. This will divide the first elements of each vector, then the second, and so on. The result is a four element vector I.

      E is given by E ← 4 8 9 12
and   R is given by R ← 2 4 3 4,

therefore I ← E ÷ R execution will be performed as follows:

```
I ←  4÷2   8÷4   9÷3   12÷4
I ←   2     2     3     3
```

MATRIX MANIPULATIONS

● **PROBLEM 14-6**

Explain, by means of examples, the following functions used in the handling of matrices:

1) Reversal function.
2) Rotation function.

Solution: APL is ideally suited for matrix manipulation. The above functions help in the storage and processing of data which is in matrix form.

Suppose we wish to represent the first 12 whole numbers as a 3×4 matrix. Key in

$$M \leftarrow 3\ 4\ \rho\ \iota\ 12 \qquad (1)$$

A matrix is entered by using ρ (rho), the shape operator. The iota function (ι) tells the computer to list the first 12 positive integers. The general form of (1) is:

$$M \leftarrow m\ n\ \rho\ x_1\ x_2\ \ldots\ x_{mn} \qquad (2)$$

Comparing (1) and (2) we see that m, the number of rows, is 3, and n, the number of columns, is 4. The matrix of (1) is:

$$M = \begin{bmatrix} 1 & 2 & 3 & 4 \\ 5 & 6 & 7 & 8 \\ 9 & 10 & 11 & 12 \end{bmatrix} \qquad (3)$$

a) Reversal function: The general form of the reversal function is $\phi[K]M$. Here K = 1 or K = 2. When K = 1, (3) becomes

$$M' = \begin{bmatrix} 9 & 10 & 11 & 12 \\ 5 & 6 & 7 & 8 \\ 1 & 2 & 3 & 4 \end{bmatrix} \qquad (4)$$

Thus, $\phi[1]M$ reverses the order of the rows. When K = 2, the order of the columns is reversed. Applying $\phi[2]M$ to (3):

$$M'' = \begin{bmatrix} 4 & 3 & 2 & 1 \\ 8 & 7 & 6 & 5 \\ 12 & 11 & 10 & 9 \end{bmatrix} \qquad (5)$$

If we apply φ[2]M to (4):

$$\begin{bmatrix} 12 & 11 & 10 & 9 \\ 8 & 7 & 6 & 5 \\ 4 & 3 & 2 & 1 \end{bmatrix} \tag{6}$$

while φ[1]M on (5) yields

$$\begin{bmatrix} 12 & 11 & 10 & 9 \\ 8 & 7 & 6 & 5 \\ 4 & 3 & 2 & 1 \end{bmatrix}. \tag{7}$$

Matrices (6) and (7) are equal.

b)   Rotation function: This is a dyadic function of the form SΦ[K]M. Here S is a vector with as many components as there are elements in the dimension being rotated. Suppose we want to shift

i)   all first elements in each row of (1) one ele- ment from top to bottom.
ii)   all second elements by two elements from top to bottom and
iii) all other elements remain the same.

Then, applying the rotation function to (1)

1 2 0 0 φ[1]M

$$\begin{bmatrix} 9 & 10 & 3 & 4 \\ 5 & 2 & 7 & 8 \\ 1 & 6 & 11 & 12 \end{bmatrix}$$

To illustrate rotation of columns apply -2 1 0 φ[2]M. The minus indicates a rotation from right to left. The effect of this function is as follows:

i)   all the first elements in each column to be cyclically shifted two elements from left to right.
ii)   all second elements in every column to be cyc- lically shifted one element from right to left.
iii) a zero shift in the third elements.

The upshot of all this on M is

$$\begin{bmatrix} 3 & 4 & 1 & 2 \\ 6 & 7 & 8 & 5 \\ 9 & 10 & 11 & 12 \end{bmatrix}$$

Thus, APL is useful for rotating matrices.

Show how

   i)   the compression function
  ii)   the expansion function
 iii) Take and Drop functions

are used in APL.

Solution: Assume the following matrix has been stored in memory

$$M = \begin{bmatrix} 6 & 1 & 220 & 144 & 153 \\ 28 & 2 & 284 & 441 & 370 \\ 496 & 145 & 1184 & 169 & 474 \\ 1729 & 40585 & 1210 & 961 & 208 \end{bmatrix} \tag{1}$$

    i) Compression is a dyadic function used to select rows or columns from a given matrix. Its general form is L/[K]M. L is a binary vector composed of ones and zeros. M is a matrix, K is an index indicating which dimension of M is to be compressed and / separates the two arguments.
    Suppose it is desired to select the first and third rows only of (1). The function 1 0 1 0/[1]M gives

      6   1   220   144   153
   496 145 1184   169   474

The K index indicates the dimension of compression, i.e., [1] = row compression and [2] = column compression. The command 0 1 0 1/[2]M yields, when applied to (1):

       1   144
       2   441
    145   169
  40585   961

(The first column here represents all numbers between 1 and 50,000 that are equal to the sum of the factorials of their digits. For example, 145 = 1! + 4! + 5!. The second column gives two pairs of numbers that are the reverse of one another and whose product is a square.)
    ii) Expansion is a dyadic function used to insert rows and columns of zeros into numeric matrices and rows and columns of blanks into character matrices. Its general form is

        L\[K]M.

Let   G = B S H A H
                T W A D E
                Q B A R T

This is a matrix of names; the first character is the initial and the remainder is the last name. To make M more legible, perform the function:

    1 0 1 1 1 1\ [2]G ,   which yields

    B S H A H
    T W A D E
    Q B A R T

    iii) Take and drop: These are dyadic functions used for selecting a submatrix from a given matrix. Their general form is L↑M and L↓M. L is a vector containing two components. The first component represents the number of rows to be taken or dropped while the second component gives the number of columns taken or dropped. Suppose we want to select Ramajunam's number (1729) from M. This is a 1×1 sub-matrix. The command 3 -4↓M causes the top three rows (3) and the right four columns (-4) to be dropped (↓). The result is 1729.

● **PROBLEM** 14-8

Find the transpose of

$$M = \begin{bmatrix} 1 & 2 \\ 3 & 5 \\ 7 & 11 \end{bmatrix}$$

Then find $M^T M$ and MM^T using the APL inner product.

Solution: Matrix transposition is accomplished in APL by means of the monadic operator ϕ. If M is a matrix, ϕ M is its transpose.

    Assuming that the values of M have already been entered, its transpose is found by: N ← ϕM

               N

$$\begin{bmatrix} 1 & 3 & 7 \\ 2 & 5 & 11 \end{bmatrix}.$$

When a matrix is transposed, the order of its rows and columns is reversed. To check this, apply the shape operator (ρ) to M and N:

               ρM

          3 2

               ρN

          2 3

The inner product function is used in APL to find the product of two matrices. Its general form is A+. × B. A and B are matrices and + and × are primitive arithmetic functions, while . is the period character. Two matrices A,B are conformable for multiplication if and only if the num-

ber of columns of A equals the number of rows of B.
    In the given problem,

$$\rho M = 3 \times 2 \quad \text{and} \quad \rho M^T = 2 \times 3.$$

Now MM^T means multiplying a (3×2) matrix by a (2×3) matrix. Since the inner numbers are equal, MM^T is conformable for multiplication. Similarly, M^TM gives $(2 \times 3)(3 \times 2)$ and is also conformable for multiplication.
    The command N+. × M gives M^TM as

$$\begin{array}{cc} 59 & 94 \\ 94 & 150 \end{array}$$

The command M+. × N gives MM^T

$$\begin{array}{ccc} 5 & 13 & 29 \\ 13 & 34 & 76 \\ 29 & 76 & 170. \end{array}$$

● **PROBLEM** 14-9

Write statements in APL to generate the identity matrix of dimension N. This matrix consists of N ones along the main diagonal and zeros everywhere else. Use the rho (ρ) and catenate (,) functions.

Solution: We first enter a value for the dimension, say
N = 10. We call the matrix V. The following statements
will do the job.

```
N ← 10
V ← (N,N)ρ(1,Nρ0)
V
```

In the above, the statement N ← 10 initializes N to a value
10.
    Now, consider the next statement

        V ← (N,N)ρ(1,Nρ0)

NρO creates a vector of 10 elements (because N = 10). Each
element is equal to 0 since the statement NρO is equivalent
to:

        N ρ 0 0 0 0 0 0 0 0 0 0

Note that there are 10 zeroes in the above. Next, (1,Nρ0)
catenates number 1 to the ten zeroes, creating a line
1 0 0 0 0 0 0 0 0 0 0. (Catenation is a procedure for linking program elements together. In APL, it is possible to
catenate

        i)   scalars to form a vector,
       ii)   a scalar and a vector to form a vector,
      iii)   several vectors to form a vector,
       iv)   matrices of the same dimension to form a matrix
        v)   N-dimensional arrays to form an array.

501

The symbol for catenation is a comma.

Then, $(N,N)\rho (1,N\rho 0)$ creates a 10 by 10 matrix, using the string 1 0 0 0 0 0 0 0 0 0 0 repeatedly. Since there are 11 elements in the string and only 10 vacant spaces in each row of the matrix, the last zero of the string will start the second row, when the string is used the first time. As a result, 1 will move one space to the right in the second row. The third row will then start with 2 zeros, etc. The 10 by 10 matrix, thus created, consists of the elements as shown below

```
                              9 zeroes
                        ⎧‾‾‾‾‾‾‾‾‾‾‾‾‾‾‾‾‾‾‾‾‾‾‾‾‾‾‾⎫
                        1 0 0 0 0 0 0 0 0 0 0        1st row
tenth zero              0 1 0 0 0 0 0 0 0 0 0        2nd row
                        0 0 1 0 0 - - - - -
                        .
                        .
                        .
```

BRANCHING

● **PROBLEM** 14-10

Explain how an unconditional branch instruction is specified in an APL program.

Solution: An unconditional branch instruction is specified in APL by means of a right pointing arrow followed by a number or a label. The number represents the program segment to which a jump is desired. If a label is used instead of a number, the label specifies the statement in the program which is thus labelled, and to which the transfer should be made. For example, in [4] → 2, the statement number 4 of a certain program instructs the computer to branch unconditionally to the statement number 2 of the same program.

● **PROBLEM** 14-11

Explain how a conditional branch instruction is specified in APL programs.

Solution: A conditional branch instruction is specified in APL by means of a right-pointing arrow followed on its right by an expression. For example:

i) [4] → (I ≤ N) × 2

In the above, a test for I is performed. Is I ≤ N? If I is indeed less than or equal to N, then the value of the test is true, i.e., 1. But if I is not less than or equal to N then the value of the test is false, i.e., 0. Now, if the result of the test is 1, the value of the expression (I ≤ N) × 2 reduces to 1 × 2, equal to 2. This means that

in the given example the statement [4] of the program reduces to the following:

$$[4] \rightarrow (I \leq N) \times 2$$
i.e., $[4] \rightarrow 1 \times 2$
i.e., $[4] \rightarrow 2.$

Thus, a branching to statement 2 is performed. However, if
the result of the test is 0, then the statement [4] of the
example reduces to the following:

$$[4] \rightarrow (I \leq N) \times 2$$
i.e., $[4] \rightarrow 0 \times 2$
i.e., $[4] \rightarrow 0.$

This means that a branching to statement 0 is to be performed. However, there is no statement 0 in the program.
Hence, the program execution halts.

ii) $[4] \rightarrow (I \leq N) \times BOB.$

The above is similar to part i) explained before, except
that instead of the statement number of the statement to
which a branch off is required, a label is specified. Labels have an advantage over numbers. If statements are
added or removed from the program, the statement numbers
change. This necessitates corrections to be made within
the statements too, in order to branch to the proper statement according to the new numbering.
     But if labels are used, corrections of the statements
are not necessary. A label takes on a value equal to the
statement number of the statement which has the given label.
In the example given above, the label is BOB.
     This means that if the test is true, the program will
jump to a statement labelled BOB. The program could be
something like the following:

[2] BOB: I ← I+1
[4]   → (I ≤ N) × BOB or,   [4]   → (I ≤ N) × BOB
                             [7]   BOB: I ← I+1

In the above, if the test is false, statement [4] becomes:

$$[4] \rightarrow 0 \times BOB,$$
i.e., $[4] \rightarrow 0.$

and the program halts.

     iii) In the above two cases, the program went to a
halt if the test was false. However, at times it is not
proper for the program to halt when the test is false. It
is just required that the program goes to the next sequential instruction if the test is false, and branch to the
statement indicated if the test is true.

     Consider the following statement, for example:

$$[4] \rightarrow 2 \times \iota (I \leq N)$$

In the above, if the test of $I \leq N$ is true, the value of

($I \leq N$) is equal to 1. Therefore the statement [4] reduces to $2 \times \iota(1) = 2 \times 1 = 2$. Thus, the program branches to statement 2. But, if the test is false, the statement [4] reduces to $2 \times \iota(0)$. Now, iota zero, i.e., $\iota 0$, generates an empty vector, and therefore the statement [4] becomes meaningless. Hence, the program goes to the next sequential statement.

iv) A label can be used, instead of a statement number, with the iota function. For example,

[4] $\rightarrow$ BOB $\times \iota(I \leq N)$.

v) Another way to specify a branch instruction is by using the compression function, which has the symbol /. It is not necessary to know the meaning of the compression function in order to understand the branching. Consider the following illustration:

[4] $\rightarrow (I \leq N)/2$.

In the above, if the test, that is, the quantity to the left of the compression function symbol is true, a transfer is made to the statement whose number is specified on the right of the compression function symbol. Thus, if $I \leq N$ is true, the program jumps to statement 2.

But, if the test is false, the program goes to the next sequential statement, i.e., to statement 5.

vi) A label can also be used on the right side of the compression function symbol instead of a number. For example,

[4] $\rightarrow (I \leq N)/$BOB.

FUNCTIONS: ACTUAL PROGRAMMING TECHNIQUES

● **PROBLEM** 14-12

Write a program using APL that evaluates the focal length of a lens.

<u>Solution</u>: The formula for the focal length of a lens is

$$F = \frac{(N)(R1)(R2)}{(N-1)((N(R1+R2)-T(N-1))}$$

where   F is the focal length
           N is the index of refraction of the glass
           T is the thickness of the lens
           R1 and R2 are the radii of curvatures.

Let us first give the program a name: LENGTH. Its

procedure looks as follows:

```
     ∇LENGTH
[1]   NUMER ← N × R1 × R2
[2]   DENOM ← (N-1) × (N×R1+R2) - T × N - 1
[3]   FOCAL ← NUMER ÷ DENOM
[4]   FOCAL
[5]   ∇
```

When writing an APL program, one must first enter the definition mode. This is achieved by typing the upside-down triangle, called "DEL", followed by a program name. The next DEL met in the procedure of the program indicates its end.

The value of the numerator is stored under NUMER, and the value obtained in the denominator-under DENOM. The solution is stored under the variable FOCAL. Line [4] tells the computer to print FOCAL when execution begins. Line [5], which contains a DEL, indicates that the definition mode is complete. The following is a sample output:

```
N ← 1.3275
T ← 0.375
R1 ← 8.0
R2 ← 7.85
LENGTH
12.16918
```

[Note that for special types of lenses, the radii of curvature can take on negative values as well. This illustration is the most general case to demonstrate the usefulness of APL.]

● **PROBLEM** 14-13

Classify the six kinds of APL functions.

Solution: In APL, functions are classified on the basis of two main criteria:

i) The number of arguments contained in the header (the header is the name of the program; it follows the ∇ operator).

ii) Whether the function is limited or unlimited. A function is limited if it cannot be used as in a compound expression. Per contra, an unlimited function can be used within another function without causing an error condition.

i) APL functions can contain zero, one or two arguments are called niladic, monadic and dyadic functions respectively. Thus we see that there are six kinds of APL functions: three kinds, depending on the number of arguments and the choice of "limited" or "unlimited" for each kind. Examples

505

of each type follow:
    a) Niladic and limited:

```
     ∇INFLATION
[1]  'ENTER BASE-YEAR INDEX'
[2]  CHEAP ← ☐
[3]  'ENTER PRESENT INDEX'
[4]  TOOMUCH ← ☐
[5]  PERCENT ← 100 × TOOMUCH ÷ CHEAP
[6]  "DISTRESS:" PERCENT
[7]     ∇
```

The function INFLATION is niladic because it has no arguments. It is limited because it is not used in the main
body of the program.
    b) Niladic and unlimited:

```
     ∇H ← HEIGHT
[1]  H ← H + 2.0
[2]     ∇
```

HEIGHT is a program concerning the effects of wearing
padded shoes. The function is unlimited because its results
will be stored in H which is contained in both the header
and main program.
    c) Monadic and limited:

```
     ∇SQUARE N
[1]  N*2
[2]     ∇
```

Here the function SQUARE which computes the square of
a number is a function of one variable. Thus it is monadic.
It is limited since it cannot be used in the program.
    d) Monadic and unlimited:

```
     ∇C ← CUBE N
[1]  C ← N*3
[2]     ∇
```

The function CUBE which computes the cube of a number
is a function of one variable and therefore monadic. Now
CUBE can be used as an argument in other APL functions.
Hence it is unlimited.
    e) Dyadic and unlimited:

```
     ∇R ← N ROUNDOFF D
[1]  M ← N + 5 × 10* - (D+1)
[2]  M ← LM × 10*D
[3]  R ← M × 10* - D
[4]     ∇
```

The roundoff function rounds off a given integer to a
required number of decimal places D. It is a function of
both N and D and is therefore dyadic.
    f) Dyadic and limited:

```
     ∇R CYVOL H
[1]  'THE VOLUME OF THE CYLINDER IS:'
[2]  V ← 3.14159 × H × R*2
```

```
[3]   V
[4]   ∇
```

Here CYVOL is a function of H and R but it does not occur in the body of the program.

Write an APL program to find the wavelengths for the first
four spectral lines of hydrogen in the Paschen series.

Solution: The Paschen series deals with the infrared region
of the hydrogen spectra. The equation used to find the lines
is given in terms of the wavelength's reciprocal.

$$NU = 109,677.58\left(\frac{1}{9} - \frac{1}{B^2}\right)cm^{-1}, \text{ for } B = 4,5,6,7.$$

APL is useful in that we can design a program, and then enter
the values for B in sequence. Remember also that in APL,
operations are performed right-to-left. The program logic is
quite simple:

```
      ∇PASCHEN
[1]   NU ← 109,677.58(÷9 - ÷B*2)
[2]   LAMBDA ← ÷NU
[3]   LAMBDA
      ∇
```

Now, when returned to the execution mode, you can enter
the integers for B. Sample output looks like this:

```
B ← 4.0
PASCHEN
0.0001875
B ← 5.0
PASCHEN
0.0001282
B ← 6.0
PASCHEN
0.0001094
B ← 7.0
PASCHEN
0.0001005
```

Note that this is the crudest way of entering the values
for B. This process can be made easier by introducing vectors. If you were to enter:

```
B ← 4.0   5.0   6.0   7.0
PASCHEN
```

the resulting output would be

```
0.0001875   0.0001282   0.0001094   0.0001005
```

Note, that only spaces are to be inserted between successive
values of B, no commas.

Write an APL program to evaluate the roots of the quadratic equation of the form $ax^2 + bx + c = 0$.

Solution: To do this, we use the quadratic formula:

$$ROOT = \frac{-B \pm \sqrt{B^2 - 4AC}}{2A}$$

The quantity given by $B^2 - 4AC$ is named the discriminant. If it is negative, then the roots are complex numbers. In that case the program will be terminated. (Complex numbers can be evaluated by a built-in library function, but we will omit this for simplicity sake.). If the discriminant is positive, then we want to calculate the roots. The program is written below:

```
     ∇QUADRATIC
[1]  DISCRIM ← (B*2) - 4 × A × C
[2]  →(0 > DISCRIM)/8
[3]  'THE ROOTS ARE'
[4]  ROOT1 ← (-B-DISCRIM*0.5) ÷ 2 × A
[5]  ROOT2 ← (-B + DISCRIM*0.5) ÷ 2 × A
[6]  ROOT1, ROOT2
[7]  →0
[8]  'THE ROOTS ARE COMPLEX'
     ∇
```

Line [2] may be translated as follows: "If zero is greater than the discriminant, then go to line [8]. If zero is less than or equal to the discriminant, proceed with the next line." This is called a branch statement. Line [7] is also a branch: after the roots have been calculated, the program goes to line [0], which actually means the end of the program. Literal text has been added to make clear the meaning of the values being computed.

Now, for the polynomial $3x^2 - 19x - 14 = 0$, we can give a sample output, with A = 3, B = -19, and C = -14. This polynomial has real roots.

```
A ← 3
B ← -19
C ← -14
QUADRATIC
```

The roots are

```
-0.666666667
+7.000000000.
```

A recursive function is the one which uses itself in the body of its definition. Use APL to write a nonrecursive and a recursive function for computing the factorial of a number.

Solution: Using the most commonly used mathematical convention, the factorial function is written as n!, where n is a
non-negative integer. n! is defined as follows:

$$n! = \begin{cases} 1 & , \text{ if } n = 0 \\ n \times (n-1) \times (n-2) \times \ldots \times 2 \times 1, & \text{ if } n \neq 0 \end{cases}$$

A nonrecursive function for computing the factorial is as
follows:

```
     ∇Z ← FAC J
[1]   Z ← I ← 1
[2]   → (I ≥ J)/6
[3]   I ← I + 1                        (1)
[4]   Z ← Z × I
[5]   → 2
[6]   Z
     ∇
```

    An explicit result function was used above to compute
factorials nonrecursively. [1] initializes both Z and I to
the value 1. If the value of I is greater than or equal to
the value of J, then Z is already the value of J! and the
program branches to statement [6]. In statement [6], the
value of Z which is computed is printed out. The program
then halts.

    But, if the value of I is smaller than J, the condition-
al branching does not take place. The program then sequences
to statement [3]. In statement [3], the value of I is incremented by 1. Statement [4] replaces the value of Z with
Z × I. Then statement [5] sends the program back to statement [2] to repeat the comparison of I and J. This process
is continued until the value of I is greater than or equal
to the value of J; J! is then Z. A jump is made to statement [6], the value of Z is printed out, and the program
ends.

    A recursive function for computing the factorial is as
follows:

```
     ∇Z ← REFAC J
[1]   → (J=0)/GO
[2]   Z ← J × REFAC J-1                (2)
[3]   → 0
[4]   GO: Z ← 1
     ∇
```

Again, an explicit result function was used. In [1], if
J=0 the program goes to the statement labelled GO. Here,
the value of Z is made equal to 1. The program ends. Thus,
the program obtains the value of 0! equal to 1. Note that
the program does not ask for the value of Z to be printed
out. The value of Z is just stored in memory for future
use when required by the programmer. If J≠0, then step [2]
indicates how J! is computed recursively. Notice how the
REFAC function calls itself in step [2].

Write a computer program in APL to analyze an electrical circuit using the AND and OR operators of Boolean algebra. Assume four switches in the circuit; two are connected in parallel and two are connected in series.

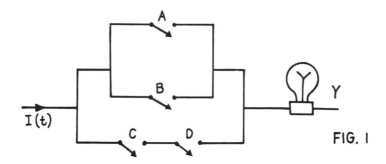

FIG. I

Solution: The circuit in fig. 1 is equivalent to the truth function $Y(A,B,C,D) = (A \lor B) \lor (C \land D)$. The complete truth table for Y is:

A	B	A∨B	C	D	C∧B	Y=A∨B∨C∧D
0	0	0	0	0	0	0
0	0	0	0	1	0	0
0	0	0	1	0	0	0
0	0	0	1	1	1	1
0	1	1	0	0	0	1
0	1	1	0	1	0	1
0	1	1	1	0	0	1
0	1	1	1	1	1	1
1	0	1	0	0	0	1
1	0	1	0	1	0	1
1	0	1	1	0	0	1
1	0	1	1	1	1	1
1	1	1	0	0	0	1
1	1	1	0	1	0	1
1	1	1	1	0	0	1
1	1	1	1	1	1	1

The truth-table is equivalent to the circuit. For example, if switches A,B,C are off and D is cn, the light will not shine. Similarly, if propositions A,B,C are false (=0) and proposition D is true (=1), the compound proposition (A or B) or (C and D) is false.

```
      ∇BOOLE
[1]   'ENTER TRUTH VALUES FOR A,B,C AND D'
[2]   L ← □
[3]   TEST ← (L[1] ∨ L[2]) ∨ L[3] ∧ L[4]
[4]   'THE VALUE OF Y IS:'; TEST
[5]   ∇
```

The header of the program is composed of ∇ (del) and BOOLE. The del operator causes the system to change to programming mode while BOOLE is the name of the program.

510

As an example, suppose the values 0,1,1,0, are entered
for A,B,C and D respectively. Then the value of Y would be
1.

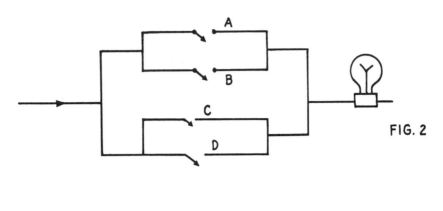

FIG. 2

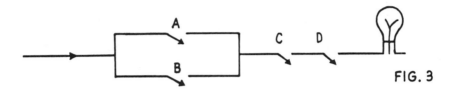

FIG. 3

The program may be modified to handle other types of
circuits. (FIG. 2)
This circuit is equivalent to the truth function Y(A,B,C,D)
= (A∨B)∨(C∨D).
To test this function replace [3] by

[3] TEST ← (L[1]∨L[2])∨ (L[3]∨L[4])

The circuit, (FIG. 3)
represents the function (A∨B)∧(C∧D). The test for this
function is

[3] TEST ← (L[1]∨L[2]) ∧ L[3]∧L[4].

● **PROBLEM** 14-18

Write an APL program to build 10 rows of Pascal's triangle.

Solution: Each row of Pascal's triangle is a set of binomial coefficients for the expansion of $(X + Y)^{n-1}$, $n > 0$.
Another way of representing these coefficients is
$\binom{N}{K}$ for N = 1,2,3,... and for K = 0,1,2,..., such that

$$\binom{N}{K} = \frac{N!}{K!\,(N-K)!}$$

or,
$$= \frac{N(N-1)\ldots(N-K+1)}{K!}.$$

511

Our strategy rests on the fact that each number in the triangle is the sum of two numbers right above it. For example, let us take rows 1 to 5.

ROWS

```
N=1                1                     K=0
N=2              1   1                   K=1
N=3            1   2   1                 K=2
N=4          1   3   3   1               K=3
N=5        1   4   6   4   1             K=4
```

To get from row 4 to row 5, we can do the following:

```
ROW 4      1  3  3  1
      +       1  3  3  1
           ─────────────
           1  4  6  4  1
```

By taking a row, moving it one place to the right, and then adding it to itself, we can generate the next row.

In APL, the symbol used for catenation is the comma. Catenation means "chaining" elements together. This can be done by the statement $P \leftarrow (0,P) + (P,0)$. This statement will do the following:

```
         0  1  3  3  1
   +     1  3  3  1  0
       ─────────────────
         1  4  6  4  1
```

A zero catenated with string P in (0,P) part, moves P one place to the right, while the zero in the second part, (P,0), just adds itself to the string P. Then, the addition is performed, and the new row is created. The program is given below:

```
      ∇PASCAL
[1]   P ← 1
[2]   P
[3]   → 2 × N ≥ ρP ← (0,P) + (P,0)
      ∇
```

Line [3] contains the symbol ρ, which is called the reshaping operator. When you enter the value for N (in this case, N = 10), ρ determines the number of times $P \leftarrow (0,P) + (P,0)$ is to be executed. When ten branches have been executed, the comparison $N \geq \rho$ will be false or, in APL, it will have the value zero. This zero will then be multiplied by 2 telling the program to branch to instruction zero, which is the way of indicating the termination of the program.

● **PROBLEM** 14-19

Write a program in APL to compute the gross pay of any number of employees.

Solution: Although APL is slanted towards mathematical problems, it may also be used in clerical functions that involve repetition.

The program below lists the name of each employee and his/her gross pay. Hours worked and rate of pay are input but do not form part of output.

```
      ∇PAYDAY
[1]   NAME ← ' '
[2]   GRS ← ' '
[3]   'ENTER THE NUMBER OF EMPLOYEES'
[4]   N ← □
[5]   I ← 0
[6]   REPEAT: 'ENTER NAME'
[7]   NAME ← NAME, 20↑□
[8]   'ENTER HOURS AND RATE'
[9]   GRS ← GRS, ×/□
[10]  I ← I + 1
[11]  → REPEAT × ι(I < N)
[12]  NAME ← (N,20)ρ NAME
[13]  GRS ← (N,1)ρGRS
[14]  ' '
[15]  'NAME ---------------- GROSS PAY'
[16]  NAME, 7 2 DEF GRS
[17]  ∇
```

Note the following points about the program: Statements [6] and [7] ensure that all names are entered. Statement [11] corresponds to the CONTINUE statement in FORTRAN. Names will continue to be entered and gross pay computed while (I < N). When I = N, ι(I < N) is 0. But since there is no statement numbered 0, the program comes to a halt. Statement [14] produces a line of blank spaces between the input and output phases of the program.

EDITING AND DEBUGGING

● **PROBLEM** 14-20

Explain how the following procedures are useful in debugging a program:

a) tracing a function
b) Stop control.

Solution: When a function returns improper or unexpected results, the programmer can investigate what is happening in each instruction of his program by tracing its execution, using the trace function.
    Consider the following program:

```
      ∇DOOMED
[1]   S ← X1,X2,...,XN
[2]   ⍋S
[3]   S[⍋]
[4]   INVS ← ÷S
[5]   PS1S2 ← ((S(I) - S(I-1)) ÷ (INVS(I) - INVS(I-1))
[6]   → [8] × ι(PS1S2 < 0)
[7]   'THE NEGATIVE PRODUCTS ARE:'; PS1S2
[8]   → [10] × ι(PS1S2 < 100)
```

```
[9]    'THE POSITIVE PRODUCTS LESS THAN 100:'; PS1S2
[10]   'THE POSITIVE PRODUCTS GREATER THAN 100:'; PS1S2
[11]   ∇
```

If we run this program through, only negative products are printed. To see what is wrong we can put the function in trace mode, i.e.

$$T\Delta DOOMED \leftarrow 1\ 2\ 3\ 4\ 5\ 6\ 7\ 8\ 9\ 10$$

where 1,2..,10 are the statement numbers. But the program is quite long. The mistake probably lies in statement [5]. Hence, instead of trying to trace the action of the system through the whole function we can concentrate on [5]. Key in $T\Delta DOOMED \leftarrow [5]$. The output is

```
        DOOMED
DOOMED[5]    -X1X2
DOOMED[5]    -X3X2
DOOMED[5]    -X4X3
     .        .
     .        .
     .        .
DOOMED[5]    -XNXN-1
```

Since all the products are negative, there is something wrong with instruction [5]. Converting into algebraic form:

$$PS1S2 = \frac{X_1 - X_2}{\frac{1}{X_1} - \frac{1}{X_2}} = \frac{X_1 - X_2}{\frac{X_2 - X_1}{X_1 X_2}} = \frac{X_1 - X_2}{X_2 - X_1}(X_1 X_2)$$

$$= \frac{X_1 - X_2}{-(X_1 - X_2)}(X_1 X_2) = -X_1 X_2.$$

Statement [5] always results in a negative product. To ensure correct calculations we can change [5] to

```
[5]   PS1S2 ← ((S(I) - S(I-1)) ÷ (INVS(I-1) - INVS(I)).
```

b) The stop control mode halts program execution at a specific instruction so the programmer can examine it. For example, suppose we wish to inspect [6] of DOOMED. To activate the stop control mode, key in

```
        S∆DOOMED ← 6
        DOOMED
```

The system responds with

```
[6]   → [8] × ι(PS1S2 < 0).
```

To end the stop control mode, key in

```
        S∆DOOMED ← ι0.
```

514

What are the common editing procedures in APL? Give examples.

Solution: Errors have to be corrected before a program becomes operational. Editing procedures help in making the
corrections. These procedures are:

- i) Open a function, display all lines of the function, then close the function.
- ii) Open a function, replace a line that contains an
error with a new line, then close the function.
- iii) Open a function, list all its instructions and
remain in definition mode.
- iv) While in programming mode, direct program control
to a specific line number.
- v) While in programming mode, direct program control
to a specific line and then eliminate that line.
- vi) Insert an instruction between two other instructions.

   To illustrate these procedures, consider the following
program:

```
      ∇TRIANGLE
[1]    'ENTER HEIGHT'
[2]    H ← □
[3]    'ENTER BASE'
[4]    B ← □
[5]    A ← .5 × H × B
[6]    'THEAREA IS:';A
```

   i) To display the total program (assuming it has been
keyed in) key in

        ∇TRIANGLE[□]∇.

This command causes a listing of the program to be made at
the users terminal. Note that [6] has an error.

   ii) 'THEAREA...' should be 'THE AREA...'. To make
this correction, type in

        ∇TRIANGLE[6]'THE AREA IS:';A∇.

   iii) To remain in definition mode, type
        ∇TRIANGLE[□]

(the ∇ has not yet been added).

   iv) Suppose we want to add more information so as to
calculate the perimeter of the triangle. Then [3] and [4]
can be deleted. Key in [3] and depress ATTN and RETURN keys.
This action deletes [3]. Similarly, key in [4] and depress
ATTN and RETURN keys. The program now looks like this:

```
     ∇TRIANGLE[□]
     ∇TRIANGLE
[1]    'ENTER HEIGHT'
[2]    H ← □
[3]    A ← .5 × H × B
[4]    'THE AREA IS:';A
[5]
```

v,vi) Of course. the program does not make any sense
right now. We must key in the three sides, replace B in
[3] by the side corresponding to B and add a line for calculating the perimeter. To add the three sides:

```
     ∇TRIANGLE[2.1]
[2.1]  'ENTER LEFT SIDE'
[2.2]  L ← □
[2.3]  'ENTER BASE'
[2.4]  B ← □
[2.5]  'ENTER RIGHT SIDE'
[2.6]  R ← □
[2.7]  P ← L + B + R
[2.8]  ∇
```

Note that there is no need to change B. However, since
P should be printed, add another line after [6]:

```
          ∇TRIANGLE[6.1]

[6.1]  'THE PERIMETER IS:';P
[6.2]  ∇
```

The command NUM will renumber the statements. The final result is:

```
     ∇TRIANGLE
 [1]   'ENTER HEIGHT'
 [2]   H ← □
 [3]   'ENTER LEFT SIDE'
 [4]   L ← □
 [5]   'ENTER BASE'
 [6]   B ← □
 [7]   'ENTER RIGHT SIDE'
 [8]   R ← □
 [9]   P ← L + B + R
[10]   A ← .5 × H × B
[11]   'THE AREA IS:';A
[12]   'THE PERIMETER IS:';P
       ∇
```

● **PROBLEM** 14-22

Give examples of the following editing procedures in APL.

    i)   Perform editing on a single instruction of a
        function.
   ii)   Change the name of the header of a given function.
  iii)   Open a function, exhibit a specific line, then
        direct program control to this line.
   iv)   Erase a function that is contained in your active
        workspace.

Solution: Assume the following program is in the active workspace:

```
      ∇ VARIANCE
 [1]    'ENTER SAMPLE ELEMENTS'
 [2]    S ← X1 X2 ... XN
 [3]    AVG ← (+/S) ÷ ρS
 [4]    RANGE ← (⌈/S) - L/S
 [5]    NS ← AVG × (+/S)
 [6]    S
 [7]    S2 ← S*2
 [8]    SSQ ← (+/S2)
 [9]    VAR ← SS2 - NS
[10]    'THE VARIANCE IS:';VAR
[11]    ∇
```

This program finds the variance of a set of numbers. The procedure is as follows:

1) Let $X_1, X_2, \ldots, X_n$ be a series of observations:

$$\bar{X} = \sum_{i=1}^{N} \frac{X_i}{N}$$

$$VAR = \frac{\Sigma (x_i - \bar{x})^2}{N} = \sum x_i^2 - \frac{[\sum x_i]^2}{N} \; .$$

The second expression is more easily evaluated and is also more amenable to treatment by APL than the first.

i) Suppose it is desired to change NS to MSQ (Mean Squares), a more descriptive acronym. Key in ∇ VARIANCE[5▢10]. Here [5] is the line number and 10 is the print position, where editing is to begin. Actually NS may be in any print position (<10). Backspace until the type ball is below N and enter two slashes followed by a 3. The two slashes erase NS and the 3 allows 3 characters for MSQ. Now, depress the RETURN key. At this point, the fifth line looks as follows:

[5]   ←AVG × (+/S)

Key in MSQ and then ask for a display of [5]: [5▢], which should be

[5]   MSQ ← AVG × (+/S)

A similar procedure is followed for [9].

ii) Next, suppose it is required to find the standard deviation of the set of numbers. The header can be changed from ∇ VARIANCE to ∇SDEV as follows:

∇VARIANCE[0▢10]

[0]   VARIANCE

517

Backspace until the ball is under V and print 8 slashes, followed by 4. Depress the RETURN key to display a blank [0]-line with 4 vacant spaces for a new name.

[0]

Type SDEV and display the line [0] for a check. It should look like the following

[0]   SDEV

Type DEL to terminate the procedure.
        To add a line that finds the standard deviation, key in

∇SDEV[9.5] SDEV ← VAR*.5∇

iii)   Line [10] should be amended to

'THE STANDARD DEVIATION IS:';SDEV

Key in ∇SDEV[10⬚] to get a display of the tenth line:

[10]   'THE VARIANCE IS:';VAR

Key in

[10]   'THE SDEV IS:';SDEV
[11]   ∇

iv)   Suppose SDEV is no longer required. The command)ERASE SDEV deletes it from the active workspace.

● **PROBLEM 14-23**

How are the concepts of local and global variables useful in debugging an APL program?

Solution: Since APL is an interactive system, the negative feedback on an incorrect program is immediate. An understanding of local and global variables can help in the quick debugging of APL programs.
        Variables that retain their values only during function execution are classified as local. By contrast, global variables are retained in the workspace before, during and after the execution of a program.
        To clarify the distinction, consider the following two programs:

```
        R ← 5
        ∇CIRCLE
[1]     D ← 2 × R
[2]     C ← 3.14159 × D
[3]     A ← 3.14159 × R × R
[4]     R,D,C,A
[5]     ∇
```

Here R is a global variable because it is active before the execution of a function. That is, R has already been stored before ∇CIRCLE.

```
      ∇CIRCLE 1 R
[1]   D ← 2 × R
[2]   C ← 3.14159 × D
[3]   A ← 3.14159 × R × R
[4]   R,D,C,A
[5]   ∇
```

Now, R, the radius, is a local variable. Suppose R = 5.
Then

        CIRCLE 1 5

causes the values

            5, 10, 31.42, 78.54

to be printed. Keying in an R, after execution is completed
produces an error message:

```
    R
VALUE ERROR
      R
      ∧
```

Once the function has been executed, R is lost. D,C, and A,
however, are global variables because they were not defined
in the header.
        Since local variables save space, it is often desirable
to use them in a program. Additional local variables can be
defined by adding them to the header, with a semicolon between each pair of variables. For example,

            ∇CIRCLE R;D;C;A

will make all variables local.

CHAPTER 15

SNOBOL

● **PROBLEM** 15-1

Give a brief introduction to the operations and applications of the SNOBOL IV language.

Solution: Developed at Bell Telephone Laboratories, Inc. in 1962, SNOBOL IV is a computer programming language containing many features not commonly found in other programming languages. The basic data element of SNOBOL IV is a string of characters, such as this line of printing. The language has operations for joining and separating strings, for testing their contents, for making replacements in them, etc.
SNOBOL IV provides numerical capabilities with both integers and real numbers. Conversions among integers, real numbers, and strings representing integers or real numbers are performed automatically as required.
SNOBOL IV provides great flexibility of function usage. Functions can be defined and redefined during program execution. Function calls can be made recursively with no special program notation.
These and many other important features make this language highly applicable to such areas as compilation techniques, machine simulation, symbolic math, text preparation, natural language translation, linguistics, music analysis, and many others.
SNOBOL IV has been implemented on several different computers, including the IBM 360, UNIVAC 1108, GE 635, CDC 3600, CDC 6000, PDP-10, SIGMA 5,6,7, ATLAS 2, and RCA SPECTRA 70 series.

● **PROBLEM** 15-2

Give examples of valid variable names in SNOBOL IV. List the basic statements and briefly explain their operations.

Solution: The variable names in SNOBOL IV must begin with a letter which may be followed by any number of letters, digits, periods and underscores. Some examples of valid variable names are listed below:

> A, B1, VARIABLE, D987654321, YOU.OR.ME, K6.J2

The basic statements are as follows:

        variable = INPUT
    - Assigns the first read in string to a variable name.
        OUTPUT = string or variable
    - Prints out a given string,

```
          PUNCH = string
     - Punches the given string,
          variable = string
     - Assigns the given string to a variable.
```

● **PROBLEM** 15-3

Write a program which concatenates two strings "I LOVE" and "YOU!",
checks for presence of the character ".", replaces it with "!",
and prints out the final string.

Solution: Concatenation is the basic operation for combining two
strings to form a third.   The general form of this operation is
represented by the following statements:

```
               variable 1 = string 1
               variable 2 = string 2
               variable 3 = string 1 string 2
```

There must be at least one blank space on each side of the "=" sign
(as well as any other arithmetic operator, except the unary minus)
and between strings 1 and 2 in variable 3.
The simple pattern matching statement has the form

```
               subject pattern
```

where the two fields are separated by at least one blank.   This
statement tells the computer to check the string indicated by
subject for the occurrence of a string specified by the pattern.
A replacement statement has the form

```
               subject pattern = object
```

The left part of this statement operates identically with the pattern
matching statement.   If a match occurs, the object string replaces
the pattern string in the subject string.   The program follows:

```
          WORD 1 = 'I LOVE'
          WORD 2 = 'YOU.'
          WORDS = WORD 1   WORD 2
          WORDS '.' = ' ! '
          OUTPUT = WORDS
          END
```

Note, that END is a label, indicating the end of program.   Labels
appear before the statements and consist of a letter or a digit
followed by any number of other characters up to a blank.
Also note, that single quotation marks can be used as well as
double quotations.

● **PROBLEM** 15-4

Write a program which counts the number of times each letter is
used in input text.

Solution:
```
1          &TRIM = 1
2          CHAR = LEN(1) . CH
3          LETTERS = 'ABCDEFGHIJKLMNOPQRSTUVWXYZ'
4          COUNT = TABLE (30)
```

521

```
5  READ    OUTPUT = INPUT      : F(DISPLAY)
6          TEXT = OUTPUT
7  NEXT    TEXT CHAR =         : F(READ)
8          COUNT <CH> = COUNT <CH> + 1      : (NEXT)
9  DISPLAY OUTPUT =
10 LOOP    LETTERS CHAR =      : F (END)
11         OUTPUT = NE(COUNT<CH>) CH'OCCURS'
   +       COUNT<CH> 'TIMES'  : (LOOP)
12  END
```

The first statement includes a keyword '&TRIM'. Keywords in SNOBOL IV
allow access to several parameters and switches internal to the
SNOBOL IV system. Keywords begin with ampersand (&) followed by
certain identifiers. For example, keyword &TRIM controls the handling
of trailing blanks on input of data. If the value of &TRIM is nonzero,
trailing blanks are deleted. Other keywords will be explained upon
occurrence in the programs.

The second statement, CHAR = LEN(1). CH, includes two important features.
First, LEN(1), is an example of primitive (Built-in) functions. This
function returns a pattern that matches any string of the length
specified by the integer in parentheses. INPUT, PUNCH, and OUTPUT
are some other primitive functions. The second important feature of
the second statement is that it is an example of conditional value
assignment (in this case .CH). The conditional value assignment
operator (.) is separated from its operands by blanks. In the statement CHAR = LEN(1) . CH, variable CHAR is assigned the very first
found string of length one, and, in case of success, assigns the same
string to CH, which is used as an array subscript later in the program.
The fourth statement, COUNT = TABLE (30), introduces the use of tables.
Tables of variables can be created by using the primitive function
TABLE, for example:

$$T = TABLE ( )$$

In a very similar way arrays of variables are constructed by using the
primitive function ARRAY, for example:

$$A = ARRAY ( )$$

The arguments of an array, written in parentheses, describe the number
of dimensions, the bounds of each dimension, and the initial value of
each variable in the array. Thus

$$A = ARRAY (10,1.0)$$

creates and assigns to A a one-dimensional array of 10 variables,
each initialized to the real value 1.0.

A table is similar to a one-dimensional array. However, instead of
referencing an element with an integer, any data object can be used.
In this program, letters of the alphabet are used as subscripts for
table elements.

The fifth statement of the program introduces the most important
feature of the flow of control - a transfer to a labelled statement.
It is specified in the GOTO field which appears at the end of a
statement and is separated from the rest of the statement by a colon.
Two types of transfers can be specified in the GOTO field: conditional
and unconditional. A conditional transfer consists of letters F or
S corresponding to failure or success respectively, followed by a
label enclosed within parentheses. Thus

```
OUTPUT = INPUT                : F(DISPLAY)
```

makes the computer print out whatever appears on the data card. If,
however, there is no data in the input file, i.e., an end of file is
encountered, the transfer is made to the statement labeled display.
An unconditional transfer is indicated by the absence of an F or
S before the enclosing parentheses. For example, consider statement #8 of this program:

        COUNT<CH> = COUNT<CH> + 1   :(NEXT)
Each time this statement is executed, the transfer is made to the
statement labelled NEXT.
Statement #11 uses one of the primitive functions of a specific
group called NUMERICAL PREDICATES. The main ones include:

        LT - less than...
        LE - less than or equal to...
        EQ - equal to...
        NE - not equal to...
        GE - greater or equal to...
        GT - greater than...

Statement OUTPUT = NE (COUNT<CH>).... prints out whatever is
following the parentheses if the value of COUNT<CH> is not equal
to zero.
Finally, a statement that is longer than one line can be continued
onto successive lines by starting the continuation lines with a
period or plus sign. This program employs a plus sign for continuation of statement #11. Also note, that the statements in this
program are numbered only for easy reference. All labels in SNOBOL IV
start with a letter, as was mentioned earlier. If a statement does
not start with a label, it must start with at least one blank.
The general flow of this program is as follows:
statement 1 - deletes trailing blanks;
statement 2 - indicates that CHAR and CH will be assigned the first
one-character string matched;
statement 3 - assigns a string of the 26 letters of the alphabet to
variable LETTERS;
statement 4 - sets a 30-element table and assigns it to COUNT;
statement 5 - prints out the first card of the input text;
statement 6 - assigns it to variable TEXT;
statement 7 - tests the text for presence of the first one-character
string (which is the first letter of the first word in the text),
deletes them all one at a time, adding 1 to COUNT<CH> in statement 8
each time around;
statement 8 - goes back to statement 7 every time after adding 1 to
COUNT<CH>; statement 7 - repeats the loop until all the appearances
of each letter are counted, and the table COUNT is set up. Then
COUNT fails when no more characters are left; the transfer is made
back to statement #5; statement 5 - repeats the whole procedure for
every following input card, adding missing members (if there are any)
to the table COUNT. Finally it fails when there is no input left and
transfers the execution to statement #9; statement 9 - prints a blank
line; statement 10 - tests string LETTERS for the presence of a one-
character string, finds 26 of them, assigns the first one (i.e., A)
to CHAR and deletes it from LETTERS; statement 11 - since CH takes
the same value as CHAR, looks in the table for COUNT<A> which represents
the number of times letter A appeared in the text. If finds it,
outputs the letter A and the number of its occurrences. In any
case it goes back to statement #10; statement 10 - repeats the same
procedure for every letter. It fails when no more letters are left
and finishes the program.

● **PROBLEM** 15-5

Write a program which reads in words and prints out only those
which end with letter "K".

Solution: If we could somehow separate the last character from each word, it would be possible then to check that character and, if it were "K", output the corresponding word. Unfortunately, there is no straightforward way to perform the separation. However, SNOBOL provides a very convenient way of separating the first letter from the word. In order to apply this method, it is necessary to reverse the order of letters in the word. The format - free flow-chart of the solution is shown in the figure.

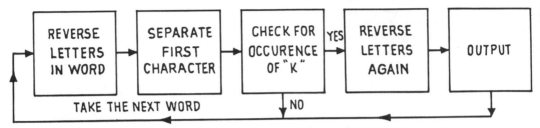

There is no primitive (built-in) function in SNOBOL IV compiler which reverses a string; therefore, it has to be defined. SNOBOL IV provides the programmer with this capability. A function is defined by executing the primitive function DEFINE to specify the function name, formal arguments, local variables, and the entry point of the function. The entry point is the label of the first of a set of statements constituting the procedure for the function. Thus:

                    DEFINE('REVERSE(W)', 'A')

defines a function REVERSE having one formal argument, W, and entry point A.

As was explained in the previous problem LEN(I) is a primitive function which returns a pattern that matches any string of the length specified by the integer I. Therefore, function LEN(1) will return the first matched string of length one, which is the first letter of the input word. Thus the statements

```
A          STRING = LEN(1) . LETTER
B          W   STRING =              : F(RETURN)
           REVERSE = LETTER   REVERSE   : (B)
```

form a procedure that reverses the string W. The first statement of this procedure (labelled) A, which indicates the entry point of the function REVERSE) indicates that both STRING and LETTER will be assigned the first one-character string found (matched). The second statement assigns the first letter of the input word under variable name W to STRING and consequently, to LETTER, and deletes that letter. The third statement concatenates values of LETTER and REVERSE (which is now just a variable with initial value 0) assigns the result to REVERSE and sends the execution back to the second statement. The next letter is taken now and the procedure repeats. When all the characters of the input word are reversed, the second statement fails and returns the execution to the main program, after hitting the RETURN label in the transfer field of the second statement. The full solution for this problem looks as follows:

```
START      WORD =  INPUT                  : F(END)
           DEFINE('REVERSE(W)', 'A')
           WORD 1 = REVERSE(WORD)
           WORD 1 LEN(1) . K
K          'K'                            : F(START)
           OUTPUT = REVERSE(WORD1)        : (START)
A          STRING = LEN(1) . LETTER
B          W   STRING =                   : F(RETURN)
           REVERSE = LETTER REVERSE       : (B)
END
```

524

The statement WORD1 = REVERSE(WORD) calls the function REVERSE, performs it for the part of the input stored in variable WORD, and assigns the final (reversed) value to the variable WORD1. The next statement, WORD1 LEN(1) . K takes the first letter of the reversed word (which is the last letter of the original word) and assigns it to variable K. The statement K 'K' :F(START), then, checks the variable K for occurrence of letter K, and transfers the execution to the first statement if it fails. .The first statement reads the next word, and the procedure repeats. However, if the check succeeds, the computer executes the next statement,

                OUTPUT = REVERSE(WORD1)   :(START),

which reverses the word for the second time to give it its original form, outputs the word, and sends the control to the first statement. The program terminates when the last word of the input is processed. Note that a function has to be defined before it is called, while the procedure statements may appear later in the program. Also note, that the entry point label in the DEFINE statement could be omitted. In that case, the entry point to the procedure is taken to be the same as the function name. For example:

                DEFINE('REVERSE(W)')

could have the procedure:

```
REVERSE        STRING = LEN(1) . LETTER
B              W     STRING =                  : F(RETURN)
               REVERSE = LETTER  REVERSE       : (B)
```

● PROBLEM 15-6

Consider the following input containing information about the players of a soccer team:
        LAST NAME   BIRTHDATE   NO.   GAMES PLAYED   GOALS SCORED

Write a program which punches cards with the same information, but in form:
        LAST NAME; BIRTH DATE: NO; GAMES PLAYED;   GOALS SCORED

Solution:
```
        &ANCHOR = 1;  &TRIM = 1
        STRING = BREAK(' ') . CHARS SPAN(' ')
NEXT    CARD = INPUT          : F(END)
LOOP    CARD STRING = CHARS ';'  : S(LOOP)
        PUNCH = CARD          : (NEXT)
END
```
The first line, &ANCHOR = 1; &TRIM = 1, introduces two new features of the SNOBOL IV language. First, it includes two separate statements. SNOBOL IV permits reordering of the several statements on one line, where each statement (except the last) ends with semicolon. Second, the first line introduces a new keyword &ANCHOR. If not otherwise specified, the initial value of &ANCHOR is zero, meaning that any pattern matching in that program will succeed whenever a pattern occurs anywhere in the subject. If the value of &ANCHOR is not zero, any pattern matching will succeed only if a pattern occurs in the beginning of the subject. Thus, in the previous problem, the two statements
```
        WORD1   LEN(1) . K
        K       'K'              : F(START)
```
could be replaced by

```
                    &ANCHOR = 1
                    WORD1     'K'              : F(START)
```

The second line includes BREAK and SPAN, the primitive functions whose
values are pattern structures that match runs of characters. Patterns
described by

```
                    A RUN OF BLANKS,
                    A STRING OF DIGITS,
                    A WORD (RUN OF LETTERS)
```

can be formed using SPAN as

```
                    SPAN (' ')
                    SPAN ('0123456789')
                    SPAN ('ABCDEFGHIJKLMNOPQRSTUVWXYZ')
```

respectively. Patterns described by
i)   Everything up to the next blank,
ii) Everything up to the next punctuation mark,
iii) Everything up to the next number, can be formed using BREAK as

```
                    BREAK (' ')
                    BREAK (',.;:!?')
                    BREAK ('+-0123456789')
```

respectively. The pattern structure for SPAN matches the longest
string that consists solely of characters, appearing in the argument.
BREAK generates a pattern structure that matches the string up to,
but not including, the break character in the argument. Thus, the
second line of this program indicates that the variable STRING will
be assigned a first matched string of characters up to a first blank
(the same string will also be assigned to CHARS), concatenated with
the run of blanks between it and the next string.
The third line of the program reads in a first input card. The
fourth line assigns the first string of the card up to a blank,
concatenated with the run of blanks following it, to STRING and
substitutes it by the same string, only now followed by a semicolon,
rather than blanks. Then it takes the next string and run of blanks
and does the same. The procedure repeats until all the strings on
the card are substituted. Then the computer punches out the first
card with the proper changes, goes back to the third line (labeled
NEXT), reads in the next card, and performs the needed substitutions
on it. The control exits from the loop and terminates the program
when there are no more cards in the input.
Considering the following input:

```
     PELE             1938            10        35            30
```

the output will be:
```
          PELE; 1938; 10; 35; 30
```

● **PROBLEM 15-7**

Let the label for an assembly language statement begin in column 1
and consist of at most eight characters, the first of which is a
letter followed by letters or digits. The label is followed by
at least one blank. A statement without a label begins with a
blank. Write a program that reads in assembly language statements
and prints those statements with invalid labels.

Solution: LETTER =   'ABCDEFGHIJKLMNOPQRSTUVWXYZ'
            DIGIT   =   '0123456789'
            LABEL   =   ' ' |ANY(LETTER) (SPAN(LETTER DIGIT)@N *LE(N,8)
        + | NULL) ' '

```
            &ANCHOR   =   1
R           CARD      =   INPUT          :F(END)
            CARD          LABEL          :S(R)
            OUTPUT    =   CARD           :(R)
      END
```

The first two statements are regular assignment statements, assigning
the string of letters to LETTER and a string of digits to DIGIT. The
third assignment statement contains alternation - the expression where
different patterns are separated by symbol | (with at least one blank
on each side). The value of the expression is a pattern structure
that matches any string specified by any of the alternative patterns.
The first alternative pattern in the third statement is ' ' - a
regular blank, while the second pattern includes a few new features.
The first of them is a primitive function ANY. ANY and the opposite
function NOTANY are primitive functions whose values are pattern
structures that match single characters. ANY matches any character
appearing in its argument, following the function in parentheses.
NOTANY matches any character not appearing in its argument. Thus
the pattern structure ANY (LETTER) matches any letter of the alphabet
(the structure ANY('ABCD...XYZ') would have the same meaning).
How ANY LETTER then concatenates with another alternative structure
needs a detailed explanation. The SPAN function returns a matched
run of characters, included in concatenated strings LETTER and DIGIT
(any other character met with indicates the end of the run).
Matching a pattern structure against a subject string, in SNOBOL IV,
is done by a procedure called the SCANNER. The scanner has a pointer
(control) called the CURSOR which is positioned to the left of the
character that the scanner must match. As the scanner matches one
by one the characters of the string, the cursor correspondingly moves
to the right. These concepts are important in understanding the
function of the next variable of the second alternative structure in
line 3 - @N. The unary operator @ is called the cursor position
operator. At any moment of the pattern matching process, it assigns
an integer, representing the cursor position at that moment, to a
variable following it (in our case, N). For example, in statement

                    'EXAMPLE' @JUNK 'L'

The cursor, at first, is located to the left of E. No match occurs;
the value 1 is assigned to the variable JUNK, and the cursor moves
to X. The process goes on until the cursor hits L. By that time
JUNK has the value of 5. Letter L matches, execution goes to the
next statement, and variable JUNK is stored with value 5.
Thus, in our problem, N indicates the position of the cursor after
the scanner matched all characters of the first string on the card
up to the first blank. In other words, N counts the number of
characters in the label.
Next comes the comparison of N. The unary operator * (asterisk)
postpones the evaluation of its operand. Thus, LE(N,8) is an unevaluated
expression until it appears as part of a pattern LABEL in statement
6. This way the expression is evaluated only when needed.
An alternative expression for concatenation in the second part of
statement 3 is a string NULL which, in SNOBOL IV indicates a string
of length zero. It is different from the strings '0' and ' ', each
of which has a length one. The NULL string consists of no characters,
no blanks, no length. A blank finishes the pattern.
It is now possible to follow through the function of the pattern
LABEL in the sixth statement. If the statement on the input card
starts with a blank, the pattern matches at once, and the execution
returns to the previous statement CARD = INPUT :F(END), reading in
the next card.

If, however, the statement on the card starts with a letter, the characters following that letter are examined. All the characters (including the initial letter) are counted up to the first blank (specified in pattern LABEL by the blank at the end). Also all those characters have to belong either to LETTER or to DIGIT. If, in fact, the cursor hits a symbol which belongs to neither of those two strings, the matching fails, and the card is printed out as having an invalid label.

Meanwhile, the integer produced by the counting procedure is assigned to N. If all the characters are legitimate, N is compared with 8. If N appears to be less than or equal to 8, the match succeeds, and the next card is considered. In case N is greater than 8, the match fails, and the card is printed out.

If the first letter is followed by no other characters (NULL string), just a blank, the match succeeds, and the next card is considered. The program terminates after consideration of the last card.

● PROBLEM 15-8

Give a list and briefly define the primitive (built in) functions of SNOBOL IV language.

Solution:

ANY	-	matches any character appearing in its argument.
APPLY	-	creates and executes a function call.
ARBNO	-	takes a value of pattern structure that matches zero or more consecutive occurrences of strings matched by its argument.
ARG	-	takes a value of the indicated argument from programmer-defined function.
ARRAY	-	creates an array of variables.
BACKSPACE	-	backspaces the indicated record.
BREAK	-	matches a string up to indicated character.
CLEAR	-	sets the values of all natural variables to the null string.
CODE	-	converts a string of characters into object code.
COLLECT	-	returns as value the amount of storage available after regeneration.
CONVERT	-	converts a given object into given datatype.
COPY	-	produces a copy of an array.
DATA	-	defines a new data type.
DATATYPE	-	identifies the type of given data.
DATE	-	gives the date of program execution.
DEFINE	-	defines a programmer defined function.
DETACH	-	removes any input and output association from the argument.
DIFFER	-	succeeds if two given arguments are not identical.
DUMP	-	lists all natural variables and their values in the program if argument ≠ 0.
DUPL	-	repeats the first argument the number of times specified by second argument.
ENDFILE	-	closes the data set, indicated by argument.
EQ	-	predicate "EQUAL".
EVAL	-	evaluates an unevaluated argument.
FIELD	-	gives function a value equal to the name of a given field of the programmer defined data type, specified in the argument.
GE	-	predicate "GREATER THAN, or EQUAL TO"

528

GT   - predicate "GREATER THAN"
IDENT   - succeeds if two given arguments are identical.
INPUT   - specifies a programmer - defined input.
INTEGER - succeeds if the value of argument is an integer.
ITEM   - assigns values to the specified members of the
              specified arrays.
LE   - predicate "LESS THAN, or EQUAL TO".
LEN   - returns a pattern structure that matches any string
              of the specified length.
LGT   - succeeds if the first argument is lexically greater
              than the second.
LOCAL   - gives function a value equal to the name of a given
              local variable from a specified defined function.
LT   - predicate "LESS THAN".
NE   - predicate "NOT EQUAL".
NOTANY   - matches any character not appearing in the argument.
OPSYN   - provides synonyms for existing functions or operators.
OUTPUT   - specifies a programmer formatted output of a pro-
              grammer defined data.
POS   - succeeds if the cursor's position is just to the right
              of the one, specified by the integer argument.
PROTOTYPE - returns a value of the dimension or range of an
              array.
REMDR   - returns an integer that is the remainder of dividing
              the first argument by the second.
REPLACE - replaces character, given in the argument, by another
              in the specified string.
REWIND   - repositions the data set associated with the given
              number to the first file.
RPOS   - succeeds if the cursor's position is just to the
              left of the one, specified by the integer argument.
RTAB   - matches all the characters of a string up to, but
              not including the one specified in the argument,
              from the right end of a subject string.
SIZE   - returns an integer equal to the length of a given
              string.
SPAN   - matches a run of characters given in the argument.
STOPTR   - cancels a single trace association.
TAB   - matches all the characters of a string up through
              the one, specified in the argument.
TABLE   - creates a table of variables.
TIME   - gives the elapsed time of program execution (in MSEC.)
TRACE   - traces a specified data segment.
TRIM   - removes trailing blanks from a string in the argument.
VALUE   - assigns a given value to a specified variable.

● PROBLEM 15-9

Write a program which, using a recursive function, determines and
prints out the steps necessary to move N discs from one needle
to another in the Tower of Hanoi game.

Solution: A Tower of Hanoi is a game where N discs of decreasing
size are stacked on a needle. There are two empty needles nearby.
The aim is to move all the discs from the original needle to a
second needle using, when necessary, the third needle as temporary
storage. Only one disc can be moved at a time, and at no time may
a larger disc rest upon a smaller disc.

A recursive procedure has the property that the function itself is called in the procedure. While convenient, recursive procedures may lead to computational inefficiencies. Nevertheless, recursion is frequently the most natural way of expressing a function, and may considerably simplify programming.

The solution of this problem is as follows:

```
*                    THE TOWER OF HANOI GAME
           DEFINE('HANOI(N,NS,ND,NI)')                    :(HANOI.END)
HANOI      EQ(N,0)                                        :S(RETURN)
           HANOI(N - 1,NS,NI,ND)
           OUTPUT = 'MOVE DISC  'N'  FROM  'NS' TO ' ND
           HANOI(N - 1,NI,ND,NS)                          :(RETURN)
HANOI.END
TEST       HANOI(5,'A','C','B')
END
```

In this case N is equal to 5. On entry to the function HANOI, the value of N is compared with zero. If N is zero, no discs are moved, and the function returns. If N is not zero, HANOI is called recursively to move N - 1 discs from the starting needle (NS) to the intermediate storage needle (NI). Having done that, the command to move the Nth disc from the starting needle to the destination needle (ND) is printed. Finally, HANOI is called a second time to move the N - 1 discs from intermediate storage to the destination needle.

The output for this program is as follows:

```
MOVE DISC  1  FROM  A  TO  C
MOVE DISC  2  FROM  A  TO  B
MOVE DISC  1  FROM  C  TO  B
MOVE DISC  3  FROM  A  TO  C
MOVE DISC  1  FROM  B  TO  A
MOVE DISC  2  FROM  B  TO  C
MOVE DISC  1  FROM  A  TO  C
MOVE DISC  4  FROM  A  TO  B
MOVE DISC  1  FROM  C  TO  B
MOVE DISC  2  FROM  C  TO  A
MOVE DISC  1  FROM  B  TO  A
MOVE DISC  3  FROM  C  TO  B
MOVE DISC  1  FROM  A  TO  C
MOVE DISC  2  FROM  A  TO  B
MOVE DISC  1  FROM  C  TO  B
MOVE DISC  5  FROM  A  TO  C
MOVE DISC  1  FROM  B  TO  A
MOVE DISC  2  FROM  B  TO  C
MOVE DISC  1  FROM  A  TO  C
MOVE DISC  3  FROM  B  TO  A
MOVE DISC  1  FROM  C  TO  B
MOVE DISC  2  FROM  C  TO  A
MOVE DISC  1  FROM  B  TO  A
MOVE DISC  4  FROM  B  TO  C
MOVE DISC  1  FROM  A  TO  C
MOVE DISC  2  FROM  A  TO  B
MOVE DISC  1  FROM  C  TO  B
MOVE DISC  3  FROM  A  TO  C
MOVE DISC  1  FROM  B  TO  A
MOVE DISC  2  FROM  B  TO  C
MOVE DISC  1  FROM  A  TO  C
```

Write a program which uses a bubble sort procedure to put given strings in lexical order.

Solution: The function of BUBBLE sort is based on the function of a simple exchange sort, i.e., when an element, compared to the previous, or next one, is found to be out of order, it is moved to a preceding or following place respectively. The described procedure is continuously performed until that element is properly placed. The solution of this problem is as follows:

```
*                 BUBBLE SORT PROGRAM
                  &TRIM = 1
                  DEFINE('SORT(N)I')
                  DEFINE('SWITCH(I)TEMP')
                  DEFINE('BUBBLE(J)')
*                     1
                  N = INPUT                          :F(ERROR)
                  A = ARRAY(N)
*                     2
READ              I = I + 1
                  A<I> = INPUT                        :F(GO)S(READ)
*                     3
GO                SORT(N)
*                     4
                  M = 1
PRINT             OUTPUT = A<M>                       :F(END)
                  M = M + 1                           :(PRINT)
*                     5
SORT              I = LT(I,N-1) I + 1                 :F(RETURN)
                  LGT(A<I>,A<I + 1>)                  :F(SORT)
                  SWITCH(I)
                  BUBBLE(I)                           :(SORT)
SWITCH            TEMP = A<I>
                  A<I> = A<I + 1>
                  A<I + 1> = TEMP                     :(RETURN)
BUBBLE            J = GT(J,1) J - 1                   :F(RETURN)
                  LGT(A<J>,A<J + 1>)                  :F(RETURN)
                  SWITCH(J)                           :(BUBBLE)
END
```

Any statement in SNOBOL IV, starting with an asterisk in column 1, is a comment (or remark) statement. These statements are not executable and are usually used to explain the functions of different parts of the program.

There are three functions used in this program, which are defined in the beginning of the program. Their procedures are given right after the comment numbered 5.

The first card of the input data for this program must contain the number of strings to be sorted, otherwise the program stalls. The part of the program between the comments numbered 1 and 2 reads that number, assigns it to N , and sets up an array of N members. The next program segment (between comments 2 and 3) fills the array with the input items. Notice that counter I is not initialized to zero, because in SNOBOL IV the initial value of the variables is a null string.

The statement between the comments 3 and 4 calls and executes the SORT function. Since the entry point label is omitted in the DEFINE

statement, the computer looks for the statement labeled SORT, as the
initial statement of the function procedure, and finds it right
after the comment 5.
The function LGT(X,Y), included in the second statement of the SORT
function procedure, compares lexically strings X and Y, and
succeeds if X follows Y alphabetically. Thus,

> LGT(SPACE,BLANK)

will succeed, while

> LGT(CAT,DOG)

will fail.
The next two statements of the SORT function procedure call and
execute functions SWITCH and BUBBLE. Function SWITCH makes the two
strings switch their places, while the BUBBLE function compares the
string with the preceding one and switches them around, if needed,
continuously, until the first string is finally properly placed.
Thus, the major function SORT works as follows:

The first statement (I = LT(I,N-1) I + 1) checks if a currently
considered string is numbered 1 through N-1 (there is no need to
specially consider the last string N, because, when the string
N-1 is considered, it is compared with the string numbered N).
The next statement checks the alphabetical order of that string
and the one following it in the array. If the order is correct,
the next string is considered. If the order is wrong, the following string moves up one place, is compared with the next string,
moves up again, if needed, and so on, until it is properly placed.
When all the input items are considered, the program execution
returns to the main part, i.e., to the section between comments 4
and 5 and one by one prints all the input strings in a just arranged
alphabetical order.

	For the input:	3
		COMPUTER
		ARRAY
		BRANCH
THE OUTPUT IS:		ARRAY
		BRANCH
		COMPUTER

CHAPTER 15A

PASCAL

INTRODUCTION TO PASCAL

● **PROBLEM** 15A-1

Explain briefly the background and applications of Pascal.

Solution: Pascal is a modern high-level programming language developed in the early 1970's in Switzerland and named in honor of 17th century French mathematician and inventor Blaise Pascal. Originally intended as a language for teaching structured programming, it is now used for a variety of scientific and commercial applications. An important boost for Pascal has come from its widespread implementation on microcomputers.

Being one of the newest general purpose programming languages, Pascal features modern control structures for sequence, selection, and iteration, which makes it particularly well-suited for structured programming, makes programs readable, and allows for implementation of various data-structures.

● **PROBLEM** 15A-2

What is the structure of a Pascal program?

Solution   A Pascal program consists of the following sections

1. Heading - The first line identifies the program and specifies input and output files.

Program example (input, output);
(All underlined words are reserved words and are required in a given situation.)

2. Label Declarations (optional)

Specifies labels used in the program.

> Label   5, 20;

3. Constant Definitions (optional)

> Defines constants used in the program.
>
> CONST   max = 80;   tax = 0.0825;

4. TYPE Definitions (optional)

> Defines data structures used in the program
>
> TYPE
>   fixed = integer;
>   string = PACKED ARRAY [1..MAX] of CHAR;

5. Variable Declarations

> Declares variables used in the program and their type.
>
> VAR
>   X: integer;
>   TEST: BOOLEAN;
>   NAME: STRING;

6. Subroutine Declarations (optional)

> Declares functions and procedures internal to the main program. Each subroutine may contain some or all of the declarations outlined above, including other subroutines.
>
>   PROCEDURE example1(var param1: real);
>
>   FUNCTION EXAMPLE2(param1: integer): integer;

7. Main body of the program always has the following form:

> BEGIN
>   .
>   .
>   .
>   .
>   .
>   Some
>   Other
>   Statements
>   .
>   .
>   .
> END.

DATA DEFINITION

● **PROBLEM** 15A-3

> Describe the data types available in Pascal.

Solution: Pascal has 4 standard data types.

1. Integer.

   Used to represent signed and unsigned integers.
   ex: -25, 600, 37523

2. Real.

   Used to represent real numbers.
   ex: -7.18, 3.1459, 2.718, 1.414, 17.0

   Also in scientific notation: 3.14E02, 3.14E-02

3. Char.

   Used to represent character data.
   ex: 'a', ' '(blank), '$', ')'

4. Boolean.

   Has only two values - TRUE and FALSE.

In addition to these four standard types, there are enumerated, or user-defined types.

```
ex:  TYPE
        DAYOFWEEK = (sun, mon, tue, wed, thu, fri, sat);
           color = (red, blue, green, yellow);
```

There are also subrange types, which are some ranges of integer, char, or enumerated types.

```
           ex:  TYPE
                   WORKDAY = (mon..fri);
                   Letters = ('A'..'Z');
                    DIGITS = (0..9);
```

All of the above types are scalar types. In addition to these, Pascal also has structured data types, composed of a number of scalar types. Examples are sets, arrays and records.

ARRAYS

● **PROBLEM** 15A-4

> How is an array declared in Pascal? Explain using examples of one-dimensional and multi-dimensional arrays.

Solution: An array is defined as follows:

TYPE
        A = ARRAY [indextype] of basetype;
        where indextype is the type of the array index,
        and basetype is the type of the array elements.
        Indextype can be any scalar type except types in-
        teger and real. Only subranges of integer are
        allowed. Basetype can be any type whatsoever.

        example: TYPE
                        A = ARRAY [1..100] of real;

        This declaration only defines type A as an array
        of 100 real numbers.

Therefore, any variable of type A will be interpreted as an
array of 100 real numbers. Alternatively, any variable
could be declared as an array by:

                VAR
                        table : ARRAY [1..100] of real;

Multidimensional arrays are essentially arrays of arrays.
Thus, having delcared TYPE

                        A = ARRAY [1..100] of real;

we can declare a matrix of size 150 x 100 by the following:

VAR
        matrix : ARRAY [1..150] of A;

This, however, is an unconventional way to declare multidimensional arrays. Usually, the same variable is delcared
by:

        VAR
                matrix : ARRAY [1..150,1..100] of REAL;

The first index parameter always refers to the number of
rows, and second refers to the number of columns. The index
parameters do not have to be of the same data type. Higher-
dimensional arrays can be declared similarly.

● **PROBLEM** 15A-5

Explain the meaning of the following functions:

   a) odd(x)   b) eoln(f)   c) eof(f)

   d) abs(x)   e) trunc(x)   f) round(x)

   g) ord(x)   h) pred(x)   i) succ(x)

Solution: a) The actual parameter of this function is an
integer. ODD(x) returns BOOLEAN value 'true' if integer x

is odd, and 'false' otherwise.
ex: odd(8) = false;   odd(9) = true

b)   eoln(f) returns value 'true' if end of a line in the
     file f has been reached, and 'false' otherwise.

c)   Similarly, returns 'true' if end of file f has been
     reached.

d)   abs(x) computes the absolute value of x.
     ex: abs(-5) = abs(5) = 5

e)   Trunc(x) - truncates the real number x.
     ex: trunc(7.98) = 7,   trunc(3.005) = 3

f)   Round(x) - rounds the real number x to the nearest inte-
     ger.
     ex: Round(7.98) = 8,   Round(3.005) = 3.
     Note that for non-negative values of x, Round (x) =
     trunc(x + 0.5), for negative values Round(x) =
     trunc(x - 0.5).

g)   ord(x) gives ordinal number of the element x in an enumer-
     ated type.   Suppose we have following declaration:

         TYPE
             DAYS = (sun, mon, tue, wed, thu, fri, sat);

     The ord values of such user-defined type are ordered
     starting with 0.   Therefore,

         ord(sun) = 0;   ord(mon) = 1;...ord(sat) = 6.

     The ord function can be applied to standard types such
     as Boolean and char, but the values will be different
     for different machines.

h)   pred(x) returns the value preceding x in an enumerated
     type.

         Thus,   pred(6) = 5,   pred(tue) = mon
                 pred(true) = false,   pred(sun) = undefined

i)   Similarly, succ(x) returns the value following x in an
     enumerated type.
     ex: succ(7) = 8;   succ(tue) = wed
           succ(false) = true,   succ(true) = undefined.

Explain why the following statements or expressions are illegal in Pascal.

   a)   Program compute-tax(input, output);

   b)   Label 2.5, 10;

   c)   CONST K: = 10.5;

   d)   VAR new : integer;

   e)   VAR Q : array [integer] of real;

   f)   VAR A : array [3.5..8.5] of integer;

   g)   TYPE REC = RECORD
                     name:packed array[1..10] of char,
                     age :real;

   h)   Y = 7.5;

   i)   VAR p : integer;
          p : = odd(x)

Solution: a) Program name is an identifier. It must start with a letter and continue with letters or digits only. No hyphen is allowed.

b)   2.5 is an invalid label. A label must be an integer.

c)   Constants are defined, not assigned. The correct form is   CONST K = 10.5;

d)   'New' is a reserved word in Pascal.

e)   The indextype of an array must be a finite subrange. 'Integer' is not a subrange.

f)   An indextype may not be a subrange of real numbers. There are infinitely many real numbers between 3.5 and 8.5.

g)   Each record definition must end with 'END' statement.

h)   Illegal assignment. Should be y:=7.5;

i)   Function odd(x) returns a boolean value, while p is

declared as an integer. Its type must be changed to boolean for the statement to be correct.

PROGRAMS IN PASCAL

Fibbonacci numbers are a sequence of numbers such that the first number is 0, the second number is 1, and each subsequent number is the sum of two preceding numbers, e.g.

$F_1 = 0$

$$Fn = Fn-1 + Fn-2, \quad n \geq 2$$

$F_2 = 1$

Write a Pascal program to print out the first 40 Fibbonacci numbers and their sum.

Solution: We will need five variables for this program:

I - to count the number of iterations. We want only 40 iterations.

SUM - to keep the current sum of numbers.

A,B - the initial two numbers (0 and 1), they will also represent the two predecessors of the current number.

X - stores the current number, the sum of the above two.

```
PROGRAM Fibbonacci (output);


VAR
     A, B, X, I, SUM:integer;

BEGIN
     A:=0;
     B:=1;
     SUM:=0; {initialize the sum and the 2 initial numbers}

     FOR I:=1 to 40 DO {Repeat 40 times}

        BEGIN
            WRITELN (A); {A is the current number}
            SUM:=SUM + A; {Update SUM}
            X:=A + B; {get the next number}
            A:=B;      {A becomes the next predecessor}
            B:=X       {transfer the current number to B}
        END;           {all 40 numbers printed out}

        WRITELN ('The sum of 40 Fibbonacci numbers is', SUM)
END.
```

What is the output of the following program:

```
PROGRAM EXAMPLE (output);

VAR A, B, C, D : integer;

PROCEDURE P1 (a,b,c,d : integer);
BEGIN
     A:=A+B+C;
     B:=C+A
END;

PROCEDURE P2 (a,b:integer; VAR C:integer);
BEGIN
     A:=A+B*C;
     B:=B-A;
     C:=A;
END;

PROCEDURE P3 (VAR a,b : integer);
VAR C : integer;
BEGIN
     C:=10;
     A:=A+C;
     B:=B+D;
     C:=A-B;
END;

BEGIN              {main part of the program}
     A:=1; B:=2; C:=3; D:=4;

     P1(a,b,c,d); writeln(a,b,c,d);

     P2(a,b,c); writeln(a,b,c,d);

     P3(a,b); writeln(a,b,c,d)
END.
```

Solution: The key to understanding what this program does is understanding the difference between calls by reference and calls by value. When procedure P1 is invoked, parameters A,B,C and D are passed to it. Since these parameters are not preceded by <u>VAR</u> in the procedure declaration, these are not variable parameters. This is known as call by value - i.e. only values of these parameters are passed to the procedure, and if their values are changed during the execution of that procedure, these changes do not become permanent. Therefore, executing procedure P1 doesn't really change the values of A, B, C, and D, and the first writeln statement prints 1 2 3 4.

In the second procedure P2, C is variable parameter-meaning that its memory location is passed to the procedure, and consequently, any changes in its value become permanent. This is an example of a call by reference. During the execution of the procedure, A becomes equal to 7, B to -5, and C to 7. Since C is variable parameter, it passes this value back to the variable C in the main program. The output after second WRITELN statement is then 1   2   7   4.

In the third procedure P3, C is declared as a local variable, and in all subsequent references to it within that procedure it is treated as such, having nothing to do with the C in the main program. Executing the statements of the procedure, we get: C:=10; A:=11, B:=6; C:=+5. A and B are variable parameters, their values are passed back to the calling variables. C is a local variable, which is "lost" after the procedure is executed, the value of C in the main program remains 7, and D retains its original value of 4. So the output of the final writeln statement is 11   6   7   4.

● **PROBLEM** 15A-9

What is the output of the following program?

```
    PROGRAM TEST (output);
    VAR I, J, K, COUNT : integer;
    BEGIN
        I:=1; J:=2; K:=3; count:=1;
        writeln (I div J, K mod J);
        while count < = 3 DO
          BEGIN
              If I < J then
              If K > J then
              If (K > I) or (I=J) then
              writeln (I)
              ELSE
                writeln (J)
              ELSE
                writeln (K);
              CASE COUNT OF
                    1:   J:=0;
                    2:   BEGIN
                            K:=K-1;
                            J:=J+K
                         END;

                    3:  I:=2*I;
              END;
              count:=count+1;
        END {while count.....}
    END.
```

Solution: The first line of output will be the results of two operations: I div J and K mod J. The first is integer division; giving the number of times I contains J. Substituting values for I and J we get 1 div 2 = 0. K mod J is defined as K-(K div J)*J, or the remainder we get when dividing K by J. 3 mod 2 = 1 Thus the first line of output is 0 1. Then, the program enters the WHILE Loop with I=1, J=2, K=3 and count=1. The first statement is true, so the THEN part

is executed. The second IF statement is also true, so the
control passes to its THEN part. For the third IF statement
to be true, at least one of the conditions, i.e. either K>I
or I=J, or both must be true. This is the case, so writeln
(I) is executed, outputting 1. Then control passes to the
CASE statement. Since COUNT=1, the statement corresponding
to 1 is executed, and J becomes equal to 0. Count is then
incremented and becomes equal to 2, going back to the beginning of the loop. Count is less than 3, so we go through the
loop again. The first IF statement is false this time, and
there is no ELSE part corresponding to it. Note that an
ELSE always corresponds to the last 'open' IF before it.
Thus the first ELSE statement corresponds to the third IF
and the second ELSE to the second IF, and there is no ELSE
corresponding to the first IF. Therefore control now passes
to the CASE statement, without printing out anything. This
time count=2, so the group of statements corresponding to 2
is executed, setting K to 2, and J to 2 (it had value 0 before). Count is then incremented to 3, which is <=3, so
we go through the loop again, with I=1, J=2, K=2, count=3.
The first IF statement is true, the second is not, so the
second ELSE is executed, printing out the value of k - 2.
Control then passes to the case statement, and the expression corresponding to 3 (the current value of count)
is executed setting I to 2. Count then becomes 4, and the
loop terminates. The total output of the program is:

              0   1

              1

              2

● **PROBLEM** 15A-10

Array A contains all odd integers from 1 to 100 (e.g.
1,3,5,7,.....99) in random order, and is declared as
follows:

        TYPE ARRAYTYPE = ARRAY [1..50] of integer;
        VAR A : ARRAYTYPE;

Write a short procedure that will accept A and return
an array with the same elements in sorted, increasing
order.

Solution: The key here is to recognize the relationship between the indices and the elements of the array. Thus,
given an element e, we can compute its correct place in the
array - let's call it X, from the following formula:

        X:=e div 2+1;

This is, then, the procedure:

```
    PROCEDURE SORT(A:ARRAYTYPE; VAR B:ARRAYTYPE);
    VAR i,X:integer;
    BEGIN
        FOR i:=1 to 50 DO
        BEGIN
            X:=A[i]div 2+1;
            B[x]:=A[i]
        END
    END;
```

Let's simulate this procedure for an Array of 5 elements containing odd integers from 1 to 10 in random order:

A | 7 | 9 | 3 | 5 | 1 |

    When i=1, x=A[1]div 2+1 = 7 div 2+1 =4.
            B[4]:=A[1]=7

The array B now looks:

| | | | 7 | |

at step 2, i=2, x=A[2]div 2+1 = 5
B[5]:=9. Array B now looks: | | | | 7 | 9 |

At step 3, i=3, x=3 div 2+1 = 2
B[2]:=3. | | 3 | | 7 | 9 |

For i=4, x=5 div 2+1 = 3
B[3]:=5. | | 3 | 5 | 7 | 9 |

Finally, for i=5, x=1 div 2+1 = 1
B[1]:=1. Now array B is in sorted increasing order:

| 1 | 3 | 5 | 7 | 9 |

The procedure works exactly like this for larger numbers.

● **PROBLEM** 15A-11

What is the output of the following program? What is
the significance of the numbers produced? What algorithm is being used to produce them?

```
    PROGRAM MYSTERY (output);
    VAR A:ARRAY[1..30]of integer;
        J,K,FLAG:Integer;
    BEGIN
        FOR J:=1 to 30 DO A[J]:=1;
        FLAG:=1; J:=1;
        WHILE FLAG = 1 DO BEGIN
```

```
              J:=J+1;
          while A[j]=0 DO J:=J+1;
          IF J=30   then FLAG=0
          ELSE BEGIN
              writeln(J);
              K:=J+J;
          while K<30 DO BEGIN
              A[K]:=0;
              K:=K+J
          END
      END
   END
END.
```

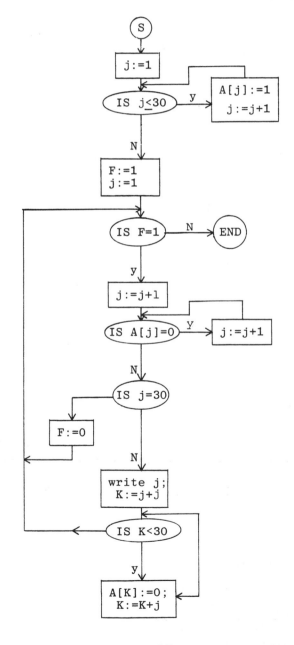

Solution: In order to determine the output of a program, it must be carefully simulated. The first executable statement of the above program, sets all elements of the array A to 1. Then, entering the WHILE Loop, J becomes 2. A[J] is not 0, so we go on to the next statement. J is not 30, and the ELSE part is executed. The value of J, 2, is printed out, K becomes 4. Entering the WHILE K<30 DO...Loop, A[4] becomes 0, K becomes 6, which is less than 30, so again A[6]=0, K=8, A[8]=0, etc. In other words, elements in all even positions starting with 4 are set to 0. When K becomes 30, the loop will terminate, returning control back to first loop. Flag is 1, so it enters the loop again, J becomes 3, A[3] is not 0, J is not 30, so 3 is printed out, K becomes 6, and similarly to the previous iteration, all muliples of 3 become 0. When K reaches 30, the control is transferred back to Loop 1. Flag is still 1, J becomes 4. A[4] is 0, J is incremented to 5, A[5] is not 0, so the second loop terminates, and the ELSE part of the next statement is executed. 5 is printed out, K becomes 10, and now all multiples of 5 are set to 0. By now, it should be clear that the program is printing out prime numbers, using the following algorithm: Set all elements of the Array to 1. Starting with J=2 if A[J] is 0, then J is a prime. Print it out and set all multiples of it to 0. Increment J by 1 and repeat the same procedure.

● **PROBLEM** 15A-12

What are Packed arrays? How do they differ from conventional arrays?

Solution: The reserved word Packed instructs the compiler to store the values of the array in memory in the most compact way. Usually, values of types char and boolean do not occupy the entire memory location provided for them. Since each element of an array of such types occupies a separate memory location, this results in a considerable waste of memory space. When PACKED ARRAY representation is used, the values are packed together as closely as possible, ignoring the borders between memory location. Therefore, a packed array takes up much less memory space than one that is not packed. On the other hand, the time required to access each individual element of an array is greatly increased, since the computer not only has to locate the memory location storing the desired value, it must also separate it from other values sharing the same memory location. Thus, what is gained in terms of memory space is lost in terms of increased processing time. This trade-off varies considerably from one machine to another, and even from one Pascal implementation to another. So the decision whether or not to use packed arrays should take that into account, as well as the requirements of the specific problem under consideration.

● **PROBLEM** 15A-13

Explain how character strings are declared and manipulated in Pascal. Give examples.

Solution: Unlike some other programming languages, Pascal has no facilities for explicit declaration of character strings. Instead, Packed arrays of characters are used to define character strings. Since the length of an array must be known at compilation time, only strings of fixed length are allowed. Thus, if we define

```
TYPE
     STRING=PACKED ARRAY[1..10] of char;
VAR
     WORD:string;
```

then the variable WORD can be assigned any value consisting of exactly ten characters. The following assignments are valid:

WORD:='HELLOⱨⱨⱨⱨⱨ';

WORD:='GOODⱨBYEⱨⱨ';

WORD:='CHARACTERS';

WORD:='#123456789'

and the following are not:

WORD:='HELLO'

WORD:='WORD'

WORD:='AVERYLONGWORD'

When a variable declared as packed array of characters appears in a WRITE or WRITELN statement, the entire array is written out. For example, the effect of these two statements

WORD:='HELLOⱨⱨⱨⱨⱨ'

writeln(word);

will be   HELLOⱨⱨⱨⱨⱨ

However, to read in a character string, the only possibility is character by character, and then only if the length of the string is exactly equal to the length of the array holding it. Thus, to read in a ten-character word, we would write

FOR I:=1 to 10 DO READ(word[I]);

Character strings can also be compared. For example, the boolean variable P will have value 'true' after the execution of any of these statements.

P:='ALEX' < 'JILL'

P:='JOHNⱨⱨⱨ' < 'JOHNSON'

P:='ZITO' > 'MARY'

P:='JACK'='JACK'

As we have seen in the previous problem, character strings in Pascal have fixed length. However, we treat a string as having a varying length if we ignore all trailing blanks. Consider, for example, the following implementation:

```
CONST STRSIZE=80;

TYPE STRING=RECORD

          WORD:PACKED ARRAY[1..STRSIZE] of
                                      CHAR;

          length:1..strsize

     END;
```

where the field length represents the position of the last non-trailing-blank character. For example, the string 'HELLObbb...' has length 5 and 75 trailing blanks, and the string 'GOODbbbBYEbbbb....' has length 10 and 70 trailing blanks. Assuming the above definitions, write

```
PROCEDURE SUBSTRING(S1:STRING;var S2:string; p,n:integer);
```

which copies the first n characters, starting with position p in the string S1 into string S2. For example, if S1='ABCDEFGHIJbbbb....', then after substring (S1, S2,4,3) S2 becomes 'DEFbbb....'.

Solution: PROCEDURE SUBSTRING(S1:string; var S2:string, p, n:integer);

```
VAR I,J:integer;
BEGIN
     IF (P+N-1) > strsize then
         writeln('ERROR-SUBSTRING is out of RANGE')
         {check to see if desired substring is within
          the first one}

     ELSE BEGIN

          J:=1;    {initial position of the second string}

          FOR I:=P to P+N-1 DO {start copying with position p}

          BEGIN
             S2.WORD[J]:=S1.WORD[I]
             J:=J+1;   {increment position count for 2 string}
          END;   {all required characters copied, pad the rest
                    of the string S2 with blanks}
          S2.length:=J-1;

          FOR I:=J to strsize  DO S2.WORD[I]:=' '
     END
END;
```

Assuming the same declarations as in Problem 14, write

    PROCEDURE CONCAT(S1,S2:string; var S3:string)

which concatenates strings S1 and S2 and puts the result
in S3.

Solution: To concatenate strings S1 and S2 means to create
a new string which consists of S1 and S2 appended to it.   In
the following program, the lengths of the two strings are
first added to see if the resulting string could fit in the
array "housing" it, which can hold only 80 characters.   If
this is the case, S3 is first set to S1, and then, starting
with position S1.length+1, the significant characters of
S2 are copied into S3.

```
PROCEDURE CONCAT(S1,S2:string:VAR S3:string);

Var
    I:integer;

BEGIN
    IF(S1.length+S2.length)>strsize THEN
      writeln('concatenation impossible-strings too
                long')

    ELSE
      BEGIN
        FOR I:=1 TO S1·length DO
          S3·Word[I]:= S1·Word[I];

        FOR I:=1 TO S2·length DO
          S3·Word[S1·length+I]:=S2·Word[I];
      END

END;
```

Assuming the same declarations as in Problem 14, write

    PROCEDURE INSERT(var S1:string; S2:string, p:integer);

which inserts string S2 into string S1 after position
p.

Solution: This is a more generalized version of the CONCAT
Procedure.   First, as usual, we check to see if the array of
size 80 can accomodate both strings.   If not, we print out
the error message.   Otherwise, we move last (length 1-p)
elements forward by the length of the second string.   This
prepares space for the insertion of the second string.   This
operation is accomplished by the first FOR loop.   Then, by
the second FOR loop, we actually move S2 into S1, starting
with position p+1.   Again, note that I-p indicates the current position of the character in S2 to be copied into S1.

The only thing remaining then is to adjust the length of the string S1.

```
PROCEDURE INSERT (var S1:string; S2:string);

VAR I:integer;
BEGIN
      IF (S1.length + S2.length)>strsize then
        writeln('insertion impossible-strings too long')
      ELSE
        BEGIN
           FOR I:=S1.length downto p+1 DO
             S1.WORD[I+S2.length]:=S1.WORD[I];

           FOR I:=p+1 to p+S2.length DO
             S1.WORD[I]:=S2.WORD[I-p];
           S1.length:=S1.length + S2.length
        END
   END;
```

● **PROBLEM** 15A-17

What are nested records? How is the WITH statement used with them? Illustrate by designing the data structure for the following problem: A school wishes to send to each of its 1,000 students the end-of-semester report, showing the courses taken and the grades received. Assume each student takes 4 courses, the name of the course is at most 80 characters long, and the grades are integers between 0 and 100. Each report must also include student's full name, address and the date of first attendance. Show how the information can be accessed in the program.

Solution: Nested Records are Records, whose fields are other records. Such records are needed to design complex data structures, such as for this problem. We know that the record must contain information on student's name, address, starting date, and grades. These are obvious choices for the fields of the record. Each of these fields must also contain sub-fields. Thus, under name, we must specify first, middle, and last name. The ADDRESS field must contain number and street, city, state and zip code. Starting date must include the date, which is an integer in the range of 1 to 31, the month and the year. The GRADEREPORT FIELD must contain the description of 4 courses and the grade associated with each. So we would need an array of 4 records - one for each course. Then the record might look like this:

```
TYPE
    STUDENTREC=RECORD

              NAME=RECORD
                    FIRST,
                    Middle,
                    Last:packed array[1..15] of char;
                  END;
              ADDRESS=RECORD
```

```
                      Number:integer;
                      Street,
                      City,
                      State:packed array[1..20] of char;
                      Zip:integer
                  END;
         STARTDATE=RECORD
                  DATE:1..31;
                  month:(jan,feb,mar,apr,may,jun,jul,
                         aug,sep,oct,nov,dec);
                  year:integer
                  END;
         GRADEREPORT:ARRAY[1..4] of
                      RECORD
                      COURSENAME=packed array[1..80]
                             of char;
                      GRADE:1..100
                      END
    END;
```

Since there are 1,000 such records, declare

VAR
     ALLRECORDS:ARRAY[1..1000]of STUDENTREC.

Here's how to initialize the complete record of, say, 66 th
student:

```
         With ALLRECORDS[66] DO

             BEGIN
                 NAME.FIRST:='JOHN       ';
                 NAME. LAST:='DOE         ';
                 NAME.MIDDLE:='PETER      ';

         With ADDRESS DO

             BEGIN
                 NUMBER:=10;
                 STREET:='PUDDLE LANE    ';
                 CITY:='New York        ';
                 STATE:='New York       ';
                 ZIP:=10010;
             END

             Startdate.DATE:=1;
             Startdate.month:=Jan;
             Startdate.year:=1981;
         GRADEREPORT[1].COURSENAME:='MATH 101    ';
         GRADEREPORT[1].GRADE:=85;
                 .
                 .
                 etc.
    END ;
```

The with statement is used instead of writing the field
designators all the time.

    Thus, without the first WITH statement, we would have
to write ALLRECORDS[66]. for each item.

Write a program to find the prime numbers between 1 and 50.

Solution: The classical algorithm for enumerating prime numbers is the sieve of Eratosthenes. Suppose that the prime numbers less than 10 are to be found. The prime numbers less than 10 can be found by writing down the numbers from 2 to 10:

2 3 4 5 6 7 8 9 10

Then the lowest number is to be removed claiming that it is prime. The multiples of 2 are also to be removed. After the first step, 2 is a prime, and the sieve contains odd numbers only.

3 5 7 9.

After the second step, 3 is a prime, and only 5 and 7 remain in the sieve. The process terminates when the sieve is empty.

Declare

CONST

maximum = 100000

VAR

Sieve:PACKED ARRAY[2..maximum] of boolean;

Initially, each component of sieve is to be set to 'true' indicating that all the numbers are present. As the numbers are removed, the corresponding components are set to 'false'. The program consists of two nested loops, one to find the lowest number still in the sieve, and the other to remove its multiples. The termination condition for the outer loop is that there are no numbers left in the sieve, and it can be expedited by maintaining a count of the numbers currently in the sieve. The program is given below.

```
PROGRAM prime numbers (input, output);
   CONST

     firstprime = 2;
     maximum = 100000;

   VAR
     sieve:PACKED ARRAY[firstprime..maximum]of boolean;

     Leftin, range, factor, multiple:0..maximum;

   BEGIN
     read(range);

     FOR factor:=firstprime To range DO
```

```
            sieve [factor]:=true;
     Leftin:=range - firstprime +1;
     factor:=firstprime - 1;
     REPEAT
          factor:=factor + 1;
          IF sieve[factor]
            THEN {factor is prime}
               BEGIN
                  writeln(factor);
                  multiple:=1;
                     WHILE factor * multiple ≤ range   DO
                        BEGIN
                           IF sieve[factor * multiple]
                             THEN {remove multiple}
                               BEGIN
                                 sieve[factor * multiple]:=false;

                                 leftin:=leftin - 1
                               END;

                           Multiple:=multiple + 1
                        END {while}

               END

        UNTIL leftin = 0

      END. {primenumbers}
  Input:
       50
  Output:
       2          41
       3
       5          43
       7
      11          47
      13
      17
      19
      23
      29
      31
      37
```

Write a program to count the number of letters and
digits in the input data.

Solution: PROGRAM CHARACTERCOUNT (INPUT, OUTPUT);

VAR

   LETTERCOUNT, DIGITCOUNT:INTEGER;

   CH : CHAR;

BEGIN

LETTERCOUNT:=0;

DIGITCOUNT:=0;

WHILE NOT EOF (INPUT) DO

   BEGIN

   READ (CH);

IF ('A'<=CH) AND (CH<='Z') OR

   ('a'<=CH) AND (CH<='z') THEN

      LETTERCOUNT:=LETTERCOUNT + 1

ELSE IF ('0'<=CH) AND (CH<='9') THEN

      DIGITCOUNT:=DIGITCOUNT + 1

END;

   WRITELN (LETTERCOUNT, 'LETTERS', DIGITCOUNT, 'DIGITS.')

END.

This program assumed that, in the lexicographic ordering,
every character between 'A' and 'Z', both inclusive is an
upper-case letter, and every character between 'a' and 'z'
both inclusive is a lower-case letter. This assumption is
valid in most character sets including ASCII, but it is not
strictly valid in the EBCDIC character set where certain
"control characters" occur among the letters. These control
characters are unlikely to occur in normal data, however, so
the assumption is not a bad one.

     The program also assumes that every character between
"0" and "9" inclusive is a digit. This assumption is in
fact valid in every character set..

Write a function to compute the Legendre polynomials.

Solution: For positive values of n, the recursive definition
to compute the Legendre polynomials is given by

$$P_n(x) = \begin{cases} 1 & \text{if } n=0 \\ x & \text{if } n=1 \\ \left((2n-1)x\, P_{n-1}(x)-(n-1)P_{n-2}(x)\right)\Big/n & \text{if } n>1 \end{cases}$$

we obtain:

```
Function P(n:integer; x:real) :real;
   BEGIN
     IF n=0
       THEN p:=1
     ELSE IF n=1
       THEN p:=x
     ELSE p:=((2*n-1)*x*p(n-1,x)-(n-1)*p(n-2,x))/n
   END;
```

In most of the cases, however, the recursive solution is not
the best because a simple solution may be obtained by iteration. The Legendre polynomials are more efficiently computed
in this way:

```
FUNCTION p(n:integer; x:real) :real;
   VAR
     prev, this, next :real;
                 count:integer;
   BEGIN
     IF n=0
       THEN p:=1
     ELSE IF n=1
       THEN p:=x
     ELSE
       BEGIN
         prev:=1;
         this:=x;
         FOR COUNT:=2  TO n DO
             BEGIN
               next:=((2*count-1)*x* this
                      -(count-1)*prev)/count;

               prev:=this;

       this:=next
       END; {for}
     p:=next
   END
END; {p}
```

Write a program, incorporating the function TAN, to compute tangents of angles 0,10,20,....,360 degrees.

Solution: PROGRAM TABLEOFTANS (OUTPUT);

```
CONST
  PI = 3.1415926536;

VAR

  DEGREES:INTEGER;

FUNCTION TAN (x:REAL):REAL;

  BEGIN
```

$$TAN:=sin(x)\Big/cos(x)$$

```
  END;(*TAN*)

BEGIN(*TABLEOFTANS*)

DEGREES:=o;

WHILE DEGREES<=360 DO

  BEGIN

  WRITE(DEGREES);

  IF DEGREES MOD 180 = 90 THEN

    WRITELN('INFINITY')

  ELSE

    WRITELN(TAN(DEGREES*PI/180));

  DEGREES:=DEGREES + 10

  END

END. (*TABLEOFTANS*).
```

Write a procedure which reads a matrix of non-negative integers and stores it in an array of type

MATRICES = ARRAY [1 . . XSIZE, 1 . . YSIZE] of
                              NONNEGINTEGER

where XSIZE and YSIZE are appropriately defined constants and NONNEGINTEGER is an appropriately defined type.

Solution: To guard against the possibility of the input data being incomplete (or there being too much input data), the matrix elements are assumed to be followed by a negative endmarker. The procedure checks every datum and, if it detects the endmarker prematurely, it writes a warning message and stops immediately.

```
      PROCEDURE READMATRIX (VAR MATRIX:MATRICES;
                            VAR VALID:BOOLEAN);

      LABEL 99;

      VAR

        DATUM:INTEGER;

        X:1 . . XSIZE;
        Y:1 . . YSIZE;

      BEGIN

      VALID:=FALSE;   (*being pessimistic!*)

      FOR X:=1 To XSIZE  DO

        FOR Y:=1 To YSIZE  DO

          BEGIN

          READ (DATUM);

      IF DATUM>=o  THEN

          MATRIX [X,Y] :=DATUM

      ELSE   (*the endmarker has been read *)

          BEGIN

          WRITELN ('DATA INCOMPLETE');

          GOTO 99;  (* leave the procedure immediately *)

          END

      END;

READ (DATUM);  (*.....this should be the endmarker *)

IF DATUM>=o  THEN

      WRITELN ('TOO MUCH DATA')

ELSE

      VALID:=TRUE;

99:

END.(* READMATRIX *)
```

The function of program copydeck is to copy a deck of cards, reading from the file indeck and writing to the file outdeck. Blank cards in indeck are not copied to outdeck. Write the program copydeck to copy a deck of cards.

Solution:

```
PROGRAM copydeck (indeck, outdeck, output);

   CONST
     maxcol=80;
      blank=' ';

   TYPE
     colindex=1 . . maxcol;
     card=PACKED ARRAY [colindex] of char;
     cardfile=FILE of card;

   VAR
     indeck, outdeck : cardfile;
     buffer, blankcard : card;

     column : colindex;

   BEGIN
     For column:=1  To  maxcol  DO
       blankcard[column]:=blank;
     reset(indeck);
     rewrite(outdeck);
     WHILE NOT eof (indeck)  DO
       BEGIN
         read(indeck, buffer);
         IF buffer<>blankcard
           THEN write (outdeck, buffer)
         END  {while}
   END. {copydeck}
```

● **PROBLEM** 15A-24

A building society lends money to house purchasers subject to a monthly payment of one per cent of the amount borrowed. This payment covers both capital repayment and interest due, interest being charged at a rate of eight per cent per annum, calculated monthly. Write a program which reads in the amount of a loan, tabulates the series of payments required, as a four column table showing the payment number, the interest due that month, the capital repayment that month, and the outstanding capital balance. The table should also show the final non-standard payment required to complete the payment.

Solution:

PROGRAM LOANPAYMENT (INPUT, OUTPUT);

```
(* This program reads in the amount of a loan *)

(* and prints the repayment table showing *)

(* the payment number, the monthly interest, *)

(* the interest repayment, and the residual *)

(* balance.                                *)

CONST ANNUALRATE = 8;  (* per cent *)

VAR NUMBER : 1 . . MAXINT;

    INTEREST, REPAYMENT,

    LOAN, PAYMENT, RESIDUE, MONTHRATE:REAL;

BEGIN

    READ (LOAN);

    WRITE ('AMOUNT BORROWED =', LOAN:12:2);

    PAYMENT := LOAN/100;

    WRITELN (' ':10, 'MONTHLY REPAYMENT =', PAYMENT:10:2);

    WRITELN; WRITELN;

    WRITELN ('NUMBER INTEREST REPAYMENT RESIDUE');WRITELN;

    MONTHRATE:=ANNUALRATE/100/12;

    NUMBER:=1;

    RESIDUE:=LOAN;

    REPEAT

     INTEREST:=MONTHRATE*RESIDUE;

     REPAYMENT:=PAYMENT-INTEREST;

     RESIDUE:=RESIDUE-REPAYMENT ;

     WRITELN(NUMBER:7, INTEREST:10:2,REPAYMENT:10:2,RESIDUE:10:2);

     NUMBER:=NUMBER+1

    UNTIL RESIDUE+RESIDUE*MONTHRATE<=PAYMENT;

    WRITELN;WRITELN;

    WRITELN ('LAST PAYMENT=', RESIDUE+RESIDUE*MONTHRATE:10:2)

END.
```

Write a program which reads an input text and prints out
the number of occurences of each adjacent letter pair
which appears within the text.

Solution:

    PROGRAM NUMBEROFOCCURENCESOFADJACENTPAIRS (INPUT,OUTPUT);

    (* This program reads an input text and *)

    (* prints out the number of occurences of *)

    (* each adjacent letter pair which appears within *)

    (* the text. This program assumes that the *)

    (* letters A to Z are 26 consecutive values *)

    (* of the type char.   *)

    TYPE letter = 'A' . . 'Z';
VAR COUNT:Array [Letter, Letter] of o . . Maxint;

    FIRST, SECOND : LETTER;

    Thisch, Lastch : char;

    Lastwasletter : Boolean;
BEGIN

    For First:='A' To 'Z' DO

    For second:='A' To 'Z' DO

        COUNT [First, second]:=o;

    While not EOF (input) DO

    BEGIN

        Lastwasletter:=False; (* At the start of a line *)

        While not EOLN (Input) DO

        BEGIN

        Read (Thisch); write (Thisch);
If (Thisch>='A') and (Thisch<='Z')
Then if lastwasletter

        Then count[Lastch, Thisch]:=count[Lastch, Thisch]+1

532-27

```
        Else lastwasletter:=True

Else lastwasletter:=False;

lastch:=Thisch

End;


Readln;writeln

End;


writeln;writeln;

writeln ('occurences of letter pairs.....');


For First :='A' to 'Z'  DO

For second:='A' to 'Z'  DO

    IF COUNT [First, second]<>o

    Then writeln (First, second, '-', count[First, second]:4)

End.
```

● **PROBLEM** 15A-26

A factory produces bars whose exact length is unknown
until after production. Its cutting shop receives
orders for cut lengths of bar which must be met by
cutting up the manufactured bars. For a given manufactured bar of length 'L' a set 'C' of orders is chosen
from the order list, which can be met by cutting up
this bar, and with minimum wastage. Design a recursive
back-tracking procedure which will construct 'C' for
given 'L' and order list.

Incorporate the procedure in a program which constructs 'C' from the following order list

order 1	773	mm
order 2	548	mm
order 3	65	mm
order 4	929	mm
order 5	548	mm
order 6	163	mm

```
        order 7            421 mm

        order 8             37 mm

and a manufactured bar length L = 1848 mm.
```

Solution:

```
  PROGRAM SETOFORDERS (input, output);

  (* This program reads a bar length and a *)

  (* list of outstanding orders for lengths to be *)

  (* cut from such bars, and chooses  by *)

  (* recursive trial and error  the set of *)

  (* ordered lengths that should be cut to minimize *)

  (* bar wastage.                              *)

  CONST  Maxsizeoforderlist = 20;

  TYPE orders = 1 . . Maxsizeoforderlist;

       orderset = set of orders;

  VAR  sizeoforderlist : orders;

       Bestset : orderset;

       Bestlength, L:o . . Maxint;

  Length:Array [orders] of 1 . . Maxint;

  I:orders;

  (* sets are used to describe the trial *)

  (* solution, best solution, and potential components, *)
```

```
     (* The length of the orders are held in the *)

     (* array length.                            *)

     (* Best set contains the indices in length of *)

     (* the orders making up the best solution *)

     (* found so far.                          *)

     (* Best length denotes the total length of *)

     (* the orders in bestset.                  *)

PROCEDURE   CONSIDER (Triallength:integer;
                      orderchosen,ordersremaining:orderset);

     (* Triallength denotes the total length of *)

     (* orders currently in the set orderchosen.*)

     (* orderchosen is a set whose members are  *)

     (* the indices in length of the orders in  *)

     (* the current trial solution.             *)

     (* ordersremaining is a set whose members  *)

     (* are the indices in length of the orders *)

     (* available for incorporation into the trail *)

     (* solution.                              *)

VAR   x: 0 . . Maxsizeoforderlist;

BEGIN

     IF triallength < = L
```

```
Then begin

    If triallength > bestlength

then begin

    bestlength := Triallength;

    bestset    := orderchosen

  End;

x:=o;

while ordersremaining < > [ ] DO

Begin

Repeat X:=X+1 until x in ordersremaining;

ordersremaining:=ordersremaining - [x];

consider (Triallength+length[x],
          orderchosen + [x],ordersremaining)

End

End
End;  (*improve*)
Begin

    Read(L);  writeln ('Manufactured bar length is', L:5,'MM');

    writeln; writeln('orderlist is');

    Read(sizeoforderlist);

    For I:=1  to sizeoforderlist   DO

    Begin read (length[I]); writeln(length[I],'MM')END;
```

```
    Bestlength :=o; Bestset := [ ];
(* Initially, trial set is empty and all *)
(* orders are available for inclusion in the *)
(* trial solution.                            *)
consider  (o,[ ] , [1 . . sizeoforderlist]);
writeln; writeln ('optimal set of orders');
For I:=1 to sizeoforderlist  DO
If I in bestset then writeln (length[I]:6,'MM');
writeln; writeln ('wastage=', L-Bestlength:4, 'MM')
End.
```

CHAPTER 15B

C LANGUAGE

INTRODUCTION TO C

● **PROBLEM** 15B-1

Write a skeletal format of C programs.

Solution: The following figure provides a skeletal format of C programs. The terms appearing within the square brackets, [ ], are optional. They can be omitted from the programs if they are not required.

    [constant declarations]

    [externals]

    main ( )

    {

    [program statements]

    }

    [additional functions]

● **PROBLEM** 15B-2

Write a program segment in C to display the following message:

        Hi from C

        C is a unique and exciting language

Solution: To display the above message the program segment is as follows:

```
main ( )

{

printf ("Hi from C\n");

printf ("C is a unique and exciting language");

}
```

The \n in the first printf ( ) statement is an escape sequence that causes the output line to be advanced. If it is not included then the program segment becomes,

```
main ( )

{

printf ("Hi from C");

printf ("C is a unique and exciting language);

}
```

and will output both messages on the same line as follows:

Hi from CC is a unique and exciting language

● **PROBLEM** 15B-3

Locate five distinct errors in the following program:

```
main

*this program prints the message*

*Hi from C on the screen*

printf ("Hi from C\n")

};
```

Solution:

1st error:

main is a function and the format (of main) is:

main ( )

2nd error:

The executable part of the function is always to be enclosed in braces { }. These braces are analogous to the 'begin-end'of Pascal, 'DO-END' of PL/I, etc.

In the given program, the terminal brace, }, is present, but the initial is missing. The initial brace, { , has to be placed in the beginning of the second line, before the first *.

3rd error:

C recognizes everything enclosed by /* and */ as a comment. There are two distinct ways by which the above given information i.e.

> *this program prints the message*

> *Hi from C on the screen*

can be represented.

1st method:

/*this program prints the message*/

/*Hi from C on the screen*/

2nd method:

/*this program prints the message

  Hi from C on the screen*/

Both the above mentioned methods are correct.

4th error:
In the statement

> printf ("Hi from C\n")

semicolon (;) at the end of line has not been given. This semicolon serves as a statement terminator to signal the compiler where an instruction ends.

5th error:
Semicolon placed after the end of main i.e.

> };

is wrong. Right brace just defines the end of function main in

this example and is never followed by a semicolon.

Therefore the correct program segment is:

> main ( )

> {

> /*this program prints the message

```
    Hi from C on the screen*/

printf ("Hi from C\n");

}
```
● **PROBLEM** 15B-4

What is the output for each of the following?

a.   printf ("%4d", 666.33);

b.   printf ("%05d", 668);

c.   putchar (67);

d.   printf ("%x", 30);

Solution: The output is as follows:

a.   Since 'd' is used for decimal integer values, the fractional part is truncated.   Therefore output is: ⌀666.

b.   Output is: 00668
     Since the width defined for 'd' is 05, hence two leading zeros.

c.   Output is: C
     67 in ASCII is C because in character I/O the data interpretation is based upon ASCII representation.

d.   Output is: 1E
     The function printf recognizes %x for hexadecimal.   So output is 1E since hexadecimal value of 30 is 1E.

● **PROBLEM** 15B-5

What is the output of the following program?

```
    main ( )
    {
      int x = 5;
      int y = 5;
      printf ("%d%d\n", x++, x);
      printf ("%d%d\n", ++y, y);
    }
```

Solution: Here it is important to distinguish between the two styles of increment operations.

1) x++: Use variable x first and then increment afterwards.

   eg. let

       z = x++;

   means

       z = x;

       x = x + 1;

2) ++y: Increment the variable y first and then use it afterwards. eg. let

   z = ++y;

   means

   y = y + 1;

   z = y;

   Therefore the output is as follows:

       5   6   /* 1st printf */

       6   5   /* 2nd printf */

VARIABLE NAME AND TYPE DEFINITION

● **PROBLEM** 15B-6

How many characters can variable names contain in C? How many letters are significant?

Solution: Variable names in C are made of letters and digits. The first character must be a letter. The underscore _ counts as a letter. Only the first eight characters of the variable name are significant. Eg., in case of the two given variables,

        value_of_1   and

        value_of_2,

C will interpret these two variable names as equivalent, i.e. referencing a variable called value_of, since their length is over eight.

● **PROBLEM** 15B-7

How does the <u>typedef</u> statement increase portability?

In C new data types can be created using <u>typedef</u> statement. Once a type is defined, it can be used in the same manner as the standard C types.

The main advantage of using <u>typedef</u> statement is for portability of code, i.e. code which can be run without change on a variety of hardware.

Some machines define the type int to contain 16 bits while other machines provide 32 bits. If we create a type called integer based on the word-size of the machine, then we can define all our integer variables in terms of this type. This is done as follows:

```
typedef long int integer;

main ( )

{

   integer x;

   integer y;

   /*statements*/

}
```

Two things are to be noted:

1) <u>typedef</u> statement is defined outside the main.

2) Qualifier <u>long</u> tells the compiler to use two words (32 bits) for storage.

Now if we want the same program to run on 16-bit machine instead of modifying variables x, y, and z, all we have to do is modify the <u>typedef</u> i.e.

```
typedef long int integer;
```

          change to

```
typedef int integer;
```

All the following integer type statements in the program will be changed automatically.

ARRAYS, LOOPS AND THEIR IMPLEMENTATION
● PROBLEM 15B-8

What is wrong in the following array declaration?

```
int my_array (200);
```

Solution: Arrays in C are created based on the four data types (int, char, float or double). The basic format of an array declaration is as follows:

<array's_type><variable_name>[number_of_subscripts];

The items appearing above i.e. array's_type and variable_name and number_of_subscripts have to be provided to declare an array. < > brackets are used only for identity purpose, but they are restricted in C (used only in defining directories).

If we check the above statement,

int my_array (200);

we note that individual items are as follows:

int: array's_type

my_array: variable_name

200: number_of_subscripts.

But the standard notation of enclosing number_of_subscripts in square brackets i.e. [ ], instead of which ( ) has been used, is missing. Therefore the correct declaration is:

int my_array [200];

● **PROBLEM** 15B-9

Write a program that

a) Reads a string from the keyboard one character at a time into an array. Maximum length of the string is 60 characters.

b) It invokes the routine printf ( ) to output the string entered.

c) It also counts the no. of characters the string contained.

Solution: Before defining the program, the following points are to be noted:

a) #include <stdio.h>: It is a standard file used for reference during character I/O

b) #define statement: It is a statement used for symbol and constant declarations.

c) Print a string using   To print a string using printf ( ),
   printf ( ):   we just have to provide the name of
                        the array (to printf ( )) containing
                        the string.

```c
#include <stdio.h>
/*constants for character I/O                              */
#define MAXLINE 61
/*maximum size of the string                              */
#define EOL '\n'
/*assume carriage return is the EOL                       */
#define NULL '\0'
/*append NULL to the end of the string                    */
main ( )
{
   int index; /*index to count characters*/
   int letter; /*letter entered by the user*/
char string [MAXLINE];
/*string to be read in and stored in an array*/
/*Following operations are to be performed*/
/*1. Read a character into string [ ] until */
/*   an EOL is encountered.                  */
/*2. Append a NULL character to the string.*/
/*3. Use printf ( ) to write the string.*/
for (index = 0; (letter = get char ( )) != EOL; ++index)
string [index] = letter;
/*put letter in the string*/

string [index] = NULL;
/*append a NULL character to the string*/
printf ("The string entered was %s\n", string);
/*write the string*/
printf ("The number of characters is %d\n", index);
/*write the no. of characters in the string*/
}
```

Write a program that performs matrix multiplication on

a) array matrix [2][4] and array vector [4].

b) Result of multiplication is to be stored in array result [ ].

c) Print the result of multiplication i.e. print each row of result [ ].

d) Assume column vector contains {1 2 3 4} and matrix contains values [0 1 2 3] and [1 2 3 4].

Solution:

```
#include <stdio.h>

#define NUM_COL 4

/*no. of columns        */

#define NUM_ROWS 2

/*no. of rows           */

main ( )

{

int matrix [NUM_ROWS][NUM_COL];

/*creates a 2 × 4 array of type integer*/

int vector [NUM_COL];

int result [NUM_ROWS];

/*To store the result of multiplication */

int i,j;

/*subscripts or counters */

/*1. Initialize the matrix, vector and result*/

for (i = 0; i < NUM_ROWS; i++)

/*Set result to zero            */

result [i] = 0;

for (i = 0; i < NUM_COL; i++)

/*set vector to 1 2 3 and 4     */

vector [i] = i + 1;
```

```
for (i = 0; i < NUM_ROWS; i++)

for (j = 0; j < NUM_COL; j++)

/*set matrix to 0 1 2 3         */

/*                1 2 3 4       */

matrix [i][j] = i + j;

/*2. Perform matrix multiplication */

for (i = 0; i < NUM_ROWS; i++)
for (j = 0; j < NUM_COL; j++)

result [i] = result [i] + matrix [i][j] * vector  [j];

printf ("The result of matrix multiplication = ");

/*Print each row of result [ ]*/

for (j = 0; j < NUM_ROWS; j++)

printf ("%d", result [j]);

/*put newline character         */

put char ('\n');

}
```

● **PROBLEM** 15B-11

Write a program that uses <u>for</u> loop to output the square of numbers 1 through 100.

Solution:

```
    main ( )

    {
  int number; /*integer whose square is calculated*/

  int square_of_number; /*storage for square of number*/

for (number = 1; number <= 100; number++)

/*for number 1 till 100 do the following*/

/*increment number only after executing following state-
                                        ments*/

  square_of_number = number * number;

printf ("The square of %d is %d\n", number,
                    square_of_number);

}
```

RECURSIVE FUNCTIONS

Write a program that

a)   Calculates factorial values.

b)   Assume that factorial of 5 is to be calculated through a routine factorial ( ).

c)   This routine should use the concept of recursion.

Solution: If a function is recursive it can call itself.   Recursion is the name given to the technique of defining a function or a process in terms of itself.

Factorial function

    0! = 1

    1! = 1

    n! = n(n - 1)!

The end condition in the recursive function is the factorial of 1.
    If this routine is invoked with a value 5, it will check if the value it received was equal to 1.   Then it carries out the required factorial functions.

```
    main ( )

    {
        int value;

        value = factorial (5);

        printf ("The factorial of 5 is = %d\n", value);

    }
    factorial (number)

      int number;

    /*number whose factorial is to be computed*/

    {
    if (number == 1)

    return (1);

    /*end condition of this recursive function*/

    else

      return (number * factorial (number - 1));

      /*calls itself until end condition occurs*/

    }
```

Write a program that

a) Has a routine fibonacci ( ). This routine calculates Fibonacci numbers using recursive algorithm.

b) Assume in the main program that 10th Fibonacci number is to be calculated.

c) Print the 10th Fibonacci number.

Solution: Fibonacci number is the sum of the previous two Fibonacci numbers. eg.

$$Fib(0) = 0$$

$$Fib(1) = 1$$

$$Fib(n+1) = Fib(n) + Fib(n-1)$$

The first two Fibonacci numbers are 1 just as factorial of 1 is 1. The algorithm followed is

1) Check if value received by fibonacci ( ) is equal to 1 or 2.

2) If value not equal to 1 or 2 the routine calls itself with (value - 1).

3) This continues until the condition value equals 1 or 2. This is the end condition.

```
main ( )

{ int Fib_num;

  Fib_num = fibonacci (10);

  printf ("The 10th Fibonacci number is = %d\n", Fib_num);

}

fibonacci (n)

  int n;

{

  int result; /*for result  */

  if (n == 1 || n == 2)

    result = 1;

  else
```

```
    result = fibonacci (n-1) + fibonacci (n-2);

    return (result);

}
```

POINTERS AND STRUCTURES

Write a program that

1) Has two routines change_values ( ) and square_of_
    number ( ).

2) Main program passes addresses of variables x and y to
    change_values ( ) and square_of_number ( ).

3) Initial values of x and y are 4 and 9. Change_values ( )
    is invoked first and it increments the value of the
    variables by 1.

4) Calculate the square of variables x and y using square_
    of_number ( ) routine. Print the squares of x and y.

Solution: Before analyzing this problem the concept of pointers
and address of variables must be made clear.

Pointers: The declaration format for a pointer is

        type *variable_name;

The * informs the compiler that the variable is actually a
pointer. eg.

    int *ptr;

Addresses: The ampersand (&) is used to specify an address
(actual memory location) of a variable. In pointers, we have
created the variable ptr. Now we can assign to it the address
of the variable integer_variable. i.e.

    ptr = &integer_variable;

In the above assignment, ptr does not contain the value that is
contained in the variable, integer_variable, but it contains the
location of integer_variable in memory i.e.

    ptr = address of integer_variable in memory

To reference the value stored in this address through ptr we
can use it as *ptr. The * (asterisk) informs the computer to
get the value contained at the location pointed by the pointer
i.e., ptr. Now if we make the following comparison that

```
    if (*ptr == integer_value)
```

the result of the above expression is true because both variables reference the same value.

```
    main ( )
  { int x = 4; /*initial value of x    */

    int y = 9; /*initial value of y    */

    /*pass addresses of x and y to change_values*/

    change_values (&x,&y)

    /*pass addresses of x and y to square_of_number*/

    square_of_number (&x,&y)

    /*print the squares of x and y  */

    printf ("Square of x = %d and y = %d\n", x,y);

    }


    change_values (xptr, yptr)

    int *xptr, *yptr;

    {

    /*modify the values of variables x and y*/

      *xptr = *xptr + 1;

      *yptr = *yptr + 1;

    }

    square_of_number (ptrx, ptry)

    int *ptrx, *ptry;

    {

    /*calculate the squares  */

      *ptrx = *ptrx * *ptrx;

    /*square of variable x   */

      *ptry = *ptry * *ptry

    /*square of variable y   */

    }
```

Explain structures in C.   Give an example and show how they can be referenced.

Solution: Structures in C are created by a <u>struct</u> statement. It is similar to the <u>typedef</u> statement in the sense that it does not create a variable we can use but provides a format for future variable declarations.

Suppose we want to create a structure of students in which we want to store their name, id and their gpa.   The following format is used.

```
#define MAX_NAME 30

#define MAX_ID 10

#define NUMBER_of_STUDENTS 100

    struct students {

char name [MAX_NAME];

char id [MAX_ID];

float gpa;

} stud[NUMBER_of_STUDENTS];
```

In the above declaration stud is the variable created that will use the structure students.   Students in this case are called a tag and each subfield within the structure i.e. name, id, gpa, etc., are called a member.

We can also define the variable NYCstud of type students for example,

```
    struct students NYCstud;
```

We can reference individual students in the following manner.

```
    stud [0].name;

    stud [0].id;

    stud [0].gpa;
```

Thus if we want to print gpa of all students along with their names then

```
    for (i = 0; i < NUMBER_of_STUDENTS; ++i)

    printf ("%s%1.1f\n", stud [i].name, stud [i].gpa);
```

prints the name and gpa of each student.

Consider the following structure.

```
struct students {
  char name [MAX_NAME];
  char id [MAX_ID];
  float gpa;
  struct students *next;
};
```

Through a program

a) create a linked list for 10 students.

b) If no memory is available for allocation then print "No memory available".

c) Use scanf to read name, id and gpa.

Solution:

```
#define NULL '\0'
#define MAX_NAME 30
#define MAX_ID 10
  struct students {
  char name [MAX_NAME];
  char id [MAX_ID];
  float gpa;
  struct students *next;
};
main ( )
{
  int i;
  struct students *start, *ptr, *new_ptr;
  char *calloc ( );
/*routine calloc returns a pointer to the location*/
```

```
/*Creating first element in the list          */

if ((ptr = (struct students *)calloc (1, sizeof (struct
                    students))) == NULL);

{

  printf ("No memory available \n");

  exit (1);

}

  ptr→next = NULL;

  start = ptr;

  scanf ("%s%s%f\n", ptr→name, ptr→id, ptr→gpa);

  /*creating 9 more elements   */

  for (i = 1; i < 10; i++)

  {

  if ((new_ptr = (struct students *)calloc (1, sizeof
                    (struct students))) == NULL)

  {

  printf ("No memory available \n");

exit (1);

}

new_ptr→next = ptr→next;

ptr→next = new_ptr;

ptr = new_ptr;

scanf ("%s%s%f\n", ptr→name, ptr→id, ptr→gpa);

}

}
```

Explanation of Related Terms

Linked List: A linked list is a list of structures. It utilizes the ability of a member of the structure to be a pointer
to a structure of the same type. Structures where member points
to a structure of the same type are known as self-referential
structures.

calloc ( ): This is a library routine that allocates space
from the heap. The function calloc ( ) returns a pointer to a
contiguous block of memory that is used for array or similar

structures. It returns NULL value if insufficient space is available for allocation.

sizeof ( ): It is an operator in C which returns the number of bytes required to store an object. eg.

number_of_bytes = sizeof (struct students);

will give us the number of bytes required to store one structure of student.

exit ( ): It provides a method of terminating a program. It is one of the library routines i.e. it is a function in the library. It returns several values but most common are 0 and 1. Value 0 is for normal termination i.e. program completes execution as required. Value 1 is for abnormal termination i.e. program terminates abnormally and does not execute as required.

Explanation of Statements

1) char *calloc ( );

The routine calloc ( ) returns a pointer to the location in memory that has been allocated. It is mainly a function which returns a pointer of the type char.

2) struct students *start, *ptr, *new_ptr

This declaration signifies that *start, *ptr and *new_ptr are pointers to the structure students.

3) ptr = (struct students *) calloc(1, sizeof (struct students));

To follow the concept in this statement we take individual parts and analyze their meaning.

a) sizeof (struct students);

will return the number of bytes required to store a structure of students.

b) calloc (1, sizeof (struct students));

Arguments required by calloc ( ) are the number of storage elements to allocate and size of storage area in bytes.

c) (struct students *)

This statement assigns the value returned from the routine calloc ( ) to a pointer to the structure of type students. The asterisk specifies that the value is to be assigned to a pointer. This assigned pointer is to a structure of type students.

d) ptr = (struct students *) calloc (1, sizeof (struct students));

The ptr is assigned to the pointer on the right side of the
assignment. i.e. pointer ptr is assigned the value calculated on the right side of the assignment.
Note: Assignment is possible only when both the pointers
are to the same structure. Here ptr is assigned to another
pointer (calculated) to a structure of type students.

4) ptr→next

ptr→name etc.

Reference to the members of the structure is through dot
notation, i.e.

(*ptr).name

(*ptr).next etc.

C provides a unique notation for pointers to structures. The
notation → is used in place of dot notation with pointers to
structures. To reference any member in a structure the → is
used. eg.

ptr→next

ptr→name

ptr→id etc.

LINKED-LIST: Represented through diagrams.

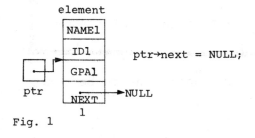

ptr→next = NULL;

Fig. 1

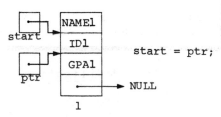

start = ptr;

Fig.2

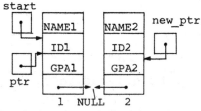

new_ptr→next = ptr→next;
Fig. 3

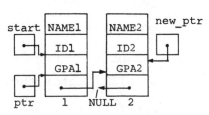

ptr→next = new_ptr;

Fig. 4

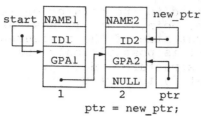

Fig. 5

Note: In element 2 the next is occupied by NULL i.e. next of element 2 is pointing to NULL.

Further expansion of this list according to the program will give the required structure. It is suggested that according to the program the whole list should be drawn to give a clear understanding of concepts involved.

● **PROBLEM** 15B-17

In question 17, a linked list for 10 students was created. Write or modify the program.

a) Delete an element if the name (member) of that element coincides with the given name.

b) Given name is to be read in.

c) The program should indicate whether it was successful or not in deleting that particular element.

Note: If element is not deleted means that particular name was not found in the linked list.

Solution: Modifications: These are all additions to be done.

```
#define TRUE 1

#define False 0

main ( )

  int not_found;

  char name [MAX_NAME];

  struct students *previous_ptr;

  printf ("Enter the student name to be deleted \n");

  scanf ("%s", name);

  not_found = TRUE; /*This segment checks 1st element */

  if (equal_string (start→name, name) == 0)
```

```
{
    not_found = FALSE;

    start = start→next;

}

else

{   ptr = start→next;

    previous_ptr = start;

    while (ptr && not_found)

    { if (equal_string (ptr→name, name) ==0)

{   not_found = FALSE;

    previous_ptr→next = ptr→next;

}

    previous_ptr = ptr;

    ptr = ptr→next;

} /*end while */

} /*end else  */

   if (not_found)

    printf ("STUDENT NOT FOUND IN THE LIST\n");

else

    printf ("STUDENT DELETED FROM THE LIST \n");

}/*end main */
```

The logic followed in this program is to

1) Locate whether the given name is in the first element of
    the list. If so delete the first element and point the
    pointer start to the second element.

2) Check the other elements. If the given name coincides with
    the name in the element then delete it from the list.

ROUTINE: equal_string ( ): This is a routine in UNIX systems
which examines two strings character by character until the
NULL value is found, or strings are found to be equal. If
strings are of equal length and contain the same sequence of
letters, value 0 is returned. If strings are unequal and contents are not the same then value -1 is returned.

Consider the following structure

```
    struct element {

    char keyfield;

    struct element *back;

    struct element *next;

    };
```

Now

1) create a doubly linked list of 5 elements.

2) Explain the logic of doubly linked lists.

Solution: In a doubly linked list the structure contains

a) pointer to the next node in the list.

b) pointer to the previous node in the list.

The logic followed is that the given structure has two pointers i.e. one for the next node and one for the back or previous node. Connecting the pointers in such a way that one single node can refer its previous and its next node is the scheme followed in the program. The first element will have in back NULL value while the next will point to the next node in the list. Similarly, the last element will have a null value in its 'next' and the 'back' will point to the previous node in the list.

```
    #define NULL '\0'

    struct element {

        char keyfield;

        struct element *back;

        struct element *next;

    };

    main ( )

    {

      int i;

      char *calloc ( );
```

```
      struct element *start, *ptr, *new_ptr;

ptr = (struct element *) calloc(1, sizeof (struct ele-
                                           ment)); */

/*following segment creates the 1st element

        ptr→next = NULL;

        ptr→back = NULL;

        start = ptr;

/*following segment creates 4 more elements */

   for (i = 1; i < 5; i++)

{

   new_ptr = (struct element *) calloc(1, sizeof (struct
                                  element));

   new_ptr→back = ptr;

   new_ptr→next = ptr→next;

    ptr→next = new_ptr

      ptr = new_ptr;

   }

   }
```

Diagram Representation:

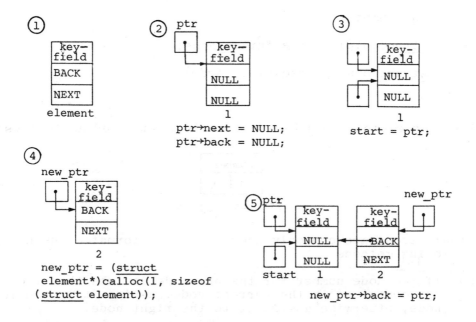

532-55

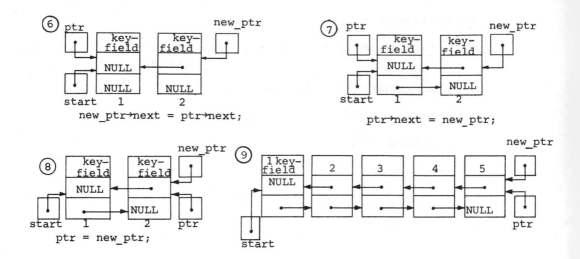

⑥ new_ptr→next = ptr→next;

⑦ ptr→next = new_ptr;

⑧ ptr = new_ptr;

⑨

SORTING

What are binary trees? Write a program that reads in 50 values and places them in a binary tree. After reading these values the program should print the values in the tree in ascending order.

Solution: Binary trees are very similar to a linked list. Consider the following structure

    struct binary_tree {

      int number;

      struct binary_tree *right_node;

      struct binary_tree *left_node;

    };

A single element in a binary tree is visualized as follows:

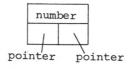

Binary trees are commonly used to sort information using the following methods

a) If the node number for the new node is less than the number contained in the current node, assign it to the left node, otherwise assign it to the right node.

b) If a pointer does not point to a node, assign NULL to that pointer.

Consider the following binary tree.

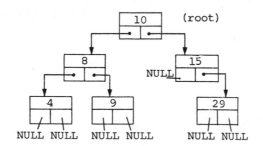

The node containing the value 10 is called the root of the tree. The nodes containing the values 8 and 15 are called the root's descendants. Each node with no descendants is termed a leaf i.e. 4, 9 and 29.

Program implementing binary tree that reads 50 values and prints them in ascending order is as follows:

```
#define TRUE 1

#define FALSE 0

#define NULL '\0'

  struct binary_tree {

    int number;

    struct binary_tree *right_node;

    struct binary_tree *left_node;

};

main ( )

{

  int number_entered; /*number entered or */

                      /*read in           */

  int number_of_values; /*number of values to be read in*/

  int i;

  int location_not_found;

  /*to track the location of the value   */
```

```
char *calloc ( );
struct binary_tree *root, *current_node, *new_node;
root = (struct binary_tree *) calloc (1, sizeof (struct
                                     binary_tree));
number_of_values = 50;
/*now get the 1st value  */
   current_node = root;
   current_node→number = get_integer ( );
   current_node→right_node = NULL;
   current_node→left_node = NULL;
/*since the 1st value has been read in   */
/*we are left with 49 more values           */
for (i = 1; i < 50; i++)
{
/*take the next value           */
   number_entered = get integer ( );
/*start at the top i.e. the root */
   current_node = root;
   location_not_found = TRUE;
new_node = (struct binary_tree *) calloc (1,sizeof (struct
                                     binary_tree));
new_node→number = number_entered;
new_node→right_node = NULL;
new_node→left_node = NULL;
/*now we have to find the location   */
/*in the tree for new value             */
while (loation_not_found)
{
if (number_entered < current_node→number)
   if (current_node→left_node == NULL)
```

```c
        location_not_found = FALSE;

    else

        current_node = current_node→left_node;

    else

        if (current_node→right_node == NULL)

        location_not_found = FALSE;
    else

        current_node = current_node→right_node;
    }/*end while */
    /*now to place the new node in the tree */
    /*at the correct location              */

    if (number_entered < current_node→number)
        current_node→left_node = new_node;


    else

        current_node→right_node = new_node
    }

    print_tree (root);
/*print_tree prints out the sorted values*/
}

    print_tree (node)
        struct binary_tree *node;
{
    if (node→left_node != NULL)
        print_tree (node→left_node);
    printf ("%d", node→number);
    if (node→right_node != NULL)
        print_tree (node→right_node);
    }
```

Explanation of Routines Used:

1) get_integer ( )

This is an assumed routine (i.e. not present in the library) which gets next integer from the input. As an excercise write this routine.

2) print_tree (node)

The function print_tree ( ) invokes itself recursively to print the values contained in the tree. This routine searches each left node until node → left equals NULL. It then prints the value contained at the node and returns up one level in the tree and prints the value at that node.

The routine further checks whether the node has a right node and if so starts the same process at that node.

● **PROBLEM** 15B-20

Write a routine that implements shell sorting. Assume there is an array of integers and size of array is known in the main program. The input parameters to the routine are

a) array.

b) size of array.

Solution: The shell sorting algorithm

1) Compares elements that are far apart and then compares adjacent elements.

2) It uses another routine, values_swaped ( ) where the values sent are interchanged.

3) The logic used is that number of elements in an array is divided by 2, then element [0] and element [no. of elements/2] are compared. The difference between [no. of elements/2 - 0] is a constant for the first pass and is referred in the program as difference.

```
shell_sort (array, number_of_elements)

int array [ ];

int number_of_elements;

{

int i;

int difference = number_of_elements/2;

int swap_occurred;
```

```
/*TRUE if a swap occurred   */

 do

   do

    {

       swap_occurred = 0;

       for (i = 0; i < number_of_elements - difference;
                              i++)

       if (array [i] > array [i + difference])

         {

            values_swaped (&(array[i]), &(array [i +
                         difference] ));

            swap_occurred = 1;

         }

    }

   while (swap_occurred);

   while ((difference/=2) > 0 );

   /*meaning (difference = difference/2) > 0  */

 }

    values_swaped (value1, value2)

     int *value1 , *value2;

    {

          int temp; /*store temporary values  */

         temp = *value1;

         *value1 = *value2;

         *value2 = temp;

      }
```

C REFERENCE GUIDE

Arithmetic Operators

    + addition.

- subtraction.

* multiplication.

/ division.

% modulus.

Operators unique to C

++ increment.

-- decrement.

Assignment operators

operator =   eg. a* = 5;   a = a * 5;

a% = 5;   a = a % 5;

Bitwise Operators

&   bitwise AND.

!   bitwise OR.

^   bitwise exclusive - or.

<<   shift left.

>>   shift right.

~   one's complement.

Break Statement:

The break statement is used within loops and the switch
statement. Within a loop the break statement causes the execution of the loop to cease and execution of the program to continue at the statement that follows the loop. Format is

break;

Global Variables:

In C the use of global variables is done using extern
statement. It is done as follows

type variable_name; /*outside of main */

main ( )

{

extern type variable_name;

/*extern tells the compiler that the */

```
/*variable is a global one              */
```

Relational Operators:

    <   less than

    >   greater than

    <=   less than or equal to

    >=   greater than or equal to

Relational operators unique to C

    ==   equal to

    !=   not equal to

Ternary Operator:

    ?:   conditional operator.

It is a conditional operator eg.

    conditional-expression:

                expression 1? expression 2: expression 3

Conditional expressions group right to left. They operate as
follows

a) If expression 1 (i.e. expression to be evaluated) is TRUE,
    expression 2 will be performed. If it is FALSE expression
    3 will be performed.

Logical AND Operator:

    logical-AND-expression

        expression 1 && expression 2

Logical OR Operator:

    logical-OR-expression

    expression 1 || expression 2.

<u>Type Specifiers</u>:

    type-specifiers are

        <u>char</u>

        <u>short</u>

        <u>int</u>

        <u>long</u>

        <u>unsigned</u>

        <u>float</u>

        <u>double</u>

        <u>struct-or-union</u> specifier

        <u>typedef</u> name.

CHAPTER 16

BUSINESS APPLICATIONS

DEPRECIATION, INTEREST AND COMMISSION PROBLEMS

● **PROBLEM** 16-1

Write a FORTRAN program to calculate depreciation by the sum of the years digits method.

<u>Solution</u>:   The Internal Revenue Service allows various methods for calculating the depreciation on a piece of machinery. The simplest is the straight-line method. According to this method, if an article costs $1000, has an estimated life of 10 years and $0 scrap value, the depreciation per year will be $100 for 10 years. The straight-line method assumes that machines wear out at a constant rate. The sum of the years digit method on the other hand, is used to compute the depreciation on articles that have the greatest rate of depreciation during the first few years of use.

For example, suppose a drilling machine costing $15,000, has a useful life of five years and can be resold for $5,000. The total depreciation is:

        15,000   cost
      - 5,000   trade-in
        10,000   depreciation

The sum of the years 1 through 5 is 1+2+3+4+5 = 15. Thus, the depreciation for the first year is 5/15, for the second year, 4/15, etc.

Year	Depreciation	Book value at end of year
1	5/15 of 10,000 = 3333.33	15,000 - 3333.33 = 11666.67
2	4/15 of 10,000 = 2666.67	11,666.67 - 2666.67 = 9000.00
3	3/15 of 10,000 = 2000	9000 - 2000 = 7000.00
4	2/15 of 10,000 = 1333.33	7000 - 1333.33 = 5666.67
5	1/15 of 10,000 = 666.67	5666.67 - 666.67 = 5000

The program follows:

```
           DIM V(100)
           READ IYR, COST, SAL
           TDEP = COST - SAL
           KSUM = 0
           JTIME = IYR
20         KSUM = KSUM + JTIME
           IF (JTIME.EQ.0) GOTO 50
           JTIME = JTIME - 1
           GOTO 20
50         DO 60 I = 1,IYR
           J = IYR - I + 1
           FRA = J/KSUM
           V(I) = COST - FRA * TDEP
60         CONTINUE
           STOP
           END
```

Program Comments: The READ statement reads in the number of years, the cost of the item, and the salvage value, respectively. TDEP stores the total value to be depreciated. The loop starting at statement 20 calculates the sum of the years. If the number of years IYR, equals 5, then JTIME = 5,4,3,2,1,0 and KSUM = 5+4+3+2+1 = 15.

When JTIME = 0, signifying that the sum of years has been calculated, the program jumps to statement 50. This loop first calculates the FRA, the fractional amount of depreciation for each year, and V(I), the book value for each year.

● **PROBLEM** 16-2

An item worth \$30,000 initially and having a life of 15 years is depreciated according to the double declining balance method. Calculate the amount of depreciation in each of the first five years.

Solution: The depreciation during the nth year can be expressed as

$$D = \frac{2C}{N}\left(1 - \frac{2}{N}\right)^{n-1} \text{ where}$$

D is the depreciation for a particular year.
C is the original cost.
N is the life span of the machine.
n is the particular year for which we are calculating the depreciation.

Hence we can write a statement function to compute D. Values of D for n = 1,2,3,4,5 will be stored in an array A.

```
           DIMENSION A (5)
           REAL D,C,N,K
           DO 100 J = 1,5
           A (J) = D (30000., 15., J)
100        CONTINUE
           END
```

```
       FUNCTION D (C,N,K)
       D = 2*C/N*(1.-2./N)**(K-1.)
       RETURN
       END
```

Write a FORTRAN program to read in an initial cost,
salvage value, expected lifetime, number of years to be
depreciated, and a code. The code indicates the function
to be performed, namely
    1 - straight-line depreciation
    2 - declining balance depreciation
    3 - sum-of-the-years-digits depreciation
The program will calculate the depreciation in accordance
with the code number you choose.

Solution: To do this problem, we assume the cost is not
equal to $999.99. (We use the value of $999.99 to indicate
that there are no more DATA cards to be read, and the
program should be terminated.) We can set up a DO-WHILE
construct here: processing will continue until all the
cards are read in. Input values as well as the output
statements have been omitted so that you may come up with
your own ideas on that.

```
       DIMENSION VALUE (100)
15     READ (3,100) COST, SALV, EXLIFE, IYRS, ICODE
       IF (COST.EQ. 999.99) GO TO 99
       IF (ICODE.EQ.1) GO TO 50
       IF (ICODE.EQ.2) GO TO 70
C      BY DEFAULT, THIS SECTION TAKES CARE OF ICODE = 3
       DEP = COST - SALV
       JSUM = 0
       KT = EXLIFE
20     JSUM = JSUM + KT
       IF (KT.EQ.0) GO TO 30
       KT = KT - 1
       GO TO 20
30     DO 40 M = 1,IYRS
       J = IYRS - 1
       FRA = J/IYRS
       VALUE (M) = FRA*DEP
40     CONTINUE
       GO TO 15
C      THIS SECTION TAKES CARE OF ICODE = 1
50     ANNDEP = DEP/ELIFE
       DO 60 K = 1,IYRS
       COST = COST - ANNDEP
60     VALUE(K) = COST
       GO TO 15
C      THIS SECTION TAKES CARE OF ICODE = 2
       DO 80 I = 1,IYRS
       DEP = VALU*.1667
       VALU = VALU - DEP
       VALUE(I) = VALU
80     CONTINUE
       GO TO 15
99     STOP
       END
```

535

Write a BASIC program to calculate the principal after
N years on a balance (original principal) of B at time
0. Assume that interest is compounded yearly at 5%
effective yield. Print the results for N = 1,3,5.

Solution: The formula we need is $P = P_o(Hi)^N$ where
$\overline{P_o = B}$, i = 0.05, and N takes on values 1,3, and 5.
This program introduces the STEP option in a FOR-NEXT loop.
Data of $P_o = B = 200$ is used.

```
1Ø REM CALCULATES PRINCIPAL ON
2Ø REM A BALANCE AT 5% INTEREST
3Ø REM B = ORIGINAL BALANCE, P = PRINCIPAL
4Ø READ B
5Ø PRINT "PRINCIPAL", "BALANCE", "YEARS"
6Ø FOR N = 1 TO 5 STEP 2
7Ø LET P = B*1.05↑N
8Ø PRINT P, B, N
9Ø NEXT N
1ØØ DATA 2ØØ
11Ø END
```

For principal P, a bank pays R interest compounded annually.
Define a function in FORTRAN which calculates the deposit
at the end of n years. Use the formula

$$\text{NEW DEPOSIT} = P((1+R)^n - 1)/R$$

Solution: Let P be the original principal. After 1
year, the new principal will be

$$P_1 = P(1+R).$$

After two years, it will be

$$P_2 = P_1(1+R) = P(1+R)(1+R) = P(1+R)^2.$$

After n years, it will be

$$P_n = P(1+R)^n.$$

By NEW DEPOSIT is understood the amount in the bank after
n years less the original principal.

In FORTRAN we can write

```
FUNCTION ND (P,R,N)
ND = P*(((1.+R)**N) - 1.)/R
RETURN
END
```

[Note: Remember to declare variables as INTEGER or REAL
in the main program.]

> Write a program in PL/I to calculate a table of returns
> on an investment of original amount A which is compounded
> yearly at P percent return, for Y years.

Solution: After Y years the original amount A will grow
to

$$T = A(1 + P/100)^Y$$

The program below reads in values of A,P, and Y.
Then it calculates the corresponding value of T and prints
out A, P, Y, and T.

```
      /*COMPOUND INTEREST*/
      ON ENDFILE (SYSIN) GO TO L60
L10:  GET LIST (A,P,Y);
L20:  T = A*(1 + P/100)**Y;
L30:  PUT EDIT (A,P,Y,T)(F(16,4));
L40:  PUT SKIP;
L50:  GO TO L10;
L60:  END
```

> Write a program in FORTRAN to prepare a payroll for a
> business employing N workers. The following computations
> must be performed: 1) regular hours and overtime must
> be totaled. 2) wages equal to regular rate times regular
> hours plus overtime rate times overtime hours. 3) Deduc-
> tions must be made for insurance taxes, and government
> income tax. 4) Net wages are printed for each worker.
> Assume that tax schedules can be accessed from secondary
> memory.

Solution: In preparing a payroll register, the first
step is collecting and processing the time cards. The
items 1) - 3) are entered by reading a card. This information is then used in calculating gross and net pay.
Since the wages values require the accuracy of only two
decimal places (cents), while the FORTRAN calculations
are much more accurate, the rounding should be made by
asking for only two places in the FORMAT statement. If
the computer uses truncation as the approximation routine,
.005 should be added to each value before truncating.

To calculate the taxes, a table look-up routine
must be performed. Assume that Table 1 has already
been loaded into an array.

Each time a card is read it will give the salary and number
of exemptions.

```
10    FORMAT (F 6.2,I2)
15    DIMENSION A(28,8)
C     READ SALARY AND EXEMPTIONS
```

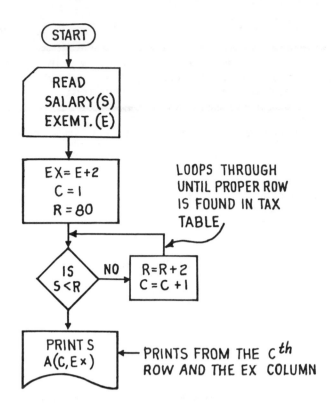

START

READ
SALARY(S)
EXEMT.(E)

EX= E+2
C = 1
R = 80

LOOPS THROUGH
UNTIL PROPER ROW
IS FOUND IN TAX
TABLE

IS
S < R

NO → R = R+2
C = C +1

PRINT S
A(C,Ex)

← PRINTS FROM THE cth
ROW AND THE EX COLUMN

```
20      READ (3,10) S,E
C       EX INDICATES WHERE THE TAX WILL BE
        EX = E + 2
C       C INDICATES ROW OF THE TAX
        C = 1
C       R IS THE LOWEST TAXABLE SALARY
        R = 80
C       TAX NOT IN TABLE
        IF (S.LT.78) GO TO 140
C       CHECKING FOR PROPER ROW
100     IF (S.LT.R) GO TO 110
C       ADVANCING TO NEXT SALARY STEP
        R = R + 2
C       ADVANCING TO NEXT ROW IN TABLE
        C = C + 1
        GO TO 100
C       PRINTS SALARY AND TAX
110     WRITE (4,120)S,A(C,EX)
120     FORMAT (F6.2,5X,F5.2)
        GO TO 20
140     WRITE (4,150)
150     FORMAT ("TAX NOT IN TABLE")
        GO TO 20
        STOP
        END
```

Note that FORTRAN is not the best choice of language for
this type of problem as evidenced by the numerous unconditional GO TO statements scattered throughout the program.
If the program had been written in COBOL, the structure
would have been easier to follow.

The wages are The number of withholding exemptions claimed

At least	But less than	0	1	2	3	4	5	6
		The amount of tax to be withheld shall be						
$ 78	$ 80	$11.10	$ 9.10	$ 7.00	$ 5.00	$ 3.00	$ 1.10	$ 0.00
80	82	11.40	9.40	7.30	5.30	3.40	1.40	0.00
82	84	11.70	9.70	7.60	5.60	3.60	1.70	0.00
84	86	12.00	10.00	7.90	5.90	3.90	1.90	0.10
86	88	12.30	10.30	8.20	6.20	4.20	2.20	0.30
88	90	12.70	10.60	8.50	6.50	4.50	2.50	0.60
90	92	13.00	10.90	8.80	6.80	4.80	2.80	0.90
92	94	13.30	11.20	9.10	7.10	5.10	3.10	1.20
94	96	13.70	11.50	9.40	7.40	5.40	3.40	1.50
96	98	14.00	11.80	9.70	7.70	5.70	3.70	1.70
98	100	14.40	12.10	10.00	8.00	6.00	4.00	2.00
100	105	15.00	12.70	10.60	8.50	6.50	4.50	2.50
105	110	15.80	13.50	11.30	9.30	7.30	5.30	3.20
110	115	16.70	14.40	12.10	10.00	8.00	6.00	4.00
115	120	17.50	15.20	12.90	10.80	8.80	6.80	4.70
120	125	18.40	16.10	13.80	11.50	9.50	7.50	5.50
125	130	19.20	16.90	14.60	12.30	10.30	8.30	6.20
130	135	20.10	17.80	15.50	13.20	11.00	9.00	7.00
135	140	20.90	18.60	16.30	14.00	11.80	9.80	7.70
140	145	21.80	19.50	17.20	14.90	12.60	10.50	8.50
145	150	22.60	20.30	18.00	15.70	13.50	11.30	9.20
150	160	23.90	21.60	19.30	17.00	14.70	12.40	10.40
160	170	25.60	23.30	21.00	18.70	16.40	14.10	11.90
170	180	27.50	25.00	22.70	20.40	18.10	15.80	13.60
180	190	29.50	26.80	24.40	22.10	19.80	17.50	15.30
190	200	31.50	28.80	26.10	23.80	21.50	19.20	17.00
200	210	33.50	30.80	28.10	25.50	23.20	20.90	18.70

● **PROBLEM** 16-8

Suppose a salesman gets $6 commission on each sale as long as the sale is under $150. However, if the sale is over $150 he gets a bonus of 2% of the amount over the $150. Write a PL/I program that will take as data the values of the amount of sale and print the commission the salesman gets.

Solution: Formally, we can express the commission C as follows. If the amount A is less than $150, then C = $6. Otherwise, if A>150, then

$$C = 6 + 2 \times (A-150)/100$$

```
      /*COMMISSION CALCULATION*/
L2Ø: GET LIST (A);
L3Ø: IF A< = 15Ø THEN GO TO L6Ø;
L4Ø: C = 6 + 2*(A-15Ø)/1ØØ;
L5Ø: GO TO L7Ø;
L6Ø: C = 6;
L7Ø: PUT EDIT (A,C) (F(7,2)F(7,2));
L8Ø: PUT SKIP;
L9Ø: GO TO L2Ø;
```

539

Write a pseudocoded program to input a sequence of numbers (representing kilowatt-hours, KWH) and output electric bills according to the following schedule:

     Each of the first 100 KWHs costs 10 cents
     Each of the next 100 costs 6 cents
     Each of the next 200 costs 8 cents
     Each KWH over 400 costs 10 cents.

The program should terminate when a negative number is inputted. Also, how could you improve this program to handle the situation in which the rate schedule changed rapidly?

Solution: The program logic is straightforward. A DO-WHILE construct is set up, so that each entry of kilowatt-hours is processed separately until a negative value is encountered.

```
real KWH, COST
input KWH (1) through KWH (N)
do while KWH>0
if 0≤KWH<100
then COST←10.0*KWH
if 100≤KWH<200
then COST←(10.0*100.0) + (6.0*(KWH-100.0))
if 200≤KWH≤400
then COST←(10.0*100.0) + (6.0*100.0) + (8.0*(KWH-200.0))
else COST←(10.0*100.0) + (6.0*100.0) + (8.0*200.0)
   + (10.0*(KWH-400.0))
output KWH, COST
end do while
endprogram
```

If the rates of the electric bills climb in price often, the program would have to be rewritten just as often. To avoid this nuisance, we could write subprograms to do the job. After each IF-THEN construct, a statement calling a particular subprogram with a certain billing schedule could be inserted. In this way, the main program is left untouched, and you would need to rewrite only a few lines of code in a subprogram. This is very often the case in programming for business applications.

An alternative way of handling the situation of rapid rate schedule changes would be to insert 2 READ statements in the program, one for inputting the KWH segments, and another for inputting the price of each segment.

The friendly neighborhood bank is planning to start a lottery to attract new customers. A new account receives a number containing three digits. The digits are between 000 and 999 and we will assume that all 1,000 combinations have been given out. Prizes are awarded according to the following scheme:

    3 numbers alike $100 gift certificate
    2 numbers alike $10 gift certificate

What will be the cost of the lottery to the bank?

Solution: There are 1000 numbers between 000 and 999.
Each occurrence of a number composed of the same digits
(like 000,111...) contributes $100 to the total cost,
while each occurrence of a number with two similar digits
(like 005, 511, 363...) adds $10 to the cost. The total
cost is composed of the cost of all "triplets" added to
the cost of all "doublets".

```
10    PRINT "GAMBLING BANKS"
20    S1 = 0
30    S2 = 0
40    FOR I = 0 TO 9
50    FOR J = 0 TO 9
60    FOR K = 0 TO 9
70    IF I = J THEN 100
80    IF J = K THEN 110
85    IF I = K THEN 110
90    GO TO 130
100   IF J = K THEN 120
110   S2 = S2 + 10
115   GO TO 130
120   S1 = S1 + 100
130   IF 100I + 10J + K<>999 THEN 150
140   S3 = S1 + S2
150   NEXT K
160   NEXT J
170   NEXT I
180   PRINT "COST OF FIRST KIND"; S1; "PLUS COST OF"
190   PRINT "SECOND KIND"; S2; "EQUALS TOTAL"
200   PRINT "COST OF LOTTERY" S3
210   END
```

● **PROBLEM 16-11**

Write a BASIC program which keeps track of the numbers of
items in stock for four different classes of items. To
be specific, let the four classes of items be denoted by
1001, 1002, 1003 and 1004. Consider the case where the
following 7 (seven) items are in stock: 1001, 1002, 1002,
1003, 1004, 1003, 1001.

Solution: It is convenient to introduce separate counters
K1, K2, K3, and K4 for the four classes. It is also
convenient to utilize the ON-GO TO statement. Thus if
we say

    50 ON X GO TO 90, 70, 110

control will be transferred to statements 90, 70, or 110
if the truncated value of X is 1, 2, or 3 respectively.

```
1Ø      REM INVENTORY PROGRAM FOR 4 CLASSES
2Ø      REM K1, K2, K3, K4 ARE THE COUNTERS
3Ø      DATA 1ØØ1, 1ØØ2, 1ØØ2, 1ØØ3, 1ØØ4, 1ØØ3, 1ØØ1
4Ø      LET K1 = K2 = K3 = K4 = Ø
5Ø      FOR I = 1 TO 7
6Ø      READ X
7Ø      ON X - 1ØØØ GO TO 8Ø, 1ØØ, 12Ø, 14Ø
8Ø      LET K1 = K1 + 1
9Ø      GO TO 16Ø
1ØØ     LET K2 = K2 + 1
11Ø     GO TO 16Ø
12Ø     LET K3 = K3 + 1
13Ø     GO TO 16Ø
14Ø     LET K4 = K4 + 1
15Ø     GO TO 16Ø
16Ø     NEXT I
17Ø     PRINT "ITEM 1ØØ1;"; K1; "IN STOCK"
18Ø     PRINT "ITEM 1ØØ2;"; K2; "IN STOCK"
19Ø     PRINT "ITEM 1ØØ3;"; K3; "IN STOCK"
2ØØ     PRINT "ITEM 1ØØ4;"; K4; "IN STOCK"
21Ø     END
```

Some computers do not accept multiple assignment statements. In that case, in statement 40 each variable should
be initialized to zero separately.

OPTIMIZING PRODUCTION

● **PROBLEM** 16-12

A steel producer uses three different processes to produce
different qualities of steel. It takes three tons of raw
material (iron, coal, oil and minor trace elements) to
produce a ton of steel in any process. The percentages
of iron, coal and oil used in each process vary and are
given below:

	Process A	Process B	Process C
Iron	40	45	25
Coal	50	25	60
Oil	10	30	15

Write a program in Basic to print the number of tons of
raw material needed to make 100, 150, 200, 250, 300 tons
of steel if the ratio of process usages A to B to C is
as 1:3:6.

Solution: We can treat the composition of each process
as a column in an input matrix. The input matrix is therefore

$$\begin{bmatrix} 40 & 45 & 25 \\ 50 & 25 & 60 \\ 10 & 30 & 15 \end{bmatrix} \tag{1}$$

The ratio of processes A, B, C is always 1 to 3 to 6.
This means that for 100 tons of steel, Method A produces

10 tons, Method B 30 tons, and Method C 60 tons. In fact,
since the ratios total 10, A will always be 10%, B 30%,
and C 60% of total output.

To find the number of tons of iron, coal and oil
used in the three processes we post multiply (1) by the
column vector $\begin{bmatrix} A \\ B \\ C \end{bmatrix}$ where A, B, C, will vary according
to total tonnage of output (100, 150, 200, 250).

A coarse flow-chart for the program is as shown in Fig. 1.

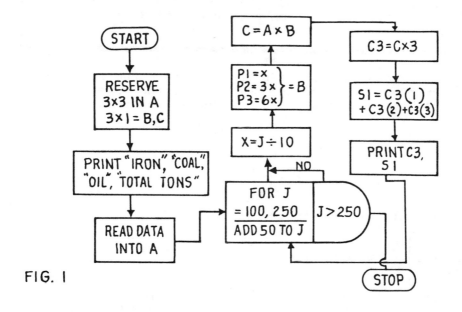

FIG. I

```
10      PRINT "STEEL PROCESSING"
20      DIM A(2,2) B(2,0) C(2,0)
30      PRINT:  PRINT "IRON," "COAL," "OIL," "TOTAL TONS"
40      MAT READ A
50      FOR J = 100 TO 250 STEP 50
60      X = J/10
70      LET B(0,0) = X
80      LET B(1,0) = 3*X
90      LET B(2,0) = 6*X
100     MAT C = A*B
110     MAT C = (3/100)*C
120     LET S1 = C(0,0) + C(1,0) + C(2,0)
130     PRINT C (0,0), C(1,0), C(2,0), S1
140     NEXT J
150     STOP
160     DATA 40, 45, 25, 50, 25, 60, 10, 30, 15
170     END
```

543

A book publisher is in the business of producing volumes in mathematics, science and the humanities. He basically uses two kinds of labor

    a) skilled for writing the books
    b) unskilled to correct the completed volumes.

His average costs per book for each type of labor and each type of book is given below:

Expenses	Mathematics	Science	Humanities
Skilled	17.00	16.00	12.00
Unskilled	6.00	5.00	4.00

Write a program in Basic to print the costs of skilled and unskilled labor needed to produce M books in math, S books in science, and H books in humanities, if M = 1, 2, 3, 4, 5; S = 2M + 1; H = 2M - 2.

Solution: We can use matrices to facilitate the solution of this problem. The command MAT X tells the compiler to operate with X according to the rules of matrix algebra.

Form the costs' matrix

$$\begin{bmatrix} 17.00 & 16.00 & 12.00 \\ 6.00 & 5.00 & 4.00 \end{bmatrix} \tag{1}$$

If we multiply (1) by the vector

$$\begin{bmatrix} M \\ 2M + 1 \\ 2M - 2 \end{bmatrix} \quad \text{we obtain:}$$

$$\begin{bmatrix} 17500 & 16200 & 12400 \\ 6200 & 5500 & 4900 \end{bmatrix} \begin{bmatrix} M \\ 2M + 1 \\ 2M - 2 \end{bmatrix}$$

$$= \begin{bmatrix} 17500M + 16200(2M+1) + 12400(2M-2) \\ 6200M + 5500(2M+1) + 4900(2M-2) \end{bmatrix} \tag{2}$$

Adding the two rows of (2) together gives the total cost of skilled and unskilled labor. Note that costs of skilled labor comprise the first row of the result in (2), while costs of unskilled labor comprise the second row.

```
10    DIM A(1,2), B(2,0), C(1,0)
15    PRINT "MATHEMATICS", "SCIENCES", "HUMANITIES",
      "SKILLED LABOR", "UNSKILLED LABOR"
20    PRINT REM L1, L2 DENOTE SKILLED AND UNSKILLED LABOR
25    LET L1 = 0
30    LET L2 = 0
35    FOR M = 0 TO 5
40    LET B(0,0) = M + 1
45    LET B(1,0) = 2*M + 1
```

```
50     LET B(2,0) = 2*M + 5
55     MAT C = A*B
60     PRINT
65     PRINT B(0,0), B(1,0), B(2,0), C(0,0), C(1,0)
66     PRINT "TOTAL COSTS", L1, L2
70     LET L1 = L1 + C(0,0)
75     LET L2 = L2 + C(1,0)
80     NEXT M
85     PRINT
90     STOP
95     DATA 17, 16, 12, 6, 5, 4
100    END
```

● **PROBLEM** 16-14

An economist suspects that a leading indicator in the
business cycle has the form xcosx. He wishes to know
when the indicator will peak, i.e. achieve a maximum,
in different time intervals. Write a FORTRAN program
to find the maximum of xcosx in interval [a,b].

Solution: There are many methods of computing the maximum of a function over its domain or a subset of its
domain (local maximum). A method particularly suited for
computer applications is the elimination scheme. To
illustrate the method, let a=o, b=π and suppose we wish
to

   Max xcosx $x\epsilon[o,\pi]$.   (1)

1) Place two search points close together at the centre
of the interval. Let the distance between the points
be $\epsilon>o$.

2) Evaluate f(x) at X_L and X_R and call the results
$f(X_L)$, $f(X_R)$. If $f(X_L) \geq f(X_R)$ Max f(X) lies between
o and X_R and the segment $[X_R, \pi]$ can be discarded.

3) Place two search points close together at the center of
the remaining interval and repeat step (2).

4) Suppose $f(X_{R_1}) \geq f(X_{L_1})$. Then Max f(X) lies in the
interval $[X_{L_1}, X_R]$ and the segment $[0, X_{L_1}]$ can be discarded.

5) The process continues until an interval less than 2ϵ
is obtained. Since the search cannot continue, the
maximum is assumed to occur at the center of this interval.

In the program, a statement function is used to define
xcosx so that it can be referred to at any further point
in the program. Also, if the search points pass a toler-
ance limit, the program halts.

```
C      DEFINE THE FUNCTION Y(X)
       Y(X) = X*COX(X)
```

545

```
        READ XL, XR, EPSI
        I = 1
C       CALCULATE INTERIOR POINTS
10      XL1 = XL + .5*(XR - XL - EPSI)
        XR1 = XL1 + EPSI
        YL1 = Y(XL1)
        YR1 = Y(XR1)
        PRINT YL1, YR1, XL, XL1, XR1, XR
        IF (YL1 - YR1) 20, 50, 30
20      XL = XL1
        GO TO 40
30      XR = XR1
C       TEST FOR END OF SEARCH
40      IF (I.GE.100) GO TO 60
        I = I + 1
        IF (XR - XL.GT.3*EPSI) GO TO 10
50      XMAX = .5*(XL1 + XR1)
        YMAX = .5*(YL1 + YR1)
        PRINT YMAX, XMAX
        GO TO 70
C       PRINT OUTPUT TERMINATED BECAUSE OF MAX-
C       IMUM ITERATION COUNT
60      WRITE (6, 300)
300     FORMAT (54HO THE SOLUTION HAS NOT CONVERGED AFTER
        100 ITERATIONS.  TERMINATE PROGRAM
70      STOP
        END
```

● **PROBLEM** 16-15

A firm is considering investing $75,000 in a new venture.
Its economists have projected the following returns over
the next five years.

Year	Return
1	20,000
2	30,000
3	35,000
4	40,000
5	50,000
Total	$175,000

Describe how the discounted cash flow interest rate would
be found, given a current interest rate of 10%.

Solution: From the given table we observe that the gross
return from the investment is $175,000 - $75,000 = $100,000.
However, this is assuming that the money invested has no
alternative uses, e.g. it could not be invested in a
bank at 10% interest. Taking the time value of money
into account, to obtain $20,000 after 1 year we would
have to invest

$$\$20,000 = X + .1X$$

now. Thus, $X = \dfrac{20,000}{1.1} = \$18182$

Similarly, $30,000 two years from now is worth

$$\$30,000 = (X+.1X)(1+.1)$$

$$= X(1+.1)(1+.1)$$
$$= X(1.1)^2$$

or, $X = \dfrac{\$30,000}{(1.1)^2} = \$24,794.$

Applying the same analysis to the remaining returns:

Year	Return	Present Value
1	20,000	$20,000/1.1 = 18,182$
2	30,000	$30,000/(1.1)^2 = 24,794$
3	35,000	$35,000/(1.1)^3 = 26,296$
4	40,000	$40,000/(1.1)^4 = 27,321$
5	50,000	$50,000/(1.1)^5 = 31,047$

Adding the present values of returns over the five years gives the present value of returns from the investment. PV = $127,640. The net present value of the investment when the current interest rate is 10% is therefore NPV = PV - I = $127,640 - $75,000 = $52,640. This means that the $100,000 return over five years is actually worth $52,640 to the firm now. Note that as the interest rate changes continuously from 0% to 100%, the NPV changes continuously from $100,000 (the gross return becomes the net present value when the interest rate is 0%) to $-59,063. Thus, there must be an interest rate at which the NPV equals zero. This interest rate value is called the DISCOUNTED CASH FLOW interest rate.

A graph of the NVP versus interest rate might look as shown in Fig. 1.

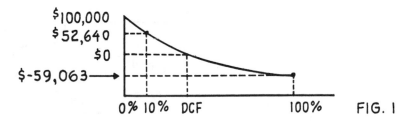

FIG. I

To actually compute the DCF we must find a root of the equation $f(r) = 0$ where NVP = $f(r)$. We cannot use the Newton-Raphson method because the functional relationship is not in polynomial form. The bisection method, however, may be applied.

The procedure is as follows: We know that $f(.10) = 52,640$ and $f(1.00) = -\$59,063$. Compute the value of f at the mid-point of the interval [.10, 1.00], $f(.55)$. If $f(.55) \geq 0$ the root must lie in the interval [.55, 1.00] (since $f(.10)$ is positive and $f(1.00)$ is negative). If $f(.55) < 0$, then the root lies in the interval [.10, .55]. In either case the interval of search has been reduced by 1/2.

Repeat the above procedure with the new interval i.e. take the mid-point and evaluate f at this point.

A flowchart for computing the DCF is as shown in Fig. 2

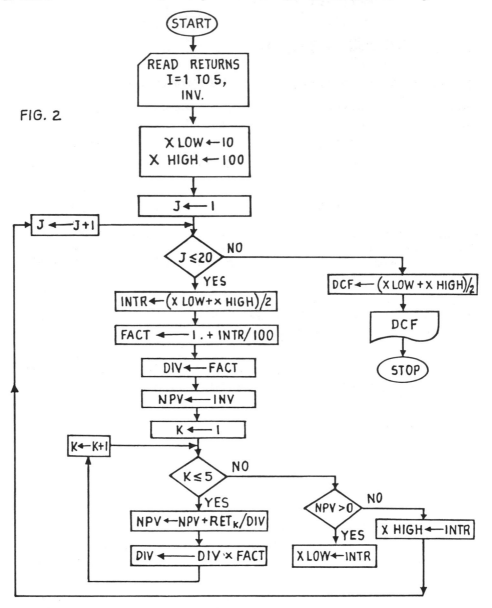

FIG. 2

● **PROBLEM** 16-16

A manufacturer can produce X units of an item at a cost given by the following equation:

$$Cost = C = 15 + 0.001x^2$$

The relationship between the number of units and price is given by $P = 35 - .1X$ (the producer is a monopolist).

How many units should the monopolist produce in order to maximize his total return?

Solution: The maximization problem may be written as follows:

Max {X.(P-C)}
X

where P = 35 - 0.1X
      C = 15 + 0.001X^2, X$\geq$0

When X, the quantity produced is zero, there is zero profit. Similarly, when the price of X equals the cost of
X, profits are zero. This occurs when P = C or,

$$35 - 0.1X = 15 + 0.001X^2$$

Solving for X gives X = 100. Thus profits are zero when
X = 0 and X = 100.

Assuming profit is a continuous function of output
Rolle's theorem may be applied to conclude that the maximum
profit point lies in the interval (0,100). Numerical
approximation of this maximum is performed on the computer
using the GOLDEN SECTION method. To illustrate the method,
suppose the graph of profit versus production looks as
follows:

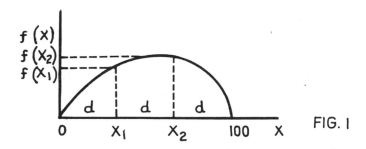

FIG. 1

In the interval [0,100] there is only one maximum. Suppose
we pick two points, X_1 and X_2 in that interval and find
their ordinates on the curve. If $f(X_2) > f(X_1)$, then the
interval of search may be reduced from [0,100] to $[X_1,100]$
and the interval $[0,X_1]$ can be eliminated.

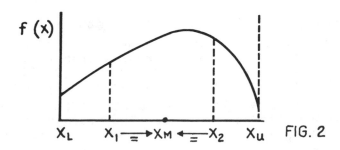

FIG. 2

The original interval $[X_L, X_u]$ is equal to 1 (Fig. 2).
Let τ equal the ratio of the long subinterval to the total

interval, i.e.

$$\frac{X_2 - X_L}{X_u - X_L} = \tau.$$

Since X_1 and X_2 have been located symmetrically about the center of the interval, the distance between X_1 and X_u is also τ. From Fig. 2, the interval $[X_L, X_1]$ will be eliminated after the first iteration since $f(X_2) > f(X_1)$. In order for X_2 to be properly located within the interval $[X_1, X_u]$ for the next iteration, the following must be true:

$$\frac{X_u - X_2}{X_u - X_1} = \tau$$

But, from Fig. 2, $X_u - X_2 = 1 - \tau$ and $X_u - X_1 = \tau$. Thus,

$$\frac{1 - \tau}{\tau} = \tau, \text{ or}$$

$$\tau^2 + \tau - 1 = 0. \tag{1}$$

Solving (1) for τ we obtain $\tau = \frac{\sqrt{5} - 1}{2} = 0.618$. Thus, according to the GOLDEN SECTION rule, X_2 should be 0.618 from X_L and X_1 should be 0.618 from X_u.

For the given problem, the selection of points in the search interval would proceed as follows:

$$X_1 = 100 - 0.618 \times 100 = 100 - 61.8 = 38.2;$$

$X_2 = 0.618 \times 100 = 61.8$. From Fig. 1, $f(X_2) > f(X_1)$ so the interval $[0, 38.2]$ is eliminated. The next point is located at $0.618 \times$ (length of interval) $= 0.618 \times (61.8) = 38.2$ from the left end of the interval, or $X_3 = 38.2 + 38.2 = 76.4$. Since $f(X_2) > f(X_3)$, $[76.4, 100]$ is eliminated.

X_4 is located at $0.618 \times$ (length of interval) $= 0.618 \times (38.2) = 23.6$ from the right end or $76.4 - 23.6 = 52.8$. After three iterations the interval within which the optimum is located has been reduced from $[0, 100]$ to $[52.8]$. These values are now assigned to X_L and X_u. The process is continued until the length of the interval is less than some preassigned $\varepsilon > 0$. The average of $f(X)$ at final X_L and X_u is then the required approximation to the optimum. The most efficient method of locating the points is the GOLDEN SECTION technique.

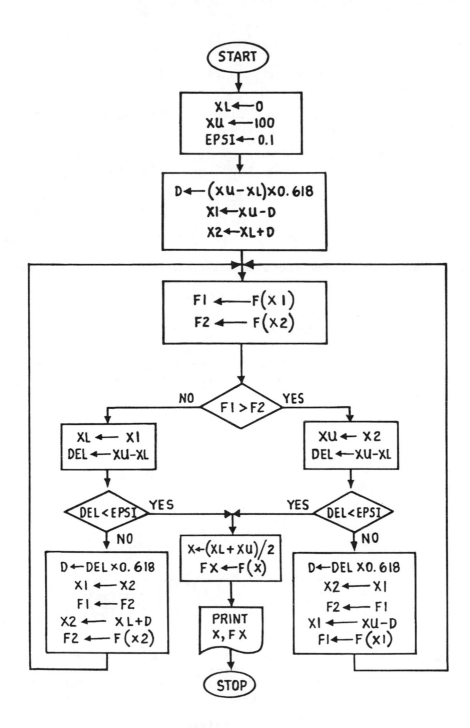

OPERATIONS RESEARCH

● **PROBLEM** 16-17

Suppose there are three typists in a typing pool. Each typist can type an average of 6 letters/hr. If letters arrive to be typed at the rate of 15 letters/hr.,

   a) What fraction of the time are all three typists

busy?

   b) What is the average number of letters waiting to
be typed?

   c) What is the average time a letter spends in the
system (waiting and being typed)?

   d) What is the probability of a letter taking longer
than 20 min. waiting to be typed and being typed?

   e) Suppose each individual typist receives letters at
the average rate of 5/hr. Assume each typist can type
at the average rate of 6 letters/hr., what is the average
time a letter would spend in the system (waiting and being
typed)?

Solution: a) The following information is given

λ = 15 letters/hr.
μ = 6 letters/hr.
S = 3

Thus, we want P(n≥3). To obtain this, we need Po, the
probability of no customers in the system given by the
equation:

$$Po = \cfrac{1}{\left\{ \left[\sum_{n=0}^{S-1} \frac{1}{n!} \left(\frac{\lambda}{\mu}\right)^n \right] + \frac{1}{S!(1 - \lambda/\mu S)} \left(\frac{\lambda}{\mu}\right)^S \right\}}$$

Substituting the given values into the above equation we
have the following:

$$Po = \cfrac{1}{\left[1 + \left(\frac{\lambda}{\mu}\right) + \frac{1}{2}\left(\frac{\lambda}{\mu}\right)^2 + \frac{1}{6}\left(\frac{\lambda}{\mu}\right)^3 \left(\cfrac{1}{\left(1 - \frac{\lambda}{3\mu}\right)}\right) \right]}$$

$$= \cfrac{1}{\left[1 + \frac{15}{6} + \frac{1}{2}\left(\frac{15}{6}\right)^2 + \frac{1}{6}\left(\frac{15}{6}\right)^3 \left(\cfrac{1}{1 - \frac{15}{18}}\right) \right]}$$

= 0.044944

Therefore, P(n≥S) = probability of the arrived letter wait-
                    ing for service
                  = probability of at least S customers in
                    the system

$$P(n≥3) = \cfrac{\left(\frac{15}{6}\right)^3 (0.044944)}{6\left(1 - \frac{15}{18}\right)}$$

= 0.70225

   b) L_q = average # of customers in queue

$$= \cfrac{\left(\frac{\lambda}{\mu}\right)^{S+1} Po}{S \cdot S!(1 - \lambda/\mu S)^2}$$

552

$$= \frac{\left(\frac{15}{6}\right)^4 (0.044944)}{(3)\ (6)\ \left(1 - \frac{15}{18}\right)^2}$$

$$= 3.51124$$

c) We first need the average number of letters in the system.

$$L = L_q + \frac{\lambda}{\mu}$$

$$= 3.51124 + \frac{15}{6}$$

$$= 6.01124$$

W = average time a customer spends in a system

$$= \frac{L}{\lambda}$$

$$= \frac{6.01124}{5}$$

$$= 0.40075 \text{ hr.}$$

$$\approx 24 \text{ min.}$$

d) The probability of a letter taking longer than 20 min. waiting to be typed and being typed

$$P(T>t) = e^{-\mu t} \left\{ 1 + \frac{(\lambda/\mu)^S P_0 \ [1 - e^{-\mu t(S-1-\lambda/\mu)}]}{S!\ (1 - \lambda/\mu S)(S - 1 - \lambda/\mu)} \right\}$$

Therefore,

$$P(T>\tfrac{1}{3}\text{hr}) = e^{-6(1/3)} \left[1 + \frac{\left(\frac{15}{6}\right)^3 (0.044944)(1-e^{-6(1/3)\left(3-1-\frac{15}{6}\right)})}{6\left(1 - \frac{15}{18}\right)\left(3 - 1 - \frac{15}{6}\right)} \right]$$

$$= 0.46198$$

e) Each queue and server can be treated as a separate single queue, single-server system so that

$$W = \frac{1}{\mu - \lambda}$$

$$= \frac{1}{6 - 5}$$

$$= 1 \text{ hr.}$$

** QUEUING PROGRAM **
** INFINITE SOURCE, INFINITE QUEUE, MULTIPLE SERVERS **

WE ASSUME
    ARRIVALS FORM A SINGLE QUEUE
    INFINITE SOURCE AND INFINITE QUEUE
    FIFO QUEUE DISCIPLINE
    THERE ARE MULTIPLE SERVERS WITH EXPONENTIAL SERVICE
    TIME
    DEPARTURES FROM SYSTEM OCCUR COMPLETELY AT RANDOM

```
      REAL*4TITLE(20), LAMBDA, MU, N, L, LQ, NFACT
5     READ(5, 10, END = 2000) TITLE
10    FORMAT (20A4)
      WRITE (6, 11) TITLE
11    FORMAT ('1', 20A4,//)
      READ (5,20) LAMBDA MU
20    FORMAT (3F10.0)
      READ (5, 20) N, S, T
      IF (LAMBDA. GE. S*MU) GO TO 700
C     ****************************************************
C     *        CALCULATE PZERO                           *
C     ****************************************************
      NS=S
      SUM=0.0
      DO 205 NK=1, NS
      SK=NK-1
      CALL FACT(SK, NFACT)
      SUM=SUM+(1/NFACT)*(LAMBDA/MU)**SK
205   CONTINUE
      CALL FACT(S, SFACT)
      PZERO=1/(SUM+(1/(SFACT*(1-LAMBDA/(MU*S))))*(LAMBDA/MU)
      **S)
C     ****************************************************
C     *        CALCULATE PN                              *
C     ****************************************************
      IF(N.GE.S) GO TO 210
      CALL FACT(N, NFACT)
      PN=(1/NFACT)*((LAMBDA/MU)**N)*PZERO
      GO TO 215
210   CALL FACT(S, SFACT)
      PN=(1/(SFACT*S**(N-S)))*((LAMBDA/MU)**N)*PZERO
C     ****************************************************
C     *        CALCULATE PS, PT, L, LQ, W, WQ            *
C     ****************************************************
215   CALL FACT(S, SFACT)
      PS=(((LAMBDA/MU)**S)*PZERO)/(SFACT*(1-LAMBDA/(MU*S)))
      PTN=((LAMBDA/MU)**S)*PZERO*(1-EXP(-MU*T*(S-1-LAMBDA/
      MU)))
      PTD=SFACT*(1-LAMBDA/MU*S))*(S-1-LAMBDA/MU)
      PT=EXP(-MU*T)*(1+PTN/PTD)
      LQ=(((LAMBDA/MU)**(S+1))*PZERO)/(S*SFACT*(1-LAMBDA/
      (MU*S))**2)
      L=LQ+LAMBDA/MU
      W=L/LAMBDA
      WQ=LQ/LAMBDA
C     ****************************************************
C     *        PRINT RESULTS                             *
C     ****************************************************
      WRITE (6,100) LAMBDA, MU, N, S, T, L, LQ, W, WQ, PT,
      PN, PZERO, PS
100   FORMAT(' LAMBDA = ', F10.5/' MU   =',F10.5/' N
      =',F10.5/' S
      * =',F10.5/'T       =',F10.5/' L   =',F10.5/' LQ
      =',F10.5
      */' W  =',F10.5/' WQ   =',F10.5/' PT   =',F10.5/' PN
      ='*,F10.5/' PZERO  =',F10.5/' PS    =',F10.5)
      GO TO 5
700   WRITE(6, 705)
705   FORMAT('QUEUING SYSTEM NOT VALID BECAUSE LAMBDA
      ≤ S*MU')
```

```
      GO TO 5
2000  STOP
      END

      SUBROUTINE FACT(P, PROD)
      NUM=P
      PROD=1.
      IF (NUM.EQ.0) GO TO 20
      DO 10 K=1, NUM
10    PROD=PROD*K
20    RETURN
      END
/DATA
      SINGLE QUEUE - MULTIPLE SERVER MODEL
      15.   6.
      1.    3.    .3333
      SINGLE QUEUE - MULTIPLE SERVER MODEL
LAMBDA = 15.00000
MU     =  6.00000
N      =  1.00000
S      =  3.00000
T      =  0.33330
L      =  6.01124
LQ     =  3.51124
W      =  0.40075
WQ     =  0.23408
PT     =  0.46198
PN     =  0.11236
PZERO  =  0.04494
PS     =  0.70225
```

A two-person barbershop has five chairs to accommodate waiting customers. Potential customers arrive at the average rate of 3.7634/hr. and spend an average of 15 min. in the barber's chair.

Assume

M = 7 (total number of persons in the system including the two barbers.)

λ = 3.7634/hr.

μ = 4/hr.

S = 2 servers.

a) What is the probability of a customer getting directly into the barber's chair upon arrival?

b) What is the expected number of customers waiting for a haircut?

c) What is the effective arrival rate assuming Pn = 1?

d) How much time can a customer expect to spend in the barbershop?

e) What fraction of potential customers are turned away?

Solution: a) The probability of a customer getting directly into the barber's chair upon arrival is the same as in the case of no customers in the system. This is computed as follows:

$$P_0 = \frac{1}{\sum\limits_{n=0}^{S}(1/n!)(\lambda/\mu)^n + (1/S!)(\lambda/\mu)^S \sum\limits_{n=S+1}^{M}(\lambda/\mu S)^{n-S}}$$

$$= \frac{1}{\sum\limits_{n=0}^{2}(1/n!)(3.7634/4)^n + \frac{1}{2}(3.7634/4)^2 \sum\limits_{n=3}^{7}(3.7634/4.2)^{n-2}}$$

$$= 0.36133$$

b) The expected number of customers waiting for a haircut:

$$L_q = \left[\frac{P_0(\lambda/\mu)^S(\lambda/\mu S)}{S!(1 - \lambda/\mu S)^2}\right]\left[1 - \left(\frac{\lambda}{\mu S}\right)^{M-S} - (M - S)\left(\frac{\lambda}{\mu S}\right)^{M-S}\left(1 - \frac{\lambda}{\mu S}\right)\right]$$

$$= \left[\frac{(0.36133)(3.7634/4)^2(3.7634/4\times2)}{2![1 - (3.7634/4\times2)]^2}\right]$$

$$\times \left[1 - \left(\frac{3.7634}{4\times2}\right)^{7-2} - (7-2)\left(\frac{3.7634}{4\times2}\right)^{7-2}\left(1 - \frac{3.7634}{4\times2}\right)\right]$$

$$= 0.2457$$

c) The effective arrival rate

$$\lambda_{eff} = \mu\left[S - \sum\limits_{n=0}^{S-1}(S-n)P_n\right]$$

where $P_n = \begin{cases} \dfrac{1}{n!}\left(\dfrac{\lambda}{\mu}\right)^n P_0 & \text{for } n \leq S \\[2mm] \dfrac{1}{S!S^{n-S}}\left(\dfrac{\lambda}{\mu}\right)^n P_0 & \text{for } S < n \leq M \\[2mm] 0 & \text{for } n > M \end{cases}$

S = number of servers
M = maximum number of persons in the system

Therefore, since $n \leq S$,

$$P_n = \frac{1}{n!}\left(\frac{\lambda}{\mu}\right)^n P_0 = \frac{1}{1}\left(\frac{3.7634}{4}\right)^1 P_0$$

$$= \frac{1}{1}\left(\frac{3.7634}{4}\right)(.36133)$$

556

$$= .2457$$

$$\lambda eff = \mu \left[S - \sum_{n=0}^{S-1} (S-n) \; Pn \right]$$

$$= 4[2 - 2(0.36133) - 0.339957]$$

$$= 3.7495$$

d) The time a customer is expected to spend in the barbershop,

$$W = \frac{L}{\lambda eff} = \frac{L_q + \left(2 - 2Po - P_1\right)}{\lambda eff}$$

$$= \frac{1.183083}{3.7495}$$

$$= 0.3155 \; hr$$

$$\cong 19 \; min$$

e) Fraction of potential customers that will be turned away

$$P(7 \; in \; the \; system) = P_7 = \frac{1}{S!S^{n-S}} \left(\frac{\lambda}{\mu} \right)^n Po$$

since $S < n \le M = 2 < 7 = 7$

$$= \frac{1}{2!2^{7-2}} \left(\frac{3.7634}{4} \right)^7 (0.36133)$$

$$= 0.00368$$

$$= 0.3 \; percent$$

Thus, only 0.3 percent of the potential customers will be turned away.

The Fortran program for the problem follows:

** INFINITE SOURCE, FINITE QUEUE, MULTIPLE SERVERS **
** QUEUING PROGRAM **

WE ASSUME
    ARRIVALS TO SYSTEM ARE COMPLETELY AT RANDOM - POISSON INPUT
    ARRIVALS FORM A SINGLE QUEUE
    INFINITE SOURCE AND FINITE QUEUE
    FIFO QUEUE DISCIPLINE
    THERE ARE MULTIPLE SERVERS WITH EXPONENTIAL SERVICE TIME
    DEPARTURES FROM SYSTEM OCCUR COMPLETELY AT RANDOM

TO CALCULATE AND PRINT
    L   AVERAGE # OF CUSTOMERS IN THE SYSTEM
    LQ   AVERAGE # OF CUSTOMERS IN QUEUE
    PN   PROBABILITY OF N CUSTOMERS IN SYSTEM AT ANY POINT IN TIME
    PZERO   PROBABILITY OF NO CUSTOMERS IN THE SYSTEM

```
          W          AVERAGE TIME CUSTOMER SPENDS IN SYSTEM
          WQ         AVERAGE TIME CUSTOMER SPENDS IN QUEUE
          LAMEFF     OVERALL EFFECTIVE ARRIVAL RATE FOR FINITE
                     QUEUE WITH INFINITE SOURCE
          REAL*4 TITLE(20), LAMBDA, MU, N, M, L, LQ, LAMEFF
5         READ(5, 10, END=2000) TITLE
10        FORMAT (20A4)
          WRITE (6, 11) TITLE
11        FORMAT ('1',20A4,//)
          READ (5, 20) LAMBDA, MU
20        FORMAT (3F10.0)
          READ (5, 20)N, M, S
C         ****************************************************
C         *       CALCULATE PZERO                            *
C         ****************************************************
          IS=S+1
          SUM=0.0
          DO 405 NK=1, IS
          SK=NK-1
          CALL FACT (SK, TFACT)
          SUM=SUM+(1/TFACT)*(LAMBDA/MU)**SK
405       CONTINUE
          SUM2=0.0
          NM=M
          DO 410 NK=IS, NM
          SUM2=SUM2+(LAMBDA/(MU*S))**(NK-S)
410       CONTINUE
          CALL FACT(S, SFACT)
          PZERO=1/(SUM+(1/SFACT)*((LAMBDA/MU)**S)*SUM2)
C         ****************************************************
C         *       CALCULATE PN AND LQ                        *
C         ****************************************************
          IF(N.LE.S) GO TO 415
          IF (N.GT.M) GO TO 420
          PN=(1/(SFACT*S**(N-S)))*((LAMBDA/MU)**N)*PZERO
          GO TO 425
415       CALL FACT(N, TFACT)
          PN=(1/TFACT)*((LAMBDA/MU)**N)*PZERO
          GO TO 425
420       PN=0.0
425       LQ=(((LAMBDA/MU)**(S+1)*PZERO)*(1-(LAMBDA/(MU*S))**
          (M-S)-(M-S)*((LAMBDA/(MU*S))**(M-S))*(1-LAMBDA/(MU*S
          ))))/(S*SFACT*(1-LAMBDA/(MU*S))**2)
C         ****************************************************
C         *       CALCULATE LAMEFF, L, W, WQ                 *
C         ****************************************************
          NS=S
          SUM=0
          DO 560 NK=1,NS
          KK=NK-1
          SKK=KK
          CALL FACT(SKK,AFACT)
          SUM=SUM+(S-KK)*PZERO*(1/AFACT)*(LAMBDA/MU)**KK
560       CONTINUE
          LAMEFF=MU*(S-SUM)
          L=LQ+LAMEFF/MU
          W=L/LAMEFF
          WQ=LQ/LAMEFF
C         ****************************************************
C         *       PRINT RESULTS                              *
C         ****************************************************
```

```fortran
      WRITE (6,810) LAMBDA, MU, L, LQ, N, PN, PZERO, W,
     WQ, LAMEFF
810   FORMAT(' LAMBDA =',F10.5/' MU   =',F10.5/' L
     =',F10.5/' LQ   =',F10.5/' N   =',F10.5/' PN
     =',F10.5/' PZERO   =',F10.5/' WQ  =',F10.5/' LAMEFF
     =',F10.5)
      GO TO 5
2000  STOP
      END

      SUBROUTINE FACT(P, PROD)
      NUM=P
      PROD=1.
      IF (NUM.EQ.0) GO TO 20
      DO 10 K=1, NUM
10    PROD=PROD*K
20    RETURN
      END
/DATA
      WITH N=1
      3.7634      4.
      1.          7.          2.

      WITH N=1
LAMBDA = 3.76340
MU     = 4.00000
L      = 1.18309
LQ     = 0.24571
N      = 1.00000
PN     = 0.33996
PZERO  = 0.36133
W      = 0.31553
WQ     = 0.06553
LAMEFF = 3.74953
```

● **PROBLEM** 16-19

Suppose a one-person tailor shop is in the business of
making men's suits. Each suit requires four distinct
tasks to be performed before it is completed. Assume all
four tasks must be completed on each suit before another
suit is started. Assume also that the time to perform
each task has an exponential distribution with a mean of
2 hours. Determine

(a) Average number of customers in the system.

(b) Average number of customers in the queue.

(c) Average time a customer spends in the system.

(d) Average time customer spends in the queue.

(e) Probability of no customers in the system.

Solution: (a) The average number of customers in the
system equals

$$L = \frac{\lambda}{\mu} + \frac{\lambda^2(1/K\mu^2) + (\lambda/\mu)^2}{2(1 - \lambda/\mu)}$$

$$= \frac{\lambda}{\mu} + \frac{[(K + 1)/K](\lambda^2/\mu^2)}{[2(\mu - \lambda)]/\mu}$$

$$= \left(\frac{K + 1}{2K}\right)\left(\frac{\lambda^2}{\mu(\mu - \lambda)}\right) + \frac{\lambda}{\mu}$$

where K is the number of stations in the service facility, where the service time T_1 at each station is independent on the service times at the other stations and has an exponential distribution with mean $1/K\mu$. Therefore, the service time for each task is

$$\frac{1}{4\mu} = 2 \text{ hr}$$

$$\mu = \frac{1}{8} \text{ order/hr}$$

$$L = \frac{5}{8} \frac{(5.5/48)^2}{\left(\frac{1}{8}\right)\left(\frac{1}{8} - 5.5/48\right)} + \frac{(5.5/48)}{\frac{1}{8}}$$

$$= 7.2188$$

(b) Average number of customers in the queue

$$L_q = \left(\frac{K + 1}{2K}\right)\left(\frac{\lambda^2}{\mu(\mu - \lambda)}\right)$$

$$= \left[\frac{4 + 1}{(2)(4)}\right]\left[\frac{\left(\frac{5.5}{48}\right)^2}{\frac{1}{8}\left(\frac{1}{8} - \frac{5.5}{48}\right)}\right]$$

$$= 6.30185$$

(c) Average time customer spends in the system

$$W = \frac{L}{\lambda}$$

$$= \frac{7.2188}{5.5/48}$$

$$= 63 \text{ hr.}$$

$$\approx 1.3 \text{ weeks}$$

(d) $\quad L_q = \left(\frac{K + 1}{2K}\right)\left(\frac{\lambda^2}{\mu(\mu - \lambda)}\right)$

$$W_q = \frac{L_q}{\lambda}$$

$$L_q = \left[\frac{4 + 1}{2(4)}\right]\left[\frac{(5.5/48)^2}{\frac{1}{8}\left(\frac{1}{8} - 5.5/48\right)}\right]$$

$$W_q = \frac{\left[\frac{5}{8}\right]\left[\frac{(5.5/48)^2}{\frac{1}{8}\left(\frac{1}{8} - 5.5/48\right)}\right]}{\frac{5.5}{48}}$$

$$= 54.99812$$

(e) Probability of no customers in the system,

$$P_o = 1 - \lambda E(T)$$

where $E(T) = \frac{1}{\mu}$

$$P_o = 1 - \left(\frac{5.5}{48}\right)(8)$$

$$= 0.08334$$

```
C                    **    QUEUING PROGRAM    **
C          **   ARBITRARY DISTRIBUTION OF SERVICE TIME    **
C
C      WE ASSUME
C          ARRIVALS TO SYSTEM ARE COMPLETELY AT RANDOM - POISSON
C          INPUT
C          ARRIVALS FORM A SINGLE QUEUE
C          INFINITE SOURCE AND INFINITE QUEUE
C          FIFO QUEUE DISCIPLINE
C          THERE IS A SINGLE SERVER IN THE SERVICE FACILITY
C          SERVICE TIME (T) HAS AN ARBITRARY DISTRIBUTION
C                    WITH MEAN ETIM AND VARIANCE VARTIM
C          1/LAMBDA > ETIM

       REAL *4 TITLE(20),L,LQ,LAMBDA
     5 READ(5,10,END=2000)TITLE
    10 FORMAT(20A4)
       WRITE(6,11)TITLE
    11 FORMAT('1',20A4,//)
       READ(5,20)LAMBDA,ETIM,VARTIM
    20 FORMAT(3F10.0)
       IF(1/LAMBDA.LE.ETIM) GO TO 40
C      ****************************************************
C      *   CALCULATE QUANTITIES AND PRINT RESULTS         *
C      ****************************************************
       PROD=LAMBDA*ETIM
```

```
      PZERO=1-PROD
      L=PROD+(LAMBDA*LAMBDA*VARTIM+PROD*PROD)/(2*PZERO)
      LQ=L-PROD
      W=L/LAMBDA
      WQ=LQ/LAMBA
      WRITE(6,30)LAMBDA,ETIM,VARTIM,L,LQ,W,WQ,PZERO
   30 FORMAT(' LAMBDA =',F10.5/' ETIM  =',F10.5/' VARTIM =',
     *    F10.5/' L
     *      =',F10.5/' LQ    =',F10.5/'   W   =',F10.5/' WQ
     *            =',F10.5*
     *  /' PZERO  =',F10.5)
      GO TO 5
   40 WRITE(6,45)
   45 FORMAT(' PROBLEM NOT VALID BECAUSE 1/LAMBDA > ETIM')
      GO TO 5
 2000 STOP
      END


      /DATA

      ERLANG SERVICE TIME
      .114583    8.    16.


      LAMBDA = 0.11458
      ETIM   = 8.00000
      VARTIM = 16.00000
      L      = 7.21852
      LQ     = 6.30185
      W      = 62.99812
      WQ     = 54.99812
      PZERO  = 0.08334
```

● **PROBLEM** 16-20

One of the first problems in linear programming was the so-called diet problem. The problem was to minimize the cost of eating three meals a day while meeting minimum daily requirements of certain essential nutrients.

Suppose we consider only the contribution of vegetables to the nutritional requirements. How many times should each vegetable be served during the next week in order to minimize cost while satisfying the nutritional and taste requirements?

Use the following information:

Units per serving

Vegetable	Iron	Phosphorus	Vitamin A	Vitamin B	Niacin	Cost/ Serving
Green beans	0.45	10	415	8	0.3	5¢
Carrots	0.45	28	9065	3	0.35	5¢
Broccoli	1.05	50	2550	53	0.6	8¢
Cabbage	0.4	25	75	27	0.15	2¢

Beets	0.5	22	15	5	0.25	6¢
Potatoes	0.5	75	235	8	0.8	3¢

Minimum daily requirements from vegetables

6.0	325	17500 USP	245 mg	5.0 mg

In addition, cabbage cannot be served more than twice during the week, and the other vegetables cannot be served more than four times each during the week. A total of 14 servings of vegetables are required during the week.

Solution: A linear programming problem is said to be in canonical form when it is in the form:

$$\text{Min } a_1 x_1 + a_2 x_2 + \ldots + a_n x_n = C \tag{1}$$

subject to

$$b_{11} x_1 + b_{12} x_2 + \ldots + b_{1n} x_n \geq C_1$$
$$b_{21} x_1 + b_{22} x_2 + \ldots + b_{2n} x\, n \geq C_2 \tag{2}$$

$$\vdots$$

$$b_{m1} x_1 + b_{m2} x_2 + \ldots + b_{mn} x_n \geq C_m$$

and $\quad x_i \geq 0 \qquad i = 1, 2, \ldots, n \tag{3}$

To convert the given problem into canonical form, let

x_1 = number of times to serve green beans

x_2 = number of times to serve carrots

x_3 = number of times to serve broccoli

x_4 = number of times to serve cabbage

x_5 = number of times to serve beets

x_6 = number of times to serve potatoes

The cost of one serving of green beans is $0.05. Thus x_1 servings will cost $5x_1$ (in cents)

Similarly, x_4 servings of cabbage will cost $2x_4$. If we multiply the number of servings for a given vegetable by the cost per serving and sum over all vegetables, we will obtain the cost function (1). Thus, we have

$$\text{Min } 5x_1 + 5x_2 + 8x_3 + 2x_4 + 6x_5 + 3x_6$$

563

Next, we hunt for the constraints. The minimum daily requirements from vegetables of iron, phosphorus, vitamin A, vitamin B and Niacin must be met or exceeded. Thus, for iron,

$$.45x_1 + .45x_2 + 1.05x_3 + .4x_4 + .5x_5 + .5x_6 \geq 42.0$$

Here the minimum daily requirement of iron, 6.0 is multiplied by 7 to give the weekly requirement. Proceeding with the other nutrients in a similar manner, we obtain the constraint inequalities

$$\text{Min} \quad 5x_1 + 5x_2 + 8x_3 + 2x_4 + 6x_5 + 3x_6$$

subject to

Iron $\quad .45x_1 + .45x_2 + 1.05x_3 + .4x_4 + .5x_5 + .5x_6 \geq 42.0$

Phos. $\quad 10x_1 + 28x_2 + 50\ x_3 + 25x_4 + 22x_5 + 75x_6 \geq 2275$

Vitamin
A $\quad 415x_1 + 9065x_2 + 2550x_3 + 75x_4 + 25x_5 + 235x_6 \geq 122500$

Vitamin
C $\quad 8x_1 + 3x_2 + 53x_3 + 27x_4 + 5x_5 + 8x_6 \geq 1715$

Niacin $\quad .3x_1 + .35x_2 + .6x_3 + .15x_4 + .25x_5 + .8x_6 \geq 35$

$$
\begin{array}{lr}
x_1 & \leq 4 \\
x_2 & \leq 4 \\
x_3 & \leq 4 \\
x_4 & \leq 2 \\
x_5 & \leq 4 \\
x_6 & \leq 4 \\
\end{array}
$$

$$x_1 \geq 0 \quad x_2 \geq 0 \quad x_3 \geq 0 \quad x_4 \geq 0 \ .$$

The next step is to convert the program into a form suitable for computer manipulation. We add slack variables S_i to convert all inequalities into equalities. The simplex algorithm is then applied to the resulting system of equations to obtain an optimal solution.

The simplex algorithm is available as a packaged program in most installations.

If the year 1975 (year 1) is started with a 2 year old truck, what decision should be made at the start of this year and the start of the next four years in order to maximize the total return.

Solution: This is a problem in dynamic optimization. A series of decisions must be made over time so as to maximize some chosen quantity. Each decision by itself may be non-optimal; the optimality of the sequence of decisions is what matters. As an example, suppose X wishes to travel from city A to city F and has the choice of routes ABCF and ADEF. It is possible for AB to cost less than AD and yet ADEF may be cheaper overall (DE is less than BC and EF is less than CF).

Going back to the initial problem, let

1) $r_i(t)$ = revenue in period i from a truck that was made in year (i - t) and is t years old at the start of period i. For example $r_3(3) = 8$.

2) $u_i(t)$ = upkeep in period i on a truck that was made in year (i - t) and is t years old at the start of period i. For example, a truck made in 1975 requires an upkeep of 2 in 1978, i.e., $u_5(3) = 2$.

3) $c_i(t)$ = cost to replace a truck that was made in year (i - t) and is t years old at the start of period i.

4) IT = age of the given truck = 2.

5) $f_i(t)$ = optimal return for periods i, i + 1,...., 5 when the i-th period is started with a truck that is t years old.

6) $X_i(t)$ = decision to make at the start of period i that will yield $f_i(t)$. The only two possible decisions are to keep the old truck or to purchase a new one.

Suppose the current truck was 2 years old at the start of 1975 (year 1), and the estimates in table I are available.

Suppose we decide to keep the current truck until 1979. Then the total revenue is

$$10 + 8 + 8 + 6 + 4 = 36.$$

Total upkeep is
$$3 + 3 + 4 + 4 + 5 = 19.$$

Thus total return is 17. On the other hand, suppose we decide to replace the 1973 truck with a truck made in 1975 at the start of 1975. Then, total revenue is

$$14 + 16 + 16 + 14 + 12 = 72$$

and the upkeep costs are

TABLE I: Truck made __ 1973 (year minus 1)

Age	2	3	4	5	6
Revenue	10	8	8	6	4
Upkeep	3	3	4	4	5
Replacement	25	26	27	28	29

Truck made in 1975 (year 1)

Age	0	1	2	3	4
Revenue	14	16	16	14	12
Upkeep	1	1	2	2	3
Replacement	20	22	24	25	26

Truck made in 1976 (year 2)

Age	0	1	2	3
Revenue	16	14	14	12
Upkeep	1	1	2	2
Replacement	20	22	24	25

Truck made in 1977 (year 3)

Age	0	1	2
Revenue	18	16	16
Upkeep	1	1	2
Replacement	20	22	24

Truck made in 1973 (year 4)

Age	0	1
Revenue	18	16
Upkeep	1	1
Replacement	21	22

Truck made in 1979 (year 5)

Age	0
Revenue	20
Upkeep	1
Replacement	21

$$1 + 1 + 2 + 2 + 3 = 9.$$

Replacement costs are 25 and hence total return is 38. Of course we could keep the truck for a year and then sell it. The total return in this case works out to 37. Clearly there is a large number of possible choices. The functional equation for period i is

$$f_i(t) = \max \begin{bmatrix} \text{purchase:} & r_i(0) - u_i(0) - C_i(t) + f_{i+1}(1) \\ \text{keep:} & r_i(t) - u_i(t) + f_i + 1(t+1) \end{bmatrix}$$

for $i = 1, 2, \ldots, 5$ and $t = 1, 2, \ldots (i-1), (i + IT - 1)$.

We now apply the functional equation working backwards. That is, assume that the fifth year is reached with a truck that is 1, 2, 3, 4, or 6 years old.

Thus, for $i = 5$ and $t = 1$

$$f_5(1) = \max \begin{bmatrix} \text{Purchase:} & r_5(0) - u_5(0) - C_5(1) + f_6(1) \\ \text{Keep:} & r_5(1) - u_5(1) + f_6(2) \end{bmatrix}$$

Note that $f_6(j) = 0$ for all j. Then

$$f_5(1) = \max \begin{bmatrix} 20 - 1 - 22 + 0 \\ 16 - 1 + 0 \end{bmatrix} = 15$$

Thus, we keep the 1978 truck in 1979, i.e., $x_5(1)$ is Keep.

At $t = 2$

$$f_5(2) = \max \begin{bmatrix} \text{Purchase:} & r_5(0) - u_5(0) - C_5(2) \\ \text{Keep:} & r_5(2) - u_5(2) \end{bmatrix}$$

$$= \max \begin{bmatrix} 20 - 1 - 24 \\ 16 - 2 \end{bmatrix} = 14$$

$x_5(2) = $ Keep

$t = 3$

$$f_5(3) = \max \begin{bmatrix} \text{Purchase:} & 20 - 1 - 25 \\ \text{Keep:} & 12 - 2 \end{bmatrix} = 10$$

$x_5(3) = $ Keep

$t = 4$

$$f_5(4) = \max \begin{bmatrix} \text{Purchase:} & 20 - 1 - 26 \\ \text{Keep:} & 12 - 3 \end{bmatrix} = 9$$

$x_5(4) = $ Keep

$t = 6$

$$f_5(6) = \max \begin{bmatrix} \text{Purchase: } 20 - 1 - 29 \\ \text{Keep: } \quad\quad 4 - 5 \end{bmatrix} = -1$$

$x_5(6) = $ Keep.

Now, assume that the start of the fourth period is reached with a 1, 2, 3, or 5 year old truck. The optimal decision to make in order to maximize the return from the last two periods is given by the functional equation:

$$f_4(t) = \max \begin{bmatrix} P: r_4(0) - u_4(0) - C_4(t) + f_5(1) \\ K: r_4(t) - u_4(t) + f_5(t + 1) \end{bmatrix}$$

$t = 1, 2, 3, 5$

Thus,

$$f_4(1) = \max \begin{bmatrix} P: 18 - 1 - 22 + 15 \\ K: 16 - 1 + 14 \end{bmatrix} = 29$$

$x_4(1) = $ Keep

$$f_4(2) = \max \begin{bmatrix} P: 18 - 1 - 24 + 15 \\ K: 14 - 2 + 10 \end{bmatrix} = 22$$

$x_4(2) = $ Keep

$$f_4(3) = \max \begin{bmatrix} P: 18 - 1 - 25 + 15 \\ K: 14 - 2 + 9 \end{bmatrix} = 21$$

$x_4(3) = $ Keep

$$f_4(5) = \max \begin{bmatrix} P: 18 - 1 - 28 + 15 \\ K: 6 - 4 + (-1) \end{bmatrix} = 4$$

$x_4(5) = $ Purchase

Moving back to the start of the third period and considering the optimal policy over the last three periods when the third period is started with a 1, 2 or 4 year old truck, we have

$$f_3(t) = \max \begin{bmatrix} P: r_3(0) - u_3(0) - C_3(t) + f_4(1) \\ K: r_3(t) - u_3(t) + f_4(t + 1) \end{bmatrix}$$

$t = 1, 2, 4$

$$f_3(1) = \max \begin{bmatrix} P: 18 - 1 - 22 + 29 \\ K: 14 - 1 + 22 \end{bmatrix} = 35$$

$x_3(1) = $ Keep

568

$$f_3(2) = \max \begin{bmatrix} P: 18 - 1 - 24 + 29 \\ \\ K: 16 - 2 + 21 \end{bmatrix} = 35$$

$x_3(2)$ = Keep

$$f_3(4) = \max \begin{bmatrix} P: 18 - 1 - 27 + 29 \\ \\ K: 8 - 4 + 4 \end{bmatrix} = 19$$

$x_3(4)$ = Purchase

Now move backwards from period 2 with t = 1,3.

$$f_2(1) = \max \begin{bmatrix} P: 16 - 1 - 22 + 35 \\ \\ K: 16 - 1 + 35 \end{bmatrix} = 50$$

$x_2(1)$ = Keep

$$f_2(3) = \max \begin{bmatrix} P: 16 - 1 - 26 + 35 \\ \\ K: 8 - 3 + 19 \end{bmatrix} = 24$$

$x_2(3)$ = Purchase or Keep

Finally, period 1 is reached where we have a 2-year old truck. To arrive at a decision whether to keep it or replace it in order to maximize the total return over the next five periods, we have

$$f_1(2) = \max \begin{bmatrix} P: 14 - 1 - 25 + 50 \\ \\ K: 10 - 3 + 24 \end{bmatrix} = 38$$

$x_1(2)$ = Purchase.

Thus, we purchase a truck at the start of 1975. We keep this truck in 1976, 1977, 1978 and 1979 in order to maximize total returns over the next four years.

● **PROBLEM** 16-22

Mrs. Jones has some money which she wants to invest in a number of activities (investment programs) in such a way that the total return is maximized.

Assume that she has $8,000 for allocation and that the investments can only be integral multiples of $1000. Three investment programs are available. The return function for each program is tabulated below:

Return Functions $h_i(x)$

X(000)	0	1	2	3	4	5	6	7	8
$h_1(x)$	0	5	15	40	80	90	95	98	100

$h_2(x)$	0	5	15	40	60	70	73	74	75
$h_3(x)$	0	4	26	40	45	50	51	52	53

Using the principles of dynamic programming, how would the optimal investment in each program be determined so as to maximize total return?

Solution: The problem can be solved recursively, i.e., the optimal solution for one stage is used as input for the next stage.

Step 1: Assume that program 3 is the only program. Then the optimal return from investing

$$X = 0,1,2,\ldots,8$$

in $h_3(x)$ is given by the last row of the table above. In particular, $h_3(8) = 53$ is the optimal return.

Step 2: Now assume only programs 2 and 3 are available and that $d_2(x)$, $d_3(y)$ can be invested in programs 2 and 3, where

$$x = 0,1,\ldots,8 \quad y = 0,1,2,\ldots,8 \quad \text{and} \quad x + y = 0,1,2,\ldots,8$$

Thus, with 8 we can invest 0 in 2 and 8 in 3, with 5 3 in 2 and 2 in 3 and so on. Find the optimum of all these choices for each x in $0,1,2,\ldots,8$. The functional equation is

$$f_2(x) = \max \left[g_2(y) + f_3(x) \right]$$

$$y = 0,1,\ldots,8 - x$$

$$x = 0,1,\ldots,8$$

Step 3: The final stage is the same as the original problem. We now assume all three programs are available. We examine the results of investing z in program 1 and 8 - z units in programs 2 and 3 (the optimal amounts for each 8 - z (z = 0,1,2,..,8) have already been found in Step 2).

The functional equation for the last stage is

$$f_i(x) = \max [g_i(z) + f_{i+1}(x - z)$$

$$x = 0,\ldots,8$$

$$z = 0,1,\ldots,x$$

$$d_i(x) = \text{value of z that yields } f_i(x)$$

where $f_i(x)$ is the optimal return from investing x units

570

in programs i, i + 1,..,3 and $d_i(x)$ is the optimal amount to invest in program i when x units are available to invest in programs i, i + 1,...,3 for i = 1,2,3.

SIMULATION

An important application of computers to market research is in computer simulation of continuous models. As an example, there appears to be a positive relationship between the number of new houses built and the sale of washing machines.

Give a differential equation connecting the growth of houses and washing machines. Illustrate with graphs.

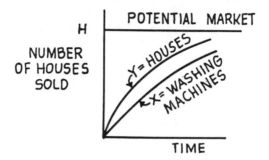

Solution: A mathematical model is said to be continuous when the variables of the system change smoothly over time. Quantities that change continuously over time are best studied with the use of differential equations.

Let H be the potential number of families and y be the number of families with houses. H is a constant upper limit on the number of houses and, thus, the number of washing machines that can be sold. Furthermore, assuming that every new house requires a washing machine, the unfilled market is the difference between houses sold and washing machines sold. Finally, as the number of new houses approaches H, the market approaches saturation and the rate of selling houses and, by extension, washing machines drops. The given figure applies:

From the figure, the slope of the function between number of houses sold and time is seen to decrease with time, reaching zero at the time when y(t) = H.

Let y = y(t). Then y(0) = 0.

If we assume that the rate of new houses sold is a constant function of the remaining potential market, the differential equation is

$$\dot{y} = k_1 (H - y) \qquad y(0) = 0 \qquad (1)$$

Give an example of a distributed lag model for the national
economy, using the national accounting scheme. Is the
computer essential for dealing with distributed lag
models?

Solution: In simulation studies, a problem in the real
world is solved using a simple mathematical model in
conjunction with the computer. Distributed lag models
belong to the class of discrete simulation models. Such
models change only at fixed intervals of time, and current
values of a given variable are determined by previous values
of the same variable.

Using Keynesian macroeconomic analysis we can construct
a model of the national economy. Let C be consumption, I
be investment, T be taxes, G be government expenditure and
Y be national income.

Then, a general macroeconomic model would be:

$$C = a + c(Y-T)$$
$$I = b + rY \tag{1}$$
$$T = tY$$
$$Y = c + I + G$$

Here, "a" represents consumption that is independent of
income while "c" is the marginal propensity to consume.
"c" represents the amount per dollar that is spent on consumption. "b" is investment that is independent of income,
and "r" is the marginal propensity to invest. Finally,
"t" is the tax rate per dollar of income. Note that
$o \leq c$, r, $t \leq 1$.

Since simulation deals with concrete situations, we
should give values to the parameters in (1). Thus,

$$C = 30 + 0.7(Y - T)$$
$$I = 3 + 0.1(Y) \tag{2}$$
$$T = .2Y$$
$$Y = C + I + G.$$

The above static model can be made dynamic by picking a
fixed time interval and then expressing the current values
of the variables in terms of values at previous intervals,
or lagging them. Thus, we can lag all the variables in
(2) by a year to obtain

$$C = 30 + 0.7(Y_{-1} - T_{-1})$$
$$I = 3 + 0.1(Y_{-1}) \tag{3}$$
$$T = 0.2Y_{-1}$$
$$Y = C_{-1} + I_{-1} + G_{-1}$$

Model (3) is to be understood as follows: Current consumption depends on disposable income from the previous year.

Investment is a function of the previous year's national income, as is taxes.

In large-scale models, like (3), most calculations can be done without the aid of the computer. But at lower levels of aggregation (say where investment in different industries is considered separately), the computer is indispensable.

● **PROBLEM** 16-25

Consider an elementary inventory control system where there is no delay between the ordering of goods and their receipt into inventory. Suppose the order rate is directly proportional to the difference between desired inventory and actual inventory, with proportionality constant 1/A, where A is the time that would be required to correct the inventory if the order rate were constant. Write a FORTRAN program to simulate this system, using modified Euler's method (the method is fully explained, and the subroutine for it is given in the SIMULATION chapter) from time $t=0$ to $t=t_f$ if $I(t)$ is the inventory level at time t and $I(0)=I_0$.

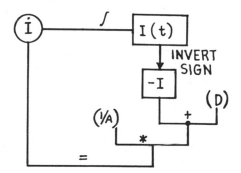

Solution: Clearly, the goal of this system is to maintain the desired inventory, D. If $\dot{I}$ is the order rate (and hence, the rate of change in inventory, since there is no delay), we can write:

$$\dot{I} = 1/A(D - I) \tag{1}$$

with block diagram as follows:

Note that this model "fills to capacity" using negative feedback control. That is, knowledge of the present system state is used to determine the future system state. If change in inventory is done continuously, the exact solution to equation (1) would be:

$$I(t) = D - (D - I_{\emptyset})e^{-t/A}$$

Note, that as $t \to \infty$, $I(t)$ approaches D, which is the steady state solution, the program looks as follows:

```
       DATA T/Ø , Ø/
       COMMON D, A
       INPUT N, TFIN, ACCUR, D, A, IØ
       OUTPUT T, I
       SPACE = D - IØ
       REALN = N
       DT = TFIN/REALN
       I = IØ
       DO 1Ø J = 1, N
            T = T + DT
            CALL MEULER (T, I, ACCUR, DT)
            EXACT = D - SPACE * EXP(-T/A)
            ERROR = ABS((EXACT - I)/EXACT)*1ØØ.
            OUTPUT T, I, EXACT, ERROR
1Ø     CONTINUE
       STOP
       END
       FUNCTION G (W)
       COMMON, D, A
       G = (D - W)/A
       RETURN
       END
```

● **PROBLEM** 16-26

Consider an elementary inventory control system where
goods are received at a rate R (units of good per time
period), where R is directly proportional to the number of
goods on order, G(t), with proportionality constant 1/L,
where L is the delay in ordering. Suppose the order rate
is directly proportional to the difference between desired
inventory and actual inventory, with proportionality constant 1/A where A is the time that would be required to
correct the inventory if the order rate were constant.
Write a FORTRAN program to simulate this system, using
modified Euler's method (the method is fully explained,
and the subroutine for it is given in the SIMULATION chapter) from time t=0 to t=t_f if I(t) is the inventory level
at time t, I(o)=Io and G(o) = Go.

Solution: Note that this system's goal is maintaining
the desired inventory. A first picture of this system
might be as shown in Fig. 1.

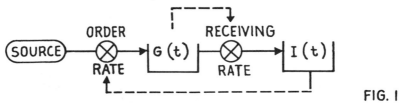

FIG. I

Where the solid arrows represent the flow of goods and the
broken arrows represent the flow of information. If $\dot{I}$
is the time rate of change of I(t):

$$\dot{I} = R = G/L \tag{1}$$

If G is the net time rate of change of G(t), W the order

574

rate, and D the desired inventory, then

$$\dot{G} = W - R$$
$$= (D-I)/A - G/L \tag{2}$$

Converting equations (1) and (2) into block diagram form
details the relationships in this coupled negative feedback system:

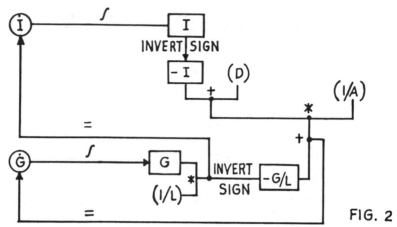

FIG. 2

The program applies the modified Euler method first to
equation (1) and then to equation (2). The variable GOODS
is used for G(t). I and GOODS are kept in a COMMON block
so that the new computed value of I will be used in
determining GOODS. A logical flag, ORDER, is used to
determine which equation is being integrated:

```
      REAL T/0, 0/, TFIN, DT, REALN, ACCUR, I, GOODS,
          IØ, GØ, L, D, A
      INTEGER J, N
      LOGICAL ORDER/. FALSE. /
      COMMON ORDER, I, GOODS, L, D, A
      INPUT N, TFIN, ACCUR, IØ, GØ, L, D, A
      OUTPUT T, IØ, GØ
      REALN = N
      DT = TFIN/REALN
      I = IØ
      GOODS = GØ
      DO 1Ø  I = 1, N
          T = T + DT
          CALL MEULER (T, I, ACCUR, DT)
          ORDER = .TRUE.
          CALL MEULER (T, GOODS, ACCUR, DT)
          ORDER = .FALSE.
          OUTPUT T, I, GOODS
1Ø    CONTINUE
      STOP
      END
      FUNCTION G(W)
      REAL G, W, I, GOODS, D, L, A

      LOGICAL ORDER
      COMMON ORDER, I, GOODS, L, D, A
      G = GOODS/L
      IF (ORDER)G = (D - I)/A - W/L
      RETURN
      END
```

575

In a competitive market (one in which no individual supplier is powerful enough to influence prices), the relation between the supply and demand of a good is assumed to be the following:

If the supply, S, exceeds the demand, D (surplus), the demand falls. If D exceeds S (shortage), the price rises.

Assuming there is no delay between the occurrence of surplus or shortage and the price change it causes, write a FORTRAN program which uses the modified Euler method (the method is fully explained, and the subroutine for it is given in the SIMULATION chapter) to simulate this system from time t=o to t=t_F, if the price of the good (in dollars per unit of good) at time t is p(t), p(o) = Po>o, and it is observed that:

Case(1): D = f(p(t)) and S = h(p(t)) where f and g are linear quantities.

Case (2): D = f(p(t)) is inversely proportional to $[p(t)]^2$ with proportionality factor d_1>2po and S is directly proportional to $[p(t)]^{0.11}$ with proportionality factor s_1.

D and S are expressed as units of good per time period. Compare the modified Euler approximations with exact values, where feasible.

Solution: First note that exogenous factors, such as government price control, will be neglected in this model. Negative demand and supply can be interpreted as return of goods, as the diagram below shows (the arrows represent flow of goods):

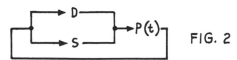

FIG. I

Also note that D = f(p), S = g(P) implies D, S vary only with price: all other influences (e.g. tastes, income, technological change, etc.) are held fixed in this model.

Since both demand and supply depend on price and both determine price, we recognize that this system has feedback. Therefore, the block diagram of the system will contain a linkage between output and input:

FIG. 2

The assumed relation between supply, demand and price can

be expressed mathematically:

$$\dot{p} = K(D - S) \tag{1}$$

where $\dot{p}$ is the time rate of change of price (in dollars per unit time period), and K is a constant of proportionality, $0<K<1$. Equation (1) is dimensionally correct only if K has dimension of dollars per (unit of good)^2. This relation can be diagrammed as:

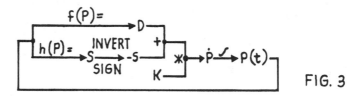

FIG. 3

The problem is to observe the system when both $D = f(p)$ and $S = h(p)$ are given first by Case 1 and then by Case 2:

Case 1: $D = f(p) = a_1 + b_1 p(t)$ $\tag{2}$

$S = h(p) = a_2 + b_2 p(t)$ $\tag{3}$

where a_2, b_2, a_1 and b_1 are constants, each with dimension:

(unit of good)^2 per dollar per time period. Substituting equations (2) and (3) into equation (1):

$$\dot{p} = K(a_1 + b_1 p - (a_2 + b_2 p))$$

$$= K (a_1 - a_2 - (b_2 - b_1)p) \tag{4}$$

If the time period becomes vanishingly small, the exact solution of equation (4) can be shown to be:

$$p(t) = \frac{A}{B} - \left(\frac{A}{B} - Po\right)e^{-Bt}$$

where $A = K(a_1 - a_2)$ and $B = K(b_2 - b_1)$. Note that as $t\to\infty$, price$\to A/B$. What would happen if the initial price were A/B? Substituting A/B for p in equation (4):

$$\dot{p} = K(a_1 - a_2 - (b_2 - b_1)(A/B))$$

$$= K\left[a_1 - a_2 - (b_2 - b_1) \frac{K(a_1 - a_2)}{K(b_2 - b_1)} \right]$$

$$= K\left[a_1 - a_2 - (b_2 - b_1) \frac{(a_1 - a_2)}{(b_2 - b_1)} \right]$$

$$= K[a_1 - a_2 - (a_1 - a_2)] = K [o] = 0$$

Therefore, if initially, $p = A/B$, then $\dot{p} = 0$ so that price will never change. In fact, whenever price reaches A/B, it will remain there. $p = A/B$ is the equilibrium price. The system is asymptotically stable (at that equilibrium point). What this means to the programmer is that if he finds that a state variable is not changing from its initial value, one possibility is that the initial value is an equilibrium point for that system. The program is as follows:

```
      DATA T/Ø.Ø/
      COMMON A, B
      INPUT N, TFIN, ACCUR, A1, A2, B1, B2, K, PØ
      OUTPUT T, PØ
      REALN = N
      DT = TFIN/REALN
      P = PØ
      A = K*(A1 - A2)
      B = K*(B2 - B1)
      SPACE = A/B - PØ
      DO 1Ø I = 1, N
           T = T + DT
           CALL MEULER (T, P, ACCUR, DT)
           EXACT = A/B - SPACE*EXP(-B*T)
           ERROR = ABS((EXACT - P)/EXACT)*1ØØ.
           OUTPUT T, P, EXACT, ERROR
1Ø    CONTINUE
      STOP
      END
      FUNCTION G (W)
      COMMON A, B
      G = A - B*W
      RETURN
      END
```

Case 2: $D = f(p) = d_1/[p(t)]^2$ $\qquad\qquad\qquad$ (5)

$\qquad\qquad S = g(p) = S_1[p(t)]^{0.11}$ $\qquad\qquad\qquad$ (6)

where d_1, S_1 are positive constants. The dimensions of d_1 and S_1 must be such that D and S will have the correct units upon dimensional analysis. Substituting equations (5) and (6) into equation (1):

$$\dot{p} = K[(d_1/p^2) - S_1p^{0.11}] \qquad\qquad\qquad (7)$$

Equation (7) is a nonlinear differential equation. In general, exact analytical solutions for nonlinear differential equations have not been found. This is where a numerical method that can be implemented on a computer, such as the modified Euler method, can be of most value. The program is as follows:

```
      DATA T/Ø.Ø/
      COMMON D1, S1, K
      INPUT N, TFIN, ACCUR, D1, S1, K, PØ
      OUTPUT T, P
      REALN = N
      DT = TFIN/REALN
      P = PØ
      DO 1Ø I = 1, N
           T = T + DT
           CALL MEULER (T, P, ACCUR, DT)
           OUTPUT T, P
```

```
1Ø      CONTINUE
        STOP
        END
        FUNCTION G(W)
        COMMON Dl, Sl, K
        G = K*((Dl/(W**2)) - (Sl*(W**0.ll)))
        RETURN
        END
```

● **PROBLEM** 16-28

Draw and explain a system dynamics diagram of a market
model.

Solution: System dynamics analyzes the forces operating
in a system in order to determine their influence on the
stability or growth of the system. Here, stability is
determined by the rates of changes of different variables.

        Consider the following system dynamics diagram of
a market model.

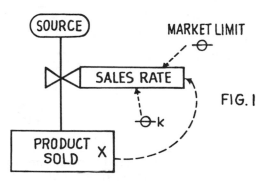

This diagram depicts a modified exponential growth model in
which a variable increases in value at first at an increasing rate and then later at a decreasing rate until it
reaches an upper limit. This corresponds to a typical
marketing situation. At first, as the product is introduced into the market, sales will increase rapidly. Later
as the saturation point is approached, the increase in
sales will gradually taper off. Next, consider the various
symbols used in the System Dynamics model. The number of
products sold can be viewed as a level in a reservoir of
products. Levels are represented by boxes. Rates are
represented by boxes with valves attached. The constants
of the system are indicated by the symbol $\ominus$.

        The differential equation corresponding to the
system diagram is:

$\dot{x} = k(X - x)$ (4)

with initial condition x(o) = 0

        The solution is $x = X(1 - e^{-kt})$ which is known as
a modified exponential curve.

579

A computer simulation model would solve (4) for various values of k, the sales rate constant, and X, the market limit.

Consider a market model showing a positive relationship between number of new houses sold and washing machines sold. Assuming that the number of households increases exponentially and that washing machines break down, draw a system dynamics model for the above system.

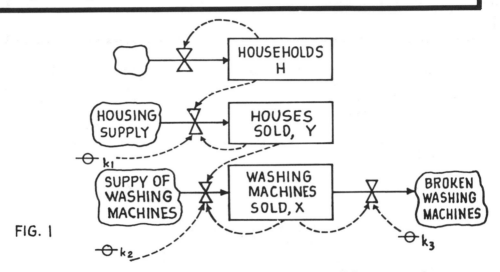

FIG. 1

Solution: Let H be the number of households, y - the number of houses sold and x - the number of washing machines installed. Since the number of houses sold increases exponentially, the differential equation that gives the rate of change of houses sold over time is

$$\dot{y} = k(H - y). \tag{1}$$

If the washing machines, once installed, never broke down, the rate of growth of washing machines would be

$$\dot{x} = k_2(y - x).$$

But washing machines do break down. This means that x, the number of washing machines in use should fall, for every level of x. A new equation needs to be given for x. Assuming that the number of breakdowns is proportional to the level of x, we have

$$\dot{x} = k_2(y - x) - k_3 x. \tag{2}$$

Next, the number of households increases exponentially. This is a more realistic assumption regarding the number of households than assuming that H is constant. The new equation for H is

$$\dot{H} = k_4 H. \tag{3}$$

A systems diagram for the decay model would trace the interdependencies in the equation system (1) - (3).

Write a CSMP111 program for the following inventory control system:

$$\dot{Y} = u - V$$

$$\dot{X} = V - S$$

$$V = \frac{Y}{T_1}$$

$$u = S + K(I - X)$$

where X - Current inventory level

Y - Outstanding level of orders placed with the suppliers

u - Rate of ordering from suppliers

V - Delivery rate from suppliers

S - Sales rate

I - Planned inventory level

T_1 - Average delivery time (= 3 days)

Let the initial conditions be

I = X = 0

Y = 12

S = 4 items/day.

Solution: The control of inventory requires a feedback system. A retailer tries to keep inventory at a level where he maintains what he views as a reasonable balance between the cost of holding goods in inventory and the penalty of losing sales if the inventory should become empty.

A simple model of the inventory control system would need two levels and three rates defined as follows:

X - Current inventory level

Y - Outstanding level of orders placed with the supplier

u - Rate of ordering from supplier

V - Rate of delivery by supplier

S - Rate of sales

Also, assume that planned inventory level and average lead time $\overline{I}$ and $\overline{T}_1$ respectively, are constant. A systems diagram for the above levels is:

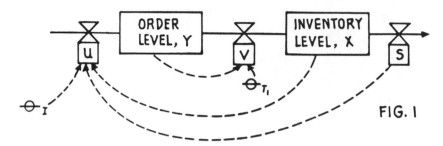

FIG. I

The rate of change of the level of orders is $\dot{Y} = u - V$ while the time derivative of X is $\dot{X} = V - S$. The rate of delivery V is inversely proportional to the outstanding level of orders placed with the suppliers. The order rate is

$$u = S + K(I - X)$$

where K is the ordering constant.

The systems diagram acts like a flowchart for the CSMPIII program. Assume that time is measured in days and let the initial conditions be, at t = 0:

$$I = X = 20$$

$$Y = 12$$

$$S = 4 \text{ items/day}$$

The program looks as follows:

```
TITLE       INVENTORY CONTROL SYSTEM
*
PARAM       K=(1.0,0.5,0.25,0.125,0.0625)
*
    S=4.0+2.0*STEP(4.0)
    V=Y/T₁
    u=S+K*(I-X)
    YDOT=u-V
    Y=INTGRL(YO,YDOT)
    XDOT=V-S
    X=INTGRL(XO,XDOT)
*
    CONST I=20.0,YO=12.0,XO=20.0,T1=3.0
*
    TIMER DELT=0.1 FINTIM=50.0 PROEL=1.0
    PRINT u,v,X,Y
    END
    STOP
```

CHAPTER 17

STATISTICS AND PROBABILITY

PROBABILITY THEORY

● **PROBLEM** 17-1

Write a program that calculates the number of permutations of N things
taken R at a time.

Solution: The factorial of N is written as N! and is equal to
$N(N-1)(N-2) \ldots (3)(2)(1)$. If N things are taken R at a time
there are N choices for the first item, N-1 choices for the second,
N-2 choices for the third, N-3 choices for the fourth and, continuing, N-R+1 choices for the Rth item. By the Fundamental principle
of Counting, the final number of permutations is $N(N-1)(N-2)(N-3)\ldots$
(N-R+1). This number is denoted by $^{N}P_{R}$. A more compact representation is $\dfrac{N!}{(N-R)!}$ since this equals $N(N-1) \ldots (N-R+1)$. The program
appears as follows:

```
1Ø          READ N,R
2Ø          IF  N < Ø  THEN 1ØØ
3Ø          LET  P = 1
4Ø          FOR  X = N  TO  N-R+1  STEP -1
5Ø          LET  P = P * X
6Ø          NEXT  X
7Ø          PRINT  N; "THINGS"; R; "AT A TIME"; P; "PERMUTATIONS"
8Ø          GO TO 1Ø
9Ø          DATA  8, 3, 4, 4, Ø, Ø
1ØØ         END
```

● **PROBLEM** 17-2

Write a program which generates the first 12 rows of Pascal's Triangle.

Solution: Pascal's triangle yields the coefficients of x^{k} and y^{k}
in the expansion of $(x+y)^{n}$. The first few rows are:

$(x+y)^{0}$:   1

$(x+y)^{1}$:   1   1

$(x+y)^{2}$:   1   2   1

583

$(x+y)^3$:   1   3   3   1

$(x+y)^4$:   1   4   6   4   1

$(x+y)^5$:   1   5   10   10   5   1

In order to find a formula for the coefficients of the nth degree expansion, consider Newton's binomial theorem:

$$(x+y)^n = \frac{x^n}{0!} + \frac{nx^{n-1}}{1!} y + \frac{n(n-1)}{2!} x^{n-2} y^2 + \frac{n(n-1)(n-2)x^{n-3}}{3!} y^3$$

$$+ \frac{n(n-1)(n-2)(n-3)}{4!} x^{n-4} y^4 + \ldots + \frac{n(n-1)\ldots(n-r+1)}{r!} x^{n-r} y^r$$

$$+ \ldots + nxy^{n-1} + y^n .$$

The coefficient of the $(n-r)$-th power of x is $\frac{n(n-1)\ldots(n-r+1)}{r!}$.

But $n(n-1)\ldots(n-r+1) = \frac{n!}{(n-r)!} = {}^nP_r$. Hence the rth coefficient where $1 \le r \le N$ is given by $\frac{n!}{r!(n-r)!}$. But this is the formula for the number of combinations of n things taken r at a time (a combination is an arrangement where order is immaterial, e.g., ABC = BAC). Thus the binomial coefficients are given by

$$\frac{n!}{r!(n-r)!} = {}^nC_r .$$

```
1Ø          FOR  N = Ø  TO  11
2Ø          FOR  R = Ø  TO  N
3Ø          LET  C = 1
4Ø          FOR  X = N  TO  N - R + 1  STEP -1
5Ø          LET  C = C * X / (N-X+1)
6Ø          NEXT  X
7Ø          PRINT  C;
8Ø          NEXT  R
9Ø          PRINT
1ØØ         NEXT  N
11Ø         END
```

● **PROBLEM** 17-3

You are in a room with 29 other people. You are asked to write a program which computes the probability of at least two people having the same birthdate.

Solution: Denote the requested probability by Q. Then $Q = 1 - P$ where P is the probability of no two identical birthdates. From elementary probability theory

$$P = \frac{365}{365} \times \frac{(365-1)}{365} \times \ldots \times \frac{(365-29)}{365}$$

$$= \frac{365 \times 364 \times 363 \times \ldots \times 336}{365^{30}}$$

Here, the probability is $365/365$ that one person will not have two identical birthdates. Given two people, the probability is $364/365$ since the first person has 365 choices and the second only has 364. Continuing, we obtain P.

The program appears as follows:

```
10              LET  P = 1
20              FOR  D = 365  TO  336  STEP -1
30              LET  P = P * D/365
40              NEXT  D
50              LET  Q = 1 - P
60              PRINT "THE PROBABILITY OF TWO OR MORE"
70              PRINT "IDENTICAL BIRTHDATES AMONG 30 PEOPLE IS"; Q
80              END
```

● PROBLEM 17-4

Insurance companies have worked out probability tables to estimate the chances a person has of living until a certain age. A study of just over a million people was made, and in 1941, a mortality table was published. It listed the number of persons still alive at age 0,1,2,3, ..., 99.
  Let
then, $L(X)$ = number of persons living at age X
                 $P(X)$ = probability that a person of age X will live
                          for one more year
                        $= \dfrac{L(X+1)}{L(X)}$

Develop a program in BASIC that allows the user to input the year of birth, the present age, and some year after the year of birth. The output should list the age, the year, and the chances of that person living until that year.

Solution: To make the problem more meaningful, let us present a concrete example. Suppose we want to calculate the chances of a 35-year old born in 1945 living until the year 2000. Adding the person's age to his birthdate gives us the year 1980. This person must live for 20 more years to reach 2000. His chances of making it are

$$\frac{L(35+20)}{L(35)} = \frac{L(55)}{L(35)} = P(X)$$

If we look at the data tables given in the program, we find that $L(55) = 754191$ and $L(35) = 906554$. So the answer is

$$\frac{754191}{906554} = .8319316$$

or, approximately 0.83.
  The strategy for our computer program is fairly easy. The program reads in the values, figures out the probability, and returns the answer. To terminate the procedure, input a negative value for the year of birth.
  We list the data (as it is stored in array L) in a DATA statement at the end of the program. The first entry is $L(0)$, the total number of persons included in the study.

```
10              DIM M(99,4)
15              FOR  J = 0  TO  99
20              READ  M(J,0)
25              IF  J = 0  THEN  30
28              LET  M(J-1,1) = M(J-1,0) - M(J,0)
30              NEXT  J
```

585

```
32          LET  M(99,1) = M(99,0)
33          REM INPUT YEAR OF BIRTH, AGE, AND EXPECTED YEAR
35          PRINT "INPUT YEAR OF BIRTH, AGE, AND EXPECTED YEAR"
4Ø          INPUT  B,A,X
45          IF  B < 0  THEN  99
48          REM  N  IS THE PRESENT YEAR; M  IS THE
49          REM YEARS BETWEEN PRESENT AND EXPECTED.
5Ø          LET  N = B + A
52          LET  M = X - N
55          LET  P = L(A+M)/L(A)
58          PRINT
6Ø          PRINT "CHANCES OF LIVING UNTIL YEAR"; X; "ARE"; P
65          GO TO 35
7Ø          DATA 1023102, 1000000, 994230, 990114, 986767
72          DATA 983817, 981102, 978541, 976124, 973869
74          DATA 971804, 969890, 968038, 966179, 964266
76          DATA 962270, 960201, 958098, 955942, 953743
78          DATA 951483, 949171, 946789, 944337, 941806
8Ø          DATA 939197, 936492, 933692, 930788, 927763
82          DATA 924609, 921317, 917880, 914282, 910515
84          DATA 906554, 902393, 898007, 893382, 888504
86          DATA 883342, 877883, 872098, 865967, 859464
87          DATA 852554, 845214, 837413, 829114, 820292
88          DATA 810900, 800910, 790282, 778981, 766967
89          DATA 754191, 740631, 726241, 710990, 694843
9Ø          DATA 677771, 659749, 640761, 620782, 599824
91          DATA 577882, 554975, 531133, 506403, 480850
92          DATA 454548, 427593, 400112, 372240, 344136
93          DATA 315982, 287973, 260322, 233251, 206989
94          DATA 181765, 157799, 135297, 114440, 93378
95          DATA 78221,  63036,  49838,  38593,  29215
96          DATA 21577,  15514,  10833,  7327,   4787
97          DATA 3011,   1818,   1005,   454,    125
99          END
```

● **PROBLEM** 17-5

Write a BASIC program to obtain the relative frequencies of the three
genotypes to be found in the next generation of a large Drosophila
population. Assume the population is subject to the Hardy-Weinberg
criteria. Use the general binomial equation $(pA + qa)^2$ to design a
table for the number of individuals with AA, Aa, and aa genotypes.

Solution: The Hardy-Weinberg law states that a large population having
completely random matings maintains a constant genotypic frequency over
every generation. This law is actually an idealized picture of reality,
because it neglects the possibilities of natural selection, mutation,
migration, and genetic drift.
    We want to design a program to simulate the genetic makeup of a suc-
ceeding generation. First, recognize that $(pA + qa)^2 = p^2 AA + 2pqAa +$
$q^2 aa$. Now, if we assume that the population contains 1000 individuals,
choose the value for p-the frequency of a given allele A, to equal .7,
and q-the frequency of the allele a, to equal .3, we can obtain three
numbers which will describe the genotypes of the next generation. P^2 will
be the number of homozygous dominants, 2pq will be the number of heterozygous dominants, and q^2 will be the number of homozygous recessives.
When each of these numbers are multiplied by the total population, the
number of individuals of each genotype is obtained. AA is homozygous

dominant, A is heterozygous dominant, and SMA is homozygous recessive.

```
1Ø          REM HARDY-WEINBERG EQUATION
2Ø          READ  P,Q
3Ø          PRINT "P", "Q", "HOMO.DOM.", "HETERO.DOM.", "HOMO.REC."
4Ø          LET  AA = (P ↑ 2) * 1000.0
5Ø          LET   A = (2 * P * Q) * 1000.0
6Ø          LET  SMA = (Q ↑ 2) * 1000.0
7Ø          PRINT  P,Q,AA,A,SMA
8Ø          DATA  Ø.7Ø, Ø.3Ø
9Ø          END
```

● **PROBLEM 17-6**

The binomial distribution is given by $b(x) = \binom{n}{x} p^x q^{n-x}$ where $\binom{n}{x} = \dfrac{n!}{x!(n-x)!}$ for integers n and x, and q = 1-p. Write a function that computes b for given n,x, and p. Feel free to use the factorial function developed in chapter 19.

<u>Solution</u>: A straightforward answer is based on the notion of a function.

```
FUNCTION B(P,N,X)
INTEGER  X
Z = P ** X * ((1.0-P) ** (N-X))
B = Z * FACT(N)/(FACT(X) * FACT(N-X))
RETURN
END
```

● **PROBLEM 17-7**

Design a FORTRAN function to simulate trials according to the geometric distribution $f(x) = pq^x$, where p is the probability of success on any trial, and q = 1 - p is the probability of failure.

<u>Solution</u>: This perfectly binary probability structure is derived from the notion of Bernoulli trials, in which the only two possible outcomes are "success" and "failure". If a sequence of these independent trials is performed, the probability of obtaining X failures before reaching a success can be exhibited by the geometric distribution.

There are two approaches to this problem, both depending on the value of p. If p is close to 0 or 1, we can generate a series of independent trials, and count the number of trials necessary before a success appears. As q = 1 - p, we can generate a series of random numbers between 0 and 1 and can call the series S. Let Si be the i-th term of the series S. As we generate a new term Si, we compare its value with q. As soon as Si > q at any point during iteration, procedure stops, and i - 1 turns out to be the value of the geometric variable X.

The alternate approach, when p is not close to 0 or 1, uses the formula
$$\left[i = \frac{\log r}{\log q} \right],$$

in which i is the geometric variable, r is a random number such that

587

$0 \leq r \leq 1$, $q = 1 - p$, and the brackets indicate that only the integer part of the result is desired. This method is unreliable when p is close to 0 or 1 because the ALOG library function is computed with a power series that, on most machines, is imprecise when calculating values near the parameters of the chosen interval.

The function procedure is described below. Comments highlight the two different methods of solution.

```
            INTEGER FUNCTION BERN(P)
C           RETURN TO THE MAIN PROGRAM IS CONTINGENT
C           UPON FINDING THE FIRST SUCCESS
            IF (P.LE. .Ø5 .OR. P. GE. .95) GO TO 1Ø
C           LOGARITHMIC METHOD
            X = RNDM (NUM)
            BERN = INT(1.Ø + (ALOG 1Ø(X)/ALOG 1Ø(1.Ø - P)))
            RETURN
C           THIS IS THE COUNTING METHOD, WHICH
C           AVOIDS THE AFOREMENTIONED PRECISION DIFFICULTIES
1Ø          DO 2Ø  J = 1, 1ØØØ
            X = RNDM (NUM)
            IF (X.LT.P)   GO TO 3Ø
2Ø          CONTINUE
C           IF NO SUCCESSES, BERN = 1ØØØØ
            BERN = 1ØØØØ
            RETURN
C           SUCCESS!
3Ø          BERN = J
            RETURN
            END
```

Some FORTRAN compilers contain random number generation function as a library function. For those which do not, the function has to be defined and called. In this program, the random number generation function is called by means of X = RNDM (NUM) statement and has the following (generally used) procedure:

```
            FUNCTION RNDM (NUM)
            IF (NUM. GT. 0) INUM = NUM
            INU = 65539 * INUM
            IF (INU.LT. 0) INU = INU + 2147483647 + 1
            RNDM = .4656613E - 9 * FLOAT (INU)
            INUM = INU
            RETURN
            END
```

● **PROBLEM** 17-8

Write a FORTRAN program segment to compute values of the POISSON distribution given by
$$P(X) = e^{-m} m^X/x!$$

Assume (1) that X and m are integer variables; (2) that X and m are small enough that no term will exceed the size permitted for a real variable in your computer; and (3) that the function FACT(n) for computing n! is available.

Solution: Remember that the library function e^y is defined for real y, so we set y = FLOAT(m) to convert the integer m to a real

variable when evaluating P. The rest of the integer expressions,
need not be FLOATED since the FORTRAN compiler allows mixing of modes
in a product expression of real * integer; the result being converted
to a real number. Bearing the above in mind, we can write out the
program below:

```
FUNCTION P(X,M)
INTEGER  X
Y = FLOAT (M)
P = EXP(-Y) * M ** X / FACT (X)
RETURN
END
```

The factorial function, FACT (X), is defined in chapter 19.

BASIC STATISTICS

● **PROBLEM** 17-9

Design a BASIC program to calculate the mean, variance, and standard
deviation for a number of observations.

<u>Solution</u>: The arithmetic mean is known as the first moment about the
origin, a measure of central tendency. The standard deviation is the
second moment about the origin, and it is a measure of dispersion.
The variance is simply the square of the standard deviation. The
equations are given below, with M as the mean, V as the variance,
S as the standard deviation, and N as the number of observations,
or sample size:

$$M = \sum_{i=1}^{N} x_i/N$$

$$V = \left(\sum_{i=1}^{N} x_i^2 /N \right) - M^2$$

$$S = \sqrt{\left(\sum_{i=1}^{N} x_i^2 /N \right) - M^2}$$

The variance is actually the average of squared deviations from the
mean, i.e.,

$$V = \frac{\sum_{i}^{N} (x - \bar{x})^2}{N} .$$

This may be rewritten as

$$V = \frac{\sum_{i}^{N} x^2}{N} - 2 \frac{\sum_{i}^{N} x\bar{x}}{n} + \frac{n\bar{x}^2}{n} = \frac{\sum_{i}^{N} x^2}{N} - 2\bar{x}^2 + \bar{x}^2$$

$$= \frac{\sum_{i}^{N} x^2}{N} - \bar{x}^2 .$$

This form is easier for computations. Remember that these formulae

589

are to be applied only for observed, ungrouped data. Other formulae
are needed for other types of data.

```
1Ø          REM  N  WILL BE COMPUTED BY KEEPING
11          REM  A  COUNT OF THE NUNBER OF TIMES WE GO THROUGH
12          REM THE LOOP BELOW (STEPS 5Ø  TO  1ØØ).  T  REPRESENTS THE
13          REM SUM Σx_i , AND  D  REPRESENTS THE SUM OF THE SQUARES
14          REM Σx_i^2 .  N,T  AND  D  ARE INITIALIZED TO ZERO.
15          REM x ONLY TAKES POSITIVE VALUES.  HENCE, ON THE LAST DATA CARD
16          REM A NEGATIVE VALUE OF x  IS USED TO INSTRUCT THE COMPUTER
17          REM TO EXIT FROM THE
18          REM LOOP AND GO TO STEP 12Ø.
2Ø          LET  N = Ø
3Ø          LET  T = Ø
4Ø          LET  D = Ø
5Ø          READ  X
6Ø          IF  X < Ø  THEN  12Ø
7Ø          LET  T = T + X
8Ø          LET  D = D + X ↑ 2
9Ø          LET  N = N + 1
1ØØ         GO TO 5Ø
11Ø         REM NOW COMPUTE MEAN, VARIANCE, AND STD.DEV.
12Ø         LET  M = T/N
13Ø         LET  V = D/N - M ↑ 2
14Ø         LET  S = SQR(V)
15Ø         REM PRINT OUT RESULTS
16Ø         PRINT "N ="; N
17Ø         PRINT "MEAN ="; M
18Ø         PRINT "VARIANCE ="; V
19Ø         PRINT "STANDARD DEVIATION ="; S
2ØØ         DATA 75, 22, 14, 83, 16, 12, 17, -1
21Ø         END
```

[Note: for small samples, N may have to be amended to N - 1.]

● PROBLEM 17-10

Develop a BASIC program that produces a horizontal bar graph for some
given distribution. Use the DIM statement to dimension any arrays that
might occur.

Solution: This program will produce a bar graph (a histogram) of a
distribution. In this case, the distribution will represent student's
grades for a math course. The frequency of a particular grade will be
given in the graph as a series of x's. The array A(J) will serve
as the counter for each class mark. The program terminates upon the
reading of a negative data point.

```
1Ø          REM  GRADE DISTRIBUTION GRAPH
2Ø          DIM A(4)
25          REM     INITIALIZE ALL  A(L)  TO ZERO
3Ø          FOR  L = 1  TO  4
4Ø          LET  A(L) = Ø
5Ø          NEXT  L
6Ø          READ  X
7Ø          IF  X = -1  THEN 12Ø
75          REM  STANDARDIZE  X  VALUES
```

```
8Ø              LET   J = (X/10) - 5
9Ø              LET   A(J) = A(J) + 1
1ØØ             GO TO 6Ø
11Ø             FOR   G = 1  TO  4
12Ø             PRINT 5Ø + 1Ø * G; "TO"; 5Ø + 1Ø * G + 9;
13Ø             FOR   W = 1  TO  A(G)
14Ø             PRINT "X";
15Ø             NEXT  W
16Ø             PRINT
17Ø             NEXT  G
18Ø             DATA 77, 85, 96, 75, 81, 68, 73, 78
19Ø             DATA 91, 72, 82, 74, 61, -1
2ØØ             END
```

Sample Output:
```
                RUN
6Ø              TO  69  XX
7Ø              TO  79  XXXXXX
8Ø              TO  89  XXX
9Ø              TO  99  XX
                READY
```

A word about format: you may wish to include letter correlates for the
number grades, such as A = 90 - 100, etc. This will make clear the
ranges for the various class marks. By adding a PRINT statement with
this information, you can make clear to the reader what the histogram
is trying to show.

● **PROBLEM** 17-11

Write a FORTRAN program to compute the arithmetic mean of N real
numbers. You may assume that the numbers have been read into an
array X having members X(1), X(2),...,X(N).

Solution: We apply the formula

$$\bar{X} = \left(\sum_{i=1}^{N} X(i) \right) / N = (X(1) + X(2)+...+X(N))/N .$$

The variable SUM is used to accumulate the value of the sum of the
X(i)'s. The variable AVG (the mean value) is set equal to SUM/N.

```
                DIMENSION X(N)
                SUM = 0.0
                READ (5,20) N
2Ø              FORMAT (2X,I5)
                DO 50  I = 1,N
5Ø              SUM = SUM + X(I)
                AVG = SUM/FLOAT(N)
                STOP
                END
```

● **PROBLEM** 17-12

Write a FORTRAN program to compute the standard deviation of N real
numbers. Again, you may assume that these numbers have already been
read into an array X having members X(1), X(2),...,X(N).

591

Solution: We apply the formula

$$\sigma = \sqrt{\sum_{N=1}^{N} (X_i - \bar{X})^2 / (N - 1)}$$

$$= \sqrt{\{(X_1 - \bar{X})^2 + (X_2 - \bar{X})^2 + \ldots + (X_N - \bar{X})^2\} / (N - 1)}.$$

To further simplify the calculation we will assume that $\bar{X}$, the mean, has already been calculated as the variable AVG from the preceding problem (#12). Let SIGMA stand for σ. The program would then be:

```
       DIMENSION X(N), Y(N)
       READ, N
       SUMSQ = Ø.Ø
       DO 5Ø  I = 1,N
       Y(I) = X(I) - AVG
       SUMSQ = SUMSQ + Y(I) ** 2
5Ø     CONTINUE
       A = FLOAT (N)
       SIGMA = SQRT (SUMSQ/(A-1.0))
       STOP
       END
```

● **PROBLEM** 17-13

Using the pertinent information from the previous problem, find the third and fourth standard moments of ungrouped data in an observed distribution.

Solution: The third and fourth standard moments are dimensionless. Unlike the first and second moments, these incorporate the fraction $(X_i - M)/S$, which renders these moments independent of units.

The third standard moment, W, is a measure of asymmetry or skewness of the distribution, and the formula is given as:

$$W = \frac{\sum_{i=1}^{N} [(X_i - M)/S]^3}{N} = \frac{1}{S^3} \frac{\sum_{i=1}^{N} (X_i - M)^3}{N} = \frac{\sum_{i=1}^{N} (X_i - M)^3}{S^3 N}$$

The fourth standard moment, K, is a measure of peakedness of the distribution curve, and is given by:

$$K = \frac{\sum_{i=1}^{N} [(X_i - M)]^4}{N} = \frac{1}{S^4} \frac{\sum_{i=1}^{N} (X_i - M)^4}{N} = \frac{\sum_{i=1}^{N} (X_i - M)^4}{S^4 N}$$

These equations will now be translated into BASIC, assuming that the mean M and the standard deviation S are known:

```
1Ø       REM COMPUTE THIRD AND FOURTH STANDARD
2Ø       REM MOMENTS
3Ø       LET  Y = Ø
4Ø       LET  Z = Ø
6Ø       READ  X
7Ø       IF  X < Ø  THEN 12Ø
```

```
80          LET  Y = Y + (X - M)↑ 3
90          LET  Z = Z + (X - M)↑ 4
110         GO TO 60
120         LET  W = Y/(S↑3 * N)
130         LET  K = Z/(S↑4 * N)
140         REM PRINT OUT RESULTS
150         PRINT "N ="; N
160         PRINT "3RD STANDARD MOMENT ="; W
170         PRINT "4TH STANDARD MOMENT ="; K
180         DATA 75, 22, 14, 83, 16, 12, 17, -1
190         END
```

Note, that the value of N is not specified in the program. One can either substitute N with a specific value, or add a READ N and DATA... statements.

● **PROBLEM** 17-14

Develop a BASIC program to compute the least-squares regression line $Y = A + BX$ corresponding to data points (X_i, Y_i) for $i = 1, 2, \ldots, N$.

Apply the program to the five data points (X_i, Y_i) given by $(1,1)$, $(2,2.5)$, $(1.8,2)$, $(3.1,2.9)$, and $(0.9,1.1)$.

Solution: We quote without proof the basic results needed from the statistical theory of regression analysis. The coefficients of the least squares line are given by

$$A = \frac{\sum Y \sum X^2 - \sum XY \sum X}{N\sum X^2 - (\sum X)^2}, \quad B = \frac{N \sum XY - \sum X \sum Y}{N\sum X^2 - (\sum X)^2}$$

It is understood that all sums (Σ) apply for $i = 1, 2, \ldots, n$. The program should allow for the input of N, to be followed by N pairs of data, each pair consisting of a value of X and the associated value of Y. Then, compute the least squares approximation to the data. Since we cannot use the sigma notation for variable names in BASIC, we will use the symbol substitution as follows:

S1 for $\sum X$, S2 for $\sum Y$, S3 for $\sum XY$, S4 for $\sum X^2$, S5 for $(\sum X)^2$, S6 for $N\sum X^2$.

```
100         REM  LEAST SQUARES ANALYSIS
110         LET  S1 = 0
111         LET  S2 = 0
112         LET  S3 = 0
113         LET  S4 = 0
120         READ  N
131         FOR  I = 1  TO  N
140         READ  X,Y
150         LET  S1 = S1 + X
151         LET  S2 = S2 + Y
152         LET  S3 = S3 + X * Y
153         LET  S4 = S4 + X ↑ 2
154         NEXT  I
160         LET  S5 = S1 ↑ 2
161         LET  S6 = N * S4
170         LET  A = (S2*S4-S3*S1)/(S6-S5)
171         LET  B = (N*S3-S1*S2)/(S6-S5)
```

593

```
184          PRINT "FOR"; N; "SETS OF DATA"
181          PRINT "THE LEAST SQUARES LINEAR"
182          PRINT "EQUATION IS"
183          PRINT "Y ="; A; "+"; B; "X"
800          DATA 5
801          DATA 1,1
802          DATA 2,2.5
803          DATA 1.8,2
804          DATA 3.1,2.9
805          DATA 0.9,1.1
999          END
```

● **PROBLEM** 17-15

Let (X_i, Y_i) be a set of points in the X,Y plane. Devise a flow-chart for a program that will find the regression line $\hat{y} = \hat{\alpha} + \hat{\beta}x_i$ that minimizes the sum of the squared deviations from the line.

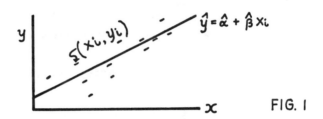

FIG. I

Solution: The simple linear regression model is as shown in Fig. 1

It is required to find the equation of the straight line, $\hat{y} = \hat{\alpha} + \hat{\beta}x_i$. The unknowns are $\hat{\alpha}$, the y-intercept and $\hat{\beta}$-the slope of the line, or the regression coefficient. Assuming that such a line exists, it is required to minimize

$$\sum_{i=1}^{n} (y_i - \hat{y})^2 ,$$

the sum of squared y_i deviations. But $(y_i - \hat{y}) = y_i - (\hat{\alpha} + \hat{\beta}x_i)$.
Thus, the problem is to

$$\text{Minimize} \sum_{i=1}^{n} (y_i - \hat{\alpha} + \hat{\beta}x_i)^2 \tag{1}$$

where x_i, y_i are known data points and $\hat{\alpha}, \hat{\beta}$ are the variables.
Taking the partial derivatives of (1) with respect to $\hat{\alpha}, \hat{\beta}$, setting them equal to zero to find the minimum of (1) and solving the resulting set of linear equations yields

$$\hat{\beta} = \frac{\sum_{i=1}^{n} (y_i - \bar{y})(x_i - \bar{x})}{\sum_{i=1}^{n} (x_i - \bar{x})^2}$$

$$\hat{\alpha} = \bar{y} - \hat{\beta} \bar{x}$$

594

where

$$\bar{y} = \frac{1}{n} \sum_{i=1}^{n} y_i \quad \text{and} \quad \bar{x} = \sum_{i=1}^{n} x_i \quad .$$

In order to convert the above program from algebraic to computer form, the following steps must be performed:

1. The points x_i, y_i are read and stored in arrays X and Y.
2. $\bar{X}, \bar{Y}$ are calculated.
3. $\Sigma(x_i - \bar{x})^2$, $\Sigma(y_i - \bar{y})^2$, $\Sigma(y_i - \bar{y})(x_i - \bar{x})$ are calculated.
4. $\hat{\alpha}, \hat{\beta}$ and $\Sigma(y_i - (\hat{\alpha} + \hat{\beta}x_i))^2$ are computed.

The flow-chart of the procedure is as shown in Fig. 2

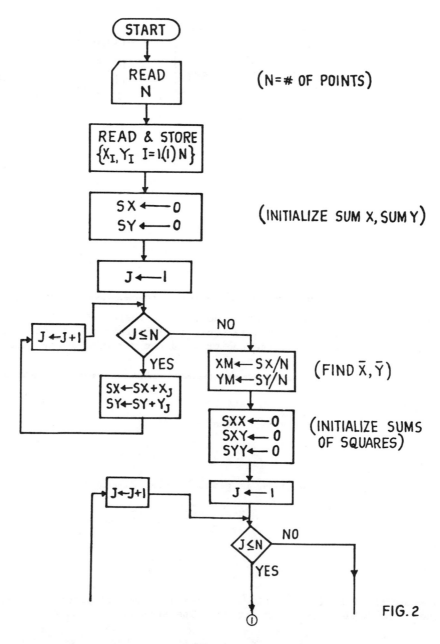

FIG. 2

595

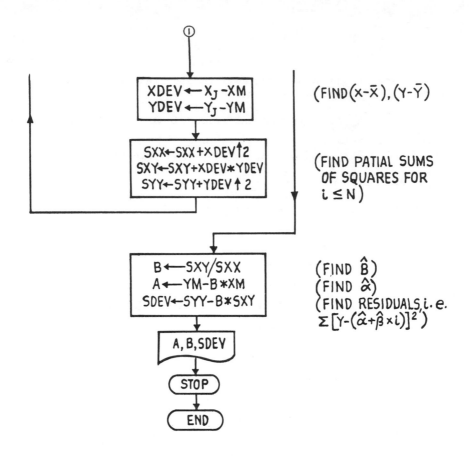

Fig. 2 – Continued

Consider the simple regression model. When there is a large number of observations, storage in single subscripted arrays can create problems. Devise a flowchart and write the program for performing the linear regression without using arrays.

Solution: Let (x_i, y_i) be data points. The simple regression problem is to find numbers $\hat{\alpha}$, $\hat{\beta}$ such that

$$\sum_{i=1}^{n} [y_i - (\hat{\alpha} + \hat{\beta}x_i)]^2$$

is minimized. The solution is given by the formulae

$$\hat{\beta} = \frac{\Sigma(x - \bar{x})(y - \bar{y})}{\Sigma(x - \bar{x})^2} \qquad \hat{\alpha} = \bar{y} - \hat{\beta}\,\bar{x}$$

where

$$\bar{x} = \frac{1}{n} \sum_{1}^{n} x_i, \qquad \bar{y} = \frac{1}{n} \sum_{1}^{n} y_i$$

One method of performing linear regression on a computer is to read and store the data (x_i, y_i) in arrays. The sums of squares and means are

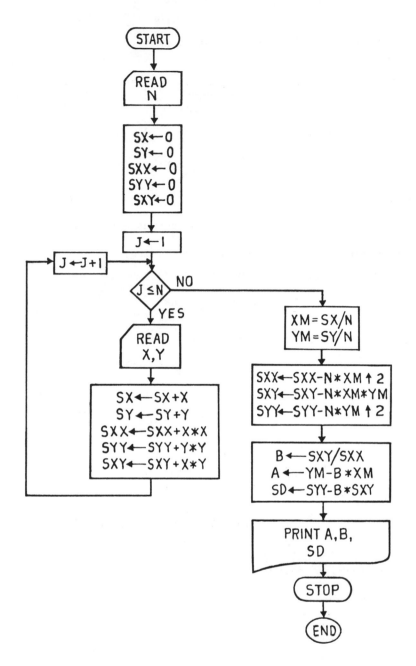

then found by operating with these arrays. However, the regression formulae can be rewritten so that $\Sigma(x-\bar{x})^2$, $\Sigma(y-\bar{y})^2$, $\Sigma(x-\bar{x})(y-\bar{y})$ can be expressed in terms of

$$\sum_{1}^{n} x_i, \ \sum_{1}^{n} y_i, \ \sum_{1}^{n} y_i^2 \ \text{ and } \ \sum_{1}^{n} x_i^2 \ .$$

These latter sums can be computed directly from the observations without storing them in arrays. To clarify, consider $\Sigma(x-\bar{x})^2$:

$$\sum_{i=1}^{n} (x_i-\bar{x})^2 = \sum_{1}^{n} x_i^2 - 2\bar{x} \sum_{1}^{n} x_i + \sum_{1}^{n} \bar{x}^2 \qquad (1)$$

But $2\bar{x} \sum\limits_1^n x_i = 2\bar{x}n\bar{x}$ $(\sum\limits_1^N x_i = n\bar{x} = 2n\bar{x}^2$. Also,

$$\sum_1^n \bar{x}^2 = \underbrace{\bar{x}^2 + \bar{x}^2 + \ldots + \bar{x}^2}_{\text{n times}} = n\bar{x}^2$$

Thus, (1) is equal to

$$\sum_1^n (x_i-\bar{x})^2 = \sum_1^n x_i^2 - n\bar{x}^2 \qquad (2)$$

To compute (2), all we need is $\sum\limits_1^n x_i^2$ and $\bar{x}$. No array is necessary for either of these since $\sum\limits_1^n x_i^2$ can be computed directly by squaring each observation, as it is read in, and summing. Similarly, $\bar{x} = \frac{1}{n} \sum x_i$ can be computed directly. From (1) and (2) above,

$$\sum(y_i-\bar{y})^2 = \sum_1^n y_i^2 - n\bar{y}^2 \quad . \qquad (3)$$

To simplify $\sum(x-\bar{x})(y-\bar{y})$ consider the following:

$$\sum_1^n (x_i-\bar{x})(y_i-\bar{y}) = x_1y_1-x_1\bar{y}-\bar{x}y_1 + \bar{x}\bar{y}$$
$$+ x_2y_2-x_2\bar{y} - \bar{x}y_2+\bar{x}\bar{y}+\ldots+x_ny_n-x_n\bar{y}-\bar{x}y_n+\bar{x}\bar{y}$$
$$= \sum_1^n x_iy_i - \bar{y}\sum_1^n x_i - \bar{x}\sum_1^n y_i + n\bar{x}\bar{y} \qquad (4)$$

But $-\bar{y}\sum\limits_1^n x_i = -\bar{y}n\bar{x} = -\bar{x}\sum\limits_1^n y_i$. Thus (4) equals

$$\sum_1^n (x_i-\bar{x})(y_i-\bar{y}) = \sum_1^n x_iy_i - n\bar{x}\bar{y} \qquad (5)$$

The program looks as follows:

```
            READ, N
            SX = 0
            SY = 0
            SXX = 0
            SYY = 0
            SXY = 0
            J = 1
1           IF (J.GT.N) GO TO 2
            READ, X,Y
            SX = SX + X
            SY = SY + Y
            SXX = SXX + X*X
            SYY = SYY + Y*Y
            SXY = SXY + X*Y
            J = J + 1
            GO TO 1
2           XM = SX/N
            YM = SY/N
            SXX = SXX - N*XM**2
            SXY = SXY - N*XM*YM
```

```
SYY = SYY - N*YM**2
B = SXY/SXX
A = YM - B* XM
SD = SYY - B*SXY
PRINT, A,B,SD
STOP
END
```

NON-PARAMETRIC AND HYPOTHESIS TESTS

The following table gives the number of items sold daily at a super-market.

	Week 1	Week 2
Sunday	900	800
Monday	400	500
Tuesday	500	300
Wednesday	600	300
Thursday	300	400
Friday	700	600
Saturday	1100	900

Write a FORTRAN program to compute a seven day moving average.

Solution: Observations taken over periods of time typically show seasonal variability. The purpose of moving averages is to reduce these variations to enable us to spot the trend.

First, find the average daily sales from Sunday to Saturday of the first week. This figure is placed in the table next to Wednesday - the midpoint of the examined period. Then find the average from Monday of the first week to Sunday of the second week, etc. Proceeding in this way we obtain the seven-day moving average for the given data.

	7 day M.A.	7 day M.A.
Sunday		571
Monday		586
Tuesday		571
Wednesday	643	543
Thursday	629	
Friday	643	
Saturday	614	

From the table, it can be seen that the sales are falling. Perhaps the supermarket should start an advertising campaign.

The program looks as follows:

```
DIMENSION X(14), AV(7)
L = 1
M = 7
SUM = 0
DO 2  I = 1,14
```

```
            READ X(I)
2           CONTINUE
10          DO L   J = L,M
            SUM = X(J) + SUM
1           CONTINUE
            AV(L) = SUM/7
            L = L + 1
            M = M + 1
            IF (M.EQ. 15) GO TO 11
            GO TO 10
11          DO 12   I = 1,7
            PRINT AV(I)
12          CONTINUE
            STOP
            END
```

● **PROBLEM** 17-18

Write a FORTRAN program to compute the coefficient of rank correlation
for the following data:

	X	Y
1.	.3	10
2.	.6	15
3.	.9	30
4.	1.2	35
5.	1.5	25
6.	1.8	30
7.	2.1	50
8.	2.4	45

Solution: The correlation coefficient r is an appropriate measure
of association between two variables when cardinal ordering is in-
appropriate. Sometimes scores can only be ranked in order without
any information concerning the distance between two elements in the
ranking. For example, two judges in a beauty contest may give different rankings. The correlation between them will depend on ordinal
properties (first, second, third, etc.), not on cardinal properties
(1, 1.5, 2.3, etc.).

To find the coefficient of rank correlation between X and Y,
first order Y's from smallest to largest, provided that X's are
initially given in increasing order.

X	Rank of X	Y	Rank of Y
.3	$X_1 = 1$	10	$Y_1 = 1$
.6	$X_2 = 2$	15	$Y_2 = 2$
.9	$X_3 = 3$	20	$Y_3 = 3$
1.2	$X_4 = 4$	35	$Y_4 = 6$
1.5	$X_5 = 5$	25	$Y_5 = 4$
1.8	$X_6 = 6$	30	$Y_6 = 5$
2.1	$X_7 = 7$	50	$Y_7 = 8$
2.4	$X_8 = 8$	45	$Y_8 = 7$

600

The correlation coefficient r is equal to

$$r = \Sigma(x-\bar{x})(y-\bar{y}) / (\Sigma(x-\bar{x})^2)^{\frac{1}{2}} (\Sigma(y-\bar{y})^2)^{\frac{1}{2}}$$

This formula can be modified into a rank correlation coefficient. Omitting the details of the transformation:

$$r_s = 1 - \frac{6 \sum_{i=1}^{n} d^2}{n(n^2-1)} \tag{2}$$

where $d^2 = (x_i - y_i)^2$, the difference in ranks between the i-th x score and i-th y score squared. The 6 in the numerator arises from the sum

$$\sum_{i=1}^{n} i^2 = \frac{n(n+1)(2n+1)}{6}$$

which is computed during the transformation. Observe that if the rankings of x_i and y_i are identical,

$$r_s = 1 - \frac{6(0)}{n(n^2-1)} = 1.$$

For the given data

$x_i - y_i$	$(x_i - y_i)^2$
0	0
0	0
0	0
-2	4
1	1
+1	1
-1	1
1	1

$$\Sigma(x_i-y_i)^2 = 8 \qquad\qquad n = 8$$

and

$$r_s = 1 - \frac{6(8)}{8(63)} = .873$$

The first task of the FORTRAN program for computing the rank correlation coefficient is the ordering of the given y's in ascending order. This can be accomplished using the subroutine "SORT", developed in the chapter named "DATA STRUCTURES". Assuming this is already done, the program looks as follows:

```
        INTEGER YFIN(N), XFIN(N)
        DIMENSION Y(N),YFIN(N), XFIN(N), M(N)
        READ, N
        READ, Y(I)
        CALL SORT (Y(J))
        I = 1
        J = 1
10      IF(Y(J) - Y(I)) 2,3,2
2       K = 0
6       IF(Y(J) - Y(I+1). EQ.0) GO TO 5
        K = K + 1
        I = I + 1
        GO TO 6
```

```
5              YFIN(J) = I
               I = I - K
               GO TO 7
3              YFIN(J) = I
7              I = I + 1
               J = J + 1
               IF(J.EQ.N+1) GO TO 11
               GO TO 10
11             M(N) = 0
               DO 12  L = 1,N
               M(L) = (XFIN(L) - YFIN(L))**2
               M(N) = M(N) + M(L)
12             CONTINUE
               RCC = 1 - 6*M(N)/(N*(N**2 - 1))
               PRINT, RCC
               STOP
               END
```

● **PROBLEM** 17-19

A doctor is testing the potency of a new drug. He compares two groups of samples, an experimental group and a control group. Each group contained 10 samples and yielded 10 results. Every result was assigned a number from 1 to 10 according to the degree of success. Do the two means of these groups differ significantly? Write a FORTRAN program to find out.

Control	Experimental
10	7
5	3
6	5
7	7
10	8
6	4
7	5
8	6
6	3
5	2

Solution: This is a problem in hypothesis testing for the difference between means of two sets of data. The test used is the t-test and the t-statistic is computed according to the formula

$$t = \frac{\bar{x}_1 - \bar{x}_2}{\sqrt{\left[\Sigma x_1^2 - \frac{(\Sigma x_1)^2}{N_1} + \Sigma x_2^2 - \frac{(\Sigma x_2)^2}{N_2}\right]\left[\frac{1}{N_1} + \frac{1}{N_2}\right]}}$$

where $\bar{x}_i$ – mean of i-th group i = 1,2 ;

Σx_i^2 – sum of squared score values of i-th group ;

$(\Sigma x_i)^2$ – square of the sum of scores in i-th group;

N_i : the number of scores in the i-th group.

602

The summary statistics for the given problem are:

$$\Sigma x_1 = 70; \quad \Sigma x_2 = 50; \quad \Sigma x_1^2 = 520; \quad \Sigma x_2^2 = 286$$

$$(\Sigma x_1)^2 = 4900; \quad (\Sigma x_2)^2 = 2500; \quad N_1 = 10 \quad N_2 = 10 \ .$$

Using these the calculated t-value is found to be

$$t = \frac{7 - 5}{1.82} = 1.10 \ .$$

This calculated t-value is compared with the t-value for $N_1 + N_2 - 2$ degrees of freedom at the 5% level of significance (i.e., if $t_{calculated} < t_{table}$ then the two means do not differ and the observed difference is due to sampling variability). If the calculated t-value exceeds the value in the table for a 5% level, this indicates that the observed difference in means would occur less than 5 times out of 100. Note that the 5% level is the usual level adopted in statistical testing.

   We conclude that at the 5% level, the two means do not differ significantly. The new drug does not indicate increased potency.

   The general program for a test of hypothesis involving two means is given below.

```
C          T-TEST FOR INDEPENDENT MEANS
           DIM X1(N), X2(M), KF(L)
           READ (2,100) N1, N2, KF
100        FORMAT (2I3/20A4)
C          INITIALIZE VARIABLES
           SUM1  = 0
           SQ1   = 0
           SQ2   = 0
C          USING THE FORMAT THAT WAS READ IN, READ
C          THE DATA FOR BOTH GROUPS
           READ (2,KF) (X1(J), J = 1,N1)
           READ (2,KF) (X2(K), K = 1,N2)
           DO 10  J = 1,N1
                 SUM1 = SUM1 + X1(J)
10         SQ1 = SQ1 + X1(J)**2
C          CHANGE THE  N'S TO FLOATING POINT
              DN1 = N1
              DN2 = N2
           S1SQ = SUM1 **2
            S1 = S1SQ/DN1
           SN1 = SQ1 - S1
           DO 20  J = 1,N2
                 SUM2 = SUM2 + X2(J)
20         SQ2 = SQ2 + X2(J)**2
           S2SQ = SUM2**2
            S2 = S2SQ/DN2
           SN2 = SQ2 - S2
           SN  = SN1 + SN2
           SS = SN/(DN1 + DN2 - 2.0)
           SSQ = SS*((1.0/DN1) + (1.0/DN2))
           SD = SQRT(SSQ)
           GM1 = SUM1/DN1
           GM2 = SUM2/DN2
           DIFF = GM1 - GM2
```

```
           WRITE (6,200) T
200        FORMAT (1H1, 7H THE T-VALUE IS T = , F 10.4 ,
    1      67H LOOK IN THE T-TABLES TO SEE WHETHER THE
           HYPOTHESIS CAN BE REJECTED.)
           STOP
           END
```

● **PROBLEM** 17-20

The "Meat is Neat" company wishes to enter the frozen shrimp market. They contract a researcher to investigate various methods of growing shrimp in large tanks. The researcher suspects that temperature and salinity are important factors influencing shrimp yield and conducts a factorial experiment with three levels of temperature and salinity. That is, each combination of temperature and salinity are employed and the shrimp yield for each (from identical 80 gallon tanks) is measured.

The recorded yields are given in the following chart:

Salinity (in ppm)

		700	1400	2100
	60	3	5	4
Temperature	70	11	10	12
	80	16	21	17

Write a computer program that computes the ANOVA(analysis of variance) tables.

Solution: This is a two factor factorial design experiment. The logic of the program is best illustrated by showing how the above problem is solved.

The interaction model is

$$Y_{ij} = \mu + \alpha_i + \beta_j + \epsilon_{ij} \qquad \begin{aligned} i &= 1,2,3 \\ j &= 1,2,3 \end{aligned}$$

The construction of the ANOVA table requires the computation of various sums of squares. If α_i is the effect due to temperature, then the row averages are:

$$\bar{Y}_{1\cdot} = \frac{3 + 5 + 4}{3} = 4$$

$$\bar{Y}_{2\cdot} = \frac{11 + 10 + 12}{3} = 11$$

$$\bar{Y}_{3\cdot} = \frac{16 + 21 + 17}{3} = 18$$

The column averages are:

$$\bar{Y}_{\cdot 1} = \frac{3 + 11 + 16}{3} = 10$$

$$\bar{Y}_{\cdot 2} = \frac{5 + 10 + 21}{3} = 12$$

$$\bar{Y}_{\cdot 3} = \frac{4 + 12 + 17}{3} = 11$$

$$\bar{Y}_{\cdot\cdot} = \frac{4 + 11 + 18}{3} = 11 = \frac{10 + 12 + 11}{3}$$

(The dots represent the index over which summation is taking place). The sum of squares about the origin is:

$$\sum_{i=1}^{3} \sum_{j=1}^{3} Y_{ij}^2 = 3^2 + 5^2 + 4^2 + 11^2 + \ldots + 21^2 + 17^2$$

$$= 9 + 25 + 16 + 121 + \ldots + 441 + 289 = 1401.$$

The sum of squares due to variation in temperature is:

$$SSA = \sum_{i=1}^{3} \sum_{j=1}^{3} (\bar{Y}_{i.} - \bar{Y}_{..})^2$$

$$= 3 \sum (\bar{Y}_{i.} - \bar{Y}_{..})^2$$

$$= 3[(4 - 11)^2 + (11 - 11)^2 + (18 - 11)^2]$$

$$= 3[49 + 49] = 294.$$

The sum of squares due to variation in salinity is:

$$SSB = \sum_{i=1}^{3} \sum_{j=1}^{3} (\bar{Y}_{.j} - \bar{Y}_{..})^2$$

$$= 3 \sum_{j=1}^{3} (\bar{Y}_{.j} - \bar{Y}_{..})^2$$

$$= 3[(10 - 11)^2 + (12 - 11)^2 + (11 - 11)^2] =$$

$$= 3[1 + 1 + 0] = 6$$

The total sum of squares is:

$$SSTO = \sum_{i=1}^{3} \sum_{j=1}^{3} (Y_{ij} - \bar{Y}_{..})^2$$

$$= \sum_{i=1}^{3} \sum_{j=1}^{3} Y_{ij}^2 - 9 \cdot \bar{Y}_{..}^2$$

$$= 1401 - 9 \cdot 11^2 = 1401 - 1089 = 312.$$

Thus, the sum of squares due to the error is

$$SSE = SSTO - SSA - SSB$$
$$= 312 - 6 - 294 = 12 .$$

The ANOVA table (Analysis of Variance)

Source of Variation	Sum of Squares	Degrees of Freedom	Mean Squares
Temperature	294	3 - 1 = 2	147
Salinity	6	3 - 1 = 2	3
Error	12	(9-1) - 4 = 4	3

The program looks as follows:

```
C       PROGRAM FOR FACTORIAL DESIGN: TWO FACTORS
C       SUBPROGRAMS FOLLOW AFTER MAIN PROGRAM
        DIMENSION A(2Ø), B(2Ø), C(2Ø,2Ø), LA(2Ø), LB(2Ø)
        DIMENSION SN(2Ø,2Ø), SA(2Ø), AM(2Ø), SB(2Ø), BM(2Ø)
        DIMENSION CLM(2Ø,2Ø), KH(5), K1(4), K2(4), K3(4),
```

```
    1   N(2Ø,2Ø), KF(2Ø), D(1Ø,2Ø,5Ø)
        ND = 20
99      READ (2,1ØØ) KH, K1, K2, K3, K,L, ((N(I,J), J = 1,K), I = 1,L)
        WRITE (3,2ØØ) KH, K1, K2, K3, K,L, ((N(I,J), J = 1,K), I = 1,L)
1ØØ     FORMAT (5A4, 3(4A4), 2I3/4ØI2)
2ØØ     FORMAT ('1', 5A4, 3(4A4), 2I3/4ØI2)
        READ (2,3ØØ) KF
        WRITE (3,3ØØ) KF
3ØØ     FORMAT (2ØA4)
        T = 0
        XX = 0
        NC = 0
        DO 1Ø  J = 1,L
        A(J) = 0
1Ø      LA(J) = 0
        DO 2Ø  M = 1,K
        B(M) = 0
        LB(M) = 0
        DO 3Ø J = 1,L
        DO 3Ø M = 1,K
3Ø      C(J,M) = 0
        DO 4Ø J = 1,L
        DO 4Ø M = 1,K
        NUM = N(J,M)
        DO 4Ø  I = 1,NUM
        T = T + D(J,M,I)
        XX = XX + D(J,M,I) ** 2
        B(M) = B(M) + D(J,M,I)
        A(J) = A(J) + D(J,M,I)
4Ø      C(J,M) = C(J,M) + D(J,M,I)
        DO 5Ø  I = 1,L
        DO 5Ø  J = 1,K
        LA(I)  = LA(I) + N(I,J)
        LB(J) = LB(J) + N(I,J)
        NC = NC + N(I,J)
5Ø      SN(I,J) = N(I,J)
        AA = 0
        BB = 0
        CLL = 0
        DO 6Ø  I = 1,L
        SA(I) = LA(I)
        AM(I) = A(I)/SA(I)
        AA = AA + A(I) ** 2/SA(I)
        DO 6Ø  J = 1,K
        CLM(I,J) = C(I,J)/SN(I,J)
6Ø      CLL = CLL + C(I,J) ** 2/SN(I,J)
        DO 7Ø  J = 1,K
        SB(J) = LB(J)
        BM(J) = B(J)/SB(J)
7Ø      BB = BB + B(J) ** 2/SB(J)
C       COMPUTE  SS, DF, MS, F
        CCC = T ** 2/NC
        BETA = AA - CCC
        BETB = BB - CCC
        BETC = CLL - CCC
        AB = BETC - BETA - BETB
        TOT = XX - CCC
        ERR = TOT - BETC
        DT = NC - 1
        DA = L - 1
```

606

```
        DB = K - 1
        DC = L * K - 1
        DAB = DA * CB
        DER = DT - DC
        AMS = BETA/DA
        BMS = BETB/DB
        ABMS = AB/DAB
        ERMS = ERR/DER
        FA = AMS/ERMS
        FB = BMS/ERMS
        FAB = ABMS/ERMS
        PA = PRBF(CA,DER,FA)
        PB = PRBF(CAB,DER,FB)
        WRITE (3,400) KH, TOT, DT, K1, BETA, DA, AMS, FA,
   1    PA, K2, BETB, BMS, FB, PB,K3, AB, DAB, ABMS, FAB, PAB,
   2    ERR, DER, ERMS
 400    FORMAT
        CALL PRTS (AM, L, 1, 7H AMEANS, ND)
        CALL PRTS (BM, K, 1, 7H BMEANS, ND)
        CALL PRTS (CLM, L, K, 8H ABMEANS, ND)
        END
        SUBROUTINE PRTS (X,N,M,KH,ND)
 C      PRINT A MATRIX OR VECTOR IN 10-COLUMN PARTITIONS
        DIMENSION X(20,20) KH(2)
        IF (M.GT.1) GO TO 20
        DO 10  I = 1,N,10
        J = MINO (I + 9,N)
        WRITE (3,5) KH, (K,K = I,J)
   5    FORMAT (2A4, 10I11)
  10    WRITE (3,15) (X(K,1), K = I,J)
  15    FORMAT (119X, 10F11.4)
        RETURN
  20    DO 25  I = 1,N
  25    WRITE (3,30) I, (x(I,J), J = K,L)
  30    FORMAT (11 I6, 4X, 10F 11.4)
        RETURN
        END
```

● **PROBLEM** 17-21

Write a computer program in FORTRAN to find the correlation coefficient
r of the two variables. What is r for the data below?

X	Y
30	.9
20	.8
10	.5
30	1.0
10	.8

Solution: Answering the second question first, the correlation coefficient
r of the given data is

$$r = \frac{n \sum xy - (\sum x)(\sum y)}{[\sqrt{n\sum x^2 - (\sum x)^2}][\sqrt{n\sum y^2 - (\sum y)^2}]} \qquad (1)$$

$$= \frac{5(86) - (100)(4.0)}{[\sqrt{5(2400) - (100)^2}][\sqrt{5(3.34) - 4^2}]} = .80$$

To understand what r is and what it measures, suppose that a regression line is drawn through the given data.

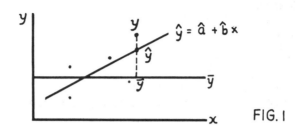

FIG. 1

Also, let $\bar{y}$ be drawn through the points. The regression line and the sample average line are predictors of how y varies when x varies. Note that $(y - \bar{y}) = (y - \hat{y}) + (\hat{y} - \bar{y})$ (see Fig. 1) The explained variation of y is defined as $\Sigma(\hat{y} - \bar{y})^2$. The unexplained variation is then $\Sigma(y - \hat{y})^2$. The coefficient of variation, r^2 is defined as

$$r^2 = \frac{\text{Explained Variation of } y}{\text{Total Variation of } y}$$

or,

$$r^2 = \frac{\Sigma(\hat{y} - \bar{y})^2}{\Sigma(y - \bar{y})^2} \qquad (2)$$

The correlation coefficient r is the square root of equation (2). The computational formula for r, (1), follows from (2).

Thus, r measures how much of the variation in y is explained by the regression line, in this case - 80%. This means that 20% of the variation is due to chance or other factors

The program looks as follows:

```
C        PROGRAM TO FIND CORRELATION COEFFICIENT
         DIMENSION  KF(2Ø), A(1ØØ), S(1ØØ), R(1ØØ,1ØØ)
1        READ (5,3) NV, NS, KF
3        FORMAT (2I5)/2ØA4)
         DO 5  I = 1,NV
         A(I) = 0
         DO 5  J = 1,NV
5        R(I,J) = 0
         DO 15  J = 1,NS
         READ (5,KF)(S(J), J = 1,NV)
         DO 15  J = 1,NV
         A(J) = A(J) + S(J)
         DO 15  K = J,NV
15       R(J,K) = R(J,K) + S(J) * S(K)
         T = NS
         DO 2Ø  I = 1,NV
         A(I) = A(I)/T
2Ø       S(I) = SQRT(R(I,I)/T - A(I) ** 2)
         DO 25  I = 1,NV
         DO 23  J = I,NV
         IF (S(I) * S(J).EQ.0.0) GO TO 23
         R(J,I) = (R(I,J)/T - A(I)* A(J))/S(I)*S(J))
```

```
23      R(I,J) = R(J,I)
25      R(I,I) = 1.0
        WRITE (6,3Ø)(A(I), I = 1,NV)
3Ø      FORMAT (8H1 x MEANS., (/1  OF  10.4))
        WRITE (6,31)(S(I), I = 1,NV)
31      FORMAT (8H SIGMAS.,(1 1 OF 10.4))
        DO 4Ø  K = 1,NV, 1Ø
        L = K + 9
        IF (NV - L)  32, 33, 32
32      L = NV
33      WRITE (6,35) K,L
35      FORMAT (14H1R MATRIX. COL, I3, 3H  TO  I3)
        DO 4Ø  I = 1,NV
4Ø      WRITE (6,45) I, (R(I,J),J = K,L)
45      FORMAT (I5, 10F 10.4)
        STOP
        END
```

CHAPTER 18

MATRICES, SYSTEMS OF EQUATIONS

COMPUTER OPERATIONS WITH VECTORS AND ARRAYS

● **PROBLEM** 18-1

Design a FORTRAN program segment to do the following:
a) Find the sum of vectors A and B, and store the sum in X .
b) Find the scalar product of vector A and scalar D, and store the product in Y.
c) Find the length (or norm) of scalar A, and store it in ALENG.

Solution: First remember that the sum of two vectors is obtained by $A + B = (A_1 + B_1, A_2 + B_2, \ldots, A_N + B_N)$, where N is the total number of vector elements. The scalar (or dot) product of vector A by scalar D is $D \cdot A = (DA_1, DA_2, DA_3, \ldots, DA_N)$. Finally, the length of

a scalar is written as

$$|A| = \sqrt{A_1^2 + A_2^2 + A_3^2 + \ldots + A_N^2} \, .$$

All three calculations can be made in one program segment:

```
      C       FIND VECTOR SUM, SCALAR PRODUCT, SCALAR NORM
              ALENG = 0.0
              DO 20 I = 1,N
                 X(I) = A(I) + B(I)
                 Y(I) = D*A(I)
                 ALENG = ALENG + A(I)**2
      20      CONTINUE
              ALENG = SQRT(ALENG)
              WRITE (5,100) X(I),Y(I),ALENG
      100     FORMAT (1X,'VECTOR SUM =', F10.4, 'SCALAR PRODUCT =',
         1    F10.4,'SCALAR NORM =', F10.4)
```

Note that N should be defined in the program before the above segment occurs.

A is any 20 × 20 array. Write a FUNCTION subprogram to compute

$$PD(A,I,J) = \frac{A(I-1,J) + A(I+1,J) + A(I,J-1) + A(I,J+1)}{4}$$

Then use it to compute

$$B_{ij} = (1-\alpha) B_{ij} + \alpha \left\{ \frac{B_{i-1,j} + B_{i+1,j} + B_{i,j-1} + B_{i,j+1}}{4} \right\} .$$

Solution: There are no special tricks involved here. The function looks as follows:

```
FUNCTION PD(A,I,J)
DIMENSION A(20,20)
PD =(A(I-1,J) + A(I+1,J) + A(I,J-1) + A(I,J+1))/4.0
RETURN
END
```

To compute B_{ij} the following statement will appear in the main program.
Note, that ALPHA has to be defined before this statement occurs.

```
B(I,J) = (1.-ALPHA)*B(I,J) + ALPHA*PD(B,I,J).
```

A two-dimensional array named RST has twenty rows and twenty columns. Use FORTRAN to compute the product of the main diagonal elements of RST and store it in DPROD. A main diagonal element is the one that has the same row and column number, so that

$$DPROD = \prod_{i=1}^{20} RST(I,I) .$$

Solution: The essential trick is to initialize DPROD = 1.0 and then set up a loop which computes DPROD by multiplying its previous value by RST(I,I).

```
        DIMENSION  RST(20,20)
        DPROD = 1.0
        DO 30  I = 1,20
        DPROD = DPROD*RST(I,I)
30      CONTINUE
        STOP
        END
```

Given a two-dimensional array AMATR which contains 10 rows and 10 columns and a one-dimensional array called DIAG which contains 10 elements, write a program segment in FORTRAN to compute the elements of DIAG from

$$DIAG(I) = AMATR(I,I)$$

for I = 1,2,...,10. Then compute the trace of AMATR, which is defined as

$$\text{trace}(AMATR) = \sum_{i=1}^{10} AMATR(I,I) = \sum_{i=1}^{10} DIAG(I) .$$

Solution:

```
            DIMENSION AMATR (10,10), DIAG (10)
            TRACE = 0.0
            DO 100  I = 1,10
            DIAG(I) = AMATR(I,I)
            TRACE = TRACE + DIAG(I)
100         CONTINUE
            STOP
            END
```

● **PROBLEM** 18-5

Write a FORTRAN subroutine to determine the largest element (in absolute value) in the ith row of N x N array called ARRAY.

Solution: Let the arguments of the subroutine be denoted by ARRAY, N,I,BIG,J. Here ARRAY stands for a square array whose dimensions are N x N, I stands for the row in which we wish to determine the maximum element, denoted by BIG, is to be found and J stands for the column in which BIG is located. The only trick to the algorithm is to implement a sequential comparison of each element of the ith row to the largest preceding value.
The subroutine looks as follows:

```
            SUBROUTINE LARGE (ARRAY,N,I,BIG,J)
            DIMENSION ARRAY (N,N)
            BIG = ABS (ARRAY (I,1))
            J = 1
            DO 9  K = 2,N
            IF (ABS(ARRAY(I,K)).LT.BIG) GO TO 9
  C         SET BIG TO THE NEW VALUE
            BIG = ABS (ARRAY(I,K))
  C         UPDATE THE COLUMN OF THE NEW BIG ELEMENT.
            J = K
  9         CONTINUE
            RETURN
            END
```

● **PROBLEM** 18-6

Four thieves have just robbed a bank of all its $100 bills. They decide to hide out for the night in an old man's cabin. While the other three are asleep, one of them wakes up and decides to be greedy by dividing the money into four equal piles, hiding one pile for himself and leaving one $100 bill for the old man. Then he recombines the 3 remaining piles and goes back to sleep.

Well, it seems that each of the other three thieves has a similar idea. In separate turns, each awakens, divides the remaining money into 4 equal piles, takes a pile for himself, and slips a left over bill to the old man.

When they awaken in the morning, they again divide the considerably smaller pile into four equal piles, with a single bill left over for the old man.
Write a FORTRAN program to determine the minimum number of bills in the original pile.

Solution: First, let us look at an algebraic interpretation of the night's festivities:

$$\begin{aligned} T &= 4N + 1 & &\text{first portion} \\ 3N &= 4P + 1 & &\text{second portion} \\ 3P &= 4Q + 1 & &\text{third portion} \\ 3Q &= 4R + 1 & &\text{fourth portion} \\ 3R &= 4S + 1 & &\text{final portion} \end{aligned}$$

To begin, let $S = 1$ and evaluate the final expression $(4S + 1)$ to see if it is a multiple of 3. If so, the value of R can be substituted in the next from the last equation. This upward climb is continued as long as integers that are multiples of 3 are being obtained. If this condition fails somewhere, S is increased to the next trial value, and the process is repeated until the top equation of the system is reached.

To program this brain teaser, two arrays, K and L, are needed. The equations become

$$\begin{aligned} L(1) &= 4K(1) + 1 = 3K(2) \\ L(2) &= 4K(2) + 1 = 3K(3) \\ L(3) &= 4K(3) + 1 = 3K(4) \\ L(4) &= 4K(4) + 1 = 3K(5) \\ T &= 4K(5) + 1 \;. \end{aligned}$$

The following flowchart will illustrate the program logic:

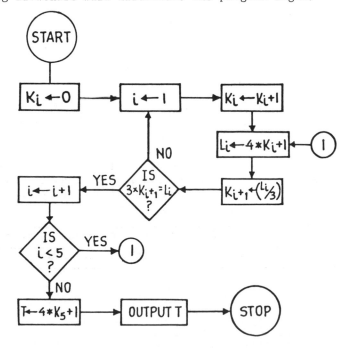

The answer for T is 1021 \$100 bills, or \$102,100 (quite a haul!)
The components of the arrays are

K :	80	107	143	191	255
L :	321	429	573	765	

```
          INTEGER T, K, L
          DIMENSION  K(5), L(4)
5         K(1) = 0
10        I = 1
          K(I) = K(I) + 1
40        L(I) = 4*K(I) + 1
          K(I+1) = L(I)/3
          IF (3*K(I+1) - L(I)) 10,50,60
60        PRINT "ERROR - TRY AGAIN"
          GO TO 5
50        I = I + 1
          IF (I - 5) 40, 90, 60
90        J = 4*K(5) + 1
          PRINT 100, T, K, L
100       FORMAT (I8//5I8//5I8)
          STOP
          END
```

● **PROBLEM** 18-7

Write a BASIC program which multiplies a polynomial of degree 2 by
a polynomial of degree 1.

Solution: It is instructive to study a concrete example.   Consider

$$3X^2 + 11X - 5$$

$$\underline{\; 2X + 7}$$

$$21X^2 + 77X - 35$$

$$\underline{6X^3 + 22X^2 - 10X}$$

$$6X^3 + 43X^2 + 67X - 35$$

or simply

$$3 + 11 - 5$$

$$\underline{\; 2 + 7}$$

$$21 \quad 77 - 35$$

$$\underline{6 + 22 - 10}$$

$$6 + 43 + 67 - 35$$

The program can be set up by putting 3, 11, and -5 in one computer
list, and   2   and   7   in a second list, while leaving room for the
product coefficients   6,43,67, and -35   in a third list.   The columns
are labeled as below

3	2	1	0	Col. no. if zero subscript allowed
4	3	2	1	Col. no. with no zero subscript

$$
\begin{array}{ccc}
 & 3 & 11 & -5 \\
 & & 2 & +7 \\
\hline
21 & + 77 & -35 \\
\underline{6 \;\; +22} & - 10 \\
6 \;\; +43 & + 67 & -35
\end{array}
$$

In general, multiplying a number in column I by a number in column J
results in a product in column I + J - 1 (unless zero subscript or a
zero column is allowed, in which case the product column is   I + J).
Thus, product totals can be accumulated with a statement of the form

614

```
XXX    LET P(I+J-1) = P(I+J-1) + F(I)*S(J)
```

where the P list is initialized to 0.

```
8       REM LINES 10 THRU 40 READ AND
9       REM PRINT THE FIRST POLYNOMIAL
10      FOR  X = 3  TO 1 STEP - 1
20      READ F[X]
30      PRINT F[X];
40      NEXT X
50      PRINT "TIMES";
51      REM LINES 60 THRU 90 READ AND
59      REM PRINT THE SECOND POLYNOMIAL
60      FOR  Y = 2  TO  1 STEP - 1
70      READ S[Y]
80      PRINT S[Y];
90      NEXT Y
98      REM 100 THRU 120 SET THE RESULT LIST
99      REM TO ALL ZEROS
100     FOR W = 1  TO  4
110     LET P(W) = 0
120     NEXT  W
128     REM LINES 130 THRU 170 DO THE
129     REM ACTUAL MULTIPLYING
130     FOR I = 1  TO  3
140     FOR  J = 1  TO  2
150     LET P(I+J-1) = P(I+J-1) + F(I)*S(J)
160     NEXT  J
170     NEXT  I
180     PRINT "YIELDS";
188     REM AND NOW THE
189     REM 'ANSWER LIST' IS PAINTED
190     FOR Z = 4  TO  1 STEP - 1
200     PRINT P(Z);
210     NEXT  Z
218     REM THE FIRST 3 NOS. REP. 3X↑2 + 11X - 5
219     REM THE NEXT 2 NOS. REP. 2X + 7
220     DATA 3,11,-5,2,7
230     END
```

COMPUTER MANIPULATIONS WITH MATRICES

● **PROBLEM** 18-8

Write a FORTRAN program to load and add two given $m \times n$ matrices.

Solution: An $m \times n$ matrix is an ordered array of real numbers containing m rows and n columns. Let $A = [a_{i,j}]$, $B = [b_{i,j}]$
$(i = 1,\ldots,m; j = 1,\ldots,n)$ be the two matrices to be added. Their sum $C = [c_{i,j}] = A + B = [a_{i,j} + b_{i,j}]$.
To load the matrices, a dimension statement reserving two sets of mn places each is required. Also, one more set of mn places must be dimensioned for the finally obtained array. Then, two nested DO-loops must be constructed to read in the values of $a_{i,j}$ and $b_{i,j}$.

615

After that, the two arrays are added using two nested DO-loops again. Finally, the resulting array is printed out by the similar method.

Note, that the format statements 20 and 30 are left out because they depend on the actual data used.

```
        DIMENSION A(10,15), B(10,15), C(10,15)
C       THE ARRAY C(10,15) WILL CONTAIN THE SUM
C       OF ARRAYS A(10,15) AND B(10,15).
C       LOAD THE ARRAYS
        DO 50 I = 1,10
        DO 50 J = 1,15
        READ (5,20) A(I,J), B(I,J)
50      CONTINUE
C       ADD THE ARRAYS
        DO 60 I = 1,10
        DO 60 J = 1,15
        C(I,J) = A(I,J) + B(I,J)
60      CONTINUE
C       OUTPUT THE RESULT
        DO 70 I = 1,10
        DO 70 J = 1,15
        WRITE (6,30) C(I,J)
70      CONTINUE
        STOP
        END
```

● **PROBLEM** 18-9

Write a FORTRAN program which determines whether or not the given square matrix(up to 20x20) is symmetrical.

Solution: By definition, a matrix is symmetric if $A(i,j) = A(j,i)$ for all i and j. Hence our approach is to use two nested DO loops to check this condition. In statement number 8, an implied DO loop is used to read in the elements of the matrix. The program looks as follows:

```
        INTEGER  X(20,20)
6       READ (2,31) N,ID
C       N  IS MATRIX SIZE, ID IS THE IDENTIFICATION OF THE MATRIX
        IF (N) 99,99,8
8       READ (2,32) ((X(I,J), I = 1,N), J = 1,N)
        DO 10 I = 1,N
        DO 10 J = 1,N
        IF (X(I,J) - X(J,I)) 9,10,9
10      CONTINUE
        WRITE (3,33) ID
        GO TO 6
9       WRITE (3,34) ID
        GO TO 6
31      FORMAT (I2, 3X, I3)
32      FORMAT (I4)
33      FORMAT (8H1MATRIX I3, 13H IS SYMMETRIC)
34      FORMAT (8H1MATRIX I3, 17H IS NOT SYMMETRIC)
99      STOP
        END
```

Write a FORTRAN program to multiply two matrices.

Solution: It is desired to compute the matrix product $AB = C$, where A is dimensioned $L1 \times L2$, B is dimensioned $L2 \times M2$, and C is dimensioned $L1 \times M2$. Note that the column dimension of A must equal the row dimension of B. This program illustrates the concept of nested DO loops. In terms of subscripts,

$$C_{ij} = \sum_{k=1}^{L2} A_{ik} \times B_{kj}$$

Thus, subscript k forms the innermost loop, while i and j are the subscripts of the outer loops.

```
            DIMENSION A(L1,L2), B(L2,M2), C(L1,M2)
            DO 100 I = 1,L1
            DO 100 J = 1,M2
            C(I,J) = 0.0
            DO 100 K = 1,L2
            C(I,J) = A(I,K)*B(K,J) + C(I,J)
      100   CONTINUE
            STOP
            END
```

Write a program in BASIC to compute the n-th power of a square $n \times n$ matrix A.

Solution: A concept of identity matrix will be used in the solution of this problem. An identity matrix in BASIC is the matrix in which all the elements in the leading diagonal are 1 and all other elements are zero. A 3×3 identity matrix, for example, looks as follows:

$$\begin{pmatrix} 1 & 0 & 0 \\ 0 & 1 & 0 \\ 0 & 0 & 1 \end{pmatrix}$$

An identity matrix multiplied by another matrix M (of the same dimensions) produces a matrix identical to M. This property is used in the solution in the following way: Matrix B is made into an identity matrix. Then matrix A is multiplied by B to produce another matrix C equal to A. After that, matrix C is assigned into B, and the multiplication of B and A is repeated. The new value of C is again assigned into B and $B \times A$ is executed again. This procedure repeats n times, where n is the desired power of A (as well as the matrix dimensions in this case). The final value of the matrix C is equal to $(A)^n$.
Note, that this is not the only possible solution to the problem. The program looks as follows:

```
      10        DIM A(N,N), B(N,N), C(N,N)
      20        INPUT N
      30        MAT B = IDN
      40        FOR I = 1 TO N
```

```
50        MAT C = B*A
60        MAT B = C
70        NEXT  I
80        MAT PRINT C;
90        END
```

● **PROBLEM** 18-12

Write a BASIC program to compute the inverse and the transpose of
a 3×3 matrix A. Apply the program to the case where

$$A = \begin{bmatrix} 1 & -1 & 2 \\ 2 & 0 & 1 \\ 0 & 3 & 1 \end{bmatrix}$$

Solution: The inverse of a matrix A is another matrix B such
that, when multiplied by A, gives an identity matrix. The statement in BASIC which results in forming of an inverse matrix B of
matrix A is as follows:

MAT B = INV (A)

A transpose C of the matrix A is a matrix with rows identical
to the respective columns of A, and columns identical to the
respective rows of A. For example, suppose that

$$A = \begin{bmatrix} 1 & 2 & 3 \\ 7 & 11 & 0 \\ -6 & 4 & 5 \end{bmatrix}$$

Then the transpose of A is:

$$\begin{bmatrix} 1 & 7 & -6 \\ 2 & 11 & 4 \\ 3 & 0 & 5 \end{bmatrix}$$

The corresponding BASIC statement is:

MAT C = TRN(S)

After generating the inverse and the transpose matrices of A, the
following program also checks if B is really an inverse by multiplying A and B to form matrix I. If I comes out to be an
identity matrix, then B is indeed an inverse of A.
The program looks as follows:

```
100       DIM A(3,3), B(3,3), C(3,3), I(3,3)
110       MAT READ A
120       MAT B = INV(A)
121       PRINT
122       PRINT
130       MAT PRINT B;
140       MAT C = TRN(A)
141       PRINT
150       MAT PRINT C;
160       MAT I = A*B
161       PRINT
170       MAT PRINT I;
800       DATA 1,-1,2,2,0,1,0,3,1
999       END
```

618

SOLVING SYSTEMS OF EQUATIONS
ON THE COMPUTER

Develop a BASIC program to solve two simultaneous linear equations,
AX + BY = C and DX + EY = F. Apply the result to the case
A = B = 1, C = 3, D = 1, E = F = -1.

Solution: Consider the pair of equations

$$AX + BY = C \qquad\qquad (1)$$

$$DX + EY = F \qquad\qquad (2)$$

Solving (1) for X yields $X = (C - BY)/A$, and substituting this
result into (2) gives:

$$D(C - BY)/A + EY = F$$

or

$$Y\{E - BD/A\} = F - CD/A$$

or

$$Y\{AE - BD\} = AF - CD$$

or

$$Y = (AF - CD)/(AE - BD) = (CD - AF)/(BD - AE).$$

Similarly $X = (BF - CE)/(BD - AE)$, provided $BD - AE \neq 0$.

Based on the above, the program looks as follows:

```
100        REM SIMULTANEOUS EQUATIONS
110        READ A,B,C,D,E,F
120        LET  Z = (B*D - A*E)
130        IF  Z = 0  THEN 160
140        LET  X = (B*F - C*E)/Z
141        LET  Y = (C*D - A*F)/Z
150        PRINT "ROOTS ARE", X,Y
151        GO TO 999
160        PRINT "NO UNIQUE SOLUTION OR INCONSISTENT EQUATIONS"
180        DATA 1,1,3,1,-1,-1
999        END
```

Write a BASIC program to solve the system of equations:

$$a_{11}x_1 + a_{12}x_2 + a_{13}x_3 + a_{14}x_4 = y_1$$
$$a_{21}x_1 + a_{22}x_2 + a_{23}x_3 + a_{24}x_4 = y_2$$
$$a_{31}x_1 + a_{32}x_2 + a_{33}x_3 + a_{34}x_4 = y_3$$
$$a_{41}x_1 + a_{42}x_2 + a_{43}x_3 + a_{44}x_4 = y_4$$

Hint: feel free to make use of built-in matrix instructions.

Solution: The above system of equations can be written in the matrix
form as $A \cdot X = Y$, and the solution is $X = (A^{-1}) \cdot Y$, where A is a
4×4 matrix of the coefficients of X's, and both X and Y are 4×1
vectors. The symbol A^{-1} stands for the inverse matrix of A.

Here is an example of the validity of the above procedure:
The system of equations

$$x_1 - x_2 = 5$$
$$2x_1 - 3x_2 = 13$$

is solved to obtain the values of x_1 and x_2:

$$x_1 = 5 + x_2 \ ; \ 2(5 + x_2) - 3x_2 = 13 \ ; \ x_2 = \frac{13 - 10}{-1} = -3$$

$$\therefore \quad x_1 = 5 - 3 = 2 \ .$$

Now, using the matrix procedure:

$$A = \begin{pmatrix} 1 & -1 \\ 2 & -3 \end{pmatrix} ; \quad A^{-1} = \begin{pmatrix} 3 & -1 \\ 2 & -1 \end{pmatrix} \quad Y = \begin{pmatrix} 5 \\ 13 \end{pmatrix}$$

$$X = (A^{-1}) \cdot Y = \begin{pmatrix} 3 & -1 \\ 2 & -1 \end{pmatrix} \cdot \begin{pmatrix} 5 \\ 13 \end{pmatrix} = \begin{pmatrix} 3 \times 5 + (-1)13 \\ 2 \times 5 + (-1)13 \end{pmatrix} = \begin{pmatrix} 15 - 13 \\ 10 - 13 \end{pmatrix}$$

$$X = \begin{pmatrix} 2 \\ -3 \end{pmatrix} \Rightarrow 7 \ , \ X_1 = 2, \ X_2 = -3.$$

Both methods yield the same results.
The program looks as follows:

```
10          DIM X(4,1),Y(4,1),A(4,4),B(4,4)
20          MAT READ Y
30          MAT READ A
40          MAT B = INV(A)
50          MAT X = B*Y
60          MAT PRINT X;
70          END
```

● **PROBLEM** 18-15

Write an APL program to solve the following system of equations in three unknowns using Cramer's Rule.

$$x + y + z = 6$$
$$x + y - 2z = -3$$
$$2x + y - z = 1$$

Also, show an easier method of solving the above system using the symbol ⊟ from APL.

<u>Solution</u>: The determinant A of the form

$$A = \begin{vmatrix} a_{11} & a_{12} & a_{13} \\ a_{21} & a_{22} & a_{23} \\ a_{31} & a_{32} & a_{33} \end{vmatrix}$$

can be evaluated as follows:

$$|A| = a_{11}a_{22}a_{33} + a_{12}a_{23}a_{31} + a_{13}a_{21}a_{32}$$
$$- a_{11}a_{23}a_{32} - a_{12}a_{21}a_{33} - a_{13}a_{22}a_{31}$$

According to Cramer's Rule, the system

$$a_1 x + b_1 y + c_1 z = d_1$$
$$a_2 x + b_2 y + c_2 z = d_2$$
$$a_3 x + b_3 y + c_3 z = d_3$$

has the following solutions in terms of determinants:

$$x = \frac{\begin{vmatrix} d_1 & b_1 & c_1 \\ d_2 & b_2 & c_2 \\ d_3 & b_3 & c_3 \end{vmatrix}}{\begin{vmatrix} a_1 & b_1 & c_1 \\ a_2 & b_2 & c_2 \\ a_3 & b_3 & c_3 \end{vmatrix}}, y = \frac{\begin{vmatrix} a_1 & d_1 & c_1 \\ a_2 & d_2 & c_2 \\ a_3 & d_3 & c_3 \end{vmatrix}}{\begin{vmatrix} a_1 & b_1 & c_1 \\ a_2 & b_2 & c_2 \\ a_3 & b_3 & c_3 \end{vmatrix}}, z = \frac{\begin{vmatrix} a_1 & b_1 & d_1 \\ a_2 & b_2 & d_2 \\ a_3 & b_3 & d_3 \end{vmatrix}}{\begin{vmatrix} a_1 & b_1 & c_1 \\ a_2 & b_2 & c_2 \\ a_3 & b_3 & c_3 \end{vmatrix}}$$

Thus, a defined function for the evaluation of a determinant must be developed first:

$$\nabla Z \leftarrow \text{Determinant} \quad X$$

[1]   A ← 3 3 ρ C

[2]   Z ← ((A[1;1]×A[2;2]×A[3;3])+(A[1;2]×A[2;3]×A[3;1])
          +A[1;3]×A[2;1]×A[3;2])

[3]   Z ←Z-(A[1;1]×A[2;3]×A[3;2])+
          (A[1;2]×A[2;1]×A[3;3])+A[1;3]×A[2;2]×A[3;1]
          ▽

Note that this defined function comes directly from the method of evaluation of the determinant explained previously. The following function computes the values of x,y,z.

          ▽ Solution

[1]   'Enter the coefficients and constants'
[2]   So ← 3 4 ρ ☐
[3]   D ← E ← F 3 3 ↑ So
[4]   R ← Determinant D
[5]   → (R = 0)/ END
[6]   X ← (Determinant D[;1] ← So[;4]) ÷ R
[7]   Y ← (Determinant E[;2] ← So[;4]) ÷ R
[8]   Z ← (Determinant F[;3] ← So[;4]) ÷ R
[9]   'The Solution is: ' ;x,y,z
[10]   → 0
[11]   End: "No unique solutions'
[12]   ▽

Note that the function solution uses the function Determinant in steps [4], [6], [7] and [8]. Applied to the given system of equations

$$x + y + z = 6$$
$$x + y - 2z = -3 \qquad\qquad (1)$$
$$2x + y - z = 1$$

The function solution works as follows: The coefficients and values of system's equations

          1   1   1   6   1   1   -2   -3   2   1   -1   1 .

are entered first;
Step [2] reshapes the vector:

621

$$So = \begin{bmatrix} 1 & 1 & 1 & 6 \\ 1 & 1 & -2 & -3 \\ 2 & 1 & -1 & 1 \end{bmatrix}$$

Step [3] takes the 3×3 matrix from So :

$$D = \begin{bmatrix} 1 & 1 & 1 \\ 1 & 1 & -2 \\ 2 & 1 & -1 \end{bmatrix}$$

Step [4] computes the determinant of D. Steps [6], [7], and [8] are all very similar. The fourth column of So is replaced with the appropriate column of D. (For x, it is the first column, for y, it is the second column, for z, it is the third column.) Dividing the determinants of D by R will yield the appropriate solutions. The symbols A $\boxed{\div}$ B are used in APL for solving systems of equations. A is a vector that contains the constant term (value) from each equation in the system. B is a matrix that contains all the co-efficients of the system's variables. ($\boxed{\div}$ is formed by typing in $\square$, backspacing, and typing in $\div$). To solve the given system, (1), one just types the following statements:

        A ← 6 -3 1
        B ← 3 3 ρ 1 1 1 1 1 -2 2 1 -1
        A $\boxed{\div}$ B .

● **PROBLEM** 18-16

Write a FORTRAN program to implement Gauss's elimination method for solving the systems of equations.

Solution: Consider the system of n linear equations with n unknowns:

$$a_{11}x_1 + a_{12}x_2 + \ldots + a_{1n}x_n = b_1$$
$$a_{21}x_1 + a_{22}x_2 + \ldots + a_{2n}x_n = b_2 \qquad (1)$$
$$\vdots \qquad\qquad \vdots$$
$$a_{n1}x_1 + a_{n2}x_2 + \ldots + a_{nn}x_n = b_n$$

Gauss's elimination method is used to find a solution of (1) i.e., a set $\{x_1, \ldots, x_n\}$ such that when it is substituted into (1), all the equations are satisfied. The method is as follows:

1) Divide the first equation by a_{11} to obtain

$$x_1 + \frac{a_{12}}{a_{11}} x_2 + \ldots + \frac{a_{1n}}{a_{11}} x_n = b_1/a_{11} . \qquad (2)$$

2) Now subtract a_{21} times the first equation from row 2, a_{31} times the first equation from row 3,..., a_{n1} times the first equation from row n to obtain

$$x_1 + \frac{a_{12}}{a_{11}} x_2 + \ldots + \frac{a_{1n}}{a_{11}} x_n = b_1/a_{11}$$
$$w_{22}x_2 + \ldots + w_{2n}x_n = c_2 \qquad (3)$$
$$\vdots$$
$$w_{n2}x_2 + \ldots + w_{nn}x_n = c_n .$$

where the result of adding $- (a_{j1} (a_{1j}/a_{11}) x_j)$ from $a_{ij}x_i$ has been written as $w_{ij}x_j$ and the result of adding $-(a_{i1}b_1/a_{11})$ to b_i has been written as c_i $(i = 2,\ldots,n)$. The method is applied again to eliminate x_2 from the third, fourth,$\ldots$,n-th equations. Repeated application yields the tridiagonal system:

$$
\begin{aligned}
x_1 + v_{12}x_2 + \ldots + v_{1n}x_n &= d_1 \\
x_2 + v_{23}x_3 + \ldots + v_{2n}x_n &= d_2 \\
\cdot \quad \cdot \quad \cdot \quad \cdot \\
x_{n-1} + v_{n-1,n}x_n &= d_{n-1} \\
x_n &= d_n
\end{aligned}
\qquad (4)
$$

Now the system can be solved by back-substituting. The X,Y and Z's need not be presented to solve such systems on a computor. The coefficients can be loaded into an array $A(N,N+1)$ and solved in a similar manner.

```
        DIMENSION  A(N,N+1)
C       AN EXTRA COLUMN IS NEEDED FIRST TO STORE
C       THE CONTINUOUSLY CHANGING VALUES (b_1...b_n) OF THE
C       EQUATIONS, AND THEN THE ROOTS OF THE SYSTEN.
        READ (5,10)N
        DO 40 I = 1,N
        DO 40 J = 1,N+1
        READ (5,20) A(I,J)
40      CONTINUE

        M = N - 1
        L = N + 1
        DO 60 K = 1,M
        K1 = K + 1
        DO 60 J = K1,L
        DO 60 I = K1,N
        A(I,J) = A(I,J) - A(I,K)/A(K,K)*A(K,J)
60      CONTINUE
        I = N
        J = I + 1
        DO 70 I1=1,N
        DO 70 J1=1,J
        A(I1,N + 1) = A(I1,N + 1)/A(I1,I1)
70      CONTINUE
100     I = I - 1
110     J = J - 1
        B(I,N + 1) = B(I,N + 1) + A(I,J)*A(J,N + 1)
        IF (J.EQ.0) GO TO 120
        GO TO 100
120     I=N
        I=I-1
        J=J-1
        A(I,N + 1) = 1/A(I,I)*(A(I,N + 1) - B(I,N + 1))
130     IF (I.EQ.0) GO TO 140
        GO TO 120
140     WRITE (3,30) (A(I,N + 1), I = 1,N)
        STOP
        END
```

Note: The formats 10,20,30 are not included because they depend on actual data.

Write a program in PL/I to use the Gauss-Seidel method for solving linear equations. Specialize to 3 equations with 3 unknowns.

<u>Solution</u>: Consider the system

$$a_{11}x_1 + a_{12}x_2 + a_{13}x_3 = b_1$$
$$a_{21}x_1 + a_{22}x_2 + a_{23}x_3 = b_2$$
$$a_{31}x_1 + a_{32}x_2 + a_{33}x_3 = b_3$$

The solution algorithm is based on rewriting this system to a form

$$a_{11}x_1 = b_1 - (a_{11}^*x_1 + a_{12}x_2 + a_{13}x_3)$$
$$a_{22}x_2 = b_2 - (a_{21}x_1 - a_{22}^*x_2 + a_{23}x_3)$$
$$a_{33}x_3 = b_3 - (a_{31}x_1 + a_{32}x_2 + a_{33}^*x_3)$$

Let us introduce a P matrix associated with the A matrix, but modified so that the diagonal elements of the matrix A are replaced by 0.
Using the new matrix P, one can rewrite the system as

$$a_{11}x_1 = b_1 - (P_{11}x_1 + P_{12}x_2 + P_{13}x_3)$$
$$a_{22}x_2 = b_2 - (P_{21}x_1 + P_{22}x_2 + P_{23}x_3)$$
$$a_{33}x_3 = b_3 - (P_{31}x_1 + P_{32}x_2 + P_{33}x_3)$$

or in compact summation notation

$$a_{ii}x_i = b_i - \sum_j P_{ij}x_j \quad \text{for } i = 1,2,3.$$

In PL/I notation this last equation becomes

$$X(I) = (B(I) - SUM(P(I,*)*X))/A(I,I).$$

Note that we SUM over the subscript * corresponding to j. Also note that $P_{ij} = a_{ij}$, $i \neq j$; $P_{ii} = 0$.

For this program we read in the dimension N of the square matrix A, and the value of K - the number of iterations.
The program looks as follows:

```
       START: PROCEDURE;
       /*GAUSS-SEIDEL*/
RPT:   GET LIST (N,K);
       BEGIN;
       DECLARE A(N,N), B(N),X(N),P(N,N);
       GET LIST (A,B);
       P = A;
       X = 0;
       DO I = 1  TO  N;
       P(I,I) = 0;
       END;
       DO J = 1  TO  K;
       DO I = 1  TO  N;
       X(I) = (B(I) - SUM(P(I,*)*X))/A(I,I);
       END;
       PUT SKIP EDIT (X) (F(10,4));
       END;
       END;
```

```
PUT SKIP (2);
GO TO RPT;
END START;
```

Develop a FORTRAN program which solves a system of linear simultaneous
equations according to the GAUSS-SEIDEL method.

Solution: To apply the Gauss-Seidel method, the system of linear
equations $AX = C$ is rewritten in the form:

$$x_1 = \frac{1}{a_{11}} (c_1 - a_{12}x_2 - a_{13}x_3 - \ldots - a_{1n}x_n) \qquad (1)$$

$$x_2 = \frac{1}{a_{22}} (c_2 - a_{21}x_1 - a_{23}x_3 - \ldots - a_{2n}x_n) \qquad (2)$$

$$\vdots$$

$$x_n = \frac{1}{a_{nn}} (c_n - a_{n1}x_1 - a_{n2}x_2 - \ldots - a_{n,n-1}x_{n-1}) \qquad (n)$$

Next, a set of starting values $x_1^0, x_2^0, \ldots, x_n^0$ is chosen. While the
program developed will take 0 as starting values, $x_i^0 = c_i/a_{ii}$ are
also frequently used as starting values. Substituting $x_2 = x_3 = \ldots = x_n = 0$
into (1) yields an approximation for x_1. This approximation is used
in (2) where $x_3 = x_4 = \ldots = x_n = 0$. Now we have approximations for
x_1 and x_2. Continuing, observe that x_n is found by substituting
the approximations for $x_1, x_2, \ldots, x_{n-1}$ into (n). This completes
the first iteration. For the k-th iteration:

$$x_1^{k+1} = \frac{1}{a_{11}} (c_1 - a_{12}x_2^k - a_{13}x_3^k - \ldots - a_{1n}x_n^k)$$

$$x_2^{k+1} = \frac{1}{a_{22}} (c_2 - a_{21}x_1^{k+1} - a_{13}x_3^k - \ldots - a_{2n}x_n^k)$$

$$\vdots$$

$$x_n^{k+1} = \frac{1}{a_{nn}} (c_n - a_{n1}x_1^{k+1} - a_{n2}x_2^{k+1} - \ldots - a_{n,n-1}x_{n-1}^{k+1}).$$

A sufficient condition for convergence (and the one which will be
assumed to hold) is that

$$\sum_{j \neq i} |a_{ij}| < |a_{ii}| \quad \text{for} \quad i = 1, 2, \ldots, n$$

As an illustrative example, let

$$x_1 = \frac{1}{10} (9 - 2x_2 - x_3)$$

$$x_2 = \frac{1}{20} (-44 - 2x_1 + 2x_3)$$

$$x_3 = \frac{1}{10} (22 + 2x_1 - 3x_2) .$$

These equations correspond to the determinant system

$$\begin{bmatrix} 10 & 2 & 1 \\ 2 & 20 & -2 \\ -2 & 3 & 10 \end{bmatrix} \begin{bmatrix} x_1 \\ x_2 \\ x_3 \end{bmatrix} = \begin{bmatrix} 9 \\ -44 \\ 22 \end{bmatrix}$$

For $x_i^{(0)} = 0$ we have

$$x_1^{(1)} = 9/10$$

$$x_2^{(1)} = \frac{1}{20}(-44-2x_1^{(1)} + 3x_3^{(0)}) = +\frac{1}{20}(-44-\frac{18}{10}) = -2.29$$

$$x_3^{(1)} = \frac{1}{10}(22 + 2x_1^{(1)} - 3x_2^{(1)}) = \frac{1}{10}(22 + \frac{18}{10} - 3(-2.29))$$

$$= 3.067$$

etc.

The program itself is given below.

```
C       GAUSS-SEIDEL ITERATION OF SIMULTANEOUS EQUATIONS
        DIMENSION A(30,30), X(30), Y(30)
1       READ 999, N, ITLAST,((A(I,J),J = 1,N), Y(I),I = 1,N)
        PUNCH 996, N,((A(I,J),J = 1,N), I = 1,N)
        PUNCH 995, (Y(I),I = 1,N)
        DO 10 I = 1,N
10      X(I) = 0.
        IT = 1.
20      PUNCH 994, IT
        DO 60 I = 1,N
        P = Y(I)
        DO 50 J = 1,N
        IF (I - J) 40,50,40
40      P = P - A(I,J)*X(J)
50      CONTINUE
        X(I) = P/A(I,I)
60      PUNCH 998, I, X(I)
        IT = IT + 1
        IF (IT - ITLAST) 20,20,1
994     FORMAT(/24X, 9HITERATION I2)
995     FORMAT(/22X,15HCONSTANT VECTOR/(3E18.7)//22X,
     1  15HSOLUTION VECTOR)
996     FORMAT(//21X, 15HMATRIX OF ORDER 12 //(3E18.7))
998     FORMAT(20X, I2, E16.7)
999     FORMAT(2I5/(8F10.0))
        END
```

CHAPTER 19

NUMERICAL METHODS

SUMS AND DIFFERENCES

● **PROBLEM** 19-1

Design a program that can guess any integer from 100 to 999999999 by asking questions of the user about the sums of certain digits. Use BASIC.

<u>Solution:</u> Let us choose 718999 as our number to be "guessed." The algorithm we shall use requires several pieces of information. First, you must type in the number of digits, which in this case is 6. Then you must type in the sums of adjacent digits starting from the left, until you reach the last digit. Finally, the sum of the second and the last digits from the left are needed if the number is even; the sum of the first and last digits, if the number is odd. At this point, the array T has stored the following quantities:

T (0) = 8	T (3) = 18
T (1) = 9	T (4) = 18
T (2) = 17	T (5) = 16

Now we hit the loop in which S is computed. Let us write down these steps as they will be executed:

S = 0 + (9 * 1) = 9
S = 9 + (17 * (-1)) = -8
S = -8 + (18 * 1) = 10
S = 10 + (-18) = -8
S = -8 + 10 = 2

S is then divided by 2 and stored in T(6).

The final loop calculates each digit, multiplies by the appropriate factor of 10, and adds the totals to give the answer.

```
5    DIM T(15)
7    PRINT
9    PRINT "WRITE ANY NUMBER FROM 3 TO 9 DIGITS ON A PIECE OF PAPER"
10   PRINT "WHEN READY, TYPE A ZERO AND RETURN"
11   INPUT W
12   IF  W < > 0 THEN 65
13   LET S = 0
14   LET E = 0
15   LET H = -1
16   MATT = ZER
17   PRINT "TYPE IN THE NUMBER OF DIGITS IN YOUR NUMBER"
18   PRINT
19   INPUT N
```

```
20    LET G = N/2
21    IF  G < > INT(N/2) THEN 23
22    LET E = 1
23    FOR  J = 0  TO  N - 2
24    LET K = J + 1
25    PRINT
26    PRINT "WHAT IS SUM OF DIGIT" K "AND DIGIT" K + 1 "?"
27    PRINT
28    INPUT T(J)
29    NEXT J
30    PRINT "WHAT IS SUM OF DIGIT" E + 1 "AND LAST DIGIT?"
31    PRINT
32    INPUT T(K)
36    FOR  J = E  TO  N - 1
38    LET  H = -1 * H
40    LET  S = S + T(J) * H
41    NEXT J
42    LET  S = S/2
43    LET  T(K + 1) = S
44    LET  G = 1
45    LET  S = 0
46    FOR  J = 0  TO  N - 1
50    LET  L = N - J - 1
52    LET  T(L) = T(L) - T(L + 1)
53    LET  S = S + T(L) - T(L + 1)
54    LET  G = 10 * G
56    NEXT J
58    PRINT
60    PRINT "I BET YOUR NUMBER IS" S
62    GO TO  7
65    END
```

● **PROBLEM** 19-2

Write a PL/I procedure that reads an integer $N > 1$ and calculates the sequence

$$Y = \frac{\sum\limits_{i=1}^{N} i(N - i)^2}{N}$$

The program should output N and the corresponding Y on each line.

Solution: We will set up a DO loop to calculate the terms as indicated by the summation symbol, (Σ). Program control passes to the end of the program when the value of N is less than or equal to zero.

In this example, we will input $N = 2$, $N = 10$, and $N = 25$.

```
SEQ: PROC OPTIONS (MAIN);
     DCL  Y  FIXED (10,3);
LOOP:  GET DATA (N);
/ *  TEST FOR END OF DATA * /
     IF N < = 0 THEN GO TO FINISH;
/ * INITIALIZE Y AND COMPUTE THE SUM * /
     Y = 0;
SUMLOOP: DO  J = 1  TO N;
         Y = Y + J * (N - J) * (N - J);
         END SUMLOOP;
         Y = Y/N;
```

```
/ * PRINT ANSWERS * /
    PUT SKIP DATA (N,Y);
    GO TO LOOP;
FINISH:  END SEQ;
```

Sample input: N = 2; N = 10; N = 25; N = 0;

Sample output:

N =	2	Y =	0.500;
N =	10	Y =	82.500;
N =	25	Y =	1300.000;

● **PROBLEM** 19-3

If we have a list of tabular values represented by a one-dimensional array, then the first differences of the list are formed by subtracting each element except the last [since nothing follows the last element] from the element immediately following it. Suppose we have a one-dimensional array named X that contains 50 elements. Compute the 49 elements of another array named DX from

$$DX(I) = X(I + 1) - X(I)$$
$$I = 1,2,\ldots,49.$$

Write a program segment to perform this calculation.

Solution: Dimension both arrays according to the given dimensions and then write a simple DO loop to define the difference array DX. Thus we get:

```
           DIMENSION X(50), DX(49)
           DO 50 I = 1, 49
50     DX(I) = X(I + 1) - X(I)
       STOP
       END
```

● **PROBLEM** 19-4

Given a one-dimensional array Y with 50 elements, and numbers U and I, write statements to compute the value of S from the following equation:
$$S = y_i + U \left(\frac{y_{i+1} - y_{i-1}}{2}\right) + \frac{U^2}{2} (y_{i+1} - 2y_i + y_{i-1})$$

Solution: Note that since the subscripts on Y can be i+1, i, or i-1 where the Y array is dimensioned 50, then we must restrict I to being an integer from 2 to 49, i.e., there are 48 possible values of I. With this restriction in mind we can simply write:

```
       DIMENSION  Y(50)
       DO 100 I = 2,49
           S = Y(I) + U * (Y(I + 1) - Y(I - 1)/2.0)
1              + U * U * (Y(I + 1) - 2*Y(I)
1              + Y(I - 1))/2.0
100    CONTINUE
       STOP
       END
```
   Further remarks on interpretation: This formula is called Stirling's interpolation formula [S stands for Stirling!] through second dif-

629

ferences and is described below. We have three points on a curve: (X_{i-1}, Y_{i-1}), (X_i, Y_i), and (X_{i+1}, Y_{i+1}) such that $X_{i+1} - X_i = X_i - X_{i-1} = h$ (i.e., the x coordinates are equally spaced) and have a value of x for which we want to guess $Y(x)$. We write $U = (x - x_i)/h$. Then the formula stated gives the interpolated value of Y corresponding to x, found by passing a quadratic through the three given points.

FINDING ROOTS OF EQUATIONS

● **PROBLEM** 19-5

A cylinder is designed to hold one quart of liquid (or 58 cubic inches). What should the dimensions of the cylinder be in order to minimize the amount of material necessary to construct it?

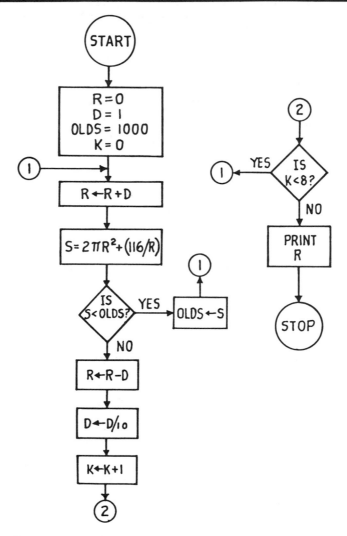

Solution: We use an approximation method known as bracketing. Of course, calculus could give us a precise solution, but we will demonstrate the usefulness of this method. First we know that the surface area S of the cylinder is given by $S = 2\pi R^2 + 2\pi RH$, where R is the radius and H is the height. We also know that volume $V = 58$ in.$^3 = \pi R^2 H$. We can solve for H by dividing both sides by πR^2 :

$$H = V/\pi R^2 = 58 \text{ in.}^3/\pi R^2$$

Substituting into the surface area formula, we have
$$S = 2\pi R^2 + 2\pi R(58/\pi R^2)$$
After combining terms,
$$S = (2\pi R^2) + (116/R)$$
We seek to minimize S by trying various values for R. We begin with very small and very large R's, and we gradually approach the solution from both sides. A flow chart illustrates the plan of the program: K is a counter; D is the increment on radius R. We begin by initializing the radius to 1, and then we calculate the surface area. If the calculated S is less than OLDS, an arbitrary initial guess at the surface area, OLDS is replaced by the calculated S, and the radius is incremented again. If S is greater than or equal to OLDS, the radius is too big. In this case, the increment D must be reduced to one-tenth its previous size. The variable K serves as a counter of precision. When 8 digits of precision have been reached, the solution of R is printed.
Below is the program segment:

```
          R = 0.0
          D = 1.0
          OLDS = 1000.0
          K = 0
2∅        R = R + D
          S = (2.0*3.14159*R**2) + (116.0/R)
          IF (S.GE.OLDS) GO TO 3∅
          OLDS = S
          GO TO 2∅
3∅        R = R - D
          D = D/10.0
          K = K + 1
          IF (K.GE.8) GO TO 4∅
          GO TO 2∅
4∅        WRITE (5,*) R
          [Note use of FORMAT-free WRITE statement.]
```

● **PROBLEM** 19-6

Write a FORTRAN program segment to find a root of the continuous function f(x) via the bisection method.

Solution: The bisection method starts with two values of X, called HI and LO, for which the values of f(x) have opposite signs. The object is to find X when f(x) = 0. We do this by halving the interval between HI and LO, alternately from the negative side (LO) and from the positive side (HI). As we continue the process, we can approach X until we reach an approximation with any desired degree of accuracy. [Note that rounding errors can alter the accuracy of the approximation.] The program logic is given below, using the function

$X^3 + 3X - 5$ (Figure)

as a sample f(x). We have chosen

HI = 2.0, so $f(HI) = (2)^3 + 3(2) - 5 = 9$, and
LO = 0.0, so $f(LO) = (0)^3 + 3(0) - 5 = -5$.

```
         REAL F, X, HI, LO, ERROR
C        CHOOSE SOME INITIAL  HI  AND  LO  VALUES,
C        SUCH AS  HI = 2.0  AND  LO = 0.0.
C        ALSO CHOOSE ERROR TO BE, SAY, = .002.
         DO 20 J = 1, 1000
         IF ((HI - LO). LE. ERROR) GO TO 30
         X = (LO + HI)/2.0
         F = (X ** 3) + (3.0 * X) - 5.0
         IF (F.GT.0.0) GO TO 15
         LO = X
         GO TO 20
15       HI = X
20       CONTINUE
30       WRITE (5,*) X
```

[Note: This WRITE statement includes an asterisk, a feature provided on some machines. It simply indicates that only variables are to be outputted, without any literals. Its purpose is to save time by eliminating a FORMAT statement.]

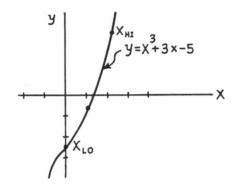

● **PROBLEM** 19-7

Solve $f(x) = x^2 - e^x = 0.$
(a)   graphically
(b)   using the Newton-Raphson method of iteration (program in BASIC)

Solution: Observe that $f(x)$ is a continuous function and that $f(-1) = 1 - e^{-1} = 0.632 > 0$ and $f(0) = -1 < 0$ so that $f(x)$ has a root between -1 and 0. By graphing $f(x)$ we can get a good preliminary estimate of where the root lies. Values plotted are given in the Figure.

Note that there is a root near $x = -0.7$.
We can use this root as an input estimate to the Newton-Raphson method. This is an iterative method in which we solve the equation

$$x_{n+1} = x_n - f(x_n)/f'(x_n),$$

where

$$f(x_n) = x_n^2 - e^{x_n} \quad \text{and} \quad f'(x_n) = 2x_n - e^{x_n}.$$

We make an initial guess x_0 (in this case, $x_0 = -0.7$), and evaluate the function. Next, we compute the error as an absolute value. This value is compared to the convergence condition, a previously established number that we have chosen. If our error is less than the convergence condition, then we write the solution x_{n+1}. If not, we return to the start of the loop and continue. A sample program solution is

632

x	$f(x)$
-1	.632
-0.9	.403
-0.8	.191
-0.7	-0.007
-0.6	-0.189
-0.5	-0.357
-0.4	-0.510
-0.3	-0.651
-0.2	-0.779
-0.1	-0.895
0.0	-1

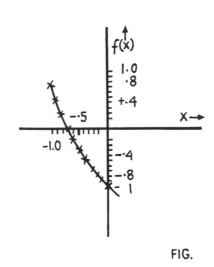

FIG.

given below:

PROGRAM		EXPLANATION
0010	INPUT X,L	Input initial guess x_0 and limiting no. of iterations
0020	F = (X↑2 - EXP(X))	Evaluate $f(x)$
0030	D = (2*X - EXP(x))	Evaluate D = $f'(x)$
0040	A = F/D	Evaluate $f(x)/f'(x)$
0050	E = ABS(A)	E = $\lvert A \rvert$ = $\lvert x_{n+1} - x_n \rvert$ = error
0060	IF E < 0.000005 THEN 110	Convergence condition
0070	X = X - A	$x_{n+1} = x_n - f(x_n)/f'(x_n)$
0080	N = N + 1	Increment loop counter
0090	IF N = L THEN 110	Check for limit on iterations
0100	GO TO 20	loop back
0110	PRINT X,N,A	output results
0120	END	end of program

● **PROBLEM** 19-8

Write a function which utilizes the Newton-Raphson method to compute the square root of a number.

Solution: By applying the Newton-Raphson method

$$x_{n+1} = x_n - \frac{f(x_n)}{f'(x_n)}$$

to the case of $f(x) = x^2 - (root)^2 = 0$ (where $(root)^2$ is the given number), one arrives at the algorithm below:

$$x_{n+1} = x_n - \left(\frac{x_n^2 - (root)^2}{2x_n}\right) = \tfrac{1}{2}\left(x_n + \frac{(root)^2}{x_n}\right) .$$

```
FUNCTION ROOT (WORK)
ARG = ABS (WORK)
ROOT = ARG/2.0
DO 6 IDX = 1,100
```

```
       ROOT = (ROOT + ARG/ROOT)/2.0
       IF(ABS((ROOT**2 - ARG)/ARG) - 0.000001) 7,7,6
6      CONTINUE
7      RETURN
       END
```

Write a subroutine which computes the roots of the quadratic equation
$a_1x^2 + a_2x + a_3 = 0$ according to the quadratic formula:

$$x_{1,2} = \frac{-a_2}{2a_1} \pm \sqrt{\left(\frac{a_2}{2a_1}\right)^2 - \frac{a_3}{a_1}} \left(= \frac{-a_2 \pm \sqrt{a_2^2 - 4a_1a_3}}{2a_1} \right)$$

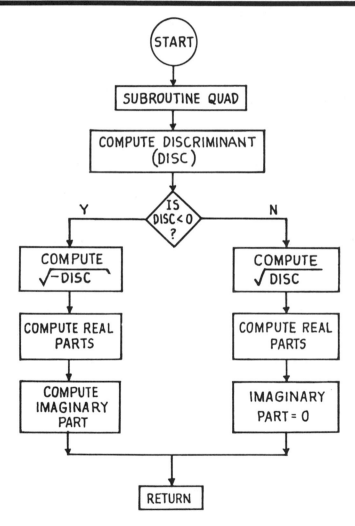

Solution: The only difficult part to this problem is taking into account the fact that the character of the solution changes according to
the sign of the discriminant, which we define as $\left[a_2/\, 2a_1\right]^2 - a_3/a_1$.

If the discriminant is positive, then the solutions are real numbers
given by the above formula. If the discriminant is negative, then the
solution consists of the pair of complex conjugate numbers

$$x_{1,2} = -\frac{a_2}{2a_1} \pm i \, |\text{DISC}|$$

where DISC is the discriminant. In this latter case, the subroutine should return the value of the real part and $|\text{DISC}|$ for the absolute value of the imaginary part. The flowchart illustrates the required logic.

```
C    SOLUTION OF THE QUADRATIC EQUATION
C    A(1) x X x X + A(2) x X + A(3) = 0
     SUBROUTINE QUAD (A, XR1, XR2, X1)
     DIMENSION A(3)
     X1 = -A(2)/(2.*A(1))
     DISC = X1*X1 - A(3)/A(1)
     IF (DISC) 10, 20, 20
10   X2 = SQRT (-DISC)
     XR1 = X1
     XR2 = X1
     XI = X2
     GO TO 30
20   X2 = SQRT (DISC)
     XR1 = X1 + X2
     XR2 = X1 - X2
     XI = 0.0
30   RETURN
     END
```

● **PROBLEM** 19-10

Write a subroutine in FORTRAN to compute the square root of the complex number $w = u + iv$ (where $i = \sqrt{-1}$ and where u and v are any real numbers) according to the formula

$$w^{\frac{1}{2}} = + \sqrt{w} = \left[\frac{(u^2 + v^2)^{\frac{1}{2}} + u}{2}\right]^{\frac{1}{2}} \pm i\left[\frac{(u^2 - v^2)^{\frac{1}{2}} - u}{2}\right]^{\frac{1}{2}}$$

Note that the imaginary part of $w^{\frac{1}{2}}$ is positive if $v > 0$, but negative if $v < 0$.

Solution: It is convenient to begin the calculation by first computing the modulus of w, which is defined as

$$|w| = R = (u^2 + v^2)^{\frac{1}{2}} .$$

Once R is evaluated, it is simple to calculate the real part of $w^{\frac{1}{2}}$, denoted by the variable REAL, as

$$\text{REAL} = ((R + u)/2)^{\frac{1}{2}} .$$

Then one calculates the imaginary part of $w^{\frac{1}{2}}$, denoted by AMAG, as AMAG = $((R - U)/2)^{\frac{1}{2}}$. If $v < 0$, one must then change the sign of AMAG from positive to negative. This completes the calculation of the real and imaginary parts of w. The logic of these calculations is presented in the flowchart.

COMPUTER PROGRAM SOLUTION
[Note all FORTRAN statements begin in column 7.]

```
     SUBROUTINE COMSQ (U,V,REAL,AMAG)
C    SQRT IS A LIBRARY FUNCTION FOR TAKING THE
C    SQUARE ROOT OF A REAL NUMBER
     R = SQRT (U * U + V * V)
```

635

```
      REAL = SQRT ((R + U)/2.)
      AMAG = SQRT ((R - U)/2.)
      IF (V.LT.0.0) AMAG = -AMAG
C     ABOVE STATEMENT SWITCHES SIGN OF
C     IMAGINARY PART IF  V  IS LESS THAN ZERO
      RETURN
      END
```

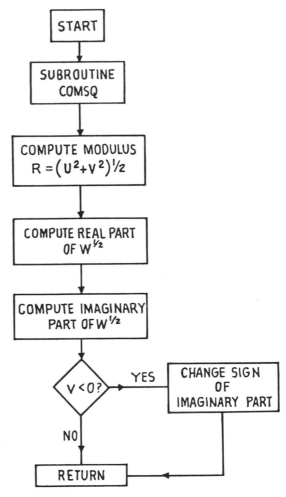

● **PROBLEM** 19-11

Write a program to solve for integral zeros of a third-degree polynomial.

Solution: The flowchart illustrates the basic program.

Now we give an explanation of the theory behind our search. Which integers do we try for Z to test P(z) for 0? Let us assume that there are N complex zeros denoted by $Z_N, Z_{N-1}, \ldots, Z_2, Z_1$. The factor theorem for polynomials states that if $f(z_1) = 0$, i.e., z_1 is a root of $f(z)$, then $f(z) = (z - z_1)g(z)$ where $g(z)$ is a polynomial one degree lower than $f(z)$. Then, by repeated applications of the factor theorem, we obtain

$$(X - Z_N)(X - Z_{N-1}) \ldots (X - Z_2)(X - Z_1)$$

$$= A_N X^N + A_{N-1} X^{N-1} + \ldots + A_1 X + A_0 . \qquad (1)$$

Multiplying out the left hand side of (1), we see that the only constant term in the product is

$$(-1)^n (Z_1) \cdot (Z_2) \ldots (Z_N) = A_0 .$$

Hence, we can conclude that if a polynomial has any integral zeros, they must be factors of the constant term A_0. Note that the converse need not be true, i.e., a factor of A_0 need not be a root. Note, however, that any factor of $P(1) = A_0$ will lie in the interval $-|P(1)|$ to $|P(1)|$. The actual program makes use of the sign function SGN to assure stopping in the right direction.

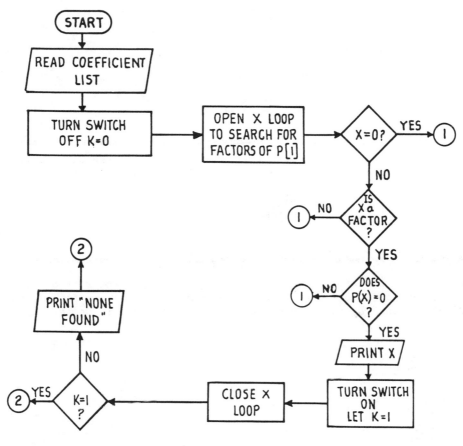

```
10    DEF FNP(X) = P(4)*X↑3 + P(3)*X↑2 + P(2)*X + P(1)
20    PRINT
25    FOR S = 4  TO 1 STEP - 1
30    READ P(S)
40    PRINT P(S);
50    NEXT S
60    PRINT "INTEGRAL ZERO(S): " ;
68    REM TURN SWITCH OFF
70    LET  K = 0
78    REM STUDY LINE 80 CAREFULLY
80    FOR  X = -P(1)  TO  P(1) STEP SGN (P(1))
```

```
88      REM LINE 90 PREVENTS ERROR MSG CAUSED BY
89      REM DIVIDING BY ZERO
90      IF  X = 0  THEN 140
98      REM IS  X  A FACTOR OF  P(1)?
100     IF  P(1)/X = INT(P(1)/X) THEN 140
108     REM IS THE REMAINDER ZERO?
110     IF  FNP(X) < > 0 THEN 140
118     REM IF THE COMPUTER GETS THROUGH HERE, THE
119     REM VALUE OF  X  IS A ZERO OF THE FUNCTION
120     PRINT X;
128     REM TURN THE SWITCH ON - WE HAVE A ZERO
130     LET  K = 1
140     NEXT X
150     IF  K = 1  THEN 20
160     PRINT "NONE FOUND";
165     GO TO 20
170     DATA 1, -2, -11, 12
180     DATA 1, 1, -5, -2
190     DATA 1, -2, 3, -4
200     DATA 2, -3, -10, 3
210     END
```

EVALUATING FUNCTIONS

● **PROBLEM** 19-12

Write two FORTRAN programs which will compute n! in two different ways:
(a) First according to the standard formula for a positive integer
n ≥ 1,

$$n! = n(n-1) \cdots (3)(2)(1)$$

(b) then use Stirling's approximation formula

$$n! \cong (2\pi)^{\frac{1}{2}} n^{n+\frac{1}{2}} e^{-n}$$

Solution: We will formulate the answers as two function routines which
will be used in later work. Denote these two functions by FACT(N) and
FACTST(N). Then by applying the above formulas directly we get the
programs below:

```
        INTEGER FUNCTION FACT(N)
        IPROD = 1
        IF (N.LE.1) GO TO 200
        DO 100 I = 2,N
        IPROD = IPROD*I
100     CONTINUE
        FACT = IPROD
        GO TO 300
200     FACT = 1
300     RETURN
        END

        FUNCTION FACTST(N)
        Z1 = EXP(-FLOAT(N))
        Z2 = (FLOAT(N))**(FLOAT(N) + 0.5)
C       FLOAT CONVERTS INTEGERS TO REALS
        Z3 = SQRT(2*3.14159)
        FACTST = Z1*Z2*Z3
        RETURN
        END
```

Write a FORTRAN program to evaluate the polynomial expression

$$a_1 x^{n-1} + a_2 x^{n-2} + \ldots + a_n$$

for given values of n, a_1, a_2,...,a_n using various values of x which are read in. Let the program terminate when a zero value of x is read in.

Solution: The most efficient polynomial evaluation procedure is based on the nesting

$$(\ldots((a_1 x + a_2)x + a_3)x + \ldots + a_{n-1})x + a_n \; .$$

We assume $n \le 25$. The data deck consists of a value for n followed by the n coefficients a_i on one or more data cards. These are followed by successive data cards, each with a value for x; the final card contains the zero value.

This nesting procedure is known as Horner's method for evaluating polynomials. We present the program segment below.

```
C       POLYNOMIAL EVALUATION
        DIMENSION A(25)
        READ, N,(A(J), J = 1,N)
16      READ, X
        IF (X.EQ.0.) STOP
        POLY = A(1)
        DO 12 I = 2,N
12      POLY = POLY*X + A(1)
        GO TO 16
        STOP
        END
```

Write in FORTRAN a complex function to find the complex number of largest magnitude in an array of complex numbers.

Solution: Our function will make use of a complex array A dimensioned size N. In addition, the complex absolute value library function is used. Otherwise no new concepts are involved.
Let $z = x + iy$ where x,y are real numbers and $i^2 = -1$. The modulus or absolute value of z is given by

$$|z| = \sqrt{x^2 + y^2} \; .$$

Since x,y are real, there are an infinite number of complex numbers of a given magnitude.

```
        COMPLEX FUNCTION MAX(N,A)
        COMPLEX A(N)
        MAX = A(1)
        IF (N.EQ.1) RETURN
        DO 7 I = 1,N
        IF (ABS(A(I)). LE. ABS(MAX)) GO TO 7
        MAX = A(I)
7       CONTINUE
        RETURN
        END
```

639

Develop a FORTRAN program to use Lagrangian interpolation to evaluate $F(x) = x^3$ at $x = 3$, given the table below:

i	1	2	3	4
x_i	1	2	4	7
f_i	1	8	64	343

$$f_i \equiv f(x_i)$$

Solution: The Lagrange polynomials of degree m are defined as

$$P_j(x) = A_j \prod_{\substack{k=1 \\ k \neq j}}^{m+1} (x - x_k) \quad \text{where} \quad A_j = \prod_{\substack{k=1 \\ k \neq j}}^{m+1} \frac{1}{(x_j - x_k)}$$

Here $m = 3$ and we approximate $f(x)$ by $\sum_{i=1}^{4} f(x_i) P_i(x)$. The evaluations of $P_j(x)$ are shown below, for $x = 3$.

$$P_1(x) \equiv P(x,1) = \frac{(x-2)(x-4)(x-7)}{(x_1-x_2)(x_1-x_3)(x_1-x_4)} = \frac{(x-2)(x-4)(x-7)}{-18}$$

$$P_2(x) \equiv P(x,2) = \frac{(x-1)(x-4)(x-7)}{(x_2-x_1)(x_2-x_3)(x_2-x_4)} = \frac{(x-1)(x-4)(x-7)}{10}$$

$$P_3(x) \equiv P(x,3) = \frac{(x-1)(x-2)(x-7)}{(x_3-x_1)(x_3-x_2)(x_3-x_4)} = \frac{(x-1)(x-2)(x-7)}{18}$$

$$P_4(x) \equiv P(x,4) = \frac{(x-1)(x-2)(x-4)}{(x_4-x_1)(x_4-x_2)(x_4-x_3)} = \frac{(x-1)(x-2)(x-4)}{90}$$

Thus $F(3) \approx \sum_{i=1}^{4} f(x_i) P(3,I)$

$$= 1(-2/9) + 8(4/5) + 64(4/9) + 343(-2/90)$$

$$= 26.9999980 \quad \text{which is very close to} \quad 3^3 = 27.$$

The program and sample output are given below:

```
C       PROGRAM 3.3
C       PROGRAM FOR LAGRANGIAN INTERPOLATION
C       UNEVENLY SPACED PIVOTAL POINTS
        DIMENSION X(50), P(50), F(50)
        PUNCH 994
        READ 999, N, (X(I), F(I), I = 1,N)
1       READ 998, XO
        DO 10 J = 1,N
        P(J) = 1
        DO 10 I = 1,N
        IF (I - J) 9, 10, 9
9       P(J) = P(J) * (XO - X(I))/(X(J) - X(I))
10      CONTINUE
        FO = 0
        DO 20 I = 1,N
20      FO = FO + P(I) * F(I)
        PUNCH 997
        PUNCH 996, (I,X(I),F(I), P(I), I = 1,N)
        PUNCH 995, XO, FO
```

```
      GO TO 1
994   FORMAT (//, 19X, 24H RESULTS FROM PROGRAM 3.3)
995   FORMAT (19X, 6H AT X = F5.2, 21H THE VALUE OF F(X) IS F12.7)
996   FORMAT (I10, 3F14.7)
997   FORMAT (//, 9X, 1H1, 8X, 4HX(I), 10X, 4HF(I), 9X, 6HP(X,I))
998   FORMAT (8F10.0)
999   FORMAT (I5/8F10.0)
      END
```

[SAMPLE] RESULTS FROM PROGRAM 3.3

	X(I)	F(I)	P(X,I)
1	1.0000000	1.0000000	-0.2222222
2	2.0000000	8.0000000	0.8000000
3	4.0000000	64.0000000	0.4444444
4	7.0000000	343.0000000	-0.0222222

AT X = 3.00 THE VALUE OF F(X) IS 26.9999980

APPROXIMATE INTEGRATION

● **PROBLEM** 19-16

Using power series, find an approximate solution to the definite integral
$$\int_0^1 \sin x \, dx \, .$$
Write a FORTRAN program segment.

Solution: First, we must remember that
$$\sin x = x - \frac{x^3}{3!} + \frac{x^5}{5!} - \frac{x^7}{7!} \cdots$$

We may then write the integral like this:
$$\int_0^1 \sin x \, dx \approx \int_0^1 \left(x - \frac{x^3}{3!} + \frac{x^5}{5!} - \frac{x^7}{7!}\right) dx \, ,$$

assuming we want to compute only 4 terms. The generalized expansion would be
$$\int_0^1 \left(x - \frac{x^3}{3!} + \frac{x^5}{5!} - \frac{x^7}{7!} \cdots - \frac{x^{2n+1}}{(2n+1)!} + \ldots\right) dx \, .$$

When integration is performed, we get the generalized primitives as
$$\left[\frac{x^2}{2!} - \frac{x^4}{4(3!)} + \frac{x^6}{6(5!)} - \frac{x^8}{8(7!)} \cdots \frac{x^{2n+2}}{(2n+2)((2n+1)!)}\right]_0^1$$

We can make use of the FACT(N) function to calculate the integral. Notice that we have not defined the accuracy parameter ERROR. You may choose that value and insert it at the start of the program. Since the lower boundary of this integral is zero, you need only compute the terms for x = 1.

```
      SINDX = (X**2)/2.0
      I = 1
```

641

```
20      IF (ABS(TERM).LT.ERROR) GO TO 50
        N = FLOAT (I)
        SINDX = SINDX + TERM
        TERM = -1.0*(X**(2*N + 2)/(2*N+2)*(FACT(2*N+1)))
C       IF  I  IS ODD, TERM IS NEGATIVE.  IF I  IS
C       EVEN, TERM IS POSITIVE.
        IF (2*(I/2).EQ.I) ABS(TERM) = TERM
        I = I + 1
        GO TO 20
50      WRITE (S,*) SINDX
```

Compute the sin(x) function, using the notion of the power series
$$\sin(x) = x - x^3/3! + x^5/5! - x^7/7! + \ldots$$

Solution: Power series may also be evaluated via Horner's method. When it is decided how many terms are to be evaluated, the series may be treated as a polynomial. However, this illustration will be useful to introduce the idea of precision. Since the computer performs its own rounding operations, we want to be able to control the degree of precision. First, let us look at what can happen if we do not specify precision:

```
C       COMPUTE EIGHT TERMS OF THE POWER SERIES SIN(PI/4)
C       AND PRINT OUT SIN(X), EACH TERM, AND SIN(PI/4)
        REAL PI, XSQ, SINE, TERM, REALI
        INTEGER I
        PI = 3.141592
        X = PI/4.0
        XSQ = X**2
        WRITE (5,100)
100     FORMAT (1X, 'SIN(X)        ', 'TERM')
        TERM = X
        SINE = TERM
C       DO LOOP IS INDENTED FOR CLARITY
        DO 20 I = 2, 16, 2
        WRITE (5,101) SINE, TERM
101     FORMAT (1X, E10.9, 14X, E10.9)
        REALI = I*(I+1)
        TERM = -1.0*(TERM*XSQ)/REALI
        SINE = SINE + TERM
20      CONTINUE
        WRITE (5,102) X
102     FORMAT (1X,'VALUE OF SIN(PI/4) EQUALS ',E10.9)
        STOP
        END
```
Sample output:

SIN(X)	TERM
0.7853980E 00	0.7853980E 00
0.7046525E 00	-0.8074546E-01
0.7071429E 00	0.2490392E-02
0.7071063E 00	-0.3657614E-04
0.7071066E 00	0.3133609E-06
0.7071066E 00	-0.1757242E-08
0.7071066E 00	0.6948429E-11
0.7071066E 00	-0.2041018E-13

VALUE OF SIN(PI/4) EQUALS 0.7071069E00

Notice that after the fifth term, the value of sin(x) does not change. We choose the number of terms to be evaluated, but the computer will round off each term, thereby creating an accumulation of errors. The convention chosen here to avoid this error propagation is the DOUBLE PRECISION statement. Let us declare DOUBLE PRECISION SINE, TERM at the beginning of the program. Now, SINE and TERM will be represented internally by a bit string which is twice as long as in single precision. The round-off error will accumulate in the least significant bits of the double precision number. Finally, when the result is returned to single precision at the end of the computation, only one round-off operation is performed. The other modification needed in double precision is in the FORMAT statement: the letter D must replace the exponential notation E.

• **PROBLEM** 19-18

Given 25 equally spaced data points x_i (i = 1,...,25) and 25 functional values $y_i = f(x_i)$ [arranged in ascending order], write a program to evaluate

$$\int_{X_1}^{X_{25}} f(x)\,dx$$

using the trapezoidal rule.

Solution: According to the trapezoidal rule of integration,

$$\int_{X_1}^{X_{25}} f(x)\,dx = \text{Area} \approx \frac{h}{2}(y_1 + 2y_2 + 2y_3 + \ldots + 2y_{24} + y_{25}) \; .$$

We adopt the following computational strategy: accumulate $\sum_{i=2}^{24} y_i$ in a DO loop, double the result, add it to $(y_1 + y_{25})$, and multiply by h = X(2) - X(1). The program (which assumes values of X and Y have already been read in) is given below.

You should also remember that the error margin for the trapezoid rule is given by

$$E \le \frac{1}{12}(b - a)h^2 |f''(\xi)| \quad X_n \le \xi \le X_1 \; .$$

Knowing this, you can use a suitable N to calculate the integration to a close approximation.

```
      REAL H
      SUM = 0.0
      DO 50 I = 2,24
50    SUM = SUM + Y(I)
      H = X(2) - X(1)
      AREA = 0.5*H*(Y(1) + 2.0*SUM+Y(25))
```

• **PROBLEM** 19-19

Write a trapezoidal integration routine in FORTRAN to evaluate

$$\int_0^{.4} \sin^2 x \, dx + \int_{.1}^{.3} \cos^2 x \, dx \; .$$

Solution: Let us structure the problem as follows: there shall be a main routine which calls a trapezoid function routine, which in turn

643

references two function routines defining the functions $\sin^2 x$ and $\cos^2 x$. First note that according to the trapezoid rule

$$\int_a^b f(x)dx \approx \frac{h}{2} [f(a) + 2f(a+h) + 2f(a+2h) + \ldots + 2f(a+(n-1)h) + f(b)],$$

where $h = (b-a)/n$ is the number of trapezoids. Thus we have

```
      FUNCTION TRAP(A,B,N,FX)
      H = (B - A)/N
      SUM = 0
      K = N - 1
      DO 6 I = 1,K
6     SUM = SUM + FX(A + I*H)
      TRAP = (FX(A) + FX(B) + 2.*SUM)*(H/2.)
      RETURN
      END
```

The main calling program and function routines are given below.

```
      EXTERNAL FX1, FX2
      APPROX = TRAP(0.,.4,5,FX1) + TRAP(.1,.3,5,FX2)
      PRINT, APPROX
      STOP
      END
      FUNCTION FX1(X)
      FX1 = (SIN X)**2
      RETURN
      END
      FUNCTION FX2(X)
      FX2 = (COS X)**2
      RETURN
      END
```

Notice that the main program uses an EXTERNAL statement. This declaration must be used in every calling program which passes the name of a subprogram or built-in function to another subprogram. Also remember that the main program is entered first. After the END statement in the main program, all subroutines may be entered.
In this program, it is up to you to define the accuracy of the integration. In other words, you choose the value of N, which determines the number of iterations to be done.

● **PROBLEM** 19-20

Develop a FORTRAN subprogram to evaluate the integration of $f(x)dx$ between the limits of A and B using GAUSSIAN quadrature, which is expressible as

$$\int_A^B f(x)dx = \frac{B - A}{2} \sum_{i=1}^N w_i f\left[\frac{(B - A)t_i + (B + A)}{2}\right]$$

where $w_1, w_2, \ldots, w_N$ are the weighting coefficients and $t_1, t_2, \ldots, t_N$ are the roots of the Legendre polynomial $P_N(t) = 0$

Solution: We need the result from elementary numerical analysis that the weights w_K can be expressed in the form

644

$$w_K = \int_{-1}^{1} L_K(x)\,dx = \frac{1}{P_{n+1}(x_K)} \int_{-1}^{1} \frac{P_{n+1}(x)\,dx}{x - x_K}$$

where $L_K(x)$ is a Lagrange polynomial and $P_n(x)$ is a Legendre polynomial.

Our program will let the value of N range from 3 to 6. The computation starts with $N = 3$. The program will compare the result based on $N = 3$ with that based on $N = 4$. The results must satisfy the criterion

$$\epsilon \geq \frac{A_{n+1} - A_n}{A_n}$$

where A_{n+1} is the answer based on $N + 1$ points, and A_n is the answer based on N points, and ϵ is taken to be 10^{-4}. If the result fails to pass the above test, the value of N will be increased by one. The maximum value of N is set to be 6.

```
      SUBROUTINE GAUSS(A, B, X, F, KOUNT)
C     INTEGRATION OF  F(X). DX BY GAUSSIAN QUADRATURE
C     BETWEEN LIMITS OF  A  AND  B
C     NOMENCLATURE
C     F = F(X) UNDER INTEGRAL SIGN
C     KOUNT = INTEGER USED TO CONTROL METHOD
C     OF EXECUTION
C     ANS = ANSWER TO INTEGRATION
      DIMENSION W(4,6), T(4,6)
      IF (KOUNT) 8, 10, 8
    8 GO TO 30
   10 ANS = 1.0
      IPOINT = 3
      EPS = 10.E - 05
C     STORE WEIGHT COEFF AND LEGENDRE ROOTS
      DO 2 I = 1,4
      IP2 = I + 2
    2 READ 1, (W(I,K), K = 1,IP2), (T(I,K), K = I,IP2)
    1 FORMAT (5F15.10)
C     CHANGE INTEGRATION LIMITS TO (-1  TO  +1).
C     EVALUATE COEFF OF NEW FUNCTION
      C = (B - A)/2.
   18 IPOINT = IPOINT + 1
      TEMP = ANS
      ANS = 0
      IPM2 = IPOINT - 2
      KOUNT = 1
C     EVALUATE NEW VARIABLES WHICH ARE EXPRESSED
C     IN TERMS OF LEGENDRE ROOT.
   20 X = C*T(IPM2,KOUNT) + (B + A)/2.
      RETURN
C     CARRY OUT INTEGRATION BY CALCULATING
C     ANS = C*(W1*F(X1) + W2*F(X2)+ ...).
   30 ANS = ANS + C*W(IPM2,KOUNT)* F
      KOUNT = KOUNT + 1
      IF (KOUNT - IPOINT) 20,20,40
   40 IF (IPOINT - 3) 18, 18, 50
C     NEXT DETERMINE WHETHER THE DEVIATION
C     OF ANSWER IS WITHIN THE LIMIT
C     IF NOT, TAKE 1 MORE INTEGRATION POINT
   50 DELT = ABSF(ANS - TEMP)
```

```
       RATIO = DELT/TEMP
  7    IF (RATIO-EPS) 70, 70, 80
C      PUNCH OUT ANS IF DEVIATION WITHIN LIMIT
 70    PUNCH 72, IPOINT, ANS
 72    FORMAT (///5X, 16H BY CONVERGENCE, , I2, 24H
     1 POINT GAUSS.  QUADRATURE, 15H GIVES ANSWER = ,
     2 E14.8//)
       KOUNT = 7
       RETURN
 80    IF (IPOINT - 6) 18, 100, 100
100    PUNCH 102, IPOINT, ANS
C      ANSWER PUNCHED OUT AFTER 6 POINT
C      GAUSSIAN INTEGRATION IS STILL NOT
C      WITHIN THE LIMIT.
102    FORMAT (///5X, 22H BY LIMITS OF PROGRAM, , I2,
     1 14H POINT GAUSS., 23H QUADRATURE GIVES ANS. =,
     2 E14.8//)
       KOUNT = 7
       RETURN
C      DATA FOR WEIGHTING COEFFICIENTS
C      AND LEGENDRE ROOTS
       END
```

● **PROBLEM 19-21**

Write a PL/I program to integrate a general function $D(X)$ over $A \le X \le B$. Illustrate for $D(X) = (1 - X)^{-2}$.

Solution: We slice the interval $[a,b]$ into n equal parts. The size of the slices is $h = (b - a)/n$. The area under the curve is given according to Simpson's rule by

$$S = \frac{h}{3} [f(a) + 4f(a+h) + 2f(a+2h) + 4f(a+3h) + 2f(a+4h)+\ldots+ f(b)]$$

```
/* SIMPSON RULE INTEGRATION */
RPT: GET LIST (A,B,N);
     H = (B - A)/N;
     X = A;
     S = 0;
     DO I = 1 TO N/2;
     S = S + H/3*(D(X) + 4*D(X+H) + D(X+2*H));
     X = X + 2*H;
     END;
     PUT SKIP EDIT (A,B,N,S) (2F(10,4)),
     F(10), F(10,4));
     GO TO RPT;
D:   PROCEDURE (X);
     RETURN (1/1 - X)**2);
     END D;
```

SOLUTIONS OF DIFFERENTIAL EQUATIONS

● **PROBLEM 19-22**

Consider the following differential equation with the initial condition $y(0) = 1$:

$$\frac{dy}{dx} = y^2 - x^2 \qquad\qquad (1)$$

Develop a FORTRAN program to get a solution for $y = y(x)$ in the interval $0 \le x \le .5$ applying the increment method. Let $dx = \Delta x = 0.05$, and output a table containing the following quantities:

$$x, \; y, \; y^2, \; x^2, \; y^2 - x^2, \; dy \; .$$

Solution: Let us first develop the problem from a mathematical viewpoint. Before we begin solving the equation we must know that a solution exists. Furthermore, this solution should be unique. The existence and uniqueness conditions for the solution of a given differential equation are contained in the following theorems:

1) Existence:

Let $y' = \varphi(x,y)$. $0 \le x \le 1$, $-\infty < y < \infty$, $y(0) = c$

If φ is continuous and bounded, then $y = y(x)$ is a solution of $\frac{dy}{dx} = \varphi(x,y)$.

2) Uniqueness:

If there exists a constant A (Lipschitz number) such that

$$\left| \varphi(x, y_2) - \varphi(x, y_1) \right| \le A \left| y_2 - y_1 \right|$$

(where (x, y_1), (x, y_2) are in the domain), then $y = y(x)$ is a unique solution to

$$y' = \varphi(x,y).$$

The given differential equation is

$$\varphi(x,y) = \frac{dy}{dx} = y^2 - x^2 \qquad 0 \le x \le 0.5, \; y(0) = 1$$

$\varphi(x,y)$ is a difference of continuous functions; hence it is continuous. Clearly $\left| y^2 - x^2 \right|$ is bounded (i.e., less than some constant K) in $[0, 0.5]$. Thus a solution exists.

Let $A = .3$. Then $\left| \varphi(x, y_2) - \varphi(x, y_1) \right| \le .3(y_2 - y_1)$ for all (x, y_1), (x, y_2) in the domain. Thus the solution is unique. We can rewrite equation (1) in the differential form

$$dy = (y^2 - x^2)dx \qquad\qquad (2)$$

The increment method entails the use of differentials to find approximate values of y. Thus, let $\Delta x = dx$, $\Delta y = dy$. Since the initial condition is $y(0) = 1$, we can substitute into equation (2) and obtain

$$\Delta y = (1^2 - 0^2)(0.05)$$
$$\Delta y = 0.05$$

thus, at $x = 0.05$, $y = y_0 + \Delta y$ becomes $1 + 0.05 = 1.05$. This means that now $y(1.00)$ becomes 1.05. The next value of Δy becomes, therefore

$$\Delta y = ((1.05)^2 - (0.05)^2)(0.05)$$
$$\Delta y = 0.055$$

As you can see, the method readily lends itself to computer implementation. We can use a FORTRAN main program to print the values in tabular form. A subroutine, INCR, can do each calculation and pass the values back to the main program for output.

```
       Y = 1.000
       DX = 0.05
C      WRITE TABLE HEADINGS
       WRITE (5,100)
100    FORMAT (2X,'X', 5X, 'Y', 6X, 'Y**2', 3X,
      1 'X**2', 3X, 'Y**2-X**2', 3X, 'DY')
C      DO FOR  X  FROM  1  TO  10  BY  0.05
```

```
      DO 10 I = 1,10
      X = (FLOAT (I) - 1.0)*0.05
      CALL INCR (DX, DY, X, Y)
      XX = X**2
      YY = Y**2
      DYDX = YY - XX
      WRITE (5,101) X, Y, YY, XX, DYDX, DY
101   FORMAT (1X, F4.2,3(2X,F5.3), 4X, F5.3, 5X, F5.3)
10    CONTINUE

C     END DO - FOR
      STOP
      END
C     SUBROUTINE INCR TO PERFORM CALCULATIONS
      SUBROUTINE INCR (DX, DY, X, Y)
      Y = Y + DY
      DY = ((Y**2) - (X**2))*DX
      RETURN
      END
```

● PROBLEM 19-23

Use the Euler method to solve the equation of motion of a damped harmonic oscillator. Let the initial conditions be that at t = 0, x(0) =
10 cm and dx/dt = v = 0.

Solution: The equation of motion is given by

$$\frac{md^2 x}{dt^2} = -\frac{cdx}{dt} - kx$$

where $\frac{-cdx}{dt}$ is the damping force and $-kx$ is the restoring force.
Since Euler's method is based on first order differential equations, we
rewrite the equation of motion as two first order equations:

$$\frac{dx}{dt} = v \tag{1}$$

$$\frac{dv}{dt} = -\frac{c}{m} v - \frac{k}{m} x \tag{2}$$

According to Euler's method, the solution is given by

$$dx \approx \Delta x = x_{new} - x_{old}; \; dx = vdt)$$

$$x_{new} = x_{old} + v_{old} \Delta t \tag{1'}$$

$$v_{new} = v_{old} + \left(\frac{-c}{m} v_{old} - \frac{k}{m} x_{old}\right)\Delta t \tag{2'}$$

Here we have used the general result that if $dy/dx = f(x,y)$, then

$$y_{i+1} = y_i + y_i'\Delta x, \text{ where } y_i' = f(x_i, y_i).$$

For the sake of concreteness we use the following data:

$$m = k = 10, \; c = 2, \; x_0 = 10, \; v_0 = 0, \; D \equiv \Delta t = 0.1$$

and we follow the motion for 2 seconds.

```
100   REM DAMPED HARMONIC OSCILLATOR
101   REM EULER'S METHOD
105   PRINT "TIME", "VELOCITY", "POSITION"
```

```
106    PRINT
110    READ M, K, C, XØ, VØ, D
120    LET X1 = XØ
121    LET V1 = VØ
130    FOR T = Ø  TO  2   STEP D
140    PRINT T, V1, X1
150    LET X2 = X1 + V1*D
151    LET V2 = V1 + (-C*V1/M - K*X1/M)*D
160    LET X1 = X2
161    LET V1 = V2
162    NEXT T
800    DATA 1Ø, 1Ø, 2, 1Ø, Ø, 0.1
999    END
```

Note that the exact solution of $t = 2$ gives $x = -2.5807$, compared with the Euler method result of -2.96507. More sophisticated numerical methods (such as the improved Euler method or Runge-Kutta type methods) are necessary for better accuracy.

Finally, v_{new} can also be solved with the quadratic equation. If you rearrange the equation of motion, you can obtain

$$m \frac{d^2 x}{dt^2} + c \frac{dx}{dt} + kx = 0 \ ,$$

which is the quadratic form. This equation has a solution of the form $x = e^{\alpha t}$. If we substitute x into the first equation and divide by $e^{\alpha t}$, we get the simpler form $m\alpha^2 + c\alpha + k = 0$. By using the discriminant $c^2 - 4mk$, we can determine what type of motion is present:

If $c^2 - 4mk$ is	the motion is
positive	over-damped
zero	critically-damped
negative	oscillatory-damped

● **PROBLEM** 19-24

Solve the heat flow equation $K \frac{\partial T}{\partial t} = \frac{\partial^2 T}{\partial x^2}$, where K is the thermal diffusivity of the homogeneous medium. Apply the algorithm to the case of a copper bar of thermal diffusivity of $1.14 \ cm^2/sec$ with 1 end maintained at $100°C$ while the other end is held at $0°C$. Let the bar be 8 cm long.

Solution: The solution can be derived from a central finite difference approximation for the spatial derivative and a forward difference approximation for the time derivative. Thus we make use of

$$\frac{\partial^2 T}{\partial x^2} = \frac{T_{i-1,j} - 2T_{i,j} + T_{i+1,j}}{\Delta x^2}$$

$$\frac{\partial T}{\partial t} = \frac{T_{i,j+1} - T_{i,j}}{\Delta t}$$

(These results derive from Taylor's formula.) So that the heat flow equation becomes

$$\frac{T_{i-1,j} - 2T_{i,j} + T_{i+1,j}}{\Delta x^2} = K \left(\frac{T_{i,j+1} - T_{i,j}}{\Delta t} \right)$$

which can be solved for $T_{i,j+1}$ to give

$$T_{i,j+1} = \alpha(T_{i-1,j} + T_{i+1,j}) + (1 - 2\alpha) T_{i,j}$$

where $\alpha = \Delta t/(K\Delta x^2)$.

This last equation is self-starting in that if the boundary conditions on the space-time grid are known, that is, if the values of the function are known for all positions at $t = 0$, and for all times at $x = 0$ and $x = L$, then the remainder of the solution can be produced from the algorithm.

An illustrative program which takes $\Delta x = 1$ cm and $\Delta t = 0.4$ sec is given below. Note that the dummy variable V_i is used to handle intermediate results for T. This process lets us avoid storing values of T in a large two-dimensional array.

```
100    REM PARABOLIC PARTIAL DIFFERENTIAL EQUATION
101    REM HEAT TRANSFER PROBLEM
102    PRINT
110    READ F0, D, X1, K, T2
120    LET F(1) = F0
121    LET F(9) = 0
130    LET A = D*K/X1↑2
140    FOR I = 2 TO 8
150    LET F[I] = 0
151    NEXT I
160    LET C = 5
170    FOR T = 0 TO T2 STEP D
180    IF C < 5 THEN 220
190    PRINT "AT"; T; "SEC,THE TEMP DISTRIBUTION IS"
191    PRINT
200    FOR I = 1 TO 9
201    PRINT F[I],
202    NEXT I
203    PRINT
210    LET C = 0
220    FOR I = 2 TO 8
230    LET V[I] = A*(F(I - 1) + F(I + 1)) + (1 - 2*A)*F(I)
231    NEXT I
240    FOR I = 2 TO 8
250    LET F[I] = V[I]
251    NEXT I
260    LET C = C + 1
261    NEXT T
800    DATA 100, 0.2, 1, 1.14, 5
999    END
```

● **PROBLEM** 19-25

Write a BASIC program to solve Laplace's equation

$$\frac{\partial^2 V}{\partial x^2} + \frac{\partial^2 V}{\partial y^2} = 0 .$$

Consider a rectangular 8 by 8 grid with boundary conditions such that 3 sides are assumed to be at a potential of 100. The remaining side is at zero potential as shown.

Solution: We use the replacement of partial derivatives by central differences

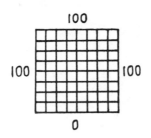

$$\frac{\partial^2 V}{\partial x^2} = \frac{V_{i-1,j} - 2V_{i,j} + V_{i+1,j}}{\Delta x^2}$$

and

$$\frac{\partial^2 V}{\partial y^2} = \frac{V_{i,j-1} - 2V_{i,j} + V_{i,j+1}}{\Delta y^2}$$

Thus

$$\frac{V_{i-1,j} - 2V_{i,j} + V_{i+1,j}}{\Delta x^2} + \frac{V_{i,j-1} - 2V_{i,j} + V_{i,j+1}}{\Delta y^2} = 0 \; .$$

But, in the given rectangular grid of little squares, $\Delta x = \Delta y$ and hence we obtain simply

$$V_{ij} = \tfrac{1}{4} \left[V_{i-1,j} + V_{i+1,j} + V_{i,j-1} + V_{i,j+1} \right] \; .$$

Thus when Laplace's equation is satisfied, the value of the function at each grid point is the average of the values of the function at the four closest neighbors. When exterior boundary conditions are specified, the solution, by repeated applications of this algorithm flows out from the boundary and stabilizes when the above condition for $V_{i,j}$ is met. Initial values of the potential are given in the data statements within the program. Each line represents one row of data in the grid. The problem specified the boundary values of the potential. Interior values of the potential are guesses.
Convergence is studied by considering

$$d = V_{ij \; new} - V_{ij} = \tfrac{1}{4}[V_{i+1,j} + V_{i,j+1} + V_{i-1,j} + V_{i,j-1} - 4V_{ij}].$$

S is used to accumulate the sum of all changes as we sweep over the grid. In addition, the counter K is used to accumulate the number of passes over the grid. The process is repeated until the total change in any sweep (the variable S) is less than some arbitrary amount.

```
100   REM ELLIPTIC PARTIAL DIFFERENTIAL EQUATION
101   REM LAPLACE'S EQUATION
110   FOR I = 1 TO 8
111   FOR J = 1 TO 8
112   READ V(I,J)
113   NEXT J
114   NEXT I
120   LET K = 0
130   LET S = 0
140   FOR I = 2 TO 7
150   FOR J = 2 TO 7
160   LET D = (V(I+1,J) + V(I,J+1) + V(I-1,J) + V(I,J-1) - 4*V(I,J))/4
161   LET S = S + ABS(D)
162   LET V(I,J) = V(I,J) + D
163   NEXT J
```

```
164     NEXT I
170     LET K = K + 1
180     IF S > 2 THEN 130
200     PRINT
202     FOR I = 1 TO 8
203     FOR J = 1 TO 8
204     PRINT INT(V(I,J));
205     NEXT J
206     PRINT
208     NEXT I
209     PRINT
212     PRINT "NUMBER OF PASSES FOR CONVERGENCE = "; K
801     DATA 100, 100, 100, 100, 100, 100, 100, 100
802     DATA 100,  90,  90,  90,  90,  90,  90, 100
803     DATA 100,  80,  80,  75,  75,  80,  80, 100
804     DATA 100,  75,  60,  50,  50,  60,  75, 100
805     DATA 100,  60,  50,  30,  30,  50,  60, 100
806     DATA 100,  50,  30,  15,  15,  30,  50, 100
807     DATA 100,  40,  20,   5,   5,  20,  40, 100
808     DATA 100,   0,   0,   0,   0,   0,   0, 100
999     END
```

Sample output is given below.

```
100     100     100     100     100     100     100     100
100      97      95      94      94      95      97     100
100      94      90      88      88      90      94     100
100      90      83      80      80      83      90     100
100      84      73      68      68      74      84     100
100      73      58      52      52      58      73     100
100      52      34      29      29      35      52     100
100       0       0       0       0       0       0     100
```

NUMBER OF PASSES FOR CONVERGENCE = 22

● **PROBLEM** 19-26

Write a BASIC program to express current as a function of time for the circuit below. Assume that the switch is closed at time $t = 0$ and that the resistance R is given as a function of current by

$$R = a + bi^2 .$$

Let $E = 100$ volts; $L = 2$ henries; $a = 50$ ohms, $b = 25$ ohms/amp^2 Use the 4th order Runge-Kutta method.

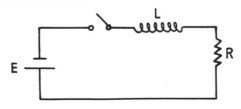

Solution: According to Kirchhoff's voltage law, the total number of voltage gains and drops around a circuit must be zero. Hence:

$$E - L\frac{di}{dt} - Ri = E - L\frac{di}{dt} - (a + bi^2)i = 0.$$

Isolating the rate of change of current, we get

652

$$\frac{di}{dt} \equiv \frac{E}{L} - \frac{b}{L} i^3 - \frac{a}{L} i \; .$$

A straightforward application of the fourth order Runge-Kutta method yields

$$i_{new} = i_{old} + \frac{\Delta t}{6} (k_1 + 2k_2 + 2k_3 + k_4)$$

where

$$k_1 = \frac{E}{L} - \frac{b}{L} i_{old}^3 - \frac{a}{L} i_{old}$$

$$k_2 = \frac{E}{L} - \frac{b}{L}(i_{old} + \tfrac{1}{2} k_1 \Delta t)^3 - \frac{a}{L}(i_{old} + \tfrac{1}{2} k_1 \Delta t),$$

$$k_3 = \frac{E}{L} - \frac{b}{L}(i_{old} + \tfrac{1}{2} k_2 \Delta t)^3 - \frac{a}{L}(i_{old} + \tfrac{1}{2} k_2 \Delta t)$$

$$k_4 = \frac{E}{L} - \frac{b}{L}(i_{old} + k_3 \Delta t)^3 - \frac{a}{L}(i_{old} + k_3 \Delta t)$$

In the program below D is the increment on the time value.

```
100    REM CIRCUIT ANALYSIS
101    REM RUNGE KUTTA METHOD
105    PRINT "TIME", "CURRENT"
106    PRINT "(SEC)", "(AMPERES)"
107    PRINT
110    READ E,L,A,B
120    READ D, T2
130    LET I1 = 0
140    FOR T = 0 TO T2 STEP D
150    PRINT T, I1
160    LET K1 = E/L - B*I1↑3/L - A*I1/L
161    LET K2 = E/L - B*(I1+.5*K1*D)↑3/L - A*(I1+.5*K1*D)/L
162    LET K3 = E/L - B*(I1+.5*K2*D)↑3/L - A*(I1+.5*K2*D)/L
163    LET K4 = E/L - B*(I1+K3*D)↑3/L - A*(I1+K3*D)/L
170    LET I2 = I1 + D*(K1+2*K2+2*K3+K4)/6.0
180    LET I1 = I2
181    NEXT T
800    DATA 100, 2, 50, 25
801    DATA 5.0E-3, 0.1
999    END
```

Computer output reveals that a steady state current of about 1.18 amps is reached in 0.1 sec. Note that with no current dependence in the resistance this steady state current would be somewhat higher, namely 2 amps = E/a .

● **PROBLEM** 19-27

Develop a flow-chart for evaluating the Fourier coefficients of the periodic waveform $f(t)$ in the given figure. The values measured for $f(t)$ are $f(0) = 0$, $f(0.05) = 0.25$, $f(0.1) = 0.3$, $f(0.15) = 0.5$, $f(0.2) = f(0.25) = f(0.3) = 1.0$, $f(0.35) = 0.55$, $f(0.4) = 0.3$, $f(0.45) = 0$, $f(0.5) = -0.25$, $f(0.55) = f(0.6) = -0.3$, $f(0.65) = -0.2$, $f(0.7) = -0.1$, $f(0.75) = f(0.8) = f(0.85) = f(0.9) = f(0.95) = 0$.

Solution: The waveform in the figure can be expressed as a Fourier series:

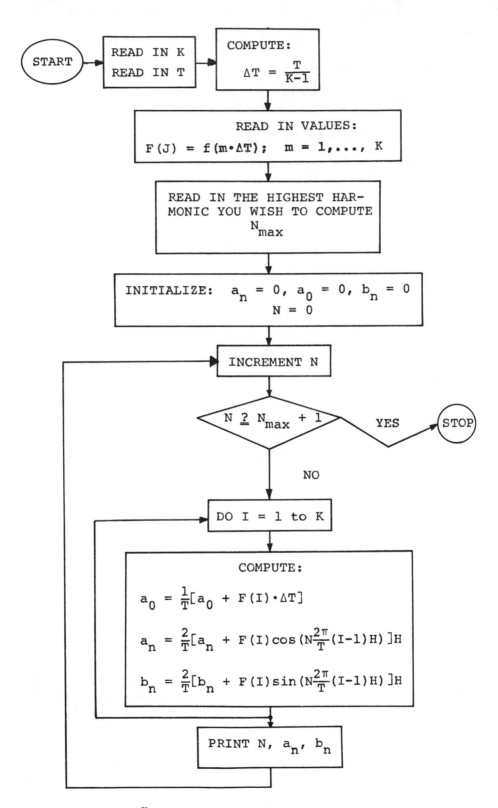

$$f(t) = a_0 + \sum_{n=1}^{\infty} (a_n \cos n\omega t + b_n \sin n\omega t) \qquad (1)$$

where,

$$a_0 = \frac{1}{T} \int_0^T f(t) \, dt \tag{2}$$

$$a_n = \frac{2}{T} \int_0^T f(t) \cos n\omega t \, dt \tag{3}$$

$$b_n = \frac{2}{T} \int_0^T f(t) \sin n\omega t \, dt . \tag{4}$$

Equations (2)-(4) are the Fourier coefficients. We approximate the integrals by dividing $f(t)$ into small pulses of width ΔT and summing:

$$a_0 = \frac{1}{T} \sum_{m=1}^{K} f(m\Delta T) \, \Delta T \tag{5}$$

$$a_n = \frac{2}{T} \sum_{m=1}^{K} f(m\Delta T) \cos(n(2/T)m\Delta T) \, \Delta T \tag{6}$$

$$b_n = \frac{2}{T} \sum_{m=1}^{n} f(m\Delta T) \sin(n(2/T)m\Delta T) \, \Delta T \tag{7}$$

Equations (5)-(7) must be evaluated for each (harmonic) value of n. The period T of the waveform is broken into $(K-1)$ parts such that $(K-1)\Delta T = T$. Then using the values found for $f(m\Delta T)$, $m = 1$ to K and setting a limit for n, say 20, a computer program can be developed for evaluating the Fourier coefficients from the flow-chart.

Note, finally, that a subroutine can process the coefficients found by the program into magnitude and phase form for the plotting of spectral lines.

CHAPTER 20

NUMBER THEORY

ELEMENTARY NUMBER THEORY

● **PROBLEM** 20-1

Write a FORTRAN program to determine the greatest integer that does not exceed a given real number X.

Solution: The greatest integer function f: R → Z has as domain the real numbers and co-domain the integers. It is denoted by [X] where X is a real number. For example,

$$[\pi] = [3.1415...] = 3$$
$$[e] = [2.7128...] = 2$$
$$[-6.01] = -7 \; ; \; [8] = 8 \; .$$

Thus, for X ≥ 0, [X] is the integer part of X (it is immaterial whether the decimal part of X is greater than .5 or not). For X < 0, [X] is the integer part of X minus 1.

Thus, to find [X], we proceed as follows:
1) Truncate X to an integer, NX
2) If X is nonnegative, [X] = NX.
3) If X is negative [X] = NX - 1.

```
C           PROGRAM TO DETERMINE THE LARGEST
C           INTEGER THAT DOES NOT EXCEED A GIVEN
C           REAL NUMBER X.
            READ (5,1) X
     1      FORMAT (F 10.4)
            NX = X
            IF (X) 5,3,3
C           IF X  IS NEGATIVE, IS IT AN INTEGER?
C           IF SO, PROCEED DIRECTLY TO WRITE.
C           IF NOT, SUBTRACT 1 FROM NX.
     5      Y = NX
            IF (X - Y) 7,3,7
     7      NX = NX - 1
     3      WRITE (6,9) X
     9      FORMAT (1HO, 14H REAL NUMBER =    , F 14.4)
            WRITE (6,11) NX
    11      FORMAT (1H  , 19H GREATEST INTEGER = ,I6)
            STOP
            END
```

Find all three-digit numbers with non-zero first digit that are equal to the sum of the cubes of their digits.

<u>Solution</u>: The solution is based upon having the computer check each three-digit number HTU = 100*H + 10*T + U to see if the condition HTU = $H^3 + T^3 + U^3$ is satisfied. [Note that H stands for hundreds, T stands for tens, and U-for units].
Since we want all possible combinations of H,T, and U where U = 0,1,2,...,9; T = 0,1,2,...,9; and H = 1,2,3,...,9 - there are 10 × 10 × 9 = 900 numbers to check.
We do this checking with three nested DO loops. The DO LOOP parameters take on values

$$1,2,\ldots,10; \quad 1,2,\ldots,10; \quad \text{and} \quad 1,2,\ldots,9,$$

progressing from the inner to the outer loops.
Since 1 is the lowest possible integer to be assigned to any DO-LOOP index, the program subtracts 1 from indexes TP1 and UP1 to initiate them at zero. Meanwhile, the final values of TP1 and UP1 are set to 10, which become 9's after the same subtraction. The program looks as follows:

```
          INTEGER  H,T,U,TP1, UP1
          DO 10   H = 1,9
          DO 10   TP1 = 1,10
          T = TP1 - 1
          DO 10   UP1 = 1,10
          U = UP1 - 1
          IF(100*H + 10*T + U.EQ. H**3 + T**3 + U**3) GO TO 1
          GO TO 10
1         WRITE (6,100) H,T,U
10        CONTINUE
100       FORMAT (3I1)
          STOP
          END
```

Consider the following problem: Find all integers less than 50,000 that equal to the sum of the factorials of their digits. Write a computer program to solve this problem.

<u>Solution</u>: To gain a better understanding of the problem, consider the following examples:

1) The number 7666 is not equal to the sum of its factorial digits since
$$7! + 6! + 6! + 6! = 5040 + 720 + 720 + 720$$
$$= 7200 \neq 7666.$$

2) Let n = 145. Then
$$1! + 4! + 5! = 1 + 24 + 120 = 145.$$

Hence 145 is equal to the sum of the factorials of its digits.

In the writing of the program, first store the value of $n!$ up to $9!$ in the memory. Then store each digit of the given number in a location cell.

Actually there are only 4 numbers that satisfy the above property: 1,2,145 and 40585. But this is a problem in programming as well as number theory; so, on with the program.

```
  5         DIM D(4), F(9)
 10         MAT D = ZER
REM         EACH DIGIT OF N (5 DIGITS FOR EVERY NUMBER)
REM         IS STORED IN D(J).  BEGIN WITH 00001.
 15         LET D(4) = 1
REM         NOW STORE FACTORIAL VALUES.
 20         LET  F(0) = 1
 25         LET F(1) = 1
 30         LET F(2) = 2
 35         LET F(3) = 6
 40         LET F(4) = 24
 45         LET F(5) = 120
 50         LET F(6) = 720
 55         LET F(7) = 5040
 60         LET F(8) = 40320
 65         LET F(9) = 362,880
 70         PRINT "NUMBER IS", " " , " SUM OF FACTORIALS OF ITS DIGITS IS"
 75         PRINT
REM         NOW ADD UP THE DIGITS IN EACH
REM         D(J), MULTIPLYING BY CORRESPONDING POWERS OF TEN FOR
REM         INCREASING  J.
 80         LET S = D(4) + 10* D(3) + 100* D(2) + 1000* D(1) + 10000* D(0)
 85         LET S1 = 0
 90         LET W = 0
 95         FOR  J = 0 TO  4
100         IF  W < > 0   THEN 115
105         IF D(J) = 0   THEN   140
110         LET  W = 1
115         LET  V = D(J)
120         IF  V = 9   THEN   160
125         IF  V < > 8 THEN    135
130         IF  S < 40000   THEN 160
            REM NOW ADD THE FACTORIAL OF  V  TO S1
135         LET  S1 = S1 + F(V)
140         NEXT  J
            REM NOW WE TEST FOR EQUALITY OF  S  AND  S1
145         IF  S < > S1   THEN 160
150         PRINT
155         PRINT  S, " ", " ", S1
160         LET D(4) = D(4) + 1
165         FOR  J = 0  TO  4
170         IF D(J) = 0   THEN 200
175         IF D(J) < 10   THEN 200
180         LET D(J) = D(J) - 10
190         LET D(J-1) = D(J-1) + 1
195         GO TO 165
200         NEXT  J
205         IF D(0) < 5 THEN   80
210         STOP
215         END
```

Write a FORTRAN program to print all pairs of amicable numbers
up to 10,000. Amicable numbers are defined as pairs of integers,
the sum of the factors of one of them being equal to the other.

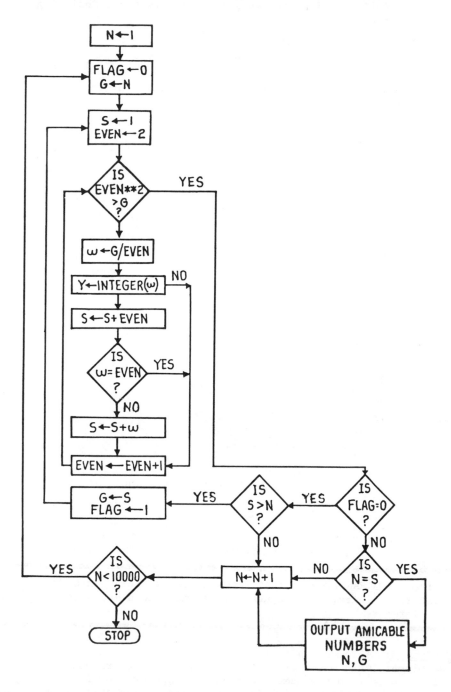

Solution: An example of one such pair is 220 and 284. The
factors of 220 summed up equal
$$1 + 2 + 4 + 5 + 10 + 11 + 20 + 22 + 44 + 55 + 110, \text{ or } 284,$$

while the factors of 284 summed up equal

$1 + 2 + 4 + 71 + 142$, or 220.

Note that 1 is included as a factor, but the number itself is not!

To find all amicable pairs up to 10,000, use the following algorithm: for every N from 1 to 10,000

1) Factor N and find the sum, S, of its factors, including 1, but excluding N.

2) If S is greater than N, find the sum of the factors of S.

3) If this second sum equals N, print the pair N,S, for they are amicables.

The flowchart will illustrate the actions taken by the program.
The program looks as follows:

```
         INTEGER FLAG,Y
         N = 1
12       FLAG = 0
         G = FLOAT (N)
16       S = 1.0
         EVEN = 2.0
20       IF ((EVEN**2).GT.G) GO TO 55
         W = G/EVEN
         Y = IFI x (W)
         IF (Y.NE.W) GO TO 45
         S = S + EVEN
         IF (W.EQ. EVEN) GO TO 45
         S = S + W
45       EVEN = EVEN + 1.0
         GO TO 20
55       IF (FLAG.NE.0) GO TO 72
         IF (S.LE.N) GO TO 76
         G = S
         FLAG = 1
         GO TO 16
72       IF (N.EQ.S) GO TO 90
76       N = N + 1
         IF (N.LT.10000) GO TO 12
         GO TO 99
90       WRITE (6, 100) N,G
100      FORMAT (1X,'AMICABLE PAIR IS', I4, 'AND', I4)
         GO TO 76
99       STOP
         END
```

● **PROBLEM** 20-5

Write a FORTRAN program that reads in two positive integers of at most five digits, and outputs all palindromic numbers lying between the integers.

Solution: A famous palindrome in English is the line spoken by Napoleon: 'Able was I ere I saw Elba'. The letters occur from right to left in the same order as they appear from left to right. Palindromic numbers are positive integers having this "mirror property", such as 44, 2992, and 75757. The integers 1,2,...,9 are also included as palindromic numbers.

We want to search for all palindromic numbers between two positive integers which lengths are at most 5 digits. The approach used in solving this problem is to store the first integer in array K, digit-by-digit in reverse order. Then a comparison is made to determine whether the integer is equal to its "mirror image", the reversed-order integer. If so, the palindromic number is printed out. This process continues until the upper parameter is exceeded. If, after all the integers between the parameters are checked, there exist no palindromic numbers, a message is printed out indicating this fact.

The program terminates when a number less or equal to zero appears on the data card as one of the two parameters.

```
        DIMENSION K(5), L(500)
10      READ (5,100) KONE, KTWO
100     FORMAT (2I5)
C       DO WHILE KONE OR KTWO IS GREATER THAN ZERO
        IF (KONE.LE.0.OR.KTWO.LE.0) GO TO 99
        J = 0
C       TEST THE INTEGERS KONE, KONE + 1,... KTWO
        DO 60 NTEST = KONE, KTWO
        NTEMP = NTEST
C       STORE NTEMP DIGIT-BY-DIGIT IN REVERSE ORDER
C       IN ARRAY K
        DO 40 I = 1,5
        M = 6 - I
        KTEMP = NTEMP/10
        K(M) = NTEMP-(KTEMP*10)
        IF (KTEMP.LE.0) GO TO 20
        NTEMP = KTEMP
40      CONTINUE
20      M2 = (M + 5)/2
        DO 30 JTEMP = M,M2
        LTEMP = 5 + M - JTEMP
        IF (K(JTEMP).NE.K(LTEMP)) GO TO 60
30      CONTINUE
        J = J + 1
        L(J) = NTEST
60      CONTINUE
        IF(J.GT.0) GO TO 70
        WRITE (5,101) KONE, KTWO
101     FORMAT (1X,'NO PALINDROMES BETWEEN', I5 ,'AND', I5)
        GO TO 10
70      WRITE (5,102)(L(N), N = 1,J)
102     FORMAT (10(1X,I6)/)
        GO TO 10
99      STOP
        END
```

● **PROBLEM** 20-6

Write a FORTRAN program that accepts two positive integers and outputs a message indicating whether the integers between the two limits are perfect, abundant, or deficient.

Solution: The proper divisors of a positive integer include all divisors except the integer itself. For instance, the proper divisors of 12 are 1,2,3,4, and 6.
We use three terms to classify integers according to the sums of

their divisors. An integer is perfect if the sum of its proper
divisors is equal to that integer. There exist only 6 perfect
numbers less than 10 billion, all of which are even. One of them
is integer 6. Its proper divisors are 1,2 and 3, the sum of
which is equal to $1 + 2 + 3 = 6$. The rest of the integers may be
either abundant or deficient. An integer is abundant if the sum of
its proper divisors is greater than that integer. Conversely, an
integer is deficient if the sum of its proper divisors is less than
an integer itself.

Perfect numbers are related to Mersenne primes, which take the form
$2^K - 1$. We can say that if $2^K - 1$ is prime, then $n = 2^K - 1(2^{K-1})$

is perfect. Note that we refer only to even perfect numbers. No odd
perfect numbers have yet been demonstrated.

The program uses a subprogram called NSIGMA, named for the σ-function.
If q is a prime, then $\sigma(q) = q + 1$. In general,

$$\sigma(q^K) = \frac{q^{K+1} - 1}{q - 1} \quad \text{for} \quad q = 1,2,3,\ldots$$

An array, NPRIM, is used to store all primes between 2 and 181.
Although this example uses a DATA statement for the primes, you could
also use a subprogram for the Sieve of Eratosthenes to generate
primes. The main program reads in upper and lower bounds (HI and LO,
respectively), an increment term (I), and a case number (K), which
indicates the following according to the values assigned to it:

K = -2   output deficient numbers only
K = -1   output deficient and perfect numbers only
K = 0   output all numbers
K = 1   output abundant and perfect numbers only
K = 2   output abundant numbers only

Since the highest prime number stored in NPRIM is 181, the upper bound
cannot exceed $(181)^2 = 32761$, otherwise some of the divisors may end
up missing. The program looks as follows:

```
          INTEGER  HI
          READ (5,100) LO, HI, I, K
   100    FORMAT (4(I5))
          DO 60  N = LO, HI, I
C         USE NSIGMA TO CHECK FACTORS
          IF (NSIGMA (N) - 2*N) 15, 20, 25
    15    IF (K) 30, 30, 60
    20    IF (IABS(K) - 1) 40, 40, 60
    25    IF (K) 60, 50, 50
    30    WRITE (6,101) N
   101    FORMAT (1H, I5, 13H  IS DEFICIENT)
          GO TO 60
    40    WRITE (6, 102) N
   102    FORMAT (1H , I5, 11H  IS   PERFECT)
          GO TO 60
    50    WRITE (6, 103) N
   103    FORMAT (1H , I5, 12H   IS ABUNDANT)
    60    CONTINUE
          STOP
          END
C         FUNCTION SUBPROGRAM NSIGMA
          FUNCTION NSIGMA
          DIMENSION NPRIM (42)
C         FILL ARRAY WITH PRIMES FROM 2 TO 181
          DATA NPRIM/2,3,5,7,11,13,17,19,23,29,31,37,41,
     1    43,47,53,59,61,67,71,73,79,83,89,97,101,103,107,109,113,
```

```
2   127,131,137,139,149,151,157,163,167,173,179,181/
    INT = N
    RN = INT
    NROOT = SQRT(RN)
    NSIGMA = 1
    MSIGMA = 1
    DO 40  I = 1,42
    NF = 0
    NP = NPR(I)
    IF (NP - NRT) 32, 32, 50
32  KINT = INT/NP
    IF (INT-KINT*NP) 36, 34, 36
34  INT = KINT
    NF = 1
    WSIGMA = NSIGMA*NP + MSIGMA
    GO TO 32
36  IF (NF) 40, 40, 38
38  MSIGMA = NSIGMA
    RN = INT
    NROOT = SQRT (RN)
40  CONTINUE
50  IF (INT-1) 60, 60, 56
56  NSIGMA = NSIGMA*INT + NSIGMA
60  RETURN
    END
```

● **PROBLEM** 20-7

Write a BASIC program to obtain unit fractions. Any proper fraction
can be expressed as the sum of unit fractions, as in the example

$$\frac{17}{21} = \frac{1}{2} + \frac{1}{4} + \frac{1}{17} + \frac{1}{1428}$$

Solution: For this problem, you can enter any two numbers to represent
the numerator and denominator of the fraction you choose. Then, by
factoring the fraction continually, the program will print out the
unit fraction's denominators. If the fraction has too many factors
(i.e., more than 29), the program will print out a message telling
you to try again. The flowchart will illustrate the procedure.
Based on the flowchart, the program looks as follows:

```
10    REM UNIT FRACTIONS BY FACTORING
11    DIM M(29)
15    PRINT "TYPE N AND D, REMEMBERING THAT D MUST BE GREATER THAN  N."
16    PRINT
18    INPUT  N,D
19    FOR  J = 0  TO  29
20    LET  M(J) = 0
21    NEXT  J
22    IF  D < = N  THEN  14
23    LET  K = 0
24    LET  P = INT(D/N) + 1
35    LET  M(K) = P
38    LET  K = K + 1
40    IF  K < 30  THEN  50
44    PRINT "TOO MANY FACTORS: TRY AGAIN"
45    PRINT
```

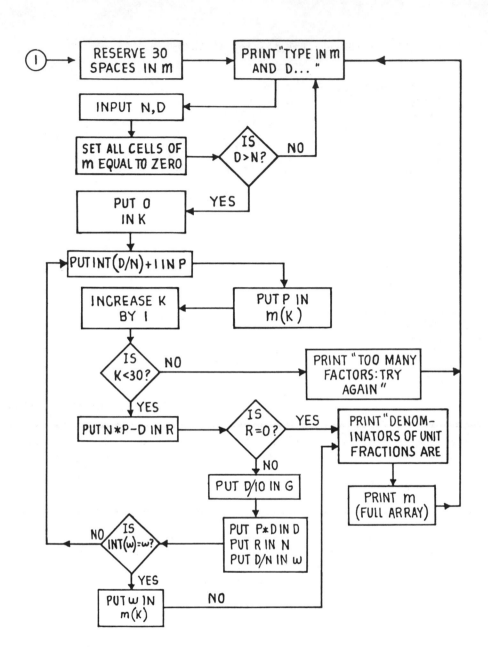

```
48      GO TO  14
50      LET   R = N*P - D
55      IF  R = 0  THEN  75
56      LET   G = D/10
58      LET   D = P*D
60      LET   N = R
62      LET   W = D/N
64      LET   Y = INT(W)
66      IF  Y < > W  THEN  24
70      LET   M(K) = W
75      PRINT
76      PRINT "DENOMINATORS OF UNIT FRACTIONS ARE:"
77      PRINT
80      LET   K = 0
```

```
84      IF  M(K) = 0  THEN  96
86      PRINT
88      PRINT M(K)
92      LET  K = K + 1
94      GO TO 84
96      PRINT "---------------------"
97      PRINT
98      GO TO 15
99      END
```

A magic square looks as follows:

$$I_1 \quad\quad I_2 \quad\quad I_3 \cdot\; \circ\; \circ$$

$$J_1 \quad\quad J_2 \quad\quad J_3 \cdot\; \circ\; \cdot$$

$$K_1 \quad\quad K_2 \quad\quad K_3 \cdot\; \cdot\; \cdot$$

$$\begin{matrix} \circ & \circ & \cdot \\ \cdot & \circ & \cdot \\ \cdot & \circ & \cdot \end{matrix}$$

where I_s, J_s, K_s ... are integers, and all rows, columns, and diagonals have the equal integer sums.
Write a program to create three 3 × 3 magic squares using a random number generator. Integers may range from 0 to 100. Use BASIC.

Solution: The statement INT(100*RND(X)) gives the programmer random integer numbers between 0 and 100. This statement is repeated 3 times to generate the three random integers L, K, J. The magic square is built then on the basis of those numbers by arranging them in the following manner:

```
J + L              L - (J+K)          K + L
K + L - J              L              J + L - K
L - K              J + K + L          L - J
```

Now, if you sum the numbers in rows, columns, and diagonals it will be seen that all the sums are the same and equal to 3L! For example, row 1: (J+L) + L-(J+K) + (K+L) =

$$= J + L + L - J - K + K + L = L + L + L = 3L$$

The program looks as follows:

```
10      LET  N = 1
15      LET  J = INT(100*RND(X))
20      LET  K = INT(100*RND(X))
25      LET  L = INT(100*RND(X))
30      LET  P1 = J + L
35      LET  Q1 = L - (J+K)
40      LET  R1 = K + L
45      LET  P2 = K + L - J
50      LET  Q2 = L
55      LET  R2 = J + L - K
60      LET  P3 = L - K
65      LET  Q3 = J + K + L
70      LET  R3 = L - J
75      PRINT P1, Q1, R1
```

```
80      PRINT P2, Q2, R2
85      PRINT P3, Q3, R3
90      LET  N = N + 1
95      IF  N < = 3  THEN 15
100     STOP
105     END
```

● **PROBLEM** 20-9

Write a program in FORTRAN that prints a calendar for any month of
the year from March 1600 to year N.

Solution: To grasp a thorough theoretical knowledge of the procedure
behind this problem, one needs to know something about congruence and
modulo arithmetic. Here, we will try to minimize the theoretical discussion and simply state some pertinent theorems.
We will look at the Gregorian calendar, first implemented on October
15, 1582. Let N be any year later than 1600. Then, between the
year 1600 exclusive, and the year N inclusive, there are

$$\left[\frac{N}{4}\right] - 400 \text{ years divisible by } 4$$

To prove this let y be any year such that $1600 < y \le N$. Year y
is divisible by 4 only if y = 4x, where x is an integer. Thus,
the number of years divisible by 4 is the same as the number of
integers x satisfying $1600 < 4x \le N$, or $400 < x \le N/4$. There are
clearly [N/4] - 400 of such integers.

$$\left[\frac{N}{400}\right] - 4 \text{ years divisible by } 400$$

$$\left[\frac{N}{100}\right] - 16 \text{ century-beginning years}$$

$$\left[\frac{N}{100}\right] - \left[\frac{N}{400}\right] - 12 \text{ century-beginning years that are not leap}$$
years

$$\left[\frac{N}{4}\right] - \left[\frac{N}{100}\right] + \left[\frac{N}{400}\right] - 388 \text{ leap years}$$

$$\left[\frac{A}{4}\right] + \left[\frac{B}{4}\right] + 24A - 388 \text{ leap years, where A and B are integers}$$
governed uniquely by the restrictions
$N = 100A + B$ and $0 \le B < 100$

(Brackets are used to express the greater integer part of the division.)
These relations tell us that leap years, containing 366 days, are those
divisible by 4, and that century-beginning years are leap years only
if divisible by 400. Thus, 1600, 2000, 2400,... are century-beginning
leap years.
Since February is a troublesome month, especially during leap years,
we rearrange our calendar so that March is the first month of the year
N. January and February of year N become the eleventh and twelfth
months of year N - 1. Then, April through the following February
become the second through twelfth months of year N. This places
February at the end of the year, a manipulation which will make the
program simpler to follow.
We must also consider the days of the week. Starting with Sunday, we
number the days 0,1,2,3,4,5,6, ending with Saturday. The theorem

666

which gives the weekday number of the Kth day of month M of year N (known as Zeller's congruence) is

$$K + [2.6M - 0.2] + B + \left[\frac{B}{4}\right] + \left[\frac{A}{4}\right] + 2A \pmod{7}.$$

To understand the derivation of this formula, consider the following: Since March 1, 1600 fell on a Wednesday, its weekday number is $W = 3$. Since $365 \equiv 1 \pmod{7}$ ($365 - 1 = 364$ is divisible by 7), March 1, 1601 has weekday number 4. March 1, 1602 has number 5 and March 1, 1603 has number 6. But March 1, 1604 has number 1, not 0 because it is a leap year. In general, the weekday number W_N of March 1 of year N is:

$$W_N = W + t + e \pmod{7}, \text{ where } W = 3 \qquad (1)$$

where t is the total number of years and e is the number of leap years between 1600 exclusive and N inclusive.
Now, $t = N - 1600$, $N = 100A + B$, and,

$$e = \left[\frac{A}{4}\right] + \left[\frac{B}{4}\right] + 24A - 388.$$

Thus, equation (1) is:

$$W_N \equiv 3 + 100A + B - 1600 + \left[\frac{B}{4}\right] + \left[\frac{A}{4}\right] + 24A - 388 \pmod{7}$$

or, after simplification,

$$W_N \equiv 3 + B + \left[\frac{B}{4}\right] + \left[\frac{A}{4}\right] - 2A \pmod{7}. \qquad (2)$$

Equation (2) gives the weekday number of March 1 for any N. Since April 1 occurs 31 days after March 1, and $31 \equiv 3 \pmod{7}$, its weekday number is 3 more than the weekday number of March 1, i.e., 6. Continuing for the other months we obtain the sequence of constants
W: 3, 6, 8, 11, 13, 16, 19, 21, 24, 26, 29, 32
   ↑ ↑
  Mar Apr ....
Reverend Zeller noticed that the arithmetic function $1 + [2.6m - 0.2]$ assumes exactly this sequence of integers for $m = 1, 2, ..., 12$. Hence, the weekday number of the first day of any month, m, of the Nth year is given by

$$W_N \equiv 1 + [2.6m - 0.2] + B + \left[\frac{B}{4}\right] + \left[\frac{A}{4}\right] - 2A \pmod{7} \qquad (3)$$

Finally, if, instead of the first day, we consider the kth day, Zeller's congruence is obtained:

$$W_N \equiv k + [2.6m - 0.2] + B + \left[\frac{B}{4}\right] + \left[\frac{A}{4}\right] - 2A \pmod{7}.$$

Take for example November 1, 2060. K is 1, M is 9 (according to our renumbering scheme), B is 60, and A is 20 (since $N = 2060$, and $N = 100A + B$). Plugging in the values, we get
$$1 + 23 + 60 + 15 + 5 - 40 = 64.$$
To complete the problem, we find that

$$64 \equiv 1 \pmod{7}$$
since $64 - 1$ is divisible by 7. Hence, 1 corresponds to Monday, and the answer is obtained.
We present the program forthwith, high-lighting control sections with comments.

```
C     CALENDAR PROGRAM
      INTEGER BLANK, DATE, YEAR, RMTHS
C     THE ELEMENTS OF DATE, ALONG WITH THE
C     CHARACTER BLANK, ARE USED TO PRINT CALENDAR
```

```
C       IF FIRST DAY OF MONTH IS NOT SUNDAY.
        DIMENSION RMTHS (12), DATE (6)
        DATA RMTHS/'JAN ', 'FEB ', 'MAR ', 'APR ', 'MAY ', 'JUN ',
1       'JUL ', 'AUG ', 'SEP ', 'OCT ', 'NOV ', 'DEC '/
        DATA BLANK, DATE/' ', '1', '2', '3', '4', '5', '6'/
C       INPUT MONTH (JAN = 1, FEB = 2,..., DEC = 12) AND YEAR
 10     READ (5,100) MONTH, YEAR
100     FORMAT (I2, I4)
C       DO WHILE YEAR GREATER THAN ZERO
        IF (YEAR.LE.0) GO TO 99
C       NOW, MONTHS ARE RENUMBERED SUCH THAT
C       M = 1 FOR MAR, M = 2 FOR APR, AND SO ON UNTIL
C       M = 10 FOR DEC. FOR JAN AND FEB, M = 11 AND M = 12
C       OF PRECEDING YEAR.
 20     NEWYR = YEAR
        IF (MONTH - 2) 25, 30, 35
C       JANUARY SECTION
 25     M = 11
        NEWYR = NEWYR - 1
C       NDIM EQUALS NUMBER OF DAYS IN MONTH
        NDIM = 31
        GO TO 40
C       FEBRUARY SECTION
 30     M = 12
        NEWYR = NEWYR - 1
C       DETERMINE WHETHER NYEAR IS A LEAP YEAR
        IF (YEAR.NE. (YEAR/4)*4) GO TO 33
        IF (YEAR.NE. (YEAR/100)*100) GO TO 34
        IF (YEAR.EQ. (YEAR/400)*400) GO TO 34
C       IF YEAR IS NOT A LEAP YEAR
 33     NDIM = 28
        GO TO 40
C       IF YEAR IS A LEAP YEAR
 34     NDIM = 29
        GO TO 40
C       NOW COMPUTE MARCH THROUGH DECEMBER
        M = MONTH - 2
C       CASE STRUCTURE TO DETERMINE DAYS IN MONTH
        GO TO (36, 37, 36, 37, 36, 36, 37, 36, 37, 36), M
 36     NDIM = 31
        GO TO 40
 37     NDIM = 30
C       NOW CALCULATE WEEKDAY NUMBER FOR THE
C       FIRST DAY OF THE MONTH
 40     NC = NEWYR/100
        ND = NEWYR - 100*NC
        NW = 1 + (26*M-2)/10 + ND + ND/4 + NC/4 - 2*NC
C       DO LOOP REDUCES WEEKDAY NUMBER MODULO 7
C       TO ONE OF THE VALUES 0, 1, 2,...,6.
        DO 41  I = 1,7
        NWKDAY = I - 1
        NDIFF = NW - NWKDAY
        IF (NDIFF.EQ.(NDIFF/7)*7) GO TO 45
 41     CONTINUE
C       WRITE HEADINGS
 45     WRITE (6, 101) RMTHS (MONTH), YEAR
101     FORMAT (1H0, 10X, A4, I4)
        WRITE (6, 102)
102     FORMAT (1H0, 27HSUN MON TUE WED THU FRI SAT/)
        IF (NWKDAY.EQ.0) GO TO 52
```

668

```
C        THIS SECTION PRINTS THE FIRST WEEK OF THE
C        MONTH IF SUNDAY IS NOT THE FIRST DAY
         LIM = 7 - NWKDAY
         WRITE (6, 103)(BLANK, I = 1, NWKDAY),(DATE(I), I = 1, LIM)
  103    FORMAT (7(3X,A1))
         LIM = LIM + 1
         GO TO 53
   52    LIM = 1
C        FINISH PRINTING CALENDAR
   53    WRITE (6, 104)(I, I = LIM,NDIM)
  104    FORMAT (7I4)
         GO TO 10
C        END DO-WHILE
   99    STOP
         END
```

● **PROBLEM** 20-10

Develop a BASIC program to use Euclid's Algorithm to find the greatest common divisor of the two positive integers A   and B.

<u>Solution</u>:   Briefly, Euclid's Algorithm is a method which takes the smaller of two numbers and divides it into the larger number.   The remainder from this division then becomes the smaller number, and the process is repeated.   When the remainder reaches zero, the last smaller number is the greatest common divisor.
A flowchart of the program's logic is given below.

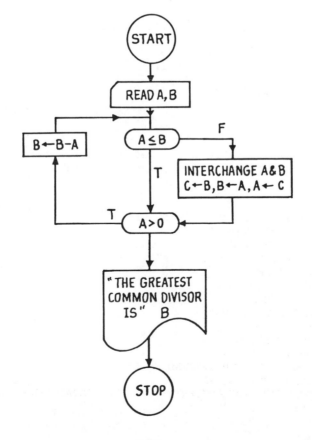

The program is given below:

```
100    REM GREATEST COMMON DIVISOR
110    READ A,B
120    IF  A < = B   THEN 130
125    GO TO 140
130    IF  A > 0   THEN 150
131    GO TO 160
140    LET  C = B
141    LET  B = A
142    LET  A = C
143    GO TO 130
150    LET  B = B - A
151    GO TO 120
160    PRINT "THE GREATEST COMMON DIVISOR IS", B
800    DATA  16,36
999    END
```

● **PROBLEM** 20-11

Write a program that finds, for integers m and n, the quotient and remainder when m is divided by n.

Solution: The Fundamental Theorem of Arithmetic states that if m and n are any integers with $n \neq 0$, then there exist unique integers q and r, $0 \leq r < |n|$ such that $m = qn + r$.
As examples:

1) $m = 43$ $n = 5$; using the division algorithm $q = 8$ $r = 3$ and
     $m = nq + r$, or $43 = 8(5) + 3$.
2) $m = -43$ $n = -5$ $q = 9$ $r = 2$
     $m = nq + r$, or $-43 = 9(-5) + 2$
     Here $r = 2 < |n| = |-5| = 5$.
3) $m = 8$ $n = 32$;
     $8 = 0(32) + 8$.

The following computer program accepts any integers m,n $(n \neq 0)$ and computes the quotient and remainder of m/n.

```
C         INPUT INTEGERS  M  AND  N.   IF  N  IS
C         ZERO, READ ANOTHER PAIR.
   5      READ (5,10) M,N
          IF (N.EQ.0) GO TO 5
   10     FORMAT (2I6)
C         FIND THE QUOTIENT
          IQ = INT(M/N)
C         FIND THE REMAINDER
          IR = M - IQ*N
C         OUTPUT RESULTS
          WRITE (6,60) M,N
   60     FORMAT (1H0, 10HDIVIDEND =, I6, 10H DIVISOR =, I8)
   70     WRITE (6,80) IQ, IR
   80     FORMAT (1H, 10HQUOTIENT =, I6, 12H REMAINDER =, I6)
   90     STOP
          END
```

670

PRIME NUMBERS AND FACTORS

> Write a FORTRAN program that generates the prime numbers in the
> 1-2000 interval, using an ancient method known as the SIEVE of
> ERATOSTHENES.

Solution: A prime is a number which has only 2 divisors: 1 and
itself. There is an ancient method for finding the primes from
2 (the smallest prime) to some number N, called the SIEVE of
ERATOSTHENES. This method works as follows: First, the integers
from 2 to N are written down. Then, the multiples of the smallest available integer, 2, greater than this integer, are crossed
out. This step, obviously, eliminates all the even numbers except
2. The procedure is then repeated for the next smallest available
integer - 3, and then next - 5, because 4 is not available, since
it was eliminated during the first step, and so on...
Thus, the initial list is scanned repeatedly, and the appropriate
integers are crossed off, until the next least remaining integer
considered is greater than $\sqrt{N}$. At this point, all the remaining
integers are indeed all the primes between 2 and N.
The program is created based upon the above discussion. First, an
array of integers from 2 to 2000 is generated. Next, this
array is scanned repeatedly, deleting the appropriate integers by
replacing them with zeros. At the point when the considered integer
is greater than $\sqrt{2000}$, all the nonzero elements of the array are
placed left justified within the array and then printed.
The program looks as follows:

```
      DIMENSION N(2000)
      K = 2000
      RK = K
      KROOT = SQRT (RK)
      KK = K - 1
C     GENERATE ARRAY OF INTEGERS FROM  2  TO  2000
      DO 10  I = 1,KK
 10   N(I) = I + 1
      J = 1
C     SECTION OF REPEATED ELIMINATION PROCESS
 15   INC = N(J)
      JJ = J + INC
      DO 20  L = JJ, K, INC
 20   N(L) = 0
 25   J = J + 1
      IF (N(J).LE.0) GO TO 25

      IF (N(J).LE.KROOT)  GO TO 15

C     PLACE THE PRIMES LEFT JUSTIFIED
C     IN THE ARRAY N.
      J = 0
      DO 45  I = 1, KK
      IF (N(I).LE.0) GO TO 45
      J = J + 1
      N(J) = N(I)
 45   CONTINUE
C     OUTPUT THE PRIMES
      WRITE (6,50)(N(I), I = 1,J)
 50   FORMAT (1H, 10I6)
      STOP
      END
```

671

Develop a program to find rare prime decades. Consider a decade
to be a series of numbers between and including 10a + 1 and 10a +
10, where a = 0,1,2,3... Rare decades are those which contain four
primes. Output such decades less than 5000.

Solution: The rarity of this occurrence is due to the fact that in
any decade, there can be at most four primes. If you consider that
in each decade there are five even numbers and one odd number that
is a multiple of five, you should recognize that the remaining four
possible primes must end with 1,3,7, or 9. The only exception to
this rule is the first decade, the primes of which are 2,3,5 and 7.
The needed algorithm must check the odd integers between 3 and
5000 to establish the existence of primes. To do this task, a FUNCTION
subprogram IPRIME is used. This subprogram may use the Sieve of
Eratosthenes (developed earlier) or some other method. It is
assumed that the subprogram returns either of the two values: a 1 if
the integer is a prime, a 0 if it is composite.

The main program makes use of a four element queue. Each time a
prime is found, it is stored in the array K. When four consecutive
primes are in the queue, a check is made to see if they are included
in one decade. If so, the entire queue is printed out. If not, the
first prime in the queue is removed, the remaining three elements
move up one position, and the next prime is inserted at the end of
the queue. This process continues until I reaches 5000.
The program looks as follows:

```
        DIMENSION K(4)
        K(1) = 2
        ISUM = 1
        J = 2
        I = 3
        II = 1
C       DO WHILE  I  IS LESS THAN 5000
 20     IF (I.GE. 5000) GO TO 60
C       ASSIGN A NEW DECADE TO ISUM IF II = 5
        IF (II.LT.5) GO TO 5
        ISUM = ISUM + 10
        II = 0
C       IF  I  IS A PRIME, ASSIGN IT TO  K(J)
 5      CALL IPRIME (I)
        IF (IPRIME.EQ. 0) GO TO 57
        K(J) = I
        J = J + 1
        I = I + 2
        II = II + 1
        IF (J.LE.4) GO TO 20
C       CHECK IF ALL 4 PRIMES IN ARRAY  K  ARE WITHIN
C       THE SAME DECADE
        IF (K(1).LT.ISUM) GO TO 30
        IF (K(4).GE.ISUM + 10) GO TO 30
C       IF, IN FACT, THEY ARE - OUTPUT THE ARRAY  K
        WRITE (5,100)(K(J), J = 1,4)
 100    FORMAT (4(2X,I4)/)
        J = 1
        GO TO 20
C       IF THEY ARE NOT WITHIN ONE DECADE
```

```
30    DO 35  N = 2,4
35    K(N-1) = K(N)
      J = 4
      GO TO 20
57    I = I + 2
      II = II + 1
      GO TO 20
60    STOP
      END
```

• **PROBLEM** 20-14

Write a program to determine the prime factorizations of integers
greater than 1.

Solution: According to the Fundamental Theorem of Arithmetic any
integer can be expressed as the product of primes. Some examples
are:

$$108 = 2 \times 2 \times 3 \times 3 \times 3 = 2^2 \times 3^3$$

$$390 = 2 \times 3 \times 5 \times 13$$

$$-210 = -(2 \times 3 \times 5 \times 7)$$

The algorithm for computing the prime factors of a positive integer
greater than 1 is based on the following facts:
1) Let p be a prime $\leq \sqrt{n}$. If n is divisible by no such p,
then n is a prime.
2) Let p be a divisor of n. Then $q = n/p$ is an integer, and
any other prime divisor of n divides q.
3) n has at most one prime factor greater than $\sqrt{n}$.

Using these facts we can construct the following computer program.
The program assumes that a table of primes for the range 1-1000
was developed earlier and can be obtained from the secondary memory
files. Thus, the program can find prime factorizations for all
numbers less than $(1000)^2 = 1,000,000$. Execution terminates when
the considered integer N is 1 or less.
The program looks as follows:

PRIME FACTORIZATION

```
C     RESERVE MEMORY FOR PRIME DIVISORS (NPR),
      FOR PRIME FACTORS (NFAC), AND FOR THE NUMBER OF TIMES EACH PRIME
      FACTOR OCCURS (NBR).
      DIMENSION NPR(168), NFAC(8), NBR(8).
C     READ IN THE PRIMES LESS THAN 1000.
C     (THERE ARE 168 OF THEM)
      READ (5,5)(NPR(I), I = 1, 168)
 5    FORMAT (20I4)
10    READ (5,15) N
15    FORMAT (I7)
      IF (N - 2) 85,75,20
C     COPY  N  INTO INT FOR TESTING PURPOSES.
20    INT = N
      RN = INT
      NRT = SQRT(RN)
C     START A COUNTER FOR THE NUMBER OF DIFFERENT PRIMES THAT DIVIDE  N.
      J = 0
      DO 45  I = 1, 168
```

```
C       NF COUNTS THE OCCURRENCES OF EACH PRIME FACTOR
        NF = 0
C       BRANCH OUT OF THE DO LOOP IF
C       THE CURRENT PRIME IS GREATER
C       THAN THE SQUARE ROOT OF INT.
        IF (NPR(I) - NRT) 25,25,50
 25     KINT = INT/NPR(I)
        IF (INT - KINT*NPR(I)) 35,30,35
C       IF NPR(I) DIVIDES INT, STORE THE
C       QUOTIENT KINT IN INT.  THUS, THIS
C       QUOTIENT IS NOW THE DIVIDEND FOR FURTHER TESTING.
 30     INT = KINT
        NF = NF + 1
        GO TO 25
 35     IF (NF) 45,45,40
C       INCREMENT  J  BY  1  IF  NF   IS POSITIVE
C       AND IF NPR(I) DOES NOT DIVIDE INT.
C       THEN STORE THE PRIME NPR(I), AS THE
C       J-TH MEMBER OF NFAC AND STORE
C       THE MULTIPLICITY  NF  IN  NBR(J).
 40     J = J + 1
        NFAC(J) = NPR(I)
        NBR(J) = NF
        RN = INT
        NRT = SQRT(RN)
 45     CONTINUE
C       N  IS PRIME IF AND ONLY IF  J = 0
 50     IF (J) 75,75,55
 55     IF (INT-1) 65,65,60
 60     J = J + 1
        NFAC(J) = INT
        NBR(J) = 1
C       PRINT PRIME FACTORIZATION
 65     WRITE (6,70) N, (NFAC(I),NBR(I), I = 1,J)
 70     FORMAT (1H0, I7, 3H =  , 8(I5, 1H( ,I2, 1H)))
        GO TO 10
 75     WRITE (6,80) N
 80     FORMAT (1H0, I7, 9H  IS PRIME)
        GO TO 10
 85     STOP
        END
```

● **PROBLEM** 20-15

Write a program in BASIC to find the sum and number of factors for
the integers between 1000 and 1050, not including 1 and the integer
itself.

Solution: As an example, consider the integer 36. It has 7 factors:
2,3,4,6,9,12,18, the sum of which is 54.
The presented program outputs the considered integer, sum of its
factors, and the number of factors. The program terminates when the
considered number is greater than 1050.
The program looks as follows:

```
15     LET  F = 1133
20     LET  F = F + 1
25     IF  F < 1175  THEN  30
```

```
28    STOP
30    LET   M = 0
32    LET   N = 0
34    LET   D = 2
35    LET   Y = F/D
40    LET   W = INT(Y)
45    IF   W < > Y   THEN   70
50    LET   M = M + D
55    LET   N = N + 1
60    IF   D = Y   THEN   70
65    LET   M = M + Y
68    LET   N = N + 1
70    LET   D = D + 1
75    IF   D*D < = F   THEN   35
80    PRINT F,M,N
90    GO TO   20
95    END
```

DIOPHANTINE EQUATIONS

Write a FORTRAN program that calculates the coefficients of a linear Diophantine equation of the form MX + NY = (M,N).

Solution: A Diophantine equation of this type is a polynomial with integer coefficients for which only integer solutions are permitted. The set (M,N) is called the solution of the equation. The simplest Diophantine equation is the one-variable, first-degree equation of the form

$$MX = p$$

where M, p are integers, and neither is equal to 0. By definition, this equation has an integer solution if and only if p/M is an integer.

Two-variable linear Diophantine equations may be solved by applying Euclid's algorithm for finding the greatest common divisor (GCD). The program used incorporates Euclid's algorithm into the following main algorithm:

1) Input coefficients M and N.
2) Check integers; if M = 0, exit, else, continue.
3) Initialize: $M0 = N1 = 1$, and $N0 = M1 = 0$.
4) Divide M by N; store quotient in Q and remainder in R.
5) Calculate two new coefficients for M and N, which are, respectively
    $M2 = M0 - Q*M1$
    $N2 = N0 - Q*N1$
6) Redefine the variables according to the following schedule:
    $M0 = M1$
    $N0 = N1$
    $M1 = M2$
    $N1 = N2$
7) Redefine the dividend as the previous divisor and the divisor as the previous remainder (this is Euclid's strategy).
8) Loop back to step (4).
9) The final nonzero remainder is (M,N); if the first remainder is zero, $(M,N) = |N|$. Output M,N,M1,N1 and (M,N) in the form
    $M \cdot M1 + N \cdot N1 = (M,N)$

One more operation must be performed. The absolute values of M   and

675

N must be stored in MABS and NABS, respectively, so that the signs of the solutions can be included in the output.
Thus, the program is presented below. Comments are added to make it easier to follow the prose description of the algorithm. The program is terminated when 0 is entered as the value of M.
Also note, that the program assumes M and N ≤ 99999.

```
                    INTEGER  Q,R
5       READ (5,100) M,N
100     FORMAT (2I5)
C       DO WHILE  M  NOT EQUAL TO ZERO
        IF (M.EQ.0) GO TO 99
C       INITIALIZE VARIABLES
        M0 = 1
        M1 = 0
        N0 = 1
        N1 = 0
C       FIND ABSOLUTE VALUES TO OBTAIN SIGNS OF  M,N
        MABS = IABS(M)
        NABS = IABS(N)
        MSIGN = M/MABS
        NSIGN = N/NABS
C       CALCULATE QUOTIENT AND REMAINDER
20      Q = MABS/NABS
        R = MABS - NABS * Q
C       IF  R  GREATER THAN ZERO, REAPPLY EUCLID'S
C       ALGORITHM
        IF (R.LE.0) GO TO  30
        M2 = M0 - Q * M1
        N2 = N0 - Q * N1
C       REDEFINE VARIABLES
        M0 = M1
        N0 = N1
        M1 = M2
        N1 = N2
        MABS = NABS
        NABS = R
        GO TO  20
C       GIVE COEFFICIENTS OF  M  AND  N  WITH
C       THEIR PROPER SIGNS
 30     M1 = MSIGN * M1
        N1 = NSIGN * N1
C       OUTPUT RESULTS; NABS IS THE FINAL NON-
C       ZERO REMAINDER
        WRITE (6,101) M,M1,N,N1,NABS
101     FORMAT (1X,'(' ,I6, ') * (', I6,') + (', I6, ') * (',
     1  I6, ') = ', I5)
        GO TO  5
 99     STOP
        END
```

● **PROBLEM** 20-17

Write a FORTRAN program to solve linear congruences of the form

$$ax \equiv b \ (\text{mod } m).$$

Solution: Two integers are said to be congruent modulo an integer m if their difference is divisible by m. Thus a ≡ b (mod m) means (a-b)/m is an integer. For example, 3 ≡ 8 (mod 5) since

$$\frac{3-8}{5} = \frac{-5}{5} = -1 \text{ (an integer).}$$

Congruences are similar to equations and linear congruences are similar to linear equations. The linear congruence

$$ax \equiv b \text{ (mod m)}$$

has a solution if and only if (a,m) (the greatest common divider of a and m) divides b, i.e., (a,m)/b. Furthermore if x_0 is such a solution, then

$$x \equiv x_0 \text{ (mod m/(a,m))}$$

is also a solution.
For example, solve the linear congruence

$$8x \equiv 4 \text{ (mod 6).} \tag{1}$$

By definition, (1) means

$$\frac{8x - 4}{6} = \text{integer}$$

When x = 2, 8x - 4 = 12, and six divides twelve. Now, (8,6) = 2. Hence any x satisfying

$$x \equiv 2 \text{ (mod 6/(8,6)),}$$

or

$$x \equiv 2 \text{ (mod 3)}$$

is also a solution of 8x ≡ 4 (mod 6). Thus, 5,8,-1,-4,...etc. are solutions. To prove the above (first part) note that ax ≡ b (mod m) means

$$\frac{ax - b}{m} = r \text{ (an integer),}$$

or

$$ax - b = rm$$

or

$$ax - rm = b. \tag{2}$$

Equation (2) is a linear Diophantine equation and is solvable for r and x if and only if (a,m) divides b.

The strategy in the presented computer program is as follows:
1) Read in values of a,b and m (< 10000).
2) Call a subroutine that solves the linear Diophantine equation described above.
3) Return to main program.

The program terminates when the value of M read in is less than, or equal to 0 .

```
5     READ (5,10) IA,M,IB
10    FORMAT (3I4)
      IF (M.LE.0) GO TO 99
20    CALL GLDE(IA,M,IB,M1,N1,NA,INDEX)
      IF (INDEX) 30,30,22
22    WRITE (6,25)
25    FORMAT (1H0,45HNO VALUE OF  X  SATISFIES
   1  THE LINEAR CONGRUENCE)
      GO TO  40
```

```
30     WRITE (6,35) IX
35     FORMAT (1H0,3HX =,  I6,32H  SATISFIES  THE  LINEAR  CONGRUENCE)
40     WRITE (6,44), IA,IB,M
44     FORMAT (1H  , I6, 5HX (=), I6, 4H(MOD,I6,1H))
       GO TO 5
99     STOP
       END




          SUBROUTINE GLDE(M,N,K,M1,N1,NA,INDEX)

C     THIS SUBROUTINE RECEIVES INTEGERS FROM
C     MAIN PROGRAM.  FIRST, ANOTHER SUBROUTINE LDE IS CALLED, THAT FINDS
          THE GCD NA OF (N,M),
C     AND DETERMINES VALUES M1  AND  N1  THAT SATISFY THE LINEAD
C     DIOPHANTINE EQUATION M*M1 + N * N1 = K.
C     THE VALUE OF   M1   RETURNED HAS THE LEAST
C     POSSIBLE ABSOLUTE VALUE.  INDEX IS SET
C     TO  0  IF A SOLUTION EXISTS, TO / IF NOT,
C     AND TO  -1  IF THE VALUE RECEIVED FOR
C     K  IS, SAY, 30000.  USE  K = 30000 IF A
C     SOLUTION TO THE EQUATION
C     M*M1 + N*N1 = NA (GCD OF  M  AND  N)
C     IS DESIRED.  NOTE:  THE NUMBER 30000
C     IS SOMEWHAT ARBITRARILY CHOSEN.  IT IS
C     ASSUMED THAT ONE WOULD NEVER WISH
C     TO SOLVE THE EQUATION  MX + NY = 30000.
       CALL LDE (M,N,M1,N1,NA)
       IF (K - 30000) 22,21,22
 21    INDEX = -1
       K = NA
       GO TO  27
 22    MULT = K/NA
       IF (K - MULT * NA) 23,25,23
 23    INDEX = 1
       RETURN
 25    M1 = M1 * MULT
       N1 = N1 * MULT
 27    MTEST = M1
       ND = N/NA
       MD = M/NA
       MX = M1
 30    MX = MX + ND
       IF (IABS(MX) - IABS(M1)) 35,40,40
 35    M1 = MX
       N1 = N1 - MD
       GO TO  30
 40    IF (MTEST - M1) 65,45,65
 45    MX = M1
 50    MX = MX - ND
       IF (IABS(MX) - IABS(M1)) 55,65,65
 55    M1 = MX
       N1 = N1 + MD
       GO TO  50
 65    INDEX = 0
       RETURN
       END
```

```
                  SUBROUTINE LDE(M,N,M1,N1,NA)
      MO = 1
      NO = 0
      M1 = 0
      N1 = 1
      MA = IABS(M)
      NA = IABS(N)
      MS = M/MA
      NS = N/NA
25    IQUOT = MA/NA
      IREM = MA - NA * IQUOT
      IF (IREM) 35,35,30
30    M2 = MO - IQUOT * M1
      N2 = NO - IQUOT * N1
      MO = M1
      NO = N1
      M1 = M2
      N1 = N2
      MA = NA
      NA = IREM
      GO TO 25
35    M1 = MS * M1
      N1 = NS * N1
      RETURN
      END
```

CHAPTER 21

GAMES OF AMUSEMENT

GAMBLING AND CASINO

● PROBLEM 21-1

Simulate a game of American roulette with a Basic program.

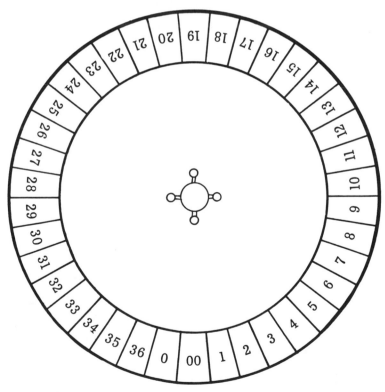

Solution: American roulette is played on a wheel with 38 compartments numbered 1 to 36, 0 and 00. Odd and even numbers alternate around the wheel as do red and black. In the simulation bets can range from $5 to $500 and you may bet on red or black, odd or even, first or second 18 numbers, a column or a single number. Place bets according to the following payoffs:

1) The numbers 1 to 36 signify a straight bet on that number and the payoff is 35:1 (i.e. 35 dollars return for a
$1 bet).
2) If you bet that the ball will land in the column or on
groups of numbers 1 - 12 or 13 - 24 or 25 - 36, the bets
are 2:1. In the program, the bet numbers are 1 - 36 for
single numbers and 37 for 1 - 12, 38 for 13 - 24, 39 for
25 - 36.
3) If you bet that the ball will land on
        i)   a number from groups 1 - 18 or 19 - 36
       ii)   even or odd
      iii)   red or black
the payoff is 1:1 ($1 additional for every $1 bet). The
even money bet numbers are 43 for 1 - 18, 44 for 19 - 36,
45 for even, 46 for odd, 47 for red and 48 for black.
4) 0 and 00 pay off 35:1 and count only when they are explicitly betted upon: The bet number for 0 is 49 and 50 for
00.

```
10   PRINT "ROULETTE"
20   PRINT "MINIMUM BET IS $5, MAXIMUM IS 500"
30   PRINT "WHEN I ASK FOR EACH BET, TYPE";
40   PRINT "THE NUMBER AND THE AMOUNT, SEPARATED BY A";
50   PRINT "COMMA. FOR EXAMPLE: TO BET $500 ON BLACK,";
60   PRINT "TYPE 48,500"
70   DIM B(100), C(100), T(100), X(38)
80   DIM A(50)
90   FOR I = 1 TO 38: X(I) = 0: NEXT I
100  REM MAT X = ZER
110  P = 1000
120  D = 100000
130  PRINT "HOW MANY BETS";
140  INPUT Y
150  IF Y < 1 OR Y <> INT(Y) THEN 130
160  FOR I = 1 TO 50: A(I) = 0: NEXT I
170  FOR C = 1 TO Y
180  PRINT "NUMBER"; C;
190  INPUT X,Z
200  B(C) = Z: T(C) = X
220  IF X < 1 OR X > 50 OR X <> INT(X) THEN 180
230  IF Z < 1 OR Z <> INT(Z) THEN 180
240  IF Z < 5 OR Z > 500 THEN 180
250  IF A(X) = 0 THEN 280
260  PRINT "YOU ALREADY MADE THAT BET"
270  GOTO 180
280  A(X) = 1: NEXT C
300  PRINT "SPINNING"
310  PRINT: PRINT
330  S = INT(100*RND(1))
340  IF S = 0 OR S > 38 THEN 330
350  X(S) = X(S) + 1
360  IF S < 37 THEN 420
370  IF S = 37 THEN 400
380  PRINT "00"
390  GOTO 520
400  PRINT "0"
410  GOTO 520
420  RESTORE
430  FOR I = 1 TO 18: READ R: IF R = S THEN 500: NEXT I
470  A$ = "BLACK"
480  PRINT S; A$
```

```
490    GOTO 520
500    A$ = "RED"
510    GOTO 480
520    PRINT
530    FOR C = 1 TO Y: IF T(C) < 37 THEN 1210
540    ON T(C) - 36 GOTO 590, 690, 720, 750, 800, 850, 900, 970,
       1000
560    ON T(C) - 45 GOTO 1030, 1060, 1130
570    GOTO 1210
580    STOP
590    REM 1-12(37) 2:1
600    IF S < = 12 THEN 650
610    PRINT "YOU LOSE"; B(C); "DOLLARS ON BET"; C
620    D = D + B(C)
630    P = P - B(C)
640    GOTO 680
650    PRINT "YOU WIN"; B(C)*2; "DOLLARS ON BET"; C
660    D = D - B(C)*2: P = P + B(C)*2
680    GOTO 1310
690    REM 13-24(38) 2:1
700    IF S > 12 AND S < 25 THEN 650
710    GOTO 610
720    REM 25 - 36(39) 2:1
730    IF S > 24 AND S < 37 THEN 650
740    GOTO 610
750    REM FIRST COLUMN (40) 2:1
760    FOR I = 1 TO 34 STEP 3: IF S = I THEN 650: NEXT I
790    GOTO 610
800    REM SECOND COLUMN (41) 2:1
810    FOR I = 2 TO 35 STEP 3: IF S = I THEN 650: NEXT I
840    GOTO 610
850    REM THIRD COLUMN (42) 2:1
860    FOR I = 3 TO 36 STEP 3: IF S = I THEN 650: NEXT I
890    GOTO 610
900    REM 1 - 18 (43) 1:1
910    IF S < 19 THEN 930
920    GOTO 610
930    PRINT "YOU WIN"; B(C); "DOLLARS ON BET"; C
940    D = D - B(C)
950    P = P + B(C)
960    GOTO 1310
970    REM 19-36(44) 1:1
980    IF S < 37 AND S > 18 THEN 930
990    GOTO 610
1000   REM EVEN (45) 1:1
1010   IF S/2 = INT(S/2) AND S < 37 THEN 930
1020   GOTO 610
1030   REM ODD (46) 1:1
1040   IF S/2 <> INT(S/2) AND S < 37 THEN 930
1050   GOTO 610
1060   REM RED (47) 1:1
1070   RESTORE
1080   FOR I = 1 TO 18
1090   READ R: IF S = R THEN 930: NEXT I
1120   GOTO 610
1130   REM BLACK (48) 1:1
1140   RESTORE
1150   FOR I = 1 TO 18: READ R: IF S = R THEN 610: NEXT I
1190   IF S > 36 THEN 610
1200   GOTO 930
1210   REM 1 TO 36, 0,00 (1-36,49,50) 35:1
```

```
1220   IF T(C) < 49 THEN 1260
1230   IF T(C) = 49 AND S = 37 THEN 1280
1240   IF T(C) = 50 AND S = 38 THEN 1280
1250   GOTO 610
1260   IF T(C) = S THEN 1280
1270   GOTO 610
1280   PRINT "YOU WIN"; B(C)*35; "DOLLARS ON BET"; C
1290   D = D - B(C)*35: P = P + B(C)*35
1310   NEXT C
1330   PRINT "TOTALS:", "ME", "YOU"
1340   PRINT " ", D, P
1350   IF P > 0 THEN 1380
1360   PRINT "YOU JUST SPENT YOUR LAST DOLLAR"
1370   GOTO 1470
1380   IF D > 0 THEN 1420
1390    PRINT "YOU BROKE THE HOUSE!"
1410   GOTO 1480
1420   PRINT "AGAIN";
1430   INPUT Y$
1440   IF LEFT $(Y$,1) = "Y" THEN 130
1450   DATA 1,3,5,7,9,12,14,16,18,19,21,23,25,27,30,32,34,36
1470   PRINT "THANKS FOR YOUR MONEY"
1480   END.
```

● **PROBLEM** 21-2

Simulate a game of draw poker between a player and the computer.
Use the Basic language.

Solution: In the game, both players (i.e. the computer vs the
operator) start with a fixed stake (say $200 each). The com-
puter accepts IOUs for certain personal items.

```
10   PRINT "POKER"
20   DIM A(50), B(15)
30   DEF FNA(X) = INT(10*RND(1))
40   DEF FNB(X) = X - 100 * INT(X/100)
50   PRINT "WELCOME TO THE TABLE. I WILL OPEN THE";
60   PRINT "BETTING BEFORE THE DRAW; YOU OPEN AFTER. WHEN";
70   PRINT "YOU FOLD, BET 0; TO CHECK, BET .5"
80   PRINT: LET O = 1
90   LET C = 200: LET S = 200
95   LET P = 0
100  PRINT: IF C < = 5 THEN 3340
110  PRINT "THE ANTE IS $5. I WILL DEAL"
120  PRINT: IF S > 5 THEN 140
130  GOSUB 3490
140  LET P = P + 10: LET S = S - 5: LET C = C - 5
150  FOR Z = 1 TO 10: GOSUB 1460: NEXT Z
160  PRINT "YOUR HAND:"
170  N = 1
180  GOSUB 1580
190  N = 6: I = 2
200  GOSUB 1830
210  PRINT: IF I <> 6 THEN 330
220  IF FNA(0) < = 7 THEN 250
230  LET X = 11100
240  GOTO 300
250  IF FNA(0) < = 7 THEN 280
```

683

```
260    LET X = 11110
270    GOTO 300
280    IF FNA(0) > = 1 THEN 320
290    X = 11111
300    I = 7: Z = 23
310    GOTO 430
320    Z = 1: GOTO 365
330    IF U > = 13 THEN 390
340    IF FNA(0) > = 2 THEN 360
350    GOTO 300
360    Z = 0
365    K = 0
370    PRINT "I CHECK"
380    GOTO 465
390    IF U < = 16 THEN 420
400    Z = 2
410    IF FNA(0) > = 1 THEN 430
420    Z = 35
430    V = Z + FNA(0)
440    GOSUB 3130
450    PRINT "I OPEN WITH" V
460    K = V
465    GOSUB 2700
470    GOSUB 490
480    GOTO 630
490    IF I <> 3 THEN 580
500    PRINT: PRINT "I WIN"
510    C = C + P
520    PRINT "NOW I HAVE $ "C" AND YOU HAVE $" S
530    PRINT "DO YOU WISH TO CONTINUE";
540    INPUT H$
550    IF H$ = "YES" THEN 95
560    IF H$ = "NO" THEN 3750
570    GOTO 530
580    IF I <> 4 THEN 620
590    PRINT: PRINT "YOU WIN"
600    S = S + P
610    GOTO 520
620    RETURN
630    PRINT: PRINT "NOW WE DRAW. HOW MANY CARDS DO YOU WANT?";
640    INPUT T
650    IF T = 0 THEN 780
660    Z = 10
670    IF T < 4 THEN 700
680    PRINT "YOU CAN'T DRAW MORE THAN THREE CARDS"
690    GOTO 640
700    PRINT "WHAT ARE THEIR NUMBERS?"
710    FOR Q = 1 TO T
720    INPUT U
730    GOSUB 1450
740    NEXT Q
750    PRINT "YOUR NEW HAND:"
760    N = 1
770    GOSUB 1580
780    Z = 10 + T
790    FOR U = 6 TO 10
800    IF INT(X/10↑(U-6)) <> 10*INT(X/10↑(U-5)) THEN 820
810    GOSUB 1450
820    NEXT U
830    PRINT: PRINT "I AM TAKING" Z - 10 - T "CARD";
```

```
 840    IF Z = 11 + T THEN 860
 850    PRINT "S": PRINT: GOTO 860
 860    N = 6: V = I: I = 1
 870    GOSUB 1830
 880    B = U: M = D
 890    IF V <> 7 THEN 920
 900    Z = 28
 910    GOTO 1060
 920    IF I <> 6 THEN 950
 930    Z = 1
 940    GOTO 1060
 950    IF U > = 13 THEN 1000
 960    Z = 2
 970    IF FNA(0) <> 6 THEN 990
 980    Z = 19
 990    GOTO 1060
1000    IF U > = 16 THEN 1050
1010    Z = 19
1020    IF FNA(0) <> 8 THEN 1040
1030    Z = 11
1040    GOTO 1060
1050    Z = 2
1060    K = 0
1070    GOSUB 2700
1080    IF T <> .5 THEN 1170
1090    IF V = 7 THEN 1130
1100    IF I <> 6 THEN 1130
1110    PRINT "I'LL CHECK"
1120    GOTO 1180
1130    V = 2 + FNA(0)
1140    GOSUB 3130
1150    PRINT "I BET" V
1160    K = V: GOSUB 2710
1170    GOSUB 490
1180    PRINT: PRINT "NOW WE COMPARE HANDS"
1190    J$ = H$
1200    K$ = I$
1210    PRINT "MY HAND:"
1220    N = 6
1230    GOSUB 1580
1240    N = 1
1250    GOSUB 1830
1260    PRINT: PRINT "YOU HAVE";
1270    K = D
1280    GOSUB 3360
1290    H$ = J$
1300    I$ = K$
1310    K = M
1320    PRINT "AND I HAVE";
1330    GOSUB 3360
1340    IF B > U THEN 500
1350    IF U > B THEN 590
1360    IF H$ = "A FLUSH" THEN 1420
1370    IF FNB(M) < FNB(D) THEN 590
1380    IF FNB(M) > FNB(D) THEN 500
1390    PRINT "THE HAND IS DRAWN"
1400    PRINT "ALL $" P "REMAINS IN THE POT"
1410    GOTO 100
1420    IF FNB(M) > FNB(D) THEN 500
1430    IF FNB(D) > FNB(M) THEN 590
```

```
1440    GOTO 1390
1450    Z = Z + 1
1460    A(Z) = 100 * INT(4*RND(1)) + INT(100*RND(1))
1470    IF INT(A(Z)/100) > 3 THEN 1460
1480    IF A(Z) - 100 * INT(A(Z)/100) > 12 THEN 1460
1490    IF Z = 1 THEN 1570
1500    FOR K = 1 TO Z - 1
1510    IF A(Z) = A(K) THEN 1460
1520    NEXT K
1530    IF Z < = 10 THEN 1570
1540    N = A(U)
1550    A(U) = A(Z)
1560    A(Z) = N
1570    RETURN
1580    FOR Z = N TO N + 4
1590    PRINT Z "--    ";
1600    GOSUB 1660
1610    PRINT "OF";
1620    GOSUB 1750
1630    IF Z/2 <> INT(Z/2) THEN 1640
1640    PRINT: NEXT Z: PRINT
1650    RETURN
1660    K = FNB(A(Z))
1670    IF K <> 9 THEN 1690
1680    PRINT "JACK";
1690    IF K <> 10 THEN 1700: PRINT "QUEEN";
1700    IF K <> 11 THEN 1710: PRINT "KING";
1710    IF K <> 12 THEN 1720: PRINT "ACE";
1720    IF K > = 9 THEN 1740
1730    PRINT K+2;
1740    RETURN
1750    K = INT(A(Z)/100)
1760    IF K <> 0 THEN 1780
1770    PRINT "CLUBS",
1780    IF K <> 1 THEN 1800
1790    PRINT "DIAMONDS",
1800    IF K <> 2 THEN 1810: PRINT "HEARTS",
1810    IF K <> 3 THEN 1820: PRINT "SPADES",
1820    RETURN
1830    U = 0
1840    FOR Z = N TO N+4
1850    B(Z) = FNB(A(Z))
1860    IF Z = N+4 THEN 1890
1870    IF INT(A(Z)/100) <> INT(A(Z+1)/100) THEN 1890
1880    U = U+1
1890    NEXT Z
1900    IF U <> 4 THEN 1970
1910    X = 11111
1920    D = A(N)
1930    H$ = "A FLUS"
1940    I$ = "H IN"
1950    U = 15
1960    RETURN
1970    FOR Z = N TO N+3
1980    FOR K = Z+1 TO N+4
1990    IF B(Z) < = B(K) THEN 2050
2000    X = A(Z)
2010    A(Z) = A(K)
2020    B(Z) = B(K)
2030    A(K) = X
```

```
2040    B(K) = A(K) - 100 * INT(A(K)/100)
2050    NEXT K
2060    NEXT Z
2070    X = 0
2080    FOR Z = N TO N+3
2090    IF B(Z) <> B(Z+1) THEN 2130
2100    X = X + 11 * 10↑(Z - N)
2110    D = A(Z)
2120    GOSUB 2420
2130    NEXT Z
2140    IF X <> 0 THEN 2280
2150    IF B(N) + 3 <> B(N+3) THEN 2180
2160    X = 1111
2170    U = 10
2180    IF B(N+1) + 3 <> B(N+4) THEN 2280
2190    IF U <> 10 THEN 2260
2200    U = 14
2210    H$ = "STRAIG"
2220    I$ = "HT"
2230    X = 11111
2240    D = A(N+4)
2250    RETURN
2260    U = 10
2270    X = 11110
2280    IF U > = 10 THEN 2350
2290    D = A(N+4)
2300    H$ = "SCHMAL"
2310    I$ = "TZ,"
2320    U = 9
2330    X = 11000
2340    GOTO 2400
2350    IF U <> 10 THEN 2380
2360    IF I = 1 THEN 2400
2370    GOTO 2410
2380    IF U > 12 THEN 2410
2390    IF FNB(D) > 6 THEN 2410
2400    I = 6
2410    RETURN
2420    IF U > = 11 THEN 2470
2430    U = 11
2440    H$ = "A PAIR"
2450    I$ = "OF"
2460    RETURN
2470    IF U <> 11 THEN 2570
2480    IF B(Z) <> B(Z-1) THEN 2530
2490    H$ = "THREE"
2500    I$ = "   "
2510    U = 13
2520    RETURN
2530    H$ = "TWO P"
2540    I$ = "AIR,"
2550    V = 12
2560    RETURN
2570    IF U > 12 THEN 2620
2580    U = 16
2590    H$ = "FULL H"
2600    I$ = "OUSE,"
2610    RETURN
2620    IF B(Z) <> B(Z-1) THEN 2670
2630    U = 17
```

```
2640   H$ = "FOUR"
2650   I$ = "    "
2660   RETURN
2670   U = 16
2680   H$ = "FULL H": I$ = "OUSE,"
2690   RETURN
2700   G = 0
2710   PRINT "WHAT IS YOUR BET?";
2720   INPUT T
2730   IF T - INT(T) = 0 THEN 2790
2740   IF K <> 0 THEN 2770
2750   IF G <> 0 THEN 2770
2760   IF T = .5 THEN 3060
2770   PRINT "NO SMALL CHANGE, PLEASE"
2780   GOTO 2710
2790   IF S-G-T >=0 THEN 2820
2800   GOSUB 3490
2810   GOTO 2710
2820   IF T <> 0 THEN 2850
2830   I = 3
2840   GOTO 3030
2850   IF G+T > = K THEN 2880
2860   PRINT "IF YOU CAN'T SEE MY BET, THEN FOLD"
2870   GOTO 2710
2880   G = G+T
2890   IF G = K THEN 3030
2900   IF Z <> 1 THEN 3070
2910   IF G > 5 THEN 2950
2920   IF Z > = 2 THEN 3000
2930   V = 5
2940   GOTO 3070
2950   IF Z = 1 THEN 2970
2960   IF T < = 25 THEN 3000
2970   I = 4
2980   PRINT "I FOLD"
2990   RETURN
3000   IF Z = 2 THEN 3080
3010   PRINT "I'LL SEE YOU"
3020   K = G
3030   S = S-G
3040   C = C-K
3050   P = P+G+K
3060   RETURN
3070   IF G > 3*Z THEN 3000
3080   V = G-K + FNA(0)
3090   GOSUB 3130
3100   PRINT "I'LL SEE YOU, AND RAISE YOU" V
3110   K = G+V
3120   GOTO 2710
3130   IF C-G-V > = 0 THEN 3330
3140   IF G <> 0 THEN 3170
3150   V = C
3160   RETURN
3170   IF C-G > = 0 THEN 3010
3180   IF (O/2) <> INT(O/2) THEN 3260
3190   PRINT "WOULD YOU LIKE TO BUY BACK YOUR SHIRT?";
3200   PRINT "AND COAT FOR $50?";
3210   INPUT J$
3220   IF J$ = "NO" THEN 3260
3230   C = C+50
```

```
3240    O = O/2
3250    RETURN
3260    IF O/3 <> INT(O/3) THEN 3340
3270    PRINT "WOULD YOU LIKE TO BUY BACK YOUR GOLD";
3280    PRINT "CHAIN FOR $50?";
3290    INPUT J$
3300    IF J$ = "NO" THEN 3340
3310    C = C + 50
3320    O = O/3
3330    RETURN
3340    PRINT "I'M BUSTED. CONGRATULATIONS!"
3350    STOP
3360    PRINT H$; I$;
3370    IF H$ <> "A FLUS" THEN 3410
3380    K = INT(K/100)
3390    GOSUB 1760
3400    PRINT: RETURN
3410    K = FNB(K)
3420    GOSUB 1670
3430    IF H$ = "SCHMAL" THEN 3450
3440    IF H$ <> "STRAIG" THEN 3470
3450    PRINT "HIGH"
3460    RETURN
3470    PRINT "S"
3480    RETURN
3490    PRINT: PRINT "YOU CAN'T BET WHAT YOU DON'T HAVE"
3500    IF O/2 = IN(O/2) THEN 3620
3510    PRINT "WOULD YOU LIKE TO SELL YOUR SHIRT AND COAT?";
3520    INPUT J$
3530    IF J$ = "NO" THEN 3620
3540    IF FNA(0) > = 7 THEN 3580
3550    PRINT "I WILL GIVE YOU $75 FOR IT"
3560    S = S + 75
3570    GOTO 3600
3580    PRINT "THIS COAT LOOKS MOTHEATEN - I'LL GIVE YOU $25"
3590    S = S + 25
3600    O = O*2
3610    RETURN
3620    IF O/3 <> INT(O/3) THEN 3740
3630    PRINT "WILL YOU PART WITH YOUR GOLD CHAIN?";
3640    INPUT J$
3650    IF J$ = "NO" THEN 3730
3660    IF FNA(0) > = 6 THEN 3700
3670    PRINT "YOU ARE NOW $100 RICHER"
3680    S = S + 100
3690    GOTO 3720
3700    PRINT "THIS IS ROLLED GOLD. $25"
3710    S = S + 25
3720    O = O*3
3730    RETURN
3740    PRINT: PRINT "YOU'RE BUSTED.  HAVE A REVOLVER"
3750    END
```

● PROBLEM 21-3

Using APL, simulate the game of craps.

Solution: First of all, let us describe how the game of
craps is played: A player rolls two dice. If the sum of

the two faces on the first throw is 7 or 11, he wins the a-
mount bet. If the sum turns up to be a 4, 5, 6, 8, 9 or 10,
the player continues to roll until he obtains (1) a 7 in
which case he loses, or (2) the sum he obtained on the first
throw; in this case he wins. Our APL program for craps is:

```
        ∇CRAPS

[1]             A ← ι0
[2]     AGAIN: A ← A, B ← +/?2ρ6
[3]             → (((1 = ρA) ∧ ∿ B ε 7 11 2 3 12) ∨ (1 ≠ ρA)
                ∧ ∿ B ε (A[1],7))/AGAIN
[4]             → (((1 = ρA) ∧ B ε 7 11)∨(1 ≠ ρA) ∧ B
                = A[1])/WIN
[5]             'YOU LOSE WITH'; A
[6]             → 0
[7]     WIN: 'YOU WIN WITH'; A
[8]             ∇
```

In step [1] we intialize the vector A to be the null vector. In [2] we find the sum of two random numbers. The
random numbers are positive integers between 1 and 6. We
catenate all sums in the vector A. Step [3] checks two
things: (1) whether it was the first roll and if the roll
automatically gave you a win (7 or 11) or a loss (2, 3,
12), (2) whether you rolled more than once, and if the
last roll gave you a 7 (loss) or the same sum as the one
obtained on the first throw (win). If you do not win or
lose in step [3] you must roll again (go to step 2). In
step 4: If you won, you are sent to step 7, where it is
printed out that you win and vector A is also printed out.
If you do not win, step [5] will indicate that you are a
loser.

● **PROBLEM 21-4**

Write a Fortran program to calculate the odds of winning in a
game of craps.

Solution: Craps is played with a pair of dice. The rules
are as follows:

1) If, on his first throw a player throws a 7 or 11 he wins
   the bet.
2) If, on his first throw, a player throws a 2, 3, or 12 he
   loses the bet.
3) If, on his first throw, a player throws any of the remaining points he continues to throw:
   a) If he obtains the same score as on the first throw
      before throwing a 7, he wins.
   b) If he throws a 7 before obtaining the same score as
      on the first throw, he loses.

   The program is written using a function to generate random numbers arising out of a uniform distribution on]0,1[.
   Once the random number generator has been created, another function subprogram uses it to obtain two random numbers between zero and 1. These represent the throw of the
dice as follows:

X∈	[0,1/6]	(1/6,2/6]	(2/6,3/6]	(3/6,4/6]	(4/6,5/6]	(5/6,1]
V(x)	1	2	3	4	5	6

Thus X = .45820000 corresponds to a spot value of 3. A single throw of the dice is obtained by adding the two functional values of X. Finally, one sequence of throws resulting in either a win or a loss will be done by a third function subprogram.

In the program, note the following:

1) The number of games is G.
2) The seed for the random number generator is KSEED.

```
10   READ(5,100)G, KSEED, IOUT
     WRITE(6,200)G, KSEED
     X = XRAND(KSEED)
C    GENERATE G RANDOM PLAYS
      KSUM = 0
      DO 15 I = 1,G
       K = KSCORE(0)
      KSUM = KSUM + K
     IF (IOUT. EQ. 1) WRITE(6,300)I, K
15   CONTINUE
C    CALCULATE FINAL PERCENTAGE OF WINS
      XNUM = FLOAT(KSUM)
      XDENOM = FLOAT(G)
      FRACT = XNUM/XDENOM
      WRITE(6,400)G, FRACT
100    FORMAT(3I10)
200    FORMAT(41H1 COMPUTER SIMULATION OF
     1 A GAME OF CRAPS/,25H0 SIMULATION
     2 BASED UPON, I5, 13H RANDOM PLAYS/,
     3 9H0 KSEED =, I10//)
300    FORMAT(10X, 2HI =, I5, 10X, 7HKSCORE =
     1 I1)
400    FORMAT(32H0 THE PERCENTAGE OF WINS
     1 AFTER, I5, 10H PLAYS IS, F8.6)
      GO TO 10
      END


      FUNCTION KSCORE(KSEED)
C   THIS SUBPROGRAM GENERATES THE OUTCOME OF
C   ONE PLAY OF CRAPS.  KSCORE = 0 IMPLIES A
C   LOSS AND KSCORE = 1 IMPLIES A WIN.
     K = KTOSS(KSEED)
     IF((K.EQ.7).OR.(K.EQ.11)) GO TO 2
     IF((K.EQ.2).OR.(K.EQ.3).OR.(K.EQ.12)) GO TO 3
C   IF K DOES NOT EQUAL 2, 3, 12, 7 OR 11,
C   THE PLAY CONTINUES
      G = K
10 K = KTOSS(KSEED)
    IF(K.EQ.G) GO TO 2
    IF(K.EQ.7) GO TO 3
     GO TO 10
 2 KSCORE = 1
    RETURN
 3 KSCORE = 0
    RETURN
    END
```

```
      FUNCTION KTOSS(KSEED)
C   THIS FUNCTION GENERATES THE OUTCOME OF A
C   RANDOM TOSS OF TWO DICE
      KTOSS = 0
      DO 10 I = 1,2
      X = XRAND(KSEED)
      IF(X.GT. 0.1666667) GO TO 1
      KTOSS = KTOSS + 1
      GO TO 10
      IF(X.GT. 0.33333333) GO TO 2
      KTOSS = KTOSS + 2
      GO TO 10
    2 IF(X.GT. 0.5) GO TO 3
      KTOSS = KTOSS + 3
      GO TO 10
    3 IF(X.GT. 0.6666667) GO TO 4
      KTOSS = KTOSS + 4
      GO TO 10
    4 IF(X.GT. 0.8333333) GO TO 5
      KTOSS = KTOSS + 5
      GO TO 10
    5 KTOSS = KTOSS + 6
   10 CONTINUE
      RETURN
      END

      FUNCTION XRAND(KX)
C   THIS FUNCTION GENERATES A UNIFORMLY
C   DISTRIBUTED RANDOM NUMBER BETWEEN ZERO
C   AND ONE.
      IF(KX. GT. 0) IX = KX
      IY = 65539 *IX
      IF(IY.LT.0) IY = IY + 2147483647 + 1
      XRAND = .4656613E - 9*FLOAT(IY)
      IX = IY
      RETURN
      END
```

● **PROBLEM** 21-5

Design a program to play a simple game of solitaire. The game should begin with a deal of nine cards, face up. If any two have the same face value, they are covered with two new cards, also face up. This step is repeated until the deck has been exhausted, except for one card. If this occurs, the dealer wins. If there are no more pairs showing, the dealer loses. The program should determine an approximation to the probability of winning.

Solution: To start, we must decide upon how the individual cards are to be represented. We will use an array of 52 components, the numbers 1, 2, 3, ... representing the Ace, two, three, ... of spades, and the numbers 14, 15, 16, ... representing the Ace, two, three, ... of hearts, and so on. To determine the suit of a particular card, the expression [(CARD(I)-1)/13] can be used; a quotient of 0 means spades, a 1 means hearts, and so on. We may find the face value of a particular card via the expression [CARD(I)-13×IS], where IS is the suit. If this expression equals, say, 11, the card

692

is a Jack.   (Brackets signify the integer part of the expressions.)

To shuffle the deck, we can use "pseudo-pointers." Start by filling the array CARD with the integers 1 through 52.   Then, fill another array, RANPTR, with random digits between 1 and 52, including duplicates.   Then the shuffling consists of making interchanges, such as CARD (1) with CARD (RANPTR(1)), CARD (2) with CARD(RANPTR(2)), etc.   You can generate a new set of random digits for each game to re-shuffle the deck.

The program is presented below.   Comments explain some of the major control sections.   The probabilities outputted at the end are meaningful only if a sufficient number of games are played.   Play 25 games and see what outcomes you get.

```
      INTEGER RANPTR, CARD, PILE, CHOICE
      DIMENSION PILE(52), CARD(52), RANPTR(52)
      DO 10 N = 1,52
      CARD(N) = N
10    CONTINUE
C     GENERATE RANDOM NUMBERS TO SHUFFLE DECK
12    DO 15 J = 1,52
      RANPTR(J) = INT(52*RANDOM(X) + 1)
      ITEMP = CARD(J)
      CARD(J) = CARD(RANPTR(J))
      CARD(RANPTR(J)) = ITEMP
15    CONTINUE
C     TYPE PLAY IF YOU WISH TO CONTINUE
20    READ (5,100) CHOICE
100   FORMAT(A5)
      IF(CHOICE.NE.'PLAY') GO TO 95
      I = 1
C     REPEAT UNTIL I IS GREATER THAN 9
21    CONTINUE
      PILE(I) = CARD(I)
      I = I + 1
      IF(I.LE.9) GO TO 21
25    K = 1
26    L = K + 1
28    IF(PILE(K).NE.PILE(L)) GO TO 30
C     THEN DEAL TWO CARDS TO COVER PAIR
      PILE(K) = CARD(I)
      PILE(L) = CARD(I + 1)
      I = I + 2
      IF(I.LT.51) GO TO 25
      NGAME = NGAME + 1
      NWIN = NWIN + 1
      WRITE(5,101)
101   FORMAT(1X, 'DEALER WINS!')
      GO TO 12
C     CHECK ALL VALUES OF K AND L
      L = L + 1
      IF(L.LE.9) GO TO 28
      K = K + 1
      IF(K.LE.8) GO TO 26
      NGAME = NGAME + 1
      NLOSS = NLOSS + 1
      WRITE(5,102)
102   FORMAT(1X, 'SORRY, DEALER LOSES.')
      GO TO 12
```

```
 95    PWIN = FLOAT(NWIN)/FLOAT(NGAME)
       PLOSS = FLOAT(NLOSS)/FLOAT(NGAME)
       WRITE(5,103) NGAME, PWIN
103    FORMAT(1X, 'PROBABILITY OF WINNING AFTER',
     1I5, 'GAMES IS', F5.4)
       WRITE(5,104) PLOSS
104    FORMAT(1X, 'PROBABILITY OF LOSING IS', F5.4)
       STOP
       END
```

LOGIC

Write a Basic program that allows a player to play Tic-Tac-Toe with a computer.

Solution: The game board is numbered

$$1 \quad 2 \quad 3$$

$$4 \quad 5 \quad 6$$

$$7 \quad 8 \quad 9$$

The program is as follows:

```
  5    PRINT TAB(30); "TIC TAC TOE"
 10    REM THE MACHINE PLAYS FIRST
 20    PRINT "THE GAME BOARD IS NUMBERED:": PRINT
 30    PRINT "1 2 3": PRINT "4 5 6": PRINT "7 8 9"
 40    DEF FNT(X) = X - 8 * INT((X-1)/8)
 50    REM MAIN PROGRAM FOLLOWS
 60    A = 9
 70    T = A
 80    GOSUB 460
 90    P = T
100    B = FNT(P+1)
110    T = B
120    GOSUB 460
130    Q = T
140    IF Q = FNT(B+4) THEN 190
150    C = FNT(B+4)
160    T = C
170    GOSUB 500
180    GOTO 520
190    C = FNT(B+2)
200    T = C
210    GOSUB 460
220    R = T
230    IF R = FNT(C+4) THEN 280
240    D = FNT(C+4)
250    T = D
260    GOSUB 500
270    GOTO 520
280    IF P/2 <> INT(P/2) THEN 330
290    D = FNT(C+7)
300    T = D
```

```
310   GOSUB 500
320   GOTO 520
330   D = FNT(C+3)
340   T = D
350   GOSUB 460
360   S = T
370   IF S = FNT(D+4) THEN 410
380   E = FNT(D+4)
390   T = E
400   GOSUB 500
410   E = FNT(D+6)
420   T = E
430   GOSUB 500
440   PRINT "THE GAME IS A DRAW"
450   GOTO 60
460   GOSUB 500
470   PRINT "YOUR MOVE"
480   INPUT T
490   RETURN
500   PRINT "COMPUTER MOVES"; T
510   RETURN
520   PRINT "AND WINS *****"
530   GOTO 60
540   END
```

● **PROBLEM** 21-7

The game of Reverse is played as follows: A list of numbers
(1 through 9) is given. The object is to arrange the numbers
in ascending order. A move is made by specifying how many
numbers (starting from the left) are to be placed in reverse
order. For example, suppose 214356789 is the starting position. Then "reverse 2" gives 124356789. "Reverse 5" gives
534126789. Write a Basic program to play Reverse with the
computer.

Solution: There are two approaches to the game - one algorithmic, and the other heuristic. The algorithmic solution
guarantees a win in a certain number of moves (if there are
N numbers, it takes 2N - 3 moves). The heuristic method
takes advantage of the information at any moment to improve
the strategy for minimizing the number of moves. The player
decides which method to pursue. Here is the program for this
game:

```
  5   PRINT "REVERSE - A GAME OF SKILL"
 10   DIM A(20)
 20   REM                N = NUMBER OF NUMBERS
 30   N = 9
 40   REM             MAKE A RANDOM LIST A(1) TO A(N)
 50   A(1) = INT((N-1)*RND(1) + 2)
 60   FOR K = 2 TO N
 70   A(K) = INT(N*RND(1) + 1)
 80   FOR J = 1 TO K -1
 90   IF A(K) = A(J) THEN 70
100   NEXT J
110   NEXT K
120   REM PRINT ORIGINAL LIST AND START GAME
130   PRINT "THE LIST IS:"
```

```
140   T = 0
150   GOSUB 430
160   PRINT "HOW MANY TO BE REVERSED?"
170   INPUT R
180   IF R = 0 THEN 370
190   IF R < = N THEN 240
200   REM THE COMPUTER CANNOT REVERSE MORE THAN
210   REM N NUMBERS
220   PRINT "TOO MANY. I CAN REVERSE AT MOST";N
230   GOTO 160
240   T = T + 1
250   REM REVERSE R NUMBERS AND PRINT NEW LIST
260   FOR K = 1 TO INT(R/2)
270   Z = A(K)
280   A(K) = A(R-K+1)
290   A(R-K+1) = Z
300   NEXT K
310   GOSUB 430
320   REM CHECK FOR A WIN
330   FOR K = 1 TO N
340   IF A(K) <> K THEN 160
350   NEXT K
360   PRINT "YOU WON IT IN"; T; "MOVES!"
370   PRINT "TRY AGAIN (YES OR NO)";
380   INPUT A$
390   IF A$ = "YES" THEN 50
400   PRINT "GOOD GAME, THANKS."
410   GOTO 470
420   REM SUBROUTINE TO PRINT LIST
430   FOR K = 1 TO N
440   PRINT A(K)
450   NEXT K
460   RETURN
470   END
```

● **PROBLEM** 21-8

Write a Basic program to solve the following puzzle: A and
B are the players. A tells B to pick a number between 1 and
100. He then asks B to tell him the remainders when the
secret chosen number is divided successively by 3, 5 and 7.
A then tells B the number he originally chose.

Solution: The game is centered on the notion of congruence.
Let x be the unknown number chosen by B, $1 \leq x \leq 100$. Now x
divided by 3 can give a remainder of 0, 1 or 2. The numbers
between 1 and 100 can be arranged in three sets

$$S_0 = \{3,6,9,\ldots,90,93,96,99\}$$
$$S_1 = \{1,4,7,\ldots,94,97,100\}$$
$$S_2 = \{2,5,8,\ldots,92,95,98\}$$

Note that $\{S_0,S_1,S_2\}$ forms a partition of 1 - 100.

Similarly, on division by 5, the possible remainders
0,1,2,3,4 give rise to the disjoint sets

$$S_0 = \{ \ ,5,10,\ldots,90,95,100\}$$
$$S_1 = \{1,6,11,\ldots,91,96\}$$
$$S_2 = \{2,7,12,\ldots,92,97\}$$
$$S_3 = \{3,8,13,\ldots,93,98\}$$
$$S_4 = \{4,9,14,\ldots,94,99\}$$

Finally division by 7 yields the following

Sets:
$$S_0 = \{7,14,\ldots,91,98\}$$
$$S_1 = \{1,8,15,\ldots,92,99\} \qquad S_2 = \{2,9,16,\ldots,93,100\}$$
$$S_3 = \{3,10,17,\ldots,87,94\} \qquad S_4 = \{4,11,\ldots,88,95\}$$
$$S_5 = \{5,12,\ldots,89,96\} \qquad S_6 = \{6,13,\ldots,90,97\}.$$

To be concrete, suppose x = 41. Then the remainders are 2,1, 6 when 41 is divided by 3,5 and 7 respectively. Thus, x = 41 lies in $S_2 = \{2,5,8,\ldots,95,98\}$ $S_1 = \{1,6,11,\ldots,91,96\}$ and $S_6 = \{6,13,\ldots,90,97\}$. In fact, 41 is the only number that simultaneously lies in these three sets!

Now memorizing the above sets is one way of mastering this puzzle but fortunately, a much simpler algorithm exists. It uses the fact that $3 \times 5 \times 7 = 105$. Let the secret number be x and let A, B, C be the remainders. Then

$$x \equiv D = 70A + 21B + 15C \quad (\text{mod } 105) \tag{1}$$

Thus, for x = 41, 70(2) + 21(1) + 15(6) = 140 + 21 + 90 = 251. But we need $x \le 100$. Note that 251 - 105 = 146 and 146 - 105 = 41. Thus, 251 when divided by an integral multiple of 105 leaves a remainder of 41. We say 251 is congruent to 41 modulo 105 and write $41 \equiv 251 \ (\text{mod } 105)$.

The program follows:

```
10    PRINT "THINK OF A NUMBER BETWEEN 1 and 100."
20    PRINT "YOUR NUMBER DIVIDED BY 3 HAS A REMAINDER OF";
30    INPUT A
40    PRINT "YOUR NUMBER DIVIDED BY 5 HAS A REMAINDER OF";
50    INPUT B
60    PRINT "YOUR NUMBER DIVIDED BY 7 HAS A REMAINDER OF";
70    INPUT C
80    D = 70*A + 21*B + 15*C
90    IF D < = 105 THEN 120
100   D = D - 105
110   GOTO 90
120   PRINT "YOUR NUMBER WAS"; D;", RIGHT?";
130   INPUT A$
140   IF A$ = "YES" THEN 170
150   REM SOMETIMES HUMANS MAKE ERRORS
160   IF A$ = "NO" THEN 190
165   PRINT "VERY FUNNY! NOW TRY 'YES' OR 'NO'."
166   GO TO 120
170   PRINT "HAL HAS SPOKEN TRULY"
180   GOTO 200
190   PRINT "CHECK YOUR ARITHMETIC"
200   PRINT "LET'S TRY AGAIN."
210   GOTO 10
220   END
```

Design a computer program to play Hexapawn. What is unusual
about this program?

Solution: Hexapawn is played on a 3 × 3 chess board. There
are six pieces - three white pawns and three black pawns.
The movements of the pawns are the same as in chess. The
initial position is

B	B	B
W	W	W

The object of the game is to get a passed pawn i.e. a pawn
on the enemy's last rank. The first one to obtain a passed
pawn (i.e. to place his pawn to any starting position of his
opponent's pawns) wins. Alternatively, if no more moves are
possible, (the position is totally blocked), then the person
who made the last move is the winner. The squares are numbered as follows:

$$1 \quad 2 \quad 3$$
$$4 \quad 5 \quad 6$$
$$7 \quad 8 \quad 9$$

The program for Hexapawn is an application of cybernetics.
The computer records every unfamiliar position in its memory
including all the moves that follow. Now assume that the
computer loses a game. It erases the move that led to defeat. As an example:

B			Computer
	W	B	
W			You

Here, with the computer to move, it could win by playing 6
to 9 (or even 1 to 5). However, if it plays 1 to 4 then you
can win by moving 5 to 2. If this same position occurs in
another game, the computer (assuming it played the losing
move in the first game) will not even consider 1 to 4 but
will play 6 to 9 or 1 to 5 instead. The computer has learned from the first game.

   If the computer gets a position from which all moves
have been deleted (they all led to defeat) it erases the
move that got it there and resigns. In this way it saves
only winning sequences of moves. If it plays long enough
and encounters a great variety of unfamiliar positions it
will become unbeatable. Note that this method of "learning"
cannot be used to create an unbeatable program in chess. The
number of different positions in chess is of astronomical order
and the chances of a computer encountering an exactly similar
position twice are vanishingly small (apart from the opening

and elementary end-game positions). Thus the program would
have to be modified with strategical concepts and evaluation of
pieces.

```
10    PRINT "HEXAPAWN"
20    DIM B(19,9) M(19,4), S(9), P$(3)
30    W = 0: L = 0
40    DEF FNR(X) = -3*(X=1) - (X=3) - 4*(X=6) - 6*(X=4) -
      7*(X=9) - 9*(X=7) + FNS(X)
60    DEF FNS(X) = -X*(X=2 OR X=5 OR X=8)
70    DEF FNM(Y) = Y - INT(Y/10)*10
80    P$ = "X•O"
90    FOR I=1 TO 19: FOR J=1 TO 9: READ B(I,J): NEXT J:
      NEXT I
100   FOR I=1 TO 19: FOR J=1 TO 4: READ M(I,J): NEXT J: NEXT
      I
110   X = 0: Y = 0
120   S(4) = 0: S(5) = 0: S(6) = 0
130   S(1) = -1: S(2) = -1: S(3) = -1
140   S(7) = 1: S(8) = 1: S(9) = 1
150   GOSUB 1200
160   PRINT "YOUR MOVE";
170   INPUT M1,M2
180   IF M1 = INT(M1) AND M2 = INT(M2) AND M1 > 0 AND M1 < 10
      AND M2 > 0 AND M2 < 10 THEN 220
200   PRINT "ILLEGAL COORDINATES".
210   GOTO 160
220   IF S(M1) = 1 THEN 240
230   PRINT "ILLEGAL MOVE.": GOTO 160
240   IF S(M2) = 1 THEN 230
250   IF M2-M1 <> -3 AND S(M2) <> -1 THEN 230
260   IF M2 > M1 THEN 230
270   IF M2-M1 = -3 AND (S(M2) <> 0) THEN 230
280   IF M2-M1 < -4 THEN 230
290   IF M1 = 7 AND M2 = 3 THEN 230
300   S(M1) = 0
310   S(M2) = 1
320   GOSUB 1200
330   IF S(1) = 1 OR S(2) = 1 OR S(3) = 1 THEN 960
340   FOR I = 1 TO 9
342   IF S(I) = -1 THEN 348
344   NEXT I
346   GOTO 960
348   FOR I = 1 TO 9
350   IF S(I) <> -1 THEN 420
360   IF S(I+3) = 0 THEN 440
370   IF FNR(I) = I THEN 410
380   IF I > 3 THEN 396
390   IF S(5) = 1 THEN 440
393   GOTO 420
396   IF S(8) = 1 THEN 440
400   GOTO 420
410   IF S(I+2) = 1 OR S(I+4) = 1 THEN 440
420   NEXT I
430   GOTO 960
440   FOR I = 1 TO 19
450   FOR J = 1 TO 3
460   FOR K = 3 TO 1 STEP -1
470   T((J-1)*3+K) = B(I,(J-1)*3+4-K)
480   NEXT K
490   NEXT J
```

```
500    FOR J = 1 TO 9
510    IF S(J) <> B(I,J) THEN 542
520    NEXT J
530    R = 0
540    GOTO 590
542    FOR J = 1 TO 9
544    IF S(J) <> T(J) THEN 550
546    NEXT J
548    R = 1
549    GOTO 590
550    NEXT I
560    REM THE TERMINATION OF THIS LOOP IS IMPOSSIBLE
570    PRINT "ILLEGAL BOARD PATTERN."
580    STOP
590    X = I
600    FOR I = 1 TO 4
610    IF M(X,I) <> 0 THEN 650
620    NEXT I
630    PRINT "I RESIGN"
640    GOTO 960
650    Y = INT(RND(1)*4+1)
660    IF M(X,Y) = 0 THEN 650
670    IF R <> 0 THEN 730
680    PRINT "I MOVE FROM"; STR$ (INT(M(X,Y)/10)); "TO";
       STR$(FNM(M(X,Y)))
700    S(INT(M(X,Y)/10)) = 0
710    S(FNM(M(X,Y))) = -1
720    GOTO 770
730    PRINT "I MOVE FROM"; STR$(FNR(INT(M(X,Y)/10))); "TO";
740    PRINT STR$(FNR(FNM(M(X,Y))))
750    S(FNR(INT(M(X,Y)/10))) = 0
760    S(FNR(FNM(M(X,Y)))) = -1
770    GOSUB 1200
780    IF S(7) = -1 OR S(8) = -1 OR S(9) = -1 THEN 1020
790    FOR I = 1 TO 9
800    IF S(I) = 1 THEN 830
810    NEXT I
820    GOTO 1020
830    FOR I = 1 TO 9
840    IF S(I) <> 1 THEN 930
850    IF S(I-3) = 0 THEN 160
860    IF FNR(I) = I THEN 920
870    IF I < 7 THEN 900
880    IF S(5) = -1 THEN 160
890    GOTO 930
900    IF S(2) = -1 THEN 160
910    GOTO 930
920    IF S(I-2) = -1 OR S(I-4) = -1 THEN 160
930    NEXT I
940    PRINT "YOU CAN'T MOVE, SO";
950    GOTO 1020
960    PRINT "YOU WIN"
970    M(X,Y) = 0
980    L = L + 1
990    PRINT "I HAVE WON"; W;" AND YOU"; L;
1000   "OUT OF"; L + W; "GAMES."
1010   PRINT: GOTO 30
1020   PRINT "I WIN"
1030   W = W + 1
1040   GOTO 990
```

```
1050   DATA -1,-1,-1,1,0,0,0,1,1,-1,-1,-1,0,1,0,1,0,1
1060   DATA -1,0,-1,-1,1,0,0,0,1,0,-1,-1,1,-1,0,0,0,1
1070   DATA -1,0,-1,1,1,0,0,1,0,-1,-1,0,1,0,1,0,0,1
1080   DATA 0,-1,-1,0,-1,1,1,0,0,0,-1,-1,-1,1,1,1,0,0
1090   DATA -1,0,-1,-1,0,1,0,1,0,0,-1,-1,0,1,0,0,0,1
1100   DATA 0,-1,-1,0,1,0,1,0,0,-1,0,-1,1,0,0,0,0,1
1110   DATA 0,0,-1,-1,-1,1,0,0,0,-1,0,0,1,1,1,0,0,0
1120   DATA 0,-1,0,-1,1,1,0,0,0,-1,0,0,-1,-1,1,0,0,0
1130   DATA 0,0,-1,-1,1,0,0,0,0,0,-1,0,1,-1,0,0,0,0
1140   DATA -1,0,0,-1,1,0,0,0,0
1150   DATA 24,25,36,0,14,15,36,0,15,35,36,47,36,58,59,0
1160   DATA 15,35,36,0,24,25,26,0,26,57,58,0
1170   DATA 26,35,0,0,47,48,0,0,35,36,0,0,35,36,0,0
1180   DATA 36,0,0,0,47,58,0,0,15,0,0,0
1190   DATA 26,47,0,0,47,58,0,0,35,36,47,0,28,58,0,0,15,47,0,0
1200   PRINT: FOR I = 1 TO 3
1210   FOR J = 1 TO 3
1220   PRINT TAB(10); MID$(P$,S((I-1)*3+J) + 2,1);
1230   NEXT J
1240   PRINT: NEXT I
1250   PRINT
1260   RETURN
1270   END
```

● **PROBLEM** 21-10

Design a program to move a knight around a chessboard so
that in 63 moves, it will have touched each square once on
a regular 8 × 8 chessboard. It is assumed that there are
no other pieces on the board during the movement.

Solution: This is a classical problem first demonstrated by
Leonard Euler in the 18th century. We define this sequence
of moves as a "knight's tour." The length of the tour is
the total number of squares visited, which, including the
starting square, we want to be 64.
    We need an 8 × 8 matrix to represent the chessboard.
The tour begins from position (1,1), and only the characteristic L-shaped move of the knight is allowed.
    We will use what is known as an heuristic strategy.
The major problem in the tour occurs when the knight must
move into the corner positions. To avoid getting trapped,
we define an array of weights to give higher priority to the
squares farthest from the center of the board. Thus, in
Figure 1, we have the array of weights.

7	6	5	4	4	5	6	7
6	5	4	3	3	4	5	6
5	4	3	2	2	3	4	5
4	3	2	1	1	2	3	4
4	3	2	1	1	2	3	4
5	4	3	2	2	3	4	5
6	5	4	3	3	4	5	6
7	6	5	4	4	5	6	7

Figure 1

Notice that when the knight comes closer to the center, it can move in eight possible directions, as shown in Figure 2:

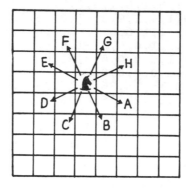

FIG. 2

Each time the knight is to move, we should check each of the potential moves starting from direction A and moving clockwise. After looking at the eight possibilities, we save the positions of the directions having the highest weights. If two possibilities have equal weight, we introduce a random generator to break the tie between them. Of course, the random process means that several tours will have to be attempted before a complete tour is realized.

A successful knight's tour produced by the heuristic method is given in Figure 3:

1	38	3	18	35	40	13	16
4	19	36	39	14	17	34	41
37	2	57	54	59	42	15	12
20	5	62	43	56	53	60	33
49	44	55	58	61	64	11	26
6	21	48	63	52	27	32	29
45	50	23	8	47	30	25	10
22	7	46	51	24	9	28	31

Figure 3

Note that it is not the only possible solution. Other successful tours do exist.

The program requires a 12 × 12 array to create a buffer zone around the board. Then we fill the border rows 1, 2, 11, and 12 with nonzero values, and the board squares are filled with zeros. This is done to insure that no moves go off the board.

A flowchart will help you to visualize the actions taken during execution of the program:

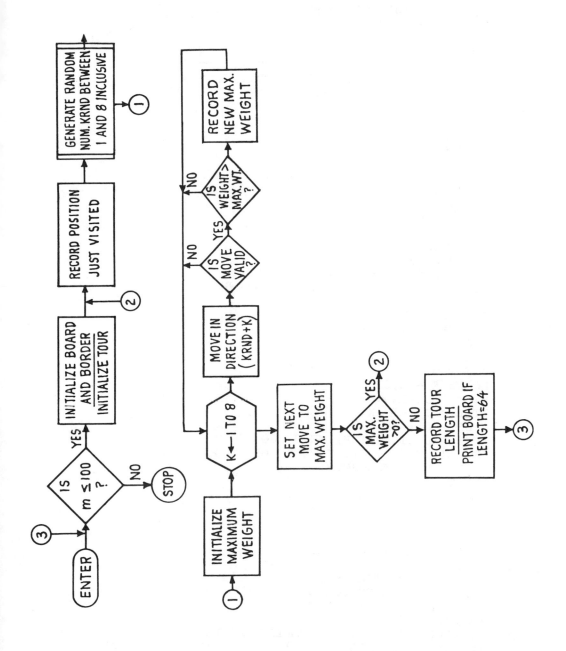

703

```
      INTEGER IM(8), JM(8), BOARD (12,12)
      INTEGER HIST(64), WGT(12,12)
      DATA(IM(K), K = 1,8)/1,2,2,1,-1,-2,-2,-1/
      DATA(JM(K), K = 1,8)/2,1,-1,-2,-2,-1,1,2/
      DATA(HIST(I), I = 1,64)/64*0.0/
      X = 0.5
   C  DO WHILE M < 101
   5  IF (M.GE. 101) GO TO 99
      DO 10 I = 1,12
      DO 15 J = 1,12
      BOARD(I,J) = 0
      IF(I.LT.3. OR. I.GT.10) BOARD(I,J) = 99
      IF(J.LT.3. OR. J.GT.10) BOARD(I,J) = 99
      WGT(I,J) = (IABS(2*I-13) + IABS(2*J-13))/2
  15  CONTINUE
  10  CONTINUE
   C  INITIALIZE TOUR
      ITUR = 3
      JTUR = 3
      N = 0
  20  CONTINUE
      N = N+1
      IF(N.GT.64) GO TO 30
      I = ITUR
      J = JTUR
      BOARD(I,J) = N
   C  NOW CHECK OTHER POSSIBLE MOVES BY
   C  GENERATING A RANDOM INTEGER BETWEEN
   C  1 AND 8 AND MOVE CLOCKWISE
      CALL RAND(X)
      KRND = INT(8.0*X) + 1
      MWGT = 0
      IMWGT = 0
      JMWGT = 0
      DO 25 K = 1,8
      K1 = MOD(KRND+K-2,8) + 1
      ITUR = I + IM(K1)
      JTUR = J + JM(K1)
      IF(BOARD(ITUR,JTUR).NE.0) GO TO 25
      IF(WGT(ITUR,JTUR).LT.MWGT) GO TO 25
      MWGT = WGT(ITUR,JTUR)
      IMWGT = ITUR
      JMWGT = JTUR
  25  CONTINUE
      ITUR = IMWGT
      JTUR = JMWGT
      IF(MWGT.NE.0) GO TO 20
  30  CONTINUE
      HIST(N) = HIST(N) + 1
   C  OUTPUT COMPLETED BOARD
      IF(N.LT.64) GO TO 99
      WRITE(6,100)
 100  FORMAT(7X,'THIS IS A COMPLETED TOUR')
      WRITE(6,101) ((BOARD(I,J), J = 3,10), I = 3,10)
 101  FORMAT(1X,8I4)
      M = M+1
      GO TO 5
  99  CONTINUE
      WRITE(6,102)M
 102  FORMAT(1X,'TOTAL NUMBER OF TRIALS = ',I4)
```

```
      WRITE(6,101)(HIST(I), I = 1,64)
      WRITE(6,103)
103   FORMAT(7X, 'THIS IS THE TABLE OF WEIGHTS')
      WRITE(6,101)((W(I,J), J = 3,10), I = 3,10)
      STOP
      END
```

Write a PL/I program that will simulate the moves of disks
in the Towers of Hanoi Game.

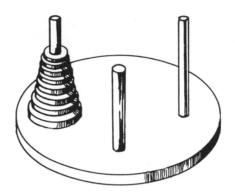

Solution: This is an ancient puzzle, in which there are
three pegs and 64 disks with holes through the center. The
object is to move the entire tower of disks from one peg to
another in the fewest possible numbers of moves. Disks must
always be stacked so that a larger disk is never on top of a
smaller disk. We have chosen a stack of eight disks, which
requires 255 moves, because to move 64 disks, you have to
make 18, 446, 744, 073, 709, 551, 615 moves - a formidable
task even for a computer. In general, 2^n-1 moves are required to transfer the tower to another peg (where n is the number of disks in the tower). The recursively defined solution
in PL/I follows:

```
/* MOVE N DISKS FROM POLE X TO POLE Y.  USE POLE Z TO */
/* STORE DISKS IF NECESSARY */
HANOI: PROCEDURE(X, Y, Z, N) RECURSIVE;
   DECLARE (X, Y, Z, N) FIXED;
   IF N = 1
      THEN PUT SKIP LIST('MOVE DISK FROM',X,'TO',Y);
      ELSE DO;
           CALL HANOI(X, Z, Y, N-1);
           PUT SKIP LIST('MOVE DISK FROM', X, 'TO', Y);
           CALL HANOI(Z, Y, X, N-1);
           END;
   END HANOI;
```

MATRIX MANIPULATION

Write a Basic program for the following computer game: A physicist is trying to locate a sub-atomic particle. Using diffraction theory he obtains information as to where his plotted coordinates are in relation to the particle. For example, suppose the particle is at (11, 9, 32) and the physicist bombards (2, 16, 21). His experimental data then tells him that he is to the North-west and too low.
   The physicist (player) specifies the dimension of the search area and the number of trials allowed before the particle disintegrates without being observed.

Solution: In the program, the dimension of the search area is left variable, as are the number of trials. The directions are given according to the orientation.
(0,0,0) is the origin of the grid and all coordinates are positive.

```
         N
      W ─┼─ E
         S
```

```
 10   PRINT "QUIRKY QUARKS"
 20   INPUT "DIMENSION OF SEARCH AREA"; S: PRINT
 30   N = INT(LOG(S)/LOG(2)) + 1
 40   PRINT "YOU ARE AN EXPERIMENTAL PHYSICIST,";
 50   PRINT "TRYING TO LOCATE A SUB-ATOMIC PARTICLE."
 60   PRINT "YOU HAVE";N;"TRIES. SPECIFY GUESS OF
 70   PRINT "LOCATION WITH A TRIO OF INTEGERS."
 80   A = INT(S*RND(1)): B = INT(S*RND(1)): C = INT(S*RND(1))
 90   FOR D = 1 TO N: PRINT: PRINT "TRIAL #";D;: INPUT X1,X2,
      X3
100   IF ABS(X1-A) + ABS(X2-B) + ABS(X3-C) = 0 THEN 150
110   GOSUB 190: PRINT: NEXT D
120   PRINT: PRINT "PARTICLE HAS DISINTEGRATED.DON RADIATION";
130   PRINT "SUIT"
140   PRINT "THE PARTICLE WAS AT" A;",",B;",";C
150   PRINT: PRINT "YOU FOUND THE PARTICLE IN";D;"TRIES"
160   PRINT: PRINT: INPUT "ANOTHER GAME(Y OR N)";A$
170   IF A$ = "Y" THEN 80
180   PRINT "OK.SEE YOU IN OSLO": GO TO 290
190   PRINT "CALCULATIONS SHOW, THAT YOUR TRY IS";
200   IF X2 > B THEN PRINT "NORTH";
210   IF X2 < B THEN PRINT "SOUTH";
220   IF X1 > A THEN PRINT "EAST";
230   IF X1 < A THEN PRINT "WEST";
240   IF X2 <> B OR X1 <> A THEN PRINT "AND";
250   IF X3 > C THEN PRINT "TOO LOW."
260   IF X3 < C THEN PRINT "TOO HIGH."
270   IF X3 = C THEN PRINT "HEIGHT OK"
280   RETURN
290   END
```

PLOTTING AND PICTURES

Write a computer program in Basic that plays the computer game of LIFE.

Solution: The game of life can be played either manually on a checkerboard square or on a CRT terminal.

The game may be interpreted as a dynamic example of the laws of genetics. The rules of the game are as follows:

1) The game is played on a chessboard (imagined infinite) with counters. An initial distribution of counters is assumed. The pattern of the initial distribution changes according to the number of survivals, deaths and births.
2) Survivals: Every counter with two or more neighboring counters survives for the next generation. Neighbors are defined by the diagram

$$
\begin{array}{|c|c|c|}
\hline
7 & 6 & 5 \\
\hline
8 & C & 4 \\
\hline
1 & 2 & 3 \\
\hline
\end{array}
$$

We see that counter C has eight potential cells on which neighbors may sprout.
3) Deaths: Each counter with four or more neighbors dies (is removed) because of over-population. Every counter with one or no neighbors dies from isolation

Fig. 2

In Fig. 2 the circled counters die from isolation and are removed. The squared counter dies from lack of resources.
4) Births: Each empty cell adjacent to three and only three neighbors is a birth cell. A counter is placed on it on the next move.

◯
X X X

Fig. 3

In Fig. 3 the circled cell will have a counter placed on it in the next generation (move).

Finally, note that births, deaths and survivals constitute a move. The game continues until a stable population is reached (no more births or deaths) or until the population dies out. An oscillating population is also possible. As an example, consider the following part game:

707

```
Initial        X X
Distribution:    X X X
                   X
                   X
Generation 1:  X X
               X X X X
                   X X
                   X

Generation 2:  X X
               X         X X
                 X         X
                         X X

Generation 3:  X X
               X   X X
                     X
                   X X
Generation 4:  X X   X
               X X     X
                   X
```

The program follows:

```
 10    PRINT "LIFE"
 20    PRINT "ENTER YOUR PATTERN.   TYPE 'DONE' WHEN FINISHED."
 30    X1 = 1: Y1 = 1: X2 = 24: Y2 = 70
 40    DIM A(24,70), B$(24)
 50    C = 1
 60    INPUT B$(C)
 70    IF B$(C) = "DONE" THEN B$(C) ="": GO TO 120
 80    IF LEFT $(B$(C),1) ="." THEN B$(C) = "" + RIGHT $(B$(C),
       LEN(B$(C)) - 1)
100    C = C+1
110    GOTO 60
120    C = C-1: L = 0
130    FOR X = 1 TO C-1
140    IF LEN(B$(X)) > L THEN L = LEN(B$(X))
145    REM SEE END OF PROGRAM
150    NEXT X
160    X1 = 11-C/2
170    Y1 = 33-L/2
180    FOR X = 1 TO C
190    FOR Y = 1 TO LEN(B$(X))
200    IF MID$(B$(X),Y,1) <> " " THEN A(X1+X, Y1+Y) = 1: P = P+1
220    NEXT Y
230    NEXT X
240    PRINT: PRINT: PRINT
250    PRINT "GENERATION:";G,  "POPULATION:";P;
260    IF I9 THEN PRINT "INVALID";
270    X3 = 24: Y3 = 70: X4 = 1: Y4 = 1: P = 0
280    G = G+1
290    FOR X = 1 TO X1-1: PRINT: NEXT X
300    FOR X = X1 TO X2
310    FOR Y = Y1 TO Y2
320    IF A(X,Y) = 2 THEN A(X,Y) = 0: GOTO 400
330    IF A(X,Y) = 3 THEN A(X,Y) = 1: GOTO 350
340    IF A(X,Y) <> 1 THEN 400
350    PRINT TAB(Y); "*";
```

708

```
360   IF X < X3 THEN X3 = X
370   IF X > X4 THEN X4 = X
380   IF Y < Y3 THEN Y3 = Y
390   IF Y > Y4 THEN Y4 = Y
400   NEXT Y
410   NEXT X
420   FOR X = X2+1 TO 24: PRINT: NEXT X
430   X1 = X3: X2 = X4: Y1 = Y3: Y2 = Y4
440   IF X1 < 3 THEN X1 = 3: I9 = -1
450   IF X2 > 22 THEN X2 = 22: I9 = -1
460   IF Y1 < 3 THEN Y1 = 3: I9 = -1
470   IF Y2 < 68 THEN Y2 = 68: I9 = -1
480   P = 0
490   FOR X = X1-1 TO X2+1
500   FOR Y = Y1-1 TO Y2+1
510   C = 0
520   FOR I = X-1 TO X+1
530   FOR J = Y-1 TO Y+1
540   IF A(I,J) = 1 OR A(I,J) = 2 THEN C = C+1
550   NEXT J
560   NEXT I
570   IF A(X,Y) = 0 THEN 610
580   IF C < 3 OR C > 4 THEN A(X,Y) = 2: GOTO 600
590   P = P+1
600   GOTO 620
610   IF C = 3 THEN A(X,Y) = 3: P = P+1
620   NEXT Y
630   NEXT X
640   X1 = X1-1: Y1 = Y1-1: X2 = X2+1: Y2 = Y2+1
650   GOTO 250
660   END
```

If your computer does not accept conditional execution,
change it into few simple statements with the same meaning.
For example: 140 IF LEN(B$(X)) > L THEN L = LEN(B$(X)) can
be changed into:

```
140   IF LEN(B$(X)) > L THEN 142
141   GOTO 150
142   L = LEN(B$(X))
```

REMOVE AN OBJECT

● **PROBLEM** 21-14

Consider the following variant of Nim. A pile of N objects is
given. Two players take turns removing 1, 2 or 3 objects
from the pile. The person who has to take the last object,
loses. Write a Basic program which enables you to play this
game with a computer.

Solution: Let us consider 2 players: you and the computer.
The computer loses if it takes the last object. The question
now is: How many objects must you leave to the computer at
its penultimate move to ensure your win? The answer is:
1 + the maximum number of objects always possible to remove
in one move by each you and the computer. This number is 4,

because if the computer removes the minimum possible number of objects (i.e., 1), and you - the maximum (i.e., 3) - that will give you the desired number. So, by leaving the computer with 5 objects at its penultimate move, you ensure your win (providing you do not make a mistake). In fact, if you leave the computer with 1 + 4N (where N = 0,1,2,3...) objects before every move, you guarantee yourself a win by removing (4-A) objects, where "A" is the number of objects removed by the computer. Using this strategy and providing that you move first, you are guaranteed to win every time, except when there are 4N objects in a pile. In that case, by using the same strategy, the computer can beat you.

```
10    PRINT "31 OBJECTS GAME"
20    PRINT "LET'S FLIP A COIN TO SEE WHO GOES FIRST."
25    PRINT "IF IT COMES UP HEADS, I WIN THE TOSS."
30    N = 31
40    Q = INT(2*RND(5))
50    IF Q = 1 THEN 80
60    PRINT "TAILS! YOU GO FIRST"
70    GOTO 140
80    PRINT "HEADS! I GO FIRST"
90    PRINT "I TAKE TWO OBJECTS"
100   N = N-2
110   PRINT "THE NUMBER OF OBJECTS IS NOW" N
120   PRINT "YOUR TURN. YOU MAY TAKE 1,2 OR
130   3 OBJECTS."
140   PRINT "HOW MANY DO YOU WISH TO REMOVE?",
150   INPUT K
160   IF K > 3 THEN 360
170   IF K < = 0 THEN 360
180   N = N-K
190   PRINT "THERE ARE NOW";N;"OBJECTS REMAINING."
200   IF N = 4 THEN 260
210   IF N = 3 THEN 280
220   IF N = 2 THEN 300
230   IF N < = 1 THEN 400
240   Z = 4-K
250   GOTO 320
260   Z = 3
270   GOTO 320
280   Z = 2
290   GOTO 320
300   Z = 1
320   PRINT "MY TURN. I REMOVE" Z "OBJECTS"
330   N = N-Z
340   IF N < = 1 THEN 380
350   GOTO 110
360   PRINT "IMPOSSIBLE. HOW MANY; 1,2 OR 3"
370   GOTO 150
380   PRINT "YOU LOST"
390   GOTO 410
400   PRINT "YOU WERE LUCKY, YOU WON"
410   STOP
420   END
```

Write a program in Basic to play the game of Nim with a computer.

Solution: The traditional game of Nim is played in the following manner: There are four rows of stones arranged as
shown:

```
0                                              (1)
0 0 0                                          (3)
0 0 0 0 0                                      (5)
0 0 0 0 0 0 0                                  (7)
```

Let A and B be the two players. The players play according
to the 3 rules below:

1) On any given turn only objects from one row may be re-
   removed. There is no restriction on which row or on how
   many objects you remove.
2) You cannot skip a move or remove zero objects or remove
   more objects than there are in a row.
3) Opponents take turns removing objects until there are
   none left. The win option should be specified in the
   program.

The program below allows the number of piles to be variable,
the pile sizes to be variable and also the win option to be
either taking the last stone(s) or being left with the last
stone(s).

```
 10    PRINT "THE GAME OF NIM"
 20    DIM A(100), B(100,10), D(2)
 30    PRINT "ENTER WIN OPTION - 1 TO TAKE LAST,
 40    2 TO AVOID LAST";
 50    INPUT W
 60    IF W = 1 THEN 80
 70    IF W <> 2 THEN 30
 80    PRINT "ENTER NUMBER OF PILES";
 90    INPUT N
100    IF N > 100 THEN 80
110    IF N < 1 THEN 80
120    IF N <> INT(N) THEN 80
130    PRINT "ENTER PILE SIZES"
140    FOR I = 1 TO N
150    PRINT I;
160    INPUT A(I)
170    IF A(I) > 2000 THEN 150
180    IF A(I) <> INT(A(I)) THEN 150
190    NEXT I
200    PRINT "DO YOU WANT TO MOVE FIRST?";
210    INPUT A$
220    IF A$ = "YES" GOTO 1000
230    IF A$ = "NO" GOTO 250
235    PRINT "PLEASE, YES OR NO";
240    GOTO 210
250    IF W = 1 THEN 490
260    LET C = 0
```

```
270    FOR I = 1 TO N
280    IF A(I) = 0 THEN 320
290    LET C = C+1
300    IF C = 3 THEN 390
310    LET D(C) = I
320    NEXT I
330    IF C = 2 THEN 470
340    IF A(D(1)) > 1 THEN 370
350    PRINT "MACHINE LOSES"
360    GOTO 1190
370    PRINT "MACHINE WINS"
380    GOTO 1190
390    LET C = 0
400    FOR I = 1 TO N
410    IF A(I) > 1 THEN 490
420    IF A(I) = 0 THEN 440
430    LET C = C+1
440    NEXT I
450    IF C/2 <> INT(C/2) THEN 350
460    GOTO 490
470    IF A(D(1)) = 1 THEN 370
480    IF A(D(2)) = 1 THEN 370
490    FOR I = 1 TO N
500    LET E = A(I)
510    FOR J = 0 TO 10
520    LET F = E/2
530    LET B(I,J) = 2*(F-INT(F))
540    LET E = INT(F)
550    NEXT J
560    NEXT I
570    FOR J = 10 TO 0 STEP - 1
580    LET C = 0
590    LET H = 0
600    FOR I = 1 TO N
610    IF B(I,J) = 0 THEN 660
620    LET C = C+1
630    IF A(I) < = H THEN 660
640    LET H = A(I)
650    LET G = I
660    NEXT I
670    IF C/2 <> INT(C/2) THEN 740
680    NEXT J
690    LET E = INT(N*RND(1) + 1)
700    IF A(E) = 0 THEN 690
710    LET F = INT(A(E)*RND(1) + 1)
720    LET A(E) = A(E) - F
730    GOTO 930
740    LET A(G) = 0
750    FOR J = 0 TO 10
760    LET B(G,J) = 0
770    LET C = 0
780    FOR I = 1 TO N
790    IF B(I,J) = 0 THEN 810
800    LET C = C+1
810    NEXT I
820    LET A(G) = A(G) + 2*(C/2-INT(C/2))*2↑J
830    NEXT J
840    IF W = 1 THEN 930
850    LET C = 0
860    FOR I = 1 TO N
```

```
870   IF A(I) > 1 THEN 930
880   IF A(I) = 0 THEN 900
890   LET C = C+1
900   NEXT I
910   IF C/2 <> INT(C/2) THEN 930
920   LET A(G) = 1 - A(G)
930   PRINT "PILE SIZE"
940   FOR I = 1 TO N
950   PRINT I; A(I)
960   NEXT I
970   IF W = 2 THEN 1000
980   GOSUB 1120
990   IF Z = 1 THEN 370
1000  PRINT "YOUR MOVE - PILE, NUMBER TO BE REMOVED";
1010  INPUT X,Y
1020  IF X > N THEN 1000
1030  IF X < 1 THEN 1000
1040  IF X <> INT(X) THEN 1000
1050  IF Y > A(X) THEN 1000
1060  IF Y < 1 THEN 1000
1070  IF Y <> INT(Y) THEN 1000
1080  LET A(X) = A(X) - Y
1090  GOSUB 1120
1100  IF Z = 1 THEN 350
1110  GOTO 250
1120  LET Z = 0
1130  FOR I = 1 TO N
1140  IF A(I) = 0 THEN 1160
1150  RETURN
1160  NEXT I
1170  LET Z = 1
1180  RETURN
1190  PRINT "DO YOU WANT TO PLAY ANOTHER GAME"
1200  INPUT A$
1210  IF A$ = "YES" THEN 1240
1220  IF A$ = "NO" THEN 1250
1230  GOTO 1200
1240  GOTO 30
1250  END.
```

● **PROBLEM** 21-16

Write a Basic program to simulate the game of Awari.

Solution: Awari is an African game played with seven sticks and 36 beans, laid out as shown:

Y

	6	5	4	3	2	1	
Y's Home Away From Home	000	000	000	000	000	000	X's Home
	000	000	000	000	000	000	
	1	2	3	4	5	6	

X

713

In the given diagram X and Y are the two players. Suppose X
has the first move. A move is made by taking all the beans
from any non-empty pit on X's side and sowing them in a
counterclockwise direction, one in each pit. A turn consists
of one or two moves. If the last bean of X's move is sown in
his own home he can take another move.

Also, if the last bean sown in a move lands in an empty
pit and the pit opposite is not empty, then all the beans in
that pit (together with the last bean sown) are captured and
moved to the player's home.

When either side is empty, the game is finished and the
player with the most beans is the winner.

Consider the following sample part game:

```
                    Y

          3   3   3   3   3   3
    0                             0
          3   3   3   3   3   3

                    X
```

X starts sowing from 4

```
          3   3   3   3   3   3
    0                             1
          3   3   3   0   4   4
```

Y starts sowing from 2:

```
          3   4   4   4   0   3
    0                             1
          3   3   3   0   4   4
```

X starts from 1

```
          3   4   4   4   0   3
    0                             1
          0   4   4   1   4   4
```

(He now captures the 4 stones on Y(3) and his X(4) to obtain

```
          3   4   4   0   0   3
    0                             6
          0   4   4   0   4   4
```

Y plays from 4:

```
          0   4   0   0   0   3
    5                             6
          0   4   4   0   4   4
```

X starts from 3 to obtain

```
          0   4   0   0   0   3
    5                             7
          0   4   0   1   5   5
```

Since he finished at home he can play again. He plays from
5:

714

```
          0   4   0   1   1   4
  5                                  8
          0   4   0   0   0   6
```

and so on...

The program follows:

```
 10    PRINT "AWARI"
 15    DATA 0
 20    DIM B(13), G(13), F(50): READ N
 30    E = 0
 40    FOR I = 0 TO 12
 50    B(I) = 3
 60    NEXT I
 70    C = 0
 80    F(N) = 0
 90    B(13) = 0
100    B(6) = 0
110    GOSUB 540
120    PRINT "YOUR MOVE";
130    GOSUB 310
140    IF E = 0 THEN 210
145    IF M = H THEN GOSUB 300
146    IF E = 0 THEN 210
150    PRINT "MY MOVE IS";
160    GOSUB 820
170    IF E = 0 THEN 210
180    IF M = H THEN PRINT ","
190    GOSUB 820
200    IF E > 0 THEN 110
210    PRINT "GAME OVER"
220    D = B(6) - B(13)
230    IF D < 0 THEN PRINT "I WIN BY"; -D; "POINTS"
240    GOTO 30
250    N = N+1
260    IF D = 0 THEN PRINT "DRAWN GAME"
270    GOTO 30
280    PRINT "YOU WIN BY";D;"POINTS"
290    GOTO 30
300    PRINT "AGAIN";
310    INPUT M
320    IF M < 7 THEN IF M > 0 THEN M = M-1
330    GOTO 360
340    PRINT "ILLEGAL MOVE"
350    GOTO 300
360    IF B(M) = 0 THEN 340
370    H = 6
380    GOSUB 400
390    GOTO 540
400    K = M
410    GOSUB 680
420    E = 0
430    IF K > 6 THEN K = K-7
440    C = C+1
450    IF C < 9 THEN F(N) = F(N)*6+K
460    FOR I = 0 TO 5
470    IF B(I) <> 0 THEN 500
480    NEXT I
490    RETURN
500    FOR I = 7 TO 12
```

```
510   IF B(I) <> 0 THEN E = 1
520   RETURN
530   GOTO 480
540   FOR I = 12 TO 7 STEP - 1
550   GOSUB 650
560   NEXT I
570   PRINT: I = 13
580   GOSUB 650
590   PRINT "           ";
600   PRINT B(6)
610   PRINT "        ";
620   FOR I = 0 TO 5: GOSUB 650
630   NEXT I
640   RETURN
650   IF B(I) < 10 THEN PRINT "      ";
660   PRINT B(I);
670   RETURN
680   P = B(M)
690   B(M) = 0
700   FOR P = P TO 1 STEP - 1
710   M = M+1
720   IF M > 13 THEN M = M - 14
730   B(M) = B(M)+1
740   NEXT P
750   IF B(M) = 1 THEN IF M <> 6 THEN IF M <> 13 THEN IF
      B(12-M) <> 0 THEN 780
770   RETURN
780   B(H) = B(H) + B(12-M) + 1
790   B(M) = 0
800   B(12-M) = 0
810   RETURN
820   D = -99
830   H = 13
840   FOR I = 0 TO 13
850   G(I) = B(I)
860   NEXT I
870   FOR J = 7 TO 12
880   IF B(J) = 0 THEN 1110
885   G = 0: M = J: GOSUB 680
886   FOR I = 0 TO 5: IF B(I) = 0 THEN 970
890   L = B(I) + I
900   R = 0
910   IF L > 13 THEN L = L - 14
920   R = 1
930   GOTO 910
940   IF B(L) = 0 THEN IF L <> 6 THEN IF L <> 13 THEN
      R = B(12-L) + R
960   IF R > Q THEN Q = R
970   NEXT I
980   Q = B(13) - B(6) - Q
990   IF C > 8 THEN 1050
1000  K = J
1010  IF K > 6 THEN K = K-7
1020  FOR I = 0 TO N-1
1030  IF F(N)*6 + K = INT(F(I)/6↑(7-C)+.1) THEN Q = Q-2
1040  NEXT I
1050  FOR I = 0 TO 13
1060  B(I) = G(I)
1070  NEXT I
1080  IF Q > = D THEN A = J
```

```
1090    D = Q
1100    NEXT J
1110    M = A
1120    PRINT CHR$(42+M);
1130    GOTO 400
1140    FOR I = 0 TO N-1
1150    PRINT B(I)
1160    NEXT I
1170    END
```

CHAPTER 22

SIMULATION

BASIC SIMULATION PROBLEMS

Although different simulation studies require variations in procedure, certain basic steps are usually followed. State the steps of the general procedure.

Solution: 1) Definition of the problem.

2) Planning the study (considering the exogenous factors that will affect the system; deciding if such factors will be included in the study; etc.)

3) Formulation of a mathematical model. Simplifying assumptions about the system components and their behavior are usually made at this stage.

4) Gathering of relevant data.

5) Construction of a computer program for the model.

6) Validation of the model.

7) Design of experiments.

8) Execution of simulation run and analysis of results.

In common use, there are two different types of simulation, continuous and discrete. Continuous simulation deals with variables (such as velocity, current, work, etc.) that take on real values and change continuously with time. These changes are defined as being smooth and nonabrupt. In discrete simulation, the model deals with random events that occur at isolated times. For example, the arrivals of motorists at a gas station could be considered random, and the simulation model might have to determine the average waiting time per

customer under various organizations of attendants and gas pumps.
This process of using random variables is called a stochastic process.

There exists a problem-oriented programming language called GPSS
(General Purpose System Simulation) which can be used for solving
the simulation problems.

● **PROBLEM 22-2**

Assume that the Gross National Product (GNP) is now 1×10^{12} dollars,
and is increasing by 4% each year. Also assume that the gross output
of the computing industry (GOC) is now 6×10^{9} dollars, and is increasing by 17% each year. If these growth rates are continuous, starting
from this year, in how many years will GOC exceed GNP?

Solution: The answer to this problem is a fictional one, since GOC
will never exceed GNP in reality. Projections such as these are
interesting brain-teasers. The logic is straightforward, and the
program is presented below:

```
10      REM GNP VS. GOC
20      READ GNP, GOC
25      YEAR = 0
30      NUP = 0.0
40      NUC = 0.0
50      NUP = GNP* .04
60      GNP = GNP + NUP
70      NUC = GOC* .17
80      GOC = GOC + NUC
90      YEAR = YEAR + 1
100     IF GOC ≤ CNP THEN 5∅
110     PRINT YEAR
120     DATA 1000, 6
130     END
```

● **PROBLEM 22-3**

Write a FORTRAN program to simulate the daily activity at a gas
station. Assuming that one customer is served every six minutes,
what is the average waiting time per customer?

Solution: This is a problem in discrete simulation. A random number
generator is used in the program to model the arrival of customers.
Since the gas station attendant cannot know if the stream of customers
will be continuous, randomness of arrivals is assumed.

To calculate the average waiting time, the program should compute the
waiting time of each individual car, add the times, and divide that
sum by the total number of cars. The first arrival incurs no waiting
time, but all subsequent arrivals must wait six minutes for each car
in front of them. To obtain an average the service time remaining
for each car, the total waiting time for all the cars, and the number
of cars that are lined up must be found.

For each simulated minute, the program must reduce the service time
SERV by one and check to see if another car has arrived. If so, the
waiting time for that last car is given by SERV. WAIT - the total
waiting time, is increased by adding SERV to it, while the number

719

of cars, CARTOT, is increased by one, and SERV is increased by six minutes. The parameter N is the number of minutes to be simulated (N cannot contain more than 6 digits).

Another assumption made is that customers arrive each minute with a probability of 0.1. To simplify the problem, it is assumed that there is only one gas pump at this station.

Note, that several values of N can be entered in the DATA section. The program procedure will be done for each of those time intervals. In order to end the program, enter N ≤ 0 as the last value.

```
C          GASOLINE LINE SIMULATION
           INTEGER WAIT, SERV, CARTOT, TIME
5          READ (5,1)N
         1 FORMAT (I6)
C          DO WHILE  N  GREATER THAN ZERO
           IF (N. LE. 0) GO TO 99
           SERV = 0
           WAIT = 0
           CARTOT = 0
           DO 10 TIME = 1,N
           SERV = MAX (SERV - 1,0)
22       2 CALL RAND (X)
           IF (X.GT.0.1) GO TO 22
           CARTOT = CARTOT + 1
           WAIT = WAIT + SERV
           SERV = SERV + 6
10         CONTINUE
           AVWAIT = FLOAT (WAIT)/FLOAT (CARTOT)
           WRITE (6,101) CARTOT,AVWAIT
101        FORMAT (1X,'AVERAGE WAIT FOR EACH OF THE',
           I6,'CUSTOMERS IS', F6.2,'MINUTES.')
           GO TO 5
C          END DO-WHILE
99         STOP
           END
```

● **PROBLEM** 22-4

A chemist has two reactants, P and Q, dissolved in one liter of water. The amounts of P and Q present are p grams and q grams, respectively, and they are combining to form 2 apq grams of the product R each second. It is also known that the reaction is reversible: in each second, 2br grams of R are breaking up into br grams of each P and Q. In summary, the change in one second is: - amount of P increases by br - apq
    - amount of Q increases by br - apq
    - amount of R increases by 2apq - 2br .
Design a program to simulate this reaction.

Solution: This reaction is actually continuous. One second divisions are used for convenience. In general, at any time interval h, the amounts of P,Q, and R are as follows:

$$p(t + h) = p(t) + hbr(t) - hap(t)q(t)$$
$$q(t + h) = q(t) + hbr(t) - hap(t)q(t)$$
$$r(t + h) = r(t) - 2hbr(t) + 2hap(t)q(t)$$

As h becomes smaller, the numerical solutions converge to the continuous functions, yielding as close an approximation as desired. In fact, they converge to the solution of the following differential equations:

$$\frac{dp}{dt} = br - apq$$

$$\frac{dq}{dt} = br - apq$$

$$\frac{dr}{dt} = -2br + 2apq \ .$$

Let us now declare all variables to avoid confusion:

P,Q - number of grams of reactants.

R - number of grams of product.

A,B - stoichiometric coefficients for P and Q, respectively in the equation $AP + BQ \rightleftarrows R$.

H - reciprocal of the desired time interval. (in $\sec^{-1}$.)

T - total time of simulated reaction (in sec.)

C - control number. This variable allows the user to change desired parts of the data.

D - rate of change in 1/H seconds.

The program looks as follows:

```
10      PRINT "INPUT THE DESIRED CONTROL NUMBER"
11      PRINT "0: STOP"
12      PRINT "1: INITIAL GRAMS", "2: NEW COEFFICIENTS"
13      PRINT "3: NEW TIME STEPS", "4: SIMULATE"
20      INPUT C
30      IF  C = 0  THEN  280
40      IF  C = 1  THEN  120
50      IF  C = 2  THEN  140
60      IF  C = 3  THEN  160
70      IF  C = 4  THEN  180
110     GO TO 10
120     PRINT "INPUT INITIAL AMOUNTS OF P,Q, AND R"
125     INPUT P,Q,R
130     GO TO 10
140     PRINT "INPUT MOLAR COEFFICIENTS FOR  P  AND  Q"
145     INPUT A,B
150     GO TO 10
160     PRINT "INPUT DESIRED AND TOTAL TIME INTERVALS"
165     INPUT H,T
170     GO TO 10
180     PRINT "TIME", "P", "Q", "R"
190     REM SIMULATION OF REVERSIBLE REACTION
200     FOR  I = 1  TO  T
210     FOR  J = 1  TO  H
220     LET  D = (B*R - A*P*Q)/H
230     LET  P = P + D
240     LET  Q = Q + D
250     LET  R = R - (2.0*D)
260     NEXT  J
270     PRINT  I,P,Q,R
275     NEXT  I
280     END
```

Write a PL/I program to simulate the computer dating service. The
following factors will be used in the selection process:
A) The sex of a person looking for a date.
B) Interest of the person in the following fields:
  1) Theatre   2) Sports   3) Politics
     Movies   Dancing   Social events
     Opera
C) The minimum and maximum acceptable ages of the person(s)
selected.

Solution: This data must be available for each person on record
and for the person looking for a date. The following rules are
used for selecting a possible date.

  1) The person selected must be of an opposite sex from the
person looking for a data.

  2) They must have at least one common interest in the first set
of activities (Theatre, Movies, Opera).

  3) They must have at least one common interest in either the
second or the third set of activities.

  4) The age of the partner selected must be greater than or equal
to a minimum age, and less then or equal to a maximum age, specified
by the original client looking for a date.

The program procedure looks as follows:

```
            DATING : PROCEDURE OPTIONS(MAIN);
      /* READ THE PERSONAL DATA OF THE PERSON LOOKING FOR DATE */
      GET LIST (/*GENERAL INFO */ IDENTIFICATION, INF_SEX,
      /*SPECIAL INTERESTS */THEATRE, MOVIE, OPERA, SPORTS, DANCING
                       POLITICS, SOC_EVENTS,
      /* THE AGE RANGE */ MIN_AGE, MAX_AGE );
      /* THE HEADINGS FOR THE OUTPUT ARE CONSTRUCTED BY THE NEXT
            THREE STATEMENTS */
      PUT LIST('THESE ARE SELECTED PARTNERS FOR', IDENTIFICATION)
                       PAGE LINE(5);
      PUT LIST ('IDENTIFICATION', 'SEX OF PARTNER', 'AGE OF PARTNER')
                       SKIP (2);
      T = 0; /* T  IS VARIABLE USED TO TEST FOR THE END OF INPUT STREAM*/
NEXT: IF  T = 1  THEN GO·TO TERMINATE; /* THE VARIABLE  T  WILL
ONLY BE CHANGED BY THE VERY LAST PART OF THE INPUT STREAM.  IN OTHER
CASES, TWO COMMAS (,,) IN THE INPUT STREAM ENSURES THAT THE VALUE OF
T  IS NOT ALTERED */
      /* ACQUIRE THE DATA OF THE INDIVIDUAL KEPT ON FILE */
      GET LIST (IDENTIFICATION_P, INF_SEX_P, THEATRE_P, MOVIE_P,
      OPERA_P, SPORTS_P, DANCING_P, POLITICS_P, SOC_EVENTS_P,
      INDIVIDUAL_AGE, T);
      IF  INF_SEX = INF_SEX_P THEN GO TO NEXT;
      IF THEATRE ¬ = THEATRE_P THEN
                                   IF MOVIE ¬ = MOVIE_P  THEN
                                   IF OPERA ¬ = OPERA_P THEN
                                   GO TO NEXT;
      /* AT LEAST ONE OF THE NEXT FOUR INTERESTS MUST BE SHARED */
      IF SPORTS ¬ = SPORTS_ P THEN
         IF DANCING ¬ = DANCING_P THEN
            IF POLITICS ¬  = POLITICS_P THEN
               IF SOC EVENTS ¬  = SOC_EVENTS_P THEN GO TO NEXT;
      /* NOW TEST WHETHER THE PERSON IN OUR FILE FITS INTO THE PROPER
```

AGE GROUP. A SELECTED CANDIDATE IS PRINTED IN THE OUTPUT */
        IF INDIVIDUAL_AGE > = MIN_AGE THEN
            IF INDIVIDUAL_AGE < = MAX_AGE THEN
                PUT LIST (IDENTIFICATION_P, INF_SEX_P, INDIVIDUAL_AGE)
                                                    SKIP;
    GO TO NEXT;
    TERMINATE : END DATING;

For identification of a person, the integer numbers that may represent
driver's license numbers or social security numbers are used. The
input data for persons on file consists of the following information:

        nnnn, S, YYYYYYY, ZZ, m

where nnnn indicates identification number, S shows the sex of the
person (the digit 1 indicates female and 0 - male), specification
of personal interest in activities follows, ZZ is the age of
potential partner, and m is used to indicate the end of file.
The person looking for a date is described by the following input
format:

        nnnn, S, YYYYYYY, Z1, Z2

Last two items specify the desired minimum age (Z1) and the maximum
age (Z2) of the future date.

EULER'S METHODS-THEORY AND SUBPROGRAMS

● **PROBLEM** 22-6

(a) Write a FORTRAN program to find approximate solutions to the
first order differential equation $dy/dx = f(x,y)$ with initial
condition $y(x_0) = y_0$, using Euler's method.

(b) Write a FORTRAN program to find approximate solutions to the
second order differential equation $d^2y/dx^2 = g(x,y,y')$ with initial
conditions $y(x_0) = y_0$ and $y'(x_0) = y_0'$, using Euler's method.

Solution: (a) Euler's method assumes that during the interval
$[x, x+\Delta x)$, dy/dx remains constant and that

$$\Delta y/\Delta x = dy/dx \equiv f(x,y) \Rightarrow \Delta y = \Delta x f(x,y).$$

Thus,

$$y_{new} = y_{old} + \Delta y = y_{old} + \Delta x f(x_{old}, y_{old}).$$

Or, stating this as a difference equation:

$$y_{n+1} = y_n + \Delta x f(x_n, y_n) \tag{1}$$

for $n = 0, 1, \ldots, N$.
The FORTRAN main program is:

```
    READ N, DELTAX,X,Y
    PRINT, T,X,Y
    DO 1Ø I = 1,N
    X = X + DELTAX
 C  USE EQUATION (1)
    Y = Y + DELTAX * F(X,Y)
    PRINT, X,Y
1Ø  CONTINUE
    STOP
    END
```

723

Note: F(X,Y) must be defined in a FUNCTION subprogram

(b) Rewrite the equation as a system of simultaneous first-order
equations: $y' = dy/dx = z$
$z' = dz/dx = g(x,y,z)$
with initial conditions $y(x_0) = y_0$ and $z(x_0) = y'(x_0) = y_0'$.

The FORTRAN main program is:

```
     READ, N, DELTAX,X,X,Z
     PRINT, X,Y,Z
     DO 1Ø I = 1,N
     ZPRIME = G(X,Y,Z)
     X = X + DELTAX
     Y = Y + DELTAX * Z
     Z = Z + DELTAX * ZPRIME
     PRINT, X,Y,Z
10   CONTINUE
     STOP
     END
```

Note: Again, G(X,Y,Z) must be defined. Also, for a fixed value of
Δx, the error increases as $|x - x_0|$ increases. In addition, for
a fixed value of x_n, the error increases as Δx increases and is
of order $(\Delta x)^2$.

● **PROBLEM 22-7**

Write FORTRAN subprograms to simulate the action of the following
forcing inputs, E(t):
Case 1: $E_1(t) = h$ where h is constant.

Case 2: $E_2(t) = \begin{cases} 0 & \text{if } t < t_1 \\ h & \text{if } t_1 \leq t < t_2, \text{ h-constant} \\ 0 & \text{if } t \geq t_2 \end{cases}$

$E_2(t)$ is a pulse of height h and width $(t_2 - t_1)$.

Case 3: $E_3(t) = A \sin(\omega t + \varphi)$ where A, ω, φ are constants. $E_3(t)$
is a sinusoid of amplitude A, period $2\pi/\omega$ and phase angle φ.

Case 4: $E_4(t) = \begin{cases} 0 & \text{if } t < t_1 \\ h & \text{if } t_1 \leq t < t_1 + W \\ 0 & \text{if } t_1 + W \leq t < t_1 + PW \end{cases}$

and $E_4(t) = E_4(t-PW)$, if $t \geq t_1 + PW$. $E_4(t)$ is a pulse train
with height h, width W and period PW.

Solution: Use FUNCTION subprograms with t as the argument. The
parameters can be read in,
Case 1:   FUNCTION CONST(T)
           READ, H

724

```
CONST = H
RETURN
END
```

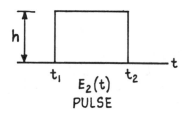

$E_2(t)$
PULSE

FIG. I

PULSE TRAIN $E_4(t)$

Case 2:
```
FUNCTION PULSE (T)
READ, H, T1, T2
PULSE = 0
IF(T.GE.T1. AND. T.LT.T2)PULSE = H
RETURN
END
```

Case 3:
```
FUNCTION SINE (T)
READ A, OMEGA, PHI
SINE = A * SIN(OMEGA*T + PHI)
RETURN
END
```

Case 4:   The formula for $E_4(t)$ is a recursion formula that defines $E_4(t)$ for $t < t_1 + PW$ and equates $E_4(t)$ with $E_4(t-PW)$ for $t \geq t_1 + PW$, thus requiring repeated subtraction of PW until $t < t_1 + PW$. Then t will be mapped into t* where $t_1 \leq t^* < t_1 + PW$. This mapping is a translation of t along the time axis to the point t*; and the distance of the translation is

$$t - t^* = nPW \tag{1}$$

where n is the number of subtractions required. (See Fig. 2).

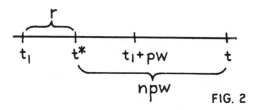

FIG. 2

But repeated subtraction is the operation of division. Therefore, the same translation mapping can be achieved by dividing the distance $t - t_1$ by PW:

$$(t - t_1)/PW = n + (r/PW) \tag{2}$$

725

where r is the remainder. Multiplying both sides of equation (2)
by PW:

$$t - t_1 = nPW + r .$$

Substituting, using equation (1)

$$t - t_1 = t - t^* + r$$
$$- t_1 = -t^* + r$$
$$r = t^* - t_1 \tag{3}$$

Equation (3) indicates that the remainder gives t^*'s distance from
t_1. Therefore, adding r to t_1 gives the absolute location of
t^*.

```
           FUNCTION TRAIN(T)
           READ H, T1, W, P
           TIME = T
           IF (T.GE.(T1 + P*W)) GO TO 5
           GO TO 6
      5    TIME = AMOD((T-T1)/(P*W))*P*W + T1
      6    IF((TIME.LT.T1).OR. (TIME.GE.(T1+W))) TRAIN = 0 .
           IF((TIME.GE.T1). AND. (TIME.LT.(T1+W))) TRAIN = H.
           RETURN
           END
```

● **PROBLEM** 22-8

(a) Write a FORTRAN subroutine to find approximate solutions to the
initial-value problem: dy/dx = f(x,y), $y(x_0) = y_0$ using modified
Euler's (predictor-corrector) method.

(b) Write a FORTRAN program to find an approximate solution to the
initial-value problem: dy/dx = g(y), $y(x_0) = y_0$, using modified
Euler's method.

Solution: The modified Euler's method uses Euler's formula:

$$y_{n+1} = y_n + \Delta x f(x_n, y_n), \tag{1}$$

to obtain a predicted value $y_{i+1,p}$ of y_{i+1} and then iterates
the following formula to obtain (k+1) corrected values $y_{i+1,c}$:

$$y_{i+1,c}^{(k+1)} = y_i + \tfrac{1}{2}[f(x_i, y_i) + f(x_{i+1}, y_{i+1}^{(k)})](x_{i+1} - x_i) \tag{2}$$

The iterative process is stopped as soon as $y_{i+1}^{(k+1)} = y_{i+1}^{(k)}$ to the
required degree of accuracy. The following flowchart details the
programming of this method:

726

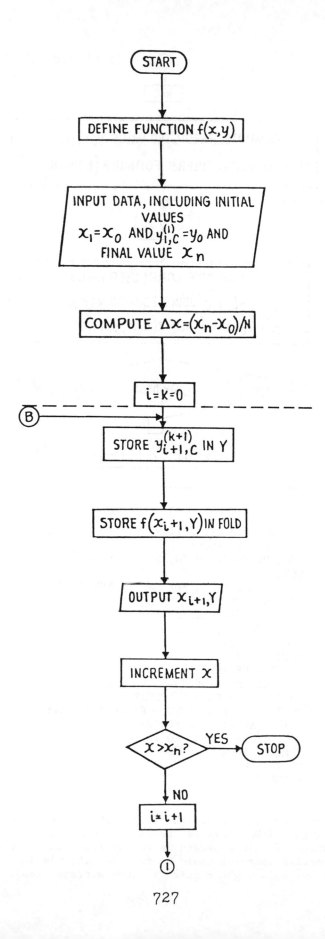

727

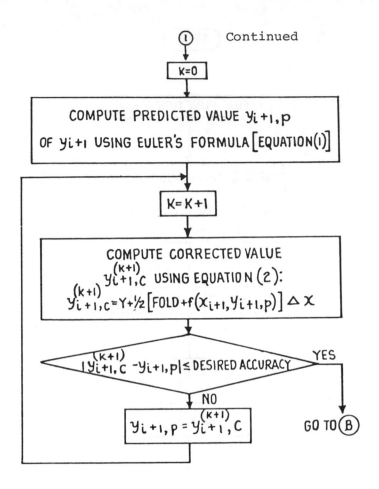

Continued

```
                        k = 0
```

COMPUTE PREDICTED VALUE $y_{i+1,p}$

OF y_{i+1} USING EULER'S FORMULA [EQUATION(1)]

```
                        K = K + 1
```

COMPUTE CORRECTED VALUE

$y_{i+1,c}^{(k+1)}$ USING EQUATION (2):

$$y_{i+1,c}^{(k+1)} = Y + \tfrac{1}{2}\left[FOLD + f(x_{i+1}, y_{i+1,p})\right]\Delta x$$

$|y_{i+1,c}^{(k+1)} - y_{i+1,p}| \le$ DESIRED ACCURACY

YES

NO

$y_{i+1,p} = y_{i+1,c}^{(k+1)}$

GO TO (B)

(a) The subroutine closely follows the flowchart, but the indices i and k have been omitted:

```
          SUBROUTINE EULER (N,XN,X,YCOR,ACCUR)
          REAL N
    C     USE A REAL VALUE FOR  N  TO AVOID MIXED
    C     MODE ARITHMETIC
          DELTAX = (XN - X)/N
    50    Y = YCOR
          FOLD = F(X,Y)
          PRINT, X,Y
          X = X + DELTAX
          IF(X.GT.XN) STOP
          YPRED = Y + FOLD * DELTAX
   100    YCOR = Y + Ø.5*(FOLD + F(X,YPRED))*DELTAX
          YDIF = ABS(YCOR - YPRED)
          IF(YDIF.LE.ACCUR) GO TO 50
          YPRED = YCOR
          GO TO 100
          RETURN
          END
```

(b) A subroutine to perform the loop that computes the corrected value, leaving I/O tasks to the main program will be used here. The advantage of this approach is the availability of each y(x). (An alternative approach would be to store the y's in an array, but for large N this might require a large storage area). The dis-

advantage is the increased execution time required to pass arguments back and forth.
The program looks as follows:

```
C         MAIN PROGRAM
          READ, N,XN,X,YCOR,ACCUR
          PRINT, X, XCOR
          REALN = FLOAT(N)
          DELTAX = (XN - X)/REALN
          DO 10 I = 1,N
          X = X + DELTAX
          CALL MEULER(X,YCOR,ACCUR,DELTAX)
          PRINT, X,YCOR
10        CONTINUE
          STOP
          END
          SUBROUTINE MEULER(X,YCOR,ACCUR,DELTAX)
          Y = YCOR
          GOLD = G(Y)
          YPRED = Y + GOLD * DELTAX
100       YCOR = Y + 0.5*(GOLD + G(YPRED))*DELTAX
          YDIF = ABS(YCOR - YPRED)
          IF (YDIF.LE.ACCUR) GO TO 11
          YPRED = YCOR
          GO TO 100
11        RETURN
          END
```

● **PROBLEM** 22-9

Write a FORTRAN subroutine to find approximate solutions to the second-order initial-value problems:

i) $\quad d^2y/dx^2 = g_1(y)$; $y(x_0) = y_0$, $y'(x_0) = y'_0$ $\hspace{2cm}$ (1)

ii) $\quad d^2y/dx^2 = g_2(y,y')$; $y(x_0) = y_0$, $y'(x_0) = y'_0$ $\hspace{1.5cm}$ (2)

iii) $d^2y/d_x^{\,2} = g_3(x,y,y')$; $y(x_0) = y_0$, $y'(x_0) = y'_0$ $\hspace{1cm}$ (3)

using the modified Euler (predictor-corrector)method.

Solution: The difference equation to approximate y_{i+1} using the modified Euler method is:

$$y_{i+1,c}^{(k+1)} = y_i + \tfrac{1}{2}[f(x_i,y_i) + f(x_{i+1},y_{i+1}^{(k)})]\Delta x \quad \text{where}$$

$$y_{i+1}^{(0)} = y_i + f(x_i + y_i)\Delta x \ .$$

i) Rewrite equation (1) as a system of simultaneous first-order equations:

$$y' = dy/dx = z \hspace{3cm} (4)$$

$$z' = dz/dx = g_1(y) \hspace{2.5cm} (5)$$

with initial conditions $y(x_0) = x_0$, $z(x_0) = y'(x_0) = y'_0$. Now use the modified Euler method to find solutions to both equations (4) and (5):

729

```
            SUBROUTINE EULER1(N,XN,X,YCOR,ZCOR,ACCUR)
            REAL N
            DELTAX = (XN - X)/N
50          Y = YCOR
            Z = ZCOR
            G1OLD = G1(Y)
            PRINT X,Y,Z
            X = X + DELTAX
            IF(X.GT.XN) GO TO 5
            YPRED = Y + Z * DELTAX
            ZPRED = Z + G1(YPRED)*DELTAX
100         YCOR = Y + 0.5 *(Z + ZPRED)*DELTAX
            ZCOR = Z + 0.5 *(G1OLD + G1(YPRED))*DELTAX
            YDIF = ABS(YCOR - YPRED)
            ZDIF = ABS(ZCOR - ZPRED)
            IF(YDIF.LE.ACCUR.AND.ZDIF.LE.ACCUR) GO TO 50
            YPRED = YCOR
            ZPRED = ZCOR
            GO TO 100
5           RETURN
            END
```

ii) Rewrite equation (2) as a system of simultaneous first-order equations:

$$y' = dy/dx = z, \quad z(x_0) = y'(x_0) = y'_0 . \tag{6}$$

$$z' = dz/dx = g_2(y,z); \quad y(x_0) = y_0 \tag{7}$$

Now use the modified Euler method to find approximate solutions to both (6) and (7):

```
            SUBROUTINE EULER2(N,XN,X,YCOR,ZCOR,ACCUR)
            REAL N
            DELTAX = (XN - X)/N
50          Y = YCOR
            Z = ZCOR
            G2OLD = G2(Y,Z)
            PRINT,X,Y,Z
            X = X + DELTAX

            IF(X.GT.XN) GO TO 5
            YPRED = Y + Z*DELTAX
            ZPRED = Z + G2(YPRED,Z)*DELTAX
100         YCOR = Y + 0.5*(Z + ZPRED)*DELTAX
            ZCOR = Z + 0.5*(G2OLD + G2(YPRED,ZPRED))*DELTAX
            YDIF = ABS(YCOR - YPRED)
            ZDIF = ABS(ZCOR - ZPRED)
            IF(YDIF.LE.ACCUR.AND.ZDIF.LE.ACCUR) GO TO 50
            YPRED = YCOR
            ZPRED = ZCOR
            GO TO 100
5           RETURN
            END
```

iii) Rewrite equation (3) as a system of simultaneous first-order equations:

$$y' = dy/dx = z; \quad z(x_0) = y'(x_0) = y'_0 \tag{8}$$

$$z' = dz/dx = g_3(x,y,z); \quad y(x_0) = y_0 \tag{9}$$

Now use the modified Euler method to find approximate solutions to both (8) and (9):

```
            SUBROUTINE EULER3(N,XN,X,YCOR,ZCOR,ACCUR)
            REAL N
            DELTAX = (XN - X)/N
50          Y = YCOR
            Z = ZCOR
            G3OLD = G3(X,Y,Z)
            PRINT,X,Y,Z
            X = X + DELTAX
            IF(X.GT.XN) GO TO 5
            YPRED = Y + Z*DELTAX
            ZPRED = Z + G2(X,YPRED,Z)*DELTAX
100         YCOR = Y + 0.5*(Z + ZPRED)*DELTAX
            ZCOR = Z + 0.5*(G2OLD + G2(X,YPRED,ZPRED))*DELTAX
            YDIF = ABS(YCOR - YPRED)
            ZDIF = ABS(ZCOR - ZPRED)
            IF(YDIF.LE.ACCUR.AND.ZDIF.LE.ACCUR) GO TO 50
            YPRED = YCOR
            ZPRED = ZCOR
            GO TO 100
5           RETURN
            END
```

APPLICATIONS OF EULER'S METHODS TO THE FIRST ORDER FEEDBACK PROBLEMS

● **PROBLEM** 22-10

(a) Water flows into a tank at a constant rate Q. Q is determined by the position of a valve connected to the inflow pipe. Write a FORTRAN program to simulate this system, using Euler's method, from time $t = 0$ to $t = t_f$ if $V(0) = V_0$ and the capacity of the tank is C units of volume. Compare the Euler approximations with the exact values.

(b) A hole is made in the bottom of the tank allowing water to flow out at a constant rate, Q_1. Modify the program of part (a) to simulate this system.

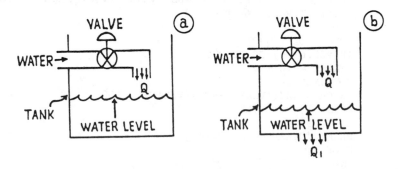

Solution: (a) Changes in this system's state can be viewed through changes in the volume of water in the tank, V. Note that once the valve position is set, Q is determined and remains unchanged for the length of the simulation. Therefore the valve is external to the system and does not effect the system during the time we are observing it in any given simulation run. The behavior of the system can be diagrammed as shown in Fig. 3

FIG. 3

meaning V is the accumulation of the rate of change, Q(when $\dot{Q}$ has units of volume/time). If $\dot{V} = dV/dt = $ constant, Q, then the complete mathematical model looks as shown in Fig. 4,

FIG. 4

meaning $\dot{V} = Q$ or $dV/dt = Q$ (1)

Using Euler's method to simulate this system means observing changes in V for small, discrete changes in t:

$$V_{new} = V_{old} + V_{added}$$
$$= V_{old} + Q *(t_{new} - t_{old})$$ (2)

The exact solution of equation (1) is:

$$V(t) = Q*t + V_0$$ (3)

Note that substituting zero for t_{old} and $V(0) = V_0$ for V_{old} in equation (2) yields equation (3). The following program uses TFIN for t_F and DT for Δt:

```
C            PROGRAM WATERFLOW
             DATA T/0.0/
             READ,N, TFIN,Q,V0,C
             REALN = N
             DT = TFIN/REALN
             VOL = V0
             VEXACT = V0
             DO 10 I = 1,N
             IF(VEXACT.NE.0.)ERROR = ABS((VEXACT-VOL)/VEXACT)* 100.
             PRINT, T,VOL,VEXACT,ERROR
             T = T + DT
             VOL = VOL + Q*DT
             IF(VOL.GT.C) GO TO 999
             VEXACT = V0 + Q*T
10           CONTINUE
             ERROR = ABS((VEXACT-VOL)/VEXACT)* 100.
             PRINT,T, VOL, VEXACT,ERROR
             GO TO 99
999          PRINT,'OVERFLOW AT TIME', T
99           STOP
             END
```

(b) Since Q_1 is the rate of flow out of the tank, it tends to

decrease V, and so it has a negative sign. V is the accumulation
of the net flow,

$$Q + (-Q_1) \quad \text{(see Fig. 5)}$$

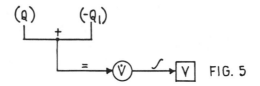

FIG. 5

From this, the following equation can be written:

$$\dot{V} = Q - Q_1 \tag{1}$$

Since both Q and Q_1 are constant, $Q - Q_1$ is constant and equation (1) can be written:

$$\dot{V} = Q_2 \quad \text{where} \quad Q_2 = Q - Q_1$$

Hence, the programmer needs only to substitute the value of Q_2
for Q in his input data for the program of part (a).

● **PROBLEM** 22-11

Water flow into a tank is regulated by the position of a valve. The
position of the valve is controlled by the height of a float: as the
float drops, the valve is turned on to admit the water, while the
rising water level causes the float to rise, which gradually shuts
off the valve, stopping the flow of water. Write a FORTRAN program
to simulate this system, using the modified Euler's method, from
time $t = 0$ to $t = t_f$, if the volume at time t is $V(t)$, $V(0) = 0$,
and the capacity of the tank is C units of volume.

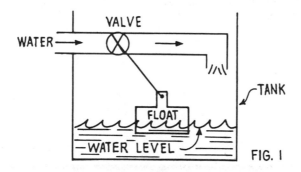

FIG. I

Solution: If $\dot{V}$ is the flow rate, the behavior of the system can be
diagrammed as shown in Fig. 2.

FIG. 2

The present water level is an accumulation of all past flow-rates.

The next flow rate is determined by the present water level. Mathematically expressed: $\dot{V} = f(V)$. But note that the flow rate is the greatest when the tank is empty and decreases to zero as the tank fills up. Stating this mathematically:

$$\dot{V} = K(C - V(t)) \tag{1}$$

where $0 < K < 1$. K is a constant of proportionality, expressed in $(time)^{-1}$ units. The complete schematic diagram of the process is shown in Fig. 3.

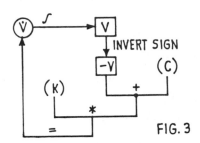

FIG. 3

Note that V (and therefore $\overset{\circ}{V}$) actually changes continuously. Using the modified Euler's method to simulate this system means observing changes in V for small, discrete changes in time. The program looks as follows:

```
C        MAIN PROGRAM
         DATA VOL/0.0/,T/0.0/
         COMMON C,K
         READ, N, TFIN, ACCUR, C,K
         PRINT, T, VOL
         REALN = N
         DT = TFIN/REALN
         DO 10 I = 1,N
         T = T + DT
         CALL MEULER(T,VOL,ACCUR,DT)
         PRINT,T, VOL
10       CONTINUE
         END
         FUNCTION G(W)
         COMMON C,K
         G = K*(C - W)
         RETURN
         END
```

● **PROBLEM** 22-12

Radioactive material spontaneously disintegrates at a rate that depends on the amount of material that remains. That is, a given fraction of the remaining material disintegrates each day. Write a FORTRAN program to simulate this system, using the modified Euler's method, from time $t = 0$ to time $t = t_f$ if the amount of material remaining at time t is $N(t)$; $N(0) = N_0$; and P is the percentage (per unit of time) of the remaining material that decays. Compare the modified Euler approximations with the exact values.

Solution: If $\dot{N}$ is the rate of disintegration the behavior of the system can be diagrammed as in Fig. 1.

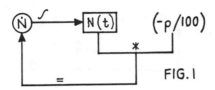

FIG. I

The amount of material that remains is a result of past disintegration, and the present decay rate is a negative percentage of the amount of remaining material. Stating this mathematically:

$$\dot{N} = (-P/100)*N(t) \tag{1}$$

The exact solution of equation (1) is:

$$N(t) = N_0 e^{-Pt/100} \tag{2}$$

Note that, as $t \to \infty$, $N(t) \to 0$ as expected since the "goal" of this system is complete disintegration of the material. The program uses the variable AMOUNT for $N(t)$.

```
            DATA T/0.0/
            COMMON P
            READ,N,TFIN,ACCUR,P,NO
            PRINT,T,NO
            REALN = N
            DT = TFIN/REALN
            AMOUNT = NO
            DO 10 I = 1,N
            T = T + DT
            CALL MEULER(T,AMOUNT,ACCUR,DT)
            EXACT = NO*EXP(-P*T/100.)
            ERROR = ABS((EXACT-AMOUNT)/EXACT)*100.
            PRINT,T,AMOUNT,EXACT,ERROR
10          CONTINUE
            STOP
            END
            FUNCTION G(W)
            COMMON P
            G = (-P/100)*W
            RETURN
            END
```

● **PROBLEM** 22-13

The "law of cooling" states that the temperature of a body, warmer than the surrounding substance, decreases at a rate proportional to the difference in temperature between the body and the surrounding substance. If the difference in temperature at time t is $D(T)$, the constant of proportionality is r (the so-called "rate of cooling") and $D(0) = D_0$, use the modified Euler's method to simulate this system in FORTRAN, from time $t = 0$ to $t = t_f$. Compare the approximations with the exact values.

Solution: If $\dot{D}$ is the rate of change of temperature difference, a
process diagram looks as shown in Fig. 1.

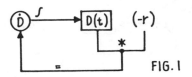

FIG.1

The corresponding equation is:

$$\dot{D} = -r * D(T) \tag{1}$$

The minus sign is included because the temperature difference decreases
at the rate r. The "goal" of this system is to reach a state of zero
temperature difference (i.e., equilibrium). The exact solution of
equation (1) is:

$$D(T) = D_0 e^{-rt}$$

Note that $t \rightarrow \infty \Rightarrow D(T) \rightarrow 0$ as expected. The program looks as
follows:

```
            DATA T/0.0/
            COMMON R
            READ,N,TFIN,ACCUR,R,DO
            PRINT,T,DO
            REALN = N
            DT = TFIN/REALN
            D = DO
            DO 10 I = 1,N
            T = T + DT
            CALL MEULER(T,D,ACCUR,DT)
            EXACT = DO * EXP(-R*T)
            ERROR = ABS((EXACT-D)/EXACT)*100.
            PRINT,T,D,EXACT,ERROR
    10      CONTINUE
            STOP
            END
            FUNCTION G(W)
            COMMON R
            G = -R*W
            RETURN
            END
```

● **PROBLEM** 22-14

Write a FORTRAN program which uses the modified Euler method to
simulate the growth of an isolated species from time $t = 0$ to
$t = t_f$; if the population growth rate (per unit of time) is directly
proportional to the additional number of individuals the environment could support. Let the number of individuals at time t be
$N(t)$, $N(0) = N_0$, and the constant of proportionality - k, $0 < k < 1$.
Compare the modified Euler approximations with the exact value.

Solution: Let S equal the total number of individuals the environment could support (saturation population). Then, at any time t,
the additional number of individuals the environment could support

is $S - N(t)$. Thus, if $\dot{N}$ is the population growth rate, the block diagram for this system would look as shown on figure #1.

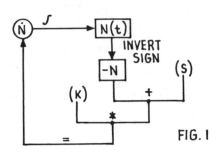

FIG. I

Or:
$$\dot{N} = k(S - N(t)) \tag{1}$$

This population model "fills to capacity" using negative feedback control. Also note that equation (1) is dimensionally correct only if k has units $(time)^{-1}$. It can be shown that the exact solution of equation (1) is:

$$N(t) = S - (S - N_0)e^{-kt} \tag{2}$$

Note that $t \to \infty \Rightarrow N(t) \to S$ and since $N_0 \le S \Rightarrow S - N_0 \ge 0$ and $e^{-kt} > 0$, $(S - N_0)e^{-kt} \ge 0 \Rightarrow N(t) \le S$ for all t, which represents the idea of population "saturation". The program uses POP for $N(t)$, POPO for $N(0)$.

```
            DATA T/0,0/
            COMMON S,K
            READ, N,TFIN,ACCUR,S,K,POPO
            PRINT,T,POPO
            REALN = N
            DT = TFIN/REALN
            POP = POPO
            SDIF = S - POPO
            DO 10 I = 1,N
            T = T + DT
            CALL MEULER(T,POP,ACCUR,DT)
            EXACT = S - SDIF*EXP(-K*T)
            ERROR = ABS((EXACT-POP)/EXACT)*100
            PRINT,T,POP,EXACT,ERROR
    10      CONTINUE
            STOP
            END
            FUNCTION G(W)
            COMMON S,K
            G = K*(S-W)
            RETURN
            END
```

Write a FORTRAN program which uses the modified Euler method to simulate the growth of an isolated species from time $t = 0$ to $t = t_f$, if the number of individuals at time t is $N(t)$, $N(0) = N_0$ and the birth rate B and the mortality rate M (per unit of population per unit of time) are given by:

Case (1): $B = b_1$; $M = m_1$ where b_1 and m_1 are positive constants.

Case (2): $B = b_2 > 0$. Competition for food causes the death rate to increase in direct proportion to the ratio $N(t)/2N_0$ with the constant of proportionality equal to m_2 where $0 < m_2 < 1$, and $N_0 > 0$. Compare the approximations with the exact values.

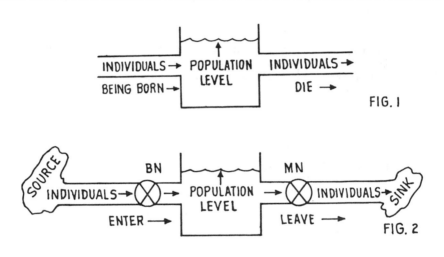

INDIVIDUALS → POPULATION LEVEL   INDIVIDUALS →

BEING BORN →   DIE →

FIG. 1

SOURCE INDIVIDUALS → ⊗ → BN POPULATION LEVEL → MN ⊗ INDIVIDUALS → SINK

ENTER →   LEAVE →

FIG. 2

Solution: An initial schematic diagram of the system looks as shown in figure #1.
The rate of flow of individuals into and out of the system (per unit of time) is given by BN and MN respectively. Thus, B and M act as valves (see Fig. #2). Thus, the net rate of change in population, $\dot{N}$, is the difference between the entrance and exit rates:

$$\dot{N} = BN - MN = (B - M)N, \tag{1}$$

and the block diagram of the process is shown in figure #3.

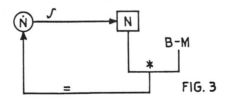

$\dot{N}$ ∫ → N

B-M

*

=

FIG. 3

Case (1): If $B = b_1$ and $M = m_1$ are positive constants, B-M = $b_1 - m_1 = r$ will also be a constant. If $b_1 > m_1$, then $r > 0$ and

the population will rise indefinitely. If $b_1 < m_1$, then $r < 0$ and
the population will continuously decrease to zero. If $b_1 = m_1$,
$r = 0$ and there will be no change in population. In any case, one
can write:

$$\dot{N} = (B - M)N = rN \qquad (2)$$

The exact solution to equation (2) is

$$N(t) = N_0 e^{rt}$$

Note that when $r > 0$, $t \to \infty \Rightarrow N(t) \Rightarrow \infty$. When $r < 0$, $t \to \infty \Rightarrow$
$N(t) \Rightarrow 0$. When $r = 0$, $N(t) = N_0 e^0 = N_0(1) = N_0$. The program uses
POP for $N(t)$.

```
           REAL T/0.0/, M1
           COMMON R
           READ,N,TFIN,ACCUR,B1,M1,POPO
           PRINT,T,POPO
           REALN = N
           DT = TFIN/REALN
           POP = POPO
           R = B1 - M1
           DO 10 I = 1,N
           T = T + DT
           CALL MEULER(T,POP,ACCUR,DT)
           EXACT = POPO*EXP(R*T)
           ERROR = ABS((EXACT-POP)/EXACT)*100
           PRINT,T,POP,EXACT,ERROR
10         CONTINUE
           STOP
           END
           FUNCTION G(W)
           COMMON R
           G = R*W
           RETURN
           END
```

Case (2): In this case, equation (1) becomes:

$$\dot{N} = (b_2 - m_2 N/2N_0)N$$
$$= b_2 N - (m_2 N^2/2N_0) \qquad (3)$$

Equation (3) is a nonlinear differential equation (because of the
N^2 term). Though, generally, solutions for nonlinear equations
are not easy to find, equation (3) is known as the Bernoulli
equation with the solution:

$$N(t) = \frac{2b_2 N_0}{m_2 + (2b_2 - m_2)e^{-b_2 t}} \qquad (4)$$

There are three possible cases:

(i) $m_2 = 2b_2$.

Substituting for m_2 in equation (3) at time $t = 0$ when $N = N_0$

739

gives:

$$\dot{N} = b_2 N_0 - (2b_2 N_0^2 / 2N_0) = b_2 N_0 - b_2 N_0 = 0$$

which means population remains at initial level. This can also be seen by substituting for m_2 in equation (4):

$$N(t) = \frac{2b_2 N_0}{2b_2 + (2b_2 - 2b_2)e^{-b_2 t}} = \frac{2b_2 N_0}{2b_2} = N_0. \tag{5}$$

Since t does not appear in equation (5), in this case, $N(t)$ is the constant function, $N(t) = N_0$. What this means to the programmer is that for the pair of parameters (b_2, m_2), where $m_2 = 2b_2$, any initial population will be an equilibrium point; and the system is stable at this point.

(ii) $m_2 < 2b_2$.

$$m_2 < 2b_2 \Rightarrow 2b_2 - m_2 > 0 \Rightarrow \text{ as } t \to \infty :$$

$$(2b_2 - m_2)e^{-bt} \to 0^+$$

$$m_2 + (2b_2 - m_2)e^{-bt} \to m_2$$

$$\frac{2b_2}{m_2 + (2b_2 - m_2)e^{-bt}} \to \frac{2b_2}{m_2} > 1 \text{ (since } m_2 < 2b_2)$$

$$N(t) \to \frac{2b_2}{m_2} N_0 > N_0 \tag{6}$$

From equation (6), we see that population will increase to the equilibrium value $2b_2 N_0 / m_2$.

(iii) $m_2 > 2b_2$.

An analysis similar to that used in case (ii) yields:

$$N(t) \to \frac{2b_2}{m_2} N_0 < N_0 \text{ (since } m_2 > 2b_2 \Rightarrow \left(2b_2 / m_2\right) < 1) \tag{7}$$

as $t \to \infty$. From equation (7), the population will decrease to the equilibrium level $2b_2 N_0 / m_2$. It follows that the system is assymptotically stable, since it converges back to its equilibrium point as a result of any arbitrary disturbance:

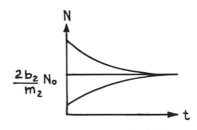

For this first-order case, the equilibrium point could also have been found by the graphical method, plotting B and M as functions of N:

The equilibrium point is the point of intersection, where the birth

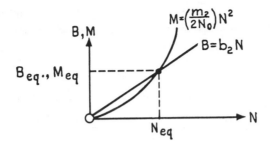

rate just equals the death rate, since the net rate of change in population, $\dot{N} = (B - M)N$, will be zero. But

$$B - M = 0 \Rightarrow b_2 N - \left(m_2/2N_0\right)N^2 = 0$$

$$N(b_2 - \left(m_2/2N_0\right)N) = 0 \Rightarrow N = 0$$

or if $N > 0$, $b_2 - \left(m_2/2N_0\right)N = 0$

$$\left(m_2/2N_0\right)N = b_2 \Rightarrow N = \left(2b_2/m_2\right)N_0$$

which is the same result obtained in equations (6) and (7), using the exact solution. Some sort of analysis of the system under study is an invaluable aid to the programmer in distinguishing between peculiar system behavior due to system stability or instability and peculiar results due to programming or logical errors. The program uses POP for $N(t)$, POP0 for N_0.

```
        REAL T/0.0/, NUMBER,M2
        COMMON B2,M2,POP0
        READ,N,TFIN,ACCUR,B2,M2,POP0
        PRINT,T,POP0
        REALN = N
        DT = TFIN/REALN
        POP = POP0
C       CONSTANT TERMS IN EXPRESSION FOR EXACT
        NUMER = 2.*B2*POP0
        DENOM = 2.*B2 - M2
        DO 10 I = 1,N
        T = T + DT
        CALL MEULER(T,POP,ACCUR,DT)
        EXACT = NUMER/(M2+(DENOM*EXP(-B2*T)))
        ERROR = ABS((EXACT-POP)/EXACT)*100.
        PRINT,T,POP,EXACT,ERROR
10      CONTINUE
        STOP
        END
        FUNCTION G(W)
        COMMON B2,M2,POP0
        REAL M2
        G = (B2-(M2*W)/(2.*POP0))*W
        RETURN
        END
```

Write a FORTRAN program which uses the modified Euler method to simulate the growth of an isolated species from time $t = 0$ to $t = t_f$, if the number of individuals at time t is $N(t)$, $N(0) = N_0$ and the rate of population change (per unit of time), $\dot{N}$, is given by:

$$\dot{N} = (K + E(t) - N/M)N \qquad (1)$$

where K and M are positive constants and $E(t)$ is a periodic forcing input resulting from seasonal cycles, given by:

Case 1: $E(t)$ is sinusoidal with amplitude $= A$, period $= 2\pi/\omega$, and phase angle φ .

Case 2: $E(t)$ is a pulse train of width w, height, h and period Pw, P, h, $w > 0$, and starting at time $t = t_1$.

Solution: Equation (1) is a nonlinear differential equation, for which a numerical method is most appropriate. Since t appears explicitly, the EULER (not MEULER!) subroutine is used.

Case 1: $E(t) = A \sin(\omega t + \varphi)$.

Substituting into equation (1),

$$\dot{N} = (K + A \sin(\omega t + \varphi) - N/M)N$$

The program uses POPO for $N(0) = N_0$; omega for ω, PHI for φ :

```
REAL T/0.0/,M,K,N
COMMON K,A,OMEGA,PHI,M
READ,N,TFIN,ACCUR,K,A,OMEGA,PHI,M,POPO
CALL EULER(N,TFIN,T,POPO,ACCUR)
STOP
END
FUNCTION F(T,W)
COMMON K,A,OMEGA,PHI,M
REAL M,K
F = (K+A*SIN(OMEGA*T+PHI) - W/M)*W
RETURN
END
```

Case 2: $E(t)$ is a pulse train. The derivation of the TRAIN subprogram to evaluate the pulse train function was given earlier. The program uses POPO for N_0 :

```
REAL T/0.0/,M,K
COMMON K,M,H,T1,W,P
READ,N,TFIN,ACCUR,K,M,POPO,A,T1,W,P,H
CALL EULER(N,TFIN,T,POPO,ACCUR)
STOP
END
FUNCTION F(T,Z)
COMMON K,M,H,T1,W,P
REAL M,K
F = (K+TRAIN(T) - Z/M)*Z
RETURN
END
FUNCTION TRAIN(T)
COMMON K,M,H,T1,W,P
```

```
            TIME = T
            IF(T.GE.(T1 + P*W))
            TIME = AMOD((T-T1)/(P*W))*P*W + T1
            IF ((TIME.LT.T1).OR. (TIME.GE.(T1+W)))TRAIN = 0
            IF ((TIME.GE.T1).AND.(TIME.LT.(T1 + W)))TRAIN = H
            RETURN
            END
```

● PROBLEM 22-17

A room is heated by a heating system controlled by an on-off thermostat, which will turn the heat on when the room temperature drops h degrees below its set point, T_s, and cuts heat off at a temperature h degrees higher than T_s. The system heats at a constant rate Q (thermal units per time unit), and the volume of the room is V, so, if the room were perfectly insulated, the heating system would raise the temperature of the room at the rate KVQ (degrees per time unit), where K is a constant of proportionality giving the change in temperature per thermal unit per unit volume. However, there is a heat loss to the outside that is proportional to the difference in temperature between the room and the outside. Using the modified Euler method, write a FORTRAN program to simulate this system, if the room temperature at time is $T(t)$, $T(0) = T_0$, and the outside temperature, T_{out}, is given by:

Case (1) : T_{out} is constant $< T_s$

Case (2) : $T_{out} = |A \sin(\omega t + \varphi)|$, reflecting daily cycles. A is temperature range, $2\pi/\omega$ is the period of a cycle, and φ is the time lag (or lead).

Solution: First, note that a typical thermostat consists of a bimetallic strip, whose elastic reaction to transient heating or cooling is used to control a triggering mechanism controlling the heating system. Thus, the internal components of the thermostat make it a dynamic element, and it can be considered a subsystem. The internal workings of the thermostat could be included in the simulation. Here we will ignore the internal operations that determine the action of the thermostat and take a "black box approach". That is, we know that information fed into the thermostat will determine whether or not it will switch, but we do not care <u>how</u> that mechanism operates:

Note that the thermostat's behavior will be nonlinear. An initial picture of the system is shown in figure #1.

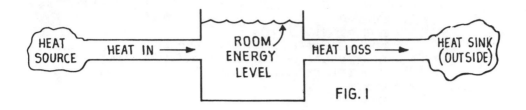

FIG. I

Since the rate of heat loss, L, acts as a valve, and the thermostat acts as a switch, we can draw them as shown in figure #2.

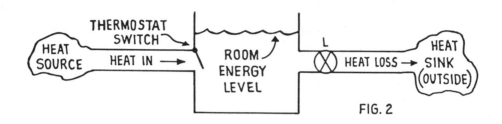

FIG. 2

Now $L = C(T-T_{out})$ where C is a constant of proportionality which represents change in heat per degree per time unit. Note that $T_{out} > T \Rightarrow L < 0$ and $T_{out} < T \Rightarrow L > 0$. Let $U(T)$ be the heating function:

$$U(T) = \begin{cases} Q, & \text{if switch is on} \\ 0, & \text{if switch is off} \end{cases}$$

Then the net rate of heat flow is H-L, and the net rate of room temperature change is given by:

$$T = KV(U-L)$$
$$= KV(U-C(T-T_{out})) \qquad (1)$$

Arbitrarily, the switch is considered off initially, U changes when $T(t)$ deviates from T_s by h degrees. Otherwise, U remains the same. Also, the programs use TEMP for $T(t)$, TMPOUT for T_{out}, TMPSET for T_s and TEMPO for T_0 :

Case (1) :

```
        REAL T/0.0/,K,V,H,C,TEMP,TMPOUT,TEMPO,
          ACCUR,TFIN,DT,TMPSET,Q,U/0.0/
        INTEGER I,N
        COMMON U, TMPOUT,K,V,C
        READ,N,TFIN,ACCUR,TEMPO,K,V,H,C,TMPOUT, TMPSET,Q
        PRINT T, TEMPO
        REALN = N
        DT = TFIN/REALN
        TEMP = TEMPO
        DO 10 I = 1,N
```

```
            T = T + DT
            IF (TEMP.LE.(TMPSET-H))U = Q
            IF (TEMP.GE.(TMPSET+H))U = 0.0
            CALL MEULER (T,TEMP,ACCUR,DT)
            PRINT T, TEMP
10          CONTINUE
            STOP
            END
            FUNCTION G(W)
            COMMON U, TMPOUT,K,V,C
            REAL K,V,C,U,TMPOUT,W,G
            G = K*V*(U-C*(W-TMPOUT))
            RETURN
            END
```

Case (2) : Using OMEGA for ω, and PHI for φ :

```
            REAL T/0.0/,K,V,H,C,TEMP,TMPOUT,TEMPO,ACCUR,TFIN,DT,
               TMPSET,Q,A,OMEGA,PHI,U/0.0/
            INTEGER I,N
            COMMON U,TMPOUT,K,V,C
            READ,N,TFIN,ACCUR,TEMPO,K,V,H,C,TMPOUT,TMPSET,Q,A,OMEGA,PHI
            PRINT,T,TEMPO
            REALN = N
            DT = TFIN/REALN
            TEMP = TEMPO
            DO 10 I = 1,N
            T = T + DT
            IF (TEMP.LE.(TMPSET-H))U = Q
            IF (TEMP.GE.(TMPSET+H))U = 0.0
            TMPOUT = A*SIN(OMEGA*T+PHI)
            CALL MEULER (T,TEMP,ACCUR,DT)
            PRINT T,TEMP
10          CONTINUE
            STOP
            END
            FUNCTION G(W)
            COMMON U, TMPOUT,K,V,C
            REAL K,V,C,U,TMPOUT,W,G
            G = K*V*(U-C*(W-TMPOUT))
            RETURN
            END
```

APPLICATIONS OF EULER'S METHODS
TO THE SECOND ORDER FEEDBACK
PROBLEMS

● **PROBLEM** 22-18

A free harmonic oscillator (FHO) is a system whose behavior can be
described by a second-order, linear differential equation of the
form:
$$\ddot{y} = -Ay(t) \tag{1}$$
where A is a positive constant. Two FHO systems are a spring-
mass system and an LC electric circuit:

745

FHO	$y(t)$	$\dot{y} = dy/dt$	A
Spring-mass	x-displacement	v = velocity	K/M
LC circuit	q-charge in coulombs	i = current in amperes	1/LC

Given the initial conditions $y(0) = y_0$ and $\dot{y}(0) = z_0$, write a FORTRAN program that uses the modified Euler method to simulate this system from $t = 0$ to $t = t_f$.

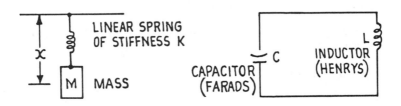

Solution: Since equation (1) is of the form $d^2y/dx^2 = g_1(y)$, we can use the EULER1 subroutine developed in a previous problem. First, rewrite equation (1) as a system of simultaneous first-order equations:

$$\dot{y} = dy/dt = z \tag{2}$$

$$\dot{z} = dz/dt = -Ay \tag{3}$$

with initial conditions $y(0) = y_0$ and $z(0) = y'(0) = z_0$. Now use the modified Euler method to find solutions to both equations (2) and (3):

```
REAL T/0.0/,TFIN,N,ACCUR,YO,ZO,A
COMMON A
READ,N,TFIN,ACCUR,YO,ZO,A
CALL EULER1(N,TFIN,T,YO,ZO,ACCUR)
STOP
END
FUNCTION G1(W)
REAL G1,W,A
COMMON A
G1 = -A*W
RETURN
END
```

Two species form a predator-prey pair. Their relation is expressed by the rule:
    The rate of predator population increase is proportional to an excess in prey population and the rate of decrease of the prey population is proportional to the increase of its enemy's population.

Let $N_1(t)$, $N_2(t)$ be the prey and predator populations, respectively and A_1, A_2, are positive constants for natural (i.e., in absence of other species) rates of birth (per unit of population per unit of time). Write a FORTRAN program which uses the modified Euler method to simulate this system from time $t = 0$ to $t = t_f$ if $N_1(0) = N_{10}$ and $N_2(0) = N_{20}$.

Solution: Proceeding directly to the mathematical model, one can express the predator-prey relation as:

$$\dot{N}_1 = -A_2 N_2 \tag{1}$$

$$\dot{N}_2 = A_1 N_1 \tag{2}$$

The program applies the modified Euler method first to equation (1) and then to equation (2). N1 and N2 are kept in a COMMON block so that the new computed value of N1 could be used in determining N2. A logical flag, TWO, is used to determine which equation is being integrated:

```
            REAL T/0.0/,TFIN,DT,REALN,ACCUR,N1,N2,N10,N20,A1,A2
            INTEGER I,N
            LOGICAL TWO/.FALSE./
            COMMON TWO,N1,N2,A1,A2
            READ,N,TFIN,ACCUR,N10,N20,A1,A2
            PRINT,T,N10,N20
            REALN = N
            DT = TFIN/REALN
            N1 = N10
            N2 = N20
            DO 10 I = 1,N
            T = T + DT
            CALL MEULER(T,N1,ACCUR,DT)
            TWO = .TRUE.
            CALL MEULER (T,N2,ACCUR,DT)
            TWO = .FALSE.
            PRINT,T,N1,N2
10          CONTINUE
            STOP
            END
            FUNCTION G(W)
            REAL G,W,N1,N2,A1,A2
            LOGICAL TWO
            COMMON TWO,N1,N2,A1,A2
            G = (-A2)*N2
            IF (TWO) G = A1*N1
            RETURN
            END
```

Note, that if equation (1) is differentiated, the result is:

$$\ddot{N}_1 = -A_2\dot{N}_2 \tag{3}$$

Substituting equation (2) into equation (3) one gets:

$$\ddot{N}_1 = -A_2A_1N_1 \tag{4}$$

Differentiating equation (2) and substituting equation (1) into the result yields:

$$\ddot{N}_2 = -A_2A_1N_2 \tag{5}$$

Equations (4) and (5) are of the form $\ddot{y} = -Ay$ where $A = A_2A_1$ is constant. The conclusion can be made that this is a free harmonic oscillating system.

● **PROBLEM 22-20**

A damped harmonic oscillator (DHO) is a system whose behavior can be described by a second-order, linear differential equation of the form:

$$\ddot{y} = -A_1\dot{y} - A_2y(t) \tag{1}$$

where A_1, A_2 are positive constants. One DHO system is a spring-mass-damper system shown in Figure #1.

This could be a simple model of an automobile wheel suspension system (assuming the automobile's body is immobile in a vertical direction). Then the damper acts as a shock absorber.

Another DHO system is an RLC electric circuit:

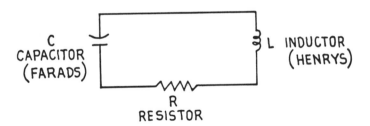

The analogy between these two DHO systems is given in Table #1.

DHO	$y(t)$	$\dot{y} = dy/dt$	A_1	A_2
Spring-mass-damper	x-displacement	v = velocity	D/M	K/M
RLC circuit	q-charge in coulombs	i = current in amperes	R/L	1/LC

Given the initial conditions $y(0) = y_0$ and $\dot{y}(0) = z_0$, write a FORTRAN program that uses the modified Euler method to simulate this system from $t = 0$ to $t = t_f$.

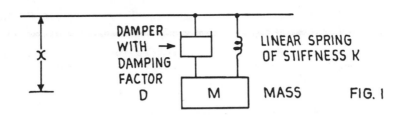

DAMPER WITH DAMPING FACTOR D

LINEAR SPRING OF STIFFNESS K

M   MASS   FIG. 1

Solution: Note that equation (1) is of the form $d^2y/dx^2 = g(y,y')$. The modified Euler subroutine will be written for this form. First, rewrite equation (1) as a system of simultaneous first-order equations:

$$\dot{y} = dy/dt = z, \quad z(0) = y'(0) = z_0 \tag{2}$$

$$\dot{z} = dz/dt = -A_1 z - A_2 y \, , \, y(0) = y_0 \tag{3}$$

Now, use the modified Euler method to find approximate solutions to both (3) and (4).

```
      REAL T/0.0/,TFIN,N,ACCUR,YO,ZO,A1,A2
      COMMON A1,A2
      READ,N,TFIN,ACCUR,YO,ZO,A1,A2
      CALL EULER2(N,TFIN,T,YO,ZO,ACCUR)
      STOP
      END
      FUNCTION G2(W,X)
      REAL G2,W,A1,A2
      COMMON A1,A2
      G2 = -A1*X-A2*W
      RETURN
      END
      SUBROUTINE EULER2(N,XN,X,YCOR,ZCOR,ACCUR)
      REAL N
      DELTAX = (XN - X)/N
50    Y = YCOR
      Z = ZCOR
      G2OLD = G2(Y,Z)
      PRINT,X,Y,Z
      X = X + DELTAX
      IF (X.GT.XN)STOP
      YPRED = Y + Z*DELTAX
      ZPRED = Z + G2(YPRED,Z)*DELTAX
100   YCOR = Y + 0.5*(Z + ZPRED)*DELTAX
      ZCOR = Z + 0.5*(G2OLD + G2(YPRED,ZPRED))*DELTAX
      YDIF = ABS(YCOR - YPRED)
      ZDIF = ABS(ZCOR - ZPRED)
      IF(YDIF.LE.ACCUR.AND.ZDIF.LE.ACCUR) GO TO 50
      YPRED = YCOR
      ZPRED = ZCOR
      GO TO 100
      RETURN
      END
```

A forced oscillator is a system whose behavior can be described by a second-order linear differential equation of the form:

$$\ddot{y} + A_1\dot{y} + A_2 y(t) = E(t) \qquad (1)$$

where A_1, A_2 are positive constants and $E(t)$ is an external forcing input. An automobile suspension system, with the road as a vertical forcing input, is a forced oscillator, for example, as shown in Figure #1.

Another example is an RLC circuit connected in series with an electromotive force generator $E(t)$, as shown in Figure #2.

Given the initial conditions $y(0) = y_0$ and $\dot{y}(0) = z_0$, write a FORTRAN program that uses the modified Euler method to simulate this system from $t = 0$ to $t = t_f$ if:

Case 1: $E(t) = h$ where h is constant

Case 2: $E(t)$ is a pulse of height h and width $(t_2 - t_1)$.

Case 3: $E(t)$ is a sinusoid of amplitude A, period $2\pi/\omega$ and phase angle φ .

Case 4: $E(t)$ is a pulse train with height h, width W, period pW and beginning at time $t = t_1$.

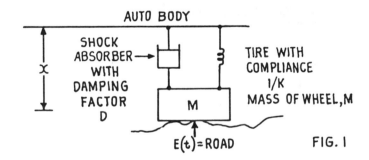

AUTO BODY

SHOCK ABSORBER→ WITH DAMPING FACTOR D

TIRE WITH COMPLIANCE 1/K MASS OF WHEEL, M

M

x

$E(t)$ = ROAD   FIG. I

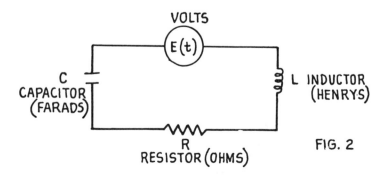

VOLTS

$E(t)$

C CAPACITOR (FARADS)

L INDUCTOR (HENRYS)

R RESISTOR (OHMS)   FIG. 2

<u>Solution:</u> If equation (1) is rearranged to the form

$$\ddot{y} = E(t) - A_1\dot{y} - A_2 y$$

it can be seen to be of the form $d^2y/dx^2 = g_3(x,y,y')$, so one can use the Euler 3 subroutine developed earlier in this chapter.

Case 1: This is the CONST FUNCTION also developed earlier in the chapter. The parameters need to be read in only once: they are read in the main program and kept in a COMMON block.

```
REAL T/0.0/,TFIN,N,ACCUR,YO,ZO,A1,A2,H
COMMON A1,A2,H
READ,N,TFIN,ACCUR,YO,ZO,A1,A2,H
CALL EULER3(N,TFIN,T,YO,ZO,ACCUR)
STOP
END
FUNCTION G3(T,V,W)
REAL G3,T,V,W,A1,A2,H
COMMON A1,A2,H
G3 = H - A1*W - A2*V
RETURN
END
```

Case 2: This is the PULSE FUNCTION developed earlier.

```
REAL T/0.0/,TFIN,N,ACCUR,YO,ZO,A1,A2,H,T1,T2
COMMON A1,A2,H,T1,T2
READ,N,TFIN,ACCUR,YO,ZO,A1,A2,H,T1,T2
CALL EULER3(N,TFIN,T,YO,ZO,ACCUR)
STOP
END
FUNCTION G3(T,V,W)
REAL G3,T,V,W,A1,A2,H,T1,T2
COMMON A1,A2,H,T1,T2
G3 = -A1*W - A2*V
IF(T.GE.T1.AND.T.LT.T2)G = H - A1*W - A2*V
RETURN
END
```

Case 3: This is the SINE FUNCTION developed earlier. The variable OMEGA is used for ω and PHI is used for φ.

```
REAL T/0.0/,TFIN,N,ACCUR,YO,ZO,A1,A2,A,OMEGA,PHI
COMMON A1,A2,A,OMEGA,PHI
READ N,TFIN,ACCUR,YO,ZO,A1,A2,A,OMEGA,PHI
CALL EULER3(N,TFIN,T,YO,ZO,ACCUR)
STOP
END
FUNCTION G3(T,V,W)
REAL G3,T,V,W,A1,A2,A,OMEGA,PHI
COMMON A1,A2,OMEGA,PHI
G3 = A*SIN(OMEGA*T + PHI) -A1*W - A2*V
RETURN
END
```

Case 4: This is the TRAIN FUNCTION developed earlier. The parameters for the G3 FUNCTION subprogram (A1,A2) are kept in the COMMON block named G, while the parameters for the TRAIN FUNCTION subprogram (H,T1,W,P) are kept in the COMMON block named TRANE. The subprogram calling sequence is as follows: The main program calls the EULER3 subroutine, EULER3 calls the G3 FUNCTION subprogram, and G3 calls the TRAIN FUNCTION subprogram.

```
C          MAIN PROGRAM
           REAL T/0.0/,TFIN,N,ACCUR,YO,ZO,A1,A2,H,T1,W,P)
           COMMON /G/A1,A2/TRANE/H,T1,W,P
           READ,N,TFIN,ACCUR,YO,ZO,A1,A2,H,T1,W,P
           CALL EULER3(N,TFIN,T,YO,ZO,ACCUR)
           STOP
           END
           FUNCTION G3(T,V,U)
           REAL G3,T,V,U,A1,A2,TRAIN
           COMMON /G/A1,A2
           G3 = TRAIN(T) -A1*U - A2*V
           RETURN
           END
           FUNCTION TRAIN(T)
           REAL TRAIN,T,H,T1,W,P
           COMMON/TRANE/H,T1,W,P
           TIME = T
           IF(T.GE.(T1 + P*W))
              TIME = AMOD((T - T1)/(P*W))*P*W + T1
           IF((TIME.LT.T1).OR.(TIME.GE.(T1 + W)))TRAIN = 0.
           IF((TIME.GE.T1).AND.(TIME.LT.(T1 + W)))TRAIN = H
           RETURN
           END
```

Write a FORTRAN program which uses the modified Euler method to simulate the competition of two species of population, $N_1(t)$ and $N_2(t)$, isolated from the environment, from time $t = 0$ to $t = t_f$, if it is observed that:

$$\dot{N}_1 = (A_1 - K_{11}N_1 - K_{12}N_2)N_1 \qquad (1)$$

$$\dot{N}_2 = (A_2 - K_{21}N_1 - K_{22}N_2)N_2 \qquad (2)$$

where $\dot{N}_1, \dot{N}_2$ are the time rates of change of $N_1(t)$ and $N_2(t)$, respectively. A_1 and A_2 are positive constants involving natural birth/death rates for each species when isolated. The K_{ij} are positive constants involving cross-effects between species. Initially, $N_1(0) = N_{10}$, and $N_2(0) = N_{20}$.

Solution: First, note that equations (1) and (2) are coupled, non-linear, first-order differential equations. Since exact solutions of such equations are rare, a numerical method, such as the modified Euler's method, is essential. The program first applies the modified method to equation (1), then to equation (2). By putting N1 and N2 in a COMMON block, the new computed value of N1 will be used in determining N2. A logical flag, TWO, is used to determine which equation is being integrated:

```
           REAL T/0.0/,TFIN,DT,REALN,ACCUR,N1,
       1       N2,N10,N20,A1,A2,K11,K12,
       1       K21,K22
           INTEGER I,N
           COMMON TWO,N1,N2,A1,A2,K11,K12,K21,K22
           LOGICAL    TWO/.FALSE./
```

```
          READ,N,TFIN,ACCUR,N10,N20,A1,A2,K11,K12,K21,K22
          PRINT,T,N10,N20
          REALN = N
          DT = TFIN/REALN
          N1 = N10
          N2 = N20
          DO 10 I = 1,N
          T = T + DT
          CALL MEULER(T,N1,ACCUR,DT)
          TWO = .TRUE.
          CALL MEULER(T,N2,ACCUR,DT)
          TWO = .FALSE.
          PRINT,T,N1,N2
10        CONTINUE
          STOP
          END
          FUNCTION G(W)
          COMMON TWO,N1,N2,A1,A2,K11,K12,K21,K22
          REAL G,W,N1,N2,A1,A2,K11,K12,K21,K22
          LOGICAL TWO
          G = (A1 - K11*W - K12*N2)*W
          IF(TWO)  G = (A2 - K21*N1 - K22*W)*W
          RETURN
          END
```

● **PROBLEM** 22-23

The population flow between two regions, A and B, is assumed to be proportional to the difference in population density between the areas. Let $N_1(t)$, $N_2(t)$ be the populations in regions A and B respectively, with $N_1(0) = N_{10}$ and $N_2(0) = N_{20}$. The natural (i.e., in absence of immigration) rates of growth of the regions (per unit of time) are given by the following formulas:

Case (1): $\dot{N}_1 = rN_1$ $\hspace{3cm}$ (1)

$\hspace{2.2cm} \dot{N}_2 = (b - mN_2/2N_{20})N_2$ $\hspace{1.5cm}$ (2)

Case (2): $\dot{N}_1 = k(S - N_1)$ $\hspace{2.5cm}$ (3)

$\hspace{2.2cm} \dot{N}_2 = r_2 N_2$ $\hspace{3.3cm}$ (4)

Case (3): $\dot{N}_1 = k(S - N_1)$ $\hspace{2.5cm}$ (5)

$\hspace{2.2cm} \dot{N}_2 = (b - mN_2/2N_{20})N_2$ $\hspace{1.5cm}$ (6)

where r, r_2, b, m, k are positive constants, $0 < k < 1$.

Write a FORTRAN program which uses the modified Euler method to simulate this system from $t = 0$ to $t = t_f$.

Solution: A first representation of the system might be the flow graph on figure #1.

The rates of flow out of the sources and into the sinks are determined by natural "valves". The rates of flow between N_1 and N_2 are determined by valves which are controlled by density levels. Using this information, a detailed diagram of the system is shown on figure #2.

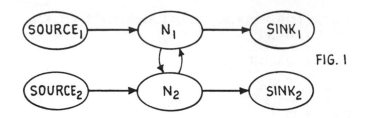

FIG. 1

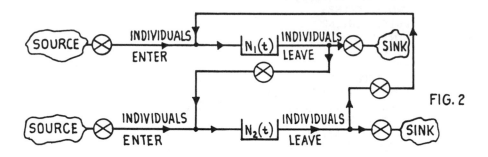

FIG. 2

The equations for the natural valves are equations (1)-(6). The equation for the inter-region population flow is

$$Q = C(N_1/A - N_2/B) \qquad (7)$$

where C is a proportionality constant. Density at A > Density at $B \Rightarrow Q > 0$. Therefore, the arbitrarily assumed direction of Q is toward B, away from A, and the complete state equations are

$$\dot{N}_1^* = \dot{N}_1 - Q \qquad (8)$$

$$\dot{N}_2^* = \dot{N}_2 + Q \qquad (9)$$

Case (1): Substitution of equations (1) and (2) into equations (8) and (9), respectively, yields:

$$\dot{N}_1^* = rN_1 - Q$$

$$\dot{N}_2^* = (b - mN_2/2N_{20})N_2 + Q$$

Substituting the formula for Q given by equation (7):

$$
\begin{aligned}
\dot{N}_1^* &= rN_1 - C(N_1/A - N_2/B) \\
&= (r - C/A)N_1 + (C/B)N_2 \\
&= C_{11}N_1 + C_{12}N_2 \qquad (10)
\end{aligned}
$$

where $C_{11} = r - C/A$ and $C_{12} = C/B$ can be evaluated outside of the simulation loop, reducing the number of operations per iteration by three:

$$
\begin{aligned}
\dot{N}_2^* &= (b - mN_2/2N_{20})N_2 + C(N_1/A - N_2/B) \\
&= (C/A)N_1 + (b - C/B)N_2 - (m/2N_{20})N_2^2 \\
&= C_{21}N_1 + C_{22}N_2 - C_3N_2^2 \qquad (11)
\end{aligned}
$$

where $C_{21} = C/A$, $C_{22} = b - C/B$, $C_3 = m/2N_{20}$. For this coupled, non-linear first-order system, the modified method is first applied to equation (10) and then to equation (11). A logical flag, TWO, is used to determine which equation is being integrated. The variable BIRTH is used for b:

```
         REAL T/0.0/,TFIN,DT,REALN,ACCUR,N1,N2,
            N10,N20,A,B,BIRTH,C,C11,C12,C21
            C22,C3,M,R
         INTEGER I,N
         LOGICAL TWO/.FALSE./
         COMMON N1,N2,TWO,C11,C12,C21,C22,C3
         READ,N,TFIN,ACCUR,N10,N20,A,B,BIRTH,C,M,R
         PRINT,T,N10,N20
         REALN = N
         DT = TFIN/REALN
         C11 = R - C/A
         C12 = C/B
         C21 = C/A
         C22 = BIRTH - C/B
         C3 = M/(2.*N20)
         N1 = N10
         N2 = N20
         DO 10 I = 1,N
            T = T + DT
            CALL MEULER(T,N1,ACCUR,DT)
            TWO = .TRUE.
            CALL MEULER(T,N2,ACCUR,DT)
            TWO = .FALSE.
            PRINT,T,N1,N2
10          CONTINUE
         STOP
         END
         FUNCTION G(W)
         REAL G,W,N1,N2,C11,C12,C21,C22,C3
         LOGICAL TWO
         COMMON N1,N2,TWO,C11,C12,C21,C22,C3
         G = C11*W + C12*N2
         IF (TWO) G = C21*N1 + C22*W - C3*W**2
         RETURN
         END
```

Case (2): Substituting equations (3) and (4) into equations (8) and (9), respectively, yield:

$$\overset{.*}{N}_1 = K(S - N_1) - Q$$

$$\overset{.*}{N}_2 = r_2 N_2 + Q$$

Substituting the formula for Q gives:

$$\overset{.*}{N}_1 = K(S - N_1) - C(N_1/A - N_2/B)$$

$$= -(K + C/A)N_1 + (C/B)N_2 + KS$$

$$= C_{11}N_1 + C_{12}N_2 + C_3$$

where $C_{11} = -(K + C/A)$, $C_{12} = C/B$, $C_3 = KS$

$$\overset{.*}{N}_2 = r_2 N_2 + C(N_1/A - N_2/B)$$

$$= (C/A)N_1 + (r - C/B)N_2$$

$$= C_{21}N_1 + C_{22}N_2$$

where $C_{21} = C/A$, $C_{22} = r - C/B$. Using the same procedure as used in Case (1):

```
        REAL T/0.0/,TFIN,DT,REALN,ACCUR,N1,N2,
1          N10,N20,A,B,C,K,R,S,C11,C12,C21
1          C22,C3
        INTEGER I,N
        LOGICAL TWO/.FALSE./
        COMMON N1,N2,TWO,C11,C12,C21,C22,C3
        READ,N,TFIN,ACCUR,N10,N20,A,B,C,K,R,S
        PRINT,T,N10,N20
        REALN = N
        DT = TFIN/REALN
        C11 =-(K + C/A)
        C12 = C/B
        C3 = K*S
        C21 = C/A
        C22 = R - C/B
        N1 = N10
        N2 = N20
        DO 10 I = 1,N
        T = T + DT
        CALL MEULER (T,N1,ACCUR,DT)
        TWO = .TRUE.
        CALL MEULER (T,N2,ACCUR,DT)
        TWO = .FALSE.
        PRINT,T,N1,N2
10      CONTINUE
        STOP
        END
        FUNCTION G(W)
        REAL G,W,N1,N2,C11,C12,C21,C22,C3
        LOGICAL TWO
        COMMON N1,N2,TWO,C11,C12,C21,C22,C3
        G = C11*W + C12*N2 + C3
        IF (TWO)G = C21*N1 + C22*W
        RETURN
        END
```

Case (3): Substituting equations (5) and (6) into equations (8) and (9), respectively, yield:

$$\dot{N}_1^* = K(S - N_1) - Q = -(K + C/A)N_1 + (C/B)N_2 + KS$$
$$= C_{11}N_1 + C_{12}N_2 + C_3$$

where $C_{11} = -(K + C/A)$, $C_{12} = C/B$, $C_3 = KS$

$$\dot{N}_2^* = (b - mN_2/2N_{20})N_2 + Q$$
$$= (C/A)N_1 + (b - C/B)N_2 - (m/2N_{20})N_2^2$$
$$= C_{21}N_1 + C_{22}N_2 - C_4N_2^2$$

where $C_{21} = C/A$, $C_{22} = b - C/B$, $C_4 = m/2N_{20}$. Using the same procedure

756

as used in Case (1), and using the variable BIRTH for b:

```
       REAL T/0.0/,TFIN,DT,REALN,ACCUR,N1,N2,N10,
1        N20,A,B,BIRTH,C,C11,C12,C21,C22,C3,C4,
1        K,M,S
       INTERGER I,N
       LOGICAL TWO/.FALSE./
       COMMON N1,N2,TWO,C11,C12,C21,C22,C3,C4
       READ,N,TFIN,ACCUR,N10,N20,A,B,BIRTH,C,K,M,S
       PRINT,T,N10,N20
       REALN = N
       DT = TFIN/REALN
       C11 = -(K + C/A)
       C12 = C/B
       C3 = K*S
       C21 = C/A
       C22 = BIRTH - C/B
       C4 = M/(2*N20)
       N1 = N10
       N2 = N20
       DO 10 I = 1,N
       T = T + DT
       CALL MEULER (T,N1,ACCUR,DT)
       TWO = .TRUE.
       CALL MEULER (T,N2,ACCUR,DT)
       TWO = .FALSE.
       PRINT,T,N1,N2
10     CONTINUE
       STOP
       END
       FUNCTION G(W)
       REAL G,W,N1,N2,C11,C12,C21,C22,C3,C4
       LOGICAL TWO
       COMMON N1,N2,TWO,C11,C12,C21,C22,C3,C4
       G = C11*W + C12*N2 + C3
       IF (TWO) G = C21*N1 + C22*W - C4*W**2
       RETURN
       END
```

CHAPTER 23

GENERAL TRACING
AND DEBUGGING

● **PROBLEM** 23-1

What are the main methods used for debugging a program and what are their advantages?

Solution: DEBUGGING is the procedure of eliminating bugs (errors) that almost every program has the first time it is run through the computer. These are some of the indications that the program does indeed have mistakes:
1)   The computer halts before completing the program and provides no answers.
2)   The computer gets caught in a loop and may never stop.
3)   The computer starts printing, but prints nonsense.
4)   The computer prints out what appears to be a good set of answers; but closer inspection reveals the answers to be wrong.

The following is a list of some of the most commonly used debugging methods:
1)   Preparing test data
2)   Having someone else look over the program
3)   Running the program to see what happens
4)   Planning ahead
5)   Running the program step by step
6)   Debugging with the automonitor
7)   Memory dumps
8)   On-line trouble shooting program (OTP) . Since 1) to 3) are common-sense methods little explanation is required for them. In preparing test-data one should be sure to include extreme values so that truncations can be noticed and at least allowed for. Also, the computer output should be compared with output computed by hand, if possible. This, of course, assumes the program is fit enough to generate output.
4)   Planning ahead is based upon occasionally including output statements into the program. Those output statements usually print intermediate results obtained up to that point. This allows the programmer to follow the execution of his program and check the intermediate results, accuracy of which is essential.
5) Running the program step by step: When the computer is in its MANUAL condition, pushing the SINGLE STEP key makes the computer perform one instruction. Each time this key is pushed, the computer will perform the instruction and change the lights on the control panel to indicate the address of the next instruction. In this way, the entire program is performed step by step. This method can only be used when working

directly with the central processing unit of the computer.
6) The automonitor program is an external program used to control the computer while the programmer is trying to run the program he is debugging. The automonitor program executes one instruction of the user program at a time. The result of what was just done is printed out and so, at the end, a complete printed record of what the program did is available (unlike method 5). Now, it is simply a matter of checking what was done incorrectly.
7) Using memory dumps means printing all or part of the computer memory at selected points along the program to see what is where, what data have been generated or used, whether the program is still there, etc.
8) OTP. Here, the programmer can sit at the computer keyboard and work out small sections of a program at a time. He can run small sections, add, remove, or change portions, trace the printout, etc. The programmer communicates with the computer via the conversational program (OTP). This means that the program gives and receives information in English. The advantages and disadvantages of methods 5) to 8) are as follows:
5) Running the program step by step ensures complete knowledge and, hence, the malfunctioning of the program can always be detected. But the method is time-consuming and expensive.
6) The automonitor is very slow in printing output. Since each step must be executed, a multi step DO loop for example, will take a lot of time to be printed (and to be read). Thus this method is useful only for short programs on inexpensive systems.
7) Memory dumps are rather complicated and require experience.
8) This method is useful for programs with many decisions and jumps since it allows the programmer to trace all these decisions and see how the program reacted to them. It is also faster than the auto-monitor.

● **PROBLEM** 23-2

How are tracers useful as a debugging aid?

Solution: Suppose a computer runs and executes a program but produces incorrect results. If the programmer is unable to locate the bugs by the usual methods (running test data, checking size dimensions, etc.), an emergency technique called tracing can be applied. Tracing is usually done with an interpreter, whose routine dissects, analyzes and executes pseudo-instructions. (Pseudo-instructions do not form part of the program but are necessary for its execution).
The tracer is an interpretive routine that analyzes and executes real machine instructions one at a time. To understand its operation consider the following problem:
The trouble with the program being debugged is suspected to be in the action of a loop. While the loop is being executed, the values of some variables go out of bounds. Using the tracer routine, the contents of the accumulator are printed out before each instruction in the loop is executed. The point at which the variables misbehave can thus be located.
The advantage of the trace routine is that the complete internal program is available for external inspection. This is, at the same time, its disadvantage. A series of nested loops may require a few thousand iterations. All these iterations will be executed and printed at printer speed. Clearly, the computer time involved is prohibitive. Hence, tracing functions have been modified to execute

only non-branch commands, attached to high speed printers. If a branch is met, selected registers are printed before execution of the branch.

Debug the following FORTRAN program for finding the roots of a quadratic equation:

```
         $ JOB
     C    PROGRAM TO CALCULATE ROOTS OF QUADRATIC EQN.
     C    ASSUME POSITIVE DISCRIMINANT
     C    READ INPUT DATA
1)        READ (5,100),A,B,C
2)   100  FORMAT (3E12.5)
     C    CALCULATE ROOTS
3)        DISC = (B**2 - 4.*A*C)**.5
4)        X1 = (-B + DISH)/2.*A
5)        X2 = (-B - DISC)/2.*A
     C    WRITE OUTPUT
6)        WRITE (6,300) A,B,C,X1,X2
7)   200  FORNAT (5(5X,E12.5))
8)        STOP
9)        END
```

Solution: The two most common kinds of errors that a programmer can commit are 1) syntax errors. 2) logical errors. Syntax errors are detected by the compiler when translating from the source language to the machine language. Thus the data will not be processed and no results will be obtained. On the other hand, if a program is free of syntax errors but contains logical errors, the machine will process the program. The output obtained will be an incorrect solution to the problem the program was designed to solve. Going through the program, note the following syntax errors:

Statement (1) contains an extra comma after (5,100).
Statement (4) defines the discriminant as DISH instead of DISC (presumably what the programmer meant.) However, this is not recognized as an error by the compiler, which interprets DISH as a correct variable name.

Statement (6) is the WRITE statement with the format label 300, while statement (7) is the corresponding format statement labelled 200. This error can be corrected by changing the value of either of those two labels to be identical to the other one.

Statement (7) has the word FORMAT incorrectly spelled as FORNAT, which the compiler cannot decode.

If any of these errors remain uncorrected (except for the one in statement (4)) the compiler cannot finish its task of translating the FORTRAN program into the machine language.

Assuming there are no syntax errors, the program will be processed by the compiler and passed to memory from where the central processing unit will manipulate the data according to the program instructions. It will then transmit the results of these manipulations to the external output device.

If logical errors are present, the output is suspect. The given program contains the following logical errors:

(4)   DISH has not been defined anywhere. Thus X1 cannot be evaluated.

(5)   Note that according to the statement
$$X2 = ((-B - DISC)/2.)*A$$

This gives the wrong result since we want
$$X2 = (-B - DISC)/(2.*A).$$

This error can be easily detected after a few sample runs of the program. However, if the calculated roots formed part of the input to a minor subroutine in a huge program, extensive logical debugging would be required to locate the error.

● **PROBLEM 23-4**

Debug the following programs, written in FORTRAN and BASIC respectively.

```
      C     FORTRAN PROGRAM TO SOLVE COMPOUND
            INTEREST PROBLEM
      100   FORMAT (F9.2,F5.4,I3)
      200   FORNAT (5X,'P = ', F9.2,5X'I = ',F5.4,
            5X,'N = ',I3,5X,'A = ',F9.2)
            REAL I
            READ,(5,100) P,I,N
            A = (P*(1. + I)**N
            WRITE (6,20) P,I,N,A
            STOP
            END
      10    REM BASIC PROGRAM TO SOLVE COMPOUND
      20    REM INTEREST PROBLEM
      30    INPUT P,I,N
      40    LET A = P*(1 + I)*N
      50    PRINT "P = ";P,"I = ";I, "N = "; N, "A = "; A
      60    END
```

Solution: When a computer program is written, it usually contains two different types of errors. The first kind are grammatical (or syntactical) errors, the second kind are logical errors. Syntactical errors are caused by incorrectly written program statements. These errors are easily detected since a program containing such errors usually cannot be executed. In addition, the computer prints out a diagnostic message that identifies the location and nature of each error.

When the program contains a logical error the computer correctly carries out the given instructions, but the wrong instructions produce incorrect results.

Turning to the given problem, the FORTRAN program has the following errors:

1) FORMAT has been misspelled as FORNAT in statement 200. Since FORNAT is not part of the compiler's vocabulary, an error message

761

is printed. The program cannot be executed because the nature of the input has not been specified (this is, of course, done by the FORMAT statement).

2) In FORTRAN, instructions must correspond exactly to a given prototype. Any deviation results in an error message. Here, the READ statement has a comma after it. In FORTRAN, READ is followed by a comma only in the unformatted input statement. Since the READ statement in the given program is formatted, there should be no comma after READ.

3) The statement $A = (P*(1 + I)**N$ is missing a right parenthesis. Some compilers (PL/I for example) may make the insertion, but

FORTRAN is strict. An error message is sent out, and the program 'bombs'.

4) The WRITE (6,20) P,I,N,A statement contains a reference to a statement labelled 20 (the alleged FORMAT statement). But since the corresponding FORMAT statement is labelled 200, the compiler is stymied. It prints an error message.
Note that all of the above errors were syntactical errors.
Consider the BASIC program for solving the compound interest problem. Statement 40 is

$$40 \quad \text{LET A = P*(1 + I)*N} \tag{1}$$

Algebraically, the formula for the amount A from a given principal P held for N years at interest I is
$$A = P(1 + I)^N.$$

But statement 40 says
$$A = P(1 + I)N .$$

Hence it should be changed to
$$A = P*(1 + I)\uparrow N. \tag{2}$$

Comparing (1) and (2) one is tempted to think that the $\uparrow$ was mistyped as $*$ and that this is a syntax error. But the compiler will accept (1) as a valid BASIC statement. The CPU will execute it and print the results which, unfortunately, are useless to the programmer. Hence this is a logical, not a syntactical error.

● **PROBLEM** 23-5

The following BASIC program is supposed to calculate the sum of the squares of the first 10 digits. Find the syntactical and logical errors.

```
10    PROGRAM TO CALCULATE SUM OF SQUARES OF
20    FIRST TEN DIGITS.
30    LET SUM = 0
40    LET J = 1
50    LET S = J
60    IF J = 10 THEN GO TO 90
70    LET J = J + 1
80    GO TO 50
90    PRINT S
100   END.
```

<u>Solution</u>: Syntax errors are errors in the grammar of the programming language being used. They are detected by the compiler and hence the program is returned even before it is executed, i.e., no output is printed.

Statements 10 and 20 are comment lines. But they are not prefaced by REM (the obligatory method of informing the BASIC compiler that a remark is forthcoming). Hence the compiler treats 10 and 20 as instructions, which cannot be done. Compilation stops and the program is ejected at line 10.

Statement 30 initializes the variable SUM. Unfortunately BASIC allows only two character variable names (of the form <u>letter</u> <u>digit</u>). Hence SUM is an invalid variable name and compilation ceases. Statement 60 is:

$$60 \quad \text{IF } J = 10 \text{ THEN GO TO } 90 \tag{1}$$

Now when the compiler begins translation of this statement into machine language it classifies 60 as of the form

$$60 \quad \text{IF } X = 10 \text{ THEN } 90 \tag{2}$$

Comparing (2) and (1), the place where 90 should be is taken by GO. Thus the compiler reads

$$60 \quad \text{IF } X = 10 \text{ THEN GO}$$

Since GO is not a statement number the instruction is nonsense. The program remains uncompiled.

Finally in 100, END is succeeded by a period. The compiler is aware that END signifies that compilation is over and execution can begin but END. is not recognized.

(Note that this last is an error only if, when the compiler has started on a line, it works through to the last column. If the compiler stops translating a line after receiving a sound construction, then the period will make no difference.)
After all the above errors have been corrected the program is ready for execution. It looks like this:

```
10    REM PROGRAM TO CALCULATE SUM OF SQUARES OF
20    REM FIRST TEN DIGITS
30    LET S = 0
40    LET J = 1
50    LET S = J
60    IF J = 10 THEN 90
70    LET J = J + 1
80    GO TO 50
90    PRINT S
100   END
```

The program is executed, but the output is 10. The program gives a wrong result. Logical errors are errors in the meaning of the program. The program is grammatically sound (otherwise the compiler would have rejected it). But its meaning is not what the programmer intended. As an analogy consider the English language sentence

The selfish house slept furiously.

The statement has nouns and verbs in the right order and the
descriptive words are acceptable too. The punctuation is accurate.
But the total sentence is almost meaningless. ('Almost' since it
could appear in a poem or modern novel).

Examining the program for logical flaws, observe that squares have
not been calculated. Thus the program must be corrected if the
desired result is to be obtained:
    Statement 50 should be as follows:

```
50    LET S = S + J↑2   or
50    LET S = S + J*J .
```

APPENDIX

PROGRAMMING CONCEPTS (PART I)

Programming is, simply, the process of planning the solution to a problem. Thus, by writing:

1. Take the reciprocal of the resistance of all resistors (expressed in ohms);
2. Sum the values obtained in step 1;
3. Take the reciprocal of the sum derived in step 2. A generalized process or program for finding the total resistance of a parallel resistance circuit has now been derived.

To progress from this example to preparing a program for a computer is not difficult; however, one basic characteristic of the computer must be kept in mind. It cannot think. It can only follow certain commands and these commands must be correctly expressed and must cover all possibilities. Thus, a program, if it is to be useful in a computer, must be broken down into specifically defined operations or steps. Then the instructions, along with other data necessary for performing these operations or steps, must be communicated to the computer in the form of a language or code that is acceptable to the machine. In broad terms, the steps that the computer follows in executing a program are as follows: It reads the instructions (sequentially unless otherwise programmed), and in accordance with these instructions it (1) locates the parameters (constants) and such other data as may be necessary for problem solution, (2) transfers the parameters and data to the point of manipulation, (3) manipulates the parameters and data in accordance with certain rules of logic, (4) stores the results of such manipulations in a specific location, and (5) provides the operator (user) with a useful output. Even in a program of elementary character such as the one above, this would involve breaking each of the steps down into a series of machine operations. Then these instructions and the parameters and data necessary for problem solution must be translated into a language or code that the computer can accept.

Consideration of these steps indicates that programming a fairly complex problem will involve writing a large number of instructions and keeping track of the great many memory cells that are used for storage of these instructions and the data necessary for problem solution. This is time consuming and could lead to error.

To reduce the amount of time required for writing a complex program and the possibility of error, an aid called the compiler has been developed. The compiler is, itself, a program which takes certain orders and then writes, in a form the machine understands, the instructions necessary for a given computer to execute these orders. Compilers are built at various levels, or degrees of complexity. The simplest form of compiler takes one mnemonic phrase and writes one machine instruction, e.g.,

RSH.A9

would cause the compiler to write an instruction which would shift the contents of the A register right 11_8 places. Note the advantages: (1) no opportunity to use the wrong function code; and (2) no necessity to convert to the shift count to octal.

Note: A computer written on this level is commonly referred to as an "Assembler."

A more sophisticated compiler may take a statement such as "MULTIPLY PRINCIPAL BY

765

PROGRAMMING CONCEPTS (PART I)

RATE" and generate all the instructions necessary for the computer to

1. Locate the factors involved (in this case the principal and the rate)
2. Transfer these factors to the arithmetic unit.
3. Perform the indicated arithmetic (or logical) operation (in this case the multiplication of the principal by the rate)
4. Start the resultant (which in this case will be the interest or the principal).

Further, the compiler would keep track of all memory allocations, whether being used for data or instructions. Compilers will be discussed at greater length in the next chapter.

PROGRAMMING FUNDAMENTALS

Depending on the complexity of the problem to be solved, programs may vary in length from a very few instructions to many thousands of instructions. Ultimately, the program could begin to occupy a significant portion, perhaps even an excessive portion, of computer memory. One method used to preclude this possibility is to segment the program, storing seldom used portions in an auxiliary storage and reading these portions into main memory only when they are required. In any event, the program should be written in as concise a form as possible in order to prevent wasting valuable memory space.

SUBROUTINES

An important method of developing this conciseness is through the use of subroutines.

Obviously, as a program grows larger certain functions will be repeated. If the instructions necessary to perform each of these repeated functions are grouped to form subroutines, these subroutines may then be referenced by a relatively few instructions in the main program each time one of the functions is to be repeated. Thus obviating the necessity of writing into the main program all of the instructions necessary to perform a function each time it is to be repeated.

Dependent upon the function being performed, a subroutine may contain other subroutines or be part of a larger subroutine.

EXECUTIVE ROUTINES

The instructions which control access to the various subroutines are referred to as the executive routine or the main program. Dependent upon the complexity of the program, there may also be subexecutive routines, within the executive routines.

Housekeeping is a term frequently used with subroutines. At the time of entry into a subroutine, the contents of the various addressable registers may or may not be of value. Hence, the programmer will, unless he is sure they are of no value, take steps to preserve the contents of these registers upon entry into a subroutine and restore them prior to exit. This process is termed housekeeping.

The Jump and Return Jump Instructions

The Jump and Return Jump instructions are a special type of instruction included in the computer's repertoire to facilitate construction of executive routines. These instructions provide the computer with the means to leave the sequential execution of the main program or executive routine, execute any of the subroutines stored in its memory then return to the execution of the main program once the subroutine has been executed. The process is as follows:

Execution of a Return Jump instruction causes the address of the next instruction to be executed in the main program to be stored (usually in the entry cell of the subroutine). Then it causes the instruction contained in the second cell of the subroutine to be executed. The last instruction to be executed in a subroutine will usually be a straight Jump to the address contained in the entry cell. Since a Jump instruction specifies the address of the next instruction to be executed, the computer is then provided with a means for returning to the main program once the subroutine has been executed.

ROGRAM CONSTRUCTION

The process of writing a program can be oken down into six basic steps:

1. Statement—Form a clear, comprehensive atement of the problem. It may seem contra-ctory to say that stating the problem is, in 'fect, one step in solving it. However, consider e following statements: (1) Solve to find the arallel resistance of a circuit; (2) Solve to find e total resistance of a circuit containing as any as ten parallel resistors having values arying between 10Ω and 1000Ω, all values to e correct to three decimal places. Now, it is bvious that the second statement is much more eaningful and will contribute more to laying ut the problem for solution.

2. Analysis—Analysis consists of laying out e problem in a form susceptible to arith-etical and/or logical computation, determining /hat logical decisions must be made, and what caling is required. (Scaling is discussed as a eparate topic later in this chapter.) Depending pon the programmer and the problem, outside ssistance may be required. This step is occasion-lly referred to as "making a model." For the roblem under consideration, the first step is to etermine the proper method for calculating arallel resistance. This equation is readily vailable either from the programmer's own xperience or a basic text. Then considering the quation and the statement of the problem the ollowing equation can be written:

$$R_t = \cfrac{1}{\cfrac{1}{R} + \cfrac{1}{R_2} \cdots \cdots \cfrac{1}{R_{10}}}$$

where the resistors, R1 to R10, could be any value between 10.000_{10} ohms and 1000.000_{10} ohms, and R_t, the total resistance, could be any value between 1.000_{10} ohms and 1000.000_{10} ohms.

The next step is to note that a programmed test must be made to discover how many branch values must be determined. Finally, the pro-grammer must determine how many binary places must be retained to give the required base 10 accuracy. A good analysis of the problem leads directly to the next step in construction.

3. Flow diagram—A flow diagram, or chart, is an elaboration of step two in which special symbols are used to denote the various oper-ations to be performed and the sequence in which they fall. Later in this chapter a flow chart will be developed for the problem just analyzed.

4. Encoding—Encoding is the process of converting the operations listed in the flow-chart into the language the computer will use, either machine instructions, words, or compiler state-ments.

5. Debugging—Debugging is the process of locating errors in the program. Various tech-niques are available for this purpose. A program may be written to include some aids itself or a separate debugging program may be run to test the operation of a malfunctioning program. Additionally for a very simple program, a trial solution may be done on paper and the computed results compared with those actually obtained at each step.

6. Documentation—It is not sufficient to merely write a program which runs properly. Changes may be necessary later or it may be desirable to use the program or subroutines from within another program. This requires that a program be documented. Minimum documenta-tion should include:

a. Title of program
b. Statement of the problem (abstract)
c. Programmer's name
d. Date
e. Memory area used and/or number of cells used
f. Registers used
g. I/0 devices required
h. Flow diagrams
i. Hard copy (program listings, especially a listing of the machine coded instruc-tions)
j. Program tapes

Documentation

A full documentation requires that each document be structured from the following components in the sequence listed.

a. Front Cover (Mandatory)
b. Title Page (Mandatory)
c. Special Notices (As required)
d. Abstract (Mandatory in FD, CM, PM and TR)[1]
e. Table of Contents (Mandatory)
f. List of Figures (As required)
g. Record of Changes (As required)
h. List of Effective Pages (As required)
i. Text (Mandatory)
j. Appendixes (As required)
  (1) Glossary (As required)
  (2) References (As required)
  (3) Bibliography (As required)
  (4) Other Appendixes (As required)
k. Index (Optional)
l. Distribution List (Mandatory)
m. Back Cover (Mandatory)

Note 1: Two-letter mnemonic identifier of the name of the document type.

FD   Functional Description
RD   Data Requirements Document
SS   System/Subsystem Specification
PS   Program Specification
DS   Data Base Specification
PM* Project Manual
CM   Command/Management Manual
OM   Computer Operation Manual
MM   Program Maintenance Manual
PT   Test and Implementation Plan
RT   Test Analysis Report
TN   Technical Note
TR   Technical Report

*Project manual mnemonic assignment occurs only when the Command/Management, Computer Operation, and Program Maintenance manuals are bound as a single document of under 200 pages for small projects.

FRONT COVER.—The front cover of each document shall display the following information, as shown in the layout in figure 9-1.

a. Activity name.
b. Activity seal.
c. Document type (use mnemonic identifier, see note 1 above).

d. Document title and subtitle (may include superseding statement).
e. Document number.
f. Security identification (including classification of the document, downgrading notice, distribution notice, and espionage law notation), if classified.

TITLE PAGE.—The title page shall contain only the following information:

a. Activity name.
b. Document title and subtitle (may include superseding statement).
c. Document type.
d. Date.
e. Document number.
f. User designator if the document is prepared for a specific user.
g. Contractor and contract number designation, if the document has been prepared by a contractor under the guidance of the approving activity.
h. Security identification (including classification of the document, downgrading notice, distribution notice, and espionage law notation), if classified.
i. Copy number, if required.

The layout of a title page is shown in figure 9-2. The actual layout of the above items may be varied when circumstances require the use of a "window" front cover which displays a portion of the title page as part of the front cover.

SPECIAL NOTICES.—Special notices may contain information concerning the status of a document, instructions for its handling, letters of promulgation, the status of the contents of the document, the date the provisions of the document become effective, credit to an individual or organization for the preparation of the document or such other information as may be pertinent.

ABSTRACT.—The abstract is a brief summary (not to exceed 250 words), preferably unclassified, of the function, purpose, scope, and content of the computer program/system or study

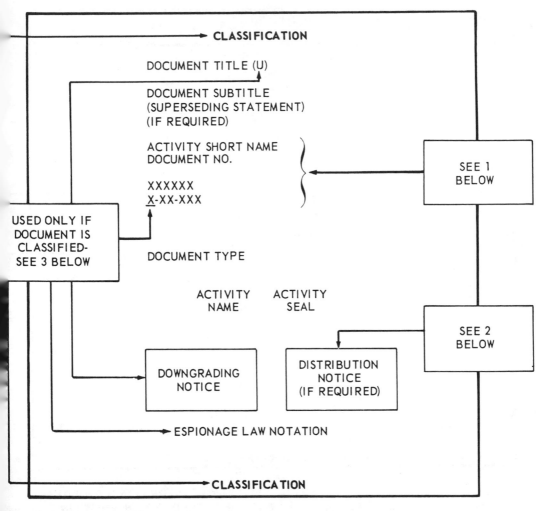

CLASSIFICATION

DOCUMENT TITLE (U)

DOCUMENT SUBTITLE
(SUPERSEDING STATEMENT)
(IF REQUIRED)

ACTIVITY SHORT NAME
DOCUMENT NO.

XXXXXX
X-XX-XXX

SEE 1
BELOW

USED ONLY IF
DOCUMENT IS
CLASSIFIED-
SEE 3 BELOW

DOCUMENT TYPE

ACTIVITY   ACTIVITY
NAME   SEAL

SEE 2
BELOW

DOWNGRADING
NOTICE

DISTRIBUTION
NOTICE
(IF REQUIRED)

ESPIONAGE LAW NOTATION

CLASSIFICATION

1. THE DOCUMENT NUMBER SHALL CONSIST OF TWO LINES OF INFORMATION BENEATH
THE DESIGNATOR OF THE COMMAND PREPARING THE DOCUMENT. THE FIRST LINE
SHALL BE THE PROJECT NUMBER UNDER WHICH THE DOCUMENT IS PRODUCED. THE
SECOND LINE CONTAINS THE CONTROL NUMBER IDENTIFYING THE INDIVIDUAL
DOCUMENT.
2. DISTRIBUTION STATEMENT APPEARING ON THE DOCUMENT ARE THE RESPONSIBILITY
OF THE DOCUMENT ORIGINATOR AND WILL BE ASSIGNED IN ACCORDANCE WITH THE
APPROPRIATE NAVMAT INSTRUCTIONS.
3. DOCUMENT CLASSIFICATION AND AUTOMATIC DOWNGRADING ARE THE RESPONSIBILITY
OF THE ORIGINATOR AND WILL BE ASSIGNED IN ACCORDANCE WITH THE APPROPRIATE
OPNAV INSTRUCTIONS.

Figure 9-1.—Layout of front cover.

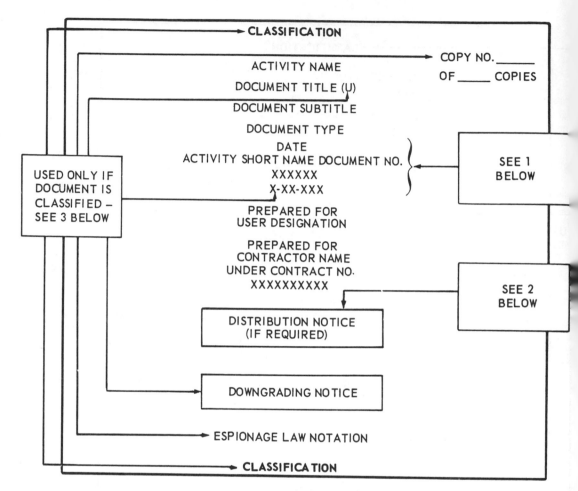

1. THE DOCUMENT NUMBER SHALL CONSIST OF TWO LINES OF INFORMATION BENEATH THE DESIGNATOR OF THE COMMAND PREPARING THE DOCUMENT. THE FIRST LINE SHALL BE THE PROJECT NUMBER UNDER WHICH THE DOCUMENT IS PRODUCED. THE SECOND LINE CONTAINS THE CONTROL NUMBER IDENTIFYING THE INDIVIDUAL DOCUMENT.

2. DISTRIBUTION STATEMENTS APPEARING ON THE DOCUMENT ARE THE RESPONSIBILITY OF THE DOCUMENT ORIGINATOR AND WILL BE ASSIGNED IN ACCORDANCE WITH THE APPROPRIATE NAVMAT INSTRUCTIONS.

3. DOCUMENT CLASSIFICATION AND AUTOMATIC DOWNGRADING ARE THE RESPONSIBILITY OF THE ORIGINATOR AND WILL BE ASSIGNED IN ACCORDANCE WITH APPROPRIATE OPNAV INSTRUCTIONS.

Figure 9-2.—Layout of title page.

escribed in the document. Included in the abstract of computer programs/systems must be information concerning inputs, processing, and outputs. An abstract of study must summarize essential facts, findings, conclusions, and recommendations. The purpose of the abstract is to assist potential users in determining the usefulness of the subject matter to their particular environment and to summarize the most significant material in the document clearly and concisely. The abstract should be in narrative form and include no special characters.

TABLE OF CONTENTS.—The table of contents shall list the identification number or code, title, and page number of each of the following:

a. Section
b. Numbered paragraph
c. Appendix

Tabulation shall ordinarily be at least to the third organizational level; e.g., 3.11.1.

LIST OF FIGURES.—The list of figures shall account for each figure included in the text and appendixes of a document. For each figure, the figure number, title, and beginning page number shall be shown.

RECORD OF CHANGES (FIG. 9-3).—A record of changes page to be used to record changes made to a document shall be included when frequent changes to the document are expected. This page shall be arranged in columnar form and provide spaces for the change number, the date of the change, the date the change was entered, and the signature of the individual making the change.

LIST OF EFFECTIVE PAGES (FIG. 9-4).—This list shall be provided when frequent changes to the document are expected or when strict page accountability is desired. Each page of the document and its change number shall be listed.

TEXT.—The text shall conform to the prescribed content for the document type being prepared. Figures may be used to clarify or illustrate the technical content.

APPENDIXES.—Appendixes shall contain material which supports, but is not readily incorporated into, the text. Included within appendixes may be narrative material or illustrations. Appendixes shall generally be ordered in the same sequence as they are referenced in the text. When classified or bulky, appendixes may be bound separately.

GLOSSARY.—This appendix shall provide definitions of acronyms and abbreviations used within the document. Also defined shall be terms and phrases that carry connotations significant to the subject being documented. These definitions shall be concise and avoid ambiguity. Terms and phrases defined in dictionaries or accepted data processing vocabularies, such as NAVSO P-3097, need not be defined.

Explanations of terms unique to specific computer programs may be provided but shall be separate from the above definitions. Item names, location tags, short program names, etc., may be included. For each, a cross reference to the full name of the computer program that uses them should be provided.

REFERENCES.—This appendix shall be provided if more than five sources are cited in the text. All references listed must be referred to in the text and shall generally be presented in the same order as they are referenced in the text. Each source listed in the appendix must be identified by an Arabic numeral. The identifying information for each reference shall be presented in the order shown in the following examples.

Example a. Books—Author's name, *name of the book,* book identification number (if any), (place of publication, name of publisher, date of edition), and pages being cited.

Example b. Periodicals—Author's name, "title of article," *name of periodical,* volume number (if any), date, and pages being cited.

BIBLIOGRAPHY.—This appendix shall provide a list of indirect references which are worthy of note by the reader. The sources listed in the bibliography shall have no identifying number, but must be listed in alphabetical order

RECORD OF CHANGES			
CHANGE NUMBER	DATE OF CHANGE	DATE ENTERED	BY WHOM ENTERED

Figure 9-3.—Layout for record of change page(s).

164.134

LIST OF EFFECTIVE PAGES			
PAGE	CHANGE NO.	PAGE	CHANGE NO.

Figure 9-4.—Layout of list of effective pages.

of the last names of the authors. References credited to no specific author shall be listed first. A short summary, usually not to exceed four lines, may be provided.

OTHER APPENDIXES.—Other appendixes may be provided as required.

INDEX.—The index shall contain an alphabetical list of names, subjects, etc. together with their paragraph numbers.

DISTRIBUTION LIST.—This list shall be composed of the names and codes of commands, activities, and offices (external to the originating organization) which are to receive copies of the document. When wide distribution will be made, Standard Navy Distribution List (SNDL) codes should be used.

BACK COVER.—The back cover shall be blank, except for security classification if the document is classified.

PROGRAMMING AIDS AND TECHNIQUES

To reduce the amount of work and, hence, the time required for programming, various programming aids may be utilized. A compiler is one such aid; other commonly used aids are described below.

Indexing

Various operations are included under the title indexing. These are: (1) counting the number of times an operation is performed; (2) the process of modifying the operand portion of an instruction word prior to its execution without modifying it as contained in memory; and (3) tagging data in a file in memory. The first two processes are of particular interest at this time.

To facilitate indexing, certain addressable registers are incorporated into the computer. The circuitry associated with each of these registers will, as a result of a comparison made between the contents of the registers and some other value, cause the count in the registers to be incremented or decremented. Also depending

on the outcome of this comparison, a program branch decision will be made.

For example, a computer might well have in its repertoire of instructions an instruction which would do the following upon execution; (1) test the contents of a specific index register for equality to zero; (2) if not equal to zero, decrement the contents by one and execute the next instruction; and (3) if equal to zero execute the instruction whose address is contained in the operand portion of the instruction. This, of course, is just one example; a great many variations are possible.

In addition to the foregoing, other circuits may be incorporated which will permit adding the contents of a specific index register to the operand portion of an instruction word after it is brought from memory and prior to its execution.

Index instructions are powerful programming tools especially in the area to be discussed next.

Loops

A loop is a sequence of instructions that are executed repeatedly until a terminal condition prevails. Thus, a loop is a group of instructions which perform a repetitive function.

PARTS OF A LOOP.—In general, a loop may be broken down into four parts. These are:

1. The instructions which initialize the loop. These instructions establish the parameters determining the number of times the loop is to be repeated and the modifications that are to be made to the loop each time it is repeated. (Note: These instructions are normally not repeated once the loop is initialized.)

2. The productive instructions. These instructions perform the desired function of the loop (computations, transfer operations, etc.).

3. Bookkeeping or indexing instructions. These instructions are used to modify the productive instructions and to keep track of the number of times the loop has been repeated.

4. Terminating instructions. These instructions are used to exit the loop once a desired terminal condition has been established.

PROGRAMMING CONCEPTS (PART I)

SAMPLE LOOP.—The following problem is posed to demonstrate more thoroughly the process of setting up a loop. It is desired to pair two sets of numbers, sum each pair and place the sum in a new location. If any sum equals zero, the loop is terminated. There will be 10_8 numbers in each set. Set one will be in memory cells M→M+7; set two in cells M+10→M+17; the sums will be stored in cells M+20→M+27.

INITIALIZE.—It is desired to go through the loop 10_8 times unless an unusual condition develops. Therefore, if the loop is indexed at the beginning, a count of 10_8 is used; if it is indexed at the end, a count of 7 will be used since the loop has already been traversed once. (Note: Using a wrong count is a very common error when programming and can cause serious confusion). This loop will be indexed at the end, so a count of 7 will be entered in index register number 1.

Index register number 2 will hold an address modifier and will be cleared prior to entering the loop.

COMPUTE.—This portion covers the addition of the pairs and storage of the sums. After each addition, a zero test is performed and the loop is terminated should the sum be zero.

MODIFY.—In this portion index register #1 is decremented by one each time the loop is completed, and after each pass index, register #2 is incremented by one.

TERMINATION.—The loop will be terminated when (1) a sum of zero is found, or (2) the count in index register #1 reaches zero. Condition (2) is the normal exit for this loop. "Normal exit" is a term sometimes used to refer to the expected or desired exit when a loop or subroutine has more than one exit. The termination instructions executed as a result of condition (1) would probably initiate a subroutine which would determine why the sum of the addition is zero, or they may even stop the computer so that the operator can make this determination. On the other hand, termination instructions executed as a result of condition (2) would probably enable the computer to continue normal operations, that is, sequential execution of the main program (executive routine).

The steps or instructions as they would be executed are stated in mnemonic form as follows:

STEP	OPERATION
1	Set index register 1 = 7
2	Clear index register 2
3	(M + IR#2)* → accumulator
4	(accum) + (M + 10 + IR#2) → accumulator
5	(accum) = 0? Yes → exit loop; No → step 6
6	(accum) → M + 20 + IR #2
7	(IR#2) + 1 → IR#2
10	IR#1 = 0? Yes → exit loop; No → step 11
11	(IR#1) - 1 → IR#1
12	Go to step 3

*(M+IR#2) is read: The contents of the memory cell whose address is M plus the value in index register 2. Thus, if M = 1004 and (IR#2 = 4), the contents of address 1010 are read.

REPEAT INSTRUCTIONS.—Another method is usually available to execute the functions of a simple loop; this is a Repeat instruction. Execution of the Repeat instruction causes the next instruction to be repeated the number of times specified in the Repeat instruction operand. Provision is generally made to permit modifications to the repeated instruction after each execution. For some repeated instructions a test may be executed after each repetition so the repeat mode may be aborted (exit from the loop prior to exhausting the repeat count.)

Scaling

Scaling was mentioned briefly as a part of the analysis of the problem. However, dependent upon the method of programming, it may be of continuing concern throughout the construction of the program. There are three different methods of scaling used: fixed point, floating point, and double precision. The selection of the system used will be based upon the range in magnitude of the numbers handled, the number of significant digits required in the solution, and the word size of the computer.

FIXED POINT ARITHMETIC.—In the situation where all numbers can be located in a register with the desired degree of accuracy, the fixed point system is used. In the fixed point system the radix is arbitrarily located and all numbers aligned accordingly.

Assume that a 30 bit word length is available, the most significant bit is the sign bit, and the radix point is located between 2^{14} and 2^{15}. Then the absolute value of the smallest number which can be entered is $00000.00001(_8)$ and the absolute value of the largest is $37777.77777(_8)$.

Any number exceeding these limits has to be multiplied by some power of two, and the programmer must keep track of the operation. If for example, it becomes necessary to add $527641.00342(_8)$ and $00153.43200(_8)$ the numbers 05276.41003 and 00001.53432 could be used, but the programmer would have to note somewhere that the numbers had been scaled down, and the solution must be scaled back up. When numbers of widely varying magnitude are encountered, the fixed point system is no longer usable and the floating point system is used.

FLOATING POINT ARITHMETIC.—All numbers in floating point arithmetic are expressed as a fraction multiplied by some power of two.

Thus:
1010011	=	.1010011	x	2^7
.000101	=	.101	x	2^{-3}
-111011	=	.111011	x	2^6
-.0001101	=	.1101	x	2^{-3}

and each data word would be broken into sign bits, fractional part (the mantissa), and exponential part (the characteristic). All rules of exponents must be observed when handling the numbers.

In some situations neither of the systems described is by itself sufficient. For example, it is possible that a calculation must be carried to 10 or 15 significant decimal places. Because it takes an average of 3.23 binary digits to write a

decimal digit, it is easy to see that a fixed length computer word will be readily exceeded.

DOUBLE PRECISION ARITHMETIC.— Double precision arithmetic is the method used to overcome this problem. Double precision indicates the use of two computer words to store a single data entry; however, in actual practice it is entirely possible that more than two words will be used. By using a combination of floating point and double precision, handling data of widely varying magnitudes and as many significant places as necessary is possible, including the foregoing example.

It is apparent that a large amount of programming is required to use these systems. Fortunately, however, the programming has already been done, and unless required as an exercise, a programmer has only to go to the program library to find the material he needs. The various compilers may have the required routines in them for performing these functions also.

Input/Output Programming

The I/O program is used to establish communications between the computer and its peripheral equipment. Communication involves not only the transfer of data, but also the commands which control the operation of the peripheral equipment. Although computers differ in the manner in which they handle the problem, certain factors are common to all.

First of all, the computer will have several I/O channels and/or provisions for multiplexing equipment on a channel. The reason is, of course, the relative slowness of the peripheral equipment. Thus, an I/O instruction will have a portion used to identify the channel or equipment.

The computer's I/O section will probably operate independent of the rest of the computer once an I/O operation has been initiated; this permits I/O operations and computations to occur simultaneously. This is particularly convenient when a large number of cells are to be filled or transmitted. (Note: Transmission of one cell's data is referred to as a single cell buffer; transmission of the data in more than one cell with a single command is called a block buffer.)

PROGRAMMING CONCEPTS (PART I)

It may be desirable to alert the main program when a block buffer is completed; if so, the I/0 instruction must be capable of performing the function. Additionally, since the peripheral equipment is relatively slow it may become necessary to hold up the main program until the buffer is completed. Instructions will probably be available to test for an I/0 channel active as part of this requirement. Different computers use different methods of defining the buffer limits (either a single cell or block). A common method is to reference an address in the I/0 word. Then stored at the referenced address is a word which defines the buffer limits.

Two additional I/0 instructions are used to control the operation of the peripheral equipment. The execution of the first of these, the external function (EXF) instruction, sets a command line and causes data to be placed on the lines to the equipment. The control section of the peripheral equipment detects the command signal, translates the data, and causes the equipment to execute the function. (Examples of these functions for a magtape unit might be rewind, write forward, read reverse, etc.) Depending upon the system used, the EXF code may occur in the operand portion of the EXF instruction or in a separate data word. If the code is in a separate data word, the operand portion of the EXF word contains the address of the cell containing the code.

It is usually desirable for the peripheral equipment to keep the computer informed of its status. It would be absurd to give the magtape unit a rewind command when it i. at the beginning of tape and then wait for it to rewind, or to give a write command when the unit is not enabled and then wait for it to write. Therefore, peripheral equipment is designed to keep the computer informed. This is done by placing a signal on a command line and a code on the data lines. When detected by the computer, the signal causes the computer to leave the main program and go to a special memory address (a separate address is usually associated with each channel) and execute the instruction contained therein. Thus, this signal is usually referred to as an interrupt since it interrupts the main program. The interrupt will occur in response to any of the following situations: (1) EXF word sent and

equipment able/unable to comply; (2) a function ordered by the computer has been completed; or (3) there is a change in the operational status of the equipment.

Since the computer jumps from the main program while processing an interrupt, steps must be taken to preserve the next program address; this is done by programmer action and with the aid of the Return Jump instruction.

The I/0 instruction, employed when an interrupt is to be honored, stores the interrupt code in a designated cell in computer memory. (This is necessary because the interrupt is usually out of sync with the timing employed for the buffer operation.) The instruction causes the information in the operational registers to be saved, then interrupts the main computer program to initiate a subroutine which will process the interrupt code and instruct the computer as to what action it must take with respect to the interrupt.

At times, it may not be desirable for the computer to honor an interrupt. For example, assume that the computer has peripheral equipment connected to all channels and that the operational program has no need to make use of all equipment and/or channels, which could very well be the case when the computer is being time shared. Inadvertent interrupts from unused equipment and/or channels could then disrupt the program. The process by which the computer is made to ignore unwanted interrupts is known as an interrupt lockout. Interrupt lockouts are usually programmed and most computers have in their repertoires certain instructions which can be modified to lockout interrupts in any of the following ways:

1. all external interrupts
2. external interrupts on all output channels
3. external interrup s on all input channels
4. external interrupts on a given output channel
5. external interrupts on a given input channel

Another concept involved in I/0 programming is that of packing and unpacking words. Because of the limited capabilities of the computer's peripheral equipment, the unit commonly used when transferring data to and from such equipment is the character. These characters have fewer bits than computer words and, in order to conserve storage space, it is common practice to assemble them to form computer words when storing them in computer memory. Conversely, when transferring data, especially to the computer's peripheral equipment, the computer words must be broken down into characters. The processes whereby this is accomplished are known as packing and unpacking. These processes must be programmed. Generally, this is done in the form of a pair of subroutines, one to do the packing and one to do the unpacking.

Flowcharting

A flow diagram, or chart, serves a multitude of purposes. As has already been noted, it serves as a map showing how the programmer intends to solve a problem. In this context, the chart illustrates the logical steps required, the decisions to be reached, and the paths to be followed as a result of these decisions. Properly annotated, it calls the programmer's attention to memory cell allocations, input/output requirements, register usage, and data accuracy considerations.

When writing a complex program, a flowchart may be used to "sectionalize" the program. Then, if necessary, each of the various sections may be assigned to a different programmer. This procedure should alert the programmer to the fact that certain parts of his program may have been previously written, either as part of another program or as a separate program.

In addition, a flowchart will be of vital importance when "debugging" a program, and when making future program changes, should they be required.

LEVELS OF FLOWCHARTING.—Flowcharts, or diagrams, may be constructed at various levels or degrees of complexity. A high level flowchart usually consists of a very few symbols and presents a broad or general overview of the problem, whereas a low level flowchart may approach a one-to-one correspondence between flowchart symbols and program instructions. There will usually be several flowcharts for a given program area. These may be compared to the prints found in a maintenance manual, i.e., the block diagram to show the relationship of major units (high level), functional block diagrams showing the major circuits in a unit (intermediate level), or the schematics of the circuits (low level). Flowcharts should always be available at a level low enough to implement all the uses previously discussed. The additional time spent flowcharting will inevitably be regained when encoding and debugging. The more complex the program, the more important is flowcharting.

FLOWCHART SYMBOLS.—Symbols are used on a flowchart to represent the functions of an information processing system. These functions are input/output, processing, flow direction, and annotation.

A basic symbol is established for each function and can always be used to represent that function. Specialized symbols are established which may be used in place of a basic symbol to give additional information.

The size of each symbol may vary, but the dimensional ratio of each symbol shall be maintained.

Basic Symbols.—The basic symbols are as follows.

The Input/Output Symbol represents the input/output function (I/O), i.e., the making available of information for processing (input), or the recording of processed information (output).

Input/Output Symbol

Dimensional Ratio

Width: Height = 1:2/3

The Process Symbol represents any kind of processing function, i.e., the process of executing a defined operation or group of operations resulting in a change in value, form, or location of information, or in the determination of which of several flow directions are to be followed.

PROGRAMMING CONCEPTS (PART I)

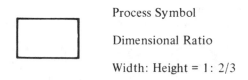 Process Symbol

Dimensional Ratio

Width: Height = 1: 2/3

The Flowline Symbol represents the function of linking symbols. It indicates the sequence of available information and executable operations. Flow direction is represented by lines drawn between symbols.

 Flowline Symbols

Normal direction of flow is from left to right and top to bottom. When the flow direction is not left to right or top to bottom. open arrowheads shall be placed on reverse direction flowlines. When increased clarity is desired, open arrowheads can be placed on normal direction flowlines. When flowlines are broken due to page limitations, connector symbols shall be used to indicate the break. When flow is bidirectional, it can be shown by either single or double lines, but open arrowheads shall be used to indicate both normal direction flow and reverse direction flow.

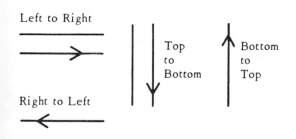

Flowlines may cross; this means they have no logical interrelation.
Example:

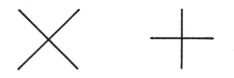

Two or more incoming flowlines may join with one outgoing flowline.
Example:

Every flowline entering and leaving a junction should have arrowheads near the junction point.
Example:

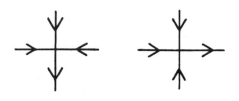

The Annotation Symbol represents the annotation function, i.e., the addition of descriptive comments or explanatory notes as clarification. The vertical line and the broken line may be drawn either on the left as shown or on the right. It is connected to any symbol at a point where the annotation is meaningful by extending the broken line in whatever fashion is appropriate.

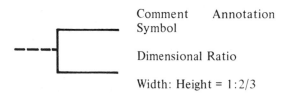 Comment Annotation Symbol

Dimensional Ratio

Width: Height = 1:2/3

Specialized Symbols.—Specialized I/0 symbols may represent the I/0 function and, in addition, denote the medium on which the information is recorded or the manner of handling the information or both. If no specialized symbol exists, the basic I/0 symbol is used.

The Punched Card symbol represents an I/0 function in which the medium is punched cards, including mark sense cards, partial cards, stub cards, mark scan cards, check of cards, bill of cards etc.

Punched Card Symbol

Dimensional Ratio

Width: Height = 1:1/2

Specialized Punched Card Symbols may be used to represent a deck of cards or a file of cards. The Deck of Cards Symbol represents a collection of punched cards.

Deck of Cards Symbol

Dimensional Ratio

Width: Height = 5/4:2/3

The File of Cards Symbol represents a collection of related punched card records.

File of Cards Symbol

Dimensional Ratio

Width: Height = 5/4:2/3

The Magnetic Tape Symbol represents an I/O function in which the medium is magnetic tape.

Magnetic Tape Symbol

Dimensional Ratio

Width: Height = 1:1

The Punched Tape Symbol represents an I/O function in which the medium is punched tape.

Punched Tape Symbol

Dimensional Ratio

Width: Height = 1:1/2

The Magnetic Drum Symbol represents an I/O function in which the medium is magnetic drum.

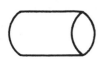

Magnetic Drum Symbol

Dimensional Ratio

Width: Height = 5/4:2/3

The Magnetic Disk Symbol represents an I/O function in which the medium is magnetic disk.

Magnetic Disk Symbol

Dimensional Ratio

Width: Height = 2/3:5/4

The Core Symbol represents an I/O function in which the medium is magnetic core.

Core Symbol

Dimensional Ratio

Width: Height = 1:1

The Document Symbol represents an I/O function in which the medium is a document.

Document Symbol

Dimensional Ratio

Width: Height = 1:2/3

The Manual Input Symbol represents an input function in which the information is entered manually at the time of processing; for example by means of online keyboards, switch settings, push-buttons.

Manual Input Symbol

Dimensional Ratio

Width: Height = 1:1/2

The Display Symbol represents an I/O function in which the information is displayed for human use at the time of processing, by means of online indicators, video devices, console printers, plotters, etc.

Display Symbol

Dimensional Ratio

Width: Height = 1:2/3

PROGRAMMING CONCEPTS (PART I)

The Communications Link Symbols represent an I/0 function in which information is transmitted by a Telecommunications link.

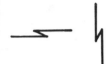 Communications Link

Symbols

Unless otherwise indicated, the direction of flow is left to right and top to bottom. Open arrowheads are necessary on symbols for which the flow opposes the above convention. An open arrowhead may also be used on any line whenever increased clarity will result.

The **Online Storage Symbol** represents an I/0 function utilizing any type of online storage, for example magnetic drums, magnetic disks, magnetic tape.

 Online Storage Symbol

Dimensional Ratio

Width: Height = 1:2/3

The Offline Storage Symbol represents the function of storing information offline, regardless of the medium on which the information is recorded.

 Offline Storage Symbol

Dimensional Ratio

Width: Height = 1:0.866

Specialized Process Symbols.—Specialized process symbols may represent the processing function and, in addition, identify the specific type of operation to be performed on the information. If no specialized symbol exists, the basic process symbol is used.

The Decision Symbol represents a decision or switching type operation that determines which of a number of alternative paths is to be followed.

 Decision Symbol

Dimensional Ratio

Width: Height = 1:2/3

The Predefined Process Symbol represents a named process consisting of one or more operations or program steps that are specified elsewhere, e.g., subroutine or logical unit. Elsewhere means not this set of flowcharts.

 Predefined Process Symbol

Dimensional Ratio

Width: Height = 1:2/3

Additional Symbols.—The additional symbols shown below are commonly used flowchart symbols not included in the categories indicated above.

The Connector Symbol represents a junction in a line of flow. A set of two connectors is used to represent a continued flow direction when the flow is broken by any limitation of the flowchart. A set of two or more connectors is used to represent the junction of several flowlines with one flowline, or the junction of one flowline with one of several alternate flowlines.

 Connector Symbol

Dimensional Ratio

Width: Height = 1:1

The Terminal Symbol represents a terminal point in a system or communication network at which data can enter or leave; e.g., start, stop, halt, delay, or interrupt.

 Terminal Symbol

Dimensional Ratio

Width: Height = 1:3/8

781

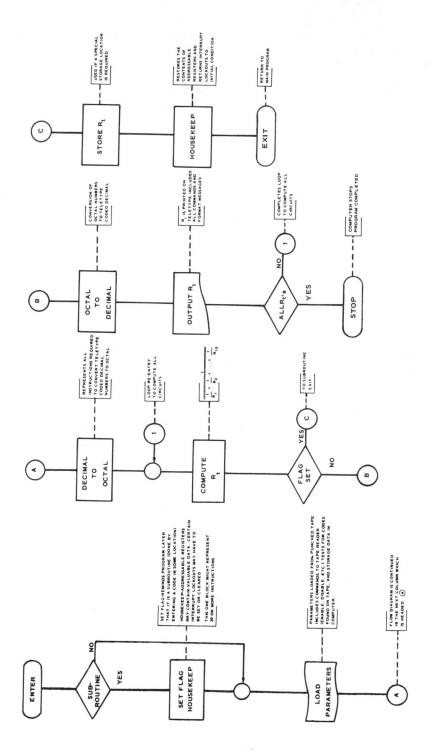

Figure 9-5.—Parallel resistance computations flow diagram.

PROGRAMMING CONCEPTS (PART I)

CONSTRUCTING A FLOWCHART.—At this point the problem previously considered will be diagramed. Certain embellishments will be added to further demonstrate the preparation and use of flowcharts. The problem is, therefore, restated.

It is desired to determine the resistance of various circuits each containing as many as ten resistors in parallel. All values will be accurate to three decimal places, and the resistors' values will range from 10.000 to 1000.000 ohms.

The values for all circuits will be entered at one time from a paper tape punched in teletype code. The resistances will be in decimal.

It is further stated that the program may be used as a subroutine if desired. When used as a subroutine, the value found for R_t will be stored and an exit made from the subroutine. If not used as a subroutine, the R_t will be typed on a teletype and the R_t for the next circuit, if any, computed. This process will continue until all circuits have been computed and typed.

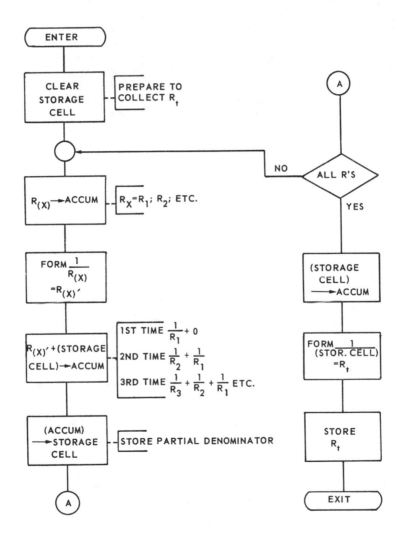

Figure 9-6.—Compute R_t.

783

Additionally, it is assumed that if the program is used as a subroutine, the programmer does not know the contents of the various registers.

Careful study of figure 9-5 should bring to light several interesting facts. The most important observation to be made is that the actual computation will comprise a relatively small portion of the instructions. The total number of instructions could be reduced, particularly by doing the octal/decimal conversions outside the computer and by making the parameter entries into the maintenance panel and reading the solution from it. These steps would, however, largely negate the advantages of the computer. The important conclusion to be drawn from these facts is that unless a relatively simple operation must be repeated a large number of times, there is no reason to program it.

A further study of this flowchart will reveal that there are many different ways in which the program could be flowcharted. For example, the load parameters and decimal/octal conversion operations might well be combined into a single operation or routine. On the other hand, the housekeeping operations to be performed on entry into the program could be charted as separate processes. That is, there could be a separate process symbol for such operations as storing the contents of the operational registers, setting the interrupt lockouts, etc. In fact, if such a problem were presented to a number of different programmers and each was allowed to devise his own flowchart, no two flowcharts would be exactly alike. Some of these flowcharts would be radically different from the one presented here. Standard symbology would be used; however, the number of symbols used and their arrangement could vary widely.

As a further illustration of flow diagraming, the compute R_t routine is reduced, without further discussion, to a low level flowchart in figure 9-6.

PROGRAMMING CONCEPTS (PART II)

After flowcharting the next step in programming is to convert the operations indicated by the flowchart into machine instructions, either by writing the necessary instructions directly in machine language or in a high level compiler language, which is then translated by the appropriate compiler program into machine language instructions. Computer instruction words on a machine language level were discussed in an earlier chapter. Compiler languages and programs commonly used by the Navy are described next.

COMPILERS (GENERAL)

When discussing operational programs, we are usually talking in terms of programs containing hundreds or thousands of machine language instructions which must be arranged in a logical sequence and stored in computer memory and/or an auxiliary memory device which is readily accessible to the computer. Designated memory cells or areas in computer memory must be set aside for the storage of operational parameters for the program and permanent or temporary storage of machine computations. From the programming it can be seen that it would be both time consuming and difficult for the programmer to write such programs using machine language and absolute addressing techniques.

To aid the programmer and facilitate the generation of these large programs compilers have been developed. Compilers are nothing more than programs fed into the computer to aid in the preparation of other programs. From information described in an English-like language, a compiler will produce an operational program complete with memory allocations suitable for use with a computer. In addition, these compiling systems can be designed to produce printed indications of errors in the source program, and a means of correcting these errors and making other program modifications as needed. Also, they can be devised to produce program listings and program diagnostic information for debugging of the object program.

In the years since the first operational data processing system utilizing a digital computer as its central processor was devised, many different compilers have been developed. The primary difference between them is the application area toward which they are oriented. Compilers are usually developed to meet specific or general needs, and are said to be oriented in the direction of this need. For example, CMS-2, COBOL, and FORTRAN are three compiler systems now finding widespread use in the Navy. CMS-2 is said to be NTDS oriented, since it was developed and is used primarily for compiling programs for the Navy's tactical data system. COBOL is said to be business oriented, since it was developed and is used to compile programs written in business oriented English. Finally, FORTRAN is oriented for formula solving. It was developed and is used to compile programs for problems stated in the form of mathematical and scientific formulas.

While the CMS-2 language was designed specifically for command and control problems, it incorporates features which make it suitable for a variety of applications. CMS-2 includes features from CS-1, FORTRAN, JOVIAL, and PL/1, all compiler languages that have been or are being used by the Navy.

Although the CMS-2 language is an extension of the CS-1 it is not compatible with the CS-1 compiler. However, the CMS-2 compiler, will accept most statements written in CS-1.

Since CMS-2 was developed primarily for Navy use and incorporates features from most of the other compilers mentioned above, it will be treated here as being representative of compilers in general. For information concerning the other compilers, refer to the appropriate texts.

Through the various years and stages of computer development a naval officer's name is prominent. Captain Grace M. Hopper began her illustrious computer oriented career as a Lieutenant (JG) in 1943. Assigned to the Bureau of Ordnance Computation Project at Harvard University, she worked with Professor Howard Aiken as a programmer for the first large-scale computer, Mark I. Her work for the Navy continued on the Mark II and Mark III computers. Captain Hopper is credited with the invention of the first practical complier for the computer. In the past 20 years. Captain Hopper has published more than 50 technical papers on automatic programming and counts the Naval Ordnance Development Award among her honors. She was retired December 1966 and recalled to active duty in August 1967 to assist in an effort to standardize the Navy's COBOL (Common Business Oriented Langauge) program. At the time of this writing, she is assigned to the Program Language Standardization Section of the Information Systems Division in the Office of the Chief of Naval Operations.

COMPILER MONITOR SYSTEM–2 (CMS-2)

Since the language is part of the total CMS-2 system, a general overview of the system is presented first, followed by a more detailed examination of the language.

SYSTEM HARDWARE

The CMS-2 system is a tape-oriented operating system currently operational on the UNIVAC CP-642B (AN/USQ-20) computer. Peripheral hardware and configuration are functions of the operating site and are thus variable. Where required for completeness of presentation, a representative operating system will be described.

SYSTEM SOFTWARE

The CMS-2 system consists of a central controlling program, called the monitor, and five

subsidiary system programs: the compiler, librarian, CP-642 loader, tape utility, and flowcharter.

MS-2 Monitor System

The MS-2 monitor system is a batch-processing operating system designed to control execution of CMS-2 subsidiary components and user jobs being run on the CP-642 Computer. The monitor coordinates all system job requests, and provides the external communication with peripheral hardware for all programs running under its control. This communication includes a control card processor; an input/output system; an operator communication package; and a debug package providing program debugging aids. In addition, the monitor maintains a library of the system component programs that can be called by the user upon request. Job accounting information is maintained and may be output for computer center use.

CMS-2 Compiler

The compiler is a multiphase language processor that analyzes a dual syntax (CS-1 and CMS-2 languages) source program and generates object code for any one of several different computers. The phases of the compiler are described below and illustrated in figure 10-1.

Syntax Analyzer–

The first phase of the compiler processes the user's source program, which consists of high-level CMS-2 or CS-1 language statements and properly bracketed machine code instructions. The source statements are checked for validity, and an internal language (IL) and symbol table are generated. The IL and symbol table are independent of the target computer for which machine code will be generated.

Code Generator–

The code generator phase processes the IL and symbol table to produce the final output listings and object code for the target computer. A separate code generator phase is used

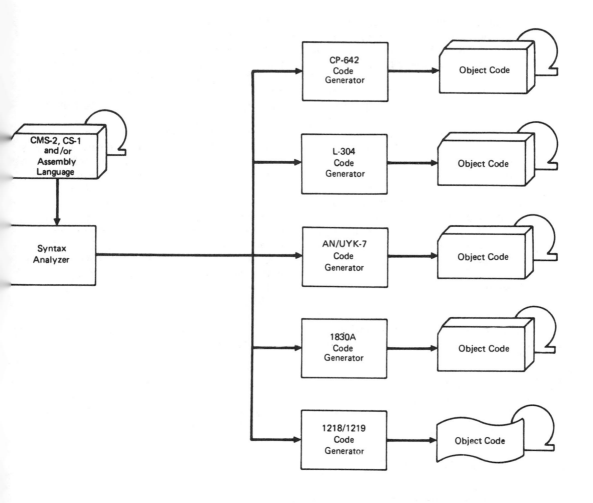

Figure 10-1.—The CMS-2 compiler.

for each target computer. The code generator outputs object code onto punched cards or magnetic tape in a format compatible with the loaders used on each machine. Each code generator locally optimizes the object code. This optimization includes utilization of instructions unique to the target computer, efficient register usage, and continuous analysis of object code strings for unnecessary or redundant instructions. Optional printed listings consist of source programs (including the side-by-side mnemonic and numeric form of instructions generated by each statement), a cross-reference listing of all identifiers and

their references, and a complete symbol analysis of the programmer's formally declared data units. The code generators produce object code in one of two compilation modes: absolute or relocatable. In an absolute compilation, all instructions and data units are assigned absolute memory locations. The resulting object code represents an executable program. In the relocatable mode, each system element being compiled is given a starting address of 0. All memory locations and symbolic references between system elements must be assigned or resolved by a linking loader program. The loader itself joins various system elements perhaps generated by separate compilations, to produce the final executable programs. The object code produced by the code generators occasionally includes references to object-time routines. These object-time routines are supplied by the CMS-2 system to perform operations requested by certain CMS-2 statements (input/output, debug, special operators). Object code for the object-time routines is linked to object code of the calling program either by the compiler (when using absolute mode), or a linking loader (when using relocatable mode). Execution of the object-time routines often requires input/output to peripheral equipment; thus, their design and operation are dependent on the monitor system of the target computer.

XCMS-2 Compiler

This compiler functions similarly to the CMS-2 compiler, but has the added capability of processing those language extension features developed for the AN/UYK-7 Computer. It is restricted to a single code generator and thus produces only relocatable AN/UYK-7 object code; it does not process CS-1 statements. Figure 10-2 presents the functional flow of the XCMS-2 compiler.

CMS-2 Librarian

The librarian is a file management system that provides storage, retrieval and correction functions for a programmer's source programs and object code. Library operations are performed by three different routines, described below.

1. The library maintenance or execution routine (LIBEXEC) is used to create, modify or reproduce libraries for CMS-2 programmers. A CMS-2 library is placed on magnetic tape and may contain source programs, object code or predefined data pools (compools).

A library translator routine, under control of LIBEXEC, is used to convert existing CS-1 program decks or libraries into a CMS-2 library format (fig. 10-3). Most CS-1 language statements are acceptable to the CMS-2 compiler. A few are converted by the library translator to equivalent acceptable statements. Those remaining CS-1 statements that cannot be processed by the CMS-2 system are identified by the library translator and must be changed by the programmer.

2. The library search routine is responsible for retrieving data from a previously created CMS-2 library (fig. 10-4). Source program and compool elements may be retrieved for input to the CMS-2 compiler. CP-642 relocatable object

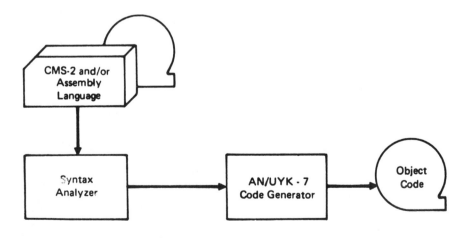

Figure 10-2.—The XCMS-2 compiler.

788

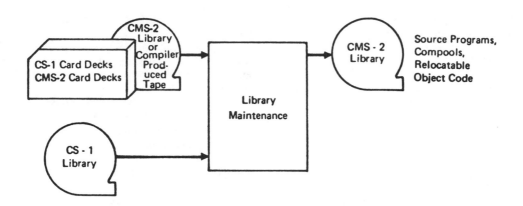

Figure 10-3.—Librarian translator (LIBEXEC)

code can be retrieved when requested by the CP-642 relocatable loader.

CP-642 Object-Code Loaders

The CMS-2 system includes two loader programs for CP-642 object code produced by the CMS-2 compiler.

1. Absolute Loader—The absolute loader accepts object code generated by a compilation in the absolute mode. All instructions and data are loaded into computer memory at the addresses assigned during the compilation.
2. Relocatable Loader—The relocatable loader processes only outputs from a relocatable compilation. Relocatable object code can come directly from the compiler or from a CMS-2 library. The relocatable loader assigns all memory addresses and links the

program segments together to produce an executable object program.

As a separate and independent function, the loader can produce relative and absolute output tapes reformatted for Naval Tactical Data System (NTDS) compability.

Tape Utility

The CMS-2 system provides a set of utility routines to assist a programmer with the manipulation of data recorded on magnetic tape. The routines provide the capability to construct, duplicate, compare, list, and reformat data files on tape.

CMS-2 Flowcharter

The flowcharter is designed to process unique flowcharter statements in a user's CMS-2 source

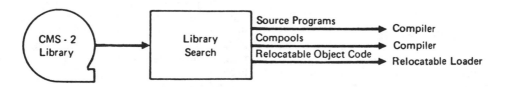

Figure 10-4.—Library search.

program and output a flowchart of the program logic to the high-speed printer.

JOB FLOW

To use the components of the CMS-2 system, a programmer must construct a job input deck to describe his requirements. The control cards in the job deck are processed by the MS-2 monitor. Based on the instructions specified on the control cards, the monitor can retrieve a CMS-2 component program from the CMS-2 system library and pass control to the component for further processing. Figures 10-5 and 10-6 illustrate the interactions among the system components.

Within a single run, several components of the CMS-2 system may be executed. Examples are:

Job 1.—Retrieve a source program from a user's library (using the library search routine) for a compile (using the compiler) and updating of the source program in the library (using the library maintenance components).

Job 2.—Compiling a source program for the CP-642 computer (using the compiler), producing a flowchart output (using the flowcharter), and loading the object code into the computer for execution (using the loader).

Job 3.—Converting a CS-1 user's library into a CMS-2 user's library (using the library translator), then listing the contents of the CMS-2 library (using the tape utility routine).

INTRODUCTION (LANGUAGE) TO THE CMS-2

The CMS-2 language is a problem-oriented compiler language developed to meet the needs of real-time data processing and scientific applications. Its major features are described below.

MAJOR FEATURES OF THE
CMS-2 LANGUAGE

CMS-2 encourages program modularization, thereby easing maintenance and modification of systems by permitting independent compilation of portions of a total system. Input to the CMS-2 compiler is statement-oriented, rather than card-oriented. The source card format is free-form and may be arranged for user convenience.

A broad range of data types is definable in CMS-2. These types include fixed-point, floating-point, Boolean, Hollerith (character), and status.

CMS-2 permits direct reference to, and manipulation of, character and bit strings. Programs may include segments of symbolic machine language, referred to as direct code.

PROGRAM STRUCTURE

A CMS-2 program is composed of an orderly set of STATEMENTS. These statements are composed of various SYMBOLS that are separated by DELIMITERS. Three categories of symbols are processed: OPERATORS, IDENTIFIERS and CONSTANTS. The operators are language primitives assigned by the compiler to indicate specific operations or definitions within a program. Identifiers are the unique names assigned by the programmer to data units, program elements and statement labels. Constants are known values, and may be numeric (decimal or octal), Hollerith strings, status values, or Boolean.

CMS-2 statements are written in a free format and terminated by a dollar sign. Several statements may be written on one card, or one statement may cover many cards. A statement label may be placed at the beginning of a statement for reference purposes.

The collection of program statements developed by the programmer for input to the CMS-2 compiler is known as the SOURCE PROGRAM and is composed of two basic types of statements: DECLARATIVE STATEMENTS provide basic control information to the compiler and define the structure of the data associated with a particular program. DYNAMIC STATEMENTS cause the compiler to generate executable machine instructions, or OBJECT CODE. These instructions, when executed at program run time, manipulate the data to solve the desired problem.

Declarative statements defining the data for a program are grouped into units called DATA DESIGNS. Data designs consist of the precise definition of temporary and permanent data storage areas, input areas, output areas, and

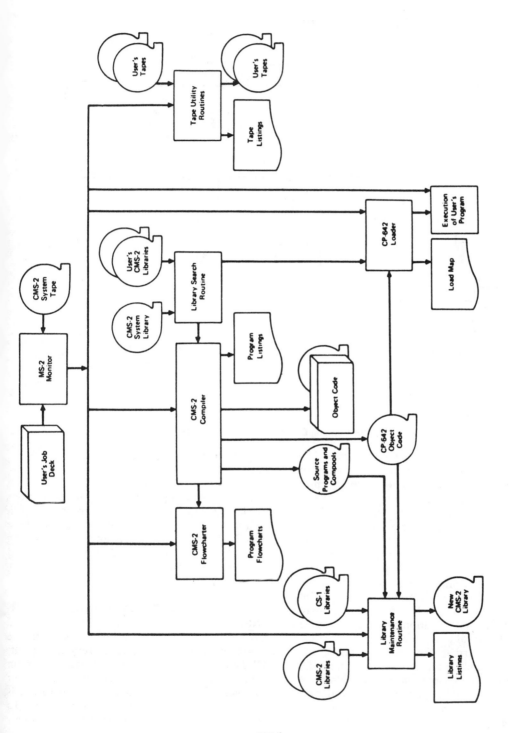

Figure 10-5.—Interaction among CMS-2 components (CMS-2 compiler).

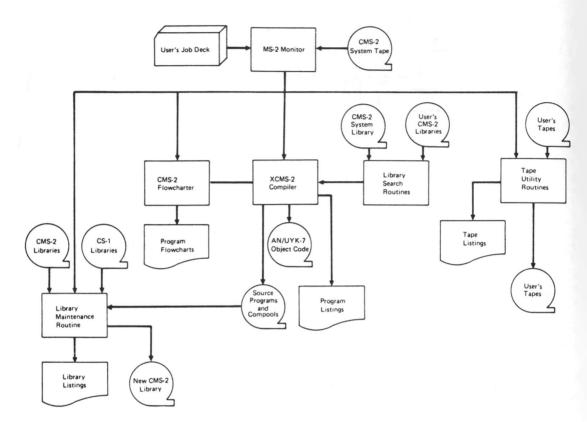

Figure 10-6.—Interaction among CMS-2 components (XCMS-2 compiler).

special data units such as program switches. The dynamic statements that cause manipulation of data or express calculations to solve the programmer's problems are grouped into PROCEDURES. These data designs and procedures must be further grouped or classified to form SYSTEM ELEMENTS of a CMS-2 program. At compile-time, the CMS-2 compiler recognizes a system as any collection of program system elements that are compiled as an entity independent of any interfacing program elements. This COMPILE-TIME SYSTEM (or system) may comprise an entire execution package or may be only a small part of a large program.

Before any further discussion concerning the classification and grouping of procedures and data designs into elements and the combining of these elements to form systems, several concepts fundamental to the CMS-2 language must be explored.

Organization and Classification of Identifiers

The CMS-2 compiler uses several conventions to classify data definitions and program identifiers that are defined in a user's program. These techniques assist the programmer in structuring his program and simplify the development and maintenance of the programs.

FORWARD AND BACKWARD REFERENCES.—The order in which definitions and references to these definitions appear in the source input to the compiler is quite important. All data units are defined in data designs. Within the data design where it is defined, an identifier may generally be referred to either before it is defined (a FORWARD reference) or after it is defined (a BACKWARD reference). However,

ferences to data from outside a data design can only be backward; that is, the data must already ave been defined before it can be referenced. ince data definitions always appear in data esigns, and since data references usually appear n procedures, procedures generally follow the ata designs defining the data referenced by the rocedure.

References to statement labels within pro-edures, calls to procedures within a system rocedure, and calls to prime procedures not aving formal parameters or abnormal exits may e forward or backward.

LOCAL AND GLOBAL DEFINITIONS.—The ompiler further structures the referencing of lentifiers by classifying all identifiers in a rogram as either local or global. LOCAL DEFINITIONS are those identifiers that can be eferenced only from within the system element vhere they are defined. GLOBAL DEFINI-TIONS are those identifiers that can be refer-nced both from inside the element where

defined and from outside by subsequent system elements in the source input stream.

Figure 10-7 is a pictorial representation of CMS-2 compile-time system consisting of three elements: A, B and C. Since definition in the CMS-2 language is said to be local if it is valid only within a single element of the system, any definition valid within element B of figure 10-7 is said to be local to element B. A global definition in the system of figure 10-7 is valid within elements A, B and C.

EXTERNAL REFERENCES AND DEFINI-TIONS.—The CMS-2 compiler provides the capability of compiling one or more elements of a large system independently. For example, all three elements of the system of figure 10-7 could be compiled together as a single compile-time system. Alternatively, elements A and B could be compiled together as a compile-time system, and then element C could be compiled separately as another compile-time system. The compiler-produced output in each case is the

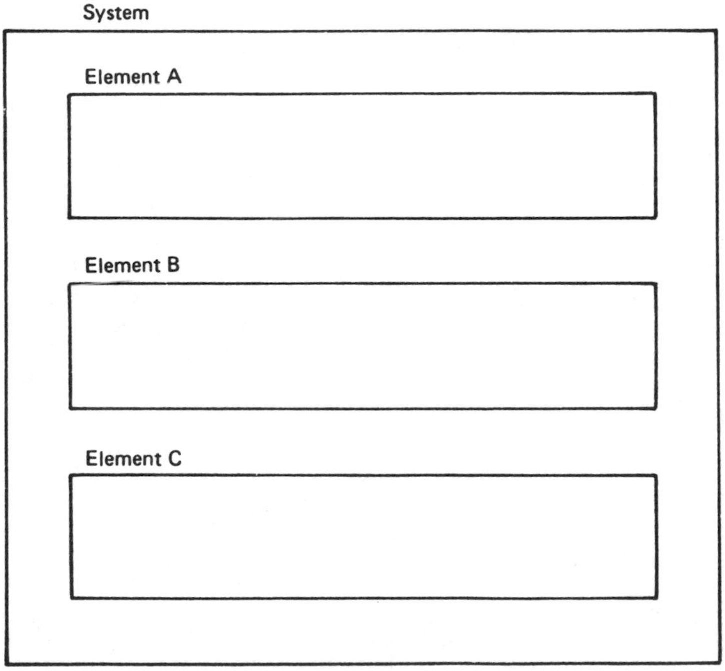

Figure 10-7.—CMS-2 compile-time system.

computer-executable instructions (object code) for the various system elements. Later, the object codes for elements A, B, and C may be combined by a "relocatable linking loader" program and executed together.

Presumably, there is some cross-referencing of data and procedures between the three elements of the example. In order to compile element C separately, any references made by element C to definitions in elements A and B must be handled in a special manner by the compiler and the loader. References of this type are called EXTERNAL REFERENCES because they involve definitions that are external to element C and, in this case, external to the compile-time system as well. Those definitions in elements A and B that are referenced externally by element C are called EXTERNAL DEFINITIONS because they are definitions that are available to elements external to A and B.

There are various ways in which definitions and references may be declared external. In some cases the compiler will automatically treat a definition or a reference as being external. In other cases, external references and definitions must be explicitly declared by the programmer. Local definitions are never valid outside, or external to, the element in which they are defined unless special compiler handling has been programmer-requested through the use of EXTDEF and EXTREF operators.

CMS-2 System Elements

As described in the previous sections, data designs and procedures may be grouped or classified to form elements of a CMS-2 program. One or more system elements then make up a compile-time system. The ordering and content of program elements is subject to the rule governing range and classification of definitions.

The two types of system elements within a compile-time system are SYSTEM DATA DESIGNS and SYSTEM PROCEDURES. System data designs contain global data definitions. System procedures contain one or more procedures and may also include local data design packages. A local data design, as the name implies, contains data definitions that are local to the system procedure in which the local data design appears. This structuring of data designs and procedures into program elements within a system is illustrated in figure 10-8. The hierarchy shown in figure 10-8 indicates that, within a system, system data designs are equal in importance to system procedures; they are the program elements of a system. Keeping in mind the restrictions against forward referencing, a source deck may take various forms, as illustrated in figure 10-9.

The technique shown in figure 10-9(A) is often used in constructing a program. Since definitions within a system data design are global to the balance of the system, system procedures may appear in any order following the system data design(s) defining the referenced data. Interspersing data designs and procedures as in figure 10-9(B) and (C), however, has an advantage, especially in a large system, of maintaining data definitions in meaningful groups close (both in core and on listings) to the associated procedures.

Note that figure 10-9 illustrates several examples of a compile-time system, but these systems might be only a small part of an entire execution package. In addition, each compile-time system of figure 10-9 might be further broken down into two or more compile-time

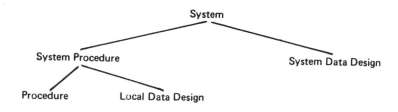

Figure 10-8.—Structuring of data designs and procedures.

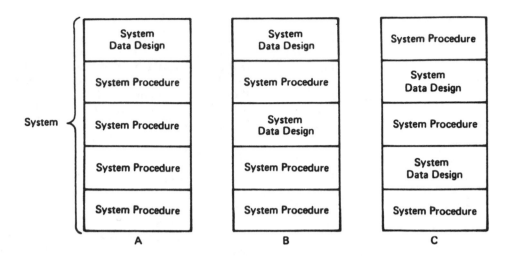

Figure 10-9.—Source deck forms.

systems. In this manner, corrections may be made to a particular system procedure, which may then be recompiled without compiling the entire execution package again.

System data designs and system procedures are the smallest program units that may be compiled individually. A compile-time system may consist of a single system data design or system procedure, but it cannot consist only of local data designs or procedures.

SYSTEM DATA DESIGNS.—Data designs contain descriptions of the attributes of the various data units (tables, variables, etc.) and their relationship to each other. As the compiler processes these descriptions, it assigns and reserves core storage locations for subsequent references to the data units. Data designs may contain value information as well, which will cause the compiler to generate object code to preset the data.

Definitions within a system data design are global to the system for backward referencing. They are all automatically externally defined by the compiler. There is, therefore, no need to specifically externally define any data within a system data design.

SYSTEM PROCEDURES.—System procedures are composed of procedures and local data designs. A system procedure may contain one procedure with a name identical to that of the system procedure name. This procedure is known as the PRIME PROCEDURE of that system procedure. The prime procedure entry point is automatically externally defined by the compiler and is global to the system. Other system procedures, procedures and data designs may reference at will prime procedures not having formal parameters or abnormal exits. Thus, the prime procedure of a system procedure may be considered a global procedure (hence, the term "system procedure"). A system procedure may contain more than one procedure, as illustrated in figure 10-10. For example, the system procedure of figure 10-10 contains three procedures and two local data designs. If this system procedure were named "B," procedure B would be the prime procedure of the system procedure, and its name would be global to the entire system. However, procedures A and C, along with the data units of the two data designs, would be local to the system procedure and could not be referenced from outside the system procedure.

Local Data Designs.—The difference between system data designs and local data designs is that, while system data design definitions are

795

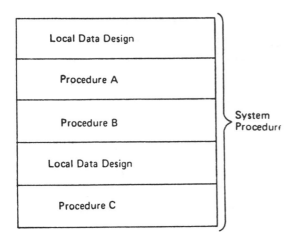

Local Data Design
Procedure A
Procedure B
Local Data Design
Procedure C

System Procedure

Figure 10-10.—System procedure design.

global to the system and automatically externally defined, local data design definitions are local to the system procedure within which they are contained; any necessary external definitions must be indicated within the data design. In addition, a local data design may not be compiled separately from its associated system procedure.

The local data design contains the definition of data units referenced only by the procedures within its system procedure. The use of local data designs reduces the possibility of duplication of data names in a large system because of their limited range of definition. The forward /backward referencing rules also apply to local data designs. For instance, definitions in the second local data design in figure 10-10 may only be referenced from procedure C. References to this data from procedures A and B would be forward references, which are not permitted.

Procedures.—Procedures contain CMS-2 dynamic statements and machine-language statements. They may not contain data definitions or data values for previously defined data. Procedures contain the statements from which the compiler generates the instructions that actually perform the steps necessary to the solution of the problem. They must be included within a system procedure element at compile time.

Range of Identifiers

As can be seen from the previous discussion, the organization of CMS-2 statements into system data designs and system procedures to form the elements of a program is closely related to the rules concerning classification of identifier definitions and references. These rules on the range of identifiers (i.e., local/global definitions and forward/backward references) are summarized, in the table, figure 10-11.

DATA DECLARATIVE STATEMENTS

The data declarative statements provide the compiler with information about data element definitions. Thus, the programmer, through the data declarative statements, defines the format, structure and order of data elements within a compile-time system. The three major data types are switches, variables, and table (or arrays).

1. VARIABLES

   Integer
   Fixed-Point   Computational
   Floating-Point

   Hollerith
   Boolean   Noncomputational
   Status

2. SWITCHES

   Statement Switches
   Procedure Switches

3. TABLES

   One-Dimensional
   Multidimensional (Array)
   Subtables
   Like-Tables
   Item-Areas
   Fields

Switches

Switches provide for the transfer of program control to one of a number of specific locations within a compile-time system, depending on

PROGRAMMING CONCEPTS (PART II)

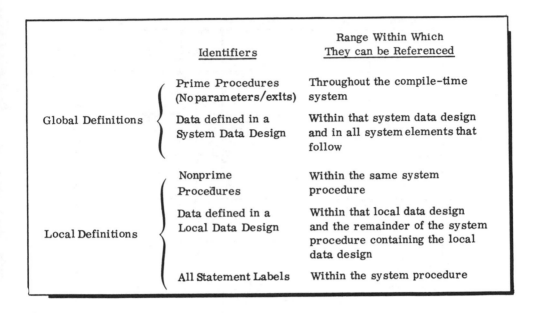

	Identifiers	Range Within Which They can be Referenced
Global Definitions	Prime Procedures (No parameters/exits)	Throughout the compile-time system
	Data defined in a System Data Design	Within that system data design and in all system elements that follow
Local Definitions	Nonprime Procedures	Within the same system procedure
	Data defined in a Local Data Design	Within that local data design and the remainder of the system procedure containing the local data design
	All Statement Labels	Within the system procedure

Figure 10-11.—Table showing range of program identifiers.

conditions or calculations made during program execution. Switches contain a set of identifiers, or switch points, to facilitate program transfers and branches. The switch points represent program addresses of statement labels or procedure names. Transfer of control to a particular switch point is usually determined by the value of a programmer-supplied index.

Variables

A variable is a single piece of data. It may consist of one bit or multiple bits or words. A variable may be preset to a desired value within the definition statement. The variable may contain a constant value, or its value may continuously change during program execution. Multiple variables having identical attributes may be defined in a single declarative statement. Data types that may be specified for a variable are arithmetic (integer, fixed- or floating-point), Hollerith (character string), status (defined states of condition), or Boolean (true or false). An initial value, or preset may be specified for the variable in the declarative statement.

Tables hold ordered sets of identically structured information. The common unit of data structure in a table is the ITEM. An item consists of k computer words, where k is selected by the programmer or compiler. A table may contain n items, where n is programmer selected. Thus, the size of the table in number of required computer words for storage becomes the product of n and k. A table structure is illustrated in figure 10-12.

Items may be subdivided into FIELDS. Fields are the smallest subdivision of a table. A field may be a partial word, a full word, or a multiword. Fields may overlap each other. An example of field assignments is illustrated in figure 10-13. Data types that may be specified for fields are arithmetic (integer, fixed- or floating-point), Hollerith (character string), status (defined states of condition), or Boolean (true or false).

CMS-2 tables may be defined as HORIZONTAL or VERTICAL. This specification by the programmer dictates the manner in which the table words will be stored in core. The words of a horizontally declared table are stored such that words 0 of all items are stored sequentially, followed by words 1 of all items, etc.

The words of a vertically defined table are stored such that all words of item 0 are stored

797

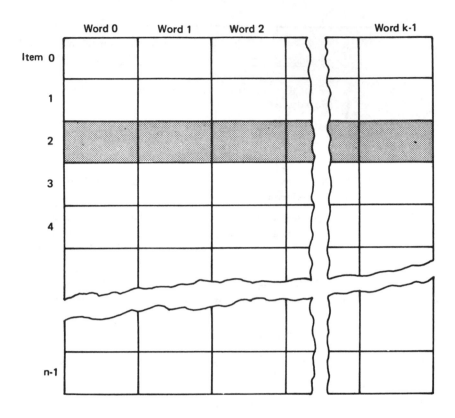

Figure 10-12.—Table structure.

sequentially, followed by all words of item 1, etc. Figure 10-14 illustrates the storage pattern for horizontal and vertical storage.

The CMS-2 table structure also allows the programmer to define a subset of adjacent items within a table as a SUBTABLE. The programmer may also allocate outside the table a working storage area designated an ITEM-AREA, which will automatically take on the same field format as that defined for the table items. Additionally, the programmer may declare tables known as LIKE-TABLES having identical field format as

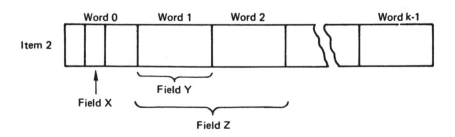

Figure 10-13.—Field assignments for a table.

164.150

798

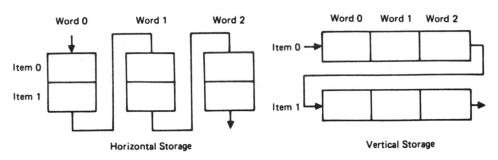

164.151

Figure 10-14.—Table storage sequence.

ie parent table but having a different number f items. Figure 10-15 illustrates these described lationships to the parent table.

rray

An array is an extension of the table concept r storing ordered sets of identically structured formation previously defined as items. Arrays ay be conceptually visualized as rows, columns, and planes of items. An example of an rray (three-dimensional) is presented in figure 0-16. As with tables, the basic structural unit f an array is the item. The array item may onsist of k computer words with fields defined s desired. The pattern for storage of an array vithin core is illustrated in figure 10-17. The ow of an array is synonymous with the item of horizontal or vertical table.

)YNAMIC STATEMENTS

CMS-2 dynamic statements specify processing perations and result in executable code generaion by the compiler. A dynamic statement onsists of an operator followed by a list of perands and additional operators. An OPERAND may be a single name, a constant, a data-element reference, or an expression.

Expressions

ARITHMETIC EXPRESSIONS may include standard addition, subtraction, multiplication, and division operators, as well as exponentiation, mixed mode values, and inline redefinition of the scaling of fixed-point numbers. An algebraic hierarchy of operation evaluation is used. A RELATIONAL EXPRESSION performs a comparison between two similar operands as specified by a RELATIONAL OPERATOR. There are four types of comparisons available:

1. Arithmetic, involving the comparison of arithmetic values (fixed, floating, or mixed)
2. Hollerith, involving a left-to-right, character-by-character comparison
3. Boolean, involving single bit comparisons
4. Status, involving the comparison of a defined status constant with the contents of the parent status data unit

Arithmetic operators used in CMS-2 are + (addition), - (subtraction), / (division), * (multiplication), ** (exponentiation), and .. (inline scaling). Relational operators are EQ (equal), NOT (not equal), LT (less than), GT (greater than), LTEQ (less than or equal) and GTEQ (greater than or equal). Boolean operators used in CMS-2 are AND, OR and COMP. A single CMS-2 expression may include arithmetic, relational and Boolean operators.

Statement Operators

The CMS-2 statement operators allow the programmer to write his program in an easy-to-learn, problem-oriented language. Major CMS-2 operators and their functions are summarized below.

PROGRAMMING CONCEPTS (PART II)

Operator	Function
SET	Performs calculations or assigns a value to one or more data units. The assignment may be arithmetic, Hollerith, status, Boolean, or multiword.
SWAP	Exchanges the contents of two data units.
GOTO	Alters program flow or calls upon a statement switch.
IF	Expresses a comparison or Boolean expression to provide conditional execution of one or more statements.
VARY	Establishes a program loop to repeat execution of a specified group of statements.
FIND	Searches a table for data that satisfies specified conditions.

Special Operators

Special operators are available in CMS-2 to facilitate references to data structures and operations on them. These operators and their functions are summarized below.

Operator	Function
BIT	References a string of bits in a data element.
CHAR	References a character string.
CORAD	References a core address.
ABS	Obtains the absolute value of an expression.
COMP	Complements a Boolean expression.

HIGH-LEVEL INPUT/OUTPUT STATEMENTS

CMS-2 high-level input/output statements permit the program to communicate with various hardware devices while running in a nonreal-time environment under a monitor system. When CMS-2 I/O statements are used by the programmer, the compiler generates specific calls to object-time routines that must be loaded with the user's program. The object-time routines are designed to link with the monitor system and communicate with its I/O drivers. I/O declarative and dynamic statement operators and their associated functions are summarized below.

Operator	Function
FILE	Defines the environment and pertinent information concerning an input or output operation and reserves a buffer area for record transmission.
OPEN	Initializes I/O object-time routines.
CLOSE	Deactivates a specified file and writes an end-of-file mark on output files.
INPUT	Directs an input operation from an external device to a FILE buffer area.
OUTPUT	Directs an output operation from a FILE buffer area to an external device.
FORMAT	Defines the desired conversion between external data blocks and internal data definitions.
ENCODE	Directs transformation of data elements into a common area, with conversion in accordance with a specified FORMAT.
DECODE	Directs unpacking of a common area and transmittal to data units as specified by a FORMAT declaration.
ENDFILE	Places an end-of-file mark on appropriate recording mediums.

800

perator	Function
)S	Special operator to position a magnetic tape file.
ENGTH	Special operator to obtain an input/output record length.

PROGRAM STRUCTURE DECLARATIVES

CMS-2 PROGRAM STRUCTURE DECLAR-ATIVES are used to define the source program organization by specifically delimiting the structure type as illustrated in the table, figure 10-18. An example of the correct organization of

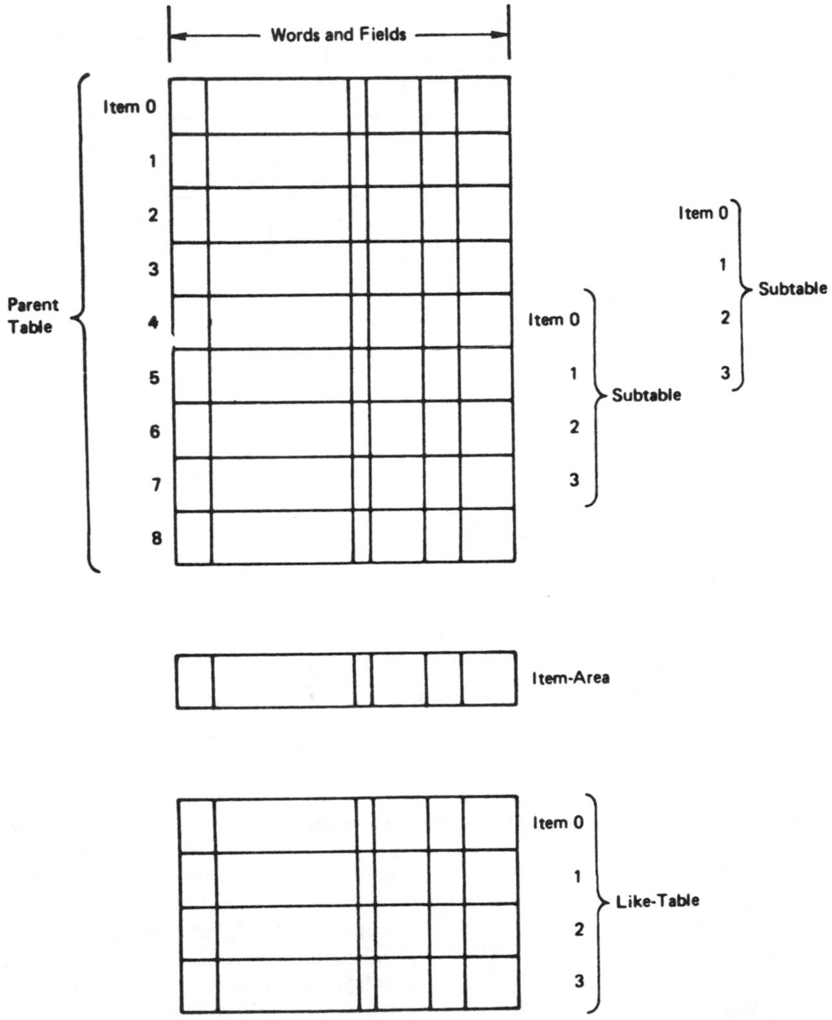

Figure 10-15.—Parent table relationships.

801

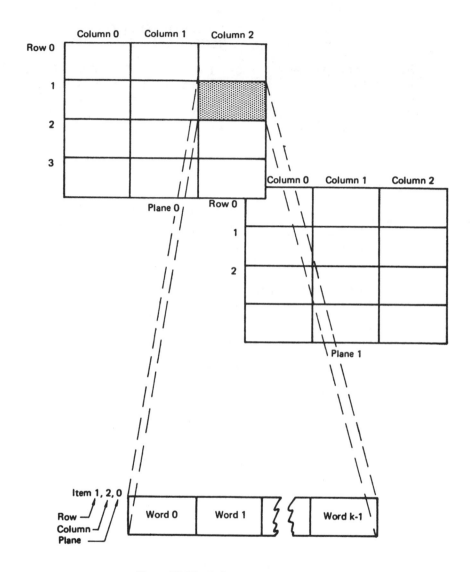

Figure 10-16.—A three-dimensional array.

program structure declaratives for a compile-time system is illustrated in figure 10-19. Figure 10-20 presents an alternate structure to accomplish the same purpose.

Procedure Structure Declarative and Linking

The dynamic statements that describe the processing operations of a program are grouped into blocks of statements called procedures. The overall purpose of a program, its design, and to some extent, its size, influence the programmer's decision as to whether one or several procedures will be declared. The transfer of program control from one procedure to another requires the observance of procedure linking rules for such transfers.

The concept of procedure linking may best be described by posing a situation from which

802

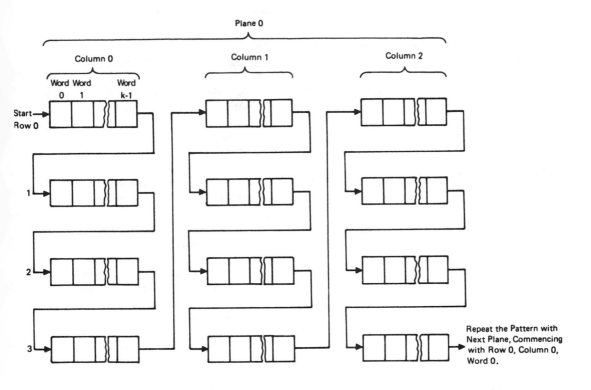

Figure 10-17.—Array storage sequence.

those linking requirements desirable for use by a programmer may be derived. As a program design develops, it becomes apparent to the programmer/designer that there is a requirement to execute a given set of statements at several points (within several procedures) in the total program. As each of these points is encountered, it would be advantageous to have a program control capability of branching to a common routine (procedure) for processing and then returning to the next instruction following the program control branch point (or PROCEDURE CALL). Along with this procedure call should be a capability of simultaneously and automatically passing that data, from the calling procedure to the CALLED PROCEDURE, which the called procedure processes. This automatic data transfer is defined as INPUT OF PARAMETERS— that is, data input to the called procedure from the calling procedure.

Upon completion of processing by the called procedure, it should also be possible to automatically pass the results of the processing from the called procedure to the calling procedure when program control is returned to the calling procedure. This is defined as OUTPUT OF PARAMETERS—that is, data output to the calling procedure from the called procedure.

Additionally, there should be a capability of specifying an instruction address (statement label) to which the called procedure may transfer program control in the event it does not perform its normal processing due to end of input, invalid input data, or processing checks indicating invalid or illogical results. This capability is defined as an ABNORMAL EXIT (abnormal return).

All of the capabilities described above are available in CMS-2 to provide linkage among procedures. Furthermore, all or part of these

Beginning Delimiter	Ending Delimiter	Purpose
SYSTEM	END-SYSTEM	Delimits a compile-time system.
SYS-DD	END-SYS-DD	Delimits a system data design within a compile-time system.
SYS-PROC	END-SYS-PROC	Delimits a system procedure within a compile-time system
LOC-DD	END-LOC-DD	Delimits a local data design within a system procedure.
PROCEDURE	END-PROC	Delimits a procedure within a system procedure.
†EXEC-PROC	END-PROC	Delimits a task-state procedure (called only from an executive-state procedure) within a system procedure.
FUNCTION	END-FUNCTION	Delimits a function within a system procedure.
†SYS-PROC-REN	END-SYS-PROC	Delimits a reentrant system procedure within a compile-time system.
†AUTO-DD	END-AUTO-DD	Delimits the dynamic data area within a reentrant system procedure that must be allocated each time the reentrant system procedure is initiated for execution.
HEAD	END-HEAD	Delimits a header package within a compile-time system.

†XCMS-2 only.

Figure 10-18.—Table showing CMS-2 program structure declaratives.

linkage capabilities may be used, depending upon the requirements of the program. Figure 10-21 is a schematic representation of the procedure linkage concept.

(XCMS-2) Reentrant System Procedures

Center programming applications require that one or more of the procedures comprising the

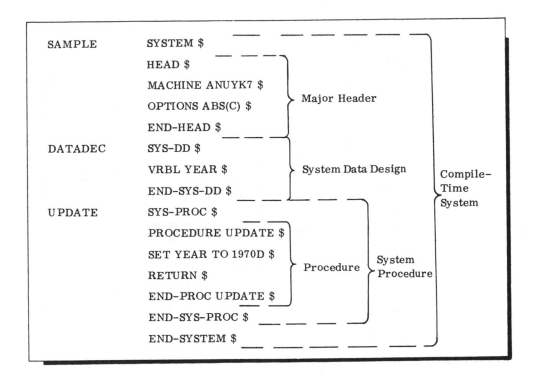

Figure 10-19.—A compile-time system structure.

program package or system for that application be structured such that they may be shared by more than one task concurrently. Procedures of this type are said to be REENTRANT procedures.

The principal characteristic of a reentrant routine is that it must be divided into two logically and physically distinct parts: a constant part and a variable part. The constant part (instruction part) is loaded into memory once and services all tasks requiring this routine. Separate copies of the variable part (data area) must be provided for each task that is being serviced. Each copy is usually created (that is, allocated memory space) when the reentrant routine is called.

Within the XCMS-2 compiler, a programmer has the capability of declaring a system procedure to be reentrant. In this case, the object code generated by the compiler for all procedures within this system procedure will be invariant (constant) under execution. In addition, a special type of local data design called an AUTOMATIC DATA DESIGN may be declared within a reentrant system procedure. An automatic data design is used for the definition of temporary storage. Procedure parameters used by the reentrant procedures are allocated within the automatic data design. Within a reentrant system procedure, the compiler automatically performs the required separation of the constant part (procedures) and the variable part (automatic data designs). Multiple copies of the variable part may then be loaded into memory along with a single copy of the constant part, and the reentrant system procedure may be executed simultaneously by more than one task or central processor.

It must be clearly understood that the compiler provides only this separation capability. The responsibility for loading these programs into memory and allocating space for automatic

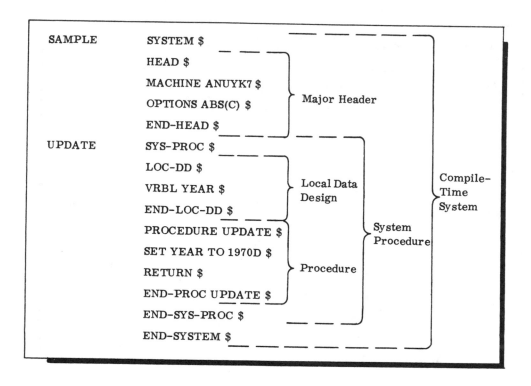

Figure 10-20.—Alternate compile-time system structure.

data designs is properly a function of loaders, monitors and executive programs. Furthermore, the XCMS-2 language and compiler provides the capability, through this separation function, of implementing such sophisticated programming techniques as recursion and reentrancy after suspension. However, much of the responsibility for this type of programming must be borne by the program designer and the executive program for the application.

COMPILER DIRECTIVE DECLARATIVES

Certain CMS-2 declarative statements specify control information to the compiler. These declaratives direct compiler action as to allocation mode, listing options, system index registers, program debug features, base numbering system interpretation, data pooling requirements, and the computer mode of operation within which the designated program is expected

to run. These declarative statements may be located in MAJOR HEADERS if the control applies to the entire compile-time system, in MINOR HEADERS if the control applies to a system element, or within a system element. The more significant compile directive operators and their functions are summarized below.

Operator	Function
MACHINE	Specifies the target machine code generator to be used.
OPTIONS	Designates:
	1. Compilation mode (absolute, relocatable or compool)
	2. Type of output listings desired

806

PROGRAMMING CONCEPTS (PART II)

Operator	Function
	3. Request to compile monitor-dependent CMS-2 statements
BASE	Specifies a starting address for an absolute compile.
TABLEPOOL LOCDDPOOL DATAPOOL	Specifies the collection of all tables or local data designs or all data beginning at a desired location in core. XCMS-2 does not recognize DATAPOOL.
DEBUG	Causes the compiler to generate object code for CMS-2 debug statements encountered in the source program.
SYS-INDEX	Assigns a unique name to a particular index register.
CSWITCH	Provides selective processing of specified sequences of source statements.

PROGRAM DEBUG FACILITIES

CMS-2 debug statements may be placed in the source language of a user's program to assist in program checkout. These statements may reference other program identifiers within the system, based on local/global regulations.

Machine code is generated by the compiler to call on object-time debug routines. The debug routines communicate with the monitor system during program execution to print the desired checkout data onto the system output.

Five program checkout statements are provided. Output code is generated only if the corresponding statements are enabled in the program header information. A programmer may then control and select the debug tools as needed. The debug operators and their functions are summarized below.

Operator	Function
DISPLAY	Causes the contents of machine registers and/or specified data

units to be formatted and printed on the system output.

Operator	Function
SNAP	The contents of a data unit are printed and stored. Subsequent executions cause a printout only when the data contents are modified.
RANGE	A high and low value are specified for a data unit. Each time the data is modified in the program, a message is printed if the value falls outside the range.
TRACE	A printout is generated for the execution of each CMS-2 statement between TRACE and END-TRACE boundaries.
PTRACE	Each CMS-2 procedure call encountered in the program being executed is identified by calling and called procedure names.

NOTE: The above debug features are not implemented in XCMS-2. XCMS-2 does not provide linkage to any object-time routines.

BASIC LANGUAGE DEFINITIONS

A CMS-2 program consists of an ordered set of statements composed of symbols and delimiters. The symbols and delimiters are formed using characters from the CMS-2 alphabet.

CMS-2 ALPHABET

The CMS-2 alphabet consists of letters, digits and marks as described below:

1. Letter—is one of the 26 letters of the English alphabet, A through Z, written in capital letter form.
2. Digit—is one of the ten Arabic numbers, 0 through 9.
3. Mark—is one of the characters listed below. The common name associated with each is indicated in parentheses.

807

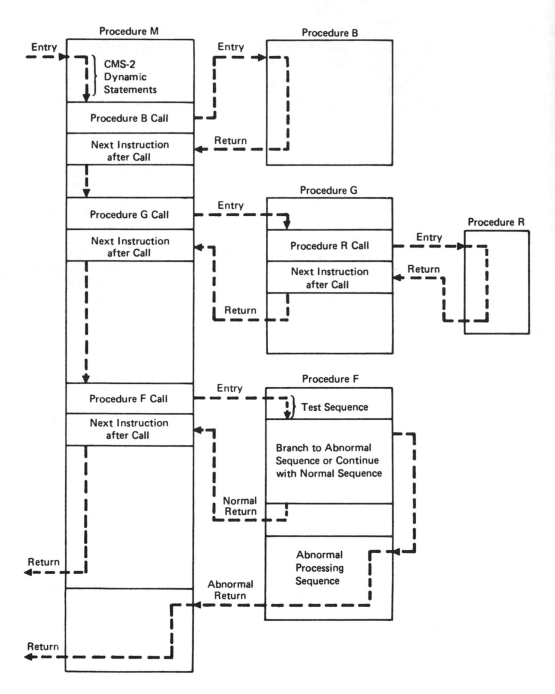

Figure 10-21.—Statement execution flow involving procedure calls.

PROGRAMMING CONCEPTS (PART II)

+ (plus)	) (right parenthesis)
- (minus)	$ (dollar sign)
/ (slash)	, (comma)
* (asterisk)	' (prime)
. (decimal point, period)	Δ (space)
((left parenthesis)	(space)

SYMBOLS

CMS-2 symbols are composed of strings of one or more letters, digits or marks from the CMS-2 alphabet. There are three types of symbols:

1. Operators—indicating operations or specifications.
2. Identifiers—names by which programs reference their environment.
3. Constants—words that represent unchanging values (constants in the mathematical sense).

Operators

Operators are symbols that denote an action or delineation to the compiler. They tell the compiler "what to do" or "what it is" as opposed to other symbols that tell "where it is" or "how much it is."

The following symbols are examples of CMS-2 operators. Symbols are classified into five categories.

Arith-metic	Rela-tional	Boolean	Proce-dural	Declara-tive
+	EQ	AND	PROCE-DURE	TABLE
-	LT	OR	FIND	FIELD
/	GT	COMP	SET	LOC-DD

A group of unique symbols constitutes a special class of operators and provides the machine control interface. These symbols, which are entirely object-machine dependent, necessarily vary from machine to machine. Each implementation for an object machine requires a specification of the complete list of associated operators.

Identifiers

Identifers are arbitrary names assigned by the user to identify various units of a CMS-2 program. A name is composed of one or more letters and digits. The first character of a name must be a letter. All CMS-2 identifiers (except statement labels, procedure names and abnormal exits) must be defined by or within a declaration that associates the identifier with its specific attribute. Statement labels, procedure names and abnormal exit names are defined to the compiler by their syntactical location within the appropriate statement.

The maximum number of characters permitted for an identifier is a machine-dependent consideration. As a general rule, however, identifiers should not exceed eight characters.

With the exception of maximum number of allowable characters, the following identifiers present legal and illegal examples.

Legal	Illegal	
A113X	5ABC	(First character is a digit)
05XY	A/BC	(Contains a mark)
X	A BC	(Embedded blank (a mark))
DATAIN		
FRIEND		
Z1234		

STATEMENT LABEL.—A statement label is a special identifier in a CMS-2 program. It is written as a prefix to a dynamic statement so that, during program execution, program control can be transferred to that statement through a reference to its label. A period immediately following the identifier (with no intervening blanks) serves to define it as a statement label and to connect it to the dynamic statement. When reference is made to the statement label, the period is omitted.

Example

```
                .
                .
                .
         IF DELTA EQ 0 THEN GOTO OK $
         SET DELTA TO 0 $
OK.      SET TIME TO INPUT $
                .
                .
                .
```

Explanation

OK is the statement label assigned to prefix the dynamic statement SET TIME TO INPUT. It is recognized by the compiler as a statement label by the period following the identifier name OK. In the IF statement a reference to the statement label OK is made; since it is a reference, a following period is not permitted.

Constants

A constant denotes a value that is known at compilation time. CMS-2 programs manipulate four types of data:

1. Numeric values—consisting of rational numbers.
2. Hollerith values—consisting of strings of characters.
3. Status values—consisting of independent sets of arbitrarily named conditions.
4. Boolean values—consisting of the two values: true or false.

NUMERIC CONSTANTS.—In the absence of unique modifiers, the CMS-2 and XCMS-2 compilers treat numeric constants as dictated by the normal mode of the compiler. The normal mode is different for each of these two compilers.

1. The CMS-2 compiler's normal numeric mode is octal. That is, all unmodified numeric constants are processed as octal, where the constant consists of one or more base-8 digits, 0 through 7. Digits greater than 7 will result in an error message. Should the user desire a numeric constant to be recognized as decimal, it may be modified by following the constant with the letter D with no intervening blanks.
2. The XCMS-2 compiler's normal numeric mode is decimal. That is, all unmodified numeric constants are processed as decimal where the constant consists of one or more base 10 digits, 0 through 9. Digits greater than 9, such as hexadecimal, will result in an error message. In addition to treating unmodified numeric constants as decimal, the XCMS-2 compiler will recognize and accept two versions of decimal constant representation. The first representation is a numeric constant immediately followed by the letter D. The second representation is a numeric constant enclosed within parentheses and immediately preceded by the letter D. Should the user desire a numeric constant to be

recognized as octal, it may be modified by enclosing the constant in parentheses with the letter O immediately preceding (no intervening blanks) the left parenthesis. For programs previously written with numeric constants in octal form, the user may achieve compatibility with the XCMS-2 compiler by utilizing the CMODE statement.

NOTE: The (XCMS-2) constant-mode (CMODE) statement may appear in a major or minor header and is used to inform the compiler that octal is to be the implied mode for numeric constants in the element or elements which follow. When this statement appears in a header, decimal constants must appear in one of two forms: a series of digits immediately followed by the letter D, e.g., 12345D; or a series of digits enclosed in parentheses and immediately preceded by the letter D, e.g., D(12345). All unmodified numeric constants or numeric constants enclosed in parentheses and immediately preceded by the letter O will be treated as octal constants, e.g., 12345 or O(12345). Any unmodified constants containing digits greater than 7 will result in a compiler-generated error message.

Numeric constants, represented according to the above rules, may be preceded by a plus sign if positive and must be preceded by a minus sign if negative. A radix point appearing within or at the beginning of the constant identifies the constant as a mixed number or fraction. If the radix point is omitted or occurs at the end of the constant, it identifies the constant as an integer (whole number).

Examples

CMS-2	XCMS-2
+77 (positive octal integer)	-94 (negative decimal integer)
98.3D (positive mixed decimal number)	O(77) (positive octal integer)
-.64 (negative octal fraction)	88.1 (positive mixed decimal number)

PROGRAMMING CONCEPTS (PART II)

CMS-2

-876D (negative decimal number)

XCMS-2

-0(.64) (negative octal fraction)

-D(492.3) (negative mixed decimal number)

239D (positive decimal number)

To avoid writing many zeros, it is sometimes convenient to express a very large or very small numeric floating-point constant as a coefficient multiplied by an exponent. For the CMS-2 compiler, when expressing decimal numbers in floating-point notation, the maximum permissible number of digits to express the mantissa is nine; the maxium value assignable as an exponent is ±25 (decimal).

Examples

CMS-2

$.00032_8$	=	$.32*10_8^{-3}$	= .32E-3
81000000_{10}	=	$81_{10}*10^5_{10}$	= 81E5D
51000_{10}	=	$5.1_{10}*10^4_{10}$	= 5.1E4D
3700_8	=	$3.7_8*10^3_8$	= 3.7E3
2500000000_8			= 25E10†
2500000000_{10}			= 25E8D†

XCMS-2

$.0023_8$	=	$.23_8*10_8^{-3}$	= 0(.23E-3)
1800000_{10}	=	$18_{10}*10^5_{10}$	= 18E5
15000_{10}	=	$1.5_{10}*10^4_{10}$	= 1.5E4
7300_8	=	$7.3_8*10^3_8$	= 0(7.3E3)
2500000000_8			= 0(25E10)†
2500000000_{10}			= 25E8†

†Both the coefficient and the exponent must have the same base.

HOLLERITH CONSTANT.—A Hollerith constant is composed of a string of characters enclosed by parentheses and preceded by the descriptor H. Any character from the MS-2 character set is a valid character in a Hollerith constant and may be used in source programs to construct character-string constants.

Examples

1. H(NOTNOW)
2. H(REWINDΔΔ)
3. H())ΔLAST)

In the second example, the two blanks are considered part of the constant. The third example illustrates the use of a right parenthesis as part of the constant within a string of characters. Each right parenthesis must be represented by two consecutive right parentheses since the string is terminated by a single right parenthesis. Encoding this constant results in the characters:

)ΔLAST

STATUS CONSTANTS.—A status constant is a mnemonic used to describe one of the possible values of a data unit. The compiler assigns a unique value to each status constant that is associated with a data unit. In subsequent statements, as the programmer sets and tests the data unit using the mnemonic, the compiler substitutes the assigned value to differentiate possible conditions. The same status constant may be assigned to more than one status data unit. However, it may not be used more than once within any given status data unit definition.

A status constant may be composed of any characters of the CMS-2 alphabet with the exception of a single prime ('). The status constant may have the same maximum number of characters as an identifier for a given machine. Status constants are always enclosed by single primes.

Examples

'REPAIR'	'5/38'
'STANDBY'	'40MM'
'ALERT'	'+'
'AIRBORNE'	'$MAX'

Status constants are represented internally as binary integers. The value of each status constant is determined by its relative position within a list of such constants. If three status constants are listed, the first is assigned a value of 1, the second a value of 2 and the third a value of 3.

BOOLEAN CONSTANTS.—A Boolean constant denotes one of the logical values of Boolean algebra (true or false) and is represented as a binary integer:

Logical	Binary
true	1
false	0

DELIMITERS

Blanks may be used to separate symbols in a CMS-2 program. When used as a separator, a single blank accomplishes the same result as a sequence of two or more blanks. All marks may be used as delimiters. Some marks, such as $, have unique delimiting uses. When a mark appears between two CMS-2 symbols, blanks are not needed as separators, although they may be used if desired.

STATEMENTS

CMS-2 statements are dynamic and declarative and are composed of a string of symbols and delimiters. In general, a declaration defines a structural configuration of data, and a dynamic statement defines the processing operation that manipulates the data. All CMS-2 statements are terminated by a dollar sign ($). More than one statement may appear on one card, and a statement may be continued on several cards. See figure 10-22 for source card format and examples of statement formulations.

COMMENTS

Comments, intended as clarifying text, have no operational effect on a program and may be included in either of two ways:
1. Within a statement by enclosing the comment with two consecutive single-prime symbols:

VRBL Z I"NTEGER" 14 "BITS" S"IGNED" $

Note

A symbol may not be broken by this type of comment; i.e., V"A"R"IA"BL"E would not result in the symbol VRBL.

2. As a separate statement by use of the operator, COMMENT:

COMMENT THIS ROUTINE COMPUTES
    SQUARE ROOTS $

Note

Since the dollar sign symbol serves as a statement terminator, it cannot be used within any comment.

Special Comments

Comments beginning in card column 11 (the first column of the statement field) are treated as special cases by the compiler. If the statement is one of the following, the compiler performs the indicated action on the listing:

Input	Action
COMMENTΔ((EJECT $	Eject to the top of the next listing page.
COMMENTΔ((LINE* $	Print a line of asterisks (*).
COMMENTΔ((SKIPn $	Skip n lines (where n is a number from 1 to 9).

If the statement is not one of the special indicators, the compiler replaces the word COMMENT with a single asterisk (*) in column 11 and lists the comment after skipping a line.

Input:

COMMENT   THIS IS AN EXAMPLE $

Output:

*   THIS IS AN EXAMPLE $

```
Card Identification Field  Statement Field
1 2 3 4 5 6 7 8 9 10       11 ... 80

XMPL     1  READIN SYS-PROC $
XMPL     2  COMMENT IN THE ABOVE STATEMENT THE SYMBOL READIN IS THE NAME
XMPL     3            IDENTIFIER ASSIGNED TO THIS COMPILE-TIME SYSTEM ELEMENT
XMPL     4            WHICH IS A SYSTEM PROCEDURE. IT IS NOT A STATEMENT LABEL
XMPL     5            AND MUST NOT BE FOLLOWED BY A PERIOD $
XMPL     6           PROCEDURE READIN EXIT NOMORE $
XMPL     7           SET WORK TO 0 $
XMPL     8             INPUT READ (WORK(TRKNO), WORK(X1), WORK(Y1), WORK(T1),
XMPL     9                                      WORK(X2), WORK(Y2), WORK(T2),
XMPL    10                                      IDEN . LOCREM) READER $
XMPL    11            IF WORK(TRKNO) EQ ENDINPUT THEN RETURN NOMORE $
XMPL    12          GOTO IDENSW $
XMPL    13   IDUNK. SET WORK(ID) TO 'UNKNOWN' $
XMPL    14          GOTO LR                          ''PROGRAM CONTROL IS TRANSFERRED
XMPL    15                                             TO STATEMENT LABELLED LR. NOTE
XMPL    16                                             THAT LR, WHEN REFERENCED, IS NOT
XMPL    17                                             FOLLOWED BY A PERIOD'' $
XMPL    18   IDFOE.     SET WORK(ID) TO 'HOSTILE' $ GOTO LR $
XMPL    19  IDFR.     SET WORK(ID) TO 'FRIEND' $
XMPL    20  LR.       IF LOCREM EQ H(NO) THEN SET WORK(REMOTE) TO 1 $
XMPL    21       RETURN$
XMPL    22            END-PROC READIN$
```

Figure 10-22.—Example of CMS-2 free-form source-card format.

These special comments allow programmers to produce listings that have a greater narrative format than listings without the special comments feature.

In addition to the above, XCMS-2 also has the following special comment.

Input	Action
COMMENTΔ- ((VERSΔABCD	The four letters or numbers represented by ABCD will be transferred to the ID card of the relocatable object deck produced by the compiler.

SOURCE CARD FORMAT

All CMS-2 source cards contain a card identification field and a statement field. The card identification field occupies columns 1 through 10; the statement field occupies columns 11 through 80. Card columns 1 through 10 have no operational effect on the compiler. The compiler does not sequence check the card sequence number. The suggested use of the card identification field is as follows:

Columns 1 through 4 = program identification
Columns 5 through 8 = card sequence number
Columns 9 through 10 = insert number

The statement field has a free format. Statement labels, operands, operators, etc., may occur anywhere in columns 11 through 80. Each statement is terminated with a $. There can be more than one statement per card, or a statement may require several cards. No continuation card indicator is needed when a CMS-2 statement exceeds one card. The statement continues in columns 11 through 80 of each succeeding card until a dollar sign is encountered. If a symbol or contiguous string of characters is to span two cards, the first part must end in column 80 of card 1, and the second part must start in column 11 of card 2. For example, if the eight-character symbol STMTLAB1 is started in column 78 of one card, the remaining five characters must begin in column 11 of the next card.

While packing of statements on cards reduces the size of the input deck, the compilers do not format the listing of the input statements. Packed statements will appear in the same form on the listing.

As a special listing option, any END statement (END, END-PROC, END-LOC-DD, etc.) beginning in card column 21 causes the compiler to skip three lines after listing the END statement.

GLOSSARY

ABSOLUTE ADDRESS—An address that is permanently assigned by the machine designer to a storage location. Synonymous with machine address, specific address.

ABSOLUTE CODING—Coding that uses machine instructions with absolute addresses.

ABSOLUTE ERROR—(1) The amount of error expressed in the same units as the quantity containing the error. (2) Loosely, the absolute value of the error, i.e., the magnitude of the error without regard to its algebraic sign.

ACCESS ARM—A part of a disc storage unit that is used to hold one or more reading and writing heads.

ACCESS TIME—(1) The time interval between the instant at which data are called for from a storage device and the instant delivery begins. (2) The time interval between the instant at which data are requested to be stored and the instant at which storage is started.

ACCUMULATOR—A register in which the result of an arithmetic or logic operation is formed.

ACCURACY—The degree of freedom from error, that is the degree of conformity to truth or to a rule.

ACOUSTIC DELAY LINE—A delay line whose operation is based on the time of propagation of sound waves in a given medium. Synonymous with sonic delay line.

ACOUSTIC MEMORY—Same as acoustic storage.

ACOUSTIC STORAGE—A storage device consisting of acoustic delay lines.

ADDER—A device whose output is a representation of the sum of the quantities represented by its inputs.

ADDRESS—(1) An identification, as represented by a name, label, or number, for a register, location in storage, or any other data source or destination such as the location of a station in a communication network. (2) Loosely, any part of an instruction that specifies the location of an operand for the instruction.

ADDRESS PART—A part of an instruction word that specifies the address of an operand, instruction, or result.

ADDRESS REGISTER—A register in which an address is stored.

ADP—Automatic data processing.

ALGOL—ALGOrithmic Language. A language primarily used to express computer programs by algorithms.

ALGORITHM—A prescribed set of well-defined rules or processes for the solution of a problem in a finite number of steps, e.g., a full statement of an arithmetic procedure for evaluating sin x to a stated precision.

ALGORITHMIC LANGUAGE—A language designed for expressing algorithms.

ALPHAMERIC—Same as alphanumeric.

GLOSSARY

ALPHANUMERIC—Pertaining to a character set that contains letters, digits, and usually other characters such as punctuation marks.

ALPHANUMERIC CHARACTER SET—A character set that contains letters, digits, and usually other characters.

ALPHANUMERIC CODE—A code whose code set consists of letters, digits, and associated special characters.

ANALOG—Pertaining to representation by means of continuously variable physical quantities.

ANALOG COMPUTER—(1) A computer in which analog representation of data is mainly used. (2) A computer that operates on analog data by performing physical processes on these data.

ANALYSIS—The methodical investigation of a problem, and the separation of the problem into smaller related units for further detailed study.

ANALYST—A person who defines problems and develops algorithms and procedures for their solution.

AND—A logic operator having the property that if P is a statement, Q is a statement, R is a statement . . . . , then the AND of P, Q, R . . . , is true if all statements are true, false if any statement is false. P AND Q is often represented by P·Q, PQ. Synonymous with logical multiply.

AND GATE—A gate that implements the logic "AND" operator.

ANNOTATION—An added descriptive comment or explanatory note.

APERTURE—An opening in a data medium or device such as a card or magnetic core; e.g., the aperture in an aperture card combining a microfilm with a punched card or a multiple aperture core.

ARITHMETIC SHIFT—(1) A shift that does not affect the sign position. (2) A shift that is equivalent to the multiplication of a number by a positive or negative integral power of the radix.

ARITHMETIC UNIT—The unit of a computing system that contains the circuits that perform arithmetic operations.

ARRAY—An arrangement of elements in one or more dimensions.

ASSEMBLE—To prepare a machine language program from a symbolic language program by substituting absolute operation codes for symbolic operation codes and absolute or relocatable addresses for symbolic addresses.

ASSEMBLER—A computer program that assembles.

ASSOCIATIVE STORAGE—A storage device in which storage locations are identified by their contents, not by names or positions.

ASYNCHRONOUS COMPUTER—A computer in which each event or the performance of each operation starts as a result of a signal generated by the completion of the previous event or operation, or by the availability of the parts of the computer required for the next event or operation. Contrast with synchronous computer.

AUTOMATIC—Pertaining to a process or device that, under specified conditions, functions without intervention by a human operator.

AUTOMATIC CARRIAGE—A control mechanism for a typewriter or other listing device that can automatically control the feeding, spacing, skipping, and ejecting of paper or preprinted forms.

AUTOMATIC CODING—The machine-assisted preparation of machine language routines.

AUTOMATIC COMPUTER—A computer that can perform a sequence of operations without intervention by a human operator.

GLOSSARY

AUTOMATIC DATA PROCESSING—Data processing largely performed by automatic means.

AUTOMATION—(1) The implementation of processes by automatic means. (2) The theory, art, or technique of making a process more automatic. (3) The investigation, design, development, and application of methods of rendering processes automatic, self-moving, or self-controlling. (4) The conversion of a procedure, a process, or equipment to automatic operation.

AUXILIARY OPERATION—An offline operation performed by equipment not under control of the central processing unit.

AUXILIARY STORAGE—(1) A storage that supplements another storage. (2) In flow-charting, an offline operation performed by equipment not under control of the central processing unit.

BASE—(1) A reference value. (2) A number that is multiplied by itself as many times as indicated by an exponent. (3) Same as radix. (4) See floating-point base.

BASE ADDRESS—A given address from which an absolute address is derived by combination with a relative address.

BATCH PROCESSING—(1) Pertaining to the technique of executing a set of computer programs such that each is completed before the next program of the set is started. (2) Pertaining to the sequential input of computer programs or data. (3) Loosely, the execution of computer programs serially.

BAUD—A unit of signalling speed equal to the number of discrete conditions or signal events per second. For example, one baud equals one-half dot cycle per second in Morse code, one bit per second in a train of binary signals, and one 3-bit value per second in a train of signals each of which can assume one of eight different states.

B BOX—Same as index register.

BCD—Binary-coded decimal notation.

BEGINNING-OF-TAPE MARKER—A marker on the magnetic tape used to indicate the beginning of the permissible recording area, e.g., a photo reflective strip, a transparent section of tape.

BINARY—(1) Pertaining to a characteristic or property involving a selection, choice, or condition in which there are two possibilities. (2) Pertaining to the number representation system with a radix of two.

BINARY CODE—A code that makes use of exactly two distinct characters, usually 0 and 1.

BINARY-CODED DECIMAL NOTATION—Positional notation in which the individual decimal digits expressing a number in decimal notation are each represented by a binary numeral. Abbreviated BCD.

BINARY DIGIT—In binary notation, either of the characters, 0 and 1.

BINARY NOTATION—Fixed radix notation where the radix is two.

BIONICS—A branch of technology relating the functions, characteristics, and phenomena of living systems to the development of hardware systems.

BIQUINARY CODE—A mixed radix notation in which each decimal digit to be represented is considered as a sum of two digits of which the first is zero or one with a significance five and the second is 0, 1, 2, 3, or 4 with significance one.

BISTABLE—Pertaining to a device capable of assuming either one of two stable states.

BIT—A binary digit.

BIT STRING—A string of binary digits in which the position of each binary digit is considered as an independent unit.

817

GLOSSARY

BLOCK DIAGRAM—A diagram of a system, instrument, or computer in which the principal parts are represented suitably associated geometrical figures to show both the basic functions and the function relationships among the parts.

BLOCK TRANSFER—The process of transmitting one or more blocks of data where the data are organized in blocks.

BOOLEAN—(1) Pertaining to the processes used in the algebra formulated by George Boole. (2) Pertaining to the operations of formal logic.

BOOLEAN ADD—Same as OR.

BOOLEAN OPERATOR—A logic operator each of whose operands and whose result have one of two values.

BOOTSTRAP—A technique or device designed to bring itself into a desired state by means of its own action e.g., a machine routine whose first few instructions are sufficient to bring the rest of itself into the computer from an input device.

BORROW—An arithmetically negative carry.

BRANCH—(1) A set of instructions that are executed between two successive decision instructions. (2) Loosely, a conditional jump.

BRANCHPOINT—A place in a routine where a branch is selected.

BREAKPOINT—A place in a routine specified by an instruction digit, or other condition, where the routine may be interrupted by external intervention or by a monitor routine.

BUFFER—(1) A routine or storage used to compensate for a difference in rate of flow of data, or time of occurrence of events, when transmitting data from one device to another. (2) An isolating circuit used to prevent a driven circuit from influencing the driving circuit.

BUG—A mistake or malfunction.

BURST—(1) To separate continuous-form paper into discrete sheets. (2) In data transmission, a sequence of signals counted as one unit in accordance with some specific criterion or measure.

BUS—One or more conductors used for transmitting signals or power.

BYTE—A sequence of adjacent binary digits operated upon as a unit and usually shorter than a computer word.

CALCULATOR—(1) A data processor especially suitable for performing arithmetical operations which require frequent intervention by a human operator. (2) Generally and historically, a device for carrying out logic and arithmetic digital operations of any kind.

CALL—To transfer control to a specified close subroutine.

CALLING SEQUENCE—A specified arrangement of instructions and data necessary to set up and call a given subroutine.

CAPACITOR STORAGE—A storage device that utilizes the capacitance properties of materials to store data.

CARD COLUMN—A single line of punch positions parallel to the short edge of a 3 1/4 by 7 3/8 inch punched card.

CARD DECK—Same as deck.

CARD HOPPER—The portion of a card processing machine that holds the cards to be processed and makes them available to a card feed mechanism.

CARD IMAGE—A one-to-one representation of the hole patterns of a punched card, e.g., a matrix in which a one represents a punch and zero represents the absence of a punch.

GLOSSARY

CARD ROW—A single line of punch positions parallel to the long edge of a 3 1/4 by 7 3/8 inch punched card.

CARD STACKER—The portion of a card processing machine that receives processed cards.

CARRIAGE CONTROL TAPE—A tape that contains line feed control data for a printing device.

CARRIAGE RETURN—The operation that prepares for the next character to be printed or displayed at the specified first position on the same line.

CARRY—(1) One or more digits, produced in connection with an arithmetic operation on one digit place of two or more numerals in positional notation, that are forwarded to another digit place for processing there. (2) The number represented by the digit or digits in (1). (3) Most commonly, a digit as defined in (1), that arises when the sum or product of two or more digits equals or exceeds the radix of the number representation system.

CASCADED CARRY—In parallel addition, a carry process in which the addition of two numerals results in a partial sum numeral and a carry numeral which are in turn added together, this process being repeated until no new carries are generated.

CATHODE RAY STORAGE—An electrostatic storage device that utilizes a cathode ray beam for access to the data.

CENTRAL PROCESSING UNIT—A unit of a computer that includes the circuits controlling the interpretation and execution of instructions. Synonymous with main frame. Abbreviated CPU.

CENTRAL PROCESSOR—A central processing unit.

CHAD—The piece of material removed when forming a hole or notch in a storage medium such as punched tape or punched cards. Synonymous with chip.

CHADLESS—Pertaining to the punching of tape in which chad does not result.

CHAIN PRINTER—A printer in which the type slugs are carried by the links of a revolving chain.

CHANGE DUMP—A selective dump of those storage locations whose contents have changed.

CHANNEL—(1) A path along which signals can be sent, e.g., data channel, output channel. (2) The portion of a storage medium that is accessible to a given reading or writing station, e.g., track, band.

CHARACTER—(1) A letter, digit, or other symbol that is used as part of the organization, control, or representation of data. A character is often in the form of a spatial arrangement of adjacent or connected strokes.

CHARACTER CHECK—A check that verifies the observance of rules for the formation of characters.

CHARACTER PRINTER—A device that prints a single character at a time.

CHARACTER RECOGNITION—The identification of graphic, phonic, or other characters by automatic means.

CHARACTER SET—A set of unique representations called characters e.g., the 26 letters of the English alphabet, 0 and 1 of the Boolean alphabet, and the set of signals in the Morse code alphabet.

CHARACTER STRING—A string consisting solely of characters.

CHARACTER SUBSET—A selection of characters from a character set, comprising all characters which have a specified common feature. For example, in the definition of character set, digits 0 through 9 constitute a character subset.

CHECK—A process for determining accuracy.

GLOSSARY

CLEAR—To place one or more storage locations into a prescribed state, usually zero or the space character.

CLOCK—(1) A device that generates periodic signals used for synchronization. (2) A register whose content changes at regular intervals in such a way as to measure time.

CLOCK PULSE—A synchronization signal provided by a clock.

CLOCK TRACK—A track on which a pattern of signals has been recorded to provide a time reference.

CLOSED SUBROUTINE—A subroutine that can be stored at one place and can be linked to one or more calling routines.

COBOL—(COmmon Business Oriented Language) A business data processing language.

CODE—In data processing, to represent data or a computer program in a symbolic form that can be accepted by a data processor.

CODER—A person mainly involved in writing but not designing computer programs.

COLLATE—To combine items from two or more ordered sets into one set having a specified order not necessarily the same as any of the original sets.

COLLATING SEQUENCE—An ordering assigned to a set of items, such that any two sets in that assigned order can be collated.

COLLATOR—A device to collate, merge, or match sets of punched cards or other documents.

COLUMN—(1) A vertical arrangement of characters or other expressions. (2) Loosely, a digit place.

COMMAND—(1) A control signal. (2) Loosely, an instruction in machine language.

COMMAND LANGUAGE—A source language consisting primarily of procedural operators, each capable of invoking a function to be executed.

COMMON FIELD—A field that can be accessed by two or more independent routines.

COMMUNICATION LINK—The physical means of connecting one location to another for the purpose of transmitting and receiving data.

COMPILE—To prepare a machine language program from a computer program written in another programming language by making use of the overall logic structure of the program, or generating more than one machine instruction for each symbolic statement, or both, as well as performing the function of an assembler.

COMPILER—A program that compiles.

COMPLEMENT—(1) A number that can be derived from a specified number by subtracting it from a second specified number. For example, in radix notation, the second specified number may be a given power of the radix or one less than a given power of the radix. The negative of a number is often represented by its complement.

COMPLETE CARRY—In parallel addition, a technique in which all of the carries are allowed to propagate.

COMPUTER—A data processor that can perform substantial computation, including numerous arithmetic or logic operations, without intervention by a human operator during the run.

COMPUTER CODE—A machine code for a specific computer.

COMPUTER INSTRUCTION—A machine instruction for a specific computer.

COMPUTER NETWORK—A complex consisting of two or more interconnected computers.

COMPUTER PROGRAM—A series of instructions or statements, in a form acceptable to a computer, prepared in order to achieve a certain result.

COMPUTER WORD—A sequence of bits or characters treated as a unit and capable of being stored in one computer location. Synonymous with machine word.

CONCURRENT—Pertaining to the occurrence of two or more events or activities within the same specified interval of time.

CONDITIONAL JUMP—A jump that occurs if specified criteria are met.

CONNECTOR—(1) On a flowchart, the means of representing the convergence of more than one flowline into one, or the divergence of one flowline into more than one. It may also represent a break in a single flowline for continuation in another area. (2) A means of representing on a flowchart a break in a line of flow.

CONSECUTIVE—Pertaining to the occurrence of two sequential events without the intervention of any other such event.

CONSOLE—That part of a computer used for communication between the operator or maintenance engineer and the computer.

CONTRAST—In optical character recognition, the differences between color or shading of the printed material on a document and the background on which it is printed.

CONTROL PANEL—A part of a computer console that contains manual controls.

CONVERT—To change the representation of data from one form to another, e.g., to change numerical data from binary to decimal or from cards to tape.

COPY—To reproduce data in a new location or other destination, leaving the source data unchanged, although the physical form of the result may differ from that of the source. For example, to copy a deck of cards onto a magnetic tape. Contrast with duplicate.

CORRECTIVE MAINTENANCE—Maintenance specifically intended to eliminate an existing fault.

CORRECTIVE MAINTENANCE TIME—Time, either scheduled or unscheduled, used to perform corrective maintenance.

COUNTER—A device such as a register or storage location used to represent the number of occurrences of an event.

CPU—Central Processing Unit.

CROSSTALK—The unwanted energy transferred from one circuit, called the "disturbing" circuit, to another circuit, called the "disturbed" circuit.

CRT DISPLAY—Cathode Ray Tube display.

CYBERNETICS—That branch of learning which brings together theories and studies on communication and control in living organisms and machines.

CYCLE—(1) An interval of space or time in which one set of events or phenomena is completed. (2) Any set of operations that is repeated regularly in the same sequence. The operations may be subject to variations on each repetition.

CYCLIC SHIFT—A shift in which the data moved out of one end of the storing register are reentered into the other end, as in a closed loop.

DATA—(1) A representation of facts, concepts, or instructions in a formalized manner suitable for communication, interpretation, or processing by humans or automatic means. (2) Any representations such as characters or analog quantities to which meaning is or might be assigned.

DATA BANK—A comprehensive collection of libraries of data.

DATA FLOW CHART—A flowchart representing the path of data through a problem solution. It defines the major phases of the processing as well as the various data media used.

DATA HIERARCHY—A data structure consisting of sets and subsets such that every subset of a set is of lower rank than the data of the set.

DATA MEDIUM—(1) The material in or on which a specific physical variable may represent data. (2) The physical quantity which may be varied to represent data.

DATA PROCESSING—The execution of a systematic sequence of operations performed upon data. Synonymous with information processing.

DATA PROCESSOR—A device capable of performing data processing, including desk calculators, punched card machines, and computers.

DATA REDUCTION—The transformation of raw data into a more useful form.

DEBUG—To detect, locate, and remove mistakes from a routine or malfunctions from a computer. Synonymous with troubleshoot.

DECIMAL—Pertaining to the number representation system with a radix of ten.

DECIMAL DIGIT—In decimal notation, one of the characters 0 through 9.

DECIMAL NOTATION—A fixed radix notation where the radix is ten.

DECIMAL NUMERAL—A decimal representation of a number.

DECIMAL POINT—The radix point in decimal representation.

DECISION—A determination of future action.

DECISION INSTRUCTION—An instruction that effects the selection of a branch of a program e.g., a conditional jump instruction.

DECK—A collection of punched cards Synonymous with card deck.

DECODE—To apply a set of unambiguous rules specifying the way in which data may be restored to a previous representation.

DECODER—(1) A device that decodes. (2) A matrix of logic elements that selects one or more output channels according to the combination of input signals present.

DECOLLATE—To separate the plies of a multipart form or paper stock.

DEFERRED MAINTENANCE—Maintenance specifically intended to eliminate an existing fault, which did not prevent continued successful operation of the device or program.

DELAY—The amount of time by which an event is retarded.

DELEAVE—Same as decollate.

DELIMITER—A flag that separates and organizes items of data. Synonymous with separator.

DESCRIPTOR—In information retrieval, a word used to categorize or index information. Synonymous with keyword.

DESTRUCTIVE READ—A read process that also erases the data from the source.

DEVELOPMENT TIME—That part of operating time used for debugging new routines or hardware.

DIAGNOSTIC—Pertaining to the detection and isolation of a malfunction or mistake.

DIGIT—A symbol that represents one of the positive integers smaller than the radix.

DIGITAL—Pertaining to data in the form of digits.

DIGITAL COMPUTER—(1) A computer in which discrete representation of data is mainly used. (2) A computer that operates on discrete data by performing arithmetic and logic processes on these data.

DIGITIZE—To use numeric characters to express or represent data.

DIGIT PUNCH—A punch in rows 1, 2, . . . , 9 of a punched card.

DIMINISHED RADIX COMPLEMENT—Same as radix-minus-one complement.

DIRECT ACCESS—(1) Pertaining to the process of obtaining data from, or placing data into, storage where the time required for such access is independent of the location of the data most recently obtained or placed in storage. (2) Pertaining to a storage device in which the access time is effectively independent of the location of the data. (3) Synonymous with random access (1).

DIRECT ADDRESS—An address that specifies the location of an operand.

DISASTER DUMP—A dump made when a nonrecoverable program error occurs.

DISCRETE—Pertaining to distinct elements or to representation by means of distinct elements such as characters.

DISPLAY—A visual presentation of data.

DOCUMENT—(1) A medium and the data recorded on it for human use. (2) By extension, any record that has permanence and that can be read by man or machine.

DOCUMENT REFERENCE EDGE—In character recognition, a specified document edge with respect to which the alignment of characters is defined.

DOCUMENTATION—(1) The creating, collecting, organizing, storing, citing, and disseminating of documents or the information recorded in documents. (2) A collection of documents or information on a given subject.

DOUBLE PRECISION—Pertaining to the use of two computer words to represent a number.

DOWNTIME—The time interval during which a device is malfunctioning.

DROP OUT—(1) In magnetic tape, a recorded signal whose amplitude is less than a predetermined percentage of a reference signal. (2) In data transmission, a momentary loss in signal, usually due to the effect of noise or system malfunction.

DUMP—(1) To copy the contents of all or part of a storage, usually from an internal storage into an external storage. (2) A process as in (1). (3) The data resulting from the process as in (1).

DUODECIMAL—(1) Pertaining to a characteristic or property involving a selection, choice, or condition in which there are twelve possibilities. (2) Pertaining to the numeration system with a radix of twelve.

DUPLICATE—To copy so that the result remains in the same physical form as the source, e.g., to make a new punched card with the same pattern of holes as an original punched card. Contrast with copy.

DYNAMIC DUMP—A dump that is performed during the execution of a computer program.

DYNAMIC STORAGE—A device storing data in a manner that permits the data to move or vary with time such that the specified data are not always available for recovery. Magnetic-drum and disc storage are nonvolatile dynamic storage. An acoustic delay line is a volatile dynamic storage.

GLOSSARY

DYNAMIC STORAGE ALLOCATION—A storage allocation technique in which the location of computer programs and data is determined by criteria applied at the moment of need.

EAM—Electrical Accounting Machine.

EDIT—To modify the form or format of data, e.g., to insert or delete characters such as page numbers or decimal points.

EDP—Electronic Data Processing.

ELECTRONIC DATA PROCESSING—(1) Data processing largely performed by electronic devices. (2) Pertaining to data processing equipment that is predominantly electronic such as an electronic digital computer.

ELECTROSTATIC STORAGE—A storage device that stores data as electrostatically charged areas on a dielectric surface.

ELEVEN-PUNCH—A punch in the second row from the top, on a Hollerith punched card. Synonymous with x-punch.

EMERGENCY MAINTENANCE—Maintenance specifically intended to eliminate an existing fault, which makes continued production work unachievable.

EMERGENCY MAINTENANCE TIME—Time, usually unscheduled, used to perform corrective maintenance.

ENCODE—To apply a set of unambiguous rules specifying the way in which data may be represented such that a subsequent decoding is possible.

END-AROUND CARRY—A carry from the most significant digit place to the least significant place.

END-OF-TAPE MARKER—A marker on a magnetic tape used to indicate the end of the permissible recording area, e.g., a photo reflective strip, a transparent section of tape, a particular bit pattern.

ENTRY CONDITIONS—The initial data and control conditions to be satisfied for successful execution of a given routine.

ENTRY POINT—In a routine, any place to which control can be passed.

ERASE—To obliterate information from a storage medium, e.g., to clear, to overwrite.

ERROR—Any discrepancy between a computed, observed, or measured quantity and the true, specified, or theoretically correct value or condition.

ERROR DETECTING CODE—A code in which each expression conforms to specific rules of construction, so that if certain errors occur in an expression the resulting expression will not conform to the rules of construction and, thus, the presence of the errors is detected. Synonymous with self-checking code.

ERROR MESSAGE—An indication that an error has been detected.

ERROR RANGE—The difference between the highest and lowest error values.

ERROR RATIO—The ratio of the number of data units in error to the total number of data units.

EXCESS THREE CODE—A binary coded decimal notation in which each decimal digit N is represented by the binary numeral of N plus three.

EXCLUSIVE OR—A logic operator having the property that if P is a statement and Q is a statement, then P exclusive OR Q is true if either but not both statements are true, false if both are true or both are false. P exclusive OR Q is often represented by $P \oplus Q$, $P \veebar Q$. Contrast with OR.

EXECUTIVE ROUTINE—A routine that controls the execution of other routines.

EXPONENT—In a floating point representation, the numeral, of a pair of numerals representing a number, that indicates the power to which the base is raised.

FALSE ADD—To form a partial sum, i.e., to add without carries.

FAULT—(1) A physical condition that causes a device, a component, or an element to fail to perform in a required manner, e.g., a short circuit, a broken wire, an intermittent connection.

FEEDBACK LOOP—The components and processes involved in correcting or controlling a system by using part of the output as input.

FERRITE—An iron compound frequently used in the construction of magnetic cores.

FIELD—In a record, a specified area used for a particular category of data, e.g., a group of card columns used to represent a wage rate, a set of bit locations in a computer word used to express the address of the operand.

FILE—A collection of related records treated as a unit.

FILE GAP—An area on a data medium intended to be used to indicate the end of a file, and possibly, the start of another. A file gap is frequently used for other purposes, in particular, as a flag to indicate the end or beginning of some other group of data.

FILE LAYOUT—The arrangement and structure of data in a file, including the sequence and size of its components. By extension, a file layout might be the description thereof.

FILE MAINTENANCE—The activity of keeping a file up to date by adding, changing or deleting data.

FILE SEPARATOR—The information separator intended to identify a logical boundary between items called "files." Abbreviated FS.

FILTER—(1) A device or program that separates data, signals, or material in accordance with specified criteria. (2) A mask.

FIXED-CYCLE OPERATION—An operation that is completed in a specified number of regularly timed execution cycles.

FIXED-POINT PART—In a floating-point representation, the numeral of a pair of numerals representing a number, that is the fixed-point factor by which the power is multiplied.

FIXED-POINT REPRESENTATION—A positional representation in which each number is represented by a single set of digits, the position of the radix point being fixed with respect to one end of the set, according to some convention.

FIXED RADIX NOTATION—A positional representation in which the significances of successive digit positions are successive integral power of a single radix. When the radix is positive, permissible values of each digit range from zero to one less than the radix, and negative integral powers of the radix are used to represent fractions.

FIXED STORAGE—Storage whose contents are not alterable by computer instructions, e.g., magnetic core storage with a lockout feature, photographic disc. Synonymous with nonerasable storage, permanent storage, read-only storage.

FLAG—(1) Any of various types of indicators used for identification, e.g., a wordmark. (2) A character that signals the occurrence of some condition, such as the end of a word. (3) Synonymous with mark, sentinel, tag.

FLIP-FLOP—A circuit or device containing active elements, capable of assuming either one of two stable states at a given time. Synonymous with toggle.

FLOATING-POINT BASE—In floating point representation, the fixed positive integer that is the base of the power. Synonymous with floating-point radix.

FLOATING-POINT REPRESENTATION—A number representation system in which each number as represented by a pair of numerals equals one of those numerals times a power of an implicit fixed positive integer base where the power is equal to the implicit base raised to the exponent represented by the other numeral.

Common Notation

0.0001234 or (O.1234) x (10⁻³)

0.0001234 or $(0.1234) \times (10^{-3})$

A Floating Representation

1234 - 03

FLOWCHART—A graphical representation for the definition, analysis, or solution of a problem, in which symbols are used to represent operations, data, flow, equipment, etc.

FLOWCHART SYMBOL—A symbol used to represent operations, data, flow, or equipment on a flowchart.

FLOWCHART TEXT—The descriptive information that is associated with flowchart symbols.

FLOW DIRECTION—In flowcharting, the antecedent-to-successor relation, indicated by arrows or other conventions, between operations on a flowchart.

FLOWLINE—On a flowchart, a line representing a connecting path between flowchart symbols.

FORMAT—The arrangement of data.

FORTRAN—(FORmula TRANSlating system) A language primarily used to express computer programs by arithmetic formulas.

FRAME—An area, one recording position long, extending across the width of a magnetic or paper tape perpendicular to its movement. Several bits or punch positions may be included in a single frame through the use of different recording positions across the width of the tape.

FUNCTION—A specific purpose of an entity, or its characteristic action.

FUNCTIONAL DESIGN—The specification of the working relations between the parts of a system in terms of their characteristic actions.

FUNCTIONAL DIAGRAM—A diagram that represents the functional relationships among the parts of a system.

GATE—A device having one output channel and one or more input channels, such as the output channel state is completely determined by the input channel states, except during switching transients, e.g., AND GATE; OR GATE.

GENERAL PURPOSE COMPUTER—A computer that is designed to handle a wide variety of problems.

GRAY CODE—A binary code in which sequential numbers are represented by binary expressions, each of which differs from the preceding expression in one place only. Synonymous with reflected binary code.

HALF-ADDER—A combinational logic element having two outputs. S and C, and two inputs, A and B, such that the outputs are related to the inputs according to the following table.

input		output	
A	B	C	S
0	0	0	0
0	1	0	1
1	0	0	1
1	1	1	0

S denotes "Sum Without Carry," C denotes "Carry." Two half-adders may be used for performing binary addition.

HALF-WORD—A contiguous sequence of bits or characters which comprises half a computer word and is capable of being addressed as a unit.

HAMMING CODE—A data code which is capable of being corrected automatically.

GLOSSARY

HARDWARE—Physical equipment, as opposed to the computer program or method of use, e.g., mechanical, magnetic, electrical, or electronic devices. Contrast with software.

HEAD—A device that reads, writes, or erases data on a storage medium, e.g., a small electromagnet used to read, write, or erase data on a magnetic drum or tape, or the set of perforating, reading, or marking devices used for punching, reading, or printing on paper tape.

HEADER CARD—A card that contains information related to the data in cards that follow.

HEXADECIMAL—Same as sexadecimal.

HIERARCHY—See data hierarchy.

HIGH-SPEED CARRY—Any technique in parallel addition for speeding up carry propagation.

HIT—A successful comparison of two items of data.

HOLE PATTERN—A punching configuration within a card column that represents a single character of a character set.

HOLLERITH—Pertaining to a particular type of code or punched card utilizing 12 rows per column and usually 80 columns per card.

HYBRID COMPUTER—A computer for data processing using both analog representation and discrete representation of data.

IDENTIFIER—A symbol whose purpose is to identify, indicate, or name a body of data.

IDLE TIME—That part of available time during which the hardware is not being used.

IDP—See Integrated Data Processing.

ILLEGAL CHARACTER—A character or combination of bits that is not valid according to some criteria, e.g., with respect to a specified alphabet a character that is not a member.

INCONNECTOR—In flowcharting, a connector that indicates a continuation of a broken flowline.

INDEX REGISTER—A register whose content may be added to or subtracted from the operand address prior to or during the execution of a computer instruction. Synonymous with B box.

INFORMATION—The meaning that a human assigns to data by means of the known conventions used in their representation.

INFORMATION PROCESSING— Same as data processing.

INFORMATION RETRIEVAL—The methods and procedures for recovering specific information from stored data.

INHERITED ERROR—An error carried forward from a previous step in a sequential process.

INHIBITING SIGNAL—A signal that prevents an operation from taking place.

INITIALIZE—To set counters, switches, and addresses to zero or other starting values at the beginning of, or at prescribed points in, a computer routine. Synonymous with prestore.

INPUT—Pertaining to a device process, or channel involved in the insertion of data or states, or to the data or states involved.

INPUT AREA—An area of storage reserved for input.

INPUT CHANNEL—A channel for impressing a state on a device or logic element.

INPUT DATA—Data to be processed.

INPUT DEVICE—The device or collective set of devices used for conveying data into another device.

GLOSSARY

INPUT/OUTPUT—Pertaining to either input or output, or both.

INSTALLATION TIME—Time spent in installing and testing either hardware, or software, or both, until they are accepted.

INSTRUCTION—A statement that specifies an operation and the values or locations of its operands.

INSTRUCTION ADDRESS—The address that must be used to fetch an instruction.

INSTRUCTION COUNTER—A counter that indicates the location of the next computer instruction to be interpreted.

INSTRUCTION REGISTER—A register that stores an instruction for execution.

INSTRUCTION REPERTOIRE—The set of operations that can be represented in a given operation code.

INTEGRATED DATA PROCESSING—Data processing in which the coordination of data acquisition and all other stages of data processing is achieved in a coherent system, e.g., a business data processing system in which data for orders and buying are combined to accomplish the functions of scheduling, invoicing, and accounting. Abbreviated IDP.

INTERFACE—A shared boundary. An interface might be a hardware component to link two devices or it might be a portion of storage or registers accessed by two or more computer programs.

INTERLEAVE—To arrange parts of one sequence of things or events so that they alternate with parts of one or more other sequences of things or events and so that each sequence retains its identity, e.g., to organize storage into banks with independent bases so that sequential data references may be overlapped in a given period of time.

INTERNAL STORAGE—Addressable storage directly controlled by the central processing unit of a digital computer.

INTERPRETER—(1) A computer program that translates and executes each source language statement before translating and executing the next one. (2) A device that prints on a punched card the data already punched in the card.

INTERRUPT—To stop a process in such a way that it can be resumed.

INVERT—To change a physical or logical state to its opposite.

I/O—An abbreviation for input/output.

ITEM—(1) In general, one member of a group, e.g., a record may contain a number of items such as fields or groups of fields: a file may consist of a number of items such as records; a table may consist of a number of items such as entries. (2) A collection of related characters, treated as a unit.

JOB—A specified group of tasks prescribed as a unit of work for a computer.

JUMP—A departure from the normal sequence of executing instructions in a computer. Synonymous with transfer.

JUSTIFY—(1) To adjust the printing positions of characters on a page so that the lines have the desired length and that both the left and right hand margins are regular. (2) By extension, to shift the contents of a register so that the most or the least significant digit is at some specified position in the register.

K—An abbreviation for the prefix kilo, i.e., 1000 in decimal notation.

KEYPUNCH—A keyboard actuated device that punches holes in a card to represent data.

LABEL—One or more characters used to identify a statement or an item of data in a computer program.

GLOSSARY

LACED CARD—A punched card that has a lace-like appearance, usually without information content.

LAG—The delay between two events.

LANGUAGE—A set of representations, conventions, and rules used to convey information.

LEADER—The blank section of tape at the beginning of a reel of tape.

LEFT-JUSTIFY—(1) To adjust the printing positions of characters on a page so that the left margin of the page is regular. (2) By extension, to shift the contents of a register so that the most significant digit is at some specified position of the register.

LEVEL—The degree of subordination in a hierarchy.

LIBRARY—(1) A collection of organized information used for study and reference. (2) A collection of related files.

LIBRARY ROUTINE—A proven routine that is maintained in a program library.

LINE PRINTER—A device that prints all characters of a line as a unit.

LINE PRINTING—The printing of an entire line of characters as a unit.

LINKAGE—In programming, coding that connects two separately coded routines.

LIST—An ordered set of items.

LOAD—In programming, to enter data into storage or working registers.

LOAD-AND-GO—An operating technique in which there are no stops between the loading and execution phases of a program, and which may include assembling or compiling.

LOCATION—Any place in which data may be stored.

LOGICAL FILE—A collection of one or more logical records.

LOGIC ELEMENT—A device that performs a logic function.

LOGIC INSTRUCTION—An instruction that executes an operation that is defined in symbolic logic, such as AND, OR, NOR.

LOGIC SHIFT—A shift that affects all positions.

LOGIC SYMBOL—(1) A symbol used to represent a logic element graphically. (2) A symbol used to represent a logic operator.

LOOP—A sequence of instructions that is executed repeatedly until a terminal condition prevails.

MACHINE CODE—An operation code that a machine is designed to recognize.

MACHINE INSTRUCTION—An instruction that a machine can recognize and execute.

MACHINE LANGUAGE—A language that is used directly by a machine.

MACHINE WORD—Same as computer word.

MACRO INSTRUCTION—An instruction in a source language that is equivalent to a specified sequence of machine instructions.

MACROPROGRAMMING—Programming with macro instructions.

MAGNETIC CARD—A card with a magnetic surface on which data can be stored by selective magnetization of portions of the flat surface.

MAGNETIC CORE—A configuration of magnetic material that is, or is intended to be, placed in a spatial relationship to current-carrying conductors and whose magnetic properties are essential to its use. It may be used to concentrate an induced magnetic field as in a transformer induction coil, or armature, to retain a magnetic polarization for the purpose of storing data, or for its nonlinear properties as in a logic element. It may be made of such material as iron, iron oxide, or ferrite and in such shapes as wires, tapes, toroids, rods, or thin film.

MAGNETIC DELAY LINE—A delay line whose operation is based on the time of propagation of magnetic waves.

MAGNETIC DISC—A flat circular plate with a magnetic surface on which data can be stored by selective magnetization of portions of the flat surface.

MAGNETIC DRUM—A right circular cylinder with a magnetic surface on which data can be stored by selective magnetization of portions of the curved surface.

MAGNETIC HYSTERESIS LOOP—A closed curve showing the relation between the magnetization force and the induction of magnetization in a magnetic substance when the magnetized field (force) is carried through a complete cycle.

MAGNETIC INK—An ink that contains particles of a magnetic substance whose presence can be detected by magnetic sensors.

MAGNETIC STORAGE—A storage device that utilizes the magnetic properties of materials to store data, e.g., magnetic cores, tapes, and films.

MAGNETIC TAPE—(1) A tape with a magnetic surface on which data can be stored by selective polarization of portions of the surface. (2) A tape of magnetic material used as the constituent in some forms of magnetic cores.

MAGNETIC THIN FILM—A layer of magnetic material, usually less than one micron thick, often used for logic or storage elements.

MAIN FRAME—Same as central processing unit.

MAIN STORAGE—The general-purpose storage of a computer. Usually, main storage can be accessed directly by the operating registers.

MAINTENANCE—Any activity intended to eliminate faults or to keep hardware or programs in satisfactory working condition, including tests, measurements, replacements, adjustments, and repairs.

MAINTENANCE TIME—Time used for hardware maintenance. It includes preventive maintenance time and corrective maintenance time.

MANTISSA—The fractional part of a logarithm.

MARGINAL CHECK—A preventive maintenance procedure in which certain operating conditions, such as supply voltage or frequency, are varied about their nominal values in order to detect and locate incipiently defective parts.

MARK—Same as flag.

MASS STORAGE DEVICE—A device having a large storage capacity, e.g., magnetic disc, magnetic drum.

MASTER FILE—A file that is either relatively permanent, or that is treated as an authority in a particular job.

MATCH—To check for identity between two or more items of data.

MATHEMATICAL MODEL—A mathematical representation of a process, device, or concept.

MATRIX—(1) In mathematics, a two-dimensional rectangular array of quantities. Matrices are manipulated in accordance with the rules of matrix algebra. (2) In computers, a logic network in the form of an array of input leads and output leads with logic elements connected at some of their intersections. (3) By extension, an array of any number of dimensions.

MATRIX STORAGE—Storage, the elements of which are arranged such that access to any location requires the use of two or more coordinates, e.g., cathode ray storage, magnetic core storage.

GLOSSARY

MEDIUM—The material, or configuration thereof, on which data are recorded, e.g., paper tape, cards, magnetic tape. Synonymous with data medium.

MEMORY—Same as storage.

MERGE—To combine items from two or more similarly ordered sets into one set that is arranged in the same order. Contrast with collate.

MESSAGE—An arbitrary amount of information whose beginning and end are defined or implied.

MISTAKE—A human action that produces an unintended result.

MNEMONIC SYMBOL—A symbol chosen to assist the human memory, e.g., an abbreviation such as "mpy" for "multiply."

MODEM—(MOdulator-DEModulator) A device that modulates signals transmitted over communication facilities.

MODULE—(1) A program unit that is discrete and identifiable with respect to compiling, combining with other units, and loading, e.g., the input to, or output from, an assembler, compiler, linkage editor, or executive routine. (2) A packaged, functional hardware unit designed for use with other components.

MONITOR—Software or hardware that observes, supervises, controls, or verifies the operations of a system.

MONOSTABLE—Pertaining to a device that has one stable state.

MULTIPLE PUNCHING—Punching more than one hole in the same column of a punched card by means of more than one keystroke.

MULTIPLEX—To interleave or simultaneously transmit two or more messages on a single channel.

MULTIPROCESSING—Pertaining to the simultaneous execution of two or more computer programs or sequences of instructions by a computer or computer network.

MULTIPROCESSOR—A computer employing two or more processing units under integrated control.

MULTIPROGRAMMING—Pertaining to the concurrent execution of two or more programs by a computer.

NAND—A logic operator having the property that if P is a statement, Q is a statement, R is a statement..., then the NAND OF P, Q, R ... is true if at least one statement is false, false if all statements are true. Synonymous with NOT-AND.

NATURAL LANGUAGE—A language whose rules reflect and describe current usage rather than prescribe usage.

N-CORE-PER-BIT STORAGE—A storage device that employs n magnetic cores for each bit to be stored.

NDR—See nondestructive read.

NEGATE—To perform the logic operation NOT.

NEST—To imbed subroutines or data in other subroutines of data at a different hierarchical level such that the different levels of routines or data can be executed or accessed recursively.

NOISE—(1) Random variations of one or more characteristics of any entity such as voltage, current, or data. (2) A random signal of known statistical properties of amplitude, distribution and spectral density. (3) Loosely, any disturbance tending to interfere with the normal operation of a device or system.

NONDESTRUCTIVE READ—A read process that does not erase the data in the source. Abbreviated NDR.

NON-RETURN-TO-ZERO (MARK) RECORDING—A method of recording in which ones are represented by a change in the condition

831

of magnetization; zeros are represented by the absence of change. Abbreviated NRZ(M).

NON-RETURN-TO-ZERO RECORDING—A method of recording in which the change between the state of magnetization representing either zero or one provides the reference condition. Synonymous with non-return-to-reference recording. Abbreviated NRZ.

NO-OP—An instruction that specifically instructs the computer to do nothing, except to proceed to the next instruction in sequence.

NOR—A logic operator having the property that if P is a statement, Q is a statement, R is a statement . . . , then the NOR of P, Q, R . . . is true if all statements are false, false if at least one statement is true. P NOR Q is often represented by a combination of "OR" and "NOT" symbols, such as ~ (P∨Q). P NOR Q is also called "neither P nor Q." Synonymous with NOT-OR.

NORMAL DIRECTION FLOW—A flow in a direction from left to right or top to bottom on a flowchart.

NORMALIZE—(1) To multiply a variable or one or more quantities occurring in a calculation by a numerical coefficient in order to make an associated quantity assume a nominated value, e.g., to make a definite integral of a variable, or the maximum member of a set of quantities, equal to unity. (2) Loosely, a scale.

NOT—A logic operator having the property that if P is a statement, then the NOT of P is true if P is false, false if P is true. The NOT of P is often represented by $\bar{P}$, ~P, ¬P, P'.

NOT-AND—Same as NAND.

NOT-OR—Same as NOR.

NRZ—Non-Return-to-Zero recording.

NRZ(M)—Non-Return-to-Zero (Mark) recording.

NUMBER—(1) A mathematical entity that may indicate quantity or amount of units. (2) Loosely, a numeral.

NUMBER REPRESENTATION—The representation of numbers by agreed sets of symbols according to agreed rules. Synonymous with numeration.

NUMBER REPRESENTATION SYSTEM—An agreed set of symbols and rules for number representation.

NUMBER SYSTEM—Loosely, a number representation system.

NUMERAL—(1) A discrete representation of a number. For example, twelve, 12, XII, 1100 are four different numerals that represent the same number. (2) A numeric word that represents a number.

NUMERIC WORD—A word consisting of digits and possibly space characters and special characters.

OBJECT CODE—Output from a compiler or assembler which is itself executable machine code or is suitable for processing to produce executable machine code.

OBJECT MODULE—A module that is the output of an assembler or compiler and is input to a linkage editor.

OBJECT PROGRAM—A fully compiled or assembled program that is ready to be loaded into the computer. Synonymous with target program.

OCR—Optical Character Recognition.

OCTAL—(1) Pertaining to a characteristic or property involving a selection, choice or condition in which there are eight possibilities. (2) Pertaining to the number representation system with a radix of eight.

GLOSSARY

OCTET–A byte composed of eight bits.

OFFLINE–Pertaining to equipment or devices not under control of the central processing unit.

OFFLINE STORAGE–Storage not under control of the central processing unit.

ONES COMPLEMENT–The radix-minus-one complement in binary notation.

ONLINE–(1) Pertaining to equipment or devices under control of the central processing unit. (2) Pertaining to a user's ability to interact with a computer.

ONLINE STORAGE–Storage under control of the central processing unit.

OPENENDED–Pertaining to a process or system that can be augmented.

OPEN SUBROUTINE–A subroutine that is inserted into a routine at each place it is used.

OPERAND–That which is operated upon. An operand is usually identified by an address part of an instruction.

OPERATING SYSTEM–Software which controls the execution of computer programs and which may provide scheduling, debugging, input/output control, accounting, compilation, storage assignment, data management, and related services.

OPERATING TIME–That part of available time during which the hardware is operating and assumed to be yielding correct results. It includes development time, production time, and makeup time.

OPERATION–A program step undertaken or executed by a computer, e.g., addition, multiplication, extraction, comparison, shift, transfer. The operation is usually specified by the operator part of an instruction.

OPERATION CODE–A code that represents specific operations. Synonymous with instruction code.

OPERATION DECODER–A device that selects one or more control channels according to the operator part of a machine instruction.

OPERATOR–(1) In the description of a process, that which indicates the action to be performed on operands. (2) A person who operates a machine.

OPTICAL CHARACTER RECOGNITION–The machine identification of printed characters through use of light-sensitive devices. Abbreviated OCR.

OPTICAL SCANNER–(1) A device that scans optically and usually generates an analog or digital signal. (2) A device that optically scans printed or written data and generates their digital representations.

OR–A logic operator having the property that if P is a statement, Q is a statement, R is a statement..., then the OR of P, Q, R..., is true if at least one statement is true, false if all statements are false. P OR Q is often represented by P + Q, P V Q. Synonymous with inclusive OR, boolean add, logical add. Contrast with exclusive OR.

OR GATE–A gate that implements the logic "OR" operator.

OUTCONNECTOR–In flowcharting, a connector that indicates a point at which a flowline is broken for continuation at another point.

OUTPUT–Pertaining to a device, process, or channel involved in an output process, or to the data or states involved.

OUTPUT AREA–An area of storage reserved for output.

OUTPUT CHANNEL–A channel for conveying data from a device or logic element.

OUTPUT DATA–Data to be delivered from a device or program, usually after some processing.

833

OUTPUT DEVICE—The device or collective set of devices used for conveying data out of another device.

OUTPUT PROCESS—The process of delivering data by a system, subsystem, or device.

OUTPUT STATE—The state occurring on a specified output channel.

OVERFLOW—That portion of the result of an operation that exceeds the capacity of the intended unit of storage.

OVERLAY—The technique of repeatedly using the same blocks of internal storage during different stages of a program. When one routine is no longer needed in storage, another routine can replace all or part of it.

PACK—To compress data in a storage medium by taking advantage of known characteristics of the data, in such a way that the original data can be recovered, e.g., to compress data in a storage medium by making use of bit or byte locations that would otherwise go unused.

PACKING DENSITY—The number of useful storage cells per unit of dimension, e.g., the number of bits per inch stored on a magnetic tape or drum track.

PARALLEL—Pertaining to the concurrent or simultaneous occurrence of two or more related activities in multiple devices or channels.

PARAMETER—A variable that is given a constant value for a specific purpose or process.

PARITY BIT—A check bit appended to an array of binary digits to make the sum of all the binary digits, including the check bit, always odd or always even.

PARITY CHECK—A check that tests whether the number of ones (or zeros) in an array of binary digits is odd or even.

PARTIAL CARRY—In parallel addition, a technique in which some or all of the carries are stored temporarily instead of being allowed to propagate immediately.

PASS—One cycle of processing a body of data.

PATCH—To modify a routine in a rough or expedient way.

PATTERN RECOGNITION—The identification of shapes, forms, or configurations by automatic means.

PATTERN SENSITIVE FAULT—A fault that appears in response to some particular pattern of data.

PERIPHERAL EQUIPMENT—In a data processing system, any unit of equipment, distinct from the central processing unit, which may provide the system with outside communication.

PINBOARD—A perforated board into which pins are manually inserted to control the operation of equipment.

PLUGBOARD—A perforated board into which plugs are manually inserted to control the operation of equipment.

POSITION—In a string each location that may be occupied by a character or binary digit and may be identified by a serial number.

POSITIONAL NOTATION—A numeration system in which a number is represented by means of an ordered set of digits, such that the value contributed by each digit depends upon its position as well as upon its value.

POSTMORTEM—Pertaining to the analysis of an operation after its completion.

POSTMORTEM DUMP—A static dump, used for debugging purposes, performed at the end of a machine run.

PRECISION—The degree of discrimination with which a quantity is stated.

PREDEFINED PROCESS—A process that is identified only by name and that is defined elsewhere.

PRESET—To establish an initial condition, such as the control values of a loop.

PRESTORE—Same as initialize.

PREVENTIVE MAINTENANCE—Maintenance specifically intended to prevent faults from occurring during subsequent operation. Contrast with corrective maintenance. Corrective maintenance and preventive maintenance are both performed during maintenance time.

PREVENTIVE MAINTENANCE TIME—Time, usually scheduled, used to perform preventive maintenance.

PROBLEM DESCRIPTION—(1) In information processing, a statement of a problem. The statement may also include a description of the method of solution, the procedures and algorithms, etc. (2) A statement of a problem. The statement may also include a description of the method of solution, the solution itself, the transformations of data and the relationship of procedures, data, constraints, and environment.

PROBLEM ORIENTED LANGUAGE—A programming language designed for the convenient expression of a given class of problems.

PROCESS—A systematic sequence of operations to produce a specified result.

PROCESSOR—(1) In hardware, a data processor. (2) In software, a computer program that includes the compiling, assembling, translating, and related functions for a specific programming language.

PROGRAM—(1) A series of actions proposed in order to achieve a certain result. (2) Loosely, a routine. (3) To design, write, and test a program as in (1). (4) Loosely, to write a routine.

PROGRAM LIBRARY—A collection of available computer programs and routines.

PROGRAM SENSITIVE FAULT—A fault that appears in response to some particular sequence of program steps.

PROGRAMMER—A person mainly involved in designing, writing and testing computer programs.

PROGRAMMING—The design, the writing, and testing of a program.

PROGRAMMING FLOWCHART—A flowchart representing the sequence of operations in a program.

PROGRAMMING LANGUAGE—A language used to prepare computer programs.

PROGRAMMING MODULE—A discrete identifiable set of instructions, usually handled as a unit, by an assembler, a compiler, a linkage editor, a loading routine, or other type of routine or subroutine.

PULSE REPETITION RATE—The number of pulses per unit time.

PUNCH—A perforation, as in a punched card or paper tape.

PUNCHED CARD—A card punched with a pattern of holes to represent data.

PUNCHED TAPE—A tape on which a pattern of holes or cuts is used to represent data.

PUNCH POSITION—A defined location on a card or tape where a hole may be punched.

QUANTIZE—To subdivide the range of values of a variable into a finite number of nonoverlapping, but not necessarily equal, subranges or intervals, each of which is represented by an assigned value within the subrange.

RADIAL TRANSFER—An input process, or an output process.

RADIX—In positional representation, that integer, if it exists, by which the significance of the digit place must be multiplied to give the significance of the next higher digit place.

GLOSSARY

RADIX COMPLEMENT—A complement obtained by subtracting each digit from one less than its radix, then adding one to the least significant digit, executing all carries required.

RADIX-MINUS-ONE COMPLEMENT—A complement obtained by subtracting each digit from one less than the radix.

RADIX NOTATION—A positional representation in which the significance of any two adjacent digit positions has an integral ratio called the radix of the less significant of the two positions; permissible values of the digit in any position range from zero to one less than the radix of that position.

RADIX POINT—In radix notation, the real or implied character that separates the digits associated with the integral part of a numeral from those associated with the fractional part.

RANDOM ACCESS—An access mode in which specific logical records are obtained from or placed into a mass storage file in a nonsequential manner.

RANDOM NUMBERS—A series of numbers obtained by chance.

READ—To acquire or interpret data from a storage device, a data medium, or any other source.

REAL TIME—Pertaining to the actual time during which a physical process transpires.

REAL TIME INPUT—Input data inserted into a system at the time of generation by another system.

REAL TIME OUTPUT—Output data removed from a system at time of need by another system.

RECORD—A collection of related items of data, treated as a unit, for example, one line of an invoice may form a record; a complete set of such records may form a file.

RECORD GAP—An area on a data medium used to indicate the end of a block or record.

RECORDING DENSITY—The number of bits in single linear track measured per unit of length of the recording medium.

RECORD LAYOUT—The arrangement and structure of data in a record, including the sequence and size of its components. By extension, a record layout might be the description thereof.

RECORD LENGTH—A measure of the size of a record, usually specified in units such as words or characters.

REGISTER—A device capable of storing a specified amount of data such as one word.

REGISTRATION—The accurate positioning relative to a reference.

RELATIVE ADDRESS—The number that specifies the difference between the absolute address and the base address.

RELATIVE CODING—Coding that uses machine instructions with relative addresses.

RELIABILITY—The probability that a device will perform without failure for a specified time period or amount of usage.

RELOCATE—In computer programming, to move a routine from one portion of storage to another and to adjust the necessary address references so that the routine, in its new location, can be executed.

REMOTE ACCESS—Pertaining to communication with a data processing facility by one or more stations that are distant from that facility.

REMOTE STATION—Data terminal equipment for communicating with a data processing system from a location that is time, space, or electrically distant.

REPERFORATOR—REceiving PERFORATOR.

REPETITION INSTRUCTION—An instruction that causes one or more instructions to be executed an indicated number of times.

RESET—(1) To restore a storage device to a prescribed initial state, not necessarily that denoting zero. (2) To place a binary cell into the state denoting zero.

RESTART—To reestablish the execution of a routine, using the data recorded at a checkpoint.

RIGHT-JUSTIFY—(1) To adjust the printing positions of characters on a page so that the right margin of the page is regular. (2) To shift the contents of a register so that the least significant digit is at some specified position of the register.

ROUNDING ERROR—An error due to roundoff.

ROUNDOFF—To delete the least significant digit or digits of a numeral, and to adjust the part retained in accordance with some rule.

ROUTINE—An ordered set of instructions that may have some general or frequent use.

ROW—A horizontal arrangement of characters or other expressions.

ROW BINARY—Pertaining to the binary representation of data on cards in which the significances of punch positions are assigned along the card rows. For example, each row in an 80-column card may be used to represent 80 consecutive binary digits.

RUN—A single, continuous performance of a computer program or routine.

SCALE—To adjust the representation of a quantity by a factor in order to bring its range within prescribed limits.

SCALE FACTOR—A number used as a multiplier, so chosen that it will cause a set of quantities to fall within a given range of values.

SCAN—To examine sequentially, part by part.

SCHEDULED MAINTENANCE—Maintenance carried out in accordance with an established plan.

SEARCH—To examine a set of items for one or more having a desired property.

SEGMENT—(1) To divide a computer program into parts such that the program can be executed without the entire program being in internal storage at any one time. (2) A part of a computer program as in (1).

SELECTION CHECK—A check that verifies the choice of devices, such as registers, in the execution of an instruction.

SELECTIVE DUMP—A dump of one or more specified storage locations.

SEQUENCE—An arrangement of items according to a specified set of rules.

SEQUENTIAL—Pertaining to the occurrence of events in time sequence, with little or no simultaneity or overlap of events.

SEQUENTIAL CONTROL—Defined sequence until a different sequence is explicitly initiated by a jump instruction.

SEQUENTIAL LOGIC ELEMENT—A device having at least one output channel and one or more input channels, all characterized by discrete states, such that the state of each output channel is determined by the previous states of the input channels.

SEQUENTIAL OPERATION—Pertaining to the performance of operations one after the other.

SERIAL—(1) Pertaining to the sequential or consecutive occurrence of two or more related activities in a single device or channel.

SET—(1) A collection. (2) To place a storage device into a specified state, usually other than that denoting zero or space character.

(3) To place a binary cell into the state denoting one.

SETUP—(1) In a computer which consists of an assembly of individual computing units, the arrangement of interconnections between the units, and the adjustments needed for the computer to solve a particular problem. (2) An arrangement of data or devices to solve a particular problem.

SETUP DIAGRAM—A diagram specifying a given computer setup.

SEXADECIMAL—(1) Pertaining to a characteristic or property involving a selection, choice, or condition in which there are sixteen possibilities. (2) Pertaining to the numeration system with a radix of sixteen. Synonymous with hexadecimal.

SHIFT—A movement of data to the right or left.

SHIFT REGISTER—A register in which the stored data can be moved to the right or left.

SIGN BIT—A binary digit occupying the sign position.

SIGN DIGIT—A digit occupying the sign position.

SIGNIFICANCE—In positional representation, the factor, dependent on the digit place, by which a digit is multiplied to obtain its additive contribution in the representation of a number.

SIGNIFICANT DIGIT—A digit that is needed for a certain purpose, particularly one that must be kept to preserve a specific accuracy or precision.

SIGN POSITION—A position, normally located at one end of a numeral, that contains an indication of the algebraic sign of the number.

SKEW—The angular displacement of a symbol or data medium from the intended or ideal placement.

SKIP—To ignore one or more instructions in a sequence of instructions.

SMOOTH—To apply procedures that decrease or eliminate rapid fluctuations in data.

SNAPSHOT DUMP—A selective dynamic dump performed at various points in a machine run.

SOFTWARE—A set of computer programs, procedures, and possibly associated documentation concerned with the operation of a data processing system, e.g., compilers, library routines, manuals, circuit diagrams.

SOLID STATE COMPONENT—A component whose operation depends on the control of electric or magnetic phenomena in solids, e.g., a transistor, crystal diode, ferrite core.

SORT—(1) To segregate items into groups according to some definite rules. (2) Same as order.

SORTER—A person, device, or computer routine that sorts.

SOURCE LANGUAGE—The language from which a statement is translated.

SOURCE PROGRAM—A computer program written in a source language.

SPECIAL CHARACTER—A graphic character that is neither a letter, nor a digit, nor a space character.

SPECIAL PURPOSE COMPUTER—A computer that is designed to handle a restricted class of problems.

SPOT PUNCH—A device for punching one hole at a time.

STATIC DUMP—A dump that is performed at a particular point in time with respect to a machine at the end of a run.

STORAGE—(1) Pertaining to a device into which data can be entered, in which they can be held, and from which they can be retrieved at a later time. (2) Loosely, any device that can store data. (3) Synonymous with memory.

STORAGE ALLOCATION—The assignment of blocks of data to specified blocks of storage.

STORAGE CAPACITY—The amount of data that can be continued in a storage device.

STORAGE CELL—An elementary unit of storage.

STORAGE DEVICE—A device into which data can be inserted, in which they can be retained, and from which they can be retrieved.

STORAGE PROTECTION—An arrangement for preventing access to storage for either reading, or writing, or both.

STORE—(1) To enter data into a storage device. (2) To retain data in a storage device.

STORED PROGRAM COMPUTER—A computer controlled by internally stored instructions that can synthesize, store, and in some cases alter instructions as though they were data and that can subsequently execute these instructions.

SUBROUTINE—A routine that can be part of another routine.

SUBROUTINE CALL—The subroutine, in object coding, that performs the call function.

SWITCH—A device or programming technique for making a selection, e.g., a toggle, a conditional jump.

SYMBOL—A representation of something by reason of relationship, association, or convention.

SYMBOLIC ADDRESS—An address expressed in symbols convenient to the computer programmer.

SYMBOLIC CODING—Coding that uses machine instructions with symbolic addresses.

SYMBOLIC LOGIC—The discipline that treats formal logic by means of a formalized artificial language or symbolic calculus, whose purpose is to avoid the ambiguities and logical inadequacies of natural languages.

SYMBOL STRING—A string consisting solely of symbols.

SYNCHRONIZATION PULSES—Pulses introduced by transmitting equipment into the receiving equipment to keep the two equipments operating in step.

SYNTAX—(1) The structure of expressions in a language. (2) The rules governing the structure of a language.

SYSTEM—An organized collection of men, machines, and methods required to accomplish a set of specific functions.

TABLE—A collection of data in which each item is uniquely identified by a label, by its position relative to the other items, or by some other means.

TAPE DRIVE—A device that moves tape past a head.

TAPE TO CARD—Pertaining to equipment or methods that transmit data from either magnetic tape or punched tape to punched cards.

TAPE TRANSPORT—Same as tape drive.

TAPE UNIT—A device containing a tape drive, together with reading, and writing heads and associated controls.

TEMPORARY STORAGE—In programming, storage locations reserved for intermediate results. Synonymous with working storage.

TERMINAL—A point in a system or communication network at which data can either enter or leave.

THIN FILM—Loosely, magnetic thin film.

TIME SHARE—To use a device for two or more interleaved purposes.

GLOSSARY

TIME SHARING—Pertaining to the interleaved use of the time of a device.

TOGGLE—(1) Same as flip-flop. (2) Pertaining to any device having two stable states.

TRACING ROUTINE—A routine that provides a historical record of specified events in the execution of a program.

TRACK—The portion of a moving storage medium, such as a drum, tape, or disc, that is accessible to a given reading head position.

TRANSFORM—To change the form of data according to specific rules.

TRANSLATE—To transform statements from one language to another without significantly changing the meaning.

TRANSMISSION—(1) The sending of data from one location and the receiving of data in another location, usually leaving the source data unchanged. (2) The sending of data.

TRANSMIT—To send data from one location and to receive the data at another location.

TROUBLESHOOT—Same as debug.

TRUNCATE—To terminate a computational process in accordance with some rule, e.g., to end the evaluation of a power series at a specified term.

TRUNCATION ERROR—An error due to truncation.

TRUTH TABLE—A table that describes a logic function by listing all possible combinations of input values and indicating, for each combination, the true output values.

TWELVE PUNCH—A punch in the top row of a Hollerith punch card. Synonymous with y-punch.

TWO-OUT-OF-FIVE CODE—A positional notation in which each decimal digit is represented by five binary digits of which two are one kind (e.g., ones) and three are the other kind (e.g., zeros).

TWOS COMPLEMENT—The radix complement in binary notation.

TYPE FONT—Type of a given size and style, e.g., 10-point Bodoni Modern.

UNIT—(1) A device having a special function. (2) A basic element.

UNPACK—To recover the original data from packed data.

UTILITY ROUTINE—Same as service routine.

VARIABLE—A quantity that can assume any of a given set of values.

VARIABLE-LENGTH RECORD—Pertaining to a file in which the records are not uniform in length.

VARIABLE-POINT REPRESENTATION—A positional representation in which the position of the radix point is explicitly indicated by a special character at that position.

VENN DIAGRAM—A diagram in which sets are represented by closed regions.

VERIFY—(1) To determine whether a transcription of data or other operation has been accomplished accurately. (2) To check the results of keypunching.

VOLATILE STORAGE—A storage device in which stored data are lost when the applied power is removed, e.g., an acoustic delay line.

WEIGHT—Same as significance.

WORD—(1) A character string or a bit string considered as an entity. (2) See alphabetic word, computer word, half-word, machine word, numeric word.

WORD LENGTH—A measure of the size of a word, usually specified in units such as characters or binary digits.

GLOSSARY

WRITE—To record data in a storage device or a data medium. The recording need not be permanent, such as the writing on a cathode ray tube display device.

X-PUNCH—Same as eleven-punch.

Y-PUNCH—Same as twelve-punch.

ZEROFILL—To character fill with the representation of zero.

ZERO SUPPRESSION—The elimination of non-significant zeros in a numeral.

ZONE PUNCH—A punch in the eleven, twelve, or zero row of a punched card.

INDEX

Numbers on this page refer to **PROBLEM NUMBERS**, not page numbers

THE PROBLEM SOLVERS